G000145506

The 1996-97 Official PFA

FOOTBALLERS FACTFILE

Edited by
Barry J Hugman

Photographs by
Empics Sports Photo Agency

Queen Anne Press

First published in 1996

© Barry J Hugman

Barry J Hugman has asserted his right under
the Copyright, Designs and Patent Act, 1988
to be identified as the author of this work

First published in Great Britain in 1996 by
Queen Anne Press
a division of Lennard Associates Limited
Mackerye End, Harpenden
Hertfordshire AL5 5DR

A CIP catalogue record for this book
is available from the British Library

ISBN 1 85291 571 4

Typeset and designed by Typecast (Artwork & Design)
West Country Marketing, 8 Mudford Road
Yeovil, Somerset BA21 4AA

Printed and bound in Great Britain by
Butler & Tanner, London and Frome

EMPICS
SPORTS PHOTO AGENCY

The editor and publishers are grateful to the
photographers of Empics Sports Photo Agency
who provided all the photographs used in this book:
Neal Simpson, Aubrey Washington, Laurence Griffiths,
Andy Heading, Steve Morton, Tony Marshall,
Matthew Ashton, Dave Tyrell, Mike Egerton
and Barry Coombes

Acknowledgements

There are so many people who have helped with this massive undertaking, it is difficult to know where to start, but I shall begin with the Professional Footballers' Association. Having known **Gordon Taylor** from way back, and recognising his great enthusiasm for the game, especially for those performing week in and week out, it was only natural that when putting together a work of this nature that I would wish to involve the PFA. Gordon and Brendan Batson's support has been magnificent. Also, once again, I am extremely grateful to **Brian Marwood**, the former Arsenal and England star, and now a PFA executive, for his painstaking work in proof-reading every page. An important job, and another instance of the PFA offering real participation in the product.

As in previous years, information was more than forthcoming from both the Football League and Premier League. My thanks go to **Sheila Andrew** and **Debbie Birch** of the former and to **Mike Foster** and **Neil Harrison** of the latter. In both instances, I was impressed by the attention to detail.

Tracking down international honours at all levels from schoolboy to senior status takes some doing and I was most grateful to have the support of **David Barber** (English FA), **Kitty Barlers** (FA of Ireland) and **Scott McIntosh** (Scottish FA). Outside of the official bodies, **Ceri Stennett** (Official FAW statistician), **Marshall Gillespie** (Editor of the *Northern Ireland Football Yearbook*) and **Sean Creedon** (Official FA of Ireland statistician), all went beyond the call of duty.

No less important were **Mike Featherstone**, who dug out missing height and weight details as well as being available to progress any other missing data, and **Alan Platt** for his timely help in construction of the final run-in of pen portraits.

Before moving on to all the club contributors, who were also quite magnificent in their application, a special thank you must go to **Jonathan Ticehurst**, managing director of Windsor Insurance Brokers' Sports Division, who has supported the Factfile from day one both financially and vocally.

For details provided on players, I have listed below, in alphabetical order, the names of the "team", without whose help this book would not have been possible to produce. I thank every one of them for all the hard work they put in.

Audrey Adams (*Watford*): Producer and statistician for BBC Radio Sport and a Watford supporter since the days of Cliff Holton, Audrey is also the club statistician for the *Ultimate Football Guide*.

Steve Adamson (*Scarborough*): A supporter for 27 years, and programme editor from 1985 and 1992, Steve continues to contribute to the latter and has also published several articles on the club.

Denise Allibone (*Aston Villa*): In her own words, Denise is a mad, crazy Villa supporter, who follows them up-and-down the country without fail. Her only previous football work was to help me with the club's profiles required for the *Premier League: The Players* publication.

Geoff Allman (*Walsall*): A university lecturer by trade, he saw his first ever game in February 1944, Walsall versus Wolves. Has written for Walsall's programme for the last 28 seasons and, at one time or another, has provided articles for more than half of the clubs currently in the Premiership and Football League. Geoff is also a Methodist local preacher and press officer.

Lawrence Appleby (*Hereford United*): In supporting Hereford for more than 25 years, for the past 16 he has collected stats and club history and has provided the data for the *Ultimate Football Guide*. Currently writing two club histories.

Stuart Basson (*Chesterfield*): Is the author of *The Definitive Chesterfield FC*, which was published in March by the Association of Football Statisticians, of which he has been a member for ten years. His comprehensive Who's Who of the club is also nearing completion.

Ian Bates (*Bradford*): Has followed City since 1951 and refereed in amateur football up until 1995-96. A member of the AFS, this is the first publication that Ian has been involved in.

David Batters (*York City*): A supporter since 1948, he is club historian, a contributor to the programme and author of *York City: The Complete Record 1922-1990*. Also commentates on matches at York Hospital.

Harry Berry (*Blackburn Rovers*): Author of the club centenary history, *A Century of Soccer* and other books on Rovers, and co-author of the *Preston North End* history, along with several books on athletics.

Peter Bishop (*Tranmere Rovers*): The club's programme editor and historian for 11 years, Peter is the author of the *A-Z of Tranmere*, the first book ever published on Rovers. Has also contributed to many other books.

Simon Bowden (*Barnet*): As sports editor of the *Barnet Advertiser*, he has followed the club home and away for the past three seasons.

Peter Bower and **Ken Craig** (*Colchester United*): The former, a life-long fan since the mid-1950s, worked with Ken to produce the input for the enclosed. The latter currently edits a monthly newsletter for all United fans living away from the area called *U's from 'Ome*.

Eddie Brennan (*Sunderland*): A regular at Roker since 1976 (aged nine) and currently the club statistician for the *Ultimate Football Guide*.

Stuart Brennan (*Stockport County*): As sports editor of the *Stockport Express* newspaper from 1989 to 1994, he covered the club's fortunes both home and away and was a programme contributor. Also County's statistician for the *Ultimate Football Guide*.

Jonathan Brewer (*Plymouth Argyle*): Currently the Argyle statistician for the *Ultimate Football Guide*, Jonathan also writes articles for the *Pasty News*, a publication run by the London branch of the supporters' club.

Jim Brown (*Coventry City*): The club's official statistician and contributor to the programme, he also pens a column for the local newspaper answering readers' queries.

Trevor Bugg (*Hull City*): Is a contributor to City's innovative matchday programme and also a committee member of the club's fund-raising "Put a Tiger in your Team Appeal".

Graham Caton (*Bournemouth*): Into his second year with the Factfile, Graham is a committed Cherries' supporter who has always enjoyed collating facts and figures relating to the club.

Wallace Chadwick (*Burnley*): A supporter for over 30 years, he has seen all the extremes in the period from the great days of the '60s, including the championship of all four divisions and a narrow escape from relegation to the Conference. Wallace is a regular contributor to the Clarets' programme.

Dennis Chapman (*Manchester City*): Now retired, Dennis has followed City since 1937-38. Has worked on several publications, including the *FA Carling Premier League: The Players* and the *Ultimate Football Guide*. Possesses possibly the largest collection of City programmes, the earliest being 1902-03.

Paul Clayton (*Charlton Athletic*): Writes in the club's matchday programme and various other publications connected with the club. A Charlton season ticket-holder, despite living in Wiltshire, and a member of the AFS, Paul also compiles the statistics for the *Ultimate Football Guide*.

Grant Coleby (*Exeter City*): A psychology graduate, Grant, a member of City's supporters' club, also belongs to the Association of Football statisticians.

Eddie Collins (*Nottingham Forest*): A Forest supporter since 1956, and a member of the Associated Football Statisticians, this is the first publication he has been involved in.

David Copping (*Barnsley*): The writer of the past meetings column in the Barnsley programme for the last seven seasons, he also commentated live hospital broadcasts from Oakwell between 1978 and 1991 and has since narrated for the club videos.

Frank Coumbe (*Brentford*): A Bees' supporter all his life, having not missed a home match since 1977, Frank has contributed to the matchday programme, along with those for other clubs, for years. For 12 years, he has also been the club statistician for the *Sky Sports Ultimate Football Guide*, formerly the *Football Club Directory*. However, the highlight of 1995-96 was when wife Susan gave birth to daughter Sally in November.

Peter Cullen (*Bury*): Aged 36, Peter is a former Bury FC supporters' club secretary, who also acted as the programme editor between 1983-1991. Editor of the *Bury Centenary Brochure* in 1985, he is currently, along with **Paul Greenless**, working on a definitive club history.

Mike Davage (*Norwich City*): Author of the ultimate who's who *Glorious Canaries*, and co-author of *Canary Citizens*. Presently involved in the eighth volume of the *Norwich City handbook* and is a regular contributor to local and national TV, radio and newspapers. As a contributor to over 60 books, Mike is currently working with Jim Creasy on a 1919-1939 supplemental book to the author's *Football League Players' Records, 1946-1992*.

Gareth Davies (*Wrexham*): Assists in the much acclaimed club programme, the editor of which, **Geraint Parry**, also helped on heights and weights, etc, for this publication. Gareth has wrtten and published the *Coast of Soccer Memories*, the centenary history of the *North Wales Coast FA (1995)*, and co-authored with Ian Garland the *Who 's Who of Welsh International Soccer Players (1991)*. Also heavily involved in Wrexham, *A Complete Record 1872-1992*, written by Peter Jones. Currently researching *Wrexham FC's Who's Who* at the moment, he still finds time to compile the club section for the *Ultimate Football Guide* and to help me with the names of all current players who have won Welsh Cup winners' medals.

David Downs (*Reading*): Teaches in a local primary school and works part-time for Reading FC at their Centre of Excellence. The official historian and statistician for the club, David is the author of *Biscuits & Royals*, the history of Reading.

Dave Drage (*Birmingham City*): A City supporter since 1966, he has contributed to the *Ultimate Football Guide* every year since its inception. Has also contributed to the *History of Birmingham City (1989)* and the *Who's Who of Birmingham City (1991)*. Is on the committee of the recently formed Blues' Collectors and Historical Society.

Ray Driscoll (*Chelsea*): Too young to see the Blues lift the league championship in 1955, he started to follow them in 1957 when Jimmy Greaves began his career in the famous blue shirt. Although watching Chelsea during the past 40 years has been frustrating, his dearest wish is to see the club win the Premiership title. A contributor to many football books, he also wrote articles for the Euro '96 programmes.

Mark Evans (*Leeds United*): Has supported United for the last 28 years and describes his association with the club as one of the loves of his life. The Leeds' statistician for the *Ultimate Football Guide* for nearly eight years, he was also involved in my two editions of the *FA Carling Premiership: The Players*.

Keith Evemy (*Fulham*): Long-standing supporter who was unfortunately away on military service when the club won its only post-war honour, the second division championship in 1948-49. Highly regarded at Craven Cottage, he contributes to the matchday programme and is never far from the ground.

Colin Faiers (*Cambridge United*): A 37-year-old chartered accountant, Colin, a fan for over 26 years, is the recognised club statisticlan and currently writes the historical features for the programme.

Harold Finch (*Crewe Alexandra*): The club's historian and a supporter for over 60 years, Harold has been the programme editor for more than 40 of them. A one-club man, he has travelled extensively to watch them play.

Paul Gilligan (*Doncaster Rovers*): A keen follower of Rovers for over 30 years, Paul has written three books on the club and is a regular contributor in the matchday programme. Also the official club photographer.

Dave Goody (*Southend United*): United historian, statistician and collector, he co-authored *Southend United: The Official History of the Blues* and is a regular contributor to the programme.

Frank Grande (*Northampton Town*): Author of *The Cobblers, A History of Northampton Town FC* and a *Who's Who* on the club. Has contributed a regular column to the club programme for the past 16 seasons.

Roy Grant (*Oxford United*): Formerly assistant secretary at Oxford and club programme editor and statistician, he also handled the Clubline telephone service. Contributes to the *Ultimate Football Guide* and, in the past, the *Official Football League Yearbook*.

Don Hales (*Leyton Orient and Luton Town*): A management consultant in financial services, Don has contributed to *World Soccer, Team Talk* and the *Ultimate Football Guide*, as well as compiling the obituary column for the AFS. In compiling the Orient and Luton information, he was assisted by life-long O's fan, **David Randlesome**, a chartered accountant, and his son, **Daniel Hales**, currently taking his A-levels, respectively.

Roger Harrison (*Blackpool*): Life-long supporter who has seen the Pool play every other league side both home and away. Joint programme editor and club statistician, Roger also contributes to other publications, including the *Ultimate Football Guide*.

Ron Hockings (*Chelsea*): Has now published five books involving the history of Chelsea, European and South American Cups. *The Nations of Europe*, currently available in two volumes, includes every line-up for all the European countries' matches up until 1993, with volume three envisaged being ready early in 1997 and has recently completed *90 Years of the "Blues"*, the statistical history of Chelsea. Provided all the international appearances for non-British teams in this year's *Factfile*.

Mike Jay (*Bristol Rovers*): Apart from helping out on other publications, notably the *Ultimate Football Guide*, Mike has had two books of his own published on Bristol Rovers, namely *The Complete Record (1883-1987)* and *Pirates in Profile, A Who's Who of the Players 1920-1995*.

Colin Jones (*Swansea City*): A fan since the early 1960s and a contributor to the club programme during the last four years. Played non-league football, also later being involved in training and coaching.

Gordon Lawton (*Oldham Athletic*): Employed as the public relations officer at the club and Athletic's official photographer. Other publications contributed to, include *Carling Premiership: The Players, Rothmans Yearbook, Ultimate Football Guide* and *News of the World* annual.

Geoffrey Lea (*Wigan Athletic*): The club statistician for the *Ultimate Football Guide*, Geoffrey has been following the Latics for over 20 years and is a major contributor to the matchday programme that won the 'Third Division Programme of the Year" in 1993-94. Also assists with the match commentary on the Clubcall.

Richard Lindsay (*Millwall*): Author of *Millwall: The Complete Record 1895-1991*, and currently in the process of helping establish the Millwall FC Museum at the New Den. If any fans or ex-players feel they can help, please ring 0171232 1222.

John Lovis (*Torquay United*): A supporter since 1955, and a regular contributor to the club programme, he is also United's statistician for the *Ultimate Football Guide*.

Steve McGhee (*Derby County*): A collector of Derby memorabilia and a fan since 1969. Earlier involved in a bi-monthly historical magazine on County, he currently compiles the club section for the *Ultimate Football Guide*.

Peter Macey (*Portsmouth*): A Pompey fan since the late 1970s, Peter, a member of the AFS, contributes to the matchday programme and also writes in the *Sky Sports' Directory*. Is currently studying for a BSC in computer science at the University of Wolverhampton.

John Maguire (*Manchester United*): A member of the AFS and a qualified FA coach, John has been working on several sports related topics during the last 12 months, including booklets on the *Busby Babes, Duncan Edwards and Eddie Coleman, England's World Cup success of 1966*, and *Manchester United's 1968 European Cup victory*, as well as a biography of the former Spurs' manager, Bill Nicholson.

Simon Marland (*Bolton Wanderers*): Club historian, statistician, and editor of Wanderers' matchday programme, he is also the author of *Bolton Wanderers: A Complete Record* and *One Hundred Years at Burnden Park, 1895-1995*.

John Martin (*Chester City*): Club statistician for both the *Rothmans Yearbook* and *Ultimate Football Guide*, he also contributes for various other publications. Was City's programme editor for ten years up until 1993-94, winning the 'Third Division Programme of the Year" award that same season.

Wade Martin (*Stoke City*): For many years a major contributor to the club programme, as well as writing *A Potters Tale* and the *Master Potters'* series of books.

Tony Matthews (*West Bromwich Albion*): Official stabstician and curator of Albion, his publications include, *the complete records of Aston Villa, Birmingham City, WBA, Wolves, Walsall and Stoke City*. Has also compiled *Who 's Whos* on the first four clubs listed above, plus Manchester United, and currently contributes to eight programmes.

Ian Mills (*Notts County*): Saw his first County game in 1959-60 when his grandfather took him and has been hooked ever since, missing just one game since 1970. Ian, who can be reached at the club shop, runs the matchday programme sales at Meadow Lane.

Ian Nannestad (*Lincoln City*): A past contributor to the Imps' programme and co-author of the *Who's Who of Lincoln City, 1892-1994*, publication.

John Northcutt (*West Ham United*): Has supported the Hammers since 1959 and is the co-author of West Ham books, *The Complete Record* and the *Illustrated History*. A regular contributor to the club programme and the club adviser to tbe *Ultimate Football Guide*.

Michael Norton *(Scunthorpe United):* Former matchday club programme editor and now a contributor, Michael is also the Irons' statistician for the *Ultimate Football Guide*. Is an avid collector of programmes and memorabilia.

Janey Orchard and **Richard Hayhoe** *(Tottenham Hotspur):* Introduced by a member of the "team", last year was the first time Janey, aided by Richard, had done anything of this nature.

Brian Pead *(Liverpool):* Author of three editions of *Liverpool, A Complete Record, Liverpool: Champion of Champions* (1990) and *Ee Aye Addio - We've Won the Cup* (1993), Brian was the statistician for the *Rush for Glory* video and has contributed to many publications, including the *Footballer* magazine and the *Ultimate Football Guide*.

Steve Peart and **Dave Finch** *(Wycombe Wanderers):* A former programme editor of the club and a supporter for over 20 years, Steve put together the player profiles, while the club statistics were supplied by Dave, the official Wycombe statistician.

Steve Phillips *(Rochdale):* A Dale fan of 30 years standing, he is the club's official statistician and author of *The Survivors: The Story of Rochdale AFC*.

Paul Plowrnan *(Swindon Town):* Football historian, statistician and freelance journalist.

Mike Purkiss *(Crystal Palace):* Having supported Palace since 1950 and produced stats on them since 1960, Mike is the author of the *Complete History of Crystal Palace, 1905-1989*, the club statistician for the *Ultimate Football Guide*, and contributed to *Premier League: The Players*.

Taff Rees and **Alan Jenkins** *(Cardiff City):* Life-long Cardiff fans. Although a contributor for the matchday programme, Taff watches City from afar these days, while Alan continues to produce copy for the *Ultimate Football Guide*.

Mike Renshaw *(Sheffield Wednesday):* Has followed Wednesday for 40 years and is a great supporter of European soccer. Currently produces the club section for the *Ultimate Football Guide*.

Jack Retter *(Mansfield Town):* First saw the team play over 60 years ago. Author of *Who's Who - The Stags,* and a regular contributor to the matchday programme. Currently working on a comprehensive centenary history of the club, due to be published next year, he is a member of the AFS and contributes to a number of publications.

Robert Ringsell and **Geoff Norcott** *(Wimbledon):* Both are life-long Dons' supporters who attend all home matches. Rob (19) is currently completing a year out before going to Roehampton University, while Geoff, also 19, has just completed his first year at Goldsmith's University, studying English.

Mick Robinson *(Peterborough United):* Another life-long fan, for a number of years Mick has contributed to the club programme and was the joint editor of the *Official Peterborough History*. Also the club statistician for the *Ultimate Football Guide*.

Phil Sherwin *(Port Vale):* As Vale's statistician, Phil works on a number of other publications and has contributed to the club programme for 15 years. A fan since 1968, he follows them home and away.

Andy Shute *(Queens Park Rangers):* Life-long QPR supporter and compiler of the QPR and Tottenham details for the *Ultimate Football Guide*.

Derrick Slasor *(Middlesbrough):* First saw the Boro play in December 1946 and, as Managing Director of Trapezium Transport Services, is well known in the area for sponsoring various club activities.

Mike Slater *(Wolverhampton Wanderers):* Having seen the majority of Wolves' home matches since 1965, Mike both wrote and published a book in 1988 on the club called *Molineux Memories*, selling all 3,600 copies over two years. Has compiled all the questions for the last seven annual *Brain of Wolves* quizzes.

Gordon Small *(Hartlepool Unlted):* Has supported United since October 1965, experiencing two promotions, two relegations, six re-elections and several close calls. Is the statistician for the *Ultimate Football Guide*.

Dave Smith *(Leicester City):* A regular columnist in the programme, co-author of *Fossils & Foxes* and the *Foxes Alphabet*, he assists with several other club handbooks.

Gerry Somerton *(Rotherham United):* Deputy sports editor of the *Rotherham Advertiser* and part-time sports reporter for the New Hallam FM local commercial radio station. Author of the *Official History of Rotherham United*, published last year.

Richard Stead *(Huddersfield Town):* Has supported his hometown team, Huddersfield, since the early '70s and, despite living in Manchester these days, continues to do so. Also contributes to the *Ultimate Football Guide*.

David Steele *(Carlisle United):* A regular contributor to the club programme for several years now, his current interest is in tracking down ex-United players.

Richard Stocken *(Shrewsbury Town):* A supporter of 38 years and a collector of club programmes and memorabilia, Richard is an annual contributor to the *Ultimate Football Guide* and other publications.

Bill Swan *(Newcastle United):* A supporter since the early 1950s, he is now a shareholder in the club, as are his wife and children. Is a keen collector of programmes and other memorabilia and long-term member of the AFS. Although the author of numerous published scientific papers, and assisting in the production of the club's volume in the *Complete Record* series, this is his first involvement of this kind of work.

Richard Swift *(Everton):* The Everton statistician for both the *FA Carling Premier League: The Players* and the *Ultimate Football Guide*, Richard is an enthusiastic Everton and Sheffield Wednesday supporter.

Alan Tait *(Scottish clubs):* A regular contributor to Tony Brown's ultimate *Scottish League* book, and a compiler of statistics appertaining to that country, Alan is currently working on a project, probably still five years down the road, that will give line-ups for all Scottish League matches since 1890.

Chris Thompson *(Arsenal):* Born in Greenwich the week before Charlton won the FA Cup, Chris has held season tickets for both the Valley and Highbury. Publications worked on, include *FA Carling Premiership: The Players* and, currently, the *Ultimate Football Guide*.

David Ticehurst *(Brighton & Hove Albion):* Author of *Brighton & Hove Albion, A Portrait in Old Picture Postcards*, secretary of the Football Postcard Collector's Club and a member of the AFS.

Andrew Treherne *(Sheffield United):* Contributor to the *Ultimate Football Guide, The Premier League: The Players* and *Sheffield United: The first Hundred Years*. Also a member of the AFS.

Les Triggs *(Grimsby Town):* First became involved with the statistical side of the club when asked to assist with Town's centenary exhibition in 1978. A retired librarian, Les, who first saw the Mariners in a wartime league match, is the co-author of the Grimsby Town volume in the *Complete Record* series and has been club statistician to the *Ultimate Football Guide* since its inception.

Roger Triggs *(Gillingham):* Has written three books on the club, *Gillingham FC - A Chronology 1893-1984, Priestfield Profiles 1950-1988* and the centenery publication, *Home of the Shouting Men*, which he co-authored with Andy Bradley. Also a feature writer in the programme since 1975.

Frank Tweddle *(Darlington):* The club's official historian and statistician, Frank is the author of *Darlington's Centenary History* and the programme editor since 1975. Also a contributor for various other publications, including the *Ultimate Football Guide*.

Paul Voller *(Ipswich Town):* A Town supporter since 1963-64, Paul works at the ground on matchdays and is a member of the supporters' management committee. Other publications worked on include the *FA Carling Premier League: The Players* and the *Ultimate Football Guide*.

Dick Wright *(Southampton):* A Saints' supporter since 1977, he is a local amateur referee and president of a youth football club that he co-founded in 1983. Is also assisting with the squad that will take the club into senior football for the first time next season.

Tony Woodburn and **Martin Atherton** *(Preston North End):* Tony started watching the club in the late 1960s and is a life member of the AFS, the Ninety-Two club and the Scottish 38 club. Martin, a fan for over 30 years, lives within a long throw-in of Deepdale and has been able to watch the development of the ground from his front doorstep.

David Woods *(Bristol City):* A life member of the AFS and a member of the Ninety-Two club, David has been watching City on a regular basis since 1958. Has also written two books on his favourite team.

Finally, on the production side of the book, all the photo's were supplied by Neal Simpson and his team at Empics Photo Agency, 26 Musters Road, West Bridgford, Nottingharn NG2 7PL. Tel: (0115) 945 5885. As in previous books of mine, they have been more than helpful. Last, but not least, my thanks go to Jean Bastin, of Typecast (Artwork & Design), for her patience and diligent work on the typesetting and design, which again went far beyond the call of normal duty and was much appreciated.

Insure You Achieve Your Goals

Insurance Brokers and Insurance Consultants to the:-
Football Association, F.A. Premier League, Football League,
British Boxing Board of Control, British Olympic Association,
Cricketer's Association, Professional Board Sailors Association,
Spanish Basketball Association, St Moritz Tobogganing Club.

Windsor is one of the world's largest specialist sports, leisure and entertainment brokers, servicing national sports associations, leagues, clubs and players throughout the U.K., Europe, and North America.

While Personal Accident forms the major part of our sports related business, the group can also offer many other types of insurance cover, including Stadium Risks, Commercial Fire, High-Risk Liability, Professional Indemnity, Marine and Aviation - at highly competitive rates.

For sponsors and event organisers we offer wide experience of contingency risks such as Event Cancellation/Abandonment, Prize Indemnity, Death and Disgrace, Bonus Protection, and other insurance-protected sponsorship enhancements and marketing initiatives.

A separate group company provides consultancy on Life Assurance, Group Pensions and Personal Financial Planning.

WINDSOR

Windsor Insurance Brokers Ltd

Lyon House, 160/166 Borough High Street, London SE1 1JR
Tel: 0171 - 407 7144 Fax: 0171 - 378 6676 Telex: 889360
For further infomation ring Jonathan Ticehurst on:
+44(0)171 - 407 7144

Forewords

Once again, I am extremely pleased to give the PFA's full endorsement and recommendation to *Footballers' Factfile*. I consider it the finest work of its kind, and one that presents a comprehensive coverage on statistics and profiles for every one of the 2,000 plus members of the PFA who played in first team football throughout the Premier League and Football League in England and Wales during 1995-96.

As in the first edition, the publication has been sponsored by Windsor Insurance Brokers, the key figures in our industry with regard to the protection of players against injury, and written by Barry Hugman, whose record in this field is unsurpassed. Barry has a team of over 90 people who provided him with the invaluable aspects of local information that gives this book such credibility and makes it a must for every enthusiast, administrator and commentator on our great game. It will occupy the most prominent position on my desk.

Gordon Taylor,
Chief Executive of the Professional Footballers' Association.

Last year's first edition of the *Footballers' Factfile* drew deserved acclaim from those associated with the world of professional football throughout the country. Indeed, it is difficult to remember a similar publication that has been so instantly recognised as a definitive authority on the players currently in the game.

Of particular interest, of course, are the facts and figures relating to the European and other overseas stars who, during the last couple of years, have made such an impact upon football in England. Long may it continue, and long may they grace our stadia with their particular brand of skill and elegance.

The mix of our own clearly identifiable English style of play with the continental style has given enormous enjoyment to football lovers of all ages in recent years and Windsor are very pleased to be able to continue to support and again lend our name as sponsors to this excellent publication.

The Windsor Insurance Group has been closely involved with professional football for over 20 years. Every registered contract professional player, all of whom appear in this book, are, or have been at some time, insured for injury and sickness through the Premier League and Football League Basic Scheme that we arrange.

Additionally, the great majority of players in this book are able to look to a more secure future once their playing days are over, by virtue of the Players' Cash Benefit Scheme and Retirement Income Scheme that we set up jointly with the Football League and the Professional Footballers' Association in the mid-1980s. Undoubtedly, this was one of the PFA's greatest achievements and a shining example to all employee groups who look to provide for the welfare of their members.

Jonathan Ticehurst,
Managing Director of the Sports Division, Windsor Insurance Brokers Limited.

Editorial Introduction

Following on from the success of last year, the *Factfile* portrays the statistical career record of every FA Carling Premiership and Endsleigh League player who made an appearance in 1995-96, whether it be in league football, the Football League (Coca Cola) Cup, FA Cup (Sponsored by Littlewoods Pools), Charity Shield, European Cup, European Cup Winners' Cup, UEFA Cup, Welsh (Allbright Bitter) Cup, Anglo-Italian Cup, Auto Windscreen's Shield, or in the Play-Offs. Not included are the Inter-Toto Cup matches in June/July 1995, which took in many guest appearances. It goes beyond mere statistics, however, with a write-up on all of the 2,300 plus players involved and also records faithfully last season's playing records separately by club.

The work falls into two sections, both inter-relating. Firstly, the main core, PFA Footballers' Factfile: A-Z (pages 9-270), and secondly, FA Carling Premiership and Endsleigh League Clubs: Summary of Appearances and Goals for 1995-96 (pages 271-284). Below is an explanation on how to follow the PFA Footballers' Factfile.

As the title suggests all players are listed in alphabetical order and are shown by Surnames first, followed by full Christian names, with the one the player is commonly known by shown in **bold**. Any abbreviation or pseudonym is bracketed.

Birthplace/date: you will note that several players, who would be predominately classified as British, were born in places like Germany and India, for example. My book, Football League Players' Records (last edition: 1992), which covered every man who had played league football since the war, has, in the past, used the family domicile as a more realistic "birthplace". But, for our purposes here, I have reverted to that which has been officially recorded.

Height and Weight: Listed in feet and inches, and stones and pounds, respectively. It must be remembered that a player's weight can frequently change and, on that basis, the recorded data should be used as a guide only, especially as they would have been weighed several times during the season.

Club Honours: Those shown, cover careers from the Conference and FA Trophy upwards. For abbreviations, read:- European Honours: EC (European Cup), ESC (European Super Cup), ECWC (European Cup Winners' Cup). English Honours: FAC (FA Cup), FLC (Football League Cup), CS (Charity Shield), FMC (Full Members Cup, which takes in the Simod and Zenith Data sponsorships), AMC (Associated Members Cup - Freight Rover, Sherpa Van, Leyland DAF, Autoglass and Auto Windscreen), AIC (Anglo-Italian Cup), GMVC (GM Vauxhall Conference), FAT (FA Trophy), FAYC (FA Youth Cup). Scottish Honours: SPD (Scottish Premier Division), S Div 1/2 (Scottish Leagues), SC (Scottish Cup), SLC (Scottish League Cup). Welsh Honours: WC (Welsh Cup).

International Honours: For abbreviations, read:- E (England), NI (Northern Ireland), S (Scotland), W (Wales) and Ei (Republic of Ireland). Under 21 through to full

internationals give total appearances (inclusive of subs), while schoolboy (U16s and U18s) and youth representatives are just listed. The cut-off date used for appearances was 30 June, following the completion of the European Championships.

Player Descriptions: Gives position and playing strengths and, in keeping the work topical, a few words on how their season went in 1995-96. This takes into account, in a positive fashion, key performances, along with value to the team, injuries, honours, and other points of interest, etc. To allow for play-off and Euro '96 input to be included, and the publication date to be maintained, the cut-off date used was 30 June. Transfers, however, are shown as stop press if they took place after 18 May, the cut-off date used by the Football and Premier Leagues to produce the close season retained and free transfer lists. The decision was taken on the grounds that the May/June Registration and Transfer booklets would not be available until after going to press.

Career Records: Full appearances, plus substitutes and goals, are given for all Premiership and Endsleigh League games and, if a player who is in the book has played in any of the senior Scottish Leagues, his appearances with the club in question will also be recorded. Other information given, includes the origination of players (clubs in the non-leagues, junior football, or from abroad), registered signing dates (if a player signs permanently following a loan spell, for our purposes, we have shown the initial date as being the point of transfer. Also, loan transfers are only recorded if an appearance is made), transfer fees (these are the figures that have been reported in newspapers and magazines and should only be used as a guide to a player's valuation), and a breakdown of matches by P/FL (Premiership and Football League), PL (Premier League), FL (Football League), FLC (Football League Cup), FAC (FA Cup), and Others. As mentioned in the first paragraph, other matches will take in the Welsh Cup, play-offs, Anglo-Italian Cup, Auto Windscreen Shield, Charity Shield, and any major European competition. All of these matches are lumped together for reasons of saving space. Scottish appearances for players on loan to P/FL clubs in 1995-96 are shown at the point of transfer and do not include games following their return to Scotland.

Career statistics are depicted as
Appearances + Substitutes/Goals

Whether you wish to analyse someone for your fantasy football team selection or would like to know more about a little known player appearing in the lower reaches of the game, the *PFA Footballers' Factfile* should provide you with the answer.

Barry J. Hugman, Editor,
PFA Footballers' Factfile

PFA Footballers' Factfile : A-Z

ABBOTT Gregory (Greg) Stephen
Born: Coventry, 14 December 1963
Height: 5'9" Weight: 10.7
Club Honours: Div 3 '85
An excellent midfield distributor who often advances into goalscoring positions, and an inspirational captain, he was sorely missed by Hull at the start of the 1995-96 campaign after snapping ankle ligaments in a pre-season warm-up. Later, despite his typical grit and determination, his leadership qualities could not lift City out of their relegation worries. Was controversially released during the summer.
Coventry C (From apprentice on 5/1/82)
Bradford C (Free on 10/9/82) FL 256+25/38 FLC 22+3/6 FAC 15+1/3 Others 19+2/5
Halifax T (£25,000 on 22/7/91) FL 24+4/1 FLC 2 FAC 2 Others 2 (Free to Guisley on 18/9/92)
Hull C (Free on 14/12/92) FL 120+4/16 FLC 5/1 FAC 3+1 Others 6+2/2

ABLETT Gary Ian
Born: Liverpool, 19 November 1965
Height: 6'2" Weight: 12.7
Club Honours: Div 1 '88, '90; CS '88, '90, '95; FAC '89; '95
International Honours: E: B-1; U21-1
Distinguished Everton central defender who provides emergency cover to any defensive position when injuries necessitate. Clears his lines well when required, but frequently plays the ball out of defence with accurate passes, especially with his left foot, and rarely gives away possession. Began last season as a regular in the Blues' defence, missing only four games towards the end of September through injury. However, with increased competition, he lost his place during November and, unable to force his way back, joined Sheffield United on loan in March, a move that coincided with the club's end of term surge and led to attempts to sign him on a permanent basis. *Stop Press:* According to newspaper reports, Gary moved to Birmingham on 18 June, a £400,000 fee required to bring him to St Andrews.
Liverpool (From apprentice on 19/11/83) FL 103+6/1 FAC 10+2 Others 9
Derby Co (Loaned on 25/1/85) FL 3+3 Others 2
Hull C (Loaned on 10/9/86) FL 5
Everton (£750,000 on 14/1/92) F/PL 128/5 FLC 12 FAC 12/1 Others 4
Sheffield U (Loaned on 1/3/96) FL 12

ABRAHAMS Paul
Born: Colchester, 31 October 1973
Height: 5'9" Weight: 11.3
Tricky right footer who plays on the right wing or just behind the central strikers. Hardly selected for Brentford in the first few months of 1995-96, making just one start, he went on loan to his first club, Colchester,

where, in his third match, he scored twice in a 3-2 home win over Barnet. Returned to the Bees in February, impressing with three goals in his first two games, and was a regular for the rest of the season.
Colchester U (From trainee on 11/8/92) FL 30+25/8 FLC 2+3 FAC 4/2 Others 3/2
Brentford (£30,000 on 9/3/95) FL 21+6/6 Others 1
Colchester U (Loaned on 29/12/95) FL 8/2 Others 1

ADAMS Darren Stephen
Born: Bromley, 12 January 1974
Height: 5'7" Weight: 10.7
Hailed as a great investment when signed from non-league, Danson Furnace, early in 1994, Darren has not yet made it for Cardiff in Endsleigh League football, but has superb pace for a striker. Failed to start more than 13 games in 1995-96, despite scoring five times, before being loaned to Woking at the end of March.
Cardiff C (Free from Danson Furnace on 21/1/94) FL 21+13/4 FLC 1+1 FAC 2 Others 4+2/2

ADAMS Derek Watt
Born: Aberdeen, 25 June 1975
Height: 5'10" Weight: 11.6
A prolific scorer from midfield in Burnley's reserves, Derek was an occasional member of the first team pool and made his debut as substitute just before last Christmas. Clearly one to watch for the future.
Aberdeen (Signed from Deeside on 5/9/91)
Burnley (Signed on 24/1/95) FL 0+2

ADAMS Kieran Charles
Born: Cambridge, 20 October 1977
Height: 5'11" Weight: 11.6
From Barnet's first batch of YTS trainees, Kieran continued to improve in the reserves last season, again, making just one start for the first team as a skilful midfielder.
Barnet (Trainee) FL 3+2

ADAMS Michael (Micky) Richard
Born: Sheffield, 8 November 1961
Height: 5'8" Weight: 11.11
International Honours E: Yth
Top scorer at Fulham in his first season, left-sided midfielder Micky was sorely missed in 1995-96 after being injured in early September. His frustration at being on the sidelines for so long was eased, however, by looking after the reserve side (which finished third in the Capital League and reached the cup final), before he stepped up to become manager/coach for the first team, slumped in 23rd position in February, and easing them six places up the table by the end of play.
Gillingham (From apprentice on 1/11/79) FL 85+7/5 FLC 5 FAC 6
Coventry C (£75,000 on 19/7/83) FL 85+5/9 FLC 9/1 FAC 7 Others 2
Leeds U (£110,000 on 23/1/87) FL 72+1/2 FLC 4 FAC 6/1 Others 6
Southampton (£250,000 on 14/3/89) F/PL 141+3/7 FLC 16 FAC 8 Others 6
Stoke C (Free on 24/3/94) FL 10/3
Fulham (Free on 14/7/94) FL 23+3/8 FLC 3 FAC 2/4 Others 2/1

ADAMS Neil James
Born: Stoke, 23 November 1965
Height: 5'8" Weight: 10.8
Club Honours: CS '86; Div 1 '87, Div 2 '91
International Honours: E: U21-1
Almost an orthodox outside right, Neil has proved his versatility at Norwich with fine performances on the wing, in midfield, and even at full back. A blistering 30-yarder in the opening match of last season at Luton and a half volley at WBA were his only goals, although he hit the bar with other shots. Made the 250th league appearance of his career in the derby match versus Ipswich and left supporters wanting more after a 50-yard run past a host of defenders in the last match of 1995.
Stoke C (Signed on 1/7/85) FL 31+1/4 FLC 3 FAC 1 Others 3
Everton (£150,000 on 7/7/86) FL 17+3 FLC 4+1/1 Others 5+1
Oldham Ath (Loaned on 11/1/89) FL 9
Oldham Ath (£100,000 on 21/6/89) F/PL 93+36/23 FLC 13+2/1 FAC 10+2/2 Others 1+1
Norwich C (£250,000 on 17/2/94) P/FL 74+15/5 FLC 10+1/1 FAC 4

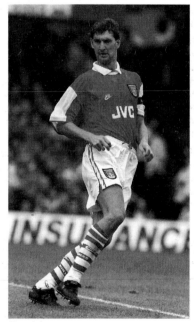

Tony Adams

ADAMS Tony Alexander
Born: Romford, 10 October 1966
Height: 6'3" Weight: 13.11
Club Honours: Div 1 '89, '91; FLC '87, '93; FAC '93; ECWC '94
International Honours: E: 45; B-4; U21-5; Yth
Unfortunately, for both club and country, Arsenal's inspirational centre back failed to make the first team after the middle of last

January, when a persistent cartilage injury eventually necessitated surgery. Even that failed to clear the problem up completely and Tony required another operation before he could make his comeback in the reserves at the end of April, in an effort to be available to serve England in Euro '96. Prior to that, however, he managed his usual quota of goals and his time honoured partnership with Steve Bould laid the foundations for the Gunners' ultimately having the best defensive record in the Premiership for 1995-96. Commanding as ever, his aerial power dominating both boxes, and difficult to pass on the ground, he was elected by his fellow professionals to the award winning Premier League side. Although England lost to Germany on a penalty shoot-out in the semi finals of the European Championships, the captain, despite carrying an injury, performed heroics throughout the tournament and could rightly be proud of his efforts.
Arsenal (From apprentice on 30/1/84) F/PL 364+3/24 FLC 53+1/5 FAC 31+1/5 Others 28/3

ADCOCK Anthony (Tony) Charles
Born: Bethnal Green, 27 February 1963
Height: 5'10" Weight: 11.9
As a former Colchester hero, he returned to his spiritual home during the 1995 close season, after nine years absence, and immediately picked up where he left off. Scored his 100th league goal for the club at Cambridge in August, only the second player to achieve three figures for the U's, and led the goalscoring charts throughout 1995-96.
Colchester U (From apprentice on 31/3/81) FL 192+18/98 FLC 16+1/5 FAC 12+2/3 Others 9/6
Manchester C (£75,000 on 1/6/87) FL 12+3/5 FLC 2+1/1 FAC 2 Others 2/3
Northampton T (£85,000 on 25/1/88) FL 72/30 FLC 6/3 FAC 1 Others 4/1
Bradford C (£190,000 on 6/10/89) FL 33+5/6 FLC 1 FAC 0+1 Others 2
Northampton T (£75,000 on 11/1/91) FL 34+1/10 FLC 1 FAC 1/1 Others 2/1
Peterborough U (£35,000 on 30/12/91) FL 107+4/35 FLC 8+1/3 FAC 5/1 Others 3+2
Luton T (£20,000 on 4/8/94) FL 0+2 FAC 0+1
Colchester U (Free on 3/8/95) FL 41/12 FLC 2/1 FAC 1 Others 3+1/4

ADEBOLA David Adeolu (Dele)
Born: Lagos, Nigeria, 23 June 1975
Height: 6'3" Weight: 12.8
Still developing as a striker with Crewe, in 1995-96 he found the mark with headers, although his strength was normally from left-foot shots. His height causes defenders problems, and he is very mobile with a deceptive turn of speed.
Crewe Alex (From trainee on 21/6/93) FL 45+21/15 FLC 2+2/1 FAC 5+1/2 Others 6+1/2

ADEKOLA David Adeolu
Born: Nigeria, 18 May 1968
Height: 5'11" Weight: 12.2
International Honours: Nigeria: 1
Strong, direct forward signed by Cambridge United on non-contract terms from Bath City at the start of last season, as cover for Steve Butler and Carlo Corazzin. However, with appearances limited to mainly those of

a substitute, David was loaned to Bishops Stortford, where he scored regularly, before a surprise move in December saw him join Cologne.
Bury (Signed on 15/1/93) FL 21+14/12 FLC 0+1 FAC 1 Others 3+1
Exeter C (Loaned on 18/2/94) FL 1+2/1
Bournemouth (Free on 29/9/94) FLC 0+1
Wigan Ath (Free on 14/10/94) FL 1+3 FAC 0+1 Others 0+1
Hereford U (Free on 2/2/95. Free to Bath C during 1995 close season)
Cambridge U (Free on 18/8/95) FL 1+4/1 FLC 2 Others 1+1/1

AGANA Patrick Anthony (Tony)
Born: Bromley, 2 October 1963
Height: 6'0" Weight: 12.2
Club Honours: AIC '95
International Honours: E: SP-1
Although signed as a goalscoring forward from Sheffield United five years ago, Tony has never showed similar striking form for Notts County and in recent seasons has been relegated to substitute as often as he made the starting line up. His 1995-96 season followed a similar pattern, being in and out of the team until March, when he reverted to a left wing position, to replace the departed Andy Legg. Enjoying a reasonable run, including the three play-off matches, although County did not make the first division, it was his cross that supplied the goal that took them to Wembley.
Watford (£35,000 from Weymouth on 13/8/87) FL 12+3/1 FLC 1+1/2 FAC 2 Others 1
Sheffield U (£45,000 on 19/2/88) FL 105+13/42 FLC 12/3 FAC 14/5 Others 4+1/1
Leeds (Loaned on 27/2/92) FL 1+1
Notts Co (£750,000 on 12/11/91) FL 97+25/12 FLC 8+1/2 FAC 5+2/2 Others 17+1/3

AGNEW Paul
Born: Lisburn, 15 August 1965
Height: 5'9" Weight: 10.12
International Honours: NI: U23-1; Yth; Sch
Sadly, WBA left back Paul missed most of the 1995-96 season through a knee injury, but is hoping to be back in contention for a first team place at The Hawthorns this coming campaign. An experienced defender, he was sorely missed by Albion until manager, Alan Buckley, recruited Shane Nicholson to fill the number three berth. Is a good tackler who likes to get forward on the overlap.
Grimsby T (£4,000 from Cliftonville on 15/2/84) FL 219+23/3 FLC 17+1 FAC 23+1 Others 12+2
West Bromwich A (£65,000 on 23/2/95) FL 17/1 FLC 1

AGNEW Stephen (Steve) Mark
Born: Shipley, 9 November 1965
Height: 5'10" Weight: 11.9
Club Honours: Div 1 '96
Midfielder Steve suffered his share of injuries in 1995-96, but still returned to enjoy his third promotion to the Premier League with a first division championship medal. Operated mostly as an outside right, and weighed in with some memorable goals, most notably, Sunderland's first strike of the season against his old club, Leicester, at Roker, and the equaliser at Old Trafford in the FA Cup-tie against Manchester United.

Barnsley (From apprentice on 10/11/83) FL 186+8/29 FLC 13/3 FAC 20/4 Others 6+1
Blackburn Rov (£700,000 on 25/6/91) FL 2 FLC 2
Portsmouth (Loaned on 21/11/92) FL 3+2 Others 2
Leicester C (£250,000 on 9/2/93) F/PL 52+4/4 FLC 4+1 FAC 2 Others 2
Sunderland (£250,000 on 11/1/95) FL 52+3/7 FLC 1 FAC 1+1/1

AGOSTINO Paul
Born: Woodville, Australia, 9 June 1975
Height: 6'0" Weight: 12.12
International Honours: Australia: 2
A skilful young forward signed from Young Boys of Berne during the 1995 close season, after having a ten-day trial at Ashton Gate the previous campaign, Paul was thrust into the Bristol City side at the outset. He equipped himself well and whilst he did not look to be an out-and-out goalscorer, his ability in holding the ball to set up chances for others, together with his excellent workrate, saw him develop into a valuable member of the Robins' team. Scored with a brilliant header against local rivals, Bristol Rovers, at Twerton Park towards the end of the campaign, and his growing stature within the game was rewarded when he won his first full international cap, as a substitute for Australia in their friendly against Chile in April.
Bristol C (£50,000 from Young Boys of Berne on 18/7/95) FL 29+11/10 FLC 4/1 Others 2+1

AINSWORTH Gareth
Born: Blackburn, 10 May 1973
Height: 5'10" Weight: 12.5
Unable to force his way into the Preston side in 1995-96, after recovering from injury, he joined his former mentor, John Beck, at Lincoln last October. A hard-working and speedy right winger, who was also used as a central striker on occasions, Gareth became a favourite with the fans, who voted him "Player of the Season", after he finished the club's leading scorer.
Preston NE (Signed from Northwich Vic, via Blackburn Rov YTS, on 21/1/92) FL 2+3 Others 1/1
Cambridge U (Free on 17/8/92) FL 1+3/1 FLC 0+1
Preston NE (Free on 23/12/92) FL 76+6/12 FLC 3+2 FAC 3+1 Others 8+1/1
Lincoln C (£25,000 on 31/10/95) FL 31/12 FAC 1 Others 3/1

AISTON Samuel (Sam) James
Born: Newcastle, 21 November 1976
Height: 6'2" Weight: 11.0
Club Honours: Div 1 '96
International Honours: E: Sch
A great future is predicted for left winger Sam. Made his league debut for Sunderland against Ipswich at Portman Road last September and immediately impressed with his ball-playing skills. Only 19, he has drawn several favourable comparisions with the young Chris Waddle, and it is undoubtedly only a matter of time before he becomes a regular at Roker. His 15 league appearances, including 11 as a sub, also entitled him to a championship medal as the club gained promotion to the Premiership.
Sunderland (Free from Newcastle U juniors on 14/7/95) FL 4+10 FLC 0+1

AKINBIYI Adeola (Ade) Peter
Born: Hackney, 10 October 1974
Height: 6'1" Weight: 12.8

Eight goals in 16 reserve games during last season meant that, given patience, his chance would come. Confident of his pace and physical strength, he opened his Norwich goal account with two in the resounding 6-1 Coca Cola Cup win over Torquay. Another important strike was his injury-time equalizer at Grimsby, with his most impressive performance coming in the vital April win over Huddersfield.
Norwich C (From trainee on 5/2/93) P/FL 19+18/3 FLC 2+2/2 FAC 1+2 Others 0+1
Hereford U (Loaned on 21/1/94) FL 3+1/2
Brighton & Hove A (Loan. d on 24/11/94) FL 7/4

ALBERT Philippe
Born: Bouillon, Belgium, 10 August 1967
Height: 6'3" Weight: 13.7
International Honours: Belgium: 39

A popular Newcastle central defender, comfortable on the ball and composed under pressure, whose majestic, long-striding sorties upfield, backed by explosive shooting, spell danger for the opposition, Philippe began last season recovering from cruciate ligament surgery and was unable to break into a team playing well until John Beresford was dismissed against Everton in December. Brought on as a substitute, he immediately demonstrated his class to become a key member of the side for the rest of the campaign, scoring six times, two of them plus an assist, away to Manchester City.
Newcastle U (£2,650,000 from Anderlecht on 10/8/94) PL 36+4/6 FLC 6+1/2 FAC 2/1 Others 4

Philippe Albert

ALCIDE Colin James
Born: Huddersfield, 14 April 1972
Height: 6'2" Weight: 12.4
Solid left-sided midfield man plucked from

non-league Emley last December and pitched straight into Lincoln's first team squad. Also used as a central striker, finishing as second top scorer, he is still very raw, but extremely powerful, and one to watch for the future.
Lincoln C (£15,000 from Emley on 5/12/95) FL 22+5/6 Others 1

ALDRIDGE John William
Born: Liverpool, 18 September 1958
Height: 5'11" Weight: 12.3
Club Honours: WC '80; Div 2 '85, Div 1 '88; FLC '86; CS '88; FAC '89
International Honours: Ei: 68

Tranmere's inspirational captain and goal-scorer became the club's player/manager in mid-April 1996, following the departure of previous boss, John King. Despite having a lean time for the team, "Aldo" topped the first division's scoring charts with 27 goals. The ultimate penalty box poacher, who is now on his way to 450 career goals, he unusually scored in ones and twos without a single hat trick. Needs just two more to become Ireland's record scorer, and hopes to continue playing international football.
Newport Co (£3,500 from South Liverpool on 2/5/79) FL 159+11/69 FLC 11/5 FAC 12+1/7 Others 4/2
Oxford U (£78,000 on 21/3/84) FL 111+3/72 FLC 17/14 FAC 5/2 Others 5/2
Liverpool (£750,000 on 27/1/87) FL 69+14/50 FLC 7+1/3 FAC 12/8 Others 1/2 (£1,000,000 to Real Sociedad on 1/9/89)
Tranmere Rov (£250,000 on 11/7/91) FL 182+3/115 FLC 21/20 FAC 7+1/4 Others 18/10

John Aldridge

ALDRIDGE Martin James
Born: Northampton, 6 December 1974
Height: 5'11" Weight: 12.2
Striker signed by Oxford on a free from Northampton last December, when Wayne Biggins left, having made just two substitute

appearances for the Cobblers in 1995-96 and been on loan at non-league Dagenham & Redbridge. It was his breakthrough into the side which helped to transform United's fortunes, when showing all the predatory instincts of namesake, John, in scoring nine in a ten goal spell, before injury ended his season.
Northampton T (From trainee on 27/8/93) FL 50+20/17 FLC 1+2 FAC 1+1/1 Others 5+2/4
Oxford U (Free on 22/12/95) FL 15+3/9 FAC 1+2

ALEXANDER Graham
Born: Coventry, 10 October 1971
Height: 5'10" Weight: 12.7

Having joined Luton from Scunthorpe during the 1995 close season, Graham proved to be a hard-tackling, determined character, operating on the right flank, either in midfield or defence. Following a hesitant start, he claimed a regular place and added muscle to the team. Although a danger at set pieces, with power-packed shooting ability, his only goal came when he ran through a retreating Grimsby defence last February.
Scunthorpe U (From trainee on 20/3/90) FL 149+10/18 FLC 11+1/2 FAC 12/1 Others 13+2/3
Luton T (£100,000 on 8/7/95) FL 35+2/1 FLC 2 FAC 0+1 Others 1+1

ALEXANDER Keith
Born: Nottingham, 14 November 1958
Height: 6'4" Weight: 13.6
International Honours: St Lucia: 3

Striker. As Mansfield's assistant manager, Keith was called upon to play in just one match last season, having the misfortune to suffer a broken leg during injury time. Five weeks later and still not walking, he accepted the hot seat with ambitious non-league outfit, Ilkeston Town.
Grimsby T (£11,500 from Barnet on 11/7/88) FL 64+19/26 FLC 4+2/1 FAC 8/1 Others 4+1/1
Stockport Co (£8,500 on 10/9/90) FL 9+2 FAC 1 Others 0+1
Lincoln C (£7,000 on 12/12/90) FL 26+19/4 FLC 1+4 FAC 1 Others 1 (Free to Malta during 1994 close season)
Mansfield T (Free on 26/8/94) FL 0+3 FLC 0+1 Others 0+1/2

ALLAN Derek Thomas
Born: Irvine, 24 December 1974
Height: 6'0" Weight: 12.1
International Honours: S: Yth

A Scottish central defender, Brighton obtained his services on loan from Southampton just before last March's transfer deadline. Just back from hernia surgery, he made his Albion FL debut at Swindon on 3 April 1996, coming through safely. Although good in the air, very quick on the ground, and a ball winner, he was deemed surplus to requirements and given a free transfer during the summer.
Ayr U (Trainee) SL 5
Southampton (£75,000 on 16/3/93) PL 0+1
Brighton & Hove A (Loaned on 28/3/96) FL 8

ALLARDYCE Craig Samuel
Born: Bolton, 9 June 1975
Height: 6'3" Weight: 13.7
Blackpool defender. Having done well in the reserves, Craig finally broke his duck after 15 months at Bloomfield Road, when coming off the bench for David Linighan in

the match against Bradford last December. Is the son of former 'Pool manager, Sam.
Preston NE (From trainee on 16/7/93) FL 0+1 (Free to Macclesfield T on 16/4/94)
Blackpool (Free from Northwich Vic on 20/9/94) FL 0+1

ALLEN Bradley James
Born: Romford, 13 September 1971
Height: 5'7" Weight: 10.0
International Honours: E: U21-8; Yth
Skilful Charlton centre forward who is aware of team mates' positions and both lively and sharp around the penalty area. Prior to his move to the Valley last March, Bradley's early season form at QPR was punctuated by injury, with four hernia operations early on. Came back to the side during the New Year, scoring in his second game against Chelsea, before signing for Charlton after six further appearances. Following an excellent start for the Addicks, with a goal at Norwich on his debut, he became the fifth different player to score from the penalty spot, when netting against Luton. Will prove a valuable asset when fully settled in.
Queens Park R (From juniors on 30/9/88) F/PL 56+25/27 FLC 5+2/5 FAC 3+2 Others 1
Charlton Ath (£400,000 on 28/3/96) FL 10/3 Others 1+1

ALLEN Christopher (Chris) Anthony
Born: Oxford, 18 November 1972
Height: 5'11" Weight: 12.2
International Honours: E: U21-2
Speedy Oxford winger or central striker, who had an eventful season. Started 1995-96 "on fire" and was top scorer until the home defeat by Wycombe, after which he lost his place. Struggling to reclaim his wide berth, the former England U21 and Endsleigh representative player went on loan to the Premiership's Nottingham Forest, for whom he scored on his full debut at Middlesbrough. Chris had hoped for a permanent move, but no fee could be decided prior to transfer deadline day and he remained at the Manor Ground.
Oxford U (From trainee on 14/5/91) FL 110+40/12 FLC 11+2/4 FAC 5+5/1 Others 5+3
Nottingham F (Loaned on 24/2/96) PL 1+2/1

ALLEN Clive Darren
Born: Stepney, 20 May 1961
Height: 5'10" Weight: 12.3
Club Honours: Div 2 '83
International Honours: E: 5; U21-3; Fl Rep; Yth; Sch
A former England international and a highly experienced forward and proven goalscorer, who made three appearances for Carlisle last autumn while on a short-term contract, he showed some class touches, but was unable to add to his considerable goal tally. At his peak, Clive, more often than not, had the uncanny knack of being in the right place at the right time.
Queens Park R (From trainee on 20/9/78) FL 43+6/32 FLC 5/2 FAC 1
Arsenal (£1,250,000 on 13/6/80)
Crystal Palace (£1,250,000 on 14/8/80) FL 25/9 FLC 4/2
Queens Park R (£700,000 on 8/6/81) FL 83+4/40 FLC 7/2 FAC 8/7
Tottenham H (£750,000 on 16/8/84) FL 97+8/60

FLC 13+1/3 FAC 12+1/9 Others 9/3 (£1,000,000 to Bordeaux on 10/5/88)
Manchester C (£1,100,000 on 18/8/89) FL 31+22/16 FLC 5+2/4 FAC 4+2/1 Others 2
Chelsea (£250,000 on 6/12/91) FL 15+1/7 FAC 4+1/2 Others 3
West Ham U £275,000 on 27/3/92) F/PL 36+2/17 FLC 2 FAC 2+2/1 Others 6/3
Millwall (£75,000 on 25/3/94) FL 11+1 Others 1
Carlisle U (Free on 7/9/95) FL 3

ALLEN Gavin
Born: Bangor, 17 June 1976
Height: 5'8" Weight: 10.5
International Honours: W: Yth
Forward. Snapped up by Stockport on a free transfer from Tranmere in the 1995 close season, despite being a mainstay in the successful reserve side at Edgeley Park, his only first team outing came as a substitute in the Coca Cola Cup draw with Ipswich. Joined Runcorn on transfer deadline day in 1996.
Tranmere Rov (From trainee on 12/7/94)
Stockport Co (Free on 21/6/95) FLC 0+1

ALLEN Martin James
Born: Reading, 14 August 1965
Height: 5'10" Weight: 11.0
International Honours: E: U21-2; Yth
After playing three early season games for West Ham in 1995-96, and scoring one goal, Martin was loaned to Portsmouth in September, where he produced a number of key performances that resulted in the move being firmed up in February, albeit with him having had to spend a month back at Upton Park in the meantime. Captaining the side in Guy Butters' absence, the midfielder showed all the battling and shooting skills for which he is recognised. From the famous "Allen" footballing family, his father, Dennis, played for Charlton, Reading and Bournemouth.
Queens Park R (From apprentice on 27/5/83) FL 128+8/16 FLC 15+3/1 FAC 9/1 Others 2/1
West Ham U (£675,000 on 24/8/89) F/PL 163+27/26 FLC 15+3/5 FAC 14/4 Others 10
Portsmouth (Loaned on 11/9/95) FL 15/3
Portsmouth (£500,000 on 22/2/96) FL 12/1

ALLEN Paul Kevin
Born: Aveley, 28 August 1962
Height: 5'7" Weight: 11.4
Club Honours: FAC '80, '91; CS '91; Div 2 '96
International Honours: E: U21-3; Yth (UEFAYC '80)
Signed on a free transfer from Southampton last October, Paul immediately became a favourite with Swindon fans with his foraging runs down the right flank. Although approaching the veteran stage, his commitment and thirst for the game was an inspiration to the younger members of the side and winning a second division championship medal was a fitting reward.
West Ham U (From apprentice on 29/8/79) FL 149+3/6 FLC 20+4/2 FAC 15+3/3 Others 2+1
Tottenham H (£400,000 on 19/6/85) FL 276+16/23 FLC 42+2/4 FAC 26+1/1 Others 12+2
Southampton (£550,000 on 16/9/93) PL 40+3/1 FLC 4 FAC 2
Luton T (Loaned on 9/12/94) FL 4
Stoke C (Loaned on 20/1/95) FL 17/1 Others 2
Swindon T (Free on 11/10/95) FL 25+2 FAC 5/1 Others 1

ALLINSON Jamie
Born: Stockton, 15 June 1978
Height: 6'1" Weight: 12.7
A promising left-sided defender, and a second year trainee with Hartlepool, Jamie was thrown in at the deep end, late in 1995, his second game being an important FA Cup-tie against local rivals, Darlington. Rated a good prospect, he was not rushed, but got few opportunities because of Sean McAuley's consistency.
Hartlepool U (Trainee) FL 3+1 FAC 1 Others 1

ALLISON Neil James
Born: Hull, 20 October 1973
Height: 6'2" Weight: 11.10
With Gary Hobson moving to Brighton, this stopper centre half became Hull's current longest serving player, along with Steve Wilson (both aged 22). Relying on his right foot, and strong in the air, "Spanner" added the occasional vital goal to his repertoire. Suspensions disrupted an encouraging campaign and a crucial 1996-97 awaits.
Hull C (From trainee on 13/7/92) FL 84+11/3 FLC 7/1 FAC 3 Others 6+1

ALLISON Wayne Anthony
Born: Huddersfield, 16 October 1968
Height: 6'1" Weight: 13.5
Club Honours: Div 2 '96
A 1995 close season signing from rivals, Bristol City, the big Yorkshireman enjoyed an outstanding season with Swindon at the County Ground, finishing as top scorer with 20 goals and winning a second division championship medal. Strong and brave, with an exceptional workrate, he lead the line well and was a valuable extra defender when needed.
Halifax T (From trainee on 6/7/87) FL 74+10/23 FLC 3/2 FAC 4+1/2 Others 8+1/3
Watford (£250,000 on 26/7/89) FL 6+1
Bristol C (£300,000 on 9/8/90) F/PL 149+46/48 FLC 4+5/2 FAC 12+1/5 Others 6+2/2
Swindon T (£475,000 on 22/7/95) FL 43+1/17 FLC 3/1 FAC 6/2 Others 3

Wayne Allison

Joe Allon

ALLON Joseph (Joe) Ball
Born: Gateshead, 12 November 1966
Height: 5'11" Weight: 12.2
Club Honours: FAYC '85
International Honours: E: Yth

Natural goalscorer who had a difficult 1995-96. Having been signed during the summer from Port Vale, he began a brief but unhappy spell with Lincoln City, before re-joining Hartlepool on a three year contract in October. His return to the scene of former glories was not an immediate success, and for much of the season he was not fully fit, however, he proved he was still a fine opportunist by scoring nine goals to finish the club's joint top scorer.

Newcastle U (From trainee on 16/11/84) FL 9/2 FLC 1
Swansea C (Free on 6/8/87) FL 27+7/11 FLC 2 FAC 2 Others 2/1
Hartlepool U (Free on 29/11/88) FL 112/48 FLC 5/2 FAC 6+1/5 Others 7/2
Chelsea (£250,000 on 14/8/91) FL 3+11/2 FLC 0+2 Others 1+1/1
Port Vale (Loaned on 27/2/92) FL 2+4
Brentford (£275,000 on 19/11/92) FL 38+7/19 FLC 2 FAC 2/2 Others 7/7
Southend U (Loaned on 16/9/93) FL 2+1
Port Vale (Signed on 24/3/94) FL 13+10/9 FLC 0+1 FAC 2/1
Lincoln C (£42,500 on 17/7/95) FL 3+1 FLC 1
Hartlepool U (£42,500 on 13/10/95) FL 22/8 Others 2/1

ALSFORD Julian
Born: Poole, 24 December 1972
Height: 6'2" Weight: 13.7

Chester City central defender who turned in some solid performances during 1995-96. Strong in the air, Julian also made a few appearances in the right back position as cover for injuries.

Watford (From trainee on 30/4/91) FL 9+4/1 FLC 1 Others 2
Chester C (Free on 11/8/94) FL 54+5 FLC 4+1 FAC 3 Others 4

AMMANN Michael (Mike) Anton
Born: California, USA, 8 February 1971
Height: 6'2" Weight: 14.4

An American goalkeeper regarded by many as being worthy of a regular place at Charlton, Mike had only limited opportunities in the first team last season. Having enjoyed a run of nine consecutive games in late 1995, culminating in a superb performance at Barnsley which earned him rave reviews, he was surprisingly dropped, in favour of fit again Mike Salmon. Although he played a couple more times later in the campaign, injury limited his appearances.

Charlton Ath (Free from LA Cobras on 20/7/94) FL 28+2 FLC 1

AMOKACHI Daniel Owofen
Born: Groko, Nigeria, 30 December 1972
Height: 5'10" Weight: 13.0
Club Honours: FAC '95, CS '95
International Honours: Nigeria: 27

Lightening fast Everton striker, who combines speed and strength with good skills, often bringing the ball under control with various parts of the body. Following an inconsistent first season, he began 1995-96 initially on the subs' bench, before grabbing his chance with three goals in four games. Unfortunately, a barren scoring spell, along with indifferent performances, later saw him in and out of the side. However, back in favour in the New Year, a good understanding firstly with Paul Rideout and then Duncan Ferguson, finally established him as a first team regular.

Everton (£3,000,000 from FC Bruges on 27/8/94) PL 34+9/10 FLC 3 FAC 2+3/2 Others 3/1

AMPADU Patrick Kwame
Born: Bradford, 20 December 1970
Height: 5'10" Weight: 11.10
Club Honours: AMC '94
International Honours: Ei: U21-4; Yth

With injuries decimating the Swansea squad last season, Kwame's form throughout the campaign was affected, as he was switched between left back and the left side of midfield. An exciting player going forward, he also possesses sound defensive qualities.

Arsenal (From trainee on 19/11/88) FL 0+2
Plymouth Arg (Loaned on 31/10/90) FL 6/1 Others 1
West Bromwich A (£50,000 on 24/6/91) FL 27+22/4 FLC 6+1 FAC 1 Others 5/1
Swansea C (£15,000 on 16/2/94) FL 87+13/8 FLC 5+1/1 FAC 3/1 Others 12/1

ANDERSEN Lief Erik
Born: Fredrickstad, Norway, 19 April 1971
Height: 6'5" Weight: 14.1

Tall Norwegian central defender who joined Crystal Palace from Norwegian club, Moss FK, last January, following a two month trial. Made his Palace debut in mid-February versus Watford in a 4-0 victory and was a regular performer as first choice or as a substitute to the end of the season, before losing his place to Robert Quinn in the division one play-off final. At 6ft 5ins, he is believed to be Palace's tallest ever player!

Crystal Palace (£120,000 from Moss FK on 18/1/96) FL 12+4

ANDERSON Colin Russell
Born: Newcastle, 26 April 1962
Height: 5'8" Weight: 10.8

Left-footed defender. Troubled by injuries again last season, Colin did not have a consistent spell in the team and could not show the Exeter City fans how good a performer he is. Has twice won the club's "Player of the Year" award.

Burnley (From apprentice on 29/4/80) FL 3+3
Torquay U (Free on 18/9/82) FL 107+2/11 FLC 5 FAC 7/1 Others 3
West Bromwich A (£20,000 on 27/3/85) FL 131+9/10 FLC 5+2 FAC 2/2 Others 2+1
Walsall (Free on 22/8/91) FL 25+1/2 FAC 2 Others 4
Hereford U (Free on 13/8/92) FL 67+3/1 FLC 4+1 FAC 2+2 Others 5
Exeter C (Free on 14/7/94) FL 26+8/1 FLC 1

ANDERSON Ijah Massai
Born: Hackney, 30 December 1975
Height: 5'8" Weight: 10.6

A talented left-sided player with plenty of pace as well as defensive awareness, Ijah joined Brentford in the 1995 close season and started on the left wing. Was out of the side for a while before returning firstly as a left back, and then as a wing/back when the formation changed. Had an excellent second half to the season, allowing the Bees to sell Martin Grainger to Birmingham.

Southend U (Free from Tottenham H juniors on 2/8/94)
Brentford (Free on 31/7/95) FL 25/2 FLC 2/1 FAC 1+2 Others 0+1

ANDERSSON Karl Magnus
Born: Koping, Sweden, 7 August 1975
Height: 6'4" Weight: 13.0

On trial from Norkoping, the tall Swedish striker made just one subs' appearance for Darlington in the AWS competition at home to Lincoln last November, before returning home.

Darlington (Free from Norkoping on 6/11/95) Others 0+1

ANDERTON Darren Robert
Born: Southampton, 3 March 1972
Height: 6'1" Weight: 12.0
International Honours: E: 16; U21-12; Yth

A brilliant winger whose club season was ruined by a succession of niggling injuries, starting with a groin strain, Darren's absence from the Tottenham team began in the summer and, despite making a comeback for the home victory over Leeds last September, it was only two and a half games later that he was pulled off at Queens Park Rangers with a re-occurrence of the injury which was to lead to a spell of treatment and operations that would keep him out of the first team for a period of nearly eight months. However, on returning to first team action against Arsenal at Highbury in April, he was quick to show that his long spell out of action had not eroded his talent, nor was he going to take things easy on his return, proving this emphatically against Leeds at Elland Road in May, when he scored two goals of great quality. Happily, this was enough to convince England manager, Terry Venables, of his fitness and he made a triumphant return to international football with two

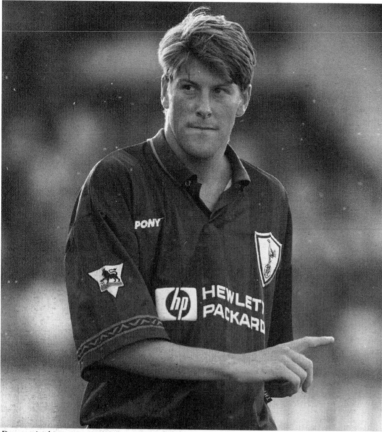

Darren Anderton

goals in the 3-0 victory over Hungary in May and booked his passage to the European Championship finals, where he played in all five matches.

Portsmouth (From trainee on 5/2/90) FL 53+9/7 FLC 3+2/1 FAC 7+1/5 Others 2
Tottenham H (£1,750,000 on 3/6/92) PL 110+6/19 FLC 10/2 FAC 13+1/2

ANDREWS Ian Edmund
Born: Nottingham, 1 December 1964
Height: 6'2" Weight: 12.13
International Honours: E: U21-1; Yth
Started last season as Bournemouth's first choice goalkeeper and started every game until the end of October when he suffered a broken finger. A vastly experienced player, after returning in December he played a further 13 games until matters off the field saw him replaced by the newly signed, Jimmy Glass. Good with crosses, and cutting an imposing figure between the sticks, Ian is extremely agile for a big man.
Leicester C (From apprentice on 6/12/82) FL 126 FLC 6 FAC 7
Swindon T (Loaned on 1/1/84) FL 1
Glasgow Celtic (£300,000 on 26/7/88) SL 5 SLC 2 Others 1
Leeds U (Loaned on 15/12/88) FL 1
Southampton (£200,000 on 22/12/89) F/PL 10 Others 1
Bournemouth (£20,000 on 5/9/94) FL 64 FLC 7 FAC 2 Others 3

ANDREWS Philip (Phil)
Born: Andover, 14 September 1976
Height: 5'11" Weight: 11.0
As a keen and energetic young reserve striker, he had several first team Brighton appearances in 1995-96. Set up the winner for Junior McDougald after coming off the bench in the home league match against Notts County on 2 September 1995 and has a promising future.
Brighton & Hove A (From trainee on 17/5/95) FL 1+17 FLC 1+2 FAC 1+2 Others 1+2

ANDREWS Wayne Michael Hill
Born: Paddington, 25 November 1977
Height: 5'10" Weight: 11.2
Seventeen-year-old powerful Watford YTS striker who was given an early first team chance in 1995-96 as a substitute, because of injuries.
Watford (Trainee) FL 0+1

ANGEL Mark
Born: Newcastle, 23 August 1975
Height: 5'8" Weight: 11.1
A tricky Oxford winger signed in the summer of 1995 from Sunderland on a free, Mark did well in pre-season, sporting a Gazza like haircut, and earned a contract. With Chris Allen in form, however, he had to wait on the bench for a game, but when in

the side he held a place for a long spell and was equally at home on either side. Used trickery to get in his crosses and worked hard. Is very popular with the fans.
Sunderland (From Walker Central on 31/12/93)
Oxford U (Free on 9/8/95) FL 16+11/1 FLC 0+1 FAC 4+1 Others 2+1/1

ANGELL Brett Ashley
Born: Marlborough, 20 August 1968
Height: 6'2" Weight: 13.11
1995-96 was a frustrating season for Brett. After opening his Sunderland goalscoring account at Preston, in the Coca Cola Cup, the powerful centre forward found himself out of favour and was allowed to go on loan to Sheffield United and then West Bromwich Albion. Required by United, following the sale of Nathan Blake, despite scoring in successive games against WBA and Barnsley, his one month loan period was not extended and after arriving at Albion, this time for two months, as back-up for Andy Hunt and Bob Taylor, he made just two subs' appearances.
Portsmouth (From trainee on 1/8/86)
Derby Co (£40,000 from Cheltenham T on 19/2/88)
Stockport Co (£33,000 on 20/10/88) FL 60+10/28 FLC 3 FAC 3/1 Others 8/4
Southend U (£100,000 on 2/8/90) FL 109+6/47 FLC 7+1/4 FAC 3/2 Others 9+1/10
Everton (£500,000 on 17/1/94) PL 16+4/1 FLC 0+1
Sunderland (£600,000 on 23/3/95) FL 10 FLC 1/1
Sheffield U (Loaned on 30/1/96) FL 6/2
West Bromwich A (Loaned on 28/3/96) FL 0+3

ANGUS Terence (Terry) Norman
Born: Coventry, 14 January 1966
Height: 6'0" Weight: 13.9
For a long period in 1995-96, the central defender was one of Fulham's most consistent players. Never giving less than a 100 per cent and a great favourite with the crowd, he has not found it easy to adapt to the passing game introduced by Micky Adams, but his superb run and pass, which set up the winner against Wigan, showed he is getting there.
Northampton T (£15,000 from VS Rugby on 22/8/90) FL 115+1/6 FLC 7 FAC 5+1 Others 9
Fulham (Free on 12/7/93) FL 79+11/4 FLC 5+1 FAC 6/2 Others 11

ANNON Darren Carlton
Born: Chelsea, 17 February 1972
Height: 5'5" Weight: 10.11
A tricky winger who can operate down either flank, he made just one appearance for Brentford in 1995-96 before being released on a free transfer. Joined Stevenage Borough, the GMVC League leaders, in February 1996 on trial.
Brentford (£20,000 from Carshalton on 8/3/94) FL 14+6/2 FAC 1/1 Others 1+1/1

ANSAH Andrew (Andy)
Born: Lewisham, 19 March 1969
Height: 5'10" Weight: 11.1
Loaned out to Brentford last November, Andy was released by Southend in mid-March, trialing at Peterborough, before signing for Gillingham on transfer deadline day. A slightly built right winger, there were few chances to impress as Gillingham went for one of the promotion spots. Hard-

working, and always looking to take full backs on, he can be a thorn in the opposition's side, with early crosses from either foot.

Brentford (Free from Dorking on 21/3/89) FL 3+5/2 FLC 0+1
Southend U (Free on 29/3/90) FL 141+16/33 FLC 7+2 FAC 4 Others 7+3/5
Brentford (Loaned on 4/11/94) FL 2+1/1 Others 2/1
Brentford (Loaned on 15/11/95) FL 6/1 Others 1
Peterborough U (Free on 15/3/96) FL 0+2/1
Gillingham (Free on 28/3/96) FL 0+2

ANTHONY Graham John
Born: South Shields, 9 August 1975
Height: 5'10" Weight: 10.8
A young, slightly-built Sheffield United midfielder, who spent the summer of 1995 in Finland on loan to further his football education, his only first team appearance last season came in the Coca Cola Cup against Bury, before he returned to the reserves to continue gaining experience. Having signed a one year contract in January, Graham had another spell on loan, this time at Scarborough in March, and looked confident on the ball, but struggled to make an impact.
Sheffield U (From trainee on 7/7/93) FL 0+1 FLC 1 Others 2
Scarborough (Loaned on 1/3/96) FL 2

ANTHROBUS Stephen (Steve) Anthony
Born: Lewisham, 10 November 1968
Height: 6'2" Weight: 12.13
Striker. Signed by Shrewsbury immediately prior to 1995-96 getting underway, following few chances at Wimbledon, "Throb" quickly became a firm crowd favourite. Physically strong on the ball, good in the air, and a continual threat to defences, he improved as the season developed. Scored most of his goals in the second half of the campaign and is a real 110 per center.
Millwall (From juniors on 4/8/86) FL 19+2/4 FLC 3 Others 1
Wimbledon (£150,000 on 16/2/90) F/PL 27+1 FLC 1 FAC 2
Peterborough U (Loaned on 21/1/94) FL 2
Chester C (Loaned on 26/8/94) FL 7
Shrewsbury T (£25,000 on 8/8/95) FL 27+12/10 FLC 2+1 FAC 3+3/1 Others 5+1

APPLEBY Matthew (Matty) Wilfred
Born: Middlesbrough, 16 April 1972
Height: 5'10" Weight: 11.5
Outstanding in Darlington's defence and midfield all last season, Matty was voted "Player of the Year", having already announced that his last game for the club would be at Wembley in the third division play-off final, his contract having expired.
Newcastle U (From trainee on 4/5/90) F/PL 18+2 FLC 2+1 FAC 2 Others 2+2
Darlington (Loaned on 25/11/93) FL 10/1 Others 1
Darlington (Free on 15/6/94) FL 77+2/7 FLC 2 FAC 4 Others 8/3

APPLEBY Richard Dean
Born: Middlesbrough, 18 September 1975
Height: 5'8" Weight: 10.6
International Honours: E: Yth
The younger brother of Darlington's Matthew, and a left-sided midfielder with

the ability to dribble past defenders, Richard joined Ipswich from Newcastle last December. However, after failing to establish himself at Portman Road, following just four appearances, three of them from the bench, he was released at the end of the season.
Newcastle U From trainee on 12/8/93) Others 2
Ipswich T (Free on 12/12/95) FL 0+3 Others 1

APPLETON Michael Antony
Born: Salford, 4 December 1975
Height: 5'9" Weight: 11.13
A teenage midfielder brought in on loan from Manchester United last September, Michael had little chance to shine in a struggling Lincoln team, after making his league debut in a 5-1 defeat at Chester. Returning to Old Trafford when his loan period was up, he has yet to make a United debut.
Manchester U (From trainee on 1/7/94)
Lincoln C (Loaned on 15/9/95) FL 4 Others 1

ARCHDEACON Owen Duncan
Born: Greenock, 4 March 1966
Height: 5'7" Weight: 11.0
Club Honours: SPD '86
International Honours: S: U21-1; Yth
Having put the nightmare of 1994-95 behind him by reclaiming his Barnsley left back position, his ability to get into the opposition's penalty area unmarked was shown on a number of occasions last season, although his final goal tally was disappointing.
Glasgow Celtic (From Gourock U on 20/8/82) SL 38+38/7 SLC 1+4/1 SC 3+1 Others 1+3
Barnsley (£80,000 on 7/7/89) FL 222+11/23 FLC 15+1/2 FAC 14+1/2 Others 9+1/4

ARCHER Lee
Born: Bristol, 6 November 1972
Height: 5'9" Weight 11.4
An attacking left winger, Lee's probing runs were badly missed by Bristol Rovers for most of last season, after he suffered an unfortunate knee injury which required surgery in November. He recovered to play in Rovers' final dozen matches, with his crossing ability being an added bonus, as the club unsuccessfully strived for a second division play-off place.
Bristol Rov (From trainee on 18/7/91) FL 86+19/13 FLC 5 FAC 5+1/2 Others 9+2/1

ARDLEY Neil Christopher
Born: Epsom, 1 September 1972
Height: 5'11" Weight: 11.9
International Honours: E: U21-10
A very skilful young Wimbledon player who is a good option for Joe Kinnear, in that he is useful in both full back or midfield positions, Neal made a late start to last season after first twisting an ankle and then pulling a hamstring. Building up his strength with the reserves, he came back to make six first team appearances and still looks on target for a promising future, provided he can maintain match fitness. Not just a strong tackler, but a man who also likes to get forward.
Wimbledon (From trainee on 29/7/91) F/PL 59+12/6 FLC 9+2/2 FAC 8+2

ARKINS Vincent (Vince)
Born: Dublin, 18 September 1970
Height: 6'2" Weight: 11.10
International Honours: Ei: B-1; U21-8: Yth
Forward. Signed by Notts County from Irish League club, Shelbourne, last September, making his league debut soon afterwards at Shrewsbury, he began brightly with seven goals in his first 15 games, but in the closing weeks of the campaign was eclipsed by later signings, Tony Battersby, Gary Jones, and Gary Martindale, and spent most games on the bench. Although he possesses a strong shot, he was felt to lack a little pace, which may be remedied in time for 1996-97, and did not make the play offs.
Dundee U (Signed from Home Farm on 9/12/87. Transferred back on 11/10/89)
St Johnstone (Signed on 25/11/91) SL 38+10/11 SLC 1 SC 7/2 (Transferred to Shelbourne on 15/10/93)
Notts Co (£100,000 on 12/9/95) FL 17+6/7 FLC 1+1 FAC 3 Others 4

Alun Armstrong

ARMSTRONG Alun
Born: Gateshead, 22 February 1975
Height: 6'1" Weight: 11.13
Stockport's young blond Geordie striker continued to mature in 1995-96, topping the goalscoring charts for the second season running. Despite the club's failure to find him a regular up-front partner, Alun attracted a host of Premership scouts after scoring at Everton in the FA Cup draw and again in the replay.
Newcastle U (From trainee on 1/10/93)
Stockport Co (£50,000 on 23/6/94) FL 84+7/27 FLC 8/3 FAC 4+1/3 Others 4

ARMSTRONG Christopher (Chris) Peter
Born: Newcastle, 19 June 1971
Height: 6'0" Weight: 13.3
Club Honours: Div 1 '94
International Honours: E: B-1
A striker who joined Tottenham from Crystal Palace in the summer of 1995, with the unenviable task of replacing Jurgen Klinsmann, the early part of 1995-96 saw Chris struggling to adapt to Spurs'

formation. However, after opening his account with two fine goals against Chester City in the Coca Cola Cup, he went on to score 22 goals in all competitions. Extremely dangerous when heading the ball with terrific pace, the now confident front man produced some of his best goals against the top 'keepers, aptly demonstrated with a terrific lob over Neville Southall against Everton in October and a well timed header to beat Shaka Hislop in the 1-1 draw with Newcastle in October. He undoubtedly benefited from the support of Teddy Sheringham, the partnership's strike total being second only to that of Robbie Fowler and Stan Collymore for Liverpool, and his winner against Arsenal in November will be remembered fondly by Tottenham fans as a season's highlight. Almost certainly on the brink of an England call-up next season.
Wrexham (Free from Llay Welfare on 3/3/89) FL 40+20/13 FLC 2+1 FAC 0+1 Others 5+1/3
Millwall (£50,000 on 16/8/91) FL 11+17/5 FLC 3+1/2 FAC 0+1 Others 0+1
Crystal Palace (£1,000,000 on 1/9/92) F/PL 118/45 FLC 8/6 FAC 8/5 Others 2/1
Tottenham H (£4,500,000 on 30/6/95) PL 36/15 FLC 3/3 FAC 6/4

ARMSTRONG Steven Craig
Born: South Shields, 23 May 1975
Height: 5'11" Weight: 12.4
A confident, attacking left back, unable to make the Nottingham Forest first team, despite being a named substitute for the UEFA Cup tie against Bayern Munich, Craig had two separate loan spells at Bristol Rovers in 1995-96. Initially arriving in January, following Andy Gurney's unavailability, he played four games, before coming back again in March, where he saw out the remainder of the season. Impressed both management and fans during his stays.
Nottingham F (From trainee on 2/6/92)
Burnley (Loaned on 10/7/85) FL 4
Bristol Rov (Loaned on 8/1/96) FL 4
Bristol Rov (Loaned on 28/3/96) FL 9+1

ARMSTRONG Gordon Ian
Born: Newcastle, 15 July 1967
Height: 6'0" Weight: 12.11
Club Honours: Div 3 '88
As Sunderland's longest-serving player, Gordon made only two substitute appearances last term, before enjoying loan spells at Bristol City, where he displayed good form in the six games played, and then at Northampton. A revelation on the left side of the Cobblers' midfield, he crowned a great performance on his home debut with a brilliant free kick winner against Cardiff.
Sunderland (From apprentice on 10/7/85) FL 331+18/50 FLC 25+4/3 FAC 19/4 Others 18+1/4
Bristol C (Loaned on 24/8/95) FL 6
Northampton T (Loaned on 5/1/96) FL 4/1 Others 1

ARNOTT Andrew (Andy) John
Born: Chatham, 18 October 1973
Height: 6'1" Weight: 12.0
Having lost his place in the centre of Gillingham's defence early last season, Andy took in a number of trials before joining Leyton Orient in January. Playing mainly in defence, but equally impressive as

a striker, especially when scoring a late equaliser against his former club, he appeared in every available game and definitely looks to be one to watch out for.
Gillingham (From trainee on 13/5/91) FL 50+23/12 FLC 2+3 FAC 10+2/1 Others 3+2
Leyton Orient (£15,000 on 25/1/96) FL 19/3

ASABA Carl
Born: London, 28 January 1973
Height: 6'2" Weight: 13.0
Hard-running, bustling Brentford centre forward, who is a useful target man. Had an early run-in the side last season with 11 starts, but despite some good play he did not score a goal and thereafter dropped out of contention. Came back, however, to score twice in the final game, a 2-0 home win over Bournemouth.
Brentford (Free from Dulwich Hamlet on 9/8/94) FL 5+5/2 FLC 1 FAC 1 Others 2/1
Colchester U (Loaned on 16/2/95) FL 9+3/2

ASHBY Barry John
Born: Park Royal, 21 November 1970
Height: 6'2" Weight: 13.2
Club Honours: FAYC '89
Steady and reliable Brentford central defender who is good in the air. Although never quite hitting the peak form of the previous season, 1995-96 saw him continue to build up a good understanding with team mate, Jamie Bates, even though the Bees struggled throughout the campaign.
Watford (From trainee on 1/12/88) FL 101+13/3 FLC 6 FAC 4 Others 2+1
Brentford (Signed on 22/3/94) FL 79+2/3 FLC 7 FAC 6/1 Others 8

ASHCROFT Lee
Born: Preston, 7 September 1972
Height: 5'10" Weight: 11.2
International Honours: E: U21-1
A right or left winger with good pace and ability, who had a mixed season at WBA, eventually being loaned out to Notts County (from March), he was never able to hold down a regular place in the side and was always struggling to find his form. Very tricky, he can overdo it at times, but can score valuable goals, especially when turning up in the penalty area unnoticed. Also, has a terrific right-footed shot.
Preston NE (From trainee on 16/7/91) FL 78+13/13 FLC 3 FAC 5 Others 6+2/1
West Bromwich A (£250,000 on 1/8/93) FL 64+21/17 FLC 2+2 FAC 3+1/1 Others 8+3
Notts Co (Loaned on 28/3/96) FL 4+2

ASHLEY Kevin Mark
Born: Birmingham, 31 December 1968
Height: 5'7" Weight: 11.10
Having fought his way back into the Peterborough side at right back last October, and then playing 14 consecutive games, he was replaced first by Carl Hooper and then by Lee Williams, before joining Doncaster on transfer deadline day. Signed on a three month contract, the tidy Kevin will be a useful acquisition if his long-standing injury problems are behind him.
Birmingham C (From apprentice on 7/1/87) FL 56+1/1 FLC 5 FAC 3 Others 1+1
Wolverhampton W (£500,000 on 13/9/90) FL 87+1/1 FLC 5 FAC 1+1 Others 4

Peterborough U (Free on 10/8/94) FL 36 FLC 3 FAC 4 Others 2
Doncaster Rov (Free on 28/3/96) FL 3

ASPIN Neil
Born: Gateshead, 12 April 1965
Height: 6'0" Weight: 12.6
Club Honours: AMC '93
Excellent Port Vale defender who suffered a bad dislocation of the shoulder in only the third game of last season. Returned to the first team ahead of schedule against leaders, Derby County, which coincided with the club's best run of the season in reaching the fifth round of the FA Cup and a place in the top half of the table. Neil, who was re-appointed team captain in March 1995 soon after playing at Wembley in the Anglo-Italian Cup Final, can play at full back or in the centre of defence with equal reliability.
Leeds U (From apprentice on 6/10/82) FL 203+4/5 FLC 9/1 FAC 17 Others 11
Port Vale (£200,000 on 28/7/89) FL 257+2/3 FLC 13 FAC 20 Others 18

Neil Aspin

ASPINALL Warren
Born: Wigan, 13 September 1967
Height: 5'9" Weight: 11.12
Club Honours: AMC '85
International Honours: E: Yth
Signed from Bournemouth during the 1995 close season after several games for Carlisle on loan towards the end of 1994-95. A midfielder, who likes to get into forward positions, he featured in the majority of the club's fixtures and was voted "Away Player of the Season" by supporters. Despite the sobriquet of "Sumo", he possesses good acceleration and his goals included Carlisle's first ever on live TV in the 4-2 defeat of Wycombe.
Wigan Ath (From apprentice on 31/8/85) FL 21+12/10 FLC 1 FAC 2+3/2 Others 1+5/2
Everton (£150,000 on 4/2/86) FL 0+7 FLC 0+1 Others 0+2
Wigan Ath (Loaned on 6/2/86) FL 18/12 Others 2/2
Aston Villa (£300,000 on 19/2/87) FL 40+4/14 FLC 4/2 FAC 1+1
Portsmouth (£315,000 on 26/8/88) FL 97+35/21 FLC 8+3/3 FAC 4+5/2 Others 6+1/2

Bournemouth (Loaned on 27/8/93) FL 4+2/1
Swansea C (Loaned on 14/10/93) FL 5 Others 1
Bournemouth (£20,000 on 31/12/93) FL 26+1/8 FLC 4 FAC 1 Others 1
Carlisle U (Free on 8/3/95) FL 42+7/7 FLC 2/1 FAC 1 Others 4+1/1

ASPRILLA Hinestroza **Faustino (Tino)** Hernan
Born: Tulua, Colombia, 10 November 1969
Height: 5'9" Weight: 11.9
Internationa Honours: Colombia: 39

After a prolonged transfer, Tino flew into Teeside from Parma, Italy only four hours before making his Newcastle debut against Middlesbrough last February and, introduced as a substitute, he made an early impact, turning the game by creating an equaliser for Steve Watson. Playing alongside Les Ferdinand, his nonchalant, loose-limbed grace and skills tended to disguise his deceptive pace, but, as an exciting and unpredictable player with a keen eye for goal, he also worked unselfishly to provide opportunities for team mates and quickly established himself as a favourite with the supporters. Was found guilty of misconduct by the FA, following clashes with Keith Curle during the game at Manchester City, in which he scored his first goal for the club. Is a former Colombian "Footballer of the Year" and a current international.
Newcastle U (£7,500,000 from Parma, via Cueuta Deportivo and Atletico Nacional de Medellin, on 10/2/96) PL 11+3/2

ATHERTON Peter
Born: Orrell, 6 April 1970
Height: 5'11" Weight: 13.12
International Honours: E: U21-1; Sch

Strong, no-nonsense Sheffield Wednesday defender, average in height but solid in the tackle, Peter had another sound season in 1995-96. Making quite a few of his appearances as a right back, although favouring the central defensive position alongside Des Walker and latterly, Jon Newsome, his steadiness and courageous play prompted David Pleat to switch the captaincy from Des Walker, the reasoning behind the move being that Peter could inspire his team mates by his never-say-die attitude. Has proved a very good signing, his forward runs and crosses from defensive positions merely an added bonus.
Wigan Ath (From trainee on 12/2/88) FL 145+4/1 FLC 8 FAC 7 Others 12+1
Coventry C (£300,000 on 23/8/91) F/PL 113+1 FLC 4 FAC 2
Sheffield Wed (£800,000 on 1/6/94) PL 77/1 FLC 8 FAC 4

ATKIN Paul Anthony
Born: Nottingham, 3 September 1969
Height: 6'0" Weight: 12.11
International Honours: E: Yth; Sch

At Bootham Crescent since 1991, Paul continued to be a valuable member of York's first team squad in 1995-96 as a consistent and steady central defender. Has captained the side on a number of occasions in the past.
Notts Co (From trainee on 6/7/87)
Bury (Signed on 22/3/89) FL 14+7/1 Others 2+1
York C (Free on 1/7/91) FL 125+16/3 FLC 4+4 FAC 6 Others 10+1

ATKINS Mark Nigel
Born: Doncaster, 14 August 1968
Height: 6'0" Weight: 12.5
Club Honours: PL '95
International Honours: E: Sch

Signed from Blackburn last September, the tall, steady midfielder, booked for a foul on his Wolves' debut against Luton, thought he had scored at Ipswich two weeks later when appearing to get the last touch, only for it to be credited to Mark Williams. Despite that, and being used in the centre of defence and at full back, he managed the occasional goal. Has had three good runs in the team, but sometimes looked out of sorts, and was dropped for the third time after the visit to Grimsby on 12 March, before coming back to play in five of the last eight matches.
Scunthorpe U (From juniors on 9/7/86) FL 45+5/2 FLC 3+1 FAC 5 Others 6+1
Blackburn Rov (£45,000 on 16/6/88) F/PL 224+33/35 FLC 20+2/4 FAC 11+3 Others 17+2/1
Wolverhampton W (£1,000,000 on 21/9/95) FL 26+6/2 FLC 5/2 FAC 4

ATKINSON Brian
Born: Darlington, 19 January 1971
Height: 5'10" Weight: 12.5
International Honours: E: U21-6

The aggressive, ball-winning Sunderland midfielder must be wondering why fate appears to have dealt him such a bad hand in 1995-96. Brian's season was once again ruined by injury and even a loan spell at Carlisle United had to be curtailed after just three appearances. A former England U21 international, and at one time one of the club's most promising young players, it is to be hoped that he can get back to full fitness and force his way into the first team this coming term.
Sunderland (From trainee on 21/7/89) FL 119+22/4 FLC 8+2 FAC 13/2 Others 2+3
Carlisle U (Loaned on 19/1/96) FL 2 Others 1

ATKINSON Graeme
Born: Hull, 11 November 1971
Height: 5'8" Weight: 11.7
Club Honours: Div 3 '96

Early season injuries at Preston in 1995-96 meant a move to central midfield for Graeme, where he blossomed. His strong running in support of attack and defence, combined with accurate passing, dangerous dead ball kicks with either foot, and powerful shooting, made him a vital part of the team that won the third division championship last term.
Hull C (From trainee on 6/5/90) FL 129+20/23 FLC 6+3/2 FAC 4+1/1 Others 9
Preston NE (Signed on 7/10/94) FL 50+9/6 FLC 2 FAC 2 Others 3/1

ATKINSON Patrick (Paddy) Darren
Born: Singapore, 22 May 1970
Height: 5'9" Weight: 11.0

Joined York midway through last term on recommendation from Kevin Keegan, having played a number of games for Newcastle United reserves. Paddy eventually settled in well at left back after initially taking time to adjust to full-time football again.
Hartlepool U (Free from Sheffield U juniors on 23/8/88) FL 9+12/3 FLC 0+1 FAC 2 Others 1+1
(Free to Gateshead during 1990 close season)
York C (Free from Workington, via Newcastle Blue Star and Barrow on 17/11/95) FL 20+2 Others 2

AUSTIN Dean Barry
Born: Hemel Hempstead, 26 April 1970
Height: 5'11" Weight: 12.4

Right-sided Spurs' defender whose speed and confidence both improved during 1995-96. Solid in the air, Dean was often at the start of many productive, attacking moves as demonstrated in the 4-1 defeat of Manchester United in April. Very cool under pressure, and an inspiration to his colleagues in defence, always committed in challenges for 50/50 balls, he was unfortunate to miss the closing stages of the season with an ankle injury sustained in training.
Southend U (£12,000 from St Albans C on 22/3/90) FL 96/2 FLC 4/1 FAC 2 Others 7
Tottenham H (£375,000 on 4/6/92) PL 104+5 FLC 7+2 FAC 15+1

AUSTIN Kevin Levi
Born: London, 12 February 1973
Height: 6'0" Weight: 14.0

A product of non-league football, Kevin plays mainly at left back for Leyton Orient, but is more than competent in central defence. Although showing his inexperience at times, he is robust and has good pace to get down the flank where he possibly needs to work on the final ball. Continued to improve and remains a good bet for the future.
Leyton Orient (Free from Saffron Walden on 19/8/93) FL 101+8/3 FLC 4/1 FAC 6 Others 7

AWFORD Andrew (Andy) Terence
Born: Worcester, 14 July 1972
Height: 5'10" Weight: 12.0
International Honours: E: U21-9; Yth; Sch

Portsmouth central defender with good tackling ability and an understanding of the game. Having recovered from a broken leg, Andy started last season, appearing in the first four games, before another break forced him onto the sidelines yet again. Absent until February, he came into the side, although out of position, at left back, but being the player he is, continued to produce good performances, finally getting on the scoresheet for Pompey with a goal in his 200th game for the club.
Portsmouth (From trainee on 24/7/89) FL 155+9/1 FLC 18+1 FAC 10 Others 12

AYORINDE Samuel (Sammy) Tayo
Born: Lagos, Nigeria, 20 October 1974
Height: 5'10" Weight: 12.5

Having announced himself at Leyton Orient, after coming from Nigeria, the enthusiastic young striker impressed enough to warrant trials and repaid the club's faith in him by scoring regularly for the reserves. Made an eagerly awaited league debut in the final game of last season, just days after receiving his work permit, and impressed. Much is expected of him.
Leyton Orient (Signed from Nigerian amateur football on 24/4/96) FL 1

THE ⚜ TIMES

WHAT'S YOURS CALLED?

BRENTFORD'S NYLON SHIRTS

RUSHDEN AND DIAMOND GEEZERS

CATHARTIC THISTLE

BARRY FRY'S REVOLVING DOOR

NOTTINGHAM FOREST GATEAUX

CHARLTON ARTHRITIC

CREW CUT ALEXANDRA

HUDDERSFIELD OF DREAMS

PLAY UP POMPEII

A BRIDGE TOO FORFAR

Play Interactive Team Football in The Times every Tuesday. Pick your ultimate team and you can win cash prizes every week. Enter your team name now. It's really time that Wrexham's Sheeping Giants won something.

http://www.the-times.co.uk

CHANGING TIMES

B

BABB Philip (Phil) Andrew
Born: Lambeth, 30 November 1970
Height: 6'0" Weight: 12.3
Club Honours: FLC '95
International Honours: Ei: 20; B-1

An automatic choice for Liverpool as one of the three central defenders for most of last season, although he occasionally found it difficult to come to terms with the formation, he continued to prove both stylish, distributing the ball with immaculate precision, and a good tackler. At the same time, he added four more caps to his Republic of Ireland collection, despite a toe injury ruling him out of action for most of March and April. Back for the last three Premiership games, he booked his place in the FA Cup final, only to be disappointed by the result, a 1-0 win for Manchester United.
Millwall (From trainee on 25/4/89)
Bradford C (Free on 10/8/90) FL 73+7/14 FLC 5+1 FAC 3 Others 3+1
Coventry C (£500,000 on 21/7/92) PL 70+7/3 FLC 5/1 FAC 2
Liverpool (£3,600,000 on 1/9/94) PL 61+1 FLC 11 FAC 10 Others 4

Phil Babb

BADDELEY Lee Matthew
Born: Cardiff, 12 July 1974
Height: 6'1" Weight: 12.7
International Honours: W: U21-2; Yth
Cardiff City central defender in the Kevin Moran mould (he always seems to pick up head injuries!). Again missed a lot of games through injury in 1995-96, but had his most reliable season at the heart of the defence

and earned the confidence of the long suffering fans. Capped twice for the Welsh U21 side.
Cardiff C (From trainee on 13/8/91) FL 108+16/1 FLC 4+2 FAC 8 Others 23

BAILEY Danny Stephen
Born: Leyton, 21 May 1964
Height: 5'8" Weight: 11.6
Club Honours: Div 4 '90
Virtually an ever present in Exeter's midfield last season, Danny gave many excellent performances and looked to be back to his old best. Re-signed by City after being given a free transfer in May 1995, he prospered as a ball winner who could occasionally score spectacular goals.
Bournemouth (Apprentice) FL 1+1
Torquay U (Free from Walthamstow Ave on 1/3/84) FL 1
Exeter C (Free from Wealdstone, via Grays Ath, Harringey Bor and Kingsbury T, on 1/8/89) FL 63+1/2 FLC 8 FAC 7/1 Others 4+1/1
Reading (£50,000 on 26/12/90) FL 49+1/2 FAC 3
Fulham (Loaned on 29/7/92) FL 2+1
Exeter C (Free on 7/12/92) FL 111+6/2 FLC 8 FAC 7/1 Others 14/1

BAILEY Dennis Lincoln
Born: Lambeth, 13 November 1965
Height: 5'10" Weight: 11.6
Signed from Brentford last August, this gifted striker, soon became the favourite of the Gillingham fans, with his close control and ability to take on defenders in tight situations. Scored on his league debut at Lincoln and came good again, as far as finding the net was concerned, in the latter part of the season, after he had gone 27 games without a goal! Described by manager, Tony Pulis, as the man who makes the team tick, he was an integral member of the promotion winning side.
Fulham (Free from Barking on 8/11/86)
Crystal Palace (£10,000 from Farnborough T on 2/12/87) FL 0+5/1
Bristol Rov (Loaned on 27/2/89) FL 17/9 Others 1+1/1
Birmingham C (£80,000 on 3/8/89) FL 65+10/23 FLC 6/2 FAC 6 Others 3+3
Bristol Rov (Loaned on 28/3/91) FL 6/1
Queens Park R (£175,000 on 2/7/91) FL 32+7/10 FLC 5/3 FAC 1+1 Others 1
Charlton Ath (Loaned on 29/10/93) FL 0+4 Others 2
Watford (Loaned on 24/3/94) FL 2+6/4
Brentford (Loaned on 26/1/95) FL 6/3
Gillingham (£25,000 on 15/8/95) FL 40+5/8 FLC 2/1 FAC 4/1

BAILEY John Andrew
Born: London, 6 May 1969
Height: 5'8" Weight: 10.8
John easily made the transition from non-league football after joining Bournemouth from Enfield in the summer of 1995. Playing on the right-hand side, either in a more attacking winger's role, or as a more defensive wing/back, he proved to be fast, not afraid to tackle, and able to deliver telling crosses. Opened his goalscoring account at Stockport and added three more before the season was over.
Bournemouth (£40,000 from Enfield on 5/7/95) FL 36+8/4 FLC 2+1 FAC 3 Others 2+1

BAIRD Ian James
Born: Rotherham, 1 April 1964
Height: 6'2" Weight: 12.12
Club Honours: Div 2 '90
International Honours: E: Sch
Plymouth centre forward. Signed in a deal which took Kevin Nugent to Bristol City, early last season, Ian is a much travelled player with a great will to win. With a terrific shot, and very dangerous from set pieces, he led the line well and brought others into play, scoring twice in just his second game. Also spent a time in midfield before suffering a groin injury.
Southampton (From apprentice on 5/4/82) FL 20+2/5 FLC 1+1
Cardiff C (Loaned on 1/11/80) FL 12/6
Newcastle U (Loaned on 1/12/86) FL 4+1/1
Leeds U (£75,000 on 10/3/85) FL 84+1/33 FLC 4 FAC 5/4 Others 7
Portsmouth (£285,000 on 12/8/87) FL 20/1 FLC 1 FAC 1
Leeds U (£120,000 on 4/3/88) FL 76+1/17 FLC 5/1 FAC 3/2 Others 6
Middlesbrough (£500,000 on 29/1/90) FL 60+3/19 FLC 5+1 FAC 3/1 Others 4/1
Heart of Midlothian (£400,000 on 31/7/91) SL 64/15 SLC 5/2 SC 7/1 Others 3/1
Bristol C (£295,000 on 6/7/93) FL 45+12/11 FLC 3 FAC 2/1 Others 2
Plymouth Arg (Free on 29/9/95) FL 24+3/6 FAC 1+1/1

BAKER Joseph (Joe) Philip
Born: London, 19 April 1977
Height: 5'7" Weight: 10.4
Not offered professional terms by Charlton after finishing his YTS period, Joe moved across the river to sign for Leyton Orient during the 1995 close season. Although making just four starts, the diminutive forward came off the bench 21 times to become a crowd favourite, his speed and enthusiasm winning them over, despite a lack of goals.
Leyton Orient (Free from Charlton Ath juniors on 24/5/95) FL 4+16 FLC 0+2 FAC 0+1 Others 0+2

BAKER David Paul
Born: Newcastle, 5 January 1963
Height: 6'1" Weight: 13.2
Starting last season with York where he left off in 1994-95, the experienced striker added strength to the forward line when scoring four times in the first four games, before being transferred to Torquay in Janaury. Although keeping the momentum going with a strike on his United debut, in 20 games he managed just four as the club remained slumped at the bottom of the third division.
Southampton (£4,000 from Bishop Auckland on 1/7/94)
Carlisle U (Free on 2/7/85) FL 66+5/11 FLC 4/1 FAC 3 Others 2+1
Hartlepool U (Free on 31/7/87) FL 192+5/67 FLC 12/4 FAC 16/6 Others 16/5
Motherwell (£77,500 on 1/8/92) SL 5+4/1 SLC 1
Gillingham (£40,000 on 7/1/93) FL 58+4/16 FAC 5/1 Others 2
York C (£15,000 on 1/10/94) FL 36+12/18 FLC 2+2/2 FAC 3 Others 5+1/1
Torquay U (£25,000 on 19/1/96) FL 20/4

BALDRY Simon
Born: Huddersfield, 12 February 1976
Height: 5'11" Weight: 11.0

Huddersfield born and bred, Simon played on the left wing for Town, using his pace to good effect. Although finding it difficult to establish himself in the first team, he was able to make an impact as a substitute. Has good passing skills.

Huddersfield T (From trainee on 14/7/94) FL 21+14/2 FLC 2+1 Others 1+2/1

BALL Kevin Anthony
Born: Hastings, 12 November 1964
Height: 5'10" Weight: 12.6
Club Honours: Div 1 '96

Sunderland midfielder and captain, "Bally" showed all his inspirational qualities last season, leading from the front in the club's successful championship campaign. Moving into midfield from his more familiar central defensive position, Kevin formed a formidable partnership with Paul Bracewell, and weighed in with four goals in seven games in the promotion run-in. A great favourite with the Roker supporters, for his tenacity and will to win, and the proud possessor of a first division championship medal, he will no doubt be relishing the opportunity to once again pit his wits against the best teams in the country.

Portsmouth (Free from Coventry C juniors on 6/10/82) FL 96+9/4 FLC 8+1 FAC 8 Others 6
Sunderland (£350,000 on 16/7/90) FL 220+3/13 FLC 15/2 FAC 15 Others 4/1

BALL Steven (Steve) John
Born: Colchester, 2 September 1969
Height: 6'0" Weight: 13.0

On his day a powerful and skilled Colchester midfield playmaker, Steve missed all of the 1994-95 season through injury. Returning to action last season, he immediately picked up a broken jaw before finally getting back into the first team in December. Scoring one goal in ten appearances, he was released in March and is now with Beazer Homes League side, Sudbury Town.

Arsenal (From trainee on 29/9/87)
Colchester U (Free on 29/12/89) FL 3+1 Others 1/1
Norwich C (Free on 18/9/90) FL 0+2 FLC 0+2
Cambridge U (Free on 7/8/92)
Colchester U (Free on 14/9/92) FL 52+12/7 FLC 2 FAC 2/3 Others 3+2/1

BALMER Stuart Murray
Born: Falkirk, 20 September 1969
Height: 6'1" Weight: 12.4
International Honours: S: Yth; Sch

Charlton defender who can play either at right back or in the centre of the defence. Was a regular in the side until suffering a punctured lung against Grimsby last October, but returned in December and played regularly from then on, being captain on several occasions. In forming a solid and reliable defensive partnership with Richard Rufus, his experience being invaluable to the younger man, Stuart is good in the air and an adept passer.

Glasgow Celtic (From juniors in 1987)
Charlton Ath (£120,000 on 24/8/90) FL 160+19/6 FLC 10 FAC 9 Others 11+1

BANGER Nicholas (Nicky) Lee
Born: Southampton, 25 February 1971
Height: 5'9" Weight: 11.6

Made his debut for Oldham last season when coming off the bench to score the opening goal in the 2-1 home win over Sheffield United and another against Crystal Palace, before sustaining a serious back injury in the September league fixture at Birmingham. Unfortunately, he did not return to action until the FA Cup match at Swindon in February and even then things went wrong, a groin strain putting him out of action for a further eight matches. A winger who twists and turns well, his probing runs often finding him in a striking position, he is now fully fit and raring to go in 1996-97.

Southampton (From trainee on 25/4/89) F/PL 18+37/8 FLC 2+2/3 FAC 0+2 Others 1
Oldham Ath (£250,000 on 4/10/94) FL 28+13/5 FLC 2 FAC 1+1 Others 0+1

BANKS Steven (Steve)
Born: Hillingdon, 9 February 1972
Height: 6'0" Weight: 13.2

Blackpool goalkeeper. Signing from Gillingham, with a tribunal fixing the price two games into last season, Steve was soon in action, keeping a clean sheet on his debut at home to Wrexham. Continued as first choice until the arrival of Eric Nixon on loan from Tranmere in February. Is an improving player who remains cool under pressure.

West Ham U (From trainee on 24/3/90) Others 1
Gillingham (Free on 25/3/93) FL 67 FAC 7 Others 2
Blackpool (£60,000 on 18/8/95) FL 24 FLC 1 FAC 3 Others 4

Steve Banks

BANNISTER Gary
Born: Warrington, 22 July 1960
Height: 5'8" Weight: 11.10
International Honours: E: U21-1

Signed from Lincoln prior to the start of 1995-96, the vastly experienced Darlington player/coach was instrumental in the club reaching the play-off final at Wembley. The former forward, now operating in midfield,

was also the only member of the side to have played on the hallowed turf previously.

Coventry C (From apprentice on 10/5/78) FL 17+5/3 FLC 2 FAC 2
Sheffield Wed (£100,000 on 3/8/81) FL 117+1/55 FLC 13/6 FAC 12/4
Queens Park R (£200,000 on 13/8/84) FL 136/56 FLC 23/9 FAC 9/1 Others 4/6
Coventry C (£300,000 on 10/3/88) FL 39+4/11 FLC 5/2
West Bromwich A (£250,000 on 9/3/90) FL 62+10/18 FLC 3+1/1 FAC 1+1 Others 2+1/1
Oxford U (Loaned on 19/3/92) FL 7+3/2
Nottingham F (Free on 1/8/92) FL 27+4/8 FLC 2+1/1 FAC 3/1
Stoke C (Free on 21/5/93) FL 10+5/2 FAC 2 Others 0+1
Lincoln C (Free from Hong Kong R on 14/9/94) FL 25+4/7 FLC 2 FAC 1+1/1 Others 1
Darlington (Free on 4/8/95) FL 39+2/10 FLC 2 FAC 3/1 Others 4+1

BARACLOUGH Ian Robert
Born: Leicester, 4 December 1970
Height: 6'1" Weight: 12.2
International Honours: E: Yth

An inspired signing by Colin Murphy for Notts County from neighbours, Mansfield Town, last October, the left back took over from the injured Richard Walker and held his place to the end of the season, missing just four games. An attacking player, with good tackling ability, he can cross the ball well from open play and corners, and also possesses a good long throw to compensate for the departure of Andy Legg.

Leicester C (From trainee on 15/12/88) FAC 1 Others 0+1
Wigan Ath (Loaned on 22/3/90) FL 8+1/2
Grimsby T (Loaned on 21/12/90) FL 1+3
Grimsby T (Free on 13/8/91) FL 1
Lincoln C (Free on 21/8/92) FL 68+5/10 FLC 7/1 FAC 4 Others 7
Mansfield T (Free on 6/6/94) FL 47/5 FLC 7 FAC 4 Others 4
Notts Co (Signed on 13/10/95) FL 35/2 FAC 3

Ian Baraclough

BARBER Frederick (Fred)
Born: Ferryhill, 26 August 1963
Height: 5'10" Weight: 12.10
With Ian Feuer and Kelvin Davis leading the goalkeeping pecking order at Luton last season, Fred was loaned out to Ipswich (November) and Blackpool (December), before signing for Birmingham in January, following injuries to both of the club's leading 'keepers. However, rushed into action at Tranmere as a last minute replacement for Bart Griemink, the experienced shot stopper suffered a similar hand injury to that of Ian Bennett and was ruled out for the rest of the campaign.
Darlington (From apprentice on 27/8/81) FL 135 FLC 9 FAC 12 Others 7
Everton (£50,000 on 8/4/86)
Walsall (£100,000 on 20/10/86) FL 153 FLC 9 FAC 12 Others 15
Peterborough U (Loaned on 16/10/89) FL 6
Chester C (Loaned on 18/10/90) FL 3
Blackpool (Loaned on 29/11/90) FL 2
Chester C (Loaned on 28/3/91) FL 5
Peterborough U (£25,000 on 15/8/91) FL 63 FLC 8 FAC 5 Others 10
Chesterfield (Loaned on 1/2/93) Others 2
Colchester U (Loaned 19/3/93) FL 10
Luton T (£25,000 on 12/8/94)
Peterborough U (Loaned on 23/12/94) FL 5
Ipswich T (Loaned on 10/11/95) FL 1
Blackpool (Loaned on 15/12/95) FL 1
Birmingham C (Free on 15/1/96) FL 1

BARBER Philip (Phil) Andrew
Born: Tring, 10 June 1965
Height: 5'11" Weight: 12.6
Much was expected of the left-sided defender at Bristol City, after he joined from Millwall during the summer of 1995, but despite a promising pre-season start, he made just five appearances for the club, and was loaned to Mansfield (November) and Fulham (January), prior to being released in April.
Crystal Palace (£7,500 from Aylesbury U on 14/2/84) FL 207+27/35 FLC 13+6/3 FAC 14/1 Others 19+2/2
Millwall (£100,000 on 25/7/91) FL 104+6/12 FLC 7 FAC 2 Others 2+1
Plymouth Arg (Loaned on 23/12/94) FL 4 FAC 1
Bristol C (Free on 15/7/95) FL 3 FLC 2
Mansfield T (Loaned on 3/11/95) FL 4/1 Others 1
Fulham (Loaned on 19/1/96) FL 13

BARCLAY Dominic Alexander
Born: Bristol, 5 September 1976
Height: 5'10" Weight: 11.9
After bursting on to the Bristol City first team scene at the end of the 1993-94 season, this talented forward has had to be content with reserve team action until near the close of the last campaign when he twice came off the substitutes' bench. Much is still expected of this young player and 1996-97 may give some answers.
Bristol C (From trainee on 3/7/95) FL 0+2

BARDSLEY David John
Born: Manchester, 11 September 1964
Height: 5'10" Weight: 11.0
International Honours: E: 2; Yth
An attacking right back, with a wonderful right foot, who is brilliant at striking long balls behind the opposing full backs. Also very effective when going forward, David

began the first six games for QPR last season, but injury ruled him out of the next five. Returning for four games, before being controversially sent off at Southampton, after suspension, he played a major part in the club's ultimately vain struggle to avoid relegation from the Premiership.
Blackpool (From apprentice on 5/11/82) FL 45 FLC 2/1 FAC 2
Watford (£150,000 on 23/11/83) FL 97+3/7 FLC 6/1 FAC 13+1/1 Others 1
Oxford U (£265,000 on 18/9/87) FL 74/7 FLC 12 FAC 5 Others 3
Queens Park R (£500,000 on 15/9/89) F/PL 240+1/4 FLC 20/1 FAC 19 Others 3/1

BARKER Richard Ian
Born: Sheffield, 20 May 1975
Height: 6'0" Weight: 11.6
International Honours: E: Yth; Sch
Tall central striker who spent a period on loan to Doncaster Rovers from Sheffield Wednesday during the opening months of the 1995-96 season. Unfortunately, he failed to impress, and failed to score in seven first team appearances. Has yet to make the first team at Hillsborough.
Sheffield Wed (From trainee on 27/7/93)
Doncaster Rov (Loaned on 29/9/95) FL 5+1 Others 0+1

BARKER Simon
Born: Farnworth, 4 November 1964
Height: 5'9" Weight: 11.0
Club Honours: FMC '87
International Honours: E: U21-4
Good battling, box-to-box midfielder, Simon likes to get forward, but rarely receives the praise his consistent performances warrant. Having nearly left QPR during the 1995 close season, he became a major influence in the centre of the midfield, scoring the winning goal against Manchester City and starring in the opening 24 games of the season until injury ruled him out. It was no coincidence that during the bad run, (Rangers suffered seven straight league defeats in January and February), Simon was out injured in six of them. returning as stand in captain at Sheffield Wednesday, he scored two goals to help Rangers win 3-1 and was finally rewarded for his excellent season with a new two year contract, despite the club being relegated.
Blackburn Rov (From apprentice on 6/11/82) FL 180+2/35 FLC 11/4 FAC 12 Others 8/2
Queens Park R (£400,000 on 20/7/88) F/PL 233+21/26 FLC 25+2/5 FAC 20+1/3 Others 7

BARKUS Lea Paul
Born: Reading, 7 December 1974
Height: 5'6" Weight: 9.13
A right-sided midfielder, whose career at Reading was blighted by injury, Lea signed for Fulham in the summer of 1995, but, despite scoring twice in August, spent most of last season in the reserves or on the bench.
Reading (From trainee on 13/8/92) FL 8+7/1 FAC 0+1 Others 1
Fulham (Signed on 1/7/95) FL 3+6/1 FLC 1+1/1 FAC 2+1 Others 2

BARLOW Andrew (Andy) John
Born: Oldham, 24 November 1965
Height: 5'9" Weight: 11.1
Club Honours: Div 2 '91

An attacking left back with two good feet. Freed after serving 13 years at Oldham, Andy joined Blackpool during the 1995 close season on a three month contract, which was extended when his long-standing problem knee stood up to the rigours of second division football. Consistent and cool under pressure, he came through 1995-96 with flying colours. Has a good long throw.
Oldham Ath (From juniors on 31/7/84) F/PL 245+16/5 FLC 22 FAC 19 Others 6
Bradford C (Loaned on 1/11/93) FL 2
Blackpool (Free on 13/7/95) FL 34/1 FLC 2 FAC 2 Others 3

BARLOW Brett
Born: Stoke, 6 September 1977
Height: 6'0" Weight: 12.2
The Chester trainee defender made just one appearance last season from the subs' bench when coming on in the Coca Cola Cup match at home to Spurs. A promising young player, Brett's YTS contract expired during the summer.
Chester C (Trainee) FLC 0+1

BARLOW Martin David
Born: Barnstaple, 25 June 1971
Height: 5'7" Weight: 10.3
Although out of favour for most of last season, Martin came back well to give some excellent performances in Plymouth's midfield. Able to play either in the centre or in a wide position, he is a good passer of the ball and gives the club a new dimension when selected. Always gives 100 per cent and will fight for everything.
Plymouth Arg (From trainee on 1/7/89) FL 152+28/14 FLC 6+1/2 FAC 7 Others 12+1

BARLOW Neil Keith
Born: Bury, 24 March 1978
Height: 6'0" Weight: 12.0
Powerful Rochdale YTS defender, who can play either at right back or more usually in the centre, he was offered pro terms last April and almost immediately made his FL debut, giving an encouraging performance as a substitute against Cambridge. Unfortunately, his full debut in the next game lasted only five minutes when he was carried off, following an over ambitious sliding tackle.
Rochdale (Trainee) FL 1+1

BARLOW Stuart
Born: Liverpool, 16 July 1968
Height: 5'10" Weight: 11.0
A fringe player at Everton, he failed to claim a place in any of the starting line-ups in 1995-96, making his six appearances from the subs' bench before signing for Oldham in November. A tricky forward who Latics' fans have yet to see the best of, despite him scoring seven goals since joining, his greatest asset is his pace. He is also hard-working, runs off the ball well and gets in a surprising number of headers for such a small man.
Everton (Free from Sherwood Park on 6/6/90) F/PL 24+47/10 FLC 3+5/1 FAC 4+3/2 Others 0+2
Rotherham U (Loaned on 10/1/92) Others 0+1
Oldham Ath (£450,000 on 20/11/95) FL 21+5/7 FAC 3 Others 1

BARMBY Nicholas (Nick) Jonathan
Born: Hull, 11 February 1974
Height: 5'7" Weight: 11.3
International Honours: E: 9; B-1; U21-3; Yth; Sch

On 8 August 1995, Nick became Middlesbrough's record signing, (manager Bryan Robson, quadrupled Boro's record transfer fee to get him) and arrived on Teeside in a blaze of publicity, due entirely to his price tag and certain remarks made by Spurs' chairman, Alan Sugar. Made his debut in the pre-season friendly against Hibs, but gave no hint of the awesome displays that he was about to treat the Boro fans to at the new Riverside Stadium. Once into Premiership football, however, he scored on his league debut against the Gunners and was involved in every goal in the first dozen or so matches played, either as scorer or provider, and quickly established himself as a firm favourite at the new Holgate end with his exciting midfield displays. His inclusion in the national squad for Euro '96, following a hat trick against China, endorses the prediction of Pele, who considers Nick to be a future world star. Made three subs' appearances in the European Championship as England reached the semi-final stage, only to lose to Germany.
Tottenham H (From trainee on 9/4/91) PL 81+6/20 FLC 7+1/2 FAC 12+1/5
Middlesbrough (£5,250,000 on 8/8/95) PL 33+7 FLC 4/1 FAC 3/1

BARNARD Darren Sean
Born: Rintein, Germany, 30 November 1971
Height: 5'10" Weight: 12.0
International Honours: E: Sch
Unable to get a Premiership game with Chelsea in 1995-96, Darren signed for Bristol City in October. At first, he appeared to be more suited to a central midfield role, but eventually found his niche in the City side at left back, linking up well with Brian Tinnion, to give the Robins good balance on the left-hand side. With the skill to go past opponents, and a good crosser of the ball, who ably demonstrated his excellent long-range shooting ability, the Bristol City Fanzine, "One Team in Bristol", made him their "Player of the Year"!
Chelsea (£50,000 from Wokingham T on 25/7/90) F/PL 18+11/2 FLC 1+1 FAC 1+1
Reading (Loaned on 18/11/94) FL 3+1
Bristol C (£175,000 on 6/10/95) FL 33+1/4 FAC 2 Others 2

BARNARD Mark
Born: Sheffield, 27 November 1975
Height: 6'0" Weight: 11.10
A fine young left back who joined Darlington after the start of last season, Mark contributed three goals through his powerful surges up the left flank. A great start to his league career was capped with an appearance at Wembley in the play-off final.
Rotherham U (From trainee on 13/7/94. Free to Worksop T during 1995 close season)
Darlington (Free on 27/9/95) FL 37/3 FLC 1 Others 3

BARNES David
Born: Paddington, 16 November 1961
Height: 5'10" Weight: 11.4
International Honours: E: Yth (UEFAYC '80)
Strong, athletic Watford left back. Given a belated run-in the first team after overcoming an achilles injury, and being unsettled for the early part of last season, he was a revelation, prior to being given a free transfer in the summer.
Coventry C (From apprentice on 31/5/79) FL 9 FAC 4
Ipswich T (Free on 12/4/82) FL 16+1
Wolverhampton W (£35,000 on 3/10/84) FL 86+2/4 FLC 7 FAC 6 Others 6
Aldershot (£25,000 on 22/8/87) FL 68+1/1 FLC 2 FAC 2+2 Others 4
Sheffield U (£50,000 on 11/7/89) F/PL 82/1 FLC 6 FAC 14 Others 4
Watford (£50,000 on 14/1/94) FL 16 FAC 1+1

BARNES David Oswald (**Bobby**)
Born: Kingston, 17 December 1962
Height: 5'7" Weight: 11.0
Club Honours: FAYC '81
International Honours: E: Yth
Striker. One of football's travellers, and 15 years in the game, Bobby went on trial to Torquay last September, having arrived back from Hong Kong, and a day later came on as a substitute in the home game against Mansfield. His brief stay lasted just 21 minutes and at the time of writing he was playing for non-league, Hendon.
West Ham U (From apprentice on 23/9/80) FL 31+12/5 FLC 2+1 FAC 5+1/1 Others 0+1
Scunthorpe U (Loaned on 28/11/85) FL 6
Aldershot (Free on 14/3/86) FL 49/26 FLC 2 FAC 5/1 Others 11/5
Swindon T (Signed on 16/10/87) FL 43+2/13 FLC 2 FAC 1 Others 4
Bournemouth (£100,000 on 23/3/89) FL 11+3 FLC 1
Northampton T (£70,000 on 13/10/89) FL 97+1/37 FLC 5/3 FAC 9/3 Others 6/1
Peterborough U (£35,000 on 7/2/92) FL 42+7/9 FLC 4+3 FAC 0+1 Others 3
Partick Thistle (Signed on 1/1/94) SL 3+4 (Free to Kettering on 26/8/94)
Torquay U (Signed from Hong Kong on 1/9/95) FL 0+1

Nick Barmby

John Barnes

BARNES John Charles Bryan
Born: Jamaica, 7 November 1963
Height: 5'11" Weight: 12.7
Club Honours: FAYC '82; Div 1 '88, '90;
FAC '89; CS '88, '89, '90; FLC '95
International Honours: E: 79; U21-3
Although it might appear that he had a quiet season in 1995-96, with only three goals in 36 Premiership games, this was simply a reflection of his new role as a midfield anchor man in the Liverpool team, a role played by Ronnie Whelan with such distinction in the club's glory years of the 80s. With Steve McManaman, Jason McAteer and Jamie Redknapp all capable of carrying the ball forward, there was less call for John, by now a veteran, to play up front and he was rarely seen in the opposition penalty area. Instead, he played deep, winning the ball in his own half and becoming the springboard for the attacks with his quick and accurate distribution. Although retaining his England place for the first half of the season, by the end of the campaign it seemed that his international career was over.
Watford (Free from Sudbury Court on 14/7/81) FL 232+1/65 FLC 21/7 FAC 31/11 Others 7
Liverpool (£900,000 on 19/6/87) F/PL 276+3/80 FLC 23/3 FAC 49/16 Others 9/2

BARNES Paul Lance
Born: Leicester, 16 November 1967
Height: 5'10" Weight: 10.9
After hitting the national headlines last season as the scorer of two goals in York's shock Coca Cola Cup win at Manchester United, Paul moved to Birmingham in March, having been trailed by Barry Fry for some time. Remained the club's leading scorer for the fourth year in succession, even though leaving Bootham Crescent, and quickly got going for Brum with seven goals in 15 matches, despite carrying a knee injury. Due to have had an operation during the summer, he will be favoured to be among the division's leading scorers this

season. Not only a natural goalscorer, but a skilful player who holds the ball up well for others.
Notts Co (From apprentice on 16/11/85) FL 36+17/14 FAC 0+1 Others 4+6/5
Stoke C (£30,000 on 23/3/90) FL 10+14/3 FLC 0+2 Others 3+1/2
Chesterfield (Loaned on 8/11/90) FL 1 FAC 1/1
York C (£50,000 on 15/7/92) FL 147+1/76 FLC 10/5 FAC 5 Others 16/4
Birmingham C (£350,000 on 4/3/96) FL 15/7

BARNES Richard Ian
Born: Wrexham, 6 September 1975
Height: 5'10" Weight: 11.6
International Honours: W: Yth
As a promising Wrexham full back who was still learning his trade, he was restricted to just one substitute appearance in 1995-96, the ECWC Preliminary Round second-leg tie against Petrolul Ploiesti in Romania, before being released during the summer.
Wrexham (From trainee on 31/5/94) FL 0+1 Others 0+1

BARNES Steven (Steve) Leslie
Born: Harrow, 5 January 1976
Height: 5'4" Weight: 10.5
One of a number of men to join Birmingham from non-league soccer last season, Steve's appearances were limited to five from the bench, without ever getting a proper run-in the side. A small and nippy winger, the coming campaign will be make or break for him.
Birmingham C (£75,000 from Welling U on 9/10/95) FL 0+3 FLC 0+1 Others 0+1

BARNESS Anthony
Born: Lewisham, 25 March 1973
Height: 5'10" Weight: 13.1
Promising left back who was Scott Minto's predecessor at Charlton Athletic. Chelsea's surfeit of players in that position have barred his way to a regular first team place – only making 12 league starts in his three seasons at Chelsea. His only match during 1995-96 being the Coca Cola Cup-tie, which saw the Blues eliminated 1-0 by first division, Stoke City. Later, in February, Anthony joined Southend on loan in an attempt to replace the departed Chris Powell. However, although he showed up as a strong tackler with good distribution, who fitted into the pattern of play, he could not convince the manager, Ronnie Whelan, and returned to Stamford Bridge after five outings.
Charlton Ath (From trainee on 6/3/91) FL 21+6/1 FLC 2 FAC 3 Others 1+1/1
Chelsea (£350,000 on 8/9/92) PL 12+2 FLC 2 Others 2+1
Middlesbrough (Loaned on 12/8/93) Others 1
Southend U (Loaned on 2/2/96) FL 5

BARNETT Jason Vincent
Born: Shrewsbury, 21 April 1976
Height: 5'9" Weight: 10.10
Released by Wolves, the busy midfield player signed for Lincoln after scoring twice in a trial for the reserves, before netting on his league debut at Exeter five days later. A long-throw specialist, with the ability to fire in crosses from either flank, Jason won the club's "Young Player of the Season" award.
Wolverhampton W (From trainee on 4/7/94)

Lincoln C (£5,000 on 26/10/95) FL 27+5/2 FAC 1 Others 3

BARNHOUSE David John
Born: Swansea, 19 March 1975
Height: 5'9" Weight: 10.9
International Honours: W: U21-3; Yth; Sch
Despite starting last season as first choice full back, David struggled to command a regular place in the Swansea first team. A gritty defender, who also played twice for the Welsh U21 side, he was unable to maintain the consistency required for league football and was released during the summer.
Swansea C (From trainee on 8/7/93) FL 18+5 FLC 2 FAC 2 Others 5

BARNWELL-EDINBORO Jamie
Born: Hull, 26 December 1975
Height: 5'10" Weight: 11.6
A product of Coventry's youth policy, Jamie made his first team debut in 1995-96 when coming on at Middlesbrough in September. Following that, a shortage of opportunities saw him going on loan to Swansea (December) and Wigan (February), where he impressed as a striker with great pace and aerial strength before signing for Cambridge United, who he had scored against while playing for Wigan, on transfer deadline day. Although his United start was temporarily delayed through injury, he found the net in his first game and will be the main man up front this season.
Coventry C (From trainee on 1/7/94) PL 0+1
Swansea C (Loaned on 15/12/95) FL 2+2
Wigan Ath (Loaned on 2/2/96) FL 2+8/1
Cambridge U (Signed on 29/3/96) FL 7/2

BARR William (Billy) Joseph
Born: Halifax, 21 January 1969
Height: 5'11" Weight: 10.8
Was unfortunate not to be fit for Crewe in time for the start of the 1995-96 season and had to wait a long time before getting his chance. Eventually selected, he played in a defensive role, read the game well and was always a consistent performer.
Halifax T (From trainee on 6/7/87) FL 178+18/13 FLC 8+1/2 FAC 11+1/2 Others 14+3
Crewe Alex (Free on 17/6/94) FL 44+7/2 FLC 2 FAC 2 Others 6+1

BARRAS Anthony (Tony)
Born: Billingham, 29 March 1971
Height: 6'0" Weight: 12.9
A generally strong and commanding figure in the centre of York's defence last season, Tony also scored a number of important goals, including one at Old Trafford in the 3-0 victory over Manchester United.
Hartlepool U (From trainee on 6/7/89) FL 9+3 FLC 2 FAC 1 Others 1
Stockport Co (Free on 23/7/90) FL 94+5/5 FLC 2 FAC 7 Others 19+1
Rotherham U (Loaned on 25/2/94) FL 5/1
York C (Signed on 18/7/94) FL 59+4/4 FLC 7/1 FAC 3 Others 5+1/1

BARRETT Earl Delisser
Born: Rochdale, 28 April 1967
Height: 5'10" Weight: 11.2
Club Honours: Div 2 '91; FLC '94; CS '95
International Honours: E: 3; B-4; U21-4

An athletic and very quick Everton defender, who is adept enough to slot in either at centre back or right back, Earl likes to pass the ball out of defence and is equally capable of coming out to set up attacks. He is also excellent in recovery. Made the right back spot his own early on last season with encouraging team performances, and moved into the middle when David Watson and Dave Unsworth were unavailable. Unlucky to sustain a bad knee injury against Feyenoord, after recovering he struggled to regain his place following the arrival of Marc Hottiger and will again have a fight on his hands in 1996-97.

Manchester C (From trainee on 26/4/85) FL 2+1 FLC 1
Chester C (Loaned on 1/3/86) FL 12
Oldham Ath (£35,000 on 24/11/87) FL 181+2/7 FLC 20/1 FAC 14/1 Others 4
Aston Villa (£1,700,000 on 25/2/92) F/PL 118+1/1 FLC 15/1 FAC 9 Others 7
Everton (£1,700,000 on 30/1/95) PL 25 FLC 2 Others 3

Earl Barrett

BARRETT Scott
Born: Ilkeston, 2 April 1963
Height: 6'0" Weight: 13.8
Club Honours: GMVC '92; FAT '92
Experienced Cambridge United goalkeeper, signed at the start of last season from Gillingham, he immediately became first choice until the end of November when suffering an abdominal injury. Back into action in mid-March, Scott remained between the posts, his experience proving invaluable in front of a young defence.

Wolverhampton W (Signed from Ilkeston T on 27/9/84) FL 30 FLC 1 FAC 1 Others 3
Stoke C (£10,000 on 24/7/87) FL 51 FLC 2 FAC 3 Others 4

Colchester U (Loaned on 10/1/90) FL 13
Stockport Co (Loaned on 22/3/90) FL 10 Others 2
Gillingham (Free on 14/8/92) FL 51 FLC 7 FAC 4 Others 4
Cambridge U (Free on 2/8/95) FL 31 FLC 2 FAC 1 Others 1

BARRICK Dean
Born: Hemsworth, 30 September 1969
Height: 5'9" Weight: 11.9
Club Honours: Div 3 '96
Signed from Cambridge in a straight swap for Paul Raynor last September, "Deano" soon became a favourite of the Preston crowd. Excellent tackling at left back, and an ability to provide telling crosses in support of the attack, were the main features of his game. Ended the campaign with a third division championship medal as North End achieved what they had set out to do.

Sheffield Wed (From trainee on 7/5/88) FL 11/2
Rotherham U (£50,000 on 14/2/91) FL 96+3/7 FLC 6 FAC 8 Others 5/1
Cambridge U (£50,000 on 11/8/93) FL 90+1/3 FLC 7/1 FAC 7/1 Others 6
Preston NE (Signed on 11/9/95) FL 39+1 FAC 2 Others 2

BARRON Michael James
Born: Chester le Street, 22 December 1974
Height: 5'11" Weight: 11.9
A strong-tackling young Middlesbrough defender (from Bryan Robson's home town), Michael is a good all-rounder who displays sound defensive qualities, is both quick and determined, and very good in the air. The reserve team captain, and a first class product of the club's youth teams, he made his Premiership debut in the 2-0 home defeat against Everton last April and will come again.

Middlesbrough (From trainee on 2/2/93) P/FL 2+1 FLC 1 Others 2+1

BARROW Lee Alexander
Born: Belper, 1 May 1973
Height: 5'11" Weight: 13.0
Almost a permanent fixture in the centre of Torquay's defence in 1995-96, Lee gave everything and more. Dependable and consistent in a season of struggle, his pace and ability to read the game were one of the club's few assets.

Notts Co (From trainee on 9/7/91)
Scarborough (Free on 3/8/92) FL 11 FLC 2 Others 1
Torquay U (Free on 18/2/93) FL 109+7/5 FLC 9/2 FAC 9/1 Others 5

BARTLEY Carl Alexander
Born: Lambeth, 6 October 1976
Height: 6'3" Weight: 13.5
Well-built young striker who came through the Fulham YTS ranks to sign professional forms during the 1995 close season. Although finding the net nine times in 15 reserve matches, Carl was only given one substitute appearance for the first team and was released in March.

Fulham (From trainee on 1/7/95) FL 1 FLC 1 Others 0+1

BARTON Warren Dean
Born: Stoke Newington, 19 March 1969
Height: 6'0" Weight: 11.0
International Honours: E: 3; B-3

Warren proved to be a sound technical player, able to perform in defence or midfield, although his pace, good distribution, and attacking flair, fit him well for the modern role of wing/back, where he operated on the right for United. Transferred from Wimbledon during the 1995 close season, he was Newcastle's record signing for just two days, but quickly established himself in the side, and was an ever present until the defeat by Arsenal in March, following which he lost his place to Steve Watson. Is bound to be a force in the club's efforts to win the Premiership.

Maidstone U (£10,000 from Leytonstone on 28/7/89) FL 41+1 FLC 0+2 FAC 3/1 Others 7
Wimbledon (£300,000 on 7/6/90) F/PL 178+2/10 FLC 16/1 FAC 11 Others 2
Newcastle U (£4,500,000 on 5/6/95) PL 30+1 FLC 5/1 FAC 2

BART-WILLIAMS Christopher (Chris) Gerald
Born: Freetown, Sierra Leone, 16 June 1974
Height: 5'10" Weight: 11.11
International Honours: E: B-1; U21-16; Yth
Probably the best of Frank Clark's 1995 summer signings, the midfield player from Sheffield Wednesday was not an immediate Nottingham Forest first team choice but, after displacing David Phillips in September, he held his place to the end of the season. Disappointingly, he failed to score, although in mitigation he was employed as the midfield anchor, rather than in the more forward role he was used to at Hillsborough. A product of the modern game, Chris has terrific stamina, keeps his passing simple, and is not afraid to get his foot in. Won two more caps for the England U21 side.

Leyton Orient (From trainee on 18/7/91) FL 34+2/2 FLC 4 Others 2
Sheffield Wed (£275,000 on 21/11/91) F/PL 95+29/16 FLC 10+6/4 FAC 9+3/2 Others 1+3/2
Nottingham F (£2,500,000 on 1/7/95) PL 33 FLC 2 FAC 7 Others 7+1

Christopher Bart-Williams

BASHAM Michael (Mike)
Born: Barking, 27 September 1973
Height: 6'2" Weight: 12.8
Club Honours: AMC '94
International Honours: E: Yth; Sch
The stylish central defender was given a free transfer by Swansea last October, having failed to settle in South Wales, following his transfer from West Ham United in April 1994. After a trial period, Mike signed a contract with Peterborough United, where he was in and out due to injury.
West Ham U (From trainee on 3/7/92)
Colchester U (Loaned on 18/11/93) FL 1
Swansea C (Free on 24/3/94) FL 27+2/1 FAC 6 Others 8+2
Peterborough U (Free on 18/12/95) FL 13+1/1

BASS Jonathan (Jon) David
Born: Bristol, 1 January 1976
Height: 6'0" Weight: 12.2
International Honours: E: Sch
Young Birmingham right back who made his league debut last season, having played in the Coca Cola Cup in 1994-95. Actually made his first appearance for 1995-96 in the same competition, deputising for Gary Poole, in the home leg of the semi final against Leeds in February and showed great maturity in a pressure situation. A rarity among the current Blues' players, in that he came through the junior sides, Jon uses the ball well and rarely dives in.
Birmingham C (From juniors on 27/6/94) FL 5 FLC 2

BATES James (Jamie) Alan
Born: Croydon, 24 February 1968
Height: 6'1" Weight: 13.0
Club Honours: Div 3 '92
Powerful Brentford centre half and captain who has now completed ten seasons at Griffin Park. Despite Brentford's poor time of it in 1995-96, Jamie played as well as in the previous season and was a good influence on his team mates. Scored twice in a game for the first time in his career against Peterborough.
Brentford (From trainee on 1/6/87) FL 295+20/14 FLC 25+3/2 FAC 12+1/1 Others 35/1

BATTERSBY Anthony (Tony)
Born: Doncaster, 30 August 1975
Height: 6'0" Weight: 12.7
A reserve striker for Sheffield United who spent the summer of 1995 in Finland, he made his league debut at Barnsley last September, later scoring his first goal in the win over Portsmouth, but was given few opportunities by Howard Kendall and joined Notts County, together with Paul Rogers, in January for a modest fee. Scored seven useful goals to assist County's push for promotion, which ended in the play-off final, despite facing severe competition for places, following the later signings of Gary Jones and Gary Martindale. A powerful header of the ball and a good future prospect.
Sheffield U (From trainee on 5/7/93) FL 3+7/1 FLC 1+1 Others 2+1/1
Southend U (Loaned on 23/3/95) FL 6+2/1
Notts Co (£200,000 on 8/1/96) FL 14+7/7 Others 4

BATTY David
Born: Leeds, 2 December 1968
Height: 5'7" Weight: 12.0
Club Honours: Div 2 '90, Div 1 '92
International Honours: E: 17; B-5; U21-7
An energetic player, renowned as a combative ball-winning anchorman, whose terrier-like style tends to obscure his skills, David has a cool footballing brain, and distributes the ball well over both short and long distances. Returning to Blackburn's midfield after a year's absence, he was unable to strike up his old partnership with Tim Sherwood and was employed wide on the left when Lars Bohinen was introduced. Unhappy with team selections, he transferred to Newcastle last March, his departure from Rovers being precipitated by a much publicised fracas with Graeme le Saux in a European Cup match. Slotting straight into the United team, playing in front of the back four, he was chosen "Man of the Match" on his debut against Manchester United, and followed that up by displaying excellent form for the rest of the season, always available to receive the ball from colleagues and use it constructively. Criticised at Blackburn for not scoring enough, he netted on his return there a month after his transfer.
Leeds U (From trainee on 3/8/87) F/PL 201+10/4 FLC 17 FAC 12 Others 17
Blackburn Rov (£2,750,000 on 26/10/93) PL 53+1/1 FLC 6 FAC 5 Others 6
Newcastle U (£3,750,000 on 2/3/96) PL 11/1

Ashley Bayes

BAYES Ashley John
Born: Lincoln, 19 April 1972
Height: 6'1" Weight: 13.5
International Honours: E: Yth
Torquay United shot-stopping goalkeeper. Although conceding many goals in a very bad season, Ashley could be blamed for very few, before losing his place in the side to Ray Newland and being released during the summer.

Brentford (From trainee on 5/7/90) FL 4 FLC 5 FAC 2 Others 1
Torquay U (Free on 13/8/93) FL 97 FLC 7 FAC 9 Others 6

BAYLISS David (Dave) Anthony
Born: Liverpool, 8 June 1976
Height: 5'8" Weight: 11.0
Former Rochdale YTS central defender who signed professional forms in the summer of 1995. With just one previous first team appearance behind him, he was thrust into the side in only the second game and injuries to Peter Valentine gave him the chance of an extended run-in which he more than held his own. Voted the club's "Young Player of the Year".
Rochdale (From trainee on 10/6/95) FL 26+3 FLC 2 FAC 1+1 Others 2

BAZELEY Darren Shaun
Born: Northampton, 5 October 1972
Height: 5'10" Weight" 11.2
International Honours: E: U21-1
Made the Watford right back spot his own after the departure of Gerard Lavin to Millwall last November. As a former winger, especially effective on his forward runs and capable of putting over accurate crosses, Darren again proved to have an eye for goal, scoring an important equaliser at Sheffield United in January.
Watford (From trainee on 6/5/91) FL 99+44/13 FLC 9+4/2 FAC 7+1 Others 3+1

BEADLE Peter Clifford
Born: Lambeth, 13 May 1972
Height: 6'1" Weight: 11.12
Having made just four appearances at Watford in 1995-96, Peter, a strong effective target man, signed for Bristol Rovers in November. Immediately forming a good goalscoring partnership with Marcus Stewart, he became a firm crowd favourite after scoring arguably Rovers' best goal of the season – a superb strike at Bristol City in an exciting 2-0 victory in January.
Gillingham (From trainee on 5/5/90) FL 42+25/14 FLC 2+4/2 FAC 1+1 Others 1
Tottenham H (£300,000 on 4/6/92)
Bournemouth (Loaned on 25/3/93) FL 9/2
Southend U (Loaned on 4/3/94) FL 8/1
Watford (Signed on 12/9/94) FL 12+11/1 FLC 1
Bristol Rov (£50,000 on 17/11/95) FL 26+1/12 Others 3

BEAGRIE Peter Sydney
Born: Middlesbrough, 28 November 1965
Height: 5'8" Weight: 9.10
International Honours: E: B-2; U21-2
The beginning of last season brought this highly skilled traditional Manchester City winger a worrying start. After summer surgery to rectify a double hernia, Peter failed to recapture his past level of consistency, starting only four Premier League and two Coca Cola Cup games and looking only a shade of his old self. Unfortunately, more leg problems developed, effectively bringing his season to an end. City can only hope that they get back on song, a player who can deceive the opposition with trickery, often feinting to cross and then going on with the ball, checking from one foot to the other.

Middlesbrough (From juniors on 10/9/83) FL 24+9/2 FLC 1 Others 1+1
Sheffield U (£35,000 on 16/8/86) FL 81+3/11 FLC 5 FAC 5 Others 4
Stoke C (£210,000 on 29/6/88) FL 54/7 FLC 4 FAC 3/1
Everton (£750,000 on 2/11/89) F/PL 88+26/11 FLC 7+2/3 FAC 7+2 Others 5+1/1
Sunderland (Loaned on 26/9/91) FL 5/1
Manchester C (£1,100,000 on 24/3/94) F/PL 46+5/3 FLC 8/1 FAC 4/1

BEALL Matthew John
Born: Enfield, 4 December 1977
Height: 5'7" Weight: 10.6
A product of Cambridge United youth policy, "Billy" made his debut at Hereford last January and scored his first league goal at Fulham two months later. Small in stature, and a reminder of Steve Spriggs who served the club well in the 1970s and 80s, he finished with three goals, his ability to score from midfield being a boost to the club.
Cambridge U (From trainee on 28/3/96) FL 15/5 Others 0+1

BEARD Mark
Born: Roehampton, 8 October 1974
Height: 5'10" Weight: 10.12
Young Sheffield full back or midfielder signed from Millwall at the beginning of last season, Mark played seven games at the back before losing his place. Returned to the squad towards the end of the campaign, but struggled, and will continue to struggle to hold down a regular place following the acquisition of Chris Short. He still has time on his side, however, and his undoubted versatility, including a reserve spell up front, is in his favour.
Millwall (From trainee on 18/3/93) FL 32+13/2 FLC 3+1 FAC 4/1
Sheffield U (£117,000 on 18/8/95) FL 13+7 FLC 2

BEARDSLEY Peter Andrew
Born: Newcastle, 18 January 1961
Height: 5'8" Weight: 11.7
Club Honours: Div 1 '88, '90; FAC '89; CS '88, '89, '90
International Honours: E: 59; B-2
Now in his second spell with Newcastle, Peter was at his best in 1995-96, playing just behind the strikers, linking midfield and attack, dictating the tempo of the game, and finding scope for his own strikes on goal. His excellent close control and quick feet enabled him to find space in the most crowded of penalty areas and create opportunities for himself and others and as the club captain his hard-working, enthusiastic, unselfish attitude set an inspiring example to his colleagues. Continued to score fine goals and passed 100 in the league for United during the season, during which he became the club's seventh highest league and cup goalscorer. Was awarded the MBE in the 1995 Queen's Birthday Honours List.
Carlisle U (Free from Wallsend BC on 9/8/79) FL 93+11/22 FLC 6+1 FAC 15/7 (£275,000 to Vancouver Whitecaps on 1/4/82)
Manchester U (£300,000 on 9/9/82) FLC 1 (Free to Vancouver Whitecaps on 1/3/83)
Newcastle U (£150,000 on 23/9/83) FL 146+1/61 FLC 10 FAC 6 Others 1
Liverpool (£1,900,000 on 24/7/87) FL 120+11/46 FLC 13+1/1 FAC 22+3/11 Others 5/1

Everton (£1,000,000 on 5/8/91) F/LP 81/25 FLC 8/5 FAC 4/1 Others 2/1
Newcastle U (£1,400,000 on 16/7/93) PL 104/43 FLC 9/3 FAC 8/3 Others 4/2

Peter Beardsley

BEARDSMORE Russell Peter
Born: Wigan, 28 September 1968
Height: 5'6" Weight 9.0
Club Honours: ESC '91
International Honours: E: U21-5
Russell made the Bournemouth left back position his own in 1995-96, missing only one game all season, while consistently performing well and showing excellent ability in his defensive role. As a former midfielder, who can get forward and support the attack, he also took on the role as captain on the field after club captain, Mark Morris, was injured in February. Is a very experienced player, despite his lack of league games, having spent seven years at the Old Trafford academy.
Manchester U (From apprentice on 2/10/86) FL 30+26/4 FLC 3+1 FAC 4+4 Others 2+5
Blackburn Rov (Loaned on 19/12/91) FL 1+1
Bournemouth (Free on 29/6/93) FL 102+9/3 FLC 11/1 FAC 7 Others 5

BEASANT David (Dave) John
Born: Willsden, 20 March 1959
Height: 6'4" Weight: 14.3
Club Honours: Div 4 '83, Div 2 '89; FAC '88; FMC '90
International Honours: E: 2; B-7
Big Dave, nicknamed "Lurch", made the goalkeeping spot his own at Southampton last season, keeping Bruce Grobbelaar on the bench for all but two games and putting together an impressive 13 clean sheets. Despite Saints' sometimes erratic defensive play, he stated that he had never played better and many felt the club might have

been in worse trouble than they were, but for his outstanding displays, particularly his shot stopping, as in the home game against Manchester United. Also capable of kicking long distances and setting up attacks with accurate throws.
Wimbledon (£1,000 from Edgware T on 7/8/79) FL 340 FLC 21 FAC 27 Others 3
Newcastle U (£800,000 on 13/6/88) FL 20 FLC 2 FAC 2 Others 1
Chelsea (£725,000 on 14/1/89) F/PL 133 FLC 11 FAC 5 Others 8
Grimsby T (Loaned on 24/10/92) FL 6
Wolverhampton W (Loaned on 12/1/93) FL 4 FAC 1
Southampton (£300,000 on 4/11/93) PL 73+1 FLC 4 FAC 8

BEASLEY Andrew (Andy)
Born: Sedgley, 5 February 1964
Height: 6'2" Weight: 13.8
After the disappointment of missing out on the 1994-95 play-off final, Andy resumed as Chesterfield's first choice goalkeeper at the start of last season and performed to his usual high standards. Two injury spells unfortunately restricted his opportunities, though, and he is now second choice behind Billy Mercer. Is a commanding and imposing last line of defence.
Luton T (From apprentice on 23/2/82)
Mansfield T (Free on 6/7/84) FL 94 FLC 5 FAC 3 Others 7
Peterborough U (Loaned on 28/7/86) FL 7 FLC 3
Scarborough (Loaned on 1/3/88) FL 4
Bristol Rov (Loaned on 25/3/93) FL 1
Doncaster Rov (Free on 30/7/93) FL 37 FLC 2 FAC 1 Others 2
Chesterfield (Free on 12/8/94) FL 31+1 FLC 3 FAC 2 Others 6

BEAUCHAMP Joseph (Joey) Daniel
Born: Oxford, 13 March 1971
Height: 5'10" Weight: 11.10
The return of the prodigal son last October, following a move from Swindon where he had been struggling, was an inspired move by Oxford's manager, Denis Smith, although it was not until the latter third of the season that the wide midfielder showed his best form. Who knows how United's season would have gone if Bobby Ford had not been inured to allow Joey in. Scored seven times in the last 17 games, including three headers – rare for a player who does the damage down on the floor – and hit a wonderful 35-yard volley to beat Blackpool, a crucial result which, in the end, saw United promoted.
Oxford U (From trainee on 16/5/89) FL 117+7/20 FLC 6+1/2 FAC 8/3 Others 5+1
Swansea C (Loaned on 30/10/91) FL 5/2 Others 1
West Ham U (£1,000,000 on 22/6/94)
Swindon T (£850,000 on 18/8/94) FL 39+5/3 FLC 7+2/1 FAC 2 Others 4
Oxford U (£300,000 on 4/10/95) FL 25+7/7 FAC 2+2/1 Others 0+2

BEAUMONT Christopher (Chris) Paul
Born: Sheffield, 5 December 1965
Height: 5'11" Weight: 11.7
Stockport's longest-serving player, Chris continued to play a key part in the club's challenge for honours last season. Used in several positions in the past, he appeared in a right-sided midfield role and, although the

leading goalscorer in 1990-91, he has now gone 15 months without finding the net.
Rochdale (Free from Denaby U on 21/7/88) FL 31+3/7 FLC 0+1/1 FAC 2/1 Others 2
Stockport Co (£8,000 on 21/7/89) FL 238+20/39 FLC 14+3/3 FAC 15/2 Others 34+2/7

BECKFORD Darren Richard
Born: Manchester, 12 May 1967
Height: 6'1" Weight: 13.6
International Honours: E: Yth; Sch

Desperate for regular first team football, and despite being offered a new contract by Oldham, Darren has turned it down in the hope that he can get his career back on the rails elsewhere. A busy, bustling centre forward, who is great in the air, he got few chances to shine in 1995-96, making just 14 starts. However, having failed to score in the home game against Wolves towards the end of the season, he proved his versatility when taking over from the injured Paul Gerrard in goal for the remaining 17 minutes and preserving a 0-0 scoreline.
Manchester C (From apprentice on 21/8/84) FL 7+4 FLC 0+1
Bury (Loaned on 10/10/85) FL 12/5
Port Vale (£15,000 on 26/3/87) FL 169+9/72 FLC 12/3 FAC 14/4 Others 9+1/3
Norwich C (£925,000 on 14/6/91) F/PL 32+6/8 FLC 3+2/3 FAC 4+1/1 Others 1/1
Oldham Ath (£300,000 on 25/3/93) P/FL 31+21/11 FLC 2/1 FAC 6+3/4 Others 1+1

BECKFORD Jason Neil
Born: Manchester, 14 February 1970
Height: 5'9" Weight: 12.13
International Honours: E: Yth; Sch

Right-sided Northampton midfield attacking player and one of Ian Atkins' first signings. Failed to break into the first team in 1995-96, then picked up an injury that saw him restricted to just a handful of substitute appearances, before being released in the summer.
Manchester C (From trainee on 18/8/87) FL 8+12/1 FLC 1+4/1
Blackburn Rov (Loaned on 14/3/91) FL 3+1
Port Vale (Loaned on 26/9/91) FL 4+1/1
Birmingham C (£50,000 on 2/1/92) FL 5+2/2 Others 1
Bury (Loaned on 24/3/94) FL 3
Stoke C (Free on 10/8/94) FL 2+2 Others 1
Millwall (Free on 15/12/94) FL 6+3
Northampton T (Signed on 15/5/95) FL 0+1 FAC 0+1 Others 0+2

BECKHAM David Robert
Born: Leytonstone, 2 May 1975
Height: 6'0" Weight: 11.2
Club Honours: FAYC '92; PL '96; FAC '96
International Honours: E: U21-9; Yth

Having broken into the Manchester United first team at the end of 1994-95, David continued to earn rave reviews last season, firstly as an admirable deputy for Ryan Giggs and later as Andy Cole's partner up front for an extended period in December. With eight goals to his credit from a total 40 games, his most important strike came against Chelsea in the FA Cup semi final at Villa Park – a goal which put United through to their 14th FA Cup final. Generally seen as a midfielder, with a whole range of passing skills to go with good engines, his first full season brought him both championship and

FA Cup winners' medals, a tremendous achievement for a 21 year old. A regular for the England U21 side, he added five more caps to his growing collections.
Manchester U (From trainee on 29/1/93) PL 28+9/7 FLC 5+1 FAC 4+1/1 Others 3/1
Preston NE (Loaned on 28/2/95) FL 4+1/2

BEDEAU Anthony (Tony) Charles Osmond
Born: Hammersmith, 24 March 1979
Height: 5'10" Weight: 11.0

Young Torquay YTS who was blooded last season, unfortunately making his first team debut when coming off the bench at Walsall in the 8-4 FA Cup defeat. However, on the brief occasions he played, he produced some bright touches from midfield.
Torquay U (Trainee) FL 1+3 FAC 0+1

BEECH Christopher (Chris) Stephen
Born: Blackpool, 16 September 1974
Height: 5'11" Weight: 11.4
International Honours: E: Sch; Yth

Blackpool midfielder who can also play as a sweeper. Failed to start many games last season, although making useful contributions when coming on as a substitute, expecially when scoring the opening goal in a 2-1 AWS win over Hull in November. Takes the eye when joining the attack.
Blackpool (From trainee on 9/7/93) FL 53+29/4 FLC 4+4 FAC 1 Others 3+3/2

BEENEY Mark Raymond
Born: Tunbridge Wells, 30 December 1967
Height: 6'4" Weight: 14.7
Club Honours: GMVC '89
International Honours: E: SP-1

A good shot stopper, he began last season as Leeds' second choice goalkeeper, but got his chance in December when John Lukic made way following the 6-2 defeat at Sheffield Wednesday. Retained his place for eight games, only to be replaced by Lukic following three straight away defeats, culminating in a poor team performance at Aston Villa. Is sure to be given further opportunities.
Gillingham (From juniors on 17/8/85) FL 2 FLC 1
Maidstone U (Free on 31/1/87) FL 50 FLC 3 FAC 11 Others 6
Aldershot (Loaned on 22/3/90) FL 7
Brighton & Hove A (£30,000 on 28/3/91) FL 68+1 FLC 6 FAC 7 Others 6
Leeds U (£350,000 on 22/4/93) PL 33 FLC 3 FAC 4

BEESLEY Paul
Born: Liverpool, 21 July 1965
Height: 6'1" Weight: 12.6

Joined Leeds prior to 1995-96 getting underway in something of a shock move from neighbouring Sheffield United. This uncompromising, and steady central defender, was used in the main as a squad player but, following injuries to Richard Jobson and John Pemberton, he came into the side in February, looking comfortable and assured alongside David Wetherall. Impressed during the club's cup runs, but did not play in the Wembley Coca Cola final against Aston Villa.
Wigan Ath (Free from Marine on 22/9/84) FL 153+2/3 FLC 13 FAC 6 Others 11
Leyton Orient (£175,000 on 20/10/89) FL 32/1 FAC 1 Others 2/1

Sheffield U (£300,000 on 10/7/90) F/PL 162+6/7 FLC 12+1 FAC 9+2/1 Others 3/1
Leeds U (£250,000 on 2/8/95) PL 8+2 FLC 4+1 FAC 4 Others 2+2

BEESTON Carl Frederick
Born: Stoke, 30 June 1967
Height: 5'10" Weight: 12.4
Club Honours: Div 2 '93
International Honours: E: U21-1

Talented local Stoke City midfielder who returned to the team in the second half of last season after shrugging off a long-standing ankle complaint. Not yet back to his sharpest, but he injected some much needed flair with his great vision.
Stoke C (From apprentice on 1/7/85) FL 207+11/13 FLC 12/1 FAC 7+1/1 Others 15/2

Carl Beeston

BELL Michael (Mickey)
Born: Newcastle, 15 November 1971
Height: 5'10" Weight: 11.4

Began 1995-96 as a left winger, but soon lost his Wycombe place to new signing, David Farrell, before taking over from the injured left back Paul Hardyman and playing in every match until the end of the campaign. Immensely popular with the supporters for his driving runs upfield, he was one of the outstanding players of the season.
Northampton T (From trainee on 1/7/90) FL 133+20/10 FLC 7+1 FAC 5/1 Others 9+2/1
Wycombe W (£45,000 on 21/10/94) FL 71+1/4 FLC 1 FAC 5/2 Others 2+1

BELLAMY Gary
Born: Worksop, 4 July 1962
Height: 6'2" Weight: 11.5
Club Honours: Div 4 '85, '88, Div 3 '89; AMC '88; WC '92

Vastly experienced, tall Leyton Orient central defender who, despite lacking a touch of pace, performed creditably in 36 matches last season. Although still dominant in the air and a threat to opponents at set pieces, with his contract up, and at the age of 34, he was released during the summer.

Chesterfield (From apprentice on 25/6/80) FL 181+3/7 FLC 12 FAC 7/1 Others 4/1
Wolverhampton W (£17,000 on 21/7/87) FL 133+3/9 FLC 9 FAC 3 Others 16
Cardiff C (Loaned on 18/3/92) FL 9
Leyton Orient (£30,000 on 10/9/92) FL 129+3/6 FLC 2 FAC 7 Others 14

BELSVIK Petter
Born: Lillehammer, Norway, 2 October 1967
Height: 6'3" Weight: 12.7

Joined Southend from Norwegian side, IFK Start, last November, in an attempt to solve the Blues' striking problems. Tall, with good ability in the air, Petter scored on his full debut, but, although he won most of the aerial duels he contested, his ability on the ground was not really good enough to make the grade and he eventually returned to Norway.

Southend U (Free from IK Start on 3/11/95) FL 3/1 Others 1

BENALI Francis (Franny) Vincent
Born: Southampton, 30 December 1968
Height: 5'10" Weight: 11.0
International Honours: E: Sch

A strong, competitive Southampton player, Franny had an in and out time of it in 1995-96, while competing for the left back spot with Simon Charlton. However, also able to play at the centre of the defence, and in midfield, he had useful games in those positions. An excellent striker of the ball, and a bit more adventurous than normal during the campaign, but is still looking for his first goal after nearly 250 games.

Southampton (From apprentice on 5/1/87) F/PL 179+23 FLC 17+6 FAC 18 Others 3+1

BENJAMIN Ian Tracey
Born: Nottingham, 11 December 1961
Height: 5'11" Weight: 13.1
Club Honours: Div 4 '87
International Honours: E: Yth

A highly experienced, old style centre forward whose appearances were restricted to just two starts, due to the large squad at Wigan, he scored in the 1-1 draw against Scunthorpe. Released when his contract was paid up towards the end of the season, he joined GM Vauxhall Conference side, Kettering Town.

Sheffield U (From apprentice on 26/5/79) FL 4+1/3 FLC 1+1
West Bromwich A (£100,000 on 31/8/79) FL 1+1
Notts Co (Free on 5/2/82)
Peterborough U (Free on 12/8/82) FL 77+3/14 FLC 7+1/1 FAC 5
Northampton T (Free on 20/8/84) FL 147+3/59 FLC 12/4 FAC 9/3 Others 9/5
Cambridge U (Free on 29/10/87) FL 20+5/2 FAC 2/1
Chester C (Free on 28/7/88) FL 18+4/2 FLC 2 FAC 2/1 Others 2/1
Exeter C (Free on 2/2/89) FL 30+2/4 FLC 2/1 FAC 4+1/4 Others 4/1
Southend U (Free on 2/3/90) FL 122/33 FLC 8/1 FAC 2 Others 7/4
Luton T (£50,000 on 20/11/92) FL 7+6/2 FLC 2 FAC 2
Brentford (Signed on 24/9/93) FL 13+2/2 FLC 0+1 Others 2
Wigan Ath (Free on 30/9/94) FL 13+7/6 FAC 0+1 Others 1+1/1

BENJAMIN Trevor Junior
Born: Kettering, 8 February 1979
Height: 6'2" Weight: 13.2

First year Cambridge United trainee and yet another youth team player introduced into the first team in 1996. Nicknamed "Fash", because of the similarity in style to John Fashanu, the left-footed centre forward was limited to five substitute appearances, but played most of the last game of the season and on that showing will be a handful for many defences.

Cambridge U (Trainee) FL 0+5

BENNETT Frank (Frankie)
Born: Birmingham, 3 January 1969
Height: 5'7" Weight: 11.8

A Southampton striker, who generally plays in a wide position, with tremendous strength and pace and the ability to get past defenders into scoring positions, as yet, Frankie has been unable to translate his potential into solid first team performances. Made just 12 appearances last season, and although seven of them were from the bench, he failed to score. Perhaps the fans will see the best of him if and when he is given an extended run.

Southampton (£7,500 from Halesowen T on 24/2/93) PL 5+14/1 FLC 1+2 FAC 0+1

BENNETT Gary Ernest
Born: Manchester, 4 December 1961
Height: 6'1" Weight: 13.0
Club Honours: Div 3 '88

Powerful central defender who joined Carlisle last November on a free transfer from Sunderland, where he had been based for over a decade. Strong in the air and a determined tackler, his presence brought authority to the heart of the defence. Nor was he afraid to cross the halfway line and he scored a number of valuable goals. But for injuries he would have made more appearances, before his release during the summer.

Manchester C (Free from Ashton U on 8/9/79)
Cardiff C (Free on 16/9/81) FL 85+2/11 FLC 6/1 FAC 3
Sunderland (£65,000 on 26/7/84) FL 362+7/23 FLC 34+1/1 FAC 17+1 Others 21/1
Carlisle U (Free on 16/11/95) FL 26/5 Others 5/1

BENNETT Gary Michael
Born: Liverpool, 20 September 1962
Height: 5'11" Weight: 12.0
Club Honours: AMC '85; WC '95

Prolific goalscorer bought from Wrexham during the summer of 1995, Gary had a disappointing season at Tranmere and ended up being re-sold to Preston North End just before the transfer deadline. Signed to play alongside John Aldridge, the two never clicked and Gary was subsequently moved wide on the right where he had played previously at Chester and Wigan. In his 33 matches he scored just nine goals, but most were vital and brought important victories. As Preston's record signing, his deadly finishing and creative play was soon in evidence when scoring on his debut at Scarborough.

Wigan Ath (Free from Kirby T on 9/10/84) FL 10+10/3 FAC 1 Others 3+1/1
Chester C (Free on 22/8/85) FL 109+17/36 FLC 6+4/1 FAC 8+1/5 Others 10/5

Southend U (Signed on 11/11/88) FL 36+6/6 FLC 4/4 FAC 1 Others 2+1
Chester C (£20,000 on 1/3/90) FL 71+9/15 FLC 8/2 FAC 5/1 Others 4+1/1
Wrexham (Free on 12/8/92) FL 120+1/77 FLC 17/9 FAC 7/3 Others 9/9
Tranmere Rov (£300,000 on 13/7/95) FL 26+3/9 FLC 4
Preston NE (£200,000 on 27/3/96) FL 5+3/1

BENNETT Ian Michael
Born: Worksop, 10 October 1971
Height: 6'0" Weight: 12.0
Club Honours: Div 2 '95; AMC '95

Continuing where he left off the previous season, Ian began 1995-96 with a string of top-class displays which not only brought the League scouts flocking to Birmingham, but produced results. His superb reflexes, agility and positional skills gave great confidence to the defence and it was hardly a surprise that City's fall from grace coincided with the bad hand injury which was to keep him out for the rest of the term.

Newcastle U (Free from Queens Park R juniors on 20/3/89)
Peterborough U (Free on 22/3/91) FL 72 FLC 10 FAC 3 Others 4
Birmingham C (£325,000 on 17/12/93) FL 92 FLC 12 FAC 7 Others 11

Ian Bennett

BENNETT Michael (Micky) Richard
Born: Camberwell, 27 July 1969
Height: 5'11" Weight: 11.11

A strong Millwall player who liked to get forward to put over well-placed crosses, Micky signed during the summer of 1995 from neighbours, Charlton Athletic. Capable of playing in midfield or at right back, in which position he started 1995-96, he picked up a thigh strain in training, with just one game under his belt, and failed to get his place back. Further injuries decimated his season, apart from the odd reserve match, and he was released during the summer.

Charlton Ath (From apprentice on 27/4/87) FL 24+11/2 FLC 4 FAC 1 Others 6+1
Wimbledon (£250,000 on 9/1/90) FL 12+6/2 FLC 1+1 FAC 0+1 Others 1+1
Brentford (£60,000 on 14/7/92) FL 40+6/4 FLC 4+1 FAC 1 Others 6+1
Charlton Ath (Free on 24/3/94) FL 19+5/1 FAC 1
Millwall (Free on 16/5/95) FL 1+1

BENNETT Thomas (Tom) McNeill
Born: Falkirk, 12 December 1969
Height: 5'11" Weight: 11.8

Signed from Wolves during the summer, the cultured midfielder looked to be a real bargain in Stockport's opening games of 1995-96. Unfortunately, though, he was plagued by injury and loss of form and, just when he was getting back to his best, an ankle injury, which required surgery, brought his season to a premature end in January.
Aston Villa (From apprentice on 16/12/87)
Wolverhampton W (Free on 5/7/88) FL 103+12/2 FLC 7 FAC 5+2 Others 1
Stockport Co (£75,000 on 23/6/95) FL 24/1 FLC 5 FAC 3 Others 2

BENT Junior Antony
Born: Huddersfield, 1 March 1970
Height: 5'5" Weight: 10.6

Potentially the best player on Bristol City's books, Junior missed only six matches last season, his excellent turn of pace often leaving opposing defenders chasing shadows as he sped down the wide right. Although his earlier goalscoring record suggests he should be getting on the scoresheet more often, it is his value to provide chances for others, especially the front men, that the manager relies upon. Undoubtedly the fastest player on City's books and a great favourite of the younger fans.
Huddersfield T (From trainee on 9/12/87) FL 25+11/6 FLC 1 FAC 3+1/1 Others 4
Burnley (Loaned on 30/11/89) FL 7+2/3
Bristol C (£30,000 on 22/3/90) FL 125+34/17 FLC 9+1 FAC 11+3/2 Others 5+2
Stoke C (Loaned on 26/3/92) FL 1

BENT Marcus Nathan
Born: Hammersmith, 19 May 1978
Height: 6'0" Weight: 12.0

Exciting, tall wide player, equally at home with either foot. A former trainee who signed professional forms for the club during the 1995 close season, he came into the Brentford team when the side struggled, but his natural ability shone through. Scored his first three senior goals for the club in FA Cup-ties.
Brentford (From trainee on 21/7/95) FL 8+4/1 FAC 4/3 Others 1

BERESFORD David
Born: Middlesbrough, 11 November 1976
Height: 5'8" Weight: 11.4
International Honours: E: Yth; Sch

Affectionately known as "The Flying Midget" at Oldham, David started last season on loan at Swansea, making six appearances before returning to Boundary Park, following a spate of injuries. Very quick and tricky on the wide right and capable of delivering quality crosses, he was mainly used from the subs' bench, making

12 starts in all. Faster than a cruise missile was how the former England manager, Graham Taylor, described him after he had scored against Wolves in November.
Oldham Ath (From trainee on 22/7/94) P/FL 8+23/2 FLC 1+1 Others 3
Swansea C (Loaned on 11/8/95) FL 4+2

BERESFORD John
Born: Sheffield, 4 September 1966
Height: 5'6" Weight: 10.12
Club Honours: Div 1 '93
International Honours: E: B-2; Yth; Sch

Compact left back whose overlapping runs were a feature of Newcastle's attacking style in 1995-96, John's consistent performances brought him selection for the England squad for the Norway game, his second such call-up, although he has yet to make the team. With a desire to get forward to deliver pin-point crosses into the box, he was an integral member of the side that stormed to the top of the Premiership, before being substituted early during the home game with Villa in April, following a verbal dispute with Kevin Keegan, and losing his place to Robbie Elliott for the remainder of the term.
Manchester C (From apprentice on 16/9/83)
Barnsley (Free on 4/8/86) FL 79+9/5 FLC 5+2/2 FAC 5/1
Portsmouth (£300,000 on 23/3/89) FL 102+5/8 FLC 12/2 FAC 11 Others 2
Newcastle U (£650,000 on 2/7/92) F/PL 141+1/1 FLC 14 FAC 12/1 Others 6

BERESFORD Marlon
Born: Lincoln, 2 September 1969
Height: 6'1" Weight: 13.1

Consistent, sometimes spectacular and, on more than one occasion, the saviour of a poor defence last season, Marlon remains one of Burnley's most valuable assets and one of the best goalkeepers in the Endsleigh League. He was missed during two lengthy absences, the first following a hernia operation and the second as a result of a back injury.
Sheffield Wed (From trainee on 23/9/87)
Bury (Loaned on 25/8/89) FL 1
Northampton T (Loaned on 27/9/90) FL 13 Others 2
Crewe Alex (Loaned on 28/2/91) FL 3
Northampton T (Loaned on 15/8/91) FL 15
Burnley (£95,000 on 28/8/92) FL 166 FLC 12 FAC 14 Others 11

BERG Henning
Born: Eidsvell, Norway, 1 September 1969
Height: 6'0" Weight: 12.7
Club Honours: PL '95
International Honours: Norway: 38

Ultra-cool Blackburn full back with great positional sense and a rare ability to slide inside and cover. Also, probably the best tackler in the Premiership, who has no fears when isolated one on one against even the best of wingers. Utilised early last season as a replacement for the injured Ian Pearce in the centre of the defence, a position he plays for Norway, this was abandoned when Graeme le Saux was also put out of action. Superbly steady throughout the campaign, as an ever present, although he was not as evidenced in the attack, possibly because of changes in personnel in front of him.

Blackburn Rov (£400,000 from Lillestrom on 26/1/93) PL 218+5/2 FLC 13 FAC 8 Others 9

BERGKAMP Dennis
Born: Amsterdam, Holland, 18 May 1969
Height: 6'0" Weight: 12.5
International Honours: Holland: 47

Signed from Inter Milan during the 1995 close season, Dennis proved the classiest player to have graced Highbury since Liam Brady, with superb first touch and powerful shooting ability. Not an out-and-out striker, although he scored 16 goals, some of them quite breathtaking, but having more of a supporting role sitting in the hole just off the front man, Ian Wright, he was effectively Arsenal's playmaker, holding the ball up and looking for Wright, David Platt or Paul Merson to make runs, or going through on his own. Missed most of December with calf problems, but otherwise an ever present, Dennis adapted to English football brilliantly and is sure to be the fulcrum of the "new" Arsenal, following his impressive displays for Holland in Euro '96.
Arsenal (£7,500,000 from Inter Milan, via Ajax, on 3/7/95) PL 33/11 FLC 7/5 FAC 1

Dennis Bergkamp

BERGSSON Gudni
Born: Iceland, 21 July 1965
Height: 6'1" Weight: 12.3
Club Honours: CS '91
International Honours: Iceland: 68

The captain of the Icelandic national side, Gudni was a steady influence in the Bolton defence throughout last season in both right back and central positions. Missing just four league games, which were down to a suspension after being sent off at Queens Park Rangers in December and to injury two months later, his four Premiership goals were a good return, with the highlight being the equaliser he hit at White Hart Lane against his former club, Spurs.

Tottenham H (£100,000 from Valur on 15/12/88) F/PL 51+20/2 FLC 4+2 FAC 2+2 Others 5+1
Bolton W (£65,000 on 21/3/95) P/FL 42/4 FLC 6+1 Others 3

BERKLEY Austin James
Born: Dartford, 28 January 1973
Height: 5'9" Weight: 10.10
Shrewsbury left winger who signed on a free from Swindon during the 1995 close season, Austin loves to run at a defence and is equally dangerous from the line or cutting inside, being the provider of numerous strikes. Hopefully, his personal goal tally will improve.
Gillingham (From trainee on 13/5/91) FL 0+3 Others 0+3
Swindon T (Free on 16/5/92) FL 0+1 FLC 0+1 Others 3+1/1
Shrewsbury T (Free on 29/7/95) FL 36+2/1 FLC 3 FAC 5 Others 6

BERNAL Andrew (Andy)
Born: Canberra, Australia, 16 May 1966
Height: 5'10" Weight: 12.5
International Honours: Australia: 18
Confirmed his reputation at Reading in 1995-96 as a strong, yet stylish defender, capable of playing anywhere along the back line, and the scorer of vital goals in the away games at Leicester and Ipswich. Captained the side on occasions, and also regained his place in the Australian national team, with an appearance against Chile in Santiago.
Ipswich T (Free from Sporting Gijon on 24/9/87) FL 4+5 Others 0+2
Reading (£30,000 from Sydney Olympic on 26/7/94) FL 67/2 FLC 7 FAC 2 Others 3

BERNARD Paul Robert
Born: Edinburgh, 30 December 1972
Height: 5'11" Weight: 11.8
International Honours: S: 2; B-1; U21-15
Having played in nine of Oldham's opening ten fixtures last season, Paul, highly rated by Scotland manager, Craig Brown, moved to Aberdeen for £850,000 at the end of September. His great attitude had earlier seen him come back strongly from a disastrous injury packed 1994-95, to show just what he was capable of in Latics' midfield. A strong tackler, and skilful when in possession, his ability to use either foot is a real plus.
Oldham Ath (From trainee on 16/7/91) F/PL 105+7/18 FLC 11+1/2 FAC 11/1 Others 1+1

BERRY Gregory (Greg) John
Born: Grays, 5 March 1971
Height: 5'11" Weight: 12.0
Attacking wide left-sided Millwall midfielder with good speed and control. Unfortunately, a spell on loan at Brighton last August ended when he was stretchered off with damaged ankle ligaments at Bournemouth, restricting his season to just two appearances for the Lions and a seven match temporary transfer period at Leyton Orient in March.
Leyton Orient (£2,000 from East Thurrock on 3/7/89) FL 68+12/14 FLC 6/3 FAC 8+2/2 Others 5+3/1
Wimbledon (£250,000 on 17/8/92) PL 6+1/1 FAC 0+1
Millwall (£200,000 on 24/3/94) FL 10+10/1 FLC 1/2 FAC 1 Others 1/1

Brighton & HA (Loaned on 24/8/95) FL 6/2
Leyton Orient (Loaned on 22/3/96) FL 4+3

BERRY Trevor John
Born: Haslemere, 1 August 1974
Height: 5'7" Weight: 10.8
Club Honours: AMC '96
International Honours: E: Yth
Signed from Aston Villa early in 1995-96, after an initial loan spell, this speedy winger made an immediate impact for Rotherham when scoring the only goal of the game on his debut against Brentford in September. A former England youth international, Trevor is a workhorse who will run all day and his ability to track back opposing forwards proved invaluable. Mainly regarded as a wide right-sided player, he also played on the left as well as in a more central midfield role, missing only a handful of games throughout the season, and picking up an AWS winners' medal following the 2-1 Wembley win over Shrewsbury.
Aston Villa (£50,000 from Bournemouth juniors on 3/4/92)
Rotherham U (£20,000 on 8/9/95) FL 33+3/7 FAC 1 Others 7/1

BETTS Simon Richard
Born: Middlesbrough, 3 March 1973
Height: 5'7" Weight: 11.4
Simon is a dependable full back who can play down either flank. Almost ever present for Colchester last season, he revealed a hitherto unsuspected goalscoring prowess, both from set pieces and from open play. Now past the 150 appearance mark for the U's in all competitions.
Ipswich T (From trainee on 2/7/91)
Wrexham (Free on 13/8/92)
Scarborough (Free on 3/11/92)
Colchester U (Free on 11/12/92) FL 133+3/8 FLC 3 FAC 6+1 Others 10/2

BIGGINS Wayne
Born: Sheffield, 20 November 1961
Height: 5'11" Weight: 13.0
Club Honours: AMC '92
A veteran striker, who did not have the best of times at Oxford, Wayne was signed from Stoke during the 1995 close season to replace another experienced striker, John Byrne, but was only on the spot twice, with penalties, before joining Wigan in November. Recruited by Athletic manager, John Deehan, for the third time in his career, injuries unfortunately restricted his appearances to just 15 starts and two goals.
Lincoln C (From apprentice on 22/11/79) FL 8/1 (Free to Kings Lynn during 1981 close season)
Burnley (£7,500 from Matlock on 4/2/84) FL 78/29 FLC 3/1 FAC 3/1 Others 7/5
Norwich C (£40,000 on 17/10/85) FL 66+13/16 FLC 6/2 FAC 4 Others 6+2/3
Manchester C (£150,000 on 15/7/88) FL 29+3/9 FLC 4/1 FAC 2
Stoke C (£250,000 on 10/8/89) FL 120+2/46 FLC 10/2 FAC 6 Others 10/5
Barnsley (£200,000 on 2/10/92) FL 44+3/16 FAC 3+1
Glasgow Celtic (Signed on 25/11/93) SL 4+5 SC 0+1
Stoke C (£125,000 on 24/3/94) FL 18+9/6 FLC 1+1 Others 3+1/2
Luton T (Loaned on 20/1/95) FL 6+1/1 FAC 2/1
Oxford U (Free on 6/7/95) FL 8+2/1 FLC 3+1/1 Others 0+1
Wigan Ath (Free on 17/11/95) FL 15+3/2

BILIC Slaven
Born: Croatia, 11 September 1968
Height: 6'2" Weight: 13.8
International Honours: Croatia: 23
Having joined West Ham last February from Karlsruhe, his fierce tackling and heading ability were quickly evidenced in victories over Newcastle and Spurs. Slotting in well with Marc Rieper at the back, and helping the Hammers to finish in the top ten, he is a current Croatian international who played against England at Wembley in April. Is also a legend in the making and probably West Ham's next captain. Had an excellent Euro '96 as Croatia reached the quarter final stage before going out to Germany.
West Ham U (£1,300,000 from Karlsruhe on 4/2/96) PL 13

BILLING Peter Graham
Born: Liverpool, 24 October 1964
Height: 6'2" Weight: 13.6
Club Honours: AMC '93
Experienced central defender signed from Port Vale during the summer of 1995 to steady a young Hartlepool defence. Early in 1995-96, he was critical of his own form, but by mid-season he had settled well and was proving to be a popular acquisition. Overall he did the job expected, but towards the end of the campaign he lost favour with manager, Keith Houchen, and was told he would be released.
Everton (Free from South Liverpool on 15/1/86) FL 1 Others 4
Crewe Alex (£12,000 on 23/12/86) FL 83+5/1 FLC 1+1 FAC 5 Others 9
Coventry C (£120,000 on 28/6/89) F/PL 51+7/1 FLC 9+1 FAC 7 Others 2
Port Vale (£35,000 on 26/2/93) FL 23+3 FLC 1 Others 3+2
Hartlepool U (Free on 8/8/95) FL 35+1 FLC 4 FAC 1 Others 2

BILLY Christopher (Chris) Anthony
Born: Huddersfield, 2 January 1973
Height: 5'11" Weight: 11.8
Signed from Huddersfield Town, prior to the start of 1995-96, Chris usually played for Plymouth as a right-sided midfielder, but also turned out at right back and in central midfield on occasion. Is a young man with plenty of potential and a good squad member.
Huddersfield T (From trainee on 1/7/91) FL 76+18/4 FLC 8+2 FAC 5 Others 15+2/2
Plymouth Arg (Signed on 10/8/95) FL 22+10/4 FLC 2 FAC 3 Others 2

BIMSON Stuart James
Born: Liverpool, 29 September 1969
Height: 5'11" Weight: 11.12
The adventurous left back began as the Bury's first choice last season, but fractured an elbow in a Coca Cola Cup-tie at Reading and was sidelined for several weeks. Made a brief re-appearance for two games during February, but then lost his place to the ever-green Nicky Reid.
Bury (£12,500 from Macclesfield T on 6/2/95) FL 35 FLC 4 Others 3

BIRCH Paul
Born: Birmingham, 20 November 1962
Height: 5'6" Weight: 11.0
Club Honours: FAYC '80; ESC '82

The right-sided Wolves' midfield man was not called upon until last October, having been injured, but he looked sharp at Watford and was involved in ten out of 13 games. The latter saw him come on as substitute in Mark McGhee's first match in charge, and he has not played since, going out on loan to Preston. At Deepdale, he was used as cover for the injured Lee Cartwright and slotted in well in midfield. Widely experienced, his busy, bustling style helped put North End back on course after faltering in the New Year.

Aston Villa (From apprentice on 15/7/80) FL 153+20/16 FLC 21+4/5 FAC 9+5/3 Others 5+2/1
Wolverhampton W (£400,000 on 1/2/91) FL 128+14/15 FLC 11+1/3 FAC 2+1 Others 8+1/1
Preston NE (Loaned on 7/3/96) FL 11/2

BIRD Anthony (Tony)
Born: Cardiff, 1 September 1974
Height: 5'10" Weight: 10.7
International Honours: W: U21-8; Yth

A striker, who was given early opportunities for Cardiff and the Welsh U21 side last season, Tony scored three times in City's opening two games, but was one of the first to go during a cost cutting exercise at the end of 1995. Is now a prolific scorer for Barry Town in the Konica League.

Cardiff C (From trainee on 4/8/93) FL 44+31/13 FLC 8/2 FAC 4+1/1 Others 12+4/3

BISHOP Charles (Charlie) Darren
Born: Nottingham, 16 February 1968
Height: 6'0" Weight: 13.7

The burly, no-nonsense defender started last season as one of Barnsley's first choice centre backs, where his pace made him an ideal man marker. However, after the signings of Peter Shirtliff and Arjan de Zeeuw he found first team opportunities few and far between. He then spent loan spells at Preston and Burnley. Played four games at right back at the former and then went to Turf Moor on transfer deadline day to fill in at left back for the injured Chris Vinnicombe, proving a key member of the defensive line up.

Watford (Free from Stoke C juniors on 17/4/86)
Bury (Free on 10/8/87) FL 104+10/6 FLC 5 FAC 4/1 Others 12+1
Barnsley (£50,000 on 24/7/91) FL 124+6/1 FLC 11+1 FAC 9 Others 5
Preston NE (Loaned on 12/1/96) FL 4
Burnley (Loaned on 28/3/96) FL 9

BISHOP Edward (Eddie) Michael
Born: Liverpool, 28 November 1962
Height: 5'10" Weight: 12.6
Club Honours: AMC '90

Having re-signed for Chester immediately prior to 1995-96 getting underway, Eddie started in fine style, scoring in the opening five games. A tough-tackling midfielder, he unfortunately missed the second half of the season due to injury and was released during the summer.

Tranmere Rov (Signed from Northwich Vic on 17/3/88) FL 46+30/19 FLC 8+3/3 FAC 2+2 Others 2+4
Chester C (£70,000 on 28/12/90) FL 100+18/28 FLC 14/3 FAC 3+3 Others 4+2
Crewe Alex (Loaned on 19/3/92) FL 3

BISHOP Ian William
Born: Liverpool, 29 May 1965
Height: 5'9" Weight: 10.12
International Honours: E: B-1

The classy West Ham midfielder had an excellent season in 1995-96 and was ever present for 35 league games before sustaining a groin injury which forced him to miss the remaining programme. Scored a blistering 25-yarder at Bolton, leaving one to wonder why he cannot get on the scoresheet more often, while his crisp passing makes many goals like the well weighted through ball which set up Tony Cottee in the home win over Coventry.

Everton (From apprentice on 24/5/83) FL 0+1
Crewe Alex (Loaned on 22/3/84) FL 4
Carlisle U (£15,000 on 11/10/84) FL 131+1/14 FLC 8/1 FAC 5/1 Others 4
Bournemouth (£35,000 on 14/7/88) FL 44/2 FLC 4 FAC 5 Others 1
Manchester C (£465,000 on 2/8/89) FL 18+1/2 FLC 4/1 Others 1
West Ham U (£500,000 on 28/12/89) F/PL 211+11/11 FLC 16/1 FAC 20+1/3 Others 4+1/1

Ian Bishop

BJORNEBY Stig-Inge
Born: Norway, 11 December 1969
Height: 5'10" Weight: 11.9
Club Honours: FLC '95
International Honours: Norway: 49

After coming back from injury, at Bolton last December, he played just once more for the Liverpool first team, spending most of his time in the reserves. His place at left back being taken first by Steve Harkness and later by Rob Jones. Prior to last season, the Norwegian international had proved to

be an excellent tackler with the ability to use his speed to good effect on the overlap.

Liverpool (£600,000 from Rosenborg on 18/12/92) PL 50+3 FLC 7 FAC 7+2

BLACK Anthony (Tony)
Born: Barrow, 15 July 1969
Height: 5'9" Weight: 11.1

Speedy, and direct Wigan right winger whose 1995-96 season came to a tragic end in March when he suffered a broken fibula and ankle at Mansfield Town. Scored his first goals for the club, following a brace of strikes in the second round FA Cup-tie against his home town club, Barrow, at the start of December in a 4-0 victory and continued to impress, albeit most of his games coming from the bench.

Wigan Ath (£12,500 from Bamber Bridge on 22/3/95) FL 17+13/2 FAC 2/2 Others 0+1

BLACK Kingsley Terence
Born: Luton, 22 June 1968
Height: 5'8" Weight: 10.11
Club Honours: FLC '88; FMC '92
International Honours: E: Sch. NI: 30; B-2; U21-1

For the second consecutive season the Northern Ireland international winger was left out in the cold by Nottingham Forest, starting only one game against Arsenal last February and only once used as a substitute. On the transfer list, he had a short loan spell with Millwall in October and made an immediate impact, scoring with an exquisitely flighted free kick on his debut at Derby. However, back at the City Ground, Kingsley had little chance to display his all-round skills, including the ability to deliver telling crosses from often extreme angles. *Stop Press:* Signed for Grimsby during the summer.

Luton T (From juniors on 7/7/86) FL 123+4/26 FLC 16+2/1 FAC 5+1/2 Others 3+2/1
Nottingham F (£1,500,000 on 2/9/91) F/PL 80+18/14 FLC 19+1/5 FAC 4 Others 4+2/1
Sheffield U (Loaned on 2/3/95) FL 8+3/2
Millwall (Loaned on 29/9/95) FL 1+2/1 FLC 0+1

BLACKMORE Clayton Graham
Born: Neath, 23 September 1964
Height: 5'8" Weight: 11.12
Club Honours: FAC '90; CS '90; ECWC '91; ESC '91; PL '93; Div 1 '95
International Honours: W: 38; U21-3; Yth; Sch

Very versatile, Clayton is equally at home in Middlesbrough's defence or midfield, having helped Manchester United to win many honours, including the famous victory against Barcelona in the European Cup Winners Cup in 1990. Although his first team appearances were strictly limited last season, only being drafted into action during January and February during an injury crisis, he mainly lent his vast experience to the reserves, where his contribution helped Boro win the Pontins League second division championship.

Manchester U (From apprentice on 28/9/82) F/PL 150+36/19 FLC 23+2/3 FAC 15+6/1 Others 19/4
Middlesbrough (Free on 11/7/94) P/FL 30+5/2 FLC 1+1 Others 1

Clayton Blackmore

BLACKWELL Dean Robert
Born: Camden, 5 December 1969
Height: 6'1" Weight: 12.7
International Honours: E: U21-6
Dean is another in the Wimbledon back four who is totally reliable in the air. After a long period out of the game with an ongoing injury problem, he returned last February, an event that coincided with an upturn in the team's fortunes. Perhaps one of the most promising aspects of his comeback was the partnership that he and Chris Perry formed at the back at the tail-end of the season. However, the outstanding facet of his play, apart from his aerial strength, is an ability to attack the ball and to make space for himself.
Wimbledon (From trainee on 7/7/88) F/PL 75+17/1 FLC 3 FAC 10+1 Others 1
Plymouth Arg (Loaned on 15/3/90) FL 5+2

BLACKWELL Kevin Patrick
Born: Luton, 21 December 1958
Height: 5'11" Weight: 12.10
Club Honours: GMVC '87
Goalkeeper. One of four Huddersfield players to follow former manager, Neil Warnock, to Plymouth last season, having arrived in order to run the youth team he found himself playing over 20 games and performing admirably. An excellent organiser on and off the field, interestingly, Kevin has spent his entire Football League career playing under Warnock.
Scarborough (Signed from Barnet on 1/11/86) FL 44 FLC 11 FAC 2 Others 2
Notts Co (£15,000 on 8/11/89)

Torquay U (Free on 15/1/93) FL 18 Others 2
Huddersfield T (Free on 5/8/93) FL 3+2 FLC 0+1 FAC 1 Others 3
Plymouth Arg (Free on 11/8/95) FL 20 FAC 3

BLADES Paul Andrew
Born: Peterborough, 5 January 1965
Height: 6'0" Weight: 11.0
Club Honours: Div 2 '87; AMC '96
International Honours: E: Yth
Having joined Rotherham in the 1995 close season from Wolves as a central defender, a club injury crisis saw him playing most of the latter part of the season at right back, where he showed his ability to support the attack, providing many goalscoring opportunities with his crosses. Paul was the second most expensive signing in the club's history and proved a good asset after taking a little while to settle in. Finished the campaign with a medal, following the 2-1 Wembley AWS win over Shrewsbury.
Derby Co (From apprentice on 29/12/82) FL 157+9/1 FLC 9+3 FAC 12 Others 8+2
Norwich C (£700,000 on 18/7/90) FL 47 FLC 8 FAC 2 Others 5
Wolverhampton W (£325,000 on 14/8/92) FL 103+4/2 FLC 4+1 FAC 9/1 Others 6
Rotherham U (£110,000 on 18/7/95) FL 34/1 FLC 3 FAC 1 Others 7

BLAKE Mark Antony
Born: Nottingham, 16 December 1970
Height: 5'11" Weight: 12.9
International Honours: E: U21-9; Yth; Sch
One time Leicester City's record signing, he briefly displaced Julian Joachim on the right side of midfield last October. After occasional selections as substitute once Martin O'Neill took charge, he was transfer listed just before deadline day. Mainly recognised as a midfielder, he has, in the past, played a number of roles, including full back. Released during the summer.
Aston Villa (From trainee on 1/7/89) FL 26+5/2 FLC 1+1 FAC 2 Others 2
Wolverhampton W (Loaned on 17/1/91) FL 2
Portsmouth (£400,000 on 5/8/93) FL 15 Others 4+1
Leicester C (£360,000 on 24/3/94) F/PL 42+7/4 FLC 4 Others 3

BLAKE Mark Christopher
Born: Portsmouth, 17 December 1967
Height: 6'1" Weight: 12.8
International Honours: E: Yth
A reliable Fulham central defender who missed two months of last season through injury, Mark is dangerous at set pieces, and an excellent reader of the game, being rarely caught out of position. In short, he is one of the club's most consistent players.
Southampton (From apprentice on 23/12/85) FL 18/2 FLC 2 FAC 3 Others 1+2
Colchester U (Loaned on 5/9/89) FL 4/1
Shrewsbury T (£100,000 on 22/3/90) FL 142/3 FLC 12 FAC 9 Others 11
Fulham (Free on 16/9/94) FL 69+4/8 FLC 6/1 FAC 6/1 Others 4

BLAKE Nathan Alexander
Born: Cardiff, 27 January 1972
Height: 5'11" Weight: 13.12
Club Honours: WC '92, '93; Div 3 '93
International Honours: W: 6; B-1; U21-5; Yth

Continuing his goalscoring run for Sheffield United in 1995-96, and continuing to feature for Wales, following Howard Kendall's appointment as manager, Nathan played only 45 minutes at Ipswich for the new regime before joining Bolton and making his debut in a 2-2 draw at Tottenham in December. A strong front runner, he showed plenty of reasons why he had been the Blades' leading scorer the previous season, but could only find the net once for the Wanderers. That came in the club's 4-1 win at Middlesbrough, their first away victory in the top flight since April 1979. Became Bolton's first Welsh international since Wyn Davies represented the principality during the 1960s.
Cardiff C (Free from Chelsea juniors on 20/8/90) FL 113+18/35 FLC 6+2 FAC 10/4 Others 13+2/1
Sheffield U (£300,000 on 17/2/94) P/FL 55+14/34 FLC 3+1/1 FAC 1 Others 1
Bolton W (£1,500,000 on 23/12/95) PL 14+4/1 FAC 2

BLAKE Noel Lloyd George
Born: Jamaica, 12 January 1962
Height: 6'0" Weight: 13.5
A no-nonsense Exeter central defender, Noel's arrival from Dundee last summer helped to improve the club's defensive record. This was no coincidence as his presence undoubtedly rubbed off on his defensive team mates. Is also the assistant manager.
Aston Villa (Signed from Sutton Coldfield T on 1/8/79) FL 4
Shrewsbury T (Loaned on 1/3/82) FL 6
Birmingham C (£55,000 on 15/9/82) FL 76/5 FLC 12 FAC 8
Portsmouth (£150,000 on 24/4/84) FL 144/10 FLC 14/1 FAC 10/2 Others 5/1
Leeds U (Free on 4/7/88) FL 51/4 FLC 4+1 FAC 2 Others 4
Stoke C (£175,000 on 9/2/90) FL 74+1/3 FLC 6 FAC 3+1 Others 4+1
Bradford C (Loaned on 27/2/92) FL 6
Bradford C (Free on 20/7/92) FL 38+1/3 FLC 2+1 FAC 5/1 Others 4
Dundee (Free on 10/12/93) SL 52+2/2 SLC 2 SC 5 Others 3
Exeter C (Free on 18/8/95) FL 44/2 FLC 2 FAC 1

BLAKE Robert James
Born: Middlesbrough, 4 March 1976
Height: 5'11" Weight: 12.0
Local striker who came through Darlington's youth side to make his mark last season as the club's top scorer with 12 goals, all coming since the turn of the year. Now attracting the attention of bigger clubs, following his fine display in the Wembley play-off final.
Darlington (From trainee on 1/7/94) FL 26+12/11 FLC 0+2 FAC 1+1 Others 3/1

BLATHERWICK Steven (Steve) Scott
Born: Nottingham, 20 September 1973
Height: 6'1" Weight: 12.12
Yet to play for Nottingham Forest, Steve was loaned out to Hereford last September in order to gain experience. Given an extended run of 12 matches, and playing in the defence, he showed himself to be both creative and consistent, also finding time to score in the 2-2 draw at home to Exeter.

Nottingham F (Free from Notts Co juniors on 2/8/92) FL 3 Others 2
Wycombe W (Loaned on 18/2/94) FL 2 Others 1
Hereford U (Loaned on 11/9/95) FL 10/1 Others 2

BLINKER Reginald (Regi) Waldie
Born: Surinam, 4 June 1969
Height: 5'8" Weight: 10.11
International Honours: Holland: 3

Signed from Dutch side, Feyenoord, last March, this pacy, skilful Dutch international winger quickly made an impact with two goals on his Sheffield Wednesday debut. Owls' fans took him to their hearts immediately because he added flair and exuberance at a time when the play was becoming dull and predictable. A good money spinner for the club has been "Regi" wigs, based on his unusual hairstyle, and great things are expected from him in the coming season.
Sheffield Wed (£275,000 from Feyenoord on 5/3/96) PL 9/2

BLISSETT Gary Paul
Born: Manchester, 29 June 1964
Height: 6'0" Weight: 12.7
Club Honours: Div 3 '92

A proven Wimbledon striker who has scored at every level, Gary continues to show many inventive and skilful touches as well as being able to spot an opening to finish clinically. Came off the bench for Dons' first four games last season, before going on loan to Wycombe in December, where two goals from four appearances whetted local appetites. Although returning to Selhurst Park, there was to be no more action there and he ended the campaign at Crewe, playing 12 times in all.
Crewe Alex (Signed from Altrincham on 23/8/83) FL 112+10/39 FLC 9/3 FAC 4 Others 6+1/4
Brentford (£60,000 on 26/3/87) FL 220+13/79 FLC 16+3/9 FAC 14/7 Others 23+2/10
Wimbledon (£350,000 on 23/7/93) PL 10+21/3 FLC 1+2 FAC 1+2
Wycombe W (Loaned on 7/12/95) FL 4/2
Crewe Alex (Loaned on 11/3/96) FL 10/1 Others 1+1

BLOUNT Mark
Born: Derby, 5 January 1974
Height: 5'10" Weight: 12.0

Young Sheffield United defender who played several games at centre back and full back at the start of last season but, following criticism, probably unwarranted, in the Coca Cola Cup defeat by Bury, he returned to the reserves. One of eight players to have his contract cancelled by the club in March, he had a trial spell with Scarborough, where he failed to make an appearance, before joining Peterborough United and making four starts.
Sheffield U (£12,500 from Gresley Rov on 11/2/94) FL 11+2 FLC 2 Others 2
Scarborough (Free on 2/3/96)
Peterborough U (Free on 28/3/96) FL 4+1

BLUNT Jason
Born: Penzance, 16 August 1977
Height: 5'8" Weight: 10.10
International Honours: E: Yth

Only 18 years old, Jason, a local product, impressed in 1995-96, playing in midfield for Leeds' youth and reserve sides, before

making his full debut against Middlesbrough, in the game immediately following the Coca Cola Cup final. Gave an inspiring performance and should have a bright future in the game.
Leeds U (From trainee on 1/1/95) PL 2+1

BOARDMAN Craig George
Born: Barnsley, 30 November 1970
Height: 6'0" Weight: 11.8

Strong central defender, and the son of former Barnsley player, George, Craig joined Scarborough on a free transfer from Halifax Town in the summer of 1995. Unfortunately, his time at the club was blighted by injury problems and a three month absence due to a hernia, which severely restricted his opportunities to impress, and he was given a free transfer at the end of the season.
Nottingham F (From trainee on 20/5/89) FLC 0+1
Peterborough U (Free on 5/8/93) Others 1 (Free to Halifax T on 6/11/93)
Scarborough (Free on 8/8/95) FL 6+3 FAC 2 Others 1+1

BOCHENSKI Simon
Born: Worksop, 6 December 1975
Height: 5'8" Weight: 11.13

Barnsley striker who made a couple of substitutional appearances during last season. As the reserves' top scorer, Simon showed plenty of pace and an obvious eye for goal and, with more experience, could claim a regular place in the side.
Barnsley (From trainee on 6/7/94) FL 0+1 FAC 0+1

BODEN Christopher (Chris) Desmond
Born: Wolverhampton, 13 October 1973
Height: 5'9" Weight: 11.0

A left-sided defender who was restricted to Derby's reserves except for a short spell at left back last November as replacement for Shane Nicholson, Chris proved a useful player to have as cover at the back or in midfield. Loaned to Shrewsbury in January, he played five games and looked comfortable on the ball as a provider to the flank.
Aston Villa (From trainee on 3/12/91) PL 0+1
Barnsley (Loaned on 15/10/93) FL 4
Derby Co (£150,000 on 24/3/95) FL 8+2
Shrewsbury T (Loaned on 19/1/96) FL 5

BODIN Paul John
Born: Cardiff, 13 September 1964
Height: 6'0" Weight: 13.1
Club Honours: Div 2 '96
International Honours: W: 23; U21-1; Yth

Experienced Welsh international who was second choice for Swindon's left back slot at the start of last season, but once in the side, impressed enough to be chosen by his fellow professionals for the PFA division two side. Although ultimately celebrating the winning of a division two championship medal as Town gained promotion, following the arrival of Alex Smith in March, however, it was clear that there was no future for "Zippy" and he was given a free transfer in May.
Newport Co (Free from Chelsea juniors on 28/1/82)
Cardiff C (Free on 1/8/82) FL 68+7/4 FLC 11 FAC 4 (Free to Bath C during 1985 close season)

Newport Co (£15,000 on 27/1/88) FL 6/1
Swindon T (£30,000 on 7/3/88) FL 87+6/9 FLC 12 FAC 6 Others 8/1
Crystal Palace (£550,000 on 20/3/91) FL 8+1 FLC 1
Newcastle U (Loaned on 5/12/91) FL 6
Swindon T (£225,000 on 10/1/92) F/PL 140+6/28 FLC 14 FAC 10/1 Others 8/1

BODLEY Michael (Mick) John
Born: Hayes, 14 September 1967
Height: 6'1" Weight: 13.2
Club Honours: GMVC '91

Mick was given the Southend captaincy by manager, Ronnie Whelan, at the start of last season and he responded in magnificent style with performances at centre half that won the hearts of the Blues' faithful and culminated in him being voted as runner-up in the "Player of the Year" poll. Dominant in the air, and strong on the ground, he added excellent distribution to his repertoire and his never-say-die attitude was an example to all around him.
Chelsea (From apprentice on 17/9/85) FL 6/1 FLC 1 Others 1
Northampton T (£50,000 on 12/1/89) FL 20 Others 2
Barnet (£15,000 on 1/10/89) FL 69/3 FLC 2 FAC 10 Others 9
Southend U (Free on 15/7/93) FL 66+1/2 FLC 3 FAC 2 Others 7
Gillingham (Loaned on 23/11/94) FL 6+1 Others 1
Birmingham C (Loaned on 23/1/95) FL 3

BOERE Jeroen Willem
Born: Arnhem, Holland, 18 November 1967
Height: 6'3" Weight: 13.5

The Dutch striker moved to Crystal Palace from West Ham last September, in an exchange deal involving Iain Dowie, yet scored only once in eight substitute appearances, before signing for Southend. Unfortunately for the Blues, just when their plight was desperate and he looked to have fitted the bill well, a badly broken finger ended his season early. Tall and strong in the air, Jeroen also looked more than competent on the ground and could easily be the foil that allows Mike Marsh and Paul Byrne to show their skills to the full this coming season.
West Ham U (£250,000 from Go Ahead Eagles on 22/9/93) PL 15+10/6 FLC 1+1/1 FAC 2
Portsmouth (Loaned on 24/3/94) FL 4+1
West Bromwich A (Loaned on 8/9/94) FL 5
Crystal Palace (£375,000 on 7/9/95) FL 0+8/1
Southend U (£150,000 on 1/3/96) FL 6/2

BOGIE Ian
Born: Newcastle, 6 December 1967
Height: 5'7" Weight: 12.0
International Honours: E: Sch

Ball-playing Port Vale central midfielder with an excellent shot. Endeared himself to the fans by scoring the winning goal in each of the local derbys against Stoke City in 1995-96, one of them being the division's quickest goal of the season after just 12 seconds. He also scored in each of the epic FA Cup-ties against Everton and, overall, had a very satisfactory campaign.
Newcastle U (From apprentice on 18/12/85) FL 7+7 FLC 0+1 FAC 1+2 Others 3/1
Preston NE (Signed on 9/2/89) FL 67+12/12 FLC 3+1 FAC 3 Others 4+1

Millwall (£145,000 on 16/8/91) FL 44+7/1 FLC 1 FAC 2 Others 3
Leyton Orient (Signed on 14/10/93) FL 62+3/5 FLC 2 FAC 2 Others 8+1
Port Vale (£50,000 on 23/3/95) FL 34+7/5 FLC 2 FAC 5+1/2 Others 8

BOHINEN Lars
Born: Vadso, Norway, 8 September 1966
Height: 5'11" Weight: 12.2
International Honours: Norway: 46

Central midfielder who was much missed when leaving Nottingham Forest last October, bound for Blackburn. On his day a world class player, with natural ball skills that buy him time, and the vision and ability to dominate, Lars transformed Rovers' play immediately, scoring on his debut and helping to drive the club into fifth place in the Premiership. The huge influence he exerted on the team was not totally apparent until he was forced out, after just 20 games, following an injured calf picked up in an international match for Norway. Unable to replace him effectively, the club can only hope that he comes back with renewed vigour at the start of 1996-97.
Nottingham F (£450,000 from Young Boys of Berne on 5/11/93) F/PL 59+5/7 FLC 7+1/2 FAC 2/1 Others 1
Blackburn Rov (£700,000 on 14/10/95) PL 17+2/4 FAC 1

Lars Bohinen

BOLAND William (Willie) John
Born: Ennis, Ireland, 6 August 1975
Height: 5'9" Weight: 11.2
International Honours: Ei: U21-6; Yth; Sch

Outstanding Coventry prospect who is a product of the club's youth scheme, Willie is a skilful innovative midfielder who rarely wastes the ball, but was given limited opportunities to shine in 1995-96. He played in the excellent draw at Anfield and the win

at Bolton and returned, as substitute at Old Trafford, never letting the side down. Also added to his Republic U21 caps when playing in Austria last September.
Coventry C (From juniors on 4/11/92) PL 35+8 FLC 4

BOLESAN Mirko
Born: Genoa, Italy, 6 May 1975
Height: 5'11" Weight: 11.4

Central defender who came to Cardiff as a trialist from the Italian club, Sestrese, last October. Coming off the bench in the home game with Scunthorpe, when replacing Derek Brazil in the second minute, he qualified to be included in the *Factfile*, before returning home.
Cardiff C (Free from Sestrese on 26/10/95) FL 0+1

BOLT Daniel (Danny) Anthony
Born: Wandsworth, 5 February 1976
Height: 5'7" Weight: 11.8

As a left-sided Fulham midfielder who can also fill in at left back, Danny had an extended run-in 1995-96, due to Micky

Adams' injury, proving to be a good crosser and having powerful shot from dead ball situations. Given a free transfer at the end of the season.
Fulham (From trainee on 15/7/94) FL 9+4/2 FAC 4+1 Others 2+1

BONETTI Ivano
Born: Brescia, Italy, 1 August 1964
Height: 5'10" Weight: 11.0
International Honours: Italy: 1

An inspired Brian Laws signing last September, in order to bring the highly experienced Serie "A" veteran to Grimsby, the supporters contributed $50,000 to an American management company. As an attacking left-sided midfielder with incredible ball skills, and the provider of pin-point crosses into the box, Ivano quickly established himself as a folk hero. Unfortunately, both his and the supporters' season was soured by an unsavoury dressing room incident, which saw him leaving the club at the end of 1995-96.
Grimsby T (Signed from Torino, via Brescia, Atalanta and Sampdoria, on 29/9/95) FL 19/3 FLC 1 FAC 2/1

Ivano Bonetti

BONNER Mark
Born: Ormskirk, 7 June 1974
Height: 5'10" Weight: 11.0
Skilful Blackpool midfielder. Was one of the club's successes in 1995-96, his hard-working displays and intelligent forward runs winning him many friends. Has become an important part of the club's plans.
Blackpool (From trainee on 18/6/92) FL 99+18/11 FLC 7+3 FAC 7 Others 8+3/1

BOOGERS Marco
Born: Dordrecht, Holland, 12 January 1967
Height: 6'1" Weight: 12.0
Signed from Sparta Rotterdam during the 1995 close season, after making his West Ham debut as a sub in the opening match of 1995-96 at home to Leeds, the big striker was sent off in the very next game, having come off the bench just 15 minutes earlier. Following a further couple of appearances as a sub, the unfortunate Marco had a cartilage operation in January, before going back to Holland on loan to Groningen, with a view to a cut price permanent move.
West Ham U (£1,000,000 from Sparta Rotterdam on 14/7/95) PL 0+4

BOOTH Andrew (Andy) David
Born: Huddersfield, 6 December 1973
Height: 6'0" Weight: 11.2
International Honours: E: U21-3
As an outstanding striker who shot to prominence for Huddersfield in 1994-95, he had Premier League scouts flocking to watch him in the first division and was the subject of a £2.5m bid from Crystal Palace that was turned down. Good in the air, Andy had little difficulty in finding goals at a higher level, being amongst the front-runners in the goalscoring charts all season. Continued to be selected for the England U21 side. *Stop Press:* Reported to have signed for Sheffield Wednesday, a fee of £2,700,000 securing the deal.
Huddersfield T (From trainee on 1/7/92) FL 109+14/54 FLC 6+1/3 FAC 8/3 Others 12+1/4

BOOTHROYD Adrian (Aidey) Neil
Born: Bradford, 8 February 1971
Height: 5'10" Weight: 11.6
Full back Aidey enjoyed a mixed season in 1995-96, losing his Mansfield Town place for a short period early on, followed by a suspension in February. Came back strongly to end the campaign, but was released during the summer due to financial considerations.
Huddersfield T (From trainee on 1/7/89) FL 9+1
Bristol Rov (£30,000 on 20/6/90) FL 10+6 FLC 1 FAC 0+1
Heart of Midlothian (Free on 19/11/92) SL 0+4 SC 0+2/2
Mansfield T (Free on 9/12/93) FL 99+3/3 FLC 7 FAC 6 Others 5+1

BOOTY Martyn James
Born: Kirby Muxloe, 30 May 1971
Height: 5'8" Weight: 11.2
Signed from Crewe Alexandra last January, with 30 games already under his belt in 1995-96, he proved to be a versatile, pacy defender, who did much to bolster Reading's

rearguard after he settled into the side. Missed games at the end of the season because of a hernia operation, but had already won over the fans with his tough-tackling displays at the back.
Coventry C (From trainee on 30/5/89) FL 4+1 FLC 2 FAC 2
Crewe Alex (Free on 7/10/93) FL 95+1/5 FLC 6 FAC 8/1 Others 13
Reading (£75,000 on 18/1/96) FL 17/1

BORLAND John Robert
Born: Lancaster, 28 January 1977
Height: 5'8" Weight: 11.6
One of the few members of Burnley's successful 1994 youth side to graduate to first team status, John impressed in his few appearances in 1995-96, with his non-stop, tigerish approach to his midfield duties and has plenty of time to make a bigger impression.
Burnley (From trainee on 6/7/95) FL 1 FLC 2 FAC 0+1

BORROWS Brian
Born: Liverpool, 20 December 1960
Height: 5'10" Weight: 10.12
International Honours: E: B-1
Mr Consistency, a full back who started 1995-96, his 11th season with Coventry, as first choice right back. Injuries to others forced him to play in the centre of defence and occasionally at left back, but he never let the side down. Suffered an injury in November, which kept him out for two months and, on his return, there were some signs that he was slowing down slightly, prior to damaging a rib against Liverpool at Easter and being ruled out for the rest of the season. Still extremely comfortable on the ball, he is close to 450 league and cup appearances for City.
Everton (From juniors on 23/4/80) FL 27 FLC 2
Bolton W (£10,000 on 24/3/83) FL 95 FLC 7 FAC 4 Others 4
Coventry C (£80,000 on 6/6/85) F/PL 380+6/11 FLC 38/1 FAC 23/1 Others 10+1
Bristol C (Loaned on 17/9/93) FL 6

BOS Gijsbert
Born: Spakenburg, Holland, 22 February 1973
Height: 6'4" Weight: 12.0
A talented striker with superb heading ability, he joined Lincoln last March from the 1994-95 Netherlands amateur champions, Ijsselmeervogels, after manager, John Beck's contracts in Holland advised him of the player's availability. Scored within four minutes of coming on for his league debut as a substitute against Barnet and his 30-yard shot which provided the winner against Mansfield, was City's "Goal of the Season".
Lincoln C (£10,000 from Ijsselmeervogels on 19/3/96) FL 10+1/5

BOSNICH Mark John
Born: Sydney, Australia, 13 January 1972
Height: 6'2" Weight: 13.7
Club Honours: FLC '94, '96
International Honours: Australia: 9
Another marvellous season for Aston Villa's Australian national team goalkeeper, confirming his reputation as one of the safest custodians in the Premier League,

conceding only 35 goals in 38 games, the second best defensive record in the league. Ever present in 1995-96, for the first time in all games, he collected his second Coca Cola Cup winners' medal in three years, following an assured display in the 3-0 defeat of Leeds in the final. An excellent shot stopper who dominates his penalty area.
Manchester U (Free from Sydney Croatia on 5/6/89) Fl 3
Aston Villa (Free on 28/2/92) F/PL 114 FLC 18+1 FAC 10 Others 2

BOULD Stephen (Steve) Andrew
Born: Stoke, 16 November 1962
Height: 6'4" Weight: 14.2
Club Honours: Div 1 '89, '91; ECWC '94
International Honours: E: 2; B-1
As Tony Adams' long-standing partner at the centre of the Arsenal defence, 1995-96 was not one of his better seasons. Forced out by suspension in mid-December, he then suffered a badly gashed thigh on his return to the Premiership at Newcastle on 2 January, and eight days later, when playing against the same team in the Coca Cola Cup, he pulled the hamstring part of the groin, which put him out of action for the rest of the season. A good healer, Steve is sure to be back in time for the new season, his reliability and aerial strengths at both ends of the park, being relished.
Stoke C (From apprentice on 15/11/80) FL 179+4/6 FLC 13/1 FAC 10 Others 5
Torquay U (Loaned on 19/10/82) FL 9 FAC 2
Arsenal (£390,000 on 13/6/88) F/PL 203+8/5 FLC 27/1 FAC 17 Others 13+3/2

BOUND Matthew Terence
Born: Melksham, 9 November 1972
Height: 6'2" Weight: 14.6
Earlier last season, Stockport's tough-tackling defender had looked to be on his way out of Edgeley Park after requesting a transfer and going on loan to Lincoln. The break obviously did him good, as he looked like a new player on his return and became a permanent fixture after replacing broken leg victim, Jim Gannon. Scored against Everton in the FA Cup.
Southampton (From trainee on 3/5/91) F/PL 2+3
Hull C (Loaned on 27/8/93) FL 7/1
Stockport Co (£100,000 on 27/10/94) FL 40/5 FAC 3/1 Others 2/1
Lincoln C (Loaned on 11/9/95) FL 3+1 Others 1

BOWEN Jason Peter
Born: Merthyr Tydfil, 24 August 1972
Height: 5'6" Weight: 9.0
Club Honours: AMC '94
International Honours: W: 1; B-1; U21-5; Yth; Sch
Signed during the 1995 close season from Swansea, Jason made an immediate impact for Birmingham, scoring some spectacular goals before an unfortunate series of injuries ultimately cost him his place in the side. At home in midfield or on the wing, where his speed takes him past defenders and into shooting positions, although not playing for Wales in 1995-96 he seems likely to figure in Bobby Gould's plans for years to come. However, following an operation, one can only hope that the problems that have

disrupted the last two years of a career that promises much, are well and truly behind him.

Swansea C (From trainee on 1/7/90) FL 93+31/26 FLC 6+1/2 FAC 9+2/1 Others 15+3/8
Birmingham C (£350,000 on 24/7/95) FL 16+7/4 FLC 3+5/2 FAC 0+2 Others 2/2

BOWEN Mark Rosslyn
Born: Neath, 7 December 1963
Height: 5'8" Weight: 11.11
International Honours: W: 37; U21-3; Yth; Sch

Still a polished defender, continuing his international career with Wales, he increased his Norwich total of goals to 27 in 1995-96, with second half efforts against Oldham and Charlton. A kick in the kidneys in November saw him miss 11 consecutive games before regaining his place from Robert Ullathorne. Unfortunately, his season ended controversially when he was axed from the first team squad, given a free transfer, and left tantalisingly on 399 club appearances.

Tottenham H (From apprentice on 1/12/81) FL 14+3/2 FAC 3 Others 0+1
Norwich C (£97,000 on 23/7/87) F/PL 315+5/24 FLC 34/1 FAC 30/1 Others 17/1

BOWER Daniel (Danny) Neil
Born: Woolwich, 20 November 1976
Height: 5'11" Weight: 12.11

Teenage central defender who made a big impression at Fulham as a stand in for Mark Blake during five games in 19 days last October. Surprisingly, he did not feature in the line up again until the final game of the season and was then freed.

Fulham (From trainee on 22/11/95) FL 4 Others 2

BOWLING Ian
Born: Sheffield, 27 July 1965
Height: 6'3" Weight: 14.8

Giant of a goalkeeper who was loth to handle the ball early on last season and conceded some goals as a result. Signed by Mansfield immediately prior to the start of 1995-96, having been released by Bradford, he had overcome this problem by mid-term and subsequently gave some outstanding and brave displays. The supporters' choice for "Player of the Year", Ian played for part of the time with a broken finger.

Lincoln C (£2,000 from Gainsborough Trinity on 23/10/88) FL 59 FLC 3 FAC 2 Others 4
Hartlepool U (Loaned on 17/8/89) FL 1
Bradford C (Loaned on 25/3/93) FL 7
Bradford C (£27,500 on 28/7/93) FL 29 FLC 2 FAC 2+1 Others 1
Mansfield T (Free on 11/8/95) FL 44 FLC 2 FAC 2 Others 1

BOWMAN Robert (Rob)
Born: Durham City, 1975
Height: 6'0½" Weight: 11.12
International Honours: E: Yth

After making his PL debut as a 17 year old, and playing twice more, this young central defender's appearances for Leeds had been for the reserves, where he is a regular performer. However, 1995-96 saw him make his full European debut at PSV Eindhoven, with his only performance in the Premier League coming in the poor defeat at Aston

Villa. A good passer of the ball, who can break forward if the need be, he is equally at home in the full back positions.

Leeds U (From trainee on 20/11/92) PL 4+3 FLC 0+1 Others 1

BOWRY Robert (Bobby)
Born: Croydon, 19 May 1971
Height: 5'8" Weight: 10.8
Club Honours: Div 1 '94

A midfielder who belies his slim appearance with strong-running displays, he signed for Millwall from Crystal Palace during the summer of 1995 and played a starring role against his old club, showing fine passing qualities in Millwall's 2-1 victory at Selhurst Park. Broke his goalscoring duck in games against Norwich and Birmingham, which were incidentally, two of Millwall's three home wins during the second half of the season.

Queens Park R (Signed on 8/8/90)
Crystal Palace (Free from Carshalton on 4/4/92) F/PL 36+14/1 FLC 10 FAC 1
Millwall (£220,000 on 5/7/95) FL 33+5/2 FLC 3 FAC 2

BOWYER Gary David
Born: Manchester, 22 June 1971
Height: 6'0" Weight: 12.13
Club Honours: WFAC '90; AMC '96

The son of Ian, who played for a number of clubs, including Manchester City and Nottingham Forest between 1968 and 1989, Gary had an injury troubled 1995-96 for Rotherham, having signed during the close season, which meant he did not play as many games as he would have liked to have done and he finished up battling for the left back spot with Paul Hurst. A strong, powerful player, his surges upfield to support his attack deserved better reward as he came close to grabbing that elusive first goal on several occasions. A member of the side that defeated Shrewsbury 2-1 at Wembley in the final of the AWS competition, he was also used as a left-sided midfielder.

Hereford U (Free from Westfields on 2/12/89) FL 12+2/2
Nottingham F (Free on 15/9/90)
Rotherham U (Free on 2/8/95) FL 23+4 FLC 3 Others 5

Lee Bowyer

BOWYER Lee David
Born: London, 3 January 1977
Height: 5'9" Weight: 9.11
International Honours: E: U21-4; Yth

Classy young midfield player who became Charlton's most valuable asset in 1995-96. Found the net regularly in the early part of the season, including a hat trick at Wimbledon in the Coca Cola Cup, uses the ball well, is extremely comfortable in possession, and strong in the tackle. Has amazing vision for a player of his age and has already represented the England U21 side.

Charlton Ath (From trainee on 13/4/94) FL 46/8 FLC 6+1/5 FAC 3/1 Others 2

BOXALL Daniel James
Born: Croydon, 24 August 1977
Height: 5'8" Weight: 10.5

Local born Crystal Palace defender who turned professional at the end of last April. Made his Palace debut in the final league game of the season, deputising for Marc Edworthy at right back, in May at home to Norwich, and was voted "Man of the Match". A good prospect for the future.

Crystal Palace (From trainee on 19/4/95) FL 1

BOYCE Robert Alexander
Born: Islington, 7 January 1974
Height: 5'11" Weight: 11.12

Young Colchester striker signed from non-league Enfield Town early last season, as "one for the future", his limited chances were not helped by a long-term shoulder injury. Released during the summer.

Colchester U (Signed from Enfield on 17/10/95) FL 0+2

BRABIN Gary
Born: Liverpool, 9 December 1970
Height: 5'11" Weight: 14.8
International Honours: E: SP-4

The transfer of the burly Doncaster midfielder to Bury on transfer deadline day last March, came as a big surprise, particularly as he was skipper of the side. He improved his dismal disciplinary record of the previous season but did not seem to make quite the same impact on games. Nevertheless, a great trier. Suffered an ankle injury on his Bury debut, before being sent off at Scarborough and subsequently handed a four match ban.

Stockport Co (From trainee on 14/12/89) FL 1+1 Others 1+1
Doncaster Rov (£45,000 from Runcorn on 26/7/94) FL 58+1/11 FLC 2 FAC 2 Others 4
Bury (£125,000 on 29/3/96) FL 5

BRACE Deryn Paul John
Born: Haverfordwest, 15 March 1975
Height: 5'9" Weight: 10.6
Club Honours: WC '95
International Honours: W: U21-5; Yth

Continued to impress in 1995-96, his wholehearted attitude endearing him to the Wrexham fans. A keen-tackling right back, Deryn was always aware of a scoring opportunity, a good example being a 25-yarder against Peterborough in February. Although unlucky with injuries and illness, he is now well established at the club with the Welsh team manager, Bobby Gould, keeping a keen eye on his progress.

Norwich C (From trainee on 6/7/93)
Wrexham (Free on 28/4/94) FL 27+4/1 FLC 1 FAC 1 Others 5

BRACEWELL Paul William
Born: Heswall, 19 July 1962
Height: 5'8" Weight: 10.9
Club Honours: CS '84, '85; ECWC '85; Div 1 '85, '93, '96
International Honours: E: 3; U21-13 (UEFAC '84)

A recognised ball winner, "Brace" returned to Sunderland in the summer of 1995 for his third spell at the club, when he transferred from Newcastle as player/assistant manager. His experience and calming influence proved vital and he filled the midfield holding role with ease. Despite serious injury problems in the past, the ex-England international missed only eight league games and was able to add yet another medal to his substantial collection when Sunderland went back to the elite as first division champions.

Stoke C (From apprentice on 6/2/80) FL 123+6/5 FLC 6 FAC 6/1
Sunderland (£250,000 on 1/7/83) FL 38/4 FLC 4 FAC 2
Everton (£425,000 on 25/5/84) FL 95/7 FLC 11/2 FAC 19+2 Others 17+2/1
Sunderland (£250,000 on 23/8/89) FL 112+1/2 FLC 9 FAC 10 Others 6
Newcastle U (£250,000 on 16/6/92) F/PL 64+9/3 FLC 3+1/1 FAC 6+2 Others 2
Sunderland (£100,000 on 23/5/95) FL 38 FLC 4 FAC 2

Paul Bracewell

BRACEY Lee Michael Ian
Born: Barking, 11 September 1968
Height: 6'1" Weight: 13.5
Club Honours: WC '89

Bury's popular goalkeeper grasped his chance when it came in 1995-96, playing in 24 league and cup games and keeping nine clean sheets. He gained a regular place in the early weeks of the season when the team was struggling to find its form, but lost out to rival custodian, Gary Kelly, from October onwards. Regained his spot in March and played no small part in the run up to promotion.

West Ham U (From trainee on 6/7/87)
Swansea C (Free on 27/8/88) FL 99 FLC 8 FAC 11 Others 10
Halifax T (£47,500 on 17/10/91) FL 73 FLC 2 FAC 1 Others 2
Bury (£20,000 on 23/8/93) FL 65+2 FLC 4 FAC 2 Others 1

BRADBURY Lee Michael
Born: Isle of Wight, 3 July 1975
Height: 6'0" Weight: 12.7

A bustling centre forward, Lee came out of non-league football to sign for Portsmouth at the start of 1995-96, making his first team debut as a sub at Leicester six games into the season. Later, in order to gain experience, he took in a three month loan spell with Exeter in December and contributed with five goals before returning to Fratton Park.

Portsmouth (Free from Cowes on 14/8/95) FL 3+9
Exeter C (Loaned on 1/12/95) FL 14/5

BRADLEY Darren Michael
Born: Birmingham, 24 November 1965
Height: 5'11" Weight: 11.10
International Honours: E: Yth

After nine seasons with WBA, Darren joined Walsall on a free transfer at the start of last season. Though still seeming to be slowed down by the cruciate knee injury that had kept him out of the Baggies' side for most of his last campaign there, Darren's shrewd positional play and use of the ball from midfield won round fans and he missed only one game, that being in the Auto Windscreen at Fulham. Excelled in the 3-1 FA Cup win at Burnley in November, scoring the opening goal and having a hand in the other two.

Aston Villa (From apprentice on 19/12/83) FL 16+4 FLC 3
West Bromwich A (Signed on 14/3/86) FL 236+18/9 FLC 13/1 FAC 10/2 Others 11/1
Walsall (Free on 3/8/95) FL 45/1 FLC 2 FAC 5/2 Others 2

BRADLEY Russell
Born: Birmingham, 28 March 1966
Height: 6'2" Weight: 13.0
Club Honours: WC '90

The solid, if unspectacular Scunthorpe central defender, was sidelined by a groin injury late in the 1995-96 season, but quickly regained his place on recovery. Does not miss much in the air and can be relied upon to get his tackles in.

Nottingham F (Signed from Dudley T on 20/5/88)
Hereford U (Loaned on 13/11/88) FL 12/1 FAC 1 Others 3
Hereford U (£15,000 on 26/7/89) FL 75+2/3 FLC 7 Others 5+1
Halifax T (£45,000 on 6/9/91) FL 54+2/3 FLC 2 FAC 3 Others 4
Scunthorpe U (Free on 30/6/93) FL 94+3/4 FLC 4 FAC 10 Others 9

BRADSHAW Carl
Born: Sheffield, 2 October 1968
Height: 6'0" Weight: 11.6
International Honours: E: Yth

Although showing wholehearted commitment performed with fairness, it is a rule of thumb, however, that you do not linger on the ball when he is around. Martin O'Neill hardly ever included him in the Norwich side early last season, but he was a regular when Gary Megson was awarded the managerial hot seat. Now recognised mainly as a right back, Carl started his career further afield, often playing as a striker, where he used his pace to good advantage.

Sheffield Wed (From apprentice on 23/8/86) FL 16+16/4 FLC 2+2 FAC 6+1/3 Others 1
Barnsley (Loaned on 23/8/86) FL 6/1
Manchester C (£50,000 on 30/9/88) FL 1+4 FAC 0+1 Others 0+1
Sheffield U (£50,000 on 7/9/89) F/PL 122+25/8 FLC 10+1/2 FAC 12+1/3 Others 4
Norwich C (£500,000 on 28/7/94) P/FL 43+4/2 FLC 5/1 FAC 2

BRADSHAW Darren Shaun
Born: Sheffield, 19 March 1967
Height: 5'11" Weight: 11.4
International Honours: E: Yth

Midfielder, cum defender. Started last season for Blackpool on the left side of the defence until losing his place through injury. Subsequently came back when Jason Lydiate was unfit to play, forming a solid and reliable partnership with David Linighan until struck down again. Always appears to have time on the ball.

Chesterfield (On trial from Matlock T on 12/8/87) FL 18 FLC 2
York C (Free from Matlock T on 14/11/87) FL 58+1/3 FLC 2 FAC 2 Others 3
Newcastle U (£10,000 on 16/8/89) FL 32+6 FLC 3 FAC 2+1 Others 3
Peterborough U (Free on 13/8/92) FL 70+3/1 FLC 7/1 FAC 4 Others 2
Plymouth Arg (Loaned on 18/8/94) FL 5+1/1 FLC 1
Blackpool (£35,000 on 20/10/94) FL 51/1 FLC 2 FAC 3 Others 5

BRADY Matthew John
Born: London, 27 October 1977
Height: 5'11" Weight: 11.0

Striker. Another Barnet trainee whose chances to break into the first team were limited last season, but is one for the future.

Barnet (Trainee) FL 1+2

BRAITHWAITE Leon Jerome
Born: Hackney, 17 December 1972
Height: 5'11" Weight: 12.0

Forward. Having arrived at Exeter during last season from Bishops Stortford, he immediately became the fan's favourite. Leon's pace made him a danger to teams and if his other skills can be honed he could turn out to be a real threat in 1996-97. Is the brother of sprinter, Darren.

Exeter C (Free from Bishops Stortford on 3/11/95) FL 14+9/3

BRAMMER David
Born: Bromborough, 28 February 1975
Height: 5'10" Weight: 11.5

Began last season in superb form for Wrexham, justifying Brian Flynn's faith in him, but a niggling injury in November restricted his appearances from then on. Has all the potential to be a top class central midfielder, who can also score some cracking goals, as seen by his effort against Carlisle United in October.

Wrexham (From trainee on 2/7/93) FL 41+10/3 FLC 4 FAC 3 Others 5+2

BRANAGAN Keith Graham
Born: Fulham, 10 July 1966
Height: 6'0" Weight: 13.2
International Honours: Ei: B-1

Agile Bolton goalkeeper who looked to be on his way to ever-present status for the season until a training injury forced him out of action last March. Despite the club's poor defensive record, his performances were good enough to put him on the fringe of a call up to the Irish international squad prior to his injury. A crowd favourite at Burnden, he should have an easier ride this time round.

Cambridge U (From juniors on 4/8/83) FL 110 FLC 12 FAC 6 Others 6
Millwall (£100,000 on 25/3/88) FL 46 FLC 1 FAC 5 Others 1
Brentford (Loaned on 24/11/89) FL 2 Others 1
Gillingham (Loaned on 1/10/91) FL 1
Bolton W (Free on 3/7/92) P/FL 130 FLC 22 FAC 10 Others 6

BRANCH Graham
Born: Liverpool, 12 February 1972
Height: 6'2" Weight: 12.2

Tall, fast Tranmere wing forward whose career took a distinct upturn in 1995-96 after a proposed £100,000 transfer to Stockport broke down. The cousin of Everton's Michael Branch, Graham enjoyed a prolonged spell of first team action and scored his first goals for Tranmere. Occasionally brilliant, sometimes frustrating, he nevertheless has all the attributes to be a top striker.

Tranmere Rov (Free from Heswall on 2/7/91) FL 17+25/2 FLC 0+4 FAC 0+1 Others 2+1
Bury (Loaned on 20/11/92) FL 3+1/1 Others 1

BRANCH Paul Michael
Born: Liverpool, 18 October 1978
Height: 5'10" Weight: 11.7
International Honours: E: U21-1; Yth; Sch

Seventeen-year-old Everton forward who made a name for himself in 1995-96 with some outstanding performances in the reserves. A good striker of the ball and able to find space behind defenders, Michael made his full first team debut against Sheffield Wednesday late in April and impressed. Having won his first England U21 cap, he will be looking for more top level experience this coming season.

Everton (From trainee on 24/10/95) PL 1+2

[BRANCO] LEAL Claudio Ibraim Vaz
Born: Brazil, 4 April 1964
Height: 5'11" Weight: 12.6
International Honours: Brazil: 72

The world famous Brazilian left back followed his campatriot Juninho to Middlesbrough last February after buying out his contract from the Italian club, Genoa. A veteran of three World Cup campaigns for Brazil, plus additional European experience

with Brescia (Italy) and Porto (Portugal), he is a dead ball specialist with many remarkable goals from free kicks and equally proficient in midfield. Made his Boro' debut in March as a substitute and played five full games at the end of the season, showing occasional flashes of his skill, but the fans and manager, Bryan Robson, expect to see a fully fit Branco to make an enormous contribution to the coming campaign.

Middlesbrough (Free from Genoa, via Fluminese, Porto Alegre, FC Porto and Brescia, on 2/3/96) PL 5+2

BRANNAN Gerard (Ged) Daniel
Born: Prescot, 15 January 1972
Height: 6'0" Weight: 12.3

A strong, powerhouse Tranmere player who is equally comfortable in central midfield or in either of the full back spots. Ged is strongest on his right side and is particularly adept at making late surging runs into the box, though that failed to bring him more than one goal last term.

Tranmere Rov (From trainee on 3/7/90) FL 196+8/14 FLC 23/4 FAC 9+1 Others 26+1/1

BRASS Christopher (Chris) Paul
Born: Easington, 24 July 1975
Height: 5'10" Weight: 11.8

Strong-tackling, speedy Burnley right back who looked set to make the number two shirt his own in 1995-96, before sustaining a groin injury at Rotherham which kept him out for some time. Still improving, he is capable of becoming a first team regular on his return to full fitness. Chris, a confident youngster, can also play on the other flank.

Burnley (From trainee on 8/7/93) FL 9+5 Others 2
Torquay U (Loaned on 14/10/94) FL 7 FAC 2 Others 1

BRAYSON Paul
Born: Newcastle, 16 September 1977
Height: 5'4" Weight: 10.10
International Honours: E: Yth

An exciting Newcastle prospect with the single minded focus and awareness of a natural scorer, Paul is cool in the penalty area with a good first touch enabling him to beat defenders in tight situations. He was not overawed when brought into the pre-1995-96 season games for first team experience, playing well on his debut against Bristol City in the Coca Cola Cup until a hamstring injury caused his withdrawal. Continued to score prolifically at reserve and junior levels, leading to his selection for the England youth side.

Newcastle U (From trainee on 1/8/95) FLC 1

BRAZIER Matthew Ronald
Born: Whipps Cross, 2 July 1976
Height: 5'8" Weight: 10.7

Midfielder who is full of running and always looking to be involved with the play. Played his first game for QPR in the Coca Cola Cup win against Oxford as a substitute last October, while his Premiership debut, also as a substitute, followed later that month against Nottingham Forest. His battling qualities soon enabled him to establish himself in Rangers' first team squad and despite all the relegation problems, Matthew

look composed enough to mount a serious challenge for a first team place this season.

Queens Park R (From trainee on 1/7/94) PL 6+5 FLC 1+1 FAC 1

BRAZIL Derek Michael
Born: Dublin, 14 December 1968
Height: 5'11" Weight: 10.6
Club Honours: Div 3 '93; WC '93
International Honours: Ei: B-1; U23-2; U21-7; Yth; Sch

As the Cardiff fans' favourite, and normally very reliable in defence or in midfield, "Brazza" did not have the best of times in 1995-96, the season probably being his least productive due to injury. Playing in less than half the available games, he was released during the summer.

Manchester U (Free from Rivermount BC on 12/3/86) FL 0+2
Oldham Ath (Loaned on 20/11/90) FL 1 Others 1
Swansea C (Loaned on 12/9/91) FL 12/1 FLC 2 Others 2
Cardiff C (£85,000 on 26/8/92) FL 109+6/1 FLC 8 FAC 9 Others 13+3/1

BRAZIL Gary Nicholas
Born: Tunbridge Wells, 19 September 1962
Height: 5'11" Weight: 11.3

Despite being Fulham's current leading goalscorer, Gary was rarely used as an out-and-out striker in 1995-96, before sustaining a bad injury in November and being only able to play two more games. When Alan Cork was appointed assistant manager, he took over running the youth team before being given a free transfer at the end of the season.

Sheffield U (Free from Crystal Palace juniors on 11/8/80) FL 39+23/9 FLC 4+1 FAC 4+5/1 Others 1+1
Port Vale (Loaned on 24/8/84) FL 6/3
Preston NE (£12,500 on 15/2/85) FL 163+3/58 FLC 13/6 FAC 10/3 Others 13/5
Newcastle U (Signed on 9/2/89) FL 7+16/2 FLC 1+1/1 FAC 0+1 Others 0+1
Fulham (£110,000 on 6/9/90) FL 207+7/48 FLC 13+1/4 FAC 9/5 Others 17/3

Gary Brazil

BREAKER Timothy (Tim) Sean
Born: Bicester, 2 July 1965
Height: 6'0" Weight: 13.0
Club Honours: FLC '88
International Honours: E: U21-2

West Ham right back who makes very important interceptions and last ditch tackles. He also loves to attack, getting forward to put in some excellent crosses which cause trouble for opposing defences. Was badly missed last October and November, when he had a cartilage operation, and again during January and February with a groin injury, before coming back into the side for the final seven games of the season.
Luton T (From apprentice on 15/5/83) FL 204+6/3 FLC 22+2 FAC 21 Others 7
West Ham U (£600,000 on 12/10/90) F/PL 187+5/8 FLC 13 FAC 22 Others 7

BRECKIN Ian
Born: Rotherham, 24 February 1975
Height: 6'1" Weight: 12.9
Club Honours: AMC '96

The nephew of former Rotherham skipper, John (1971-82), Ian might not have been considered an automatic choice at the start of last season, but the tall central defender finished up as one of Rotherham's most frequent players. When injuries took its toll on the squad, he played several games at right back and, being locally born, took particular pleasure in playing in the Auto Windscreen Shield winning team at Wembley.
Rotherham U (From trainee on 1/11/93) FL 88+2/3 FLC 4 FAC 4 Others 10

BREEN Gary Patrick
Born: Hendon, 12 December 1973
Height: 6'1" Weight: 12.0
International Honours: Ei: 6; U21-9

Stylish central defender with a great turn of pace, Gary signed for Birmingham last February in the deal that took Ken Charlery in the opposite direction. Having missed only one game for Posh in 1995-96, he was felt to be the obvious replacement for Liam Daish, who transferred to Coventry two weeks later, and so it proved to be. Captaining the side in Gary Poole's absence, and also turning out at full back, his sound performances saw him selected for the Eire squad, where he looks to have a future following six impressive displays.
Maidstone U (Free from Charlton Ath juniors on 6/3/91) FL 19
Gillingham (Free on 2/7/92) FL 45+6 FLC 4 FAC 5 Others 1
Peterborough U (£70,000 on 5/8/94) FL 68+1/1 FLC 6 FAC 6 Others 6/1
Birmingham C (£400,000 on 9/2/96) FL 17+1/1

BREMNER Kevin Johnston
Born: Banff, 7 October 1957
Height: 5'9" Weight: 12.3
Club Honours: Div 3 '86

Striker. Appointed Gillingham youth team coach during the summer of 1995, having spent the previous three years in Scottish non-league football, he came on as substitute in the AWS home game against Hereford United. And, apart from being a regular playing member of the reserve side in the Capital League, that was it as far as first team football was concerned. A very experienced goalscorer, Kevin recorded 128 in the Football League between 1980 and 1992.
Colchester U (£40,000 from Keith on 10/10/80) FL 89+6/31 FLC 5+2/3 FAC 10/2
Birmingham C (Loaned on 8/10/82) FL 3+1/1
Wrexham (Loaned on 30/12/82) FL 4/1
Plymouth Arg (Loaned on 27/1/83) FL 5/1
Millwall (£25,000 on 25/2/83) FL 87+9/32 FLC 8 FAC 4+1/1 Others 6+1/2
Reading (£30,000 on 13/8/85) FL 60+4/21 FLC 4/1 FAC 6 Others 3
Brighton & Hove A (£65,000 on 8/7/87) FL 125+3/36 FLC 2 FAC 7/1 Others 4/4
Peterborough U (£18,000 on 27/7/90) FL 13+4/3 FLC 2/3 FAC 3 Others 2
Dundee (Free during 1991 close season) SL 15+9/6 SLC 1 SC 0+1 (Free to Inverness during 1992 close season)
Shrewsbury T (Loaned on 27/3/92) FL 7/2
Gillingham (Free from Deveronvale on 7/9/95) Others 0+1

BRENCHLEY Scott Alan
Born: Hull, 22 November 1976
Height: 5'11" Weight: 11.5

Freed by Liverpool during the 1995 close season, having finished his YTS period, Scott joined Chester on a month by month basis, coming off the bench in the Coca Cola Cup game at home to Wigan. Prior to being released in early November, although not doing enough to be offered a contract, he had shown himself to be a constructive midfielder.
Chester C (Free from Liverpool juniors on 11/8/95) FLC 0+1

BRENNAN Mark Robert
Born: Rossendale, 4 October 1965
Height: 5'10" Weight: 11.1
International Honours: E: U21-5; Yth

Although making 31 appearances for Oldham last season, Mark found himself unlucky to be handed a free transfer in the summer. Prior to being replaced towards the end of February, as tired legs took their toll, he proved as skilful as ever in providing from the wide left of midfield, his superb left foot picking players out and giving the side balance. Would surely provide good service for any number of teams.
Ipswich T (From apprentice on 7/4/83) FL 165+3/19 FLC 21+1/2 FAC 12/3 Others 11/1
Middlesbrough (£375,000 on 27/7/88) FL 61+4/6 FLC 6 FAC 4 Others 8/1
Manchester C (£500,000 on 25/7/90) FL 25+4/6 FLC 4 FAC 1 Others 2
Oldham Ath (£200,000 on 24/11/92) P/FL 82+8/7 FLC 7+1 FAC 6 Others 2

BREVETT Rufus Emanuel
Born: Derby, 24 September 1969
Height: 5'8" Weight: 11.0

Very quick left-sided QPR player who is strong in the tackle and eager to get forward. With the departure of Clive Wilson to Tottenham, Rufus claimed the left back position as his own in 1995-96 and began the season well, before an injury in the televised game against Coventry City ruled him out for seven matches. After this, he struggled to hold down his place under competition from Trevor Challis, but eventually regained his form and came back from March onwards, scoring his first ever goal for the club in the 3-0 win against Southampton.
Doncaster Rov (From trainee on 8/7/88) FL 106+3/3 FLC 5 FAC 4 Others 10+1
Queens Park R (£250,000 on 15/2/91) F/PL 77+8/1 FLC 5+1 FAC 2

BRIDGES Michael
Born: North Shields, 5 August 1978
Height: 6'1" Weight: 10.11
Club Honours: Div 1 '96

A 17-year-old Sunderland striker who burst onto the scene last term and looks to have a fantastic future. Pacy, skilful, and adept at holding the ball up, Michael scored four crucial goals when coming off the substitutes' bench, never more so than the late brace against Huddersfield at Roker in March, that turned a 1-2 deficit into a 3-2 win. Although 13 of his 15 appearances were from the bench, they were enough to give him a first division championship medal as the club went back to the top flight.
Sunderland (From trainee on 9/11/95) FL 2+13/4

BRIEN Anthony (Tony) James
Born: Dublin, 10 February 1969
Height: 6'0" Weight: 13.0
International Honours: Ei: Yth

Having been released by Rotherham during the summer of 1995, the utility defender was brought to WBA by manager, Alan Buckley, primarily as a squad player. A solid tackler, Tony was troubled by injuries during the first half of the season and never figured in Albion's plans after November. Thereafter, had spells on loan at Mansfield (February) and Chester (March), before returning to the Hawthorns where he will start 1996-97.
Leicester C (From apprentice on 13/2/87) FL 12+4/1 FLC 1 FAC 1 Others 3
Chesterfield (£90,000 on 16/12/88) FL 201+3/8 FLC 14 FAC 7 Others 14
Rotherham U (Signed on 8/10/93) FL 41+2/2 FLC 2 FAC 4 Others 6
West Bromwich A (Free on 13/7/95) FL 2 FLC 1 Others 1
Mansfield T (Loaned on 16/2/96) FL 4
Chester C (Loaned on 22/3/96) FL 8

BRIGHT Mark Abraham
Born: Stoke, 6 June 1962
Height: 6'0" Weight: 12.12
Club Honours: FMC '91

An unselfish striker who has given Sheffield Wednesday great service during his time at the club. Overall, 1995-96 was a disappointing season for him, making just 18 starts and not being part of the squad for the last few months of the campaign. However, he is still a good competitor and his goals per game ratio bears comparison with most, his ten scored included Wednesday's only hat trick in the 5-2 Coca Cola Cup win at home to Crewe. At the same time there have been no histrionics from this very good professional who just gets on with the job of playing football to the best of his ability.
Port Vale (Free from Leek T on 15/10/81) FL 18+11/10 FLC 1+1 FAC 0+1/1 Others 2
Leicester C (£33,000 on 19/7/84) FL 26+16/6 FLC 3+1 FAC 1

Crystal Palace (£75,000 on 13/11/86) F/PL 224+3/92 FLC 22/11 FAC 13+1/2 Others 23/9
Sheffield Wed (£1,375,000 on 11/9/92) PL 112+20/48 FLC 20+1/11 FAC 13/7

BRIGHTWELL David John
Born: Lutterworth, 7 January 1971
Height: 6'2" Weight: 13.5
Unable to get a place in the Manchester City squad at the start of last season, David was despatched on loan first to Lincoln (August) and then Stoke (September), as cover for injuries, before signing permanently for Bradford in December, seven days after another loan spell had started. Proved a great buy for City, playing consistently well at full back or centre half as the club fought their way into the first division, via the play offs. Is the brother of Manchester City's Ian.
Manchester C (From juniors on 11/4/88) F/PL 35+8/1 FLC 2+1 FAC 5+2/1
Chester C (Loaned on 22/3/91) FL 6
Lincoln C Loaned on 11/8/95) FL 5 FLC 2
Stoke C (Loaned on 11/9/95) FL 0+1 Others 1
Bradford C (£30,000 on 22/12/95) FL 21+1 FAC 1 Others 2

BRIGHTWELL Ian Robert
Born: Lutterworth, 9 April 1968
Height: 5'10" Weight: 11.7
International Honours: E: U21-4; Yth
Continuing his role in Manchester City's midfield, Ian again showed consistent form in 1995-96. Although preferring to be in support of the big central defenders, following the transfer of Terry Phelan to Chelsea, and Richard Edghill being out with a long-term injury, he was utilised at full back, where by his own admission he did not feel he did justice to himself. However, he still made a major contribution to City's performances and continued to be a much valued member of the squad. Normally good for scoring a goal or two, with last season being a "backs to the wall" situation, opportunities up front did not materialise. As befits the brother of David, now with Bradford, and the son of the famous 1964 Olympians, the former Ann Packer and Robbie Brightwell, he has great stamina to compliment his tackling and passing skills.
Manchester C (From juniors on 7/5/86) F/PL 230+33/16 FLC 27+2 FAC 15+4/1 Others 4+3

BRISCOE Lee Stephen
Born: Pontefract, 30 September 1975
Height: 5'10" Weight: 10.9
International Honours: E: U21-4
A talented, young left-sided Sheffield Wednesday player, mainly appearing at full back, but equally at home in midfield, Lee made the breakthrough as a true first team player in 1995-96. The side always seemed to have more balance with him appearing and he added drive and pace down the left. Will be looking to concentrate more on defensive duties in 1996-97, something that should see him make the transition from a good player to one who really takes the eye and, at the same time, resolving a long-standing problem position at Hillsborough. His good form also saw him win four England U21 caps.
Sheffield Wed (From trainee on 22/5/94) PL 28+5 FLC 1

BRISSETT Jason Curtis
Born: Wanstead, 7 September 1974
Height: 5'11" Weight: 12.7
It was another impressive campaign for Jason, who continued to torment defenders on the Bournemouth left wing in 1995-96 with his speed and fast footwork. Quite capable of scoring goals, with five to his credit during the season, he also undertook defensive duties when called upon, which added another dimension to his play. Can play on either flank if required and can be relied upon for an accurate supply of crosses.
Peterborough U (Free from Arsenal juniors on 14/6/93) FL 27+8 FLC 5+1/1 FAC 2+1/1 Others 3+1/1
Bournemouth (Free on 23/12/94) FL 67+1/3 FLC 4 FAC 3 Others 3/2

BRODIE Stephen (Steve) Eric
Born: Sunderland, 14 January 1973
Height: 5'6" Weight: 10.6
Unable to find a place in the first team squad, the Sunderland striker started last season on loan at Doncaster, playing five times and scoring the only goal of the game on his debut against Hartlepool, before returning home. Very small for a front man, he makes up for his lack of height and weight, by his pace and ability to move defenders out of position. Also has two good feet.
Sunderland (From trainee on 1/7/91) FL 1+11
Doncaster Rov (Loaned on 31/8/95) FL 5/1

BROLIN Tomas
Born: Sweden, 29 November 1969
Height: 5'8" Weight: 12.2
International Honours: Sweden: 52
The "blue eyed boy" of Swedish football became Leeds United's record signing last November, when completing a transfer from Parma, Italy, where he had suffered a long lay off following an ankle injury. Made his full debut with a tremendous performance in the Coca Cola Cup victory against Blackburn, but after that he was in and out of the side with reasons given, such as struggling to adapt to pace of the English game and injuries. Following a brief substitute role at Wembley in the Coca Cola Cup final, and being dropped from the Swedish squad, this highly intelligent player appears ready to return to the continent (especially after his "April Fools'" prank on Swedish TV was not taken too kindly at Elland Road).
Leeds U (£4,500,000 from Parma on 25/11/95) PL 17+2/4 FLC 2+2 FAC 1+1

BROOKER Paul
Born: Hammersmith, 25 November 1976
Height: 5'5" Weight: 9.10
A right-sided Fulham midfielder or striker, Paul made an immediate impact when coming on against Swansea in the FA Cup and playing a big part in Fulham's 7-0 win, the highest ever by a league side against one from a higher division. Paul loves taking players on and is a great favourite of the crowd.
Fulham (From trainee on 1/7/95) FL 9+11/2 FAC 1+2/1 Others 0+1

BROOKS Shaun
Born: London, 9 October 1962
Height: 5'8" Weight: 11.0
International Honours: E: Yth; Sch
The son of the former Spurs and England star, Johnny, Shaun has always been a skilful ball-playing midfielder in his own right, his good distribution, particularly from long range, and free kicks that are placed rather than blasted, often seeming out of place in the lower reaches. Although missing very few matches for Leyton Orient last season, following the expiry of his contract during the summer, and being the wrong side of 30, he was released. Scored Orient's first goal in 1995-96.
Crystal Palace (From apprentice on 16/10/79) FL 47+7/4 FLC 5+1/1 FAC 5
Leyton Orient (Free on 17/10/83) FL 140+8/26 FLC 10/1 FAC 12/4 Others 7+3/1
Bournemouth (£20,000 on 22/6/87) FL 114+14/13 FLC 12 FAC 4+1/1 Others 3
Bournemouth (Free from Dorchester T on 6/10/94) FL 1
Leyton Orient (Free on 18/11/94) FL 42+8/2 FLC 2 FAC 1+1 Others 4/1

BROUGH John Robert
Born: Ilkeston, 8 January 1973
Height: 6'0" Weight: 12.10
Eventually becoming the third man at the heart of Hereford's defence last season, John proved to be an aggressive tackler and a player who could be relied upon to win more than his fair share of aerial battles. In and out of the side earlier, his drive and determination still shone through.
Notts Co (From trainee on 9/7/91)
Shrewsbury T (Free on 6/7/92) FL 7+9/1 FLC 1+1 FAC 1 Others 1
Hereford U (Free from Telford on 4/11/94) FL 38+2/2 FLC 1 FAC 3/1 Others 3+3

John Brough

BROWN Grant Ashley
Born: Sunderland, 19 November 1969
Height: 6'0" Weight: 11.12
Central defender and Lincoln's longest-serving player. Missed the start of last

season with a toe injury, but became an automatic choice once fit. Appointed club skipper by new manager, John Beck, Grant performed consistently well, his play continuing to show a greater maturity.
Leicester C (From trainee on 1/7/88) FL 14 FLC 2
Lincoln C (£60,000 on 20/8/89) FL 354/11 FLC 13/1 FAC 10 Others 16/2

BROWN Gregory (Greg) Jonathan
Born: Manchester, 31 July 1978
Height: 5'10" Weight: 11.6
A highly promising Chester midfielder. Still a YTS, Greg, an excellent passer of the ball who likes to join up with the attack, made his first full league appearance at Cardiff last Boxing Day and impressed. However, while looking for further chances, a broken ankle sustained in a reserve fixture put him out of circulation towards the end of the season. He will be back, though.
Chester C (Trainee) FL 1+2 Others 0+1

BROWN Kenneth (Kenny) James
Born: Upminster, 11 July 1967
Height: 5'8" Weight: 11.6
The likeable West Ham full back, and son of a famous Hammer, again never let the side down when called upon to make three appearances at the beginning of the year, but that was it as far as United were concerned, Kenny spending the rest of his time on loan at Huddersfield, Reading, Southend and Crystal Palace. Wherever he went he impressed. Certainly, at Reading he greatly contributed to their battle for first division survival, while at the other end of the table, he scored on his debut for Palace at Millwall, and then at Derby, before thumping in an equaliser at Charlton that ultimately took the club to the play-off final. Apart from scoring vital goals, is also a good passer who likes to join up with the play.
Norwich C (From juniors on 10/7/85) FL 24+1 Others 3
Plymouth Arg (Free on 10/8/88) FL 126/4 FLC 9 FAC 6 Others 3
West Ham U (£175,000 on 2/8/91) F/PL 55+8/5 FLC 2+1 FAC 7+2/1 Others 2+2
Huddersfield T (Loaned on 7/9/95) FL 5
Reading (Loaned on 27/10/95) FL 12/1 FLC 3
Southend U (Loaned on 1/3/96) FL 6
Crystal Palace (Loaned on 28/3/96) FL 5+1/2 Others 3/1

BROWN Linton James
Born: Hull, 12 April 1968
Height: 5'9" Weight: 11.0
A groin and hip strain, sceptic foot, and pulled hamstring, plus personal problems, highlighted a difficult time last season for the Hull City man, culminating in a pre-deadline move to Swansea in March. Sadly, he suffered a hamstring injury in his third outing for the Swans, forcing him to miss the rest of the campaign, apart from the final game. Linton will be an asset to the club in 1996-97, with his ability to play in numerous positions.
Halifax T (Free from Guisley on 18/12/92) FL 3
Hull C (Free on 8/1/93) FL 111+10/23 FLC 6 FAC 4+1/1 Others 4
Swansea C (£60,000 on 22/3/96) FL 3+1

BROWN Michael (Mickey) Antony
Born: Birmingham, 8 February 1968
Height: 5'9" Weight: 10.12
Club Honours: Div 3 '94
Preston right winger. Excellent at getting down the line and crossing the ball, he had to wait nine months for his club debut last September, due to injury, and was then unable to secure a regular spot. Scored within 30 seconds of coming on as substitute on New Year's Day.
Shrewsbury T (From apprentice on 11/2/86) FL 174+16/9 FLC 17/2 FAC 10/1 Others 11
Bolton W (£100,000 on 15/8/91) FL 27+6/3 FLC 0+1 FAC 3 Others 2
Shrewsbury T (£25,000 on 23/12/92) FL 66+1/11 FLC 8/1 FAC 3 Others 2
Preston NE (£75,000 on 30/11/94) FL 6+4/1 Others 1

BROWN Michael Robert
Born: Hartlepool, 25 January 1977
Height: 5'7" Weight: 10.6
International Honours: E: U21-4
Is a product of Manchester City's excellent youth programme. Having developed into a firm-tackling and committed midfield player, Michael came into the senior squad in 1995-96 and earned his place during a difficult time for the club by his attitude and skill with the ball, as encouraged and demanded by manager, Alan Ball. Given another season, his enthusiasm and contribution should see him become an ideal clubman and a player to be watched. Most definitely a comer. Played four times for the England U21 side.
Manchester C (From trainee on 13/9/94) PL 16+5 FLC 0+2 FAC 5

BROWN Philip (Phil)
Born: South Shields, 30 May 1959
Height: 5'11" Weight: 11.8
Club Honours: AMC '89
Blackpool full back who favours the right side. Appointed player/coach and assistant manager last season, Phil spent most of his time in the reserves. Still showing great enthusiasm, as befits one who has played more than 600 league games, he filled in admirably when called upon, prior to being released in the summer to re-join Bolton as the club coach.
Hartlepool U (Signed on 7/7/78) FL 210+7/8 FLC 12 FAC 11 Others 3/1
Halifax T (Free on 30/7/85) FL 135/19 FLC 6/1 FAC 8/1 Others 9
Bolton W (£17,000 on 23/6/88) FL 254+4/14 FLC 25/1 FAC 23/1 Others 28/1
Blackpool (Free on 25/7/94) FL 33+11/5 FLC 2/1 FAC 2+2 Others 2+1

BROWN Richard Anthony
Born: Nottingham, 13 January 1967
Height: 5'10" Weight: 11.2
Full back. Having played for Stockport in 1994-95, he joined Blackpool on a short-term contract for last season, playing in the first four games at right back before being released.
Sheffield Wed (£10,000 from Ilkeston T on 8/1/85)
Blackburn Rov (£15,000 from Kettering, via Ilkeston T, Grantham and Boston U, on 26/9/90) F/PL 26+2 FLC 1+1 FAC 2 Others 1

Maidstone U (Loaned on 21/2/91) FL 3
Stockport Co (Free on 3/3/95) FL 1
Blackpool (Free on 10/8/95) FL 2+1 FLC 2

BROWN Steven (Steve) Byron
Born: Brighton, 13 May 1972
Height: 6'1" Weight: 13.10
Missed the first half of last season due to injury before regaining his place in the Charlton side in February. Steve played in both full back positions, centre half and in midfield, and even took the goalkeeper's jersey at Southend, when Mike Salmon was injured, giving an impressive performance, while keeping a clean sheet. Possesses a very strong right foot, and likes to get in early crosses.
Charlton Ath (From trainee on 3/7/90) FL 77+4/3 FLC 3 FAC 9 Others 3

BROWN Steven (Steve) Ferold
Born: Northampton, 6 July 1966
Height: 6'1" Weight: 11.4
Very talented Wycombe left-footed, central midfielder, fearsome in the tackle and, on occasions, the outstanding player on the pitch last season. An elegant performer with the ability to drift past players, his failure to score in his 38 league appearances was a disappointment, however.
Northampton T (From juniors on 11/8/83) FL 14+1/3 (Free to Irthlingborough T in December 1985)
Northampton T (Free on 21/7/89) FL 145+13/19 FLC 10/1 FAC 12/2 Others 10+1/1
Wycombe W (£60,000 on 9/2/94) FL 84+3/2 FLC 5+1 FAC 5 Others 3+1

BROWN Steven (Steve) Robert
Born: Southend, 6 December 1973
Height: 6'0" Weight: 12.7
A hard-working striker, he came on as substitute in Gillingham's opening game last season against Wigan, but the signing of Dennis Bailey restricted his chances and he moved to Lincoln in October, quickly becoming a favourite with the Imps' supporters for his willingness to chase a lost cause. Netted a great 20-yard last minute goal to beat Northampton at Sincil Bank, but failed to score on a regular basis.
Southend U (From trainee on 10/7/92) FL 10/2 FAC 0+1 Others 1
Scunthorpe U (Free on 5/7/93)
Colchester U (Free on 27/8/93) FL 56+6/17 FLC 2 FAC 5/1 Others 4/1
Gillingham (Signed on 22/3/95) FL 8+1/2
Lincoln C (£20,000 on 6/10/95) FL 22+4/3 FAC 1 Others 3/1

BROWNE Paul
Born: Glasgow, 17 February 1975
Height: 6'1" Weight: 12.0
A regular fixture in central defence for Aston Villa's reserve team, he finally made his PL debut last March, deputising for Ugo Ehiogu at home to Middlesbrough, and followed this up with two further appearances in the last two games of the season. An excellent tackler, with a good recovery rate, he may receive further opportunities in 1996-97.
Aston Villa (From trainee on 7/7/93) PL 2

BROWNING Marcus Trevor
Born: Bristol, 22 April 1971
Height: 6'1" Weight: 12.10
International Honours: W: 2

Some remarkably consistent performances by the midfield powerhouse before last Christmas, saw him elevated into the full Welsh International squad, winning his first cap against Italy in November. A fine athlete and confident runner with the ball, Marcus was an integral part of the Bristol Rovers' team, the one disappointment being a lack of goals.
Bristol Rov (From trainee on 1/7/89) FL 128+20/11 FLC 5+3 FAC 7/1 Others 12+5/3
Hereford U (Loaned on 18/9/92) FL 7/5

Marcus Browning

BRUCE Stephen (Steve) Roger
Born: Corbridge, 31 December 1960
Height: 6'0" Weight: 13.0
Club Honours: Div 2 '86, PL '93, '94, '96; FLC '85, '92; FAC '90, '94; CS '90, '93, '94; ECWC '91; ESC '91;
International Honours: E: B-1; Yth

One of the great competitors, a man who competes for everything, both in the air and on the ground, and a scorer of vital goals, the central defender's decision to turn down Derby's tempting offer to become their new manager in the 1995 close season was like music to the ears of Alex Ferguson and the Manchester United faithful. Unfortunately, 1995-96 was blighted by several lay offs from injuries, although he still played a major part in helping the club to another successful league and cup double, despite not being deemed fit enough to play at Wembley. *Stop Press:* Rejecting the prospect of a lucrative testimonial at Old Trafford, Steve opted to sign a two year contract for Birmingham, where he will start 1996-97 as club captain under new manager, Trevor Francis.
Gillingham (From apprentice on 27/10/78) FL 203+2/29 FLC 15/6 FAC 14/1

Norwich C (£125,000 on 24/8/84) FL 141/14 FLC 20/5 FAC 9/1 Others 10
Manchester U (£800,000 on 18/12/87) F/PL 309/36 FLC 32+2/6 FAC 41/3 Others 32+9/7

BRUMWELL Phillip (Phil)
Born: Darlington, 8 August 1975
Height: 5'8" Weight: 11.0

Unable to get a first team opportunity at Sunderland, Phil, a local boy, joined Darlington prior to the start of 1995-96 and deputised in midfield and at right back throughout the campaign. Proving to be a strong tackler, he crowned a fine start in league football by starting the Wembley play-off final.
Sunderland (From trainee on 30/6/94)
Darlington (Free on 11/8/95) FL 16+12 FLC 1+1 FAC 3/1 Others 3+2

BRYAN Marvin Lee
Born: Paddington, 2 August 1975
Height: 6'0" Weight: 12.2

A right winger at Queens Park Rangers, he transferred to Blackpool for a bargain basement fee prior to the start of last season, immediately settling down in the right back position. Proved extremely popular with the crowd with great attacking runs made at every opportunity. Very quick and strong, he is sure to improve further.
Queens Park R (From trainee on 17/8/92)
Doncaster Rov (Loaned on 8/12/94) FL 5/1
Blackpool (£20,000 on 10/8/95) FL 44+2/1 FLC 0+2 FAC 3 Others 6

BRYANT Matthew (Matt)
Born: Bristol, 21 September 1970
Height: 6'1" Weight: 12.11

Another good campaign in 1995-96, in spite of still suffering problems with his back, for this popular player at the heart of the Bristol City defence. His wholehearted commitment to the cause is appreciated by the fans, who would also welcome him being used more often to attack the ball in the opposition's box, something that could well improve City's poor strike record from corner kicks.
Bristol C (From trainee on 1/7/89) FL 201+2/7 FLC 9+1 FAC 11 Others 9
Walsall (Loaned on 24/8/90) FL 13 FLC 4

BRYSON James Ian Cook
Born: Kilmarnock, 26 November 1962
Height: 5'11" Weight: 11.11
Club Honours: Div 3 '96

Preston's captain, Ian was still a threat on the left-hand side of midfield in 1995-96, even at 33, his form good enough to see him elected to the PFA division three side on awards night, followed by a league title winners' medal as North End gained promotion to the second division. His ability to cut in and provide dangerous shots and crosses, supplemented his pivotal role in many of the team's set pieces. Also has a powerful shot from the edge of the area, as Torquay fans can testify. Is training to become a qualified referee.
Kilmarnock (Signed from Hurlford in 1981) SL 194+21/40 SLC 12+7/1 SC 14+2/3
Sheffield U (£40,000 on 24/8/88) F/PL 138+17/36 FLC 11+2/1 FAC 18+4/4 Others 7/3
Barnsley (£20,000 on 12/8/93) FL 16/3 FLC 2/1 Others 2

Preston NE (£42,500 on 29/11/93) FL 109+1/16 FLC 3+1/1 FAC 6+1 Others 10/1

BUCKLE Paul John
Born: Hatfield, 16 December 1970
Height: 5'8" Weight: 10.8
Club Honours: Div 3 '92

Arriving on a free transfer from neighbours, Torquay, early last season, Paul was an ever present in the Exeter side until an injury (medial ligament) picked up playing against his former club in March ruled him out for the rest of the season. An excellent passer of the ball from midfield.
Brentford (From trainee on 1/7/89) FL 42+15/4 FLC 5+1 FAC 3+1 Others 6+5
Torquay U (Free on 3/2/94) FL 57+2/9 FLC 8 FAC 3 Others 1
Exeter C (Free on 13/10/95) FL 22/2 FAC 1 Others 2

BULL Garry William
Born: West Bromwich, 12 June 1966
Height: 5'8" Weight: 11.7
Club Honours: GMVC '91

As the cousin of the more famous Steve Bull, and unable to get a look in at Nottingham Forest, Garry was loaned out to Brighton at the start of last season, scoring four times in 11 appearances before returning to the City Ground. Eventually allowed to leave, he signed for Birmingham in December, but after just one goal, and that in an AWS match, he moved to York City as part of the deal that brought Paul Barnes to St Andrews in March. Proved most popular at Bootham and quickly settled down to snap up goals, including a hat trick at Wrexham in the closing weeks. Not from the same mould as Steve, he effectively plays off the target man.
Southampton (Signed from Paget R on 15/10/86)
Cambridge U (Signed on 29/3/88) FL 13+6/4 FLC 0+1 Others 0+2
Barnet (£2,000 on 1/3/89) FL 83/37 FLC 4/4 FAC 11/3 Others 8/2
Nottingham F (Free on 21/7/93) F/PL 4+8/1 FLC 2 FAC 0+3
Birmingham C (Loaned on 12/9/94) FL 10/6 Others 2/1
Brighton & Hove A (Loaned on 17/8/95) FL 10/2 Others 1/2
Birmingham C (Free on 29/12/95) FL 3+3 FLC 0+1 FAC 0+2 Others 1/1
York C (Free on 4/3/96) FL 15/8

BULL Stephen (Steve) George
Born: Tipton, 28 March 1965
Height: 5'11" Weight: 12.11
Club Honours: Div 4 '88, Div 3 '89; AMC '88
International Honours: E: 13; B-5; U21-5

The hard-working Wolves' striker nearly went to Coventry during the summer of 1995 and struggled in the first ten games of 1995-96. This culminated in him being sent off against Norwich, though he should not have taken all the blame for the incident. Suspended, and with the team doing well without him, he initially returned as substitute. Had only scored four times when Graham Taylor departed in November, but looked better under caretaker manager, Bobby Downes, before the new man in charge, Mark McGhee, re-instated him as captain on Boxing Day versus Millwall.

Within 11 minutes, Steve had promptly chested the ball down, turned and scored from edge of area. Other memorable goals ensued as he returned to form, reaching the 15 mark for the tenth season running on 2 March.

West Bromwich A (Free from Tipton T on 24/8/85) FL 2+2/2 FLC 2/1 Others 1+2
Wolverhampton W (£35,000 on 21/11/86) FL 383+2/217 FLC 23+1/13 FAC 16/7 Others 31+1/32

Steve Bull

BULLIMORE Wayne Alan
Born: Sutton in Ashfield, 12 September 1970
Height: 5'9" Weight: 11.7
International Honours: E: Yth
Skilful, ball-playing midfielder who can score great goals. Started 1995-96 with Scunthorpe, but his talents were often nullified by the more physical approach at lower level, although dangerous with free kicks around the 20-yard mark, he was allowed to move to Bradford City in December. Unfortunately, one minute into his home debut against Oxford, he was stretchered off, requiring a cruciate ligament operation that put him out of action for the rest of the season as far as the first team was concerned.

Manchester U (From trainee on 16/9/88)
Barnsley (Free on 9/3/91) FL 27+8/1 FLC 2+1 FAC 1+1
Stockport Co (Free on 11/10/93)
Scunthorpe U (Free on 19/11/93) FL 62+5/10 FLC 2+2/1 FAC 7/1 Others 5/1
Bradford C (£40,000 on 15/12/95) FL 1+1

BULLOCK Darren John
Born: Worcester, 12 February 1969
Height: 5'8" Weight: 12.4
Darren was one of Huddersfield's revelations last season, giving some outstanding performances from midfield. Originally signed from non-league circles, he has made substantial progress in little over two years as a tough tackler with an eye for goal. His progress has led to offers from the Premier League and he is sure to be one of the stars of the coming campaign. Represented the Endsleigh League U21 side against an Italian Serie "B" XI in November.

Huddersfield T (£55,000 from Nuneaton Borough on 19/11/93) FL 101/15 FLC 7/1 FAC 6/2 Others 9/1

BULLOCK Martin John
Born: Derby, 5 March 1975
Height: 5'5" Weight: 10.7
This Barnsley livewire midfielder's 1995-96 season was a mixture. The manager decided that he was a better option as a substitute to be brought on to attack tiring defences when his dribbling skills could be seen to the full, something superbly illustrated when he netted against Leicester. Will be looking to gain a regular place in the side in 1996-97.

Barnsley (£15,000 from Eastwood T on 4/9/93) FL 42+28/1 FLC 2+1 FAC 0+3 Others 1

BURGESS Daryl
Born: Birmingham, 24 January 1971
Height: 5'11" Weight: 12.3
During the 1995-96 season, Daryl played at right back, centre half, and as a sweeper for WBA and did supremely well, being one of the most consistent members of the team, especially when forming a dual partnership at the heart of the defence with Paul Raven. His pace, heading ability, and strong tackling, once more received high praise from his manager.

West Bromwich A (From trainee on 1/7/89) FL 218+5/7 FLC 12+2/3 FAC 7 Others 14

Craig Burley

BURLEY Craig William
Born: Irvine, 24 September 1971
Height: 6'1" Weight: 11.7
International Honours: S: 12; U21-7; Yth; Sch

A hard-working midfielder with a tremendous shot, Craig has been particularly unfortunate with injuries in 1995-96 and has missed most of Chelsea's matches over the past two seasons, having had to watch impatiently from the sidelines as Ruud Gullit, Eddie Newton and Dennis Wise pulled the strings for them in midfield. Nevertheless, he has still managed to impress Scotland manager, Craig Brown, and was an integral part of the Scottish squad for Euro '96. Coming from a footballing family, as the nephew of Ipswich Town boss, George Burley, he has been capped at all levels by Scotland and is now hoping for an injury-free run-in the first team.

Chelsea (From trainee on 1/9/89) F/PL 59+23/5 FLC 5 FAC 11+2/3 Others 3

BURNETT Wayne
Born: Lambeth, 4 September 1971
Height: 6'0" Weight: 12.6
International Honours: E: Yth
A gifted midfielder who has the ability to pick out excellent passes, but can sometimes drift in and out of games, Wayne came to Bolton from Plymouth Argyle, initially on loan, before completing a permanent transfer at the turn of the year. Although a regular in the reserve side, he made just one Premiership appearance when he came on as substitute against Leeds United at Burnden and will step up this season.

Leyton Orient (From trainee on 13/11/89) FL 34+6 FLC 3+1/1 FAC 3+1 Others 4
Blackburn Rov (£90,000 on 19/8/92)
Plymouth Arg (Signed on 9/8/93) FL 61+9/3 FLC 3 FAC 3 Others 4+1
Bolton W (£100,000 on 12/10/95) PL 0+1

BURNHAM Jason John
Born: Mansfield, 8 May 1973
Height: 5'10" Weight: 13.3
In his second season at Chester, Jason missed only six league games in 1995-96, playing mainly at left back where he continued to enjoy his forays down the flank to join up with the forwards. Freed during the summer.

Northampton T (From trainee on 23/7/91) FL 79+9/2 FLC 4+2 FAC 6 Others 8
Chester C (Free on 29/7/94) FL 62+2/1 FLC 6 FAC 2 Others 4

BURNS Christopher (Chris)
Born: Manchester, 9 November 1967
Height: 6'0" Weight: 12.0
Attacking Northampton midfielder, who was at his most dangerous in 1995-96 with free kicks and corners, where his accurate pin-point passes led to many goals for his team mates. Will be well remembered for the home match against Cardiff, when he appeared as substitute goalkeeper!

Portsmouth (£25,000 from Cheltenham T on 15/3/91) FL 78+12/9 FLC 7+2/2 FAC 7 Others 9+1/1
Swansea C (Loaned on 17/12/93) FL 4 Others 1/1
Bournemouth (Loaned on 11/3/94) FL 13+1/1
Swansea C (Free on 25/11/94) FL 3+2 FAC 0+1
Northampton T (Free on 13/1/95) FL 56+4/9 FLC 2/1 FAC 2 Others 3/1

BURRIDGE John

Born: Workington, 3 December 1951
Height: 5'11" Weight: 13.3
Club Honours: FLC '77; Div 2 '79; SLC '91

During 1995-96, the veteran goalkeeper was registered with Notts County, Witton Albion, Darlington, Grimsby, Gateshead and Northampton, before surely bowing out of the game for good. Darlington were the only league club who benefited from his services at first team level and "Budgie", at 45 years of age, became their oldest ever player when standing in for the recently transferred Michael Pollitt for five games.

Workington (From apprentice on 2/1/70) FL 27 FLC 1 FAC 4
Blackpool (£10,000 on 1/4/71) FL 134 FLC 10 FAC 4 Others 17
Aston Villa (£100,000 on 1/9/75) FL 65 FLC 9 FAC 6
Southend U (Loaned on 20/1/78) FL 6
Crystal Palace (£65,000 on 9/3/78) FL 88 FLC 7 FAC 7
Queens Park R (£200,000 on 19/12/80) FL 39 FLC 4 FAC 2
Wolverhampton W (£75,000 on 26/8/82) FL 74 FLC 2 FAC 5
Derby Co (Loaned on 21/9/84) FL 6 FLC 2
Sheffield U (£10,000 on 26/10/84) FL 109 FLC 6 FAC 6 Others 4
Southampton (£30,000 on 11/8/87) FL 62 FLC 7 FAC 4 Others 2
Newcastle U (£25,000 on 3/10/89) FL 67 FLC 4 FAC 7 Others 5
Hibernian (Free during 1991 close season) SL 65 SLC 5 SC 5 Others 2
Newcastle U (Free on 13/8/93)
Scarborough (Free on 29/10/93) FL 3 Others 1
Lincoln C (Free on 24/12/93) FL 4 (Free to Enfield in February 1994)
Aberdeen (Free in March 1994) SL 3 SC 1 (Free to Barrow in September 1994)
Dumbarton (Free in October 1994) SL 3
Falkirk (Free in November 1994) SL 3
Manchester C (Free on 15/12/94) PL 3+1
Notts Co (Free on 11/8/95. Free to Witton A on 1/10/95)
Darlington (Free on 17/11/95) FL 3 FAC 2
Grimsby T (Free on 20/12/95. Free to Gateshead in January 1996)
Northampton T (Free on 26/1/96)

BURROWS David

Born: Dudley, 25 October 1968
Height: 5'10" Weight: 11.8
Club Honours: CS '89 '90; Div 1 '90; FAC '92
International Honours: E: B-3; U21-7

Coventry left back who had a miserable season in 1995-96 with hamstring injuries. Injured in the Forest home game early on, he recovered only to exacerbate the problem in a reserve game and, after returning to first team action in February, he played just six games before breaking down at Tottenham. Sorely missed by the team, which always looked vulnerable without him, David can also play in central defence and midfield, if required, his powers of recovery and ability to get down the flank holding him in good stead.

West Bromwich A (From apprentice on 8/11/86) FL 37+9/1 FLC 3+1 FAC 2 Others 1
Liverpool (£550,000 on 20/10/88) F/PL 135+11/3 FLC 16 FAC 16+1
West Ham U (Signed on 17/9/93) PL 29/1 FLC 3/1 FAC 3
Everton (Signed on 6/9/94) PL 19 FLC 2 FAC 2
Coventry C (£1,100,000 on 2/3/95) PL 22 FAC 1

BURTON Deon John

Born: Reading, 25 October 1976
Height: 5'8" Weight: 11.9

The talented Portsmouth centre forward again improved on the previous season in 1995-96, but his progress continued to be held up by poor team performances. However, his seven goals put him only behind Paul Hall and Alan McLoughlin, scoring both in the 2-1 home win over Charlton, and he will be looking to find the net on a more regular basis this coming season. It was his effort in a 1-0 win at Huddersfield on the last day of the campaign that kept Pompey in the first division on goal difference.

Portsmouth (From trainee on 15/2/94) FL 30+11/9 FLC 1+2 FAC 0+1

BUSHELL Stephen (Steve) Paul

Born: Manchester, 28 December 1972
Height: 5'9" Weight: 11.6

York midfield dynamo who also has an abundance of skill. Towards the end of the 1995-96 campaign, Steve was showing signs of returning to his best form, having had to battle against injuries during the last couple of seasons.

York C (From trainee on 25/2/91) FL 90+13/5 FLC 3 FAC 2 Others 9+2/1

BUSST David John

Born: Birmingham, 30 June 1967
Height: 6'1" Weight: 12.10

Dominant Coventry centre half who always looked good in the air and improved his play on the ground in 1995-96. Very important at set pieces where most of his goals come from, he proved to be an outstanding club-man who, in a season when a lot of goals were conceded, was rarely exposed. Was the hero and villain in the pulsating Coca Cola Cup match with Tottenham, scoring an own goal then popping up to score the equaliser. He also scored two good headed goals against Blackburn and Everton at home. Tragically suffered a compound fracture of his right leg at Old Trafford on Easter Monday only two days after an outstanding display against Liverpool and is likely to be out of action until well into 1997.

Coventry C (Free from Moor Green on 14/1/92) F/PL 48+2/4 FLC 5+1/1 FAC 3+1

BUTLER Philip Anthony (Tony)

Born: Stockport, 28 September 1972
Height: 6'2" Weight: 12.0

A tall, commanding central defender, and not yet 24, he has now made nearly 200 first team appearances for Gillingham since turning professional. Absent for most of September 1995, through a back injury sustained at Scunthorpe, Tony came back as a regular in the promotion winning side, only missing further games due to suspension. Not many centre forwards got the better of him, especially in the air, during 1995-96.

Gillingham (From trainee on 13/5/91) FL 142+6/5 FLC 12 FAC 12+1 Others 5+1/1

BUTLER John Edward

Born: Liverpool, 7 February 1962
Height: 5'11" Weight: 11.7
Club Honours: AMC '92; Div 2 '93

A consistent and dependable Wigan defender, John signed for the club after being freed by Stoke during the summer of 1995 and coped with playing in both full back positions like a true professional. In his second spell with the club, he has now completed well over 250 league games for the Latics and throughout his career has also performed at centre back and midfield when required.

Wigan Ath (Free from Prescot Cables on 15/1/82) FL 238+7/15 FLC 17+1 FAC 20+1/2 Others 18
Stoke C (£75,000 on 23/12/88) FL 258+4/7 FLC 19 FAC 11 Others 26+1/2
Wigan Ath (Free on 17/6/95) FL 33/1 FLC 1 FAC 3 Others 3

BUTLER Lee Simon

Born: Sheffield, 30 May 1966
Height: 6'2" Weight: 14.4

Goalkeeper. Because of the form of David Watson in goal in 1995-96, Lee was restricted to just one start and that due to suspension. His season's highlight probably came at Watford when, because of injuries, he made an appearance as an outfield substitute in a winning team. Loaned to Scunthorpe as cover for Mark Samways, but, not seen at his best, he was released during the summer.

Lincoln C (Free from Haworth Colliery on 16/6/86) FL 30 FLC 1 FAC 1
Aston Villa (£100,000 on 21/8/87) FL 8 Others 2
Hull C (Loaned on 18/3/91) FL 4
Barnsley (£165,000 on 22/7/91) FL 118+2 FLC 5 FAC 9 Others 4
Scunthorpe U (Loaned on 5/2/96) FL 2

BUTLER Martin Neil

Born: Wordsley, 15 September 1974
Height: 5'11" Weight: 11.3

Striker who has been with Walsall from his trainee days and enjoyed his most successful season to date in 1995-96. A great chaser of lost causes, he netted twice in last season's 3-2 defeat at Oxford in February and scored with a fine chip in the win at Blackpool at the end of the season that robbed the Seasiders of automatic promotion. Can also play on the left flank.

Walsall (From trainee on 24/5/93) FL 23+28/7 FLC 0+1 FAC 2+5/2 Others 2+2/2

Paul Butler

BUTLER Paul John
Born: Manchester, 2 November 1972
Height: 6'2" Weight: 13.0
Centre back and pillar of the Rochdale defence in 1995-96, he assumed the senior role when Peter Valentine was injured and replaced by "rookie", Dave Bayliss. Still only 22, he has now passed 150 FL appearances for Dale and scored numerous vital goals from set pieces. Outstanding in the air, he was voted "Player of the Year" for the second season running.
Rochdale (From trainee on 5/7/91) FL 151+7/10 FLC 8+1 FAC 6+2 Others 12+1

BUTLER Peter James
Born: Halifax, 27 August 1966
Height: 5'9" Weight: 11.1
An all-round midfielder with good ball winning and passing ability, surprisingly, Peter was not required to play for Notts County last season, instead, spending much of his time on loan at Grimsby (January) and WBA (March). Although making no real impression at Grimsby, he was instrumental in helping Albion string together some important results as they pulled away from the relegation zone.
Huddersfield T (From apprentice on 21/8/84) FL 0+5
Cambridge U (Loaned on 24/1/86) FL 14/1 Others 1
Bury (Free on 8/7/86) FL 9+2 FLC 2/1 FAC 1
Cambridge U (Free on 10/12/86) FL 55/9 FLC 4 FAC 2 Others 2
Southend U (£75,000 on 12/2/88) FL 135+7/9 FLC 12/1 FAC 2 Others 11/2
Huddersfield T (Loaned on 24/3/92) FL 7
West Ham U (£125,000 on 12/8/92) F/PL 70/3 FLC 4 FAC 3 Others 1
Notts Co (£350,000 on 4/10/94) FL 20 FLC 2 FAC 2 Others 3
Grimsby T (Loaned on 30/1/96) FL 3
West Bromwich A (Loaned on 28/3/96) FL 9

BUTLER Stephen (Steve)
Born: Birmingham, 27 January 1962
Height: 6'2" Weight: 13.6
Club Honours: GMVC '89
International Honours: E: SP-3
Experienced centre forward. Having signed from Cambridge in December 1995, in only his fifth game for Gillingham he scored a hat trick in 17 minutes against Chester City. Missed five weeks of the season late on, after having an operation for a persistent groin injury. Interestingly, he had trials with Gillingham in 1982 and 1983, only to be told that the club could not afford to buy him out of the army!
Brentford (Free from Windsor & Eton on 19/12/84) FL 18+3/3 Others 2
Maidstone U (Free on 1/8/86) FL 76/41 FLC 4/3 FAC 18/7 Others 10/4
Watford (£150,000 on 28/3/91) FL 40+22/9 FLC 4+3 FAC 1 Others 2+1
Bournemouth (Loaned on 18/12/92) FL 1
Cambridge U (£75,000 on 23/12/92) FL 107+2/51 FLC 4+1 FAC 6/5 Others 3
Gillingham (£100,000 on 15/12/95) FL 14+6/5

BUTT Nicholas (Nicky)
Born: Manchester, 21 January 1975
Height: 5'10" Weight: 11.3
Club Honours: FAYC '92; CS '94; PL '96; FAC '96
International Honours: E: U21-5; Yth (UEFA Yth '93); Sch

The shock departure of Paul Ince to Inter Milan in the 1995 close season, rankled hard with some of United's most vociferous supporters, but the elevation of Nicky to the former maestro's number eight Manchester United jersey soon silenced the critics. The young central midfielder has certainly come on leaps and bounds since emerging from the youth team in 1992, his neat skills, hardened edge, and ever growing maturity, making him one of the most constructive players in the Premiership throughout the 1995-96 campaign. Although not an avid scorer, he did add some important contributions during the season. His first goal of the campaign against Liverpool at Old Trafford was somewhat overshadowed by the return of Eric Cantona, but his contribution against Sunderland in the FA Cup at Old Trafford helped to keep United in the competition when they appeared to be going out. A regular in the England U21 side, and a constant inspiration in the latter stages, he could rightly be proud of his championship and FA Cup winning medals, having been a professional for less than four years.
Manchester U (From trainee on 29/1/93) PL 42+14/3 FLC 3 FAC 10+2/1 Others 7+1

Nicky Butt

BUTTERS Guy
Born: Hillingdon, 30 October 1969
Height: 6'3" Weight: 13.0
International Honours: E: U21-3
Good, solid and dependable no thrills Portsmouth central defender with a great attitude and a left foot to match. Started last season as captain and led by example through difficult times, forming a great partnership with first, Adrian Whitbread and

subsequently, Andy Thomson, as Pompey ultimately finished one place above the relegation zone.
Tottenham H (From trainee on 5/8/88) FL 34+1/1 FLC 2+1 FAC 1
Southend U (Loaned on 13/1/90) FL 16/3 Others 2
Portsmouth (£375,000 on 28/9/90) FL 141+6/6 FLC 13+1/1 FAC 7 Others 7+2
Oxford U (Loaned on 4/11/94) FL 3/1 Others 1

BYNG David Graeme
Born: Coventry, 9 July 1977
Height: 6'1" Weight: 13.0
The strong, bustling striker made 20 appearances for Torquay last season, of which 13 were from the bench, scoring just one goal, before being signed by Doncaster in February. Yet to play for Rovers, he is still very much a player for the future.
Torquay U (From trainee on 7/7/95) FL 12+12/3 FLC 1+3 FAC 1+1/1 Others 1
Doncaster Rov (Free on 6/2/96)

BYRNE John Frederick
Born: Manchester, 1 February 1961
Height: 6'0" Weight: 12.13
Club Honours: Div 4 '84
International Honours: Ei: 23
It was a frustrating 1995-96 for Brighton's popular striker. Sidelined for chunks of the season with sciatica, he struggled to regain peak form, with the Brighton fans only seeing glimpses of his neat ball control and eye for goal. Nicknamed "Budgie", he was released during the summer.
York C (From apprentice on 31/1/79) FL 167+8/55 FLC 10+2/5 FAC 10+1/3 Others 1
Queens Park R (£115,000 on 30/10/84) FL 108+18/30 FLC 12+1/4 FAC 7+2/2 Others 1 (£175,000 to Le Havre in May 1988)
Brighton & Hove A (£120,000 on 1/9/90) FL 47+4/14 FLC 2/2 FAC 2/2 Others 2+1
Sunderland (£225,000 on 23/10/91) FL 33/8 FLC 2 FAC 8/7
Millwall (£250,000 on 28/10/92) FL 12+5/1
Brighton & Hove A (Loaned on 25/3/93) FL 5+2/2
Oxford U (£50,000 on 1/11/93) FL 52+3/18 FLC 4 FAC 5/2 Others 2
Brighton & Hove A (Free on 24/2/95) FL 29+10/6 FLC 1+1 FAC 3/2 Others 0+1

BYRNE Paul Peter
Born: Dublin, 30 June 1972
Height: 5'11" Weight: 13.0
International Honours: Ei: U21-1; Yth; Sch
One of Southend manager, Ronnie Whelan's best buys of last season, Paul's undoubted skill on the right side of midfield was one of the highlights of 1995-96 for Blues' fans. Certainly, the £50,000 fee paid to Celtic seemed a bargain after many exciting moments, his ball control and jinking wing runs always causing defences' problems. His 30-yard drive at home to Norwich was one of the best goals ever seen at Roots Hall and the Blues may have trouble holding onto him if he continues where he left off this coming season.
Oxford U (From trainee on 4/7/89) FL 4+2 (Free to Bangor in September 1991)
Glasgow Celtic (Signed on 26/5/93) SL 24+4/4 SLC 1+1 SC 1 Others 2
Brighton & Hove A (Loaned on 10/3/95) FL 8/1
Southend U (£50,000 on 25/8/95) FL 38+3/5 FLC 2/1 FAC 1 Others 4

Carling Black Label

CARLING Black. Label
Position: No. 1
Nationality: British
Strength: 4.1% volume
Appearances: Every Carling Premiership game
Record: Sponsor of the Carling Premiership: 1993 to present. Sponsor of the Professional Footballers' Association: 1993 to present.
Honours: The Carling No.1 Awards - the only football awards in which fans representatives get a vote
The Carling Manager of the Month
The Carling Player of the Month
The Carling No.1 Award
The Carling Manager of the Year
The Carling Player of the Year

Ever-present in the top flight since 1993, Carling is a natural leader and a consistent crowd pleaser. Carling's main assets are: pace - 44 pints are served every second; strength - 4.1%abv and its distribution - 27,000 pubs and clubs nationwide. Constantly in demand, Carling is a refreshing all-rounder suited to all occasions.

CARLING BLACK LABEL, THE BEST SELLING BEER IN BRITAIN...
A FACT WORTH REMEMBERING NEXT TIME YOU HIT THE BAR

carling net @
www.fa-carling.com

CADETTE Richard Raymond
Born: Hammersmith, 21 March 1965
Height: 5'8" Weight: 12.0
Club Honours: B&QC '94

Speedy Millwall forward who is adept at close control and shielding the ball from defenders. Since coming back to London, Richard has been unlucky with injuries, last season being no exception. On the bench for the opening game, he later suffered a knee condition that kept him out until April and will be hoping for better fortune in 1996-97.
Leyton Orient (Free from Wembley on 25/8/84) FL 19+2/4 FLC 4 FAC 1/1 Others 2
Southend U (Free on 15/8/85) FL 90/48 FLC 5+1/1 FAC 4/5 Others 5/1
Sheffield U (£130,000 on 20/7/87) FL 26+2/7 FLC 1 FAC 2 Others 2
Brentford (£80,000 on 22/7/88) FL 67+20/20 FLC 10+3/6 FAC 9/1 Others 14/4
Bournemouth (Loaned on 22/3/90) FL 4+4/1
Falkirk (Signed on 9/1/92) SL 82+10/31 SLC 6/7 SC 4/2 Others 4/6
Millwall (£135,000 on 13/10/94) FL 12+5/4 FLC 2/1 FAC 1

CAESAR Gus Cassius
Born: Tottenham, 5 March 1966
Height: 6'0" Weight: 12.7
International Honours: E: U21-3

In his third year at the heart of Colchester's defence, Gus is a former England U21 cap with experience at the top level. Always a solid and reliable defender, he also doubled his English goalscoring record, with the winner against Bury last March and added another at Exeter in April for good measure. Released during the summer.
Arsenal (From apprentice on 10/2/84) FL 27+17 FLC 2+3 FAC 0+1
Queens Park R (Loaned on 28/11/90) FL 5
Cambridge U (Free on 31/7/91)
Bristol C (Free on 6/9/91) FL 9+1 FLC 1 FAC 1 Others 1
Airdrie (Free on 30/1/92) SL 57/1 SLC 3 SC 5+1 Others 1
Colchester U (Free on 11/8/94) FL 62/3 FLC 4 FAC 5 Others 5

CAHILL Oliver (Ollie) Francis
Born: Clonmell, 29 September, 1975
Height: 5'10" Weight: 11.2

Left-sided Northampton midfield player who likes to take on opposing defenders rather than beat them with speed. His first team outings were somewhat restricted last season, but earmarked him as one for the future.
Northampton T (Signed from Clonmel on 2/9/94) FL 7+4/1 FAC 0+1 Others 1+2

CAIG Antony (Tony)
Born: Whitehaven, 11 April 1974
Height: 6'1" Weight: 13.4
Club Honours: Div 3 '95

Carlisle's first choice goalkeeper in 1994-95, he again played in the majority of the club's matches last season, despite two spells as understudy to Tony Elliott. Has a deserved reputation as a shot stopper and worked to improve other areas of his game, notably his kicking. He even ventured into his opponents' area on occasions and almost scored at Brighton when his last minute header was cleared off the line.
Carlisle U (From trainee on 10/7/92) FL 94 FLC 6 FAC 7 Others 17

CALDERWOOD Colin
Born: Stranraer, 20 January 1965
Height: 6'0" Weight: 12.12
Club Honours: Div 4 '86
International Honours: S: 13; Sch

Spurs' central defender who continued to improve in fitness and consistency of performance last season. Colin's height and strong build made him an ideal partner for Sol Campbell, where the pair could cope with crosses both high and low and shut down attacks from midfield. Continued to demonstrate a good awareness of the game by bringing the ball out from defence and passing intelligently to both wings as well as central players. Consistency and enthusiasm helped him become an almost automatic choice for Scotland and he was rewarded with selection for their European Championship squad.
Mansfield T (Signed on 19/3/82) FL 97+3/1 FLC 4 FAC 6/1 Others 7
Swindon T (£30,000 on 1/7/85) FL 328+2/20 FLC 35 FAC 17/1 Others 32
Tottenham H (£1,250,000 on 22/7/93) PL 87+4/3 FLC 9 FAC 13

Colin Calderwood

CALDWELL Garrett Evan James
Born: Princeton, USA, 6 November 1973
Height: 6'2" Weight: 13.0

Young goalkeeper, already with Canadian junior representative honours, who joined Colchester last September after impressing in the World Student Championships. With one AWS appearance behind him, Garrett missed his big league chance after Carl Emberson broke his thumb in March, being away on international duty, again!
Colchester U (Free from Princeton, USA on 25/9/95) Others 1

CALDWELL Peter James
Born: Dorchester, 5 June 1972
Height: 6'1" Weight: 13.0
International Honours: E: Sch

A goalkeeper signed by Leyton Orient from QPR during the 1995 close season to stand in for Paul Heald, he made his debut on day one after the latter had been sold to Wimbledon. Tall and agile, in the Chris Woods' mould, Peter made a promising start before missing several weeks, having unfortunately contracted glandular fever.
Queens Park R (From trainee on 9/3/90)
Leyton Orient (Free on 3/7/95) FL 28 FLC 2 Others 1

CAME Mark Raymond
Born: Exeter, 14 September 1961
Height: 6'1" Weight: 13.0

Centre half and team captain, Mark had another superb season for Exeter in 1995-96, alongside Noel Blake and Jon Richardson, shoring up the centre of the City defence. Scored the first goal of 1996 among the four divisions, against Plymouth on New Year's Day. Excellent in the air and dangerous at set pieces, he was good value for the "Player of the Year" award.
Bolton W (Signed from Winsford U on 28/4/84) FL 188+7/7 FLC 15+4/2 FAC 16+2 Others 27/2
Chester C (Signed on 4/12/92) FL 47/1 FLC 2 FAC 3 Others 6/1
Exeter C (Free on 14/7/94) FL 70/5 FLC 4 FAC 2 Others 3/1

CAMPBELL Andrew (Andy) Paul
Born: Stockton, 18 April 1979
Height: 5'11" Weight: 11.7

One of Middlesbrough's youngest ever first timers, and still a trainee professional, Andy made his debut as a substitute last April against Sheffield Wednesday, a few days short of his 17th birthday, followed up by a first full appearance against Liverpool at Anfield. Clearly, he is highly regarded by manager, Bryan Robson, as a player of high potential and is certainly one to note for the future.
Middlesbrough (Trainee) PL 1+1

CAMPBELL Jamie
Born: Birmingham, 21 October 1972
Height: 6'1" Weight: 11.3

Freed by Cambridge during the summer of 1995, Jamie signed for Barnet and proved reliable in the left back slot until Alex Dyer arrived before Christmas. As a player who is equally at home in midfield or attack, he still remained a regular substitute and squad member.
Luton T (From trainee on 1/7/91) FL 10+26/1 FLC 1+1 FAC 1+3 Others 1+2
Mansfield T (Loaned on 25/11/94) FL 3/1 FAC 2
Cambridge U (Loaned on 10/3/95) FL 12
Barnet (Free on 11/7/95) FL 14+10/1 FLC 2 FAC 2

Jamie Campbell

CAMPBELL Kevin Joseph
Born: Lambeth, 4 February 1970
Height: 6'1" Weight: 13.8
Club Honours: FAYC '88; FLC '93; FAC '93; ECWC '94
International Honours: E: B-1; U21-4
After a disappointing season with Arsenal in 1994-95, Kevin was given the chance of a fresh start by Nottingham Forest, who signed him in the summer as a replacement for Stan Collymore. Sadly, he failed to deliver, with only six league and cup goals from a total of 31 games played. However, in mitigation, it should be pointed out that he suffered from a long-standing back problem which kept him out of action from September to December. Forest fans must be hoping that 1996-97 will see a change of fortune for a player who, at his best, combines strength with pace and fine aerial ability.
Arsenal (From trainee on 11/2/88) F/PL 124+42/46 FLC 14+10/6 FAC 13+6/2 Others 15+4/5
Leyton Orient (Loaned on 16/1/89) FL 16/9
Leicester C (Loaned on 8/11/89) FL 11/5 Others 1/1
Nottingham F (£30,000 on 1/7/95) PL 21/3 FAC 7/3 Others 3

CAMPBELL Sulzeer (Sol) Jeremiah
Born: Newham, 18 September 1974
Height: 6'2" Weight: 14.1
International Honours: E: 2; B-1; U21-11; Yth (UEFA Yth '93)
This versatile player, who can play at full back or in midfield, now seems to be established in the centre of Tottenham's defence. Overcoming a pre-season injury to have a highly successful 1995-96 campaign for Tottenham, which was rewarded by England international honours, he also proved his ability to score goals with a fine

low drive beating Peter Schmeichel for Spurs' second in the 4-1 defeat of Manchester United in January. Solid defensive performances enhanced his reputation as a mature and reliable anchor man at the heart of Tottenham's vastly improved defence. Comfortable on the ball, and a player who looks to come out of defence to set up an attack, he was selected for England's final 22, making his European Championship debut as a sub in the match against Scotland.
Tottenham H (From trainee on 23/9/92) PL 87+9/2 FLC 10/1 FAC 10+2

CANHAM Anthony (Tony)
Born: Leeds, 8 June 1960
Height: 5'8" Weight: 11.4
An experienced midfielder who can also play in defence, Tony joined Hartlepool in the 1995 close season from York, but unfortunately struggled to find his best form, before suffering a serious knee ligament injury in mid-term which could easily have finished his career. Returning after a lengthy spell out, although playing some of his best football, he was never seen as a long-term signing, and was released during the summer.
York C (Free from Harrogate RI on 16/1/85) FL 309+38/57 FLC 18/2 FAC 20/6 Others 24+4/4
Hartlepool U (Free on 8/8/95) FL 25+4/1 FLC 3 Others 1

CANHAM Scott Walter
Born: Newham, 5 November 1974
Height: 5'7" Weight: 11.7
A talented, skilful West Ham playmaker who specialises with set pieces and who passes and moves well. Unable to break into the Hammers' first team squad in 1995-96, Scott had two loan periods at Torquay (November) and Brentford (January), turning in impressive displays for both clubs. Still highly thought of at Upton Park, the coming season may see the big opportunity coming his way, after three years as a pro.
West Ham U (From trainee on 2/7/93)
Torquay U (Loaned on 3/11/95) FL 3
Brentford (Loaned on 19/1/96) FL 14

CANTONA Eric
Born: Nimes, France, 24 May 1966
Height: 6'2" Weight: 14.3
Club Honours: Div 1 '92; PL '93, '94, '96; CS '93, '94; FAC '94, '96
International Honours: France: 45
One of the most naturally gifted strikers ever to play in the English League, he combines great skill and vision to plain, hard work. Sees chances and takes them, often spectacularly. After frantic negotiations by Alex Ferguson to keep Eric at Manchester United during the 1995 close season, the enigmatic Frenchman celebrated his much awaited comeback with a vital equalising goal against Liverpool in October. Such was the manager's faith in his undoubted talents, he promoted him to team captain in the absence of Steve Bruce, a task which he carried out with much aplomb, often acting as peacemaker during volatile disputes

between team mates and opponents. With him in the side, United looked a different proposition and his influence, goalscoring prowess and deft skills helped the Reds towards a second league and cup challenge, just when it appeared to be a losing cause. Having won a league championship medal, the double was achieved when he fittingly scored the only goal of the game against Liverpool in the FA Cup final. With the much publicised incident at Crystal Palace now well and truly behind him, Eric was honoured by the Football Writers' Association in May when he was named "Footballer of the Year". Has now pledged to stay at the club for the remainder of his career.
Leeds U (£900,000 from Nimes on 6/2/92) F/PL 18+10/9 FLC 1 Others 6/5
Manchester U (£1,200,000 on 27/11/92) PL 106+1/53 FLC 6/1 FAC 14/10 Others 8/3

Eric Cantona

CAPLETON Melvyn (Mel) David
Born: London, 24 October 1973
Height: 5'11" Weight: 12.0
Blackpool goalkeeper. Started last season as first choice, playing in the opening two matches, before being displaced by Steve Banks, a recent arrival from Gillingham. With Lee Martin ensconced as the regular reserve goalie, he had a spell on loan at Cork City, prior to being released in the summer.
Southend U (From trainee on 1/7/92)
Blackpool (Free on 1/8/93) FL 9+2 FLC 1

CARBON Matthew (Matt) Phillip
Born: Nottingham, 8 June 1975
Height: 6'2" Weight: 12.4
International Honours: E: U21-1
Talented youngster who missed the start of last season with an ankle injury and when fit again rarely found his best form. Appeared for Lincoln in a variety of positions during the campaign, including centre back, central midfield, left-sided midfield and central

striker, also having a short spell as club captain. Moved to Derby in March and finished the campaign on a high note, winning an England U21 cap against Croatia when he came on as a second half substitute.

Lincoln C (From trainee on 13/4/93) FL 66+3/10 FLC 4/1 FAC 3 Others 4+3
Derby Co (£385,000 on 8/3/96) FL 2+4

CAREY Brian Patrick
Born: Cork, 31 May 1968
Height: 6'3" Weight: 14.4
International Honours: Ei: 3; U21-1

Right-footed Leicester central defender. Regained a first team place last October, when Steve Walsh was injured, then held it until suspension at Christmas. Denied his first goal for the club on his seasonal debut as a substitute, when players voted Steve Walsh as the scorer at Barnsley, after both men had appeared to head simult-aneously. Incidentally, David Lowe had also claimed a faint touch en-route to the net. Eventually got on the scoresheet against Millwall in March with a first minute header.

Manchester U (£100,000 from Cork C on 2/9/89)
Wrexham (Loaned on 17/1/91) FL 3
Wrexham (Loaned on 24/12/91) FL 13/1 FAC 3 Others 3
Leicester C (£250,000 on 16/7/93) F/PL 51+7/1 FLC 3 FAC 0+1 Others 4

CAREY Louis Anthony
Born: Bristol, 22 January 1977
Height: 5'10" Weight: 11.10

One of the Bristol City youngsters of whom much is expected in the future. Louis made his league debut in City's 1-0 success at York early last season and went on to have a lengthy run at right back, before making way for Gary Owers. This coming season will be a crucial one for this cool-headed player, when improvement in distribution and pace should see him ensconced in the side as a regular.

Bristol C (From trainee on 3/7/95) FL 22+1 FAC 2 Others 1

CAREY Shaun Peter
Born: Kettering, 13 May 1976
Height: 5'9" Weight: 10.6
International Honours: Ei: U21-2

Shaun graduated through the Norwich City youth scheme, having played 54 games for the reserves in the last two seasons. Neat and accurate distribution skills, allied to determined midfield tackling, saw him make his debut for City from the subs' bench during the 6-1 Coca Cola Cup defeat of Torquay last September. Eleven stitches in a head wound in a New Year's Day clash with Derby's Marco Gabbiadini delayed his progress, but he returned to play particularly well at Leicester and Derby and has a very promising future. Selection for the Republic of Ireland U21 side against Russia in March would seemingly support that view.

Norwich C (From trainee on 1/7/94) FL 6+3 FLC 2+1

CARMICHAEL Matthew (Matt)
Born: Singapore, 13 May 1964
Height: 6'2" Weight: 12.4

Freed by Preston during the summer of 1995, he spent a week at Mansfield on trial prior to signing for Doncaster and playing in a variety of positions during the 1995-96 season, before moving to Darlington in the second half of the campaign. Perhaps at his best as a central defender, but has a more than reasonable games per goal ratio up front, where his strength and aerial ability make him a real handful for the opposition.

Lincoln C (Free from Basingstoke T on 8/8/89) FL 113+20/18 FLC 9+1/1 FAC 4+1 Others 7+1/2
Scunthorpe U (Signed on 16/7/93) FL 51+11/20 FLC 1+1 FAC 4+3/2 Others 5/5
Barnet (Loaned on 23/9/94) FL 2+1
Preston NE (Free on 10/3/95) FL 7+3/3
Mansfield T (Free on 11/8/95) FL 1/1
Doncaster Rov (Free on 18/8/95) FL 19+8/4 FLC 0+1 FAC 0+1/1 Others 2+1
Darlington (Free on 29/2/96) FL 11+2/2 Others 2+1

CARPENTER Richard
Born: Sheerness, 30 September 1972
Height: 6'0" Weight: 13.0

Strong-tackling Gillingham midfielder, who is equally at home in the right back position, he was on the fringes of the first team squad for most of last season, playing very few games. Is dangerous at free kicks with an explosive right foot.

Gillingham (From trainee on 13/5/91) FL 106+15/4 FLC 2+1 FAC 9+1 Others 7/1

CARR Darren John
Born: Bristol, 4 September 1968
Height: 6'2" Weight: 13.0

Chesterfield's Darren began and ended 1995-96 recovering from knee injuries, his only appearance coming in a bizarre game at Swindon when he gave away a throw-in at the stroke of half time and was promptly sent off. His return to the dressing rooms summed up what, all in all, was rather a sad season for the big man. As the club's "Player of the Year" in 1994-95, and the cornerstone of the defence, much more was expected.

Bristol Rov (From trainee on 20/8/86) FL 26+4 FLC 2+2 FAC 3 Others 2
Newport Co (£3,000 on 30/10/87) FL 9
Sheffield U (£8,000 on 10/3/88) FL 12+1/1 FLC 1 FAC 3+1 Others 1
Crewe Alex (£35,000 on 18/9/90) FL 96+8/5 FLC 8 FAC 12/2 Others 10
Chesterfield (£30,000 on 21/7/93) FL 64/3 FLC 8 FAC 3 Others 7

CARR Franz Alexander
Born: Preston, 24 September 1966
Height: 5'7" Weight: 10.12
Club Honours: FMC '89; FLC '90
International Honours: E: U21-9; Yth

Another season in the wilderness for the one time mercurial winger. After occasional selections as a non-playing substitute, he finally started a match in the FA Cup sixth round-tie away to Nottingham Forest last March where he scored the only goal to secure Aston Villa's place in the semi final. Although it was not to be the start of a "fairy tale" comeback, with Franz returning to obscurity after just one more game, at his best there are still few full backs who can live with his pace.

Blackburn Rov (From apprentice on 30/7/84)
Nottingham F (£100,000 on 2/8/84) FL 122+9/17 FLC 16+2/5 FAC 4 Others 5+2/1
Sheffield Wed (Loaned on 22/12/89) FL 9+3 FAC 2
West Ham U (Loaned on 11/3/91) FL 1+2
Newcastle U (£250,000 on 13/6/91) FL 20+5/3 FLC 2+2 Others 3+1
Sheffield U (£120,000 on 12/1/93) P/FL 18/4 FAC 4 Others 1/1
Leicester C (£100,000 on 8/9/94) PL 12+1/1
Aston Villa (£250,000 on 10/2/95) PL 1+2 FAC 1/1

Franz Carr

CARRAGHER Matthew
Born: Liverpool, 14 January 1976
Height: 5'9" Weight: 10.7

Wigan Athletic right back who celebrated a century of league games in 1995-96, in only his second full season as a professional. A strong tackler, his appearances, however, were somewhat restricted due to the return to the club of John Butler. Predominantly an attacking player, he should continue to progress at a satisfactory rate.

Wigan Ath (From trainee on 25/11/93) FL 90+11 FLC 4+1/1 FAC 10/2 Others 7+1

CARROLL David (Dave) Francis
Born: Paisley, 20 September 1966
Height: 6'0" Weight: 12.0
Club Honours: FAT '91, '93; GMVC '93
International Honours: E: Sch

Deservedly voted Wycombe's 1995-96 "Player of the Season" by the supporters, he was the only player to start and finish every game last season. Very comfortable on the ball, and a good passer, this skilful right winger scored nine valuable league goals, and in the dearth of flair in the second division, his long, mazy runs towards goal were a delight. Is only a handful of appearances away from reaching 400 for the club.

Wycombe W (£6,000 from Ruislip Manor in 1988 close season) FL 128/21 FLC 10 FAC 17/3 Others 10/3

CARROLL Roy Eric
Born: Belfast, 30 September 1977
Height: 6'2" Weight: 11.9

As the third youngest ever Hull goalkeeper, Roy is aiming to follow former colleague, Alan Fettis, into Northern Ireland's goal. Twice called up for the national U18 squad before making a terrific Tigers' debut at Swindon in January, he retained his place with a series of eye-catching performances, displaying a presence and maturity way beyond his years. Attracted many scouts, Bolton showing particular interest, Roy was City's find of the season, being voted "Player of the Year".

Hull C (From trainee on 7/9/95) FL 23

CARRS Anthony John
Born: Alnwick, 31 March 1976
Height: 5'11" Weight: 12.0

A promising left-sided midfielder who came from Blackburn prior to 1995-96 getting underway, he never really established a regular first team place at Darlington, despite an ability to score stunning goals. He did, however, end the season by starting at Wembley in the play-off final.

Blackburn Rov (Free from Bradford C juniors on 29/8/94)
Darlington (Free on 11/8/95) FL 13+15/2 FLC 2/1 FAC 1+1 Others 3

CARRUTHERS Martin George
Born: Nottingham, 7 August 1972
Height: 5'11" Weight: 11.9

A clearly determined striker who had another frustrating season at Stoke in 1995-96, he sometimes displays a lack of composure in front of goal. Linked with a move to Burnley before the transfer deadline, and Fortuna Sittard in the Dutch League earlier in the season, Martin is still only 23 and can continue to develop into a first class forward.

Aston Villa (From trainee on 4/7/90) F/PL 2+2 FAC 0+1 Others 0+1
Hull C (Loaned on 31/10/92) FL 13/6 Others 3
Stoke C (£300,000 on 5/7/93) FL 60+30/13 FLC 7+2/1 FAC 3+1 Others 10+4/6

CARSLEY Lee Kevin
Born: Birmingham, 28 February 1974
Height: 5'11" Weight: 11.11
International Honours: Ei: U21-1

An effective and versatile Derby youngster who can play either at the back or in a midfield role, Lee confirmed his high rating with a series of cultured displays at whatever role he was asked to play last season and, in doing so, obtained a regular first team spot. Having won his first Republic of Ireland U21 cap, he now looks to become a key player in County's long-term future plans.

Derby Co (From trainee on 6/7/92) FL 53+5/3 FLC 5+1 FAC 1 Others 3

CARTER Darren (Danny) Stephen
Born: Hackney, 29 June 1969
Height: 5'11" Weight: 11.12

A wide, attacking midfielder, who only showed on odd occasions for Peterborough last season, having been signed from Leyton Orient the previous June, Danny has the ability to get behind defenders to whip in telling crosses. Played the first half of the campaign on the right, before moving to the opposite flank.

Leyton Orient (Signed from Billericay T on 4/7/88) FL 168+20/22 FLC 13+3/2 FAC 10/3 Others 17+2/1
Peterborough U (£25,000 on 21/6/95) FL 30+7/1 FLC 3 FAC 2 Others 3

CARTER James (Jimmy) William Charles
Born: Hammersmith, 9 November 1965
Height: 5'10" Weight: 11.1
Club Honours: Div 2 '88

A free transfer signing from Arsenal during the 1995 close season, Jimmy started 1995-96 erratically for Portsmouth and his performances took time to get going. However, once the tricky wingman found his pace and switched to the right flank, he was soon one of the greatest contributors to the team, also scoring four goals. His ability to go past the full back to release great crosses augurs well for the new season, that is if the supply line holds up.

Crystal Palace (From apprentice on 15/11/83)
Queens Park R (Free on 30/9/85)
Millwall (£15,000 on 12/3/87) FL 99+11/10 FLC 6+1 FAC 6+1/2 Others 5+1
Liverpool (£800,000 on 10/1/91) FL 2+3 FAC 2 Others 0+1
Arsenal (£500,000 on 8/10/91) F/PL 18+7/2 FLC 1 FAC 2+1
Oxford U (Loaned on 23/3/94) FL 5
Oxford U (Loaned on 23/12/94) FL 3+1
Portsmouth (Free on 6/7/95) FL 31+4/4 FLC 1+1 FAC 0+1

CARTER Mark Colin
Born: Liverpool, 17 December 1960
Height: 5'9" Weight: 12.6
International Honours: E: SP-11

Finished last season as Bury's top scorer with 18 league and cup goals, despite suffering a recurring hamstring injury in mid-term. The striker came back in emphatic style, though, recapturing his best form and his scoring touch, and is a proven goalscorer who promises to be around a little while longer yet.

Barnet (£40,000 from Runcorn on 20/2/91) FL 62+20/30 FLC 5/2 FAC 4+1/6 Others 7+2/8
Bury (£6,000 on 10/9/93) FL 85+9/50 FLC 6+1/3 FAC 4 Others 9+1

Mark Carter

CARTER Timothy (Tim) Douglas
Born: Bristol, 5 October 1967
Height: 6'2" Weight: 13.11
International Honours: E: Yth

Fearless, experienced goalkeeper who is very confident, especially with crosses. Freed by Millwall at the end of 1994-95, Tim trialed at Blackpool before signing for Oxford, where he played in the first 17 matches of last season. Having kept six clean sheets, prior to being replaced by Phil Whitehead, he re-signed for Millwall in December as cover for when Kasey Keller was called up for international duty. Performed admirably in his five games for the Lions.

Bristol Rov (From apprentice on 8/10/85) FL 47 FLC 2 FAC 2 Others 2
Newport Co (Loaned on 14/12/87) FL 1
Sunderland (£50,000 on 24/12/87) FL 37 FLC 9 Others 4
Carlisle U (Loaned on 18/3/88) FL 4
Bristol C (Loaned on 15/9/88) FL 3
Birmingham C (Loaned on 21/11/91) FL 2 FLC 1
Hartlepool U (Free on 1/8/92) FL 18 FLC 4 FAC 1 Others 2
Millwall (Free on 6/1/94) FL 4 FLC 0+1
Blackpool (Free on 4/8/95)
Oxford U (Free on 18/8/95) FL 12 FLC 4 Others 1
Millwall (Free on 6/12/95) FL 4 FAC 1

CARTWRIGHT Lee
Born: Rawtenstall, 19 September 1972
Height: 5'10" Weight: 11.0
Club Honours: Div 3 '96

Lee's move from the centre of Preston's midfield to the wide right last season was an inspired move, his pace and accurate crossing leading to many goals for the strikers. It was a tragedy for himself and the club when a serious knee injury at Scunthorpe in February sidelined him until at least Christmas, 1996, although by then he had played enough games to qualify for a third division championship medal when the title was eventually won. Is North End's longest serving player.

Preston NE (From trainee on 30/7/91) FL 160+22/13 FLC 7/2 FAC 12+1/1 Others 10+4

CASE James (Jimmy) Robert
Born: Liverpool, 18 May 1954
Height: 5'9" Weight: 12.12
Club Honours: Div 1 '76, '77, '79, '80; ESC '77; EC '77, '78, '81; FLC '81
International Honours: E: U23-1

This veteran midfielder made only two first team Brighton appearances in 1995-96, before hanging up his boots after being stretchered off in a reserve game with a neck injury. A hugely experienced player, he was not lost to Albion, however, taking over as manager following the departure of Liam Brady in November 1995.

Liverpool (Signed from South Liverpool on 1/5/73) FL 170+16/23 FLC 21+1/3 FAC 20+1/7 Others 28+3/13
Brighton & Hove A (£350,000 on 19/8/81) FL 124+3/10 FLC 8 FAC 13+1/5
Southampton (£30,000 on 20/3/85) FL 213+2/10 FLC 34/2 FAC 15/1 Others 7/1
Bournemouth (Free on 25/7/91) FL 38+2/1 FLC 3 FAC 5 Others 2/1
Halifax T (Free on 16/5/92) FL 17+4/2 FLC 1 FAC 1
Wrexham (Free on 26/2/93) FL 1+3
Darlington (Free on 22/10/93) FL 1 (Free to Sittingbourne in December 1993)
Brighton & Hove A (Free on 30/12/93) FL 30+2 FLC 2

CASKEY Darren Mark
Born: Basildon, 21 August 1974
Height: 5'8" Weight: 11.9
International Honours: E: Yth (UEFAYC '93); Sch

Naturally a right-sided midfielder, Darren found the start of last season frustrating at Spurs, with a loan spell at Watford in October, followed by half a dozen starts when brought in to replace the missing Darren Anderton and David Howell. However, with the arrival of Ruel Fox and Andy Sinton making it even more difficult to find a place at White Hart Lane, he became Reading's record signing last February, when agreeing to a four year contract. Instrumental in keeping the Royals out of division two, he almost scored with his first touch for the club, while his two goals came in away defeats at Tranmere and Watford.

Tottenham H (From trainee on 6/3/92) PL 20+12/4 FLC 3+1/1 FAC 6+1
Watford (Loaned on 27/10/95) FL 6/1
Reading (£700,000 on 28/2/96) FL 15/2

CASPER Christopher (Chris) Martin
Born: Burnley, 28 April 1975
Height: 6'0" Weight: 11.11
Club Honours: FAYC '92; CS '94
International Honours: E: U21-1; Yth (EUFAC '93)

Unable to break in to the first team squad at Old Trafford, the elegant Manchester United central defender spent three months on loan at Bournemouth last season, after arriving in January. An excellent reader of the game, and very composed for one so young, Chris turned in some excellent displays for the Cherries, scoring in the memorable 5-4 win at Peterborough. Is the son of the former Burnley player, Frank.

Manchester U (From trainee on 3/2/93) FLC 1
Bournemouth (Loaned on 11/1/96) FL 16/1

CASTLE Stephen (Steve) Charles
Born: Barking, 17 May 1966
Height: 5'11" Weight: 12.10

An experienced midfielder with a proven goalscoring record, Steve left Plymouth during the 1995 close season bound for Birmingham as a replacement for the injured Peter Shearer. Playing mainly on the left-hand side, his finishing touch seemed to have deserted him and he quickly fell victim to the Blues' injury curse which was to ultimately cost him his place. Eventually loaned to Gillingham (February), he scored a spectacular 30-yarder on his debut against Hereford, before returning to St Andrews.

Leyton Orient (From apprentice on 18/5/84) FL 232+11/55 FLC 15+1/5 FAC 23+1/6 Others 18+2
Plymouth Arg (£195,000 on 30/6/92) FL 98+3/35 FLC 5/1 FAC 8/2 Others 6/1
Birmingham C (£225,000 on 21/7/95) FL 12+3/1 FLC 7 FAC 1 Others 3/1
Gillingham (Loaned on 15/2/96) FL 5+1/1

CASTLEDINE Stewart Mark
Born: Wandsworth, 22 January 1973
Height: 6'1" Weight: 12.13

An influential loan signing from Wimbledon at the beginning of last season, Stewart proved to be a forceful central midfielder at

Wycombe, having a happy knack of producing late runs into the box and scoring three times in seven games before being recalled. Back at Selhurst Park, he only featured on six occasions, but struck a valuable well taken goal at Everton when Dons were 2-1 down and staring defeat in the face. Is another of the club's youngsters capable of stepping up in the future.

Wimbledon (From trainee on 2/7/91) F/PL 10+5/3 FAC 1+1
Wycombe W (Loaned on 25/8/95) FL 7/3

CAWLEY Peter
Born: Walton on Thames, 15 September 1965
Height: 6'4" Weight: 14.6

The rock at the heart of the Colchester defence, Peter is inevitably labelled "towering" or "commanding" by the Press. Previously a much travelled player, he has now settled down with United and replaced the injured Tony English as captain in the middle of last season. His many outstanding displays became even more notable during his rare absences from the team.

Wimbledon (Signed from Chertsey T on 26/1/87) FL 1 Others 1
Bristol Rov (Loaned on 26/2/87) FL 9+1
Fulham (Loaned on 14/12/88) FL 3+2
Bristol Rov (Free on 17/7/89) FL 1+2
Southend U (Free on 6/7/90) FL 6+1/1 FLC 1 FAC 1 Others 1
Exeter C (Free on 22/11/90) FL 7
Barnet (Free on 8/11/91) FL 3
Colchester U (Free on 9/10/92) FL 123+2/7 FLC 2 FAC 8 Others 9/1

CECERE Michele (Mike) Joseph
Born: Chester, 4 January 1968
Height: 6'0" Weight: 11.4

In a season disrupted by injury, Mike, who was Exeter's top scorer the previous term, only managed to play a handful of games and unfortunately none of them were during 1996. He will be hoping for better luck this season to show the fans what he can do in front of goal.

Oldham Ath (From apprentice on 17/1/86) FL 35+17/8 FLC 4+1 FAC 1+2/1 Others 2+1/1
Huddersfield T (£100,000 on 11/11/88) FL 50+4/8 FLC 4/1 FAC 7+1/3 Others 5/1
Stockport Co (Loaned on 22/3/90) FL 0+1
Walsall (£25,000 on 23/8/90) FL 92+20/32 FLC 10+1 FAC 4+2 Others 12/2
Exeter C (Signed on 13/1/94) FL 34+9/11 FLC 3/1 FAC 1/1 Others 3+1/2

CHALK Martyn Peter Glyn
Born: Louth, 30 August 1969
Height: 5'6" Weight: 10.0

The little winger suffered a loss of confidence, and consequently a loss of form last season at Stockport, which saw him hovering on the fringes of the first team squad before leaving to join Wrexham in February, in an exchange deal that took former Wrexham wide-right midfielder, Kieran Durkan, to Edgeley Park. Proved to be a fast, tricky little player who could put over some useful crosses for his hungry strikers and also contributed a few goals himself. The right-sided attacking position has not been the most productive in recent years at the Racecourse Ground, but, along with the signing of Craig Skinner, this might now be put right!

Derby Co (£10,000 from Louth U on 23/1/90) FL 4+3/1 FAC 3/1 Others 0+1
Stockport Co (£40,000 on 30/6/94) FL 29+14/6 FLC 7+1/2 FAC 2+3 Others 2+2
Wrexham (Signed on 19/2/96) FL 19/4

CHALLIS Trevor Michael
Born: Paddington, 23 October 1975
Height: 5'7" Weight: 10.0
International Honours: E: U21-1; Yth

QPR Left back who is strong in the tackle and likes to get forward to supply the front men. An ex-youth team captain, Trevor made his league debut as a substitute in the televised game versus Coventry City and started the following match at Everton at left back, being in and out of the side, rotating with Rufus Brevett. Having made the step up during difficult times, the club ultimately being relegated, the young man can only have benefited from the experience. A rising star, his impressive start in league football saw him win an England U21 cap.

Queens Park R (From trainee on 1/7/94) PL 10+1 FAC 2

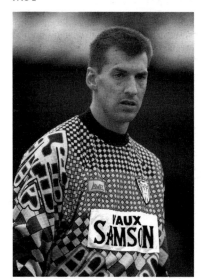

Alec Chamberlain

CHAMBERLAIN Alec Francis Roy
Born: March, 20 June 1964
Height: 6'2" Weight: 13.9
Club Honours: Div 1 '96

Goalkeeper Alec was unfortunate to lose his Sunderland place to Shay Given last January, but returned to play a vital part in securing promotion and then the championship. His razor-sharp reflexes and impressive tally of clean sheets, surely make him one of the best free transfer signings the club has ever made.

Ipswich T (Free from Ramsey T on 27/7/81)
Colchester U (Free on 3/8/82) FL 188 FLC 11 FAC 10 Others 12
Everton (£80,000 on 28/7/87)
Tranmere Rov (Loaned on 1/11/87) FL 15
Luton T (£150,000 on 27/7/88) FL 138 FLC 7 FAC 7 Others 7
Sunderland (Free on 8/7/93) FL 89+1 FLC 9 FAC 8 Others 1

CHAMBERLAIN Mark Valentine
Born: Stoke, 19 November 1961
Height: 5'9" Weight" 10.7
International Honours: E: 8; U21-4 (UEFA U21 '84); Sch

Signed from Brighton immediately prior to the start of last season, Mark was used by Exeter in his favourite position on the wing and as an emergency full back – where he played out the latter half of the campaign. A former England international, he is still a superb crosser of the ball.

Port Vale (From apprentice on 1/5/79) FL 90+6/17 FLC 4 FAC 10/2
Stoke C (£135,000 on 24/8/82) FL 110+2/17 FLC 9 FAC 4/1
Sheffield Wed (£300,000 on 13/9/85) FL 32+34/8 FLC 5+2/1 FAC 1+11/1 Others 2+1
Portsmouth (£200,000 on 2/8/88) FL 143+24/20 FLC 11+2/1 FAC 7+1/1 Others 9+1
Brighton & Hove A (Free on 20/8/94) FL 12+7/2 FLC 3/1 FAC 1 Others 1
Exeter C (Free on 11/8/95) FL 29+4/1 FLC 2 Others 1

CHAMBERS Leroy Dean
Born: Sheffield, 25 October 1972
Height: 5'11" Weight: 12.0

A pacy forward who made ten appearances for Chester last season, scoring his only goal in the final game, the first in a 2-1 home win over Mansfield, he was freed during the summer.

Sheffield Wed (From trainee on 13/6/91)
Chester C (Free on 12/8/94) FL 8+13/1 FLC 2/1 Others 2+1

CHANDLER Dean Andrew Robert
Born: Ilford, 6 May 1976
Height: 6'2" Weight: 11.10

As cover for the central defenders, Dean's only appearance for Charlton last season was as a substitute against Ipswich in December. A strong tackler, who is commanding in the air, and dangerous at set pieces, he looks capable of earning a regular first team spot this term.

Charlton Ath (From trainee on 13/4/94) FL 1+1/1

CHANNING Justin Andrew
Born: Reading, 19 November 1968
Height: 5'10" Weight: 11.7
International Honours: E: Yth

Despite being on a week to week contract throughout last season, he continued to hold down a regular place in the Bristol Rovers' line-up. At the same time, the hard-working Justin completed a century of league appearances for the club, during which he performed consistently well at full back or on occasions, on the left-hand side of midfield. Has tremendous pace which gives him the ability to get forward to deliver quality crosses.

Queens Park R (From apprentice on 27/8/86) F/PL 42+13/5 FLC 4+1 FAC 2 Others 5
Bristol Rov (£250,000 on 24/10/92) FL 121+9/10 FLC 5 FAC 4+1 Others 11+1

CHAPMAN Daniel (Danny) Graham
Born: Deptford, 21 November 1974
Height: 5'11" Weight: 13.6

A free transfer signing for Leyton Orient in the 1995 close season after playing just 13 times for Millwall, Danny showed up well

as a tenacious right-sided midfielder who was totally committed. Quickly made himself a regular place in the side, missing only a handful of games, and seems sure to carry on where he left off.

Millwall (From trainee on 18/3/93) FL 4+8 FLC 0+1
Leyton Orient (Free on 3/7/95) FL 38/2 FLC 2 FAC 1 Others 2

CHAPMAN Ian Russell
Born: Brighton, 31 May 1970
Height: 5'9" Weight: 12.5

Left-footed Brighton defender who has also played in midfield. A hard-working player, who again produced solid defensive displays and likes to get forward to support the attack, Ian was stretchered off at the Goldstone on 17 October 1995 in a Auto Windscreens Shield match against Bristol Rovers with knee ligament damage leading to an eight match lay off. Given a free transfer during the summer.

Brighton & Hove A (From trainee on 5/6/87) FL 265+16/14 FLC 18+2 FAC 12+2/2 Others 12+4

CHAPMAN Lee Roy
Born: Lincoln, 5 December 1959
Height: 6'2" Weight: 13.0
Club Honours: FLC '89; FMC '89; Div 2 '90, Div 1 '92
International Honours: E: B-1; U21-1

Son of a former Aston Villa and Lincoln player, Roy, and still very much an old-fashioned centre forward himself, Lee was involved in Ipswich's start to last season, either deputising for Ian Marshall or coming off the bench to use his aerial ability to good effect. However, eventually falling out of favour, he went to Leeds on loan in January as cover for Brian Deane, but was sent off after just 26 minutes of his debut match against West Ham, having already instigated the opening goal. Played just once more before returning to Portman Road and being transferred on deadline day to Swansea,

Ian Chapman

where, despite being unable to halt the relegation slide, he quickly proved his worth with four goals in seven games.

Stoke C (From juniors on 22/6/78) FL 95+4/34 FLC 5/3 FAC 3/1
Plymouth Arg (Loaned on 5/12/78) FL 3+1
Arsenal (£500,000 on 25/8/82) FL 15+8/4 FLC 0+2 FAC 0+1 Others 2/2
Sunderland (£200,000 on 29/12/83) FL 14+1/3 FAC 2/1
Sheffield Wed (£100,000 on 24/8/84) FL 147+2/63 FLC 17/6 FAC 17+1/10 Others 2+1 (£350,000 to Niort on 1/6/88)
Nottingham F (£350,000 on 17/10/88) FL 48/15 FLC 12/6 FAC 5/3 Others 6/3
Leeds U (£400,000 on 11/1/90) F/PL 133+4/62 FLC 15/10 FAC 11/4 Others 10/4
Portsmouth (£250,000 on 11/8/93) FL 5/2 Others 1
West Ham U (£250,000 on 16/9/93) PL 33+7/7 FLC 4+1/2 FAC 6/2
Southend U (Loaned on 13/1/95) FL 1/1
Ipswich T (£70,000 on 19/1/95) P/FL 11+11/1 FLC 1 Others 2
Leeds U (Loaned on 11/1/96) PL 2
Swansea C (Free on 28/3/96) FL 7/4

CHAPPLE Philip (Phil) Richard
Born: Norwich, 26 November 1966
Height: 6'2" Weight: 12.7
Club Honours: Div 3 '91

Right-sided Charlton central defender, who tackles well, is good in the air, and dangerous at corners and set pieces, especially with knock-backs from the far post. Unfortunately, he suffered bad knee ligament damage in the fine win at Millwall last December and took no further part in the season.

Norwich C (From apprentice on 10/7/85)
Cambridge U (Signed on 29/3/88) FL 183+4/19 FLC 11/2 FAC 23/1 Others 17
Charlton Ath (£100,000 on 13/8/94) FL 74+7/9 FLC 7 FAC 5 Others 5

CHAPPLE Shaun Ronald
Born: Swansea, 14 February 1973
Height: 5'11" Weight: 12.3
International Honours: W: B-1; U21-10; Sch

Despite missing the first half of last season through a cartilage operation, Shaun showed excellent touches in midfield for Swansea, following the appointment of Jan Molby as manager. A good passer of the ball, he also scored some vital goals.

Swansea C (From trainee on 15/7/91) FL 59+26/9 FLC 3+1/1 FAC 8+2 Others 8+2/1

CHARLERY Kenneth (Kenny)
Born: Stepney, 28 November 1964
Height: 6'1" Weight: 13.3

An experienced striker with a proven scoring record in the lower divisions, Kenny moved from Peterborough to Birmingham during the 1995 close season. However, in taking time to settle down, his confidence was affected and, although scoring six goals in 24 games, he was unable to gain a regular place in the side and spent a spell on loan at Southend in January. Following that, Posh fans were delighted to welcome him back as the new player/coach and he obliged by giving the team added stability in attack and also playing deeper when required.

Maidstone U (£35,000 from Beckton on 1/3/89) FL 41+18/11 FLC 1+3/1 FAC 0+3 Others 5+4

Peterborough U (£20,000 on 28/3/91) FL 45+6/19 FLC 10/5 FAC 3/1 Others 11/7
Watford (£350,000 on 16/10/92) FL 45+3/13 FLC 3 FAC 1+1
Peterborough U (£150,000 on 16/12/93) FL 70/24 FLC 2 FAC 2+1/3 Others 2/1
Birmingham C (£350,000 on 4/7/95) FL 8+9/4 FLC 3+1/2 Others 2+1
Southend U (Loaned on 12/1/96) FL 2+1
Peterborough U (Signed on 9/2/96) FL 19/7 Others 1

Kenny Charlery

CHARLES Gary Andrew
Born: Newham, 13 April 1970
Height: 5'9" Weight: 11.2
Club Honours: FMC '92; FLC '96
International Honours: E: 2; U21-4

Confirmed his place at right back in 1995-96, playing a more aggressive wing/back role in Aston Villa's new defensive formation of three centre backs, and enjoyed his most consistent season since his entry to top flight football, scoring his first goal for the club in the 3-0 defeat of Southampton in April. He might have been considered for a return to international duty but for a tragic injury at home to West Ham at the end of the campaign, when he suffered a broken ankle which is likely to keep him out of action for most of the coming season. Earlier, had received his first winners' medal in the Coca Cola Cup final victory over Leeds. Has great pace and balance.

Nottingham F (From trainee on 7/11/87) F/PL 54+2/1 FLC 9 FAC 8+2/1 Others 4+2
Leicester C (Loaned on 16/3/89) FL 5+3
Derby Co (£750,000 on 29/7/93) FL 61/3 FLC 5+1 FAC 1 Others 9
Aston Villa (Signed on 6/1/95) PL 48+2/1 FLC 8 FAC 5

CHARLES Lee
Born: Hillingdon, 20 August 1971
Height: 5'11" Weight: 12.4

Pacy QPR forward player with a good first touch, who likes to run at defenders. A 1995 summer signing from Chertsey Town, he made his Premier League debut at West

Ham as a substitute, and also appeared from the bench at Tottenham. His best moment of the season was in the final home match against West Ham, a game the club had to win, when his introduction helped Rangers to a 3-0 win. Earlier, in September, Lee failed to make an impact on loan at Barnet, having gone there in order to gain experience.

Queens Park R (£67,500 from Chertsey on 4/8/95) PL 0+4
Barnet (Loaned on 22/9/95) FL 2+3 Others 0+1

CHARLES Stephen (Steve)
Born: Sheffield, 10 May 1960
Height: 5'9" Weight: 11.12
Club Honours: Div 4 '82; WC '86
International Honours: E: Sch

Having re-signed for Scarborough during the summer of 1995, the classy midfielder completed his 17th season as a professional last term, playing the 600th league match of his career against Cardiff City in February. A great servant for the club during his time with them, he was released on a free transfer in the summer, which will possibly bring to an end a distinguished career at the age of 36.

Sheffield U (Free from Sheffield University on 16/1/80) FL 112+11/10 FLC 12/1 FAC 9+1/1 Others 3/1
Wrexham (£10,000 on 2/11/84) FL 111+2/37 FLC 8 FAC 4+1/1 Others 11+1/5
Mansfield T (£15,000 on 3/8/87) FL 231+6/39 FLC 16/1 FAC 12/4 Others 12+1/4
Scunthorpe U (Loaned on 20/11/92) FL 4 Others 2
Scarborough (Free on 26/2/93) FL 134/20 FLC 7/1 FAC 8 Others 5/1

CHARLTON Simon Thomas
Born: Huddersfield, 25 October 1971
Height: 5'8" Weight: 11.1
International Honours: E: Yth

A strong-running, naturally left-sided player, Simon had some excellent games at full back and in midfield for Southampton in 1995-96. Competing with Francis Benali for the left back spot, in which he may have played more games except for injury, he often got forward well and his powerful runs and accurate crosses created a number of scoring opportunities, although unable to find the net himself. Is also the possessor of a long throw.

Huddersfield T (From trainee on 1/7/89) FL 121+3/1 FLC 9/1 FAC 10 Others 14
Southampton (£250,000 on 8/6/93) PL 78+6/2 FLC 3+2 FAC 8

CHARNOCK Philip (Phil) Anthony
Born: Southport, 14 February 1975
Height: 5'11" Weight: 11.2

A young Liverpool player, who is still waiting in the wings for his Premier League debut, having had just one selection for the subs' bench in 1995-96, Phil was loaned out to Blackpool in February, making just three brief appearances as a substitute before returning to Anfield. An elegant left-sided midfielder, very much in the Ray Kennedy mould, he is always looking to set up attacks and is still highly regarded at the club.

Liverpool (From trainee on 16/3/93) FLC 1 Others 0+1
Blackpool (Loaned on 9/2/96) FL 0+4

CHEETHAM Michael Martin
Born: Amsterdam, Holland, 30 June 1967
Height: 5'10" Weight: 12.2
Club Honours: Div 3 '91

Experienced Colchester winger who grabbed a few goals (all away from home!) early last season, but later lost his place due to a combination of lapse in form and injury and was released during the summer. On his day, his pacy runs often threatened.

Ipswich T (Free from Basingstoke T on 10/10/88) FL 1+3 Others 0+1
Cambridge U (£50,000 on 11/10/89) FL 123+9/22 FLC 8+1/1 FAC 17/1 Others 12+1/3
Chesterfield (Free on 15/7/94) FL 5 FLC 2/1 Others 0+1
Colchester U (Free on 23/3/95) FL 33+4/3 FLC 2/1 FAC 1 Others 3

CHENERY Benjamin (Ben) Roger
Born: Ipswich, 28 January 1977
Height: 6'1" Weight: 12.0

Young Luton defender who made his league debut last April at home to Port Vale, after the club had already been relegated. Following a nervous start, when the opposition scored through an attack down his flank, Ben grew in confidence and composure and did well enough to earn a further first team outing. Comfortable at right back or in the centre of the defence, he could be one for the future.

Luton T (From trainee on 3/3/95) FL 2 FAC 1

CHERRY Steven (Steve) Reginald
Born: Nottingham, 5 August 1960
Height: 6'1" Weight: 13.0
Club Honours: AIC '95
International Honours: E: Yth

Sound, very experienced goalkeeper who made a handful of appearances as Kevin Miller's deputy after joining Watford on a free transfer from Notts County in the summer of 1995. Finished the season on a monthly contract at Plymouth, his second spell at the club, where he was confident on crosses and a good organiser.

Derby Co (From apprentice on 22/3/78) FL 77 FLC 5 FAC 8
Port Vale (Loaned on 26/11/80) FL 4 FAC 4
Walsall (£25,000 on 10/8/84) FL 71 FLC 10 FAC 7 Others 6
Plymouth Arg (£17,000 on 23/10/86) FL 73 FLC 4 FAC 5 Others 1
Chesterfield (Loaned on 1/12/88) FL 10 Others 3
Notts Co (£70,000 on 16/2/89) FL 266 FLC 17 FAC 14 Others 31
Watford (Free on 14/7/95) FL 4
Plymouth Arg (Signed on 19/2/96) FL 16 Others 3

CHETTLE Stephen (Steve)
Born: Nottingham, 27 September 1968
Height: 6'1" Weight: 13.3
Club Honours: FMC '89, '92; FLC '90
International Honours: E: U21-12

The experienced central defender was once again Nottingham Forest's most consistent performer, missing just one game throughout 1995-96, while continuing to form a highly effective defensive partnership with Colin Cooper. There was nothing spectacular or extraordinary about Steve, who went about his job in a very quiet and efficient manner with a minimum of bookings and therefore suspensions – which

is relatively rare for a defender. The highlight of his season was his only goal – scored early in the away leg of the UEFA Cup-tie with Bayern Munich – which seemed vital at the time, but was rendered academic by Bayern's crushing 5-1 victory in the second-leg at the City Ground. For a big man, he is extremely comfortable on the ball, which is no more than you would expect from a 27 year old who has played nearly 400 first team games, many of them in the top flight.

Nottingham F (From apprentice on 28/8/86) F/PL 280+13/7 FL 38+3/1 FAC 31+1 Others 21+2/2

CHILDS Gary Paul Colin
Born: Birmingham, 19 April 1964
Height: 5'7" Weight: 10.9
International Honours: E: Yth

A skilful, intuitive, and creative Grimsby midfielder, cum forward, who makes the side tick when on song, Gary enjoys getting wide where he can run past defenders to get accurate crosses into the box. Ever since player/manager, Brian Laws, established himself at right back the pairing has provided a most effective partnership, with 1995-96 being one of the best to date. An improved goal tally saw him netting five, including the winner at Sheffield United, before his season was curtailed by injury.

West Bromwich A (From apprentice on 13/2/82) FL 2+1
Walsall (£15,000 on 7/10/83) FL 120+11/17 FLC 14+2/2 FAC 9+1/2 Others 7/2
Birmingham C (£50,000 on 8/7/87) FL 39+16/2 FLC 0+2 FAC 3 Others 2
Grimsby T (Free on 20/7/89) FL 185+21/25 FLC 14/1 FAC 14/1 Others 7+2

CHRISTIE Iyseden
Born: Coventry, 14 November 1976
Height: 6'0" Weight: 12.2

Coventry striker with a lot of promise. A product of the club's youth policy, Iyseden made two appearances in 1995-96, totalling 33 minutes as a substitute against Blackburn and Hull City. Suffered injuries to stomach muscles and shin, but when fit played in the reserve side, scoring regularly.

Coventry C (From trainee on 22/5/95) PL 0+1 FLC 0+1

CLARE Daryl Adam
Born: Jersey, 1 August 1978
Height: 5'9" Weight: 11.0

A former Grimsby trainee and a promising wide midfielder who likes taking players on, he had a brief taste of first team football at Blundell Park in 1995-96, when coming on as a substitute in the Coca Cola Cup-tie against Birmingham and the league game versus Sheffield United. Is a promising young player.

Grimsby T (From trainee on 9/12/95) FL 0+1 FLC 0+1

CLARIDGE Stephen (Steve) Edward
Born: Portsmouth, 10 April 1966
Height: 5'11" Weight: 11.8
Club Honours: Div 3 '91, Div 2 '95; AMC '95

Bustling, hard-working striker, signed from Birmingham in March 1996 for an initial fee

of £1m, with an extra £200,000 due depending on appearances made and Leicester achieving promotion by the end of 1997-98. His hard running and experience proved invaluable in taking the weight off young Emile Heskey. Hit the woodwork in each of his first two appearances, before scoring a spectacular winner at Charlton to keep City in the play-off hunt. All of that paled into insignificance, however, when he cracked in the goal that took the club back into the top flight, a 90th minute winner breaking Crystal Palace's hearts at Wembley.

Bournemouth (Signed from Fareham on 30/11/84) FL 3+4/1 Others 1 (£10,000 to Weymouth in October 1985)
Crystal Palace (Signed on 11/10/88)
Aldershot (£14,000 on 13/10/88) FL 58+4/19 FLC 2+1 FAC 6/1 Others 5/2
Cambridge U (£75,000 on 8/2/90) FL 56+23/28 FLC 2+4/2 FAC 1 Others 6+3/1
Luton T (£160,000 on 17/7/92) FL 15+1/2 FLC 2/3 Others 2/1
Cambridge U (£195,000 on 20/11/92) FL 53/18 FLC 4/3 FAC 4 Others 3
Birmingham C (£350,000 on 7/1/94) FL 86+2/35 FLC 14+1/2 FAC 7 Others 9+1/5
Leicester C (£1,000,000 on 1/3/96) FL 14/5 Others 3/1

Steve Claridge

CLARK Anthony John
Born: London, 7 April 1977
Height: 5'7" Weight: 10.7

Forward. Although starting the league game at Brighton and making two more substitute appearances for Wycombe, he was released at the end of last season. In his first year as a professional, prior to his release, Anthony showed up well in the reserves and during a loan spell at Hitchin.

Wycombe W (From school on 5/7/95) FL 2+2

CLARK Ian David
Born: Stockton, 23 October 1974
Height: 5'11" Weight: 11.7

Promising young Doncaster winger who was given his first taste of FL action during the course of the 1995-96 season, after arriving during the summer from non-league football. Good coaching should bring out the best in a youngster who has bags of potential.

Doncaster Rov (Free from Stockton on 11/8/95) FL 14+9/1 FLC 0+2 FAC 1 Others 3/1

CLARK Lee Robert
Born: Wallsend, 27 October 1972
Height: 5'8" Weight: 11.7
Club Honours: Div 1 '93
International Honours: E: U21-11; Yth; Sch

Lee always seems to have time and space on the ball and combines this with astute vision and accurate passing. A local lad, and a favourite with the Newcastle fans, he withdrew a transfer request during the summer of 1995, signing a new contract, and given the chance to claim the holding role in front of the back four he turned in some outstanding pre-season displays to establish himself as first choice. Was a significant influence on the early form of the side and held his place until March when he was unlucky to be dropped in favour of the new arrival, David Batty.

Newcastle U (From trainee on 9/12/89) F/PL 144+26/21 FLC 16 FAC 12+1/2 Others 5+2/1

Lee Clark

CLARK Paul Peterson
Born: Benfleet, 14 September 1958
Height: 5'9" Weight: 13.7
International Honours: E: Yth; Sch

As Cambridge's assistant manager, Paul was brought out of retirement on two separate occasions in 1995-96 to boost a young defence, playing at Mansfield at the age of 37 years and 131 days and becoming the second oldest player to turn out for United in the league.

Southend U (From apprentice on 1/7/76) FL 29+4/1 FLC 0+1 FAC 1
Brighton & Hove A (£55,000 on 16/11/77) FL 69+10/9 FLC 7+2 FAC 4+1
Reading (Loaned on 1/10/81) FL 2

Southend U (Free on 13/8/82) FL 269+7/3 FLC 15+1/1 FAC 12+1/1 Others 14+1/1
Gillingham (Free on 18/7/91) FL 87+3/1 FLC 6+1 FAC 9/1 Others 4+1 (Free to Chelmsford C during 1994 close season)
Cambridge U (Free on 24/10/95) FL 2

CLARK Simon
Born: Boston, 12 March 1967
Height: 6'1" Weight: 12.6

A tough-tackling Peterborough player who is equally at home at full back or in central defence, Simon missed very few games in 1995-96, proving to be both strong and dependable. He also scored the opening goal of the season for Posh, his first for the club.

Peterborough U (Free from Stevenage Borough on 25/5/94) FL 72+1/1 FLC 5 FAC 6 Others 4+1/1

CLARK William (Billy) Raymond
Born: Christchurch, 19 May 1967
Height: 6'0" Weight: 12.3

Billy is a resolute central defender who, in 1995-96, enjoyed probably one of his best seasons in the decade he has been with Bristol Rovers. Although scoring on the opening day in a fine 2-1 victory at Carlisle, it was the ability to stop goals being conceded that was his main achievement, his aerial strengths and man-marking skills proving supreme. The loyal defender has now completed over 200 league appearances and is the Pirates' longest serving player.

Bournemouth (From apprentice on 25/9/84) FL 4
Bristol Rov (Signed on 16/10/87) FL 209+12/13 FLC 9+1 FAC 8+1 Others 18+2/1

CLARKE Adrian James
Born: Cambridge, 28 September 1974
Height: 5'10" Weight: 11.0
International Honours: E: Yth; Sch

A young Arsenal winger who broke into the first team last December, making eight appearances, he impressed with his pace and crossing ability and will be looking for more opportunities this season. Appeared on both flanks, but probably favours the left.

Arsenal (From trainee on 6/7/93) PL 4+3 FAC 1+1

CLARKE Andrew (Andy) Weston
Born: Islington, 22 July 1967
Height: 5'10" Weight: 11.7
Club Honours: GMVC '91
International Honours: E: SP-2

Having burst on the Wimbledon scene at the end of 1990-91, when he was widely recognised to be one of the most exciting players to have come out of the non-leagues for some time, Andy is the possessor of an explosive pace and, in often coming on as substitute for the last 20 minutes or so, he terrorises defences with his ability to latch on to long balls. Last season, he made a habit of scoring important winning goals late on in games, obviously making him very popular with Dons' supporters.

Wimbledon (£250,000 from Barnet on 21/2/91) F/PL 69+76/16 FLC 9+7/3 FAC 8+4/2

CLARKE Christopher (Chris) John
Born: Barnsley, 1 May 1974
Height: 6'1" Weight: 12.10

Chris briefly won back his place in the Rochdale goal when Ian Gray was injured in 1995-96. However, unable to recapture the form he had showed prior to his serious head injury the previous season, he returned to the reserves to regain confidence, before being released in the summer.

Bolton W (From trainee on 13/7/92)
Rochdale (Free on 4/7/94) FL 30 FLC 2 FAC 1 Others 3

CLARKE Darrell James
Born: Mansfield, 16 December 1977
Height: 5'9" Weight: 11.0

Young Mansfield midfielder who made his first team debut when coming on as substitute to replace the injured Petrescu against Hereford last April. One of Town's more promising youngsters, Darrell's trainee period expired at the end of June.

Mansfield T (Trainee) FL 1+2

CLARKE Dean Brian
Born: Hereford, 28 July 1977
Height: 5'9" Weight: 10.10

Having signed professional forms prior to the start of 1995-96, Dean played a handful of games for Hereford in the early part of the season, proving that he could be relied upon to fill in at the back when needed. Also showed as an excellent tackler, before being surprisingly released during the summer.

Hereford U (From trainee on 12/7/95) FL 8+3 FLC 0+1

CLARKE Matthew (Matt) John
Born: Sheffield, 3 November 1973
Height: 6'3" Weight: 11.7

A highly-rated goalkeeper who skippered Rotherham for the second half of last season, becoming only the second 'keeper to lead a team out at Wembley, culminating in the 2-1 AWS victory over Shrewsbury. His ability to pull off magnificent saves frequently attracted attention from some top clubs and he is expected to go on to much bigger things. An injury ruled him out of a probable place in the England U21 team, after being on standby the previous season.

Rotherham U (From trainee on 28/7/92) FL 123+1 FLC 4 FAC 3 Others 10

CLARKE Stephen (Steve)
Born: Saltcoats, 29 August 1963
Height: 5'9" Weight: 11.10
Club Honours: Div 2 '89
International Honours: S: 6; B-3; U21-8; Yth

Steve's days as a first team regular looked to be numbered when Chelsea signed right back Dan Petrescu from Sheffield Wednesday last November. But Chelsea's longest serving player showed his adaptability by moving across to occupy the left hand position in the Blues' three-man central defensive formation. His experience and ability to read the game were crucial in the club's improved form either side of Christmas. Restored to his former berth at right back to replace the suspended Petrescu for the FA Cup semi final, his first half departure through injury severely disrupted the side's wing/back strategy and allowed

Manchester United to exploit the space down their left flank.

St Mirren (Free from Beith Juniors in 1981) SL 151/6 SLC 21 SC 19/1 Others 6
Chelsea (£422,000 on 19/1/87) F/PL 268+5/6 FLC 17/1 FAC 26+2/1 Others 21/1

CLARKE Timothy (Tim) Joseph
Born: Stourbridge, 19 September 1968
Height: 6'3" Weight: 13.7
Club Honours: AMC '96

Shrewsbury Town goalkeeper. Presents an imposing figure, looks comfortable with crosses, and has a tremendous kick which is useful in an attacking role! Had a good run of 14 games at the start of last season, but was restricted thereafter to just a handful due to the excellent form of Paul Edwards and was released in the summer.

Coventry C (£25,000 from Halesowen T on 22/10/90)
Huddersfield T (£15,000 on 22/7/91) FL 70 FLC 7 FAC 6 Others 8 (Free to Halesowen on 19/8/93)
Rochdale (Loaned on 12/2/93) FL 2
Shrewsbury T (Free on 21/10/93) FL 30+1 FLC 3 Others 1

CLARKSON Ian Stewart
Born: Solihull, 4 December 1970
Weight: 5'11" Weight: 12.0
Club Honours: AMC '91

Right back. Ian was virtually ever present for Stoke City during the 1995-96 season, after the summer sale of John Butler to Wigan. Keen to get forward, and a committed tackler, he was unfortunate to be sent off in the Coca Cola Cup-tie against Newcastle United for two innocuous challenges on David Ginola.

Birmingham C (From trainee on 15/12/88) FL 125+11 FLC 5+1 FAC 5+1 Others 17+1
Stoke C (£40,000 on 13/9/93) FL 72+3 FLC 6 FAC 5 Others 8+2

CLARKSON Philip (Phil) Ian
Born: Garstang, 13 November 1968
Height: 5'10" Weight: 12.5

A utility player who has in the past proved adept in midfield and up front, Phil made only two starts for Crewe last season and spent a period on loan at Scunthorpe towards the end of October, before going back to sign permanently in February. Good in the air and with a penchant to get forward from midfield, he made some timely runs into the box to score vital goals for the Irons.

Crewe Alex (£22,500 from Fleetwood T on 15/10/91) FL 76+22/27 FLC 6+2/1 FAC 3+2/2 Others 7+6/1
Scunthorpe U (Loaned on 30/10/95) FL 4/1
Scunthorpe U (Free on 13/2/96) FL 17+3/5

CLAYTON Gary
Born: Sheffield, 2 February 1963
Height: 5'10" Weight: 12.3
International Honours: E: SP-1

Along with Chris Billy, Gary moved from Huddersfield during the 1995 close season as a utility player, with a view to giving a greater depth to the Plymouth squad. However, his good form made him a regular in the side, mainly as a central defender, from where he scored an excellent goal in the Devon derby against Exeter.

Doncaster Rov (Signed from Burton A on 23/8/86) FL 34+1/5 FLC 2 FAC 3 Others 2
Cambridge U (£10,000 on 2/7/87) FL 166+13/17 FLC 17+1/3 FAC 9 Others 7/2
Peterborough U (Loaned on 25/1/91) FL 4
Huddersfield T (£20,000 on 18/2/94) FL 15+4/1 FAC 0+1 Others 4/2
Plymouth Arg (Signed on 10/8/95) FL 32+4/2 FLC 2 FAC 2 Others 1

CLODE Mark James
Born: Plymouth, 24 February 1973
Height: 5'10" Weight: 10.10
Club Honours: AMC '94

An exciting Swansea full back going forward, Mark displayed more consistency during the second half of last season. A talented defender, who links up well with his midfield, he is capable of playing in a higher standard of football.

Plymouth Arg (From trainee on 30/3/91)
Swansea C (Free on 23/7/93) FL 84+7/2 FLC 6+2 FAC 3 Others 8

Nigel Clough

CLOUGH Nigel Howard
Born: Sunderland, 19 March 1966
Height: 5'9" Weight: 11.8
Club Honours: FLC '89, '90; FMC '89, '92
International Honours: E: 14; B-3; U21-15

An attractive signing from Liverpool in mid-January 1996, having made just one start for the Reds in 1995-96, Nigel settled in well to the Manchester City manager's blueprint for his midfield artistry and support of the front men. Every time he pulled the shirt on he produced skilful, ball-winning performances that were an object lesson for all the young midfielders competing for regular selection at the club, while his three goals came in matches where the result had a significant bearing on further progress in the FA Cup and Premier League survival. Graham Souness once said of Nigel: "Playing under such a dominating and forceful character as his father, Brian, proved him to have a

strong character". He certainly showed that attribute in abundance in what was a most difficult season.

Nottingham F (Free from Heanor T on 15/9/84) F/PL 307+4/101 FLC 46/22 FAC 28/6 Others 11+3/1
Liverpool (£2,275,000 on 7/6/93) PL 29+10/7 FLC 3/2 FAC 2
Manchester C (£1,500,000 on 24/1/96) PL 15/2 FAC 3/1

COATES Jonathan Simon
Born: Swansea, 27 June 1975
Height: 5'8" Weight: 10.4
International Honours: W: U21-2; Yth

Surprisingly offered a free transfer by Swansea last March after showing impressive form on the wing earlier in 1995-96. A regular goalscorer at reserve level, Jonathan also possesses an ability to beat his opposing defender, being capped last season for the Wales U21 side against Moldova and Germany.

Swansea C (From trainee on 8/7/93) FL 7+20/1 FLC 1+1 FAC 1 Others 2

COCKERILL Glenn
Born: Grimsby, 25 August 1955
Height: 5'10" Weight: 12.4

The veteran midfielder continued as an inspirational captain for Leyton Orient last season, even though, at the age of 37, he had slowed appreciably, leading by example, showing great enthusiasm, and only missing games through injury or suspension. However, time waiteth for no man and with his contract at an end he was released during the summer.

Lincoln C (Free from Louth U on 1/11/76) FL 65+6/10 FLC 2 FAC 2
Swindon T (£11,000 on 6/12/79) FL 23+3/1 FLC 3
Lincoln C (£40,000 on 12/8/81) FL 114+1/25 FLC 16/1 FAC 7 Others 1
Sheffield U (£125,000 on 23/3/84) FL 62/10 FLC 6/1 FAC 1
Southampton (£225,000 on 17/10/85) F/PL 272+15/32 FLC 35+2/5 FAC 20+2/2 Others 12
Leyton Orient (Free on 10/12/93) FL 89+1/7 FLC 4/1 FAC 3 Others 10

CODNER Robert George
Born: Walthamstow, 23 January 1965
Height: 5'11" Weight: 11.8
International Honours: E: SP-1

Released by Brighton during the 1995 close season, Robert went to Reading on trial and did well enough in the reserves to earn a handful of first team appearances, before moving on at the end of December, having been unable to impose himself in Royals' midfield. Following another trial, this time at Peterborough, he signed for Barnet on transfer deadline day and quickly showed up with excellent distribution and a cool head.

Leicester C (Free from Tottenham H juniors on 17/9/83)
Brighton & Hove A (£125,000 from Barnet, via Dagenham, on 8/9/88) FL 257+9/39 FLC 18+2/1 FAC 11+1/4 Others 16+1/3
Reading (Free on 22/9/95) FL 3+1 FLC 1
Peterborough U (Free on 8/3/96) FL 1+1
Barnet (Free on 28/3/96) FL 8

COLCOMBE Scott
Born: West Bromwich, 15 December 1971
Height: 5'5" Weight: 10.6

Nippy little winger who has yet to cement his place in the Doncaster Rovers' first team. A willing runner who came on a free transfer from Torquay during the 1995 close season, he has much to offer the team, having also featured at full back during 1995-96.

West Bromwich A (From trainee on 5/7/90)
Torquay U (Free on 14/8/91) FL 78+11/1 FLC 8+1 FAC 4+1/1 Others 5
Doncaster Rov (Free on 10/7/95) FL 21+9/3 FAC 1 Others 2/1

COLDICOTT Stacy
Born: Redditch, 29 April 1974
Height: 5'11" Weight: 11.2

Stacy produced several competent displays at both right back and in midfield for WBA during 1995-96, being determined, aggressive, and totally committed every time he took the field. Vied for a place in the side with at least six other players of similar style, and was never a regular in the first team ranks.

West Bromwich A (From trainee on 4/3/92) FL 47+19 FLC 7+1 FAC 2+1/1 Others 7+3

Andy Cole

COLE Andrew (Andy) Alexander
Born: Nottingham, 15 October 1971
Height: 5'11" Weight: 11.2
Club Honours: Div 1 '93; PL '96; FAC '96
International Honours: E: 1; B-1; U21-8; Yth, Sch

A quick and elusive striker with skill to match, his speed off the mark can often leave defenders struggling, especially around the six yard box. Although his strike rate for Manchester United in 1995-96 failed to reach the dizzy heights he sustained at Newcastle his all-round team play improved immeasurably. One of the reasons for this has been his tremendous understanding with Eric Cantona, which has gone from strength

to strength. Having scored just two goals, his most prolific spell came in December when he hit the net in four successive matches, including a majestic strike against his former club, Newcastle. However, at the end of a season where he won both championship and FA Cup winners' medals, he would probably claim his equaliser in the FA Cup semi final against Chelsea to be his most important.

Arsenal (From trainee on 18/10/89) FL 0+1 Others 0+1
Fulham (Loaned on 5/9/91) FL 13/3 Others 2/1
Bristol C (£500,000 on 12/3/92) FL 41/20 FLC 3/4 FAC 1 Others 4/1
Newcastle U (£1,750,000 on 12/3/93) F/PL 69+1/55 FLC 7/8 FAC 4/1 Others 3/4
Manchester U (£6,000,000 on 12/1/95) PL 49+3/23 FLC 1 FAC 7/2 Others 1

COLEMAN Christopher (Chris)
Born: Swansea, 10 June 1970
Height: 6'2" Weight: 14.6
Club Honours: WC '89, '91; Div 1 '94
International Honours: W: 14; U21-3; Yth; Sch

A splendidly built Welsh international centre back who was signed by Blackburn from Crystal Palace last December, when it became apparent that Ian Pearce was not going to return early, he has all the attributes of a top class defender. Would probably have been introduced slowly, but for an injury to Graeme le Saux forcing his inclusion. Took some time to settle in alongside Colin Hendry and after a difficult start he improved rapidly as the season progressed, having an outstanding game in the Easter Monday defeat of Newcastle, when handling Les Ferdinand and Tino Asprilla with some comfort.

Swansea C (From from Manchester C juniors on 1/9/87) FL 159+1/2 FLC 8 FAC 13/1 Others 15
Crystal Palace (£275,000 on 19/7/91) F/PL 143+11/13 FLC 24+2/2 FAC 8/1 Others 2
Blackburn Rov (£2,800,000 on 16/12/95) PL 19+1 FAC 2

COLEMAN Simon
Born: Worksop, 13 March 1968
Height: 6'0" Weight: 10.8

One of the success stories of last season for Bolton was the return to action of their central defender, after he suffered a broken leg at Derby in February 1995. His comeback, against one of his former clubs, Middlesbrough, came in February and he celebrated by scoring one of the goals in a 4-1 win. A steady player capable of causing problems in opponents' penalty areas, his experience in the Premiership will prove invaluable.

Mansfield T (From juniors on 29/7/85) FL 96/7 FLC 9 FAC 7 Others 7/1
Middlesbrough (£600,000 on 26/9/89) FL 51+4/2 FAC 5 Others 10/1
Derby Co (£300,000 on 15/8/91) FL 62+8/2 FLC 5+1 FAC 5 Others 12
Sheffield Wed (£250,000 on 20/1/94) PL 11+5/1 FLC 3 FAC 2
Bolton W (£350,000 on 5/10/94) P/FL 34/5 FLC 4 FAC 1

COLKIN Lee
Born: Nuneaton, 15 July 1974
Height: 5'11" Weight: 12.0

Left-sided Northampton defender, cum midfielder, with speed, who finally worked his way through the ranks to become a first team regular, before a bad leg injury kept him out for most of last season. Admired by the fans for his aggressive never-say-die approach, he will undoubtedly be back.

Northampton T (From trainee on 31/8/92) FL 73+20/3 FLC 5/1 FAC 2+1 Others 3

COLL Owen Oliver
Born: Donegal, 9 April 1976
Height: 6'1" Weight: 11.7
International Honours: Ei: U21-3

Signed from Spurs on transfer deadline day in March 1996, the youngster was drafted straight into Bournemouth's first team for the game against Bristol Rovers and secured a place at centre back through to the end of the season. As well as his defensive abilities he looked comfortable when coming forward with the ball and dangerous at set pieces. Very impressive during his time on the south coast, prior to his move, Owen had made his debut for the Republic of Ireland's U21 side.

Tottenham H (From Enfield R on 1/7/94)
Bournemouth (Signed on 28/3/96) FL 8

COLLETT Andrew (Andy) Alfred
Born: Stockton, 28 October 1973
Height: 6'0" Weight: 13.2

Andy grasped the chance to become Bristol Rovers' first choice goalkeeper last January, showing himself to be a brave shot stopper who commanded his goal area and was confident with left-footed clearances. Earlier, he had been involved in a much publicised event on 28 October at Brighton, when the Seagulls' George Parris crept up from behind his goal line to net an improbable goal.

Middlesbrough (From trainee on 6/3/92) PL 2 Others 3
Bristol Rov (£10,000 on 18/10/94) FL 30 FAC 1 Others 6

COLLIER Daniel (Danny) Joseph
Born: Eccles, 15 January 1974
Height: 6'3" Weight: 12.8

Central defender. Just as in 1994-95, Danny was never a contender for a regular first team spot at Crewe. An injury crisis brought him into the side for just a few outings, in what was the last year of his current contract, before he was released during the summer.

Wolverhampton W (From trainee on 7/7/92)
Crewe Alex (Free on 15/6/94) FL 5+6 FLC 1 FAC 1 Others 0+2

COLLINS Lee
Born: Bellshill, 3 February 1974
Height: 5'8" Weight: 9.12

A Swindon midfielder in the Steve McMahon mould, Lee was signed from Scottish League basement club, Albion Rovers, last February. Although he will need to adjust to the pace of first division football, at 22, however, time is on his side, and he should prove a real asset.

Albion Rov (Signed from Pollock on 25/11/93) SL 43+2 SLC 2 SC 2 Others 2
Swindon T (£15,000 on 15/11/95) FL 2+3 FAC 1 Others 1

COLLINS Simon
Born: Pontefract, 16 December 1973
Height: 5'11" Weight: 13.0

Once again on the fringe of first team selection for Huddersfield in 1995-96, he is a combative and skilful midfielder who performed well when selected and showed an eye for goal, with three in four games early on. Is quite happy to have a "pop" from long range.

Huddersfield T (From trainee on 1/7/92) FL 21+15/3 FLC 4+1/1 FAC 1+2 Others 1+3

COLLINS Wayne Anthony
Born: Manchester, 4 March 1969
Height: 6'0" Weight: 12.0

Until last season, Wayne had been considered by Crewe to be a midfielder, but has now been converted into a full back with success. Very mobile, he likes to attack whenever the opportunity arises.

Crewe Alex (£10,000 from Winsford U on 29/7/93) FL 102+15/14 FLC 5/1 FAC 8+1 Others 14+1/2

COLLYMORE Stanley (Stan) Victor
Born: Stone, 22 January 1971
Height: 6'4" Weight: 13.11
International Honours: E: 2

Despite scoring two outstanding goals, one on his Liverpool debut, early last season, having been signed from Nottingham Forest during the summer, Britain's most expensive player to date struggled to make any impact in his first three months at Anfield and was relegated to the bench, an outburst in the media in October further diminishing his reputation. Fortunate to regain his first team place in November, due to an injury to Ian Rush, he at last showed that he could be a team player, in the home match with Arsenal, when he laid on two goals for Robbie Fowler. Following this, his partnership with Fowler became the most deadly in the Premiership, the pair scoring 42 of the club's 70 league goals. Such form may yet herald a return to the England national squad, where his pace and strength, allied to his aerial ability, could still make an impact.

Wolverhampton W (From trainee on 13/7/89)
Crystal Palace (£100,000 from Stafford R on 4/1/91) FL 4+16/1 FLC 2+3/1
Southend U (£100,000 on 20/11/92) FL 30/15 FAC 3/3
Nottingham F (£2,000,000 on 5/7/93) F/PL 64+1/41 FLC 9/2 FAC 2/1 Others 2/1
Liverpool (£8,500,000 on 3/7/95) PL 30+1/14 FLC 2+2 FAC 7/5 Others 1+1

COMYN Andrew (Andy) John
Born: Wakefield, 2 August 1968
Height: 6'1" Weight: 11.12

As a strong, well-built central defender, he played one league match in WBA's defence, replacing the injured Paul Raven against Millwall. Probably needs a change of direction to put his career back on track.

Manchester U (From juniors on 5/8/86)
Aston Villa (£34,000 from Alvechurch on 22/8/89) FL 12+3 FLC 2+1 FAC 2 Others 1
Derby Co (£200,000 on 8/8/91) FL 59+4/1 FLC 7 FAC 3+1/1 Others 9/2
Plymouth Arg (£200,000 on 1/8/93) FL 76/5 FLC 4 FAC 7 Others 6
West Bromwich A (Free on 28/3/96) FL 3

CONLON Paul Robert
Born: Sunderland, 5 January 1978
Height: 5'9" Weight: 11.7

Exciting young forward who is a second year trainee with Hartlepool. A leading goalscorer with the juniors, Paul got his chance in the first team last season due to other players injuries, proving to be a real opportunist, scoring four goals in six games, and finishing the campaign an established member of the first team squad. Has now signed full professional forms and should really make his mark in 1996-97.

Hartlepool U (Trainee) FL 11+4/4

CONNELLY Sean Patrick
Born: Sheffield, 26 June 1970
Height: 5'10" Weight: 11.10

Kept a firm hold on his right back position at Stockport with some steady displays last season. Combines his playing duties with the the job of assistant physio to Roger Wylde, after passing his final exams. Can also play in a more central role if required.

Stockport Co (Free from Hallam on 12/8/92) FL 116+5 FLC 9 FAC 6+1 Others 10

CONNELLY David James
Born: Willesden, 6 June 1977
Height: 5'8" Weight: 11.4
International Honours: Ei: 4

Watford striker, with an emerging reputation, who missed the first five months of last season with a serious ankle injury which required surgery. Having put his enforced rest to good use by studying the leading strikers, especially Ian Wright, David got off the mark in league football with a hat trick against Port Vale. Repeated the feat two matches later against Grimsby, and ended 1995-96 with a tally of eight goals in just seven games. Was included in the full Irish squad for their end of season tour, playing in four matches.

Watford (From trainee on 15/11/94) FL 7+6/8 FAC 1+2

Stan Collymore

CONNOLLY Karl Andrew
Born: Prescot, 9 February 1970
Height: 5'11" Weight: 11.2
Club Honours: WC '95

Still the "gem" of the Wrexham side in 1995-96 and even more so with the sad departure of goalscoring hero, Gary Bennett, to Prenton Park. After moving from his wide-left position to central striker, much onus was put on Karl to become a prolific goalscorer. To a point, he obliged, being leading scorer by a mile, but at times the pressure told which affected his skilful general play that was so beneficial to the team. However, his form was such that, come the end of the season, he was elected by his fellow professionals as being worthy of a place in the PFA award winning second division team.
Wrexham (Free from Napoli, in local Sunday League, on 8/5/91) FL 201+7/47 FLC 14/21 FAC 16/4 Others 24+1/5

CONNOR James (Jim) Richard
Born: Twickenham, 22 August 1974
Height: 6'0" Weight: 13.0

All-round Millwall midfielder, with good passing skills, neat control and one who tackles hard. A substitute appearance against Derby last December was a personal milestone for Jim, after a recurring shoulder problem had almost wrecked his career, while his first full game at home to Portsmouth won him the sponsor's "Man of the Match" award, the first of two last season, for his tireless midfield display. Is equally at home at right back or centre back.
Millwall (From trainee on 21/11/92) FL 8+1

CONROY Michael (Mike) Kevin
Born: Glasgow, 31 December 1965
Height: 6'0" Weight: 12.7
Club Honours: Div 4 '92

Fulham's leading scorer in 1995-96 with 15 goals, after joining from Preston during the close season, a return of nine goals from 40 league appearances was disappointing, considering his record at Burnley and Preston. Now on the transfer list, the lack of a settled partner did not help his cause.
Clydebank (Free from Coventry C juniors in 1984) SL 92+22/38 SLC 4+1 SC 5+2
St Mirren (Signed in Dec 1987) SL 9+1/1 SC 0+1
Reading (£50,000 on 28/9/88) FL 65+15/7 FLC 3+2 FAC 8+2/1 Others 2+2
Burnley (£35,000 on 16/7/91) FL 76+1/30 FLC 4/1 FAC 9+1/4 Others 7+1/4
Preston NE (£85,000 on 20/8/93) FL 50+7/22 FLC 2+1 FAC 7/2 Others 2+3
Fulham (£75,000 on 9/8/95) FL 38+2/9 FLC 4/2 FAC 4+1/3 Others 3/1

CONWAY Paul James
Born: London, 17 April 1970
Height: 6'1" Weight: 12.6
Club Honours: Div 3 '95
International Honours: USA: U21

A talented Carlisle midfielder of whom much was expected last season, Paul was very unlucky with injuries which restricted his appearances. Though more renowned as a striker of the ball than for his heading skills, his diving header brought a late victory over Crewe in one of the club's best performances of the campaign. A naturalised US citizen, he is the son of Jimmy Conway (ex-Fulham and Manchester City).
Carlisle U (Signed on 29/10/93) FL 53+11/13 FLC 1+1 FAC 4+1/2 Others 9+3/1

COOK Andrew (Andy) Charles
Born: Romsey, 10 August 1969
Height: 5'9" Weight: 12.0

Niggling injuries at various times throughout last season prevented Andy from consolidating his Swansea place at left back. However, he continually showed his versatility by alternating between full back and midfield.
Southampton (From apprentice on 6/7/87) FL 11+5/1 FLC 4 FAC 1 Others 1
Exeter C (£50,000 on 13/9/91) FL 70/1 FLC 2 FAC 7/1 Others 6/1
Swansea C (£125,000 on 23/7/93) FL 54+8 FLC 2 FAC 3 Others 9+1/2

COOK Mitchell (Mitch) Christopher
Born: Scarborough, 15 October 1961
Height: 6'0" Weight: 12.3
Club Honours: GMVC '87

An experienced and skilful left-sided midfielder who returned to Scarborough as director of coaching late last season, having been previously player/manager of Unibond League club, Guiseley, Mitch made a couple of appearances as the club struggled with injury problems.
Darlington (Signed from Scarborough on 13/8/84) FL 34/4 FLC 1 FAC 6 Others 3
Middlesbrough (Signed on 13/9/85) FL 3+3 Others 1+1
Scarborough (Free on 1/8/86) FL 61+20/10 FLC 6+2/4 FAC 3/1 Others 7+1
Halifax T (£25,000 on 2/8/89) FL 52+2/2 FLC 7/1 Others 5/2
Scarborough (Loaned on 1/10/90) FL 9/1 FAC 1
Darlington (Free on 26/3/91) FL 35+1/3 FLC 2/1 FAC 2
Blackpool (Signed on 26/3/92) FL 66+2 FLC 6 FAC 1 Others 5
Hartlepool U (Free on 18/11/94) FL 22+2 (Free to Guiseley during 1995 close season)
Scarborough (Free on 26/3/96) FL 2

COOK Paul Anthony
Born: Liverpool, 22 February 1967
Height: 5'11" Weight: 11.0

After finding himself on the sidelines at Coventry, having made just two starts and showing patchy form, the talented left-sided schemer arrived at Prenton Park, initially on loan, eventually becoming a fully-fledged Tranmere man on transfer deadline day last March. A player who likes to make probing passes from deep positions and pepper the opposition goal with long-range shots, he hit his first goal for Rovers, a cheeky free kick at Derby County.
Wigan Ath (Signed from Marine on 20/7/84) FL 77+6/14 FLC 4 FAC 6+1 Others 5+1/1
Norwich C (£73,000 on 23/5/88) FL 3+3 Others 1+1
Wolverhampton W (£250,000 on 1/11/89) FL 191+2/19 FLC 7/1 FAC 5+2 Others 6+1/1
Coventry C (£600,000 on 18/8/94) FL 35+2/3 FLC 3 FAC 3
Tranmere Rov (£250,000 on 29/2/96) FL 15/1

COOKE Andrew (Andy) Roy
Born: Shrewsbury, 2 January 1974
Height: 6'0" Weight: 12.0

Signed from League of Wales club, Newtown, at the end of 1994-95, Andy's scoring feats proved hard to repeat at second division level last season. Perfectly built for a striker, he seemed the ideal foil for the more skilful Kurt Nogan but, used mainly as a substitute, seemed to need more time to impose himself on the game than he was sometimes allowed. However, given the opportunity he may yet become the player many Burnley fans believe he can be.
Burnley (Signed from Newtown on 1/5/95) FL 10+13/5 FAC 0+1 Others 2+2

COOKE Jason
Born: Birmingham, 13 July 1971
Height: 6'3" Weight: 14.0

A tall, bustling striker, Jason arrived at Torquay last October from non-league Bilston Town and, after scoring a hat trick in the reserves, he was quickly promoted to the first team for the home game against Preston, a club he had previously trialed with. Unfortunately not given much opportunity to settle, he was released following a subs' appearance in the AWS competition.
Torquay U (Free from Bilston T on 10/10/95) FL 1 Others 0+1

COOKE Terence (Terry) John
Born: Birmingham, 5 August 1976
Height: 5'7" Weight: 9.9
Club Honours: FAYC '95
International Honours: E: U21-4; Yth

Talented young Manchester United right winger who possesses an excellent repertoire of skills and lightening pace. Terry's introduction on the Old Trafford stage came last September against Bolton when he manufactured a Maradona-style back pass for Paul Scholes to score in United's 3-0 win. Despite his initial success, the lack of opportunities resigned him to reserve team football and he went on loan to Sunderland in January, where he impressed in six matches, mainly with his tenacious tackling and willingness to cover back in defence. Won four England U21 caps during the season and looks a good bet to go on to bigger and better things.
Manchester U (From trainee on 1/7/94) PL 1+3 FLC 1+1/1 Others 0+1
Sunderland (Loaned on 29/1/96) FL 6

COOPER Colin Terence
Born: Sedgefield, 28 February 1967
Height: 5'11" Weight: 11.5
International Honours: E: 2; U21-8

As a strong-tackling central defender, partnering Steve Chettle in Nottingham Forest's defence, Colin enjoyed another consistent season in 1995-96, missing only four games (in March) due to injury, and scoring five goals, mostly from set pieces, into the bargain. Although his unexpected England call up for two games last summer was not repeated, he continued to build on past performances and as the club's vice captain he no doubt looks forward to taking over the full responsibility if and when Stuart Pearce retires.
Middlesbrough (From juniors on 17/7/84) FL 183+5/6 FLC 18 FAC 13 Others 19+1/2

Millwall (£300,000 on 25/7/91) FL 77/6 FLC 6 FAC 2 Others 2
Nottingham F (£1,700,000 on 21/6/93) F/PL 108+1/13 FLC 10/1 FAC 8/1 Others 7

Colin Cooper

COOPER Gary

Born: Hammersmith, 20 November 1965
Height: 5'8" Weight: 11.3
Club Honours: Div 2 '95; AMC '95
International Honours: E: Yth; Sch

A versatile player who can slot into midfield or at full back without undue worry, he began last season as a Birmingham regular until injuries, suspensions, and the excellent form of John Frain put him out of contention. Used from then on to fill in mainly during regular injury crisis, the lack of further opportunities saw him freed in April.

Queens Park R (From apprentice on 2/6/83) FL 1 FLC 1+1 Others 0+1 (Free to Fisher Ath in February 1986)
Brentford (Loaned on 1/9/85) FL 9+1
Maidstone U (Signed on 1/3/89) FL 53+7/7 FLC 3 FAC 3+1 Others 10/1
Peterborough U (£20,000 on 28/3/91) FL 83+5/10 FLC 12/1 FAC 5/2 Others 9/1
Birmingham C (Free on 17/12/93) FL 58+4/2 FLC 6+1/1 FAC 4+1/1 Others 6+2

COOPER Kevin Lee

Born: Derby, 8 February 1975
Height: 5'6" Weight: 10.7

A left winger in Derby's reserve side who, like others, found his progress limited at the club in 1995-96, as they pushed for promotion. Notable for his pace and ability to cross the ball on the run, he made one substitute appearance on the last day of the season. Still young enough to be patient for further chances.

Derby Co (From trainee on 2/7/93) FL 0+2 Others 0+1

COOPER Mark David

Born: Watford, 5 April 1967
Height: 6'1" Weight: 13.0

The big Barnet centre forward weighed in with nine goals before having to take a back seat to the Lee Hodges and Sean Devine partnership in the final third of the season. Although having over 100 first team goals behind him, Mark was deemed to be surplus to requirements and released in the summer.

Cambridge U (From apprentice on 16/10/84) FL 62+9/17 FLC 7/3 FAC 4 Others 2
Tottenham H (Signed on 2/4/87)
Shrewsbury T (Loaned on 10/9/87) FL 6/2
Gillingham (£105,000 on 9/10/87) FL 38+11/11 FLC 2+1 FAC 3+1 Others 4
Leyton Orient (Signed on 2/2/89) FL 117+33/45 FLC 6/2 FAC 8+2/4 Others 10+2/4
Barnet (Free on 13/7/94) FL 58+9/19 FLC 2+3/2 FAC 4/2 Others 3/2

COOPER Mark Nicholas

Born: Wakefield, 18 December 1968
Height: 5'8" Weight: 11.4
Club Honours: Div 4 '90

Son of the former City manager, Terry, Mark had another good season in 1995-96 as Exeter's penalty taker and it is surprising that the club have managed to hang onto his services without other teams enquiring after him. A good passer who can also tackle well in midfield, another of his specialities is at dead ball situations.

Bristol C (From trainee on 10/9/87)
Exeter C (Free on 3/10/89) FL 46+4/12 FLC 4+1 FAC 3+1/1 Others 5
Southend U (Loaned on 22/3/90) FL 4+1
Birmingham C (Signed on 5/9/91) FL 30+9/4 FAC 2 Others 3/1
Fulham (£40,000 on 21/11/92) FL 10+4 FLC 2 Others 3
Huddersfield T (Loaned on 25/3/93) FL 10/4
Wycombe W (Free on 10/1/94) FL 0+2/1
Exeter C (Free on 11/2/94) FL 78+10/20 FLC 3 FAC 2 Others 4/1

COPE James Andrew

Born: Solihull, 4 October 1977
Height: 6'0" Weight: 11.0

Still a trainee, the young Shrewsbury midfielder made his first team debut in 1995-96, when coming on for the last ten minutes of the season at Burnley. Obviously a promising player, his YTS contract was due to expire at the end of June.

Shrewsbury T (Trainee) FL 0+1

CORAZZIN Giancarlo (Carlo) Michele

Born: Canada, 25 December 1971
Height: 5'9" Weight: 12.7
International Honours: Canada: 15

Finished 1995-96 as Cambridge United's top scorer, this after leaving on transfer deadline day for Plymouth. A constant threat to defences, Carlo was always likely to move on in a season that saw him win further Canadian international honours and also score for the national team. With Argyle ultimately promoted to the second division, via the play offs, he spent most of his time on the subs' bench, causing the strike force to look over their shoulders and to improve on performances.

Cambridge U (£20,000 from Vancouver 86ers on 10/12/93) FL 104+1/39 FLC 4/2 FAC 5 Others 3/2
Plymouth Arg (£150,000 on 28/3/96) FL 1+5/1 Others 0+1

CORDEN Simon Wayne

Born: Leek, 1 November 1975
Height: 5'9" Weight: 10.6

A promising Port Vale left winger who spent much of 1995-96 in the reserves, Simon made his full league debut in the April home game against Luton, playing on the right flank, before switching to his favoured side for the Charlton match. The winner of Vale's "Young Player of the Year" award, he should have a bright future ahead of him.

Port Vale (From trainee on 20/9/94) FL 2+1

CORICA Stephen (Steve) Christopher

Born: Cairns, Australia, 24 March 1973
Height: 5'8" Weight: 10.7
International Honours: Australia

Skilful right-sided midfielder. Signing for Leicester on the eve of last season from Marconi of Sydney, the fee being eventually settled by a FIFA tribunal, he was the first player to be capped at every level by Australia, and appeared against Scotland in March. Scored a cracking goal on his debut at Roker Park, before breaking a leg at Port Vale in September and returning after just 11 weeks. Unsettled by Mark McGhee's defection to Molineux, Steve eventually followed his former manager to Wolves in February for an initial fee of £1.1 million, which could eventually rise by another £400,000. Missing just one match, the main purpose of his signing was to speed up the link between midfield and attack.

Leicester C (£325,000 from Marconi on 11/8/95) FL 16/2 FAC 2
Wolverhampton W (£1,100,000 on 16/2/96) FL 17

CORNFORTH John Michael

Born: Whitley Bay, 7 October 1967
Height: 6'1" Weight: 12.11
Club Honours: Div 3 '88; AMC '94
International Honours: W: 2

A major influence in the Swansea midfield last season, and a regular inclusion in the Welsh international squad, his knee injury coincided with the club's slide down the table. Although a star in the valleys, following a return to fitness he transferred to Birmingham in March, thus adding to the Welsh colony at St Andrews. Very constructive, with super passing skills, despite finding it difficult to settle into his new team, John promises much for 1996-97.

Sunderland (From apprentice on 11/10/85) FL 21+11/2 FLC 0+1 Others 1+3
Doncaster Rov (Loaned on 6/11/86) FL 6+1/3 Others 2
Shrewsbury T (Loaned on 23/11/89) FL 3 Others 2
Lincoln C (Loaned on 11/1/90) FL 9/1
Swansea C (£50,000 on 2/8/91) FL 147+2/16 FLC 14 FAC 11/1 Others 19/1
Birmingham C (£350,000 on 26/3/96) FL 8

COTTEE Anthony (Tony) Richard

Born: West Ham, 11 July 1965
Height: 5'8" Weight: 11.5
International Honours: E: 7; U21-8; Yth

The experienced West Ham striker finished joint top scorer for the club last season, with ten league goals. Although not as consistent as in previous years, he contributed a great deal to the team's play and built up a good understanding alongside Iain Dowie, with

Tony Cottee

vital winning goals coming against Wimbledon, QPR and Bolton, whilst his best came against Coventry when he raced clear, rounded the 'keeper, and slotted the ball home. Capable of losing his marker in tight situations, Tony has the knack of getting in on the end of chances.

West Ham U (From apprentice on 1/9/82) FL 203+9/92 FLC 19/14 FAC 24/11 Others 1/1
Everton (£2,300,000 on 2/8/88) F/PL 161+23/72 FLC 19+4/11 FAC 15+6/4 Others 11+2/12
West Ham U (Signed on 7/9/94) PL 61+3/23 FLC 6/3 FAC 5/1

COUGHLAN Derek James
Born: Cork, 2 January 1977
Height: 6'3" Weight: 14.0

Having exchanged his YTS agreement for that of a full-time contract during this 1995 close season, this young Irish central defender made an encouraging league debut

for Brighton at home against Oxford on 12 March 1996, prior to being released during the summer.
Brighton & Hove A (From trainee on 17/5/95) FL 1

COUGHLIN Russell James
Born: Swansea, 15 February 1960
Height: 5'8" Weight: 11.12
Club Honours: WC '91
International Honours: W: Yth; Sch

Transferred to Torquay from Exeter last October, having played little more than a handful of games in 1996-97 after being re-signed during the summer, Russell provided most of United's craft. A very experienced midfield operator, who has spent more than 18 years in the professional game, he was freed during the close season.
Manchester C (From apprentice on 3/3/78)
Blackburn Rov (£40,000 on 26/3/79) FL 22+2 FLC 1+1

Carlisle U (£20,000 on 30/10/80) FL 114+16/13 FLC 5+1/1 FAC 12
Plymouth Arg (£20,000 on 25/7/84) FL 128+3/18 FLC 8/2 FAC 8/1 Others 5/1
Blackpool (£75,000 on 11/12/87) FL 100+2/8 FLC 9/1 FAC 13 Others 10/1
Shrewsbury T (Loaned on 11/9/90) FL 4+1 FLC 1
Swansea C (£30,000 on 17/10/90) FL 99+2/2 FLC 4+1 FAC 8 Others 10+1
Exeter C (Signed on 12/7/93) FL 64+4 FLC 5 FAC 5 Others 4
Torquay U (Free on 13/10/95) FL 22+3 FAC 3 Others 1

COUSINS Jason Michael
Born: Hayes, 14 October 1970
Height: 5'11" Weight: 12.4
Club Honours: GMVC '93; FAT '93

Began last season for Wycombe in his usual right back role and then, after an injury, filled in as a central defender for Terry Evans, before returning at right back in March. However, after a run of ten games he was surprisingly dropped and put on the transfer list. A very hard tackler, and renowned for his commitment and desire to win, his demise unsettled the supporters.
Brentford (From trainee on 13/7/89) FL 20+1 Others 2+2
Wycombe W (Free on 1/7/91) FL 106+2/3 FLC 9/1 FAC 13 Others 12

COUZENS Andrew (Andy)
Born: Shipley, 4 June 1975
Height: 5'10" Weight: 11.11
Club Honours: FAYC '93
International Honours: E: U21-3

Having made his Leeds' PL debut in 1994-95, the talented 20-year-old defender, cum midfielder, who was capped at England U21 level in the annual Toulon tournament during the summer, continued to progress well last season by forcing his way into the first team picture. Tigerish and tenacious, he scored his first senior goal in the Coca Cola Cup victory at Notts County.
Leeds U (From trainee on 5/3/93) PL 10+8 FLC 1+1/1 Others 0+2

COWAN Thomas (Tom)
Born: Bellshill, 28 August 1969
Height: 5'8" Weight: 10.8

The Huddersfield left back who, despite his lack of height, is extraordinarily good in the air, a fact pointed out by no less an authority than Alan Hansen on *Match of the Day*. Remarkably consistent, and a player who likes to get forward to put in crosses for the forwards, and always in close attendance for corners and set pieces, he managed to contribute a couple of goals last season. Naturally left footed, Tom is a good passer of the ball and a reliable tackler.
Clyde (Free from Netherdale BC in 1988-89) SL 16/2 SC 2
Glasgow R (Signed in February 1989) SL 8+4 SC 0+1 Others 2
Sheffield U (£350,000 on 1/8/91) F/PL 45 FLC 5 FAC 2 Others 1
Stoke C (Loaned on 1/10/93) FL 14 FLC 1 Others 3
Huddersfield T (£150,000 on 24/3/94) FL 90/4 FLC 8 FAC 6/1 Others 6

COWANS Gordon Sidney
Born: Cornforth, 27 October 1958
Height: 5'7" Weight: 10.6

Club Honours: FLC '77; Div 1 '81; CS '81; EC '82; ESC '82
International Honours: E: 10; B-2; U21-5; Yth

An inspired Howard Kendall signing when obtained on a free transfer from Wolves last December, Gordon gave some masterful midfield displays for Sheffield United, including "Man of the Match" performances which belied his advancing years. Also showed his commitment to the cause by playing the second half against Southend with six stitches in a head gash. By the time you read this, he is more than likely to have taken up a management or coaching role, following his release at the end of the campaign.

Aston Villa (From apprentice on 1/9/76) FL 276+10/42 FLC 23+4/5 FAC 19+1/3 Others 23+1/2 (£500,000 to Bari on 1/7/85)
Aston Villa (£250,000 on 13/7/88) FL 114+3/7 FLC 15 FAC 9 Others 11+1
Blackburn Rov (£200,000 on 28/11/91) F/PL 49+1/2 FLC 4 FAC 5/1 Others 3
Aston Villa (Free on 5/7/93) PL 9+2 FLC 2 Others 4
Derby Co (£80,000 on 3/2/94) FL 36 FLC 3 Others 5+1/1
Wolverhampton W (£20,000 on 19/12/94) FL 31+6 FLC 2 FAC 5/1 Others 2
Sheffield U (Free on 29/12/95) FL 18+2 FAC 3

COWE Steven (Steve) Mark
Born: Gloucester, 29 September 1974
Height: 5'7" Weight: 10.2

Busy little striker signed from Aston Villa on transfer deadline last March after impressing Swindon during a brief loan spell. Making quick, darting runs and showing excellent skills on the ball, he was reminiscent of a Town striker of an earlier era, in Alan Mayes. Scored on his full debut at Chesterfield and is definitely one to watch for the future.

Aston Villa (From trainee on 7/7/93)
Swindon T (£100,000 on 22/3/96) FL 4+7/1

COX Ian Gary
Born: Croydon, 25 March 1971
Height: 6'0" Weight: 12.2

Ian never quite made the grade with Crystal Palace, following his transfer from neighbouring Carshalton two years ago and, as in 1994-95, most of his appearances last season were from the bench. His only start being at Barnsley in January after he had scored an FA Cup goal in the replay at Port Vale, which Palace lost 3-4 after extra time. Transferred to Bournemouth in March on transfer deadline day, he quickly settled in central midfield, showing pace, control, and dribbling qualities, and impressed in eight matches played.

Crystal Palace (£35,000 from Carshalton on 8/3/94) F/PL 2+13 FAC 1+2/1
Bournemouth (Free on 28/3/96) FL 8

COX Neil James
Born: Scunthorpe, 8 October 1971
Height: 6'0" Weight: 13.2
Club Honours: FLC '94; Div 1 '95
International Honours: E: U21-6

Middlesbrough's first £1m player, "Coxy" is currently enjoying life in the Premiership where his strong tackling and determined defending, allied to his attacking runs into enemy territory, laid the very foundations on which the Boro's early 1995-96 season supremacy was founded. A brilliant defender with an eye for goal (his home goal in 120 seconds against Liverpool may well be the fastest yet by a defender in the Premiership), he turned in some magnificent performances, in spite of carrying injuries that lesser players would have yielded to. Neil plays the wing/back role to perfection in his manager's chosen formation and was probably the club's most consistent player in a roller-coaster season, missing only three games.

Scunthorpe U (From trainee on 20/3/90) FL 17/1 FAC 4 Others 4+1
Aston Villa (£400,000 on 12/2/91) F/PL 26+16/3 FLC 5+2 FAC 4+2/1 Others 2
Middlesbrough (£1,000,000 on 19/7/94) P/FL 74+1/3 FLC 7+1 FAC 2 Others 2

Neil Cox

COYLE Owen Columba
Born: Glasgow, 14 July 1966
Height: 5'11" Weight: 11.2
International Honours: Ei: 1; B-3; U23-1; U21-2

The Scottish striker, who has played for the Republic of Ireland, made just two Premiership starts for Bolton last season, before moving north of the border to join Dundee United for a fee of £380,000 in October. Before leaving, and very much in keeping with 1994-95, he scored three goals in five Pontins League appearances.

Dumbarton (Signed from Renfrew YM in 1985) SL 85+18/36 SLC 4 SC 2
Clydebank (Signed on 1/8/88) SL 63/33 SLC 2 SC 3/1
Airdrie (£175,000 on 1/2/90) SL 116+7/50 SLC 6/2 SC 9+1/1 Others 4
Bolton W (£250,000 on 30/6/93) P/FL 35+19/12 FLC 5+3/1 FAC 8/5 Others 7+1/5

COYNE Daniel (Danny)
Born: Prestatyn, 27 August 1973
Height: 5'11" Weight: 12.7
International Honours: W: 1; U21-9; Yth; Sch

Tranmere Rovers' goalkeeper. Having displaced Eric Nixon as the number one at the end of 1994-95, Danny kept his place throughout last season, becoming an ever present in the side and ended the campaign by winning his first full Welsh cap against Switzerland. A brilliant 'keeper, whose bravery, handling, and agility, suggest he will be Neville Southall's successor for many years to come, he produced several outstanding displays which brought the scouts flocking to Prenton Park.

Tranmere Rov (From trainee on 8/5/92) FL 56+1 FLC 4 FAC 1 Others 2

CRADDOCK Jody Darryl
Born: Bromsgrove, 25 July 1975
Height: 6'0" Weight: 12.4

Still not 21 years old, the right-footed Cambridge United defender was virtually ever present throughout last season, with a composed style that belied his age. Commanding in the air, he also went forward to score vital goals and was rewarded for his consistency by being named the club's "Player of the Year".

Cambridge U (Free from Christchurch on 13/8/93) FL 101+3/3 FLC 3/1 FAC 4 Others 4

CRAMB Colin
Born: Lanark, 23 June 1974
Height: 5'11" Weight: 11.13
Club Honours: B&Q '93

Young Doncaster striker with a talent for scoring spectacular goals. Signed from Scottish side, Hearts, last December, his fiery temper sometimes got him into hot water, but he should be amongst the goals again this season. Has a good touch and the ability to hold the ball up for others to arrive.

Hamilton Academical (From juniors on 1/6/93) SL 27+18/8 SC 0+1 Others 1+3
Southampton (£75,000 on 8/6/93) PL 0+1
Falkirk (Signed on 30/8/94) SL 6+2/1 SLC 0+1
Heart of Midlothian (Signed on 1/3/95) SL 3+3/1
Doncaster Rov (£25,000 on 15/12/95) FL 20+1/7

CRANSON Ian
Born: Easington, 2 July 1964
Height: 5'11" Weight: 13.4
Club Honours: AMC '92; Div 2 '93
International Honours: E: U21-5

An immensely experienced and reliable central defender, Ian returned to the Stoke team midway through last season after battling back from a third serious knee injury, his commanding presence in the side's back line being fundamental to their climb up the table. At £450,000, along with Mike Sheron, he is Stoke City's record signing.

Ipswich T (From apprentice on 5/7/82) FL 130+1/5 FLC 15 FAC 11+1 Others 7
Sheffield Wed (£450,000 on 24/3/88) FL 29+1 FLC 2 FAC 2 Others 1
Stoke C (£450,000 on 25/7/89) FL 214+3/9 FLC 16+1/1 FAC 14/1 Others 27/1

CRAWFORD James (Jimmy)
Born: Chicago, USA, 1 May 1973
Height: 5'11" Weight: 11.6
International Honours: Ei: U21-2

In 1995-96, Jimmy became the first player born in the USA to play for Newcastle, although he was also qualified for the

Republic of Ireland, being called into their U21 squad early in the season, being twice called upon. Made his debut when coming on as a substitute in the Coca Cola Cup-tie against Bristol City, and is considered a midfield player for the future.
Newcastle U (£75,000 from Bohemians on 23/3/95) FLC 0+1

CREANEY Gerard (Gerry) Thomas
Born: Coatbridge, 13 April 1970
Height: 5'11" Weight: 12.7
International Honours: S: B-1; U21-11
Although a proven striker with his previous clubs, Gerry was still a surprise Manchester City acquisition last September, coming from Portsmouth by way of cash, plus Paul Walsh. With no experience of Premier League football, on the occasions selected, he showed he could forage and screen the ball under tight marking. He also showed he could score at the highest level, a finely placed header at Newcastle which lifted the morale of the team and, more importantly, the winner at Leeds to continue the excellent December form. However, without a proper run-in the side, in order to fulfil his potential, he finished the last few weeks of the season on loan at Oldham. Was capped by Scotland at "B" level last October.
Glasgow Celtic (From juniors on 15/5/87) SL 85+28/36 SLC 9+1/7 SC 9/8 Others 6+3/3
Portsmouth (£500,000 on 25/1/94) FL 60/32 FLC 7/3 FAC 2/1
Manchester C (£2,000,000 on 8/9/95) PL 6+9/3 FAC 0+3/1
Oldham Ath (Loaned on 28/3/96) FL 8+1/2

Gerry Creaney

CRESSWELL Richard Paul Wesley
Born: Bridlington, 20 September 1977
Height: 6'0" Weight: 11.0
Highly-rated young York striker who created a big impression when he made a number of senior appearances in the second half of last season. A former YTS, Richard turned professional in November.
York C (From trainee on 15/11/95) FL 9+7/1 Others 1

CRICHTON Paul Andrew
Born: Pontefract, 3 October 1968
Height: 6'0" Weight: 12.1
Grimsby Town goalkeeper with good positional sense and who is quick off his line. Showing remarkable consistency, Paul has made the position almost his own since joining the club and had another good season in 1995-96, missing just two league games and keeping 11 clean sheets, three of them in successive games.
Nottingham F (From juniors on 23/5/86)
Notts Co (Loaned on 19/9/86) FL 5
Darlington (Loaned on 30/1/87) FL 5
Peterborough U (Loaned on 27/3/87) FL 4
Darlington (Loaned on 28/9/87) FL 3 FLC 1 Others 1
Swindon T (Loaned on 24/12/87) FL 4
Rotherham U (Loaned on 9/3/88) FL 6
Torquay U (Loaned on 25/8/88) FL 13 FLC 2
Peterborough U (Signed on 3/11/88) FL 47 FAC 5 Others 3
Doncaster Rov (Free on 25/9/90) FL 77 FLC 5 FAC 3 Others 5
Grimsby T (Free on 9/7/93) FL 133 FLC 7 FAC 8 Others 2

CROFT Brian Graham
Born: Chester, 27 September 1967
Height: 5'9" Weight: 11.6
Freed by QPR during the 1995 close season, Brian initially signed on for a month with Blackpool, before moving on to Torquay as a non-contract player at the start of 1995-96 and making two subs' appearances. His next stop was at Vauxhall Conference side, Southport, and then Stockport, whose manager, Dave Jones, was spreading the net for good wide men. However, after four reserve games, and three from the bench for the first team, he was released. Still only 28, earlier in his career, he had shown much potential on the left wing, especially in his ability to pass defenders and cross accurately.
Chester C (From trainee on 23/7/86) FL 36+23/3 FLC 1 FAC 2+3/1 Others 7+3
Cambridge U (£10,000 on 23/10/88) FL 12+5/2 FAC 3/2 Others 3/1
Chester C (£3,000 on 17/8/89) FL 90+24/3 FLC 7+1/2 FAC 9/3 Others 9+1
Queens Park R (£60,000 on 21/8/92)
Shrewsbury T (Loaned on 10/12/93) FL 4
Blackpool (Free on 13/7/95)
Torquay U (Free on 14/8/95) FL 0+1 FLC 0+1 (Free to Southport in September 1995)
Stockport Co (Free on 10/10/95) FL 0+3

CROFT Gary
Born: Burton on Trent, 17 February 1974
Height: 5'9" Weight: 10.8
International Honours: E: U21-4
Having represented his country at U21 level, Gary was largely ignored by the selectors last season, although his potential for a higher grade of football was eventually realised when Grimsby sold him to Blackburn on transfer deadline day. Yet to make an appearance for Rovers, prior to the move, he had been ever present for Town, playing mainly in the left back position where his tackling ability held him in good stead. A versatile player, who can play anywhere in defence and also further afield if required, his ability to go past defenders wide on the flanks has often reaped dividends.

Grimsby T (From trainee on 7/7/92) FL 139+10/3 FLC 7 FAC 8+2/1 Others 3
Blackburn Rov (£1,700,000 on 29/3/96)

CROOK Ian Stuart
Born: Romford, 18 January 1963
Height: 5'8" Weight: 10.6
International Honours: E: B-1
With 1995-96 being his testimonial season, the sweet-passing midfielder was voted "Man of the Match" in four games by the local newspaper and became only the 13th man to play 300 league games for Norwich City. Apart from that, it was an up-and-down campaign, that saw him miss 17 matches between November and February and, like so many of the side, he did not enjoy his first spell outside of the Premiership. However, sparkling late form saw him spraying the ball around to great effect, with his free kicks from around the box continuing to cause opposing goalkeepers concern. Surprisingly released in the summer.
Tottenham H (From apprentice on 1/8/80) FL 10+10/1 FLC 1 FAC 0+1 Others 1+1
Norwich C (£80,000 on 13/6/86) F/PL 281+23/16 FLC 29+5/4 FAC 18+4/1 Others 16+1/1

CROSBY Andrew (Andy) Keith
Born: Rotherham, 3 March 1973
Height: 6'2" Weight: 13.0
Having finally scored his first goal for Darlington at Orient in 1995-96 after some 70 games, the strong central defender and club captain crowned a great season by leading the team out at Wembley for the third division play-off final against Plymouth. Despite the 1-0 defeat, Andy and the team could be proud of their performance.
Doncaster Rov (Free from Leeds U juniors on 4/7/91) FL 41+10 FLC 1+1 FAC 2 Others 4+1/1
Darlington (Free on 10/12/93) FL 105/1 FLC 4 FAC 5 Others 7

CROSBY Gary
Born: Sleaford, 8 May 1964
Height: 5'7" Weight: 9.13
Club Honours: FLC '90; FMC '92
A skilful midfield player, Gary struggled to establish himself in the Huddersfield first team last season. As a result he played out his time in the reserves and spent a considerable amount of 1995-96 on the transfer list. Remembered from his Nottingham Forest days as a wide player who delivered pin-point early crosses to the forwards.
Lincoln C (Free from Lincoln U on 23/8/86) FL 6+1 FLC 2 (Free to Grantham in November 1986)
Nottingham F (£20,000 on 21/12/87) F/PL 139+13/12 FLC 29+1/6 FAC 18+3/3 Others 10+1/4
Grimsby T (Loaned on 23/8/93) FL 2+1
Huddersfield T (Free on 27/9/94) FL 16+4/4 FLC 2 FAC 1 Others 5+2/1

CROSS Jonathan Neil
Born: Wallasey, 2 March 1975
Height: 5'10" Weight: 11.4
Another Wrexham player who has great potential but, as yet, has not produced the goods consistently, he is able to play on the wide right, as a central striker, or in defence, and is strong running and hard to shake off

the ball. Unfortunately hampered by injury for much of last season, Jonathan was loaned out to Irish League club, Cliftonville, to help restore his confidence.

Wrexham (From trainee on 15/11/92) FL 79+20/10 FLC 4+2/1 FAC 4+1/1 Others 9+6/1

CROSS Nicholas (Nicky) Jeremy
Born: Birmingham, 7 February 1961
Height: 5'9" Weight: 11.12
Club Honours: AMC '93

Nicky continued his understanding up front at Hereford with Steve White in 1995-96, his "old" head allowing him to play in a cool and calculating fashion. Always a joy to watch, with his control and passing superb, he had a spell later on playing a little deeper than usual and was a major influence on the club reaching the third division play-off stage, prior to being released during the summer.

West Bromwich A (From apprentice on 12/2/79) FL 68+37/15 FLC 6+2/2 FAC 5/1 Others 0+1
Walsall (£48,000 on 15/8/85) FL 107+2/45 FLC 10/2 FAC 12+1/3 Others 6+1/1
Leicester C (£65,000 on 21/1/88) FL 54+4/15 FLC 3+2/1 FAC 1 Others 1
Port Vale (£125,000 on 28/6/89) FL 120+24/39 FLC 2+4 FAC 12/1 Others 12+1/2
Hereford U (Free on 13/7/94) FL 56+9/14 FLC 4+2 FAC 6/1 Others 9+1/3

CROSS Ryan
Born: Plymouth, 11 October 1972
Height: 6'0" Weight: 13.10

The Bury right back was a regular performer in the opening three months of last season, before he suffered a hamstring injury the day before the away game at Cardiff on 18 November, which allowed Dean West to claim the position for himself. Although not particularly attack minded, Ryan was a little unlucky to be released during the summer.

Plymouth Arg (From trainee on 30/3/91) FL 18+1 FLC 2 Others 1
Hartlepool U (£75,000 on 11/6/92) FL 49+1/2 FLC 8 FAC 5 Others 5
Bury (Signed on 7/12/93) FL 40+2 FLC 6 FAC 5 Others 3

CROSSLEY Mark Geoffrey
Born: Barnsley, 16 June 1969
Height: 6'0" Weight: 13.9
International Honours: E: U21-3

Enjoyed another excellent season in the Nottingham Forest goal, being ever present for their 56 match programme. Disappointed at being overlooked by the England management, he declared his eligibility for Scotland through a Scottish grandmother, although Craig Brown has yet to take up the offer! A hero in the FA Cup fifth round replay at Tottenham, when he saved three penalties in the shoot-out which decided the outcome, and also a major factor in Forest's "backs to the wall" progress in the UEFA Cup after doing so much to keep them in the competition, it was unfortunate that his mistake in the second-leg of the quarter final with Bayern Munich opened the floodgates for their crushing defeat by the German team. Signed a new four year contract during the summer.

Nottingham F (From trainee on 2/7/87) F/PL 237+1 FLC 31 FAC 29 Others 18

CROSSLEY Matthew (Matt) John William
Born: Basingstoke, 18 March 1968
Height: 6'2" Weight: 13.4
Club Honours: FAT '91, '93; GMVC '93

A very consistent, two-footed Wycombe central defender with fine anticipation and strong in the air, he picked up a serious back injury in the fourth game of last season, which prevented his return until April. Managed two goals in his 15 appearances though.

Wycombe W (Signed from Overton U in 1987-88) FL 86+1/3 FLC 7/1 FAC 14 Others 9

CROWE Glen Michael
Born: Dublin, 25 December 1977
Height: 5'9" Weight: 12.7
International Honours: Ei: Yth

A determined left-footed Wolves' striker, and still a trainee, Glen made a surprise impact in the final two games of last season. Came on as a sub at Reading and was immediately booked, and then started the game at Charlton, lashing in a superb equaliser to give the club their first goal in five outings. Is undoubtedly one to look out for.

Wolverhampton W (Trainee) FL 1+1/1

CULVERHOUSE Ian Brett
Born: Bishops Stortford, 22 September 1964
Height: 5'10" Weight: 11.2
Club Honours: Div 2 '86, '96
International Honours: E: Yth

One of two ever presents in Swindon's second division championship winning side last season, Ian's experience at a higher level was clearly evident. His performances as a sweeper were simply immaculate, being the fulcrum around which the defence functioned so well. Cool and calm when put under pressure, he showed excellent vision and clearly enjoyed the occasional surge forward to set up an attack. Was one of three Town players to be elected by their fellow professionals to the PFA second division team.

Tottenham H (From apprentice on 24/9/82) FL 1+1
Norwich C (£50,000 on 8/10/85) F/PL 295+1/1 FLC 23 FAC 28 Others 22/1
Swindon T (£250,000 on 9/12/94) FL 55 FLC 5 FAC 8 Others 1

CUNDY Jason Victor
Born: Wandsworth, 12 November 1969
Height: 6'1" Weight: 13.7
International Honours: E: U21-3

The forgotten player at White Hart Lane since a disastrous game at Sheffield United in March 1993, the powerfully-built central defender was shut out of first team action by Spurs' for the third consecutive season. However, he enjoyed a successful loan with Crystal Palace last December and January, playing four games from which Palace took ten points. Strong in the air, with a good turn of pace, sadly, no transfer fee could be agreed between the two clubs, and Jason returned to reserve team football.

Chelsea (From trainee on 1/8/88) FL 40+1/2 FLC 6 FAC 6 Others 4

Tottenham H (£750,000 on 26/3/92) F/PL 23+3/1 FLC 2
Crystal Palace (Loaned on 14/12/95) FL 4

CUNNINGHAM Kenneth (Kenny) Edward
Born: Dublin, 28 June 1971
Height: 6'0" Weight: 11.8
International Honours: Ei: 6; B-2; U21-4; Yth

A reliable, attacking right back who, barring six games, was an ever present for Wimbledon last season. After the Christmas period, Kenny's form improved markedly and he ended the campaign in fine form, his well-timed tackling and important over-lapping runs earning him a surprise call up to the Eire squad. Still a young man, he now has the chance to not only establish himself in Premiership football, but to also go on and make a name for himself on the international stage.

Millwall (Signed from Tolka Rov on 18/9/89) FL 132+4/1 FLC 10 FAC 1 Others 5+1/1
Wimbledon (Signed on 9/11/94) PL 60+1 FLC 2 FAC 12

CUNNINGTON Shaun Gary
Born: Bourne, 4 January 1966
Height: 5'9" Weight: 11.12
Club Honours: WC '86

Having signed from Sunderland prior to the start of 1995-96, knee and ankle injuries completely ruined the season for Shaun, whose aggressive style of play in midfield was missed by WBA during the club's disastrous spell between November and January, when they won only one game in 14 starts. He made three separate attempts at a comeback during the campaign, but each time he was forced to not undergo treatment for long periods. Favours the right-hand side of the pitch and can be expected to get on the scoresheet occasionally.

Wrexham (From juniors on 11/1/84) FL 196+3/12 FLC 13 FAC 9/1 Others 21/2
Grimsby T (Signed on 19/2/88) FL 182/13 FLC 11 FAC 11/3 Others 9
Sunderland (£650,000 on 17/7/92) FL 52+6/8 FLC 3 FAC 2/1 Others 2
West Bromwich A (£220,000 on 11/8/95) FL 8+1 FLC 1 Others 2

CURCIC Sasa
Born: Belgrade, Yugoslavia, 14 February 1972
Height: 5'9" Weight: 10.7
International Honours: Yugoslavia: 10

One of the finds of last season as far as Bolton supporters were concerned, the Yugoslav international added another dimension to the team's midfield after coming from Partizan Belgrade for a club record fee in October. Capable of beating defenders with his silky skills, he made the headlines with some memorable goals, notably against Chelsea. At Stamford Bridge he made a dazzling run from the half way line that culminated in a spectacular strike and, later in the campaign, at Burnden, hit the winner against the Blues with a powerful drive. Celebrated his first season in English football by becoming the club's "Player of the Season".

Bolton W (£1,500,000 from Partizan Belgrade on 28/10/95) PL 28/4 FLC 3/1 FAC 2/2

CURETON Jamie
Born: Bristol, 28 August 1975
Height: 5'8" Weight: 10.7
International Honours: E: Yth
Striker. Last season, Jamie became the first Norwich player since 1972 to score in consecutive matches from the substitutes' bench. Sporting green hair for the day he struck a fine goal at Ipswich within a minute of coming on to the field, and followed it up the next match by harassing WBA's Nigel Spink into miskicking a clearance. Martin O'Neill appeared not to like his style of play, but his improved attitude is bringing its reward and in one-on-one situations you would invariably give him more than a 50 per cent chance of success in finding the net. Had a spell on loan at Bournemouth in September, making six substitute appearances without scoring, and apart from his two City league goals, he also struck 13 in 24 games for the reserves.
Norwich C (From trainee on 5/2/93) P/FL 13+16/6 FLC 0+1 FAC 0+2
Bournemouth (Loaned on 8/9/95) FL 0+5 Others 0+1

Keith Curle

CURLE Keith
Born: Bristol, 14 November 1963
Height: 6'0" Weight: 12.7
Club Honours: AMC '86; FMC '88
International Honours: E: 3; B-4

Captain of Manchester City, Keith is a central defender with the skills of a winger, his great pace allowing him to break out of defence to set up chances for the forwards. Diversely, he is also quick in recovery, often covering fellow defenders against breakaways. Missed the first five league games in 1995-96, due to a broken ankle received in a pre-season friendly at Wolverhampton, but, on coming back, was as consistent as ever. As the regular penalty taker, his only goal of a tough campaign came from the spot against Wycombe in the Coca Cola Cup, while his only other attempt, a miss at West Ham, proved costly. Undoubtedly, still at the forefront of Premier League defenders.
Bristol Rov (From apprentice on 20/11/81) FL 21+11/4 FLC 3 FAC 1

Torquay U (£5,000 on 4/11/83) FL 16/5 FAC 1/1 Others 1
Bristol C (£10,000 on 3/3/84) FL 113+8/1 FLC 7+1 FAC 5 Others 14+1
Reading (£150,000 on 23/10/87) FL 40 FLC 8 Others 5
Wimbledon (£500,000 on 21/10/88) FL 91+2/3 FLC 7 FAC 5 Others 6/1
Manchester C (£2,500,000 on 14/8/91) F/PL 171/11 FLC 18/2 FAC 14 Others 1

CURRAN Christopher (Chris)
Born: Birmingham, 17 September 1971
Height: 5'11" Weight: 12.4
The former Torquay captain missed only two games for the Gulls last season, prior to signing for Plymouth in December, having scored in 1-1 draws against Wigan and Swindon (AWS). Brought to Home Park as a squad player, although mainly appearing on the bench, in the games he did play, Chris proved versatile and combative right across the defence and looked a useful acquisition.
Torquay U (From trainee on 13/7/90) FL 144+8/4 FLC 15 FAC 8 Others 10/1
Plymouth Arg (£40,000 on 22/12/95) FL 6+2 Others 3

CURRIE Darren Paul
Born: Hampstead, 29 November 1974
Height: 5'9" Weight: 11.7
Shrewsbury left winger who was signed from West Ham last February following two successful loan spells the previous season. Again proving to be a real crowd pleaser, with obvious ability on the ball in taking defenders on and providing pin-point crosses, Darren also found time to score two goals as an added bonus. Earlier, in November, he had played ten games for Leyton Orient, also on a temporary basis.
West Ham U (From trainee on 2/7/93)
Shrewsbury T (Loaned on 5/9/94) FL 10+2/2
Shrewsbury T (Loaned on 3/2/95) FL 5
Leyton Orient (Loaned on 16/11/95) FL 9+1
Shrewsbury T (£70,000 on 7/2/96) FL 11+2/2

CURRIE David Norman
Born: Stockton, 27 November 1962
Height: 6'0" Weight: 12.9
Club Honours: Div 2 '91, Div 3 '95
A gifted Carlisle forward who, after a slow start in 1995-96, again emerged as one of the most influential players at the club. Blessed with the ability to both make and score goals, his hard-working performances were one of the highlights of the second half of the campaign and he was deservedly voted "Player of the Season" by the club's followers. Second top goalscorer behind David Reeves, his 30-yard strike against Brighton in November was reminiscent of his "Goal of the Season" the previous term.
Middlesbrough (Signed on 5/2/82) FL 94+19/31 FLC 6/1 FAC 5+1 Others 2
Darlington (Free on 17/6/86) FL 76/33 FLC 6 FAC 3 Others 5/3
Barnsley (£150,000 on 26/2/88) FL 80/30 FLC 3/1 FAC 5 Others 3
Nottingham F (£750,000 on 19/1/90) FL 4+4/1
Oldham Ath (£460,000 on 23/8/90) FL 17+14/3 FLC 2+1/2 FAC 1 Others 0+1
Barnsley (£250,000 on 5/9/91) FL 53+22/12 FLC 2+1 FAC 4+1 Others 1+1/1
Rotherham U (Loaned on 15/10/92) FL 5/2
Huddersfield T (Loaned on 10/1/94) FL 7/1 Others 1

Carlisle U (Free on 18/7/94) FL 79+1/13 FLC 5+1 FAC 4/1 Others 13+1/5

CURTIS Andrew
Born: Doncaster, 2 December 1972
Height: 5'8" Weight: 12.0
Signed from Peterborough during the 1995 close season, the speedy right winger found his opportunities at York City limited by the form of Jon McCarthy and Rob Matthews, and was freed by the Minstermen in January 1996 to link up with Scarborough on non-contract terms. Unlucky to break his leg for the third time in his career, in a training accident in April, he was released by the club at the end of the season.
York C (From trainee on 1/7/91) FL 6+6 FLC 0+1
Peterborough U (Free on 16/9/92) FL 8+3/1 FLC 0+1 Others 1
York C (Free on 14/7/95) FL 0+1 FAC 0+1 Others 0+1
Scarborough (Free on 22/1/96) FL 3+2

CURTIS Thomas (Tommy) David
Born: Exeter, 1 March 1973
Height: 5'8" Weight: 11.4
The tough-tackling midfielder came to terms with a higher standard of opposition in Chesterfield's return to division two last season and shone as the only ever present. His passing developed well and, with his university course over and full-time training on the agenda, he will continue to improve. He was, apparently, the subject of an unsuccessful six-figure bid from WBA during 1995-96.
Derby Co (From juniors on 1/7/91)
Chesterfield (Free on 12/8/93) FL 120+2/5 FLC 10+1 FAC 5 Others 10

CUSACK Nicholas (Nicky) John
Born: Maltby, 24 December 1965
Height: 6'0" Weight: 11.13
As a striker, Nicky just could not hit it off with Fulham's new signing, Mike Conroy, in 1995-96, but when tried in a central midfield role he showed exceptional ability. His form was such that he ended the season being voted Fulham's "Player of the Year".
Leicester C (Signed from Alvechurch on 18/6/87) FL 5+11/1 FAC 0+1 Others 1+1
Peterborough U (£40,000 on 29/7/88) FL 44/10 FLC 4/1 FAC 4/1 Others 2
Motherwell (£100,000 on 2/8/89) SL 68+9/17 SLC 5/4 SC 3+1/2 Others 1+1/1
Darlington (£95,000 on 24/1/92) FL 21/6
Oxford U (£95,000 on 16/7/92) FL 48+13/10 FLC 3/2 FAC 4+2/1 Others 2+1
Wycombe W (Loaned on 24/3/94) FL 2+2
Fulham (Free on 4/11/94) FL 64+5/12 FLC 1+3/1 FAC 6+1/1 Others 4+2/2

CUTLER Neil Anthony
Born: Birmingham, 3 September 1976
Height: 6'1" Weight: 12.0
International Honours: E: Yth; Sch
Capped by England at schoolboy and youth level, the giant West Bromwich Albion goalkeeper, yet to figure at the Hawthorns, was loaned out to Chester last March as cover for the indisposed Billy Stewart. Making just one appearance, he impressed in a 1-1 draw at Torquay. Earlier in the season, Neil spent some time at non-league Tamworth.
West Bromwich A (From trainee on 7/9/93)
Chester C (Loaned on 27/3/96) FL 1

Another good idea for

BUSINESS GROWTH

Could the right banking services help your business flourish? At the Royal Bank we take a more flexible attitude, providing business banking that grows as you do. From specialist loans to expert advice, the Royal Bank gives you the best answers to the complex problems faced by any growing company.

For more information on how the Royal Bank can help, call free on **0800 880880**.

The Royal Bank of Scotland

Another Good Idea For Business Growth

The Royal Bank of Scotland plc. Registered in Scotland Number 90312. Registered Office: 36 St Andrew Square Edinburgh EH2 2YB.

D

DAISH Liam Sean
Born: Portsmouth, 23 September 1968
Height: 6'2" Weight: 13.5
Club Honours: Div 3 '91, B-1; Div 2 '95;
AMC '95
International Honours: Ei: 5; B-1; U21-5
Central defender with good organisational
ability, a good left-foot, and a no-nonsense
approach, Liam was signed by Coventry
from Birmingham last February to bolster
their shaky defence. Had an immediate
impact, scoring with an excellent header
from a corner at Everton and always looked
dangerous at set pieces. Recalled to the
Republic of Ireland squad by Mick
McCarthy soon after joining City, his best
will probably be seen by the fans next
season.
Portsmouth (From apprentice on 29/9/86) FL 1
Others 1+1
Cambridge U (Free on 11/7/88) FL 138+1/4 FLC
11 FAC 17 Others 15/3
Birmingham C (£50,000 on 10/1/94) FL 72+1/3
FLC 10/3 FAC 7 Others 8
Coventry C (£1,500,000 on 24/2/96) PL 11/1

DAKIN Simon Mark
Born: Nottingham, 30 November 1974
Height: 5'9" Weight: 11.2
Used at right back and in midfield by Hull,
"Biscuit", who saved his more impressive
performances for the sweeper role, was
lucky to see the 1995-96 season after a
death-defying 50-foot plunge down a lift
shaft whilst on holiday in Tenerife. After
fracturing two ribs, suffering a collapsed
lung and cuts to his knee, arms, and head, he
made a remarkable recovery to be back in
action by November. Released during the
summer.
Hull C (Free from Derby Co juniors on 24/3/94)
FL 29+7/1 FLC 1+1 FAC 2 Others 2

DALE Carl
Born: Colwyn Bay, 29 April 1966
Height: 6'0" Weight: 12.0
Club Honours: WC '92, '93; Div 3 '93
Back to his brilliant best in 1995-96, and
voted into the divisional side by his fellow
professionals, Carl scored 30 goals, 21 in the
Endsleigh League and nine in the cups,
including a hat trick in Cardiff's 3-2 win
over Doncaster at Ninian Park in February.
His super form in a poor side saw him sign
a new two year deal on transfer deadline
day, having struggled for two seasons to
make it back to the form of the 1992-93
championship season.
Chester C (£12,000 from Bangor C on 19/5/88)
FL 106+10/41 FLC 7+1 FAC 9/5 Others 6/2
Cardiff C (£100,000 on 19/8/91) FL 144+11/59
FLC 9+1/4 FAC 6/2 Others 17+1/18

DALEY Anthony (Tony) Mark
Born: Birmingham, 18 October 1967
Height: 5'8" Weight: 11.7
Club Honours: FLC '94
International Honours: E: 7; B-1; Yth

The fast winger made his full Wolves' debut
a year after he intended, due to injury, but
was then involved in all but two matches
under Graham Taylor in 1995-96. Helped
create three goals against Grimsby and
among the ones he scored was a 25-yarder at
Watford. Inconsistent, however, he lost his
place, making a brief return over the
Christmas period, before receiving his fifth
booking of a frustrating season. His only
interest in 1996 was in coming on as
substitute against Tottenham in an FA Cup
replay.
Aston Villa (From apprentice on 31/5/85) F/PL
189+44/31 FLC 22+2/4 FAC 15+1/2 Others
15+2/1
Wolverhampton W (£1,250,000 on 6/6/94) FL
16+3/3 FLC 4/1 FAC 0+1

Tony Daley

DALEY Philip (Phil)
Born: Liverpool, 12 April 1967
Height: 6'2" Weight: 12.9
Bulky Lincoln striker who suffered a thigh
injury in a pre-season match and missed the
start of 1995-96. When eventually fit he
found himself unable to win a regular place
and spent most of the season either in the
reserves or on the substitutes' bench, prior
to being freed in the summer.
Wigan Ath (Signed from Newtown on 12/10/89)
FL 152+9/39 FLC 16/1 FAC 11+1 Others 15/6
Lincoln C (£40,000 on 1/8/94) FL 25+7/5 FLC
2+1 FAC 1+1 Others 2+2/1

DALTON Paul
Born: Middlesbrough, 25 April 1967
Height: 5'11" Weight: 12.7
Signed from Plymouth at the beginning of
1995-96, in a swap deal which reunited last
years play-off scorer, Chris Billy, with
former manager, Neil Warnock, he is
predominantly left footed, can play on either
wing, and has an eye for goal when cutting
inside opposing full backs. Was unluckily
ruled out of Huddersfield's end of season

run-in due to injury. Excellent at dead ball
situations.
Manchester U (£35,000 from Brandon U on
3/5/88)
Hartlepool U (£20,000 on 4/3/89) FL 140+11/37
FLC 10/2 FAC 7/1 Others 9/3
Plymouth Arg (£275,000 on 11/6/92) FL 93+5/25
FLC 5/2 FAC 7/5 Others 6
Huddersfield T (Signed on 11/8/95) FL 29+5 FLC
4/1 FAC 3+1

[DANI] CARVALHO Daniel Da Cruz
Born: Lisbon, Portugal, 2 November 1976
Height: 5'8" Weight: 10.13
International Honours: Portugal: U21
Having paid Sporting Lisbon £130,000 last
February to secure him on loan until the end
of the season, the skilful young striker
proceeded to score the only goal of the game
at White Hart Lane on his full West Ham
debut, a header that left Spurs reeling.
Reckoned by Hammers' manager, Harry
Redknapp, to have a left foot like a magic
wand, the Portuguese star of the future
surprisingly managed to make only three
starts before going home. Showed his real
quality, however, in Portugal's 3-1 defeat of
England in the Toulon U21 tournament at
the end of May.
West Ham U (Loaned from Sporting Lisbon on
3/2/96) PL 3+6/2

DANIEL Raymond (Ray) Christopher
Born: Luton, 10 December 1964
Height: 5'8" Weight: 12.2
Signed on a free transfer from Portsmouth at
the start of last season, the left flank
defender soon won the hearts of Walsall fans
with his firm-tackling, positional play, and
readiness to overlap, before losing out to
Lee Rogers, having been injured in October.
Eventually regained his place in February,
after tussling with Lee, and went on to play
in exactly half the Endsleigh fixtures.
Luton T (From apprentice on 7/9/82) FL 14+8/4
FLC 2 FAC 5+1
Gillingham (Loaned on 1/9/83) FL 5
Hull C (Free on 30/6/86) FL 55+3/3 FLC 1 FAC
1+1 Others 0+1
Cardiff C (£40,000 on 22/8/89) FL 56/1 FLC 5
FAC 5 Others 1
Portsmouth (£80,000 on 9/11/90) FL 91+9/4 FLC
7+2 FAC 6 Others 6+1/1
Notts Co (Loaned on 28/10/94) FL 5 Others 1
Walsall (Free on 9/8/95) FL 23+2 FLC 2 FAC 1

DARBY Duane Anthony
Born: Birmingham, 17 October 1973
Height: 5'11" Weight: 12.13
The bustling striker did not enjoy a
particularly happy stay at Doncaster, having
signed during the 1995 close season, a
mixture of injuries and poor form restricting
his appearances. Transferred to Hull, along
with Scott Maxfield, on transfer deadline
day, he proved to be sorely missed during
the Tigers' relegation term. Not scared to get
hurt, in addition to his own solid scoring
record, his bravery created opportunities for
others.
Torquay U (From trainee on 3/7/92) FL 60+48/26
FLC 4+3/1 FAC 1+4 Others 5+3/2
Doncaster Rov (£60,000 on 19/7/95) FL 8+9/4
FLC 2 FAC 0+1 Others 1+1
Hull C (Signed on 27/3/96) FL 8/1

DARBY Julian Timothy
Born: Bolton, 3 October 1967
Height: 6'0" Weight: 11.4
Club Honours: AMC '89
International Honours: E: Sch

Out of contention for a Coventry place in 1995-96, this hard-working midfielder signed for WBA in November, being introduced to Albion's engine room at a time when the team was going through a difficult patch. He did well, initially, but then faded from the scene and was mainly on the substitutes' bench during the last two months of the season following the arrival of the Dutchman, Richard Sneekes.
Bolton W (From trainee on 22/7/86) FL 258+12/36 FLC 25/8 FAC 19/3 Others 31+1/5
Coventry C (£150,000 on 28/10/93) PL 52+3/5 FLC 3/1 FAC 2+2
West Bromwich A (£200,000 on 24/11/95) FL 19+3/1 FAC 1 Others 4

DARTON Scott Richard
Born: Ipswich, 27 March 1975
Height: 5'11" Weight: 11.3

Blackpool left back who failed to start many games in 1995-96 due to the consistent form of Andy Barlow. However, converted to midfield in the reserves, he scored several goals, including a hat trick against Hull City and has the ability to sort out a regular first team place for himself.
West Bromwich A (From trainee on 28/10/92) FL 15 FLC 1 Others 5/1
Blackpool (£7,500 on 20/1/95) FL 23+4 Others 0+1

D'AURIA David Alan
Born: Swansea, 26 March 1970
Height: 5'9" Weight: 11.8
Club Honours: WC '94
International Honours: W: Yth

A stylish midfielder, who was a revelation for Scarborough in season 1994-95, he was allowed to join Scunthorpe last November when the Boro were struggling financially. Quickly settled with his new club as an attacking central or wide midfielder, with a penchant for getting forward, David showed himself to be good on the ball, especially with his distribution.
Swansea C (From trainee on 2/8/88) FL 27+18/6 FLC 2+2 FAC 1 Others 4 (Free transfer to Merthyr Tydfil during 1991 close season)
Scarborough (Signed from Barry T on 22/8/94) FL 49+3/8 FLC 3+2/1 FAC 4+1 Others 2
Scunthorpe U (£40,000 on 6/12/95) FL 27/5

DAVEY Simon
Born: Swansea, 1 October 1970
Height: 5'10" Weight: 11.2
Club Honours: Div 3 '95, '96

Influential Preston midfielder, who was elected to the PFA award winning third division team last season, Simon brings aggression to his ball-winning skills. Dangerous when running directly at players, he has an eye for goal, as his goals tally testifies, while his passing ability opens up many opposition defences. Missed just eight games as North End stormed to the league title.
Swansea C (From trainee on 3/7/89) FL 37+12/4 FLC 1 FAC 1+2/1 Others 2+3

Carlisle U (Free on 5/8/92) FL 105/18 FLC 10/1 FAC 7/2 Others 15/2
Preston NE (£125,000 on 22/2/95) FL 50+1/13 FAC 2 Others 5

DAVIDSON Ross James
Born: Chertsey, 13 November 1973
Height: 5'10" Weight: 12.4

Young right back who played one league game for Sheffield United in 1995-96. After an early season trial with Blackpool, Lincoln showed interest in signing him, but a change in management there led to a cooling off. Following his release by Howard Kendall in March he signed for Chester City on a permanent basis, following a loan period, having already made the number two shirt his own in showing himself to be an excellent crosser of the ball from wide positions.
Sheffield U (Signed from Walton & Hersham on 5/6/93) FL 2 Others 1
Chester C (Free on 26/1/96) FL 19/1

Ross Davidson

DAVIES Gareth Melville
Born: Hereford, 11 December 1973
Height: 6'1" Weight: 11.12
International Honours: W: U21-8

A Welsh U21 central defender who joined Crystal Palace in the summer of 1995 from Hereford United. Had to wait until last November to make his debut and for the remainder of the season he was in and out of the team, alternating with Lief Andersen, Tony Gale, and David Tuttle, and missing out on a Wembley appearance in the division one play-off final. Very strong in the tackle, and a player who has also impressed in an attacking midfield role, Gareth will be expected to hold down a regular place this coming term.
Hereford U (From trainee on 10/4/92) FL 91+4/1 FLC 5+2 FAC 4 Others 5
Crystal Palace (£120,000 on 1/7/95) FL 17+3/2 FAC 2

DAVIES Kevin Cyril
Born: Sheffield, 26 March 1977
Height: 6'2" Weight: 12.12
International Honours: E: Yth

Kevin's skilful, pacy, right-sided attacking play was at the forefront of Chesterfield's surprisingly good early season showing in 1995-96. A pelvic strain, sustained during an icy Christmas game, kept him out of the side as the Spireites tried for the play offs and, with him absent, the attack lost spontaneity and slipped out of contention. Has excellent control and first touch.
Chesterfield (From trainee on 18/4/94) FL 85+10/19 FLC 6+1/1 FAC 3/2 Others 9+2/1

DAVIES Martin Lemuel
Born: Swansea, 28 June 1974
Height: 6'2" Weight: 13.7
International Honours: W: Yth

Cambridge United goalkeeper. Signed from Coventry during the 1995 close season as cover for Scott Barrett, he achieved a first team place in December, following an injury to the latter, and in the next 15 games showed consistently good form, being in the side that earned the first clean sheet of the campaign.
Coventry C (From trainee on 2/7/92)
Cambridge U (Free on 2/8/95) FL 15 Others 1

DAVIES Simon Ithel
Born: Winsford, 23 April 1974
Height: 6'0" Weight: 11.8
Club Honours: FAYC '92
International Honours: W: 1

Simon made only one full appearance for Manchester United last season in the ill-fated Coca Cola Cup-tie against York City at Old Trafford in September and, although he remained an active member of the first team squad, most of his other appearances came as a substitute in the Premiership and UEFA Cup. A midfield player who can run all day, and who possess both skill and vision in his footballing make up, he was recognised by Wales for the Switzerland game, winning his first full cap along with three other newcomers.
Manchester U (From trainee on 6/7/92) PL 4+7 FLC 4 Others 2+1/1
Exeter C (Loaned on 17/12/93) FL 5+1/1 FAC 1

DAVIS Craig
Born: Rotherham, 12 October 1977
Height: 6'4" Weight: 11.6

As the Rotherham junior team goalkeeper, Craig was suddenly thrust into the limelight when injuries to the two recognised first teamers meant he had to play in the FA Cup first round at Rochdale, where he was unfortunate to concede five goals in his only appearance of the season.
Rotherham U (Trainee) FAC 1

DAVIS Darren John
Born: Sutton in Ashfield, 5 February 1967
Height: 6'0" Weight: 11.0
International Honours: E: Yth

An experienced central defender brought in during the 1995 close season from non-league, Grantham Town, on a non-contract basis, for his second spell at Lincoln, he assisted with coaching during Steve Wicks' short spell in charge, but left when John Beck was appointed manager. Later appeared for Leicester United, before linking up again with Wicks in January when he signed as a player for Woodlands Wellington in the newly formed Singapore S-League.

Notts Co (From apprentice on 5/2/85) FL 90+2/1 FLC 6 FAC 6/1 Others 7
Lincoln C (Signed on 25/8/88) FL 97+5/4 FLC 8/1 FAC 4/1 Others 6/1
Maidstone U (£27,500 on 28/3/91) FL 31/2 FLC 2 FAC 2 Others 1 (Free to Frickley Ath during 1992 close season)
Scarborough (Free on 1/8/93) FL 46+2/3 FLC 2+1 FAC 6 Others 4/1 (Free to Grantham T during 1995 close season)
Lincoln C (Free on 6/7/95) FL 3 Others 1

DAVIS Kelvin Geoffrey
Born: Bedford, 29 September 1976
Height: 6'1" Weight: 13.2
International Honours: E: U21-3; Yth

Started last season as Luton's first choice goalkeeper but, despite his shot-saving ability, his inexperience showed behind a hesitant defence and he was immediately replaced by Juergen Sommer, following the 3-1 home defeat at the hands of Norwich. Even allowing for the departure of Sommer, the arrival of Ian Feuer made further opportunities decidedly tough, and although Kelvin played a few more games he was mainly consigned to the reserves. Still a great prospect, however, as his inclusion in the Endsleigh League U21 squad and two further England U21 caps would denote.

Luton T (From trainee on 1/7/94) FL 16 Others 4
Torquay U (Loaned on 16/9/94) FL 2 FLC 1 Others 1

Kelvin Davis

DAVIS Michael (Mike) Vernon
Born: Bristol, 19 October 1974
Height: 6'0" Weight: 12.0

A hard-working striker, Mike was a regular goalscorer in the Bristol Rovers' reserve side, but could only add a further three league appearances to his career total in 1995-96. He did, however, manage a goal in an Auto Windscreen Shield victory at Brighton, before having a loan spell at Irish club, Bangor City, and being released in the summer.

Bristol Rov (Free from Yate T on 26/4/93) FL 3+14/1 FLC 0+1 Others 0+2/1
Hereford U (Loaned on 19/8/94) FL 1/1

DAVIS Neil
Born: Bloxwich, 15 August 1973
Height: 5'8" Weight: 11.0

Aston Villa reserve team striker for three years, he finally made his first team debut with a brief substitute appearance last March in the FA Cup sixth round-tie at Nottingham Forest, followed up by two further substitute appearances in the Premier League. A player who is very quick off the mark and can finish strongly, he will be looking to build on those performances in 1996-97.

Aston Villa (£25,000 from Redditch on 4/5/91) PL 0+2 FAC 0+1

DAVIS Paul Vincent
Born: Dulwich, 9 December 1961
Height: 5'10" Weight: 10.13
Club Honours: FLC '87, '93; Div 1 '89, '91; FAC '93; ECWC '94
International Honours: E: B-1; U21-11

In his heyday a superb passer from midfield, he joined Brentford early in the 1995-96 campaign from Arsenal on a free transfer. Played in seven consecutive games, but was unable to make his mark with well below par performances. At the age of 35, Paul would appear to be nearing the end of his FL career.

Arsenal (From apprentice on 11/7/79) F/PL 331+20/30 FLC 47+5/4 FAC 22+5/3 Others 19+1/1
Brentford (Free on 12/9/95) FL 5 FLC 2 Others 1

DAVIS Stephen (Steve) Mark
Born: Hexham, 30 October 1968
Height: 6'2" Weight: 14.7
Club Honours: Div 4 '92

Commanding Luton centre back whose fee from Burnley was fixed by the Tribunal, following his 1995 close season move. Although more than Town had expected, it proved to be worth every penny as he quickly took over the role as captain and acted as a colossus in an otherwise unsteady defence. Suspended three times during the campaign, his value was illustrated by the fact that all the club's best performances came when he was in the side, while they invariably lost when he was missing.

Southampton (From trainee on 6/7/87) FL 5+1
Burnley (Loaned on 21/11/89) FL 7+2
Notts Co (Loaned on 28/3/91) FL 0+2
Burnley (£60,000 on 17/8/91) FL 162/22 FLC 10/2 FAC 18/1 Others 13
Luton T (£750,000 on 13/7/95) FL 36/2 FLC 2 Others 4

DAVIS Steven (Steve) Peter
Born: Birmingham, 26 July 1965
Height: 6'0" Weight: 12.12
International Honours: E: Yth

Carried on with his impressive form of the previous season at the heart of Barnsley's defence in 1995-96, while his ability in the opposition's penalty area was clearly shown with four goals in the opening eight games, before a knee injury in late February ended his season early. At the back, he marshalled superbly, his great experience shining through. Is always a danger at set pieces.

Crewe Alex (Free from Stoke C juniors on 17/8/83) FL 140+5/1 FLC 10 FAC 3 Others 7+1
Burnley (£15,000 on 3/10/87) FL 147/11 FLC 7 FAC 9 Others 19/1
Barnsley (£180,000 on 26/7/91) FL 79+4/7 FLC 5 FAC 3

DAVISON Aidan John
Born: Sedgefield, 11 May 1968
Height: 6'1" Weight: 13.12
International Honours: NI: 1; B-1

Goalkeeping understudy to Keith Branagan for most of last season at Bolton, his performances in the reserves alerted the Northern Ireland manager, Bryan Hamilton, to his credentials. Despite making just two Premiership appearances, and letting in four goals, he went on to make his full international debut against Sweden at Windsor Park. Now appears to be third in the Wanderers' pecking order behind Gavin Ward and Branagan.

Notts Co (Signed from Billingham Synthonia on 25/3/88) FL 1
Bury (£6,000 on 7/10/89)
Millwall (Free on 14/8/91) FL 34 FLC 3 FAC 3 Others 2
Bolton W (£25,000 on 26/7/93) P/FL 35+2 FAC 8 Others 4

DAVISON Robert (Bobby)
Born: South Shields, 17 July 1959
Height: 5'9" Weight: 11.9
Club Honours: Div 2 '87, '90

This vastly experienced striker was restricted to just a single Rotherham first team appearance in 1995-96, before being loaned to Hull City. There, at 36 years, 131 days, he became the third oldest player to make his debut for the club, his vast experience benefiting a very young strikeforce, especially the precocious Paul Fewings. Returning to Millmoor, he continued to turn out for the reserve team, where he always gave maximum effort and was a perfect example to the youngsters playing around him, prior to being released in the summer.

Huddersfield T (£1,000 from Seaham Colliery on 2/7/80) FL 1+1
Halifax T (£20,000 on 28/8/81) FL 63/29 FLC 4/4 FAC 2
Derby Co (£90,000 on 2/12/82) FL 203+3/83 FLC 18/6 FAC 11/7 Others 4/2
Leeds U (£350,000 on 27/11/87) FL 79+12/31 FLC 4/1 FAC 2+4/1 Others 7+2/3
Derby Co (Loaned on 19/9/91) FL 10/8
Leicester C (£50,000 on 12/8/92) FL 21+4/6 FLC 3/1 Others 3/2
Sheffield U (Loaned on 6/3/92) FL 6+5/4
Sheffield U (Free on 4/11/93) P/FL 9+3/1 FLC 2/1 Others 2
Rotherham U (Free on 14/10/94) FL 20+2/4 FLC 1 FAC 2/3 Others 2
Hull C (Loaned on 24/11/95) FL 11/4 Others 1

DAWE Simon
Born: Plymouth, 16 March 1977
Height: 5'11" Weight: 11.0
Having been given a first team opportunity for Plymouth in 1994-95, while still a trainee, Simon turned professional during the summer. Although the young midfielder appeared as a substitute in the Auto Windscreen competition, he failed to make the progress expected of him and was released during the summer.
Plymouth Arg (From trainee on 10/7/95) FL 3+1 Others 0+1

DAWS Anthony (Tony)
Born: Sheffield, 10 September 1966
Height: 5'8" Weight: 11.10
International Honours: E: Yth; Sch
A Lincoln striker with a good goals record, he was given few opportunities to show what he could do in 1995-96 and was loaned to Halifax Town in March, before being allowed to leave on a free transfer shortly after his return in mid-April.
Notts Co (From apprentice on 18/9/84) FL 6+2/1
Sheffield U (Free on 21/8/86) FL 7+4/3 FAC 1 Others 0+1
Scunthorpe U (Free on 2/7/87) FL 166+17/63 FLC 15+1/4 FAC 9/2 Others 23+1/3
Grimsby T (£50,000 on 25/3/93) FL 14+2/1 FLC 2 Others 1+1/1
Lincoln C (£50,000 on 15/2/94) FL 42+9/13 FAC 1+1 Others 2

DAWS Nicholas (Nick) John
Born: Manchester, 15 March 1970
Height: 5'11" Weight: 13.2
Midfield man who spent the opening three months of 1995-96 on the Bury substitutes' bench, before gaining his chance, initially in an unfamiliar wide-right role, prior to holding down a regular spot in central midfield and playing in the closing 27 fixtures. Is a much improved player.
Bury (£10,000 from Altrincham on 13/8/92) FL 131+13/5 FLC 8+3/1 FAC 9 Others 10+2

DEAN Michael James
Born: Weymouth, 9 March 1978
Height: 5'10" Weight: 11.12
Made the transition last season from Bournemouth's youth team to the first team squad, playing in the centre of midfield and showing good control and distribution in four starts. With a bright future ahead of him, and still a trainee, Michael will be looking for further first team opportunities in the coming season.
Bournemouth (Trainee) FL 4+1

DEANE Brian Christopher
Born: Leeds, 7 February 1968
Height: 6'3" Weight: 12.7
International Honours: E: 3; B-3
Highly popular Leeds' striker, who was voted the club's "Player of the Year" in 1994-95. A regular member of the side last season, who always gave 100 per cent, he was used in a wide, left-sided role and as a central striker, where he looks much more at home. This was highlighted by his two goal performance against Everton in March. Very skilful for a big man, he unsettles defenders with his style of play, but still has a poor goals per game ratio.

Brian Deane

DEARDEN Kevin Charles
Born: Luton, 8 March 1970
Height: 5'11" Weight: 12.8
Sound Brentford goalkeeper and an excellent shot stopper. Another steady season for Kevin in the Bees' goal in 1995-96, with a number of superb saves that secured vital points. Left out for a spell in November, he quickly regained the number one spot and was soon back to his best. Impressed with his early use of the ball.
Tottenham H (From trainee on 5/8/88) PL 0+1 FLC 1
Cambridge U (Loaned on 9/3/89) FL 15
Hartlepool U (Loaned on 31/8/89) FL 10
Swindon T (Loaned on 23/3/90) FL 1
Peterborough U (Loaned on 24/8/90) FL 7
Hull C (Loaned on 10/1/91) FL 3
Rochdale (Loaned on 16/8/91) FL 2
Birmingham C (Loaned on 19/3/92) FL 12
Brentford (Free on 30/9/93) FL 119 FLC 8 FAC 7 Others 11

DEARY John Steele
Born: Ormskirk, 18 October 1962
Height: 5'10" Weight: 12.4
Club Honours: Div 4 '92
All-action Rochdale midfielder, and latterly a defender, who had more trouble with referees than opponents in 1995-96, clocking up four separate suspensions. His finest hour came in the cup-tie against Darlington, when his two goals earned Dale a second chance and, ultimately, the money spinning game at Anfield.
Blackpool (From apprentice on 13/3/80) FL 285+18/43 FLC 20/5 FAC 16+2/4 Others 14/1

Doncaster Rov (From juniors on 14/12/85) FL 59+7/12 FLC 3 FAC 2+1/1 Others 2+2
Sheffield U (£30,000 on 19/7/88) F/PL 197/82 FLC 16/11 FAC 23+1/11 Others 2/2
Leeds U (£2,900,000 on 14/7/93) PL 104+6/27 FLC 8+3/2 FAC 9+3/3 Others 3

DEBONT Andrew (Andy) Cornelius
Born: Wolverhampton, 7 February 1974
Height: 6'2" Weight: 15.6
A third choice goalkeeper at Wolves who joined Hartlepool on loan last October, gave a confident display in his one first team appearance, before being recalled. Later had a loan spell with Hereford United in March as cover for Chris MacKenzie, showing himself to be strong and confident in the air and an excellent shot stopper.
Wolverhampton W (From trainee on 7/7/92)
Hartlepool U (Loaned on 13/10/95) FL 1
Hereford U (Loaned on 21/3/96) FL 8

DE FREITAS Fabian
Born: Paramaribo, 28 July 1972
Height: 6'1" Weight: 12.9
Bolton's pacy Dutch forward made a great start to last season with a couple of goals in the opening three games, but, unfortunately, could not sustain the effort. Drifting in and out of the side, he did score a memorable goal against Nottingham Forest at Burnden, from what seemed an almost impossible angle, and it was a great source of disappointment at Burnden that "Fab" did not get on the scoresheet more often in order to treat the fans with his out of the ordinary celebrations.
Bolton W (£400,000 from Vollendam on 19/8/94) P/FL 24+16/7 FLC 2+4 FAC 1 Others 0+2/2

DEGRYSE Marc
Born: Roeselare, Belgium, 4 September 1965
Height: 5'8" Weight: 10.9
International Honours: Belgium: 60
The 1995 close season signing of this often capped Belgium international midfielder excited the Sheffield Wednesday supporters and he went about his job with the minimum of fuss, scoring a fair ratio of goals. Neat in control, and very thoughtful in his distribution, he almost appeared to be playing at half throttle on occasion and can feel very content with his first season in English football. As proof of his popularity in Belgium, a party of fans came over at Easter to see the home match against Arsenal, and were overjoyed as Marc went on to score the only goal of the game.
Sheffield Wed (£1,500,000 from Anderlecht on 23/8/95) PL 30+4/8 FLC 3/4 FAC 1

DELAP Rory John
Born: Sutton Coldfield, 6 July 1976
Height: 6'0" Weight: 11.13
International Honours: Ei: U21-1
A Carlisle forward who has come up through the youth ranks, he made a number of appearances during last season, scoring his first league goal at Crewe. His ability to deliver a long throw gave an extra dimension to his game and his progress was rewarded with a call up to the Eire U21 side.
Carlisle U (From trainee on 18/7/94) FL 7+17/3 Others 3+2

DEMPSEY Mark Anthony
Born: Dublin, 10 December 1972
Height: 5'7" Weight: 11.10
International Honours: Ei: U21-5; Yth
A Shrewsbury left winger equally at home in midfield, Mark arrived in the 1995 close season from Leyton Orient and held a regular place until a broken toe ended his season and caused him to miss the Auto Windscreens Shield final at Wembley. Earlier, he had shown a keen eye for a goal, scoring the FA Cup third round winner against Fulham that set up a home game against Liverpool.
Gillingham (From trainee on 9/8/90) FL 27+21/2 FLC 0+1 FAC 5 Others 6
Leyton Orient (Free on 4/7/94) FL 43/1 FLC 2 FAC 1+1 Others 5/1
Shrewsbury T (£25,000 on 4/7/95) FL 17+11/2 FLC 2+2 FAC 3+3/2 Others 4+1/1

DENNIS John Anthony (Tony)
Born: Maidenhead, 1 December 1963
Height: 5'8" Weight: 13.0
Club Honours: Div 3 '91
An experienced Colchester midfield dynamo and ball winner, Tony was disappointed to be left out for the opening games of 1995-96 and made his point forcibly with two goals within ten minutes of his first start. Developed more of a holding role as the season developed, allowing his younger midfield colleagues more scope to attack, prior to being freed during the summer.
Plymouth Arg (From apprentice on 3/12/81) FL 7+2 FLC 1/1 FAC 0+1
Exeter C (Free on 15/8/83) FL 3+1 FLC 1 (Free to Bideford on 1/10/83)
Cambridge U (£15,000 from Slough T, via Taunton, on 22/9/89) FL 89+22/10 FLC 6+2 FAC 2+4 Others 7+2/1
Chesterfield (£20,000 on 15/6/93) FL 4+6 FLC 2 Others 2
Colchester U (Free on 10/8/94) FL 56+9/5 FLC 2 FAC 1+3 Others 5+1

DENNISON Robert (Robbie)
Born: Banbridge, 30 April 1963
Height: 5'7" Weight: 12.0
Club Honours: AMC '88; Div 4 '88, Div 3 '89
International Honours: NI: 17; B-1; Yth
Despite the long absence of Steve Froggatt, there was no place at Wolves for the left-sided winger last season and he had a two month loan spell at the Vetch Field, alternating between the left wing and left back for Swansea. An excellent crosser of the ball, Robbie set up many chances for the Swans' front runners before returning to Molineux and playing in the last 20 minutes of the Coca Cola Cup quarter final against Aston Villa.
West Bromwich A (£40,000 from Glenavon on 13/9/85) FL 9+7/1 FLC 1 FAC 2 Others 1
Wolverhampton W (£20,000 on 13/3/87) FL 255+24/40 FLC 12+4/3 FAC 15+2/2 Others 24+2/4
Swansea C (Loaned on 5/10/95) FL 9 Others 2

DERRY Shaun Peter
Born: Nottingham, 6 December 1977
Height: 5'10" Weight: 10.13
Right back Shaun made his debut for Notts

County last March against York City, whilst still a trainee, and performed so impressively that he held his place till the end of the season and signed a two year professional contract in April. Clearly a player with a bright future ahead of him.
Notts Co (From trainee on 13/4/96) FL 12 Others 3

DESOUZA Miquel Juan
Born: Newham, 11 February 1970
Height: 6'1" Weight: 12.6
Striker. Began last season in prolific form for Wycombe, scoring eight times in the first seven games, but had a rather barren spell, before returning to form in February, with hat tricks in the league, both remarkably against Bradford, and finishing with 20 goals. At his most dangerous on the break, where his speed can outstrip any defender, he possesses good close control, a fierce shot, and the ability to fend off any challenge.
Charlton Ath (Signed from Clapton on 4/7/89)
Bristol C (Free on 1/8/90)
Birmingham C (£25,000 from Dagenham & Redbridge, via Yeovil T, Dorchester T and Bashley, on 1/2/94) FL 5+10 FLC 2 Others 1
Bury (Loaned on 25/11/94) FL 2+1
Wycombe W (£80,000 on 27/1/95) FL 44+6/24 FLC 4/2 FAC 2 Others 2

DEVINE Sean Thomas
Born: Lewisham, 6 September 1972
Height: 6'0" Weight: 13.0
Signed from the continent last October, Sean became Barnet's top scorer with a tremendous flourish to the season. Super-quick, he was especially effective away from home when played as a solo striker, scoring on his debut.
Barnet (£10,000 from Famagusta on 5/10/95) FL 35/19 FAC 2/1 Others 2

DEVLIN Mark Andrew
Born: Irvine, 18 January 1971
Height: 5'10" Weight: 11.3
International Honours: S: Yth
Young Scottish midfielder who made a handful of substitute appearances for Stoke early last season. A product of the club's youth policy, who has yet to establish a regular first team spot under Lou Macari, he has done well to return to contention following a serious leg injury.
Stoke C (From trainee on 6/4/91) FL 26+8/2 FLC 1+1 Others 2+2

DEVLIN Paul John
Born: Birmingham, 14 April 1972
Height: 5'9" Weight: 10.5
Club Honours: AIC '95
Starting last season for Notts County on the right wing, he opened his scoring account in the 1-0 home win over Stockport and notched a further seven before signing for Birmingham in February, at the same time as Andrew Legg. A life-long City fan, who can play either on the wide right or down the middle, he quickly slotted into the latter alongside Paul Barnes, proving a lethal finisher, especially around the six yard box. His arrival also solved an acute problem for Brum, in that he could score from the penalty spot.

Notts Co (£40,000 from Stafford R on 22/2/92) FL 132+9/25 FLC 11+1/1 FAC 8/3 Others 17+2/4
Birmingham C (Signed on 29/2/96) FL 16/7

DEWHURST Robert (Rob) Matthew
Born: Keighley, 10 September 1971
Height: 6'3" Weight: 12.0
Dominant in the air, the strong left-sided centre back stopper was just returning to form for Hull after the early season was disrupted by controversial disciplinary setbacks, being sent off at Rotherham and Coventry, when his season effectively ended on 23 December, after breaking his left tibia and fibula at Bournemouth. His lengthy absence must count as a vital factor in the club's poor campaign.
Blackburn Rov (From trainee on 15/10/90) FL 13 FLC 2 Others 1
Darlington (Loaned on 20/12/91) FL 11/1 Others 1
Huddersfield T (Loaned on 2/10/92) FL 7
Hull C (Free on 5/11/93) FL 84/10 FLC 5 FAC 5 Others 4

DE WOLF John
Born: Schiedam, Holland, 10 December 1962
Height: 6'2" Weight: 14.6
International Honours: Holland: 8
The big Dutch defender's long lay off ended early last season, but he was not fully match fit and just when he was re-establishing himself in the Wolves' side he was injured again. Also around this time, he ended all speculation about him becoming player/manager. After more fitness problems he came back strongly at Derby in February and helped Wolves keep a clean sheet, only to limp off against Norwich the following week. Appearing twice more, although only partially, at his best he had a huge influence on the team, and even when struggling he looked to be the best passer at the club.
Wolverhampton W (£600,000 from Feyenoord on 6/12/94) FL 27+1/5 FLC 1 FAC 4

DE ZEEUW Adrianus (Arjan) Johannes
Born: Holland, 16 April 1970
Height: 6'1" Weight: 13.11
Signed at the start of last November from Holland, the central defender made an immediate impact on his Barnsley debut when he snuffed out the considerable threat of Wolves' Steve Bull and Don Goodman. Good in the air, a strong tackler, and an accurate passer of the ball, all in all, he looked to be an excellent purchase.
Barnsley (£250,000 from Telstar on 3/11/95) FL 31/1 FAC 2

DIAZ Isidro (Izzy)
Born: Valencia, Spain, 15 May 1972
Height: 5'2" Weight: 9.6
One of three Spaniards, two of them from Balaguer, who arrived at Wigan in the summer of 1995, Izzy showed himself to be a pacy, right-sided, wide forward, who quickly became a crowd pleaser with his ability to take on defenders at speed. Often a matchwinner, with a tally of 12 goals from all games, he ended the season as the club's leading league scorer with ten.
Wigan Ath (Free from Balaguer on 25/7/95) FL 31+6/10 FLC 2 FAC 4/2 Others 3

Danny Dichio

DICHIO Daniele (Danny) Salvatore Ernest
Born: Hammersmith, 19 October 1974
Height: 6'3" Weight: 12.0
International Honours: E: U21-1; Sch

Tall centre forward who is not only excellent in the air, but also possesses a fierce shot. With the departure of Les Ferdinand to Newcastle, Danny started last season alongside Kevin Gallen as one of QPR's main strikers, and although beginning slowly, after scoring two goals at Leeds in a 3-1 win, he went on to find the net seven times in six games. However, his form and confidence was affected as Rangers slid down the league table and apart from a few substitute appearances, he did not start a match between the end of November and mid-February, when he returned with a goal against Liverpool. Capped for England at U21 level, he was voted the club's "Young Player of the Season" and has the ability to set division one alight in 1996-97.
Queens Park R (From trainee on 17/5/93) PL 25+13/14 FLC 4/1 FAC 1+1
Barnet (Loaned on 24/3/94) FL 9/2

DICKINS Matthew (Matt) James
Born: Sheffield, 3 September 1970
Height: 6'4" Weight: 14.0

Stockport goalkeeper. With a good pair of hands and cutting a commanding figure between the sticks, he lost his battle with Neil Edwards for the club jersey, his only first team game in 1995-96 being a disastrous 4-1 defeat at Wycombe in February and was released during the summer.
Sheffield U (From trainee on 1/7/89)
Lincoln C (Free on 27/2/91) FL 27 FLC 1 FAC 1 Others 2
Blackburn Rov (£250,000 on 27/3/92) FL 1
Blackpool (Loaned on 22/1/93) FL 19
Lincoln C (Loaned on 19/11/93) Others 1
Rochdale (Loaned on 14/10/94) FL 4 Others 1
Stockport Co (Signed on 13/2/95) FL 12+1

DICKOV Paul
Born: Livingston, 1 November 1972
Height: 5'6" Weight: 11.9
Club Honours: ECWC '94
International Honours: S: U21-4; Yth; Sch

Tiny Arsenal striker who, although determined and confident, again had limited opportunities last season and has yet to make the breakthrough that many were expecting. However, in making seven appearances, six of them from the bench, Paul managed a goal in the 4-2 defeat of Sheffield Wednesday at Highbury.
Arsenal (From trainee on 28/12/90) PL 6+14/3 FLC 2+2/3
Luton T (Loaned on 8/10/93) FL 8+7/1
Brighton & Hove A (Loaned on 23/3/94) FL 8/5

DICKS Julian Andrew
Born: Bristol, 8 August 1968
Height: 5'10" Weight: 13.0
International Honours: E: B-2; U21-4

West Ham's left back had a great season in 1995-96, and there were some who felt that he was unlucky not to be included in the England squad. The tough-tackling defender was in top form throughout, never wasting possession, passing accurately, heading well, and generally leading by example. Having been sent off at Arsenal in September, Julian cleaned up his act and did not receive a single booking during the remaining 22 games, while finishing as the club's joint top scorer, with superb headers against Chelsea and Wimbledon, and a thundering shot against Manchester City, included among his 11 goals. Deservedly won the fans' "Hammer of the Year" award.
Birmingham C (From apprentice on 12/4/86) FL 83+6/1 FLC 5+1 FAC 5 Others 2
West Ham U (£300,000 on 25/3/88) FL 159/29 FLC 19/5 FAC 14/2 Others 11/4
Liverpool (£1,500,000 on 17/9/93) PL 24/3 FLC 3 FAC 1
West Ham U (£1,000,000 on 20/10/94) PL 63/15 FLC 5/1 FAC 5

DIGBY Fraser Charles
Born: Sheffield, 23 April 1967
Height: 6'1" Weight: 12.12
Club Honours: Div 2 '96
International Honours: E: U21-5; Yth; Sch

Injury, illness and a contractual dispute kept the experienced former England U21 goalkeeper on Swindon's sidelines at the start of last season but, after being recalled in October, he impressed on many occasions and only twice in 25 league appearances did he concede more than a single goal. The winner of a second division championship medal after Town gained promotion, he is now the longest serving player at the County Ground and has been awarded a testimonial.
Manchester U (From apprentice on 25/4/85)
Swindon T (£32,000 on 25/9/86) F/PL 348 FLC 32 FAC 19 Others 33+1

DINNING Anthony (Tony)
Born: Wallsend, 12 April 1975
Height: 6'2" Weight: 12.11

Unlucky to miss out, due to the fierce competition for central defensive places at Stockport in 1995-96, he spent the first half of the season on the subs' bench, making just one start. In a lighter moment, Tony

made an impeccable appearance as the emergency goalkeeper against Carlisle and kept a clean sheet!
Newcastle U (From trainee on 1/10/93)
Stockport Co (Free on 23/6/94) FL 39+11/2 FLC 2+2 FAC 0+3 Others 2/1

DIXON Andrew Paul
Born: Hartlepool, 5 August 1968
Height: 5'9" Weight: 11.4

A useful deep-lying forward who re-joined Hartlepool as a trialist last November, seven years after first leaving the club, having made a name for himself in Belgian football. However, problems with his registration meant he was forced to turn out as an amateur and although showing some promise in three games, he was then released and finished the season with Bishop Auckland.
Hartlepool U (From juniors on 7/7/87) FL 7+7/1 FLC 0+2 (Free to Bishop Auckland during the 1988 close season)
Hartlepool U (Free from RAEC Mons on 8/11/95) FL 3

DIXON Benjamin (Ben) Marcus
Born: Lincoln, 16 September 1974
Height: 6'1" Weight: 11.0

Lincoln winger who converted to left back during the 1995 close season. Started 1995-96 as first choice in the number three position, but made only one appearance as a substitute in the first team after the arrival of John Beck as manager, before having trials with both Birmingham and Norwich City towards the end of the campaign.
Lincoln C (From trainee on 4/11/92) FL 33+10 FLC 2 FAC 0+1 Others 2+1

DIXON Kerry Michael
Born: Luton, 24 July 1961
Height: 6'0" Weight: 13.0
Club Honours: Div 2 '84, '89; FMC '90
International Honours: E: 8; U21-1

A very experienced and much travelled ex-England striker, Kerry joined Watford from Millwall last January. The fans were unsure of him at first, not least because of his Luton connections, but his astute positional sense and clever lay offs for his colleagues soon proved him to be an asset. Earlier in 1995-96, he had shown that he had lost none of his appetite for the game, when outscoring both of Millwall's big money summer signings. Still very good in the air.
Tottenham H (From apprentice on 1/7/78)
Reading (£20,000 from Dunstable on 22/7/80) FL 110+6/51 FLC 6+1 FAC 2+1
Chelsea (£175,000 on 4/8/83) FL 331+4/147 FLC 40+1/24 FAC 18+2/8 Others 25/12
Southampton (£575,000 on 19/7/92) PL 8+1/2 FLC 2 FAC 1
Luton T (Free on 19/2/93) FL 66+9/19 FLC 2 FAC 7+2 Others 2/1
Millwall (£5,000 on 23/9/95) FL 24+7/9 FLC 1+2 FAC 1
Watford (£25,000 on 12/1/96) FL 8+3

DIXON Lee Michael
Born: Manchester, 17 March 1964
Height: 5'9" Weight: 11.8
Club Honours: Div 1 '89, '91; FAC '93; ECWC '94
International Honours: E: 21; B-4

Lee Dixon

Arsenal right back and, along with David Seaman and Paul Merson, an ever present in 1995-96. Lee continued as a superb attacking wing/back who delivered quality crosses with either foot and with the new defensive formation in place under Bruce Rioch, he was able to get into the opposition's area much more frequently, striking two glorious goals from open play, the equaliser against Chelsea and the other in a 3-1 win over his boyhood side, Manchester City. Also defended well, as the likes of David Ginola discovered to their cost, and when things were not going well he never hid, his attitude being an example to every youngster in the game.

Burnley (From juniors on 21/7/82) FL 4 FLC 1
Chester C (Free on 16/2/84) FL 56+1/1 FLC 2 FAC 1 Others 3
Bury (Free on 15/7/85) FL 45/5 FLC 4 FAC 8/1 Others 1
Stoke C (£40,000 on 18/7/86) FL 71/5 FLC 6 FAC 7 Others 4
Arsenal (£400,000 on 29/1/88) F/PL 289+3/18 FLC 39 FAC 28/1 Others 28

DOBBIN James (Jim)
Born: Dunfermline, 17 September 1963
Height: 5'9" Weight: 10.7
International Honours: S: Yth

After an intermittent start to 1995-96, Jim was effectively a regular on the right side of Grimsby's midfield from the middle of September through to the end of January, until losing his place during the club's indifferent mid-season run. At his best, his movement and passing skills, coupled to an ability to score from long-range efforts, made him extremely popular. However, despite brief returns to the side near the end of the campaign, and bearing in mind that he was 32 years of age, he was released.

Glasgow Celtic (Free from Whitburn BC on 9/10/80) SL 1+1 SLC 4/1
Motherwell (Loaned on 1/2/84) SL 1+1
Doncaster Rov (£25,000 on 19/3/84) FL 56+8/13 FLC 5/1 FAC 2 Others 3
Barnsley (£35,000 on 19/9/86) FL 116+13/12 FLC 3+1 FAC 11 Others 4/1
Grimsby T (£200,000 on 15/7/91) FL 154+10/21 FLC 13/33 FAC 7+1/1 Others 5/1

DOBBS Gerald Francis
Born: Lambeth, 24 January 1971
Height: 5'8" Weight: 11.7

An enthusiastic Wimbledon midfielder who is always looking to get his foot in, moves about well, and has the ability to take on defenders and beat them, Gerald was loaned out to Cardiff last September in an effort to kick-start his flagging career, after failing to appear in 1994-95. Unfortunately, after just four games he was forced to return to London, having aggravated a previous injury, and spent the rest of the campaign on the sidelines. Released during the summer.

Wimbledon (From trainee on 21/7/89) F/PL 21+12/1 FLC 2 FAC 1+1/1
Cardiff C (Loaned on 8/9/95) FL 3 FLC 1

DOBSON Anthony (Tony) John
Born: Coventry, 5 February 1969
Height: 6'1" Weight: 13.6
Club Honours: FAYC '87
International Honours: E: U21-4

Portsmouth central defender, who can also play at left back, where his penchant for strong tackling rarely goes unnoticed. Unable to hold down a regular spot last season, even with the injury to Andy Awford, he merely filled in for others, before being loaned to Peterborough in January. Certainly impressed in his four appearances there, making everything look easy and never seeming to be stretched, but returned to Fratton Park when Posh could not afford to meet the asking price.

Coventry C (From apprentice on 7/7/86) FL 51+3/1 FLC 5+3 Others 0+1
Blackburn Rov (£300,000 on 17/1/91) F/PL 36+5 FLC 5 FAC 2 Others 1
Portsmouth (£150,000 on 22/9/93) FL 44+3/2 FLC 5 FAC 1+1 Others 4/1
Oxford U (Loaned on 15/12/94) FL 5
Peterborough U (Loaned on 29/1/96) FL 4

DODD Jason Robert
Born: Bath, 2 November 1970
Height: 5'11" Weight: 11.10
International Honours: E: U21-8

An outstanding Southampton right back, who also gave some first class displays in the centre of defence last season, Jason missed just one Premiership game during the same period, yet again proving to be a very good reader of situations, a facet of his play that allows him to gain possession cleanly and move forward to lay off intelligent passes and crosses. Although Saints' fans feel he has not received the recognition his ability deserves, his current form, if maintained, could see him breaking into the full England squad in the not too distant future.

Southampton (£50,000 from Bath C on 15/3/89) F/PL 156+16/5 FLC 22+1 FAC 21/1 Others 5

DOHERTY Neil
Born: Barrow, 21 February 1969
Height: 5'8" Weight: 10.9

Neil again failed in his attempt to gain a regular place among the forwards at Birmingham last season, playing mainly as a substitute, and was loaned out to Northampton in February. Returned to St Andrews without ever setting Sixfields alight and has since quit the professional game to concentrate on an accountancy course.

Watford (From trainee on 5/3/87)
Birmingham C (£40,000 from Barrow on 9/2/94) FL 15+8/2 FLC 2+1 FAC 0+1 Others 0+3
Northampton T (Loaned on 16/2/96) FL 3+6/1

DOLBY Tony Christopher
Born: Greenwich, 16 June 1974
Height: 5'11" Weight: 13.0
Club Honours: FAYC '91

Left-sided Millwall midfielder who fought his way back to first team football at the Den in 1995-96, after two years in the reserves. The boss, Jimmy Nicholl, played Tony in a wide-left role, where his neat ball control and clever feints were often seen to good effect, and as a member of the first team squad he will obviously be looking for a run-in the side this coming season.

Millwall (From trainee on 29/10/91) FL 23+22/1 FLC 4 Others 1+1
Barnet (Loaned on 16/2/94) FL 13+3/2

DOLING Stuart James
Born: Newport, IOW, 28 October 1972
Height: 5'6" Weight: 11.6
International Honours: E: Yth

Released by Portsmouth during the 1995 close season, he was snapped up by non-league Lymington. Had an unsuccessful trial with Torquay, before joining Doncaster in October, but suffered throughout the season with hernia and groin injuries, so much so that his first team involvement was limited to one appearance as substitute. Strong in the tackle, with good passing skills in midfield, if he can regain fitness, Rovers could get the benefit of his potential.

Portsmouth (From trainee on 25/6/90) FL 20+17/4 FLC 4+3 FAC 1 Others 4+3/1 (Free to Lymington on 3/7/95)
Doncaster Rov (Free on 30/10/95) FL 0+1

DONACHIE Daniel James
Born: Manchester, 17 May 1973
Height: 6'1" Weight: 12.6

The son of the ex-Manchester City defender, Willie, Danny is a full back who was Mervyn Day's first Carlisle signing, joining the club from non-league circles. Making one appearance as a substitute, he showed promise, before being released during the summer.

Carlisle U (Signed from Radcliffe Borough on 22/1/96) FL 0+1

DONALDSON O'Neill McKay
Born: Birmingham, 24 November 1969
Height: 6'1" Weight: 11.8

A talented, pacy striker, in his second season at Sheffield Wednesday, who, because of injuries and the need for experience in a struggling team, has not made the impact at first team level expected of him. On one of his few outings in 1995-96, he scored in a fine win at Queens Park Rangers, but unfortunately suffered the first of a few niggling injuries which delayed his progress. Will be hoping to claim a more regular starting place in 1996-97.

Shrewsbury T (Free from Hinckley T on 13/11/91) FL 15+13/4 Others 3
Doncaster Rov (Free on 10/8/94) FL 7+2/2 FLC 2 Others 0+1
Mansfield T (Loaned on 23/12/94) FL 4/6 FAC 1/1
Sheffield Wed (£50,000 on 9/1/95) PL 1+3/1

DONOVAN Kevin
Born: Halifax, 17 December 1971
Height: 5'8" Weight: 11.0

Determination was once again one of Kevin's main attributes as he battled away on the right side of WBA's midfield last season. His probing runs, dangerous crosses, and shooting power, often put defenders under pressure, before an ankle injury disrupted his form from March onwards.

Huddersfield T (From trainee on 11/10/89) FL 11+9/1 FLC 1+1 FAC 1/2 Others 4
Halifax T (Loaned on 13/2/92) FL 6
West Bromwich A (£70,000 on 1/10/92) FL 122+14/19 FLC 9/5 FAC 7+1/3 Others 15+1/4

Kevin Donovan

DONOWA Brian Louis (Louie)
Born: Ipswich, 24 September 1964
Height: 5'9" Weight: 12.2
Club Honours: FAYC '83; FLC '85; Div 2
'95; AMC '95
International Honours: E: U21-3

A fast-raiding Birmingham left winger, albeit having lost some of the devastating pace he enjoyed in earlier days, Louie found first team opportunities limited last season, mainly due to injury, and made most of his appearances from the bench. The fact that City fielded a different team almost every week did not help his cause either.

Norwich C (From apprentice on 28/9/82) FL 56+6/11 FLC 13+2/3 FAC 1+2/1 (£400,000 to Real Deportivo on 1/2/86)
Stoke C (Loaned on 23/12/85) FL 4/1 FAC 0+1
Ipswich T (Free from Willem 11 on 14/8/89) FL 17+6/1 FLC 0+2 FAC 2 Others 2+1/1
Bristol C (£55,000 on 10/8/90) FL 11+13/3 FLC 1 FAC 0+1
Birmingham C (£60,000 on 30/8/91) FL 78+34/18 FLC 14+6 FAC 8/1 Others 9+3/2
Burnley (Loaned on 15/1/93) FL 4 Others 2
Shrewsbury T (Loaned on 27/1/94) FL 4

DOOLAN John
Born: Liverpool, 10 November 1968
Height: 5'10" Weight: 10.12

A right-footed utility player who impressed in Wigan's pre-1995-96 season matches before injuries early into the campaign restricted his appearances to just three starts. Able to play in midfield or at full back, John has now been beset by injuries for the past three years and was released during the summer.

Wigan Ath (Free from Knowsley U on 18/3/92) FL 29+9/1 FLC 5 Others 2

DOOLAN John
Born: Liverpool, 7 May 1974
Height: 6'1" Weight: 12.10

Had a very good season in Mansfield's midfield in 1995-96, playing in a poor side that would have suffered even more had it not been for his talented play. Despite having a temporary loss of form in the remaining weeks of the campaign, he was still the club's most outstanding outfielder, before sadly breaking an ankle in the final game. Can also perform in central defence and both full back positions, his energy and enthusiasm superb.

Everton (From trainee on 1/6/92)
Mansfield T (Free on 2/9/94) FL 63+3/3 FLC 4 FAC 3/1 Others 4/1

DORIGO Anthony (Tony) Robert
Born: Australia, 31 December 1965
Height: 5'9" Weight: 10.7
Club Honours: Div 2 '89, Div 1 '92; FMC '90; CS '92
International Honours: E: 15; B-7; U21-11

Another season hampered by injuries for this unlucky left back. Began 1995-96 in splendid form for Leeds, before sustaining an injury at Monaco in September, forcing him to miss the next six games. On returning to the side, he played his way into Terry Venables' Euro '96 plans, when called up for an England get-together. Unfortunately, suffered further problems in the Coca Cola semi final, which was a shame; he would

have been ideally suited to the wing/back role, in the 3-5-2 system then operated by the side.

Aston Villa (From apprentice on 19/7/83) FL 106+5/1 FLC 14+1 FAC 7 Others 2
Chelsea (£475,000 on 3/7/87) FL 146/11 FLC 14 FAC 4 Others 16/1
Leeds U (£1,300,000 on 6/6/91) F/PL 153/5 FLC 12+1 FAC 12 Others 9/1

DOUGLAS Stuart Anthony
Born: Enfield, 9 April 1978
Height: 5'9" Weight: 11.5

Luton youth team striker, with pace and power, who made a scoring league debut as a 17 year old last November against Oldham and won the "Man of the Match" award. Wisely used in his first season, he should prove to be a great prospect as he builds up his strength, stamina and experience.

Luton T (From trainee on 2/5/96) FL 3+5/1 Others 0+1

DOW Andrew (Andy) James
Born: Dundee, 7 February 1973
Height: 5'9" Weight: 10.7
International Honours: S: U21-3

Another Chelsea full back surplus to requirements after the Dan Petrescu and Terry Phelan acquisitions, Andy made just one Premiership start in 1995-96 against Liverpool in the 2-2 draw at Stamford Bridge on 30 December – before a £125,000 transfer to Hibernian in January. During his time at the Bridge, he proved to be a skilful, rather than tough-tackling, defender, and should do well back in Scottish football.

Dundee (From Sporting Club 85 on 10/11/90) SL 8+10/1 SC 1
Chelsea (£250,000 on 15/7/93) PL 14+1 FLC 2 FAC 1
Bradford C (Loaned on 14/10/94) FL 5

DOWELL Wayne Anthony
Born: Durham, 28 December 1973
Height: 5'10" Weight: 11.2

The consistency of Chris Vinnicombe at left back for Burnley last season allowed Wayne only one first team outing before a loan move to Carlisle in March, just two days before the former's injury. Having missed the opportunity to step into his rival's boots, he made several appearances for United in midfield or defensive positions, mainly as a substitute.

Burnley (From trainee on 27/3/93) FL 6 FLC 1 FAC 2
Carlisle U (Loaned on 29/3/96) FL 2+5

DOWIE Iain
Born: Hatfield, 9 January 1965
Height: 6'1" Weight: 13.11
International Honours: NI: 36; U23-1; U21-1

Returned to West Ham from Crystal Palace last September, having scored twice in the opening game of the season. The big Northern Ireland striker quickly won over the fans with his all-round commitment, non-stop running, and workrate, in forming a good partnership with Tony Cottee, his height making him an excellent target man. Scored important winning goals against Coventry and Southampton, not forgetting two outstanding headers against Manchester City. Runner up in the "Hammer of the

Year" awards, Iain also added to his collection of international caps during the campaign.

Luton T (£30,000 from Hendon on 14/12/88) FL 53+13/16 FLC 3+1 FAC 1+2 Others 5/4
Fulham (Loaned on 13/9/89) FL 5/1
West Ham U (£480,000 on 22/3/91) FL 12/4
Southampton (£500,000 on 3/9/91) F/PL 115+7/30 FLC 8+3/1 FAC 6/1 Others 4
Crystal Palace (£400,000 on 13/1/95) P/FL 19/4 FAC 6/4
West Ham U (£500,000 on 8/9/95) PL 33/8 FLC 3 FAC 3/1

Iain Dowie

DOWNING Keith Gordon
Born: Oldbury, 23 July 1965
Height: 5'8" Weight: 11.0
Club Honours: Div 4 '88, Div 3 '89; AMC '88

Freed by Stoke during the summer of 1995, Keith found himself without a club, before featuring in Cardiff's pre-season games and being given four league opportunities early on. His monthly contract ran, however, and he signed for Hereford in September and, as a fiercely competititve midfield dynamo, struck up a good understanding with Richard Wilkins, missing few games other than through injury and proving instrumental in the run-in to the play offs.

Notts Co (Free from Mile Oak Rov on 16/5/84) FL 23/1
Wolverhampton W (Free on 6/8/87) FL 169+22/8 FLC 9+3 FAC 7/2 Others 15+3/1
Birmingham C (Free on 22/7/93) FL 1 FLC 1
Stoke C (Free on 9/8/94) FL 16 FLC 2 FAC 1 Others 3+2
Cardiff C (Free on 21/8/95) FL 3+1 FLC 0+1
Hereford U (Free on 15/9/95) FL 29 FAC 3 Others 4

DOYLE Maurice
Born: Ellesmere Port, 17 October 1969
Height: 5'8" Weight: 10.7

Tenacious midfielder with fine ball control and passing ability, Maurice joined Millwall from Queens Park Rangers during the summer of 1995. Started last season as first choice, but found stiff competition from Bobby Bowry hard to overcome and was in and out of the side. With great stamina, he has all the ingredients, but needs regular first team football.

Crewe Alex (From trainee on 11/7/88) FL 6+2/2
Queens Park R (£120,000 on 21/4/89) PL 6
Crewe Alex (Loaned on 17/1/91) FL 6+1/2 FAC 2
Millwall (Signed on 16/5/95) FL 15+3 FLC 2

DOZZELL Jason Alvin Winans
Born: Ipswich, 9 December 1967
Height: 6'1" Weight: 13.8
Club Honours: Div 2 '92
International Honours: E: U21-9; Yth

The forgotten man at White Hart Lane in 1994-95, Jason made a remarkable return to grace last season, playing in 34 games. A Tottenham midfielder who often scores a crucial goal to turn a game, and confident on the ball, his first touch is usually good and allows him to take time to spread the play from midfield where he likes to run at opponents and get forward. Has matured to become a consistently good player and scored two quality goals in 1995-96, the first being the equaliser against Queens Park Rangers in September, Tottenham having been 2-0 behind went on to win 3-2, and the second came in the final game at Newcastle when he gathered the ball in the 18 yard box with his back to goal turned and placed it beautifully inside the far post, leaving Shaka Hislop stranded and Newcastle's title dreams in tatters. He also scored the only goal in the narrow home win over Southampton.

Ipswich T (From apprentice on 20/12/84) F/PL 312+20/52 FLC 29+1/3 FAC 22/12 Others 22/4
Tottenham H (£1,900,000 on 1/8/93) PL 58+9/11 FLC 7+2 FAC 4+1/1

DRAPER Mark Andrew
Born: Long Eaton, 11 November 1970
Height: 5'10" Weight: 12.0
Club Honours: FLC '96
International Honours: E: U21-3

A key midfield player whose consistent performances for Aston Villa in 1995-96 fully lived up to his advance billing and justified his large transfer fee when signed from Leicester during the previous summer, so much so that he was on the threshold of an international call up by England which, in the event, did not materialise. Scored some spectacular long-range goals during the season, most notably against Manchester United in the opening game, Wimbledon in September, and Ipswich in the FA Cup in February, and provided Villa with more creativity than in recent seasons. A Coca Cola Cup winners' medal in March was a deserved reward for an outstanding campaign.

Notts Co (From trainee on 12/12/88) FL 206+16/40 FLC 14+1/2 FAC 10/2 Others 21+2/5
Leicester C (£1,250,000 on 22/7/94) PL 39/5 FLC 2 FAC 2
Aston Villa (£3,250,000 on 5/7/95) PL 36/2 FLC 8/1 FAC 5/2

DREYER John Paul
Born: Alnwick, 11 June 1963
Height: 6'1" Weight: 13.2

The experienced and versatile Stoke defender who can play all along the back four, despite being more comfortable on the left side. In and out of the team all last season, John still played his part in a number of makeshift roles as the regular substitute, starting on six times in all. And, always to be relied upon, he even turned up with the equaliser against Brescia in the Anglo-Italian Cup in November.

Oxford U (Signed from Wallingford on 8/1/85) FL 57+3/2 FLC 10+1 FAC 2 Others 3
Torquay U (Loaned on 13/12/85) FL 5
Fulham (Loaned on 27/3/88) FL 12/2
Luton T (£140,000 on 27/6/88) FL 212+2/13 FLC 13+1/1 FAC 14 Others 8/1
Stoke C (Free on 15/7/94) FL 20+17/2 FLC 2 FAC 1 Others 4+1/1
Bolton W (Loaned on 23/3/95) FL 1+1 Others 1+1

DRUCE Mark Andrew
Born: Oxford, 3 March 1974
Height: 5'11" Weight: 11.11

Missing the opening third of last season with an achilles tendon injury, sustained during the previous campaign, Mark made a first team return, albeit brief, and, as in previous years, most of his Oxford appearances were as a substitute. The signing of Martin Aldridge pushed him further down the line for places up front and he needs to get a run-in the side to show his pace off.

Oxford U (From trainee on 3/12/91) FL 18+34/4 FLC 1+3 Others 2+1

DRURY Adam James
Born: Cambridge, 29 August 1978
Height: 5'9" Weight: 10.13

Having been an unused sub earlier in the season, the young Peterborough trainee midfielder was eventually given a taste of league football when coming off the bench for the last 13 minutes of the final game of 1995-96. Having been blooded, one can only assume he will be offered professional terms during the summer.

Peterborough U (Trainee) FL 0+1

DRYDEN Richard Andrew
Born: Stroud, 14 June 1969
Height: 6'0" Weight: 12.0
Club Honours: Div 4 '90

A disappointing campaign for this experienced Bristol City central defender. Manager, Joe Jordan, persevered with him throughout the first half of last season, but the return to fitness of Alan McLeary brought only places on the substitutes' bench thereafter. A centre half of the old school, who clears his lines without undue fuss, he could never be faulted for lack of effort.

Bristol Rov (From trainee on 14/7/87) FL 12+1 FLC 2+1 FAC 0+2 Others 2
Exeter C (Loaned on 22/9/88) FL 6
Exeter C (Signed on 8/3/89) FL 86/13 FLC 7/2 FAC 2 Others 4
Notts Co (£250,000 on 9/8/91) FL 30+1/1 FLC 1+1 FAC 2+1 Others 2
Plymouth Arg (Loaned on 18/11/92) FL 5 Others 1
Birmingham C (£165,000 on 19/3/93) FL 48 FLC 5 FAC 1
Bristol C (£140,000 on 16/12/94) FL 32+5/2 FLC 4 FAC 1+1 Others 2

DRYSDALE Jason
Born: Bristol, 17 November 1970
Height: 5'10" Weight: 12.0
Club Honours: FAYC '89; Div 2 '96
International Honours: E: Yth

An opening day injury at Hull last season set the pattern for a frustrating time for the Swindon left back. Returned to the side in November, but his price tag seemed to be weighing heavily at times and he soon lost his place to Paul Bodin. Was recalled in February for six games and although unable to fulfil his true potential at the County Ground, a second division championship medal was a fine reward for just 13 league appearances, three of them from the subs' bench.

Watford (From trainee on 8/9/88) FL 135+10/11 FLC 8+1/2 FAC 2 Others 4
Newcastle U (£425,000 on 2/8/94)
Swindon T (£340,000 on 23/3/95) FL 11+3 FAC 2+2 Others 2

DUBERRY Michael Wayne
Born: Enfield, 14 October 1975
Height: 6'1" Weight: 12.13

One of the discoveries of last season, young Michael was recalled from a loan spell at Bournemouth in November due to an injury crisis amongst Chelsea's central defenders. He came into the side at Leeds for only his second Premiership match and showed such maturity and assurance that he kept his place for the rest of the season. Fast and powerful, he is also a threat at dead ball situations, scoring his first two senior goals against Grimsby and Wimbledon during Blue's FA Cup run to the semi finals against Manchester United, and nearly added a third with a sweetly placed chip which rocked the United crossbar. Such was his impact that Chelsea had to refuse at least one £2m bid before he had even played ten Premiership matches. The youngster's rapid progression was recognised with a call up for England's U21 squad for May's Toulon tournament – the only uncapped player in the squad. Also voted as London's "Young Player of the Year" by *Capital Gold* Radio.

Chelsea (From trainee on 7/6/93) PL 23 FAC 8/2
Bournemouth (Loaned on 29/9/95) FL 7 Others 1

DUBLIN Dion
Born: Leicester, 22 April 1969
Height: 6'1" Weight: 12.4
Club Honours: Div 3 '91; CS '94

Centre forward and Coventry captain. The tall, skilful striker, with excellent heading ability, had another good goalscoring season in 1995-96. Was a major influence on the side's performances in the first half of the season and City did not win any of the four league games they played whilst he was out injured in September and October. Returned in the momentous Coca Cola Cup-tie against Tottenham as a substitute and inspired the team to go on and win the game. He scored many outstanding goals, including a superb header to grab a point at QPR, a thunderous volley at White Hart Lane and one of the skilful variety in the 5-0 drubbing of Blackburn, when he struck out a seemingly telescopic leg to control the ball and finish

Dion Dublin

with deadly accuracy. His hat trick at Hillsborough in the 3-4 defeat marked him out as one of the top strikers around, but he lost some of his form around the end of January, before rumours linked him with a big money move in the summer.

Norwich C (From trainee on 24/3/88)
Cambridge U (Free on 2/8/88) FL 133+23/52 FLC 8+2/5 FAC 21/11 Others 14+1/5
Manchester U (£1,000,000 on 7/8/92) PL 4+8/2 FLC 1+1/1 FAC 1+1 Others 0+1
Coventry C (£2,000,000 on 9/9/94) PL 65/27 FLC 4+1/2 FAC 7/3

DUBLIN Keith Barry
Born: High Wycombe, 29 January 1966
Height: 6'0" Weight: 12.10
International Honours: E: Yth

Keith was continually moved around in the Southend team in 1995-96 to compensate for injuries, appearing at centre half, right and left back and, later on, at centre forward. Although he looks more comfortable at centre half, where his aerial ability is at its best, he always gives 100 per cent wherever he is asked to play and is a useful member of the squad. Also showed he had lost none of his pace.

Chelsea (From apprentice on 28/1/84) FL 50+1 FLC 6 FAC 5 Others 5+1
Brighton & Hove A (£3,500 on 14/8/87) FL 132/5 FLC 5 FAC 7/1 Others 7
Watford (£275,000 on 17/7/90) FL 165+3/2 FLC 12 FAC 4 Others 6
Southend U (Signed on 21/7/94) FL 82+1/5 FLC 4 FAC 2 Others 2

DUGUID Karl Anthony
Born: Hitchin, 21 March 1978
Height: 5'11" Weight: 11.7

Midfielder and captain of Colchester's youth team, Karl burst into the 1995-96 first team picture with a vital goal at Torquay on New Year's Day, before making the right wing position his own for a couple of months. Unlucky not to add to his goals total, he is a great prospect for the coming seasons.

Colchester U (Trainee) FL 7+9/1 Others 0+1

DUMITRESCU Ilie
Born: Bucharest, Romania, 6 January 1969
Height: 5'9" Weight: 10.7
International Honours: Romania: 54

Loaned by Tottenham to Spanish side, Seville, in December 1994, it had been felt that the move would be made permanent at some stage. However, when that failed to materialise, Ilie came back to White Hart Lane last season, but apart from the odd match or two, spent most of his time in the reserves as Spurs' need for an attacking midfielder was outweighed by the need for a defensive one. Nonetheless, he showed great enthusiasm and ball control in the side that beat Manchester United in January, prior to signing for West Ham, a transfer that was not made official until March due to work permit legislation being unwieldy. A player with the ability to both run at and turn defenders, unfortunately, after making just two starts, he was forced to miss the remainder of the programme because of injury.

Tottenham H (£2,600,000 from Steau Bucharest on 3/8/94) PL 16+2/4 FLC 2/1
West Ham U (£1,500,000 on 9/3/96) PL 2+1

DUNGEY James Andrew
Born: Plymouth, 7 February 1978
Height: 5'8" Weight: 10.1
International Honours: E: Yth; Sch

Although lacking in inches, Plymouth's youth team goalkeeper appears to have a big future in the game, as an excellent shot stopper who exudes confidence. Made his 1995-96 debut in the Auto Windscreen Shield, but will see bigger games in the near future. Is still a trainee.

Plymouth Arg (Trainee) FL 3+1 Others 1

Iain Dunn

DUNN Iain George
Born: Howden, 1 April 1970
Height: 5'10" Weight: 11.7
International Honours: E: Sch

A forward who has spent much of his career at Huddersfield, Ian remained on the fringe of the first team in 1995-96. Despite this, he still continued to be a trump card when brought on as substitute, with his tricky play and eye for shooting chances. A scorer of outstanding goals and more at home in a left-sided position.

York C (From juniors on 7/7/88) FL 46+31/11 FLC 3+1 FAC 3+1 Others 1+3
Chesterfield (Free on 14/8/91) FL 8+5/1
Scarborough (Free on 27/8/92)
Peterborough U (Free on 29/9/92) Others 0+1
Scarborough (Free on 9/10/92)
Huddersfield T (Free from Goole T on 4/12/92) FL 61+54/14 FLC 6+4/3 FAC 7+3/3 Others 11+7/9

DUNNE Joseph (Joe) John
Born: Dublin, 25 May 1973
Height: 5'9" Weight: 11.6
International Honours: Ei: U21-1; Yth; Sch

Able to perform at right back or in midfield, he found his first team chances limited at Gillingham and moved to Colchester on transfer deadline day in March 1996, as defensive cover. Looking useful in the games that he was called upon, Joe was one of several former Irish U21 internationals on duty at Layer Road last season. Scored his first goal for the club in injury time at Mansfield.

Gillingham (From trainee on 9/8/90) FL 108+7/1 FLC 7 FAC 5+1 Others 4+2
Colchester U (Free on 27/3/96) FL 2+3/1

DUNWELL Richard Kirk
Born: Islington, 17 June 1971
Height: 5'10" Weight: 11.0

Brought in from non-league Collier Row last October, Richard scored on his Barnet debut at Fulham after coming off the bench. He eventually went on to make a handful of appearances at centre forward without finding the net again.

Millwall (From trainee on 6/7/89)
Aldershot (Free on 19/11/90) FL 0+1 (Released during 1991 close season)
Barnet (Free from Collier Row on 5/10/95) FL 3+10/1

DURKAN Kieran John
Born: Chester, 1 December 1973
Height: 5'11" Weight: 12.0
Club Honours: WC '95
International Honours: Ei: U21-3

The Republic of Ireland U21 international winger was found to be surplus to requirements at Wrexham, and Stockport boss, Dave Jones, snapped him up in a deal which saw Martyn Chalk move the other way, along with £70,000, last February. A fine crosser of the ball, Edgeley Park fans have yet to see the best of him, something that will be remedied as he continues to improve.

Wrexham (From trainee on 16/7/92) FL 43+7/3 FLC 3+1 FAC 4+2/2 Others 15/1
Stockport Co (£95,000 on 16/2/96) FL 11+5

DURNIN John Paul
Born: Bootle, 18 August 1965
Height: 5'10" Weight: 11.10

Battling Portsmouth midfielder who is impressive when going forward, John played in many positions during last season, from right back to all over the midfield and also up front, producing a number of good performances and never giving less than 110 per cent. Netted at Tranmere in a 2-1 win on

9 December and 14 days later scored the only goal of the game at home to Norwich, a result that would ultimately prove vital to Pompey maintaining their first division status.

Liverpool (Free from Waterloo Dock on 29/3/86) FLC 1+1
West Bromwich A (Loaned on 20/10/88) FL 5/2
Oxford U (£225,000 on 10/2/89) FL 140+21/44 FLC 7/1 FAC 7/1 Others 4+1/1
Portsmouth (£200,000 on 15/7/93) FL 61+24/11 FLC 9+1/2 FAC 2+1 Others 4+2

DURRANT Lee Roger
Born: Great Yarmouth, 18 December 1973
Height: 5'10" Weight: 11.7
International Honours: E: Sch

A right-sided midfielder with good ball skills and crossing ability, Lee first came to notice when playing a handful of matches for Ipswich towards the end of 1993-94. Unfortunately, with competition for places hotting up, he failed to make an impact, making just one subs' appearance last season, before being released in the summer.

Ipswich T (From trainee on 13/7/92) PL 3+4 Others 0+1

DUXBURY Lee Edward
Born: Keighley, 7 October 1969
Height: 5'8" Weight: 11.13

After failing to establish himself at Huddersfield, having been the mainstay of the promotion winning side of 1994-95, Lee returned to his first club, Bradford, as their record signing last November. Very impressive when played in central midfield, and acting as captain when Eddie Youds was unavailable, he was an ever present as the side battled into the first division, via the play offs. Incidentally, two of his four league goals during the season proved to be match winners.

Bradford C (From trainee on 4/7/88) FL 204+5/25 FLC 18+1/3 FAC 11 Others 13
Rochdale (Loaned on 18/1/90) FL 9+1 FAC 1
Huddersfield T (£250,000 on 23/12/94) FL 29/2 FLC 1 Others 3
Bradford C (£135,000 on 15/11/95) FL 30/4 FAC 2 Others 3

DYCHE Sean Mark
Born: Kettering, 28 June 1971
Height: 6'0" Weight: 13.2

This distinctive, determined man added to his reputation in 1995-96. Pressed into service as an emergency centre half at the start of the season, he excelled in that position and played his best football there as Chesterfield showed up well amongst the early front runners. Thankfully, Sean enjoyed a largely injury-free campaign – his first in three years. His tough tackling and crossing skills saw him perform in defence and attack with equal confidence.

Nottingham F (From trainee on 20/5/89)
Chesterfield (Free on 1/2/90) FL 183+12/8 FLC 7 FAC 7 Others 16

DYER Alexander (Alex) Constantine
Born: Forest Gate, 14 November 1965
Height: 5'11" Weight: 12.0

Having been freed by Oxford at the end of 1994-95, he was given a trial by Lincoln's Sam Ellis last August, but made little

impression during his short stay at Sincil Bank and moved on to Barnet. Soon found his feet at Underhill, slotting into the left back position superbly and becoming a vital link in a formidable defence as the team found its form after Christmas.

Blackpool (Free from Watford Juniors on 20/10/83) FL 101+7/19 FLC 8+1/1 FAC 4+1 Others 7/1
Hull C (£37,000 on 13/2/87) FL 59+1/14 FLC 2 FAC 4/1
Crystal Palace (£250,000 on 11/11/88) FL 16+1/2 FLC 3+1 FAC 1+1 Others 3+1/3
Charlton Ath (£100,000 on 30/11/90) FL 60+18/13 FLC 2+1 FAC 1/1 Others 3+1
Oxford U (Free on 26/7/93) FL 62+14/6 FLC 4/1 FAC 5/1 Others 5
Lincoln C (Free on 21/8/95) FL 1 FLC 1
Barnet (Free on 1/9/95) FL 30+5/2 Others 1

DYER Bruce Antonio
Born: Ilford, 13 April 1975
Height: 6'0" Weight: 11.3
International Honours: E: U21-7

A skilful, attacking winger or forward, with England U21 honours, Bruce seemed to be the natural replacement for Chris Armstrong at Crystal Palace at the start of last season but soon lost his place to Gareth Taylor and thereafter was in and out of the starting line-up. Despite this, he was Palace's second highest scorer with 13 league goals, which included a hat trick against Birmingham in February. He is still trying to live up to his initial potential which prompted Palace to pay over £1m for his services.

Watford (From trainee on 19/4/93) FL 29+2/6 FLC 4/2 FAC 1 Others 2/1
Crystal Palace (£1,100,000 on 10/3/94) F/PL 30+32/14 FLC 5+2/1 FAC 1+3/1 Others 0+2

DYKSTRA Sieb
Born: Kerkrade, Holland, 20 October 1966
Height: 6'5" Weight: 14.7

Although failing to put in an appearance for QPR last season, the colourful goalkeeper tasted league football in loan spells at Bristol City (September) and Wycombe (March). Proved an instant hit at Ashton Gate as a replacement for Phil Kite, his short spell there allowing the fans to appreciate the capabilities of a top flight 'keeper who commands the area with aplomb, while at Wycombe, in putting his great height and size to good effect in 13 games he also kept the crowd on their toes.

Motherwell (From Roda JC on 14/8/91) SL 80 SLC 3 SC 4
Queens Park R (£250,000 on 22/7/94) PL 11 FLC 1
Bristol C (Loaned on 22/9/95) FL 8 Others 2
Wycombe W (Loaned on 7/3/96) FL 13

DYSON Jonathan (Jon) Paul
Born: Mirfield, 18 December 1971
Height: 6'1" Weight: 12.0

A versatile Huddersfield player whose most natural position is at right back. Given an extended run-in the side at the beginning of last season, he then found himself out of favour before making a handful of appearances in midfield, covering for injuries and suspensions. Is an intelligent player, having obtained a degree from Huddersfield University.

Huddersfield T (From juniors on 29//12/90) FL 72+10/2 FLC 11 FAC 3 Others 7+4

EADEN Nicholas (Nicky) Jeremy
Born: Sheffield, 12 December 1972
Height: 5'10" Weight: 11.9
As Barnsley's only ever present, it was another steady season for the right-sided wing/back in 1995-96. Suffered a little early on from the absence on the pitch of player/manager, Danny Wilson, but recovered and again gave the Reds balance on the right with his assured passing and crossing. Not afraid to have a shot, Nicky scored at Norwich with a cracker from the edge of the box.
Barnsley (From juniors on 4/6/91) FL 127+3/5 FLC 6+1 FAC 7 Others 2

EADIE Darren Malcolm
Born: Chippenham, 10 June 1975
Height: 5'8" Weight: 11.6
International Honours: E: U21-2; Yth
A left winger, capable of intimidating defenders with his terrific pace, Darren finally discovered the art of scoring in 1995-96, netting four in his first 20 Norwich appearances. Spectacular goals too – an arrowed shot into the top corner against Leicester and scorching runs past defenders to score against Wolves and Reading. Unfortunately, he continued to suffer from injuries, including a pulled thigh and calf, and knee problems, such troubles causing him to pull out of an England U21 squad versus Croatia. Sent off at Grimsby for an ill-timed tackle, he nonetheless enhanced his reputation during the season and could shine under new manager, Mike Walker.
Norwich C (From trainee on 5/2/93) P/FL 60+12/11 FLC 15+1/2 FAC 4+1/1 Others 1+1

Robbie Earle

EARLE Robert (Robbie) Gerald
Born: Newcastle under Lyme, 27 January 1965
Height: 5'9" Weight: 10.10
The lynchpin of the Wimbledon midfield. Since his transfer to the Dons in 1991, Robbie has been one of the most free-scoring midfielders in the Premiership, netting an astonishing 14 goals from a midfield position in 1995-96. Although he is currently on a long-term contract, transfer speculation continually surrounds him and he remains a target of many of the top clubs.
Port Vale (From juniors on 5/7/82) FL 284+10/77 FLC 21+2/4 FAC 20+1/4 Others 18+1/5
Wimbledon (£775,000 on 19/7/91) F/PL 170/41 FLC 14/5 FAC 21/3 Others 1/1

EBBRELL John Keith
Born: Bromborough, 1 October 1969
Height: 5'7" Weight: 10.0
Club Honours: CS '95
International Honours: E: B-1; U21-14; Yth; Sch
Everton central midfield anchorman in the same mould as ex-Blues' star, Peter Reid. Crucial to the team's balance, he tends to sit in front of the back four, where his tenacity and strong tackling breaks up opposition advances and, in possession, accuracy is his main asset. Injury frustrated John's first three months of last season, but when full fitness was regained he did not look back, achieving his 200th league appearance for the club against Middlesbrough at Goodison on Boxing Day. A fixture in the side from the end of October, he also scored some important goals, including a strike in each of the Toffees' 3-2 wins over Reykjavic and Wimbledon.
Everton (From trainee on 7/11/86) F/PL 200+10/13 FLC 16/1 FAC 20/3 Others 9+2/2

EBDON Marcus
Born: Pontypool, 17 October 1970
Height: 5'8" Weight: 12.4
International Honours: W: U21-2; Yth
A ball-playing Peterborough midfielder, who is possibly the best passer at the club. Marcus missed very few games in 1995-96, normally being at the hub of things on the right-hand side of the park. Is also Posh's free kick specialist.
Everton (From trainee on 16/8/89)
Peterborough U (Free on 15/7/91) FL 124+3/14 FLC 12+1 FAC 10+1/1 Others 11+1

ECKHARDT Jeffrey (Jeff) Edward
Born: Sheffield, 7 October 1965
Height: 6'0" Weight: 11.7
His non-stop style and ability to slot into any position continued to endear him to the Stockport fans in 1995-96 and, at the same time, he also showed a knack of scoring important goals, notching a hat trick against Lincoln in the FA Cup in November. Although used in more forward positions recently, his tackling and recovery strengths make him a formidable defender.
Sheffield U (From juniors on 23/8/84) FL 73+1/2 FLC 7 FAC 2 Others 5
Fulham (£50,000 on 20/11/87) FL 245+4/25 FLC 13 FAC 5+1 Others 15/3
Stockport Co (£50,000 on 21/7/94) FL 56+6/7 FLC 6+2/1 FAC 5/4 Others 2

EDGHILL Richard Arlon
Born: Oldham, 23 September 1974
Height: 5'9" Weight: 10.6
International Honours: E: B-1; U21-3
Stylish Manchester City full back who shows great promise. Made a confident start to last season, his only blemish being a sending off at Newcastle in September and he continued in a determined vein until receiving a serious knee injury – the dreaded cruciate ligament – at Leeds in December. With City having a difficult time of it and Richard pushing for an international opportunity, it was a huge blow for both player and club. Thankfully, he is progressing well and the early signs are that he will be fit in time for next season. One can only hope that his ability to get forward quickly has not been impaired.
Manchester C (From trainee on 15/7/92) PL 49 FLC 10 FAC 1

EDINBURGH Justin Charles
Born: Brentwood, 18 December 1969
Height: 5'10" Weight: 11.6
Club Honours: FAC '91; CS '91
Spurs' first choice left back for several seasons, Justin found competition for places hot up following the arrival of Clive Wilson in the summer of 1995, but, nonetheless, proved reliable when called upon. In and out of the side throughout the campaign, his longest run-in the team was ten games from December to February, although he was recalled to replace the injured Dean Austin for the final few matches. Always enthusiastic and committed, he linked up well with attacking moves, providing width and depth by his presence.
Southend U (From trainee on 5/8/88) FL 36+1 FLC 2+1 FAC 2 Others 4+1/1
Tottenham H (£150,000 on 30/7/90) F/PL 135+14/1 FLC 15+4 FAC 21 Others 3

Justin Edinburgh

EDMONDSON Darren Stephen
Born: Coniston, 4 November 1971
Height: 6'0" Weight: 12.2
Club Honours: Div 3 '95

The longest serving player at Carlisle, Darren has now settled at right back where his assets of speed and strength in the tackle can best be deployed. With his committed approach to the game, he relishes coming forward and against Burnley in the AWS last season he scored two goals from open play before retiring through injury – all in the first 20 minutes. One of the successes of a disappointing season, he narrowly missed being voted the club's "Player of the Year".
Carlisle U (From trainee on 17/7/90) FL 186+8/8 FLC 13/3 FAC 12/1 Others 20/2

EDWARDS Andrew (Andy) David
Born: Epping, 17 September 1971
Height: 6'3" Weight: 13.7

Birmingham central defender who was signed from Southend during the 1995 close season. At various times playing alongside Liam Daish, Michael Johnson and Gary Breen, despite the lack of a regular partner, Andy showed considerable form before injury and suspension temporarily cost him his place. Strong in the air and good at blocking an opponent's way to goal, he also turned out at full back during an injury crisis.
Southend U (From trainee on 14/12/89) FL 141+6/5 FLC 5 FAC 4 Others 9/2
Birmingham C (£400,000 on 6/7/95) FL 36+1/1 FLC 11/1 FAC 2 Others 5/1

EDWARDS Christian (Chris) Nicholas Howells
Born: Caerphilly, 23 November 1975
Height: 6'3" Weight: 11.9
International Honours: W: 1; U21-1

Swansea central defender. Christian's in-experience showed last season as the Swans' defence was continually changed in an attempt to arrest the flood of goals being conceded. The experience should stand him in good stead, however, as he is certainly one for the future. Made his first appearance for the Welsh U21 team against Germany in October, and in April came on as a substitute for the full Welsh international side in the friendly game against Switzerland.
Swansea C (From trainee on 20/7/94) FL 45+2/2 FLC 2 FAC 1 Others 4+1

EDWARDS Neil Ryan
Born: Aberdare, 5 December 1970
Height: 5'10" Weight: 11.10
International Honours: W: U21-1; Yth; Sch

Having re-established himself as the undisputed first choice goalkeeper at Stockport in 1995-96, with some brilliant displays early in the season, he continued to perform steadily throughout the campaign. Although on the small side for a 'keeper, his positional sense and agility more than compensate for any deficiency and the failure of the Welsh management team to recognise his ability with an international squad call remains a mystery.
Leeds U (From trainee on 10/3/89) Others 1
Stockport Co (£5,000 on 3/9/91) FL 163+1 FLC 11 FAC 11 Others 29

EDWARDS Paul
Born: Liverpool, 22 February 1965
Height: 5'11" Weight: 11.5
Club Honours: Div 3 '94

Custodian for most of last season, the Shrewsbury goalkeeper was more confident on the ground than in the air with an excellent record for saving penalties, stopping one in the Auto Windscreens regional final to set up the day at Wembley. Reflex saves are second nature, although kicking sometimes not.
Crewe Alex (Free from Leek T on 24/8/88) FL 29 FLC 4 FAC 3 Others 4
Shrewsbury T (Free on 6/8/92) FL 146 FLC 11 FAC 13 Others 14

EDWARDS Paul Ronald
Born: Birkenhead, 25 December 1963
Height: 5'11" Weight: 12.2
Club Honours: FLC '85

Ginger-haired WBA left back who struggled throughout last season with injury (back and then a hernia operation). When he did appear, Paul gave a good account of himself, tackling consistently well, although perhaps lacking pace at crucial times, before being given the chance to take over from the injured Paul Agnew. More than capable of playing in the centre of defence, if the occasion demands, he was loaned to Bury in February. Released during the summer.
Crewe Alex (Free from Altrincham on 12/1/88) FL 82+4/6 FLC 6 FAC 8 Others 7+1/1
Coventry C (£350,000 on 16/3/90) FL 32+4 FLC 6 FAC 2 Others 2
Wolverhampton W (£100,000 on 13/8/92) FL 43+3 FLC 2 FAC 2 Others 1
West Bromwich A (£80,000 on 19/1/94) FL 48+3 FLC 4 FAC 3 Others 2
Bury (Loaned on 5/2/96) FL 4

EDWARDS Robert (Rob)
Born: Manchester, 23 February 1970
Height: 5'8" Weight: 11.7

As Crewe's longest serving player last season, Rob hit a golden scoring run with 21 goals to his credit, including a hat trick at Wrexham, following which he signed for Huddersfield in early March. Continuing his goal surge in Town's colours from the right wing, with seven in 13 games, the fans considered him a "steal" and remain convinced that he could be the missing ingredient that will help the club attain promotion in 1996-97.
Crewe Alex (From trainee on 11/7/88) FL 110+45/44 FLC 8/5 FAC 13+5/5 Others 9+8/4
Huddersfield T (£150,000 on 8/3/96) FL 13/7

EDWARDS Robert (Rob) William
Born: Kendal, 1 July 1973
Height: 6'0" Weight: 11.10
International Honours: W: B-2; U21-17; Yth

Rob was settling nicely into the Bristol City side at left back in 1995-96, when illness in the guise of glandular fever intervened. Appeared very capable in this position and if he can recapture his form this coming season, perhaps Darren Barnard can be utilised in a more influential midfield role. Has a sweet left foot and, hopefully, he will at last consistently demonstrate to Ashton Gate fans the ability that brought about his signing from Carlisle United over five years ago.
Carlisle U (From trainee on 10/4/90) FL 48/5 FLC 4 FAC 1 Others 2+1
Bristol C (£135,000 on 27/3/91) FL 104+21/3 FLC 8+1/1 FAC 10+1 Others 8+1/2

EDWORTHY Marc
Born: Barnstaple, 24 December 1972
Height: 5'8" Weight: 11.10

Young right back who was signed by Crystal Palace from Plymouth Argyle in the summer of 1995 to replace the departed John Humphrey and Darren Patterson. A great success in his first season at Selhurst Park, missing only two matches of Palace's 55 match programme, his exciting runs down the flanks and accurate crosses made him a crowd favourite. Unfortunate to concede the penalty in the division one play-off final that led to Leicester's equaliser, and ultimate despair for Palace with defeat from the last kick of the game, Marc's ability to perform strongly in midfield as well as in defence should prove to be a real asset.
Plymouth Arg (From trainee on 30/3/91) FL 52+17/1 FLC 5+2 FAC 5+2 Others 2+2
Crystal Palace (£350,000 on 9/6/95) FL 44 FLC 4 FAC 2 Others 3

EHIOGU Ugochuku (Ugo)
Born: Hackney, 3 November 1972
Height: 6'2" Weight: 13.3
Club Honours: FLC '96
International Honours: E: 1; B-1; U21-15

A strong player with good pace and dominant in the air. As one of Aston Villa's central defensive triumvirate with Gareth Southgate and Paul McGrath, he enjoyed another excellent season in 1995-96 and was rewarded by two call ups to the England international squad, winning his first cap as a substitute in the 3-1 win over China towards the end of May. Played in all but two games of Villa's highly successful campaign and won his first medal after the comprehensive victory over Leeds in the Coca Cola Cup final. Elected by his fellow professionals to the Premier League side on the PFA Awards Night.
West Bromwich A (From trainee on 13/7/89) 0+2
Aston Villa (£40,000 on 12/7/91) F/PL 93+11/4 FLC 12+1/1 FAC 7+2 Others 5/1

EKELUND Ronald (Ronnie) Michael
Born: Denmark, 21 August 1972
Height: 5'11" Weight: 12.8
International Honours: Denmark: 2

A skilful midfielder, Ronnie, who was well known to Alan Ball from their days together at Southampton in 1994-95, joined Manchester City on a two month loan from Barcelona last December. Showed promise in two starts at Blackburn and Leicester, before returning to Spain after four weeks. Earlier, with the relaxing of the foreign player ruling, allowing his appearance as a substitute against Chelsea, City created history when having four foreign players on the field at the same time. Came back on loan with Coventry in March, without appearing.
Southampton (Loaned from Barcelona on 15/9/94) PL 15+2/5 FLC 2+1
Manchester C (Loaned on 23/12/95) PL 2+2 FAC 1+1

Efan Ekoku

EKOKU Efangwu (Efan) Goziem
Born: Manchester, 8 June 1967
Height: 6'1" Weight: 12.0
International Honours: Nigeria: 4
When the strong Wimbledon striker runs at defences it is easy to recognise the kind of form that once netted him four goals in a single game for Norwich. Although his strike rate has not been as proficient since his move, his burly strength going forward has been an important outlet for the midfield and his goals in 1995-96 were crucial to the club reaching the FA Cup quarter final.
Bournemouth (£100,000 from Sutton U on 11/5/90) FL 43+19/21 FLC 0+2 FAC 5+2/2 Others 3+1/2
Norwich C (£500,000 on 26/3/93) PL 26+11/15 FLC 3/1 FAC 1+1 Others 3/1
Wimbledon (£900,000 on 14/10/94) PL 52+3/16 FLC 1 FAC 10/3

ELKINS Gary
Born: Wallingford, 4 May 1966
Height: 5'9" Weight: 11.13
International Honours: E: Yth
Wimbledon left back who started last season in fine fettle, playing in 11 of the first 19 games, before being put out of action with a bad knee injury. Robust and determined, with plenty of pace enabling him to get forward on the overlap, Gary fitted in well with Dons' new approach to play and his ability to pass the ball to feet enables him to play in midfield when required. Is also dangerous at set plays, especially with free kicks and corners.
Fulham (From apprentice on 3/12/83) FL 100+4/2 FLC 6 FAC 2+2 Others 7+1
Exeter C (Loaned on 23/12/89) FL 5
Wimbledon (£20,000 on 20/8/90) F/PL 100+10/3 FLC 8 FAC 7/1 Others 1+1

ELLIOTT Anthony (Tony) Robert
Born: Nuneaton, 30 November 1969
Height: 6'0" Weight: 13.7
Club Honours: WC '90
International Honours: E: Yth; Sch
A talented Carlisle goalkeeper with a good command of his area, he began last season as second choice before taking over from Tony Caig in October. Unfortunately, injuries sustained at Bournemouth caused him to lose his place, but he returned in February for a longer spell in the side.
Birmingham C (From apprentice on 3/12/86) FLC 1
Hereford U (Free on 22/12/88) FL 75 FLC 5 FAC 6 Others 9

Huddersfield T (Free on 29/7/92) FL 15 FLC 2 FAC 3 Others 3
Carlisle U (Free on 28/6/93) FL 21+1 FAC 1 Others 5

ELLIOTT Matthew (Matt) Stephen
Born: Wandsworth, 1 November 1968
Height: 6'3" Weight: 14.5
A classy centre back who will not be out of place in the first division, following Oxford's promotion in 1995-96. Dominating the airways and good on the ground, he notched up eight goals to deservedly win the supporters' "Player of the Year" award. Surprisingly overlooked by his fellow pros for a place in the division two PFA team, a sure sign of his presence can be gleaned from the fact that the team conceded just eight goals in their final 16 games, and half of those came in the only game Matt missed during the season!
Charlton Ath (£5,000 from Epsom & Ewell on 9/9/88) FLC 1
Torquay U (£10,000 on 23/3/89) FL 123+1/15 FLC 9/2 FAC 9/2 Others 16/1
Scunthorpe U (£50,000 on 26/3/92) FL 61/8 FLC 6 FAC 2 Others 3
Oxford U (£150,000 on 5/11/93) FL 122+17 FLC 8 FAC 11/2 Others 6

ELLIOTT Robert (Robbie) James
Born: Newcastle, 25 December 1973
Height: 5'10" Weight: 11.6
International Honours: E: U21-2; Yth
Robbie made a good recovery from the injuries which disrupted his progress at Newcastle over the last two seasons, playing in central defence or midfield, but probably showed up best at left back, where he made his debut for the England U21 team. A strong tackler, who is cool under pressure with excellent distribution and a keen eye for goal, he made few appearances during last season, but after being brought on as a substitute for John Beresford against Villa he kept his place from the last four games with a series of accomplished performances.
Newcastle U (From trainee on 3/4/91) F/PL 42+8/2 FLC 3 FAC 6+2 Others 1

ELLIS Anthony (Tony) Joseph
Born: Salford, 20 October 1964
Height: 5'11" Weight: 11.0
Blackpool's proven goalscorer again consistently found the net in 1995-96, even though he had a lean spell and was left out, leading to him being placed on the transfer list at his own request. As the scorer of superb goals, although overhauled as the club's number one by Andy Preece during the tense promotion run-in, he continued to present problems for opposing defences.
Oldham Ath (Free from Northwich Victoria on 22/8/86) FL 5+3 FLC 1 FAC 1
Preston NE (£23,000 on 16/10/87) FL 80+6/27 FLC 3 FAC 5 Others 11+1/5
Stoke C (£250,000 on 20/12/89) FL 66+11/19 FLC 5+1/1 FAC 1+4 Others 3+2
Preston NE (£140,000 on 14/8/92) FL 70+2/48 FLC 4/2 FAC 6/3 Others 6/3
Blackpool (£165,000 on 25/7/94) FL 81+2/31 FLC 4/3 FAC 4 Others 6/1

ELLISON Anthony **Lee**
Born: Bishop Auckland, 13 January 1973
Height: 5'11" Weight: 12.3
Club Honours: Div 4 '91

Forward. Previously with Darlington and Leicester City, Lee started 1995-96 on trial at Crewe before signing a contract for the season. Unfortunately, he was unable to force himself into the team, with just one substitute appearance and a seat on the bench in a non-playing capacity at the end of the season and was released in the summer. Also played on loan at Stalybridge Celtic.
Darlington (From trainee on 8/11/90) FL 54+18/17 FLC 2+1 FAC 4+2/2 Others 3+1/1
Hartlepool U (Loaned on 25/3/93) FL 3+1/1
Leicester C (Free on 12/8/94)
Crewe Alex (Free on 23/8/95) FL 0+1 Others 0+1

EMBERSON Carl Wayne
Born: Epsom, 13 July 1973
Height: 6'2" Weight: 14.7
Having won his Colchester first team place in 1994-95, Carl made the goalkeeper's position his own, following a string of impressive performances during last season. Ever present, until breaking a thumb at Orient in March, he missed five games, then returned with two more clean sheets to further the U's play-off challenge. Has great presence and is a young 'keeper with loads of potential.
Millwall (From trainee on 4/5/91) Others 1
Colchester U (Loaned on 17/12/92) FL 13
Colchester U (£25,000 on 6/7/94) FL 60+1 FLC 3 FAC 2 Others 5

EMBLEN Neil Robert
Born: Bromley, 19 June 1971
Height: 6'2" Weight: 13.11
Returning from injury, Neil seemed to lack stamina in Wolves' midfield during the opening games of last season, and from 2 September was to start only one match in over two months. However, back in the team when Mark McGhee arrived, he then appeared to be out of position and the manager reverted him to centre half after just one match. From then on he was in good form until he received a head injury at Birmingham, although he soon returned to action, even being deployed at right back one afternoon. Another distinction, of sorts, was that he was the only Wolves' outfield regular not to be booked all season.
Millwall (£175,000 from Sittingbourne on 8/11/93) FL 12 Others 1
Wolverhampton W (£600,000 on 14/7/94) FL 53+7/9 FLC 2+2/1 FAC 6+2 Others 2+1

ENGLISH Anthony (Tony) Karl
Born: Luton, 19 October 1966
Height: 6'1" Weight: 12.10
Club Honours: GMVC '92; FAT '92
International Honours: E: Yth
Versatile Colchester club captain, Tony, played in central midfield and at centre half in 1995-96, during which he made his 400th club appearance. Sent off in the opening game, he bounced back until his season was ended by injury at Peterborough in the Auto Windscreen Shield.
Colchester U (Free from Coventry C juniors on 24/12/84) FL 345+6/42 FLC 16/1 FAC 29/2 Others 22+2

EUELL Jason Joseph
Born: London, 6 February 1977
Height: 6'2" Weight: 12.7

A young right-sided midfielder, cum attacker, and a product of the Wimbledon youth policy, Jason is dangerous with the ball at his feet in wide positions with defenders to beat. Making his debut last October, he burst on the scene in spectacular style, scoring from a phenomenal overhead kick against Southampton and swiftly gained a cult following. Although following that goal up with another against Manchester United, from an acute angle, he still has a long way to go, but he has made a great start and, at the same time, impressed a few good judges in the game.

Wimbledon (From trainee on 1/6/95) PL 4+5/2 FAC 1+5

EUSTACE Scott Douglas
Born: Leicester, 13 June 1975
Height: 6'0" Weight: 13.12
Central defender. After signing for Mansfield during the 1995 close season, having been released by Leicester City, Scott had to wait some time before he was given his opportunity. However, when it came he took it with both feet and progressed following some excellent performances, improving in every match. Suffered a knee injury in February which sidelined him for several games.

Leicester C (From trainee on 9/7/93) FL 0+1
Mansfield T (Free on 9/6/95) FL 25+2/1 FAC 1 Others 2

EVANS David Andrew (Andy)
Born: Aberystwyth, 25 November 1975
Height: 6'1" Weight: 12.1
International Honours: W: Yth
A prolific scorer in the junior side, he made only one appearance for Cardiff in 1995-96, as a last minute replacement for Carl Dale at Cambridge in October. In February, Andy became yet another of the players released in the economy drive, joining Cambridge United on trial but being injured on his first day of training and returning to Wales.

Cardiff C (From trainee on 19/12/94) FL 5+10 FLC 0+2 FAC 0+1 Others 1+3

EVANS Darren
Born: Wolverhampton, 30 September 1974
Height: 5'10" Weight: 11.0
Signed on a free transfer from Aston Villa last September, Darren quickly made the Hereford right back position his own. A very good ball winner, with an all-round game, who can also play further afield, his prospective appearances were impaired by a bout of flu and a sore foot. Was surprisingly freed during the summer.

Aston Villa (From trainee on 7/7/93)
Hereford U (Free on 13/9/95) FL 24 FAC 4 Others 5

EVANS Michael (Micky) James
Born: Plymouth, 1 January 1973
Height: 6'0" Weight: 13.4
A much improved Plymouth player who, in 1995-96, showed the consistency he lacked in previous years. This resulted in his first long run-in the team where he formed a good partnership with Adrian Littlejohn in his favoured centre forward position. More than capable of scoring spectacularly, Micky

opened his account last season with five from his first four games. Can also play on the wide right.

Plymouth Arg (From trainee on 30/3/91) FL 97+33/26 FLC 4+1 FAC 7+2 Others 7/2

Micky Evans

EVANS Paul Simon
Born: Oswestry, 1 September 1974
Height: 5'6" Weight: 10.8
Club Honours: Div 3 '94
International Honours: W: U21-4; Yth
Hard-tackling Shrewsbury midfield man with a strong shot. Always at the hub of things, although needing a little more composure at times, he was in and out of the side on a few occasions last season as his form fluctuated, but always gave total commitment. Won two more caps for the Welsh U21 side.

Shrewsbury T (From trainee on 2/7/93) FL 67+18/8 FLC 7+2/1 FAC 7+1/2 Others 7/1

EVANS Terence (Terry)
Born: Pontypridd, 8 January 1976
Height: 5'8" Weight: 10.7
International Honours: W: U21-4
Another of the Cardiff youngsters who left the club last season due to the economy drive. So reliable when called upon to play full back in the senior side, Terry made just one appearance in 1995-96, the home draw with Barnet in October, before being dispatched to play Abacus League football, despite the fact that he had represented the Welsh U21 side earlier.

Cardiff C (From trainee on 8/7/94) FL 12+2 FLC 2+1 FAC 1 Others 2+2

EVANS Terence (Terry) William
Born: Hammersmith, 12 April 1965
Height: 6'5" Weight: 15.7
Club Honours: Div 3 '92
Injured at the start of last season with a shoulder ligament problem, he scored as a substitute on his comeback in October against Hull, before turning his ankle in his next game and being out of action until returning in December for the remaining programme. His role as captain and centre half has always been crucial to Wycombe, his great height virtually winning all balls in

the air, and for his size he is surprisingly adept at containing the quicker forwards. Also has a fierce desire to win.

Brentford (£5,000 from Hillingdon Borough on 22/7/85) FL 228+1/23 FLC 15+1/4 FAC 17/2 Others 23/1
Wycombe W (£40,000 on 26/8/93) FL 90+4/13 FLC 4/1 FAC 6 Others 4/1

EVANS Duncan Wayne
Born: Abermule, 25 August 1971
Height: 5'10" Weight: 12.0
Tenacious defender who had mixed fortunes in what was his third season with Walsall in 1995-96. Having scored his first ever goal in the early season Coca Cola Cup game at Brentford, after three colleagues had bet that he would not find the net all season, Wayne was called into the Welsh squad by Bobby Gould, but broke a bone in his foot in the game at Bristol City in October and after that found Charlie Ntamark difficult to displace on the right flank. However, he showed his versatility in April when playing three games in midfield during Chris Marsh's suspension.

Walsall (Free from Welshpool on 13/8/93) FL 97+4/1 FLC 7+1/1 FAC 8 Others 4

EVERS Sean Anthony
Born: Hitchin, 10 October 1977
Height: 5'9" Weight: 9.7
A spindly-legged, but hard-tackling Luton midfielder, Sean was introduced to the league side after relegation was a certainty last April against Port Vale and proved himself able to do a man's job. His promise was suitably recognised when he was voted "Young Player of the Year" by the club's coaching staff.

Luton T (From trainee on 16/5/96) FL 1 Others 1

EYRE John Robert
Born: Hull, 9 October 1974
Height: 6'1" Weight: 11.3
Having been on loan from Oldham the previous season, John signed for Scunthorpe on a permanent basis prior to the start of 1995-96. A central or right-sided attacker, who was expected to notch 20 goals for the club, niggling injuries meant he rarely hit peak form. Relies on skill and positional play rather than the physical approach.

Oldham Ath (From trainee on 16/7/93) P/FL 4+6/1 FLC 0+2
Scunthorpe U (Loaned on 15/12/94) FL 9/8
Scunthorpe U (£40,000 on 4/7/95) FL 36+3/10 FLC 2/2 FAC 3/1 Others 2/1

EYRES David
Born: Liverpool, 26 February 1964
Height: 5'10" Weight: 11.8
Seldom out of the Burnley side last season, David was not only employed in his normal left wing role, but also as a central striker, an emergency left back, or wing/back, and even once between the sticks following Wayne Russell's sending off against Bournemouth. His killer instinct near goal was seen less often than before, but his contribution in a struggling side was seldom in doubt.

Blackpool (£10,000 from Rhyl on 15/8/89) FL 147+11/38 FLC 11+1/1 FAC 11/2 Others 13+2/4
Burnley (£90,000 on 29/7/93) FL 122+4/33 FLC 9/3 FAC 10/7 Others 7/2

F

FAIRCLOUGH Courtney (Chris) Huw
Born: Nottingham, 12 April 1964
Height: 5'11" Weight: 11.7
Club Honours: Div 2 '90, Div 1 '92; CS '92
International Honours: E: B-1; U21-7
Bolton's first signing for the 1995-96 season was the experienced defender from Leeds United. An honest hard-working player, Chris produced many consistent displays with his strong tackling giving a number of opposing forwards a torrid time and he appeared to have lost none of his zest for the game. After two defeats by his former club at Burnden in league and cup games, he was a cornerstone of the Wanderers' side that went to Elland Road and won with their first clean sheet on away territory in the Premiership.
Nottingham F (From apprentice on 12/10/81) FL 102+5/1 FLC 9+1/1 FAC 6 Others 9+2
Tottenham H (£387,000 on 3/7/87) FL 60/5 FLC 7 FAC 3
Leeds U (£500,000 on 23/3/89) FL 187+6/21 FLC 17+2/2 FAC 14+1 Others 14
Bolton W (£500,000 on 4/7/95) PL 33 FLC 6 FAC 2

Chris Fairclough

FAIRCLOUGH Wayne Ricks
Born: Nottingham, 27 April 1968
Height: 5'10" Weight: 12.2
The fine form showed by the likes of Sean Dyche and Mark Williams in Chesterfield's defence last season, left Wayne with few opportunities, and he was allowed to go on loan to Scarborough in March, giving some steady performances during his one month spell. An experienced defender, he can also adapt to a central defensive role if required. Released during the summer.
Notts Co (From apprentice on 28/4/86) FL 39+32 FLC 1+2 FAC 3 Others 10+3

Mansfield T (£80,000 on 5/3/90) FL 131+10/12 FLC 5 FAC 4+1/1 Others 10
Chesterfield (Free on 23/6/94) FL 12+3 FLC 3 FAC 2 Others 3+1
Scarborough (Loaned on 28/3/96) FL 7

FARNWORTH Simon
Born: Chorley, 28 October 1963
Height: 6'0" Weight: 11.13
International Honours: E: Sch
Experienced shot-stopping goalkeeper now in his third season at Wigan Athletic. After missing the first five matches of last season, he regained his first team place from David Felgate, producing the best form of his career, before going on to pass a century of league appearances for the club.
Bolton W (From apprentice on 5/9/81) FL 113 FLC 11 FAC 6 Others 8
Stockport Co (Loaned on 11/9/86) FL 10 FLC 2
Tranmere Rov (Loaned on 9/1/87) FL 7
Bury (Free on 12/3/87) FL 105 FLC 11 FAC 3 Others 5
Preston NE (Free on 1/7/90) FL 81 FLC 6 FAC 3 Others 7
Wigan Ath (Free on 27/7/93) FL 126 FLC 6 FAC 10 Others 9

FARRELL Andrew (Andy) James
Born: Colchester, 7 October 1965
Height: 5'11" Weight: 11.0
Club Honours: Div 4 '92
A solid if unspectacular Wigan performer, either in defence or midfield, his opportunities last season were restricted simply by the strength of competition at the club. Never let the side down when playing and scored his first league goal for Latics at Plymouth in December.
Colchester U (From apprentice on 21/9/83) FL 98+7/5 FLC 9 FAC 8 Others 6
Burnley (£13,000 on 7/8/87) FL 237+20/19 FLC 17+4/1 FAC 19+2 Others 27+3/3
Wigan Ath (£20,000 on 22/9/94) FL 51+3/1 FLC 3 FAC 4+1 Others 5/1

FARRELL David (Dave) William
Born: Birmingham, 11 November 1971
Height: 5'11" Weight: 11.9
An early season signing from Aston Villa in 1995-96, he quickly established himself at Wycombe and became widely regarded as the best left winger in the division, having the speed to beat defenders and deliver good crosses with either foot. Suffered a loss of form in March, but returned as an effective striking partner for John Williams, scoring three goals in the process.
Aston Villa (£45,000 from Redditch U on 6/1/92) F/PL 5+1 FLC 2
Scunthorpe U (Loaned on 25/1/93) FL 4+1/1 Others 2
Wycombe W (£100,000 on 14/9/95) FL 27+6/5 FLC 2 FAC 2 Others 2

FARRELL Sean Paul
Born: Watford, 28 February 1969
Height: 6'0" Weight: 13.7
Second only to Gary Martindale in the Peterborough goalscoring stakes in 1995-96, the young striker was just running into a good vein of form early on when injury put him out of the game for quite a chunk of the season. However, 13 goals from 35 games, nine of them as a substitute, was not bad by any standards.

Luton T (From apprentice on 5/3/87) FL 14+11/1 FAC 2+1/1 Others 1+2/2
Colchester U (Loaned on 1/3/88) FL 4+5/1
Northampton T (Loaned on 13/9/91) FL 4/1
Fulham (£100,000 on 19/12/91) FL 93+1/31 FLC 5+1/3 FAC 2/3 Others 8/1
Peterborough U (£120,000 on 5/8/94) FL 45+14/17 FLC 3+1 FAC 4+1/3 Others 3+1/1

FARRELLY Gareth
Born: Dublin, 28 August 1975
Height: 6'1" Weight: 12.7
International Honours: Ei: 3; U21-4; Yth; Sch
A midfield player with Irish Republic U21 honours, he was added to the Aston Villa first team squad in mid-season, making three appearances as substitute before starting his first full game away to Liverpool last March. This proved to be a real "baptism of fire", as Villa were three goals down within eight minutes before recovering to prevent further damage. A player for the future and likely to make further progress in 1996-97, Gareth graduated to full international status with his first cap for Ireland versus Portugal in late May, before going on to play twice more.
Aston Villa (From trainee on 21/1/92) PL 1+4 FLC 0+1
Rotherham U (Loaned on 21/3/95) FL 9+1/2

FEAR Peter Stanley
Born: Sutton, 10 September 1973
Height: 5'10" Weight: 11.7
International Honours: E: U21-3
Following a good start to last season, Peter was unable to hold his place in the centre of Wimbledon's midfield and was consigned to reserve team football for the remainder of the campaign. However, his ability to tackle and cut down opponents' space, coupled to speed and good passing skills, make him a huge asset for the club, both financially and on the field of play if used, and he is bound to be back before long.
Wimbledon (From trainee on 2/7/92) PL 37+8/2 FLC 3+2 FAC 2

FEARON Ronald (Ron) Thomas
Born: Romford, 19 November 1960
Height: 6'0" Weight: 12.2
An experienced goalkeeper, Ron joined Leyton Orient prior to the start of 1995-96, having previously been playing five-a-side football in America. A good shot stopper, he stepped in to replace the struggling Peter Caldwell in November and, despite his lack of inches occasionally being a handicap, he performed well in his 20 appearances, before being released at the end of the season.
Reading (Signed from Dover on 23/2/80) FL 61 FLC 4 FAC 2 (Free to San Diego Sockers during 1983 close season)
Ipswich T (Signed from Sutton U on 9/9/87) FL 28 FAC 1 Others 2 (Free to Sutton U on 8/2/93)
Brighton & Hove A (Loaned on 23/9/88) FL 7
Walsall (Loaned on 1/2/93) FL 1
Southend U (Free on 22/10/93 - Released in January 1994)
Leyton Orient (Free from Ashford T and American Five-a-Side soccer on 10/8/95) FL 18 FAC 1 Others 1

FELGATE David Wynne
Born: Blaenau, Ffestiniog, 4 March 1960
Height: 6'1" Weight: 15.0
Club Honours: AMC '89
International Honours: W: 1; Sch

Reunited with his former manager, Graham Barrow, at Wigan prior to the start of last season, having been freed by Chester, he appeared in the first five games. However, a freak injury during the kick about before a league match against his former club on the 29 August, saw the return of Simon Farnworth, while David, when fit again, played out the rest of the campaign in the reserves. Was released during the summer.

Bolton W (From Blaenau Ffestiniog on 1/8/78)
Rochdale (Loaned on 7/10/78) FL 35
Crewe Alex (Loaned on 27/9/79) FL 14
Rochdale (Loaned on 9/3/80) FL 12
Lincoln C (£25,000 on 5/9/80) FL 198 FLC 16 FAC 10 Others 2
Cardiff C (Loaned on 1/12/84) FL 4
Grimsby T (£27,000 on 23/2/85) FL 36 FLC 2 FAC 1
Bolton W (Loaned on 14/2/86) FL 15 Others 4
Bolton W (£15,000 on 17/2/87) FL 223 FLC 14 FAC 17 Others 27
Bury (Free on 17/7/93)
Wolverhampton W (Free on 12/8/93)
Chester C (Free on 1/10/93) FL 71+1 FLC 2 FAC 6 Others 5
Wigan Ath (Free on 4/7/95) FL 3 FLC 2

FENSOME Andrew (Andy) Brian
Born: Northampton, 18 February 1969
Height: 5'8" Weight: 11.2
Club Honours: Div 3 '91, '96

"Player of the Year" at the end of the previous campaign, Andy had a more in and out time at Preston in 1995-96. Never letting North End down from right back, combining well with Lee Cartwright on that flank, his exclusion from the team in mid-season was a mystery to many fans. Good on the overlap, and sound defensively, he is also a long-throw specialist. Was released during the summer, despite playing 20 league games and winning a third division championship medal.

Norwich C (From apprentice on 16/2/87)
Cambridge U (Free from Bury T on 21/11/89) FL 122+4/1 FLC 11 FAC 17+2 Others 9+1
Preston NE (Signed on 8/10/93 FL 93/1 FLC 3/1 FAC 9 Others 11

FENTON Graham Anthony
Born: Wallsend, 22 May 1974
Height: 5'10" Weight: 11.9
Club Honours: FLC '94, '96
International Honours: E: U21-1

Starting last season with Aston Villa, following just five appearances from the bench, he moved to Blackburn in November. A quick and forceful utility forward who likes to get into the box, he shows great coolness when given a scoring chance. Disconsolately, after signing for Rovers, he twice developed hamstring problems that retarded his progress and consequently had to settle for a substitute spot. However, he became the most visible sub of the campaign when his two goals in the last five minutes helped defeat Newcastle on Easter Monday and virtually handed the title to Manchester United.

Aston Villa (From trainee on 13/2/92) PL 16+16/3 FLC 2+5
West Bromwich A (Loaned on 10/1/94) FL 7/3
Blackburn Rov (£1,500,000 on 7/11/95) PL 4+10/6

FERDINAND Leslie (Les)
Born: Acton, 8 December 1966
Height: 5'11" Weight: 13.5
Club Honours: Turkish Cup '89 (During loan spell in 1988-89 with Besiktas)
International Honours: E: 10

Having signed from QPR during the 1995 close season, possessing great natural strength and electrifying pace, Les led the Newcastle attack well, coming short off defenders and using the ball unselfishly to bring colleagues into the game. Good in the air, where his spring enabled him to outjump taller defenders, his all-round game brought an extra dimension to the Newcastle attack and he set a new post-war club record by scoring in eight consecutive matches, while breaking his personal record haul for a season when netting 29 times. His good form was rewarded by a recall to the England team after a wait of two years and he scored against Bulgaria, his excellent performances leading to his selection as Newcastle's "Player of the Year". Also chosen as the PFA "Player of the Year", he was the first United player to win the award which was presented to him by the legendary Pele.

Queens Park R (£15,000 from Hayes on 12/3//87) F/PL 152+11/80 FLC 11+2/7 FAC 6+1/3 Others 1
Brentford (Loaned on 24/3/88) FL 3
Newcastle U (£6,000,000 on 7/6/95) PL 37/25 FLC 5/3 FAC 2/1

Les Ferdinand

FERDINAND Rio Gavin
Born: London, 7 November 1978
Height: 6'2" Weight: 12.1
International Honours: E: Yth

A young West Ham centre back who is calm under pressure and strong in the air, Rio was given his first taste of Premiership football in the last 22 minutes of the final game of the 1995-96 season against Sheffield Wednesday. Looking to have a promising future, he also played a big part in getting the Hammers to the FA Youth Cup final. Is the cousin of Newcastle's Les.

West Ham U (From trainee on 27/11/95) PL 0+1

FERGUSON Darren
Born: Glasgow, 9 February 1972
Height: 5'10" Weight: 11.10
Club Honours: PL '93
International Honours: S: U21-5; Yth

Wolves' midfielder. Missed the opening three games of 1995-96, but replaced Gordon Cowans for the following 11 until 14 October. His next start was in November when he got a superb opening goal for the club in the Coca Cola Cup against Coventry, beating two players and giving the goalkeeper no chance. This began a 16-match run, before being dropped, prior to coming back strongly to be involved in seven of the last eight matches. Is the son of Manchester United manager, Alex.

Manchester U (From trainee on 11/7/90) F/PL 20+7 FLC 2+1
Wolverhampton W (£250,000 on 13/1/94) FL 60+11/1 FLC 7/1 FAC 7+1/1 Others 4

FERGUSON Duncan
Born: Stirling, 27 December 1971
Height: 6'4" Weight: 14.6
Club Honours: SL '94; SLC '94; FAC '95
International Honours: S: 5; B; U21-7; Yth; Sch

Extremely physical Everton target man in the traditional sense. Putting his size to good use when getting in front of defenders, and a master of the flick on, he is lethal at set pieces where his presence unnerves the coolest of stoppers. He also holds the ball up well. Unfortunately, the 1995-96 season emerged as a personal nightmare as continual niggling injuries dogged him from the beginning of the campaign. This was nothing compared to unceremoniously being imprisoned for two months, following a violent conduct charge whilst with Glasgow Rangers, and then suspended for a number of games. Having returned to first team action in December, and scoring a brace against Wimbledon on New Year's Day, he was again unable to shake off persistent injury problems and can only hope of getting back to full fitness this summer.

Dundee U (Signed from Carse Thistle on 1/2/90) SL 75+2/27 SLC 2+1/2 SC 6/4
Glasgow R (£4,000,000 on 20/7/93) SL 8+6/2 SLC 2+2/3 SC 0+3 Others 1
Everton (£4,400,000 on 4/10/94) PL 38+3/12 FLC 1 FAC 5+1/3

FERNANDES Tamer Hasan
Born: Paddington, 7 December 1974
Height: 6'3" Weight: 13.7
International Honours: E: Yth

Tall Brentford reserve goalkeeper. In 1995-96, he again proved a good understudy to Kevin Dearden, keeping a clean sheet at Farnborough in the FA Cup-tie shown live

on Sky Sports, during a spell of six successive games for the club.
Brentford (From trainee on 12/7/93) FL 8+2 FAC 2 Others 1+1

FETTIS Alan William
Born: Belfast, 1 February 1971
Height: 6'1" Weight:11.4
International Honours: NI: 15; B-2; Yth; Sch

The Northern Ireland international goal-keeper began 1995-96 in dispute at Hull City, playing just nine times and being loaned to WBA in November, where he conceded eight goals in three games, before being transferred to Nottingham Forest to understudy Mark Crossley in January. An excellent shot stopper with great reflexes, Alan has yet to make his debut for Forest.
Hull C (£50,000 from Ards on 14/8/91) FL 131+4/2 FLC 7+1 FAC 5 Others 7
West Bromwich A (Loaned on 20/11/95) FL 3
Nottingham F (£250,000 on 13/1/96)

Alan Fettis

FEUER Anthony **Ian**
Born: Las Vegas, USA, 20 May 1971
Height: 6'7" Weight: 14.0

Supremely tall and able Luton goalkeeper, originally signed on loan from West Ham last September to take over from fellow American, Juergen Sommer, who had been sold to QPR. Ian enjoyed tremendous form in his first season at Town and must be favoured to eventually take over from Kasey Keller and Sommer in the pecking order for a place in the USA national team. When his loan period ended, Luton were forced to spend virtually all the Sommer fee to secure him, but the general consensus felt that it was money well spent. Despite occasional lapses as the last line in a bottom of the table club, his form shone through in a poor side, where he used his height to great advantage and was regularly the best player. Was elected "Player of the Year" by the supporters.
West Ham U (£70,000 on 23/3/94)
Peterborough U (Loaned on 20/2/95) FL 16
Luton T (£580,000 on 11/9/95) FL 38 FAC 1

FEWINGS Paul John
Born: Hull, 18 February 1978
Height: 5'11" Weight: 11.7

After breaking into the first team towards the end of the previous season, Paul continued his sensational progress as a right-footed striker by being awarded a three year professional contract at the age of 17 – a unique offer by the Hull club. Still learning his trade, he admirably carried the heavy burden of City's attacking hopes for much of 1995-96 and as a sharp finisher and intelligent runner, Fewings is a name to look out for in the future.
Hull C (From trainee on 4/8/95) FL 16+11/2 FLC 3+1/1 FAC 2 Others 0+1/1

FICKLING Ashley
Born: Sheffield, 15 November 1972
Height: 5'10" Weight: 11.6
International Honours: E: Sch

A hard-tackling Grimsby full back, who can also play in central defence if required, his opportunities for first team football were limited due to the club's strength in the defensive department. However, drafted in for the fourth round FA Cup replay against West Ham, Ashley gave a sterling per-formance, his through ball creating the opening goal in a 3-0 victory. Has a great enthusiasm for the game.
Sheffield U (From juniors on 26/7/91) FLC 2+1 Others 3
Darlington (Loaned on 26/11/92) FL 14 Others 1
Darlington (Loaned on 12/8/93) FL 1 FLC 1
Grimsby T (Free on 23/3/95) FL 6+6 FLC 2 FAC 1+1

FIDLER Richard Michael
Born: Sheffield, 26 October 1976
Height: 5'9" Weight: 10.7
International Honours: E: Sch

Having signed from Leeds United, where he was a YTS, last December, Richard made his only Hull City appearance in the home 2-5 drubbing by Carlisle United the day after he had been snapped up. Although a talented and composed youngster who can fill any of the left-flank positions, he was released in March.
Hull C (Free from Leeds U juniors on 8/12/95) FL 0+1

FILAN John Richard
Born: Sydney, Australia, 8 February 1970
Height: 5'11" Weight: 13.2
International Honours: Australia: U21

Australian goalkeeper who played the first 12 league games of last season for Coventry whilst Steve Ogrizovic was injured. A good kicker, who handles crosses confidently, he could not be faulted for any of the 24 goals conceded during that period, but, recalled at Villa Park when "Oggy" was suspended, John was left badly exposed in the 1-4 defeat. Spent the remainder of the campaign on the bench.
Cambridge U (£40,000 from Budapest St George on 12/3/93) FL 68 FLC 6 FAC 3 Others 3
Coventry C (£300,000 on 2/3/95) PL 15 FLC 2

FINN Neil Edward
Born: London, 29 December 1978
Height: 6'0" Weight: 12.4

At 17 years of age, the West Ham youth team goalkeeper became the youngest player ever to appear in the Premiership when called into the side on New Year's Day, 1996, after both Ludo Miklosko and Les Sealey had been pronounced unfit for duty. Acquitting himself well in the 2-1 defeat, he would later be a member of the junior team that lost in the FA Youth Cup final against Liverpool.
West Ham U (Trainee) PL 1

FINNAN Stephen (Steve) John
Born: Limerick, 20 April 1976
Height: 6'0" Weight: 12.0
International Honours: Ei: U21-1

Another Birmingham find from non-league soccer during the 1995 close season, Steve made a dramatic introduction to league football when scoring from a free kick at Watford. However, with so many mid-fielders at the club, and opportunities limited, he had a three month spell on loan at Notts County in March, playing on the wide right and proved to be pacy and skilful, while always looking to float the ball in to the main strikers. His good form did not go unnoticed and he was selected for the Republic of Ireland U21 squad, making his debut against Norway at the end of May, scoring the equaliser in a 1-1 draw. Also has an excellent long throw.
Birmingham C (£100,000 from Welling U on 12/6/95) FL 6+6/1 FLC 2+2 Others 2+1
Notts Co (Loaned on 5/3/96) FL 14+3/2 Others 3/1

FINNEY Stephen (Steve) Kenneth
Born: Hexham, 31 October 1973
Height: 5'10" Weight: 12.0
Club Honours: Div 2 '96

Plucked from Central League football during the 1995 close season, Steve scored twice on his home debut for Swindon and never looked back. Having signed from a free transfer from Manchester City, he was only in the side due to an injury to Peter Thorne, but he soon endeared himself to Town fans and had bagged 15 goals by Christmas. Left out for almost three months, before a broken leg at Burnley finally ended his campaign, a second division championship medal went some way to rewarding him for his efforts.
Preston NE (From trainee on 2/5/92) FL 1+5/1 FAC 0+1 Others 1+1
Manchester C (Free on 12/2/93)
Swindon T (Free on 15/6/95) FL 22+8/12 FLC 4/1 FAC 2+4/2 Others 2+1/1

FINNIGAN Anthony (Tony)
Born: Wimbledon, 17 October 1962
Height: 6'0" Weight: 12.0
International Honours: E: Yth

The experienced defender continued as a non-contract player for Fulham in 1995-96, making four first team appearances at right back in October, before travelling north to sign for Falkirk in February. Comfortable on the ball with a fierce shot, he still has something to offer, despite off the field problems.
Fulham (From apprentice on 3/11/80)
Crystal Palace (Free from Corinthian Casuals on 5/2/85) FL 94+11/10 FLC 7+1 FAC 2+1 Others 2

Blackburn Rov (£45,000 on 29/7/88) FL 21+14 FLC 3 FAC 5/1 Others 3/1
Hull C (£30,000 on 3/8/90) FL 15+3/1 FLC 2+1
Swindon T (Free on 18/3/91) FL 2+1
Brentford (Free on 17/1/92) FL 3 Others 1
Barnet (Signed on 28/9/93) FL 5+1/1 FLC 0+1 (Free to Enfield in February 1994)
Fulham (Free on 30/9/94) FL 8+5 FLC 1 FAC 1 Others 3

FISHER Neil John
Born: St Helens, 7 November 1970
Height: 5'10" Weight: 10.9

A skilful and creative midfielder, Neil signed for Chester during the 1995 close season, having been released by Bolton. Missing just three games and looking a class above the third division, he seems sure to return to a higher level before too long.
Bolton W (From trainee on 12/7/89) FL 17+7/1 FLC 4 FAC 1
Chester C (Free on 5/6/95) FL 43+1/2 FLC 4 FAC 1 Others 1

FISHLOCK Murray Edward
Born: Marlborough, 23 September 1973
Height: 5'8" Weight: 10.8

Another Hereford player to suffer from injury problems in 1995-96, he started the season on the left wing before returning to left back when Kevin Lloyd was injured. Continuing to tousle with the latter for the position throughout the campaign, Murray impressed with his linking play and excellent ability.
Hereford U (Free from Trowbridge on 30/9/94) FL 38+3/3 FLC 3 FAC 3 Others 6

FITZGERALD Scott Brian
Born: Westminster, 13 August 1969
Height: 6'0" Weight: 12.12
International Honours: Ei: B-1; U21-4

One of a crop of very promising Wimbledon centre backs, Scott made two subs' appearances, followed by full games against Newcastle and Southampton last October, before having a six month spell on loan at Sheffield United a month later. A tidy player and a good man-to-man marker, who takes up good covering positions and defends well, he ended the season a fixture in Dons' reserves.
Wimbledon (From trainee on 13/7/89) F/PL 95+11/1 FLC 13 FAC 5 Others 1
Sheffield U (Loaned on 23/11/95) FL 6

FJORTOFT Jan-Aage
Born: Aalesund, Norway, 10 January 1967
Height: 6'3" Weight: 13.4
International Honours: Norway: 69

Middlesbrough's record signing when joining towards the end of 1994-95, although Premiership goals were scarce in 1995-96, he never stopped trying to find the net. His value to the team goes beyond scoring, his deft touches, determination, and ability to shield the ball from defenders, allied to his enthusiasm, make him a clubman in the real sense of the word.
Swindon T (£500,000 from Rapid Vienna on 29/7/93) P/FL 62+10/28 FLC 9/9 FAC 3+1/2 Others 1+1
Middlesbrough (£1,300,000 on 31/3/95) P/FL 35+1/9 FLC 6/2

Jan Fjortoft

FLACK Steven (Steve) Richard
Born: Cambridge, 29 May 1971
Height: 6'3" Weight: 14.4

Joining Cardiff in the autumn of 1995 from non-league Cambridge City, he proved to be a big, bustling centre forward, mainly used as a late substitute. Scored his one and only goal for the club, in the 88th minute from a yard out, in a 3-1 defeat at Wigan last March.
Cardiff C (£10,000 from Cambridge C on 13/11/95) FL 5+5/1

FLATTS Mark Michael
Born: Islington, 14 October 1972
Height: 5'6" Weight: 9.8
International Honours: E: Yth

Quick, two-footed Arsenal wide midfielder who has been on the fringe of the first team for several years without receiving too many opportunities. Having starred in a pre-season match at Kettering, Mark's hopes were high for 1995-96, especially with a new manager on board, but it was not to be, and he even failed to be selected for the bench. Loaned to Grimsby in March, he impressed on his Blundell Park debut despite a hesitant start, but failed to live up to expectations and returned to Highbury abruptly, prior to being given a free transfer in the summer.
Arsenal (From trainee on 28/12/90) PL 9+7 FLC 1 FAC 0+1
Cambridge U (Loaned on 14/10/93) FL 5/1
Brighton & Hove A (Loaned on 31/12/93) FL 9+1/1
Bristol C (Loaned on 23/3/95) FL 4+2
Grimsby T (Loaned on 28/3/96) FL 4+1

FLECK Robert William
Born: Glasgow, 11 August 1965
Height: 5'10" Weight: 10.8
Club Honours: SPD '87; SLC '87, '88
International Honours: S: 4; U21-6; Yth

The once free-scoring centre forward rejoined his old club, Norwich, last August, having spent three fruitless years at Chelsea, and quickly proved that the absence had not dimmed his ability to find a Norwich City

shirt and talk a good, smiling game to all and sundry. Maybe Robert was not the player he was previously, but a respectable 12 goal tally in a dismal team season saw him net his 50th Canary league goal and he is now lying fourth in the club's all-time list of goalscorers. Among his strikes were trademark volleys and half volleys, but his 20 withdrawals from the field of play drew questions over his lasting power, something that will have been hopefully sorted out during the summer.
Glasgow R (Free from Possil YM in 1983) SL 61+24/29 SLC 3+5/2 SC 1+1 Others 3+4/3
Partick Thistle (Loaned in November 1983) SL 1+1/1
Norwich C (£580,000 on 17/12/87) FL 130+13/40 FLC 13/11 FAC 16+2/11 Others 7/4
Chelsea (£2,100,000 on 13/8/92) PL 35+5/3 FLC 7/1 FAC 1
Bolton W (Loaned on 17/12/93) FL 6+1/1 Others 1
Bristol C (Loaned on 12/1/95) FL 10/1
Norwich C (£650,000 on 29/8/95) FL 37+4/10 FLC 5+2/2 FAC 1

FLEMING Craig
Born: Halifax, 6 October 1971
Height: 6'0" Weight: 11.7

Sidelined on and off for a good five months last season with a recurring groin strain, Oldham's hard-man came back strongly in the last four games of the campaign to strengthen the back four tremendously. This following just five appearances in 1994-95. The club's man-marker, Craig takes up excellent positions and is always prepared to accept the ball no matter where and is very difficult to dispossess. Hopefully, 1996-97 will be injury free.
Halifax T (From trainee on 21/3/90) FL 56+1 FLC 4 FAC 3 Others 2
Oldham Ath (£80,000 on 15/8/91) F/PL 114+6/1 FLC 8+1 FAC 10 Others 4

FLEMING Curtis
Born: Manchester, 8 October 1968
Height: 5'11" Weight: 12.8
Club Honours: Div 1 '95
International Honours: Ei: 7; U23-2; U21-5; Yth

Brilliant Middlesbrough full back who, because of injury, struggled through 1995-96, a season that should have heralded the peak of his career, after he had occupied the left back position with absolute authority in 1994-95. Renowned for his strong tackling and coming away with the ball from the most impossible situations to set up counter attacks from which forwards were able to take full advantage, Curtis battled hard to regain his fitness and his place. However, he finished the season in style, culminating in his first ever Boro goal, and his first full cap for the Republic of Ireland versus Czechoslovakia shortly afterwards, followed by six more.
Middlesbrough (£50,000 from St Patricks on 16/8/91) F/PL 114+12/1 FLC 8+2 FAC 8 Others 7+1

FLEMING Gary James
Born: Londonderry, 17 February 1967
Height: 5'9" Weight: 11.9
International Honours: NI-31; U23-1

After losing out at the heart of the Barnsley

defence at the beginning of 1995-96, he had just fought his way back into the team in September when a serious knee injury ended his season. As an international class player, with the ability to read the game from his role in the side as sweeper, he was sorely missed.

Nottingham F (From apprentice on 19/11/84) FL 71+3 FLC 5+1 FAC 2+1 Others 0+1
Manchester C (£150,000 on 17/8/89) FL 13+1 FLC 4 Others 1
Notts Co (Loaned on 8/3/90) FL 3 Others 1
Barnsley (£85,000 on 23/3/90) FL 236+3 FLC 14 FAC 12 Others 6

FLEMING Haydn Valentine
Born: Islington, 14 March 1978
Height: 5'5" Weight: 9.11
Promoted from the Cardiff junior ranks, where he had started last season at full back with attacking ambitions, Haydn made his debut at Plymouth in November. Still a trainee, he had games where he was inspired, but also showed that he had a lot still to learn in others. All in all an excellent prospect.
Cardiff C (Trainee) FL 20+2 FAC 2 Others 1

FLEMING Terence (Terry) Maurice
Born: Marston Green, 5 January 1973
Height: 5'9" Weight: 10.9
Lincoln utility player used on the right side of defence and in midfield after signing from Preston last December. One of four North End men who moved to Sincil Bank during the season to link up again with the Deepdale club's former boss, John Beck, Terry managed to put a lack of first team opportunities and off the field problems, behind him.
Coventry C (From trainee on 2/7/91) F/PL 8+5 FLC 0+1
Northampton T (Free on 3/8/93) FL 26+5/1 FLC 2 FAC 0+1 Others 0+1
Preston NE (Free on 18/7/94) FL 25+7/2 FLC 4 FAC 0+1 Others 3+2
Lincoln C (Signed on 7/12/95) FL 17+5

FLETCHER Steven (Steve) Mark
Born: Hartlepool, 26 June 1972
Height: 6'2" Weight: 14.0
Had a miserable season in 1995-96, being dogged by a persistent knee injury which limited his appearances to 11, with four of those a substitute, and scoring just one goal. Having started training again, Bournemouth will look forward to his return this coming season and a sight of the aerial power that they missed throughout the last campaign.
Hartlepool U (From trainee on 23/8/90) FL 19+13/4 FLC 0+2/1 FAC 1+2 Others 2+2/1
Bournemouth (£30,000 on 28/7/92) FL 100+14/7 FLC 11/1 FAC 4 Others 3

FLITCROFT David John
Born: Bolton, 14 January 1974
Height: 5'11" Weight: 13.5
Starting last season to great effect, playing wide on the right of Chester's midfield, David delighted in delivering excellent crosses which produced many goals. Unfortunately, however, knee problems sustained in October, brought his flourish to a halt and it can only be hoped that the brother of Blackburn's Garry will be fit in time for 1996-97.

Preston NE (From trainee on 2/5/92) FL 4+4/2 FLC 0+1 Others 0+1
Lincoln C (Loaned on 17/9/93) FL 2 FLC 0+1
Chester C (Free on 9/12/93) FL 31+18/2 FLC 4 FAC 2 Others 3

FLITCROFT Garry William
Born: Bolton, 6 November 1972
Height: 6'0" Weight: 11.8
International Honours: E: U21-10; Yth; Sch
Having been at Manchester City since the age of 12, Garry joined the Premiership champions, Blackburn Rovers, immediately prior to last March's transfer deadline. Even though he had failed to score in his 25 league games in 1995-96, and the fact that City were well endowed with midfielders, it still came as a shock to the fans. As a hard tackler, and a fluid mover who is very comfortable on the ball and covers vast areas of the field, he made the shortest debut in Rovers' history when being dismissed after 87 minutes, and a subsequent three game suspension virtually closed his season. However, he made an outstanding contribution to the victory over Newcastle when successfully contesting the midfield with David Batty and will be raring to go this coming term.
Manchester C (From trainee on 2/7/91) PL 109+6/13 FLC 11+1 FAC 14/2
Bury (Loaned on 5/3/92) FL 12
Blackburn Rov (£3,200,000 on 26/3/96) PL 3

Garry Flitcroft

FLO Jostein
Born: Eid, Norway, 3 October 1964
Height: 6'4" Weight: 13.12
International Honours: Norway: 44
A regular member of the Sheffield United team during the Dave Bassett era, Jostein continued to give his best up front and scored five goals in the various competitions last season. A problem over the final instalment of his transfer fee led to the

eventual cancellation of his contract in January and his release back to Norway, but, prior to that, had become the club's second most capped international during his time at Bramall Lane.
Sheffield U (£400,000 from Songdal on 10/8/93) P/FL 74+10/19 FLC 4/3 FAC 1+1

FLOWERS Timothy (Tim) David
Born: Kenilworth, 3 February 1967
Height: 6'2" Weight: 14.0
Club Honours: PL '95
International Honours: E: 7; U21-3; Yth
Blackburn and England goalkeeper. A good shot stopper with great concentration, and seldom surprised when suddenly called into action, Tim is a positive influence on the team with his enthusiasm and commitment. Following an indifferent start to last season, he came back in tip-top fashion, giving many impressive displays. Seen to best effect in the game against Newcastle that virtually decided the championship, although some might well remember the freak bounce that let Liverpool in.
Wolverhampton W (From apprentice on 28/8/84) FL 63 FLC 5 FAC 2 Others 2
Southampton (£70,000 on 13/6/86) F/PL 192 FLC 26 FAC 16 Others 8
Swindon T (Loaned on 23/3/87) FL 2
Swindon T (Loaned on 13/11/87) FL 5
Blackburn Rov (£2,400,000 on 4/11/93) PL 105 FLC 7 FAC 8 Others 10

FLYNN Michael (Mike) Anthony
Born: Oldham, 23 February 1969
Height: 6'0" Weight: 11.0
Ever present at the heart of Stockport's defence in 1995-96, as in the previous season, the skipper remained the epitome of the team's fighting spirit. A committed and fearless defender, his long throws also add to County's attacking capabilities.
Oldham Ath (From apprentice on 7/2/87) FL 37+3/1 FLC 1+1/1 FAC 1 Others 2
Norwich C (£100,000 on 22/12/88)
Preston NE (£125,000 on 4/12/89) FL 134+2/7 FLC 6 FAC 6+1/1 Others 13
Stockport Co (£125,000 on 25/3/93) FL 144+1/9 FLC 11 FAC 9 Others 14

FLYNN Sean Michael
Born: Birmingham, 13 March 1968
Height: 5'8" Weight: 11.8
Signed for Derby in the 1995 close season from Coventry, for whom he had been a first team regular, as part of the deal which took Paul Williams to City. A right-sided utility player at home in a defensive or attacking role, his determination to win the ball and use it positively epitomised the spirit that won promotion.
Coventry C (£20,000 from Halesowen T on 3/12/91) F/PL 90+7/9 FLC 5/1 FAC 3
Derby Co (£250,000 on 11/8/95) FL 29+13/2 FLC 3 FAC 1

FOLEY Dominic Joseph
Born: Cork, 7 July 1976
Height: 6'1" Weight: 12.8
International Honours: Ei: U21-2
Wolves' rangy forward. Signed from the Irish team, St James' Gate, during the 1995 close season, he came on twice as a

substitute before starting the game at Huddersfield in November. In January he was to come on in three successive away matches, all of which were local derbies in different competitions. Definitely one for the future, his progress was rewarded by selection for the Eire U21 side.

Wolverhampton W (Signed from St James' Gate on 31/8/95) FL 1+4 FLC 0+1 FAC 0+1

FOLEY Stephen (Steve)
Born: Liverpool, 4 October 1962
Height: 5'7" Weight: 11.3
Club Honours: AMC '92; Div 2 '93

A tough-tackling midfielder who was released by Lincoln during the 1995 close season, Steve arrived at Bradford on a month's trial and made just one appearance from the bench in the home game against Wycombe before leaving in October.

Liverpool (From apprentice on 2/9/80)
Fulham (Loaned on 16/12/83) FL 2+1
Grimsby T (Free on 20/8/84) FL 31/2 FLC 6/2 FAC 3/1
Sheffield U (Free on 20/8/85) FL 56+10/14 FLC 5/3 FAC 5/1 Others 2+1
Swindon T (£40,000 on 24/6/87) FL 142+9/23 FLC 14+2/1 FAC 10/2 Others 12+1/3
Stoke C (£50,000 on 16/1/92) FL 106+1/10 FLC 8 FAC 6 Others 14/3
Lincoln C (Free on 14/7/94) FL 15+1 FLC 1 FAC 2 Others 2
Bradford C (Free on 11/8/95) FL 0+1

FORAN Mark James
Born: Aldershot, 30 October 1973
Height: 6'4" Weight: 13.12

Young Sheffield United defender who started last season on loan at Wycombe to gain experience and played in seven of the first eight matches at centre back before returning to Bramall Lane. Given a further six starts for United, he was later made available by Howard Kendall, and signed for Peterborough in February, immediately settling into Posh's rearguard and impressing in aerial battles.

Millwall (From trainee on 3/11/90)
Sheffield U (£25,000 on 28/8/93) FL 10+1/1 FLC 1 Others 0+1
Rotherham U (Loaned on 26/8/94) FL 3
Wycombe W (Loaned on 11/8/95) FL 5 FLC 2
Peterborough U (£40,000 on 8/2/96) FL 17/1 Others 1

FORBES Steven (Steve) Dudley
Born: Stoke Newington, 24 December 1975
Height: 6'2" Weight: 12.6

Tireless Millwall midfield player who can also play in defence. Good in the air and when surging forward, first team games were limited, by the strong competition for midfield places, to a handful of substitute appearances in 1995-96. Yet to make a start for the club, he will be hoping for better under Jimmy Nicholl.

Millwall (£45,000 from Sittingbourne on 11/7/94) FL 0+5 FLC 0+1 FAC 0+1

FORD Anthony (Tony)
Born: Grimsby, 14 May 1959
Height: 5'9" Weight: 12.7
Club Honours: Div 3 '80; FLGC '82
International Honours: E: B-2

Player/coach who performed consistently well on the right side of Scunthorpe's midfield in 1995-96. Gets forward well and retains the goalscorer's instinct from his days as a right winger, while a lack of pace is countered by sound positional sense. Hampered by groin strain in late season.

Grimsby T (From apprentice on 1/5/77) FL 321+34/54 FLC 31+3/4 FAC 15+4/2 Others 2
Sunderland (Loaned on 27/3/86) FL 8+1/1
Stoke C (£35,000 on 8/7/86) FL 112/13 FLC 8 FAC 9 Others 6/1
West Bromwich A (£145,000 on 24/3/89) FL 114/14 FLC 7 FAC 4/1 Others 2+1
Grimsby T (£50,000 on 21/11/91) FL 59+9/3 FLC 1 FAC 3
Bradford C (Loaned on 16/9/93) FL 5 FLC 2
Scunthorpe U (Free on 2/8/94) FL 73+3/9 FLC 4/1 FAC 7/1 Others 4

FORD Gary
Born: York, 8 February 1961
Height: 5'8" Weight: 12.5
Club Honours: Div 4 '84

An experienced midfielder who returned to England last September after a lengthy spell playing in Norway, he joined Hartlepool as a non-contract player, linking up with ex-York team mates, Keith Houchen and Tony Canham. Not really up to the rigours of Endsleigh League football, he made just four appearances, not lasting a full game, and was released after a month.

York C (From apprentice on 7/2/79) FL 359+7/52 FLC 24/4 FAC 36/7 Others 9
Leicester C (£25,000 on 19/7/87) FL 15+1/2 FLC 1+1 Others 2/1
Port Vale (Signed on 6/1/88) FL 66+9/12 FLC 6 FAC 7 Others 3/1
Walsall (Loaned on 22/3/90) FL 13/2
Mansfield T (Signed on 22/3/91) FL 88/7 FLC 4 FAC 2 Others 4 (Free to Telford during 1993 close season)
Hartlepool U (Free from Harstad IL on 7/9/95) FL 2+1 FLC 0+1

FORD Jonathan (Jon) Steven
Born: Birmingham, 12 April 1968
Height: 6'0" Weight: 12.0
Club Honours: AMC '94

Signed from Swansea during the 1995 close season, Jon missed many games for Bradford in 1995-96, following two separate operations on his right knee. A strong and determined centre half, who also played at left back, he actually carried on for six weeks, using pain killers, after being injured in a friendly against Manchester United. Hopes to be properly fit in time for the new season.

Swansea C (£5,000 from Cradley T on 19/8/91) FL 145+15/7 FLC 12+1 FAC 8+5/2 Others 15+5
Bradford C (£210,000 on 26/7/95) FL 18+1 FLC 4 FAC 2 Others 1

FORD Mark
Born: Pontefract, 10 October 1975
Height: 5'8" Weight: 10.8
Club Honours: FAYC '93
International Honours: E: U21-1; Yth

Local-born midfielder who captained Leeds' 1993 FA Youth Cup winning side. Having made his solitary league appearance at Swindon in the final game of the 1993-94 season, he took his 1995-96 bow at Newcastle last November, and stayed in the

first team picture for the rest of the season. His size, style, and performances in the midfield holding role were in so many ways reminiscent of old crowd favourite, David Batty, and allowed Gary McAllister to play in a more forward position, even more so in the cup runs. Unfortunately, his tigerish approach and will to win resulted in a suspension for passing the 45 point mark. His good form, however, saw him win his first England U21 cap, hopefully the start of a long international career.

Leeds U (From trainee on 5/3/93) PL 12+1 FLC 4 FAC 5 Others 0+1

FORD Michael (Mike) Paul
Born: Bristol, 9 February 1966
Height: 6'0" Weight: 11.6
Club Honours: WC '88

The full back, who also doubles up as the Oxford skipper and is an excellent motivator known to the fans as "Mr Busy", missed just three games in 1995-96. Likes nothing more than to link up with the attack and scored a vital late equaliser against Rotherham with a long-range strike. Has just completed his eighth season at the Manor Ground.

Leicester C (From apprentice on 11/2/84)
Cardiff C (Free from Devizes T on 19/9/84) FL 144+1/13 FLC 6 FAC 9 Others 7
Oxford U (£150,000 on 10/6/88) FL 209+16/12 FLC 17+1/1 FAC 10+1/1 Others 8/1

FORD Robert (Bobby) John
Born: Bristol, 22 September 1974
Height: 5'8" Weight: 11.0

Last season was to have been Bobby's coming of age and he was a vital member of the Oxford midfield until an ankle injury forced him to sit out United's most productive spell of the campaign. A talented player, who should shine in division one next season, he is still only 21 and remains one for the future. Is a good dead ball kicker.

Oxford U (From trainee on 6/10/92) FL 58+7/5 FLC 3+1 FAC 9/2 Others 7/1

FOREMAN Matthew
Born: Newcastle, 15 February 1975
Height: 6'0" Weight: 12.1

A 21-year-old midfielder, who can also play at full back, Matthew joined Scarborough as a non-contract player on transfer deadline day last March, having been unable to break into the first team at Sheffield United, and made just three appearances before moving on. With good feet and a tremendous appetite for work, he is sure to be heard from again.

Sheffield U (From trainee on 5/7/93) Others 1+2
Scarborough (Free on 22/3/96) FL 1+3

FORMBY Kevin
Born: Ormskirk, 22 July 1971
Height: 5'11" Weight: 12.0

Rochdale's first choice left back in 1995-96, he missed just a couple of games through suspension before being ruled out in mid-season with a long-term muscle injury that eventually required a hernia operation. Famed at the club for his Rob Jones-like inability to get on the score sheet!

Rochdale (Free from Burscough on 24/3/94) FL 47+4 FLC 4 FAC 5 Others 10

FORREST Craig Lorne
Born: Vancouver, Canada, 20 September 1967
Height: 6'4" Weight: 14.4
Club Honours: Div 2 '92
International Honours: Canada: 31
Started last season as Ipswich's number one goalkeeper, despite the fact that he was initially on a weekly contract. That, however, did not detract from his performances. Showing excellent reflexes and judgement, he performed consistently well until sidelined with a neck injury that forced him to leave the field during the home game against Charlton in September. Soon regained his place from Richard Wright but, following an international call up in January, and with the latter playing so well, he was forced to sit out the rest of the campaign.
Ipswich T (From apprentice on 31/8/85) F/PL 257 FLC 14 FAC 11 Others 14
Colchester U (Loaned on 1/3/88) FL 11

FORRESTER Jamie Mark
Born: Bradford, 1 November 1974
Height: 5'6" Weight: 10.4
Club Honours: FAYC '93
International Honours: E: Yth (UEFAYC '93); Sch
Surprisingly released by Leeds last October, having failed to make the first team in 1995-96, Jamie joined Grimsby permanently, following a spell on loan the previous season. A small, but compact striker, with a good footballing brain and an excellent turn of speed, both on and off the ball, he quickly capitalised on the long-term absence of Clive Mendonca to command a regular place and, at the same time, established himself as a firm favourite with the fans.
Leeds U (£60,000 from Auxere on 20/10/92) PL 7+2 FAC 1+1/2
Southend U (Loaned on 1/9/94) FL 3+2
Grimsby T (Loaned on 10/3/95) FL 7+2/1
Grimsby T (Signed on 17/10/95) FL 23+5/5 FAC 3+1/3

FORSTER Nicholas (Nicky) Michael
Born: Caterham, 8 September 1973
Height: 5'10" Weight: 11.5
International Honours: E: U21-4
Brentford striker blessed with considerable pace. A disappointing last season for Nicky, following a superb 1994-95, not helped by the constant press speculation concerning his future. Scored in the opening two games before his goal tally dried up, with just three more from his next 20 matches, prior to being ruled out of action for two months with a leg injury. Hopefully, next season will see him back to his best.
Gillingham (Signed from Horley T on 22/5/92) FL 54+13/24 FLC 3+2 FAC 6/2
Brentford (£100,000 on 17/6/94) FL 83+1/29 FLC 8/2 FAC 5 Others 6+1/3

FORSYTH Richard Michael
Born: Dudley, 3 October 1970
Height: 5'11" Weight: 12.4
International Honours: E: SP-2
Signed from non-league Kidderminster during the summer of 1995, Richard managed to bridge the gap between part-time and full-time football successfully, often giving sterling displays, when called

upon, in Birmingham's midfield. Strong in the tackle, and carrying a fierce shot, the former England semi-pro international slotted in at full back on occasions, before losing favour towards the end of the season.
Birmingham C (£50,000 from Kidderminster Hrs on 13/7/95) FL 12+14/2 FLC 7+2 FAC 2 Others 3+1

FORTUNE-WEST Leo Paul D
Born: Stratford, 9 April 1971
Height: 6'4" Weight: 13.10
Aggressive and skilful on the ball for a big man, this centre forward was signed by Gillingham from Stevenage Borough in June 1995 in return for a fee, which was paid for by the Gill's supporters club. In his first full season, he finished as top scorer with 15 goals, including two at home to Bury, the side that eventually gained promotion to the second division in third place behind Preston and Gillingham. An unknown quantity at the start of 1995-96, his form now attracts the big boys.
Gillingham (£5,000 from Stevenage Borough on 12/7/95) FL 36+4/12 FLC 2/1 FAC 3/2

Leo Fortune-West

FOSTER Adrian Michael
Born: Kidderminster, 19 March 1971
Height: 5'9" Weight: 11.0
Striker. A hard-working inside forward, he lost his place in the Gillingham team to Dennis Bailey, after scoring the club's first goal of the Football League programme on the opening day of last season against Wigan Athletic. Top scorer for the reserve team in the Capital League, he spent March onwards on loan to Exeter City, prior to being released in the summer.
West Bromwich A (From trainee on 20/7/89) FL 13+14/2 FLC 1+3 FAC 0+2
Torquay U (Free on 3/7/92) FL 55+20/24 FLC 5+1/3 FAC 3/1 Others 4+3
Gillingham (£60,000 on 11/8/94) FL 28+12/9 FLC 2+2 FAC 3 Others 3/2
Exeter C (Loaned on 22/3/96) FL 4+3

FOSTER Colin John
Born: Chislehurst, 16 July 1964
Height: 6'4" Weight: 14.1
Dominant and surprisingly skilful Watford central defender who continued to use his six feet four inches to good effect at both ends of the pitch last season. Despite being prone to niggling injuries, Colin has now made over 400 league appearances in a career encompassing five clubs. Never a crash-bang-wallop merchant, he always looks to pass the ball out of defence.
Leyton Orient (From apprentice on 4/2/82) FL 173+1/10 FLC 12 FAC 19/5 Others 5/1
Nottingham F (Signed on 4/3/87) FL 68+4/5 FLC 8/1 FAC 5 Others 2
West Ham U (Signed on 22/9/89) F/PL 88+5/4 FLC 5 FAC 9/2 Others 2+2
Notts Co (Loaned on 10/1/94) FL 9 Others 2
Watford (£100,000 on 23/3/94) FL 66/7 FLC 6/1 FAC 6

FOSTER John Colin
Born: Manchester, 19 September 1973
Height: 5'11" Weight: 11.2
International Honours: E: Sch
Very promising Manchester City full back with a strong physique who can perform well in any of the back five positions. Having already shown great promise, especially when coming out of defence looking to pass the ball, it was thought that he would play a significant part in the club's hoped-for recovery in 1995-96. Unfortunately, after getting over a training accident that occurred at the end of the previous season, and impressing in the opening four matches, John was first hindered and then eventually sidelined by a shoulder injury. Must surely be hoping that 1996-97 brings better fortune.
Manchester C (From trainee on 15/7/92) PL 14+2 FLC 2+1 FAC 2+1

FOSTER Lee
Born: Bishop Auckland, 21 October 1977
Height: 5'9" Weight: 11.7
A right-sided forward, this second-year trainee showed good form for Hartlepool juniors at the start of 1995-96 and was rewarded with an early promotion to the first team, making his debut in August as substitute, playing just 18 minutes. Surprisingly, not recalled later in the season as manager, Keith Houchen, was forced to play a number of youngsters.
Hartlepool U (Trainee) FL 0+1

FOSTER Stephen (Steve) Brian
Born: Portsmouth, 24 September 1957
Height: 6'1" Weight: 14.0
Club Honours: FLC '88
International Honours: E: 3; U21-1
Sadly, the veteran Brighton central defender was absent for most of 1995-96 with knee ligament damage that required surgery and, not surprisingly, his commanding presence and leadership qualities were greatly missed. "Fozzie's" long service was rewarded with a benefit match at the end of the season, prior to him being released during the summer.
Portsmouth (From apprentice on 1/10/75) FL 101+8/6 FLC 10 FAC 8/2

Brighton & Hove A (£150,000 on 6/7/79) FL 171+1/6 FLC 13/2 FAC 16
Aston Villa (£200,000 on 3/3/84) FL 15/3 FLC 2
Luton T (£150,000 on 29/11/84) FL 163/11 FLC 20/1 FAC 27/2 Others 2
Oxford U (£175,000 on 13/7/89) FL 95/9 FLC 9/2 FAC 5 Others 4/1
Brighton & Hove A (Free on 14/8/92) FL 115/7 FLC 9 FAC 2 Others 3

FOWLER Jason Kenneth
Born: Bristol, 20 August 1974
Height: 6'0" Weight: 11.12
After showing much promise in 1994-95, the left-sided midfielder was given a run-in the Bristol City side towards the end of last season without suggesting he was going to lay claim to a permanent position. With obvious competition for places in 1996-97, Jason must look to recapture some of his earlier form in order to claim further opportunities.
Bristol C (From trainee on 8/7/93) FL 16+9 FLC 1+2 Others 1+1

FOWLER John Anthony
Born: Preston, 27 October 1974
Height: 5'10" Weight: 12.3
A young central midfielder, John was limited to just four appearances for Cambridge United in 1995-96 and, following a loan spell at Cambridge City, joined Kettering in December.
Cambridge U (From trainee on 18/4/92) FL 30+11 FLC 2+5/1 FAC 4+1 Others 4+1
Preston NE (Loaned on 19/2/93) FL 5+1

FOWLER Robert (Robbie) Bernard
Born: Liverpool, 9 April 1975
Height: 5'11" Weight: 11.10
Club Honours: FLC '95
International Honours: E: 5; B-1; U21-8; Yth (UEFAYC '93)
Following an outstanding season for Liverpool in 1994-95, when he scored 31 goals in all competitions at the age of 19, it did not seem credible that he could maintain such a high-performance level at such a tender age, yet he topped this with 36 goals in all competitions in 1995-96 and was rewarded with a full game for England against Croatia in April, playing four more times, including an appearance as a sub in the European Championships. Relegated to the bench for the opening games of last season, he responded with four goals against Bolton in September and re-established himself as an automatic first choice. Perhaps the most remarkable feature of his game is his ability to perform on the big occasion and score against the tightest defences in the Premier League – four in two games against Manchester United, a second hat trick against Arsenal, five in three games with Aston Villa, and two in the 4-3 classic with Newcastle. Robbie is not only lethal in the six yard box, but can score stunning goals from anywhere around the penalty area, such is his power and accuracy. Whilst not yet an all-round player in the Ian Rush mould, there is little doubt that he will be a more than worthy successor to his mentor.
Liverpool (From trainee on 23/4/92) FL 105+3/65 FLC 17/12 FAC 15/8 Others 3+1

Robbie Fowler

FOX Mark Stephen
Born: Basingstoke, 17 November 1975
Height: 5'11" Weight: 10.9
Although a promising Brighton reserve midfield player, opportunities for the youngster last season were restricted because of the club's precarious league position. Is the elder brother of Simon.
Brighton & Hove A (From trainee on 21/7/94) FL 8+15/1 Others 1

FOX Peter David
Born: Scunthorpe, 5 July 1957
Height: 5'11" Weight: 12.4
Club Honours: AMC '92; Div 2 '93
Having been appointed Exeter's player/manager during the 1995 close season (replacing Terry Cooper, who resigned due to ill health), he was the only ever present in the side and had another superb season, saving many points with his consistent goalkeeping. Is the holder of a full FA coaching badge.
Sheffield Wed (From apprentice on 1/6/75) FL 49 FAC 3
Barnsley (Loaned on 22/12/77) FL 1 FLC 1
Stoke C (£15,000 on 4/3/78) FL 409 FLC 32 FAC 22 Others 4
Exeter C (Free on 15/7/93) FL 102+1 FLC 7 FAC 6 Others 4

FOX Ruel Adrian
Born: Ipswich, 14 January 1968
Height: 5'6" Weight: 10.0
International Honours: E: B-2
A lively winger or forward, who can play on either flank, Ruel joined Tottenham last October from Newcastle, after finding his first team chances diminished by the good form of Keith Gillespie and the arrival of David Ginola. He quickly added pace and width to Spurs' midfield and demonstrated deadly accuracy in providing crosses for Teddy Sheringham and Chris Armstrong, as well as showing great confidence on the ball in taking on opponents to surge forward and create chances for his colleagues, or taking shots at goal himself. Missing just four games due to injury, his consistency, and his ability to score valuable goals, along with all his other attributes, had manager, Gerry Francis, extolling his virtues as a future England player.
Norwich C (From apprentice on 20/1/86) F/PL 148+24/22 FLC 13+3/3 FAC 11+4 Others 12+4
Newcastle U (£2,250,000 on 2/2/94) PL 56+2/12 FLC 3/1 FAC 5 Others 4/1
Tottenham H (£4,200,000 on 6/10/95) PL 26/6 FAC 6

FOX Simon Mark
Born: Basingstoke, 28 August 1977
Height: 5'11" Weight: 10.2
Reserve Brighton forward. As the younger brother of Mark, he is yet another Albion player of potential awaiting his chance of an extended run-in the first team after useful appearances as a substitute in 1995-96. Signed professional forms during the summer of 1995.
Brighton & Hove A (From trainee on 17/5/95) FL 1+8 FLC 0+1 Others 0+1

FOYLE Martin John
Born: Salisbury, 2 May 1963
Height: 5'10" Weight: 11.2
Club Honours: AMC '93
Once again amongst the leading goalscorers at Port Vale. A central striker, he missed a large part of the first half of last season with a foot injury and it was no coincidence that the team's fortunes improved after he returned. He notched seven goals in 11 games as the team moved out of the relegation zone and then scored twice at Wembley in the final of the Anglo-Italian Cup.
Southampton (From apprentice on 13/8/80) FL 6+6/1 FLC 0+2/2
Aldershot (£10,000 on 3/8/84) FL 98/35 FLC 10/5 FAC 8/5 Others 6
Oxford U (£140,000 on 26/3/87) FL 120+6/36 FLC 16/4 FAC 5/3 Others 3+1/1
Port Vale (£375,000 on 25/6/91) FL 153+10/56 FLC 13/6 FAC 13+1/9 Others 13+3/9

FRAIN John William
Born: Birmingham, 8 October 1968
Height: 5'9" Weight: 11.9
Club Honours: AMC '91
Birmingham's longest serving player, having started at St Andrews for ten years, John started last season plagued by a series of injuries, prior to making a welcome return to first team action in November and turning in a top-class display at left back. The recipient of a well earned testimonial in 1996-97, he is one of the few Brummies in the side and has always worn the shirt with pride in any number of positions.
Birmingham C (From apprentice on 10/10/86) FL 264+9/23 FLC 28/1 FAC 12 Others 22/2

FRANCIS John Andrew
Born: Dewsbury, 21 November 1963
Height: 5'8" Weight: 12.13
Club Honours: Div 4 '92
A regular on the Burnley subs' bench in 1995-96, before being laid low by cartilage problems, when coming on he was almost invariably employed on the wing. Can still

cause problems for opponents, but has not yet recovered the speed that was his greatest asset prior to his injury in the 1994 play offs.
Halifax T (On trial from Emley on 8/2/85) FL 1+3 Others 2
Sheffield U (£10,000 from Emley on 15/9/88) FL 14+28/6 FLC 0+2 FAC 0+1 Others 3+2/1
Burnley (£90,000 on 24/1/90) FL 99+2/26 FLC 6 FAC 8 Others 11+1/4
Cambridge U (£95,000 on 13/8/92) FL 15+14/3 FLC 2+2/1 FAC 0+1 Others 0+1
Burnley (£70,000 on 25/3/93) FL 44+32/10 FLC 3+4/1 FAC 4+2 Others 4+4/2

FRANCIS Kevin Michael
Born: Birmingham, 6 December 1967
Height: 6'7" Weight: 15.8
Club Honours: Div 2 '95; AMC '95
Big Kev suffered an injury plagued season for Birmingham in 1995-96, although doing extremely well to come back so soon from serious ligament damage sustained at the end of 1994-95. Despite playing inter-mittently, he still managed to score spec-tacularly and strikes against Middlesbrough and Leeds will long be remembered by the fans. Hopefully, over the worse of it, 1996-97 will see the tallest striker in the game back to his very best and while his ability in the air is unquestioned, he is more than skilful on the ground, also.
Derby Co (Free from Mile Oak Rov on 2/2/89) FL 0+10 FLC 1+2 FAC 1+2/1 Others 0+1
Stockport Co (£45,000 on 21/2/91) FL 147+5/88 FLC 12/5 FAC 9/6 Others 25/18
Birmingham C (£800,000 on 20/1/95) FL 26+8/11 FLC 6/4 FAC 2 Others 4/1

FRANCIS Stephen (Steve) Stuart
Born: Billericay, 29 May 1964
Height: 5'11" Weight: 11.5
Club Honours: FMC '86, '88
International Honours: E: Yth
Huddersfield Town goalkeeper. Carrying on where he left off in 1994-95, his perform-ances last season were rewarded with a Wilkinson Sword award. Recognised for his ability to make outstanding "last ditch" saves and very consistent, although he lost his place for a couple of games to Tony Norman, he soon re-established himself.
Chelsea (From apprentice on 28/4/82) FL 71 FLC 6 FAC 10 Others 1
Reading (£20,000 on 27/2/87) FL 216 FLC 15 FAC 15 Others 13
Huddersfield T (£150,000 on 1/8/93) FL 132 FLC 11 FAC 8 Others 12

FREEDMAN Douglas (Dougie) Alan
Born: Glasgow, 21 January 1974
Height: 5'9" Weight: 11.2
International Honours: S: U21-8; Sch
Probably the find of last season for Crystal Palace, his 20 goals helped to propel the team from near the foot of division one to the play offs. Signed from Barnet in September, having already scored three goals in five league games, the Scottish U21 striker made a slow start at Selhurst Park but never looked back after a hat trick against Wolves in November, which he repeated in the space of 12 minutes against Grimsby in March. Released on a free transfer by Gerry Francis, the then manager at QPR, the intelligent ball-playing striker added to

Scottish U21 caps and seems almost certain to win full honours in the future.
Queens Park R (From trainee on 15/5/92)
Barnet (Free on 26/7/94) FL 47/27 FLC 6/5 FAC 2 Others 2
Crystal Palace (£800,000 on 8/9/95) FL 37+2/20 FAC 2 Others 3

FREEMAN Andrew (Andy) James
Born: Reading, 8 September 1977
Height: 5'10" Weight: 10.6
YTS midfield player who graduated through the Reading youth and reserve sides in 1995-96 to earn a place on the bench in two first team games, playing for the last five minutes at Watford. Has a superb attitude towards the game and will be taken on as a professional for the 1996-97 season, having shown that he is ready for senior football.
Reading (Trainee) FL 0+1

FREEMAN Darren Barry Andduet
Born: Brighton, 22 August 1973
Height: 5'11" Weight: 13.0
Injured almost before he started at Gillingham in 1994-95, on recovery he established himself as a member of the reserve side in the Capital League, but failed to gain a regular position in the first team, being used mainly from the bench. A fleet-footed right winger, or central striker, Darren spent a period on loan to Glenavon in December 1995.
Gillingham (Free from Worthing on 31/1/95) FL 4+8 FAC 0+1 Others 2/1

FREESTONE Christopher (Chris) Mark
Born: Nottingham, 4 September 1971
Height: 5'11" Weight: 11.7
A speedy young striker, snapped up from minor league football in Nottingham, Chris was leading scorer for the Middlesbrough reserve team which won the Pontins League division two championship last season. Following some excellent performances, he fully merited his call up to the senior squad with a goal in his first full Premiership game versus Sheffield Wednesday in April, having made two brief appearances as a substitute earlier on.
Middlesbrough (£10,000 from Arnold T on 2/12/94) P/FL 2+2/1 FAC 0+1

FREESTONE Roger
Born: Newport, 19 August 1968
Height: 6'3" Weight: 14.6
Club Honours: Div 2 '89; AMC '94
International Honours: W: U21-1; Yth; Sch
Yet another consistent season for Swansea in 1995-96, despite playing behind an unsettled defence. On standby for the Welsh international squad, Roger missed just one league game last season, even scoring two goals from penalty kicks during the first month.
Newport Co (From trainee on 2/4/86 FL 1 Others 1
Chelsea (£95,000 on 10/3/87) FL 42 FLC 2 FAC 3 Others 6
Swansea C (Loaned on 29/9/89) FL 14 Others 1
Hereford U (Loaned on 9/3/90) FL 8
Swansea C (£45,000 on 5/9/91) FL 223+1/3 FLC 14 FAC 16 Others 27

Roger Freestone

FRENCH Jonathan (Jon) Charles
Born: Bristol, 25 September 1976
Height: 5'10" Weight: 10.10
A young and talented striker, Jon made his Bristol Rovers' league debut in the absence of Marcus Stewart, against Peterborough and three days later scored against Cambridge in an Auto Windscreen Shield-tie. He then went on to open his league goal account with a fine opportunist effort at Crewe Alexandra in March.
Bristol Rov (From trainee on 15/7/95) FL 3+7/1 Others 2+1/1

FROGGATT Stephen (Steve) Junior
Born: Lincoln, 9 March 1973
Height: 5'10" Weight: 11.11
International Honours: E: U21-2
Wolves' left winger. Out since September 1995 with a serious ankle injury, and missing the start of last season, after a quiet period Steve showed signs of returning to form at Southend on September, making a goal and netting in the last minute, only for it to be disallowed. However, he had been tiring easily and the mystery ailment was diagnosed as a blood clot, which could have had terrible consequences. It was exactly six months before he figured in the starting line up again, and it was a nice moment when he scored against Watford a fortnight later. With pace and skill, he is capable of both scoring and creating goals. Also dangerous at corner kicks.
Aston Villa (From trainee on 26/1/91) F/PL 30+5/2 FLC 1+1 FAC 5+2/1
Wolverhampton W (£1,000,000 on 11/7/94) FL 33+5/3 FLC 3/1 Others 2

FRONTZECK Michael
Born: Germany, 24 April 1964
Height: 5'11" Weight: 12.12
International Honours: Germany: 19

A seasoned German international left back who joined Manchester City from Borussia Munchengladbach last January, he came partly as cover for the injured Richard Edghill and the transfer of Terry Phelan to Chelsea. Made a very impressive home debut against QPR, showing himself to be a natural defender, and one who timed his tackles well. Also likes to go forward wide on the wing, an asset that was employed in the last few games of the season.

Manchester C (£350,000 from Borussia Munchengladbach on 31/1/96) PL 11+1 FAC 1

FRY Christopher (Chris) David
Born: Cardiff, 23 October 1969
Height: 5'10" Weight: 10.2
International Honours: W: Yth

Colchester right winger, cum wing/back, Chris started 1995-96 out of the team, but quickly won a place at right back, then on the right wing, before establishing himself as a regular choice for the rest of the campaign. Very much a crowd favourite, he also popped up with a couple of picture-book goals to complete an excellent season.

Cardiff C (From trainee on 3/8/88) FL 22+33/1 FLC 1+2 FAC 0+2 Others 0+2
Hereford U (Free on 2/8/91) FL 76+14/10 FLC 6+2 FAC 8+2/1 Others 6+1
Colchester U (Signed on 24/10/93) FL 71+17/10 FLC 1+1 FAC 2+1 Others 6+1

FUCHS Uwe
Born: Kaiserslautern, Germany, 23 July 1966
Height: 6'2" Weight: 14.1
Club Honours: Div 1 '95

A Millwall 1995 close season signing from Germany, although having spent the second half of 1994-95 with Middlesbrough, Uwe proved himself yet again to be a strong-running striker whose deft ball control stands him in good stead when he goes surging goalwards. Unfortunately, a knee injury prevented "Oovey" being 100 per cent fit, although he never gave any less when on the field.

Middlesbrough (Loaned from Kaiserslautern on 27/1/95) FL 13+2/9
Millwall (£750,000 from Kaiserslautern on 8/7/95) FL 21+11/5 FLC 2+1 FAC 0+1

FURLONG Paul Anthony
Born: Wood Green, 1 October 1968
Height: 6'0" Weight: 12.11
Club Honours: FAT '88
International Honours: E: SP-5

Another disappointing season for big "Furs", who found his opportunities to play for Chelsea limited by the signing of Mark Hughes and the form of Scotland's John Spencer. He started only 14 league matches in 1995-96 and scored just three goals, the first of those not coming until 2 January against QPR at Loftus Road. His only other goal was a nicely taken effort in the FA Cup fourth round – once again at Loftus Road. Is a wholehearted trier whose luck in front of goal doesn't reflect the contribution he makes to the team. Everybody at The Bridge will be hoping that things go better for the big fellow in 1996-97.

Coventry C (£130,000 from Enfield on 31/7/91) FL 27+10/4 FLC 4/1 FAC 1+1 Others 1
Watford (£250,000 on 24/7/92) FL 79/37 FLC 7/4 FAC 2 Others 4
Chelsea (£2,300,000 on 26/5/94) PL 44+20/13 FLC 3+1 FAC 5+4/1 Others 7/3

FURNELL Andrew (Andy) Paul
Born: Peterborough, 13 February 1977
Height: 5'10" Weight: 13.7
International Honours: E: Yth

With opportunities in 1995-96 having been hard to come by, the skilful young Peterborough midfielder was released during the summer. Also able to play as a forward, he made just three subs' appearances in mid-season, before being loaned out to VS Rugby and Chertsey Town, both non-league sides.

Peterborough U (From trainee on 31/12/94) FL 9+10/1 FLC 1 FAC 0+1 Others 0+1

FUTCHER Stephen (Steve) Arron
Born: Chester, 24 October 1976
Height: 6'0" Weight: 11.7
International Honours: W: Yth

Midfielder. Related to Ron and Paul (his uncles) who played in the 1970s, Steven only made two first team appearances for Wrexham in 1995-96, both in the European Cup Winners' Cup preliminary round against Petrolul Ploiesti (Romania). Still learning his trade, he qualified for the ECWC games as one of his grandmothers is Welsh and has also represented Wales at youth under 18 level.

Wrexham (From trainee on 4/7/95) Others 2

Paul Furlong

G

GABBIADINI Marco
Born: Nottingham, 20 January 1968
Height: 5'10" Weight: 13.4
Club Honours: Div 3 '88
International Honours: E: B-1; FL-1; U21-2
Bustling and combative Derby striker who is a great favourite with the home fans. A first team regular who linked up well with Dean Sturridge and Paul Simpson in 1995-96, he was on the scoresheet with less regularity than in previous seasons only due to the fact he played more as a provider for others. However, his non-stop movement will make him a handful even for Premiership defenders. The brother of former pro, Riccardo, Marco enjoyed a purple patch of nine goal in 11 games midway through the campaign.
York C (From apprentice on 5/9/85) FL 42+18/14 FLC 4+3/1 Others 4/3
Sunderland (£80,000 on 23/9/87) FL 155+2/74 FLC 14/9 FAC 5 Others 9/4
Crystal Palace (£1,800,000 on 1/10/91) FL 15/5 FLC 6/1 FAC 1 Others 3/1
Derby Co (£1,000,000 on 31/1/92) FL 158+16/50 FLC 12/7 FAC 8/3 Others 16+1/8

GAGE Kevin William
Born: Chiswick, 21 April 1964
Height: 5'10" Weight: 12.11
Club Honours: Div 4 '83
International Honours: E: Yth
The previous season's Sheffield United "Player of the Year", Kevin missed the start of 1995-96 due to a minor knee operation, but came back to play at full back against Wolves and Portsmouth, before further damage to his knee necessitated a cartilage operation. Following his recovery, he failed to regain a first team spot under Howard Kendall and signed for Preston North End in March on a free transfer, appearing in seven of the remaining eight games.
Wimbledon (From apprentice on 4/1/82) FL 135+33/15 FLC 7+2/1 FAC 8+3/1 Others 0+1
Aston Villa (£100,000 on 17/7/87) FL 113+2/8 FLC 13/3 FAC 9/1 Others 8
Sheffield U (£150,000 on 15/11/91) F/PL 107+5/7 FLC 6 FAC 10+2 Others 1
Preston NE (Free on 28/3/96) FL 4+3

GALE Anthony (Tony) Peter
Born: Westminster, 19 November 1959
Height: 6'1" Weight: 13.7
Club Honours: PL '95
International Honours: E: U21-1; Yth
Veteran central defender. The former West Ham stalwart was signed as cover by Crystal Palace last September from Premier League champions, Blackburn, but sadly spent most of the season on the treatment table. Starting only three games for Palace in January and February, he was released in March and is now expected to retire from the playing side.
Fulham (From apprentice on 5/8/77) FL 277/19 FLC 22/2 FAC 16

West Ham U (£200,000 on 1/8/84) F/PL 293+7/5 FLC 28+2/1 FAC 29/1 Others 9
Blackburn Rov (Free on 11/8/94) PL 15 FLC 2 Others 3
Crystal Palace (Free on 5/9/95) FL 2 FAC 1

GALE Shaun Michael
Born: Reading, 8 October 1969
Height: 6'0" Weight: 11.6
Having suffered from injury in 1994-95, Shaun settled in effectively at right back, missing just two league games last season. Great at getting down the touchline, his crosses led to many a Barnet goal.
Portsmouth (From trainee on 12/7/88) FL 2+1 Others 0+1
Barnet (Free on 13/7/94) FL 69+2/3 FLC 6 FAC 2 Others 3

GALLACHER Kevin William
Born: Clydebank, 23 November 1966
Height: 5'8" Weight: 11.0
International Honours: S: 23; B-2; U21-7; Yth
Quick, busy little Blackburn forward who is difficult to mark because of his good ball skill and ability to drift into unexpected positions. Came back in 1995-96 from a twice-broken leg, but then developed hamstring trouble in the first league game, which put him out until Christmas. Able to play wide on either flank, or up front, because of his injury problems, he has yet to regain full confidence and fitness, having made so few appearances. A talented player, no doubt about it, what he needs is an injury-free run-in the side. Appeared for Scotland in the European Championships.
Dundee U (Signed from Duntocher BC in 1983) SL 118+13/27 SLC 13/5 SC 20+3/5 Others 15+6/3
Coventry C (£900,000 on 29/1/90) F/PL 99+1/28 FLC 11/7 FAC 4 Others 2
Blackburn Rov (£1,500,000 on 22/3/93) PL 51+5/15 FLC 4 FAC 6/1 Others 1+1

Kevin Gallacher

GALLAGHER Ian
Born: Hartlepool, 30 May 1978
Height: 5'10" Weight: 11.7
Promising young midfielder, who made his debut for Hartlepool in the last game of 1995-96. Like several other trainees, he got his chance as Keith Houchen struggled to assemble a fully-fit team. Ian followed his brother Micky as a 'Pool trainee, but has now gone one better by playing in the first team.
Hartlepool U (Trainee) FL 1

GALLAGHER Thomas (Tommy) Duncan
Born: Nottingham, 25 August 1974
Height: 5'10" Weight: 11.8
Club Honours: AIC '95
Tommy won a regular place in the Notts County line up last September, firstly at right back and, subsequently, in right midfield, until a tragic accident in training left him with a broken leg and ended his season in March. A tough-tackling ball winner, hopefully, he is young enough to make a complete recovery and resume his career in 1996-97.
Notts Co (From trainee on 1/6/92) FL 41+1/2 FLC 1 FAC 3 Others 8+2/1

GALLEN Kevin Andrew
Born: Chiswick, 21 September 1975
Height: 6'0" Weight: 12.3
International Honours: E: U21-4; Yth (EUFAC '93); Sch
Centre forward who is very sharp in and around the box and has a good eye for goal. After his excellent first season at QPR last year, a lot was expected of Kevin in 1995-96, but he struggled to find his form and managed just two goals before the end of 1995, although both of them were winners, against Oxford United in the Coca Cola Cup and Aston Villa in the league. Losing his first team place at the turn of the year, fortunately he regained his form in March, scoring seven times in ten games, but it was not enough to keep Rangers in the Premiership. Was included in the England U21 squad throughout the campaign.
Queens Park R (From trainee on 22/9/92) PL 57+10/18 FLC 3+1/2 FAC 4/1

GALLIMORE Anthony (Tony) Mark
Born: Crewe, 21 February 1972
Height: 5'11" Weight: 11.10
Club Honours: Div 3 '95
An automatic choice at left back for Carlisle until his move to Grimsby last March, Tony is a stylish defender who likes to overlap down the flank when the opportunity permits. The possessor of a powerful left-foot shot, he was also the club's penalty taker, a task he carried out with coolness and competence. Signed by Town to replace Gary Croft, he had little time to adjust to the higher level, but performed reasonably well.
Stoke C (From trainee on 11/7/90) FL 6+5
Carlisle U (Loaned on 3/10/91) FL 8
Carlisle U (Loaned on 26/2/92) FL 8
Carlisle U (£15,000 on 25/3/93) FL 124/9 FLC 8/1 FAC 8 Others 24/1
Grimsby T (£125,000 on 28/3/96) FL 10/1

GALLOWAY Michael (Mick) Anthony
Born: Nottingham, 13 October 1974
Height: 5'11" Weight: 11.5
The homegrown Notts County midfielder was a regular choice as substitute for the first half of last season, but was overlooked in the second half with all the new signings arriving at Meadow Lane. More at home on the left-hand side of the park, he should make a renewed challenge for first team action this coming term.
Notts Co (From trainee on 15/6/93) FL 13+3 FLC 2 Others 3

GAMBARO Enzo
Born: Genoa, Italy, 23 February 1966
Height: 6'0" Weight: 12.7
An experienced Serie "A" midfielder, previously with AC Milan, Enzo, not taken on by Bolton following a trial last January, eventually signed for Grimsby until the end of the season, making just one brief substitute appearance at Leicester.
Bolton W (Free from AC Milan on 15/1/96)
Grimsby T (Free on 8/3/96) FL 0+1

GANNON James (Jim) Paul
Born: Southwark, 7 September 1968
Height: 6'2" Weight: 13.0
The long-serving Stockport defender's luck in avoiding serious injury ran out last December when he broke his leg against Shrewsbury – and was booked by the referee as he was stretchered away! The injury was a bad blow to a composed and effective defender, who had established a firm partnership with Mike Flynn in the first half of the season. Returned to action in April.
Sheffield U (Signed from Dundalk on 27/4/89)
Halifax T (Loaned on 22/2/90) FL 2
Stockport Co (£40,000 on 7/3/90) FL 233+7/47 FLC 18/2 FAC 11/1 Others 33+2/8
Notts Co (Loaned on 14/1/94) FL 2

GANNON John Spencer
Born: Wimbledon, 18 December 1966
Height: 5'9" Weight: 11.10
Very much a fetcher and carrier in midfield, John started last season in plaster following an achilles problem, before regaining his Sheffield United place in October. However, on the arrival of a new management team, he played just four games, being substituted in every one of them, and, following a transfer listing, was signed by Oldham in March. Having created a favourable impression, unfortunately, four appearances into his new career, he picked up a thigh strain and missed the rest of the campaign. Could prove invaluable with all the youngsters now in Latics' first team.
Wimbledon (From apprentice on 19/12/84) FL 13+3/2 FLC 1+1 Others 1
Crewe Alex (Loaned on 19/12/86) FL 14+1 Others 1
Sheffield U (Free on 23/2/89) F/PL 162+12/6 FLC 13+1 FAC 14 Others 6/1
Middlesbrough (Loaned on 5/11/93) FL 6+1 Others 2
Oldham Ath (Free on 8/3/96) FL 5

GARDNER James (Jimmy)
Born: Dunfermline, 27 September 1967
Height: 5'10" Weight: 10.2
Freed by Scottish club, St Mirren, in the summer of 1995, the orthodox winger had a brief spell with Scarborough early last season, playing five games, before signing for Cardiff in September. Able to play on either flank and a quality crosser of the ball, Jimmy had impressed City when playing for Scarborough against them and once settled at Ninian Park looked to be a bargain.
Queens Park (Free from Ayresome North AFC on 1/4/87) SL 0+1
Motherwell (Signed on 1/7/88) SL 8+8 SC 0+1
St Mirren (Signed on 7/9/93) SL 31+10/1 SLC 1 SC 0+2 Others 2
Scarborough (Free on 25/8/95) FL 5+1/1
Cardiff C (Free on 28/9/95) 32+3/4 FAC 2 Others 2

GARLAND Peter John
Born: Croydon, 20 January 1971
Height: 5'9" Weight: 12.0
International Honours: E: Yth
Charlton midfielder. It was another disappointing time for Peter in 1995-96, as his season was again plagued by injuries. A scorer of long-range, eye-catching goals from the right side of midfield, he had his best game for the club at Wimbledon in the Coca Cola Cup in September, scoring the first goal. His contract was cancelled by mutual consent in April.
Tottenham H (From trainee on 1/7/89) FL 0+1
Newcastle U (£35,000 on 24/3/92) FL 0+2 Others 0+1
Charlton Ath (Signed on 18/12/92) FL 40+13/2 FLC 5/1 FAC 2 Others 4+1/1
Wycombe W (Loaned on 18/3/95) FL 5

Darren Garner

GARNER Darren John
Born: Plymouth, 10 December 1971
Height: 5'6" Weight: 10.1
Club Honours: AMC '96
After slipping into non-league football, Darren made a return to the top when he joined Rotherham from Dorchester Town prior to the start of last season. Settling into a midfield position, his ball-winning ability proved invaluable to the team and though he would have liked to have scored more goals, being ever willing to have a shot, he established a good partnership with Shaun Goodwin. The winner of an AWS medal, following the 2-1 Wembley win over Shrewsbury, he was sadly missed when out of the side through injury.
Plymouth Arg (From trainee on 15/3/89) FL 22+5/1 FLC 2+1 FAC 1 (Free to Dorchester T on 19/8/94)
Rotherham U (£20,000 on 26/6/95) FL 31/1 FLC 3 FAC 1 Others 6/1

GARNER Simon
Born: Boston, 23 November 1959
Height: 5'9" Weight: 12.11
Club Honours: FMC '87
In spite of his very infrequent appearances in 1995-96 – the manager was reluctant to rely on a player who could not last 90 minutes – he still had an almost mesmeric hold on the Wycombe supporters. Skilful, subtle, inventive, his forward play was a joy to watch and he is still one of the best brains in the game. Loaned out to Torquay in January, he retains a first-class attitude and strong desire to win, and will continue to be an excellent influence on whichever team captures him on a free transfer.
Blackburn Rov (From apprentice on 5/7/78) FL 455+29/168 FLC 32+2/11 FAC 24+5/7 Others 17+1/6
West Bromwich A (£30,000 on 6/8/92) FL 25+8/8 FLC 3 FAC 3 Others 4+2/1
Wycombe W (Free on 4/2/94) FL 53+13/15 FLC 2+2 FAC 4+1/3 Others 6/4
Torquay U (Loaned on 19/1/96) FL 10+1/1

GARNETT Shaun Maurice
Born: Wallasey, 22 November 1969
Height: 6'3" Weight: 13.4
Club Honours: AMC '90
A tall, dominant centre half with a useful turn of pace, Shaun was never able to secure a regular position in Tranmere's defence, once Shaun Teale arrived, and last March he moved to South Wales to join Swansea's ultimately fruitless battle against relegation. Nevertheless, his 19 appearances during the season characterised his total commitment to the club and it was a matter of real regret to Shaun that he had to move for the sake of his career, which had gone into reverse. Soon made his presence felt at his new club, being appointed captain in April.
Tranmere Rov (From trainee on 15/6/88) FL 110+2 FLC 13/1 FAC 4 Others 15+2
Chester C (Loaned on 1/10/92) FL 9
Preston NE (Loaned on 11/12/92) FL 10/2 Others 1
Wigan Ath (Loaned on 26/2/93) FL 13/1
Swansea C (£200,000 on 11/3/96) FL 9

GARVEY Stephen (Steve) Hugh
Born: Stalybridge, 22 November 1973
Height: 5'9" Weight: 11.1
Steve has been with Crewe for almost five years as a professional and normally plays in about half the games available, operating either on the left or right flanks and causing problems for defenders with his attacking style. Not high on the goalscoring lists, he opened his 1995-96 account in the 8-0 AWS win over Hartlepool.
Crewe Alex (From trainee on 25/10/91) FL 51+28/6 FLC 6+4/2 FAC 2+3/1 Others 7+1/1

GAUGHAN Steven (Steve) Edward
Born: Doncaster, 14 April 1970
Height: 5'11" Weight: 11.2

A powerhouse in Darlington's midfield, Steve had a tremendous season in 1995-96, his strong running and tenacity being vital to the drive towards the play offs. Also scored spectacularly on occasion from outside the box.

Doncaster Rov (Free from Hatfield Main Colliery on 21/1/88) FL 42+25/3 FLC 2+2 FAC 4+1 Others 5+1
Sunderland (Free on 1/7/90)
Darlington (£10,000 on 21/1/92) FL 159+12/15 FLC 8 FAC 6/1 Others 10+1

GAVIN Mark Wilson
Born: Bailleston, 10 December 1963
Height: 5'8" Weight: 10.7

Mark was troubled by injuries last season, hence his lack of Exeter appearances. Still as tricky as ever, one of the highlights of 1995-96 for City fans was the goal he scored at home against Rochdale. Loves taking on defenders.

Leeds U (From apprentice on 24/12/81) FL 20+10/3 FLC 4+1/1 FAC 0+1
Hartlepool U (Loaned on 29/3/85) FL 7/1
Carlisle U (Free on 4/7/85) FL 12+1/1 FLC 2/1 Others 1
Bolton W (Free on 27/3/86) FL 48+1/3 FLC 1 FAC 5/1 Others 10/1
Rochdale (£20,000 on 14/8/87) FL 23/6 FLC 3 FAC 1 Others 2
Heart of Midlothian (£30,000 on 3/2/88) SL 5+4
Bristol C (£30,000 on 4/10/88) FL 62+7/6 FLC 8 FAC 13/1 Others 6/1
Watford (Signed on 9/8/90) FL 8+5
Bristol C (£60,000 on 6/12/91) FL 34+7/2 FLC 0+1 FAC 4 Others 4
Exeter C (Signed on 11/2/94) FL 73+4/4 FLC 3 FAC 3 Others 5

GAYLE Brian Wilbert
Born: Kingston, 6 March 1965
Height: 6'1" Weight: 12.7

As Sheffield United club captain and centre half, Brian returned from injury at the start of last season only to be sent off in his first full appearance at Oldham, after just 26 minutes. He then required a fourth operation on his knee and spent the rest of the term regaining full fitness in the reserves, until an emotional 15 minute appearance in the last game brought his United career to a close.

Wimbledon (From apprentice on 31/10/84) FL 76+7/3 FLC 7/1 FAC 8/1 Others 2
Manchester C (£325,000 on 6/7/88) FL 55/3 FLC 8 FAC 2 Others 1
Ipswich T (£330,000 on 19/1/90) FL 58/4 FLC 3 FAC 0+1
Sheffield U (£750,000 on 17/9/91) F/PL 115+2/9 FLC 9 FAC 11/1 Others 1/1

GAYLE John
Born: Bromsgrove, 30 July 1964
Height: 6'2" Weight: 15.4
Club Honours: AMC '91

Towering Stoke striker. Having burst into the City side midway through last season, following an injury to the regular striker, Paul Peschisolido, even though scoring twice in a 3-3 draw at Portsmouth, his long-overdue run-in the team was derailed by suspension after just five games. He ended the campaign, being loaned out to Gillingham until the end of the season, scoring the winning goal on his debut at Mansfield Town.

Wimbledon (£30,000 from Bromsgrove on 1/3/89) FL 17+3/2 FLC 3
Birmingham C (£175,000 on 21/11/90) FL 39+5/10 FAC 2 Others 8+1/4
Walsall (Loaned on 20/8/93) FL 4/1
Coventry C (£100,000 on 13/9/93) PL 3 FLC 1+2
Burnley (£70,000 on 17/8/94) FL 7+7/3 FLC 1+1/1 FAC 1+1/1
Stoke C (£70,000 on 23/1/95) FL 6+8/3 FAC 0+1 Others 3+1
Gillingham (Loaned on 14/3/96) FL 9/3

GAYLE Marcus Anthony
Born: Hammersmith, 27 September 1970
Height: 6'1" Weight: 12.9
Club Honours: Div 3 '92
International Honours: E: Yth

A left-sided Wimbledon midfielder, Marcus is always a threatening prospect with the ball at his feet, bearing down on a defender. Last season, he started to find the net more frequently and with this added facet to his game he may yet become a fixture on the Dons' team-sheet. Tall and powerful, and crucial to set piece routines, in many ways he has filled the void in the air following John Fashanu's departure.

Brentford (From trainee on 6/7/89) FL 118+38/22 FLC 6+3 FAC 6+2/2 Others 14+6/2
Wimbledon (£250,000 on 24/3/94) PL 53+14/7 FLC 4/1 FAC 6+2

GAYLE Mark Samuel Roye
Born: Bromsgrove, 21 October 1969
Height: 6'2" Weight: 12.3

Since coming back into the Crewe first team in April 1995, Mark has not missed a game either in the league or cups. Gaining in confidence all the time and is determined to keep his goalkeeping spot in the team. An excellent shot stopper who can get down quickly to block close-range efforts, he is a good talker and reader of penalties.

Leicester C (From trainee on 1/7/88)
Blackpool (Free on 15/8/89) FLC 1 (Free to Worcester C in July 1990)
Walsall (£15,000 on 8/5/91) FL 74+1 FLC 8 FAC 1 Others 8
Crewe Alex (£35,000 on 21/12/93) FL 78+1 FLC 4 FAC 5 Others 9

GEE Philip (Phil) John
Born: Pelsall, 19 December 1964
Height: 5'11" Weight: 12.6
Club Honours: Div 2 '87

Right-footed Leicester City forward. A substitute in the televised game away to former club, Derby, he only received one further outing during the first half of last season, before being injured in a reserve match and hardly figuring thereafter. Released during the summer.

Derby Co (£5,000 from Gresley Rov on 2/9/85) FL 107+17/26 FLC 11+2/3 FAC 6+1/2 Others 7+1
Leicester C (Signed on 11/3/92) P/FL 35+18/9 FLC 2+3 Others 5+1/4
Plymouth Arg (Loaned on 27/1/95) FL 6

GEMMILL Scot
Born: Paisley, 2 January 1971
Height: 5'11" Weight: 11.0
Club Honours: FMC '92
International Honours: S: 6; B-2; U21-4

Displaced by Lars Bohinen at the start of 1995-96, Scot returned to first team duty with Nottingham Forest when the Norwegian departed in October and held his place in midfield, barring injury and suspension, for the remainder of the season. Although, by his own standards it was a quiet and unspectacular campaign, his hard-working displays impressed the Scottish manager, Craig Brown, and following an earlier selection against San Marino he received two more caps on his way to Euro '96. Is the son of Archie, former Forest and Scotland star, and new manager of Rotherham United.

Nottingham F (From trainee on 5/1/90) F/PL 149+8/19 FLC 22+1/3 FAC 17/1 Others 13+1/4

Scot Gemmill

GERMAINE Gary
Born: Birmingham, 2 August 1976
Height: 6'2" Weight: 14.0

A young West Bromwich goalkeeper who had yet to be given an opportunity to show what he was made of, mainly because Stuart Naylor and Nigel Spink were ahead of him in the pecking order, he was loaned to Scunthorpe last March, following a similar stay at non-league, Telford. Having figured in Scotland's U21 squad, without being called upon, Gary looked an exciting prospect in his 11 games with the Irons and with Naylor given a free transfer during the summer he could be pushing for an Albion place in the very near future.

West Bromwich A (From trainee on 5/7/94)
Scunthorpe U (Loaned on 8/3/96) FL 11

GERRARD Paul William
Born: Heywood, 22 January 1973
Height: 6'2" Weight: 12.3
International Honours: E: U21-18

Without a doubt, Oldham's Paul is one of

the best young goalkeepers around, as his England U21 caps have proved, but, with Jon Hallworth snapping at his heels last season, he still had to work hard to maintain his place. Daring and agile, he missed six games earlier on due to suspension and then the last five after breaking his jaw at home to Wolves, his good form in between fuelling speculation that he would join either Everton or Celtic in a £2m deal.

Oldham Ath (From trainee on 2/11/91) P/FL 118+1 FLC 7 FAC 7 Others 2+1

GIBB Alistair (Ally) Stuart
Born: Salisbury, 17 February 1976
Height: 5'9" Weight: 10.8

Right-sided midfield player who came to Northampton on loan from Norwich earlier last season, and returned on a permanent basis in February. Has already become a great favourite with the crowd, and is yet another free kick specialist.

Norwich C (From trainee on 1/7/94)
Northampton T (Loaned on 22/9/95)
Northampton T (£30,000 on 5/2/96) FL 12+11/2 Others 2

GIBBS Nigel James
Born: St Albans, 20 November 1965
Height: 5'7" Weight: 11.11
Club Honours: FAYC '82
International Honours: E: U21-5; Yth

Watford's club captain, and a stalwart defender, who started last season strongly but then made only a handful of appearances because of knee problems, prior to being released in the summer. His ability to read the game and his leadership qualities enable him to play anywhere in defence, although right back is his favoured position.

Watford (From apprentice on 23/11/83) FL 285+6/3 FLC 15/2 FAC 30+1 Others 13

GIBBS Paul Derek
Born: Gorleston, 26 October 1972
Height: 5'10" Weight: 11.3

Initially signed by Colchester as a left back, Paul's early 1995-96 season was interrupted by injury. However, on returning to fitness in February, he won a place on the left of the forward line in a major change of tactics and scored his first league goals as the play-off race intensified. Has, arguably, the most skilful left foot seen at Layer Road for years.

Colchester U (Signed from Diss T on 6/3/95) FL 21+12/3 FAC 0+1 Others 3

GIGGS Ryan Joseph
Born: Cardiff, 29 November 1973
Height: 5'11" Weight: 10.9
Club Honours: ESC '91; FAYC '92; FLC '92; PL '93, '94, '96; CS '93, '94; FAC '94, '96
International Honours: W: 16; U21-1; Yth. E: Sch

Skilful Manchester United left winger who runs at defenders and goes past them effortlessly to look for the cross or to get on target with a tremendous left-foot shot. The re-emergence of Ryan as a major force was one of the main reasons for United's continued quest for honours in 1995-96. Although his wing play was beyond reproach, he actually won greater super-

latives when Alex Ferguson was forced to pull him back into midfield alongside Roy Keane after the club was hit by a series of injuries earlier on. Scoring a goal a month on average, his best strike came against Manchester City during the all-important Easter game, while his final one, in a 3-0 win at Middlesbrough, assured United of their third Premiership title in four years. A regular for Wales, he brought his season to an end with an FA Cup winners' medal, following the 1-0 defeat of Liverpool.

Manchester U (From trainee on 1/12/90) F/PL 164+17/39 FLC 16+4/6 FAC 24+2/5 Others 13+1/2

Ryan Giggs

GILBERT David (Dave) James
Born: Lincoln, 22 June 1963
Height: 5'4" Weight: 10.8
Club Honours: Div 4 '87

Following his transfer from Grimsby, immediately prior to the start of 1995-96, Dave gave WBA much needed width down the left-hand side, performing exceedingly well at times in front of a number of different left backs! His close-dribbling skills and creativeness caused opponents plenty of trouble and he was always a tireless worker when things were not going all that well for the team. Perhaps lacking that little extra pace at times, nevertheless, he had a fine season.

Lincoln C (From apprentice on 29/6/81) FL 15+15/1 FLC 5 FAC 3
Scunthorpe U (Free on 18/8/82) FL 1 FLC 1 (Free to Boston U in 1982-83)
Northampton T (Signed on 30/6/86) FL 120/21 FLC 10/2 FAC 6/3 Others 9/1
Grimsby T (£55,000 on 23/3/89) FL 259/41 FLC 18/4 FAC 11/2 Others 9
West Bromwich A (Signed on 8/8/95) FL 35+5/5 FLC 4 FAC 1 Others 7

GILBERT Kenneth (Kenny) Robert
Born: Aberdeen, 8 March 1975
Height: 5'8" Weight: 11.4
International Honours: S: Yth; Sch

Usually seen on the right-hand side of Hull's midfield, although he also filled in at full back, Kenny was signed from Aberdeen on the recommendation of their boss, Roy Aitken (following a loan period), shortly after Dean Windass moved in the opposite direction for £700,000. A tenacious battler, he provided valuable back up to City's injury ravaged squad.

Aberdeen (Free from East End "A" on 7/6/91)
Hull C (Free on 12/1/96) FL 6+7

GILCHRIST Philip (Phil) Alexander
Born: Stockton on Tees, 25 August 1973
Height: 5'11" Weight: 11.12

The other half (with Matthew Elliott) of one of the best central defensive partnerships in the second division, Phil is smaller than his partner but compliments him with his tremendous pace and good-tackling ability, scoring some important goals for Oxford early last season. Is also the long-throw expert and should excel in division one next season, following the club's promotion as runners up to Swindon.

Nottingham F (From trainee on 5/12/90)
Middlesbrough (Free on 10/1/92)
Hartlepool U (Free on 27/11/92) FL 77+5 FLC 4+1 FAC 4 Others 5
Oxford U (£100,000 on 17/2/95) FL 60/4 FLC 4 FAC 5 Others 3

GILKES Michael Earl
Born: Hackney, 20 July 1965
Height: 5'8" Weight: 10.10
Club Honours: FMC '88; Div 3 '86, Div 2 '94

Having spent 11 seasons at Reading and due a well deserved testimonial during 1996-97, Michael showed he had lost none of his pace in 1995-96 and, despite failing to get on the score sheet during the campaign, created many goals with his speedy runs and whipped in crosses, especially down the left flank. Captained the side during the latter part of the season.

Reading (Free from Leicester C juniors on 10/7/84) FL 321+40/42 FLC 25+6/6 FAC 29+2/1 Others 26+2/2
Chelsea (Loaned on 28/1/92) FL 0+1 Others 0+1
Southampton (Loaned on 4/3/92) FL 4+2

GILLESPIE Keith Robert
Born: Bangor, 18 February 1975
Height: 5'10" Weight: 11.3
Club Honours: FAYC '92; CS '94
International Honours: NI: 12; U21-1; Yth; Sch

Although he can operate on either flank, it was on the right wing that Keith displayed outstanding early season form for Newcastle in 1995-96. Well balanced with searing pace, he can drop his shoulder to deceive the full back and race to the goal line before producing a fine cross at full speed. His groin injury at Old Trafford at Christmas was a blow, and the importance of his contribution was demonstrated when he was recalled to the team much earlier than expected. Later lost his place on the arrival of Tino Asprilla, a controversial decision which caused much debate amongst supporters and the media as United ultimately failed to land the Premiership title. Continued as a Northern Ireland regular with four more caps.

Keith Gillespie

Manchester U (From trainee on 3/2/93) PL 3+6/1 FLC 3 FAC 1+1/1
Wigan Ath (Loaned on 3/9/93) FL 8/4 Others 2
Newcastle U (£1,000,000 on 12/1/95) PL 41+4/6 FLC 4/1 FAC 3/2

GINOLA David
Born: Gossin, France, 25 January 1967
Height: 6'0" Weight: 11.10
International Honours: France:16

David enriched the Premiership with flair and inventiveness, operating primarily from Newcastle's left midfield. Gifted with wonderful technique, his instant control and silky skills enabled him to turn full backs at will and leave them trailing, a feature of his play being the long crossfield pass from one touchline to the other, delivered to the foot of a team mate. He also likes to cut in and go for goal, and possesses a powerful shot. Very confident on the ball, he settled well following his transfer and was Carling "Player of the Month" in August. Although often accused of theatricals, his skills are highly regarded by his fellow professionals and he was third in the PFA "Player of the Year" poll, as well as making the representative XI. However, despite his fine form for Newcastle, he was surprisingly overlooked by the French national side this year.
Newcastle U (£2,500,000 from Paris St Germain, via Toulon, Racing Paris and Brest, on 6/7/95) PL 34/5 FLC 4 FAC 2

GITTENS Jonathan (Jon) Antoni
Born: Mossley, 22 January 1964
Height: 5'11" Weight: 12.10
Tough-tackling Portsmouth central defender who came into the side during Andy Awford's enforced absence at the beginning of last season. Although producing some good performances, he was replaced by Russell Perrett, following suspension, and never really regained his place. A good man to have in the wings, Jon is an excellent marker, his pace making him difficult to pass, and strong in the air. Despite that, he was released during the summer.

Southampton (£10,000 from Paget R on 16/10/85) FL 18 FLC 4 FAC 1
Swindon T (£40,000 on 22/7/87) FL 124+2/6 FLC 15+1 FAC 9 Others 13+1/1
Southampton (£400,000 on 28/3/91) FL 16+3 FLC 4 Others 1
Middlesbrough (Loaned on 19/2/92) FL 9+3/1
Middlesbrough (£200,000 on 27/7/92) PL 13 FLC 0+1 FAC 1
Portsmouth (Free on 9/8/93) FL 81+2/2 FLC 10 FAC 3 Others 3/1

GIVEN Seamus (Shay) John
Born: Lifford, 20 April 1976
Height: 6'2" Weight: 13.4
Club Honours: Div 1 '96
International Honours: Ei: 7; U21; Yth

A 19-year-old goalkeeper who arrived at Sunderland on loan from Blackburn last January and departed in April as a Roker cult hero. Displaying ultra-confidence, Shay played 17 games, keeping 12 clean sheets, conceding only 11 goals, and appearing to have no visible flaws to his game. Having come to the club as a virtual unknown, he not only picked up a first division championship medal, but won his first full caps for the Republic of Ireland, having earlier played at U21 level – a first for a player on loan? Whilst Shay's valuation in the transfer market will now have rocketed, all Roker fans hope that the young 'keeper will return permanently. Yet to appear for Rovers, earlier in the season he played five games on loan at Swindon, conceding just one goal.
Blackburn Rov (Free from Glasgow Celtic juniors on 8/8/94)
Swindon T (Loaned on 4/8/95) FL 5
Sunderland (Loaned on 19/1/96) FL 17

GLASS James (Jimmy) Robert
Born: Epsom, 1 August 1973
Height: 6'1" Weight: 13.4
Although a professional at Crystal Palace since 1991, the young goalkeeper has spent the whole of that time in the wings due to the brilliant form of Nigel Martyn. Bearing that in mind, and searching for first team football, he had two periods on loan last season, at Gillingham (December) and Burnley (January), without being called upon, before signing for Bournemouth in March. Went straight into the side, replacing the injured Ian Andrews, and quickly showed himself to be a brave 'keeper who was not afraid to come off his line and one who was in command of the penalty area.
Crystal Palace (From trainee on 4/7/91)
Portsmouth (Loaned on 10/2/95) FL 3
Bournemouth (Free on 8/3/96) FL 13

GLEGHORN Nigel William
Born: Seaham, 12 August 1962
Height: 6'0" Weight: 13.2
Club Honours: AMC '91; Div 2 '93

An experienced midfielder whose switch from the left wing to the centre of midfield was the turning point in Stoke's season in 1995-96, enabling him to use his knowledge and passing ability to great effect. Formed a well-balanced partnership with Ray Wallace and played the captain's role with distinction after Vince Overson's injury. One of the best midfielders in the Endsleigh League and a City ever present in all 56 games played.

Ipswich T (Free from Seaham RS on 30/8/85) FL 54+12/11 FLC 3+2 FAC 3+1 Others 7+2/2
Manchester C (£47,500 on 4/8/88) FL 27+7/7 FLC 2+1/2 FAC 0+1/1 Others 1/1
Birmingham C (£175,000 on 9/9/89) FL 142/33 FLC 13/5 FAC 7/3 Others 14/2
Stoke C (£100,000 on 24/10/92) FL 162+4/26 FLC 10/2 FAC 10 Others 22/3

GLOVER Dean Victor
Born: Birmingham, 29 December 1963
Height: 5'10" Weight: 11.13
Club Honours: AMC '93

Classy Port Vale central defender who was a regular during the first half of 1995-96 before injury forced him out of the team. Whilst on the sidelines, Vale embarked on a long run of improved results and Dean was unable to regain his place. Had begun the season well by scoring the club's first goal in the Coca Cola Cup-tie at Huddersfield Town.

Aston Villa (From apprentice on 30/12/81) FL 25+3 FLC 7/1 FAC 3 Others 1
Sheffield U (Loaned on 17/10/86) FL 5
Middlesbrough (Signed on 17/6/87) FL 44+6/5 FLC 4 FAC 5 Others 7/2
Port Vale (£200,000 on 3/2/89) FL 293+3/12 FLC 20/1 FAC 18/1 Others 22/3

GLOVER Edward Lee
Born: Kettering, 24 April 1970
Height: 5'10" Weight: 12.1
Club Honours: FMC '92
International Honours: S: U21-3; Yth

Port Vale striker who holds the ball up well to bring others into the game. Began last season as a regular in the side, but after three months his total of only four goals and a run of poor results led to him becoming a casualty of the manager's changes. However, having notched up three hat tricks for the reserves, Lee returned in March to score one of the goals that took the club to the Anglo-Italian Cup final at Wembley.

Nottingham F (From apprentice on 2/5/87) F/PL 61+15/9 FLC 6+5/2 FAC 8+2/1 Others 4+1/1
Leicester C (Loaned on 14/9/89) FL 3+2/1
Barnsley (Loaned on 18/1/90) FL 8 FAC 4
Luton T (Loaned on 2/9/91) FL 1
Port Vale (£200,000 on 2/8/94) FL 38+14/7 FLC 5+1/4 FAC 0+2 Others 3+2/2

GOATER Leonard Shaun
Born: Hamilton, Bermuda, 25 February 1970
Height: 6'1" Weight: 11.10
Club Honours: AMC '96
International Honours: Bermuda: 8

Bermuda's all-time leading international goalscorer, this highly talented striker topped Rotherham's scoring charts in 1995-96 for the second successive season. In developing an ability to turn past defenders and then use his speed, which often leaves his marker floundering, Shaun has improved enormously over the last couple of years and frequently attracts the attention of bigger clubs. Played in all eight AWS matches that ended in a 2-1 Wembley victory over Shrewsbury.

Manchester U (From juniors on 8/5/89)
Rotherham U (Free on 25/10/89) FL 169+40/70 FLC 13+4/4 FAC 12+3/7 Others 15+5/5
Notts Co (Loaned on 12/11/93) FL 1

Shaun Goater

GOODEN Ty Michael
Born: Canvey Island, 23 October 1972
Height: 5'8" Weight: 12.6
Club Honours: Div 2 '96

In and out of the Swindon side last season until the New Year, when he finally began to string together some impressive performances, he proved to be equally effective in midfield or on the flanks. Showed good skills to go with a powerful shot, despite missing the end of the campaign to take in a hernia operation, his 26 league appearances were enough to warrant him a second division championship medal as Town stormed back to join the Football League elite.

Swindon T (Free from Wycombe W on 17/9/93) P/FL 29+17/5 FLC 2+1/1 FAC 3+1 Others 3+1

GOODING Michael (Mick) Charles
Born: Newcastle, 12 April 1959
Height: 5'9" Weight: 10.7
Club Honours: Div 3 '81, '89, Div 2 '94

Obviously relishing the role of joint Reading player/manager, and putting unlimited effort and enthusiasm into both jobs, he led the side by example in 1995-96, being elected "Player of the Year" for the third time in five seasons. Despite his maturity, he remains one of the fittest players on the books and also finds time to move upfield to score goals as well as bolster the midfield.

Rotherham U (Signed from Bishop Auckland on 18/7/79) FL 90+12/10 FLC 9/3 FAC 3
Chesterfield (Signed on 24/12/82) FL 12
Rotherham U (Signed on 9/9/83) FL 149+7/33 FLC 18/3 FAC 13/4 Others 7
Peterborough U (£18,000 on 13/8/87) FL 47/21 FLC 8/2 FAC 1/2 Others 4/2
Wolverhampton W (£85,000 on 20/9/88) FL 43+1/4 FLC 4 Others 5+1/1
Reading (£65,000 on 26/12/89) FL 263+8/26 FLC 17 FAC 16+1/2 Others 16/2

GOODMAN Donald (Don) Ralph
Born: Leeds, 9 May 1966
Height: 5'10" Weight: 13.2
Club Honours: Div 3 '85

Continued to play behind Steve Bull and David Kelly in Wolves' first three games of

1995-96, but then replaced the latter and revelled in being an out-and-out striker, where he could use his heading power more. Scored ten goals in a 13 game spell, including a diving header to complete a good move against Grimsby, two in two minutes at Fulham, and one at Ipswich after a fine run. He then went 11 games without adding any more, but soon got his touch back, reaching 20 in his 47th appearance, before suffering a depressed fractured scull after an accidental collision in the penultimate match of the season, at home to Huddersfield.

Bradford C (Free from Collingham on 10/7/84) FL 65+5/14 FLC 5+1/2 FAC 2+3/4 Others 4+1/2
West Bromwich A (£50,000 on 27/3/87) FL 140+18/60 FLC 11/1 FAC 7/1 Others 5/1
Sunderland (£900,000 on 6/12/91) FL 112+4/40 FLC 9/1 FAC 3/1 Others 4/2
Wolverhampton W (£1,100,000 on 6/12/94) FL 67+1/9 FLC 6/3 FAC 9+1/1 Others 2

GOODMAN Jonathan (Jon)
Born: Walthamstow, 2 June 1971
Height: 5'11" Weight: 12.11

Whenever Jon has an extended run for Wimbledon he scores goals and on the strength of 12 starts in 1995-96, albeit appearing a further 19 times from the bench, he netted an impressive nine. A hard-running and quick-thinking finisher, he would be more than ready and capable of claiming a regular place in the team if the Dons were ever forced to sell one of their main line strikers.

Millwall (£50,000 from Bromley on 20/8/90) FL 97+12/35 FLC 5+4/2 FAC 5+1 Others 3
Wimbledon (Signed on 9/11/94) PL 22+24/10 FLC 0+1 FAC 3+1/3

GOODRIDGE Gregory (Greg) Ronald St Clair
Born: Barbados, 10 July 1971
Height: 5'6" Weight: 10.0
International Honours: Barbados: 2

A winger with electrifying pace, and predominantly left sided, Greg was signed from Torquay United in the summer of 1995 as one for the future and made his debut for QPR in the Coca Cola Cup against Oxford in October, followed 11 days later by his league debut against Newcastle, both appearances as a substitute. In all he appeared nine times throughout the season, all from the bench, scoring once direct from a corner at Sheffield Wednesday in a 3-1 win.

Torquay U (Free from Lambada on 24/3/94) FL 32+6/4 FLC 4/1 FAC 2+1 Others 3+1/1
Queens Park R (£350,000 on 9/8/95) PL 0+7/1 FLC 0+1 FAC 0+1

GOODWIN Shaun
Born: Rotherham, 14 June 1969
Height: 5'8" Weight: 10.11
Club Honours: Div 4 '89; AMC '96

It is often said that whenever Shaun plays well, then Rotherham play well and that certainly proved to be the case again in 1995-96. Manager's Archie Gemmill and John McGovern encouraged him to play in his preferred role, namely running from midfield at opposing defenders. Unfortunately, his season was interrupted by injury, but when he returned to full fitness in the latter part of the term he showed just how much the team missed him with some superbly worked goals. Linked together in perfect style with Nigel Jemson, especially in the 2-1 Wembley victory over Shrewsbury that brought the AWS trophy to Millmoor.

Rotherham U (From trainee on 1/7/87) FL 243+16/34 FLC 16+7/1 FAC 16+1/3 Others 20+2/4

Shaun Goodwin

GORDON Dale Andrew
Born: Great Yarmouth, 9 January 1967
Height: 5'10" Weight: 11.8
Club Honours: SC '92; SPD '92, '93; SLC '93
International Honours: E: B-2; U21-4; Yth; Sch

Skilful West Ham right winger with good pace, plus the added ingredient of being able to score vital goals. Still trying to shake off long-term injuries, Dale was not available for first team action until last February and following a couple of subs' appearances he was loaned out to Millwall, immediately prior to the transfer deadline. Showing good control, and impressing the locals, he was unlucky not to score on a couple of occasions, the ball hitting the woodwork, before returning to Upton Park, where a free transfer awaited him.

Norwich C (From apprentice on 17/1/84) FL 194+12/31 FLC 21/3 FAC 19/6 Others 14+2/3
Glasgow R (£1,200,000 on 8/11/91) SL 41+4/6 SLC 1+1/1 SC 6+1/1 Others 1
West Ham U (£750,000 on 20/7/93) PL 8+1/1 FLC 1 FAC 0+1
Peterborough U (Loaned on 23/3/95) FL 6/1
Millwall (Loaned on 21/3/96) FL 6

GORDON Dean Dwight
Born: Croydon, 10 February 1973
Height: 6'0" Weight: 13.4
Club Honours: Div 1 '94
International Honours: E: U21-13

The tall, strong Crystal Palace left back enjoyed another excellent season in 1995-96, despite being on the transfer list until March, following which he signed a new three year contract. Scored a rare hat trick (for a full back) at West Bromwich in December, although two of the goals were penalties, but missed the last part of the campaign, including the play offs, having suffered a leg injury in March. A regular member of the England U21 squad, Dean was selected as the first division's best left back in the PFA award winning XI.

Crystal Palace (From trainee on 4/7/91) F/PL 119+15/15 FLC 14+3/2 FAC 8+1/1 Others 2+1

GORDON Kenyatta Gavin
Born: Manchester, 24 June 1979
Height: 6'1" Weight: 11.5

A rangy target-man and another fledgling Tiger, just a couple of months into his YTS, Gavin became Hull's second youngest player (16 years, 88 days) when coming on as sub in the Coca Cola Cup-tie at Premiership, Coventry City, where he was partnered up front by 17-year-old Paul Fewings. Earlier "Big Fash" had been on schoolboy forms at Manchester City.

Hull C (Trainee) FL 3+10/3 FLC 0+2 Others 0+1

GORDON Neville Spencer Damian
Born: Greenwich, 15 November 1975
Height: 5'9" Weight: 10.12

Given a one year contract at Reading after leaving Millwall, immediately prior to the start of last season, Neville was unable to resurrect his career at Elm Park, making only one first team appearance, and that as an 80th minute substitute at West Bromwich. He also failed to impress in reserve fixtures, and was given a free transfer during the summer, following a loan spell at non-league Woking.

Millwall (From trainee on 24/5/94)
Reading (Free on 11/8/95) FL 0+1

GORE Ian George
Born: Prescot, 10 January 1968
Height: 5'11" Weight: 12.4

An experienced defender who slotted nicely into the Doncaster back four following his transfer from Torquay towards the end of last season. Prior to arriving at Belle Vue, after being released by Blackpool during the 1995 close season, he made his debut for United in the opening game of the campaign and quickly impressed as a regular. Will be looking to improve his goalscoring record of just two in nearly 250 league games!

Birmingham C (From trainee on 1/5/86)
Blackpool (Free from Southport on 21/1/88) FL 196+4 FLC 15+1 FAC 11 Others 20+2
Torquay U (Free on 11/8/95) FL 25/2 FLC 4 FAC 1/1 Others 2
Doncaster Rov (£5,000 on 22/3/96) FL 5

GOSS Jeremy
Born: Cyprus, 11 May 1965
Height: 5'9" Weight: 11.4
Club Honours: FAYC '83
International Honours: W: 9

Hard-working Norwich midfielder who pressures opponents into mistakes and is good on the ball, keeping the game going

with quick passing movements. Injuries and a lack of opportunity under the stewardship of Martin O'Neill meant that his first seasonal appearance in 1995-96 did not arrive until Boxing Day and this for a 200 game man for the club! New manager, Gary Megson, recalled him to the side and he busily played in 18 of the next 26 matches, his fine right-foot volleyed winner against first division runners-up, Derby County, seeing him become the club's 19th different scorer at senior level, thus breaking a record that had stood for 87 years. Was released at the end of the season, despite continuing to play for Wales.

Norwich C (From juniors on 23/3/83) F/PL 155+33/14 FLC 14+3/3 FAC 14+4 Others 15/6

GOUCK Andrew (Andy) Scott
Born: Blackpool, 8 June 1972
Height: 5'9" Weight: 11.2

Battling Blackpool midfielder who started last season in the side, but then lost his place to Andy Morrison, appearing only sparsely afterwards. Although predominately a ball winner, he is quite capable of getting forward to score the odd goal.

Blackpool (From trainee on 4/7/90) FL 121+27/12 FLC 9+3 FAC 4+1 Others 11+1/3

GOULD Jonathan (Jon) Alan
Born: Paddington, 18 July 1968
Height: 6'1" Weight: 13.7

Goalkeeping son of Bobby Gould whose strong points are his reflexes and shot-stopping ability. Made only one starting appearance for Coventry in 1995-96, at home to Hull City in the Coca Cola Cup, keeping a clean sheet, before having the misfortune to come on as a substitute at Molineux in the fourth round, after Steve Ogrizovic was sent off, and concede two goals in his first two minutes on the pitch. With his appearances restricted by the form of "Oggy" and John Filan, Jon went to Bradford City on loan on transfer deadline day, prior to being released during the summer.

Halifax T (Free from Clevedon T on 18/7/90) FL 32 FLC 2 FAC 5 Others 5
West Bromwich A (Free on 30/1/92)
Coventry C (Free on 15/7/92) PL 25 FLC 1+1
Bradford C (Loaned on 29/3/96) FL 9 Others 3

GRAHAM Deniol William
Born: Cannock, 4 October 1969
Height: 5'10" Weight: 10.7
International Honours: W: U21-1; Yth

Midfielder. Freed by Stockport at the end of 1994-95, he joined Scunthorpe on trial at the start of last season but was judged not to be worth a full contract and released. During his short stay at Glanford Park, Deniol made three appearances, two of them as a substitute, coming off the bench to score on his debut at Lincoln.

Manchester U (From trainee on 8/10/87) FL 1+1 FLC 0+1 FAC 0+1/1
Barnsley (£50,000 on 8/8/91) FL 18+20/2 FLC 1+3
Preston NE (Loaned on 24/10/92) FL 8 FAC 2/1 Others 1
Carlisle U (Loaned on 29/11/93) FL 2/1 Other 1
Stockport Co (Free on 30/6/94) FL 5+6/2
Scunthorpe U (Free on 10/8/95) FL 1+2/1

GRAHAM James (Jimmy)
Born: Glasgow, 5 November 1969
Height: 6'0" Weight: 11.8

The tough-tackling Scottish left back returned last August from a five month lay off, due to a knee ligament complaint, to recapture the impressive form of his first Hull City term, only to suffer a re-occurrence of the same injury which then needed surgery. The bald cult hero's nightmare ended in February when City were pleased to welcome back this reliable player, prior to him being released during the summer.

Bradford C (From trainee on 12/9/88) FL 6+1
Rochdale (Loaned on 3/11/89) FL 11 FAC 4 Others 3
Rochdale (£15,000 on 9/7/90) FL 120+6/1 FLC 13+1 FAC 8 Others 6/1
Hull C (Free on 5/8/94) FL 63/1 FLC 4 FAC 1 Others 2

GRAHAM Richard Ean
Born: Dewsbury, 28 November 1974
Height: 6'2" Weight: 12.1

An Oldham defender, cum midfielder, Richard played most of last season in the centre of Latics' defence, following the departure of Richard Jobson. And as you would expect for such a tall man, he is good in the air, his height being extremely useful at set piece situations, while his awkward-looking, gangling runs caused defences all kinds of problems. His good form was rewarded by selection for the England U21 squad, although not making the field of play.

Oldham Ath (From trainee on 16/7/93) P/FL 64+5/4 FLC 6 FAC 5 Others 2

GRAINGER Martin Robert
Born: Enfield, 23 August 1972
Height: 5'11" Weight: 12.0

Birmingham left back whose style is certainly uncompromising. Although continuing to give blood, sweat and tears for Brentford in 1995-96, he did not reach the peaks of the previous campaign and was sold to Birmingham during the transfer deadline week. This coming season, City will be looking to him for free kicks and penalties, as well as relying on his un-doubted defensive capabilities.

Colchester U (From trainee on 28/7/92) FL 37+9/7 FLC 3 FAC 3+2 Others 3/1
Brentford (£60,000 on 21/10/93) FL 100+1/12 FLC 6/1 FAC 9/1 Others 8/2
Birmingham C (£400,000 on 25/3/96) FL 8

GRANT Anthony (Tony)
Born: Drogheda, 20 August 1976
Height: 5'10" Weight: 11.8
International Honours: Ei: Yth; Sch

Signed from Leeds as an investment for the future last November, Tony became a favourite in the Preston reserve team, as an aggressive, powerful forward, which led to his regular inclusion in the first team squad, although usually on the bench. Great potential and one to watch for.

Leeds U (From trainee on 1/8/94)
Preston NE (Free on 13/11/95) FL 0+1

GRANT Anthony (Tony) James
Born: Liverpool, 14 November 1974
Height: 5'10" Weight: 10.2
Club Honours: CS '95

Everton central midfielder who combines sound technical ability with vision. Comfortable in possession and having the ability to deliver probing balls into danger areas, he started last season in the first team and, although only a squad player, put together a run of seven matches early on and scored against Reykjavic. Later, in order to further his experience, Tony went on loan to Swindon, scoring on his debut, and impressed the locals before coming back to Goodison where he became a regular towards the end of the campaign, working well with John Ebbrell in Joe Parkinson's absence.

Everton (From trainee on 8/7/93) PL 12+6/1 FLC 2 FAC 0+1 Others 2+2/1
Swindon T (Loaned on 18/1/96) FL 3/1

GRANT Kim Tyrone
Born: Ghana, 25 September 1972
Height: 5'10" Weight: 10.12

A hard-working striker who at last lived up to his considerable potential, Kim scored some excellent goals during last season, including spectacular solo efforts for Charlton against Wimbledon in the Coca Cola Cup, and Liverpool in the FA Cup. Surprisingly transferred to Luton just before the transfer deadline, where he scored on his debut, although his form was good there was nothing more to be done for a side already seemingly consigned to second division football. Is a threat to any defence with his speed off the mark.

Charlton Ath (From trainee on 6/3/91) FL 74+49/18 FLC 3+9/1 FAC 8+5/5 Others 5+2/1
Luton T (£250,000 on 15/3/96) FL 10/3

GRANVILLE Daniel (Danny) Patrick
Born: Islington, 19 January 1975
Height: 5'11" Weight: 12.5

A left-sided Cambridge United player, who is at home either at full back or in midfield, Danny struggled in the early part of last season, but after Christmas made the left back position his own. Incidentally, at the age of 23, he is the longest-serving player at the club.

Cambridge U (From trainee on 19/5/93) FL 52+10/7 FLC 1+2 FAC 0+2 Others 3+2

GRAY Andrew (Andy)
Born: Southampton, 25 October 1973
Height: 5'6" Weight: 10.10

An enthusiastic and nippy Leyton Orient striker who, throughout his career, has promised much in penalty area situations, but has yet to get into double figures. Unfortunately, he missed most of last season through injury and after just seven games without scoring was transferred to non-league, Slough Town, in March, following a spell on loan at Enfield.

Reading (From trainee on 3/7/92) FL 8+9/3 0+1/1 Others 1+1
Leyton Orient (Free on 20/7/94) FL 16+16/3 FLC 0+2 FAC 1/1 Others 0+1

GRAY Andrew David
Born: Harrogate, 15 November 1977
Height: 6'1" Weight: 12.8
International Honours: S: Yth

Eighteen-year-old Leeds United winger, cum striker, who has followed in the family footsteps at Elland road as the son of Frankie and the nephew of old crowd favourite, Eddie, Andy made his first team debut, coming on as a substitute against West Ham last January, and maintained his first team squad place thereafter. Selected for the Coca Cola Cup final line up, he looked to be the best Leeds' player that day. Very quick, skilful, and a superb crosser of the ball, he appears to have a big future in the game.

Leeds U (From trainee on 1/7/95) PL 12+3 FLC 1+1 FAC 0+2

GRAY Ian James
Born: Manchester, 25 February 1975
Height: 6'2" Weight: 12.0

Signed from Oldham in the 1995 close season, the young goalkeeper continued the brilliant form he had shown when on loan at Rochdale the previous term, despite carrying an injury that eventually ruled him out of the second half of the season and necessitated a hernia operation, as well as one to repair a damaged stomach muscle. Is agile, with good, safe hands, and competent on crosses.

Oldham Ath (From trainee on 16/7/93)
Rochdale (Loaned on 18/11/94) FL 12 Others 3
Rochdale (£20,000 on 17/7/95) FL 20 FLC 2 FAC 3 Others 3

GRAY Kevin John
Born: Sheffield, 7 January 1972
Height: 6'0" Weight: 13.0

Kevin had an outstanding season for Huddersfield in 1995-96, having initially struggled to establish himself in the first team, to become first choice at centre back. Despite his age, he is very experienced and his assured performances in the first division have marked him out as a quality player.

Mansfield T (From trainee on 1/7/90) FL 129+12/4 FLC 6+1 Others 12+2/2
Huddersfield T (Signed on 18/7/94) FL 43 FLC 1 FAC 4 Others 3

GRAY Martin David
Born: Stockton on Tees, 17 August 1971
Height: 5'9" Weight: 11.4

A strong tackler, and a useful squad player who could also fill in at full back, Martin turned in a particularly good performance for Sunderland when deputising for skipper, Kevin Ball, in the 6-0 home win over Millwall last December, before later joining Oxford in transfer deadline week. At the Manor Ground, he quickly fitted into the defensive area of midfield, clearing up well and feeding the wide men, in helping United to the first division as runners up. Incidentally, earlier in the season, while on loan at Fulham, in a case of mistaken identity he was sent off, something which was later rectified.

Sunderland (From trainee on 1/2/90) FL 46+18/1 FLC 6+2 FAC 0+3 Others 3+1
Aldershot (Loaned on 9/1/91) FL 3+2 Others 1
Fulham (Loaned on 20/10/95) FL 6 Others 1
Oxford U (£100,000 on 28/3/96) FL 6+1

GRAY Michael
Born: Sunderland, 3 August 1974
Height: 5'7" Weight: 10.10
Club Honours: Div 1 '96

The young outside left enjoyed a particularly satisfying season in 1995-96, playing in every game, representing a Football League U21 XI against an Italian Serie "B" side, and adding a PFA first division select XI medal to his championship gong. As well as being a potent attacker, Michael also impressed with his defensive capabilities, and formed a solid partnership with Martin Scott down Sunderland's left side. Currently attracting the attention of several leading clubs, no doubt his thunderous 30-yard goal against Birmingham at Roker in April will have added to his valuation.
Sunderland (From trainee on 1/7/92) FL 95+16/7 FLC 6+3 FAC 3+1

Michael Gray

GRAY Philip (Phil)
Born: Belfast, 2 October 1968
Height: 5'10" Weight: 12.5
Club Honours: Div 1 '96
International Honours: NI: 17; U23-1; Yth; Sch

Leading goalscorer in the previous two seasons, the Sunderland striker was injured last February and unfortunately missed out on the title run-in, although winning a first division championship medal. However, the Northern Ireland international certainly played his part in the Rokerites' success with nine goals earlier in the campaign, including a brilliant 30-yard strike at Grimsby in March. At the time of writing, Phil's future at the club is uncertain as he became a free agent in the summer, but many fans feel that he has the right credentials to succeed in the Premiership.
Tottenham H (From apprentice on 21/8/86) FL 4+5 FAC 0+1
Barnsley (Loaned on 17/1/90) FL 3 FAC 1
Fulham (Loaned on 8/11/90) FL 3 Others 2/1
Luton T (£275,000 on 16/8/91) FL 54+5/22 FLC 4/3 FAC 2/1 Others 2
Sunderland (£800,000 on 19/7/93) FL 108+7/34 FLC 9/4 FAC 8/3 Others 2

GRAYSON Neil
Born: York, 1 November 1964
Height: 5'10" Weight: 12.4
The Northampton striker, cum left-sided

midfielder, is a very busy player who buzzes in what ever position he plays. The previous season's top scorer and "Player of the Year", he is another great favourite with the crowd.
Doncaster Rov (Free from Rowntree Mackintosh on 22/3/90) FL 21+8/6 FAC 1+1 Others 2+1/1
York C (Free on 28/3/91) FL 0+1
Chesterfield (Free on 16/8/91) FL 9+6 FLC 2 FAC 1 Others 1
Northampton T (Free from Boston U, via Gateshead, on 19/6/94) FL 71+9/19 FLC 4 FAC 2 Others 5/3

GRAYSON Simon Nicholas
Born: Ripon, 16 December 1969
Height: 6'0" Weight: 12.10
Right-sided full back or midfielder for Leicester City. Regained his form and popularity with a string of consistent displays in 1995-96, scoring with a fierce drive in a televised fixture at St Andrews and also netting a last gasp equaliser in the next game home to Barnsley. Held down the right back slot for most of the season, but was occasionally pushed forward into midfield to cover for injuries.
Leeds U (From trainee on 13/6/88) FL 2 Others 1+1
Leicester C (£50,000 on 13/3/92) F/PL 139+13/4 FLC 9+2 FAC 6 Others 13+1

GRAYSTON Neil James
Born: Keighley, 25 November 1975
Height: 5'8" Weight: 10.9
Although the young left back made just two appearances for Bradford last season, with competition for places intense, he continued to remain a regular in the reserve side. Released during the summer.
Bradford C (From trainee on 27/5/94) FL 7 Others 1

GRAZIOLI Giuliano Stefano Luigi
Born: London, 23 March 1975
Height: 5'11" Weight: 12.11
Signed by Peterborough from Wembley last October, just two weeks later the young striker was loaned to Yeovil, followed by a spell at Enfield. Strange you might think for a player who had only just arrived from non-league circles. However, recalled to London Road after good reports, he returned in March to make three appearances, scoring at Crewe on his full debut.
Peterborough U (Free from Wembley T on 19/10/95) FL 2+1/1

GREEN Richard Edward
Born: Wolverhampton, 22 November 1967
Height: 6'0" Weight: 13.12
Used last season in the right back position, and occasionally at centre half, he is now approaching 200 first team appearances for Gillingham. Unfortunate to miss the last six games of 1995-96, due to a fractured arm sustained in the home game against Hartlepool, Richard's consistency was one of the main reasons for the club's promotion. Often creates havoc in the opposition's penalty area at set pieces.
Shrewsbury T (From trainee on 19/7/86) FL 120+5/5 FLC 11/1 FAC 5 Others 5/1
Swindon T (Free on 25/10/90)
Gillingham (Free on 6/3/92) FL 161+1/14 FLC 9 FAC 13+1/1 Others 6

GREEN Scott Paul
Born: Walsall, 15 January 1970
Height: 5'10" Weight: 12.5
The versatile Scott held down the Bolton right back berth for most of last season and with the Wanderers adopting a three man central defensive formation for long periods it gave him the licence to push forward into what once was more familiar territory. In finding the net three times, all away from home, at Chelsea, Spurs and Blackburn, his past experience as a forward held him in good stead. Can also play in midfield.
Derby Co (From trainee on 20/7/88)
Bolton W (£50,000 on 17/3/90) P/FL 159+49/24 FLC 19+3/1 FAC 18+2/2 Others 16+4/1

Scott Green

GREENALL Colin Anthony
Born: Billinge, 30 December 1963
Height: 5'11" Weight: 11.10
International Honours: E: Yth
Very consistent and competent Wigan centre back who was appointed club captain after he had joined his hometown side last September from Lincoln. His leadership and organisational skills, allied to the strengths of John Pender, also saw the formation of an effective partnership at the heart of Latics' defence.
Blackpool (From apprentice on 17/1/81) FL 179+4/9 FLC 12/2 FAC 9 Others 2
Gillingham (£40,000 on 10/9/86) FL 62/4 FLC 3/1 FAC 6/1 Others 9/2
Oxford U (£285,000 on 15/2/88) FL 67/2 FLC 4 FAC 1 Others 2
Bury (Loaned on 4/1/90) FL 3 Other 1
Bury (£125,000 on 16/7/90) FL 66+2/5 FLC 3 FAC 1 Others 8/1
Preston NE (£50,000 on 27/3/92) FL 29/1
Chester (Free on 13/8/93) FL 42/1 FLC 2 FAC 4/1 Others 4
Lincoln C (Free on 27/7/94) FL 43/3 FLC 6 FAC 3/1 Others 2
Wigan Ath (£45,000 on 19/9/95) FL 37/2 FAC 3 Others 2+1

GREENE David Michael
Born: Luton, 26 October 1973
Height: 6'2" Weight: 13.5
International Honours: Ei: U21-14

Eire U21 central defender who failed to break into Luton's first team in 1995-96, despite promising much the previous season. Unable to get further than the reserves, David had long-term loan spells at Colchester (November) and Brentford (March), where he added height and stability to both defences, even finding time to score a late, vital equaliser for United at Plymouth. Although offered new terms by Town, at the time of going to press, a move seemed imminent.

Luton T (From juniors on 3/9/91) FL 18+1 FLC 2 FAC 1 Others 0+1
Colchester U (Loaned on 23/11/95) FL 14/1 Others 2
Brentford (Loaned on 1/3/96) FL 11

GREGAN Sean Matthew
Born: Guisborough, 29 March 1974
Height: 6'2" Weight: 13.7
Despite being the longest-serving player at Darlington, Sean is still only 22, having first played in December 1991. A robust central defender who is tremendously strong in the air, he had a great game at Wembley in last season's third division play-off final and is now attracting the attention of bigger clubs.
Darlington (From trainee on 20/1/91) FL 113+7/4 FLC 4 FAC 6 Others 10+1/1

GREGG Matthew Stephen
Born: Cheltenham, 30 November 1978
Height: 5'11" Weight: 12.0
Deputising for Ashley Bayes, the young Torquay YTS goalkeeper impressed on his first team debut, a 1-1 home draw against Wigan last September. Is sure to be given further chances.
Torquay U (Trainee) FL 1

GREGORY David Spencer
Born: Sudbury, 23 January 1970
Height: 5'11" Weight: 11.10
Signed by Peterborough during the 1995 close season, having been freed by Ipswich, David never quite fitted in with Posh and following a limited number of appearances, joined Colchester in December, primarily as cover for a wafer-thin squad. The elder brother of Ipswich's Neil, despite the vast geographical disparity of their birthplaces, he is a versatile right-sided midfielder who can make good forward runs and moves into space well.
Ipswich T (From trainee on 31/3/87) F/PL 16+16/2 FLC 3+2 FAC 1 Others 3+2/4
Hereford U (Loaned on 9/1/95) FL 2 Others 1
Peterborough U (Free on 4/7/95) FL 0+3 FLC 1 FAC 1 Others 2
Colchester U (Free on 8/12/95) FL 7+3

GREGORY Neil Richard
Born: Ndola, Zambia, 7 October 1972
Height: 5'11" Weight: 11.10
Although being mainly on the subs' bench last season, niggling injuries to Alex Mathie and Ian Marshall gave the hard-running central striker the opportunity to score his first goals for Ipswich, a double at the expense of Watford. Also had the experience of taking over from Craig Forrest after the 'keeper was injured against Charlton, having four goals knocked past him for his

pains. As 1995-96 progressed, he invariably found himself behind James Scowcroft in the pecking order. Unfortunately, a groin injury picked up at Sunderland in February, which at the time did not seem too serious, brought his season to a premature end.
Ipswich T (From trainee on 21/2/92) P/FL 6+14/2 FLC 2 FAC 0+1 Others 3+2/2
Chesterfield (Loaned on 3/2/94) FL 2+1/1
Scunthorpe U (Loaned on 6/3/95) FL 10/7

GRIDELET Philip (Phil) Raymond
Born: Hendon, 30 April 1967
Height: 5'11" Weight: 13.0
International Honours: E: SP-5
Phil had a quieter season in the Southend midfield in 1995-96 than previously, with some of his drive and bite apparently missing, possibly caused by the crackdown on aggressive play by referees. Always willing to go into battle for the club, he is still an excellent ball winner and while not managing as many goals last season as he has in the past, he netted the winner against Leicester in December.
Barnsley (£175,000 from Barnet on 21/1/90) FL 3+3 FAC 1 Others 1
Rotherham U (Loaned on 5/3/93) FL 9
Southend U (Free on 25/9/93) FL 84+14/7 FLC 1 FAC 2 Others 7/1

GRIEMINK Bart
Born: Holland, 29 March 1972
Height: 6'4" Weight: 15.4
A goalkeeper spotted playing amateur football in Holland, while holding down a job in a furniture store, Bart hardly needed enticing when Birmingham moved in to sign him last November. Progress came quicker than he might have expected, when an unfortunate injury to Ian Bennett saw him thrust in from the bench during the 3-1 Anglo-Italian Cup win against Cesena, barely a month after arriving in England. While an inability to fully command the area was not helped by continuous defensive changes, he showed good reflexes and performed most creditably.
Birmingham C (Free from WKE Holland on 9/11/95) FL 20 FLC 3 FAC 1 Others 1+1

GRIFFITHS Carl Brian
Born: Welshpool, 16 July 1971
Height: 5'9" Weight: 10.6
International Honours: W: B-1; U21-2; Yth
Signed from Manchester City at the beginning of 1995-96, Carl went to Portsmouth in the deal that took Kit Symons to Maine Road, but never really got the opportunity of a run-in the first team, making just two starts in 15 appearances. Subsequently sold to Peterborough on transfer deadline day, and becoming their record buy, the centre forward scored within two minutes of his debut before suffering an injury three games later and missing the remainder of the campaign. Fast and direct, he will be back.
Shrewsbury T (From trainee on 26/9/88) FL 110+33/54 FLC 7+4/3 FAC 6/2 Others 7+3/3
Manchester C (£500,000 on 29/10/93) PL 11+7/4 FLC 0+1 FAC 2
Portsmouth (£200,000 on 17/8/95) FL 2+12/2 FLC 0+1
Peterborough U (£225,000 on 28/3/96) FL 4/1

GRIFFITHS Gareth John
Born: Winsford, 10 April 1970
Height: 6'4" Weight: 14.0
Tall central defender who hardly missed a game for Port Vale in 1995-96. A good header of the ball, he improved as the season went on to become the undisputed first choice centre half. Did exceptionally well against Duncan Ferguson in the FA Cup-ties against Everton and scored two goals during the campaign, at Charlton and Portsmouth. Is very highly rated.
Port Vale (Signed from Rhyl on 8/2/93) FL 63+2/4 FLC 4 FAC 6/1 Others 7

GROBBELAAR Bruce David
Born: Durban, South Africa, 6 October 1957
Height: 6'1" Weight: 14.2
Club Honours: Div 1 '82, '83, '84, '86, '88, '90; FLC '82, '83, '84, '90; FAC '86, '89, '92; CS '82, '86, '88, '89; EC '84
International Honours: Zimbabwe: 14
Eccentric and vastly experienced former Liverpool star goalkeeper who, due to Dave Beasant's outstanding form and his off-field problems, was restricted to just two first team appearances for Southampton last season. Finally getting his chance in April when preferred to the latter for the home match against Blackburn, he kept a clean sheet, but then let in three at Aston Villa, his manager being somewhat uncomplimentary about his performance. Was released during the summer.
Crewe Alex (On trial from Vancouver Whitecaps on 18/12/79) FL 24/1
Liverpool (£250,000 from Vancouver Whitecaps on 12/3/81) F/PL 440 FLC 70 FAC 62 Others 56
Stoke C (Loaned on 17/3/93) FL 4
Southampton (Free on 11/8/94) PL 32 FLC 3 FAC 5

GROVES Paul
Born: Derby, 28 February 1966
Height: 5'11" Weight: 11.5
Paul is currently Grimsby's most consistent player, having the remarkable record of appearing in every first team game during the four seasons he has been at Blundell Park. As the club captain and dominating the club's "Player of the Year" awards, his ability in midfield to both win the ball and then distribute accurately, plus his liking to get forward, enabled him to come second in the scoring stakes to Steve Livingstone, with ten goals. *Stop Press:* Out of contract at the end of June, and Town wanting £1m for his services, he moved to WBA, the fee to be decided by the tribunal.
Leicester C (£12,000 from Burton A on 18/4/88) FL 7+9/1 FLC 1/1 FAC 0+1 Others 0+1
Lincoln C (Loaned on 20/8/89) FL 8/1 FLC 2
Blackpool (£60,000 on 25/1/90) FL 106+1/21 FLC 6/1 FAC 9/4 Others 13/3
Grimsby (£150,000 on 12/8/92) FL 183+1/37 FLC 10+1/2 FAC 12/2 Others 4/1

GUDMUNDSSON Niklas
Born: Sweden, 29 February 1972
Height: 5'11" Weight: 12.9
International Honours: Sweden:10
Blackburn striker and a Swedish international, who plays wide left or up front, Niklas has good accleration, is technically gifted, and a goalscorer. Came initially on

loan from Halmstads last December and was not rushed into the team, his actions being mainly limited to the substitute position and the reserves. However, he did enough to induce the club to take him on a permanent move and is one for the future.

Blackburn Rov (Signed from Halmstads on 2/12/95) PL 1+3

GUENTCHEV Bontcho Lubomisov
Born: Tchoshevo, Bulgaria, 7 July 1964
Height: 5'10" Weight: 11.7
International Honours: Bulgaria: 12

Although a skilful, two-footed and experienced Bulgarian international, Bontcho failed to become Luton's Mesia, following his 1995 close season free transfer from Ipswich. Without the use of a central striker, he was often asked to play with inadequate support and lacked the speed and strength to be a front runner. His personal highlight of the season was a 25-yard curling free kick into the net against Sheffield United in February to complete a run of four goals in five games, with Town winning all four in which he scored and drawing the other. That was the club's best spell, but then the goals dried up for both Bontcho and Town and relegation ultimately ensued. Finished joint top league scorer with nine strikes, including four from the spot, prior to inclusion in the Bulgarian squad for Euro '96.

Ipswich T (£250,000 from Sporting Lisbon on 29/12/92) PL 39+22/6 FLC 6 FAC 6+2/5
Luton T (Free on 23/8/95) FL 25+10/9 FLC 2 FAC 1 Others 2+1/2

GUINAN Stephen (Steve)
Born: Birmingham, 24 December 1975
Height: 6'1" Weight: 12.12

Promising Nottingham Forest reserve team striker who was loaned out to Darlington last December, scoring on his debut at home to Barnet and playing three games before returning to the City Ground. The experience must have done him some good for soon after he was rewarded with his Premiership debut, deputising for Ian Woan at Wimbledon in late March. However, this appears to have been a one-off selection as he has yet to be included in the first team squad.

Nottingham F (From trainee on 7/1/93) PL 1+1
Darlington (Loaned on 14/12/95) FL 3/1

GULLIT Ruud
Born: Surinam, 1 September 1962
Height: 6'0" Weight: 13.0
International Honours: Holland: 64

Chelsea stunned the football world in June 1995 when they signed Ruud Gullit from Sampdoria on a free transfer, originally to play as a sweeper. The "Dutch Master" had suffered a series of knee injuries and had been written off by many critics, but he proved the doubters wrong with a string of performances that illuminated the Premiership. Glenn Hoddle's footballing philosophy – a belief in a patient, passing game – and London's cosmopolitan lifestyle gave Chelsea the edge over French, Japanese and Turkish clubs when Ruud was made available. In every match he produced a "cameo" – a moment to remember – utilising his repertoire of flicks, feints and

dummies. There were memorable goals also – a blistering volley against Southampton at The Bridge in September, in the return at The Dell a superb solo run and chip over Dave Beasant, a late equaliser at St James Park to send the FA Cup third round replay into extra time, and the bullet-like header past Peter Schmeichel that gave Chelsea the lead in the FA Cup semi final. Voted as runner up to Eric Cantona in the "Footballer of the Year" poll, having earlier been elected into the PFA award winning Premiership side, his influence at Chelsea is immense and to watch the man is similar to watching a maestro conduct an orchestra. He has brought the best out of youngsters such as Michael Duberry, Eddie Newton and Frank Sinclair, and when Glenn Hoddle vacated the manager's seat to manage England shortly before the final home match the crowd were unanimous in their choice of successor – Ruud Gullit. On 10 May the fans got their wish – Ruud Gullit was appointed player/manager of Chelsea.

Chelsea (Free from Sampdoria, via Haarlem, PSV Eindhoven and AC Milan, on 1/7/95) PL 31/3 FLC 2 FAC 7/3

Ruud Gullit

GUNN Bryan James
Born: Thurso, 22 December 1963
Height: 6'2" Weight: 13.13
International Honours: S: 6; B-4; U21-9; Yth; Sch

Consistent Norwich goalkeeper, who cuts a commanding figure in the penalty area and can turn defence into immediate attack with giant long-kicks. Became only the seventh man to reach 400 City appearances in 1995-96 and has moved to sixth place in their all-time charts. Missed just four matches in the relegation threatened season, a three-match ban after being sent off against Sheffield United, plus a last match rest to allow his understudy, Andy Marshall, a further game. His close range reactions are as good as ever and a memorable night, saw him saving three penalties in the Coca Cola Cup-tie at Bolton. Unusually though, he was beaten by three blockbusting 35-yarders during the

campaign and frequently tried to atone by appearing in the opposing goal mouth for City corners.

Aberdeen (Signed from Invergordon BC in 1980) SL 15 SLC 4 SC 1 Others 1
Norwich C (£150,000 on 23/10/86) F/PL 347 FLC 36 FAC 25 Others 22

Bryan Gunn

GUPPY Stephen (Steve)
Born: Winchester, 29 March 1969
Height: 5'11" Weight: 12.0
Club Honours: FAT '91, '93; GMVC '93
International Honours: E: SP-1

In a season when Port Vale's wing policy surprised a good many of their opponents, the left winger performed well, his dazzling play often receiving rave notices. Scored five goals, all before the end of last year, two of them of vital importance, and missed only two games, both as a result of suspension. Interestingly, due to heavy traffic, he had to run two miles to the ground to make the kick off for the Everton FA Cup-tie and went on to star in the 2-2 draw.

Wycombe W (Signed in 1989-90) FL 41/8 FLC 4 FAC 8/2 Others 10
Newcastle U (£150,000 on 2/8/94) FLC 0+1
Port Vale (£225,000 on 25/11/94) FL 68+3/6 FLC 2 FAC 7 Others 7+1/1

GURNEY Andrew (Andy) Robert
Born: Bristol 25 January 1974
Height: 5'11" Weight: 12.2

Enjoying a good season in 1995-96, after establishing himself in the Bristol Rovers' team, Andy's switch from left back to the right-hand side of midfield reaped six goals and he was involved in creating many others. He would probably have been the club's only ever present, albeit for two dismissals which brought untimely suspensions.

Bristol Rov (From trainee on 10/7/92) FL 79+5/7 FLC 5 FAC 5 Others 14

GUTZMORE Leon Johnson Fitzgerald
Born: St Pancras, 30 October 1976
Height: 6'0" Weight: 12.9

A former Cambridge United trainee, he was signed on non-contract terms last September. Battling back after a knee injury disrupted his season, the young striker spent time on loan at Billericay before making two substitute appearances in the last part of the campaign. Released during the summer.

Cambridge U (From trainee on 1/9/95) FL 0+2

EAT FOOTBALL.
SLEEP FOOTBALL.
DRINK COCA-COLA.©1996

Coca-Cola plays a unique role in supporting Football at all levels of the game – adding enjoyment to a young player's first kick through to the World Cup Final.

Starting with the **Coca-Cola FA Grassroots Development Programme** which invests in the future of the sport and ensures young players receive top quality coaching to improve their performance, knowledge and enjoyment of our national game.

The Coca-Cola Cup gives supporters of all the regional clubs throughout England and Scotland the chance to enjoy the excitement and calibre of play that only a cup competition can give.

Moving into the international arena, Coca-Cola supports **the England Team** which competed in **Euro 96™** – the biggest sporting event to be held in England since the 1966 World Cup. As one of the main supporters of **Euro 96™**, Coca-Cola enhanced the event by bringing fans closer to the action.

In 1998 the **World Cup** takes place in France and, as sponsors, Coca-Cola will ensure fans are given the opportunity to enjoy the World's premier sporting occasion.

HAALAND Alf-Inge Rasdal
Born: Stavanger, Norway, 23 November 1972
Height: 5'10" Weight: 12.12
International Honours: Norway: 15

The Norwegian international proved his versatility in 1995-96 by turning out for Nottingham Forest at right back and in central defence, central and wide midfield, but always as cover for other players, except at the end of the season when he replaced Des Lyttle at right back. A tough tackler who links up well with the attack, he needs to find a regular position to call his own to progress his career with Forest.
Nottingham F (Signed from Young Boys of Berne on 25/1/94) F/PL 33+7/1 FLC 0+4 FAC 2+1 Others 2+3

HACKETT Warren James
Born: Plaistow, 16 December 1971
Height: 6'0" Weight: 12.5
Club Honours: FAYC '90

Stylish full back who played ten first team games for Doncaster during the 1995-96 season before moving to Mansfield Town as a replacement for Ian Baraclough in a surprise early season move. A little uncertain in his early matches, he found his composure by the end of the year and then produced some sterling performances. An excellent player from a defensive point of view and always keen to go forward.
Leyton Orient (Free from Tottenham H juniors on 3/7/90) FL 74+2/3 FLC 4 FAC 8/2 Others 7
Doncaster Rov (Free on 26/7/94) FL 46/2 FLC 4 FAC 1 Others 4
Mansfield T (£50,000 on 20/10/95) FL 32/3 FAC 2

HADDAOUI Riffi
Born: Copenhagen, Denmark, 24 March 1971
Height: 5'10" Weight: 13.5

Partially sponsored by Carlsberg, and on loan from the Danish side, Vata, the skilful midfielder looked to be a more than useful acquisition for Torquay last March, especially with his passing skills. Unfortunately, United's backs to the wall approach did not do him justice and two subs' appearances were his sum total at Plainmoor.
Torquay U (Loaned from Vata, Denmark on 29/3/96) FL 0+2

HADLEY Stewart
Born: Dudley, 30 December 1973
Height: 6'0" Weight: 13.2

"Turbo" was nothing like as effective in his 1995-96 striking role for Mansfield as during the previous season and clearly missed the prompting he had received from the departed Paul Holland and Steve Wilkinson. At his best, Stewart is a powerful, hard-running forward who can panic defences into mistakes.
Derby Co (Free from Halesowen T on 6/7/92)

Mansfield T (Signed on 9/2/94) FL 69+17/25 FLC 5+2 FAC 5/1 Others 6+1/3

HAILS Julian
Born: Lincoln, 20 November 1967
Height: 5'10" Weight: 11.1

Julian's all-round abilities were more than useful to Southend in 1995-96, with injuries forcing him to play in defence, midfield, and attack, with the highlight being a hat trick at Filbert Street in the 3-1 victory, the first of his career. Julian's tireless running and effort, allied to his neat touches and tough tackling, made him a true team player, and his performances at right back at the end of the season were as good as any other seen during the campaign.
Fulham (Signed from Hemel Hempstead on 29/8/91) FL 99+10/12 FLC 5+1 FAC 2 Others 8+1/1
Southend U (Free on 2/12/94) FL 59+9/6 FLC 1+1 FAC 1 Others 3

HALL Derek Robert
Born: Ashton under Lyme, 5 January 1965
Height: 5'8" Weight: 12.3

Kept out of the Rochdale first team picture until near the end of last season, due to the number of other midfield men available, Derek did an excellent job as skipper of the Dale's exciting young reserve side. A very experienced player with over 400 games under his belt. he was released during the summer, having earlier had a spell on loan at non-league, Altrincham.
Coventry C (From apprentice on 8/10/82) FL 1
Torquay U (Free on 23/3/84) FL 55/6 FLC 2 FAC 2 Others 3/1
Swindon T (Free on 29/7/85) FL 9+1 FLC 2 FAC 1+1
Southend U (Free on 21/8/86) FL 120+3/15 FLC 13/1 FAC 6/2 Others 8/1
Halifax T (Free on 25/7/89) FL 48+1/4 FLC 5/1 FAC 2 Others 5/1
Hereford U (Free on 18/7/91) FL 98+5/18 FLC 8/2 FAC 11/1 Others 9/1
Rochdale (£10,000 on 8/8/94) FL 14+9/2 FLC 1+1 Others 1+2

Derek Hall

HALL Gareth David
Born: Croydon, 12 March 1969
Height: 5'8" Weight: 12.0
Club Honours: Div 2 '89; Div 1 '96; FMC 90
International Honours: E: Sch. W: 9; U21-1

Having arrived at Sunderland on loan last December, Peter Reid eventually signed the Chelsea midfielder, cum defender, on a more permanent basis in the New Year. Although Gareth found first team opportunities hard to come by, with the Kevin Ball/Paul Bracewell midfield partnership in such good form, his Premiership experience at Stamford Bridge will no doubt have him knocking on the door for a regular place next term. Prior to winning a first division championship medal with his new club, Gareth had played five times for the Londoners in 1995-96 and scored in a 3-2 win over Bolton.
Chelsea (From apprentice on 25/4/86) F/PL 120+16/4 FLC 12+1 FAC 6 Others 10+4/1
Sunderland (£300,000 on 20/12/95) FL 8+6

HALL Leigh
Born: Hereford, 10 June 1975
Height: 5'11" Weight: 11.7

Leigh, a strong, hard-working defender, was unable to break into the Hereford side last season, being limited to just one substitute appearance. Still a non-contract player.
Hereford U (Signed on 23/3/95) FL 0+2

HALL Marcus Thomas
Born: Coventry, 24 March 1976
Height: 6'1" Weight: 12.2

Outstanding local young Coventry defender who came through club's youth scheme and is able to play at left back or in central defence. Gaining a regular place in the first team last season, as a result of an injury to David Burrows, he gave some very good displays, his overlapping a major strength. His form having dipped as time went on, it was discovered he had been carrying a hernia injury. Marcus was one of Bobby Gould's tips for stardom and a great future is predicted for him, especially after an early season call up to the England U21 squad.
Coventry C (From trainee on 1/7/94) PL 26+4 FLC 4 FAC 2

HALL Mark Anthony
Born: Islington, 13 January 1973
Height: 5'7" Weight: 11.7

Freed by Southend during the 1995 close season, the diminutive striker signed for Torquay and although showing some nice touches in 27 starts, critically could not finish off his good play in front of goal. Was released during the summer.
Southend U (Free from Tottenham H juniors on 20/8/91) FL 4+8
Barnet (Loaned on 13/9/93) FL 3 FLC 1 Others 1
Torquay U (Free on 14/7/95) FL 22+7 FLC 3 FAC 2+1 Others 0+1

HALL Paul Anthony
Born: Manchester, 3 July 1972
Height: 5'9" Weight: 11.0

Predominately a right winger, Paul played most of last season for Portsmouth at centre forward, although it was apparent early on that when he was moved to a wide right position, his speed and control created additional openings. Appearing in every game, albeit two as a sub, he joint top-scored with ten goals, all of them ultimately invaluable as Pompey stayed in the first division on goal difference.

Torquay U (From trainee on 9/7/90) FL 77+16/1 FLC 7 FAC 4+1/2 Others 5+1/1
Portsmouth (£70,000 on 25/3/93) FL 90+27/19 FLC 6+2/1 FAC 1+1 Others 6+2/2

HALL Richard Anthony
Born: Ipswich, 14 March 1972
Height: 6'2" Weight: 13.11
International Honours: E: U21-11

Very promising Southampton central defender who was dogged by injuries during the second half of last season, having been ever present for the first 25 matches, when forming an excellent partnership with Ken Monkou. Big and strong, and enjoying the physical side of the game, Richard is dangerous when getting forward, especially at set pieces. This was borne out when he scored three goals during the campaign, two of them winners, as well as creating a number of opportunities for others. *Stop Press:* Out of contract, he was reported to have signed for West Ham during the summer.

Scunthorpe U (From trainee on 20/3/90) FL 22/3 FLC 2 FAC 3 Others 4
Southampton (£200,000 on 13/2/91) F/PL 119+7/12 FLC 11+1/1 FAC 15/3 Others 3

HALL Wayne
Born: Rotherham, 25 October 1968
Height: 5'8" Weight: 10.6

The regular and reliable York left back, Wayne missed the second half of the last season following a stomach injury which necessitated an operation. More at home on the left side, he can also be used to good effect further up the flank.

Darlington (From trainee on 19/12/88)
York C (Free from Hatfield Main Colliery on 15/3/89) FL 245+14/8 FLC 15+1 FAC 9+1/1 Others 19/1

Gunnar Halle

HALLE Gunnar
Born: Oslo, Norway, 11 August 1965
Height: 5'11" Weight: 11.2
Club Honours: Div 2 '91
International Honours: Norway: 53

Undoubtedly a class player, 53 caps for Norway tells it all. Injured against Sunderland last March, Gunnar did not return until the penultimate game of the season, a 2-0 win over Stoke, his presence being sorely missed. Again playing mainly on the wide right of midfield, where his pace and ability to drive forward into key positions gave Oldham a range of options, he also found time to score four goals, one of them at Luton in a 1-1 draw. Unfortunately, 1996-97 will be his last season in England as he intends playing out his career in Norway.

Oldham Ath (£280,000 from Lillestrom on 15/2/91) F/PL 167+1/14 FLC 11/2 FAC 8/2 Others 4

HALLIDAY Stephen William
Born: Sunderland, 3 May 1976
Height: 5'10" Weight: 11.11

Hartlepool wing/forward seen to best effect when running at speed at the opposition's defence. Highly rated, he consolidated his reputation in 1995-96, despite him having problems with a hernia for much of the season. Keith Houchen has gone on record as saying that one day Stephen will be worth £3m.

Hartlepool U (From trainee on 5/7/94) FL 62+16/12 FLC 6+1 FAC 2/1 Others 3+1

HALLWORTH Jonathan (Jon) Geoffrey
Born: Stockport, 26 October 1965
Height: 6'1" Weight: 14.3
Club Honours: Div 2 '91

Surely one of the best second choice goalkeepers in the first division, Jon would be the number one at many clubs, where his agility and awareness, especially in coming for crosses, would be an asset. Unfortunately for him, Paul Gerrard's good form for Oldham last season, allowed him only 12 full games, but he never let the side down, with six of them being won and three drawn. Often starts attacks with quick throws and long kicks.

Ipswich T (From apprentice on 26/5/83) FL 45 FLC 4 FAC 1 Others 6
Bristol Rov (Loaned on 1/1/85) FL 2 Others 1
Oldham Ath (£75,000 on 3/2/89) F/PL 167+3 FLC 18 FAC 20 Others 3

HAMILL Rory
Born: Coleraine, 4 May 1976
Height: 5'8" Weight: 12.3
International Honours: NI: Yth; Sch

Striker. A favourite with the Fulham fans with his pace and aggression, although Rory was leading scorer for the reserves in 1995-96, he started only six league matches, most of his time being spent on the bench. He was subsequently placed on the transfer list at the end of the season.

Fulham (Free from Southampton juniors on 18/11/94) FL 24+24/7 FLC 2 FAC 2+4/3 Others 1+3

HAMILTON Derrick (Des) Vivian
Born: Bradford, 15 August 1976
Height: 5'11" Weight: 12.9

A strong and aggressive, hard-running Bradford midfielder who makes long surging runs into the opposing territory, often with success. Unfortunate to miss 19 matches last season with a badly damaged leg muscle, he came back to play as well as ever, scoring in both the semi final and final stages of the play offs to help City into the first division. Can also be used in defence.

Bradford C (From trainee on 1/6/94) FL 43+13/5 FLC 5/1 FAC 3 Others 4+1/2

HAMILTON Ian Richard
Born: Stevenage, 14 December 1967
Height: 5'9" Weight: 11.3

Ian had perhaps his best season with WBA in 1995-96, with his prompting play and probing exploits from midfield. Although teaming up with several partners in the "engine room" he never lost his composure and produced many outstanding performances, laying on plenty of chances for his colleagues. With a powerful right-foot shot, he could and should have scored more goals himself, but that was not for the want of trying.

Southampton (From apprentice on 24/12/85)
Cambridge U (Signed on 29/3/88) FL 23+1/1 FLC 1 FAC 2 Others 2
Scunthorpe U (Signed on 23/12/88) FL 139+6/18 FLC 6 FAC 6+1 Others 14+1/3
West Bromwich A (£160,000 on 19/6/92) FL 161+3/17 FLC 8 FAC 7+1/1 Others 14+2/3

HAMMOND Nicholas (Nicky) David
Born: Hornchurch, 7 September 1967
Height: 6'0" Weight: 11.13

Signed from Swindon at the beginning of 1995-96, the long-serving goalkeeper had a difficult start with Plymouth, as other new players were also having to blend into the team. Played only six league games before going to Reading on loan in December as cover and following an impressive debut against Sunderland, the move was made permanent in January. Unfortunately, a long-term back injury saw him out of action from February until the end of the season.

Arsenal (From apprentice on 12/7/85)
Bristol Rov (Loaned on 23/8/86) FL 3
Swindon T (Free on 1/7/87) F/PL 65+2 FLC 11 FAC 10 Others 6
Plymouth Arg (£40,000 on 14/8/95) FL 4 FLC 2 Others 1
Reading (£40,000 on 13/2/96) FL 5 FAC 1

HAMSHER John James
Born: Lambeth, 14 January 1978
Height: 5'10" Weight: 10.10

A right-sided Fulham player, John played regularly in the reserves as well as captaining the youth team, proving to be an excellent crosser, who showed his best form in an attacking right back role. Rewarded with three first team substitute appearances at the end of 1995-96, he became the only member of the youth side to be offered a full contract.

Fulham (Trainee) FL 0+3

HANCOX Richard
Born: Wolverhampton, 4 October 1968
Height: 5'10" Weight: 13.0

Left-sided Torquay striker. Having a disappointing time of it in 1995-96 at

Torquay, as the club plummeted to the bottom of the Football League, and with just one goal to his credit, he was moved into defence as an emergency full back and acquitted himself well.

Torquay U (Free from Stourbridge Swifts on 18/3/93) FL 50+21/10 FLC 6+1/3 FAC 2+3/2 Others 3

HANDYSIDE Peter David
Born: Dumfries, 31 July 1974
Height: 6'1" Weight: 13.0
International Honours: S: U21-7

His excellent early 1995-96 displays for Grimsby in the centre of their defence, as a commanding presence in the air and cultured on the ball, saw him twice capped for Scotland at U21 level before injury cost him his club place in the second half of the season. Despite not recapturing his form on coming back for seven of the last eight games, the overall assessment would be that he continued to make progress and will go on doing so.

Grimsby T (From trainee on 21/11/92) FL 86+3 FLC 5 FAC 4 Others 4

HANSEN Vergard
Born: Dramen, Norway, 8 August 1969
Height: 6'1" Weight: 12.12

So impressive in the right back role for Bristol City in 1994-95, Vergard failed to recapture such form last season and lost his first team spot early during the campaign. Too good a player to remain in the reserves, he eventually went back on loan to his old club, Stromgodset.

Bristol C (£105,000 from Stromgodset on 18/11/94) FL 36+1 FLC 4 FAC 3 Others 1

HANSON David (Dave) Paul
Born: Huddersfield, 19 November 1968
Height: 6'0" Weight: 13.7

Although having experienced league football earlier in his career, Dave gave it another shot when signing for Leyton Orient last October. In 13 appearances (including four as a sub), the tall striker created a favourable impression and with the right guidance could still make an impact. Had a spell on loan at non-league Welling United in February.

Bury (Free from Farsley Celtic on 19/7/93) FL 1 FLC 2 (Free to Halifax T on 18/8/94)
Leyton Orient (£50,000 from Hednesford T on 4/10/95) FL 7+4/1 Others 2

HARDING Paul John
Born: Mitcham, 6 March 1964
Height: 5'10" Weight: 12.5
Club Honours: FAT '88

Initially seen as an inspirational Cardiff signing from Birmingham, prior to the start of 1995-96, the experienced midfielder was immediately made club captain. Unfortunately, in a side that struggled all season, it proved too difficult for him to stamp his authority on the team in lasting fashion and he must hope for better fortune this season.

Notts Co (£60,000 from Barnet on 28/9/90) FL 45+9/1 FLC 1 FAC 6 Others 7+1/2
Southend U (Loaned on 26/8/93) FL 2+3 Others 2
Watford (Loaned on 2/11/93) FL 1+1
Birmingham C (£50,000 on 3/12/93) FL 19+3 FLC 3 FAC 1/1

Cardiff C (Free on 10/8/95) FL 36 FLC 4 FAC 1 Others 2

HARDY Jason Paul
Born: Manchester, 14 December 1969
Height: 5'10" Weight: 11.4

The former Burnley man was recruited by Rochdale from non-league Halifax last August. He made a handful of appearances in place of Kevin Formby at left back, but spent most of the season playing at centre back in the reserves, prior to being released during the summer.

Burnley (From trainee on 20/7/88) FL 38+5/1 FAC 3+2/1 Others 2
Halifax T (Loaned on 30/1/92) FL 0+4
Halifax T (Free on 1/7/92) FL 20+2/2
Rochdale (Signed on 24/8/95) FL 5+2

HARDY Philip (Phil)
Born: Chester, 9 April 1973
Height: 5'8" Weight: 11.2
Club Honours: WC '95
International Honours: Ei: U21-9

Wrexham left back. Could well now be called the "Hardy Perennial", such is the time he seems to have been around at the racecourse and yet is still only a relative youngster at 23. Always reliable, Phil, in many ways missed the talented Karl Connolly down the left side in 1995-96, as they have an excellent understanding. Captain of the Republic of Ireland U21 team, he can only get better.

Wrexham (From trainee on 24/11/90) FL 217+1 FLC 15 FAC 17 Others 31

HARDYMAN Paul George
Born: Portsmouth, 11 March 1964
Height: 5'8" Weight: 11.12
International Honours: E: U21-2

Freed by Bristol Rovers during the 1995 close season, Paul was Wycombe's first choice left back at the start of 1995-96, before sustaining a bad ankle injury in October and being unable to break into the side on regaining fitness in March. Although solid and dependable, he was released at the end of the campaign.

Portsmouth (Free from Waterford on 8/7/83) FL 113+4/3 FLC 5 FAC 6 Others 8/1
Sunderland (£130,000 on 25/7/89) FL 101+5/9 FLC 11/2 FAC 8+1/1 Others 3
Bristol Rov (£160,000 on 3/8/92) FL 54+13/5 FLC 3 FAC 3+1 Others 3/1
Wycombe W (Free on 8/8/95) FL 12+3 FLC 4 Others 1

HARE Matthew
Born: Barnstaple, 26 December 1976
Height: 6'1" Weight: 12.0

Defender. Having signed professional terms during the 1995 close season, Matthew broke into the Exeter first team of a number of occasions, often being employed for his man-marking ability.

Exeter C (From trainee on 4/8/95) FL 10+3 FAC 0+1 Others 3

HARFORD Michael (Mick) Gordon
Born: Sunderland, 12 February 1959
Height: 6'2" Weight: 14.5
Club Honours: FLC '88
International Honours: E: 2; B-1

There were many eyebrows raised when

Wimbledon manager, Joe Kinnear, signed the ageing striker at the beginning of 1994-95. Since that time, however, Mick has gone on to become an important part of the Dons' set up and, at the age of 37, he was still full of enthusiasm and gritty determination, playing in the new midfield, cum defensive role, he excelled in during 1995-96. His spirit and will to win was no more in evidence than in the home game against Aston Villa, when rising in the final minute to head home a valuable equaliser to earn a crucial point in the battle against relegation. Recognised as one of the leading target men of the last decade, especially in the air, he is still a good man to have up your sleeve at set pieces.

Lincoln C (Free from Lambton Street BC on 6/7/77) FL 109+6/41 FLC 8/5 FAC 3
Newcastle U (£180,000 on 24/12/80) FL 18+1/4
Bristol C (£160,000 on 24/8/81) FL 30/11 FLC 5/1 FAC 5/2
Birmingham C (£100,000 on 26/3/82) FL 92/25 FLC 10/6 FAC 7/2
Luton T (£250,000 on 13/12/84) FL 135+4/57 FLC 16/10 FAC 27/11 Others 4/3
Derby Co (£450,000 on 18/1/90) FL 58/15 FLC 7/3 FAC 1 Others 2
Luton T (£325,000 on 12/9/91) FL 29/12 FLC 1 Others 1
Chelsea (£300,000 on 13/8/92) PL 27+1/9 FLC 5/2 FAC 1
Sunderland (£250,000 on 18/3/93) FL 10+1/2
Coventry C (£200,000 on 12/7/93) PL 0+1/1
Wimbledon (£50,000 on 18/8/94) PL 34+14/7 FLC 2+2/1 FAC 9+2/1

HARGREAVES Christian (Chris)
Born: Cleethorpes, 12 May 1972
Height: 5'11" Weight: 12.2

Released by Hull City during the 1995 close season, he was signed by WBA boss, Alan Buckley, as strike cover for Andy Hunt, Bob Taylor and Tony Rees. Finding opportunities limited, and with only two substitute games under his belt, he joined Hereford on loan in February, scoring a couple of important goals. In doing so, he impressed all with his capability for hard work and, at the same time, formed a good understanding with Steve White.

Grimsby T (From trainee on 6/12/89) FL 15+36/5 FLC 2+2/1 FAC 1+2/1 Others 2+4
Scarborough (Loaned on 4/3/93) FL 2+1
Hull C (Signed on 26/7/93) FL 34+15 FLC 1 FAC 2+1/1 Others 3+1
West Bromwich A (Free on 13/7/95) FL 0+1 Others 0+1
Hereford U (Loaned on 19/2/96) FL 15+2/2 Others 1

HARKES John Andrew
Born: New Jersey, USA, 8 March 1967
Height: 5'10" Weight: 11.10
Club Honours: FLC '91
International Honours: USA: 70

Having played eight early season games for Derby in 1995-96, the USA Soccer Federation paid around £500,000 in October to secure the versatile midfielder's services and then loaned him to West Ham until mid-March. Able to play at right back, and having explosive shooting ability, he fitted in comfortably at Upton Park whenever Tim Breaker or John Moncur were injured, following his debut against former club, Sheffield Wednesday. Now back home, John is skippering the USA national team and at the end of May, led them to a 2-1 victory over a Scotland side warming up for Euro '96.

Sheffield Wed (£70,000 from North Carolina University on 3/10/90) F/PL 59+22/7 FLC 17/3 FAC 12+1/1 Others 7
Derby Co (Signed on 17/8/93) FL 67+7/2 FLC 5 Others 6/1 (£500,000 to USSF on 27/10/95)
West Ham U (Loaned on 28/10/95) PL 6+5 FAC 1+1

John Harkes

HARKNESS Steven (Steve)
Born: Carlisle, 27 August 1971
Height: 5'10" Weight: 11.2
International Honours: E: Yth

Steve enjoyed his best Liverpool moments to date in 1995-96 as the first choice left back, before being displaced in January by Rob Jones, his fierce tackling and accurate distribution proving a great asset. A steady player who does the simple things well, and back in the side again, sadly his season ended in tragedy when he broke his leg during the match at Coventry in April, following a dreadful, but accidental tackle. The injury unfortunately dealt a death knell to any hopes Steve might have harboured for a Wembley FA Cup final place, but he will be back.

Carlisle U (From trainee on 23/3/89) FL 12+1
Liverpool (£75,000 on 17/7/89) F/PL 57+7/3 FLC 8+2/1 FAC 3 Others 8+2
Huddersfield T (Loaned on 24/9/93) FL 5 Others 1
Southend U (Loaned on 3/2/95) FL 6

HARLE Michael (Mike) James
Born: Lewisham, 31 October 1972
Height: 5'10" Weight: 11.12

Yet to play for Millwall, Mike arrived at Bury on a month's loan last December, being one of many left backs tried out

during 1995-96. Having played in just one first team fixture for the Shakers, coming on as a half time substitute at Barnet on 9 December, he returned to Millwall.

Millwall (£100,000 from Sittingbourne on 8/11/93)
Bury (Loaned on 8/12/95) FL 0+1

HARPER Alan
Born: Liverpool, 1 November 1960
Height: 5'8" Weight: 11.9
Club Honours: Div 1 '85, '87; CS '86, '87
International Honours: E: Yth

Very much a fringe member of the Burnley side in 1995-96, his midfield experience being mainly used for the benefit of younger players in the reserve side. Loaned out to Cardiff in November, there were no questions asked of his pedigree, but what was against him was his age and pace and, although the period was extended, he made just three starts before an injury saw him return to Turf Moor, prior to his summer release.

Liverpool (From trainee on 22/4/78)
Everton (£100,000 on 1/6/83) FL 103+24/4 FLC 17+2 FAC 10+8/1 Others 13+1
Sheffield Wed (£275,000 on 6/7/88) FL 32+3 FLC 1+1 FAC 1 Others 1
Manchester C (£150,000 on 15/12/89) FL 46+4/1 FLC 3/1 FAC 6 Others 3
Everton (£200,000 on 12/8/91) F/PL 45+6 FLC 5+1 FAC 2+1 Others 2
Luton T (Free on 13/9/83) FL 40+1/1 FAC 7
Burnley (Free on 11/8/94) FL 30+1 FLC 6 FAC 5
Cardiff C (Loaned on 24/11/95) FL 5 Others 1

HARPER Stephen (Steve) Alan
Born: Easington, 14 March 1975
Height: 6'2" Weight: 13.0

Tall and commanding Newcastle goalkeeper who spent three months on loan at Bradford last season. Behind Shaka Hislop, Pavel Srnicek and Mike Hooper, in the queue for places at United, and covering for Gavin Ward at City, Steve made his league debut at Valley Parade in a 1-1 draw with Hull in November before going back to Tyneside. Has good hands and comes for crosses well.

Newcastle U (Free from Seaham Red Star on 5/7/93)
Bradford C (Loaned on 18/9/95) FL 1

HARPER Steven (Steve) James
Born: Newcastle under Lyme, 3 February 1969
Height: 5'10" Weight: 11.12
Club Honours: Div 4 '92

Signed by Mansfield from Doncaster early last season for an arbitration decided fee, in an attempt to bolster a weak midfield, Steve was used mainly as part of the strike force and made a useful contribution to the team. Suffered a knee injury in January which sidelined him for some time. As a speedy, wide player he played a major part in the Stags' victory over his old club in the FA Cup.

Port Vale (From trainee 29/6/87) FL 16+12/2 FLC 1+2 Others 1+1
Preston NE (Signed on 23/3/89) FL 57+20/10 FLC 1+1 FAC 1+2 Others 6+1/1
Burnley (Free on 23/7/91) FL 64+5/8 FLC 1+2 FAC 10/3 Others 8
Doncaster Rov (Free on 7/8/93) FL 56+9/11 FLC 2+1/1 FAC 3 Others 4

Mansfield T (£20,000 on 8/9/95) FL 29/5 FAC 2/1 Others 2

HARRIS Mark Andrew
Born: Reading, 15 July 1963
Height: 6'3" Weight: 13.11
Club Honours: AMC '94

Commanding centre half who was probably the unsung hero of Gillingham's success story last season. Originally signed on loan from Swansea City in August, he became a permanent fixture a month later and went on to miss just two league games during a campaign that saw the club promoted to the second division. Unofficially the players' "Player of the Year", he scored the all-important goal in the 1-1 draw against prospective champions, Preston.

Crystal Palace (£25,000 from Wokingham T on 29/2/88) FL 0+2
Burnley (Loaned on 7/8/89) FL 4 FLC 2
Swansea C (£22,500 on 22/9/89) FL 228/14 FLC 16/1 FAC 18/1 Others 26/2
Gillingham (£15,000 on 11/8/95) FL 44/2 FLC 2 FAC 4

HARRISON Gerald (Gerry) Randall
Born: Lambeth, 15 April 1972
Height: 5'10" Weight: 12.12
International Honours: E: Sch

Probably Burnley's most improved player, particularly in the second half of last season when many around him were struggling. Looked at his best in central defence, but could also perform in both attacking and defensive midfield roles, as well as being a more than capable stand in at right back. His wholehearted efforts earned popularity with the fans, but a short fuse and occasional recklessness had to be curbed.

Watford (From trainee on 18/12/89) FL 6+3 Others 1
Cardiff C (Loaned on 24/1/92) FL 10/1
Bristol C (Free on 23/7/91) FL 24+13/1 FLC 2+2 FAC 1 Others 4+1
Hereford U (Loaned on 19/11/93) FL 6 FAC 1 Others 1
Huddersfield T (Free on 24/3/94)
Burnley (Free on 5/8/94) FL 51+3/3 FLC 3+1 FAC 2 Others 4

HARRISON Lee David
Born: Billericay, 12 September 1971
Height: 6'2" Weight: 12.0

The perfect build for a goalkeeper, Lee was unfortunate to be understudy at Fulham to Jim Stannard for two years and when the latter left for Gillingham, many thought his chance would come. Unfortunately for him, the club then signed the experienced Tony Lange and Lee only played seven games in 1995-96, before being freed at the end of the season. A very good shot stopper, he was a major reason for the reserves having a good Capital League campaign.

Charlton Ath (From trainee on 3/7/90)
Fulham (Loaned on 18/11/91) Others 1
Gillingham (Loaned on 24/3/92) FL 2
Fulham (Free on 18/12/92) FL 11+1 FAC 2 Others 6

HARTE Ian Patrick
Born: Drogheda, 31 August 1977
Height: 5'11" Weight: 11.8
International Honours: Ei: 4; U21-2

Young Irish striker who made his first team

bow for Leeds as a substitute against West Ham last January. A regular for the reserves and junior sides at Elland Road, he is yet another of a long line of trainees to break into the side. His excellent displays saw him first capped by the Republic of Ireland at U21 level, before being elevated to the full international side in June and making four appearances.

Leeds U (From trainee on 15/12/95) PL 2+2 FLC

HARTSON John
Born: Swansea, 5 April 1975
Height: 6'1" Weight: 14.6
International Honours: W: 6; U21-7; Yth

A hard-running out-and-out striker, who is fast becoming a handful for any defence, he was disappointed to have made just 16 starts for Arsenal last season. However, time is very much on his side and, still an outstanding prospect, he continued to add to his Welsh caps, while his long-range lob against Manchester City at Highbury was a goal that either Dennis Bergkamp or Ian Wright would have been proud of. Strong in the air, working on his speed, and with good first touch, John will be looking to score regularly alongside Wright in 1996-97.

Luton T (From trainee on 19/12/92) FL 32+22/11 FLC 0+1 FAC 3+3/2 Others 2
Arsenal (£2,500,000 on 13/1/95) PL 29+5/11 FLC 1+2/1 FAC 1 Others 6+1/1

HARVEY Lee Derek
Born: Harlow, 21 December 1966
Height: 5'11" Weight: 11.7
International Honours: E: Yth

Reliable right-sided Brentford player. Started last season in his usual right wing slot, but moved to right back after Brian Statham broke his leg. Although out of position, he produced a consistent run of form and captained the side when Jamie Bates was absent.

Leyton Orient (From apprentice on 5/12/84) FL 135+49/23 FLC 13+3/3 FAC 10+4/2 Others 19+4/3
Nottingham F (Free on 4/8/93) FL 0+2 FLC 0+1
Brentford (Free on 18/11/93) FL 85+6/6 FLC 6+1/1 FAC 7+1 Others 5

HARVEY Richard George
Born: Letchworth, 17 April 1969
Height: 5'10" Weight: 11.10
International Honours: E: Yth; Sch

Accomplished left-sided Luton defender, cum midfielder, with a thunderous shot, who likes to come forward to support the attack, he appeared a little uncomfortable when asked to play in a midfield role last season. A regular squad member when fit, Richard was offered fresh terms at the end of the campaign, following the expiry of his contract, and should play a major role in the bid to regain first division status. Strong in the tackle and rarely caught for pace, he is well up to the task.

Luton T (From apprentice on 10/1/87) FL 128+25/4 FLC 8/1 FAC 6+2 Others 9
Blackpool (Loaned on 30/10/92) FL 4+1

HATELEY Mark Wayne
Born: Wallasey, 7 November 1961
Height: 6'2" Weight: 13.0

Club Honours: SPD '91, '92, '93, '94, '95; SC '92, '93; SLC '90, '92, '93
International Honours: E: 32; U21-10; Yth

An experienced QPR centre forward, excellent in the air, but equally adept with the ball at his feet, Mark returned to English football from Glasgow Rangers, following spells in France and Italy, when ex-AC Milan team mate, Ray Wilkins, signed him last November. Because of injury he had to wait for his debut, at Aston Villa in the Coca Cola Cup, and then made his league start against Middlesbrough four days later. After just five games he was injured again, missing another three games, before returning as a substitute against Blackburn Rovers. Scored his first goal for Rangers at Wimbledon, but loss of form and injury ruled him out once more before he returned to the side at the end of March, playing his first game in nine, against Everton, and notching an important goal.

Coventry C (From apprentice on 1/12/78) FL 88+6/25 FLC 8/3 FAC 10+1/6
Portsmouth (£220,000 on 6/6/83) (£1,000,000 to AC Milan on 28/6/84) FL 38/22 FLC 4/2 FAC 2/1
Glasgow R (Signed from AS Monaco on 19/7/90) SL 158+7/85 SLC 15+3/11 SC 16/10 Others 17/7
Queens Park R (£1,500,000 on 3/11/95) PL 10+4/2 FLC 0+1 FAC 1

HATHAWAY Ian Ashley
Born: Wordsley, 22 August 1968
Height: 5'8" Weight: 11.4

1995-96 was a very disappointing season for this talented Torquay left winger as the club slumped to the lowest point in the league. Normally a threat with superb crosses, and a scorer of spectacular goals, Ian had just one to his tally before going on loan to Chesterfield, where he failed to make an appearance.

Mansfield T (£8,000 from Bedworth U on 8/2/89) FL 21+23/2 FLC 1+1 FAC 1 Others 3+1/1
Rotherham U (Signed on 22/3/91) FL 5+8/1 Others 0+1
Torquay U (Free on 30/7/93) FL 93+12/13 FLC 9/1 FAC 9/2 Others 4+3/1

HAWES Steven Robert
Born: Wycombe, 17 July 1978
Height: 5'8" Weight: 11.4

Just 15 days past his 17th birthday, the young Sheffield United trainee midfielder made a surprise debut as a substitute at West Bromwich Albion last September, breaking Julian Broddle's record and making him the youngest player to appear for United in a league game. Given his full debut against Derby County in October, he then returned to gain experience with the reserves and juniors, signing professional forms for the club in March.

Sheffield U (From trainee on 2/3/96) FL 1+1

HAWORTH Simon Owen
Born: Cardiff, 30 March 1977
Height: 6'3" Weight: 13.8
International Honours: W: Yth

A young Cardiff striker, Simon was pitched into the side in 1995-96 during an emergency, being given six straight starts in September after the proposed Paul Shaw deal fell through. However, after failing to

find the net and making only fleeting appearances thereafter, he missed the second half of the season through injury.

Cardiff C (From trainee on 7/8/95) FL 7+6 FLC 4 Others 2

HAWTHORNE Mark
Born: Glasgow, 31 October 1973
Height: 5'9" Weight: 10.12

Having been released at the end of 1994-95, Mark re-signed for Torquay immediately prior to the start of last season. Playing in midfield, in what turned out to be a back to the wall struggle, he showed plenty of spirit and aggression, before again being placed on the free transfer list during the summer.

Crystal Palace (From juniors on 26/6/92)
Sheffield U (Free on 16/8/94) Others 3/1
Walsall (Free on 23/1/95)
Torquay U (Free on 23/3/95) FL 18+6 FLC 3/1 FAC 2 Others 2

HAYES Adrian (Adi) Michael
Born: Norwich, 22 May 1978
Height: 6'1" Weight: 12.10

A second year Cambridge trainee, and a left-footed constructive midfielder, Adi made his first ever appearance for the club at Scarborough last April and showed some nice touches, despite being booked. Due to sign professional forms during the summer.

Cambridge U (Trainee) FL 1

HAYES Martin
Born: Walthamstow, 21 March 1966
Height: 6'0" Weight: 12.4
Club Honours: Div 1 '89; FLC '87
International Honours: E: U21-3

Freed by Swansea during the 1995 close season, the former Arsenal man briefly trialed with Southend at the start of 1995-96, playing in the Anglo-Italian Cup-tie at home to Brescia. Although showing some nice touches from the wide left of midfield, he did not impose himself on the game and moved on early in September to non-league, Dover.

Arsenal (From apprentice on 2/11/83) FL 70+32/26 FLC 14+7/5 FAC 8+1/3 Others 0+2
Glasgow Celtic (£650,000 on 1/8/91) SL 3+4 SLC 3
Wimbledon (Loaned on 22/2/92) FL 1+1
Swansea C (Free on 6/1/93) FL 44+17/8 FLC 5+1 FAC 7+1 Others 10+7/7
Southend U (Free on 18/8/95) Others 1

HAYFIELD Matthew (Matt) Anthony
Born: Bristol, 8 August 1975
Height: 5'11" Weight: 12.2

A promising first-year professional, Matt made the breakthrough into Bristol Rovers' first team last season and immediately created a good impression on the supporters with his determined all-action displays. Capable of playing in a number of positions, unfortunately, a knee injury sustained in November, restricted any further opportunities.

Bristol Rov (From trainee on 13/7/94) FL 3+3 FAC 1 Others 1+1

HAYWARD Andrew (Andy) William
Born: Barnsley, 21 June 1970
Height: 6'0" Weight: 11.2
Club Honours: AMC '96

Versatile forward who has spent most of his time at Rotherham playing wide on the right, although he came to the club as a striker. Frequently having to settle for a role on the substitutes' bench last season, Andy never let the side down when he was called into action and weighed in with a handful of vital goals. An unused sub in the 2-1 AWS win over Shrewsbury at Wembley, he will have benefited from having another season as a full-timer, after making a late entry into the Football League.
Rotherham U (Free from Frickley Ath on 10/8/94) FL 55+18/8 FLC 3+1/3 FAC 2+1 Others 6+3/2

HAYWARD Steven (Steve) Lee
Born: Pelsall, 8 September 1971
Height: 5'10" Weight: 12.5
International Honours: E: Yth

A hard-working Carlisle midfielder, he came to the fore in the second half of last season with a series of impressive all-round performances. His ability to deliver telling free kicks brought him several goals, while his strike against Rotherham in March was voted "Goal of the Season". Is an excellent passer of the ball.
Derby Co (From juniors on 17/9/88) FL 15+11/1 FLC 0+2 FAC 1 Others 3+4
Carlisle U (£100,000 on 13/3/95) FL 45+2/6 FLC 2 Others 8/1

HAZEL Desmond (Des) Lloyd
Born: Bradford, 15 July 1967
Height: 5'10" Weight: 11.5
Club Honours: Div 4 '89

Des found his opportunities limited in Chesterfield's play-off push last season until injury struck the club's other forwards, but, even then, John Duncan's tactical approach did not present him with many chances to get beyond the subs' bench. When he did, his work on the right wing was often the cause of consternation in opposing defences. Was released during the summer.
Sheffield Wed (From apprentice on 29/7/85) FL 5+1 FLC 1 Others 0+1
Grimsby T (Loaned on 23/10/86) FL 9/2
Rotherham U (£45,000 on 13/7/88) FL 204+34/30 FLC 17+1/3 FAC 17/1 Others 18/6
Chesterfield (Signed on 23/3/95) FL 16+5 FLC 1 FAC 0+1 Others 3

HEALD Gregory (Greg) James
Born: Enfield, 26 September 1971
Height: 6'1" Weight: 12.8
International Honours: E: Sch

The Peterborough man continued his improvement as a strong and effective, no-frills central defender as last season progressed to become an important team player, missing very few games. He also proved his value at both ends of the park in scoring four league goals from set pieces, two with his head, including one that earned a draw at Chesterfield. Can play at full back if needed.
Peterborough U (£35,000 from Enfield on 8/7/94) FL 67+2/4 FLC 4 FAC 3 Others 8/1

HEALD Oliver Richard
Born: Vancouver, Canada, 13 March 1975
Height: 6'0" Weight: 12.0

A free transfer signing from Port Vale during the 1995 close season, the popular striker was a regular reserve team player for Scarborough, before being released midway through the campaign. He then had a spell with non-league, Guiseley, prior to returning home to Canada to pursue his international ambitions, having represented the country at youth level and being in the current Olympic squad.
Port Vale (Free from Norvan on 6/10/93)
Scarborough (Free on 4/8/95) FL 1+8/1 FLC 0+2 FAC 0+1 Others 2/1

HEALD Paul Andrew
Born: Wath on Dearne, 20 September 1968
Height: 6'2" Weight: 14.0

Signed from London neighbours, Leyton Orient, in the 1995 close season as cover for the injured Neil Sullivan and the unfortunate Hans Segers, he immediately took up his place in the Wimbledon first team and was ever present until January. The period was a difficult one for the team in general, but Paul regularly turned in outstanding performances, which, if not match winning, certainly kept the score down, before handing out his place to the returning Sullivan.
Sheffield U (From trainee on 30/6/87)
Leyton Orient (Signed on 2/12/88) FL 176 FLC 13 FAC 9 Others 21
Coventry C (Loaned on 10/3/92) PL 2
Swindon T (Loaned on 24/3/94) PL 1+1
Wimbledon (£125,000 on 25/7/95) PL 18 FLC 2

HEANEY Neil Andrew
Born: Middlesbrough, 3 November 1971
Height: 5'9" Weight: 11.13
Club Honours: FAYC '88
International Honours: E: U21-6; Yth

Southampton winger, predominantly left sided, whose fast and skilful runs can be exciting to watch. In and out of favour at various times last season, and occasionally unavailable through injury, he was thought to be on the move when Saints signed Mark Walters. However, is still with the club and is still a useful player to bring in for specific games. On his day a match-winner, both his 1995-96 goals came in drawn away games.
Arsenal (From trainee on 14/11/89) F/PL 4+3 FLC 0+1
Hartlepool U (Loaned on 3/1/91) FL 2+1
Cambridge U (Loaned on 9/1/92) FL 9+4/2 FAC 2
Southampton (£300,000 on 22/3/94) PL 38+15/4 FLC 4+2 FAC 6/2

HEATH Adrian Paul
Born: Stoke, 11 January 1961
Height: 5'6" Weight: 11.0
Club Honours: Div 1 '85, '87; FAC '84; CS '84, '85, '86, '87
International Honours: E: B-1; U21-8 (UEFAC '82)

Jimmy Mullen's failure to include him in the Burnley side last season, following his recovery from injury, was a contributory factor to both Mullen's unpopularity and Adrian's departure to Sheffield United in December, as assistant manager to Howard Kendall. However, having made five subs' appearances, including one in the FA Cup at Arsenal where he set up the equalising goal, the offer of the manager's job at Burnley

proved too tempting. Still a highly-skilled tactician and keen motivator, his return brought changes in tactics, but little improvement, and the fans would like to see him include himself in the line up more often.
Stoke C (From apprentice on 12/1/79) FL 94+1/16 FLC 9 FAC 4/1
Everton (£700,000 on 7/1/82) FL 206+20/71 FLC 33+2/11 FAC 24+5/6 Others 14+3/5 (£600,000 to Espanol on 15/11/88)
Aston Villa (£360,000 on 14/8/89) FL 8+1 FLC 1+1 FAC 0+1
Manchester C (£300,000 on 23/2/90) FL 58+17/4 FLC 7+1/2 FAC 2+1 Others 1+2
Stoke C (£50,000 on 27/3/92) FL 5+1 Others 3+1
Burnley (Free on 21/8/92) FL 109+6/29 FLC 8+1 FAC 12/6 Others 7
Sheffield U (Free on 15/12/95) FL 0+4 FAC 0+1
Burnley (Free on 7/3/96) FL 1+2

HEATHCOTE Michael (Mick)
Born: Kelloe, 10 September 1965
Height: 6'2" Weight: 12.5

Extremely reliable central defender who came from Cambridge during the summer of 1995, Mick held Plymouth together in 1995-96 when the rest of the team were having an off day. Put in a number of outstanding performances during the season, looking after Dion Dublin with great aplomb during an FA Cup match, his excellent form seeing him elected for the PFA award winning third division team, a great honour, fully deserved.
Sunderland (£15,000 from Spennymoor on 19/8/87) FL 6+3 Others 0+1
Halifax T (Loaned on 17/12/87) FL 7/1 FAC 1
York C (Loaned on 4/1/90) FL 3 Others 1
Shrewsbury T (£55,000 on 12/7/90) FL 43+1/6 FLC 6 FAC 5 Others 4
Cambridge U (£150,000 on 12/9/91) FL123+5/13 FLC 7/1 FAC 5+2/2 Others 7/2
Plymouth Arg (£100,000 on 27/7/95) FL 44/4 FLC 2/1 FAC 3/1 Others 4

Mick Heathcote

HEGGS Carl Sydney
Born: Leicester, 11 October 1970
Height: 6'0" Weight: 11.10

Swansea striker. Signed from WBA in the summer, Carl started 1995-96 in excellent form, showing good close skills, and a capacity for hard running from wide positions in midfield. A loss of form midway through the campaign, however, saw him relegated to a substitute's role and being placed on the transfer list. His season finished in April after suffering a broken arm against Brighton.

West Bromwich A (£25,000 from Leicester U on 22/8/91) FL 13+27/3 FLC 2 FAC 0+1 Others 6+3/1
Bristol Rov (Loaned on 27/1/95) FL 2+3/1
Swansea C (£60,000 on 27/7/95) FL 28+4/5 FLC 2 FAC 1 Others 2

HELDER Glenn
Born: Leiden, Holland, 28 October 1968
Height: 5'11" Weight: 11.7
International Honours: Holland: 4

The classy Dutch left winger had an in-and-out season with Arsenal in 1995-96, starting fewer than half the games and often being used as a late substitute for tactical purposes. Very quick, and a superb crosser, unfortunately, his lightweight frame sometimes gave him problems coping with the rigours of the English game and may explain why he was often substituted. Nevertheless, Glenn scored his first goal for the club at Middlesbrough and, in future, may well be used as a wing/back in Bruce Rioch's new defensive strategy.

Arsenal (£2,300,000 from Vitesse Arnhem on 14/2/95) PL 27+10/1 FLC 4+2 FAC 2

Glenn Helder

HELLIWELL Ian
Born: Rotherham, 7 November 1962
Height: 6'3" Weight: 13.12

The archetypal big, strong centre forward played a key part in Stockport's early season success in 1995-96, scoring twice on the opening day and going on to bag 11 in all, including one against Everton in the FA

Cup. Signed by Burnley in January 1996, unfortunately, after just three games, a cartilage injury put him out of action in what was hardly an auspicious start for his new club.

York C (£10,000 from Matlock T on 23/10/87) FL 158+2/40 FLC 8/1 FAC 5 Others 9+1/7
Scunthorpe U (£80,000 on 16/8/91) FL 78+2/22 FLC 8/5 FAC 4/2 Others 9/2
Rotherham U (£50,000 on 1/8/93) FL 47+5/4 FLC 4+1 FAC 1+2/1 Others 2+1/1
Stockport Co (Signed on 12/1/95) FL 35+4/13 FLC 4/1 FAC 2/1 Others 1
Burnley (£30,000 on 9/2/96) FL 3+1

HEMMINGS Anthony (Tony) George
Born: Burton, 21 September 1967
Height: 5'10" Weight: 12.10
International Honours: E: SP-1

A fast, but unpredictable left winger, he was part of Wycombe's first team squad in the opening weeks of last season, before returning to non-league football soon afterwards, via an unsuccessful trial with Chesterfield, and enjoying considerable success with Macclesfield.

Wycombe W (£25,000 from Northwich Victoria on 8/9/93) FL 28+21/12 FLC 1+5 FAC 2+2/1 Others 3+3/1
Chesterfield (Free on 20/10/95)

HENDERSON Damian Michael
Born: Leeds, 12 May 1973
Height: 6'2" Weight: 13.8

Useful member of the Hartlepool first team squad who is able to play equally well in attacking or defensive roles. Freed by Scunthorpe during the 1995 close season, he had a lengthy spell out with a dislocated shoulder in mid-term, but then finished strongly, teaming up with Ian McGuckin at the heart of Pool's defence. Surprisingly, with Keith Houchen opting for a clean sweep, he was released at the end of the season.

Leeds U (From trainee on 5/7/91)
Scarborough (Free on 1/8/93) FL 17/5 FLC 2 FAC 2 Others 3
Scunthorpe U (Free on 10/12/93) FL 31+6/4 FLC 2/1 FAC 1 Others 1
Hereford U (Loaned on 27/1/95) FL 5
Hartlepool U (Loaned on 6/3/95) FL 12/3
Hartlepool U (Free on 11/7/95) FL 33+3/3 FLC 3+1 FAC 1 Others 2

HENDON Ian Michael
Born: Ilford, 5 December 1971
Height: 6'1" Weight: 12.10
Club Honours: FAYC '90; CS '91
International Honours: E: U21-7; Yth

Expected to sign for Birmingham during the 1995 close season, the deal failed to materialise and he immediately settled into Leyton Orient's defence, missing very few games and proving a key player. Predominately a centre back, Ian is equally at home at right back, from where he can threaten the opposition with good runs and crosses. Was the supporters' "Player of the Season".

Tottenham H (From trainee on 20/12/89) FL 0+4 FLC 1 Others 0+2
Portsmouth (Loaned on 16/1/92) FL 1+3
Leyton Orient (Loaned on 26/3/92) FL 5+1
Barnsley (Loaned on 17/3/93) FL 6

Leyton Orient (£50,000 on 9/8/93) FL 102+1/4 FLC 6 FAC 5 Others 11/1
Birmingham C (Loaned on 23/3/95) FL 4

HENDRIE John Grattan
Born: Lennoxtown, 24 October 1963
Height: 5'8" Weight: 12.3
Club Honours: Div 3 '85, Div 2 '90, Div 1 '95
International Honours: S: Yth

Highly popular with Middlesbrough fans for his thrilling pace and spectacular goals, his return to the Premier League last season was dogged by injury and his 13 outings came in three different spells, with only one goal versus West Ham in December to show for his efforts. Although his appearances always belie the fact that he has been in the treatment room, a fully fit John Hendrie would be a boon to manager, Bryan Robson, even if he is now approaching the veteran stage. Interestingly, he lined up against his cousin, Lee Hendrie, at Aston Villa in March, a 0-0 draw leaving family pride intact.

Coventry C (From apprentice on 18/5/81) FL 15+6/2 FLC 2
Hereford U (Loaned on 10/1/84) FL 6
Bradford C (Free on 2/7/84) FL 173/46 FLC 17/3 FAC 11/6 Others 11/4
Newcastle U (£500,000 on 17/6/88) FL 34/4 FLC 2/1 FAC 4 Others 3
Leeds U (£600,000 on 20/6/89) FL 22+5/5 FLC 1 FAC 1 Others 2
Middlesbrough (£550,000 on 5/7/90) F/PL 181+11/44 FLC 21+1/6 FAC 10+2/2 Others 6/3

HENDRIE Lee Andrew
Born: Birmingham, 18 May 1977
Height: 5'7" Weight: 9.0
International Honours: E: U21-1; Yth

An Aston Villa reserve forward who was unfortunate to be sent off on his Premier League debut at QPR last December when, after coming on as substitute, he was booked and later dismissed by a referee making no allowances for youthful exuberance, or anxiety. The son of Paul, a former Birmingham player, and cousin of John (Middlesbrough), he made his first full appearance at home to Middlesbrough later in the season.

Aston Villa (From trainee on 18/5/94) PL 2+1

HENDRY Edward Colin James
Born: Keith, 7 December 1965
Height: 6'1" Weight: 12.2
Club Honours: FMC '87; PL '95
International Honours: S: 21; B-1

Blackburn centre back who is an inspirational player, fiercely competitive, brilliant in the air, and able to tackle with split-second judgement and bone juddering force. Normally dominates the centre completely and is surely the most combative defender in the English game. Had a superb last season, despite having three different central partners in Ian Pearce, Henning Berg, and Chris Coleman. Unfortunate to be ordered off in Moscow, he was one of the few Rovers to enhance their reputation during the Champions' Cup campaign, going on to consolidate his place in the Scottish side and win the club's "Player of the Year" award. Ended his season with impressive European Championship displays for Scotland.

Dundee (Signed from Islavale in 1983) SL 17+24/2 SC 2+3/1
Blackburn Rov (£30,000 on 11/3/87) FL 99+3/22 FLC 4 FAC 3 Others 13/1
Manchester C (£700,000 on 16/11/89) FL 57+6/5 FLC 4+1/1 FAC 5/2 Others 4/2
Blackburn Rov (£700,000 on 8/11/91) F/PL 160+5/10 FLC 20 FAC 11+1 Others 11

Colin Hendry

HENRY Nicholas (Nicky) Ian
Born: Liverpool, 21 February 1969
Height: 5'6" Weight: 10.8
Club Honours: Div 2 '91
Having played in 17 of the opening 19 games of 1995-96, Oldham's club captain suffered a terrible back injury in the home fixture against Derby, which necessitated an operation and sidelined him for the remainder of the season. As the midfield general who kept things ticking over and generally controlled the flow of passes, it was a huge blow for the first division club and probably the main reason for them finishing in such a lowly position.
Oldham Ath (From trainee on 6/7/87) F/PL 243+8/18 FLC 27+3/3 FAC 20 Others 5

HERBERT Craig Justin
Born: Coventry, 9 November 1975
Height: 6'0" Weight: 12.0
A hard-tackling WBA central defender, unfortunately, Craig missed practically all of the 1995-96 season after breaking his leg early in the campaign while playing for the second team. His only first team outing of the season, saw him score Albion's only goal in a 2-1 Anglo-Italian Cup defeat at the hands of Foggia in October. Competent, and good on the ball, the youngster has a quiet approach to the game.
West Bromwich A (Free from Torquay U juniors on 18/3/94) FL 8 FLC 2 Others 1/1

HERRERA Roberto (Robbie)
Born: Torquay, 12 June 1970
Height: 5'7" Weight: 10.6

Robbie must be one of Fulham's best signings in recent years. His all-round ability on the left side of defence, or in midfield, made him a great favourite with the crowd and a regular candidate for "Man of the Match" honours throughout 1995-96.
Queens Park R (From trainee on 1/3/88) FL 4+2 FLC 1+2 Others 1+1
Torquay U (Loaned on 17/3/92) FL 11
Torquay U (Loaned on 24/10/92) FL 5
Fulham (Signed on 29/10/93) FL 91+2/1 FLC 7 FAC 9 Others 6+1

HESKEY Emile William Ivanhoe
Born: Leicester, 11 January 1978
Height: 6'1" Weight: 13.0
International Honours: E: Yth
Right-footed Leicester City striker. A regular substitute early last season, netting a late winner at Carrow Road, Emile came off the bench in the televised return with the Canaries to lay on the equaliser, then scored the winner, that earned both the "Man of the Match" accolade and a place in the starting line up. Won a regular slot under Martin O'Neill and continued to impress with both his strength and speed. Scored a brace to clinch victory in the win at Molineux and another to sink the Mariners at Filbert Street. Voted the club's "Young Player of the Season".
Leicester C (From trainee on 3/10/95) P/FL 21+10/7 FLC 1+1 Others 3

HESSENTHALER Andrew (Andy)
Born: Dartford, 17 August 1965
Height: 5'7" Weight: 11.5
International Honours: E: SP-1
Absent for nearly half of last season with a hairline fracture of the leg, Andy was sorely missed by Watford, both for his drive and enthusiasm in midfield and for his inspirational captaincy. His never-say-die attitude was a crucial factor in the club's determined, if fruitless, battle against relegation.
Watford (£65,000 from Dagenham on 12/9/91) FL 195/11 FLC 13/1 FAC 5/2 Others 4

HEWITT James (Jamie) Robert
Born: Chesterfield, 17 May 1968
Height: 5'10" Weight: 11.9
Jamie has now completed his tenth season with his hometown club, happily settled into the right back position. And, like almost every other Chesterfield player, he missed four months of last season through injury. Usually allowed to get forward more than his full back partners, he is also the Spireites' regular corner taker.
Chesterfield (From trainee on 22/4/86) FL 240+9/14 FLC 10/1 FAC 8+1 Others 3
Doncaster Rov (Free on 1/8/92) FL 32+1 FLC 3+1/1 FAC 1 Others 3
Chesterfield (Signed on 8/10/93) FL 89+6/8 FLC 6 FAC 2 Others 9

HEWLETT Matthew (Matt) Paul
Born: Bristol, 25 February 1976
Height: 6'2" Weight: 10.11
International Honours: E: Yth
Matt put the disappointments of the 1994-95 campaign behind him and made the impact expected of him at Bristol City last season, when he was finally able to build on the

promise shown three years ago. Coming on in leaps and bounds, his skill and confidence in midfield from December onwards saw him make the role his own in the City team.
Bristol C (From trainee on 12/8/93) FL 38+2/2 FLC 2 FAC 0+1

HICKS Stuart Jason
Born: Peterborough, 30 May 1967
Height: 6'1" Weight: 13.0
During a season when Scarborough struggled near the foot of the third division, the club skipper and stalwart of the defence, was by far the outstanding performer, easily scooping the "Player of the Year" award. He was also an excellent off the field embassador for the club.
Peterborough U (From apprentice on 10/8/84)
Colchester U (Free from Wisbech on 24/3/88) FL 57+7 FLC 2 FAC 5/1 Others 5
Scunthorpe U (Free on 19/8/90) FL 67/1 FLC 4 FAC 4/1 Others 8
Doncaster Rov (Free on 10/8/92) FL 36 FLC 2 FAC 1 Others 2
Huddersfield T (Signed on 27/8/93) FL 20+2/1 FLC 3 FAC 3 Others 1
Preston NE (Signed on 24/3/94) FL 11+1 FLC 2 Others 1/1
Scarborough (Signed on 22/2/95) FL 45+2/1 FLC 2 FAC 1 Others 2

HIGGINS David (Dave) Anthony
Born: Liverpool, 19 August 1961
Height: 6'0" Weight: 11.0
Club Honours: AMC '90
Though coming to the end of his career, and no longer a first choice for Tranmere, he provided dependable back up for the central defensive partnership and towards the end of last season won a place on merit ahead of Shaun Teale, but got sent off at Grimsby. A great man-marker, with good pace, Dave relishes a battle and has never given less than 100 per cent commitment to Rovers during his 400 plus appearances for the club.
Tranmere Rov (Free from Eagle FC on 22/8/83) FL 27+1 FAC 2 Others 5 (Free to South Liverpool during 1985 close season)
Tranmere Rov (Free from Caernarfon on 20/7/87) FL 294+2/10 FLC 25 FAC 17 Others 34

HIGNETT Craig John
Born: Prescot, 12 January 1970
Height: 5'9" Weight: 11.10
Club Honours: Div 1 '95
A speedy Middlesbrough winger with instant acceleration and a deadly free kick, his shirt number (21) suggested that he was not to be regarded as an automatic first team choice in 1995-96. However, some excellent pre-season form saw him preferred to John Hendrie at the start of the campaign and he responded with his best-ever form for Boro, scoring seven goals in 16 games in partnership with Nick Barmby, which helped the club into fourth place. Sadly, he was sidelined with injury received in the Coca Cola Cup games against Crystal Palace in November and when he returned later in the season, other players had taken their chances, forcing him on to the subs' bench. However, he never stopped trying and often produced telling performances when recalled.
Crewe Alex (Free from Liverpool juniors on

11/5/88) FL 108+13/42 FLC 9+1/4 FAC 11+1/8 Others 6+1/3
Middlesbrough (£500,000 on 27/11/92) F/PL 79+19/22 FLC 9+2/8 FAC 2+1 Others 5+1

Craig Hignett

HILEY Scott Patrick
Born: Plymouth, 27 September 1968
Height: 5'9" Weight: 10.7
Club Honours: Div 4 '90

With first team opportunities limited at Birmingham following the arrival of Gary Poole, Scott eventually moved on a three month loan to Manchester City last February, thus joining up with his former manager, Alan Ball. A stylish right back who gets forward to deliver quality crosses for the forwards to power in, his home debut for City against Newcastle brought Niall Quinn such a goal. Unfortunate to break his foot at Bolton on 30 March, two days later Scott's move was made permanent.
Exeter C (From trainee on 4/8/86) FL 205+5/12 FLC 17 FAC 14 Others 16+2
Birmingham C (£100,000 on 12/3/93) FL 49 FLC 7 FAC 1 Others 2
Manchester C (£250,000 on 23/2/96) PL 2+4

HILL Andrew (Andy) Rowland
Born: Maltby, 20 January 1965
Height: 5'11" Weight: 12.0
International Honours: E: Yth

Experienced Port Vale right back who can also play in central defence. Having moved to Vale Park from Manchester City, following an injury to Neil Aspin early in the 1995-96 campaign, he made his debut in the local derby victory at Stoke City. A very dependable defender, he hardly missed a game in helping the club to avoid relegation, apart from a couple of small injuries and a one match suspension. Looks the part when

breaking out of defence with the ball and rarely misses a passing opportunity.
Manchester U (From apprentice on 16/1/83)
Bury (Free on 4/7/84) FL 264/10 FLC 22/1 FAC 12 Others 19/1
Manchester C (£200,000 on 21/12/90) F/PL 91+7/6 FLC 1 FAC 2+1 Others 1
Port Vale (£150,000 on 25/8/95) FL 35 FAC 6 Others 6

HILL Colin Frederick
Born: Uxbridge, 12 November 1963
Height: 6'0" Weight: 12.7
International Honours: NI: 14

A right-footed Leicester City central defender, he figured regularly in a three man central defence last season, gaining regular selection for his country under former City boss, Bryan Hamilton. Unfortunate to suffer a knee injury in the win at Molineux, that sidelined him through to the spring.
Arsenal (From apprentice on 7/8/81) FL 46/1 FLC 4 FAC 1 (Free to Maritimo during 1986 close season)
Colchester U (Free on 30/10/87) FL 64+5 FLC 2 FAC 7/2 Others 3+1
Sheffield U (£85,000 on 1/8/89) FL 77+5/1 FLC 5 FAC 10+2 Others 3
Leicester C (£200,000 on 26/3/92) F/PL 134+4 FLC 9+1/1 FAC 8 Others 9+1

HILL Daniel Ronald
Born: Enfield, 1 October 1974
Height: 5'9" Weight: 11.2
International Honours: E: U21-4; Yth

Unable to make his mark at Spurs last season, the young midfielder went on loan to first Birmingham (November) and then, Watford (February). At St Andrews, although impressing with his quality passing ability, using both feet, and looking a cut above many around him, he was forced to return to White Hart Lane after City had passed their allowed quota of loan players. Just one game at Watford and that was his season over, but the experience would have done him good.
Tottenham H (From trainee on 9/9/92) PL 4+6 FLC 0+2
Birmingham C (Loaned on 24/11/95) FL 5 FLC 2
Watford (Loaned on 15/2/96) FL 1

Keith Hill

HILL Keith John
Born: Bolton, 17 May 1969
Height: 6'0" Weight: 12.6

A versatile Plymouth player, usually found in central defence, although able to play anywhere across the back four, he lost his place at the back end of the 1995-96 campaign to Richard Logan and was used quite often as a substitute. Was released during the summer.
Blackburn Rov (From juniors on 9/5/87) F/PL 89+7/4 FLC 6/1 FAC 5+1 Others 3+2
Plymouth Arg (Signed on 23/9/92) FL 117+6/2 FLC 9 FAC 10 Others 9

HILLIER David
Born: Blackheath, 19 December 1969
Height: 5'10" Weight: 12.5
Club Honours: FAYC '88; Div 1 '91
International Honours: E: U21-1

Kept out of the Arsenal midfield in 1994-95 by Ray Parlour, with the advent of David Platt and Dennis Bergkamp, there were even less opportunities last season and he made just seven appearances. A determined, strong tackler, with plenty of stamina and two footed, he is far too good a player to remain in reserve team football indefinitely.
Arsenal (From trainee on 11/2/88) F/PL 82+20/2 FLC 13+2 FAC 13+2 Others 5+4

HIMSWORTH Gary Paul
Born: Pickering, 19 December 1969
Height: 5'8" Weight: 10.6

A quick and skilful left-sided midfielder, and fully recovered from the broken leg sustained in February 1994, Gary came back into service at Darlington at the beginning of last season. In taking his appearances for the Quakers past the 100 mark, his good performances saw his old club, York, move for him in February. Sadly, after just eight appearances, he was forced onto the sidelines after suffering further injury.
York C (From trainee on 27/1/88) FL 74+14/8 FLC 5 Others 5+2
Scarborough (Free on 5/12/90) FL 83+9/6 FLC 7+2/1 FAC 1+1 Others 6+1
Darlington (Free on 16/7/93) FL 86+8/8 FLC 5+1 FAC 6 Others 7/4
York C (£25,000 on 16/2/96) FL 7+1/1

HINCHCLIFFE Andrew (Andy) George
Born: Manchester, 5 February 1969
Height: 5'10" Weight: 12.10
Club Honours: FAC '95; CS '95
International Honours: E: U21-1; Yth

As an attacking left back, Andy makes good use of possession on the overlap to provide strong, telling crosses and is adept at corners, where his swirling, powerfully hit balls cause trouble for 'keepers. Also defensively sound, he uses his speed and agility to track back and make crucial last-ditch tackles. Continued at left back for Everton last season until losing his place to another gifted left footer in David Unsworth, and thereafter being mainly relegated to the bench. He will be looking to replace the latter this coming season.
Manchester C (From apprentice on 13/2/86) FL 107+5/8 FLC 11/1 FAC 12/1 Others 4/1
Everton (£800,000 on 17/7/90) F/PL 137+10/5 FLC 16+2/1 FAC 12+2/1 Others 8

HINSHELWOOD Daniel (Danny) Martin
Born: Bromley, 12 December 1975
Height: 5'9" Weight: 10.11
International Honours: E: Yth

Unable to make a first team debut for
Nottingham Forest, the young full back
joined Portsmouth, where his father, Martin,
was reserve team coach, on a free transfer
last February. Took a while to settle before
making his debut against dad's old club,
Crystal Palace, and with relegation staring
the club in the face, he made a solid
appearance at right back, which led to four
more outings. From a footballing family,
with Martin already mentioned, his
grandfather, Wally, played for a number of
clubs immediately after the last war, and his
uncle, Paul, also played for Palace.

Nottingham F (From trainee on 14/12/92)
Portsmouth (Free on 28/2/96) FL 5

HIRST David Eric
Born: Cudworth, 7 December 1967
Height: 5'11" Weight: 13.10
Club Honours: FLC '91
International Honours: E: 3; B-3; U21-7;
Yth

This fine, exciting left-sided Sheffield
Wednesday striker surely deserves to have
an injury free run this time around.
Although playing and scoring more goals
than in his last few injury laden seasons, he
was still sidelined by minor knocks in quite
a few games, but when bearing down on the
opposition's goal there was no finer sight
and he continued to show no sign of shirking
50/50 challenges, despite the many setbacks
suffered. Although David Pleat was on the
verge of transferring him to Everton midway
through the campaign, most Owls' fans
would want him to stay and get 100 per cent
fit.

Barnsley (From apprentice on 8/11/85) FL 26+2/9
FLC 1
Sheffield Wed (£200,000 on 11/8/86) F/PL
238+25/100 FLC 25+9/11 FAC 12+5/6 Others 8/5

HISLOP Neil (Shaka)
Born: London, 22 February 1969
Height: 6'6" Weight: 12.2
Club Honours: Div 2 '94

Signed from Reading prior to the start of
1995-96, Shaka proved an agile goalkeeper
and one of the fastest players at Newcastle.
Cool under pressure, he used his height to
dominate his area, instilling confidence in
his defenders, and with Pavel Srnicek
suspended for the opening games, his early
season performances kept him in the team
until he was injured and substituted at
Chelsea in December. Recalled for the run-
in, following the defeat at Anfield, of his
many fine saves during the season, the most
memorable was one at full stretch from a
deflected Steve McManaman shot in the
home game against Liverpool. Conceded
only 20 goals in 27 games, including 11
clean sheets.

Reading (Signed on 9/9/92) FL 104 FLC 10 FAC
3 Others 9
Newcastle U (£1,575,000 on 10/8/95) PL 24 FLC 4

Shaka Hislop

HITCHCOCK Kevin Joseph
Born: Canning Town, 5 October 1962
Height: 6'1" Weight: 12.2
Club Honours: AMC '87

Reliable Chelsea goalkeeping deputy who
came in for the injured Dmitri Kharine for
the FA Cup third round replay at St James'
Park and gave the Fleet Street headline
writers an opportunity to dust off that old
cliché: *Hitchcock Thriller!* when he saved
two penalties in a shoot-out to ruin
Newcastle's 100 per cent home record. Kept
his place for the next 18 matches and played
impressively as Chelsea reached the FA Cup
semi finals. Brave, loyal and long-serving,
he has spent the majority of his eight
seasons at The Bridge understudying international 'keepers, Dave Beasant and
Kharine, but would be an automatic choice
at many other Premiership clubs.

Nottingham F (£15,000 from Barking on 4/8/83)
Mansfield T (£140,000 on 1/2/84) FL 182 FLC 12
FAC 10 Others 20
Chelsea (£250,000 on 25/3/88) F/PL 80+1 FLC 8
FAC 12 Others 13
Northampton T (Loaned on 28/12/90) FL 17
Others 1

HOBSON Gary
Born: Hull, 12 November 1972
Height: 6'1" Weight: 12.10

The left-sided centre back missed much of
Hull City's pre-1995-96 season with a jarred
knee, but was soon back in action and
splendid form before suffering a terrible
gash to his left leg at Bristol City. "Hobo"
returned to be the bright light in a dark City
season, adding growing maturity to his
unquestioned abilities, prior to a shock
deadline move to Brighton.

Hull C (From trainee on 17/7/91) FL 135+7 FLC
13+1 FAC 2+2/1 Others 6+1
Brighton & Hove A (£60,000 on 27/3/96) FL 9

HODGE John
Born: Skelmersdale, 1 April 1969
Height: 5'7" Weight: 11.3
Club Honours: AMC '94

Despite playing throughout last season on a
temporary contract, John showed glimpses
of exciting wing play on occasions for
Swansea. A difficult winger to play on his
day, his only league goal during 1995-96
was a cracker against Walsall.

Exeter C (Signed from Falmouth T on 12/9/91)
FL 57+8/10 FLC 3/1 FAC 2 Others 8+2/1
Swansea C (Signed on 14/7/93) FL 87+25/10 FLC
6+2/3 FAC 6 Others 13+4

HODGE Stephen (Steve) Brian
Born: Nottingham, 25 October 1962
Height: 5'7" Weight: 10.3
Club Honours: FLC '89, '90; FMC '89; Div
1 '92
International Honours: E: 24; B-2; U21-8
(UEFAC '84)

Experienced former England midfielder
who joined Watford from QPR last
December. Having failed to be selected for
Rangers in 1995-96, he signed a monthly
contract for the Hornets and played against
Tranmere and Oldham before leaving in
mysterious circumstances. Used only
sparingly over the last few years, he would
appear to have reached the end of the road.

Nottingham F (From apprentice on 25/10/80) FL
122+1/30 FLC 10/2 FAC 6 Others 11/4
Aston Villa (£450,000 on 27/8/85) FL 53/12 FLC
12/3 FAC 4/1 Others 1
Tottenham H (£650,000 on 23/12/86) FL 44+1/7
FLC 2 FAC 7/2
Nottingham F (£550,000 on 17/8/88) FL 79+3/20
FLC 20+1/6 FAC 11+1/2 Others 9/2
Leeds U (£900,000 on 25/7/91) F/PL 28+26/10
FLC 4+3 FAC 2+1 Others 0+3
Derby Co (Loaned on 30/8/94) FL 10/2 Others 1/2
Queens Park R (£300,000 on 28/10/94) PL 15
FAC 1
Watford (Free on 15/12/95) FL 2

HODGES Glyn Peter
Born: Streatham, 30 April 1963
Height: 6'0" Weight: 12.3
Club Honours: Div 4 '83
International Honours: W: 18; B-1; U21-5;
Yth

Signed by Derby on a free transfer from
Sheffield United last February, the left-sided
midfielder who operates best in a wide role,
made a number of effective appearances
mainly as a substitute in the promotion run-
in, before being released at the end of the
season. With his ability to cross early balls
into the danger zone, allied to a wealth of
experience, he added two more Welsh caps
to his collection before the campaign was
over.

Wimbledon (From apprentice on 3/2/81) FL
200+32/49 FLC 14+2/3 FAC 13+2/2 Others 0+1
Newcastle U (£200,000 on 15/7/87) FL 7
Watford (£300,000 on 1/10/87) FL 82+4/15 FLC
5/2 FAC 8/1 Others 2_1/1
Crystal Palace (£410,000 on 16/7/90) FL 5+2
FLC 2+2/1
Sheffield U (£450,000 on 17/1/91) F/PL 116+31/19
FLC 4+3 FAC 13+3/3 Others 1
Derby Co (Free on 15/2/96) FL 1+8

Glyn Hodges

HODGES Kevin
Born: Bridport, 12 June 1960
Height: 5'8" Weight: 10.11

Although mainly employed at Plainmoor as the youth team coach, Kevin still managed to make the 600th league appearance (including subs) of a long career when he played in Torquay's midfield in the final game of last season at Lincoln. Released during the summer.

Plymouth Arg (From apprentice on 2/3/78) FL 502+28/81 FLC 32+3 FAC 39/3 Others 9+2/2
Torquay U (Loaned on 21/1/92) FL 3
Torquay U (Free on 7/12/92) FL 49+18/4 FLC 2 FAC 2+3 Others 8/1

HODGES Lee Leslie
Born: Epping, 4 September 1973
Height: 5'9" Weight: 11.6
International Honours: E: Yth

A natural goalscoring Barnet forward with good first touch, Lee caught fire towards the end of last season, scoring eight times in three games at one stage including four at Rochdale. With a great left foot and quick-thinking brain, Ray Clemence will do well to hold onto him.

Tottenham H (From trainee on 29/2/92) PL 0+4
Plymouth Arg (Loaned on 26/2/93) FL 6+1/2
Wycombe W (Loaned on 31/12/93) FL 2+2 FAC 1 Others 1
Barnet (Free on 31/5/94) FL 66+8/21 FLC 6 FAC 2+1/2 Others 3+1

HODGSON Douglas (Doug) John
Born: Frankston, Australia, 27 February 1969
Height: 6'2" Weight: 13.10

Strong and gritty Sheffield United central defender who began last season on loan at Plymouth. Following his return, he made his full league debut, due to injuries to David Tuttle and Brian Gayle, but, destined to be a squad player, Lincoln showed interest and a £60,000 bid was accepted. However, the

change of management at Lincoln ended the deal and, offered a new 18 month contract, his game went from strength to strength, proving more than adequate cover for Michel Vonk when called upon.

Sheffield U (£30,000 from Heidelberg Alex on 22/7/94) FL 12+5 FLC 2 FAC 1+1 Others 1
Plymouth Arg (Loaned on 10/8/95) FL 3+2

HOGG Graeme James
Born: Aberdeen, 17 June 1964
Height: 6'1" Weight: 12.4
Club Honours: AIC '95
International Honours: S: U21-4; Yth

The central defender, now with Notts County, was injured early on last season and when fit again in November, was unable to displace the partnership of Shaun Murphy and Gary Strodder, spending most of the remainder of the campaign on the bench, with occasional stand-in appearances. Still a very good player, when in the side, his ability to marshal the defence, coupled to his heading and tackling qualities, make him a difficult man to pass.

Manchester U (From apprentice on 1/6/82) FL 82+1/1 FLC 7+1 FAC 8 Others 12
West Bromwich A (Loaned on 3/11/87) FL 7 Others 1
Portsmouth (£150,000 on 25/8/88) FL 97+3/2 FLC 2 FAC 6 Others 2
Heart of Midlothian (£200,000 on 23/8/91) SL 49+6/3 SLC 6 SC 1/1 Others 4
Notts Co (£75,000 on 27/1/95) FL 27 FLC 2 FAC 1 Others 3

HOLDEN Richard (Rick) William
Born: Skipton, 9 September 1964
Height: 5'11" Weight: 13.10
Club Honours: Div 2 '91

Experienced left-sided player who joined Blackpool during the 1995 close season, having been freed by Oldham. Proved to be a good acquisition, with his crosses to the forwards always liable to create danger. Sadly, a serious injury cut short his season and he was released during the summer.

Burnley (Free from Carnegie College on 27/3/86) FL 0+1
Halifax T (Free on 24/9/86) FL 66+1/12 FLC 2 FAC 7 Others 8
Watford (£125,000 on 24/3/88) FL 42+8 FLC 2 FAC 6/1 Others 3+1/1
Oldham Ath (£165,000 on 18/8/89) FL 125+4/19 FLC 15+1/4 FAC 13/2 Others 3/1
Manchester C (£900,000 on 10/7/92) PL 49+1/3 FLC 3/1 FAC 5/1
Oldham Ath (£450,000 on 11/10/93) P/FL 46+14/9 FLC 3+2 FAC 7+1/1
Blackpool (Free on 7/9/95) FL 19+3/2 FAC 2 Others 2+1

HOLDSWORTH David Gary
Born: Walthamstow, 8 November 1968
Height: 6'1" Weight: 12.4
International Honours: E: U21-1; Yth

Much admired centre half who has now made over 300 appearances for Watford, his only club, though he remains the subject of persistent transfer speculation. In the FA Cup third round last season, David was in direct opposition to his identical twin, Dean, the Wimbledon striker, who also started his career at Vicarage Road. Perhaps, unsurprisingly, the brothers knew each other's games too well and cancelled each other out.

Missed the last two months of the season with a knee injury.

Watford (From apprentice on 8/11/86) FL 249+9/10 FLC 20/2 FAC 14+1/1

HOLDSWORTH Dean Christopher
Born: Walthamstow, 8 November 1968
Height: 5'11" Weight: 11.13
Club Honours: Div 3 '92
International Honours: E: B-1

The twin brother of Watford's David, Dean is an out-and-out striker who has been top scorer at Wimbledon during the last four seasons, his main strength being his ability to snap up chances in the box. Ever since his arrival, he has had to contend with endless transfer speculation and an ongoing back problem which has slightly curtailed his goalscoring exploits. However, that does not stop him being potentially one of the top men around and, as if to prove the point last season, five of his ten league goals were either winners or equalisers against teams of real quality, including Newcastle and Liverpool, two of the top three Premiership sides.

Watford (From apprentice on 12/11/86) FL 2+14/3 Others 0+4
Carlisle U (Loaned on 11/2/88) FL 4/1
Port Vale (Loaned on 18/3/88) FL 6/2
Swansea C (Loaned on 25/8/88) FL 4+1/1
Brentford (Loaned on 13/10/88) FL 2+5/1
Brentford (£125,000 on 29/9/89) FL 106+4/53 FLC 7+1/6 FAC 6/7 Others 12+2/9
Wimbledon (£720,000 on 20/7/92) PL 134+5/53 FLC 12+1/9 FAC 10+4/5

HOLLAND Christopher (Chris) James
Born: Whalley, 11 September 1975
Height: 5'9" Weight: 11.5
International Honours: E: U21-7; Yth

Very skilful on the ball, with neat and accurate distribution, Chris is a Newcastle midfield star of the future. An unpleasant incident in a night club in which ammonia was thrown in his face almost cost him the sight in his right eye, but happily recovered, he continued to demonstrate his considerable promise. This was confirmed by his continued selection for the England U21 team and his invitation to join the training sessions of the full squad preparing for the Portugal match.

Preston NE (Trainee) FL 0+1 Others 1
Newcastle U (£100,000 on 20/1/94) PL 2+1 FLC 0+1

HOLLAND Matthew (Matt) Rhys
Born: Bury, 11 April 1974
Height: 5'9" Weight: 11.4

Matt had an excellent season for Bournemouth in 1995-96, sweeping the board in the "Player of the Year" awards. He played the majority of the campaign in central midfield, but also appeared as a sweeper, always giving 100 per cent and scoring ten goals, the majority from outside the area. With a liking to push forward, and possessing a fierce shot, he is also very effective when defending and not afraid to tackle.

West Ham U (From trainee on 3/7/92)
Bournemouth (Signed on 27/1/95) FL 52+7/11 FLC 4 FAC 2 Others 2

HOLLAND Paul
Born: Lincoln, 8 July 1973
Height: 5'11" Weight: 12.10
International Honours: E: U21-4; Yth; Sch
A midfielder signed from Mansfield during the Toulon 1995 summer tournament, he failed to shine for Sheffield United in 1995-96 and suffered an early season dislocated shoulder in the third match at Oldham, which did not help his consistency. Following a change of management, he was allowed to join Chesterfield, who had shown an earlier interest in his signature, in January, and, although his talents were not utilised early on in a deep midfield role, he began to go forward more as time progressed. Disappointingly, just as Paul was running into a good seam of form a knee injury put him out with four crucial games left.
Mansfield T (From juniors on 4/7/91) FL 149/25 FLC 11 FAC 7/3 Others 9/2
Sheffield U (£250,000 on 20/6/95) FL 11+7/1 FLC 2/1
Chesterfield (Signed on 5/1/96) FL 16+1/2 Others 1

Ian Holloway

HOLLOWAY Ian Scott
Born: Kingswood, 12 March 1963
Height: 5'8" Weight: 10.10
Club Honours: Div 3 '90
The ideal midfield type, Ian has a good footballing brain, works hard to get into good positions, and does not give the ball away easily. He was yet another QPR player whose form and number of games were greatly affected by niggling injuries in 1995-96. However, he still managed to make 30 appearances and even scored a rare goal at Newcastle, a thumping volley into the roof of the net, before returning to his old club, Bristol Rovers, as their player/manager at the end of the season.
Bristol Rov (From apprentice on 18/3/81) FL 104+7/14 FLC 10/1 FAC 8/2 Others 5

Wimbledon (£35,000 on 18/7/85) FL 19/2 FLC 3 FAC 1
Brentford (£25,000 on 12/3/86) FL 27+3/2 FLC 2 FAC 3 Others 0+1
Torquay U (Loaned on 30/1/87) FL 5
Bristol Rov (£10,000 on 21/8/87) FL 179/26 FLC 5 FAC 10/1 Others 20/3
Queens Park R (£230,000 on 12/8/91) F/PL 130+17/4 FLC 12+1 FAC 7+1/1 Others 1+1

HOLMES Matthew (Mattie) Jason
Born: Luton, 1 August 1969
Height: 5'7" Weight: 10.7
A good footballing wide midfielder who passes and moves well, and who is always dangerous at set pieces with a great left foot, Mattie joined Blackburn from West Ham immediately prior to 1995-96 getting underway. As the club's only pre-season signing, being brought in to fill the gap caused by the injury to Jason Wilcox, apart from the game against Rosenborg where early goals opened up the play and his fine cross was headed home by Mike Newell, he had too little time in the side to establish himself and will be looking for more than ten starts this coming term.
Bournemouth (From trainee on 22/8/88) FL 105+9/8 FLC 7 FAC 8+2 Others 5
Cardiff C (Loaned on 23/3/89) FL 0+1
West Ham U (£40,000 on 19/8/92) F/PL 63+13/4 FLC 4 FAC 6 Others 3/1
Blackburn Rov (£1,200,000 on 15/8/95) PL 8+1/1 Others 2+1

HOLMES Paul
Born: Stocksbridge, 18 February 1968
Height: 5'10" Weight: 11.3
Added a new dimension to WBA's play when he was brought into the side early in 1996, having been signed from Everton. An overlapping right back, with good technique, Paul centred the ball well and was always willing to get into the opposing penalty area to have a shot at goal. Suffered a minor knee injury towards the end of the season, but, nevertheless, made an excellent start to his career at The Hawthorns.
Doncaster Rov (From apprentice on 24/2/86) FL 42+5/1 FAC 3+1/1 Others 1
Torquay U (£6,000 on 12/8/88) FL 127+11/4 FLC 9 FAC 9+2 Others 13+3
Birmingham C (£40,000 on 5/6/92) FL 12 FAC 1
Everton (£100,000 on 19/3/93) PL 21 FLC 4 FAC 1 Others 0+2
West Bromwich A (£80,000 on 12/1/96) FL 18 Others 3

HOLMES Steven (Steve) Peter
Born: Middlesbrough, 13 January 1971
Height: 6'2" Weight: 13.0
Reliable right back who also performed well in the centre of defence for both Preston and Lincoln last season. Had begun his career at Sincil Bank back in Colin Murphy's time and signed twice more for the Imps during 1995-96, enjoying a three month loan period from November to January, before joining on a permanent basis in March. Particularly dangerous in the opposition's area, Steve is a strong tackler and heads powerfully.
Lincoln C (From trainee on 17/7/89)
Preston NE (£10,000 from Guisborough T, via Gainsborough Trinity, on 14/3/94) FL 13/1 FAC 3 Others 1
Hartlepool U (Loaned on 10/3/95) FL 5/2

Lincoln C (Loaned on 20/10/95) FL 12/1 Others 2
Lincoln C (£30,000 on 15/3/96) FL 11/1

HOLSGROVE Paul
Born: Telford, 26 August 1969
Height: 6'1" Weight: 11.10
Although selected to play in several positions for Reading in 1995-96, he looked most comfortable in the sweeper role, where his pace and ability to read the game got the side out of trouble on many occasions. He also scored one of his speciality long-range goals against WBA, but his form dipped at the end of the season and he was no longer an automatic choice.
Aldershot (From trainee on 9/2/87) FL 0+3 Others 1 (Free to Wokingham T in 1990 close season)
Luton T (£25,000 on 1/1/91) FL 1+1 (Free to Heracles in November 1991)
Millwall (Free on 13/8/92) FL 3+8 FLC 0+1 FAC 0+1 Others 2
Reading (Free on 10/8/94) FL 50+4/4 FLC 7+2/1 FAC 3

HOMER Christopher (Chris)
Born: Stockton, 16 April 1977
Height: 5'9" Weight: 11.5
Promising young midfielder who will be disappointed with 1995-96, his first season as a professional with Hartlepool, making only rare first team appearances, before being troubled with breathing difficulties which meant he tired easily. Towards the end of the campaign he was hospitalised in an attempt to clear up his problem and starts 1996-97 on a six month contract.
Hartlepool U (From trainee on 11/7/95) FL 2+4 FLC 0+1 Others 0+1

HONE Mark Joseph
Born: Croydon, 31 March 1968
Height: 6'1" Weight: 12.5
International Honours: E: SP-4
Never able to find a consistent place in the Southend team during last season, Mark had to be satisfied with short runs at full back in a replacement role. Never one to let the team down, his tackling was first class and his desire to get forward caused opposing defences problems on more than one occasion. Released during the summer.
Crystal Palace (From juniors on 3/11/85) FL 4 FLC 0+1
Southend U (£50,000 from Welling U on 11/8/94) FL 50+6 FLC 2+2 FAC 1 Others 2

HOOKER Jonathan (Jon) William
Born: London, 31 March 1972
Height: 5'7" Weight: 11.0
Diminutive Brentford outside left. Made a few early season appearances in 1995-96, but failed to establish a place in the squad, before being released in the summer.
Gillingham (On trial from Hertford T on 7/11/94) Others 1
Brentford (£5,000 from Hertford T on 14/11/94) FL 4+1 FLC 1 FAC 0+2

HOOPER Dean Raymond
Born: Harefield, 13 April 1971
Height: 5'11" Weight: 11.6
Little was seen of the speedy former Hayes winger, whose only full senior appearances for Swindon last season were in the Auto Windscreens Shield – at right back. Went on

loan to Peterborough in December, but injury soon curtailed his progress there after just four games.

Swindon T (£15,000 from Hayes on 3/3/95) FL 0+4 FLC 0+2 Others 2
Peterborough U (Loaned on 15/12/95) FL 4

HOPE Christopher (Chris) Jonathan
Born: Sheffield, 14 November 1972
Height: 6'1" Weight: 12.7

A regular for Scunthorpe in 1995-96 at either right back or in the centre of defence, Chris tended to be used as replacement for missing first-choice defenders, although more than capable of holding his place on merit. Strong in the air, solid on the ground, and the scorer of some useful goals.

Nottingham F (Free from Darlington juniors on 23/8/90)
Scunthorpe U (£50,000 on 5/7/93) FL 97+8/3 FLC 3+1 FAC 8/1 Others 8

HOPE Matthew (Matt) Philip
Born: Bristol, 13 October 1976
Height: 5'8" Weight: 10.0

A creative Bristol Rovers' trainee midfielder, Matt made his first team debut last October as a substitute in the 2-0 AWS win at Brighton, before having his career cut tragically short, following a serious knee injury. For both club and player, it was a huge blow.

Bristol Rov (Trainee) Others 0+1

HOPKIN David
Born: Greenock, 21 August 1970
Height: 6'0" Weight: 13.0

Scottish winger who moved from Chelsea to Crystal Palace in the summer of 1995, and proved to be a big hit with the fans, playing in nearly every game and scoring 12 goals, of which the best was a late winner with a curling shot against Tranmere in March. Hard running and direct, and a good tackler who can play further back if required, he came back from injury to play in the Wembley play-off final, that ended so disappointingly for Palace. Also possesses a good long throw.

Morton (Signed from Port Glasgow BC in 1989-90) SL 33+15/4 SLC 2/2 SC 2/1
Chelsea (£300,000 on 25/9/92) PL 21+19/1 FLC 0+1 FAC 3+2
Crystal Palace (£850,000 on 29/7/95) FL 41+1/8 FLC 4/4 FAC 1 Others 1

HOPKINS Jeffrey (Jeff)
Born: Swansea, 14 April 1964
Height: 6'0" Weight: 12.12
Club Honours: Div 2 '94
International Honours: W: 16; U21-5; Yth

Missed the first six months of last season due to a persistent achilles tendon injury, but returned for the 0-0 draw at Grimsby and gave a typically gritty performance at centre back. He remained a cornerstone of the Reading defence for the rest of the fixtures, and his experience and determination did much to ensure Royals' survival in division one.

Fulham (From apprentice on 10/9/81) FL 213+6/4 FLC 26/2 FAC 12 Others 3
Crystal Palace (£240,000 on 17/8/88) FL 70/2 FLC 7/1 FAC 4/1 Others 12

Plymouth Arg (Loaned on 24/10/91) FL 8 Others 1
Bristol Rov (Free on 5/3/92) FL 4+2
Reading (Free on 13/7/92) FL 110+3/3 FLC 8+1/1 FAC 6+1 Others 6+2

HOPPER Anthony (Tony)
Born: Carlisle, 31 May 1976
Height: 5'10" Weight: 11.13

Local Carlisle product who has developed through the youth side to become part of the first team squad. An enthusiastic performer, Tony made several appearances last season, mostly in midfield.

Carlisle U (From trainee on 18/7/94) FL 4+7 Others 1

HORLOCK Kevin
Born: Bexley, 1 November 1972
Height: 6'0" Weight: 12.0
Club Honours: Div 2 '96
International Honours: NI: 2; B-2

1995-96 was a remarkable season for the left-sided midfielder. Having missed the opening game, after undergoing a knee operation, he appeared in each of Swindon's subsequent 58 games en-route to a second division championship medal. Only Wayne

Allison finished with more goals than Kevin's 16, which included an inspirational hat trick at Bristol Rovers in September, and he looks certain to be rewarded with further caps for Northern Ireland.

West Ham U (From trainee on 1/7/91)
Swindon T (Free on 27/8/92) F/PL 123+12/14 FLC 10+2/1 FAC 11/3 Others 5+2

HORNE Barry
Born: St Asaph, 18 May 1962
Height: 5'10" Weight: 12.2
Club Honours: WC '86; FAC '95; CS '95
International Honours: W: 54

Everton midfielder with great battling and ball-winning qualities who never shirks a tackle. His great stamina enables him to move between the two penalty areas, both supporting and breaking up attacks. Last season, he again marshalled the Toffees' midfield, sitting just ahead of the back four, inevitably missing the odd match, but working well with a number of different partners, before losing his place in February. Somewhat surprisingly, although 34 years of age, Barry was allowed to move to Birmingham at the end of the campaign, a

Barry Horne

£250,000 fee securing the services of a man who only recently took his total of Welsh caps to 54.

Wrexham (Free from Rhyl on 26/6/84) FL 136/17 FLC 10/1 FAC 7/2 Others 15/3
Portsmouth (£60,000 on 17/7/87) FL 66+4/7 FLC 3 FAC 6
Southampton (£700,000 on 22/3/89) FL 111+1/6 FLC 15+2/3 FAC 15/3 Others 7/1
Everton (£675,000 on 1/7/92) PL 118+5/3 FLC 12+1 FAC 11+1 Others 3

HORNE Brian Simon
Born: Billericay, 5 October 1967
Height: 5'11" Weight: 14.6
Club Honours: Div 2 '88
International Honours: E: U21-5; Yth

An eventful season for Hartlepool's goal-keeper. Although he turned in many fine performances in 1995-96, manager, Keith Houchen, was not happy with his attitude and also publicly criticised him about his weight. Three loan 'keepers were signed to temporarily replace him, but throughout he remained popular with the public and it was somehow inevitable that he was voted the supporters' "Player of the Year".

Millwall (From apprentice on 10/10/85) FL 163 FLC 14 FAC 9 Others 10
Middlesbrough (Loaned on 28/8/92) FL 3+1
Stoke C (Loaned on 2/10/92) FL 1 FLC 1
Portsmouth (Free on 24/12/92) FL 3 Others 2
Hartlepool U (Free on 2/8/94) FL 73 FLC 5 FAC 2 Others 2+1

Marc Hottiger

HOTTIGER Marc
Born: Lausanne, Switzerland, 7 November 1967
Height: 5'10" Weight: 12.9
International Honours: Switzerland: 61

Typical European full back who relishes attacking down the right flank to provide dangerous crosses to the forwards. Determined in the tackle, and settling on the ball well, rarely surrendering possession, the arrival of Warren Barton at Newcastle last season, however, limited the first team

exposure he required to ensure selection for Switzerland and he finally moved to Everton in March, a transfer long delayed by a work permit dispute. Soon got down to business, building up an excellent partnership with Andrei Kanchelskis and making the right back position his own. Played in two of the three Euro '96 group games before the Swiss departed from the tournament.

Newcastle U (£520,000 on 4/8/94) PL 38+1/1 FLC 6+1 FAC 4/1 Others 4
Everton (£700,000 on 9/3/96) PL 9/1

HOUCHEN Keith Morton
Born: Middlesbrough, 25 July 1960
Height: 6'2" Weight: 13.7
Club Honours: FAC '87

Hartlepool United player/manager who had an eventful first season in charge at the Victoria Park in 1995-96. For a player who made his name as a striker, he will be disappointed at his own goalscoring return, but at times circumstances dictated that he played a deeper role. Next season, he will probably appear in fewer games, but is far from finished and may yet score the seven league goals he needs to beat the club's goalscoring record.

Hartlepool U (Free from Chesterfield juniors on 9/2/78) FL 160+10/65 FLC 8/1 FAC 4+1
Leyton Orient (£25,000 on 26/3/82) FL 74+2/20 FLC 3/1 FAC 3 Others 0+1
York C (£151,000 on 22/3/84) FL 56+11/19 FLC 6/3 FAC 9+2/3 Others 4/2
Scunthorpe U (£40,000 on 28/3/86) FL 9/3
Coventry C (£60,000 on 3/7/86) FL 43+11/7 FLC 2+1 FAC 5+1/5 Others 2+1
Hibernian (£100,000 on 29/3/89) SL 51+6/11 SLC 5/1 SC 6/4 Others 4/1
Port Vale (£100,000 on 9/8/91) FL 44+5/10 FLC 2+1/1 FAC 2 Others 1+1
Hartlepool U (Free on 1/8/93) FL 102+2/27 FLC 8/1 FAC 2 Others 3

HOUGHTON Raymond (Ray) James
Born: Glasgow, 9 January 1962
Height: 5'7" Weight: 10.10
Club Honours: FLC '86, '94; Div 1 '88, '90; CS '88, '90; FAC '89, '92
International Honours: Ei: 66

The veteran, hard-working Irish Republic midfielder was the brains behind Crystal Palace's great push for promotion which ended in despair in the play-off final at Wembley. Playing in all but four games of the 55-match programme, and scoring five vital goals, all of which contributed to victories, he continued to lend his vast experience to the cause, his vision still able to unlock the best of defences. His good form also won him a recall to Ireland's national side in April against the Czechs.

West Ham U (From juniors on 5/7/79) FL 0+1
Fulham (Free on 7/7/82) FL 129/16 FLC 12/2 FAC 4/3
Oxford U (£147,000 on 13/9/85) FL 83/10 FLC 13/3 FAC 3 Others 6/1
Liverpool (£825,000 on 19/10/87) FL 147+6/28 FLC 14/3 FAC 26+1/4 Others 8/3
Aston Villa (£900,000 on 28/7/92) PL 83+12/6 FLC 11+2/2 FAC 7/2 Others 4+2/1
Crystal Palace (£300,000 on 23/3/95) P/FL 51/6 FLC 4 FAC 4 Others 3/1

HOUGHTON Scott Aaron
Born: Hitchin, 22 October 1971
Height: 5'7" Weight: 12.4
Club Honours: FAYC '90
International Honours: E: Yth; Sch

Speedy winger who scored some exciting goals for Walsall in 1995-96. Showed his mettle early last season when, having been brought down heavily in the game against Swansea, he got up to bang home the free kick and after missing five matches with an injured foot he scored within nine minutes of the start of his first game back at Bristol City. His value to the side was further emphasised in March, when he netted a last minute equaliser at leaders, Swindon, and laid on both goals to turn a 2-1 deficit into a 3-2 win against promotion challengers, Crewe, all in the space of four days. Apart from a willingness to take on defenders, Scott is also a good early crosser.

Tottenham H (From trainee on 24/8/90) FL 0+10/2 FLC 0+2 Others 0+2
Ipswich T (Loaned on 26/3/91) FL 7+1/1
Gillingham (Loaned on 17/12/92) FL 3
Charlton Ath (Loaned on 26/2/93) FL 6
Luton T (Loaned on 10/8/93) FL 7+9/1 FLC 2+1 FAC 0+1 Others 2
Walsall (£20,000 on 2/9/94) FL 76+2/14 FLC 0+1/1 FAC 10/3 Others 4

HOULT Russell
Born: Leicester, 22 November 1972
Height: 6'3" Weight: 14.9

Tall and commanding goalkeeper who, after signing permanently for Derby, began last season as second choice to Steve Sutton, before taking advantage of the latter's substitution at Sheffield United to claim the first team place for the rest of the campaign. Kept a string of clean sheets, especially during County's club record of undefeated games, which was behind their eventual promotion. Should cope very well at a higher level now he has become the manager's first choice.

Leicester C (From trainee on 28/3/91) FL 10 FLC 3 Others 1
Lincoln C (Loaned on 27/8/91) FL 2 FLC 1
Bolton W (Loaned on 3/11/93) FL 3+1 Others 1
Lincoln C (Loaned on 12/8/94) FL 15 Others 1
Derby Co (£300,000 on 17/2/95) FL 55+1 FLC 2 FAC 1

HOUSHAM Steven James
Born: Gainsborough, 24 February 1976
Height: 5'10" Weight: 11.8

Forceful Scunthorpe right back who was a regular choice for the first half of 1995-96 until illness forced him out. Although returning later in the season, injury put him out for a few more games. Attracting attention from bigger clubs, he can also play on the right side of midfield.

Scunthorpe U (From trainee on 23/12/93) FL 25+7 FAC 1 Others 2+1/1

HOWARD Jonathan (Jon)
Born: Sheffield, 7 October 1971
Height: 5'11" Weight: 12.6

Jon remained on the fringe of Chesterfield's first team throughout last season, frequently claiming a place when injury hit other forwards. Often playing up the left he generally went about his business quietly, occasionally appearing to be overlooked by defenders. Sadly, he seemed to be the butt of criticism from "fans" on the terraces but, to his credit, he remained unaffected by this. Probably at his best in an old-fashioned centre forward role.

Rotherham U (From trainee on 10/7/90) FL 25+11/5 FLC 0+1 FAC 4/2 Others 3+1 (Free to Buxton on 11/11/94)
Chesterfield (Free on 9/12/94) FL 17+25/3 FLC 1 FAC 1+1 Others 5+3/2

HOWARD Steven (Steve) John
Born: Durham, 10 May 1976
Height: 6'2" Weight: 13.7

Attacking midfielder who soon adjusted to full-time training after joining Hartlepool from Tow Law Town in the 1995 close season. As a 19 year old, he may have expected a more gradual introduction to Endsleigh League football, but from the start his form earned him a regular place, and with the club having no outstanding goalscorer, his contributions saw him finishing joint top of the list with nine to his credit.
Hartlepool (Free from Tow Law on 8/8/95) FL 32+7/7 FLC 3 FAC 1 Others 2/2

HOWARD Terence (Terry)
Born: Stepney, 26 February 1966
Height: 6'1" Weight: 14.0
International Honours: E: Yth

A left-footed Wycombe central defender, whose consistent performances in 1995-96 endeared himself to the supporters, he was surprisingly dropped in April and released at the end of the season. Good at both ends of the field, especially in the air, Terry should certainly remain in league soccer.
Chelsea (From apprentice on 1/3/84) FL 6
Crystal Palace (Loaned on 9/1/86) FL 4
Chester C (Loaned on 23/1/87) FL 2 FAC 2
Leyton Orient (£10,000 on 19/3/87) FL 323+5/31 FLC 26/1 FAC 23+1/3 Others 29/1
Wycombe W (Free on 10/2/95) FL 56+3/2 FLC 3 FAC 2 Others 2/1

HOWARTH Lee
Born: Bolton, 3 January 1968
Height: 6'1" Weight: 12.3

After some rather inept displays for Mansfield last season, the central defender lost his place and Brian Kilcline was recruited to replace him. Loaned out to fellow strugglers, Barnet, in January, he impressed so much that Ray Clemence signed him permanently and when given the captaincy, the no-nonsense and no-frills Lee proved an ideal foil for Linvoy Primus.
Peterborough U (Free from Chorley on 16/8/91) FL 56+6 FLC 8 FAC 3 Others 3+2/1
Mansfield T (£15,000 on 5/8/94) FL 56+1/2 FLC 7 FAC 4 Others 5
Barnet (Signed on 26/1/96) FL 19

HOWE Edward (Eddie) John Frank
Born: Amersham, 29 November 1977
Height: 5'11" Weight: 11.10

Another product of Bournemouth's success-ful youth policy, having played at centre back for the youth team, Eddie came in as a right back when he made the step up in place of the suspended Neil Young last season. Impressed in four starts as a player with good engines, who could link between defence and attack, and one who was comfortable on the ball.
Bournemouth (Trainee) FL 4+1

HOWE Stephen Robert (Bobby)
Born: Annitsford, 6 November 1973
Height: 5'7" Weight: 10.4
International Honours: E: Yth

This young Nottingham Forest reserve striker seemed a long way from first team action at the start of last season, especially when on loan at non-league Kettering, but he forced his way into the squad in November, making his bow as a substitute in the first leg of the UEFA Cup against French club, Lyon, and his full Premier League debut versus Manchester United a week later. Thereafter, he made occasional appearances both as first choice and substitute for the remainder of the season, scoring at Sheffield Wednesday in March and at home to QPR in the final game. Fast and tricky, with a good turn of pace, following the disappointing form shown by Forest's front-line strikers during 1995-96, he may receive further opportunities during the coming campaign.
Nottingham F (From trainee on 5/12/90) P/FL 6+7/2 FLC 1 Others 1+1

HOWELLS David
Born: Guildford, 15 December 1967
Height: 5'11" Weight: 12.4
Club Honours: FAC '91; CS '91
International Honours: E: Yth

A midfielder who plays mainly defensively as anchor man in front of the Spurs' back four, his key role is in reducing the space opponents have in the middle of the field as a first line of defence, a tactic which has proved very effective in recent campaigns. Rarely spectacular and often unnoticed in games, it is a fact that the club often struggle for good results when he is absent. Scored against Leeds United last September, his powerful header from 18 yards helping Spurs gain a 2-1 victory which proved to be a turning point after a poor start to 1995-96, before missing part of the season, between the end of December and most of February, due to injury. Made a welcome return against Sheffield Wednesday, being absent just once in the remaining 14 matches.
Tottenham H (From apprentice on 28/1/85) F/PL 192+33/20 FLC 21+5/4 FAC 17+3/1 Others 7

HOWES Shaun Colin
Born: Norwich, 7 November 1977
Height: 5'10" Weight: 12.3

Second year Cambridge United trainee, and a left-footed defender, Shaun made his league debut as substitute in the penultimate game of the season at Torquay, when coming on for the last seven minutes for a side with few players over the age of 21.
Cambridge U (Trainee) FL 0+1

HOWEY Lee Matthew
Born: Sunderland, 1 April 1969
Height: 6'2" Weight: 13.9
Club Honours: Div 1 '96

A Sunderland defender, cum striker, Lee joins his younger brother Steve in the Premiership this season. Essentially a squad player, he never let anyone down when called upon, scoring some vital goals, such as the winner against Barnsley at Roker in

October and a last minute headed equaliser at Portsmouth in February that set the club off on a nine-match winning run, which ultimately ended in him winning a first division championship medal.
Sunderland (Free from Bishop Auckland on 25/3/93) FL 30+27/8 FLC 1+4/2 FAC 2+4/1 Others 0+1

HOWEY Stephen (Steve) Norman
Born: Sunderland, 26 October 1971
Height: 6'2" Weight: 11.9
Club Honours: Div 1 '93
International Honours: E: 4

Younger brother of Sunderland striker, Lee, Steve had another fine season in 1995-96 at centre back for Newcastle. Confident on the ball and good in the air, he is rarely exposed for pace, and his cultured style equips him to step forward readily out of defence into midfield more ably than most of his contemporaries. This, together with his consistent quality performances, resulted in further recognition by England, although a series of niggling injuries prevented his availability for the Norway and Croatia games and ended his season prematurely at the beginning of April. A cartilage problem may have required surgery during the summer.
Newcastle U (From trainee on 11/12/89) F/PL 127+19/5 FLC 13+2/1 FAC 11+2 Others 8

Steve Howey

HOYLAND Jamie William
Born: Sheffield, 23 January 1966
Height: 6'0" Weight: 12.8
International Honours: E: Yth

Most often used as part of a three-man Burnley defence alongside Mark Winstanley and Peter Swan in 1995-96, Jamie's role was often unclear and he was seldom as effective as in the previous season. Unfortunately, after losing his place when the side was rearranged to accommodate Steve Thompson, he suffered a cartilage injury, which then kept him out of action. Previously recognised as a midfielder. Is the son of Tommy, who played for Sheffield United and Bradford City between 1949 and 1962.

Manchester C (From apprentice on 12/11/83) FL 2 FLC 0+1/1
Bury (Free on 11/7/86) FL 169+3/35 FLC 14+1/5 FAC 6 Others 12/2
Sheffield U (£250,000 on 4/7/90) F/PL 72+17/6 FLC 5+3/1 FAC 2+2/1 Others 5/1
Bristol C (Loaned on 4/3/94) FL 6
Burnley (£130,000 on 14/10/94) FL 51+2/2 FLC 1 FAC 5 Others 3

HOYLE Colin Roy
Born: Wirksworth, 15 January 1972
Height: 5'11" Weight: 12.3

A frustrating season for the former Bradford City player who joined Notts County on a free transfer in 1994-95. Able to play in defence or midfield, he made only two starts in 1995-96, at right back in March, and only three selections as substitute, before being released on a free transfer in the summer.

Arsenal (From trainee on 29/1/90)
Chesterfield (Loaned on 8/2/90) FL 3
Barnsley (Free on 1/7/90)
Bradford C (£25,000 on 28/8/92) FL 55+7/1 FLC 1 FAC 3+1 Others 4
Notts Co (Free on 6/8/94) FL 5 Others 1
Mansfield T (Loaned on 3/10/94) FL 4+1 FLC 2 Others 1

HUCKERBY Darren Carl
Born: Nottingham, 23 April 1976
Height: 5'9" Weight: 11.2

Playing for Lincoln last season, his first as a regular, Darren attracted a clutch of admirers, including Manchester United, but it was Newcastle who secured his signature as an investment for the future in November. Although opportunities were limited, with only two substitute appearances, he impressed as a player with pace and good finishing. He prefers to play off a big striker and link others into the game, rather than as a target man.

Lincoln C From trainee on 14/7/93) FL 20+10/3 FLC 2 Others 1/2
Newcastle U (£400,000 on 10/11/95) PL 0+1 FAC 0+1

HUGHES Andrew John
Born: Manchester, 2 January 1978
Height: 5'11" Weight: 12.1

The Oldham youngster burst into first team football last season, mainly thanks to the Anglo-Italian Cup, his youthful exuberance adding much needed pace to the midfield area. Still a trainee at the time, he soon became a squad regular, making his full debut at home to Birmingham (December), signing professional forms (January), and scoring his first goal for the club in a 2-1 defeat at Sheffield United in February. Looks a very good prospect.

Oldham Ath (From trainee on 20/1/96) FL 10+5/1 FAC 3 Others 0+2

HUGHES Bryan
Born: Liverpool, 19 June 1976
Height: 5'10" Weight: 11.2
Club Honours: WC '95

Wrexham central midfielder. As is often the case, after such a brilliant first full season in the Football League, Bryan failed to do justice to himself in 1995-96. However, as a talented prospect he has time on his side and the coaching staff at the Racecourse will no doubt give him every encouragement.

Wrexham (Trainee) FL 51+20/9 FLC 2 FAC 4+3/1 Others 14/3

HUGHES Ceri Morgan
Born: Pontypridd, 26 February 1971
Height: 5'10" Weight: 11.6
International Honours: W: 5; B-2; Yth

For the second season running, injuries and suspensions restricted his appearances for Luton in 1995-96. Recalled by Wales, he ably demonstrated his talent, but two dismissals brought his career total to five, forcing him onto the sidelines, something the club could ill afford. There was no doubting that his strong, battling midfield qualities were sorely missed when he was out of the side, and surprisingly, his hard shooting saw him score just one goal, a 25-yarder in the 1-1 home draw against Leicester. Should be a dominant force in second division football.

Luton T (From trainee on 1/7/89) FL 121+18/13 FLC 7 FAC 8/1 Others 4

HUGHES Darren John
Born: Prescot, 6 October 1965
Height: 5'11" Weight: 10.11
Club Honours: FAYC '84

Signed on a free transfer from Northampton last November, the experienced Darren made the Exeter left back spot his own. This was due in no small terms to him being a stout defender who was rarely beaten. Likes to go forward on the overlap.

Everton (From apprentice on 8/10/83) FL 3
Shrewsbury T (Free on 13/6/85) FL 34+3/1 FLC 5+1 FAC 1 Others 2
Brighton & Hove A (£35,000 on 30/9/86) FL 26/2 FAC 2 Others 1
Port Vale (£10,000 on 4/9/87) FL 183+1/4 FLC 12 FAC 14 Others 12
Northampton T (Signed on 12/1/95) FL 19+2 Others 1
Exeter C (Free on 3/11/95) FL 25+1 FAC 1

HUGHES David Robert
Born: St Albans, 30 December 1972
Height: 5'10" Weight: 11.8
International Honours: W: U21-1. E: Sch

An attacking Southampton midfielder, David was unfortunate to suffer injury problems last season, particularly to his back, making only eight first team starts. Although recognised at the club for an ability to score spectacularly, his one and only goal during the campaign was a simple 74th minute tap in at home to Bolton, his first touch after coming on as a sub. Hard-working and skilful, he will no doubt develop once he can stay free of injury.

Southampton (From juniors on 2/7/91) PL 8+17/3 FLC 2 FAC 0+5/1

HUGHES Ian
Born: Bangor, 2 August 1974
Height: 5'10" Weight: 12.0
International Honours: W: U21-12; Yth

Son of a former Bury player, Ian is the Shakers' man for all seasons and he once

again demonstrated his versatility in 1995-96 by appearing at left back, centre half and in central midfield, filling each role admirably. Good on the ball, he played his last game as captain of the Wales U21 team in October, having finally reached the age of 21.

Bury (From trainee on 19/11/91) FL 111+3/1 FLC 7+1 FAC 6+2 Others 14+3/1

HUGHES Leslie Mark
Born: Wrexham, 1 November 1963
Height: 5'10" Weight: 13.0
Club Honours: FAC '85, '90, '94; ECWC '91; ESC '91; FLC '92; PL '93, '94; CS '93, '94
International Honours: W: 60; U21-5; Yth; Sch

Joined Chelsea at roughly the same time as Ruud Gullit in the summer of 1995 in a surprise double transfer swoop. A great favourite with Manchester United fans, his move came as a shock, particularly as he was thought to have signed a two year contract at Old Trafford and he received a rapturous reception when he returned there in December as captain for the day. "Sparky" proved that he is still the best target man in the business, particularly with his back to goal, although his muscular approach made life difficult for defenders it also incurred the wrath of referees and he suffered two lengthy suspensions during the season. His second league goal for Chelsea, against Southampton at the Bridge, was a typical Hughes volley and was one of eight league goals in an interrupted campaign. Mark notched his first Chelsea hat trick in the 4-1 thrashing of Leeds United in April and was top scorer with four goals in Chelsea's run to the FA Cup semi finals, where he set up Ruud Gullit's goal against his old club with a typically aggressive run and cross. Continued his Welsh career with three more caps, scoring twice in a 5-0 win over San Marino.

Manchester U (From apprentice on 5/11/80) FL 85+4/37 FLC 5+1/4 FAC 10/4 Others 14+2/2 (£2,500,000 to Barcelona on 1/7/86)
Manchester U (£1,500,000 on 20/7/88) F/PL 251+5/82 FLC 32/12 FAC 34+1/13 Others 27+1/8
Chelsea (£1,500,000 on 6/7/95) PL 31/8 FLC 2 FAC 6/4

Mark Hughes (Chelsea)

HUGHES Mark

Born: Port Talbot, 3 February 1962
Height: 6'0" Weight: 13.0
Club Honours: AMC '90
International Honours: W: Sch

Shrewsbury Town central defender or sweeper. Mark was restricted to a handful of games early last season as, sadly, he had to announce his retirement from the game through injury. His influence will be greatly missed as you would expect of a man with over 400 Football League games to his credit.

Bristol Rov (From apprentice on 5/2/80) FL 73+1/3 FLC 1 FAC 9+1 Others 3/1
Torquay U (Loaned on 24/12/82) FL 9/1 FAC 3/1
Swansea C (Free on 30/7/84) FL 12
Bristol C (Signed on 7/2/85) FL 21+1 FLC 1 Others 3
Tranmere Rov (£3,000 on 19/9/85) FL 258+8/9 FLC 27/2 FAC 12+3 Others 36+1/1
Shrewsbury T (Free on 4/7/94) FL 20+2 FAC 4 Others 1

HUGHES Michael Eamonn

Born: Larne, 2 August 1971
Height: 5'6" Weight: 10.8
International Honours: NI: 31; U23-2; U21-1; Yth; Sch

Having his second spell on loan from Strasbourg, the tricky winger, who is equally at home on either flank, had another good season for West Ham in 1995-96. For a player with a great shot, Michael surprisingly scored just one goal, in an FA Cup win over Southend, but he more than made up for that by providing excellent crosses for his fellow Northern Ireland international, Iain Dowie, and the other strikers. In full flight, his great pace and natural confidence, allied to a "sweet" left foot, takes him past defenders as if they do not exist.

Manchester C (From trainee on 17/8/88) FL 25+1/1 FLC 5 FAC 1 Others 1 (£450,000 to RS Strasbourg in 1992 close season)
West Ham U (Loaned on 29/11/94) PL 15+2/2 FAC 2
West Ham U (Loaned on 2/10/95) PL 28 FLC 2 FAC 3/1

HUGHES Stephen (Steve) John

Born: Reading, 18 September 1976
Height: 6'0" Weight: 12.12
Club Honours: FAYC '94
International Honours: E: Yth; Sch

Left-sided Arsenal midfield player who signed professional forms during the 1995 close season, having already made his Premiership debut. An unused sub for the second leg of the Coca Cola semi final against Aston Villa, Steve came off the bench on a couple of occasions in 1995-96 and will be looking to make more of an impact this term.

Arsenal (From trainee on 15/7/95) PL 1+1 FLC 0+1

HULME Kevin

Born: Farnworth, 2 December 1967
Height: 5'10" Weight: 13.2

A hard-tackling midfield man signed from Bury in exchange for Dean West last September, he was soon out of favour, following the departure of Steve Wicks as Lincoln's boss, and moved on to Macclesfield Town in December.

Bury (£5,000 from Radcliffe Borough on 16/3/89) FL 82+28/21 FLC 4+3/2 FAC 4+1/1 Others 4+8/2
Chester C (Loaned on 26/10/89) FL 4
Doncaster Rov (£42,500 on 14/7/93) FL 33+1/8 FLC 2/1 FAC 1 Others 2
Bury (£42,500 on 11/8/94) FL 24+5 FLC 2 FAC 2 Others 2
Lincoln C (Signed on 28/9/95) FL 4+1 FAC 1 Others 1+1

HUMES Anthony (Tony)

Born: Blyth, 19 March 1966
Height: 5'11" Weight: 11.0

Central defender. Captain of the Wrexham ship, Tony always gave 100 per cent in every game last season, which often meant that he received more than his fair share of injuries and suspensions. However, he would not be the fine aggressive, committed player he is by changing his style in any way and has proved a fine buy from Ipswich, being well respected at the Racecourse after four full seasons.

Ipswich T (From apprentice on 26/5/83) FL 107+13/10 FLC 6 FAC 4/1 Others 10/1
Wrexham (£40,000 on 27/3/92) FL 125+4/4 FLC 7 FAC 10 Others 13

HUMPHREY John

Born: Paddington, 31 January 1961
Height: 5'10" Weight: 11.4
Club Honours: FMC '91; Div 1 '94

Signed from Crystal Palace during the 1995 close season, the right-sided full back began his second spell at Charlton. Though not as fast as he used to be, John still reads the game well, is a steadying influence at the back, and likes to break down the wing to get in early crosses. Was a regular in the side until late February, when he suffered an ankle injury against Huddersfield. Released during the summer.

Wolverhampton W (From apprentice on 14/2/79) FL 149/3 FLC 8 FAC 7
Charlton Ath (£60,000 on 22/7/85) FL 194/3 FLC 13 FAC 9 Others 15/1
Crystal Palace (£400,000 on 16/8/90) F/PL 153+7/2 FLC 23+2 FAC 8+1 Others 8+1
Reading (Loaned on 9/12/93) FL 8 Others 1
Charlton Ath (Free on 13/7/95) FL 28 FLC 6 FAC 2

HUMPHREYS Richard (Richie) John

Born: Sheffield, 30 November 1977
Height: 5'10" Weight: 11.3

This young stocky left-sided striker broke through into the Sheffield Wednesday squad last season, making his full debut, plus several substitute appearances. Obviously hoping to become a big part of the Owls' future over the next year or so, Richie seems level headed enough to make it happen. Having also appeared on the left side of midfield and coped admirably, he obviously is a versatile player, which should help speed up his progression to the first team on a regular basis.

Sheffield Wed (From trainee on 8/2/96) PL 1+4

HUMPHRIES Glenn

Born: Hull, 11 August 1964
Height: 6'0" Weight: 12.10
International Honours: E: Yth

Right-footed central defender. Completed a surprise move to his hometown club late last August to add vast experience and competition to the young Hull defensive

ranks, giving particularly impressive performances in the Coca Cola Cup-tie against Coventry. Although Glenn's season was badly disrupted by injury and suspension, his ferocious tackling and general demeanour had already earned him the "Psycho" nickname. Was released during the summer.

Doncaster Rov (From apprentice on 19/8/82) FL 174+6/8 FLC 12+1/1 FAC 7+1
Lincoln C (Loaned on 25/3/87) FL 9
Bristol C (£20,000 on 23/10/87) FL 81+4 FLC 3 FAC 12 Others 9
Scunthorpe U (£55,000 on 7/3/91) FL 71+1/5 FLC 5/1 FAC 3+1 Others 7/1 (Freed during 1993 close season)
Hull C (Free from Gainsborough Trinity on 25/8/95) FL 9+3 FLC 2 FAC 1 Others 1

HUNT Andrew (Andy)

Born: Thurrock, 9 June 1970
Height: 6'0" Weight: 12.0

Striker. Voted WBA supporter's 1995-96 "Player of the Year", Andy's season was divided. During the first two-thirds he was in tremendous form, scoring 16 goals as the team battled to stay in touch with the leading group. But after February the goals dried up, if not his enthusiasm, as he ran his heart out covering acres of ground, thus allowing his co-attackers, Bob Taylor and Dutchman, Richard Sneekes, to hit the target instead.

Newcastle U (£150,000 from Kettering T on 29/1/91) FL 34+9/11 FLC 3/1 FAC 2/2 Others 3
West Bromwich A (£100,000 on 25/3/93) FL 121+8/48 FLC 7/2 FAC 4/2 Others 8+1/3

HUNT James Malcolm

Born: Derby, 17 December 1976
Height: 5'8" Weight: 10.3

A former trainee midfielder with Notts County, he made his league debut for the club at Bournemouth last February, after several previous appearances on the bench as an unused substitute. In a stunning introduction, the youngster scored from 25 yards in a 2-0 victory and held his place for eight more games, enforcing local belief that he is a player with a very promising future.

Notts Co (From trainee on 15/7/94) FL 10/1

HUNT Jonathan Richard

Born: Camden, 2 November 1971
Height: 5'10" Weight: 12.3
Club Honours: Div 2 '95; AMC '95

Began last season with a bang when scoring a hat trick against Norwich, his third for Birmingham, although he had a bad spell in mid-season, when he was dropped. Came back strongly, however, to finish the club's leading scorer with 15 to his credit, despite playing in midfield. Possessing a tremendous shot in either foot, and composed on the ball, he is a vital member of the side.

Barnet (From juniors in 1989-90) FL 12+21 FLC 1 FAC 0+1 Others 6+2
Southend U (Free on 20/7/93) FL 41+8/6 FLC 1+3 FAC 1 Others 6+1
Birmingham C (£50,000 on 16/9/94) FL 61+4/16 FLC 9+3/2 FAC 2+1/1 Others 8/4

HUNTER Barry Victor

Born: Coleraine, 18 November 1968
Height: 6'3" Weight: 12.0
Club Honours: WC '95
International Honours: NI: 6; B-1; Yth

It was a frustrating last season for Wrexham's Northern Ireland International. Up to November everything was going splendidly for the lad from Coleraine, with his commanding displays in the centre of defence helping the Reds to a lofty position in division two and, at the same time, playing a leading role in his country's outstanding European Championship results against Portugal and Austria (scoring one). However, having suffered a knee injury almost a year ago, but playing through it, the match at Crewe on Boxing Day on a hard frosty ground was the last straw. Since then he spent more time on the treatment table than in the first team and may have required surgery during the close season to clear up the problem. With Wrexham being a "smallish" side, Barry's height is all important and it was sorely missed towards the latter part of the season.

Wrexham (£50,000 from Crusaders on 20/8/93) FL 88+3/4 FLC 6 FAC 7+1/1 Others 15/1

HUNTER Roy Ian
Born: Middlesbrough, 29 October 1973
Height: 5'9" Weight: 10.12
A defender, or defensive midfield player, he joined Northampton at the start of last season on trial, having been released by West Bromwich. Soon earned a regular first team place and a contract with his gritty 100 per cent performances.

West Bromwich A (From trainee on 4/3/92) FL 3+6/1 Others 4+1
Northampton T (Free on 2/8/95) FL 26+8 FAC 2 Others 4/1

HURDLE Augustus (Gus) Athel
Born: Kensington, 14 October 1973
Height: 5'8" Weight: 11.11
Fast, right-footed Brentford defender. Commenced last season in midfield, playing in the first five matches, and had a few games at centre back in March, but was mostly out of the first team picture in 1995-96.

Fulham (From trainee on 3/7/92)
Brentford (Free from Dorchester T on 19/7/94) FL 18+5 FLC 4 FAC 0+1 Others 1

HURST Glynn
Born: Barnsley, 17 January 1976
Height: 5'10" Weight: 11.6
Still to make a start for Barnsley, the striker's strong running got him on and off the substitutes bench on a number of occasions during last season. Loaned to Swansea in December, he scored on his debut against Burnley, but failed to follow it up, making just one more appearance before returning to Oakwell. Can also play in defence.

Barnsley (Free from Tottenham H juniors on 13/7/94) FL 0+7
Swansea C (Loaned on 15/12/95) FL 2/1

HURST Paul Michael
Born: Sheffield, 25 September 1974
Height: 5'7" Weight: 10.4
Club Honours: AMC '96
He may not be the tallest left back in the league, but there can be few, if any, who put more effort into his game than Paul does. Some people may consider he is lacking in inches, but he more than makes up for that

with his undying appetite for the game and never knows when he is beaten – as many wingers have found out to their detriment. Played an important part in the Rotherham defence, which showed it's spirit during the closing weeks of last season as the team battled to get away from the relegation zone, having earlier won an AWS medal following the 2-1 Wembley win over Shrewsbury.

Rotherham U (From trainee on 12/8/93) FL 43+14/1 FLC 1 FAC 3/1 Others 9+1

Paul Hurst

HUTCHINGS Carl Emil
Born: Hammersmith, 24 September 1974
Height: 5'11" Weight: 11.0
Enthusiastic Brentford midfielder who beavers away. Out of the first team picture until last October, he was eventually given a long run-in the club's engine room, where he did his best to steady a rocky boat. Something of a utility player, Carl has also turned out for the Bees in both full back positions.

Brentford (From trainee on 12/7/93) FL 78+13 FLC 5 FAC 8+1 Others 7+3

HUTCHISON Donald (Don)
Born: Gateshead, 9 May 1971
Height: 6'2" Weight: 11.8
International Honours: S: B-1
After starting as first choice at West Ham last season, Don was rarely selected for first team action following the arrival of Iain Dowie and was transferred to Sheffield United in January, becoming the Blades' record signing. Prior to that, however, he had scored two goals in 12 1995-96 appearances. Took some time to settle with his new club, not relishing playing up front when pressed into service there, before some excellent performances late on won over the doubters. Although often weighing in with invaluable goals, he is predominantly a skilful and cultured midfielder, who has a good range of passing skills. Is also dangerous at set plays.

Hartlepool U (From trainee on 20/3/90) FL 19+5/2 FLC 1+1 FAC 2 Others 1
Liverpool (£175,000 on 27/11/90) F/PL 33+12/7 FLC 7+1/2 FAC 1+2 Others 3+1/1
West Ham U (£1,500,000 on 30/8/94) PL 30+5/11 FLC 3/2 FAC 0+1
Sheffield U (£1,200,000 on 11/1/96) FL 18+1/2 FAC 1

HUTT Stephen Graham
Born: Middlesbrough, 19 February 1979
Height: 6'3" Weight: 12.0
First year YTS centre back who made his debut for Hartlepool in the last game of 1995-96, coming on as substitute for just five minutes. Hopefully, he will get the chance to add to this in 1996-97 and will not be in the record books as the 'Pool player with the shortest-ever league career.

Hartlepool U (Trainee) FL 0+1

HUXFORD Richard John
Born: Scunthorpe, 25 July 1969
Height: 5'11" Weight: 12.2
Although missing much of 1995-96, following two cartilage operations, Richard again proved to be a reliable and solid utility player who was equally at home as Bradford's right back, where he started the first 18 matches, or in midfield. Back in time for the last two play-off games and happy to be part of the side that will be playing first division football this season.

Barnet (Signed from Kettering T on 6/8/92) FL 33/1 FLC 2 FAC 2 Others 2+1
Millwall (Free on 16/7/93) FL 25+7 FLC 1+1/1 FAC 1 Others 3
Birmingham C (Loaned on 21/2/94) FL 5
Bradford C (£50,000 on 7/10/94) FL 54+5/2 FLC 5 FAC 3+1 Others 7+1

HYDE Graham
Born: Doncaster, 10 November 1970
Height: 5'7" Weight: 11.7
Terrier-like midfield player who makes up for his lack of inches with wholehearted displays. Popular with the Sheffield Wednesday fans, his omission from the side at certain stages of last season mystified regular watchers, his drive and sheer capacity for hard work being so useful to the team when they were under pressure. Also, his application and dedication as one of the relatively few Yorkshire-born lads in the squad, make him one of the vital ingredients for the club's future.

Sheffield Wed (From trainee on 17/5/88) F/PL 97+33/8 FLC 16+3/2 FAC 8+5/1 Others 4/1

HYDE Micah Anthony
Born: Newham, 10 November 1974
Height: 5'9" Weight: 11.5
Right-footed Cambridge United midfielder who had a spell in Finland at the start of last season. A skilful ball player, only 21, he struggled early on, but impressed in the last months during the end of season recovery.

Cambridge U (From trainee on 19/5/93) FL 51+18/6 FLC 2 FAC 5+2 Others 3+1

HYDE Paul David
Born: Hayes, 7 April 1963
Height: 6'1" Weight: 15.5
Club Honours: GMVC '93; FAT '93
A brave and dependable Wycombe goalkeeper, he fell out with the manager over a new contract and played his final game at the end of last November, before rejoining his previous boss, Martin O'Neill, at Leicester City. Released by City at the end of the season, it was a rather sad end for one of the most popular and loyal players at the club.

Wycombe W (£15,000 from Hayes on 6/7/93) FL 105 FLC 10 FAC 13 Others 13
Leicester C (Free on 15/2/96)

IGOE Samuel (Sammy) Gary
Born: Spelthorne, 30 September 1975
Height: 5'6" Weight: 10.8
An attacking Portsmouth midfielder, small in stature, but big in heart and ability, Sammy was on the edge of the first team throughout last season and was a regular substitute, actually coming off the bench on 20 occasions. His performances in a campaign that saw the club struggling in the bottom third for much of that time, showed that he will be pushing hard for a regular place this season.
Portsmouth (From trainee on 15/2/94) FL 4+19 FLC 0+2

ILLMAN Neil David
Born: Doncaster, 29 April 1975
Height: 5'7" Weight: 11.5
Signed by Plymouth from non-league circles last February, having earlier played in the Football League with Middlesbrough, he was loaned out to Cambridge United when Carlo Corazzin travelled in the opposite direction. A hard-working striker who played four times without scoring, Neil returned to Home Park where he awaits his debut.
Middlesbrough (From trainee on 23/3/93) FL 0+1 FLC 0+1 Others 3+1 (Free to Eastwood T on 26/2/94)
Plymouth Arg (Signed on 27/3/96)
Cambridge U (Loaned on 28/3/96) FL 1+4

IMMEL Eike
Born: Marburg, Germany, 27 November 1960
Height: 6'2" Weight: 13.5
International Honours: West Germany: 19
Yet another German import at Manchester City in 1995-96, having been signed from VFB Stuttgart at the beginning of 1995-96. With three goalkeepers injured – Tony Coton, Martyn Margetson and Andy Dibble – Eike came to Maine Road after glowing references from Uwe Rosler and a former City legend between the sticks in Bert Trautmann. As one of two own presents, he turned out to be a shrewd buy, performing excellently almost every week, particularly when the defence was under abnormal pressure. His main attributes have been his calmness, positional sense, and his ability to throw the ball accurately out of defence.
Manchester C (£400,000 from VFB Stuttgart on 17/8/95) PL 38 FLC 3 FAC 5

IMPEY Andrew (Andy) Rodney
Born: Hammersmith, 30 September 1971
Height: 5'8" Weight: 10.6
International Honours: E: U21-1
Fast-raiding QPR winger, excellent at getting forward and tracking back, he will take defenders on before unloading telling crosses. As the 1995 "Player of the Year" Andy started last season promisingly, but failed to live up to expectation. Played in all but one game until mid-January, before injury and a loss of form meant he was in and out of the side from then on. When on song, however, he was still a player to be reckoned with and proved that when coming on as a substitute against Manchester United and turning the game in Rangers' favour, following this up with an important goal against Everton at Loftus Road in a 3-1 win. With the club playing in the first division this season, his talents could see them come back with a bang.
Queens Park R (£35,000 from Yeading on 14/6/90) F/PL 151+4/11 FLC 13+1/2 FAC 6+2/1 Others 0+2/1

INGESSON Klas
Born: Odeshog, Sweden, 20 August 1968
Height: 6'1" Weight: 14.0
International Honours: Sweden: 56
Never able to adapt to the English game, having struggled with a succession of injuries and being tried in midfield, Sheffield Wednesday's Swedish international was sold to the Italian side, Bari, for £900,000 last November. Ironically, the move came immediately after he had played as a sweeper and received great praise from the manager, David Pleat.
Sheffield Wed (£800,000 from PSV Eindhoven on 1/9/94) PL 12+6/2 FLC 2 FAC 1

INGLETHORPE Alexander (Alex) Matthew
Born: Epsom, 14 November 1971
Height: 5'11" Weight: 11.6
Signed from Watford at the end of 1994-95, having impressed as a goalscorer in the reserves, Alex failed to get on the Leyton Orient scoresheet until match five, but then notched six in seven games. A skilful, pacy striker who shields the ball well and gets into good positions, he scored nine times in 33 outings before injury brought his campaign to a halt.
Watford (From juniors on 1/7/90) FL 2+10/2 FLC 1+2 Others 1+1/1
Barnet (Loaned on 23/3/95) FL 5+1/3
Leyton Orient (Signed on 19/5/95) FL 30/9 FLC 2 Others 1

INGRAM Christopher (Chris) David
Born: Cardiff, 5 December 1976
Height: 5'10" Weight: 11.5
Another of the Cardiff youngsters who were called upon in 1995-96 in order to try and stop the rot and patch up the side, Chris started less than half a dozen games. Contributed a goal in a 3-0 win against Mansfield at Ninian in September. Was released during the summer.
Cardiff C (From trainee on 7/8/95) FL 4+4/1 FLC 1 Others 1+1

INGRAM Stuart Denevan (Denny)
Born: Sunderland, 27 June 1976
Height: 5'10" Weight: 11.8
Hartlepool utility player who seemed to have found his best position when playing as an attacking right back in 1995-96. Denny is barely recognisable now from the raw recruit who was blooded as a 17 year old when the club were in deep trouble in 1993-94. Progressively, he has shown greater maturity and awareness and is at last being recognised for his reliable play.
Hartlepool U (From trainee on 5/7/94) FL 80+1/2 FLC 6+1 FAC 2 Others 4

INGRAM Rae
Born: Manchester, 6 December 1974
Height: 5'11" Weight: 12.2
Manchester City full back who is good on the overlap and an excellent crosser of the ball. He can also play in the centre of the defence. Prior to 1995-96, Rae had yet to play first team football, but having come through the club's ranks was named in the squad for senior consideration. Finally made his debut at home against Everton, but, after acquitting himself well, broke a bone in his foot during a reserve match. Came back in December, making five appearances, before again being sidelined by injury. Has a promising future ahead of him.
Manchester C (From trainee on 9/7/93) PL 5 FAC 1

INMAN Niall Edward
Born: Wakefield, 6 February 1978
Height: 5'8" Weight: 10.6
One of three Peterborough trainees given first team experience in 1995-96, Niall made his debut in the penultimate game of the season at Crewe, playing on the wide left in the absence of Danny Carter. A young midfielder, his YTS period expired last June.
Peterborough U (Trainee) FL 1

IORFA Dominic
Born: Lagos, Nigeria, 1 October 1968
Height: 6'1" Weight: 12.12
International Honours: Nigeria: 3
Dominic never managed to find a regular place in the Southend team in 1995-96, although the side were desperately short of a good goalscorer and, as a consequence, failed to find the net. However, his strong running caught the eye of Scottish Premier side, Falkirk, who signed him in January after Southend intimated he could leave.
Queens Park R (£145,000 from Royal Antwerp on 23/3/90) FL 1+7 FLC 1 (Signed for Galatasaray on 1/12/91)
Peterborough U (Free on 24/10/92) FL 27+33/9 FLC 2+1 FAC 2+2 Others 1/1
Southend U (£15,000 on 3/8/94) FL 5+5/1 FLC 2 Others 0+3

IOURAN Serguei
Born: Kiev, Russia, 11 June 1969
Height: 6'1" Weight: 12.2
International Honours: Russia: 32
Recommended to Millwall, by his old manager at Porto, Bobby Robson, the Russian signed for the club last January, along with his great friend, Vassili Kulkov. It was a major coup for the Lions, even if the pair were only on short-term contracts. Having scored eight goals in 29 appearances for Russia, it was hardly a surprise that Serguei turned out to be a clever striker with immaculate ball control, who was good at holding up play and laying off short passes around the box. Looked a cut above the first division, his ability standing out for all to see.
Millwall (Loaned from Spartak Moscow on 11/1/96) FL 13/1

Ian Ironside

IRELAND Simon Piers
Born: Barnstaple, 23 November 1971
Height: 5'11" Weight: 11.12
International Honours: E: Sch

Mansfield winger who was not as sharp in 1995-96 as in the previous season, when his skilful and speedy runs down the flanks were a delight to watch. Like many of the team, he no doubt suffered from the absence of adequate replacements for the earlier departures.

Huddersfield T (From juniors on 1/7/90) FL 10+9 FLC 1/1 FAC 0+1 Others 1+1
Wrexham (Loaned on 11/3/92) FL 2+3
Blackburn Rov (£200,000 on 3/11/92) PL 0+1
Mansfield T (£60,000 on 8/3/94) FL 84+4/12 FLC 7/1 FAC 6/1 Others 4+1

IRONS Kenneth (Kenny)
Born: Liverpool, 4 November 1970
Height: 5'10" Weight: 11.2

In and out of the Tranmere side for much of last season, Kenny finally found his best form after new player/manager, John Aldridge, gave him a role operating just behind the strikers and he responded with a David Platt-like performance in the 5-2 defeat of Ipswich. Though he lacks the killing pace of top flight players, he has good touch and vision, can tackle, and knows where the goal is in a formation which allows him the freedom to get forward.

Tranmere Rov (From trainee on 9/11/89) FL 200+24/30 FLC 15+3/4 FAC 11+1/3 Others 28+3/3

IRONSIDE Ian
Born: Sheffield, 8 March 1964
Height: 6'2" Weight: 13.0

An experienced goalkeeper who did much to prevent Scarborough finishing at the foot of division three last term. Commanding his penalty area, and proving very agile, Ian was immensely popular with the supporters. Is the son of the former Rotherham and Barnsley 'keeper, Roy.

Barnsley (From juniors on 17/9/82)
Scarborough (Free from North Ferriby U on 8/3/88) FL 88 FLC 2 FAC 2 Others 10
Middlesbrough (£80,000 on 15/8/91) F/PL 12+1 FLC 2
Scarborough (Loaned on 5/3/92) FL 7
Stockport Co (Signed on 23/9/93) FL 17+2 FAC 1 Others 1
Scarborough (Free on 23/3/95) FL 49 FAC 1 Others 2

IRVING Richard James
Born: Halifax, 10 September 1975
Height: 5'7" Weight: 10.6
International Honours: E: Yth; Sch

After signing from Manchester United in the summer of 1995, surprisingly he was only given one first team opportunity for Nottingham Forest in 1995-96, ironically as a substitute against his former club in November, when he almost scored the winning goal, heading just wide in the final minute. Although on the small side for a striker, Richard is very quick and confident on the ball and can twist and turn around the box well to unsettle defences.

Manchester U (From trainee on 1/10/92)
Nottingham F (£75,000 on 19/7/95) PL 0+1

IRWIN Joseph Denis
Born: Cork, 31 October 1965
Height: 5'8" Weight: 11.0
Club Honours: CS '90, '93; ECWC '91; ESC '91; FLC '92; PL '93, '94, '96; FAC '94, '96
International Honours: Ei: 40; B-1; U23-1; U21-3; Yth; Sch

Once again, Denis proved to be Manchester United's "Mr Dependable", performing admirably both at right and left back, and missing only seven Premier League games throughout 1995-96. A model of consistency, and with a penchant to get forward, his only goal for the club, apart from a faux pas against QPR, came in the Reds' second biggest PL away win of the season at Coventry. Good value for his championship and FA Cup winners' medals, he is still recognised as a specialist at free kicks and corners, his accuracy giving United added options in dangerous areas of the pitch. Going as well as ever, the only disappointment in a highly successful campaign came when the Republic of Ireland failed to qualify for Euro '96.

Leeds U (From apprentice on 3/11/83) FL 72/1 FLC 5 FAC 3 Others 2
Oldham Ath (Free on 22/5/86) FL 166+1/4 FLC 19/3 FAC 13 Others 5
Manchester U (£625,000 on 20/6/90) F/PL 223+2/14 FLC 28+2 FAC 29/6 Others 22

ISAIAS Marques Soares
Born: Rio de Janeiro, Brazil, 17 November 1963
Height: 5'10" Weight: 12.10

Brazilian born midfield playmaker who Coventry signed from Benfica in the 1995 close season. Silky skills and fierce shooting ability were his trademarks and he impressed in the early season games at Chelsea (where he scored a good goal) and at home to Arsenal and Manchester City. Questions were later asked about his fitness though, and he lost his place after the Villa home defeat and appeared only four more times, without ever reproducing his early season form. Scored some spectacular goals for the reserves, after returning from a cartilage operation in February, as rumours of a summer return to Portugal continued to circulate.

Coventry C (£500,000 from Benfica on 2/8/95) PL 9+2/2 FLC 2

IZZET Mustafa (Muzzy) Kemmel
Born: Mile End, 31 October 1974
Height: 5'10" Weight: 10.3

Midfielder. Signed on loan from Chelsea on transfer deadline day in March 1996, he made his Leicester debut from the bench in the home debacle against Sheffield United, but did well enough to earn a place in the starting line up thereafter. Gave a particularly impressive performance in the draw at Tranmere, where he was unlucky not to open his goalscoring account and became a key member of the side that reached the Premiership, via the play offs. On the fringe of a call up to the Turkish squad through his father's qualification, Martin O'Neill was keen to sign Muzzy permanently, notwithstanding City's Wembley win having triggered a £75,000 user fee under the terms of the loan agreement.

Chelsea (From trainee on 19/5/93)
Leicester C (Loaned on 28/3/96) FL 8+1/1 Others 3

J

JACK Rodney Alphonso
Born: St Vincent, 28 September 1972
Height: 5'7" Weight: 10.9
International Honours: St Vincent: 8

Signed from Lambada last October, the St Vincent international showed enough to suggest he can succeed in English football, despite being injury hit and making just 16 starts for Torquay. Scoring twice, the speedy striker, cum midfielder's second, was the winner at Darlington, one of just five victories for the club all season.

Torquay U (Free from Lambada, St Vincent on 10/10/95) FL 12+2/2 FAC 3 Others 1

JACKSON Christopher (Chris) Dean
Born: Barnsley, 16 January 1976
Height: 6'0" Weight: 12.0
International Honours: E: Yth; Sch

Barnsley centre forward. A tragic car accident at the end of last October not only put an end to his season but put a question mark against his career. Up to then, the striker had worked hard up front for the Reds, without managing to get on the score sheet.

Barnsley (From trainee on 19/1/93) FL 16+7/2 FLC 2+1 Others 0+1

JACKSON David Kenneth George
Born: Solihull, 22 August 1978
Height: 5'9" Weight: 11.7

Another of Shrewsbury's excellent youngsters, the left back made his league debut in the final ten minutes of last season, when coming on at Burnley, and showed that he was not overawed. Only 17 years old, and a first-year trainee, he looks a good long-term bet.

Shrewsbury T (Trainee) FL 0+1

JACKSON Mark Graham
Born: Leeds, 30 September 1977
Height: 6'0" Weight: 11.3
International Honours: E: Yth

Young Leeds' defender who, along with Jason Blunt and Harry Kewell, forced himself into the first team picture at the end of last season. Made his first team debut as a substitute against Middlesbrough in March.

Leeds U (From trainee on 1/7/95) PL 0+1

JACKSON Matthew (Matt) Alan
Born: Leeds, 19 October 1971
Height: 6'0" Weight: 12.12
Club Honours: FAC '95; CS '95
International Honours: E: U21-10; Sch

Tall, right-sided Everton defender who can play at full back or in central defence. Composed both in possession, and when the team is under pressure, and good at pushing wingers out wide with accurate positioning, Matt was out of the side in the early stages of 1995-96, before taking his chance following an injury to Earl Barrett and

managing a sustained run until Marc Hottiger finally arrived. Loaned out to Charlton in March, and almost scoring on his debut at Norwich, he was later the subject of a transfer bid from Sheffield United, which, at the time of going to press, had not materialised.

Luton T (From juniors on 4/7/90) FL 7+2 FLC 2 Others 0+1
Preston NE (Loaned on 27/3/91) FL 3+1 Others 1
Everton (£600,000 on 18/10/91) F/PL 132+6/4 FLC 9 FAC 14/2 Others 4
Charlton Ath (Loaned on 26/3/96) FL 8 Others 2

JACKSON Michael James
Born: Chester, 4 December 1973
Height: 6'0" Weight: 13.8
International Honours: E: Yth

Until an away game at Cardiff last November, the central defender was unable to win a regular place in Bury's line up. Given the opportunity, he went on to strike up a superb partnership alongside Chris Lucketti, missing just one of the closing 30 fixtures. He also scored four important goals and was named as runner up in the supporters' "Player of the Season" poll.

Crewe Alex (From trainee on 29/7/92) FL 5 FLC 1 FAC 1 Others 2
Bury (Free on 13/8/93) FL 95+6/2 FLC 5 FAC 2 Others 9

JACKSON Peter Allan
Born: Bradford, 6 April 1961
Height: 6'0" Weight: 13.6
Club Honours: Div 3 '85

Influential Chester skipper and solidly reliable at the heart of their defence last season, Peter was voted "Player of the Year" by both supporters and fellow team mates. Very experienced, missing games only through injury and suspensions, it would be difficult to imagine City without him.

Bradford C (From apprentice on 7/4/79) FL 267+11/24 FLC 27/1 FAC 10+1 Others 4
Newcastle U (£250,000 on 23/10/86) FL 60/3 FLC 3 FAC 6 Others 3
Bradford C (£290,000 on 15/9/88) FL 55+3/5 FLC 7 FAC 4 Others 2

Huddersfield T (Free on 6/9/90) FL 152+3/3 FLC 11 FAC 13/1 Others 18/1
Chester C (Free on 29/9/94) FL 68/2 FLC 3 FAC 2 Others 2

JACOBS Wayne Graham
Born: Sheffield, 3 February 1969
Height: 5'9" Weight: 11.2

Yet another Bradford player to go down with a knee ligament injury in 1995-96, Wayne missed 13 matches in all, but was back in time to help the club into the first division, via the play offs. A very strong full back, who enjoys the overlap, his attacking flair was seen to good advantage when scoring two goals against Preston in the FA Cup.

Sheffield Wed (From apprentice on 3/1/87) FL 5+1 FLC 3 Others 1
Hull C (£27,000 on 25/3/88) FL 127+2/4 FLC 7 FAC 8 Others 6
Rotherham U (Free on 5/8/93) FL 40+2/2 FLC 4 FAC 1 Others 2
Bradford C (Free on 5/8/94) FL 66/1 FLC 8 FAC 4/2 Others 5

JAMES Anthony (Tony) Craig
Born: Sheffield, 27 June 1967
Height: 6'3" Weight: 14.7

Welcomed back to the heart of Hereford's defence in 1995-96, following a series of injuries, Tony scored on his return to the side and made an immediate impact. Strong and forceful, while making very few mistakes, Tony and Dean Smith made a formidable duo. Is almost as lethal from set pieces as the latter.

Lincoln C (£20,000 from Gainsborough Trinity on 22/8/88) FL 24+5 FLC 2 Others 0+1
Leicester C (£150,000 on 23/8/89) FL 79+28/11 FLC 6 FAC 2/1 Others 3+1
Hereford U (Free on 25/7/94) FL 35/4 FLC 4 FAC 1 Others 5/1

JAMES David Benjamin
Born: Welwyn Garden City, 1 August 1970
Height: 6'5" Weight: 14.5
Club Honours: FAYC '89; FLC '95
International Honours: E: B-1; U21-10

Ever present in 1995-96 for the second

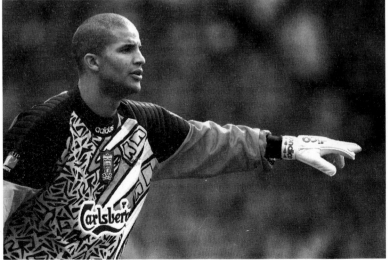

David James

consecutive season, David is now firmly established as Liverpool's first choice goalkeeper for the foreseeable future, after an indifferent start to his Anfield career four years ago. Naturally flamboyant, and keen to replace Bruce Grobbelaar in the affections of Reds' supporters by emulating his eccentricities, he curbed his natural instincts to rush off his line to deal with every high cross into the penalty area and by so doing became safer and more consistent. Recognised by his fellow professionals, when selected for the PFA award winning Premier side, a continuation of this consistency in 1996-97 could yet see him called up for international selection.

Watford (From trainee on 1/7/88) FL 89 FLC 6 FAC 2 Others 1
Liverpool (£1,000,000 on 6/7/92) PL 122+1 FLC 13 FAC 15 Others 5

JAMES Julian Colin
Born: Tring, 22 March 1970
Height: 5'10" Weight: 11.10
International Honours: E: U21-2
Resolute Luton right back with good all-round abilities, Julian had a mixed season in 1995-96. Occasional injuries and a two-match suspension at the start of the year curtailed his appearances, but, unlike the previous term, he was not necessarily an automatic choice when available. Out of contract at the end of the campaign he was offered a new contract and starts 1996-97 with a benefit match to mark his ten years with the club. Although a strong tackler, who also gets forward well, he faces stiff competition from Darren Patterson.

Luton T (From trainee on 1/7/88) FL 195+19/12 FLC 9+1 FAC 17+1 Others 10+1
Preston NE (Loaned on 12/9/91) FL 6

JAMES Martin Joseph
Born: Crosby, 18 May 1971
Height: 5'10" Weight: 11.7
Martin, who can play either at left back or on the left side of midfield, had little chance to do either as he made just one appearance for Rotherham as substitute in 1995-96. First injured in pre-season training, after battling back from that he missed the majority of the term, suffering a serious back injury which required an operation, before being released in the summer.

Preston NE (From trainee on 19/7/89) FL 92+6/11 FLC 6 FAC 4 Others 8+1
Stockport Co (£50,000 on 16/3/93) FL 13+19 FLC 2 FAC 0+1 Others 0+2
Rotherham U (£50,000 on 3/8/94) FL 40+1 FLC 2 FAC 3 Others 3

JARMAN Lee
Born: Cardiff, 16 December 1977
Height: 6'3" Weight: 12.9
International Honours: W: U21-1; Yth
Cardiff City's Welsh U21 international who was blooded early last season due to injury to Lee Baddeley and gave a competent air to the centre back position. Suspensions permitting, Lee became almost an ever present, his form being noted by a number of Premiership clubs.

Cardiff C (From trainee on 23/8/95) FL 31+1 FAC 2/1 Others 1+1

JEFFERS John Joseph
Born: Liverpool, 5 October 1968
Height: 5'10" Weight: 11.10
International Honours: E: Sch
A cunning winger, with a superb left foot, John made a big impression at Stockport after signing from Port Vale on an amazing free transfer last November. Gave the side more balance and was a key man behind the promotion push in the second half of the season.

Liverpool (From apprentice on 13/10/86)
Port Vale (£30,000 on 11/12/88) FL 147+33/10 FLC 8+1 FAC 13+2 Others 13+2/1
Shrewsbury T (Loaned on 6/1/95) FL 3/1 Others 2
Stockport Co (Free on 16/11/95) FL 21+2/3 FAC 3

JEFFREY Andrew (Andy) Samuel
Born: Bellshill, 15 January 1972
Height: 5'10" Weight: 12.7
1995-96 was another prone season for the right-footed Cambridge United defender. A first team regular for the early part of the campaign, he missed a large part after Christmas with a re-occurence of a groin injury, and not being selected in the last two months, was released during the summer.

Leicester C (From trainee on 13/2/90)
Cambridge U (£8,500 from Cambridge C on 9/7/93) FL 82+13/2 FLC 5 FAC 6 Others 5

JEFFREY Michael (Mike) Richard
Born: Liverpool, 11 August 1971
Height: 5'11" Weight: 11.6
Club Honours: AMC '96
When the striker joined Rotherham from Newcastle during the summer it was looked upon as a master stroke. However, Mike found it difficult to produce the goals that he would have hoped for and moved on to Fortuna Sittard in Holland at the beginning of January, leaving the club with a handsome profit, his £205,000 fee becoming their record sale.

Bolton W (From trainee on 9/2/89) FL 9+6 FLC 1+2 FAC 1 Others 2+1
Doncaster Rov (£20,000 on 5/3/92) FL 48+1/19 FLC 4 Others 2/1
Newcastle U (£60,000 on 4/10/93) PL 2 FLC 1/1 Others 0+2
Rotherham U (£80,000 on 22/6/95) FL 22/5 FLC 3/1 FAC 1 Others 3

JEMSON Nigel Bradley
Born: Hutton, 10 August 1969
Height: 5'10" Weight: 12.10
Club Honours: FLC '90; AMC '96
International Honours: E: U21-1
One of the forgotten men at Meadow Lane, he made only three appearances for Notts County at the start of last season and was then overlooked for the remainder of the campaign. However, he ended 1995-96 on a note of triumph, whilst on loan to Rotherham, scoring both goals in the Millers' 2-1 defeat of Shrewsbury in the Auto Windscreen Shield final at Wembley in April, following up his double against Carlisle in the northern area final. Showing class and the ability to hold the ball, how United's fans would have loved him to stay permanently.

Preston NE (From trainee on 6/7/87) FL 28+4/8 FAC 2/1 Others 5+1/5

Nottingham F (£150,000 on 24/3/88) FL 45+2/13 FLC 9/4 FAC 3+1/3 Others 1
Bolton W Loaned on 23/12/88) FL 4+1
Preston NE (Loaned on 15/3/89) FL 6+3/2 Others 2/1
Sheffield Wed (£800,000 on 17/9/91) F/PL 26+25/9 FLC 3+4 FAC 3+3/1 Others 2+2/1
Grimsby T (Loaned on 10/9/93) FL 6/2 Others 1
Notts Co (£300,000 on 8/9/94) FL 7+7/1 FLC 2+2/1 Others 1
Watford (Loaned on 12/1/95) FL 3+1
Rotherham U (Loaned on 15/2/96) FL 16/5 Others 3/4

JENKINS Iain
Born: Whiston, 24 November 1972
Height: 5'9" Weight: 11.10
A skilful and very popular Chester defender, who unfortunately missed most of 1995-96 due to injuries sustained in a car crash, he was welcomed back for the last five league games. His best position appears to be at full back, where he is difficult to pass and has an ability to mount attacks down the flank with regularity.

Everton (From trainee on 4/6/91) PL 3+2 FLC 0+1
Bradford C (Loaned on 31/12/92) FL 6 Others 1
Chester C (Free on 13/8/93) FL 82+5 FLC 4+2 FAC 6+1 Others 8

JENKINS Stephen (Steve) Robert
Born: Merthyr, 16 July 1972
Height: 5'10" Weight: 10.9
Club Honours: AMC '94
International Honours: W: 3; U21-2; Yth
After an impressive international appearance for Wales against West Germany at Cardiff, Stephen was soon on his way from Swansea to Huddersfield for a ridiculously low tribunal judgement, set at under £300,000. A solid, dependable right back, he was sorely missed by the Swans following his departure. Initially at Town, he was played on the right wing and even scored on his debut, but soon established himself in the defence, where his pace and ability to read the game were a distinct asset. Added two more caps to his collection before the season finished.

Swansea C (From trainee on 1/7/90) FL 155+10/1 FLC 12+1 FAC 10+1 Others 26
Huddersfield T (£275,000 on 3/11/95) FL 31/1 FAC 4

JENSEN John Faxe
Born: Copenhagen, Denmark, 3 May 1965
Height: 5'11" Weight: 12.4
Club Honours: FAC '93; ECWC '94
International Honours: Denmark (EC '92): 67
A hard-working central midfielder who keeps play simple and tackles with the best of them, John was more of a peripheral figure under the new regime at Arsenal last season and, although as solid and reliable as ever in making 23 appearances, he was freed in March and returned to his old club, Brondby.

Arsenal (£1,100,000 from Brondby on 1/8/92) PL 93+5/1 FLC 14+2 FAC 8+1 Others 15

JEPSON Ronald (Ronnie) Francis
Born: Stoke, 12 May 1963
Height: 6'1" Weight: 13.2
Having established a Huddersfield goal-

scoring partnership with Andy Booth in 1994-95, that relationship continued to flourish in the higher division during 1995-96. With his all-round effort and workrate, and constant cajoling of team mates, he took over the captaincy at the end of the season. His ability to hold up play and lay off at the vital moment was essential to Town's cause.

Port Vale (Free from Nantwich T on 23/3/89) FL 12+10 FLC 1+1 FAC 1+1
Peterborough U (Loaned on 25/1/90) FL 18/5
Preston NE (£80,000 on 12/2/91) FL 36+2/8 FLC 2 Others 3/4
Exeter C (£60,000 on 29/7/92) FL 51+3/21 FLC 6/2 FAC 3/1 Others 4/1
Huddersfield T (£80,000 on 7/12/93) FL 95+12/36 FLC 6+1/2 FAC 4/3 Others 6/1

JESS Eoin
Born: Aberdeen, 13 December 1970
Height: 5'9" Weight: 11.6
Club Honours: SLC '89
International Honours: S: 3; B-2; U21-14

Originally a striker, Aberdeen converted him to an attacking midfield player and Coventry paid nearly two million pounds for him last February. A slight player with a good turn of speed and excellent ball control, he took some time to adapt to the pace of the English game. Came on as a substitute in the crucial home fixture against QPR and scored the winner, following it up with an excellent game at Forest. Lost his place in the full Scotland squad, but played for the "B" team in Denmark in April and came back to appear against England in the European Championships. High expectations are held for him for this coming season.

Aberdeen (Free from Glasgow Rangers juniors on 13/11/87) SL 167+34/50 SLC 19+2/4 SC 14+2/3 Others 8+2/6
Coventry C (£1,750,000 on 24/2/96) PL 9+3/1

JEWELL Paul
Born: Liverpool, 28 September 1964
Height: 5'8" Weight: 12.1

Transfer listed at the end of 1994-95, Paul, Bradford's longest serving player, started last season on loan at Grimsby, where he scored the only goal of the game at Charlton, before returning to Valley Parade in October. A versatile performer who can play in midfield or as a striker, he signed a new contract in December, but was mainly confined to the subs' bench as City chased first division soccer.

Liverpool (From apprentice on 30/9/82) FL 117+20/35 FLC 5+2 FAC 9/5 Others 14+4/7
Wigan Ath (£15,000 on 20/12/84) FL 117+20/35 FLC 5+2 FAC 9/5 Others 14+4/7
Bradford C (£80,000 on 21/7/88) FL 217+52/56 FLC 16+1/6 FAC 12+1/3 Others 8+1/1
Grimsby T (Loaned on 16/8/95) FL 2+3/1 FLC 1

JOACHIM Julian Kevin
Born: Peterborough, 20 September 1974
Height: 5'6" Weight: 11.10
International Honours: E: U21-9; Yth (UEFAC '93)

A potentially brilliant attacking player he lost his way with Leicester during the last two seasons and his signing for Aston Villa by his former manager, Brian Little, last February, gave him the opportunity to re-activate his career. Despite scoring on his

first full appearance for Villa against Blackburn, most of his subsequent games were from the bench, and the England U21 man will be looking to rediscover his early form for Leicester in order to win a regular berth in the line up for 1996-97.

Leicester C (From trainee on 15/9/92) F/PL 77+22/25 FLC 7+2/3 FAC 4+1/1 Others 4+2/2
Aston Villa (£1,500,000 on 24/2/96) PL 4+7/2

Julian Joachim

JOBLING Kevin Andrew
Born: Sunderland, 1 January 1968
Height: 5'8" Weight: 12.0

Although a recognised midfielder, having come back to the Grimsby side as a left back in 1994-95 he started last season in the latter position, playing in the opening three games, until a serious injury put him out of action for the rest of the campaign. A good tackler, who also finds team mates with accurate passes out of defence, Kevin will be hoping to be fit in time for 1996-97.

Leicester C (From apprentice on 9/1/86) FL 4+5 FAC 0+1 Others 3/2
Grimsby T (Signed on 19/2/88) FL 210+17/9 FLC 12+1 FAC 4+3/1 Others 5+4
Scunthorpe U (Loaned on 10/1/94) Others 1

JOBSON Richard Ian
Born: Holderness, 9 May 1963
Height: 6'1" Weight: 13.5
Club Honours: Div 2 '91
International Honours: E: B-2

Classy England "B" defender who had been trailed by Leeds' Howard Wilkinson for some time and had originally signed from Oldham in the summer of 1995, only to fail a medical with blood complications, following a long lay off. Eventually, the transfer was completed last October and Richard immediately looked the part in defence. Unluckily, after 13 games, he picked up a cruciate injury at Derby in the FA Cup, which disrupted the rest of the season. An excellent professional, he is extremely comfortable on the ball and strong in the air.

Watford (£22,000 from Burton A on 5/11/82) FL 26+2/4 FLC 2 FAC 0+1 Others 5+1
Hull C (£40,000 on 7/2/85) FL 219+2/17 FLC 12 FAC 13/1 Others 9
Oldham Ath (£460,000 on 30/8/90) F/PL 188+1/10 FLC 19/1 FAC 13 Others 4
Leeds U (£1,000,000 on 26/10/95) PL 12/1 FAC 1

JOHNROSE Leonard (Lenny)
Born: Preston, 29 November 1969
Height: 5'10" Weight: 12.6

Bury's midfield general enjoyed a great season in 1995-96, having been in and out of the side in the opening months. Handed a regular place from November onwards, the determined Lenny proved to have an eye for goal and bagged his best total for the club so far.

Blackburn Rov (From trainee on 16/6/88) FL 20+22/11 FLC 2+1/1 FAC 0+3 Others 2
Preston NE (Loaned on 21/1/92) FL 1+2/1
Hartlepool U (£50,000 on 28/2/92) FL 59+7/11 FLC 5+1/4 FAC 5/1 Others 5
Bury (Signed on 7/12/93) FL 68+6/11 FLC 4+1 FAC 5/1 Others 6

JOHNSEN Erland
Born: Fredrikstad, Norway, 5 April 1967
Height: 6'1" Weight: 13.5
International Honours: Norway: 24

Chelsea's "Player of the Year" for 1995 had a disjointed season in 1995-96 as suspension and injuries cost him his place in the team. Whilst he was out, the new three-man central defensive formation functioned effectively and he was unable to reclaim a first team place. A hard-tackling, aggressive defender, who is particularly good in the air, he never let the Blues down when called upon. Started 18 league matches and came on as substitute for Steve Clarke, in the FA Cup semi final.

Chelsea (£306,000 from Bayern Munich on 6/12/89) F/PL 121+6/1 FLC 6 FAC 15+1 Others 9

JOHNSON Alan Keith
Born: Wigan, 19 February 1971
Height: 6'0" Weight: 12.0

Solid Lincoln defender who began last season on loan at Preston as cover and then found himself in and out of the team on his return. Finished the campaign as first choice centre back and was made captain for the final game of the season, only to find himself given a free transfer 48 hours later.

Wigan Ath (From trainee on 1/4/89) FL 163+17/13 FLC 7+2/2 FAC 14+2/1 Others 14+3/3
Lincoln C (Signed on 15/2/94) FL 57+6 FLC 2 FAC 3 Others 3+1/1
Preston NE (Loaned on 1/9/95) FL 2

JOHNSON Andrew (Andy) James
Born: Bristol, 2 May 1974
Height: 6'0" Weight: 12.0
International Honours: E: Yth

A good passer, and very quick in linking with the forwards, Andy enjoyed an outstanding first half of 1995-96, giving forceful displays in Norwich's midfield, laced with several important goals. Plagued by suspensions (sent off in consecutive games against Oldham and Wolves) and back and ankle injuries, the first seven games of the season saw him net three goals and hit the bar, pick up five bookings, and be withdrawn five times. When unavailable, City missed his unstinting appetite for hard work and telling midfield bursts and can only hope he continues his record of never being on the losing side when he scores. Can also play in defence.

Norwich C (From trainee on 4/3/92) F/PL 32+7/8 FLC 5+1/1 FAC 1

JOHNSON David Alan
Born: Dinnington, 29 October 1970
Height: 6'2" Weight: 14.3

Lincoln striker who had a disappointing campaign in 1995-96, failing to show the ability that had previously earned him the nickname "Magic". Scoring just one league goal, he played on a week-to-week contract, until eventually being released at the end of March.

Sheffield Wed (From trainee on 1/7/89) FL 5+1
Hartlepool U (Loaned on 31/10/91) FL 7/2 FAC 2/1
Hartlepool U (Loaned on 20/11/92) FL 3 Others 2/1
Lincoln C (Signed on 20/8/93) FL 75+14/13 FLC 5+1/4 FAC 5/2 Others 9/4

David Johnson (Lincoln C)

JOHNSON David Anthony
Born: Kingston, Jamaica, 15 August 1976
Height: 5'6" Weight: 12.3
Club Honours: FAYC '95

Powerfully built, despite his lack of height, the young striker impressed everyone with his enthusiastic, all-action style in his first full season of league football after joining Bury from Manchester United during the summer of 1995. Scored on his full debut at Cardiff in November and although facing stiff competition for his place, earned prolonged spells in the team, initially alongside Phil Stant and more latterly, Mark Carter.

Manchester U (From trainee on 1/7/94)
Bury (Free on 5/7/95) FL 21+15/4 FLC 1+2/1 FAC 0+1 Others 1+1

JOHNSON Gavin
Born: Eye, 10 October 1970
Height: 5'11" Weight: 11.12
Club Honours: Div 2 '92

A versatile left-sided player, signed from

Ipswich Town on a free transfer in the 1995 close season, Gavin looked useful in his half dozen appearances in midfield for Luton and particularly enjoyed his part in the 1-0 away victory against his previous club in October. However, he was away on loan at Wigan when Lennie Lawrence took over as manager and with Town showing a rare sign of good form he was sold to the Lancashire club, having impressed the locals. Playing at left back and pushing forward at every opportunity, Gavin scored some valuable goals, including a brace in the 2-1 home victory over Colchester in February.

Ipswich T (From trainee on 1/3/89) F/PL 114+18/11 FLC 10+1/2 FAC 12/2 Others 3+1/1
Luton T (Free on 4/7/95) FL 4+1
Wigan Ath (£15,000 on 15/12/95) FL 27/3

JOHNSON Glenn Paul
Born: Sydney, Australia, 16 July 1972
Height: 5'10" Weight: 11.1

Striker. Signed in a blaze of publicity in deadline week 1996 from Aussie club, Blacktown City, having been attracted to Cardiff by his boyhood hero, Phil Neal. Made an immediate impact by scoring in two run outs, before coming off the bench regularly in 1996-97. Definitely one to watch for in 1996-97.

Cardiff C (Free from Blacktown C, Australia on 21/3/96) FL 1+4

JOHNSON Marvin Anthony
Born: Wembley, 29 October 1968
Height: 5'11" Weight: 12.3

1995-96 was another dependable season for the hard-working, crowd-pleasing Luton central defender. Captaining the side in the absence of fellow defenders, Steve Davis and Trevor Peake, he continued to make steady progress in a struggling side, proving calm under pressure, timing his tackles well, and remaining steady in the air. Despite the evidence of the results, he formed an effective partnership with Davis and should prove the pillar of the defence in 1996-97 as the club attempts to climb back up. Although niggling injuries, including a hamstring in February, caused him to miss a few matches, it would be a surprise if his name is not one of the first on the team sheet.

Luton T (From apprentice on 12/11/86) FL 189+13/4 FLC 10+2/1 FAC 9+1 Others 10

JOHNSON Michael Owen
Born: Nottingham, 4 July 1973
Height: 5'11" Weight: 11.0
Club Honours: AIC '95

Transferred from Notts County to Birmingham last September, Michael made an immediate impression as a cultured central defender who was quick in the tackle and very rarely beaten for pace, being the perfect foil for first Liam Daish and later, Gary Breen, in 43 games. Nicknamed "Magic", he played mainly on the left-hand side and also sat in at left back when required.

Notts Co (From trainee on 9/7/91) FL 102+5 FLC 9 FAC 4 Others 15+1
Birmingham C (£225,000 on 1/9/95) FL 31+2 FLC 5 FAC 1 Others 4

JOHNSON Richard Mark
Born: Newcastle, Australia, 27 April 1974
Height: 5'10" Weight: 12.0

Combative, hard-tackling Watford midfield player who made a strong start to last season, scoring the club's second goal, before losing his place after a thigh operation. Possesses a thunderous shot and should, perhaps, figure more often on the scoresheet.

Watford (From trainee on 11/5/92) FL 67+18/4 FLC 6+1/1 FAC 4 Others 0+1

JOHNSON Ross York
Born: Brighton, 1 February 1976
Height: 6'0" Weight: 12.4

In his second season as a professional with Brighton, central defender, Ross, can be proud of his performances during difficult times in 1995-96. Strong in the air, he impressed with his coolness under pressure and grew in confidence. Has a bright future ahead.

Brighton & Hove A (From trainee on 22/7/94) FL 20+2 FAC 2 Others 2

JOHNSON Thomas (Tommy)
Born: Newcastle on Tyne, 15 January 1971
Height: 5'10" Weight: 11.2
Club Honours: FLC '96
International Honours: E: U21-7

After spending the early months of 1995-96 on the bench, he enjoyed an excellent game for Aston Villa at West Ham in November, coming on as a substitute and both scoring and creating goals. Once restored to first team duty, he notched Villa's only goals at home to Newcastle and away to Southampton and, thus rejuvenated, held his place, showing his best-ever form for Villa, with a willingness to shoot on sight from any range. Sadly, a thigh strain incurred in the FA Cup-tie at Ipswich in February, disrupted his season and, although fit in time for the Coca Cola Cup final, he remained on the bench. A classy player who keeps the line moving, he returned to duty in the closing weeks, but could not recapture the same form.

Notts Co (From trainee on 19/1/89) FL 100+18/47 FLC 7+2/5 FAC 3+2/1 Others 14+3/4
Derby Co (£1,3000,000 on 12/3/92) FL 91+7/30 FLC 9+1/2 FAC 5/1 Others 16/8
Aston Villa (Signed on 6/1/95) PL 28+9/9 FLC 4/2 FAC 3+2/1

JONES Barry
Born: Prescot, 20 June 1970
Height: 5'11" Weight: 11.7
Club Honours: WC '95

Since being converted to a central defensive position from his right back slot, Barry continued to make the Wrexham number six shirt his own as a model of consistency in 1995-96. Has missed few games since his free transfer from Liverpool in 1992 and is a vital cog in the club's plans to reach higher league status in the, hopefully, not too distant future.

Liverpool (Signed from Prescot T on 19/1/89) Others 0+1
Wrexham (Free on 10/7/92) FL 158+1/4 FLC 12/1 FAC 9 Others 21

JONES Gary
Born: Huddersfield, 6 April 1969
Height: 6'1" Weight: 12.9

A centre forward who is dangerous in the air at corners and free kicks, Gary was transferred from Southend to Notts County last March to assist in the club's promotion drive. Prior to the move, although scoring only three goals for United last season, they had all been either winners or equalisers. At his new club, he quickly got on the scoresheet with five in his first five games, before temporarily losing his place when they dried up. Played in two of the three play-off games, however.

Doncaster Rov (Free from Rossington Main Colliery on 26/1/89) FL 10+10/2 FLC 1 (£8,500 to Grantham on 1/11/89)
Southend U (£25,000 from Boston U, via Kettering T, on 3/6/93) FL 47+23/16 FLC 3/1 FAC 2 Others 6+1/2
Lincoln C (Loaned on 17/9/93) FL 0+4/2 Others 0+1
Notts Co (£140,000 on 1/3/96) FL 16+2/5 Others 1+1

JONES Gary Steven
Born: Chester, 10 May 1975
Height: 6'3" Weight: 14.0

Tranmere have three players in one with Gary. The young giant, having been successfully converted from a centre half into a centre forward the previous campaign, found himself the pivotal figure in the heart of Rovers' midfield during their best spell of last season. Blessed with great touch and passing ability for a big man, he was a revelation, "another string to his bow", said John King, but because of his size he was never cut out to be a box-to-box player, and eventually lost his place to Paul Cook and Liam O'Brien. Made a November appearance as a sub for the Football League XI that drew 1-1 with Italian Serie "B" side at Huddersfield.

Tranmere Rov (From trainee on 5/7/93) FL 25+23/6 FLC 3+1/2 FAC 2+1 Others 1+1

Graeme Jones

JONES Graeme Anthony
Born: Gateshead, 13 March 1970
Height: 6'0" Weight: 12.12

Bustling Doncaster Rovers' central striker who was leading scorer for the club for the second season in succession in 1995-96. Troubled with niggling injuries for much of the campaign, he remained a willing trier, fully deserving of the success that came his way.

Doncaster Rov (£10,000 from Bridlington T on 2/8/93) FL 80+12/26 FLC 4+1/1 FAC 2+1/1 Others 5/1

JONES Ian Michael
Born: Germany, 26 August 1976
Height: 5'5" Weight: 9.8
International Honours: W: Yth

Having made two appearances in 1993-94, but none since, the young Cardiff full back was tried out at Ninian against Exeter six games into 1995-96 and following a 1-0 defeat failed to return to the side.

Cardiff C (From trainee on 31/7/95) FL 3

JONES Jonathan (Jon) Berwyn
Born: Wrexham, 27 October 1978
Height: 5'11" Weight: 11.5

Chester midfield youngster. Only three months into a two year YTS contract, Jon was introduced to the first team in the Auto Windscreen Shield at Burnley last November as a sub and could be one for the future.

Chester C (Trainee) Others 0+1

JONES Keith Aubrey
Born: Dulwich, 14 October 1965
Height: 5'9" Weight: 10.11
International Honours: E: Yth; Sch

A tenacious midfield player who started 1995-96 as Charlton team captain, Keith mixes up his play with tackling ability and good distribution. Various injuries, including a fractured cheekbone sustained against Portsmouth, disrupted his season, but he put in some steady performances, giving probably his best one in the televised home game against Luton Town. Never gives less than his best.

Chelsea (From apprentice on 16/8/83) FL 43+9/7 FLC 9+2/3 FAC 1 Others 4+1
Brentford (£40,000 on 3/9/87) FL 167+2/13 FLC 15/2 FAC 13/4 Others 16/1
Southend U (£175,000 on 21/10/91) FL 88+2/11 FLC 4 FAC 5 Others 9/1
Charlton Ath (£150,000 on 16/9/94) FL 55+1/1 FLC 2+1 FAC 1

JONES Lee
Born: Pontypridd, 9 August 1970
Height: 6'3" Weight: 14.4
Club Honours: AMC '94

Of impressive build for a goalkeeper, with Roger Freestone so reliable, Lee had to wait a long time to make his first Swansea appearance in 1995-96. When it came, he was magnificent in the 2-1 home win over Crewe on the final day of the season. Ironically, he had been on loan at Crewe in October and November and although not playing, did well enough for an offer to be made and subsequently turned down.

Swansea C (£7,500 from AFC Porth on 24/3/94) FL 3 Others 1

JONES Philip Lee
Born: Wrexham, 29 May 1973
Height: 5'9" Weight: 10.5
International Honours: W: B-1; U21-14

Signed as an investment for the future four years ago, Lee has yet to start a first team game for Liverpool, continuing to feature in the reserves as a speedy forward and goalscorer. Had two spells on loan last season, the first at Crewe in October, where he failed to make an appearance, and then it was on to his former club, Wrexham, in January. With the Robins pushing hard for a play-off place, he duly obliged with eight goals, his pace often unsettling opposing defences, before returning to Anfield.

Wrexham (From trainee on 5/7/91) FL 24+15/10 FLC 2 FAC 1+2/1 Others 4+1/2
Liverpool (£300,000 on 12/3/92) PL 0+1 FLC 0+1
Crewe Alex Loaned on 3/9/93) FL 4+4/1
Wrexham (Loaned on 26/1/96) FL 20/8

JONES Paul Steven
Born: Chirk, 18 April 1967
Height: 6'3" Weight: 14.8

Wolves' goalkeeper. Dropped a shot to concede an opening day goal at Tranmere last season and then had to wait until Mike Stowell was hurt in October for his next chance. Back in the side, he let in just three goals in six appearances, only to struggle during the next three games and ultimately lose his place. As Stowell's capable deputy, and a fine shot stopper, Paul has now spent six years in his rival's shadow at Molineux.

Wolverhampton W (£40,000 from Kidderminster Harriers on 23/7/91) FL 33 FLC 2 FAC 5 Others 4

Rob Jones

JONES Robert (Rob) Marc
Born: Wrexham, 5 November 1971
Height: 5'11" Weight: 11.0
Club Honours: FAC '92; FLC '95
International Honours: W: Sch. E: 8; U21-2; Yth

Whilst not quite reaching the heights predicted for him after his superb first season for Liverpool, and an outstanding international debut four years ago, he remains one of the most consistent and dependable full backs in the country. A naturally right-sided player he was switched to the left wing/back position last January to make way for the mercurial Jason McAteer, without any noticeable reduction in his efficiency. However, this switch did not assist his international prospects, and his England career remains on hold as a squad member with no further caps in 1995-96. Remarkably, he has yet to score for his club, but is frequently to be found in the opposition's penalty area, only to be thwarted by the woodwork or athletic 'keeping. Is the nephew of former Red's defender, Billy, who played in their 1950 FA Cup final team.

Crewe Alex (From trainee on 20/12/88) FL 59+16/2 FLC 9 FAC 0+3 Others 3
Liverpool (£300,000 on 4/10/91) F/PL 160 FLC 18+1 FAC 27 Others 7

JONES Ryan Anthony
Born: Sheffield, 23 July 1973
Height: 6'1" Weight: 13.10
International Honours: W: 1; B-1; U21-4

Having come back from injury towards the end of 1994-95, Ryan struggled throughout last season in trying to ease his way back to fitness and, at the same time, re-establish himself at Sheffield Wednesday. Predominately recognised as a left-sided midfielder, although he can play with equal vigour at left back, at his best, Ryan is strong and athletic and possesses a sweet left foot. However, unable to stake a claim at Wednesday, he was loaned out to Scunthorpe in Janaury and scored three goals in 11 games, despite finding it difficult to adapt to lower division football. Now back at Hillsborough and raring to go.

Sheffield Wed (From trainee on 18/6/91) PL 36+5/6 FLC 5+1 FAC 3/1
Scunthorpe U (Loaned on 12/1/96) FL 11/3

JONES Scott
Born: Sheffield, 1 May 1975
Height: 5'10" Weight: 11.6

Left-sided defender who forced his way into the Barnsley first team. Proved to be a strong tackler, and the Reds will be looking for continued improvement from the youngster. As a former trainee, Scott warranted his first team opportunity, having impressed at reserve level.

Barnsley (From trainee on 1/2/94) FL 4

JONES Stephen (Steve) Gary
Born: Cambridge, 17 March 1970
Height: 6'0" Weight: 12.12

Steve was Bournemouth's leading scorer for the second season running in 1995-96, with 20 goals. Had an explosive start to the campaign, scoring ten in the first 12 games, including a hat trick against Peterborough in the first home match. Always a handful in the penalty area, he used his speed and strength to great effect and along with the easier finishes struck some spectacular goals, showing his willingness to shoot at every opportunity. His good form, saw West Ham, his old club, re-sign him in mid-June, with Mark Watson going in the opposite direction, plus cash.

West Ham U (£22,000 from Billericay T on 16/11/92) PL 8+4/4 FAC 2+2/1 Others 1+1
Bournemouth (£150,000 on 21/10/94) FL 71+3/24 FLC 4/3 FAC 3/1 Others 3
West Ham U (Signed on 16/5/96)

JONES Stephen (Steve) Robert
Born: Bristol, 25 December 1970
Height: 5'10" Weight: 12.2

Young defender signed from non-league Cheltenham Town last November, who showed plenty of promise when introduced into the Swansea first team. Played mostly at right back, but also appeared in central defence towards the end of the season.

Swansea C (£25,000 from Cheltenham T on 14/11/95) FL 16+1

JONES Steven
Born: Stockton, 31 January 1974
Height: 5'11" Weight: 13.7

Hartlepool's reserve goalkeeper who struggled in his few first team appearances in 1995-96, due to his lack of match practice, the club not having a reserve team. Although told he was to be released, Steven showed great spirit by playing in the last three games of the season when his movement was restricted by a serious calf injury.

Hartlepool U (From trainee on 7/5/92) FL 45+3 FLC 2 Others 1

Scott Jordan

JONES Thomas (Tom)
Born: Aldershot, 7 October 1964
Height: 5'10" Weight: 11.7
Club Honours: Div 2 '94
International Honours: E: SP-1

Never sure of a regular place in the Reading first team during 1995-96, he wore nine different shirt numbers, usually filling in at full back or midfield for players missing through injury or suspension, before being given a free transfer at the end of the season. Will be fondly remembered by Royals' fans for his ability to send long, penetrating passes from midfield.

Aberdeen (£30,000 from Weymouth in 1987-88) SL 14+14/3 FAC 1+2
Swindon T (Signed on 27/9/88) FL 162+6/12 FLC 14+4 FAC 10 Others 11
Reading (£125,000 on 9/7/92) FL 63+16/2 FLC 6 FAC 5 Others 1

JONES Vincent (Vinny) Peter
Born: Watford, 5 January 1965
Height: 6'0" Weight: 11.12
Club Honours: FAC '88 DIV 2 '90
International Honours: W: 5

A tough-tackling, uncompromising Wimbledon midfielder for whom every season seems to be one of on and off field controversy. However, over the last three or four years he has quietly been adding subtlety and skill to the more combative elements of his game. This was nowhere more in evidence than in the FA Cup quarter final against Chelsea at Stamford Bridge last season when he impressed as the most outstanding footballer on the day and not Ruud Gullit, as one might have imagined. Having taken the lead of Eric Cantona and let the football do the talking in 1995-96, Vinny also turned his hand to public speaking, with appearances at the Eton and Oxford student unions and a UN conference on human rights. Added to his Welsh caps with an appearance against Switzerland in April.

Wimbledon (£10,000 from Wealdstone on 20/11/86) FL 77/9 FLC 6+2 FAC 11+2/1 Others 3
Leeds U (£650,000 on 20/6/89) FL 44+2/5 FLC 2 FAC 1 Others 4
Sheffield U (£700,000 on 13/9/90) FL 35/2 FLC 4 FAC 1 Others 1
Chelsea (£575,000 on 30/8/91) F/PL 42/4 FLC 1 FAC 4/1 Others 5/2
Wimbledon (£700,000 on 10/9/92) F/PL 120+4/9 FLC 13/2 FAC 11

JORDAN Scott Douglas
Born: Newcastle, 19 July 1975
Height: 5'10" Weight: 11.2

A thoughtful midfield player and excellent passer of the ball, Scott surprisingly lost his first team place at York midway through the 1995-96 campaign. He returned in the closing weeks, however, to play an important part in City's escape from relegation. Had earlier scored the vital goal in the home game against Manchester United which knocked the Reds out of the Coca Cola Cup.
York C (From trainee on 21/10/92) FL 51+13/4 FLC 4+1/1 FAC 2 Others 3+4

JOSEPH Marc Ellis
Born: Leicester, 10 November 1976
Height: 6'0" Weight: 12.5

Promising young right-footed Cambridge United defender, who spent early last season on loan at Cambridge City, before impressing in league performances, following his debut at Doncaster in October, to earn trials and a loan spell at Coventry. Returned for the last game in order to strengthen United's defence.
Cambridge U (From trainee on 23/5/95) FL 10+2 Others 1

JOSEPH Matthew (Matt) Nathan Adolphus
Born: Bethnal Green, 30 September 1972
Height: 5'7" Weight: 10.7
International Honours: E: Yth

As Cambridge United's club captain, Matt missed only a handful of games last season, his tough tackling and aggressive style being an important part of the midfield. A versatile player, he can also play at full back or up front if required.
Arsenal (From trainee on 17/11/90)
Gillingham (Free on 7/12/92)
Cambridge U (Signed on 19/11/93) FL 108/6 FLC 4 FAC 5 Others 3

JOYCE Joseph (Joe) Patrick
Born: Consett, 18 March 1961
Height: 5'10" Weight: 11.6
Club Honours: Div 3 '95

A highly experienced Carlisle defender who is now club coach and assistant manager to Mervyn Day, Joe's only appearance last season came in the Coca Cola Cup in August 1995. Equally at home in the centre of the defence or in a full back role.
Barnsley (From juniors on 14/11/79) FL 332+2/4 FLC 26+1/1 FAC 24/1 Others 3
Scunthorpe U (Free on 20/2/91) FL 91/2 FLC 5 Others 11
Carlisle U (Free on 5/8/93) FL 45+5 FLC 5+1 FAC 4+1 Others 9/1
Darlington (Loaned on 23/9/93) FL 4

JOYCE Warren Garton
Born: Oldham, 20 January 1965
Height: 5'9" Weight: 11.11

Finally a regular Burnley first teamer in his third season at Turf Moor, Warren was often a key man with his industrious efforts in midfield and his eye for goal. Never a spectacular player, he was one of the club's most reliable men during 1995-96.
Bolton W (From juniors on 23/6/82) FL 180+4/17 FLC 14+1/1 FAC 11/1 Others 11/2
Preston NR (£35,000 on 16/10/87) FL 170+7/34 FLC 8/2 FAC 6/1 Others 19/7
Plymouth Arg (£160,000 on 19/5/92) FL 28+2/3 FLC 6/1 FAC 2 Others 2
Burnley (£140,000 on 7/7/93) FL 65+5/9 FLC 8/1 FAC 4/1 Others 8/1
Hull C (Loaned on 20/1/95) FL 9/3

JULES Mark Anthony
Born: Bradford, 5 September 1971
Height: 5'8" Weight: 11.1

As in 1994-95, Mark usually fulfilled a man

marking or full back role for Chesterfield last season, and was given little opportunity to get beyond the halfway line. When he did, however, his close control and crossing ability was an asset to the left side of the attack.
Bradford C (From trainee on 3/7/90) FLC 0+1
Scarborough (Free on 14/8/91) FL 57+20/16 FLC 6+2/2 FAC 1+1 Others 6/4
Chesterfield (£40,000 on 21/5/93) FL 66+22/3 FLC 5+2/2 FAC 1+2 Others 7

[JUNINHO] JUNIOR Oswaldo Giroldo
Born: Sao Paulo, Brazil, 22 February 1975
Height: 5'5" Weight: 9.6
International Honours: Brazil: 24

Acknowledged as one of the most gifted players in the world, the brilliant midfield maestro's signing for unfashionable Middlesbrough was the biggest British transfer coup since the arrival of the Argentinians, Ossie Ardiles and Ricardo Villa at Spurs some 18 years previously. And when Juninho announced himself at the Riverside in a blaze of samba bands and euphoria, the like of which had never been seen before in England let alone at the Boro, the whole of football were forced to recognise that the club had posted its intent. His early form was sensational, creating the opening goal for Jan Fjortoft after only nine minutes of his debut at Leeds last November, while his first half performance in the 2-1 home defeat of Liverpool was probably his best display in a Boro shirt. It was also fascinating to see his exuberance, enthusiasm and skill, coupled to perfect balance and a body swerve that frequently left opponents bemused as he rode their tackles. However, he was still trying to adjust to the pace of the English game when the team went into "free fall" after Christmas and the fans will be waiting anxiously to see if a rejuvenated Juninho and his compatriot, Branco, can raise the club to greater heights this coming season.
Middlesbrough (£4,750,000 from Sao Paulo on 3/11/95) PL 20+1/2 FLC 2 Others 3

JUPP Duncan Alan
Born: Haslemere, 25 January 1975
Height: 6'0" Weight: 12.12
International Honours: S: U21-9

Although the young Scottish U21 international right back had an excellent season for Fulham in 1994-95 and attracted considerable interest from Premiership clubs, last season was a hiatus in his career, despite being named in the PFA third division team for the second successive year. At times, his penetrating runs and crossing were top class, but occasionally his final ball let him down, while defensive slip ups gave away goals. He is only 21 though, and the best is yet to come. *Stop Press:* Reported to have signed for Wimbledon, who beat off competition from Sunderland and QPR.
Fulham (From trainee on 12/7/93) FL 101+4/2 FLC 10+2 FAC 9+1/1 Others 9+1/1

THIRST QUENCHER!
Lucozade
SPORT

LUCOZADE SPORT
THE OFFICIAL SPORT DRINK

KAAMARK Pontus Sven
Born: Vasteras, Sweden, 5 April 1969
Height: 5'11" Weight: 12.7
International Honours: Sweden: 27
Swedish international right back who signed for Leicester from IFK Gothenburg last September, having captained the former to the Swedish League title. Impressed on his debut at The Hawthorns, before suffering a knee injury in his second outing against Bolton in the Coca Cola Cup. Returning to action after eight weeks, he unfortunately broke down seconds into a reserve fixture, requiring a cruciate ligament operation that ended his season.
Leicester C (£840,000 from IFK Gothenberg on 2/11/95) FL 1 FLC 1

KAASIKMAE Scot Robert
Born: Wolverhampton, 14 December 1977
Height: 5'9" Weight: 11.2
Capable of playing in midfield or defence, the young YTS made his Torquay debut in the 5-2 AWS defeat at Colchester last September and did not let himself down. However, after suffering a fractured skull in an accident away from football and not regaining any kind of form, he was released early in March.
Torquay U (Trainee) Others 1

KALAC Zeljko
Born: Sydney, Australia, 16 December 1972
Height: 6'7" Weight: 14.3
International Honours: Australia: 14
Leicester City's Australian international goalkeeper. Signed from Sydney United in July 1995, he had to wait until the end of October before a work permit was agreed. Looked nervous on his televised debut at West Bromwich, then suffered a nightmare game in the Coca Cola Cup defeat by Bolton. Following that, Zeljko appeared set to rejoin former boss, Martin McGhee, at Wolves, but another work permit argument saw him back at Filbert Street in March. His topsy-turvey season came to a near spectacular climax when brought off the bench in the closing seconds of the Wembley play-off final, in preparation for the anticipated penalty shoot-out, which, thankfully, was not required.
Leicester C (£760,000 from Sydney U on 13/10/95) FL 1 FLC 1 Others 0+1

KANCHELSKIS Andrei
Born: Kirovograd, USSR, 23 January 1969
Height: 5'10" Weight: 13.3
Club Honours: ESC '91; FLC '92 PL '93, '94; CS '93, '94; FAC '94
International Honours: USSR: 43
An incredibly gifted right winger who uses explosive pace and direct running to leave defenders trailing in his wake, Andrei eventually joined Everton from Manchester United just after the start of last season,

following a well-publicised bust up with Alex Ferguson and protracted negotiations. Eventually making his debut against Southampton, and playing twice more, a bad rib injury kept him on the sidelines for a number of games before he came back to add a new dimension to the team and, at the same time, endear himself to the supporters. He hit two stunners to sink Merseyside rivals, Liverpool, in the November derby and carried on in similar vein throughout the campaign, adding a touch of unpredictability to his enthusiastic running. Climaxed his super season with a memorable hat trick in a 5-2 victory at Sheffield Wednesday, before going on to play for Russia in Euro '96, the Soviets going out at the group stage.
Manchester U (£650,000 from Shakhtyor Donetsk on 26/3/91) F/PL 96+27/28 FLC 15+1/3 FAC 11+1/4 Others 10/1
Everton (£5,000,000 on 25/8/95) PL 32/17 FAC 4

Andrei Kanchelskis

KANE Paul James
Born: Edinburgh, 20 June 1965
Height: 5'9" Weight: 11.0
International Honours: S: Yth
Having earlier played in the Football League with Oldham, and looking for an opportunity to return, the Scot began last season at Barnsley on loan from Aberdeen. Although the midfielder impressed with his passing and the Reds won three of the four games he took part in, he returned home once his period was up.
Hibernian (Free from Salvesen BC on 20/7/82) SL 235+9/33 SLC 21+1/6 SC 13+2/2 Others 4
Oldham Ath (£350,000 on 22/1/91) FL 13+8 FLC 2 FAC 1 Others 1
Aberdeen (Signed on 22/11/91) SL 101+18/11 SLC 6+1/1 SC 7+1 Others 5/1
Barnsley (Loaned on 3/8/95) FL 4

KAVANAGH Graham Anthony
Born: Dublin, 2 December 1973
Height: 5'10" Weight: 12.11
International Honours: Ei: U21-9; Yth; Sch

Somewhat eclipsed by all the big names arriving at Riverside Park, the talented young Middlesbrough midfielder did not figure in first team action until last February. Enjoying his best season at every level, he was even entrusted with a penalty at Leeds in the third minute, scoring with a cheeky little shuffle to secure the points and bring about Boro's first victory in 14 PL games. A current Republic of Ireland U21 international, Graham is a strong and fearless youngster who displays super ball skills and passes with great accuracy, allied to good positional sense and off the ball intelligence.
Middlesbrough (Signed from Home Farm on 16/8/91) F/PL 22+13/3 FLC 1 FAC 3+1/1 Others 7
Darlington (Loaned on 25/2/94) FL 5

KAVANAGH Jason Colin
Born: Meriden, 23 November 1971
Height: 5'9" Weight: 12.4
International Honours: E: Yth; Sch
Right-sided Derby defender who was asked to perform a role as a wing/back in a five-man midfield and kept his place in the team until last October when he was replaced by Lee Carsley. A tenacious ball winner who prefers the right back slot, but can also perform equally well alongside the centre back, Jason first came to County after passing through the FA School of Excellence.
Derby Co (From trainee on 9/12/88) FL 74+25/1 FLC 3+2 FAC 7 Others 8+8

KAVELASHVILI Mikhail
Born: Tbilisi, Georgia, 22 July 1971
Height: 6'0" Weight: 12.1
International Honours: Georgia: 2
After an anxious period trying to clear a work permit, the Georgian striker joined Manchester City on deadline transfer day last March. Coming with a good pedigree, and being a fellow countryman of Georgiou Kinkladze, it was hoped that an excellent partnership would be forthcoming. Has already showed a good head for the game and should make great strides with more sharpness, if his opportunist goal against Manchester United was anything to go by.
Manchester C (£1,400,000 from Sporting Vladikavkaz on 28/3/96) PL 3+4/1

KAY John
Born: Great Lumley, 29 January 1964
Height: 5'9" Weight: 11.6
Club Honours: Div 3 '88
Sidelined since October 1993, following a series of injuries and mishaps, Sunderland's veteran left back, cum central defender, finally came back last March on loan at Shrewsbury. With his experience, the long lay off was barely in evidence as he quickly settled down, always looking assured on the ball and playing confidently out of defence to set up the forwards. Given a free transfer during the summer.
Arsenal (From apprentice on 7/8/81) FL 13+1
Wimbledon (£25,000 on 20/7/84) FL 63/2 FLC 3 FAC 3 Others 1
Middlesbrough (Loaned on 8/1/85) FL 8
Sunderland (£22,500 on 22/7/87) FL 196+3 FLC 19 FAC 12 Others 6
Shrewsbury T (Loaned on 28/3/96) FL 7 Others 1

KEANE Roy Maurice
Born: Cork, 10 August 1971
Height: 5'10" Weight: 12.10
Club Honours: FMC '92; CS '93; PL '94, '96; FAC '94, '96
International Honours: Ei: 30; U21-4; Yth; Sch

A hard-working Manchester United midfielder who seems to cover every blade of grass, Roy also enjoys the passing game and is always prepared to play his way out of trouble. The strength to burst through from deep positions to score is yet another facet of his all-round capability. Once again, his brilliant competitive midfield performances for United and the Republic of Ireland in 1995-96 earned him a succession of rave reviews by many within the game, including a glowing tribute from the Sunderland manager, Peter Reid, who called him the best midfield player in the country, following a sparkling display against Sunderland in the FA Cup. Although Roy appeared to have a demanding time ahead of him at the start of the campaign, following the shock departure of Paul Ince to Inter Milan, his brilliant link-up play with United's new ace in the pack, Nicky Butt, made the departure of Ince look more plausible than first appeared. Although it is difficult to pick out any game in particular from so many fine displays, his greatest accolade was reserved for the FA Cup final against Liverpool when he won the prestigious Littlewoods' "Man of the Match" award. Ever present in the FA Cup, his 29 league games also brought him a championship medal as United ultimately waltzed to their second ever double.
Nottingham F (£10,000 from Cobh Ramblers on 12/6/90) F/PL 114/22 FLC 17/6 FAC 18/3 Others 5/2
Manchester U (£3,750,000 on 22/7/93) PL 86+5/13 FLC 7+2 FAC 19+1/1 Others 10/3

KEEN Kevin Ian
Born: Amersham, 25 February 1967
Height: 5'6" Weight: 10.10
International Honours: E: Yth; Sch

Right-sided Stoke City midfielder. Kevin will be remembered for a long time as the scorer of a wonderful goal against Derby at the Victoria Ground last season, when he volleyed in from a Nigel Gleghorn free kick. Although having a frustrating time, failing to consolidate his place in the team's midfield, he could always be relied upon to put in hard-working performances in linking defence to attack.
West Ham U (From apprentice on 8/3/84) FL 187+32/21 FLC 21+1/5 FAC 15+7/1 Others 14+2/3
Wolverhampton W (£600,000 on 7/7/93) FL 37+5/7 FLC 2+1 FAC 5/1 Others 4/1
Stoke C (£300,000 on 19/10/94) FL 42+12/5 FLC 2 FAC 2 Others 3

KEISTER John Edward Samuel
Born: Manchester, 11 November 1970
Height: 5'8" Weight: 11.0
International Honours: Sierra Leone: U21

A tenacious little Walsall midfielder who was in and out of the side last season, he came in to midfield several times when skipper, Martin O'Connor, was either out with injury or filling in up front. Always to be relied upon to give a battling display, John never lets the Saddlers' down.
Walsall (Free from Faweh FC on 18/9/83) FL 35+19/1 FAC 5+2 Others 2+2

KELLER Kasey
Born: Washington, USA, 27 November 1969
Height: 6'1" Weight: 13.7
International Honours: USA: 22

Cool and confident Millwall goalkeeper with very sharp reactions and reflexes in close situations. His excellent displays in 1995-96 earned him a USA international call up in January for the CONCACAF tournament, thus costing him his Millwall number one spot, which he duly won back from Tim Carter in February. Continues to improve and would not look out of place at any level.
Millwall (Free from Portland University on 20/2/92) FL 176 FLC 14 FAC 8 Others 4

KELLY Alan Thomas
Born: Preston, 11 August 1968
Height: 6'2" Weight: 12.5
International Honours: Ei: 14; U23-1; Yth

Sheffield United's Irish international once again showed he is among the top flight of goalkeepers in the country in 1995-96. Took over as captain of the club, following the injury to Brian Gayle, and was absent for only three games until a back injury in training led him to miss the run-in to the end of the season. Prior to that, he had added further international caps to his collection and had been elected to the PFA first division team by his fellow professionals.
Preston NE (From apprentice on 25/9/85) FL 142 FLC 1 FAC 8 Others 13
Sheffield U (£150,000 on 24/7/92) P/FL 133+3 FLC 8 FAC 12

Alan Kelly

KELLY Anthony (Tony) Gerald
Born: Prescot, 1 October 1964
Height: 5'10" Weight: 13.10
Club Honours: AMC '85

A former member of Wigan Athletic's 1985 Freight Rover Trophy midfield, who was recruited from Peterborough at the start of last season, Tony was unable to reproduce the passing skills and vision he showed during his first spell at the club. It therefore came as no surprise, following the appointment of John Deehan as manager, that his contract was cancelled in February and he moved on to GM Vauxhall Conference side, Altrincham.
Liverpool (From apprentice on 30/9/82)
Wigan Ath (Free from Prescot Cables on 4/1/84) FL 98+3/15 FLC 4/2 FAC 10/1 Others 12/4
Stoke C (£80,000 on 26/4/86) FL 33+3/4 FLC 2 FAC 5 Others 1
West Bromwich A (£60,000 on 13/7/87) FL 26/1 FLC 2 FAC 1 Others 1
Chester C (Loaned on 22/9/88) FL 5 FLC 2
Colchester U (Loaned on 24/10/88) FL 13/2 FAC 4 Others 3
Shrewsbury T (£30,000 on 28/1/89) FL 100+1/15 FLC 8/1 FAC 7/1 Others 4
Bolton W (£100,000 on 15/8/91) FL 103+3/5 FLC 9/2 FAC 15+3 Others 9/1
Port Vale (Free on 23/9/94) FL 3+1/1 FLC 1
Millwall (Free on 31/10/94) FL 1+1
Wigan Ath (Free on 25/11/94)
Peterborough U (Free on 9/12/94) FL 12+1/2
Wigan Ath (Free on 14/7/95) FL 2 Others 1

KELLY Nyrere Anthony (Tony)
Born: Meriden, 14 February 1966
Height: 5'11" Weight: 11.6

Capable of playing on either flank, the speedy winger joined Leyton Orient from Bury during the summer of 1995. However, as in previous seasons, following a promising start, niggling injuries slowed him down and he eventually lost his place in the side. Retained for 1996-97, hopefully, he can maintain match fitness throughout the campaign.
Bristol C (Apprentice) FL 2+4/1
Stoke C (£20,000 from St Albans C, via Dulwich Hamlet, Cheshunt and Enfield, on 29/1/90) FL 33+25/5 FLC 5+4/3 Others 3+3
Hull C (Loaned on 30/1/92) FL 6/1
Cardiff C (Loaned on 30/10/92) FL 5/1
Bury (£10,000 on 17/9/93) FL 53+4/10 FLC 0+1 FAC 1+1 Others 8/3
Leyton Orient (£30,000 on 7/7/95) FL 32+2/3 FLC 1 FAC 1 Others 2

KELLY David Thomas
Born: Birmingham, 25 November 1965
Height: 5'11" Weight: 11.3
Club Honours: Div '93
International Honours: Ei: 20; B-3; U23-1; U21-3

Signed from Wolves last September, the striker played only 12 games, before damaged ankle ligaments finished his season two months later. Despite this, the Eire international had already notched one of the most important goals of the campaign in Sunderland's 1-0 victory at would be promotion rivals, Crystal Palace. Significantly, when promotion was assured, David became the club's record signing after £100,000 – an extra payment to Wolves if Sunderland reached the Premiership – was made over.
Walsall (Signed from Alvechurch on 21/12/83) FL 115+32/63 FLC 11+1/4 FAC 12+2/3 Others 14+3/10
West Ham U (£600,000 on 1/8/88) FL 29+12/7 FLC 11+3/5 FAC 6 Others 2+1/2

Leicester C (£300,000 on 22/3/90) FL 63+3/22 FLC 6/2 FAC 1 Others 2/1
Newcastle U (£250,000 on 4/12/91) FL 70/35 FLC 4/2 FAC 5/1 Others 4/1
Wolverhampton W (£750,000 on 23/6/93) FL 76+7/26 FLC 5/2 FAC 11/6 Others 4/2
Sunderland (£1,000,000 on 19/9/95) FL 9+1/2 FLC 1 FAC 1

KELLY Garry
Born: Drogheda, 9 July 1974
Height: 5'9" Weight: 11.0
International Honours: Ei: 18; U21-5; Yth; Sch

1995-96 was yet another consistent season for the young Irishman, who remained a regular for both Leeds and the Republic of Ireland. Equally adept and pacy in defence and attack, his must be one of the first names on the team sheet. More than dangerous going forward and possessing a deft touch, while a good crosser of the ball, he has yet to score his first goal at senior level at the club. Has a tremendous future though.
Leeds U (Signed from Home Farm on 24/9/91) PL 118+2 FLC 12+1 FAC 12 Others 4

KELLY Gary Alexander
Born: Preston, 3 August 1966
Height: 5'11" Weight: 13.6
Club Honours: FAYC '85
International Honours: Ei: B-1; U23-1; U21-8

Goalkeeper. The son of former Preston and Eire 'keeper, Alan, and brother of Sheffield United and current Eire 'keeper, Alan junior, Bury's Gary was sidelined through a knee injury in the early part of 1995-96. However, he came back strongly and regaining his place went on to keep seven successive clean sheets between 14 October and 23 December – a run of 683 minutes and just outside the club record.
Newcastle U (From apprentice on 20/6/84) FL 53 FLC 4 FAC 3 Others 2
Blackpool (Loaned on 7/10/88) FL 5
Bury (£60,000 on 5/10/89) FL 236 FLC 14 FAC 13 Others 29

KELLY Gavin John
Born: Beverley, 29 September 1968
Height: 6'1" Weight: 13.0
Very capable goalkeeper who was unlucky that the outstanding form of Ian Ironside kept him out of the Scarborough first team for most of last season. Always performed well when called upon, and saved two penalty kicks in a dramatic shoot-out at Hartlepool in the Coca Cola Cup, prior to being released on a free transfer at the end of the campaign.
Hull C (From trainee on 9/5/87) FL 11 FLC 1 Others 1
Bristol Rov (Free on 1/7/90) FL 30 FAC 2
Scarborough (Free on 4/7/94) FL 30 FLC 6 FAC 3

KELLY Russell
Born: Ballymoney, 10 August 1976
Height: 5'11" Weight: 11.2
Unable to break out of Chelsea reserves in 1995-96, having signed professional forms during the previous summer, Russell spent the remaining weeks of the season on loan at Leyton Orient, following a move there in transfer deadline week. Tall and slim, he played as an attacking midfielder or wide striker, showing both pace and ball skills, before going back to Stamford Bridge and being handed a free transfer.
Chelsea (From trainee on 4/7/95)
Leyton Orient (Loaned on 28/3/96) FL 5+1

KELLY Thomas (Tom) John
Born: Bellshill, 28 March 1964
Height: 5'10" Weight: 12.7
As in keeping with several other key Torquay players, Tom was also hit by injury in 1995-96. Hard tackling and aggressive, he managed to soldier on in a variety of positions in defence and midfield before finally succumbing and missing the last five games of the season. Released during the summer.
Hartlepool U (Free from Queen of the South on 14/8/85) FL 14+1 FLC 2 Others 1
Torquay U (Free on 16/7/86) FL 116+4 FLC 7+1 FAC 7+1 Others 16
York C (Free on 1/7/89) FL 35/2 FLC 4 FAC 1 Others 3/1
Exeter C (£15,000 on 22/3/90) FL 76+12/9 FLC 5/1 FAC 5 Others 6
Torquay U (Free on 14/1/93) 109+8/8 FLC 7 FAC 7 Others 6

Jeff Kenna

KENNA Jeffrey (Jeff) Jude
Born: Dublin, 27 August 1970
Height: 5'11" Weight: 12.2
International Honours: Ei: 12; B-1; U21-8; Yth; Sch
Blackburn full back and an enthusiastic defender who is able to get forward and join in attacking movements. Naturally at home on the right, he was unfortunate to have to deputise for the injured Graeme le Saux on the other flank last season. Uncomfortable in that position, and unable to show his true ability, he never stopped trying to improve for the obvious benefit of the team and his run and shot that came back from the post at Southampton, his old club, might just have been one of the season's best goals. At international level, Jeff played in nine of the Republic's 12 matches in 1995-96.
Southampton (From trainee on 25/4/89) F/PL 114+4/3 FLC 4 FAC 10+1 Others 3
Blackburn Rov (£1,500,000 on 15/3/95) PL 41/1 FLC 4 FAC 2 Others 6

KENNEDY Mark
Born: Dublin, 15 May 1976
Height: 5'11" Weight: 11.9
International Honours: Ei: 10; U21-4; Yth; Sch
A semi-permanent fixture on the Liverpool bench in 1995-96, Mark finally made a full appearance, his only one of the season, against Southampton at Anfield in December, before falling out of contention in the New Year. His club experience did not stop him from adding ten Republic of Ireland caps to his collection of honours, but, obviously, he will be hoping for more opportunities to impress this coming season. Preferring the left flank, he has excellent pace, likes to take his man on, and is a fine crosser of the ball. Watch out for him.
Millwall (From trainee on 6/5/92) FL 37+6/9 FLC 6+1/2 FAC 3+1/1
Liverpool (£1,500,000 on 21/3/95) PL 5+5 FLC 0+1 Others 0+1

KENT Kevin John
Born: Stoke, 19 March 1965
Height: 5'11" Weight: 11.0
Club Honours: AMC '87, '93
Wholehearted Port Vale midfielder who was forced to give up the game through injury in 1995-96. A nagging back problem became worse when he was slightly injured in a coach accident on the way to a reserve game at Grimsby Town and the diagnosis led to his retirement from the professional ranks. Since then he has been coaching the clubs youngsters and venturing into local radio as a summariser.
West Bromwich A (From apprentice on 31/12/82) FL 1+1
Newport Co (Free on 9/7/84) FL 23+10/1 FLC 2 FAC 0+1 Others 3+1/1
Mansfield T (Free on 15/8/85) FL 223+6/35 FLC 10/2 FAC 13/4 Others 21+2/4
Port Vale (£80,000 on 22/3/91) FL 87+28/7 FLC 9 FAC 2 Others 7+5

KENWORTHY Jonathan (Jon) Raymond
Born: St Asaph, 18 August 1974
Height: 5'8" Weight: 10.7
International Honours: W: U21-4; Yth
A skilful winger who is prepared to tuck in and contribute to the midfield play, Jon had only brief glimpses of first team action at Tranmere in 1995-96, as Graham Branch was preferred on the left wing in the long-term absence of John Morrissey. Enjoyed a two month loan spell in mid-season at Chester City, but injuries suffered there in less than a handful of starts set back his case for inclusion on his return to Prenton Park.
Tranmere Rov (From trainee on 14/7/93) FL 14+12/2 FLC 3 Others 1+2
Chester C (Loaned on 8/12/95) FL 5+2/1

KEOWN Darren Paul
Born: Chertsey, 28 February 1978
Height: 6'1" Weight: 13.0

Left-sided Millwall striker with pace and goalscoring technique. Excellent displays in the club's youth and reserve teams won Darren a substitute appearance in the FA Cup replay at Oxford last January, coming on for Lee McRobert after 80 minutes.
Millwall (From trainee on 17/10/95) FAC 0+1

KEOWN Martin Raymond
Born: Oxford, 24 July 1966
Height: 6'1" Weight: 12.4
International Honours: E: 11; B-1; U21-8; Yth

As Arsenal's leading utility player, who is commanding in the air, a strong tackler, and has fair pace, Martin can be relied upon to fill in at full back, in central defence, and in midfield, if the need be. Used in midfield early in 1995-96, he reverted to his favoured central defensive position when injuries sidelined Tony Adams and Steve Bould, and with new manager, Bruce Rioch, electing to play the three at the back system, he ultimately resumed his old youth team partnership with the former. Probably the most improved player over the season, he was a popular captain in the latter stages of the campaign.
Arsenal (From apprentice on 2/2/84) FL 22 FAC 5
Brighton & Hove A (Loaned on 15/2/85) FL 21+2/1 FLC 2/1 Others 2/1
Aston Villa (£200,000 on 9/6/86) FL 109+3/3 FLC 12+1 FAC 6 Others 2
Everton (£750,000 on 7/8/89) F/PL 92+4 FLC 11 FAC 12+1 Others 6
Arsenal (£2,000,000 on 4/2/93) PL 96+18/1 FLC 11+2/1 FAC 5+2 Others 9+5

Martin Keown

KERNAGHAN Alan Nigel
Born: Otley, 25 April 1967
Height: 6'1" Weight: 13.0
International Honours: NI: Sch. Ei: 22

Well-built Manchester City central defender who can slot in well when called upon for first team duty. After an encouraging end to 1994-95, when he came back to form following an unsettled period, it was hoped

that he would be a strong candidate for City's rearguard last season. Unfortunately, Alan was unable to break into new manager, Alan Ball's team, and, ultimately, only played a handful of games when Keith Curle was absent. Loaned to Bradford in February, in order to keep match fit, he returned a month later, but remained a member of the Republic of Ireland squad, making nine appearances in all.
Middlesbrough (From apprentice on 8/3/85) F/PL 172+40/16 FLC 22+7/1 FAC 7+4/3 Others 14+2/2
Charlton Ath (Loaned on 17/1/91) FL 13
Manchester C (£1,600,000 on 20/9/93) PL 45+7/1 FLC 7 FAC 5/1
Bolton W (Loaned on 18/8/94) FL 9+2
Bradford C (Loaned on 2/2/96) FL 5

KERR David William
Born: Dumfries, 6 September 1974
Height: 5'11" Weight: 11.2

This young full back appeared to have an encouraging future after breaking into Manchester City's first team in 1994-95. However, he failed to capitalise on his previous good form last season, making only one substitute appearance in the Premiership and playing a handful of games in the reserves. This being mainly due to a long lay off through injuries. Also had a period on loan at Mansfield in September and October, where he was given five starts before returning to Maine Road. Hopefully, all that is behind him now and he can start again.
Manchester C (From trainee on 10/9/91) PL 4+2
Mansfield T (Loaned on 22/9/95) FL 4+1 Others 1

KERR Dylan
Born: Valetta, Malta, 14 January 1967
Height: 5'9" Weight: 11.4
Club Honours: Div 2 '94

Upset by a series of nagging injuries, which kept him out of Reading's first team action for most of 1995-96, he had a brief mid-season spell in the side and scored two spectacular goals – both 25-yard free kicks against Sunderland and Norwich, where he curled the ball over a defensive wall and into the corner of the net.
Sheffield Wed (From juniors on 1/9/84)
Leeds U (Free from Arcadia Shepherds on 8/2/89) F/PL 6+7 FLC 2 FAC 1 Others 0+4
Doncaster Rov (Loaned on 22/8/91) FL 7/1
Blackpool (Loaned on 31/12/91) FL 12/1 Others 1
Reading (£75,000 on 15/7/93) FL 84+5/5 FLC 8+1 FAC 2 Others 3+1

KERR John Joseph
Born: Toronto, Canada, 6 March 1965
Height: 5'8" Weight: 11.5
International Honours: USA: 6

Speedy USA international striker. Released by Millwall during the 1995 close season, he made a trip to the States before coming back to trial with Walsall in November, making three substitute appearances in three different competitions, playing against Brighton (AWS) at home, at Bristol Rovers (FL) and at Ipswich (FAC), where he came close to snatching a dramatic late equaliser before departing in early March.
Portsmouth (Signed from Harrow Borough on 17/8/87) FL 2+2 FLC 0+1 Others 1
Peterborough U (Loaned on 11/12/87) FL 10/1 Others 1

Millwall (Signed from Chertsey T, via Washington Stars, Wycombe W and San Sourine, on 26/2/93) FL 21+22/8 FLC 2 Others 1+2
Walsall (Free on 27/11/95) FL 0+1 FAC 0+1 Others 0+1

KERSLAKE David
Born: Stepney, 19 June 1966
Height: 5'9" Weight: 12.3
International Honours: E: U21-1; Yth; Sch

A full back who can also play in midfield, he had a disappointing season for Spurs in 1995-96, making only two starts in the opening games of the season. Thereafter, with tremendous competition for places, he was discarded from first team consideration by Gerry Francis and had little opportunity to demonstrate his skills in crossing the ball, which he does with good accuracy and pace, when running down the line to set up attacking moves.
Queens Park R (From apprentice on 1/6/83) FL 38+20/6 FLC 6+2/4 FAC 2+2 Others 2+2
Swindon T (£110,000 on 24/11/89) FL 133+2/1 FLC 12 FAC 8 Others 10
Leeds U (£500,000 on 11/3/93) PL 8
Tottenham H (£450,000 on 24/9/93) PL 34+3 FLC 5 FAC 1+1

KEWELL Harold (Harry)
Born: Smithfield, Australia, 22 September 1978
Height: 6'0" Weight: 11.10

This 17 year old, from the Australian Academy of Sport, broke into the Leeds' first team picture following the Coca Cola Cup final defeat. Although a left back for the reserves and juniors, he made his debut against Middlesbrough last March in a wide midfield role and kept his place for the next game. Highly rated at the club.
Leeds U (Signed from the Australian Academy of Sport on 23/12/95) PL 2

KEY Lance William
Born: Kettering, 13 May 1968
Height: 6'2" Weight: 14.6

Behind Kevin Pressman and Chris Woods in the pecking order at Sheffield Wednesday in 1995-96, the giant goalkeeper was again loaned out in order to gain experience and keep match fit. Following five games at Lincoln (August), he was at Hartlepool for less than a week in December, being recalled after just one appearance, prior to joining Rochdale early March and staying for the rest of the campaign, his debut at Preston helping them to their first win in 14 games. Was released during the summer.
Sheffield Wed (£10,000 from Histon on 14/4/90) FAC 0+1
Oldham Ath (Loaned on 12/10/93) PL 2
Oxford U (Loaned on 26/1/95) FL 6
Lincoln C (Loaned on 11/8/95) FL 5
Hartlepool U (Loaned on 15/12/95) FL 1
Rochdale (Loaned on 1/3/96) FL 14

KHARINE Dmitri Victorvitch
Born: Moscow, Russia, 16 August 1968
Height: 6'2" Weight: 12.4
International Honours: Russia: 34

Top class international goalkeeper who was injured in Chelsea's third round FA Cup-tie at home to Newcastle last January and was forced to watch from the sidelines as Kevin

Hitchcock stood in impressively for the next 19 matches. Brave, agile, and a good shot stopper, with excellent distribution, he has shared the Russian 'keeping duties with Stanislav Cherchesov of FC Tirol for the past two years and continued with that arrangement during Euro '96.

Chelsea (£200,000 from CSKA Moscow on 22/12/92) PL 102 FLC 8 FAC 12 Others 4

KIDD Ryan Andrew
Born: Radcliffe, 6 October 1971
Height: 6'1" Weight: 13.0
Club Honours: Div 3 '96

Sound Preston central defender or left back, who temporarily lost his place after being sent off at Colchester last October, Ryan continued to develop as a fine player whose progress will no doubt continue to interest the big clubs. A fine tackler and good in the air, he won a third division championship medal following North End's title win.

Port Vale (From trainee on 12/7/90) FL 1 FLC 0+2 Others 0+1
Preston NE (Free on 15/7/92) FL 103+10/4 FLC 5/1 FAC 5 Others 9+1/1

KIELY Dean Laurence
Born: Salford, 10 October 1970
Height: 6'1" Weight: 12.13
International Honours: E: Yth; Sch

Goalkeeper. A serious facial injury last September ended a run of 150 successive senior appearances for York. However, the popular 'keeper returned after a two month absence and proved as reliable as ever, taking over the captaincy for the last three months of the season.

Coventry C (From trainee on 30/10/87)
York C (Signed on 9/3/90) FL 210 FLC 9 FAC 4 Others 16

KILBANE Kevin Daniel
Born: Preston, 1 February 1977
Height: 6'1" Weight: 12.7
International Honours: Ei: U21-2

A left winger with a fine future in the game, Kevin broke into the Preston first team squad last season, having come up through the club's junior ranks as a YTS. With the ability to beat men at pace and whip in dangerous crosses, his good form saw him called up for the Republic of Ireland U21 squad.

Preston NE (From trainee on 6/7/95) FL 7+4/1 Others 1+1

KILCLINE Brian
Born: Nottingham, 7 May 1962
Height: 6'2" Weight: 12.0
Club Honours: FAC '87; Div 1 '93
International Honours: E: U21-2

Recognised as a central defender of proven ability, "Killer" was recruited from Swindon last November to replace the out of form Lee Howarth and bolster a Mansfield defence which was leaking goals at an alarming rate. This he helped to do to good effect, but was unable to turn round the team's fortunes as it coincided with the forwards ability to score goals virtually drying up. Added to the coaching staff in May, Brian missed a few games late in the season due to hamstring problems.

Notts Co (From apprentice on 1/4/80) FL 156+2/9 FLC 16/1 FAC 10/2
Coventry C (£60,000 on 11/6/84) FL 173/28 FLC 16+1/4 FAC 15/3 Others 8
Oldham Ath (£400,000 on 1/8/91) FL 8 FLC 2
Newcastle U (£250,000 on 19/2/92) F/PL 20+12 FLC 3+2 FAC 1+2 Others 5
Swindon T (£90,000 on 20/1/94) P/FL 16+1 FLC 3 Others 4
Mansfield T (Free on 1/12/95) FL 18+1

KILFORD Ian Anthony
Born: Bristol, 6 October 1973
Height: 5'10" Weight: 10.5

Central midfielder with a lovely touch and an eye for an opening, unfortunately, a virus effected his performances for Wigan last season and he was unable to reproduce the form of his first spell at the club. Scored the winner in the home game against Barnet in September.

Nottingham F (From trainee on 3/4/91) FL 0+1
Wigan Ath (Loaned on 23/12/93) FL 7+1/3 FAC 0+1
Wigan Ath (Free on 13/7/94) FL 53+7/8 FLC 4 FAC 3+1/1 Others 5/1

KIMBLE Alan Frank
Born: Dagenham, 6 August 1966
Height: 5'8" Weight: 12.4
Club Honours: Div 3 '91

A solid left back who is as reliable in defensive situations as he is dangerous in set piece scenarios, 1995-96 was the first injury free season at Wimbledon for the former Cambridge man, and with the freedom to hold his place he featured in most games, proving to be a mainstay of the defence. And, with his solid shooting and free kick technique, it should not be too long before his name is on the scoresheet as well as being associated with defensive excellence. Alan's twin brother, Gary, played for a number of teams between 1984-1992, after the pair had started out together at Charlton.

Charlton Ath (From juniors on 8/8/84) FL 6
Exeter C (Loaned on 23/8/85) FL 1 FLC 6
Cambridge U (Free on 22/8/86) FL 295+4/24 FLC 23+1 FAC 29/1 Others 22
Wimbledon (£175,000 on 27/7/93) PL 71 FLC 6 FAC 11

KING Nathan Paul
Born: Birmingham, 1 August 1975
Height: 6'0" Weight: 12.6

Made an assured debut in Shrewsbury's midfield at Derby County in the Coca Cola Cup 1-1 draw last October, having impressed in reserve team football. Following that, he spent some time on loan at non-league Stafford Rangers prior to being surprisingly released during the summer.

Shrewsbury T (From trainee on 4/7/94) FLC 1

KING Philip (Phil) Geoffrey
Born: Bristol, 28 December 1967
Height: 5'8" Weight: 12.7
Club Honours: FLC '91
International Honours: E: B-1

As a left back his chances of first team action with Aston Villa in 1995-96 were slim, with Alan Wright and Steve Staunton also available. With that in mind, it was felt a loan spell with neighbours, West Bromwich, who had just lost Paul Agnew

and Paul Edwards through injury, would be in his best interests. Sadly, a permanent move was torpedoed by a cruciate ligament injury in November that put him out of action until at least the start of the coming season, when he will have to start again. Seen to best effect on the overlap, Phil delivers quality passes and crosses from a superb left foot.

Exeter C (From apprentice on 7/1/85) FL 24+3 FLC 1 Others 1+2
Torquay U (£3,000 on 14/7/86) FL 24/3 FLC 2 FAC 1 Others 2
Swindon T (£155,000 on 6/2/87) FL 112+4/4 FLC 11 FAC 5 Others 13
Sheffield Wed (£400,000 on 30/11/89) F/PL 124+5/2 FLC 17 FAC 9 Others 4
Notts Co (Loaned on 22/10/93) FL 6 Others 2
Aston Villa (£250,000 on 1/8/94) PL 13+3 FLC 3 Others 4
West Bromwich A (Loaned on 30/10/95) FL 4 Others 1

Georgiou Kinkladze

KINKLADZE Georgiou
Born: Tbilisi, Georgia, 6 November 1973
Height: 5'8" Weight: 10.9
International Honours: Georgia: 15

Signed by Manchester City from Dinamo Tbilisi in time for the start of last season, the unknown Georgian international midfielder took the Premiership by storm, displaying artistry, vision, control and confidence, to create goalscoring openings for himself and his team mates. Settling down well, Georgiou propped the team up many times throughout 1995-96 as they continued to struggle, scoring his first goal for City in November against Aston Villa. His next, versus Southampton in March, was perfectly executed. Taking on the defence, he drifted past four defenders, committed Dave Beasant, before casually slipping the ball over him into the net. An outstanding talent, he was a challenger to Eric Cantona and Ruud Gullit for the sportswriters' "Footballer of the Year" award.

Manchester C (£2,000,000 from Dinamo Tbilisi on 17/8/95) PL 37/4 FLC 3 FAC 4/1

KINNAIRD Paul
Born: Glasgow, 11 November 1966
Height: 5'8" Weight: 10.10
International Honours: S: Yth

Widely travelled left winger who joined Scarborough on loan from Dunfermline last October. Unfortunately, having impressed on his debut at Bury, when sending over a steady stream of excellent crosses, he picked up a groin injury soon after and was forced to return home.

Norwich C (From apprentice on 13/11/84)
Dundee U (Free on 29/11/85) SL 12+6 SC 3 Others 1+2
Motherwell (Signed on 2/3/88) SL 34 SLC 1 SC 1
St Mirren (Signed on 24/2/89) SL 43+14/4 SLC 2+1/1 SC 2/1
Partick Thistle (Signed on 11/1/92) SL 27+6/3 SLC 0+2/1 SC 1
Shrewsbury T (Free on 9/2/93) FL 4/1
St Johnstone (Free on 1/3/93) SL 2+6
Partick Thistle (Loaned on 2/7/93) SL 2+1 SLC 0+3
Dunfermline (Signed on 27/7/95) SL 6+2 SLC 1 Others 3
Scarborough (Free on 20/10/95) FL 3 FAC 1

KINSELLA Mark Anthony
Born: Dublin, 12 August 1972
Height: 5'9" Weight: 11.8
Club Honours: GMVC '92; FAT '92
International Honours: Ei: U21-8; Yth

Central midfield star of the Colchester team and an Irish U21 cap, Mark enjoyed a superb 1995-96 season in the U's engine room, as well as covering at sweeper on occasion. He also weighed in with some spectacular goals, including one after 15 seconds at Torquay. Voted the U's "Player of the Season", the Irishman is surely destined to play at a higher level in the not-too-distant future.

Colchester U (Free from Home Farm on 18/8/89) FL 167+6/25 FLC 8/2 FAC 11/1 Others 9+1/5

KIRBY Ryan Mark
Born: Chingford, 6 September 1974
Height: 5'11" Weight: 12.0

This young Doncaster full back enjoyed a mixed season during 1995-96, when he played a number of league games in midfield – a position where he is plainly unsuited. A return to purely defensive duties, where he had earlier impressed with his sureness of tackle, should see this youngster in a better light at another club, following a free transfer during the summer.

Arsenal (From trainee on 6/7/93)
Doncaster Rov (Free on 6/7/94) FL 73+5 FLC 0+1 FAC 2 Others 5

KITE Philip (Phil) David
Born: Bristol, 26 October 1962
Height: 6'1" Weight: 14.7
International Honours: E: Yth; Sch

Goalkeeper. Despite being given a free transfer at the end of the 1994-95 campaign, Phil remained at Bristol City last term and

proved to be very effective cover for the injured Keith Welch, before he too suffered injury. Almost single handedly kept Newcastle at bay during the first half of the Coca Cola Cup match at St James Park in early October, but in the end, was unable to prevent a 3-1 defeat (8-1 on aggregate). Released during the summer.

Bristol Rov (From apprentice on 31/10/80) FL 96 FLC 12 FAC 8 Others 2
Southampton (£50,000 on 16/8/84) FL 4 Others 1
Middlesbrough (Loaned on 27/3/86) FL 2
Gillingham (Free on 7/2/87) FL 70 FLC 5 FAC 4 Others 1
Bournemouth (£55,000 on 16/8/89) FL 7 FLC 1
Sheffield U (£25,000 on 10/8/90) FL 11 FLC 5 FAC 1 Others 1
Mansfield T (Loaned on 21/11/91) FL 11 Others 1
Plymouth Arg (Loaned on 9/9/92) FL 2
Rotherham U (Loaned on 24/10/92) FL 1
Crewe Alex (Loaned on 27/11/92) FL 5 FAC 1 Others 2
Stockport Co (Loaned on 25/3/93) FL 5
Cardiff C (Free on 1/7/93) FL 17+1 FLC 2 FAC 0+1 Others 2
Bristol C (Free on 11/8/94) FL 5+1 FLC 2

KITSON Paul
Born: Peterlee, 9 January 1971
Height: 5'11" Weight: 10.12
International Honours: E: U21-7

Paul is a striker who likes to play off a target man and although good in the air, prefers the ball to be fed to his feet to allow him to use his skill and pace to beat defenders. Beginning last season at Newcastle carrying an injury from the previous year, which was eventually diagnosed as a double hernia, he underwent surgery in October and was out of action for two months, thus hampering his challenge for a first team place. Hopefully back on song for the coming campaign, despite the disappointment of 1995-96, he still managed two goals in seven Premiership appearances, five of them from the bench.

Leicester C (From trainee on 15/12/88) FL 39+11/6 FLC 5/3 FAC 1+1/1 Others 5/1
Derby Co (£1,300,000 on 11/3/92) FL 105/36 FLC 7/3 FAC 5/1 Others 13+1/9
Newcastle U (£2,250,000 on 24/9/94) PL 26+7/10 FLC 3/1 FAC 6+1/3

Mark Kinsella

KIWOMYA Andrew (Andy) Derek
Born: Huddersfield, 1 October 1967
Height: 5'9" Weight: 10.10
International Honours: E: Yth
The brother of Arsenal's Chris, he signed for Bradford during the 1995 close season, having previously played for Scunthorpe. Consigned to the bench for the majority of the campaign, his first full appearance eventually arrived towards the end of March when he stepped into the side on the right wing. Very fast and tricky, and an excellent crosser, a run of seven games ended in injury before he came back for the final two play-off fixtures and the chance of a regular spot in the first division this coming season.
Barnsley (From apprentice on 16/7/85) FL 1
Sheffield Wed (£5,000 on 7/10/86)
Dundee (Free in 1992-93) SL 11+10/1 SC 0+1
Rotherham U (Free on 1/10/93) FL 4+3 FLC 0+1 Others 0+2 (Free to Halifax during 1994 close season)
Scunthorpe U (Free on 23/3/93) FL 9/3
Bradford C (Free on 4/7/95) FL 7+9/2 FLC 0+2 Others 2+1

Andy Kiwomya

KNIGHT Alan Edward
Born: Balham, 3 July 1961
Height: 6'1" Weight: 13.1
Club Honours: Div 3 '83
International Honours: E: U21-2; Yth
The experienced Portsmouth goalkeeper mysteriously started 1995-96 as the club's number two to Mart Poom, having been "Player of the Year" the previous season. Quickly regaining his place though, he produced a number of good performances in passing Peter Bonetti's league record of goalkeeping appearances for one club (Chelsea). Still an excellent shot stopper, at the end of the campaign, Alan had played 725 first team games for Pompey, although still 145 league appearances short of breaking Jimmy Dickinson's club record.
Portsmouth (From apprentice on 12/3/79) FL 620 FLC 49 FAC 35 Others 21

KNIGHT Jason George
Born: Australia, 16 September 1974
Height: 6'1" Weight: 12.9
Signed from non-league football during the

first few weeks of last season, this midfield player had his contract paid up on the turn of the year, having failed to impress in four league appearances at Doncaster.
Doncaster Rov (Free from Hinckley Ath on 23/8/95) FL 1+3

KNILL Alan Richard
Born: Slough, 8 October 1964
Height: 6'0" Weight: 13.0
Club Honours: WC '89
International Honours: W: 1; Yth
Tall Scunthorpe central defender who is dominant in the air and not unnaturally gets his fair share of goals from set pieces. Missed the middle part of the 1995-96 campaign due to hamstring trouble, but came back to play as well as ever.
Southampton (From apprentice on 14/10/82)
Halifax T (Free on 13/7/84) FL 118/6 FLC 6 FAC 6 Others 6
Swansea C (£15,000 on 14/8/87) FL 89/3 FLC 4 FAC 5 Others 7
Bury (£95,000 on 18/8/89) FL 141+3/8 FLC 7 FAC 8/1 Others 14+1/1
Cardiff C (Loaned on 24/9/93) FL 4
Scunthorpe U (Signed on 5/11/93) FL 102/8 FLC 3 FAC 9 Others 6

KNOWLES Darren Thomas
Born: Sheffield, 8 October 1970
Height: 5'6" Weight: 10.6
Remarkably consistent full back who appeared in every match for Scarborough last season, becoming only the tenth player to reach 100 league appearances for the club. Cool under pressure, and accurate with his distribution, Darren is sure to be one of Boro's key players once again in 1996-97. Was voted the supporters' "Away Player of the Year" last season.
Sheffield U (From trainee on 1/7/89)
Stockport Co (£3,000 on 14/9/89) FL 51+12 FLC 2+4 Others 14+1
Scarborough (Free on 4/8/93) FL 127/2 FLC 8 FAC 8 Others 6

KOVACEVIC Darko
Born: Yugoslavia, 18 November 1973
Height: 6'1" Weight: 12.0
International Honours: Yugoslavia: 9
A tall, slim 22-year-old striker signed from Red Star Belgrade, along with Dejan Steranovic halfway through last season, Darko did not have too many chances to impress at Sheffield Wednesday, David Pleat insisting that both Yugoslavs had been bought with a view to the future. In the few games he played, or came on as a substitute, however, he showed that he needed to be more aware of the extra speed of English football, something that can only come with experience. Another player who the crowd have taken to, perhaps this season they will see his true worth to the side. *Stop Press:* Reported to be on his way to Real Sociedad, a £2.5m fee changing hands.
Sheffield Wed (£2,000,000 from Red Star Belgrade on 22/12/95) PL 8+8/4 FAC 1

KUBICKI Dariusz
Born: Warsaw, Poland, 6 June 1963
Height: 5'10" Weight: 11.7
Club Honours: Div 1 '96
International Honours: Poland: 49

1995-96 was another solid season for Sunderland's Polish international right back, who recorded his second successive ever-present statistic. Having tasted cup success back in his homeland, Dariusz was able to add a first division championship medal to his collection, and was also honoured by his fellow professionals by being selected for the PFA XI. Particularly impressive on the overlap, Roker fans are still willing him to score his first goal for the club.
Aston Villa (£200,000 from Legia Warsaw on 28/8/91) F/PL 24+1 FLC 3 FAC 4+1 Others 1
Sunderland (£100,000 on 4/3/94) FL 107 FLC 6 FAC 5

KUHL Martin
Born: Frimley, 10 January 1965
Height: 5'11" Weight: 11.13
After a difficult first campaign with Bristol City, Martin settled last season when, for the first time in his career, he achieved the feat of appearing in every first team game. A defensive midfielder with two good feet, he also possesses a fine shot and the occasional strike has demonstrated what he is capable of. Was voted City's "Player of the Year" by both the supporters club and the junior Reds.
Birmingham C (From apprentice on 13/1/83) FL 103+8/5 FLC 13 FAC 8/1 Others 1+1/1
Sheffield U (Signed on 20/3/87) FL 38/4 FLC 2 FAC 1 Others 1
Watford (Signed on 19/2/88) FL 4
Portsmouth (£125,000 on 30/9/88) FL 146+11/27 FLC 11/1 FAC 13 Others 3
Derby Co (£650,000 on 26/9/92) FL 68/1 FLC 6 FAC 6 Others 4/1
Notts Co (Loaned on 9/9/94) FL 2
Bristol C (£330,000 on 30/12/94) FL 63+1/6 FLC 4 FAC 4 Others 3

KULKOV Vassili
Born: Moscow, Russia, 11 June 1966
Height: 5'10" Weight: 11.7
International Honours: Russia: 41
Joined Millwall last January as part of the package that brought both himself and his great friend, Serguei Iouran, to the Den from Moscow Spartak on a short-term contract. Proved he could play with equal finesse in both defence and midfield, showing good ball control and fine passing skills. As in the case of his compatriot, Vassili looked a class above, although a knee injury kept him out of important games and curtailed his season.
Millwall (Loaned from Spartak Moscow on 11/1/96) FL 6

KYD Michael Robert
Born: Hackney, 21 May 1977
Height: 5'8" Weight: 12.10
Cambridge United forward, and still only 19, Michael broke into the first team in March 1995. Unfortunately, appearances were limited in 1995-96, due to a cartilage operation, but age is on his side and he is sure to feature in the coming season. Spent the summer playing in Australia in a bid to attain match fitness, having earlier had a spell on loan at non-league Bishops Stortford.
Cambridge U (From trainee on 18/5/95) FL 13+15/2 FLC 1+1 FAC 0+1 Others 1+1

A WARM WELCOME

TO FOOTBALL FOOTBALL™

L O N D O N

a unique footballing experience

FOOTBALL FOOTBALL ™ is an exciting new restaurant situated in the heart of Central London, close to Piccadilly Circus tube station. The aim of the restaurant is to provide a total and dynamic football experience. In addition to the internationally themed food, service and futuristic interior design, the restaurant also features a myriad of special effects. Imagine emerging from a continental style tunnel, accompanied by the sound of studs on concrete, to be welcomed by the roar of a packed stadium!

The state of the art audio visual system provides thrilling entertainment with clips from memorable matches and magical moments.

On display is one of the world's largest collections of football memorabilia, including personal mementos of the great heroes and their cup winning medals.

"Football Football"™ is open from 12 noon 7 days a week and provides a unique entertainment facility - including live football matches on two video walls and 14 TV monitors.

For football fans everywhere, "Football Football"™ is the restaurant to be seen at, with star players such as George Best, Jamie Redknapp, Chris Armstrong, Richard Gough, all being regular visitors.

BOOKINGS AND INFORMATION,
CONTACT THE RESTAURANT ON:

TEL: 0171 930 9970

FOOTBALL FOOTBALL™
57-60 HAYMARKET
LONDON
SW1Y 4QX

FOOTBALL FOOTBALL ™
supports the Bobby Moore Fund
for Imperial Cancer Research

LAIGHT Ellis Stanley
Born: Birmingham, 30 June 1976
Height: 5'10" Weight: 11.2
Striker. Having signed professional forms for Torquay during the summer of 1995, although Ellis began 1995-96 in the first team, his appearances from the bench eventually outweighed his starts. Released during the summer, he would have undoubtedly fared better in a non-struggling side.
Torquay U (From trainee on 4/7/95) FL 12+19/2 FLC 0+2 FAC 1+1 Others 0+4/1

LAKIN Barry
Born: Dartford, 19 September 1973
Height: 5'9" Weight: 12.6
A promising young Leyton Orient midfielder who unfortunately missed most of 1995-96 through injury, prior to being released during the summer. At his best when going forward from wide positions to cross the ball, or when lining up a long-range effort, he needs an injury-free season to show his true value.
Leyton Orient (From trainee on 6/7/92) FL 41+13/2 FLC 4 FAC 2+2/1 Others 3+1

LAMBERT Christopher **James** (Jimmy)
Born: Henley, 14 September 1973
Height: 5'7" Weight: 10.4
Never quite sure of a place in Reading's starting line-up in 1995-96, Jimmy faded from the picture almost completely after February, giving only glimpses of his undoubted subtlety and flair. However, he continued to score tremendous individual goals and earned an appearance as substitute for the Football League XI which drew 1-1 with the Italian Serie "B" side at Huddersfield in November.
Reading (From juniors on 3/7/92) FL 23+36/8 FLC 2+3/1 FAC 4+2 Others 2+3/1

LAMPARD Frank James
Born: Romford, 21 June 1978
Height: 5'10" Weight: 12.4
International Honours: E: Yth
The son of a former West Ham legend, Frank (junior), made his Premiership debut while still a trainee, when coming on as a sub against Coventry last January. He also came off the bench in the final game of the season at home to Sheffield Wednesday. Earlier, he had been on loan at Swansea, where he had impressed the locals as a strong, attacking midfielder with plenty of workrate and skill, even scoring in the club's first away win in 1995-96. Obviously a player with a future, on the junior front he skippered the Hammers' side that won the championship and reached the FA Youth Cup final.
West Ham U (Trainee) PL 0+2
Swansea C (Loaned on 6/10/95) FL 8+1/1 Others 1+1

LAMPKIN Kevin
Born: Liverpool, 20 December 1972
Height: 5'10" Weight: 12.0
This talented Mansfield Town midfielder played just one match early in 1995-96, before suffering a cruciate ligament injury. Sadly, it proved to be difficult to mend and after missing most of the season he only returned for the last few games, prior to being released during the summer. A ball winner and strong tackler.
Liverpool (From trainee on 17/5/91)
Huddersfield T (Free on 1/7/92) FL 13 FLC 1
Mansfield T (Free on 18/2/94) FL 35+7/3 FLC 0+1 FAC 1 Others 1+1

LAMPTEY Nii Odartey
Born: Accra, Ghana, 10 December 1974
Height: 5'6" Weight: 10.7
International Honours: Ghana: 21
Skilful, wide Coventry striker signed from Anderlecht early in 1995-96, after spending a period the previous season with Aston Villa. The Ghanaian had very few opportunities in the first team, but scored on his debut against Hull City in the Coca Cola Cup and again in the second leg. When he did play he showed a lot of skill and speed and always went for goal, giving an excellent performance at Anfield and coming close to winning the game for City. Although his future is uncertain, as he played insufficient games to qualify for a work permit, Nii was a member of the Ghanaian squad that played in the African Nations Cup, but was sent off in the semi final.
Aston Villa (Loaned from Anderlecht on 3/8/94) PL 1+5 FLC 2+1/3
Coventry C (Signed on 25/8/95) PL 3+3 FLC 3+1/2 FAC 0+1

Nii Lamptey

LANCASHIRE Graham
Born: Blackpool, 19 October 1972
Height: 5'10" Weight: 11.12
Club Honours: Div 4 '92

A poacher of goals with a great deal of speed, Graham finally broke his duck at Preston in last September's game against Cambridge. However, unable to hold down a regular place, he was loaned to Wigan in January and scored three goals during a four-match spell. A permanent move followed in March, but the unfortunate striker was ruled out for the rest of the season with damaged knee ligaments after 40 minutes of his full debut.
Burnley (From trainee on 1/7/91) FL 11+20/8 FLC 1+1 FAC 2+2/1 Others 2+4
Halifax T (Loaned on 20/11/92) FL 2 Others 1+1
Chester C (Loaned on 21/1/94) FL 10+1/7
Preston NE (£55,000 on 23/12/94) FL 11+12/2 Others 1+1
Wigan Ath (Loaned on 12/1/96) FL 4/3
Wigan Ath (£35,000 on 8/3/96) FL 1

LANCASTER David
Born: Preston, 8 September 1961
Height: 6'3" Weight: 14.0
An experienced Bury centre forward, David made just one full appearance in 1995-96, at home to Scarborough. Eventually regarded as the sixth choice striker at Gigg Lane, he was allowed to return to his former club, Rochdale, in March on loan, where his renewed partnership with Steve Whitehall helped Dale out of a drought in which they had scored just five times in 11 games.
Blackpool (Free from Colne Dynamoes on 15/8/90) FL 7+1/1 FLC 2 Others 0+1
Chesterfield (Loaned on 26/2/91) FL 12/4
Chesterfield (£70,000 on 27/8/91) FL 66+3/16 FLC 5/3 FAC 2 Others 6/3
Rochdale (£7,500 on 5/7/93) FL 37+3/14 FLC 4/1 FAC 2 Others 1 (Free to Halifax T on 20/7/94)
Bury (Free on 12/3/95) FL 4+6/1 FLC 0+1 Others 0+1
Rochdale (Loaned on 19/2/96) FL 13+1/2

David Lancaster

LANDON Richard John
Born: Worthing, 22 March 1970
Height: 6'3" Weight: 13.5

Centre forward. A pre-season injury in 1995-96 spoiled Richard's bid to establish himself at Stockport after his summer-time move from Plymouth. Constantly troubled by injury and fitness problems, he only made a handful of first team appearances, creditably scoring four goals.

Plymouth Arg (£30,000 from Bedworth U on 26/1/94) FL 21+9/12 FLC 0+1 FAC 0+1 Others 4
Stockport Co (£50,000 on 13/7/95) FL 7+4/4 FLC 0+1

LANGE Anthony (Tony) Stephen
Born: West Ham, 10 December 1964
Height: 6'1" Weight: 12.9

Joining Fulham on a free from WBA last August, the experienced goalkeeper played in 52 out of the Cottagers' 59 matches. A very confident 'keeper, Tony's best game was undoubtedly at champions elect, Preston, where, at times, he kept their forwards at bay almost single-handedly to preserve a point in a 1-1 draw.

Charlton Ath (From apprentice on 15/12/82) FL 12 Others 1
Aldershot (Loaned on 22/8/85) FL 7
Aldershot (Free on 7/7/86) FL 125 FLC 5 FAC 10 Others 16
Wolverhampton W (£150,000 on 13/7/89) FL 8 FLC 2
Aldershot (Loaned on 23/11/90) FL 2 Others 1
Torquay U (Loaned on 12/9/91) FL 1
West Bromwich A (Free on 12/8/92) FL 45+3 FLC 3 FAC 1 Others 7
Fulham (Free on 27/7/95) FL 41 FLC 4 FAC 5 Others 2

LAPPER Michael (Mike) Steven
Born: California, USA, 28 August 1970
Height: 6'0" Weight: 12.2
International Honours: USA: 59

Signed from American soccer during the summer of 1995, Southend fans really took to Mike and the decision to replace the departed Andy Edwards with him at centre half, was a masterstroke by manager, Ronnie Whelan. An American international, he began 1995-96 with a little apprehension, but by Christmas had blossomed into a powerful ball winner with excellent distribution skills. Unfortunately, his season was all but ended by a freak accident at Carrow Road, when he broke his leg in two places. Came back for the final two games and was greeted by the fans as a hero, with much expected of him in the future.

Southend U (£150,000 from USSF on 11/8/95) FL 23+1 FLC 2 Others 4

LAUNDERS Brian Terence
Born: Dublin, 8 January 1976
Height: 5'10" Weight: 11.12
International Honours: Ei: U21-9; Yth

1995-96 was a disappointing season for the Irish U21 forward, who, despite adding to his international appearances, made only three substitutions at club level for Crystal Palace and scored only twice for the reserve side. Obviously not in contention for places at Palace, he was loaned out to Oldham in March, but after failing to make the first

team and returning to Selhurst Park, he was released.

Crystal Palace (Signed on 2/9/93) P/FL 1+3 FLC 0+2

LAVIN Gerard
Born: Corby, 5 February 1974
Height: 5'8" Weight: 10.8
International Honours: S: U21-7

A regular at right back for Watford at the start of last season, missing just three games from a possible 21, Gerard transferred to Millwall in November, going straight into a team that was sitting on top of the first division. Tenacious in the tackle, and able to get forward with ease, but for a couple of injuries, he would have maintained his place throughout the campaign.

Watford (From trainee on 11/5/92) FL 121+5/3 FLC 11/1 FAC 6 Others 2+1
Millwall (£500,000 on 23/11/95) FL 18+2 FAC 1

LAW Brian John
Born: Merthyr Tydfil, 1 January 1970
Height: 6'2" Weight: 15.0
International Honours: W: 1; U21-2; Yth; Sch

Wolves' central defender. With a cloud hanging over him, he faced a possible gaol sentence (ultimately averted) for a well publicised offence away from football, caretaker manager, Bobby Downes, brought him in for the Coventry Coca Cola Cup-tie last November and he looked impressive against the Premier League team. Sent off in the FA Cup win over Birmingham, when he handled to concede a penalty, with several players doing well in that position his chances were limited. Strong in the air as you would expect from someone of his height, he is also capable of hitting the front men with long passes. Unfortunate to finish the season on the sidelines again, the latest injury was not related to the one that nearly finished his career.

Queens Park R (From trainee on 15/8/87) FL 19+1 FLC 2+1 FAC 3 Others 1
Wolverhampton W (£134,000 on 23/12/94) FL 22+2/1 FLC 1+1 FAC 7

LAW Nicholas (Nicky)
Born: Greenwich, 8 September 1961
Height: 6'0" Weight: 13.5
International Honours: E: Sch

Chesterfield's club captain sometimes seemed hard pressed by the better class of forward found in division two last season, but this was more due to his willingness to play through injury than to any short-comings on his part. Again, his inspirational qualities were as important as his solid defending and cool reading of a game. There is no doubt that if he can regain full fitness during the summer, he will continue to be an important part in the centre of the Spireities' defence in 1996-97. Possesses a dangerous long throw.

Arsenal (From apprentice on 17/7/79)
Barnsley (Free on 4/8/81) FL 113+1/1 FLC 5 FAC 6
Blackpool (Free on 28/8/85) FL 64+2/1 FLC 2 FAC 2 Others 3
Plymouth Arg (£40,000 on 12/3/87) FL 37+1/5 FLC 2 FAC 2 Others 0+1

Notts Co (£70,000 on 17/6/88) FL 44+3/4 FLC 4 FAC 1 Others 4
Scarborough (Loaned on 10/11/89) FL 12 FLC 1
Rotherham U (£35,000 on 1/8/90) FL 126+2/4 FLC 12/1 FAC 12 Others 7
Chesterfield (Signed on 8/10/93) FL 104/10 FLC 3 FAC 3 Others 10/3

LAWFORD Craig Brian
Born: Dewsbury, 25 November 1972
Height: 5'10" Weight: 11.0

One of Hull City's band of ex-Bradford players, Craig earned an extensive run at left back last season, due to the absence of the injured Jimmy Graham, only to be thwarted by an ankle injury. Versatile down the left-hand side – a useful attribute in a small squad – he was even pressed into action in central midfield on occasions. However, he struggled to recapture the form he enjoyed when first coming to Boothferry Park and was released during the summer.

Bradford C (From trainee on 2/7/91) FL 13+7/1 FLC 3 FAC 1+1 Others 1+1
Hull C (Free on 5/8/94) FL 45+17/3 FLC 5+1 FAC 1+1 Others 5/1

LAWRENCE James (Jamie) Hubert
Born: Balham, 8 March 1970
Height: 6'0" Weight:12.6

Tricky, right-footed winger. Only appeared intermittently for Leicester during the first half of last season, though his run set up Steve Corica's goal in the seasonal opener at Sunderland. However, he won a regular squad place after Martin O'Neill took charge, showing to good effect when laying on Emile Heskey's winner in the victory at Molineux during February.

Sunderland (Signed from Cowes on 15/10/93) FL 2+2 FLC 0+1
Doncaster Rov (£20,000 on 17/3/94) FL 16+9/3 FLC 2 FAC 1 Others 3
Leicester C (£125,000 on 6/1/95) P/FL 19+13/1

LAWRENCE Matthew James
Born: Northampton, 19 June 1974
Height: 6'1" Weight: 12.12

Young Wycombe striker, who was initially signed as a right-sided midfielder from Grays Athletic last January. Made his Football League debut at Crewe, but on the morning of the next match he picked up a freak training injury, cutting his knee badly on a stone. After suffering more bad luck, Matthew finally returned to first team action in April and should have a bigger part to play next season.

Wycombe W (£20,000 from Grays Ath on 19/1/96) FL 1+2

LAWS Brian
Born: Wallsend, 14 October 1961
Height: 5'10" Weight: 11.5
Club Honours: Div 3 '82; FLC '89, '90; FMC '89
International Honours: E: B-1

Just when most people felt that the Grimsby manager would be running the playing side of his career down, he actually made the right back position his own in 1995-96, until sidelined by injury. In doing so, he continued to show that he could still pass both short and long and, in getting forward, he established a most effective link with

Gary Childs down the flank. Still the subject of an FA action for his part in the Ivano Bonetti affair, it remains to be seen whether his managerial prospects will suffer interminably.

Burnley (From apprentice on 19/10/79) FL 125/12 FLC 14/2 FAC 15/1 Others 3
Huddersfield T (£10,000 on 26/8/83) FL 56/1 FLC 7 FAC 3
Middlesbrough (£30,000 on 15/3/85) FL 103+5/12 FLC 6+1/2 FAC 8+1 Others 6+1
Nottingham F (£120,000 on 7/7/88) F/PL 136+11/4 FLC 28+4 FAC 16+2/1 Others 11+1
Grimsby T (Free on 1/12/94) FL 27+16/2 FLC 2 FAC 4/1

LAWTON Craig Thomas
Born: Mancot, 5 January 1972
Height: 5'8" Weight: 10.3
International Honours: W: B-1; U21-1; Yth; Sch

Having broken a leg the previous March, following his recovery, the little midfielder spent the majority of 1995-96 in Port Vale's reserves. However, he did make his full debut for the club in a preliminary round of the Anglo-Italian Cup against Genoa and was called up for two league games against Luton and Charlton near the end of the season. A strong tackler, who can pass and move well, Craig was surprisingly released during the summer.

Manchester U (From trainee on 1/7/90)
Port Vale (Free on 2/8/94) FL 2+1 Others 1+1

LAZARIDIS Stanley (Stan)
Born: Perth, Australia, 16 August 1972
Height: 5'9" Weight: 11.12
International Honours: Australia: 9

Brought over from Australia to play for West Ham last September, the flying left winger made his debut against Chelsea just three days later. However, finding the pace of the Premiership difficult to adjust to he had a spell in the reserves before being recalled for the FA Cup-tie against Grimsby the following February. Unfortunately, when coming off the bench for Robbie Slater, he himself had to be replaced after breaking an ankle and was sidelined for the rest of the season. Must hope for better fortune this time round.

West Ham U (£300,000 from West Adelaide on 8/9/95) PL 2+2 FLC 1 FAC 0+1

LEABURN Carl Winston
Born: Lewisham, 30 March 1969
Height: 6'3" Weight: 13.0

Charlton striker who is good in the air, especially at corners and set pieces. Although not an out-and-out goalscorer, Carl has the ability to hold up the ball for others, his overall play invaluable to the well-being of the team. Opened his account last season in his first game, when coming off the bench to score the winner against Watford, and later collected his first ever hat trick in the 5-1 away win at Ipswich. Also possesses a very long throw.

Charlton Ath (From apprentice on 22/4/87) FL 123+41/42 FLC 15/4 FAC 16+2/3 Others 9+5/4
Northampton T (Loaned on 22/3/90) FL 9

LEADBITTER Christopher (Chris) Jonathan
Born: Middlesbrough, 17 October 1967
Height: 5'9" Weight: 10.6
Club Honours: Div 3 '91

After moving from Bournemouth during the 1995 close season, Chris brought versatility to Plymouth's cause when playing mainly on the left side of midfield. A sound tackler, he also came into the team at left back.

Grimsby T (From apprentice on 4/9/85)
Hereford U (Free on 21/8/86) FL 32+4/1 FLC 2 FAC 2 Others 3
Cambridge U (Free on 2/8/88) FL 144+32/18 FLC 12/3 FAC 16+2/3 Others 11+2/1
Bournemouth (£25,000 on 16/8/93) FL 45+9/3 FLC 6+1 FAC 5 Others 2
Plymouth Arg (Free on 27/7/95) FL 29+4/1 FAC 3/1 Others 4+1/1

LEANING Andrew (Andy) John
Born: Howden, 18 May 1963
Height: 6'0" Weight: 14.7

Experienced Lincoln goalkeeper who spent much of last season as second choice. Initially kept out by on loan Lance Key, after a short spell back in the first team he was dropped in favour of new signing, Barry Richardson, making just 13 appearances.

York C (Free from Rowntree Mackintosh on 1/7/85) FL 69 FLC 4 FAC 8 Others 5
Sheffield U (Free on 28/5/87) FL 21 FLC 2 FAC 2
Bristol C (£12,000 on 27/9/88) FL 75 FLC 5 FAC 7 Others 2
Lincoln C (Free on 24/3/94) FL 36 FLC 6 FAC 3 Others 6

LE BIHAN Neil Ernest
Born: Croydon, 14 March 1976
Height: 5'11" Weight: 12.13

Although never a regular for Peterborough, starting 23 times, the young midfielder continued to improve in 1995-96, his passing and control the leading components of his game. Also scored three goals, a 20-yard free kick that effectively won the Coca Cola Cup-tie against Swansea, being his first for Posh.

Peterborough U (Free from Tottenham H juniors on 13/7/94) FL 19+10 FLC 2+1/1 FAC 2+1/2 Others 3+1

LEE Christian
Born: Aylesbury, 8 October 1976
Height: 6'2" Weight: 11.7

Leggy Northampton Town striker. Signed on a free transfer from Doncaster during the summer of 1995, he had limited chances last season, but is one of the players that manager, Ian Atkins, has in mind for the future.

Northampton T (Free from Doncaster Rov YTS on 13/7/95) FL 1+4 FAC 1+1 Others 2

LEE Christopher (Chris)
Born: Halifax, 18 June 1971
Height: 5'10" Weight: 11.10

A veritable pros' pro, the son of the club coach (Jeff Lee) worked tirelessly and unselfishly for his Hull team mates in 1995-96, but after missing only two of City's 51 game 1994-95 campaign, he was hampered by injury, especially calf and groin strains and released during the summer. Often battled away in central midfield a little too much, epitomised by his sending off at

Bradford, while continuing to provide an aerial threat at set piece situations.

Bradford C (From trainee on 1/7/89)
Rochdale (Free on 14/6/90) FL 24+2/2 FLC 4/1 FAC 2 Others 3
Scarborough (Free on 14/3/91) FL 75+3/3 FLC 11/2 FAC 2 Others 4
Hull C (Free on 30/7/93) FL 104+12/5 FLC 4/1 FAC 3+1 Others 5

LEE David John
Born: Kingswood, 26 November 1969
Height: 6'3" Weight: 13.12
Club Honours: Div 2 '89
International Honours: E: U21-10; Yth

Long serving David has just enjoyed his most successful season for Chelsea after coming in against Sheffield Wednesday last November and playing in the last 36 matches. Recalled by Glenn Hoddle to play as the sweeper when Ruud Gullit was out injured, so effective was the big man that he kept his place and Gullit moved to midfield! Comfortable on the ball, with great awareness, the role suited him admirably. It also allowed him to use his dribbling skills and he was hitting 30-yard Gullit-like passes to fast-raiding full backs, Dan Petrescu and Terry Phelan, which gave an extra dimension to the club's attacking play. After being used as a utility player in either midfield, or as a conventional centre back in the past two years, David Lee's re-emergence as sweeper is great news for Chelsea – and maybe England, if he follows former boss, Hoddle, into the international set up.

Chelsea (From trainee on 1/7/88) F/PL 117+32/10 FLC 12+5/1 FAC 10+4 Others 6+2/1
Reading (Loaned on 30/1/92) FL 5/5
Plymouth Arg (Loaned on 26/3/92) FL 9/1
Portsmouth (Loaned on 12/8/94) FL 4+1

David Lee (Chelsea)

LEE David Mark
Born: Blackburn, 5 November 1967
Height: 5'7" Weight: 11.0

The flying Bolton winger's season was curtailed with a hernia problem after he had been involved in the opening 17 games of 1995-96, his best performance having come in the Wanderers 4-1 win at Middlesbrough in February, when he scored what was to be his only goal of the campaign. At his best, David can use his acceleration to go past defenders to get accurate crosses into the box, while his skilful play and indomitable spirit has undone the best of defences.

Bury (From juniors on 8/8/86) FL 203+5/35 FLC 15/1 FAC 6 Others 19+1/4
Southampton (£350,000 on 27/8/91) P/FL 11+9 FAC 0+1 Others 1+1
Bolton W (£300,000 on 2/11/92) P/FL 111+19/15 FLC 15+1/2 FAC 12+1 Others 8+1/1

LEE Graeme Barry
Born: Middlesbrough, 31 May 1978
Height: 6'2" Weight: 13.0
Central defender, and a second-year trainee with Hartlepool, Graeme had a memorable debut in 1995-96, coming on as substitute at Highbury in a Coca Cola Cup match. Although he made few appearances, when he did, he received compliments all round for his good attitude and level-headed play. From a footballing family, there are big hopes for him in 1996-97.

Hartlepool U (Trainee) FL 3+3 FLC 0+1 Others 0+1

LEE Jason Benedict
Born: Forest Gate, 9 May 1971
Height: 6'3" Weight: 13.8
Forward who, unfortunately, became more famous for his hair style than his playing ability in 1995-96! Although expected to play second fiddle to Kevin Campbell, Bryan Roy and Andrea Silenzi, he in fact enjoyed two long runs in the Nottingham Forest first team from September to December and again in the closing weeks of the season, scoring eight goals in 40 appearances. Despite his lack of deadly finishing, Jason remained popular with Forest supporters due to his enthusiasm, hard work, and 100 per cent commitment to the cause, his running off the ball always giving the side additional options.

Charlton Ath (From trainee on 2/6/89) FL 0+1 Others 0+2
Stockport Co (Loaned on 6/2/91) FL 2
Lincoln C (£35,000 on 1/3/91) FL 86+7/21 FLC 6 FAC 2+1/1 Others 4
Southend U (Signed on 6/8/93) FL 18+6/3 FLC 1 FAC 1 Others 5+3/3
Nottingham F (£200,000 on 4/3/94) F/PL 36+27/13 FLC 2+2 FAC 0+4 Others 4+2

LEE Mark
Born: Consett, 31 May 1979
Height: 6'0" Weight: 12.2
A talented young Scarborough winger, and a first-year YTS trainee, Mark made his senior debut in Auto Windscreen Shield at Preston, after just two reserve outings in the Pontins League. And, just 16 years and 160 days old, he thus became the youngest player to represent the club in first-class football.

Scarborough (Trainee) Others 1

LEE Robert Martin
Born: West Ham, 1 February 1966
Height: 5'10" Weight: 11.13
Club Honours: Div 1 '93
International Honours: E: 7; B-1; U21-2

Robert began last season for Newcastle in fine style, scoring four times in the first nine games from midfield. Although the goals became rarer thereafter, he continued to make an impressive contribution and was Carling "Player of the Month" in November. His good, tight control, strong running, and powerful shooting, made him a perfect foil for the more subtle skills of Peter Beardsley and led Kevin Keegan to describe him as the best midfield player in the country. With United leading the Premiership, his strikes in the home games against Leeds and Forest were particularly noteworthy, especially in keeping the club on target, and it was the result of performances like this that saw him rewarded with further England caps, despite missing out on Euro '96. Was elected by his fellow professionals to the PFA award winning Premiership team.

Charlton Ath (Free from Hornchurch on 12/7/83) FL 274+24/59 FLC 16+3/1 FAC 14/2 Others 10+2/3
Newcastle U (£700,00 on 22/9/92) F/PL 148/34 FLC 12/3 FAC 12/3 Others 3/4

Robert Lee

LEGG Andrew (Andy)
Born: Neath, 28 July 1966
Height: 5'8" Weight: 10.7
Club Honours: WC '89, '91; AIC '95
International Honours: W: 2
The third Notts County player to sign for Birmingham last season, Andy joined Brum, along with Paul Devlin, in February, having played 39 games in 1995-96 prior to the transfer. Also scored six goals, including the only one of the game in the FA Cup at York. Immediately settling down on the left-hand side of City's midfield, and once or twice at left back, he showed the ability to pass defenders to get the crosses in, his good form resulting in winning two Welsh caps. A long-throw expert, according to the Guinness Book of Records, he has the longest recorded throw on record.

Swansea C (Signed from Britton Ferry on 12/8/88) FL 155+8/29 FLC 9+1 FAC 16/4 Others 15+3/5
Notts Co (£275,000 on 23/7/93) FL 85+4/9 FLC 11 FAC 7+1 Others 16+2/6
Birmingham C (Signed on 29/2/96) FL 9+3/1

LEITCH Donald Scott
Born: Motherwell, 6 October 1969
Height: 5'9" Weight: 11.4
Midfielder signed by Swindon last March on loan from Hearts to cover for the the continuing absence of player/manager, Steve McMahon. Industrious, strong in the tackle, with the ability to switch play, unfortunately, he was injured in the championship showdown at Blackpool on 20 April and played no further part in the celebrations.

Dumfermline Ath (Free from Shettleston Juniors on 4/4/90) SL 72+17/16 SLC 6+1/3 SC 3 Others 1
Heart of Midlothian (Signed on 6/8/93) SL 46+9/2 SLC 1+2/1 SC 3 Others 2
Swindon T (Loaned on 29/3/96) FL 7

LENNON Neil Francis
Born: Lurgan, 25 June 1971
Height: 5'9" Weight: 12.4
International Honours: NI: 6; B-3; U23-1; U21-2; Yth
Continued where he left off in 1994-95, at the hub of Crewe's midfield, but, ambitious for a higher grade of football, he eventually signed for first division Leicester last February, having earlier rejected a move to Coventry. The tenacious midfielder made an eventful debut at Reading, where he laid on a goal before being judged to have conceded a penalty. Exerting a growing influence on the side as the campaign progressed, he scored his first goal for City in the win over Birmingham, added to his tally of Northern Ireland caps, and gave an outstanding performance at Wembley as the Foxes reached the Premiership, via the play offs. Was also elected to the PFA award winning second division team by his fellow professionals, for the third year running.

Manchester C (From trainee on 26/8/89) FL 1
Crewe Alex (Free on 9/8/90) FL 142+5/15 FLC 8+1/1 FAC 12/1 Others 15+1
Leicester C (£750,000 on 23/2/96) FL 14+1/1 Others 3

LEONARD Mark Anthony
Born: St Helens, 27 September 1962
Height: 5'11" Weight: 11.10
An endlessly enthusiastic, traditional centre forward, Mark showed great aerial ability when leading the Wigan line in 1995-96. Last season, his 14th in the Football League, also saw him complete 350 FL appearances, although he is still 11 short of 100 goals, prior to him being released during the summer.

Everton (Signed from Witton A on 24/2/82)
Tranmere Rov (Loaned on 24/3/83) FL 6+1
Crewe Alex (Free on 1/6/83) FL 51+3/15 FLC 4/2 FAC 2 Others 3+1
Stockport Co (Free on 13/2/85) FL 73/23 FLC 5/2 FAC 1 Others 2/3
Bradford C (£40,000 on 27/9/86) FL 120+37/29 FLC 13+5/6 FAC 6+3/1 Others 6+5/3
Rochdale (£40,000 on 27/3/92) FL 9/1
Preston NE (£40,000 on 13/8/92) FL 19+3/1 FLC 2

Chester C (Free on 13/8/93) FL 28+4/8 FLC 2
FAC 3/1 Others 3
Wigan Ath (Signed on 15/9/94) FL 60+4/12 FLC
2 FAC 6/2 Others 6/2

LEONHARDSEN Oyvind

Born: Norway, 17 August 1970
Height: 5'10" Weight: 11.13
International Honours: Norway: 47

The busy work-horse in the Wimbledon midfield, not only is Oyvind a tireless tackler, but he also has a significant goalscoring aspect to his game, his exploits over the last two years prompting offers reaching as much as six million pounds. "Leo", as he is known to the fans, is a firm favourite among the Selhurst faithful, and remains popular in his native Norway, where he regularly plays and scores for the national team. Last season he was invariably one of the first names on the Wimbledon team-sheet and the injury he picked up towards the tail-end of the campaign was his only major disruption.

Wimbledon (£660,000 from Rosenborg on 8/11/94) PL 46+3/8 FLC 1+1 FAC 10/2

LE SAUX Graeme Pierre

Born: Harrow, 17 October 1968
Height: 5'10" Weight: 11.2
Club Honours: PL '95
International Honours: E: 12; B-2; U21-4

Ebullient Blackburn and England left back. A multi-talented player with pace, composure on the ball, and attacking flair, allied to his ability to recover quickly and get his tackles in, make him a player of true international standing. Unfortunately, 1995-96 turned into a nightmare. Having been sidelined for a month in September with ligament damage, his return was both brief and controversial. A participant in the well documented on-field argument with team mate, David Batty, he had scarcely lived that down when an horrific injury, which saw him breaking his ankle and rupturing tendons in the game against Middlesbrough, brought his season to a halt. Rovers will be praying that Graeme is ready for the 1996-97 kick off.

Chelsea (Free from St Paul's, Jersey, on 9/12/87) F/PL 77+13/8 FLC 7+6/1 FAC 7+1 Others 8+1
Blackburn Rov (Signed on 25/3/93) PL 101+2/6 FLC 10 FAC 6 Others 6+1

LESTER Jack William

Born: Sheffield, 8 October 1975
Height: 5'10" Weight: 11.2
International Honours: E: Sch

A Grimsby striker whose 1995-96 appearances were limited to just six from the bench, Jack will probably have to bide his time a little while yet. While not bringing a lot of height to the attack, relying mainly on speed and ability to lose his marker, he continued to be effective in the Pontins League.

Grimsby T (From juniors on 8/7/94) FL 1+11 FLC 0+2 FAC 0+1

LE TISSIER Matthew (Matt) Paul

Born: Guernsey, 14 October 1968
Height: 6'1" Weight: 13.8
International Honours: E: 6; B-5; Yth

By the superbly gifted Southampton attacking midfielder's high standards, last season was perhaps a poor one, and he managed only ten goals, three on the opening day. Many theories were put forward for this downturn in form, including a supposed reaction to his exclusion from the England squad. However, whilst not scoring so regularly as in previous years, his midfield vision and passing ability was still of the highest quality and there are few around, if any, who can match him in that department. To his great credit, Matt continued to pledge his future to Saints as long as they remain in the Premiership, despite certain newspapers linking him to moves elsewhere.

Southampton (From apprentice on 17/10/86) F/PL 296+30/127 FLC 30+6/20 FAC 28+1/12 Others 11+1/9

Matt le Tissier

LEVER Mark

Born: Beverley, 29 March 1970
Height: 6'3" Weight: 13.5

The Grimsby centre back contested the number five shirt with Graham Rodger in 1995-96 and for the greater part of the campaign was the lynchpin of the defence, while making 28 appearances. Using his height to good advantage and a sure tackler, Mark had one of his best seasons since making his debut seven years earlier.

Grimsby T (From trainee on 9/8/88) FL 236+7/8 FLC 16+1 FAC 14+1 Others 9

LEWIS Benjamin (Ben)

Born: Chelmsford, 22 June 1977
Height: 6'1" Weight: 12.3

A former YTS central defender in his first year as a Colchester professional, Ben made his league debut at Scunthorpe at the end of last September and looked quite at home at that level. Unfortunately, chances were limited by a cartilage operation which brought his season to a premature end.

Colchester U (From trainee on 24/3/96) FL 1+1 Others 1

LEWIS Michael (Mickey)

Born: Birmingham, 15 February 1965
Height: 5'8" Weight: 10.10
International Honours: E: Yth

Oxford's Mickey, a committed, ball-winning midfielder, has always remained a favourite with the fans, who have nicknamed him "Mad dog" for his hard, but fair tackles. Did not feature a great deal in 1995-96, but received a great reception when coming on late in United's promotion winning game.

West Bromwich A (From apprentice on 18/2/82) FL 22+2 FLC 4+1 FAC 4
Derby Co (£25,000 on 16/11/84) FL 37+6/1 FLC 2 FAC 0+1 Others 4
Oxford U (Signed on 25/8/88) FL 276+24/7 FLC 15+2 FAC 12+1 Others 11+1

LEWIS Neil Anthony

Born: Wolverhampton, 28 June 1974
Height: 5'8" Weight: 11.1

Left-sided midfielder or full back who occasionally appeared for Leicester as a substitute during the first half of last season. Regained a regular place under Martin O'Neill, exciting the crowd with his silky dribbling skills and scoring his first goal for the club at Reading. Has outstanding potential, if only he can manage to focus on the full 90 minutes in hand.

Leicester C (From trainee on 9/7/92) F/PL 49+12/1 FLC 4+1 FAC 2 Others 2

LIBURD Richard John

Born: Nottingham, 26 September 1973
Height: 5'9" Weight: 11.1

Following a shaky start to last season, Richard became one of Bradford's most consistent players, equally at home at right or left back, and more than happy to set off on an attacking run where he could join in the play, while looking to have a crack at goal himself. Although missing the final two play-off games, he can now look forward to first division football.

Middlesbrough (£20,000 from Eastwood T on 25/3/93) FL 41/1 FLC 4 FAC 2 Others 5
Bradford C (£200,000 on 21/7/94) FL 42/2 FLC 5+2 FAC 1 Others 2

LIDDELL Andrew Mark

Born: Leeds, 28 June 1973
Height: 5'8" Weight: 10.9
International Honours: S: U21-11

As a tireless worker up front for Barnsley in 1995-96, he would probably admit that his goal tally should have been higher, but his ability to unlock defences resulted in many opportunities for his partners. Showed his quality, however, when scoring three times in matches against the first division's two leading sides, Derby and Sunderland, and was again a regular in the highly successful Scottish U21 team.

Barnsley (From trainee on 6/7/91) FL 101+25/25 FLC 5+1/1 FAC 4+1 Others 2+1

LIDDLE Craig George
Born: Chester le Street, 21 October 1971
Height: 5'11" Weight: 12.7

A promising Middlesbrough midfielder, strong in the tackle and powerful in the air, he made his Premier League debut, together with the Brazilian Juninho, against Leeds last November and held his place until February and the return of Robbie Mustoe. Craig is yet another youngster in keeping with the strong traditions of Brian Robson's hometown and is strongly tipped to go far in the game.

Middlesbrough (Free from Blyth Spartans on 12/7/94) P/FL 13+1 FLC 2+1 FAC 1 Others 2

LIGHTBOURNE Kyle Lavince
Born: Bermuda, 29 September 1968
Height: 6'2" Weight: 12.2
International Honours: Bermuda: 24

Despite carrying a groin injury for much of last season, the tall striker missed only three games and in the Auto Windscreen Shield against Wycombe he became the first Walsall player for almost ten years to score four goals in a game. With 24 goals, his powerful finishing with both feet and head over the past three years has already made him the club's ninth highest scorer of all time.

Scarborough (Signed on 11/12/92) FL 11+8/3 FLC 1 Others 0+1
Walsall (Free on 17/9/93) FL 113+7/45 FLC 6/2 FAC 12+2/8 Others 6/5

LIGHTFOOT Christopher (Chris) Ian
Born: Penketh, 1 April 1970
Height: 6'2" Weight: 13.6

As Wigan Athletic's then record signing in the 1995 close season from Graham Barrow's old club, Chester City, Chris unfortunately missed part of the 1995-96 campaign through an ankle injury and, after failing to regain regular first team action, was sold on to Crewe Alexandra in March. At Gresty Road he quickly settled into the team's style, providing both aggression and good passing skills.

Chester C (From trainee on 11/7/88) FL 263+14/32 FLC 15+2/1 FAC 16+2/1 Others 14+2/5
Wigan Ath (£87,500 on 13/7/95) FL 11+3/1 FLC 2 FAC 2 Others 3
Crewe Alex (£50,000 on 22/3/96) FL 5+1 Others 2

LIMPAR Anders Erik
Born: Solna, Sweden, 24 September 1965
Height: 5'8" Weight: 11.5
Club Honours: Div 1 '91; FAC '95; CS '95
International Honours: Sweden: 66

Everton's Swedish international left winger, who is extremely quick and skilful on the ball and has the ability to twist and turn defenders in wide positions before making his way inside. Was in and out of the team in 1995-96, due to injuries and competition for places, but early on he weighed in with two goals in three matches and, for a player who had a reputation for inconsistency, gave good, solid displays. Eventually sharing the left wing spot with Graham Stuart in midseason, manager, Joe Royle, gave him a vote of confidence by assuring him that he had a future at Goodison after press speculation

Kyle Lightbourne

suggested otherwise. Will be looking to establish himself once and for all as the perfect foil to Andrei Kanchelskis in 1996-97.

Arsenal (£1,000,000 from Cremonese on 6/8/90) F/PL 76+20/17 FLC 9 FAC 7/2 Others 4/1
Everton (£1,600,000 on 24/3/94) PL 50+14/5 FLC 1 FAC 7+3/1 Others 4

LING Martin
Born: West Ham, 15 July 1966
Height: 5'8" Weight: 10.2
Club Honours: Div 2 '96

The talented Swindon midfielder, who really blossomed in the days of Glenn Hoddle, struggled to clinch a first team slot last season, although 16 league appearances afforded him a second division championship medal as Town won promotion. Showed glimpses of his undoubted ability, but injuries and, latterly, competition for places, culminated in him being given a free transfer in May.

Exeter C (From apprentice on 13/1/84) FL 109+8/14 FLC 8 FAC 4 Others 5
Swindon T (£25,000 on 14/7/86) FL 2 FLC 1+1
Southend U (£15,000 on 16/10/86) FL 126+12/31 FLC 8/2 FAC 7/1 Others 11+1/3
Mansfield T (Loaned on 24/1/91) FL 3
Swindon T (£15,000 on 28/3/91) F/PL 132+18/10 FLC 11+1/1 FAC 10+1/1 Others 12+1/1

LINGER Paul Hayden
Born: Stepney, 20 December 1974
Height: 5'6" Weight: 10.1

Skilful Charlton midfielder. Had only limited opportunities to display his undoubted talent last season, but showed good control and a penchant for getting forward, scoring his first ever goal for the club in spectacular fashion when coming off the bench against Ipswich in September. Unfortunately, his progress was halted when suffering a broken leg at Port Vale in April.

Charlton Ath (From trainee on 1/7/93) FL 5+18/1 FLC 0+1 Others 0+3

LINIGHAN Andrew (Andy)
Born: Hartlepool, 18 June 1962
Height: 6'3" Weight: 13.10
Club Honours: FLC '93; FAC '93; ECWC '94
International Honours: E: B-4
Tough-tackling and consistent Arsenal centre back who is good in the air and more than adaptable on the ground, despite being at the veteran stage. Unable to get into the first team until last January, when injuries to the regular pairing of Tony Adams and Steve Bould gave him his opportunity, Andy adapted well to the three man defensive system and his partnership with Martin Keown was so successful that the other two were barely missed. From a footballing family, father, Brian, played for Darlington, and brothers, David and Brian, currently turn out for Blackpool and Sheffield Wednesday, respectively.
Hartlepool U (Free from Henry Smiths BC on 19/9/80) FL 110/4 FLC 7+1/1 FAC 8 Others 1/1
Leeds U (£20,000 on 15/5/84) FL 66/3 FLC 6/1 FAC 2 Others 2
Oldham Ath (£65,000 on 17/1/86) FL 87/6 FLC 8/2 FAC 3 Others 4
Norwich C (£350,000 on 4/3/88) FL 86/8 FLC 6 FAC 10 Others 4
Arsenal (£1,250,000 on 4/7/90) F/PL 91+16/4 FLC 13+1/1 FAC 12+2/1 Others 7+1/1

LINIGHAN David
Born: Hartlepool, 9 January 1965
Height: 6'2" Weight: 13.0
Club Honours: Div 2 '92
Joined Blackpool from Ipswich last January on a permanent basis, having been at the club since October on an extended loan period. Had only played twice for Town in 1995-96, but at Bloomfield Road he was a regular, his great experience and competitiveness in the centre of the defence being vital to the promotion push. Also chipped in with important goals.
Hartlepool U (From juniors on 3/3/82) FL 84+7/5 FLC 3+1/1 FAC 4 Others 2
Derby Co (£25,000 on 11/8/86)
Shrewsbury T (£30,000 on 4/12/86) FL 65/1 FLC 5 FAC 3 Others 1
Ipswich T (£300,000 on 23/6/88) F/PL 275+2/12 FLC 21 FAC 18/1 Others 11
Blackpool (£80,000 on 17/11/95) FL 29/4 Others 4

LINTON Desmond (Des) Martin
Born: Birmingham, 5 September 1971
Height: 6'1" Weight: 13.2
Having been recalled by Luton as an attacking right-sided midfielder for the match against his old club, Leicester, last August, he was unfortunately dropped after just a handful of games as the side struggled to find any semblance of form. Although injuries hampered his bid to win back his place, a committed attitude led to him being offered a new contract and he looks for better fortune in 1996-97, his ability to both win and carry the ball making him a valuable squad member.
Leicester C (From trainee on 9/1/90) FL 6+5 FLC 0+1 Others 1
Luton T (Signed on 22/10/91) FL 62+14/1 FLC 3+1 FAC 7 Others 6

LITTLE Colin Campbell
Born: Wythenshawe, 4 November 1972
Height: 5'10" Weight: 10.5

Crewe paid their highest fee to a non-league side when taking Colin from Hyde United in February 1996. With a reputation as a goalscorer, he was naturally pleased to get what proved to be the winning goal against Peterborough to secure a play-off place.
Crewe Alex (£50,000 from Hyde U on 7/2/96) FL 7+5/1 Others 1/1

LITTLEJOHN Adrian Sylvester
Born: Wolverhampton, 26 September 1970
Height: 5'9" Weight: 10.5
International Honours: E: Yth
A Plymouth centre forward with lightening speed, Adrian scared most defenders in division three in 1995-96 with his pace, having signed from Sheffield United during the summer. Started the season at a gallop, scoring regularly, but a mid-term lay off due to injury caused a slump in his output. After notching his first goal of the New Year on 8 April, like all good strikers this started him on another run with improved confidence.
Walsall (Free from West Bromwich A juniors on 24/5/89) FL 26+18/1 FLC 2+1 FAC 1+1 Others 4+1
Sheffield U (Free on 6/8/91) F/PL 44+25/12 FLC 5+1 FAC 3+2/1 Others 2/1
Plymouth Arg (£100,000 on 22/9/95) FL 40+2/17 FLC 2 FAC 3/1 Others 3

Adrian Littlejohn

LIVINGSTONE Stephen (Steve)
Born: Middlesbrough, 8 September 1969
Height: 6'1" Weight: 12.7
A bustling centre forward of the old school, Steve continued last season where he left off in 1994-95, scoring in Grimsby's opening game at Millwall. Strong in possession, and a good target man who held the ball up well, he also created danger at the far post with his aerial power and was always a handful for opposing defences. As Town's leading scorer with 13 goals, his best spell came during January with four strikes in six matches, none of them won.

Coventry C (From trainee on 16/7/86) FL 17+14/5 FLC 8+2/10 Others 0+1
Blackburn Rov (£450,000 on 17/1/91) F/PL 25+5/10 FLC 2 FAC 1/1
Chelsea (£350,000 on 23/3/93) PL 0+1
Port Vale (Loaned on 3/9/93) FL 4+1
Grimsby (£140,000 on 29/10/93) FL 89+10/22 FLC 3 FAC 4+2/2

LLOYD Kevin Gareth
Born: Llanidloes, 26 September 1970
Height: 6'0" Weight: 12.1
Kevin had to battle hard with Murray Fishlock for the Hereford left back spot in 1995-96, suffering with injuries, including an ankle problem, along the way. However, as a pacy, overlapping wing/back who enjoyed getting up with the attack, he again proved a good man to have in the side.
Hereford U (Free from Caersws on 7/11/94) FL 49+2/3 FLC 2 FAC 1 Others 6

LOCKE Adam Spencer
Born: Croydon, 20 August 1970
Height: 5'11" Weight: 12.7
Adam enjoyed a storming start to 1995-96, playing as a right wing/back, from where he scored Colchester's winner on the opening day against Plymouth – a 30-yard drive into the roof of the net, followed by two more against Hartlepool in the autumn. Struggled with injury as the season progressed and was seldom fully fit after the New Year. On song, he is a classy midfielder who can take opponents on.
Crystal Palace (From trainee on 21/6/88)
Southend U (Free on 6/8/90) FL 56+17/4 FLC 5 FAC 2+1 Others 6+1
Colchester U (Loaned on 8/10/93) FL 4 Others 1
Colchester U (Free on 23/9/94) FL 42+5/4 FLC 2 FAC 4 Others 4+2

LOGAN Richard Anthony
Born: Barnsley, 24 May 1969
Height: 6'1" Weight: 13.3
Followed former Huddersfield team mate, Gary Clayton and Chris Billy to Plymouth last October, when he signed as a squad player with a view to playing a central midfield role. However, in spending most of his time in central defence, his partnership with Mick Heathcote was a revelation and saw him gain a regular place in the team. Has a very useful long throw, which can cause havoc in the opposition's penalty area.
Huddersfield T (Free from Gainsborough Trinity on 15/11/93) FL 35+10/1 FLC 3 FAC 1 Others 9
Plymouth Arg (£20,000 on 26/10/95) FL 25+6/4 FAC 1+2 Others 4

LOMAS Stephen (Steve) Martin
Born: Hanover, Germany, 18 January 1974
Height: 6'0" Weight: 12.8
International Honours: NI: 12; B-1; Yth; Sch
This highly competitive Manchester City midfielder, with fine passing ability to match, finally made a niche for himself in the side last season as a permanent member throughout, bar injuries and suspensions. Popped up with the odd goal or two, each one of significance to the outcome of the result, showing confidence, and not being afraid to shoot on sight, thus putting the injury problems of 1994-95 well and truly behind him. Now a seasoned Northern

Ireland international, having moved into double figures, he seems sure to be a key man in Alan Ball's future plans.

Manchester C (From trainee on 22/1/91) PL 67+9/5 FLC 13/2 FAC 7+1/1

LONERGAN Darren
Born: Cork, 28 January 1974
Height: 6'0" Weight: 13.0

Having signed from the Irish club, Waterford, at the beginning of 1994-95, Darren finally made his debut last April at Port Vale when he came off the bench in a 3-1 win and started the next game at home to Wolves. More renowned in Ireland as a midfield player in gaelic football, playing in three all-Ireland cup finals, he now performs in defence, his heading ability making him a forceful centre back.

Oldham Ath (Signed from Waterford on 2/9/94) FL 1+1

LORMOR Anthony (Tony)
Born: Ashington, 29 October 1970
Height: 6'0" Weight: 13.6

The tall striker's willingness to run forever turned many lost causes into attacking opportunities for Chesterfield in 1995-96. He was a key part of the club's direct style, and was sorely missed when an ankle injury sidelined him towards the end of the season. Despite sometimes struggling against a better class of defender, Tony finished up as top scorer and was rewarded with a two-year contract in April.

Newcastle U (From trainee on 25/2/88) FL 6+2/3
Lincoln C (£25,000 on 29/1/90) FL 90+10/30 FLC 1+2/3 FAC 4/2 Others 6
Peterborough U (Free on 4/7/94) FL 2+3 FAC 1 Others 1+1
Chesterfield (Free on 23/12/94) FL 61+3/23 FLC 2 FAC 2/2 Others 6+1/3

Tony Lormor

LOVELL Stuart Andrew
Born: Sydney, Australia, 9 January 1972
Height: 5'10" Weight: 11.0
Club Honours: Div 2 '94

Recovered from the trauma of that Wembley

penalty miss to form an effective striking spearhead for Reading in 1995-96, usually alongside Jimmy Quinn or Lee Nogan, he finished as third-highest goalscorer, despite missing chunks of the season through injury. A popular figure who identifies closely with the fans, Stuart has gone close to selection for the Australian national squad.

Reading (From trainee on 13/7/90) FL 152+34/53 FLC 12/5 FAC 5+7/2 Others 7+3/2

LOW Joshua (Josh) David
Born: Bristol, 15 February, 1979
Height: 6'1" Weight: 12.0
International Honours: W: Yth

As a tall, 17-year-old winger, Josh made an historic league debut for Bristol Rovers last season in the last 90 seconds of the club's final match at Twerton Park against Wycombe Wanderers. For the first year trainee, it had been an exciting finale to the season, having made his Welsh youth international debut just weeks before his league initiation.

Bristol Rov (Trainee) FL 8 Others 2/1

LOWE David Anthony
Born: Liverpool, 30 August 1965
Height: 5'10" Weight: 11.9
Club Honours: AMC '85; Div 2 '92
International Honours: E: U21-2; Yth

A right-footed midfielder, or striker, who earned a regular place in the Leicester starting line-up last season. Although popular with the crowd for his wholehearted approach, he was allowed to rejoin former club, Wigan, on transfer deadline day, having been offered a long-term contract and possible coaching experience. Quickly settling down, David scored three goals, including the winner against Leyton Orient on his home debut.

Wigan Ath (From apprentice on 1/6/83) FL 179+9/40 FLC 8 FAC 16+1/4 Others 18/9
Ipswich T (£80,000 on 26/6/87) FL 121+13/37 FLC 10/2 FAC 3 Others 10+2/6
Port Vale (Loaned on 19/3/92) FL 8+1/2
Leicester C (£250,000 on 13/7/92) F/PL 68+26/22 FLC 4+3/1 FAC 2+2 Others 3
Port Vale (Loaned on 18/2/94) FL 18+1/5
Wigan Ath (£125,000 on 28/3/96) FL 7/3

LOWE Kenneth (Kenny)
Born: Sedgefield, 6 November 1961
Height: 6'1" Weight: 11.4
Club Honours: FAT '90
International Honours: E: SP-2

Although Barry Fry's first signing for Birmingham, Kenny was rarely able to command a regular place in the side and was loaned out to Hartlepool early last season. After an absence of 11 years he was outstanding, running the show from midfield and having great support from the fans. Unfortunately, personal terms could not be agreed and following two subs' appearances back at City, the 35 year old signed as a part-timer for Gateshead in January.

Hartlepool U (From apprentice on 14/11/78) FL 50+4/3 FLC 1+1 FAC 2 Others 1 (Free to Billingham during 1984 close season)
Scarborough (Free from Barrow, via Spearwood, Australia, Gateshead and Morecambe, on 15/1/88) FL 4 (Free to Barrow in April 1989)

Barnet (£40,000 on 1/3/91) FL 55+17/5 FLC 2+1 FAC 5 Others 4
Stoke C (Free on 5/8/93) FL 3+6 FLC 2 Others 2
Birmingham C (£75,000 on 17/12/93) FL 16+7/3 FLC 0+1 FAC 3+1 Others 2+1
Carlisle U (Loaned on 22/9/94) FL 1+1
Hartlepool U (Loaned on 28/8/95) FL 13/3 FLC 2

LOWTHORPE Adam
Born: Hull, 7 August 1975
Height: 5'7" Weight: 10.6

Hospitalised after receiving concussion and facial injuries in a Hull pre-season friendly at Leek Town, Adam, a recognised right back, was later switched to the left back berth following the arrival of Simon Trevitt. In a position he had filled regularly in the past when captaining City's junior team, he proved a willing trier. Also, the club's injury crisis meant he gave of his best in the midfield ball-winning role.

Hull C (From trainee on 2/7/93) FL 39+5 FLC 4 FAC 2 Others 1+1

LUCAS David Anthony
Born: Preston, 23 November 1977
Height: 6'2" Weight: 13.3
International Honours: E: Yth

The current England U18 goalkeeper, David made his Preston debut in the title clinching game at Hartlepool last season, where he kept a clean sheet. A great prospect for the future, he had earlier played six times for Darlington, whilst on loan last December, and impressed.

Preston NE (From trainee on 12/12/94) FL 1
Darlington (Loaned on 14/12/95) FL 6

LUCAS Richard
Born: Chapeltown, 22 September 1970
Height: 5'10" Weight: 11.4

Freed by Preston during the summer of 1995, Richard, a tough, uncompromising left back, who is also a more than useful centre back when required, was one of Scarborough's most consistent players in 1995-96, always giving total commitment. Is likely to be one of the Boro's key players once again this season.

Sheffield U (From trainee on 1/7/89) FL 8+2 FAC 1 Others 0+1
Preston NE (£40,000 on 24/12/92) FL 47+3 FAC 4 Others 4+1
Lincoln C (Loaned on 14/10/94) FL 4 Others 2
Scarborough (Free on 5/7/95) FL 44 FLC 2 FAC 1 Others 1

LUCKETTI Christopher (Chris) James
Born: Littleborough, 28 September 1971
Height: 6'0" Weight: 13.6

A commanding, powerful centre half, Chris once again enjoyed a very consistent season at the heart of Bury's defence in 1995-96. Completely dominant in the air, he also showed good skill with the ball at his feet, being surely destined for a higher grade of football, and for the second year in succession was voted Bury's "Player of the Season".

Rochdale (Trainee) FL 1
Stockport Co (Free on 23/8/90)
Halifax T (Free on 12/7/91) FL 73+5/2 FLC 2/1 FAC 2 Others 4
Bury (£50,000 on 1/10/93) FL 108/5 FLC 7 FAC 7/1 Others 12

LUDDEN Dominic James
Born: Basildon, 30 March 1974
Height: 5'9" Weight: 11.0
International Honours: E: Sch
Promising left back who broke into the Watford first team squad towards the end of last season and impressed with his pace and tidy play. Is particularly effective at going forward in support of his forwards.
Leyton Orient (From trainee on 6/7/92) FL 50+8/1 FLC 1 FAC 0+1 Others 6/1
Watford (£100,000 on 7/8/94) FL 10+3 FAC 1+1

LUKIC Jovan (John)
Born: Chesterfield, 11 December 1960
Height: 6'4" Weight: 13.12
Club Honours: Div 1 '89, '92; FLC '87; CS '89, '92
International Honours: E: B-1; EU21-7; Yth
The 35-year-old goalkeeper began last season for Leeds in consistent form, but was dropped following the 6-2 defeat at Sheffield Wednesday in December. However, after a spell of ten games, he was recalled at Birmingham in the Coca Cola Cup and looked to have regained all his old form and confidence. Indeed, from that moment on, John was one of United's most consistent performers, saving the side on more than one occasion. Despite playing in the final match, the long-serving 'keeper was released during the summer, having been at Elland Road on and off since 1975.
Leeds U (From apprentice on 16/12/78) FL 146 FLC 7 FAC 9 Others 3
Arsenal (£50,000 on 25/7/83) FL 223 FLC 32 FAC 21 Others 4
Leeds U (£1,000,000 on 14/6/90) F/PL 209 FLC 23 FAC 19 Others 15

John Lukic

LUND Gary James
Born: Grimsby, 13 September 1964
Height: 5'11" Weight: 11.0
International Honours: E: U21-1; Sch
A forward with the ability to hold the ball up for others, having failed to make an appearance for Notts County last season, he was signed by Chesterfield in December as a replacement for long-term injury victim, Andy Morris. Unfortunately, Gary soon picked up a back injury himself and

ultimately played little part in the Spireities' play-off push.
Grimsby T (From juniors on 27/7/83) FL 47+13/24 FLC 6+2/1 FAC 4/5 Others 2/1
Lincoln C (Free on 22/8/86) FL 41+3/13 FLC 4/1 FAC 1/1 Others 3/1
Notts Co (£40,000 on 17/6/87) FL 223+25/62 FLC 15+2/5 FAC 13+3/4 Others 28+6/8
Hull C (Loaned on 14/8/92) FL 11/3
Hull C (Loaned on 23/3/95) FL 11/3
Chesterfield (Free on 14/12/95) FL 6+2/1 Others 1

LYDIATE Jason Lee
Born: Manchester, 29 October 1971
Height: 5'11" Weight: 12.3
The strong Blackpool defender was committed all season to the drive for promotion, despite having two spells out of the side, firstly due to injury and then because of the general performance of the team. Continued to impress with his pace, power, and ability in the air.
Manchester U (From trainee on 1/7/90)
Bolton W (Free on 19/3/92) FL 29+1 FLC 4 FAC 2 Others 1
Blackpool (£75,000 on 3/3/95) FL 41+2/1 FLC 2 FAC 3/1 Others 3

LYNCH Christopher (Chris) John
Born: Middlesbrough, 18 November 1974
Height: 6'0" Weight: 11.0
Left-sided midfielder. Had a difficult 1995-96 with Hartlepool, being only engaged on short-term contracts, and although he had a good spell in mid-season, he otherwise struggled to win a place and was often used as substitute. Released in March, Chris later turned out for Bishop Auckland.
Hartlepool U (From trainee on 2/8/93) FL 38+12/2 FLC 3+4 FAC 0+1 Others 1

LYNCH Thomas (Tommy) Michael
Born: Limerick, 10 October 1964
Height: 6'0" Weight: 12.6
Club Honours: Div 3 '94
Shrewsbury Town left back or central defender. An honest defender who never gives less than 110 per cent, a strong tackler and sound header of the ball, Tommy can also play up front in emergencies. Very popular with the crowd, he was team captain on occasion, and showed tremendous drive and enthusiasm whenever he played last season.
Sunderland (£20,000 from Limerick on 11/8/88) FL 4 Others 1
Shrewsbury T (£20,000 on 16/1/90) FL 220+14/14 FLC 16/1 FAC 12 Others 18+2/1

LYNE Neil George Francis
Born: Leicester, 4 April 1970
Height: 6'1" Weight: 12.2
Neil's appearances for Hereford were limited last season due to a bad knee injury. Capable of turning a game, once fully fit, the pacy, skilful winger should give an added dimension to the attack with his ability to run at defenders and force errors.
Nottingham F (Signed from Leicester U on 16/8/89) FLC 0+1
Walsall (Loaned on 22/3/90) FL 6+1
Shrewsbury T (Loaned on 14/3/91) FL 16/6
Shrewsbury T (Signed on 11/7/91) FL 61+3/11 FLC 6/2 FAC 3/2 Others 3
Cambridge U (£75,000 on 15/1/93) FL 5+12
Chesterfield (Loaned on 24/9/93) FL 3/1

Chesterfield (Loaned on 24/3/94) FL 2+1
Hereford U (Free on 27/7/94) FL 49+14/2 FLC 2 FAC 5 Others 9+1/1

LYONS Andrew (Andy)
Born: Blackpool, 19 October 1966
Height: 5'10" Weight: 11.0
Although the 1994-95 leading scorer for Wigan Athletic, Andy was not able to recapture the form of the previous season in 1995-96. Short on confidence, and with just two goals from 21 starts, the nippy left winger was allowed to join Partick Thistle in March after failing to hold down a regular place.
Crewe Alex (£15,000 from Fleetwood T on 26/10/92) FL 7+4/2 FLC 1/1 Others 1+1
Wigan Ath (Signed on 1/10/93) FL 79+8/27 FLC 4+1/1 FAC 7+1 Others 7

LYONS Paul
Born: Leigh, 24 June 1977
Height: 5'8" Weight: 10.2
A former Manchester United trainee, he signed for Rochdale last September and figured in midfield as well as at left back for the reserve and "A" teams. Having earlier been named as a sub without getting on, he made a promising debut against Barnet at Easter when Dale were without most of their senior defenders.
Rochdale (Free from Manchester U juniors on 19/9/95) FL 1+2

LYTTLE Desmond (Des)
Born: Wolverhampton, 24 September 1971
Height: 5'9" Weight: 12.0
Another consistent season for the Nottingham Forest full back, who forged a useful partnerhip with Steve Stone on the right flank and scored the goal which earned a point at Villa Park last September. After missing only two games up to April he lost his place to Alf-Inge Haaland following the humiliating 5-1 home defeat by Blackburn in the closing weeks, but will doubtless again be first choice right back at the start of the coming term. Not just attack minded, Des is also sound defensively, his tackling and powers of recuperation, making things difficult for the best of wingmen.
Leicester C (From trainee on 1/9/90)
Swansea C (£12,500 from Worcester C on 9/7/92) FL 46/1 FLC 2 FAC 5 Others 5
Nottingham F (£375,000 on 27/7/93) F/PL 107+1/2 FLC 12 FAC 11 Others 8

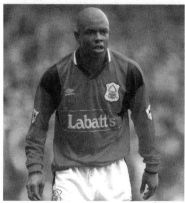
Des Lyttle

Play the world's best selling hand-held video game system with the world's biggest football team.

It's the classic Game Boy in a smart new strip. But you don't have to stick to just football.

There are over 150 games available from golf to cricket to shoot-em-ups and beat-em-ups.

Game Boy £49.99

Game Boy with "Soccer" game £59.99

Call the Manchester United hotline on (0161) 877 9777 and you can be a United player.

Nintendo®

TM and ® are trademarks of Nintendo Co., Ltd. Manchester United football badge ©1970, 1994, Manchester United plc. Soccer ©1994, Rage Software Ltd. Developed by Denton Designs Ltd. for Elite Systems Ltd. Licensed to Nintendo.

M

MABBUTT Gary Vincent
Born: Bristol, 23 August 1961
Height: 5'10" Weight: 12.9
Club Honours: UEFA '84; FAC '91; CS '91
International Honours: E: 16; B-9; U21-7; Yth

Central defender currently in his testimonial season at Tottenham. A real battler, who is a great boost for morale, Gary's dependable, consistent style of play continued to be an example to any youngster at any level in 1995-96, his strength in the air and amazing stamina still an asset even at the veteran stage of his career, while his ability to organise and remain composed under pressure was unchallenged. Has recently signed a new two-year deal which will allow him to see out his career with the club he has served magnificently for 14 seasons so far.
Bristol Rov (From apprentice on 9/1/79) FL 122+9/10 FLC 10/1 FAC 5+1/1
Tottenham H (£105,000 on 11/8/82) F/PL 449+16/27 FLC 59+2/2 FAC 45+2/3 Others 29+4/4

McALINDON Gareth Edward
Born: Hexham, 6 April 1977
Height: 5'10" Weight: 11.3
Forward. Formerly on the books of both Manchester United and Newcastle, he joined Carlisle at the start of last season, making several substitute appearances during the campaign. Scored goals in the reserves and will now be looking for the step up.
Carlisle U (Free from Newcastle U juniors on 10/7/95) FL 0+3

McALLISTER Brian
Born: Glasgow, 30 November 1970
Height: 5'11" Weight: 12.5
Like so many others at Wimbledon, Brian has found it difficult to break into the first team during the past few years. A reliable centre back who is tough tackling, but fair, he lined up twice in 1995-96 against West Ham and Newcastle, having recovered from an early season injury, before going on a three month loan to Crewe in March. Good in the air, other attributes include the ability to hit fine long passes over opposing full backs.
Wimbledon (From trainee on 1/3/89) F/PL 51+4 FLC 5 FAC 3 Others 1
Plymouth Arg (Loaned on 5/12/90) FL 7+1
Crewe Alex (Loaned on 8/3/96) FL 13/1 Others 2

McALLISTER Gary
Born: Motherwell, 25 December 1964
Height: 6'1" Weight: 11.5
Club Honours: S Div 1 '85; Div 1 '92; CS '92
International Honours: S: 44; B-2; U21-1
One of the best midfield players in the country. Captain of Leeds and Scotland, his contribution to the side last season was highlighted more than ever. An outstanding professional, Gary again contributed on the goalscoring front, including a hat trick against Coventry City and spectacular efforts such as the one in a 5-3 defeat at the hand of PSV Eindhoven and a glorious curling free kick to earn a victory in the FA Cup at Port Vale. Is on a long-term contract at Elland Road, even though he is often shrouded with transfer speculation. Had an excellent Euro '96 with Scotland, but will be mainly remembered for his penalty miss against England.
Motherwell (Signed from Fir Park BC in 1981) SL 52+7/6 SLC 3+1/1 SC 7/2
Leicester C (£125,000 on 15/8/85) FL 199+2/47 FLC 14+1/3 FAC 5/2 Others 4
Leeds U (£1,000,000 on 2/7/90) F/PL 230+1/31 FLC 26/5 FAC 24/6 Others 14/4

McANESPIE Stephen (Steve)
Born: Kilmarnock, 1 February 1972
Height: 5'9" Weight: 10.7
Club Honours: S Div 1 '95; SLC '95
International Honours: S: Yth
Purchased from Raith Rovers last September, the right back went straight into the Bolton side that went down 1-0 at home to Queens Park Rangers. After a run of nine first team games he was replaced by Scott Green and did not return until the final game of the season at Arsenal, where he looked much more comfortable in the attacking full back role that saw him making some good overlapping runs.
Aberdeen (From juniors on 12/5/88. Transferred to Vasterhaninge on 30/6/93)
Raith Rov (Signed on 25/1/94) SL 37+3 SLC 4 SC 3 Others 5
Bolton W (£900,000 on 30/9/95) PL 7+2 FLC 3

McAREE Rodney (Rod) Joseph
Born: Dungannon, 19 August 1974
Height: 5'7" Weight: 10.9
International Honours: NI: Yth; Sch
Having come to Fulham asking for a trial last December, it was soon obvious that here was a midfielder who could really distribute the ball, something the club were sadly lacking at the time. There was no doubting his upbringing at Liverpool had taught him this and he was soon fighting for a first team spot, eventually making his debut in January. Also packs a powerful shot.
Liverpool (From trainee on 21/8/91)
Bristol C (Free on 26/7/94) FL 4+2 FLC 2 (Free to Dungannon Swifts on 6/11/95)
Fulham (Free on 29/12/95) FL 16+1/2 Others 0+1

McATEER Jason Wynn
Born: Birkenhead, 18 June 1971
Height: 5'9" Weight: 11.5
International Honours: Ei: 18; B-1
His talent was well known to Roy Evans, even before his outstanding performance for Bolton against the Reds in the 1995 Coca Cola Cup final, his transfer to his home town club early last season came as no great surprise. Even so his immediate acclimatisation to Liverpool's style of play was a major bonus to the team. Although a central midfielder for the Trotters, he was deployed at Anfield as a right-sided wing/back, his ability to run at defences, deliver early pin-point crosses and pull backs from the goal line, creating several goals and marking him as a more effective player than many conventional wingers. Added to his collection of Republic of Ireland caps and if he can maintain his current form he is destined to be one of the Liverpool "greats". Interestingly, Jason hails from a family of ex-professional boxers, which includes three brothers and a cousin, two of them, Pat and Les, being former British middleweight champions.
Bolton W (Signed from Marine on 22/1/92) P/FL 109+5/8 FLC 11/2 FAC 11/3 Others 8+1/2
Liverpool (£4,500,000 on 6/9/95) PL 27+2 FLC 3+1 FAC 7/3

Jason McAteer

McAULEY Sean
Born: Sheffield, 23 June 1972
Height: 6'0" Weight: 11.7
International Honours: S: U21-1
Normally an attacking left back, but with the occasional game in midfield, Sean was Hartlepool's only ever present in 1995-96, having signed from St Johnstone during the summer. A most consistent player, and with the right temperament, although largely an unsung hero, he was rewarded at the end of the season by being named the club's ASDA "Player of the Year".
Manchester U (From trainee on 1/7/90)
St Johnstone (Signed on 22/4/92) SL 59+3 SLC 3/1 SC 3 Others 1
Chesterfield (Loaned on 4/11/94) FL 1/1 FAC 1+1 Others 2
Hartlepool U (Free on 21/7/95) FL 46 FLC 4 FAC 1 Others 2

MACAULEY Steven (Steve) Roy
Born: Lytham, 4 March 1969
Height: 6'1" Weight: 12.0
Club Honours: FAYC '86
Since March 1992, when he came from Fleetwood, Crewe had played Steve in a central defensive role but, in 1995-96, they experimented with him as a striker. A powerful header of the ball, with eight goals during the season, he is still studying to become a physiotherapist.
Manchester C (From trainee on 5/11/87)
Crewe Alex (£25,000 from Fleetwood T on 24/3/92) FL 121+2/18 FLC 10 FAC 8 Others 15/3

McCALL Stephen (Steve) Harold
Born: Carlisle, 15 October 1960
Height: 5'11" Weight: 12.6
Club Honours: UEFAC '81
International Honours: E: B-1; U21-6; Yth

A very experienced footballer, with nearly 20 years in the game behind him, Steve returned to the fray for Plymouth near the end of last season, following a long-term injury. His great passing ability and influence in midfield had been badly missed, but, despite that, at the age of 35, he was released during the summer. Had resigned the role of player/manager in 1994-95.

Ipswich T (From apprentice on 5/10/78) FL 249+8/7 FLC 29 FAC 23+1/1 Others 18+1/3
Sheffield Wed (£300,000 on 3/6/87) FL 21+8/2 FLC 2+3 FAC 1 Others 0+1
Carlisle U (Loaned on 8/2/90) FL 6
Plymouth Arg (£25,000 on 26/3/92) FL 97+3/5 FLC 5 FAC 6 Others 6

McCARTHY Alan James
Born: Wandsworth, 11 January 1972
Height: 5'11" Weight: 12.10
International Honours: E: Y-1. W: B-1; U21-3

Signed from the Premier League's QPR at the start of last season, Alan quickly settled into the centre of Leyton Orient's defence, his strong tackling and ability to bring the ball out being a real bonus for the club. Comfortable on the ball, he missed just five games throughout the campaign.

Queens Park R (From trainee on 8/12/89) F/PL 8+3 FAC 0+1 Others 1
Watford (Loaned on 26/11/93) FL 8+1
Plymouth Arg (Loaned on 11/2/94) FL 1+1
Leyton Orient (Signed on 14/8/95) FL 40+3 FLC 1 Others 2

McCARTHY Anthony (Tony) Paul
Born: Dublin, 9 November 1969
Height: 6'1" Weight: 12.10
International Honours: Ei: U21-5; Yth

The third Dubliner in the Colchester squad, and another Irish U21 cap, Tony is a commanding centre half who was successfully converted to right back when the U's went to 4-4-2 last season. A solid and consistent performer, his long throws proved a useful attacking weapon.

Millwall (£100,000 from Shelbourne on 25/6/92) FL 20+1/1 FLC 3
Crewe Alex (Loaned on 9/12/94) FL 2
Colchester U (Free on 17/3/95) FL 54/1 FLC 2 FAC 1 Others 6

McCARTHY Jonathan (Jon) David
Born: Middlesbrough, 18 August 1970
Height: 5'9" Weight: 11.0
International Honours: NI: 1; B-1

Had an excellent campaign on the Port Vale right wing, having signed from York during the 1995 close season, during which he showed a sharp turn of pace. Began 1995-96 slowly, his first experience of first division football, but as the season wore on he was one of the main reasons behind the club's upturn in form. Scored the winning goal against Everton in the FA Cup, during a spell of being on the mark five times in eight games, and earned his first international honours at Northern Ireland "B" level before

stepping up to the full squad against Sweden. Hardly surprisingly, he won the supporters' "Player of the Year" award.

Hartlepool U (From juniors on 7/11/87) FL 0+1 (Free to Shepshed Charterhouse in March 1989)
York C (Free on 22/3/90) FL 198+1/31 FLC 8/1 FAC 11/3 Others 15/3
Port Vale (£450,000 on 1/8/95) FL 44+1/8 FLC 8 FAC 6/1 Others 8/2

Jon McCarthy

McCARTHY Paul Jason
Born: Cork, 4 August 1971
Height: 6'0" Weight: 13.6
International Honours: Ei: U21-10; Yth; Sch

Solid, no frills central defender who was appointed the Brighton skipper during the prolonged absence of Steve Foster in 1995-96. Brave, strong in the air, and giving his all, he even led the attack as an emergency striker against Swindon at the Goldstone on 14 October 1995. Unfortunately, injured knee ligaments early in March 1996 meant him missing some vital matches in Albion's relegation struggle.

Brighton & Hove A (From trainee on 26/4/89) FL 180+1/6 FLC 11/1 FAC 102 Others 12/1

McCARTHY Sean Casey
Born: Bridgend, 12 September 1967
Height: 6'1" Weight: 12.5
International Honours: W: B-1

A bustling Oldham striker, despite losing his goalscoring touch when going 17 games without finding the net last season, Sean still finished with 11 goals to his credit. Good in the air, and a handful for any first division defender, he never lets up, often creating panic with his strong runs direct into danger areas. Was tracked by both Bristol City and Bradford during the campaign.

Swansea C (Signed from Bridgend T on 22/10/85) FL 76+15/25 FLC 4+1/3 FAC 5+2/4 Others 9+1/6

Plymouth Arg (£50,000 on 18/8/88) FL 67+3/19 FLC 7/5 FAC 3/1 Others 0+1/1
Bradford C (£250,000 on 4/7/90) FL 127+4/60 FLC 10+2/10 FAC 8/2 Others 8+1/7
Oldham Ath (£500,000 on 3/12/93) P/FL 84+10/32 FLC 6 FAC 3 Others 3/1

McCLAIR Brian John
Born: Belshill, 8 December 1963
Height: 5'10" Weight" 12.13
Club Honours: SC '85; SPD '86; FAC '90, '94; CS '90, '94; ECWC '91; ESC '91; FLC '91; PL '93, '94, '96
International Honours: S: 30; B-1; U21-8; Yth

Brian continued to be a man Manchester United could rely on in 1995-96, with selfless running for the good of the team his trademark and able to slot in either up front or in midfield. A great clubman, and now vying for the role of senior professional, he enjoyed another outstanding season, celebrating an extended run-in November with two opportunist goals at Coventry. Although his main role was confined to the subs' bench, he could always be relied upon to give the Reds a succession of polished performances and fully justified his third Premier League championship medal.

Motherwell (Free from Aston Villa juniors on 1/8/81) SL 33+7/15 SLC 9+1/4 SC 2/1
Glasgow Celtic (£100,000 on 1/7/83) SL 129+16/99 SLC 19+1/9 SC 14+4/11 Others 13+2/3
Manchester U (£850,000 on 30/7/87) F/PL 290+33/88 FLC 41+1/19 FAC 35+4/14 Others 23/7

McCONNELL Barry
Born: Exeter, 1 January 1977
Height: 5'10" Weight: 10.3

Forward. As a product of the Exeter City youth set up, who scored plenty of goals for the reserves, Barry made his first team debut at Rochdale last September. Will be looking for more chances this coming season.

Exeter C (From trainee on 4/8/95) FL 1+7

McDERMOTT John
Born: Middlesbrough, 3 February 1969
Height: 5'7" Weight: 10.6

As Grimsby's senior professional, and a very consistent member of the squad, John was unfortunate last season, in as much that the manager, Brian Laws, usually picked himself for the right back spot. However, on the latter's injury, he re-established himself towards the end of January, missing just two games from 25, his speed in recovery and in linking with the attack seemingly unimpaired. Is also an excellent tackler.

Grimsby T (From trainee on 1/6/87) FL 290+14/5 FLC 17+1 FAC 20+1 Others 11

McDONALD Alan
Born: Belfast, 12 October 1963
Height: 6'2" Weight: 12.7
International Honours: NI: 52; Sch

A rugged and uncompromising, strong-tackling QPR and Northern Ireland international defender, who leads by example, Alan's 1995-96 season was disrupted by injury and this was one of the main reasons behind the side's downfall in the Premier League. As club captain, he scored his only goal of the campaign in the 1-1 draw with Middlesbrough and, having returned from injury once again in mid-March, he was superb at the heart of the defence as Rangers unsuccessfully battled to avoid relegation. His experience, especially in the air at both ends of the park, will stand the team in good stead as they try and regain their place in the top flight.

Queens Park R (From apprentice on 12/8/81) F/PL 357+6/11 FLC 41/2 FAC 30/1 Others 5
Charlton Ath (Loaned on 24/3/83) FL 9

McDONALD Colin
Born: Edinburgh, 10 April 1974
Height: 5'7" Weight: 10.8
International Honours: S: U21-5; Sch

Following his transfer from Falkirk last March, Colin had few chances to impress when introduced to first team action with Swansea. A former Scottish U21 international, he is small, but quick, and can be used up front, through the centre or wide on either flank.

Hibernian (Signed from Musselburgh on 14/5/91)
Falkirk (Signed on 8/7/93) SL 31+22/10 SLC 2+2/1 SC 1+1 Others 2+2/2
Swansea C (£40,000 on 22/3/96) FL 3+5

MacDONALD David Hugh
Born: Dublin, 2 January 1971
Height: 5'11" Weight: 11.7
International Honours: Ei: B-1; U21-3; Yth; Sch

Barnet right back who always gave his all for the cause, before losing his place late last season. A hard tackler with no frills, and an excellent passer to the front men out of defence, David's forte is his dependability.

Tottenham H (From trainee on 5/8/88) PL 2
Gillingham (Loaned on 27/9/90) FL 10 Others 2
Bradford C (Loaned on 28/8/92) FL 7
Reading (Loaned on 6/3/93) FL 11
Peterborough U (Free on 13/8/93) FL 28+1 FLC 4 FAC 2 Others 1
Barnet (Free on 24/3/94) FL 75+2 FLC 6 FAC 4 Others 4

McDONALD Neil Raymond
Born: Wallsend, 2 November 1965
Height: 5'11" Weight: 11.4
International Honours: E: U21-5; Yth; Sch

After failing to get an opportunity to play in the Premier League with Bolton last season, Neil was signed by Preston in November to add class to their midfield. Undoubtedly has ability, but took some time to settle in to the style of play and has still to win over the fans. Hopefully, he will show his true form next season. One of two players at the club who are training to become qualified referees.

Newcastle U (From apprentice on 19/2/83) FL 163+17/24 FLC 12/3 FAC 10+1/1 Others 3
Everton (£525,000 on 3/8/88) FL 76+14/4 FLC 7/3 FAC 17 Others 10+1
Oldham Ath (£500,000 on 1/10/91) F/PL 19+5/1 FLC3 FAC2
Bolton W (Free on 20/7/94) FL 4 Others 2
Preston NE (£40,000 on 6/11/95) FL 8+3 FAC 1 Others 2

McDONALD Paul Thomas
Born: Motherwell, 20 April 1968
Height: 5'7" Weight: 10.0
Club Honours: S Div 1 '88; B&QC '92, '93

A typical, speedy Scottish left winger who goes past defenders looking to draw on his superb left foot. Unable to get into the Southampton squad at the start of last season, Paul had a two month spell on loan at Burnley in September before returning to the Dell and eventually making two subs' appearances. Signed by Brighton in February, he moved along the coast but, after an encouraging debut, was carried off at Wycombe with an ankle injury in his fifth game.

Hamilton Academical (Signed from Merry Street BC on 30/6/86) SL 187+28/26 SLC 8+2/2 SC 8+1 Others 8/3
Southampton (£75,000 on 8/6/93) PL 0+3 FAC 0+1
Burnley (Loaned on 15/9/95) FL 8+1/1 Others 2
Brighton & Hove A (£25,000 on 16/2/96) FL 5

McDOUGALD David Eugene Junior
Born: Big Spring, Texas, USA, 12 January 1975
Height: 5'11" Weight: 12.6
International Honours: E: Yth

Junior started last season for Brighton as a central striker, but his best performances were ultimately on the left side of midfield, where his pace unsettled defenders. Although Albion's leading goalscorer, he was allowed to depart on loan to Chesterfield just before the transfer deadline. There he quickly became a crowd favourite with his distinctive skills well suited to the club's direct style of play.

Tottenham H (From trainee on 12/7/93)
Brighton & Hove A (Signed on 12/5/94) FL 71+7/14 FLC 7/2 FAC 4/3 Others 6/3
Chesterfield (Loaned on 28/3/96) FL 9/3

McELHATTON Michael
Born: Kerry, 16 April 1975
Height: 6'1" Weight: 12.8
International Honours: Ei: Sch

Michael unfortunately had his 1995-96 season interrupted by injury, restricting his Bournemouth appearances to just four starts and three as a substitute. A combative midfielder, he will hope to be fully fit in time for the beginning of the new term in order to get his place in the side back. Can also play in defence.

Bournemouth (From trainee on 5/7/93) FL 21+21/2 FLC 3+1 FAC 1+2/1 Others 1

McFARLANE Andrew (Andy) Antonie
Born: Wolverhampton, 30 November 1966
Height: 6'3" Weight: 13.8
Club Honours: AMC '94

Signed from Swansea prior to the start of 1995-96, Scunthorpe's tall, awkward-looking striker, enjoyed the best season of his career so far. Not previously renowned as an out-and-out goalscorer, he showed his colleagues how it should be done by getting into the right position at the right time. Although let down by his first touch on occasions, his positive attitude reaped dividends. Scored four times in the 8-1 league win at Torquay in October.

Portsmouth (From apprentice on 20/11/90) FL 0+2
Swansea C (£20,000 on 6/8/92) FL 33+22/8 FLC 3/1 FAC 0+6 Others 7+4/5
Scunthorpe U (£15,000 on 4/8/95) FL 41+5/16 FLC 2/1 FAC 2/2 Others 3/2

McGARRIGLE Kevin
Born: Newcastle, 9 April 1977
Height: 5'11" Weight: 11.4

Brighton's highly-rated young central defender had a shaky start to 1995-96, due to poor form and a groin injury, before coming back well with some creditable performances late in the season. Scored his first senior goal with a fine half-volley after being called on as a substitute in Albion's 2-0 win at Wycombe on 6 March 1996.

Brighton & Hove A (From trainee on 21/7/94) FL 25+7/1 FLC 2 Others 1+1

McGAVIN Steven (Steve) James
Born: North Walsham, 24 January 1969
Height: 5'10" Weight: 10.10
Club Honours: GMVC '92; FAT '92; Div 2 '95

A skilful forward player with good close ball control, he enjoyed his best form at Wycombe towards the end of 1995-96. His season is best remembered for the many goals he laid on, rather than the ones he scored, as he appeared to be jinxed in that department.

Colchester U (£10,000 from Sudbury T on 28/7/92) FL 55+3/17 FLC 2 FAC 6/2 Others 4
Birmingham C (£150,000 on 7/1/94) FL 16+7/2 FLC 1+1/1 FAC 3+1/2 Others 1+3
Wycombe W (£140,000 on 20/3/95) FL 34+9/4 FLC 2+1 FAC 0+1 Others 1+1

McGHEE David Christopher
Born: Worthing, 16 June 1976
Height: 5'10" Weight: 11.4

Talented Brentford utility player. In the squad for nearly every game in 1995-96, playing in a variety of positions, he was usually to be found as a centre back or striker. Did well in his first full season and proved dangerous at set pieces.

Brentford (From trainee on 15/7/94) FL 32+11/6 FLC 1+1/1 FAC 4 Others 2+1

McGIBBON Patrick (Pat)
Born: Lurgan, 6 September 1973
Height: 6'2" Weight: 13.2
International Honours: NI: 4; B-3; U21-1; Sch

Promising young Manchester United central defender who looks cool and assured on the ball and commanding in the air, Pat had a bitter-sweet introduction to first team football when assuming the Steve Bruce mantle in the Coca Cola Cup-tie against York last September. During the Reds' unexpected defeat to the second division outfit, he gave away a penalty (clearly outside the box), which ultimately led to his dismissal. Highly thought of at Old Trafford, the following month he made his fourth full Northern Ireland international appearance as a sub in Liechtenstein.

Manchester U (£100,000 from Portadown on 1/8/92) FLC 1

McGINLAY John
Born: Inverness, 8 April 1964
Height: 5'9" Weight: 11.6
International Honours: S: 9; B-2

Scottish international striker who missed the start of last season through injury before recovering to become Bolton's leading goalscorer in what was a most difficult season. John often found himself as a lone striker, or even playing as a wide midfielder, as the team went through different transitions in an attempt to find their best formation. Is still a crowd favourite at Burnden Park, thanks to his wholehearted attitude to the game.

Shrewsbury T (Signed from Elgin C on 22/2/89) FL 58+2/27 FLC 4 FAC 1/2 Others 3/2
Bury (£175,000 on 11/7/90) FL 16+9/9 FLC 1 FAC 1 Others 1+1
Millwall (£80,000 on 21/1/91) FL 27+7/10 FLC 2+1 FAC 2 Others 2/1
Bolton W (£125,000 on 30/9/92) P/FL 133+9/63 FLC 16+1/7 FAC 15+1/9 Others 11/7

John McGinlay

McGLASHAN John
Born: Dundee, 3 June 1967
Height: 6'1" Weight: 13.3
International Honours: S: Yth

The strong midfielder had to miss much of last season after undergoing an operation for a torn stomach muscle which had troubled him for some time. Back again, he demonstrated that he has an eye for goal as well as hard work when he netted one of the goals which gave Rotherham an unexpected Easter Monday victory at second placed Blackpool. Also useful in the air, he reads the game very well.

Montrose (Signed from Dundee Violet in 1988-89) SL 67+1/11 SLC 2 SC 4
Millwall (£50,000 on 22/8/90) FL 9+7 FAC 0+1 Others 1
Fulham (Loaned on 11/12/92) FL 5/1 Others 1
Cambridge U (Loaned on 15/1/93) FL 0+1
Peterborough U (£75,000 on 27/1/93) FL 44+2/3 FLC 4+1/1 FAC 1 Others 2/1
Rotherham U (Free on 4/11/94) FL 40+3/5 FLC 2/1 FAC 1/1 Others 1

McGLEISH Scott
Born: Barnet, 10 February 1974
Height: 5'10" Weight: 11.7

Released by Charlton, Scott joined Peterborough during the 1995 close season, but was given only limited opportunities, despite playing well when called upon. Posh did not want to lose him and in an effort to keep match fit he spent the last three months of 1995-96 on loan at Colchester, having earlier scored the winner against them in the AWS competition. The energetic and enthusiastic striker proved to be a highly successful temporary acquisition for United, scoring several vital goals and delighting the locals with his celebratory double handspring, before arriving back at London Road.

Charlton Ath (Free from Edgware T on 24/5/94) FL 0+6
Leyton Orient (Loaned on 10/3/95) FL 4+2/1 Others 1/1
Peterborough U (Free on 4/7/95) FL 3+9 FLC 0+1 FAC 0+1 Others 3+1/2
Colchester U (Loaned on 23/2/96) FL 10+5/6 Others 2

McGOLDRICK Edward (Eddie) John
Born: Islington, 30 April 1965
Height: 5'10" Weight: 11.7
Club Honours: Div 4 '87; FMC '91; ECWC '94
International Honours: Ei: 15; B-1

Arsenal utility player, predominately left sided, who started as a winger before being used more in an attacking midfield role. Limited to a 14 minute substitute appearance at Manchester City last September, although on the transfer list, his help and encouragement to the youngsters in the reserves speak volumes for his attitude.

Northampton T (£10,000 from Nuneaton Borough on 23/8/86) FL 97+10/9 FLC 9 FAC 6+1/1 Others 7/1
Crystal Palace (£200,000 on 10/1/89) FL 139+8/11 FLC 21+1/2 FAC 5 Others 13+2/3
Arsenal (£1,000,000 on 18/6/93) PL 32+6 FLC 7+2 FAC 1+1 Others 4+4/1

McGORRY Brian Paul
Born: Liverpool, 16 April 1970
Height: 5'10" Weight: 12.8

One of Alan Smith's first signings for Wycombe early in 1995-96, when coming from Peterborough, he was part of the first team squad until September, but then had a frustrating season confined mainly in the reserves. Following a spell on loan at Cardiff in March, where he impressed as a welcome addition to their midfield, Brian was released during the summer.

Bournemouth (£30,000 from Weymouth on 13/8/91) FL 56+5/11 FLC 7 FAC 7+3/2 Others 5/1
Peterborough U (£60,000 on 10/2/94) FL 44+8/6 FLC 0+2 FAC 2 Others 2
Wycombe W (Free on 18/8/95) FL 0+4 FLC 1
Cardiff C (Loaned on 22/3/96) FL 7

McGOWAN Gavin Gregory
Born: Blackheath, 16 January 1976
Height: 5'11" Weight: 12.3
Club Honours: FAYC '94
International Honours: E: Yth; Sch

Young Arsenal full back who is equally at home on either flank. Having been on the fringe of first team football since making his debut while still a trainee, he twice deputised for Nigel Winterburn last season,

and with both the latter and Lee Dixon approaching the veteran stage, 1996 might well be his year. Can also play in central defence and midfield.

Arsenal (From trainee on 1/7/94) PL 2+2 FAC 1

McGRATH Paul
Born: Ealing, 4 December 1959
Height: 6'2" Weight: 14.0
Club Honours: FAC '85; FLC '94, '96
International Honours: Ei: 82

The evergreen Irish Republic central defender is as much an icon at Aston Villa as he is for his country and was playing as well as ever in 1995-96, at the age of 36, in a three man central defensive formation alongside Gareth Southgate and Ugo Ehiogu. He started 29 PL games and played his 80th international for Ireland against Holland in December, a remarkable achievement given his persistent knee problems and inability to train regularly, and added to his impressive list of honours with another Coca Cola Cup winners' medal, following the outstanding victory over Leeds. Having been offered a new one year contract in view of his immense contribution to establishing Villa as an elite team, he is currently considering it along with offers from Japan and the USA.

Manchester U (£30,000 from St Patricks on 30/4/82) FL 159+4/12 FLC 13/2 FAC 15+2/2 Others 9
Aston Villa (£400,000 on 3/8/89) F/PL 248+5/9 FLC 29+1/1 FAC 23+1 Others 15

Paul McGrath

McGREAL John
Born: Liverpool, 2 June 1972
Height: 5'11" Weight: 10.11

It is no coincidence that Tranmere's slump in form followed the injury to John in the last minutes of a 1-0 win at Leicester, which took Rovers into third spot. The team won just two of the next eight games without him and, by the time he returned, confidence had already ebbed away. A cultured defender who likes to carry the ball out of defence into attacking positions, he might not have had the best of seasons but he is still a highly sought after player. In short, a class act.

Tranmere Rov (From trainee on 3/7/90) FL 91+2/1 FLC 9 FAC 3 Others 7+2

McGREGOR Mark Dale Thomas
Born: Chester, 16 February 1977
Height: 5'11" Weight: 10.12
Another young player from the Wrexham youth factory, Mark has blossomed in the last 12 months and in 1995-96, his second season in the Football League, he grew more confident with every game, performing equally well at right back and as a central defender. His assured displays give one the impression that he has been around for years and a promising future lies ahead.

Wrexham (From trainee on 4/7/95) FL 28+5/1 FAC 2+1 Others 3

McGREGOR Paul Anthony
Born: Liverpool, 17 December 1974
Height: 5'10" Weight: 10.4
Reserve Nottingham Forest striker or winger who was adding to his large total of substitute appearances when he hit the headlines with the winning goal against Lyon in the UEFA Cup last November, following up Stuart Pearce's blocked penalty. Rewarded with his first full Premier League game against Manchester United a week later, he celebrated by scoring in a 1-1 draw. Further outings both as substitute and first choice followed throughout the season and he can expect further opportunities to impress in 1996-97. Has good feet and is prepared to run at defenders to force errors.

Nottingham F (From trainee on 13/12/91) F/PL 7+18/3 FAC 0+2 Others 0+4/1

McGUCKIN Thomas Ian
Born: Middlesbrough, 24 April 1973
Height: 6'2" Weight: 14.2
Strong central defender who was the Hartlepool captain throughout 1995-96. As the season progressed, Ian took on more responsibility, thus managing to curb his sometime impulsive behaviour, and although he can be content with his own performances, surprisingly, unlike previous seasons, there were no reports of bigger clubs trying to sign him.

Hartlepool U (From trainee on 20/6/91) FL 126+4/8 FLC 12/1 FAC 4 Others 6

MacKENZIE Christopher (Chris)
Born: Northampton, 14 May 1972
Height: 6'0" Weight: 12.6
The Hereford goalkeeper made a spectacular start to 1995-96, scoring directly from a goal kick in a 4-1 win over Barnet. Despite carrying a niggling back injury for most of the season, his command and authority of the penalty area was most important to the team.

Hereford U (£15,000 from Corby on 20/7/94) FL 59+1/1 FLC 1 FAC 4 Others 8

McKENZIE Leon Mark
Born: Croydon, 17 May 1978
Height: 5'7" Weight: 9.10

Crystal Palace youth team striker who was promoted to the senior side last October, after netting 14 goals in eight games, and scored in a 2-0 victory over Southend in the Coca Cola Cup. Made his league debut as substitute in the next match and his full debut in December, but after three months in the first team squad without further goals he was rested. Nevertheless, he looks a great prospect and signed a three year contract in October. Is the son of Clinton, the former British and European light-welterweight champion and the nephew of Duke, a world champion in three different weight divisions.

Crystal Palace (From trainee on 7/10/95) FL 4+8 FLC 3/1 FAC 1+1

McKINLAY William (Billy)
Born: Glasgow, 22 April 1969
Height: 5'9" Weight: 11.1
International Honours: S: 18; B-1; U21-6; Yth; Sch
Signed by Blackburn last October from Dundee United, Billy arrived at Ewood with a great reputation as a grafting central midfielder. Had to wait for several weeks to receive his debut, and had made insufficient advances, even with Lars Bohinen absent, to stop Rovers replacing David Batty with Garry Flitcroft. Although displaying an ability to get forward, he did not hit the target until April when he scored at Nottingham Forest, but continued to improve right up until the final whistle and will be a better player for the experience in 1996-97. Added to his Scottish caps when coming off the bench for 34 minutes of the Euro '96 0-0 draw against Holland.

Dundee U (Free from Hamilton Thistle on 24/6/85) SL 210+10/22 SLC 21/3 SC 23+3/4 Others 16+1/2
Blackburn Rov (£1,750,000 on 14/10/95) PL 13+6/2 FLC 2 FAC 1+1

McLAREN Paul Andrew
Born: Wycombe, 17 November 1976
Height: 6'0" Weight: 12.6
Young Luton midfielder with good ball control, plus the ability to get stuck in when necessary. Made his full debut away to Tranmere last October and scored his first goal, the winner, in a 3-2 thriller against the same team in the home fixture in December. With added confidence and experience that a longer run-in the side will bring, 1996-97 could see Paul kick-start his career as a regular.

Luton T (From trainee on 5/1/94) FL 9+4/1 FAC 1 Others 3

McLEAN Ian
Born: Paisley, 18 August 1966
Height: 6'2" Weight: 13.2
International Honours: Canada: 3
A Canadian international central defender, Ian found it difficult to establish a regular place in Bristol Rovers' line-up in 1995-96, although enjoying a two month loan spell with second division rivals, Rotherham. This was only interrupted following his dismissal in a match against Chesterfield, but not before he had shown a willingness to give his all and his left-footed ability had

brought balance to the Merry Miller's defence. On his return to Twerton Park, he was subsequently released in the summer.

Bristol Rov (Signed from Metroford on 15/9/93) FL 21+14/2 FLC 0+1 FAC 1 Others 3+2/1
Cardiff C (Loaned on 9/9/94) FL 3
Cardiff C (Loaned on 21/12/94) FL 1
Rotherham U (Loaned on 19/1/96) FL 9

McLEARY Alan Terry
Born: Lambeth, 6 October 1964
Height: 6'0" Weight: 11.9
Club Honours: FLT '83; Div 2 '88
International Honours: E: B-2; U21-1; Yth
This right-footed central defender who joined Bristol City from Charlton Athletic during the summer of 1995, amazed everyone in making a quick recovery from a serious injury sustained at Peterborough in September, that was expected to keep him sidelined for the rest of the season. Returning to the team on 4 November, Alan went on to play a major part in City's improved form during the second half of the campaign and, as a good reader of the game and strong in the air, he also proved to be an excellent choice as the club captain.

Millwall (From apprentice on 12/10/81) FL 289+18/5 FLC 16+1 FAC 24+1/2 Others 22+1/2
Sheffield U (Loaned on 23/7/92) PL 3
Wimbledon (Loaned on 16/10/92) PL 4 FLC 2
Charlton Ath (Free on 27/5/93) FL 66/3 FLC 2 FAC 6 Others 3
Bristol C (Free on 31/7/95) FL 30+1 FLC 2

Alan McLoughlin

McLOUGHLIN Alan Francis
Born: Manchester, 20 April 1967
Height: 5'8" Weight: 10.0
International Honours: Ei: 23; B-3
Portsmouth's attacking midfielder led the team in goals for most of last season, although many came from the penalty spot. Missing very few games, despite not playing

in his favoured slot for most of the time, and battling hard to produce a number of very strong performances, Alan continued to show his ability to get forward into good scoring positions and was rewarded with further Republic of Ireland international caps. At the same time, the passing side of his game remains highly valued.

Manchester U (From apprentice on 25/4/85)
Swindon T (Free on 15/8/86) FL 101+5/19 FLC 11+3/5 FAC 4+2 Others 10/1
Torquay U (Loaned on 13/3/87) FL 21+3/4
Southampton (£1,000,000 on 13/12/90) FL 22+2/1 FLC 0+1 FAC 4 Others 1
Aston Villa (Loaned on 30/9/91) Others 1
Portsmouth (£400,000 on 17/2/92) FL 171+5/33 FLC 15/3 FAC 7+1/5 Others 9/1

McMAHON Gerard (Gerry) Joseph
Born: Belfast, 29 December 1973
Height: 5'11" Weight: 11.6
International Honours: NI: 7; B-2; U21-1; Yth; Sch

The potentially gifted winger who, despite winning international selection for Northern Ireland, has found it hard to secure first team action at Tottenham. A skilful player who enjoys getting forward to have shots at goal, and who creates space in midfield by taking play wide to the wings, he started last season on the bench and enjoyed a short run of five games as first choice in September and October, but made only one further appearance thereafter. However, he did not lack confidence and first team football will surely come his way in 1996-97, wherever.

Tottenham H (£100,000 from Glenavon on 31/7/92) PL 9+7 FLC 3 FAC 0+1
Barnet (Loaned on 20/10/94) FL 10/2 FAC 2/1 Others 1

McMAHON Samuel (Sam) Keiron
Born: Newark, 10 February 1976
Height: 5'10" Weight: 11.5

Classy right-footed Leicester City midfielder. Although scoring on his seasonal debut from the bench at Port Vale in 1995-96, he failed to establish a regular place in the side. However, he continued to impress in the reserves.

Leicester C (From trainee on 10/7/94) P/FL 1+3/1 FLC 0+1

McMAHON Stephen (Steve)
Born: Liverpool, 20 August 1961
Height: 5'9" Weight: 12.1
Club Honours: Div 1 '86, '88, '90; Div 2 '96; FAC '86, '89; CS '86, '88, '89
International Honours: E: 17; B-2; U21-6

Steve had an outstanding first full season as player/manager in 1995-96, inspiring Swindon to the division two championship after the club had suffered two successive relegations. Injury forced the former England midfield hard-man to direct operations from the bench during the second half of the campaign, but his side responded magnificently and in the end won the title with something to spare.

Everton (From apprentice on 29/8/79) FL 99+1/11 FLC 11/3 FAC 9
Aston Villa (£175,000 on 20/5/83) FL 74+1/7 FLC 9 FAC 3 Others 4
Liverpool (£375,000 on 12/9/85) FL 202+2/29 FLC 27/13 FAC 30/7 Others 16/1

Manchester C (£900,000 on 24/12/91) F/PL 83+4/1 FLC 8 FAC 3
Swindon T (£100,000 on 1/12/94) FL 36+2 FLC 4 FAC 3+1 Others 0+1

McMAHON Steven (Steve)
Born: Glasgow, 22 April 1970
Height: 6'4" Weight: 14.3

The giant striker came to Darlington last January on a six month contract, following a trial at Partick Thistle, having previously spent two years in China. Never really hit it off at Feethams, despite his aerial ability and scored just once in ten outings, prior to being released during the summer.

Swansea C (Signed from Ferguslie on 16/8/91) FL 2
Carlisle U (Free on 7/7/93) FL 2 Others 0+1 (Free to Barrow on 12/2/94)
Partick Thistle (Free from Foshan, China in December 1995) SL 0+1
Darlington (Free on 15/1/96) FL 6+4/1

Steve McManaman

McMANAMAN Steven (Steve)
Born: Bootle, 11 February 1972
Height: 5'11" Weight: 10.10
Club Honours: FAC '92; FLC '95
International Honours: E: 15; U21-7; Yth

Enjoyed his best ever season for Liverpool in 1995-96 as an ever present and established himself as a regular choice for the England team. Recognised as a winger, he was given a free role in the Reds' system, similar to that of John Barnes under the management of Kenny Dalglish, thus operating mainly in centre field and carrying the ball forward from half way to the penalty area. His close control and ability to ghost around defenders, created havoc amongst opposing defences and set up numerous scoring opportunities for his colleagues. The only criticism that can be made about his game is his lack of finishing, his superb goal against Aston Villa in March being his first at Anfield for over a year! This was followed closely by two against Leeds in the

FA Cup sixth round replay. Had an excellent Euro '96 as a regular for an English side that was unlucky to lose out to the Germans at the semi-final stage.

Liverpool (From trainee on 19/2/90) F/PL 160+11/24 FLC 23+1/8 FAC 25+1/5 Others 15/2

McMILLAN Lyndon Andre (Andy)
Born: Bloemfontein, South Africa, 22 June 1968
Height: 5'11" Weight: 11.9

A matured and composed right back, Andy had a fine season as York's only ever present in 1995-96, where his coolness and authority at the back was a great asset to the defence during a difficult campaign. Currently 14 months away from completing ten years at Bootham Crescent, he was voted "Clubman of the Year" by the supporters.

York C (Signed on 17/10/87) FL 300+12/4 FLC 16 FAC 13 Others 23

McMINN Kevin (Ted) Clifton
Born: Castle Douglas, 28 September 1962
Height: 6'0" Weight: 13.8
Club Honours: SLC '86

Always a crowd pleaser, at 33, Ted often found the pace of the game too much and his wing skills were generally reserved for home matches during the first half of last season. There were still occasional flashes of brilliance, though, and many were sorry to see him go when Burnley granted his request to leave as a result of personal problems.

Queen of the South (Signed from Glenafton Ath on 1/1/82) SL 56+6/5 SLC 4+2 SC 1
Glasgow R (£50,000 on 1/10/84) SL 37+26/4 SLC 4+2/2 Others 2+3 (£225,000 to Seville on 5/2/88)
Derby Co (£300,000 on 5/2/88) FL 108+15/9 FLC 11/3 FAC 6+1/1 Others 12/1
Birmingham C (£115,000 on 28/7/93) FL 19+3 FLC 1+1 FAC 1 Others 1
Burnley (Signed on 5/4/94) FL 38+8/3 FLC 4 FAC 2+2 Others 3+1

Ted McMinn

McNALLY Mark
Born: Motherwell, 10 March 1971
Height: 5'9" Weight: 10.7
Club Honours: SC '95
International Honours: S: U21-2

Another bargain capture from Celtic by Southend manager, Ronnie Whelan, last December, Mark's natural talent on the ball was a joy to behold for the fans. Fitting in at centre half after the serious injury to Mike Lapper, he always had time on the ball and the skill to find the wide men with telling long passes, chipping in with a couple of goals as well. Is sure to be one of the men that the team will be built around next season.

Glasgow Celtic (From juniors on 15/5/87) SL 112+10/3 SLC 11+2/1 SC 10 Others 6+1
Southend U (£100,000 on 8/12/95) FL 20/2 FAC 1

McNIVEN Scott Andrew
Born: Leeds, 27 May 1978
Height: 5'10" Weight: 10.6
International Honours: S: U21-1; Yth

The son of the former Leeds' player, David, and with a twin brother also on Oldham's books, Scott developed well with Latics during 1995-96, making 22 first team appearances. Fast footed and a good passer of the ball, his impressive early form, when he played mainly at right back, saw him called up by Scotland at both youth and U21 level. Having turned professional in October, there should be no holding back for this youngster.

Oldham Ath (From trainee on 25/10/95) FL 15+1 FLC 2 FAC 1 Others 4

McPHERSON Keith Anthony
Born: Greenwich, 11 September 1963
Height: 5'11" Weight: 11.0
Club Honours: FAYC '81; Div 4 '87, Div 2 '94

Yet another former Reading first team regular, whose 1995-96 season was blighted by a long-term injury problem, pelvic instability meaning a complete rest for up to six months after his final game of the season, at Norwich in December. Thereafter, the popular centre back and captain was very much missed for his consistency and commitment in the heart of the Royals' defence.

West Ham U (From apprentice on 12/9/81) FL 1
Cambridge U (Loaned on 30/9/85) FL 11/1
Northampton T (£15,000 on 23/1/86) FL 182/8 FLC 9/1 FAC 12 Others 13
Reading (Signed on 24/8/90) FL 188+5/6 FLC 13+1 FAC 10+1 Others 9+1

McROBERT Lee Peter
Born: Bromley, 4 October 1972
Height: 5'8" Weight: 10.12

Millwall midfielder whose tenacious tackling and fine passing ability augers well for the future. Injury and competition for midfield slots restricted Lee's appearances in 1995-96, but he had a good game against Everton in the Coca Cola Cup and would hope to build on the experience.

Millwall (£35,000 from Sittingbourne on 17/2/95) FL 5+9/1 FLC 1 FAC 1

McSWEGAN Gary
Born: Glasgow, 24 September 1970
Height: 5'8" Weight: 10.9
Club Honours: SC '93
International Honours: S: Yth; Sch

Discarded by the Notts County manager, Colin Murphy, after four games from the bench at the start of last season, the lofty Scottish forward ended 15 disappointing months at Meadow Lane with a move to Dundee United for £375,000 in October. With a strike rate of 26 in 80 (including 17 as a sub) games and the ability to shoot on sight, Gary would have scored many more had it not been for injuries.

Glasgow R (From juniors in 1986) SL 9+9/4 SLC 1 SC 0+2 Others 0+3/1
Notts Co (£400,000 on 13/7/93) FL 47+15/21 FLC 6+1/3 FAC 4+1/1 Others 6/1

MADDEN Lawrence (Lawrie) David
Born: Hackney, 28 September 1955
Height 5'11" Weight: 13.1
Club Honours: FLC '91

This veteran non-contract central defender appeared just once for Chesterfield in 1995-96, in the season's opener, at Oxford. Thereafter, he concentrated on his sports journalism career and eventually moved to Unibond League side, Emley, in March, having completed 21 years in the Football League.

Mansfield T (Free from Arsenal on 1/3/75) FL 9+1 FLC 2 FAC 2 (Freed during 1976 close season)
Charlton Ath (Free from Manchester University on 4/3/78) FL 109+4/7 FLC 4+2 FAC 8
Millwall (£10,000 on 25/3/82) FL 44+3/2 FLC 2 FAC 1
Sheffield Wed (Free on 24/8/83) FL 200+12/2 FLC 26+2/3 FAC 20+1 Others 5
Leicester C (Loaned on 17/1/91) FL 3
Wolverhampton W (Free on 15/8/91) FL 62+5/1 FLC 4 FAC 3 Others 2
Darlington (Free on 3/9/93) FL 5 Others 1
Chesterfield (Free on 4/10/93) FL 37/1 FLC 2 FAC 1 Others 1

MADDISON Lee Robert
Born: Bristol, 5 October 1972
Height: 5'11" Weight: 12.4

Northampton left back with an attacking flair, he initially came on loan from Bristol Rovers before signing on a permanent basis last October. However, no sooner had he put pen to paper, he picked up a leg injury that ended his season in February. Good in the air, he can also tackle with the best of them.

Bristol Rov (From trainee on 18/7/91) FL 68+5 FLC 4 FAC 2 Others 6+1
Northampton T (£25,000 on 22/9/95) FL 21 FAC 2 Others 2

MADDISON Neil Stanley
Born: Darlington, 2 October 1969
Height: 5'10" Weight: 11.8

Southampton midfielder with high workrate qualities who can also play up front, he keeps his passing simple but effective, with running off the ball a trademark of his play. Unfortunate to miss a large part of 1995-96 due to injury, having played in the opening 11 games followed by a brief spell in mid-season, Neil made a good comeback immediately prior to the end of the campaign

and will be looking for a better return in 1996-97.

Southampton (From trainee on 14/4/88) F/PL 130+15/17 FLC 7+3 FAC 7+5 Others 1

MADDIX Daniel (Danny) Shawn
Born: Ashford, 11 October 1967
Height: 5'11" Weight: 11.7

Strong-tackling QPR central defender who is good in the air and one of the best man-for man-markers around, Danny began last season as the central defensive partner to Alan McDonald, playing in the opening 18 games of the season until injury set him back in November. Returning to the side on New Year's Day, he only played in "fits and starts", before injury once again ruled him out. With Rangers ultimately relegated, his experience will be vital as the club hunt for a quick return to the Premiership.

Tottenham H (From apprentice on 25/7/85)
Southend U (Loaned on 1/11/86) FL 2
Queens Park R (Free on 23/7/87) F/PL 163+25/7 FLC 18/2 FAC 18+2/2 Others 2+3

MAGEE Kevin
Born: Edinburgh, 10 April 1971
Height: 5'10" Weight: 11.4

Despite featuring in the squad for all of Preston's opening nine games of last season, his monthly contract was not renewed in mid-September. Following a trial for Plymouth, the flying winger joined Scarborough in December and retained a regular place for most of the term, turning in some good performances, before being released in a mass clear out of players this summer.

Partick Thistle (Signed from Armadale Thistle on 12/8/91) SL 0+11 SC 1
Preston NE (£25,000 on 5/5/93) FL 23+3/1 FLC 1+1 Others 1
Plymouth Arg (Free on 29/9/95) FL 0+4 FAC 0+1 Others 1
Scarborough (Free on 7/12/95) FL 26+2/1

MAGILTON Jim
Born: Belfast, 6 May 1969
Height: 6'0" Weight: 13.12
International Honours: NI: 32; U23-2; U21-1; Yth; Sch

Skilful Southampton midfielder, and a regular for Northern Ireland, Jim is a good link player who works well with Matt le Tissier and Barry Venison. He can also score valuable goals, the winner against Newcastle, an equaliser in a 2-2 draw with Everton and two in a 3-0 FA Cup win over Portsmouth, all at home, among his five from 40 games last season. Although left out on a couple of occasions, the side played better with him, something borne out by results when he was absent.

Liverpool (From apprentice on 14/5/86)
Oxford U (£100,000 on 3/10/90) FL 150/34 FLC 9/1 FAC 8/4 Others 6/3
Southampton (£600,000 on 11/2/94) PL 88/9 FLC 6 FAC 11/3

MAHON Alan Joseph
Born: Dublin, 4 April 1978
Height: 5'10" Weight: 11.5
International Honours: Ei: U21-1; Yth; Sch

Highly-rated Irish youth international who made his debut for the Eire U21 side last season, Alan burst on the scene for Tranmere as a substitute at Huddersfield in February. An attacking midfielder with pace, skill and tenacity, who loves to burst forward, big things are expected of him in the future. Came through the club's youth scheme.

Tranmere Rov (From trainee on 7/4/95) FL 0+2

MAHORN Paul Gladstone
Born: Leyton, 13 August 1973
Height: 5'10" Weight: 11.6

A deadline day loan signing from Tottenham, Paul was one of several players used by Burnley up front, alongside Kurt Nogan, during last season. Quite nimble, he occasionally threatened danger and scored on his Claret's debut. Failed to appear for Spurs in 1995-96, having played just one Premier League match in four years.

Tottenham H (From trainee on 31/1/92) PL 1
Fulham (Loaned on 23/9/93) FL 1+2 Others 1
Burnley (Loaned on 28/3/96) FL 3+5/1

MAKEL Lee Robert
Born: Sunderland, 11 January 1973
Height: 5'11" Weight: 11.7

Midfield playmaker signed by Huddersfield from Blackburn Rovers last October. A quality player with a good first touch, he has the ability to ghost past opposition players and dictate the play. Was told by the management that, despite his all-round play, they expected a greater contribution from him on the goals front, which he attempted to correct by pushing forward more. Prior to joining Town, Lee made just one start from six appearances for Blackburn in 1995-96. Played for the Football League U21 side against the Italian Serie "B" XI on home territory in November.

Newcastle U (From trainee on 11/2/91) FL 6+6/1 FLC 1 Others 0+1
Blackburn Rov (£160,000 on 20/7/92) PL 1+5 FLC 0+3 Others 1+3
Huddersfield T (£300,000 on 13/10/95) FL 33/2 FAC 4

MAKIN Christopher Gregory
Born: Manchester, 8 May 1973
Height: 5'10" Weight: 11.2
International Honours: E: U21-5; Yth; Sch

An extremely reliable Oldham defender, cum midfielder, who played at full back on both flanks last season, Chris again proved that he had the distribution to match his pace. Watched throughout the campaign by Manchester City and Sunderland, he missed very few games and, with his contract up in the summer, were he to move, the club would feel it most keenly, his great stamina allowing him to match anyone around. Just ask Sunderland's Alex Rae if you do not believe it. Also scored in wins at Wolves and at home to Norwich. Represented the Football League U21 side that drew 1-1 against the Italian Serie "B" XI at Huddersfield in November.

Oldham Ath (From trainee on 2/11/91) F/PL 93+1/4 FLC 7 FAC 11 Others 1+1
Wigan Ath (Loaned on 28/8/92) FL 14+1/2

MALKIN Christopher (Chris) Gregory
Born: Hoylake, 4 June 1967
Height: 6'3" Weight: 12.9
Club Honours: AMC '90

A Millwall signing from Tranmere during the 1995 close season, Chris proved to be both pacy and tireless in his role up front for the club. Having recovered from a knee operation during the summer, he opened his goalscoring account in the first game of last season against Grimsby. Continued in that vein with some lovely headers, as well as injury-time winner against Luton, when latching onto a perfect through ball and slipping it past the 'keeper. Has been an excellent buy for the Lions.

Tranmere Rov (Free from Stork AFC on 27/7/87) FL 184+48/60 FLC 20+5/6 FAC 9+4/3 Others 26+7/7
Millwall (£400,000 on 13/7/95) FL 39+4/11 FLC 3 FAC 2/1

MANN Neil
Born: Nottingham, 19 November 1972
Height: 5'10" Weight: 12.1

Neil's 1995-96 campaign got off to a heartening start when scoring for Hull in a pre-season win over his old club, Grimsby Town. Filled the left wing/back role when moved to overcome City's early malaise, but suffered his own setback when sidelined for two months with shin splints. Arthur Mann's (the WBA assistant boss) son can carry the ball and uses it to good effect, and with the loss of Dean Windass, arguably, he became the most skilful performer in the Tigers' squad.

Grimsby T (Free from Notts Co juniors on 6/9/90)
Hull C (Free from Grantham T, via Spalding, on 30/7/93) FL 65+9/3 FLC 5+2 FAC 3 Others 4+2/1

MANUEL William (Billy) Albert James
Born: Hackney, 28 June 1969
Height: 5'10" Weight: 12.8
Club Honours: Div 3 '92

Now in his second spell with Gillingham, and recognised as a biting midfielder, he returned in January 1996 to play in the unusual position of left back, having been freed by Peterborough. At London Road he had only missed one game from 18 at one stage, and had scored three goals in the first four matches, before leaving. With Dominic Naylor out injured, Billy took over in five out of the last seven games as the Gills raced into the second division.

Tottenham H (From trainee on 28/7/87)
Gillingham (Signed on 10/2/89) FL 74+13/5 FLC 2 FAC 3 Others 5
Brentford (£60,000 on 14/6/91) FL 83+11/1 FLC 7+1/1 FAC 4 Others 8+2
Peterborough U (Free on 16/9/94)
Cambridge U (Free on 28/10/94) FL 10 FAC 2
Peterborough U (Free on 28/2/95) FL 27/2 FLC 4/3 FAC 1+1 Others 2
Gillingham (Free on 26/1/96) FL 6+4

MARDENBOROUGH Stephen (Steve) Alexander
Born: Birmingham, 11 September 1964
Height: 5'7" Weight: 11.9
Club Honours: GMVC '90; Div 4 '91

Striker. Released by Swansea in 1985, Steve returned to the Vetch Field last December on non-contract terms, but made only one league appearance at Oxford. Started 1995-

96 with Scarborough, before joining Colchester on a free, and got his chance after injury to Steve Whitton and Robert Reinelt. Slightly unfortunate to be released on economic grounds.

Coventry C (From apprentice on 6/8/82)
Wolverhampton W (Free on 20/9/83) FL 9/1 FLC 0+1 FAC 0+1
Cambridge U (Loaned on 23/2/84) FL 6
Swansea C (Free on 30/7/84) FL 32+4/7 FLC 2 FAC 2 Others 3+1
Newport Co (Free on 19/7/85) FL 50+14/11 FLC 4+1 FAC 5+1/1 Others 2+1/1
Cardiff C (Free on 27/3/87) FL 18+14/1 FLC 1 FAC 0+1 Others 1+1
Hereford U (Free on 28/7/88) FL 20+7 FLC 2 FAC 1 Others 1+1 (Free to IFK Ostersund on 1/7/89)
Darlington (Free from Cheltenham T on 6/7/90) FL 79+27/18 FLC 2+5/1 FAC 3+1 Others 2/1
Lincoln C (£10,000 on 12/7/93) FL 14+7/2 FLC 2 FAC 0+1 Others 1+1
Scarborough (Free on 1/2/95) FL 0+1
Colchester U (Free on 30/8/95) FL 4+8/2 FAC 1 Others 1
Swansea C (Free on 7/12/95) FL 1

MARDON Paul Jonathan
Born: Bristol, 14 September 1969
Height: 6'0" Weight: 11.10
International Honours: W: 1

Paul had an excellent first half to last season when he teamed up with Paul Raven at the heart of WBA's defence, his good form winning him a Welsh cap against Germany at Cardiff Arms Park in October. Strong in the air, and composed on the ground, he was in dominating form as Albion held a high position in the table, but then suffered a knee injury which sidelined him for a short while before he returned to play just as well as ever. Can also contribute from midfield and full back.

Bristol C (From trainee on 29/1/88) FL 29+13 FLC 3+3/1 FAC 1
Doncaster Rov (Loaned on 13/9/90) FL 3
Birmingham C (£115,000 on 16/8/91) FL 54+10 FLC 11+1 FAC 1 Others 3
West Bromwich A (£400,000 on 18/11/93) FL 84+5/2 FLC 4 FAC 3 Others 2

Paul Mardon

MARGETSON Martyn Walter
Born: Neath, 8 September 1971
Height: 6'0" Weight: 13.10
International Honours: W: B; U21-7; Yth; Sch

With three experienced goalkeepers on Manchester City's books, Martyn has had little opportunity to play these past five years. A good shot stopper and sure kicker, he made his only appearance of last season as a forward, after being brought on as a substitute for the last five minutes in the home Coca Cola Cup game against Wycombe. And, much to the amusement of the crowd, his great enthusiasm saw him almost score with a looping header. Selected as substitute for over 20 first team games, now that Tony Coton has left, his chance will surely come.
Manchester C (From trainee on 5/7/90) F/PL 6 FLC 0+2 Others 1
Bristol Rov (Loaned on 8/12/93) FL 2+1

MARKER Nicholas (Nicky) Robert
Born: Budleigh Salterton, 3 May 1965
Height: 6'0" Weight: 12.11
Blackburn utility player and a survivor of cruciate ligament surgery who returned to star regularly for a young reserve side in 1995-96. Pressed into first team service when the club were down to a minimum of players, he filled in for Colin Hendry and also in midfield. His five games at centre back, against Tottenham, scoring his first goal for the club, Leeds, Rosenborg, Everton and Southampton, brought him the accolade that Hendry had scarcely been missed.
Exeter C (From apprentice on 4/5/83) FL 196+6/3 FLC 11/1 FAC 8 Others 8/3
Plymouth Arg (£95,000 on 31/10/87) FL 201+1/13 FLC 15/3 FAC 9/1 Others 7/1
Blackburn Rov (£500,000 on 23/9/92) PL 36+11/1 FLC 3 FAC 4 Others 1+1

MARKMAN Damien Liam
Born: Ascot, 7 January 1978
Height: 5'8" Weight: 11.1
A prolific scorer for Wycombe's youth team, this fast, compact striker was given a surprise first team debut against Brighton last March and was rewarded with a professional contract. Only a youngster, he has plenty of time to develop.
Wycombe W (Free from Slough T on 29/11/95) FL 0+2

MARKS Jamie
Born: Belfast, 18 March 1977
Height: 5'9" Weight: 10.13
International Honours: NI: Yth; Sch
Having become a Tiger early in 1996, along with former Leeds colleague, Paul Wharton, Jamie made his Hull debut a month later (with Paul) in the home draw against Bournemouth. Used in the right wing/back role and not being scared to hug the touchline, he gave a useful attacking option. Is the possessor of a powerful physique and not one to shirk a challenge.
Leeds U (From trainee on 1/4/95)
Hull C (Free on 13/2/96) FL 4

MARQUIS Paul Raymond
Born: Enfield, 29 August 1972
Height: 6'2" Weight: 14.4
Elegant Doncaster defender who enjoyed a run-in the first team towards the end of last season after a series of niggling injuries had earned him the unwanted tag of "the forgotten man of Belle Vue". Good enough to warrant a regular place now he is fully fit, earlier in the campaign he had a spell on loan with non-league Gateshead.
West Ham U (From trainee on 1/7/91) PL 0+1
Doncaster Rov (Free on 10/3/94) FL 25+1/1

MARRIOTT Andrew (Andy)
Born: Sutton in Ashfield, 11 October 1970
Height: 6'0" Weight: 12.6
Club Honours: Div 4 '92; FMC '92; WC '95
International Honours: E: U21-1; Yth; Sch. W: 1
Andy has not missed a single game for Wrexham since his transfer from Nottingham Forest in October 1993, being a superb shot stopper who, last season, emerged as a contender for the custodian's spot in the Welsh side following long-term consistent displays. Available for Wales due to his grandparents, and the fact that his England U21 appearance was a friendly, he came on for the second half against Switzerland in April and acquitted himself well.
Arsenal (From trainee on 22/10/88)
Nottingham F (£50,000 on 20/6/89) F/PL 11 FLC 1 Others 1
West Bromwich A (Loaned on 6/9/89) FL 3
Blackburn Rov (Loaned on 29/12/89) FL 2
Colchester U (Loaned on 21/3/90) FL 10
Burnley (Loaned on 29/8/91) FL 15 Others 2
Wrexham (£200,000 on 8/10/93) FL 128 FLC 6 FAC 10 Others 19

MARSDEN Christopher (Chris)
Born: Sheffield, 3 January 1969
Height: 5'11" Weight: 10.12
Initially signed on loan from Notts County last January, the move becoming permanent a month later, the astute and highly competitive player made himself a big Edgeley Park favourite with a string of "Man of the Match" awards. A midfielder who played just four times for the Magpies before his transfer, he masterminded Stockport's late-season push for the play offs, his silky passing skills giving his transfer fee a real bargain look.
Sheffield U (From apprentice on 6/1/87) FL 13+3/1 FLC 1 Others 1
Huddersfield T (Signed on 15/7/88) FL 113+8/9 FLC 15+1 FAC 6+2 Others 10
Coventry C (Loaned on 2/11/93) PL 5+2
Wolverhampton W (£250,000 on 11/1/94) FL 8 FAC 3
Notts Co (£250,000 on 15/11/94) FL 10 FLC 1 Others 1/1
Stockport Co (£70,000 on 12/1/96) FL 19+1/1

MARSH Christopher (Chris) Jonathan
Born: Sedgley, 14 January 1970
Height: 6'0" Weight: 13.2
Walsall club captain and longest serving player, having made his debut in January 1988, Chris is a splendidly versatile player who spent most of last season in midfield and would probably have been an ever

present but for an unfortunate sending off at Notts County in March. Just 12 short of 300 appearances, he looks forward to celebrating his testimonial in 1996-97.
Walsall (From trainee on 11/7/88) FL 204+32/21 FLC 13+2/1 FAC 21+1/3 Others 14+1/3

MARSH Michael (Mike) Andrew
Born: Liverpool, 21 July 1969
Height: 5'8" Weight: 11.0
Club Honours: FAC '92
Probably the most naturally skilful player to have ever worn the blue of Southend, Mike was brought from Galatasaray of Turkey for a club record last September. His continual midfield promptings were behind the majority of Blues' moves, while his partnership with Paul Byrne brought many gasps of delight from the fans, and his injury-time goal to beat Ipswich in April from 25 yards will be remembered by all those that witnessed it for many years to come. Also a firm tackler, he is the man that could lead the club to even greater heights next season.
Liverpool (Free from Kirby T on 21/8/87) F/PL 42+27/2 FLC 10+1/3 FAC 6+2 Others 12+1/1
West Ham U (Signed on 17/9/93) PL 46+3/1 FLC 6 FAC 6/1
Coventry C (£450,000 on 30/12/94) PL 15/2 FAC 4 (£500,000 to Galatasaray on 13/7/95)
Southend U (£500,000 on 4/9/95) FL 40/5 FLC 2 FAC 1 Others 3/1

Mike Marsh

MARSH Simon Thomas Peter
Born: Ealing, 29 January 1977
Height: 5'11" Weight: 11.2
Simon is a full back who did not feature as much for Oxford in 1995-96 as in the previous season, when he broke through from the youth team, largely due to the almost ever-present defence which United were able to field. However, he remains a bright hope for the future, perhaps even next season, with his ability to get forward, especially for set pieces.

Oxford U (From trainee on 22/11/94) FL 10+3 FLC 2+2 FAC 2 Others 2

MARSHALL Andrew (Andy) John
Born: Bury St Edmunds, 14 April 1975
Height: 6'2" Weight: 13.7
International Honours: E: U21-2
The promising young Norwich and England U21 international goalkeeper selected himself in a world's best team, so he does not lack confidence, although he spent another season in 1995-96 lacking opportunity behind first choice, Bryan Gunn. Manager, Martin O'Neill, invariably preferred three outfield players as substitutes so Andy only played when Gunn served a suspension, apart from a last match win at Selhurst Park when the big Scot was rested. Supplemented his meagre first team appearances with 25 outings for the high-scoring combination side.
Norwich C (From trainee on 6/7/93) P/FL 23+1 FLC 2 FAC 2+1

MARSHALL Dwight Wayne
Born: Jamaica, WI, 3 October 1965
Height: 5'11" Weight: 11.8
Right-sided Luton attacker who is fast and opportunistic and who would have undoubtedly enjoyed more success playing alongside a conventional central striker last season. Top scorer in a goal shy team struggling against relegation, Dwight unfortunately broke his leg against Sunderland in February just as Town were putting a fine run together and, without his ability to take on defenders in the box and capitalise on half chances, the Hatters fell apart to finish bottom of the table. Despite his absence, he remained the club's leading goalscorer and won three "Player of the Year" awards from the various supporters clubs.
Plymouth Arg (£35,000 from Grays Athletic on 9/8/91) FL 93+6/27 FLC 8/1 FAC 7+2/4 Others 7+1/4
Middlesbrough (Loaned on 25/3/93) PL 0+3
Luton T (£150,000 on 15/7/94) FL 59+12/20 FLC 3+1/2 FAC 5/2 Others 2+1/2

Dwight Marshall

MARSHALL Ian Paul
Born: Liverpool, 20 March 1966
Height: 6'1" Weight: 12.12
Club Honours: CS '86; Div 2 '91
Fortunately, a series of niggling injuries failed to disrupt Ian's performances for Ipswich last season and he notched up 19 goals, the same number as his strike partner, Alex Mathie, even though helping out in defence on a number of occasions. As a chaser of lost causes, his strength and deceptive pace leading defenders a merry dance, it was his role up front that took the eye, scoring the club's first goal on the opening day. He later collected braces at Sheffield United, Leicester and Barnsley, while a classic header against the Foxes earned him the club's "Goal of the Season".
Everton (From apprentice on 23/3/84) FL 9+6/1 FLC 1+1/1 Others 7
Oldham Ath (£100,000 on 24/3/88) F/PL 165+5/36 FLC 17 FAC 14/3 Others 2+1/1
Ipswich T (£750,000 on 9/8/93) P/FL 77+5/32 FLC 3/2 FAC 9/3

MARSHALL John Philip
Born: Balham, 18 August 1964
Height: 5'10" Weight: 12.6
A real pro, who has played in virtually every position for Fulham except goal, John missed half of last season recuperating from a badly broken leg, sustained in 1994-95, before coming back to play wide on the right and then taking over the right back spot for the last five games. Was released during the summer.
Fulham (From apprentice on 20/8/82) FL 393+18/28 FLC 33/2 FAC 19+1/3 Others 21/2

MARSHALL Scott Roderick
Born: Edinburgh, 1 May 1973
Height: 6'1" Weight: 12.5
International Honours: S: U21-5; Yth
Arsenal central defender who is strong in the air and looks to come out of defence with the ball, rather than clear his lines. Having made two Premiership appearances back in 1992-93, he finally managed to add to that last season, due to a mixture of injuries and the implimentation of the three man defence. Also scored his first goal for the club, a memorable header in the league victory over Newcastle, which was pure "Tony Adams". The son of former Hearts' favourite, Gordon, and brother to the current Celtic 'keeper, Gordon junior, Scott added three more Scottish U21 caps to his collection in 1995-96.
Arsenal (From trainee on 18/3/91) PL 12+1/1
Rotherham U (Loaned on 3/12/93) FL 10/1 Others 1
Sheffield U (Loaned on 25/8/94) FL 17

MARTIN Alvin Edward
Born: Bootle, 29 July 1958
Height: 6'1" Weight: 13.9
Club Honours: FAC '80; Div 2 '81
International Honours: E: 17; B-2; Yth
The veteran West Ham centre half, calling on his vast experience, helped the side recover from a bad start when coming in for ten games alongside Marc Rieper, the Hammers losing just once during that spell. Unlucky to pick up a hamstring injury, when

fit again, the brilliant form of the Croatian newcomer, Slaven Bilic, forced him to play out the rest of the season with the reserves, apart from coming on as sub in the final game of the season. Announced as being his final appearance in a United shirt, Alvin received a standing ovation before leaving during the summer to join Leyton Orient. Is still very competitive and strong, especially in aerial situations.
West Ham U (From apprentice on 1/7/76) F/PL 462+7/27 FLC 71/6 FAC 40 Others 16/1

MARTIN David
Born: East Ham, 25 April 1963
Height: 6'1" Weight: 13.1
Club Honours: FAYC '79; FLT '83; FAT '92
(On loan at Colchester U)
International Honours: E: Yth
Appointed Gillingham's club captain on his signing from Bristol City during the summer of 1995, the hard-tackling midfielder led the team to their first title success for 22 years. Although missing a large chunk of the season due to suspensions and injury, this was the sixth time he had been involved in a promotion winning side, his experience proving invaluable. Is a player who leads by example.
Millwall (From apprentice on 10/5/80) FL 131+9/6 FLC 10+2/3 FAC 7/1 Others 4/1
Wimbledon (£35,000 on 14/9/84) FL 30+5/3 FLC 21 FAC 2+1
Southend U (Free on 23/8/86) FL 212+9/19 FLC 25/4 FAC 9+1 Others 10+1/3
Bristol C (Free on 19/7/93) FL 36+2/1 FAC 5 Others 2
Northampton T (Loaned on 13/2/95) FL 7/1
Gillingham (Free on 4/8/95) FL 27+4/1 FLC 1 FAC 4/1 Others 1

MARTIN Dean Edward
Born: Islington, 31 August 1972
Height: 5'8" Weight: 11.6
Small Brentford outside right with good skill and the ability to cross the ball well. Having arrived back in this country from a spell in Iceland, he signed up at Griffin Park, becoming a regular from last October through to Christmas, before joining the subs' bench following a poor performance against Brighton. Scored his first Bees' goal with a long-range header at Wrexham.
West Ham U (£25,000 from Fisher Ath on 3/6/91) FL 1+1 FAC 0+1 (Free to Kettering on 9/9/93)
Colchester U (Loaned on 31/12/92) FL 8/2
Brentford (Signed from Iceland on 12/10/95) FL 14+5/1 FAC 4+1 Others 2

MARTIN Dean Stacey
Born: Halifax, 9 September 1967
Height: 5'11" Weight: 11.10
Dean held down a regular place in the Rochdale side last season as the midfield anchor, just occasionally dropping to substitute when the club wanted to play an extra striker. "Stud's" one goal of the term – a flying header through a crowd of players – earned Dale their big pay day at Liverpool in the FA Cup. Ruled out by injury for the final weeks of the campaign, he was one of seven players who were incapacitated.
Halifax T (From apprentice on 10/9/85) FL 149+4/7 FLC 7 FAC 10 Others 12/3

Scunthorpe U (Free on 8/7/91) FL 100+6/7 FLC 8/1 FAC 7 Others 13+1/1
Rochdale (Free on 13/1/95) FL 45+7 FLC 0+1 FAC 4/1 Others 2+1

MARTIN Jae Andrew
Born: London, 5 February 1976
Height: 5'11" Weight: 12.4

A 1995 close season signing from Southend, Jae made his Birmingham debut in October and quickly showed up as a player with pace and tremendous shooting power who looked as though he would be a permanent contender for one of the striking roles. Although contracted for two years, eight substitute appearances later he had faded from the first team scene faster than he arrived.
Southend U (From trainee on 7/5/93) FL 1+7 FLC 1+1 Others 0+1
Leyton Orient (Loaned on 9/9/94) FL 1+3 Others 1
Birmingham C (Free on 1/7/95) FL 1+6 Others 0+2

MARTIN Lee Carl
Born: Birmingham, 3 October 1976
Height: 5'10" Weight: 11.0

Still learning his trade, the young Shrewsbury trainee forward came off the bench at Derby in the second leg of the Coca Cola Cup last October. Had two loan spells with Stafford Rangers and Bridgenorth before being given a free transfer in the summer.
Shrewsbury T (From trainee on 1/7/95) FLC 0+1

MARTINDALE Gary
Born: Liverpool, 24 June 1971
Height: 5'10" Weight: 12.1

Signed on a free transfer by Peterborough from Bolton in the summer of 1995, with no previous league experience behind him, the Merseyside born striker proved to be a sensation with the Posh, and was their leading scorer with 18 goals when signed by Notts County last March. At Meadow Lane, Gary quickly got on the scoresheet with six in County's last ditch push for promotion, plus two more in the division two play offs versus Crewe Alexandra, before the team succumbed to Bradford City in the final at Wembley. Is expected to show the same goalscoring form in 1996-97.
Bolton W (Signed from Burscough on 24/3/94)
Peterborough U (Signed on 4/7/95) FL 26+5/15 FLC 4/1 FAC 4 Others 4/2
Notts Co (£175,000 on 6/3/96) FL 13+3/6 Others 2+1/2

MARTINEZ Roberto
Born: Balaguer Lerida, Spain, 13 July 1973
Height: 5'9" Weight: 12.2

Cultured right-footed midfielder with a clinical eye for finishing who ended last season as Wigan's top scorer with 13 goals. Also selected, after signing from Spanish football prior to the start of 1995-96 as the club's "Player of the Year", earlier the Spaniard had been a worthy choice for the PFA third division team, having had an excellent first year in English football.
Wigan Ath (Free from Balaguer on 25/7/95) FL 42/9 FLC 2/1 FAC 4/3 Others 2

MARTYN Antony Nigel
Born: St Austell, 11 August 1966
Height: 6'2" Weight: 14.7
Club Honours: Div 3 '90, FMC '91; Div 1 '94
International Honours: E: 3; B-6; U21-11

The Crystal Palace goalkeeper is now the longest-serving player at the club and although on the transfer list for most of last season, signed a new four year contract in February. Ever present for the fourth time in seven seasons at Selhurst Park, Nigel kept 16 clean sheets, while conceding just 48 goals – the third best defensive record in the first division. Sadly, his efforts were not rewarded with promotion to the Premier League, where his talent belongs, after watching in horror as Steve Claridge's miss-hit volley flew past him in the last minute of extra time in the Wembley play-off final to give Leicester the third promotion place. A commanding and imposing figure between the sticks, and deceptively agile, he also kicks long and hard.
Bristol Rov (Free from St Blazey on 6/8/87) FL 101 FLC 6 FAC 6 Others 11
Crystal Palace (£1,000,000 on 21/11/89) F/PL 272 FLC 36 FAC 22 Others 19

Nigel Martyn

MASINGA Philomen (Phil) Raul
Born: South Africa, 28 June 1969
Height: 6'2" Weight: 12.7
International Honours: South Africa: 23

South African striker who, in his second season at Leeds in 1995-96, struggled to make the first team. Always with an eye for goal, he weighed in with important strikes in the Coca Cola Cup victories over Reading and Birmingham, but although a member of the victorious South African, African Cup winning side, it appears highly unlikely that he will be granted a further work permit for next season.
Leeds U (£275,000 from Marmelodo Sundown on 3/8/94) PL 20+11/5 FLC 3/1 FAC 3+2/4

MASKELL Craig Dell
Born: Aldershot, 10 April 1968
Height: 5'10" Weight: 11.11

Skilful striker who twists and turns well to make room for shots at goal. Signed by Brighton from Southampton last March, following a loan period at Bristol City, where he made a scoring introduction, he made his debut at home to Brentford on 2 March 1996. Behind both goals in his second start, he opened his own account with a left-footed shot against Oxford. Weighed in with two more in the following match against Hull, including a superb 20-yard effort. A great beginning.
Southampton (From apprentice on 15/4/86) FL 2+4/1
Huddersfield T (£20,000 on 31/5/88) FL 86+1/43 FLC 6/4 FAC 8/3 Others 7/4
Reading (£250,000 on 7/8/90) FL 60+12/26 FLC 2 FAC 5+1 Others 1
Swindon T (£225,000 on 9/7/92) F/PL 40+7/22 FLC 3+1/1 FAC 2+1 Others 4+1/4
Southampton (£250,000 on 7/2/94) PL 8+9/1 FAC 1+1
Bristol C (Loaned on 28/12/95) FL 5/1
Brighton & Hove A (£40,000 on 1/3/96) FL 15/4

MASON Andrew (Andy) John
Born: Bolton, 22 November 1974
Height: 5'11" Weight: 11.11

20 goals in 30 1994-95 Bolton reserves games, tempted Hull City's boss, Terry Dolan, to sign him during the summer. Although he got off to a great start when scoring a stunning winner on his full league debut against Blackpool, he was rarely given the chance to live up to his early promise, despite the club's limited resources. A forward who shows good awareness around the goal, he was used as a central defender in the final games of the campaign.
Bolton W (From trainee on 21/5/93)
Hull C (Free on 27/6/95) FL 10+10/1 FLC 1+3 Others 1+1

MASON Paul David
Born: Liverpool, 3 September 1963
Height: 5'8" Weight: 12.1
Club Honours: SLC '90; SC '90

Began last season asking Ipswich for a transfer, but remained to make a significant contribution, scoring 13 goals from midfield. Preferring a wide role, which enables him to cut in looking for the shot, and proficient with either foot, he made his first appearance at Brescia in October and netted six times in his first five games. Also scored all of the club's FA Cup goals, one in each round, his best being the 20-yarder that clinched an extra-time victory at Blackburn in the third round.
Aberdeen (£200,000 from FC Groningen on 1/8/88) SL 138+20/27 SLC 13+2/8 SC 11+1/1 Others 7/1
Ipswich T (£400,000 on 18/6/93) P/FL 61+8/13 FLC 3/1 FAC 4+3/3 Others 3/3

MASSEY Stuart Anthony
Born: Crawley, 17 November 1964
Height: 5'11" Weight: 11.8

One of the leading lights in Oxford's midfield last season, Stuart weighed in with eight goals and would not have been far away from winning the supporters "Player of the Year" award. Adding bite to the tackle, and crossing a good ball, he also excelled at getting into the box late for his goals – the exception coming with the long-range special which knocked Millwall out of the FA Cup.

Crystal Palace (£20,000 from Sutton U on 17/7/92) F/PL 1+1 Others 1
Oxford U (Free on 5/7/94) FL 53+4/4 FLC 6/1 FAC 7/4 Others 3

MASTERS Neil Bradley
Born: Ballymena, 25 May 1972
Height: 6'1" Weight: 14.2
International Honours: NI: Yth

The Wolves' left back made a good start at Tranmere on the opening day of last season, providing corner kicks that led to both goals in a 2-2 draw, but, after the third fixture, was again thwarted by injuries. As before, what was expected one to be a short absence proved a very long one as he required surgery on his tendons. Hopefully, he can get back to full fitness in time for the coming season.

Bournemouth (From trainee on 31/8/90) FL 37+1/2 FLC 4/1 FAC 5+2/1 Others 1
Wolverhampton W (£300,000 on 22/12/93) FL 10+2

MATEU Jose Luis (Pinto)
Born: Castellon, Spain, 15 January 1966
Height: 6'0" Weight: 11.13

A Spanish striker signed from Castellon last October, Jose found the physical demands of third division football with Torquay too demanding as his seven full appearances would suggest.

Torquay U (Free from Castellon on 18/10/95) FL 5+5/1 FLC 0+1 FAC 0+2/1 Others 2

MATHIE Alexander (Alex)
Born: Bathgate, 20 December 1968
Height: 5'10" Weight: 10.7
International Honours: S: Yth

In his first full season at Ipswich, Alex continued to impress with his striking abilities, having pace, a good shot in either foot, and able to turn defenders, often beating them at will. As a result, his partnership with Ian Marshall blossomed and, whenever in tandem, goals looked to be forthcoming. Scored in each of Town's first four games, including a brace against Stoke and a hat trick in a 3-0 win over the eventual champions, Sunderland, his first for the club. Would surely have exceeded 20 had not two shoulder dislocations forced him to miss nine matches.

Glasgow Celtic (From juniors on 15/5/87) SL 7+4 SC 1 Others 0+1
Morton (£100,000 on 1/8/91) SL 73+1/31 SLC 2/1 SC 5/3 Others 7/9
Port Vale (Loaned on 30/3/93) FL 0+3
Newcastle U (£285,000 on 30/7/93) PL 3+22/4 FLC 5+2
Ipswich T (£500,000 on 24/2/95) P/FL 52/20 FLC 1 FAC 2 Others 4/1

MATTEO Dominic
Born: Dumfries, 28 April 1974
Height: 6'1" Weight: 11.8
International Honours: E: U21-3; Yth

With four experienced central defenders

ahead of him at Liverpool in 1995-96, Dominic had few opportunities to advance his career, playing in the opening two Premiership games, when deputising for Neil Ruddock, and appearing in three more towards the end of the season. Apart from occasional selections as a non-playing substitute, that was it. Is comfortable anywhere along the left flank, as a back or winger, where his skill and control allows him to run at defenders in order to get into attacking areas.

Liverpool (From trainee on 27/5/92) PL 18+5 FLC 2 FAC 1+1
Sunderland (Loaned on 28/3/95) FL 1

MATTHEW Damian
Born: Islington, 23 September 1970
Height: 5'11" Weight" 10.10
Club Honours: Div 1 '94
International Honours: E: U21-9

Yet another season in the shadows of Selhurst Park for the former England U21 midfielder. He made only five starts for Crystal Palace in 1995-96, with a further five appearances from the bench, and was loaned to Bristol Rovers in January, before a permanent deal in March was scuppered due to an injury problem. An industrious midfielder, who also shows creative skills, Damian is trying hard to get himself into shape for the coming season.

Chelsea (From trainee on 13/6/89) F/PL 13+8 FLC 5 Others 1
Luton T (Loaned on 25/9/92) FL 3+2 Others 1
Crystal Palace (£150,000 on 11/2/94) F/PL 17+7/1 FLC 2+1 FAC 1
Bristol Rov (Loaned on 12/1/96) FL 8 Others 2/1

MATTHEWS Robert (Rob) David
Born: Slough, 14 October 1970
Height: 6'0" Weight: 12.5
International Honours: E: Sch

Unable to secure a first team place at Luton, Rob moved to York last September for the then club record transfer fee, but never really settled at Bootham Crescent and joined Bury in January, coming on as substitute to score a point saving goal at Chester. Slotted in admirably up front alongside Mark Carter, scoring four goals in his first 11 appearances, but then suffered an ankle injury and could not regain his place in the closing weeks.

Notts Co (Free from Loughborough University on 26/3/92) FL 23+20/11 FLC 0+2 FAC 3+2/2 Others 4+3
Luton T (£80,000 on 17/3/95) FL 6+5 FLC 0+1
York C (£90,000 on 8/9/95) FL 14+3/1 FAC 1 Others 3
Bury (£100,000 on 12/1/96) FL 11+5/4

MATTHEWSON Trevor
Born: Sheffield, 12 February 1963
Height: 6'4" Weight: 13.6
Club Honours: GMVC '88; AMC '91

An ever reliable central defender, Trevor was drafted into Bury's side last season to add his experience to a defence which had leaked 13 goals in the opening five league games. Although the Shakers kept seven clean sheets during his 16 match run as a climb up the table began, he lost his place after a 3-0 home reverse against Hartlepool and was given a free transfer in May.

Sheffield Wed (From apprentice on 12/2/81) FL 3 FAC 2
Newport Co (Free on 15/10/83) FL 73+2 FLC 2 FAC 7 Others 6
Stockport Co (Free on 27/9/85) FL 79+1 FLC 3 FAC 2 Others 3
Lincoln C (£13,000 on 1/8/87) FL 43/2 FLC 3 FAC 3 Others 2
Birmingham C (£45,000 on 3/8/89) FL 167+1/12 FLC 11 FAC 8 Others 16/1
Preston NE (Signed on 20/8/93) FL 12/1 FLC 1 Others 1
Bury (£10,000 on 2/9/94) FL 34 FLC 4 FAC 5 Others 6

MATTISON Paul Andrew
Born: Wakefield, 24 April 1973
Height: 5'10" Weight: 11.5

The speedy, attacking right-sided midfielder started just one game for Darlington last season, although infrequently coming off the bench, and was named as a sub for the Wembley play-off final. Having made just seven starts in the past two years, he was released during the summer.

Darlington (Free from Ferrybridge Amateurs on 12/8/94) FL 5+12 FLC 1 Others 0+1

MAUGE Ronald (Ronnie) Carlton
Born: Islington, 10 March 1969
Height: 5'10" Weight: 11.10

Having moved from Bury during the 1995 close season, Ronnie proved to be a sound buy for Plymouth in central midfield and scored some excellent goals in 1995-96. His form dipped slightly during mid-term when he had a few niggling injuries, but he came back to produce some sound performances. Captained the side on a number of occasions.

Charlton Ath (From trainee on 22/7/87)
Fulham (Free on 21/9/88) FL 47+3/2 FLC 4 FAC 1 Others 2
Bury (£40,000 on 30/7/90) FL 92+16/10 FLC 8+2/2 FAC 8/2 Others 10+2
Manchester C (Loaned on 26/9/91) Others 0+1
Plymouth Arg (£40,000 on 22/7/95) FL 36+1/6 FLC 2 FAC 3 Others 3+1/1

MAXFIELD Scott
Born: Doncaster, 13 July 1976
Height: 5'8" Weight: 10.7

Talented young defender, cum midfielder, who was surprisingly transferred from Doncaster Rovers to Hull City on transfer deadline day last March. Definitely an excellent prospect for the future, this young player is sure in the tackle and quick in recovery and could well be a very astute signing for the Tigers.

Doncaster Rov (From trainee on 8/7/94) FL 22+7/1 Others 1
Hull C (Signed on 27/3/96) FL 3+1

MAY David
Born: Oldham, 24 June 1970
Height: 6'0" Weight: 12.10
Club Honours: CS '94; PL '96; FAC '96

Speed of recovery, allied to good positional play and heading ability, make him ideal for a central defender, his good passing technique an added bonus. After standing in the shadows of Steve Bruce at Manchester United for most of 1994-95, David formed a promising pairing with his captain in successive games against Chelsea, Sheffield

Wednesday and Liverpool last season, when Gary Pallister was sidelined through injury. His next big chance came in the latter stages of the campaign when Bruce sustained hamstring problems and, having played in the FA Cup semi final victory over Chelsea, he was an impressive member of the side that lifted the trophy following the 1-0 win over Liverpool. Championship and FA Cup winners' medals were a fine return for just 18 first team games and, with Bruce now departed, he will be looking to hold down a regular place in 1996-97.
Blackburn Rov (From trainee on 16/6/88) F/PL 123/3 FLC 12+1/2 FAC 10/1 Others 5
Manchester U (£1,400,000 on 1/7/94) PL 26+9/3 FLC 2/1 FAC 3 Others 5

David May

MAYBURY Alan
Born: Dublin, 8 August 1978
Height: 5'11" Weight: 11.7
International Honours: Ei: Yth
A product of Home Farm, Alan signed pro forms for Leeds during the 1995 close season after being spotted playing in local boys club football. The young Irish defender made his senior bow for the club during the poor team showing at Aston Villa last season, having been a regular in the right back slot for the juniors and reserves. Is yet another of a long list of young Irishmen to further their opportunities at Elland Road.
Leeds U (From St Kevin's BC on 17/8/95) PL 1

MAZZARELLI Giuseppe
Born: Switzerland, 14 August 1972
Height: 6'1" Weight: 12.7
International Honours: Switzerland: 1
The young midfielder came to Manchester City on loan from FC Zurich last March, with a view to build on a growing reputation and to also further his experience. Watched by Switzerland, with future European games in mind, Giuseppe showed that the glowing reports which preceded his arrival at Maine Road were not unjustified, when impressing in reserve team fixtures, but only managed a

couple of substitute appearances in the first team before going home.
Manchester C (Loaned from FC Zurich on 12/3/96) PL 0+2

MEAKER Michael John
Born: Greenford, 18 August 1971
Height: 5'11" Weight: 11.5
International Honours: W: B-1; U21-2
Signed by Reading during the 1995 close season as part of the deal which took Simon Osborn to QPR, the speedy winger spent some time trying to establish himself in the first team, and even his reserve appearances lacked consistency. Only towards the end of the campaign did he show his undoubted ability to ghost past defenders and whip over the dangerous crosses on which his reputation was built.
Queens Park R (From trainee on 7/2/90) F/PL 21+13/1 FLC 2/1 FAC 1 Others 2+1/1
Plymouth Arg (Loaned on 20/11/91) FL 4 Others 1
Reading (£550,000 on 19/7/95) FL 15+6 FAC 0+1

MEAN Scott James
Born: Crawley, 13 December 1973
Height: 5'11" Weight: 11.11
Stylish Bournemouth central midfielder who has good passing ability and can make penetrating runs with the ball deep into opposing territory, Scott's season in 1995-96 was disrupted by a knee injury that limited him to just 18 appearances and one goal. Still things did not go right for him. Having travelled on loan to West Ham in March, with a view to a permanent transfer worth £750,000 to the Cherries, the move was put on ice until everyone was happy with his fitness. Hopefully, that is now the case and, if so, he will probably start 1996-97 at Upton Park.
Bournemouth (From trainee on 10/8/92) FL 52+22/8 FLC 7+1 FAC 2+1 Others 4

MEARA James (Jim) Stephen
Born: Hammersmith, 7 October 1972
Height: 5'9" Weight: 11.2
Club Honours: FAYC '89
A young Doncaster midfielder who had promised so much with his passing abilities, Jim barely made any impact in the first team during 1995-96. Evidently out of favour with the powers that be, he was another player to be paid up during the winter months and was, at one point, considering a move to play in China.
Watford (From trainee on 30/4/91) FL 1+1
Doncaster Rov (Free on 15/7/94) FL 14+2/1 FLC 1 FAC 1 Others 1

MEASHAM Ian
Born: Barnsley 14 December 1964
Height: 5'11" Weight: 11.9
Club Honours: Div 4 '92
Despite apparently making a full recovery from his severe neck injury suffered two years ago, this classy full back failed to regain his place in the Doncaster Rovers' first team on a regular basis. Arguably the best defender at the club, he was given a free transfer last summer.
Huddersfield T (From apprentice on 16/12/82) FL 17
Lincoln C (Loaned on 18/10/85) FL 6

Rochdale (Loaned on 21/3/86) FL 12
Cambridge U (Free on 8/8/86) FL 46 FLC 6 FAC 3 Others 2
Burnley (Free on 10/11/88) FL 181+1/2 FLC 8 FAC 19 Others 19
Doncaster Rov (Signed on 16/9/93) FL 29+3 FLC 2 FAC 3 Others 4

MEDLIN Nicholas (Nicky) Ryan Maxwell
Born: Truro, 23 November 1976
Height: 5'7" Weight: 10.7
An exciting Exeter midfield prospect, Nicky is another player who broke through from the youth team in 1995-96. A tenacious ball winner, he made his debut at Colchester in November and will be looking for a regular midfield place this coming season.
Exeter C (From trainee on 4/8/95) FL 2+4 Others 1

MEGSON Gary John
Born: Manchester, 2 May 1959
Height: 5'10" Weight: 12.0
Released by Norwich during the 1995 close season, having been caretaker manager for the club's last five games in the Premiership, Gary joined Lincoln, making four appearances as a non-contract player at the beginning of 1995-96. The veteran midfield playmaker then moved to Shrewsbury on a similar basis, but spent even less time before taking up an appointment as first team coach at Bradford. Despite having moved back to manage Norwich in January, a post he later relinquished, he would have been delighted with the Bantam's rise to the first division, via the play offs.
Plymouth Arg (From apprentice on 1/5/77) FL 78/10 FLC 9 FAC 5
Everton (£250,000 on 18/12/79) FL 20+2/2 FAC 3/1
Sheffield Wed (£130,000 on 7/8/81) FL 123/13 FLC 13/2 FAC 12/5
Nottingham F (£175,000 on 28/8/84)
Newcastle U (£130,000 on 21/11/84) FL 21+3/1 FLC 1+1 FAC 2/1
Sheffield Wed (£60,000 on 20/12/85) FL 107+3/12 FLC 10 FAC 15/1 Others 3
Manchester C (£250,000 on 12/1/89) FL 78+4/2 FLC 5 FAC 7+1 Others 2
Norwich C (Free on 1/7/92) PL 42+4/1 FLC 1 FAC 4 Others 2+1
Lincoln C (Free on 26/7/95) FL 2 FLC 2
Shrewsbury T (Free on 8/9/95) FL 2

MELLON Michael Joseph
Born: Paisley, 18 March 1972
Height: 5'9" Weight: 11.3
Blackpool's midfield star of last season. Impressing with his forward runs and the knack of scoring important goals, the two against Brighton to win the game will long be remembered. Now firmly established in the midfield, Michael allied skill to terrific effort during the club's tenuous run-in. His good form saw him elected by his fellow professionals to the PFA award winning second division team.
Bristol C (From trainee on 6/12/89) FL 26+9/1 FLC 3 FAC 1+1 Others 5+3
West Bromwich A (£75,000 on 11/2/93) FL 38+7/6 FLC 3+2 FAC 0+1 Others 6/1
Blackpool (£50,000 on 23/11/94) FL 71/10 FLC 2/1 FAC 3 Others 5/1

MELVILLE Andrew (Andy) Roger
Born: Swansea, 29 November 1968
Height: 6'0" Weight: 13.3
Club Honours: WC '89; Div 1 '96
International Honours: W: 27; B-1; U21-2

The Welsh international central defender had only ever encountered relegation battles since arriving at Sunderland three years ago, so last season's promotion to the Premiership as first division champions must have been especially satisfying for him. A good distributor of the ball, and always dangerous from set pieces, Andy contributed four goals to the cause, including an important last minute equaliser at home to Reading in September.

Swansea C (From trainee on 25/7/86) FL 165+10/22 FLC 10 FAC 14+1/5 Others 13/2
Oxford U (£275,000 on 23/7/90) FL 135/13 FLC 12/1 FAC 6 Others 6/1
Sunderland (Signed on 9/8/93) FL 120/9 FLC 9+1 FAC 7 Others 2

MENDONCA Clive Paul

Born: Tullington, 9 September 1968
Height: 5'10" Weight: 12.6

After more than a season struggling against an injury which many thought had ended his career, the quick-footed Grimsby striker returned to first team football for the last eight games of 1995-96. Although not fully fit, Clive showed he had lost none of his predatory instincts in front of goal when scoring a hat trick in only his second game, a 3-1 win at home to Ipswich, and will be looking for a good start this time round.

Sheffield U (From apprentice on 10/9/86) FL 8+5/4 FLC 0+1 Others 1
Doncaster Rov (Loaned on 26/2/88) FL 2
Rotherham U (£35,000 on 25/3/88) FL 71+13/27 FLC 5+2/1 FAC 4+1/2 Others 4+2/1
Sheffield U (£110,000 on 1/8/91) FL 4+6/1 FLC 0+2 Others 0+1
Grimsby T (Loaned on 9/1/92) FL 10/3
Grimsby T (£85,000 on 13/8/92) FL 106+5/39 FLC 8+1/2 FAC 7/2 Others 2/1

MERCER William (Billy)

Born: Liverpool, 22 May 1969
Height: 6'2" Weight: 13.5

When the goalkeeper arrived from Sheffield United on a permanent basis last December, Chesterfield fans began to take seriously their club's chances of a second successive tilt at the play offs. They already knew from his loan spell earlier that he was cool, displayed great positional sense, was good in the air, and excelled at point-blank work. Billy would be a great asset to any club, and Chesterfield are fortunate to have him. Played just once for Sheffield United in 1995-96.

Liverpool (From trainee on 21/8/87)
Rotherham U (Signed on 16/2/89) FL 104 FLC 12 FAC 12 Others 10
Sheffield U (Signed on 12/10/94) FL 4
Chesterfield (Loaned on 15/9/95) FL 11 Others 2
Chesterfield (£93,000 on 12/12/95) FL 23 Others 2

MEREDITH Thomas (Tom) James Anthony

Born: Enfield, 27 October 1977
Height: 5'11" Weight: 11.7

Another of Peterborough's young trainees to break into the side in 1995-96, Tom came in for the last two matches of the season, making his full debut at right back in the final game at Oxford. Normally a central defender, he stood in for the absent Lee Williams.

Peterborough U (Trainee) FL 1+1

Paul Merson

MERSON Paul Charles

Born: Harlesden, 20 March 1968
Height: 6'0" Weight: 13.2
Club Honours: Div 1 '89, '91; FLC '93; FAC '93; ECWC '94
International Honours: E: 14; B-3; U21-4; Yth

The Arsenal midfielder, cum striker, put his well publicised problems firmly behind him in 1995-96, producing his most consistent displays since the 1988-89 championship year. Enjoying the floating role, he was asked to fill during the latter part of the season, it was perhaps fitting that he was an ever present in his testimonial year and against an International XI the fans were treated to a unique glimpse of his creative skills. A big crowd favourite, Paul remains an exciting player, who will always be looking for a crack at goal.

Arsenal (From apprentice on 1/12/85) F/PL 257+38/72 FLC 33+2/8 FAC 25+3/4 Others 16+1/3
Brentford (Loaned on 22/1/87) FL 6+1 Others 1+1

MICKLEWHITE Gary

Born: Southwark, 21 March 1961
Height: 5'7" Weight: 10.4
Club Honours: Div 2 '83, Div 1 '87

Hard-working midfielder who was employed by Gillingham last season on a number of occasions in a full back role, where he excelled. As you would expect from a man who has been a professional since 1978, his experience helped a promotion-chasing side no end but, despite that, he was released during the summer.

Manchester U (From apprentice on 23/3/78)
Queens Park R (Free on 4/7/79) FL 97+9/11 FLC 12+1/5 FAC 4+2/1 Others 1+1
Derby Co (£90,000 on 26/2/85) FL 223+17/31 FLC 23+3/2 FAC 8+3/4 Others 8+3/6
Gillingham (Free on 22/7/93) FL 78+17/3 FLC 4 FAC 10/1 Others 3+1

MIDDLETON Craig Dean

Born: Nuneaton, 10 September 1970
Height: 5'9" Weight: 10.13

A Cambridge United midfielder who missed all of 1994-95, Craig returned to action last season to provide both stability and class to the middle of the field, also proving to be an able goalscorer, finishing with nine to his credit. Unfortunately, his time at United ended prematurely with a shoulder dislocation against Preston and he was released in the summer. Is the twin brother of Lee.

Coventry C (From trainee on 30/5/89) F/PL 2+1 FLC 1
Cambridge U (Free on 20/7/93) FL 55+4/11 FLC 3 FAC 1 Others 1

MIDDLETON Lee John

Born: Nuneaton, 10 September 1970
Height: 5'9" Weight: 11.9

Having been out of football for a considerable time with a back injury, Lee joined up with his twin brother, Craig, at Cambridge United on a non-contract basis last November. At his best, a player who could read the game, and pass and intercept well, he appeared once alongside his brother in midfield, before being released.

Coventry C (From trainee on 30/5/89) FL 0+2
Swindon T (Free on 20/7/92)
Cambridge U (Free on 17/11/95) FL 1+2

MIDGLEY Craig Steven

Born: Bradford, 24 May 1976
Height: 5'8" Weight: 10.13

Unable to make a first team start for Bradford in 1995-96, having signed professional forms the previous summer, he joined Scarborough on loan in December, appearing 16 times during the next three months. Although impressed by the talented young winger, and offering £50,000 to retain his services, Boro were ultimately rebuffed after Craig decided to return to Valley Parade to fight for a place. Later voted City's "Young Player of the Year".

Bradford C (From trainee on 4/7/95) FL 0+8/1 FAC 0+2 Others 1
Scarborough (Loaned on 7/12/95) FL 14+2/1

MIHAILOV Borislav (Bobby) Biserov

Born: Bulgaria, 12 February 1963
Height: 6'0" Weight: 12.10
International Honours: Bulgaria: 96

Becoming Reading's record signing when he was transferred from Botev Plovdiv last August, the Bulgarian international goalkeeper missed many games through hamstring and back injuries, managing just 17 in all. Captained his country against England at Wembley, and when he did play for the Royals, he showed himself to be a world class custodian. Known to opposing fans as "Wiggy" because of the hairpiece he wears during games, Bobby appeared in all three of Bulgaria's Euro '96 group matches.

Reading (£300,000 from Botev Plovdiv on 19/9/95) FL 16 FAC 1

MIKE Adrian (Adie) Roosevelt

Born: Manchester, 16 November 1973
Height: 6'0" Weight: 11.9
International Honours: E: Yth; Sch

A close season signing from Manchester City, striker Adie was plagued by injury and lack of fitness, only making a handful of appearances in 1995-96 for Stockport, and failing to score. At his best, very quick and adept at making good runs of the ball, with an excellent first touch.

Manchester C (From trainee on 15/7/92) F/PL 5+11/2 FLC 1+1 FAC 0+1
Bury (Loaned on 25/3/93) FL 5+2/1
Stockport Co (£60,000 on 18/8/95) FL 4+4 FAC 0+1

MIKLOSKO Ludek (Ludo)
Born: Ostrava, Czechoslovakia, 9 December 1961
Height: 6'5" Weight: 14.0
International Honours: Czechoslovakia: 42

Giant West Ham goalkeeper who had another excellent season in 1995-96. Very agile for such a big man, a one-match ban forced him to miss the New Year's Day trip to Manchester City, his first league absence for four years. In an improving Hammers' side, he had a brilliant game in the 2-0 home win over Newcastle and saved crucial penalties at Upton Park against Chelsea and in the Manchester City return. Continues to take crosses comfortably, make difficult saves look easy, and is a good kicker.

West Ham U (£300,000 from Banik Ostrava on 19/2/90) F/PL 266 FLC 20 FAC 23 Others 8

MILDENHALL Stephen (Steve) James
Born: Swindon, 13 May 1978
Height: 6'5" Weight: 13.5

Steve was still a Swindon trainee when he was thrown in at the deep end for two Coca Cola Cup games against Cambridge last August. With first choice goalkeeper, Fraser Digby, injured and Blackburn unwilling to allow on loan Shay Given to be cup-tied, the youngster performed admirably in Town's 3-2 aggregate win.

Swindon T (Trainee) FLC 2

MILLEN Keith Derek
Born: Croydon, 26 September 1966
Height: 6'2" Weight: 12.4
Club Honours: Div 3 '92

A Watford central defender who is the soul of consistency, unobtrusive but effective, and totally reliable. Scores at the rate of one a season (last time round finding the net against Ipswich) and could perhaps increase his goals tally. With the club staring the second division in the face, Keith was unfortunate to miss the end of the campaign with a shoulder injury.

Brentford (From apprentice on 7/8/84) FL 301+4/17 FLC 26/2 FAC 18/1 Others 30+1
Watford (Signed on 22/3/94) FL 73+1/2 FLC 4 FAC 7

MILLER Alan John
Born: Epping, 29 March 1970
Height: 6'3" Weight: 14.6
Club Honours: FAYC '88; ECWC '94; Div 1 '95
International Honours: E: U21-4; Sch

Middlesbrough goalkeeper. Started last season in brilliant form, winning praise from all quarters as "Man of the Match" in the opening game at Highbury, where he

pulled off a string of fine saves to frustrate the Gunners' £12m debutantes, Dennis Bergkamp and David Platt. An agile and commanding shot stopper, whose antici- pation and ability to cover angles is superb, he was unfortunately injured after three games to let in Boro's second choice 'keeper, Gary Walsh. And, with the latter grabbing his chance to claim the number one spot for himself, his good form forced Alan onto the sidelines for all but three more games.

Arsenal (From trainee on 5/5/88) PL 6+2
Plymouth Arg (Loaned on 24/11/88) FL 13 FAC 2
West Bromwich A (Loaned on 15/8/91) FL 3
Birmingham C (Loaned on 19/12/91) FL 15 Others 1
Middlesbrough (£500,000 on 12/8/94) P/FL 47 FLC 1 FAC 2 Others 2

MILLER David Brian
Born: Burnley, 8 January 1964
Height: 5'11" Weight: 11.12

Experienced and reliable Wigan centre half who has played all of his football in the north west. A good passer of the ball, David, the son of former Burnley and England player, Brian, found it difficult to break back into central defence last season, making just six starts, due to the form of John Pender and Colin Greenall, and was released during the summer.

Burnley (From apprentice on 11/1/82) FL 27+5/3 FLC 2 FAC 1 Others 2+1
Crewe Alex (Loaned on 18/3/83) FL 3
Tranmere Rov (Free on 16/7/85) FL 25+4/1 FLC 1 FAC 4 Others 2/1 (Free to Colne Dynamoes during 1986 close season)
Preston NE (Free on 18/12/86) FL 50+8/2 FLC 6 FAC 0+2 Others 7+2
Burnley (Loaned on 16/2/89) FL 4
Carlisle U (£30,000 on 14/9/89) FL 108+1/7 FLC 6 FAC 4 Others 7
Stockport Co (£25,000 on 31/3/92) FL 72+9/1 FLC 6 FAC 5+2 Others 12+2
Wigan Ath (Signed on 6/10/94) FL 35+3/3 FLC 2 FAC 2 Others 3+1

MILLER Kevin
Born: Falmouth, 15 March 1969
Height: 6'1" Weight: 13.0
Club Honours: Div 4 '90

By his own very high standards, Kevin had a slightly disappointing season for Watford in 1995-96, partly due to defensive uncertainty in front of him and niggling injuries. Nevertheless, he remains a goalkeeper of the highest class, who commands his penalty area well and, at the same time, gives confidence to the defence. Is also one of the club's greatest assets.

Exeter C (Free from Newquay on 9/3/89) FL 163 FLC 7 FAC 12 Others 18
Birmingham C (£250,000 on 14/5/93) FL 24 FLC 4 Others 2
Watford (£250,000 on 7/8/94) FL 86 FLC 6 FAC 6

MILLER Paul Anthony
Born: Woking, 31 January 1968
Height: 6'0" Weight: 11.7

Following the transfer of Gareth Taylor, he was widely expected to move from the left- hand side of Bristol Rovers' midfield to his preferred orthodox forward role. With this move failing to materialise, Paul's goal contribution declined accordingly. Probably

at is best up front, he runs well off the ball and is good in the air.

Wimbledon (From Yeovil T on 12/8/87) F/PL 65+15/10 FLC 3+3 FAC 3 Others 1
Newport Co (Loaned on 20/10/87) FL 6/2
Bristol C (Loaned on 11/1/90) FL 0+3 Others 2
Bristol Rov (£100,000 on 16/8/94) FL 78+2/20 FLC 5/1 FAC 4/4 Others 11/2

MILLETT Michael Paul
Born: Billinge, 22 September 1977
Height: 5'10" Weight: 11.0
International Honours: E: Yth; Sch

One of Wigan's brightest prospects, Michael tragically died on Thursday, 21 September, 1995, in a car crash, a day before his 18th birthday. Rated as potentially the biggest asset the club have ever produced, Latic's season was to be overshadowed by the tragedy. Prior to the accident, the young midfielder had made just one appearance in 1995-96, when coming off the bench at home to Chester in the Coca Cola Cup.

Wigan Ath (From trainee on 1/10/94) FL 1+2 FLC 0+1

Mike Milligan

MILLIGAN Michael (Mike) Joseph
Born: Manchester, 20 February 1967
Height: 5'8" Weight: 11.0
International Honours: Ei: 1; B-2; U23-1; U21-1

The Norwich midfield general, who is both a good competitor and a reliable team player, unfortunately picked up an early season hip injury, restricting his selection chances in 1995-96, but three goals in ten reserve games showed him to be back at his warrior-like best. Although appearances were sporadic, he had a superb last two months, with goals, "Man of the Match" awards, bookings, and a stunning left-footed scoring drive against Portsmouth, followed by his 50th City league appearance against Huddersfield.

Oldham Ath (From apprentice on 2/3/85) FL 161+1/17 FLC 19+1/1 FAC 12/1 Others 4
Everton (£1,000,000 on 24/8/90) FL 16+1/1 FLC 0+1 FAC 1 Others 4+1/1
Oldham Ath (£600,000 on 17/7/91) F/PL 117/6 FLC 11/1 FAC 9 Others 1/1
Norwich C (£800,000 on 27/6/94) P/FL 46+8/4 FLC 8 FAC 3

MILLS Daniel (Danny) John
Born: Norwich, 18 May 1977
Height: 5'11" Weight: 11.9
International Honours: E: Yth

Danny made the step up from trainee status to the Norwich first team squad in 1995-96 with almost nonchalant ease. A calm and authoritative defender, he was one of eight players to wear the number two shirt during the season. Has gained plenty of youth and reserve experience at a tender age and as the only Norwich-born professional on the club's books he was thrilled to net against Torquay in the Coca Cola Cup, following a give-and-go exchange with Keith O'Neill.

Norwich C (From trainee on 1/11/94) FL 8+6 FLC 1+2/1

MILLS Daniel (Danny) Raymond
Born: Sidcup, 13 February 1975
Height: 6'0" Weight: 10.5

As the second summer signing from Charlton, following Alan Pardew, Danny joined Barnet as a tricky and speedy right-sided winger who, apart from a run of starts during last October and November, was used predominately from the bench.

Charlton Ath (From trainee on 1/7/93) Others 0+2
Barnet (Free on 29/9/95) FL 5+14 FAC 1+1 Others 0+1

MILLS Gary Roland
Born: Northampton, 11 November 1961
Height: 5'9" Weight: 11.10
Club Honours: EC '80; AIC '95
International Honours: E: U21-2; Yth; Sch

The experienced right back and midfielder started 1995-96 as Notts County's first choice right back, but lost his place to Tommy Gallagher before returning to first team action in November. Sadly, a serious injury in December ruled him out of contention for the remainder of the season. Comfortable on the ball and a good tackler, Gary is the son of the former Northampton player, Roley. Was released during the summer.

Nottingham F (From apprentice on 13/11/78) FL 113+23/12 FLC 16+5/3 FAC 5 Others 7+3
Derby Co (Loaned on 13/10/82) FL 18/2 FLC 2 FAC 3
Notts Co (Signed on 14/8/87) FL 75/8 FLC 6/1 FAC 5 Others 10
Leicester C (Signed on 2/3/89) F/PL 195+5/16 FLC 9+1/1 FAC 7 Others 15
Notts Co (£50,000 on 26/9/94) FL 44+3 FLC 5 FAC 4 Others 7/1

MILLS Rowan Lee
Born: Mexborough, 10 July 1970
Height: 6'1" Weight: 12.11

Signed from Derby during the 1995 close season, Lee proved to be an enthusiastic striker who notched double figures for Port Vale, despite spending a large part of 1995-96 out of favour. Scoring on his debut at Huddersfield meant the start of his best run-in the side, but although the goals came regularly he was left out after the club suffered some poor results. His best game came in the Anglo-Italian Cup-tie at Perugia when he scored a hat trick.

Wolverhampton W (Signed from Stocksbridge on 9/12/92) FL 12+13/2 FLC 1 FAC 3+1/1 Others 3/1
Derby Co (£400,000 on 24/2/95) FL 16/7
Port Vale (£200,000 on 1/8/95) FL 20+12/8 FLC 2/1 FAC 0+2 Others 6/4

MILNER Andrew (Andy) John
Born: Kendal, 10 February 1967
Height: 6'0" Weight: 11.0

Andy missed very few games for Chester last season, playing in either wide or central attacking roles. Very fast, and with a penchant for running at defenders, he proved more dangerous on the flanks, where his skill on the ball was seen to great effect.

Manchester C (£7,000 from Netherfield on 24/1/89)
Rochdale (£20,000 on 18/1/90) FL 103+24/25 FLC 9+4/5 FAC 6+2/1 Others 4/2
Chester C (Free on 12/8/94) FL 67+11/12 FLC 3+1/3 FAC 2+1/2 Others 2

MILOSEVIC Savo
Born: Bijeljina, Yugoslavia, 2 September 1973
Height: 6'1" Weight: 13.4
Club Honours: FLC '96
International Honours: Yugoslavia: 11

Many eyebrows were raised when Brian Little signed the little known Serbian forward from Partizan Belgrade during the 1995 close season for a huge fee, simply on the strength of a video. Such scepticism seemed well founded when he failed to score at Aston Villa until December, whereupon he notched a hat trick against Coventry! However, there was no doubting his impressive skills on the ball, or the way he linked up with his colleagues, and when he scored a brilliant solo goal from 30 yards to open the Villa account in the 3-0 Coca Cola Cup final victory over Leeds, even the doubters were convinced. If he can add a more consistent finishing ability to his deft touches on the ball, he could be a sensation in 1996-97.

Aston Villa (£3,500,000 from Partizan Belgrade on 17/7/95) PL 36+1/10 FLC 7/1 FAC 5/1

MILSOM Paul Jason
Born: Bristol, 5 October 1974
Height: 6'1" Weight: 13.4

Released by Cardiff during the 1995 close season, the young striker made just one subs' appearance in an Auto Windscreen Shield game for Oxford as a non-contract player, before leaving for non-league Gloucester City soon afterwards.

Bristol C (From trainee on 7/7/93) FL 1+2
Cardiff C (Free on 23/3/95) FL 1+2 Others 1
Oxford U (Free on 9/8/95) Others 0+1

MILTON Simon Charles
Born: Fulham, 23 August 1963
Height: 5'10" Weight: 11.5
Club Honours: Div 2 '92

Once again his goals from midfield, particularly towards the end of last season, contributed much towards Ipswich's cause. Proving versatile as well, playing wide on the right, in central midfield, and as a ball winner, it was Simon who scored the third goal at Barnsley to earn an unlikely last minute 3-3 draw, Town having been three down five minutes earlier. Voted the supporters' "Player of the Year", he also cracked in two goals at Luton, which, at the time, gave rise to a play-off place.

Ipswich T (£5,500 from Bury T on 17/7/87) F/PL 202+36/48 FLC 11+5/2 FAC 12/1 Others 14+2/3
Exeter C (Loaned on 1/11/87) FL 2/3 Others 1
Torquay U (Loaned on 1/3/88) FL 4/1

MIMMS Robert (Bobby) Andrew
Born: York, 12 October 1963
Height: 6'2" Weight: 12.10
Club Honours: Div 1 '87; CS '86, '87
International Honours: E: U21-3

Experienced Blackburn reserve goalkeeper with admirable temperament and self belief. Called upon when Tim Flowers was sent off in the first game of last season and then subsequently suspended, Bobby's performances proved the value of the club having a steady performer in the wings. However, with the advent of the brilliant youngster, Shay Given, who had a marvellous season on loan at Swindon and Sunderland, he was given a free transfer during the summer.

Halifax T (From apprentice on 5/8/81)
Rotherham U (£15,000 on 6/11/81) FL 83 FLC 7 FAC 3 Others 1
Everton (£150,000 on 30/5/85) FL 29 FLC 2 FAC 2 Others 4
Notts Co (Loaned on 13/3/86) FL 2 Others 1
Sunderland (Loaned on 11/12/86) FL 4
Blackburn Rov (Loaned on 23/1/87) FL 6
Manchester C (Loaned on 24/9/87) FL 3
Tottenham H (£325,000 on 25/2/88) FL 37 FLC 5 FAC 2
Aberdeen (Loaned on 16/2/90) SL 6 SC 2
Blackburn Rov (£250,000 on 22/12/90) F/PL 126+2 FLC 15 FAC 9 Others 4

MINETT Jason
Born: Peterborough, 12 August 1971
Height: 5'10" Weight: 10.2

Freed by Exeter during the 1995 close season, the skilful utility player only found his best form after Lincoln manager, John Beck, switched him from right to back to midfield. Is a solid tackler, with good distribution, and City's regular penalty taker.

Norwich C (From trainee on 4/7/89) F/PL 0+3
Exeter C (Free on 19/3/93) FL 83+5/3 FLC 4 FAC 6 Others 7/2
Lincoln C (Free on 10/7/95) FL 39+3/5 FLC 2 FAC 1 Others 4

MINTO Scott Christopher
Born: Heswall, 6 August 1971
Height: 5'9" Weight: 10.7
International Honours: E: U21-6; Yth

Another injury ruined season for this talented young full back, whose career at Chelsea has resulted in just 38 starts in his two years at Stamford Bridge since his move from Charlton Athletic. A fine attacking wing/back in the modern style, he made a good start to 1995-96, being involved in all three goals when Chelsea defeated Southampton at The Bridge in September, but, eight days later, picked up a nasty tendon injury at St James' Park, which sidelined him for the next 34 matches. With the arrival of Terry Phelan and a change in management, it could be a very hard struggle for Scott to fulfil his undoubted potential.

Charlton Ath (From trainee on 2/2/89) FL 171+9/7 FLC 8/2 FAC 8+2 Others 7/1
Chelsea (£775,000 on 28/5/94) PL 29 FLC 1 FAC 3 Others 5+1

MINTON Jeffrey (Jeff) Simon Thompson
Born: Hackney, 28 December 1973
Height: 5'6" Weight: 11.10
Hard-working Brighton midfield player who has still to fully realise his potential. Two footed, and a good tackler, Jeff likes to get forward and contributed some useful goals in 1995-96, something the fans are looking for again this coming season.

Tottenham H (From trainee on 11/1/92) FL 2/1 FLC 0+1
Brighton & Hove A (Free on 25/7/94) FL 74+4/13 FLC 6 FAC 5 Others 4

MISON Michael
Born: London, 8 November 1975
Height: 6'3" Weight: 13.9
After a good first season, the Fulham midfielder stagnated somewhat in 1995-96 and was in and out of the side after a promising start. It is believed at the club that his best position, in taking advantage of his height and build, might well be in central defence.

Fulham (From trainee on 15/7/94) FL 34+17/5 FLC 7/1 FAC 4+1 Others 4+1/1

MITCHELL Graham Lee
Born: Shipley, 16 February 1968
Height: 6'0" Weight: 11.4
Versatile Bradford player who started last season in central defence and later performed in midfield and at full back equally well, his passing ability giving both him and City many options. Out of action for the last four games with an ankle injury, Graham came back for the crucial two remaining play-off fixtures as an integral part of the side that attained first division status.

Huddersfield T (From trainee on 16/6/86) FL 235+9/2 FLC 13+2/1 FAC 27/1 Others 24/1
Bournemouth (Loaned on 24/12/93) FL 4
Bradford C (Signed on 23/12/94) FL 58+1/1 FLC 6 FAC 2 Others 4

MITCHELL Neil Nicholas
Born: Lytham, 7 November 1974
Height: 5'6" Weight: 10.0
International Honours: E: Sch
The young Blackpool striker who, throughout last season, remained on a week-to-week contract, ultimately failed to make a first team appearance before being released in the summer. Earlier, however, having carried a leg injury for a month or so, he had loan spells at Rochdale (December) and non-league Southport (March).

Blackpool (From trainee on 28/11/92) FL 39+28/8 FLC 0+3 FAC 2+1/1 Others 5+1/1
Rochdale (Loaned on 8/12/95) FL 3+1

MITCHELL Paul Robert
Born: Bournemouth, 20 October 1971
Height: 5'10" Weight: 12.0
International Honours: E: Yth; Sch
Unable to get a place in the West Ham squad last season, Paul moved to Bournemouth in March, having started with them as an associated schoolboy back in December 1985, the club taking over the remaining few months of his contract. Able to play on the right side of defence or in midfield, he made just four appearances before being released in the summer.

Bournemouth (From trainee on 7/8/89) FL 6+6 Others 1+1
West Ham U (£40,000 on 6/8/93) PL 0+1
Bournemouth (Free on 28/3/96) FL 2+2

MOHAN Nicholas (Nicky)
Born: Middlesbrough, 6 October 1970
Height: 6'1" Weight: 13.1
Powerful Bradford centre back whose great strength and excellent physique makes him a dominant force in the air and one who bosses the back four well. Signed from Leicester prior to the start of last season, Nicky was a driving force in the club's surge to first division football, missing very few games and always at the heart of things. Extremely dangerous when attacking free kicks and corners, he scored the only goal of the game against Oxford and two more in a 2-2 draw against York.

Middlesbrough (From juniors on 18/11/87) F/PL 93+6/4 FLC 11 FAC 9+1 Others 11
Hull C (Loaned on 26/9/92) FL 5/1
Leicester C (£330,000 on 7/7/94) PL 23 FLC 2 FAC 1
Bradford C (£225,000 on 13/7/95) FL 39/4 FLC 6 FAC 2 Others 5

MOILANEN Teuvo (Tepi) Johannes
Born: Oulu, Finland, 12 December 1973
Height: 6'5" Weight: 13.2
International Honours: Finland: U21
Signed from FF Jaro last December and immediately became the tallest goalkeeper in Preston's history. While it was hardly surprising to find that Tepi had no problem with crosses, he was also quick to get down for such a big man. Still learning about the English game, he showed that he had a bright future ahead of him before a hand injury curtailed his season.

Preston NE (£120,000 from FF Jaro on 12/12/95) FL 2

MOLBY Jan
Born: Kolding, Jutland, 4 July 1963
Height: 6'1" Weight: 14.7
Club Honours: Div 1 '86, '90; FAC '86, '92; CS '86; FLC '95
International Honours: Denmark: 67
Loaned out by Liverpool last season to both Barnsley (September) and Norwich (December), Jan made five appearances for the Yorkshire club and the same again at City, with the added bonus of a scorching goal in his farewell game at Birmingham, before deciding on a move to Swansea to become their player/manager. Although the Swans were ultimately relegated, his international pedigree stood out, whether in midfield or defence, as the players

responded to him, and the side should be in much better shape for the coming season.

Liverpool (£575,000 from Ajax on 24/8/84) F/PL 195+23/44 FLC 25+3/9 FAC 24+4/4 Others 16+2/4
Barnsley (Loaned on 22/9/95) FL 5
Norwich C (Loaned on 22/12/95) FL 3 FLC 2/1
Swansea C (Free on 22/2/96) FL 12/2

Jan Molby

MONCUR John Frederick
Born: Stepney, 22 September 1966
Height: 5'7" Weight: 9.10
Talented West Ham midfielder with excellent passing skills who loves to run with the ball. Started last season as an integral part of the team, playing in the first 14 games, before injury and suspensions saw him miss the next six. Although he came back for December and January, the groin injury which had already troubled him, proved to be the final straw, and forced him out until 13 April. As a player who cannot get enough of the ball, and who always makes himself available for others, 1995-96 was disappointing to say the least, but he will be back.

Tottenham H (From apprentice on 22/8/84) FL 10+11/1 FLC 1+2
Doncaster Rov (Loaned on 25/9/86) FL 4
Cambridge U (Loaned on 27/3/87) FL 3+1
Portsmouth (Loaned on 22/3/89) FL 7
Brentford (Loaned on 19/10/89) FL 5/1 Others 1
Ipswich T (Loaned on 24/10/91) FL 5+1
Swindon T (£80,000 on 30/3/92) F/PL 53+5/5 FLC 4 FAC 1 Others 4/1
West Ham U (£900,000 on 24/6/94) PL 49+1/2 FLC 6/2 FAC 3/1

MONINGTON Mark David
Born: Bilsthorpe, 21 October 1970
Height: 6'1" Weight: 14.0
Club Honours: AMC '96
This central defender was expected to be the one who would hold the Rotherham defence together, but 1995-96 turned out to be a season he would rather forget, as injuries restricted his appearances to around the

dozen mark. Unfortunately for him, his longest run of successive games was four and it seemed that whenever he made a return he picked up another knock.

Burnley (From juniors on 23/3/89) FL 65+19/5 FLC 5 FAC 4+1/1 Others 4+2
Rotherham U (Signed on 28/11/94) FL 32+4/2 FLC 2 Others 2

MONK Garry Alan
Born: Bedford, 6 March 1979
Height: 6'0" Weight: 12.1

A local born Torquay defender, and still a YTS, Garry was introduced to the league side last season and quickly showed that even in a struggling side he had the ability to go with his powerful physique. Could well make it before too long.

Torquay U (Trainee) FL 4+1

MONKOU Kenneth (Ken) John
Born: Surinam, 29 November 1964
Height: 6'3" Weight: 14.4
Club Honours: FMC '90
International Honours: Holland: U21

Strong Southampton central defender, who combines his aerial ability with solid tackling, Ken is also surprisingly skilful and more than capable of hitting quality long balls behind opposing defenders. Had a superb season in 1995-96, despite a couple of periods out injured, and at one stage many believed he might have a chance to make the Dutch squad for Euro '96. Continuing to attract interest from clubs further up the Premiership, Saints must hope they can hold onto him.

Chelsea (£100,000 from Feyenoord on 2/3/89) FL 92+2/2 FLC 12 FAC 3 Others 10
Southampton (£750,000 on 21/8/92) PL 130+1/8 FLC 10/1 FAC 13/1

MOODY Paul
Born: Portsmouth, 13 June 1967
Height: 6'3" Weight: 14.3

Top scorer for the second successive season, Paul notched 24 goals, including seven in the last six games, when Oxford eventually overhauled Blackpool for automatic promotion to the first division. Despite being the leading scorer at the club, he was not always a regular and spent a while on the subs' bench. In one such game against Burnley, he came on to score a 12-minute hat trick (becoming the first ever United substitute to score three goals in a match), just one of three during the campaign for the big striker.

Southampton (£50,000 from Waterlooville on 15/7/91) F/PL 7+5 FLC 1 FAC 0+1
Reading (Loaned on 9/12/92) FL 5/1 Others 1
Oxford U (£60,000 on 19/2/94) FL 79+19/45 FLC 7/2 FAC 7/5 Others 3/3

MOONEY Thomas (Tommy) John
Born: Middlesbrough, 11 August 1971
Height: 5'11" Weight: 12.6

A versatile player who can, and did, perform anywhere on the left side of the field for Watford in 1995-96. His enthusiasm and positive approach made him a great favourite with the fans and it was no surprise when he was voted Watford's "Player of the Year". Is an expert header of the ball, and

blessed with a strong shot, which was seen to particular advantage against Wimbledon in the FA Cup.

Aston Villa (From trainee on 23/11/89)
Scarborough (Free on 1/8/90) FL 96+11/30 FLC 11+2/8 FAC 3 Others 6/2
Southend U (£100,000 on 12/7/93) FL 9+5/5 FLC 1+1 Others 2+3
Watford (Signed on 17/3/94) FL 77+4/11 FLC 7/1 FAC 2+1/1

MOORE Alan
Born: Dublin, 25 November 1974
Height: 5'10" Weight: 10.7
Club Honours: Div 1 '95
International Honours: Ei: 5; U21-4; Yth; Sch

After some brilliant performances on the left wing in Middlesbrough's promotion campaign of 1994-95, Alan seemed a natural for Premier League stardom. However, in reality, he scarcely got a chance in 1995-96, making more appearances from the bench than in the starting line-up and only in the second half of the season. Some compensation came with his first Republic of Ireland cap versus the Czech Republic in April, followed by four more, and much is expected of this talented youngster who can provide magical match-winning moments on his day.

Middlesbrough (From trainee on 5/12/91) F/PL 82+11/14 FLC 7+2/1 FAC 2+1/2 Others 3+1

Alan Moore

MOORE Darren Mark
Born: Birmingham, 22 April 1974
Height: 6'2" Weight: 15.6

A 1995 close season signing from Torquay, the giant central defender won Doncaster's "Player of the Year" award by a mile in his first season at Belle Vue. Commanding in the air, and uncompromising on the deck, he has fully justified the club-record fee that Rovers paid for him.

Torquay U (From trainee on 18/11/92) FL 102+1/8 FLC 6 FAC 7/2 Others 8/2
Doncaster Rov (£62,500 on 19/7/95) FL 35/2 FLC 2 FAC 1 Others 2/1

MOORE Ian Ronald
Born: Birkenhead, 26 August 1976
Height: 5'11" Weight: 12.0
International Honours: E: U21-5; Yth

Another milestone season for Tranmere's prodigious young striker. An eight goals in 11 games burst, early last season, caught the eye of the big clubs and the son of ex-Tranmere coach, Ronnie, is now a "wanted man". An invitation to train with England's senior squad and a first U21 cap against Croatia at Sunderland, having earlier represented the Football League U21 side against an Italian Serie "B" XI, were further evidence of his growing reputation, despite a lack of goals at club level. Great in the air and on the ground, he seems to have boundless energy.

Tranmere Rov (From trainee on 6/7/94) FL 27+10/9 FLC 3+1/1 FAC 1 Others 0+1

MOORE Kevin Thomas
Born: Grimsby, 29 April 1958
Height: 5'11" Weight: 13.2
Club Honours: Div 3 '80; FLC '82
International Honours: E: Sch

Kevin took a back seat in the early stages of the 1995-96 campaign, concentrating on his new duties as Fulham's safety liaison officer, before being called into action during Mark Blake's absence through injury and playing in 14 consecutive games. Although, at times, his age caught up with him when faced by a particularly nippy forward, his vast experience and enthusiasm usually enabled him to cope. Was released at the end of the season.

Grimsby T (From juniors on 1/7/76) FL 397+3/27 FLC 41/3 FAC 25/3 Others 2
Oldham Ath (£100,000 on 20/2/87) FL 13/1 Others 2
Southampton (£125,000 on 3/8/87) F/PL 144+4/10 FLC 19+1/2 FAC 12 Others 5/1
Bristol Rov (Loaned on 9/1/92) FL 7
Bristol Rov (Loaned on 17/10/92) FL 4/1
Fulham (Free on 28/7/94) FL 48+3/4 FLC 4/2 FAC 6+2 Others 3

MOORE Neil
Born: Liverpool, 21 September 1972
Height: 6'1" Weight: 12.3

Everton centre back who is very strong in the air, aggressive in the tackle, and basically a good all-round defender. Figured less prominently in 1995-96 than in the previous season, his appearances being limited because of strong competition for places, and had extended loan periods with first Carlisle (August) and then Rotherham (March). Looked accomplished with the former and later demonstrated his versatility when playing a holding role in midfield on his debut for Rotherham, where he impressed the locals, especially with his aerial ability.

Everton (From trainee on 4/6/91) PL 4+1 FLC 0+1
Blackpool (Loaned on 9/9/94) FL 7 Others 1
Oldham Ath (Loaned on 16/2/95) FL 5
Carlisle U (Loaned on 25/8/95) FL 13 Others 2
Rotherham U (Loaned on 20/3/96) FL 10+1

MOORS Christopher (Chris)
Born: Yeovil, 18 August 1976
Height: 6'0" Weight: 11.7
Striker. Arriving at Torquay last November, at the same time as another Hammer, Scott Canham (who was on loan), Chris came on a non-contract basis after completing his period as a trainee at Upton Park. Although showing himself to be fairly quick and skilful, with the ability to hold the ball up well, he was released in February, having made just one start. Had a spell on loan at Glenavon in March, but is now back home and looking for a new club.
Torquay U (Free from West Ham U juniors on 3/11/95) FL 0+1 FAC 1

MORALEE Jamie David
Born: Wandsworth, 2 December 1971
Height: 5'11" Weight: 11.0
The Watford striker spent 1995-96 in and out of the first team, partly because of injuries, but also because his goal return – just three all season – continued to disappoint. Released during the summer, to his credit, Jamie's effort and enthusiasm were never in doubt.
Crystal Palace (From trainee on 3/7/90) FL 2+4
Millwall (Free on 3/9/92) FL 56+11/19 FLC 3+1/1 FAC 1 Others 3+1
Watford (£450,000 on 13/7/94) FL 40+9/7 FLC 6+1 FAC 5

Jamie Moralee

MORENO Jaime (Jamie)
Born: Bolivia, 19 January 1974
Height: 5'10" Weight: 11.9
Club Honours: Div 1 '95
International Honours: Bolivia: 35
Having represented Bolivia in the 1994 World Cup in the USA, Jamie is a deceptive striker who made his international debut at the tender age of 16. A product of the Tahuici Academy, renowned for teaching its students about life away from, as well as inside of, the football environment, he is a good dribbler and ball controller and has

adapted well to the way we play here, as opposed to the game back home in Bolivia. An intelligent young footballer who is trying hard to make a successful entry to the English game, he made just two starting line-ups for Middlesbrough, plus five brief subs' appearances, in the Premier League in 1995-96, to add to the six starts he made in the previous season and will be looking to make more impact in 1996-97 in order to secure a new contract.
Middlesbrough (£250,000 from Blooming on 20/9/94) P/FL 8+13/1 FLC 3 FAC 0+1 Others 3/1

MORGAN Alan Meredith
Born: Aberystwyth, 2 November 1973
Height: 5'9" Weight: 10.12
International Honours: W: U21-2; Yth; Sch
The nightmare of four years as a Tranmere professional without a league appearance finally ended for Alan in 1995-96 when new boss, John Aldridge, gave him his debut as a substitute against Ipswich at Prenton Park and within eight minutes he had scored to make it a double delight. Capped by Wales at schoolboy, youth and U21 levels, he is a skilful and versatile player, who can play up front, in midfield, or either full back position.
Tranmere Rov (From trainee on 8/5/92) FL 0+4/1

MORGAN James (Jamie)
Born: Lincoln, 11 September 1975
Height: 5'11" Weight: 11.9
Hard-working young midfield player. Signed from Plymouth during the 1995 close season, Jamie made only a couple of first team appearances for Exeter before sadly having to retire due to injury.
Plymouth Arg (From trainee on 29/6/94) FL 9+2 FLC 0+1 Others 1
Exeter C (Free on 11/8/95) FL 2+4 Others 0+1

MORGAN Simon Charles
Born: Birmingham, 5 September 1966
Height: 5'10" Weight: 11.13
International Honours: E: U21-2
Fulham skipper who leads by example. A centre back, turned central midfielder, Simon could never be accused of shirking a tackle, and is also capable of scoring spectacular goals, his buccaneering runs often causing panic in opposition defences. As in the previous season, he was again the club's second-highest scorer in 1995-96.
Leicester C (From apprentice on 15/11/84) FL 147+13/3 FLC 14/1 FAC 4+1 Others 3
Fulham (£100,000 on 12/10/90) FL 223+4/33 FLC 15 FAC 12/1 Others 14/4

MORGAN Stephen (Steve) Alphonso
Born: Oldham, 19 September 1968
Height: 5'11" Weight: 13.0
The fast and skilful, well-built Coventry left back, who can play in midfield if required, was unfortunate to suffer with back injuries last season. Struggled to regain fitness and when doing so he went on loan to Bristol Rovers in February, prior to being released during the summer. Good on the overlap and an excellent crosser.
Blackpool (From apprentice on 12/8/86) FL 135+9/10 FLC 13/2 FAC 16/1 Others 10+1/1

Plymouth Arg (£115,000 on 16/7/90) FL 120+1/6 FLC 7 FAC 6 Others 5
Coventry C (£110,000 on 14/7/93) PL 65+3/2 FLC 5/3 FAC 5
Bristol Rov (Loaned on 1/3/96) FL 5 Others 2

MORLEY Trevor William
Born: Nottingham, 20 March 1961
Height: 5'11" Weight: 12.1
Club Honours: Div 4 '87
International Honours: E: SP-6
Signed from West Ham during the 1995 close season, the striker made an immediate impact at Reading with a superb headed goal in a 3-2 victory over Derby. However, he then suffered a fractured skull at Portsmouth in only his third match and was forced to miss much of the campaign. Thankfully recovered to give glimpses of his ability to poach goals, Trevor netted five times in seven games at the turn of the year.
Northampton T (£20,000 from Nuneaton Borough on 21/6/85) FL 107/39 FLC 10/4 FAC 6/2 Others 7
Manchester C (£175,000 on 22/1/88) FL 69+3/18 FLC 7/3 FAC 5
West Ham U (£500,000 on 28/12/89) F/PL 159+19/57 FLC 10+1/5 FAC 14+5/7 Others 5+1/1
Reading (Free on 1/8/95) FL 14+3/4 FLC 2/1 FAC 2/1

MORRIS Andrew (Andy) Dean
Born: Sheffield, 17 November 1967
Height: 6'4" Weight: 15.7
A big, strong forward, remarkably skilful for such a large man, "Bruno" endured a miserable time of it for Chesterfield in 1995-96. When playing, he performed well, his height and presence causing many problems to opposing defences, but his season ended in December with persistent injuries to both ankles. Without him, the attack lacked variety and the club were nothing like as effective going forward.
Rotherham U (From juniors on 29/7/85) FL 0+7 FLC 0+1
Chesterfield (Signed on 12/1/88) FL 203+31/51 FLC 15+1/8 FAC 10+1/3 Others 17+4/3
Exeter C (Loaned on 4/3/92) FL 4+3/2

MORRIS Christopher (Chris) Barry
Born: Newquay, 24 December 1963
Height: 5'10" Weight: 11.11
Club Honours: SPD '88; SC '88, '89; Div '95
International Honours: E: Sch. Ei: 35
Happiest in the full back position on either flank, Chris is a determined professional who fights hard to win every ball, overlaps well and is an accurate passer. Another who always gives 100 per cent, he enjoyed great success as a wing/back in Middlesbrough's revised 5-2-2-1 formation last season until losing his place through injury to Curtis Fleming early in December. Having missed just one game form the first 21, he was first suspended and came back, only to twice suffer thigh strains and be sidelined for the remaining period. Hopefully, he will be recovered well in time for 1996-97.
Sheffield Wed (Signed on 1/10/82) FL 61+13/1 FLC 5+5/1 FAC 7+5
Glasgow Celtic (£125,000 on 10/8/87) SL 157+6/8 SLC 16+1 SC 22/1 Others 9
Middlesbrough (Signed on 14/8/92) F/PL 72+6/3 FLC 10 FAC 6 Others 4/1

MORRIS Jody
Born: London, 22 December 1978
Height: 5'5" Weight: 9.7
International Honours: E: Yth; Sch

Local-born England U17 captain who came on as a substitute for the last 20 minutes of Chelsea's televised 5-0 thrashing of Middlesbrough, just six weeks after his 17th birthday. A talented midfield player, Jody is a bright hope for the future.

Chelsea (From trainee on 8/1/96) PL 0+1

MORRIS Mark John
Born: Morden, 26 September 1962
Height: 6'1" Weight: 13.8
Club Honours: Div 4 '83

As club captain and Bournemouth's senior player, Mark took up his usual role as centre back at the start of last season and was going well before it ended prematurely for him, following a knee injury sustained in February. Starting to come back to fitness towards the end of the campaign, with a couple of appearances for the reserves, his strength, enthusiasm and tackling capability having been obviously missed.

Wimbledon (From apprentice on 26/9/80) FL 167+1/9 FLC 11 FAC 11 Others 1+1
Aldershot (Loaned on 5/9/85) FL 14 FAC 1
Watford (£35,000 on 21/7/87) FL 41/1 FLC 5/1 FAC 7
Sheffield U (£175,000 on 11/7/89) FL 53+3/3 FLC 5 FAC 5 Others 2
Bournemouth (£100,000 on 31/7/91) FL 190+3/8 FLC 15/2 FAC 17/1 Others 9

MORRIS Stephen (Steve)
Born: Liverpool, 13 May 1976
Height: 5'10" Weight: 11.1
Club Honours: WC '95

Striker. Short and lively, he had few opportunities to stake a regular place for Wrexham in 1995-96, but, when called upon, did not let anyone down, always being aware of the half chance. Was a regular goalscorer in the Racecourse club's successful Pontins League side last season.

Wrexham (Free from Liverpool juniors on 5/9/94) FL 14+11/5 FLC 1+1 FAC 1 Others 3+2

MORRISON Andrew (Andy) Charles
Born: Inverness, 30 July 1970
Height: 5'11" Weight: 13.10

The tough-tackling Blackpool midfielder who started last season belatedly, due to injury, eventually proved to be the ball winner needed in the centre of the field as the club strove for promotion. Still the 'Pool's record signing and a key figure in their future plans, he is equally at home in defence or midfield. *Stop Press:* Reportedly signed by Huddersfield for the sum of £500,000.

Plymouth Arg (From trainee on 6/7/88) FL 105+8/6 FLC 10+1/1 FAC 6 Others 2+1
Blackburn Rov (£500,000 on 5/8/93) PL 1+4 FAC 1
Blackpool (£245,000 on 9/12/94) FL 47/3 FAC 2 Others 4

MORRISON David Ellis
Born: Waltham Forest, 30 November 1974
Height: 5'11" Weight: 12.5

A wide, attacking player, who can operate on either flank, David started on the left

wing for Peterborough last season, before losing confidence and eventually coming back for a further spell, this time on the right side. Highly regarded by Posh, he has yet to turn potential into results.

Peterborough U (£30,000 from Chelmsford C on 12/5/94) FL 55+11/10 FLC 4+1/1 FAC 2+1 Others 4+1

MORRISSEY John Joseph
Born: Liverpool, 8 March 1965
Height: 5'8" Weight: 11.9
International Honours: E: Yth

In contractual dispute with former Tranmere manager, John King, John found himself cast into the wilderness for most of last season, with just occasional invitations to the first team, and only returned to favour when John Aldridge took over. At his best, a brilliant jinking right winger and supplier of teasing crosses, however, goalscoring has never been one of his forte – his last strike being 18 months ago. Is the son of the former Liverpool and Everton star, Johnny.

Everton (From apprentice on 10/3/83) FL 1 Others 0+1
Wolverhampton W (Free on 2/8/85) FL 5+5/1 FLC 1
Tranmere Rov (£8,000 on 2/10/85) FL 343+35/47 FLC 30+2 FAC 26+1/5 Others 39+3/6

MORROW Stephen (Steve) Joseph
Born: Belfast, 2 July 1970
Height: 6'0" Weight: 12.2
Club Honours: FAYC '88; FLC '93; ECEC '94
International Honours: NI: 19; B-1; U23-2; Yth; Sch

Captain of the Northern Ireland national side and a valuable Arsenal squad player, Steve is a left-footed central defender, who can also operate at left back or in a defensive midfield role. A good all-rounder, he filled in occasionally for Martin Keown last season.

Arsenal (From trainee on 5/5/88) F/PL 34+14/1 FLC 7+2/2 FAC 3+2 Others 1+4
Reading (Loaned on 16/1/91) FL 10
Watford (Loaned on 14/8/91) FL 7+1 Others 1
Reading (Loaned on 30/10/91) FL 3
Barnet (Loaned on 4/3/92) FL 1

MORTIMER Paul Henry
Born: Kensington, 8 May 1968
Height: 5'11" Weight: 11.3
International Honours: E: U21-2

Two seasons into his second spell at Charlton, he missed the early part of the 1995-96 campaign recovering from a ruptured achilles tendon sustained during the final week of 1994-95. As an attacking left-sided midfielder, who likes nothing better than having a crack from long range, Paul, in getting back to his best, put in some excellent performances, and was the club's main penalty taker, scoring with all four attempts.

Charlton Ath (Free from Farnborough T on 22/9/87) FL 108+5/17 FLC 4+1 FAC 8 Others 3+1
Aston Villa (£350,000 on 24/7/91) FL 10+2/1 FLC 2
Crystal Palace (£500,000 on 18/10/91) F/PL 18+4/2 FLC 1 FAC 1 Others 3
Brentford (Loaned on 22/1/93) FL 6 Others 2
Charlton Ath (£200,000 on 5/7/94) FL 39+6/9 FAC 3/1

MOSES Adrian Paul
Born: Doncaster, 4 May 1975
Height: 6'1" Weight: 12.8

Continued to develop as a central defender of note for Barnsley in 1995-96. Good in the air, and a strong tackler, he was usually used as a man marker, playing in a number of different shirts. He also netted his first ever league goal during the season.

Barnsley (From juniors on 2/7/93) FL 24+4/1 FLC 2 FAC 2

MOSS David Albert
Born: Doncaster, 15 November 1968
Height: 6'2" Weight: 13.7

Making a comeback from a long injury last February, just as the first cracks were appearing in Chesterfield's play-off chances, he was played in what was probably his least effective position, as an out-and-out forward. Far happier when coming through from midfield, where his shooting ability can be seen to good effect, David was released during the summer.

Doncaster Rov (Signed from Boston U on 10/3/93) FL 18/5 FLC 2 Others 0+1
Chesterfield (Free on 8/10/93) FL 59+12/16 FLC 2/1 FAC 2+1 Others 3

MOSS Neil Graham
Born: New Milton, 10 May 1975
Height: 6'1" Weight: 12.11

Following an injury to Bournemouth's first team goalkeeper, Ian Andrews, last October, the agile youngster immediately stepped into his shoes, keeping seven clean sheets in a row, before being transferred to Southampton after just 12 appearances. Although yet to make his Saints' debut, such was his outstanding form during that spell, and as the clear number two to Dave Beasant, following Bruce Grobbelaar's release, his chance is bound to come before too long.

Bournemouth (From apprentice on 29/1/93) FL 21+1 FLC 1 FAC 3+1 Others 2
Southampton (£250,000 on 20/12/95)

MOULDEN Paul Anthony
Born: Farnworth, 6 September 1967
Height: 5'8" Weight: 11.3
Club Honours: FAYC '86; Div 2 '91
International Honours: E: Yth; Sch

Son of 1960s Rochdale player, Tony, having been released by Huddersfield, Paul was signed on monthly terms by his dad's former club early on last season and sensationally netted a hat trick in his first full appearance, in the Autoglass Trophy. Indeed, he scored six goals in his first four starts, but did not secure a regular place in the side, though he top scored for the reserves and was freed during the summer. Not tall, he uses skill to unsettle defenders around the box.

Manchester C (From apprentice on 7/9/84) FL 48+16/18 FLC 5+1/4 FAC 2+3/1 Others 3+1/3
Bournemouth (£160,000 on 2/8/89) FL 32/13 FLC 4 FAC 0+1 Others 1
Oldham Ath (£225,000 on 23/3/90) F/PL 17+21/4 FLC 2+1/1
Brighton & Hove A (Loaned on 14/8/92) FL 11/5
Birmingham C (£150,000 on 12/3/93) FL 18+2/5 FLC 1+1 Others 1
Huddersfield T (Free on 23/3/95) FL 0+2
Rochdale (Free on 23/8/95) FL 6+10/1 FAC 3/2 Others 2/3

MOUNTFIELD Derek Neal
Born: Liverpool, 22 November 1962
Height: 6'1" Weight: 13.6
Club Honours: FAC '84; CS '84, '85; Div 1 '85, '87, Div 3 '95; ECWC '85
International Honours: E: B-1; U21-1

A key figure in Carlisle's championship winning side of 1994-95, injury confined him to a single appearance last season, before being released and playing four games for Northampton, en-route to Walsall in November. His debut at the heart of the Saddlers' defence coincided with a 5-0 Auto Windscreen Shield win over Wycombe, while his first league game took in a 3-0 victory at Brighton. After this he missed just three matches, when laid temporarily low by an injury at Notts County in February, his partnership with another newcomer, Adrian Viveash, being a key factor in the club's improved defensive record.
Tranmere Rov (From apprentice on 4/11/80) FL 26/1 FLC 2 FAC I
Everton (£30,000 on 2/6/82) FL 100+6/19 FLC 16/3 FAC 17/2 Others 14+1/1
Aston Villa (£450,000 on 6/6/88) FL 88+2/9 FLC 13/2 FAC 6/1 Others 11/5
Wolverhampton W (£150,000 on 7/11/91) FL 79+4/4 FLC 4/1 FAC 2 Others 2
Carlisle U (Free on 3/8/94) FL 30+1/3 FLC 4+1 FAC 4/1 Others 6/1
Northampton T (Free on 6/10/95) FL 4
Walsall (Free on 6/11/95) FL 28/1 FAC 3 Others 2

MOUSSADDIK Choukri (Chuck)
Born: Maknes, Morocco, 23 February 1971
Height: 5'11" Weight: 13.1
International Honours: Morocco: U21

After seven years with Wycombe as an impressive shot stopper in the reserves, he finally made his first class debut at Leyton Orient in the Coca Cola Cup last September, coming on as substitute when Paul Hyde was sent off. He then made his league debut in the next match against Peterborough, but made no further appearances and was released midway through the season, ending up at Barnet in March.
Wycombe W (Signed in 1989, following spells at Tottenham H and Wimbledon on trial) FL 1 FLC 0+1
Barnet (Free on 28/3/96)

MOWBRAY Anthony (Tony) Mark
Born: Saltburn, 22 November 1963
Height: 6'1" Weight: 13.2
International Honours: E: B-2

Having joined Ipswich from Celtic last October, Tony was immediately installed as club captain prior to making his debut at home to Wolves. An uncompromising central defender, who is powerful in the air at both ends of the pitch, he took a while to settle in, not being helped by having six different partners in as many games. However, once a fixture, the leadership qualities were there for all to see, his organisational skills invaluable to the younger players.
Middlesbrough (From apprentice on 27/11/81) FL 345+3/25 FLC 28+2/2 FAC 23/1 Others 23+1/1
Glasgow Celtic (£1,000,000 on 8/11/91) SL 75+3/6 SLC 7 SC 5 Others 6
Ipswich T (£300,000 on 6/10/95) FL 19/2 FAC 4 Others 3/1

MOYES David William
Born: Blythswood, 25 April 1963
Height: 6'1" Weight: 12.0
Club Honours: SPL '82; AMC '86; Div 3 '96
International Honours: S: Yth; Sch

Although approaching the end of his career, David continues to be a class defender. The added responsibility of being Preston's assistant manager sometimes showed in his play during 1995-96, but he always came back strongly. Still a threat at set pieces with his powerful and accurate heading, his 41 league games were good value for a third division championship medal.
Glasgow Celtic (From juniors in 1980) SL 19+5 SLC 7+1 Others 2+1
Cambridge U (Free on 28/10/83) FL 79/1 FLC 3 FAC I Others 3
Bristol C (£10,000 on 10/10/85) FL 83/6 FLC 6 FAC 5 Others 15
Shrewsbury T (£30,000 on 30/10/87) FL 91+5/11 FLC 4 FAC 3/1 Others 5
Dunfermline Ath (Signed on 1/8/90) SL 105/13 SLC 7/1 SC 5
Hamilton Academical (Signed in August 1993) SL 5
Preston NE (Free on 20/9/93) FL 108/11 FLC 4/1 FAC 9/1 Others 13/1

MUDD Paul Andrew
Born: Hull, 13 November 1970
Height: 5'9" Weight: 11.4
International Honours: E: Sch

Attacking Lincoln left back. Signed on a free transfer in the summer of 1995, having been released by Scunthorpe, Paul lost his place in the first team squad after suffering a fractured foot. Recuperating, he spent a month on loan at Halifax Town in February.
Hull C (From trainee on 1/7/89) FL 1
Scarborough (£5,000 on 25/7/90) FL 95+3/2 FLC 10 FAC 3 Others 6
Scunthorpe U (Free on 26/7/93) FL 66+2/4 FLC 4 FAC 8 Others 5
Lincoln C (Free on 28/7/95) FL 2+2 Others 1

MUGGLETON Carl David
Born: Leicester, 13 September 1968
Height: 6'2" Weight: 13.4
International Honours: E: U21-1

Athletic goalkeeper. Made only a handful of appearances at the start of 1995-96 for Stoke, before becoming one of a number of casualties axed during a shake-up by the manager after the team's poor start to the campaign. Carl was loaned out twice during the season. At Rotherham, he saved a penalty in the Auto Windscreens Shield shoot-out against Wigan, but conceded seven goals in the FL against Wrexham, before going to Sheffield United on transfer deadline day, where he made his debut as a substitute when coming on for an outfield player after 90 minutes.
Leicester C (From apprentice on 17/9/86) FL 46 FAC 3 Others 5
Chesterfield (Loaned on 10/9/87) FL 17 Others 2
Blackpool (Loaned on 1/2/88) FL 2
Hartlepool U (Loaned on 28/10/88) FL 8 Others 2
Stockport Co (Loaned on 1/3/90) FL 4
Stoke C (Loaned on 13/8/93) FL 6 FLC 1 Others 2
Glasgow Celtic (£150,000 on 11/1/94) SL 12 SC 1
Stoke C (£150,000 on 21/7/94) FL 30 FLC 3 Others 4
Rotherham U (Loaned on 1/11/95) FL 6 Others 1
Sheffield U (Loaned on 28/3/96) FL 0+1

MUIR Ian James
Born: Coventry, 5 May 1963
Height: 5'8" Weight: 11.0
Club Honours: AMC '90
International Honours: E: Yth; Sch

Vastly experienced forward who re-joined Birmingham during the 1995 close season, 11 years after leaving St Andrews bound for Brighton. Arriving at City from Tranmere, having lost his place in the side to John Aldridge, Rovers' record goalscorer was expected to add the finishing touches to chances going begging around the six-yard box. But, after appearing in the first and coming off the bench in the second, Ian went on loan to Darlington, where he scored once in four games before returning and subsequently fading from the scene completely.
Queens Park R (From apprentice on 3/9/80) FL 2/2
Burnley (Loaned on 8/10/82) FL 1+1/1
Birmingham C (Free on 27/8/83) FL 1 FLC 1
Brighton & Hove A (Free on 15/2/84) FL 3+1
Swindon T (Loaned on 28/1/85) FL 2 Others 1
Tranmere Rov (Free on 26/7/85) FL 283+31/141 FLC 22+3/6 FAC 17+1/14 Others 29+7/19
Birmingham C (£125,000 on 30/6/95) FL 1 FLC 0+1
Darlington (Loaned on 8/9/95) FL 4/1

MULLIGAN James (Jimmy)
Born: Dublin, 21 April 1974
Height: 5'6" Weight: 11.7

The diminutive Dubliner was something of an enigma at Bury in 1995-96. He could play on the right wing or at centre forward, had skill in abundance, and yet was unable to find the required consistency. Very injury prone, he made just two substitute appearances before becoming disillusioned and homesick for Dublin, having his contract mutually terminated in November.
Stoke C (From trainee on 7/7/92)
Bury (Loaned on 5/11/93) FL 2+1/1 Others 2
Bury (£15,000 on 5/7/94) FL 9+8/2 FLC 2/1 FAC 0+2 Others 1+1

MULLIN John
Born: Bury, 11 August 1975
Height: 6'0" Weight: 11.5

A leggy striker, John arrived from Burnley in the 1995 close season and made his mark early in the campaign, when scoring his first Sunderland goal in the 2-0 victory at Luton in September. Although he found first team opportunities restricted after that, to use a well-worn cliché, he is hopefully "one for the future".
Burnley (From trainee on 18/8/92) FL 7+11/2 FAC 2
Sunderland (£215,000 on 12/8/95) FL 5+5/1 FLC 1 FAC 0+1

MUNDAY Stuart Clifford
Born: Newham, 28 September 1972
Height: 5'11" Weight: 11.0

Sadly, a pre-season car crash, plus ankle injuries, meant limited opportunities to clinch a regular first team spot at Brighton in 1995-96. Transfer listed at his own request in February 1996, Stuart, who possesses a good, long throw in, can play either in defence or midfield. Was released during the summer.
Brighton & Hove A (From trainee on 6/7/90) FL 78+17/4 FLC 7+1/1 FAC 2+3 Others 7+1

MUNDEE Denny William John
Born: Swindon, 10 October 1968
Height: 5'10" Weight: 11.7

This versatile, right-footed player, noted for his shuffle, who joined Brighton in October 1995 after being released by Brentford, played a few games in attack but was mainly used on right side of midfield. Competitive and hard-working, Denny had an impressive home debut against Bristol Rovers on 28 October, which he capped with a coolly taken penalty.

Swindon T (Free from Queens Park R juniors on 21/8/86)
Bournemouth (Free on 29/3/88) FL 76+24/6 FLC 3+2 FAC 9+2/4 Others 5+1/2
Torquay U (Loaned on 7/9/89) FL 9
Brentford (Free on 12/8/93) FL 64+20/16 FLC 1+4 FAC 3 Others 5+3/2
Brighton & Hove A (Free on 19/10/95) FL 31+1/3 FAC 4 Others 2/1

MUNGALL Steven (Steve) Henry
Born: Bellshill, 22 May 1958
Height: 5'8" Weight: 11.5
Club Honours: AMC '90

A great Tranmere servant, who is now part of John Aldridge's backroom team, Steve now seems unlikely to overhaul Ray Mathias' 637-game club appearance record, of which he is 13 short. Only used as a substitute in 1995-96, he will be remembered mainly as a full back. Always willing and able, when called upon, and a shining example to the club's youngsters, Steve coaches the U15's and is set to look after the reserves next season.

Motherwell (Signed from Chapelhall in 1976) SL 14+6 SLC 11+2 SC 14+1
Tranmere Rov (Free on 3/7/79) FL 478+34/13 FLC 32+3/2 FAC 30+1 Others 43+2/1

Stuart Munro

MUNRO Stuart
Born: Falkirk, 15 September 1962
Height: 5'8" Weight: 10.5
Club Honours: SPD '87, '89, '90, '91; SLC '87, '88, '89, '91

Season 1995-96 brought the Ashton Gate career of this fine player to an end. An excellent free transfer signing from Blackburn Rovers during February 1993, Stuart made over 100 appearances for Bristol City, either at left back or in central defence, and he started the last campaign in the first team before falling out of favour. Released on a free transfer during October to join his home town club, Falkirk, as player/coach, before the end of the season he had taken on the role of caretaker manager with them in a forlorn attempt to avoid relegation from the Scottish Premier League.

St Mirren (From Bo'ness U in 1980) SL 1
Alloa (Signed during 1982 close season) SL 58+2/6 SLC 14/1 SC 2/1
Glasgow R (Signed in February 1984) SL 173+6/3 SLC 21+1 SC 13+2 Others 19+1
Blackburn Rov (£350,000 on 12/8/91) FL 1
Bristol C (Free on 4/2/93) FL 91+3 FLC 5 FAC 8 Others 1+1/1

MURFIN Andrew John
Born: Doncaster, 26 November 1976
Height: 5'10" Weight: 11.7

Having signed professional forms for Scunthorpe during the 1995 close season, the youth team left back, or left winger, was thrown in at the deep end at Exeter in September as a replacement for Max Nicholson. Has not figured in first team plans since, but is sure to come again.

Scunthorpe U (From juniors on 1/9/95) FL 1

MURPHY Daniel (Danny) Benjamin
Born: Chester, 18 March 1977
Height: 5'9" Weight: 10.8
International Honours: E: Yth; Sch

Still only 19 years of age, Danny is tipped as a player of the future. Capped by England at schoolboy and youth levels, and a very talented midfield player, he began to get on the Crewe scoring charts more regularly in 1995-96.

Crewe Alex (From trainee on 21/3/94) FL 66+23/17 FLC 5 FAC 3/1 Others 9+3/2

Danny Murphy

MURPHY James (Jamie) Anthony
Born: Manchester, 25 February 1973
Height: 6'1" Weight: 13.10

Utility player. Signed from Blackpool during the 1995 close season, he was in and out of the Doncaster league side during the course of 1995-96. Performed adequately when called upon, but a definitive decision about his role in the side could lead to a more settled existence at Belle Vue.

Blackpool (From juniors on 23/8/90) FL 48+7/1 FLC 4/1 FAC 3 Others 2+3
Doncaster Rov (Free on 14/9/95) FL 17+6 Others 2

MURPHY John James
Born: Whiston, 18 October 1976
Height: 6'1" Weight: 14.0

Young Chester forward for whom the club has high hopes, and who signed professional forms during the 1995 close season, John was involved in the first team throughout 1995-96, albeit, mainly as a substitute. Possessing a powerful shot, and using his height well, his improvement was significant, however.

Chester C (From trainee on 6/7/95) FL 1+22/3 FLC 1+2/1 FAC 0+1 Others 2+1

MURPHY Matthew (Matt) Simon
Born: Northampton, 20 August 1971
Height: 5'10" Weight: 11.5

Matt, a midfield striker, continued to impress in 1995-96, despite being a regular on the Oxford subs' bench. And, from being a fringe player almost released two seasons ago, he is now an important member of the squad, having his best season for goals, scoring eight times.

Oxford U (£20,000 from Corby T on 12/2/93) FL 32+26/12 FLC 2+2/1 FAC 2+2 Others 3+3/3

MURPHY Shaun Peter
Born: Sydney, Australia, 5 November 1970
Height: 6'1" Weight: 12.0
Club Honours: AIC '95

The Notts County "Player of the Year" for 1994-95, Shaun was also a strong contender for the same honour last season, having played in all but two games, following his return to the team after pre-season injury in September. A very reliable right-sided central defender, he forged a strong partnership with Gary Strodder in the heart of the County defence and was rewarded by a call up by Australia for their match with Scotland in March, although he remained on the bench.

Notts Co (Signed from Perth Italia on 4/9/92) FL 84+9/5 FLC 4+2 FAC 6/1 Others 12+1/1

MURRAY Edwin (Eddie) John
Born: Ilford, 31 August 1973
Height: 5'11" Weight: 12.0

Normally a left-sided defender, Eddie was drafted in as an emergency striker for Swindon's visit to Carlisle last August and responded by volleying a sensational goal that won the game. But it was not to prove a significant breakthrough, making only a handful of senior appearances, the last being at York where Town slumped to one of only four league defeats.

Swindon T (From trainee on 9/7/91) FL 7+5/1 FLC 3 FAC 1+1 Others 1

MURRAY Paul
Born: Carlisle, 31 August 1976
Height: 5'8" Weight: 10.5
International Honours: E: Yth

Already an English Youth international, Paul produced a number of impressive displays for Carlisle last season, having missed much of the previous term through injury. A talented footballer who looks comfortable in both defence and midfield, he has the ability and ambition to perform at a higher level. In March, he went to QPR in a loan deal that was eventually made permanent after he had made his debut in the final game of 1995-96 at Nottingham Forest.

Carlisle U (From trainee on 14/6/94) FL 38+8/1 FLC 2 FAC 1 Others 6+1
Queens Park R (£300,000 on 8/3/96) PL 1

MURRAY Robert (Rob) James
Born: Hammersmith, 21 October 1974
Height: 5'11" Weight: 11.7
International Honours: S; U21-1
Rob established himself at the centre of Bournemouth's defence last season, appearing in several different defensive partnerships, and would have played more games had it not been for injury. Due to his experience as a striker, he is comfortable on the ball and can also perform effectively at full back. Continues to improve at the heading and tackling side of the game.

Bournemouth (From trainee on 11/1/93) FL 68+43/10 FLC 4+5 FAC 2+2 Others 1+4/2

MURRAY Scott George
Born: Aberdeen, 26 May 1974
Height: 5'10" Weight: 11.0
As understudy to Gary Charles at right back for Aston Villa, he made his PL debut last March against Middlesbrough and replaced the unlucky Charles for the last two games of the season after the latter was incapacitated by a broken ankle. An excellent dribbler, especially when going forward on the overlap, it remains to be seen whether Brian Little will entrust him with the right back slot for the start of 1996-97, due to his limited experience. Is definitely one for the future though.

Aston Villa (£35,000 from Fraserburgh on 16/3/94) PL 3

MURRAY Shaun
Born: Newcastle, 7 December 1970
Height: 5'8" Weight: 11.2
International Honours: E: Yth; Sch
Following an indifferent start to last season, when he spent most of his time on the Bradford bench, Shaun finally got into gear, his attacking midfield play a joy to watch. Not a great goalscorer, nevertheless, he pops up with the odd goal now and again, two in away games at Doncaster (AWS) and Shrewsbury (FL) effectively saving matches that would have otherwise been lost. Unfortunate to miss the last five matches, along with the play offs, due to achilles tendon trouble.

Tottenham H (From trainee on 10/12/87)
Portsmouth (£100,000 on 12/6/89) FL 21+13/1 FLC 2+1/1 FAC 1+3 Others 2+2
Scarborough (Signed on 1/11/93) FL 29/5 FAC 2 Others 2
Bradford C (£200,000 on 11/8/94) FL 63+12/7 FLC 5+2/1 FAC 3+2 Others 4/2

MURTY Graeme Stuart
Born: Middlesbrough, 13 November 1974
Height: 5'10" Weight: 11.10
An energetic and skilful midfielder, he

operated chiefly wide on the right for York last season, but is equally at home on the other flank. Unfortunately, for club and player, a number of niggling injuries proved troublesome throughout a difficult campaign.

York C (From trainee on 23/3/93) FL 49+7/4 FLC 3 Others 4+1

MUSSELWHITE Paul Stephen
Born: Portsmouth, 22 December 1968
Height: 6'2" Weight: 12.9
Club Honours: AMC '93
Once again Port Vale's most regular goalkeeper. Beginning last season as the team's number one before being left out after a poor run of results in September, Paul returned refreshed after just six games, but was again dropped towards the end of the season. Probably his best game came against Genoa in the preliminary round of the Anglo-Italian Cup and he also performed well at Crystal Palace in the FA Cup. A tall and commanding figure, he saved a penalty on the final day at Sheffield United.

Portsmouth (From apprentice on 1/12/86)
Scunthorpe U (Free on 21/3/88) FL 132 FLC 11 FAC 7 Others 13
Port Vale (£20,000 on 30/7/92) FL 170 FLC 8 FAC 17 Others 19

MUSTOE Robin (Robbie)
Born: Witney, 28 August 1968
Height: 5'11" Weight: 11.12
Club Honours: Div 1 '95
The powerhouse midfielder was a key player in Middlesbrough's formation and his absence through injury from last November until late February was probably a vital factor in Boro's dramatic fall from grace after Christmas. His equalising goal against Nottingham Forest in March, a minute after Forest took the lead, was a vital turning point in the club's season, following a succession of heavy defeats. Always to be found in the thick of the action, he keeps running when others have stopped and is an inspiration to his team mates.

Oxford U (From juniors on 2/7/86) FL 78+13/10 FLC 2 FAC 2 Others 3
Middlesbrough (£375,000 on 5/7/90) F/PL 171+9/13 FLC 24+1/7 FAC 10 Others 12+1/1

MUTCH Andrew (Andy) Todd
Born: Liverpool, 28 December 1963
Height: 5'10" Weight: 11.3
Club Honours: Div 4 '88, Div 3 '89; AMC '88
International Honours: E: B-3; U21-1
Seemingly not part of Swindon's plans for 1995-96, Andy was loaned to Wigan five games into the season, scoring on his debut in the 1-1 home draw against Preston, before returning after the clubs had failed to agree on a fee. Eventually, after several months in the wilderness, Steve Bull's former strike partner, and a skilful penalty box poacher in his own right, accepted a move to Stockport in March and fairly burst into action with a hat trick in the important 4-2 win over promotion rivals, Oxford. Although County ultimately failed to reach the first division, there was no doubting the wisdom in the move.

Wolverhampton W (Signed from Southport on 25/2/86) FL 277+12/96 FLC 14/4 FAC 11+1/1 Others 23/4
Swindon T (£250,000 on 16/8/93) F/PL 34+16/6 FLC 6+1/3 FAC 4/1 Others 3/2
Wigan Ath (Loaned on 24/8/95) FL 7/1
Stockport Co (Free on 15/3/96) FL 11/4

MYALL Stuart Thomas
Born: Eastbourne, 12 November 1974
Height: 5'10" Weight: 12.12
As a right-footed midfielder or full back, Stuart was also pressed into action by Brighton during 1995-96 as an emergency left back for nine games and performed commendably. Is a recognised long-throw specialist and a good passer of the ball. Was given a free transfer during the summer.

Brighton & Hove A (From trainee on 9/7/93) FL 69+11/4 FLC 4 FAC 4 Others 4+1

MYERS Andrew (Andy) John
Born: Hounslow, 3 November 1973
Height: 5'8" Weight: 9.10
International Honours: E: U21-4; Yth
Speedy, accomplished left-sided utility player who was another victim of Chelsea's injury hoodoo. Since making his debut four years ago, a catalogue of various injuries has restricted his total of appearances to just 67. Until last season, Andy had been used as either a left back or left-sided midfield player, but due to an injury crisis to the Blues' central defenders, Glenn Hoddle played him on the left side of a three-man central defensive formation, alongside David Lee and Michael Duberry. The fact that this previously untried trio played together at Old Trafford in December for the first time, and Chelsea held United to a 1-1 draw, spoke volumes. His speed along the back line was crucial in tidying dangerous situations, but his bad luck with injuries continued after nine impressive matches, when he limped off at St James' Park in that titanic FA Cup replay. Forced to miss the next 14 matches, he re-appeared in the FA Cup semi final at Villa Park. Everybody at Chelsea wishes this talented young player a clear injury-free run to allow him to fulfil his potential.

Chelsea (From trainee on 25/7/91) F/PL 47+6/1 FLC 1+1 FAC 9 Others 3

MYERS Christopher (Chris)
Born: Yeovil, 1 April 1969
Height: 5'10" Weight: 11.10
Released by Dundee United early last January, Chris had a brief trial at Wrexham before joining Scarborough some three weeks later on non-contract terms. Made his debut in a 1-1 home draw against Rochdale and continued to assist the club until a change of manager in March saw him move to Exeter, where he helped bolster the midfield ranks. Is both a ball winner and a creative passer.

Torquay U (From trainee on 16/6/87) FL 8+1 (Free to Dawlish during 1988 close season)
Torquay U (Free from Waldon-junior football on 22/8/90) FL 88+8/7 FLC 8+2/1 FAC 3 Others 5+3
Dundee U (Signed on 5/8/93) SL 4+2 SLC 3+2
Torquay U (Loaned on 8/12/93) FL 6
Wrexham (Free on 8/1/96)
Scarborough (Free on 22/1/96) FL 8+1
Exeter C (Free on 28/3/96) FL 7+1

We joined in…

…so they could

Pizza Hut UK Ltd. are proud to be
the official sponsors of the Community
Programme in Professional Football.

For more information contact:
Roger Reade, The Community Programme in Professional Football,
2 Oxford Court, Bishopsgate, Off Lower Mosley Street, Manchester M2 3WQ.
Tel: (061) 236 0583 Fax: (061) 228 7229

NARBETT Jonathan (Jon) Velelzer
Born: Birmingham, 21 November 1968
Height: 5'11" Weight: 12.3

Jon operated in an attacking midfield role for most of last season, without standing out, until he scored a cracking goal for Chesterfield at Carlisle in January. After that, his confidence grew and his play became more authoritative. Sadly, injury struck in March, and he took no further part in the campaign, before being released in the summer.
Shrewsbury T (From apprentice on 19/9/86) FL 20+6/3 FLC 4 FAC 1
Hereford U (£30,000 on 6/10/88) FL 148+1/31 FLC 8/1 FAC 10/2 Others 14/3
Oxford U (£65,000 on 7/7/92) FL 13+2 FLC 1 FAC 2 Others 2+1 (Free to Kalmar FF on 30/3/94)
Chesterfield (Free from Merthyr Tydfil on 23/12/94) FL 13+7/1 FLC 1+1 FAC 1 Others 2+3

NAYLOR Anthony (Tony) Joseph
Born: Manchester, 29 March 1967
Height: 5'8" Weight: 10.8

Nippy striker who missed the first two months of Port Vale's 1995-96 season through injury. Once he regained his form, he scored in five successive league games during December and January and then cracked in a hat trick in the Anglo-Italian Cup at Ipswich Town. A hamstring injury meant another spell out of the side, but he returned to continue scoring goals and finished up as top scorer.
Crewe Alex (£20,000 from Droylsden on 22/3/90) FL 104+18/45 FLC 7+2/5 FAC 9/7 Others 12/9
Port Vale (£150,000 on 18/7/94) FL 59+13/20 FLC 3/1 FAC 6/1 Others 5+1/3

NAYLOR Dominic John
Born: Watford, 12 August 1970
Height: 5'10" Weight: 13.3
Club Honours: FAYC '89

A free transfer signing from Plymouth last August, Dominic proved his value for Gillingham as a classy left back, who was strong in the tackle and liked to get forward. Although he missed the latter part of the season through a serious knee injury, his good earlier work was a vital factor in the promotion success story. Also continued where he left off as a free kick expert, when rocketing one in at Barnet early on.
Watford (From trainee on 20/9/88)
Halifax T (Loaned on 6/12/89) FL 5+1/1 Others 1+1 (Free to Hong Kong in October 1990)
Barnet (Free on 12/8/91) FL 50+1 FLC 2 FAC 5/1 Others 4
Plymouth Arg (Free on 16/7/93) FL 84+1 FLC 2 FAC 8 Others 4+1/1
Gillingham (Free on 11/8/95) FL 30+1/1 FLC 2/1 FAC 3 Others 1

NAYLOR Glenn
Born: Howden, 11 August 1972
Height: 5'10" Weight: 11.10

Glenn did not figure for York in the first half of last season and had a spell on loan with Darlington. Struck up a good partnership with newcomer Gary Bull in the closing weeks and netted a number of goals, before returning to Bootham Crescent. Is a skilful, rather than crash-and-bash forward.
York C (From trainee on 5/3/90) FL 78+33/30 FLC 2+3 FAC 4+1/2 Others 3+4
Darlington (Loaned on 13/10/95) FL 3+1/1 Others 1+1

NAYLOR Stuart William
Born: Wetherby, 6 December 1962
Height: 6'4" Weight: 12.10
International Honours: E: B-3; Yth

In his testimonial season, Stuart started as WBA's first choice goalkeeper for the 1995-96 campaign, playing consistently well until the team started to go through a sticky patch before Christmas and then being replaced by veteran, Nigel Spink. A fine shot stopper, he has seemingly always been hesitant on crosses and the manager decided on a change between the sticks at a crucial stage in the season. Having played in more games than any other Albion goalkeeper, he was released during the summer.
Lincoln C (Free from Yorkshire Amateurs on 19/6/80) FL 49 FLC 4 FAC 2 Others 6
Peterborough U (Loaned on 23/2/83) FL 8
Crewe Alex (Loaned on 6/10/83) FL 55 FLC 2 FAC 2 Others 3
West Bromwich A (£100,000 on 18/2/86) FL 354+1 FLC 22 FAC 13 Others 20

NDAH George Ehialimolisa
Born: Dulwich, 23 December 1974
Height: 6'1" Weight: 11.4
International Honours: E: Yth

A tall winger, or striker, with Crystal Palace, George took the place of John Salako on the left wing for the opening games of last season, but was then discarded, having a loan spell at Bournemouth in October, until the arrival of Dave Bassett as manager. Restored to first team duty in February, as a striking partner for Dougie Freedman, he responded with four vital goals in the run up to the promotion play offs, including two in a 4-1 victory over Millwall. His brother Jamie is currently a Football League player with Torquay.
Crystal Palace (From trainee on 10/8/92) F/PL 26+23/5 FLC 6+4/1 FAC 1+1/1 Others 4+1
Bournemouth (Loaned on 13/10/95) FL 12/1 Others 1

NDAH Jamie Jidefor Ogoegbunan
Born: Camberwell, 5 August 1971
Height: 6'0" Weight: 12.4

Signed from non-league Kingstonian at the beginning of last season, the pacy striker opened his Torquay scoring account in a 3-0 home win against Northampton, before notching a further two at Plymouth. That was it as far as goals were concerned, but in his 19 starts he showed touches of real class until being hampered by injury. Is the brother of Crystal Palace's George.
Torquay U (£20,000 from Kingstonians on 22/8/95) FL 16/3 FLC 2+1 FAC 1

NDLOVU Peter
Born: Buluwayo, Zimbabwe, 25 February 1973
Height: 5'8" Weight: 10.2
International Honours: Zimbabwe: 13

Exciting Coventry striker or midfield player. Highly talented, with two good feet, amazing ball control, and devastating pace, following John Salako's arrival, Peter started last season up front with Dion Dublin, hoping to continue where he had left off in 1994-95. Despite playing well, the goals did not flow and his confidence was affected. He did, however, score a superb individual goal in the 5-0 win over Blackburn, but the following week picked up a nasty eye injury. Out for five games during this period, Noel Whelan arrived and took his place. After returning to the starting line-up against Chelsea, being injured near the end of a good performance, towards the end of the campaign he reverted to playing wide on the left and there were signs that he was returning to his best. Scored two stunning goals in the vital game at Wimbledon.
Coventry C (£10,000 from Highlanders on 16/8/91) F/PL 131+26/36 FLC 10/2 FAC 5+1/2 Others 0+1

NEIL James (Jimmy) Darren
Born: Bury St Edmunds, 28 February 1976
Height: 5'8" Weight: 10.5

Right-sided Grimsby defender. A very promising product of the club's youth policy, and a first-year professional, Jimmy was given a run out in the final game of 1995-96 at Barnsley and did enough to show that he has a future in the game.
Grimsby T (From trainee on 13/7/94) FL 1

NEILL Lucas Edward
Born: Sydney, Australia, 9 March 1978
Height: 6'1" Weight: 12.0

Millwall midfield player with good ball control and a strong tackling capability, who came to the club last November from the Australian Institute of Sport, and quickly progressed from the youth side to first team action at Luton in February. Has an excellent attitude to go with good engine power and is certainly one to note for the future.
Millwall (Free from AIS on 13/11/95) FL 5+8

NEILL Warren Anthony
Born: Acton, 21 November 1962
Height: 5'10" Weight: 12.5
Club Honours: Div 2 '83
International Honours: E: Sch

Formerly a right back at Portsmouth, and having retired at the end of 1994-95 with a back injury, Warren came back to play a few games for Watford reserves on a non-contract basis last season, before finding himself plunged into first team action during an injury crisis.
Queens Park R (From apprentice on 3/9/80) FL 177+4/3 FLC 18+1/1 FAC 11+1/2 Others 3/1
Portsmouth (£110,000 on 28/7/88) FL 216+2/2 FLC 20/1 FAC 14 Others 8
Watford (Free on 19/1/96) FL 1

NEILSON Alan Bruce
Born: Wegburg, Germany, 26 September 1972
Height: 5'11" Weight: 12.4
International Honours: W: 4; B-2; U21-7

A reliable and improving Southampton defender signed from Newcastle during the summer of 1995, Alan found it difficult to gain a regular first team place in 1995-96 with five other defenders to compete with. However, when called upon, usually at right back, he did rather well in 16 starts. Is a sound passer with the ability to get forward.

Newcastle U (From trainee on 11/2/91) F/PL 35+7/1 FLC 4 Others 4
Southampton (£500,000 on 1/6/95) PL 15+3 FAC 1+1

NELSON Garry Paul

Born: Braintree, 16 January 1961
Height: 5'10" Weight: 11.10
Club Honours: Div 4 '81

Recently recognised for his literary talents, Garry started 1995-96 for Charlton as their first choice striker, scoring against Birmingham in the third match, but thereafter only making limited full appearances, usually when coming on as a substitute. Also capable of playing as a left-sided midfielder, he can always be relied upon to give 100 per cent performances and made his 600th league appearance during the season, before being released and joining the Torquay management team as player/coach during the summer.

Southend U (From juniors on 9/7/79) FL 106+23/17 FLC 3+1/1 FAC 6+2
Swindon T (£10,000 on 17/8/83) FL 78+1/7 FLC 4/1 FAC 5 Others 5/1
Plymouth Arg (£15,000 on 12/7/85) FL 71+3/20 FLC 4 FAC 7/2 Others 3
Brighton & Hove A (£80,000 on 17/7/87) FL 132+7/37 FLC 7 FAC 7/6 Others 8/6
Notts Co (Loaned on 8/11/90) FL 0+2
Charlton Ath (£50,000 on 16/8/91) FL 147+38/37 FLC 17+1/2 FAC 8+3/1 Others 7+1

NETHERCOTT Stuart David

Born: Ilford, 21 March 1973
Height: 6'1" Weight: 13.8
International Honours: E: U21-8

Normally a central defender with Spurs, he was called upon in mid-1995-96 to play in midfield, in place of David Howells in an injury crisis. Extremely strong, with powerful heading ability, Stuart rarely disappointed and made more regular appearances in the centre of defence later in the season. Competition for places was very fierce at White Hart Lane, but his presence kept the other defenders on their toes. Given the opportunity, he has a lot to offer at first team level and will be looking to prove this in 1996-97.

Tottenham H (From trainee on 17/8/91) PL 29+16 FAC 5+3/1
Maidstone U (Loaned on 5/9/91) FL 13/1 Others 1
Barnet (Loaned on 13/2/92) FL 3

NEVES Rui Santos Cordeiro

Born: Portugal, 10 March 1965
Height: 6'3" Weight: 11.5

One of David Hodgson's signings from Portugal last season, the experienced striker proved excellent at holding the ball and laying it off for other Darlington forwards. However, it was short lived as Rui returned home after just nine appearances.

Darlington (Free from FC Famlicao on 11/8/95) FL 3+2 FLC 2 Others 2

NEVILLE Gary Alexander

Born: Bury, 18 February 1975
Height: 5'10" Weight: 11.10
Club Honours: FAYC '92; PL '96; FAC '96
International Honours: E: 14; Yth (UEFAC '93)

A hard-tackling defender, who can also attack the flank in some style, Gary began last season as Manchester United's regular right back, before his talents were later utilised in the centre of defence when Gary Pallister was laid off through injury. But, despite forming a promising partnership with David May in United's vital home Premiership game against Newcastle, he was confined to the bench for the final two matches of the league programme after Steve Bruce and Pallister had returned to the side, his younger brother, Philip, assuming the right back slot. However, at the end of a season that saw United do the double, his 31 league games and an 89th minute substitute appearance in the FA Cup final victory over Liverpool, ensured him medals for both competitions. Voted into the PFA award winning team, and having added further England caps to his collection, including four in Euro '96, his long-term future for both club and country seem assured.

Manchester U (From trainee on 29/1/93) PL 47+3 FLC 3+1 FAC 9+1 Others 2+3

Phil Neville

NEVILLE Philip (Phil) John

Born: Bury, 21 January 1977
Height: 5'11" Weight: 12.0
Club Honours: FAYC '95; PL '96; FAC '96
International Honours: E: 1; U21-6; Yth; Sch

After playing just two Premier League games for Manchester United prior to the start of 1995-96, the brother of the marginally more experienced Gary, attained what one can only describe as the most meteoric rise to fame of recent years. Superb

in the air and sound of tackle, he took over the regular right back spot from Gary, who was switched to a central defensive role, and established himself as a first team regular, winning league and cup medals along the way. Equally adaptable in central defence, he earned a deserved England call-up for the friendly against Belgium in April – the first occasion that two brothers have been included in the squad since the Charltons, some 30 years earlier – and was selected for the Euro '96 squad.

Manchester U (From trainee on 1/6/94) PL 22+4 FLC 1+1 FAC 7+1 Others 1

NEVIN Patrick (Pat) Kevin Francis Michael

Born: Glasgow, 6 September 1963
Height: 5'6" Weight: 11.9
Club Honours: S Div 2 '82, Div 2 '84; FMC '86
International Honours: S: 28; B-4; U21-5; Yth

In terms of goalscoring for Tranmere, the PFA chairman will admit to a disappointing season in 1995-96, having netted just three times. But those bare statistics hide some very good performances, despite being asked to perform in a variety of roles on either wing, in midfield, and in the "hole" between the front two. Through it all, Pat maintained his place in the Scotland squad, helping them to Euro '96, although not selected for the final 22. Is a great ambassador for Tranmere.

Clyde (Signed from Gartcosh in 1981) SL 60+13/17 SLC 5+3 SC 10/3
Chelsea (£95,000 on 14/7/83) FL 190+3/36 FLC 25+1/5 FAC 8+1/1 Others 13/4
Everton (£925,000 on 13/7/88) FL 81+28/16 FLC 10+1/2 FLC 12+6/2 Others 9+3/1
Tranmere Rov (Loaned on 4/3/92) FL 8 Others 9+3/1
Tranmere Rov (£300,000 on 18/8/92) FL 171+1/28 FLC 16/5 FAC 7/2 Others 14/2

NEWELL Michael (Mike) Colin

Born: Liverpool, 27 January 1965
Height: 6'1" Weight: 11.0
Club Honours: AMC '85; PL '95
International Honours: E: B-2; U21-4

Blackburn striker and a good target man who works with pride and commitment. Adept at taking the pressure in the centre and dragging play out wide, he is also a good crosser from these positions and is able to bring out the best from wide players with telling, quick balls. Unable to sustain his play as he ages, and a striker without a scoring record, Alan Shearer never misses an opportunity to tell why he prefers him as his partner. Often appears ungainly and lacks touch, but works with diligence and intelligence, and is adept at creating space for Shearer before letting him have the ball. Did not score after early December last season, but contributed a ten minute hat trick in the European Cup-tie against Rosenborg, when every goal was of the highest quality. Unluckily, his season ended early, with the first hamstring pull of his career.

Crewe Alex (Free from Liverpool juniors on 28/9/83) FL 3
Wigan Ath (Free on 31/10/83) FL 64+8/25 FLC 6/1 FAC 8/6 Others 5+1/3
Luton T (£100,000 on 9/1/86) FL 62+1/18 FAC 5/1

Leicester C (£350,000 on 16/9/87) FL 81/21 FLC 9/5 FAC 2 Others 4
Everton (£1,100,000 on 27/7/89) FL 48+20/15 FLC 7+3/4 FAC 6+4 Others 6/2
Blackburn Rov (£1,100,000 on 15/11/91) F/PL 113+17/28 FLC 14+2/8 FAC 9+2/6 Others 9+1/6

Mike Newell

NEWELL Paul Clayton
Born: Woolwich, 23 February 1969
Height: 6'1" Weight: 12.8

Having only managed one game at Barnet last season due to the good form of Maik Taylor, Paul moved to Darlington, who were short of a recognised goalkeeper, in January. Becoming the fifth 'keeper to be used, following the departure of Michael Pollitt, the agile shot stopper was only twice on the losing side in the remaining 24 games, before being released during the summer.
Southend U (From trainee on 17/6/87) FL 15 FAC 2 Others 1
Leyton Orient (£5,000 on 6/8/90) FL 61 FLC 3 FAC 3 Others 4
Colchester U (Loaned on 12/8/92) FL 14 FLC 2
Barnet (Free on 26/7/94) FL 16 Others 1
Darlington (Free on 29/1/96) FL 21 Others 3

NEWHOUSE Aidan Robert
Born: Wallasey, 23 May 1972
Height: 6'2" Weight: 13.5
International Honours: E: Yth

Never quite having made the impact initially expected of him, the tall Wimbledon striker had a spell on loan at Torquay last December, scoring on his debut at Northampton. A player who can bring his team mates into dangerous positions with good lay offs and astute passes, he picked up another goal in the 3-2 home defeat against Colchester before departing for Selhurst Park. Needs a run of games to bring out the best of him.
Chester C (From trainee on 1/7/89) FL 29+15/6 FLC 5+1 FAC 0+2 Others 2+3/1

Wimbledon (£100,000 on 22/2/90) F/PL 7+16/2 FLC 1+1 FAC 2 Others 0+1
Port Vale (Loaned on 21/1/94) FL 0+2 FAC 0+1
Portsmouth (Loaned on 2/12/94) FL 6/1
Torquay U (Loaned on 7/12/95) FL 4/2

NEWLAND Raymond (Ray) James
Born: Liverpool, 19 July 1971
Height: 6'3" Weight: 13.10

Goalkeeper. Never a first team regular at Chester, Ray made just one appearance for the side last season, before being transferred to Torquay in January and taking over from Ashley Bayes. Making several fine saves along the way, he kept four clean sheets in his 17 matches played as United vainly struggled to escape the league's lowest spot.
Plymouth Arg (Free from St Helens on 3/7/92) FL 25+1 FLC 1 FAC 2
Chester C (Free on 18/7/94) FL 9+1 Others 2
Torquay U (Free on 12/1/96) FL 17

NEWMAN Richard (Ricky) Adrian
Born: Guildford, 5 August 1970
Height: 5'10" Weight: 12.6

Versatile Millwall defender and midfielder. Having arrived at the Den from Crystal Palace during the 1995 close season, he came into the side following the injury to Micky Bennett, settling in at right back until the arrival of Gerard Lavin. Then moved into midfield, continuing to tackle well, while providing fine distribution and showed signs of his fire power when scoring an equaliser against Reading with a thunderous volley.
Crystal Palace (From juniors on 22/1/88) F/PL 43+5/3 FLC 5 FAC 5+2 Others 2
Maidstone U (Loaned on 28/2/92) FL 9+1/1
Millwall (£500,000 on 19/7/95) FL 34+2/1 FLC 3 FAC 2

NEWMAN Robert (Rob) Nigel
Born: Bradford on Avon, 13 December 1963
Height: 6'2" Weight: 13.4
Club Honours: AMC '86

Good in the air and always dangerous at set pieces, former Norwich City manager, Gary Megson, described him as having the heart of a whale. Rob endeared himself to the Canary crowd with fine end of season displays in 1995-96, both in defence and attack, his rock-like pairing with John Polston steadying the side during a campaign when he played the 650th first team game of his 14-year career. Here, there and everywhere, his 88th minute goal at Barnsley secured a valuable point as the club narrowly avoided consecutive relegations.
Bristol C (From apprentice on 5/10/81) FL 382+12/52 FLC 29+1/2 FAC 27/2 Others 33/5
Norwich C (£600,000 on 15/7/91) F/PL 127+19/13 FLC 19+1/2 FAC 11/1 Others 7

NEWSOME Jonathan (Jon)
Born: Sheffield, 6 September 1970
Height: 6'2" Weight: 13.11
Club Honours: Div 1 '92

Jon had a marvellous start to 1995-96 with Norwich, but two well-taken headers at Luton proved a false dawn for both club and player. Further goals against Barnsley, Ipswich, and Brentford, were followed by media speculation regarding his future, as

the club adjusted to life in the first division, and, to the horror of City fans, in February, he transferred to his former club, Sheffield Wednesday. The tall, strong centre back quickly settled in, alongside Des Walker, adding height and weight to a shaky defence that was being sorely tested in its efforts to retain Premiership football. Ultimately, the drop was avoided and both he and the team will be all the better for the experience.
Sheffield Wed (From trainee on 1/7/89) FL 6+1 FLC 3
Leeds U (£150,000 on 11/6/91) F/PL 62+14/3 FLC 3 FAC 3+1 Others 5
Norwich C (£1,000,000 on 30/6/94) P/FL 61+1/7 FLC 9 FAC 5/1
Sheffield Wed (£1,600,000 on 16/3/96) PL 8/1

NEWTON Edward (Eddie) John Ikem
Born: Hammersmith, 13 December 1971
Height: 5'11" Weight: 11.2
International Honours: E: U21-2

Much improved Chelsea player whose 1995-96 season was tragically curtailed in February, when, against West Ham United at Stamford Bridge, he collided with his own goalkeeper, Kevin Hitchcock, and broke his right shin. Playing in the responsible holding position in the centre of midfield, his tackling and awareness allowed Ruud Gullit and Dennis Wise greater freedom to move forward, knowing that he was there to mop up behind them. Eddie became a real hero when he kept his nerve in the pressure cooker atmosphere of St James' Park to bury the decisive penalty in that pulsating shoot-out. Had his plaster removed in May and a fully fit, top form Eddie Newton is crucial to the club's fortunes in the coming season.
Chelsea (From trainee on 17/5/90) F/PL 108+17/8 FLC 12+1/1 FAC 10+2 Others 5
Cardiff C (Loaned on 23/1/92) FL 18/4

NEWTON Shaun O'Neill
Born: Camberwell, 20 August 1975
Height: 5'8" Weight: 11.0

Charlton's right-sided midfielder. An exciting player when in possession, Shaun played further forward last season and responded with some valuable goals. At the same time, as a regular in the side, he consistently used his much vaunted speed, allied to super crossing skills, to make numerous goals for others. Such was his form, that he would have been one of the first names on the team sheet and one should expect even more progress in 1996-97. Can also play at full back if required.
Charlton Ath (From trainee on 1/7/93) FL 62+26/7 FLC 8/1 FAC 2+2 Others 4+1/1

NICHOLLS Alan
Born: Birmingham, 28 August 1973
Height: 5'11" Weight: 14.7
International Honours: E: U21-1

A talented goalkeeper, he joined Gillingham from Plymouth on a non-contract basis in November 1995 and deputised for Jim Stannard in the club's AWS home tie against Hereford United. Later that month he joined Stalybridge Celtic in the GM Vauxhall Conference, but after making his debut for them at Dover he was tragically killed in a motor-bike accident near Peterborough, when returning home. A former England U21 international, at one stage of his career it was thought he would go all the way.

Plymouth Arg (£5,000 from Cheltenham T on 1/8/93) FL 64+1 FLC 1 FAC 7 Others 6
Gillingham (Free on 11/10/95) Others 1

NICHOLSON Maximillian (Max)
Born: Leeds, 3 October 1971
Height: 5'10" Weight: 12.3

Blond-haired Scunthorpe left winger who likes to get forward and take on defenders, he is also the provider of deep crosses to the far post, and loves cutting inside to strike at goal. Inconsistent form in 1995-96 saw most of his appearances come via the substitutes' bench, before being freed in the summer.

Doncaster Rov (From trainee on 27/6/90) FL 23+4/2 FAC 0+1 Others 0+2
Hereford U (Free on 16/5/92) FL 52+11/7 FLC 4+1 FAC 4 Others 6
Torquay U (Free on 9/9/94) FL 1
Scunthorpe U (Free on 18/11/94) FL 27+24/5 FLC 2 FAC 1+2 Others 0+3

NICHOLSON Shane Michael
Born: Newark, 3 June 1970
Height: 5'10" Weight: 12.2
Club Honours: GMVC '88

After playing 24 games for Premiership hopefuls, Derby, before being displaced by the new signing, Chris Powell, Shane moved to WBA last February with a view to filling the club's problem left back position. Naturally left footed, and a good tackler who enjoys going forward to link up with the forwards, his crosses are always hit with some degree of accuracy, he immediately settled in, playing well under pressure, as the Baggies battled their way out of trouble.

Lincoln C (From trainee on 19/7/88) FL 122+11/6 FLC 8+3 FAC 6/1 Others 7+1
Derby Co (£100,000 on 22/4/92) FL 73+1/1 FLC 4 FAC 4/1 Others 5
West Bromwich A (£150,000 on 9/2/96) FL 18 Others 2

NICOL Stephen (Steve)
Born: Irvine, 11 December 1961
Height: 5'10" Weight: 12.0
Club Honours: Div 1 '84, '86, '88, '90; FAC '86, '89, '92; EC '84; CS '89
International Honours: S: 27; U21-14

Having shown excellent form in 16 games with Notts County last season, and at the age of 34, Steve joined Sheffield Wednesday on a free in November. With the side struggling it seemed that a position in the back four or just in front of them best suited him, but he also had to play in midfield and at full back, not always looking to be really at ease as a short-term attempt to add experience to the squad.

Ayr U (From juniors in 1979) SL 68+2/7 SLC 16/1 SC 3
Liverpool (£300,000 on 26/10/81) F/PL 328+15/36 FLC 42/4 FAC 50/3 Others 32+2/3
Notts Co (Free on 20/1/95) FL 32/2 FLC 1 FAC 1 Others 3/1
Sheffield Wed (Free on 25/11/95) PL 18+1

NIJHOLT Luc
Born: Amsterdam, Holland, 29 July 1961
Height: 5'11" Weight: 12.1
Club Honours: SC '91

On completing two seasons with Swindon, incidentally both of them involving relegation, he made just one subs' appearance in the Coca Cola Cup in 1995-96, before moving back to Holland as FC Volendam's player/coach at the end of August. At his best, a good all-round defender or midfielder who read the game well, Luc will mainly be remembered at Town for his comfortability on the ball.

Motherwell (£125,000 from Basle OB on 1/8/90) SL 91+5/5 SLC 6 SC 1+1 Others 2
Swindon T (£175,000 on 20/7/93) F/PL 66+1/1 FLC 11+1 FAC 3+1/1 Others 3

NILSEN Roger
Born: Tromso, Norway, 8 August 1969
Height: 5'9" Weight: 12.0
International Honours: Norway: 28

Sheffield United's Norwegian international defender put in many consistent performances throughout last season at both full back and centre back, but still awaits his first goal for the club, despite many creditable efforts both from free kicks and open play. Extremely versatile, he could be used in any number of positions if required, often playing as a sweeper.

Sheffield U (£550,000 from Viking Stavanger on 2/11/93) P/FL 93+1 FLC 3 FAC 4+1

NIXON Eric Walter
Born: Manchester, 4 October 1962
Height: 6'4" Weight: 15.7
Club Honours: AMC '90

After losing his place to Danny Coyne, and failing to make an appearance for Tranmere last season, the experienced goalkeeper was loaned to first Reading (January) and then Blackpool (February). Urgently required at Reading for service in the Coca Cola Cup-tie at Leeds, due to injuries to Bobby Mihailov and Simon Sheppard, and Nicky Hammond being cup-tied, he returned north after being judged responsible for the Premier side's winning goal. However, in 20 appearances for the Seasiders, Eric spent the last three months of the campaign giving many excellent displays.

Manchester C (£1,000 from Curzon Ashton on 10/12/83) FL 58 FLC 8 FAC 10 Others 8
Wolverhampton W (Loaned on 29/8/86) FL 16
Bradford C (Loaned on 28/11/86) FL 3
Southampton (Loaned on 23/12/86) FL 4
Carlisle U (Loaned on 23/1/87) FL 16
Tranmere Rov (£60,000 on 24/3/88) FL 316 FLC 34 FAC 18 Others 45+1
Reading (Loaned on 9/1/96) FLC 1
Blackpool (Loaned on 5/2/96) FL 20 Others 2

NOGAN Kurt
Born: Cardiff, 9 September 1970
Height: 5'11" Weight: 12.7
International Honours: W: U21-2

With 20 goals scored before last Christmas, Kurt was looking like the man capable of spearheading a Burnley promotion bid, but his fortunes slumped, along with the team's in the New Year. Much more than just a finisher, he often showed trickery and elusiveness in his dealings with bigger defenders, and his scoring touch will surely return, along with his prospects of a full Welsh international cap. Selected for the PFA award winning second division team.

Luton T (From trainee on 11/7/89) FL 17+16/3 FLC 1+3/1 Others 1+1
Peterborough U (Free on 30/9/92) Others 1
Brighton & Hove A (Free on 17/10/92) FL 97/49 FLC 10/7 FAC 5+1 Others 7/4
Burnley (£250,000 on 24/4/95) FL 57+4/23 FLC 4/3 FAC 1 Others 4/3

NOGAN Lee Martin
Born: Cardiff, 21 May 1969
Height: 5'10" Weight: 11.0
International Honours: W: 2; B-1; U21-1

Second top goalscorer behind Jimmy Quinn for Reading in 1995-96, his liveliness in front of goal earned him a recall to the Welsh team, for whom he appeared against Moldova. Notching some vital goals in the battle against relegation, including an exciting hat trick in the 3-3 draw against Southend, Lee is not the biggest of front players, but one who is very difficult to mark.

Oxford U (From trainee on 25/3/87) FL 57+7/10 FLC 4+1 FAC 2+1/1 Others 4+1/1
Brentford (Loaned on 25/3/87) FL 10+1/2
Southend U (Loaned on 17/9/87) FL 6/1 FLC 2 Others 1/1
Watford (£350,000 on 12/12/91) FL 97+8/26 FLC 5+2/3 FAC 2/1 Others 1+2
Southend U (Loaned on 17/3/94) FL 4+1
Reading (£250,000 on 12/1/95) FL 50+9/20 FLC 4/1 FAC 2 Others 3/2

Lee Nogan

NOLAN Ian Robert
Born: Liverpool, 9 July 1970
Height: 6'0" Weight: 12.1

The fast, mobile, attacking Sheffield Wednesday full back started last season once again at left back, before being switched to the right side of defence midway through the campaign. Immediately looking more at ease on his natural side, Ian helped to give the team additional attacking options and a much better balance, but, unfortunately, his fine form was brought to an end following a ligament injury at Aston Villa. The fans will be hoping that he is fit enough to continue where he left off.

Ian Nolan

Preston NE (From trainee on 31/8/88)
Tranmere Rov (£10,000 from Marine, via Northwich Victoria, on 2/8/91) FL 87+1/1 FLC 10/1 FAC 7 Others 9
Sheffield Wed (£1,500,000 on 17/8/94) PL 71/3 FLC 8 FAC 4

NORBURY Michael (Mickey) Shaun
Born: Hemsworth, 22 January 1969
Height: 6'0" Weight: 12.0
This striker was yet another player to be released from his contract by Doncaster during the course of last season. His involvement was limited to just a handful of league and cup appearances, mostly as a playing substitute. Spent a brief spell in Irish football, before returning to non-league soccer in this country.
Scarborough (Signed from Ossett T on 30/12/89)
Cambridge U (Signed from Bridlington T, via Ossett T, on 13/2/92) FL 11+15/3 Others 1+2
Preston NE (£32,500 on 23/12/92) FL 32+10/13 FLC 1+1 FAC 0+3 Others 3+1/1
Doncaster Rov (£30,000 on 21/11/94) FL 19+8/5 FLC 0+1 Others 1+1

NORFOLK Lee Richard
Born: Dunedin, New Zealand, 17 October 1975
Height: 5'10" Weight: 11.3
The tenacious right-sided Ipswich midfielder, who had impressed a few good judges with his promising displays in 1994-95, had an unfortunate follow up season, making just one Anglo-Italian Cup appearance at home to Salernitana due to hectic competition for midfield places at the club. Retained for the coming season, he is sure to be offered further opportunities.
Ipswich T (From trainee on 1/7//94) PL 1+2 Others 1

NORMAN Anthony (Tony) Joseph
Born: Deeside, 24 February 1958
Height: 6'2" Weight: 14.5
International Honours: W: 5; B-1
Huddersfield goalkeeper. Now approaching the veteran stage, he was signed on a free from Sunderland during the 1995 close season, as cover for first choice, Steve Francis. Performing admirably whenever asked to deputise, keeping a clean sheet on his debut at home to Barnsley, Tony stands up well and is still remarkably agile.
Burnley (From juniors on 1/8/76)
Hull C (£30,000 on 14/2/80) FL 372 FLC 22 FAC 26 Others 13
Sunderland (Signed on 29/12/88) FL 198 FLC 8 FAC 14 Others 7
Huddersfield T (Free on 7/7/95) FL 3 FLC 1

NORTON David Wayne
Born: Cannock, 3 March 1965
Height: 5'7" Weight: 11.8
International Honours: E: Yth

Northampton Town right back who is equally at home as either a defender or attacking down the flanks, looking to provide quality crosses for the forwards. Can also play in midfield. Was released during the summer.
Aston Villa (From apprentice on 23/3/83) FL 42+2/2 FLC 8 FAC 2+1 Others 2
Notts Co (£30,000 on 24/8/88) FL 22+5/1 FLC 3+1 Others 4+1
Rochdale (Loaned on 18/10//90) FL 9 Others 2
Hull C (Loaned on 10/1/91) FL 15
Hull C (£80,000 on 16/8/91) FL 134/5 FLC 7 FAC 7/1 Others 9/1
Northampton T (£25,000 on 15/8/94) FL 78+4 FLC 4 FAC 3 Others 4

NOTEMAN Kevin Simon
Born: Preston, 15 October 1969
Height: 5'10" Weight: 12.2
Signed from Mansfield during the 1995 close season, the speedy and skilful left-sided winger played in Doncaster's opening six games in 1995-96, before being surprisingly transferred to Chester. Quickly impressing his new team mates with a scoring debut at Hereford, Kevin set up a good number of goals for fellow team mates, whilst netting nine himself throughout the remainder of the campaign.
Leeds U (From trainee on 13/6/88) FL 0+1 Others 1
Doncaster Rov (£10,000 on 10/11/89) FL 105+1/20 FLC 4/1 FAC 5+1/2 Others 11/1
Mansfield T (£25,000 on 27/3/92) FL 77+18/15 FLC 7/1 FAC 3 Others 5+1
Doncaster Rov (Free on 4/8/95) FL 4/1 FLC 2
Chester C (Free on 1/9/95) FL 27+6/9 FAC 1 Others 1+1

NTAMARK Charles (Charlie) Batmbog
Born: Paddington, 22 July 1964
Height: 5'10" Weight: 11.12
International Honours: Cameroon: 31
The Cameroon international has now completed six years with Walsall and, after an excellent campaign in midfield in 1994-95, he underlined his versatility last season by taking over as a right-flank defender when Wayne Evans was injured in October. Skilful on the ball, Charlie is a great favourite with the fans and his overlapping set up several goals as he took his career appearances tally close to the 300 mark.
Walsall (Free from Borehamwood on 22/8/90) FL 220+18/11 FLC 15+1/1 FAC 19 Others 17+1/1

NUGENT Kevin Patrick
Born: Edmonton, 10 April 1969
Height: 6'1" Weight: 13.3
International Honours: Ei: Yth
A hard-working centre forward who was signed by Bristol City from Plymouth towards the end of last September, when Ian Baird moved in the opposite direction, he exhibited good close control and proved to be an effective leader of the line, able to bring players into the game with his passing ability. Not a prolific goalscorer, but wins enough in the air to be a source of concern, especially at free kicks and corners.
Leyton Orient (From trainee on 8/7/87) FL 86+8/20 FLC 9+3/6 FAC 9/3 Others 9+1/1
Plymouth Arg (£200,000 on 23/3/92) FL 124+7/31 FLC 11/2 FAC 10/3 Others 5+3
Bristol C (Signed on 29/9/95) FL 29+5/8 FAC 2

treat **yourself**

professional
sportscare products *for*
every **BODY**

 endorsed by **THE PROFESSIONAL FOOTBALLERS ASSOCIATION**

Milas Healthcare, Petersfield Business Park, Petersfield, Hants GU32 3QA Telephone: 01730 231132 Fax: 01730 2317

OAKES Scott John
Born: Leicester, 5 August 1972
Height: 5'10" Weight: 11.4
International Honours: E: U21-1

Injured in pre-season preparation with damaged muscle fibres, 1995-96 never really took off for Luton's former starlet. A calf muscle injury in October, and back muscle damage in February, merely added to his problems, and the campaign finished with relegation and being booed off the pitch in the last home game, a sad situation for a player whose skill as a winger and scorer of spectacular goals had made him the fans' favourite. At his best, Scott is an exciting, confident player who takes defenders on and runs set piece situations. However, with Town up against it, apart from fleeting moments of magic, he suffered as the side fell into disarray. Is the son of a member of the famous pop group, Showaddywaddy.
Leicester C (From trainee on 9/5//90) FL 1+2 Others 1
Luton T (Signed on 22/10/91) FL 136+37/27 FLC 3+3/1 FAC 12+2/5 Others 3+3/1

OAKLEY Matthew
Born: Peterborough, 17 August 1977
Height: 5'10" Weight: 11.0

Young Southampton winger who can play on either flank. Having made just one appearance as a substitute in 1994-95, Matthew was in for seven games last season, scoring in the FA Cup win over Swindon and showing promise of better things to come. Has good passing skills and gets tremendous distance on his throw-ins.
Southampton (From trainee on 1/7/95) PL 5+6/1 FAC 2+1/1

OATWAY Anthony (Charlie)
Born: Hammersmith, 28 November 1973
Height: 5'7" Weight: 10.10

A very aggressive midfielder, having been discarded by Cardiff's new management team, and back from a loan spell with Coleraine, he was transferred to Torquay last December as one of his former manager, Eddie May's first signings. With his running and passing one of the features of a dire season for the club, Charlie soon became a great favourite with Gulls' fans, the "Player of the Year" trophy being a just return.
Cardiff C (Free from Yeading on 4/8/94) FL 29+3 FLC 2/1 FAC 1+1 Others 3+1
Torquay U (Free on 28/12/95) FL 24

O'BRIEN Liam Francis
Born: Dublin, 5 September 1964
Height: 6'1" Weight: 11.10
Club Honours: Div 1 '93
International Honours: Ei: 15; U23-1; Yth; Sch

After a campaign disrupted by a niggling injury which required surgery, Liam returned to first team action for Tranmere

last April and made a huge impression, scoring some vital goals. A skilful playmaker, who likes to sit just in front of the back four and spray the ball around, he hit the first goal of the season against Wolves, but then lost his place through injury to Gary Jones. Although he could have been on his way out in the summer, but for the recent managerial changes, his good end of season form brought about a recall for the Republic of Ireland against Croatia in early June and he went on to win a further three caps.
Manchester U (£60,000 from Shamrock Rov on 14/10/86) FL 16+15/2 FLC 1+2 FAC 0+2
Newcastle U (£250,000 on 15/11/88) F/PL 131+20/19 FLC 9/1 FAC 12+2/1 Others 9+2/1
Tranmere Rov (£300,000 on 21/1/94) FL 73+4/6 FLC 7 FAC 3+1/1 Others 5+1

O'CONNELL Brendan
Born: Lambeth, 12 November 1966
Height: 5'10" Weight: 12.1

Out of action until last December due to an achilles injury, the non-stop midfielder soon fought his way back into the Barnsley team. Hard work is his biggest asset and he never hid from the action, although his form suffered a little towards the end of the season.
Portsmouth (From apprentice on 1/7/85)
Exeter C (Free on 4/8/86) FL 73+8/19 FLC 3+1/2 FAC 3 Others 4
Burnley (Free on 1/7/88) FL 62+2/17 FLC 6/3 FAC 3/1 Others 5/2
Huddersfield T (Loaned on 30/11/89) FL 11/1
Barnsley (£50,000 on 23/3/90) FL 212+28/35 FLC 10+1/1 FAC 14/1 Others 7+1/2

O'CONNOR Gary
Born: Newtongrange, 7 April 1974
Height: 6'2" Weight: 12.0
International Honours: S: Yth; Sch

Promising young Doncaster Rovers' goalkeeper, who was signed from Hearts in January, 1996. Capped by Scotland at school and youth levels, he should be pushing Dean Williams for the first team jersey before too long.
Heart of Midlothian (Signed from Dalkeith Thistle on 6/3/92) SL 3
Berwick R (Loaned on 19/2/93) SL 39 SLC 1 SC 1 Others 1
Doncaster Rov (£25,000 on 17/1/96) FL 8

O'CONNOR Jonathan
Born: Darlington, 29 October 1976
Height: 5'10" Weight: 11.3
International Honours: E: U21-3; Yth

A fixture in the Everton reserve side during 1995-96, where he showed distinct leadership qualities at centre back in marshalling the back line well, his good form pushed him into first team contention as the season wore on. Although primarily a squad player, first appearing on the bench against Wimbledon on New Years Day, he actually made his debut at Manchester United in February, facing Ryan Giggs, a 2-0 defeat dampening his display. With four Premiership appearances under his belt, he is certain to be in contention for places in 1996-97.
Everton (From trainee on 28/10/93) PL 3+1

O'CONNOR Mark Andrew
Born: Thundersley, 10 March 1963
Height: 5'7" Weight: 10.2
Club Honours: Div 3 '87

Now in his second spell with Gillingham, having signed from Bournemouth prior to the start of last season, this hard-working and stylish midfielder was just about everybody's tip to become the club's "Player of the Year", when he suffered a broken leg in the infamous game at Priestfield against Fulham in November. Until then he had impressed as the playmaker, his crossing from tight situations being superb.
Queens Park R (From apprentice on 1/6/80) FL 2+1
Exeter C (Loaned on 7/10/83) FL 38/1 FAC 2/1 Others 3/1
Bristol Rov (£20,000 on 13/8/84) FL 79+1/10 FLC 8/1 FAC 7/1 Others 4/1
Bournemouth (£25,000 on 27/3/86) FL 115+13/12 FLC 5+3 FAC 7 Others 4+1
Gillingham (£70,000 on 15/12/89) FL 107+9/8 FLC 8 FAC 7+1 Others 6+2/1
Bournemouth (Free on 5/7/93) FL 56+2/3 FLC 7+1 FAC 4 Others 1
Gillingham (Free on 4/8/95) FL 18/1 FLC 2 FAC 2

O'CONNOR Martyn John
Born: Walsall, 10 December 1967
Height: 5'9" Weight: 12.8

As the skipper and midfield general, Martyn enjoyed a highly successful second full season with Walsall. Apart from his constructive work in midfield he scored 12 times in 1995-96, including a spectacular match-winning header at Peterborough in March and a late winner at Blackpool at the end of April, which effectively robbed the Seasiders of automatic promotion. Offers from higher division clubs continue to come in, but, at the time of writing, the fans are still hoping to keep him at Bescot. Elected by his fellow professionals to the award winning PFA second division team.
Crystal Palace (£25,000 from Bromsgrove Rov on 26/6/92) FL 2 Others 1+1
Walsall (Loaned on 24/3/93) FL 10/1 Others 2/1
Walsall (£40,000 on 14/2/94) FL 94/21 FLC 6/2 FAC 10/2 Others 3/1

O'CONNOR Paul Daniel
Born: Easington, 17 August 1971
Height: 5'11" Weight: 13.5

Became the sixth recognised goalkeeper used by Hartlepool in 1995-96 when borrowed from Blyth Spartans after the transfer deadline, and being allowed to play in one game which did not affect promotion matters. Acquitting himself well, there is a good chance he will have been offered professional terms during the close season.
Hartlepool U (Loaned from Blyth Spartans on 19/4/96) FL 1

OGDEN Neil
Born: Billinge, 29 November 1975
Height: 5'10" Weight: 10.4

Neil occasionally featured in Wigan Athletic's left back position last season, but, with his appearances limited, he moved on to Vauxhall Conference side, Northwich Victoria, in the closing stages of the campaign after having his contract cancelled by mutual consent.
Wigan Ath (From trainee on 18/3/94) FL 11+4 FLC 0+1 FAC 0+2 Others 1

OGRIZOVIC Steven (Steve)
Born: Mansfield, 12 September 1957
Height: 6'5" Weight: 15.0
Club Honours: FAC '87

"Oggy" has now made more appearances for Coventry than any other goalkeeper. A broken leg sustained in an end of season friendly in 1994-95 kept him out of the side until last November and he could not have started any worse, conceding 12 goals in four league games. His return, however, brought some stability to the defence and his form inspired City to a good spell in December and January. Had outstanding games at Highbury, the Dell, Forest, and Plymouth, with some superb saves and confident handling, and kept four successive clean sheets in the final few weeks. He seems likely to go on longer and could break George Curtis' record 486 league appearances for the club.
Chesterfield (Signed from ONRYC on 28/7/77) FL 16 FLC 2
Liverpool (£70,000 on 18/11/77) FL 4 Others 1
Shrewsbury T (£70,000 on 11/8/82) FL 84 FLC 7 FAC 5
Coventry C (£72,000 on 22/6/84) F/PL 440/1 FLC 41 FAC 28 Others 11

Steve Ogrizovic

O'HAGEN Daniel (Danny) Alexander Nicholas
Born: Truro, 24 April 1976
Height: 6'1" Weight: 13.8

Young Plymouth centre forward. Very willing when he gets his chance, however, these were few and far between in 1995-96, all seven appearances coming from the subs' bench, while the signing of Carlo Corazzin merely pushed him further down the pecking order.
Plymouth Arg (From trainee on 29/6/94) FL 1+8/1 FLC 0+1 Others 1

O'HALLORAN Keith James
Born: Dublin, 10 November 1975
Height: 5'10" Weight: 12.3
International Honours: Ei: U21-1; Yth; Sch

The versatile young Middlesbrough central midfielder, or full back, won early international recognition with an appearance for the Republic of Ireland U21 team last September. Brave and determined, fast off the mark, and strong in the tackle, he made his Premier League debut as a substitute versus Southampton in January and held his place for four more games before returning to the reserves. In the last month of the season he gained more first team experience on loan to Scunthorpe, but, unfortunately, picked up a niggling back injury which restricted his mobility.
Middlesbrough (Signed from Cherry Orchard on 6/9/94) P/FL 3+1 FAC 2 Others 1
Scunthorpe U (Loaned on 25/3/96) FL 6+1

O'KANE John Andrew
Born: Nottingham, 15 November 1974
Height: 5'10" Weight: 12.2
Club Honours: FAYC '92

A Manchester United right back who is very good on the ball and a natural athlete, John made his only appearance of last season in the club's ill-fated UEFA Cup match against Rotor Vologradt at Old Trafford in September. As a regular in the Pontins Division One side, he bides his time patiently.
Manchester U (From trainee on 29/1/93) PL 0+1 FLC 1+1 FAC 1 Others 1

OLDBURY Marcus John
Born: Bournemouth, 29 March 1976
Height: 5'7" Weight: 10.2

Midfielder. Signed from Norwich in the summer of 1995, he was not given a consistent run-in Bournemouth's first team, although he impressed when played. Came off the subs' bench to score a dramatic injury time equaliser, that took the Watford Coca Cola Cup-tie to penalties and should make his mark with more experience. Is a good passer of the ball.
Norwich C (From trainee on 1/7/94)
Bournemouth (Free on 1/7/95) FL 2+11 FLC 0+1/1 FAC 0+1 Others 1

OLDFIELD David Charles
Born: Perth, Australia, 30 May 1968
Height: 5'11" Weight: 13.4
International Honours: E: U21-1

A hard-working and sometimes creative midfielder, David returned to Luton, the club where he began his career as a striker, during the 1995 close season. Not always a regular choice, he was frequently employed as a substitute, or was himself substituted. In fact, some of his best moments came when changing the pattern of the game after coming off the bench, his telling passes setting up many chances for the strikers, but, with the exception of Dwight Marshall's efforts, going largely uncapitalised.
Luton T (From apprentice on 16/5/86) FL 21+8/4 FLC 4+2/2 FAC 0+1 Others 2+1/2
Manchester C (£600,000 on 14/3/89) FL 18+8/6 FLC 2+1/2 Others 0+1/1
Leicester C (£150,000 on 12/1/90) F/PL 163+25/26 FLC 10+2/1 FAC 7/3 Others 11+3/2
Millwall (Loaned on 24/2/95) FL 16+1/6
Luton T (£150,000 on 21/7/95) FL 23+11/2 FLC 2 FAC 1 Others 2

O'LEARY Kristian Denis
Born: Neath, 30 August 1977
Height: 5'11" Weight: 12.9
International Honours: W: Yth

Swansea youth team skipper who made his Endsleigh League debut at Bradford City in a 5-1 defeat last season. A promising young defender, he is likely to figure regularly in future Swans' teams.
Swansea C (Trainee) FL 1

OLIVER Keith
Born: South Shields, 15 January 1976
Height: 5'8" Weight: 10.9

A steady player whose best position is deep in midfield, just in front of the defence, Keith had a disappointing time at Hartlepool in 1995-96. For most of the season he was a fringe first teamer who could not win a regular place, having been criticised for his lack of fitness, and finally being told he would be released. However, he finished on a high with a week's trial at Aston Villa.
Hartlepool U (From trainee 5/7/94) FL 25+7 FLC 5+3 FAC 0+1 Others 3

OLIVER Michael
Born: Cleveland, 2 August 1975
Height: 5'10" Weight: 12.4

An aggressive Stockport midfielder, he seemed to have conquered his fitness problems in 1995-96, having a run of nine first team games and scoring in the 2-2 draw at York. Unfortunately, that was not to be and he left on transfer deadline day, returning to his native north east in search of a new club.
Middlesbrough (From trainee on 19/8/92) Others 0+1
Stockport Co (£15,000 on 7/7/94) FL 17+5/1 FLC 0+2 FAC 2 Others 1

OLNEY Ian Douglas
Born: Luton, 17 December 1969
Height: 6'1" Weight: 12.4
International Honours: E: U21-10

The former England U21 striker finally came back for Oldham last October after being out of the game since sustaining an horrendous knee injury at West Ham in November 1993. Unfortunately, following three matches, the knee broke down yet again and he was forced to announce his retirement from the game. Is due a testimonial on 6 August 1996.
Aston Villa (From trainee on 25/7/88) FL 62+26/16 FLC 8+2/1 FAC 5+1/2 Others 8+2/2
Oldham Ath (£700,000 on 1/7/92) P/FL 43+2/13 FLC 4+1 FAC 2/1 Others 1

OLSSON Paul
Born: Hull, 24 December 1965
Height: 5'8" Weight: 10.11

The influential Darlington midfielder was unlucky to miss the end of last season, and a Wembley play-off appearance, after suffering a cruciate knee ligament injury in early March. Prior to that, though, he had provided his normal quota of important goals and, at the same time, produced many hard-working performances.
Hull C (From apprentice on 7/1/84) Others 1/1
Exeter C (Free on 13/3/87) FL 38+5/2 FLC 2 FAC 0+1

Scarborough (Free on 17/8/88) FL 34+14/5 FLC 5+1 FAC 2 Others 8
Hartlepool U (£5,000 on 26/12/89) FL 162+9/13 FLC 11+2 FAC 10 Others 11+1/2
Darlington (Free on 1/7/94) FL 76/8 FLC 3 FAC 5/1 Others 4/2

OMIGIE Joseph Eghodalo
Born: Hammersmith, 13 June 1972
Height: 6'2" Weight: 13.0
A tall, gangly centre forward, he signed for Brentford shortly into 1995-96. Was a regular substitute for the Bees in the second half of the season, often coming on and causing mayhem in the opposition's defence with his awkward style. Had a spell on loan at Woking in September.
Brentford (Free from Donna FC on 26/8/94) FL 3+7

O'NEILL John Joseph
Born: Glasgow, 3 January 1974
Height: 5'10" Weight: 10.4
Brought to Bournemouth on loan from Celtic last March, on transfer deadline day, John proved a quick and lively striker who was not afraid to run at defenders. Having sampled what he is about, the club signed him permanently during the summer.
Queens Park (From school on 25/7/91) SL 70+21/30 SLC 2+1 SC 2 Others 0+1
Glasgow Celtic (Signed on 16/5/94) SL 0+2
Bournemouth (Free on 29/3/96) FL 2+4

Keith O'Neill

O'NEILL Keith Padre Gerard
Born: Dublin, 16 February 1976
Height: 6'2" Weight: 12.7
International Honours: Ei: 6; U21-1; Yth; Sch
Keith provides pace, power, and accurate delivery of the ball from Norwich's left flank. Becoming more consistent in 1995-96, he had runs of six and eight consecutive games, and his flyer past four Reading

defenders was a sign that with progression he will become a star. Endeared himself to the local press with seven "Man of the Match" awards and thoroughly deserved his Republic of Ireland U21 call up against Russia in March, before going on to win full international caps against Portugal, Croatia, Holland, USA, Mexico and Bolivia, in the summer.
Norwich C (From trainee on 1/7/94) P/FL 12+8/1 FLC 4+1 FAC 1

ONUORA Ifem (Iffy)
Born: Glasgow, 28 July 1967
Height: 6'2" Weight: 13.13
Mansfield striker Iffy had another long lay off last season, due to a knee injury, following his similar misfortune of the previous term. His sharpness seemed to have eluded him this time round and he too suffered from poor midfield support. Known for his pace and skill.
Huddersfield T (Signed from Bradford University on 28/7/89) FL 115+50/30 FLC 10+6/4 FAC 11+3/3 Others 13+3/3
Mansfield T (£75,000 on 20/7/94) FL 17+11/8 FAC 0+1 Others 1

ONWERE Udo Alozie
Born: Hammersmith, 9 November 1971
Height: 6'0" Weight: 11.7
Tough-tackling Lincoln midfield man with the knack of scoring goals. One of only two players who lined up for the opening match of last season at Preston to remain on the Imps' books in May, he made 39 starts in a side that used the same amount of players. Was released during the summer.
Fulham (From trainee on 11/7/90) FL 66+19/7 FLC 4+2 FAC 1+1 Others 9
Lincoln C (Free on 12/8/94) FL 40+3/4 FLC 5 FAC 1 Others 4/1

ORD Richard John
Born: Murton, 3 March 1970
Height: 6'2" Weight: 13.5
Club Honours: Div 1 '96
International Honours: E: U21-3
1995-96 was the season when Richard came of age. Following Peter Reid's arrival at Sunderland, the centre back started to fulfil the promise he had showed as a youngster. Dominant in the air, he formed a tremendous partnership with Andy Melville at the heart of the defence, which was the rock that promotion was built on. Deceptively skilful for a big man, the club's vice captain can think himself somewhat unfortunate not to have been selected for the PFA XI. Compensation came in the shape of a first division championship medal, though.
Sunderland (From trainee on 14/7/87) FL 177+19/5 FLC 14+5 FAC 9+1/1 Others 5+1
York C (Loaned on 22/2/90) FL 3

O'RIORDAN Donald (Don) Joseph
Born: Dublin, 14 May 1957
Height: 6'0" Weight: 12.7
International Honours: Ei: U21-1; Yth
Started last season as Torquay's player/manager, before leaving the club following an 8-1 drubbing at the hands of Scunthorpe. Still a good player, who can pass and read the game well, he joined Scarborough's

coaching staff in December and made one appearance at Barnet on 23 March in a midfield with a combined age of 107 – O'Riordan (38), Steve Charles (36) and Andy Toman (33) – prior to being released upon the appointment of Mitch Cook.
Derby Co (From apprentice on 1/5/75) FL 2+4/1 FLC 0+1 (£30,000 to Tulsa Roughnecks in February 1978)
Doncaster Rov (Loaned on 21/1/78) FL 2
Preston NE (£30,000 on 13/10/78) FL 153+5/8 FLC 10 FAC 8/1
Carlisle U (£30,000 on 8/8/83) FL 84/18 FLC 4 FAC 4
Middlesbrough (£55,000 on 8/8/85) FL 41/2 FLC 2 FAC 1/1 Others 2/1
Grimsby T (Free on 22/8/86) FL 86/14 FLC 6 FAC 6 Others 3
Notts Co (£16,000 on 13/7/88) FL 102+7/5 FLC 5+1/1 FAC 6/2 Others 16+2/1
Mansfield T (Loaned on 28/9/89) FL 6
Torquay U (Free on 12/2/93) FL 76+3/3 FLC 3+1 FAC 5 Others 5
Scarborough (Free on 8/12/95) FL 1

ORLYGSSON Thorvaldur (Toddy)
Born: Odense, Iceland, 2 August 1966
Height: 5'11" Weight: 11.3
International Honours: Iceland: 41
The Icelandic midfielder, who started last season on a weekly contract at Stoke, was dropped after the club's poor start to the campaign and sold to Oldham in December, the fee being settled by a tribunal. Quickly getting into his stride at Boundary Park, Toddy was one of the main reasons for Latics' turnaround of fortunes, his strength in the tackle and distribution skills being just what the doctor ordered. Is the cousin of Stoke defender, Larus Sigurdsson.
Nottingham F (£175,000 from KA Akureyri on 9/12/89) F/PL 31+6/2 FLC 5+1/2 FAC 1 Others 0+1
Stoke C (Free on 5/8/93) FL 86+4/16 FLC 7/1 FAC 6/1 Others 7/1
Oldham Ath (Signed on 22/12/95) FL 15+1 FAC 3

ORMONDROYD Ian
Born: Bradford, 22 September 1964
Height: 6'4" Weight: 13.9
Back at Bradford after starting his career there, "Sticks", who signed from Leicester prior to the start of last season, was quickly into his stride, his awkward gangling gait causing plenty of trouble in opponent's penalty areas. A scorer of three match winning goals among his ten strikes, he may well have delivered more had he not picked up an injured ankle in January, while his second touch in the play-off final, a back header that Mark Stallard volleyed in, effectively finished Notts County off and put City into the first division.
Bradford C (Signed from Thackley on 6/9/85) FL 72+15/20 FLC 12+2/4 FAC 7/2 Others 7+2/1
Oldham Ath (Loaned on 27/3/87) FL 8+2/1
Aston Villa (£600,000 on 2/2/89) FL 41+15/6 FLC 4+2/2 FAC 5/2 Others 6+1
Derby Co (£350,000 on 19/9/91) FL 25/8 FLC 3 FAC 3/1
Leicester C (Signed on 11/3/92) F/PL 67+10/7 FLC 6/2 FAC 1+1 Others 11/3
Hull C (Loaned on 27/1/95) FL 10/6
Bradford C (£75,000 on 13/7/95) FL 28+9/6 FLC 6/3 FAC 2+1/1 Others 2+2

OSBORN Simon Edward
Born: Croydon, 19 January 1972
Height: 5'10" Weight: 11.4
Signed by Ray Wilkins from Reading, who pocketed £1m profit on the sale, during the 1995 close season, with a view to strengthening the QPR midfield, Simon never quite fitted in to his new manager's plans and after just 11 games, he was on his way to Wolves, to join up with his former boss, Mark McGhee. A player with great stamina, who is always looking for the early ball, and with a penchant for long-range strikes, two against Watford eventually getting him off the mark at Molineux, he unfortunately struggled with injury towards the latter part of the campaign. With luck, 1996-97 should see the best of him.
Crystal Palace (From trainee on 3/1/90) F/PL 47+8/5 FLC 11/1 FAC 2 Others 1+3
Reading (£90,000 on 17/8/94) FL 31+1/5 FLC 4 Others 3
Queens Park R (£1,100,000 on 7/7/95) PL 6+3/1 FLC 2
Wolverhampton W (£1,000,000 on 22/12/95) FL 21/2 FAC 4

OSBORNE Wayne
Born: Stockton, 14 January 1977
Height: 5'9" Weight: 11.0
A young York City left back in his first season as a professional, Wayne gave a number of useful performances when called up for first team action in 1995-96. A good tackler, he shows promise.
York C (From trainee on 21/6/95) FL 5+1 FAC 1 Others 1

O'SHEA Daniel (Danny) Edward
Born: Kennington, 26 March 1963
Height: 6'0" Weight: 13.0
Club Honours: Div 3 '91
Right-footed Northampton defender or midfielder. As the club's player/coach, he was a regular last season, mainly in the centre of the defence, where his experience proved invaluable. Had earlier helped out Wimbledon in the 1995 Inter-Toto Cup
Arsenal (From apprentice on 23/12/80) FL 6 FLC 3
Charlton Ath (Loaned on 23/2/84) FL 9
Exeter C (Free on 24/8/84) FL 45/2 FLC 2 FAC 2 Others 2
Southend U (£5,000 on 9/8/85) FL 116+2/12 FLC 8 FAC 5+1 Others 6
Cambridge U (Free on 18/8/89) FL 186+17/1 FLC 18+1 FAC 15+3 Others 12+2/1
Northampton T (Free on 23/3/95) FL 44+1/1 FLC 2 FAC 2 Others 2+1

OSMAN Russell Charles
Born: Repton, 14 February 1959
Height: 5'11" Weight: 12.1
Club Honours: FAYC '75; UEFAC '81
International Honours: E: 11; B-2; U21-7; Yth
Having been freed by Plymouth, the experienced central defender was drafted in by Brighton last September, due to the prolonged absence of Steve Foster. Out himself for seven games with a pulled hamstring, Russell produced some steady performances before moving on to Cardiff in February. Joining the club after Phil Neal arrived, and in an attempt to shore up the defence, he did the job really well,

becoming a favourite with the crowd and earning a contract for 1996-97.
Ipswich T (From apprentice on 1/3/76) FL 294/17 FLC 28/3 FAC 30+2/1 Others 29+1
Leicester C (£240,000 on 31/7/85) FL 108/8 FLC 8 FAC 2 Others 2
Southampton (£325,000 on 17/6/88) FL 92+4/6 FLC 18 FAC 7 Others 3
Bristol C (£60,000 on 10/10/91) FL 67+3/3 FLC 1+2 FAC 5 Others 3
Plymouth Arg (Free on 21/3/95)
Brighton & Hove A (Free on 29/9/95) FL 11+1 FAC 2 Others 3
Cardiff C (Free on 15/2/96) FL 14+1

O'SULLIVAN Wayne St John
Born: Akrotiri, Cyprus, 25 February 1974
Height: 5'11" Weight: 11.2
Club Honours: Div 2 '96
International Honours: Ei: U21-2
Tigerish Swindon midfielder with an excellent workrate who covers every blade of grass during a game. Showed good early form last season, keeping his place in the side until late November and being selected for the Eire U21 squad. Unfortunately, he failed to maintain his rhythm in the second half of the campaign. However, having come back strongly at the close to win a second division championship medal, Wayne could be a key figure in the side this time round.
Swindon T (From trainee on 1/5/93) FL 49+15/3 FLC 9 FAC 1+2 Others 3+2

Ricky Otto

OTTO Ricky
Born: Hackney, 9 November 1967
Height: 5'10" Weight: 12.10
Club Honours: Div 2 '95; AMC '95
It was hoped that 1995-96 would see the best of Ricky and he certainly started well, scoring a stunning goal in Birmingham's 3-1 win over Ipswich on the opening day of the season. Unfortunately, a mixture of injuries and loss of form saw him in and out of the side and with so many forwards at the club he found it difficult to get a run. On song, he plays with great skill and pace

down the left flank and can be relied upon for his share of goals, especially the spectacular variety.
Leyton Orient (Free from Haringey Borough on 7/11/90) FL 41+15/13 FLC 3 FAC 2+1 Others 5+1/2
Southend U (£100,000 on 9/7/93) FL 63+1/17 FLC 3 FAC 1 Others 8/2
Birmingham C (£800,000 on 19/12/94) FL 24+18/6 FLC 3+3 FAC 2/1 Others 8/1

OVERSON Vincent (Vince) David
Born: Kettering, 15 May 1962
Height: 6'2" Weight: 14.2
Club Honours: Div 3 '82, Div 2 '93; AMC '91, '92
An inspirational Stoke City central defender whose 1995-96 season was cut short with a serious achilles injury sustained against Sunderland. A towering presence on the field, with a surprising amount of skill for such a big player, his many fans hope to see him full recovered and back in the side for the start of the coming campaign.
Burnley (From apprentice on 16/11/79) FL 207+4/6 FLC 9/1 FAC 19 Others 10
Birmingham C (Free on 11/6/86) FL 179+3/3 FLC 11+1 FAC 8 Others 11/1
Stoke C (£55,000 on 29/8/91) FL 167+3/6 FLC 13/1 FAC 10 Others 23

OWEN Gareth
Born: Chester, 21 October 1971
Height: 5'8" Weight: 11.8
Club Honours: WC '95
International Honours: W: B-1; U21-8
Central midfielder. Continued to be an enigma at the Racecourse, after many had predicted he would playing at a higher level by now, with inconsistency resulting in few opportunities for the first team during 1995-96, an on-form Gareth is so beneficial to Wrexham, his strong foraging and long-passing game a notable feature of his play.
Wrexham (From trainee on 6/7/90) FL 162+29/20 FLC 6+1 FAC 12+3 Others 28+1

OWERS Gary
Born: Newcastle, 3 October 1968
Height: 5'11" Weight: 11.10
Club Honours: Div 3 '88
After a fine first campaign with Bristol City in 1994-95 it was perhaps expecting too much that Gary would be able to produce such form again. Even though he was yet another City player who had to fight back from injury, it was still a great disappointment that the zest and invention that had been such a part of his game previously was missing last season. At his best as a midfield co-ordinator, he played most of his games in the right back position.
Sunderland (From apprentice on 8/10/86) FL 259+9/25 FLC 27+1/1 FAC 10+2 Others 11+1/1
Bristol C (£250,000 on 23/12/94) FL 55+3/4 FLC 1 FAC 5 Others 3

OXLEY Scott
Born: Sheffield, 22 November 1976
Height: 5'9" Weight: 11.0
A talented young left-sided winger, Scott made his first team debut for York early last season and showed much promise as a tricky ball player before going back to reserve football. Definitely one for the future.
York C (From trainee on 5/7/95) FL 1+1 FLC 1

PAATELAINEN Mika (Mixu) Matti
Born: Helsinki, Finland, 3 February 1967
Height: 6'0" Weight: 13.11
International Honours: Finland: 50
Finland's leading striker found last season in the Premiership with Bolton a series of setbacks. Due to injuries that kept him out of action for long periods, his only goal of the campaign came at Burnden in one of his comeback games, when he found the net in the opening minute against Everton, a match that finally ended in a 1-1 draw. A powerful, well-built player, who could probably do with a bit more pace, Mixu could find himself moving into a more defensive position as time goes on.
Dundee U (Signed from Valkeakosken in October 1987) SL 101+32/33 SLC 7+2/5 SC 20+1/8 Others 8+1/1
Aberdeen (Signed on 31/3/92) SL 53+22/23 SLC 6/3 SC 7+1/1 Others 3/1
Bolton W (£300,000 on 29/7/94) P/FL 55+4/13 FLC 8+1/2 FAC 1+1 Others 3/1

PACK Leonard (Lenny) John
Born: Salisbury, 27 September 1976
Height: 5'10" Weight: 12.9
After spending the 1995 close season in Finland, in a bid to get match-fit, much was expected from this right-footed Cambridge United midfielder. Although back in the starting line up in early August, Lenny unfortunately continued to suffer from back and hamstring pain, resulting in consultants visits and limiting him to mainly substitute appearances throughout 1995-96.
Cambridge U (From trainee on 20/7/95) FL 5+9 FLC 1+1 Others 1

PAGE Donald (Don) Richard
Born: Manchester, 18 January 1964
Height: 5'10" Weight: 11.2
Very experienced in the lower divisions, the speedy striker had often impressed when playing against Scarborough in the past, Don joined them last summer after being released by Chester. Unfortunately, he found it hard to adapt in a struggling team and had difficulty establishing a regular first team place, being released on a free transfer at the end of the season.
Wigan Ath (Signed from Runcorn on 23/3/89) FL 62+12/15 FLC 5/2 FAC 5/2 Others 4+2/3
Rotherham U (Signed on 16/8/91) FL 40+15/13 FLC 2+2 FAC 3/2 Others 1+2/1
Rochdale (Loaned on 17/2/93) FL 3+1/1
Doncaster Rov (Signed on 17/11/93) FL 18+4/4
Chester C (Free on 29/7/94) FL 22+8/5 FLC 2/1 FAC 2/1 Others 3/2
Scarborough (Free on 4/8/95) FL 26+11/5 FLC 2 FAC 1 Others 1

PAGE Robert John
Born: Llwynpia, 3 September 1974
Height: 6'0" Weight: 11.8
International Honours: W: U21-6; Yth; Sch
Much improved Watford central defender who established himself in the first team towards the end of last season and even stood in as captain on one occasion. Strong in the tackle and dominant in the air, much his distribution is not yet of the same high standard, having been a regular in the Welsh U21 team, he earned a call-up to the full squad to play Switzerland. Should be ready for a full cap in 1996-97.
Watford (From trainee on 19/4/93) FL 24+4 FAC 1+1

PAINTER Peter Robert (Robbie)
Born: Wigan, 26 January 1971
Height: 5'11" Weight: 11.0
A hard-running Darlington striker who missed the first ten games of last season after recovering from a summer groin operation, he contributed nine goals to the promotion drive and achieved his ambition of playing at Wembley. Ahead after the first leg of the play-off semi final against Hereford, it was Robbie's goal that set up a 2-1 win in the return and made the dream possible.
Chester C (From trainee on 1/7/88) FL 58+26/8 FLC 2+2 FAC 7+1/3 Others 3+3
Maidstone U (£30,000 on 16/8/91) FL 27+3/5 FLC 2 FAC 1+1 Others 0+2
Burnley (£25,000 on 27/3/92) FL 16+10/2 FLC 2 FAC 1
Darlington (Signed on 16/9/93) FL 102+7/28 FLC 2 FAC 5+1/2 Others 9/3

Gary Pallister

PALLISTER Gary Andrew
Born: Ramsgate, 30 June 1965
Height: 6'4" Weight: 14.13
Club Honours: FAC '90, '94, '96; CS '90, '93, '94; ECWC '91; ESC '91; FLC '92; PL '93, '94, '96
International Honours: E: 20; B-9
Massive Manchester United and England central defender who dominates the area as you would expect from such a big man. His pace also makes him difficult to pass and, in possession, he is more than comfortable bringing the ball out to look for the right option. Although an ever present in the side at the start of last season, a series of niggling back injuries severely restricted his appearances. After missing the whole of November, and playing just once in January, he returned, only for more problems to surface. However, taking up his usual mantle in the latter stages of the campaign, he quickly formed an excellent partnership with David May as United rolled on to win both the Premiership and the FA Cup.
Middlesbrough (Free from Billingham on 7/11/84) FL 156/5 FLC 10 FAC 10/1 Others 13
Darlington (Loaned on 18/10/85) FL 7
Manchester U (£2,300,000 on 29/8/89) F/PL 254+3/9 FLC 36 FAC 34/1 Others 29+1/1

PALMER Carlton Lloyd
Born: Rowley Regis, 5 December 1965
Height: 6'2" Weight: 12.4
International Honours: E: 18; B-5; U21-4
A consistent member of Leeds United in a somewhat fragmented 1995-96 season, he was used more in midfield, where his non-stop running and defending enabled the two Garys, McAllister and Speed, to operate in more forward roles, although he did score a spectacular goal in the victory at Wimbledon. Persistently linked with being re-united with old boss, Ron Atkinson, at Coventry, throughout the season, Carlton continued to show he only had Leeds' interests at heart.
West Bromwich A (From apprentice on 21/12/84) FL 114+7/4 FLC 7+1/1 FAC 4 Others 6
Sheffield Wed (£750,000 on 23/2/89) F/PL 204+1/14 FLC 31/1 FAC 18/2 Others 8+1/1
Leeds U (£2,600,000 on 30/6/94) PL 74/5 FLC 10 FAC 9/1 Others 4/1

PALMER Charles (Charlie) Anthony
Born: Aylesbury, 10 July 1963
Height: 5'11" Weight: 13.2
This experienced central defender gave some cool displays in the first part of last season for Walsall, but after the arrival of Derek Mountfield and Adrian Viveash he found himself squeezed out, having initially been sidelined following a leg injury sustained at Bristol City in October. Relegated to the reserves, Charlie was happy to pass on his experience to the youngsters, prior to being released in the summer.
Watford (From apprentice on 13/7/81) FL 10/1 FLC 2 Others 4
Derby Co (Free on 12/7/84) FL 51/2 FLC 7 FAC 1 Others 2
Hull C (£32,000 on 13/2/87) FL 69+1/1 FLC 3 FAC 3 Others 2
Notts Co (£25,000 on 15/2/89) FL 178+4/7 FLC 9 FAC 10 Others 19/2
Walsall (Free on 30/7/94) FL 54/2 FLC 4 FAC 5 Others 2+1

PALMER Lee James
Born: Croydon, 19 September 1970
Height: 6'0" Weight: 13.0
Signed during the 1995 close season from Gillingham, Lee made Cambridge United's left back position his own for the first half of last season. He later moved into a central defensive role, his experience being vital to the many young players around him.

Gillingham (From trainee on 28/7/89) FL 109+11/5 FLC 7+1 FAC 7+1 Others 8
Cambridge U (Free on 2/8/95) FL 30/1 FLC 1 FAC 1 Others 1

PALMER Stephen (Steve) Leonard
Born: Brighton, 31 March 1968
Height: 6'1" Weight: 12.13
Club Honours: Div 2 '92
International Honours: E: Sch

Watford utility player. Signed from Ipswich last September for six figures, it proved to be money well spent, Steve being especially effective playing just in front of the back four and breaking forward on telling runs. He also stood in as a competent central defender. A graduate in computer studies from Cambridge University, his thoughtful approach was reflected on the pitch.
Ipswich T (Free from Cambridge University on 1/8/90) F/PL 87+24/2 FLC 3 FAC 8+3/1 Others 4+2
Watford (£135,000 on 28/9/95) FL 35/1 FLC 2

PARDEW Alan Scott
Born: Wimbledon, 18 July 1961
Height: 5'11" Weight: 11.0

Freed by Charlton during the 1995 close season, Alan signed for Barnet to act as a midfield prompter. However, he struggled to find his feet until a switch in the team's formation found him playing as the spare centre half of three, where he showed a quick brain and good distribution.
Crystal Palace (£7,000 from Yeovil T on 17/3/87) FL 111+17/8 FLC 9+3/1 FAC 8/1 Others 20/2
Charlton Ath (Free on 21/11/91) FL 98+6/24 FLC 3+1 FAC 9+1/1 Others 6/1
Barnet (Free on 31/7/95) FL 41 FLC 2 FAC 2 Others 2

PARKER Garry Stuart
Born: Oxford, 7 September 1965
Height: 5'11" Weight: 13.2
Club Honours: FLC '89, '90; ESC '89
International Honours: E: B-1; U21-6; Yth

Right-footed Leicester City midfielder. Enjoyed new lease of life as playmaker in 1995-96, earning a string of "Man of the Match" awards, while scoring in three successive fixtures early in the season with a spot kick and two fierce free kicks. Helped to organise affairs during the club's managerless spell in December, although a brief, but much publicised, flare up with Martin O'Neill cost him the club captaincy on the eve of the visit to Oldham in March. Suffered a calf injury upon his recall that kept him sidelined over the busy Easter period, before being recalled for the play-off semi final second-leg at Stoke where he volleyed a spectacular winner. Won the "Man of the Match" award for a commanding display at Wembley, having coolly netted the equaliser from the penalty spot and being instrumental in City reaching the Premiership. Recognised for his sterling efforts, he was voted the club's "Player of the Season" and elected by his fellow professionals to the PFA award winning first division side.
Luton T (From apprentice on 5/5/83) FL 31+11/3 FLC 1+3/1 FAC 6+2
Hull C (£72,000 on 21/2/86) FL 82+2/8 FLC 5 FAC 4 Others 2/1

Nottingham F (£260,000 on 24/3/88) FL 99+4/17 FLC 22+1/4 FAC 16/5 Others 9/3
Aston Villa (£650,000 on 29/11/91) F/PL 91+4/13 FLC 12 FAC 10/1 Others 0+2
Leicester C (£300,000 on 10/2/95) P/FL 50+4/5 FLC 4 FAC 3 Others 2+1/2

PARKER Paul Andrew
Born: West Ham, 4 April 1964
Height: 5'7" Weight: 11.11
Club Honours: FLC '92; PL '93, '94; CS '93; FAC '94
International Honours: E: 19; B-3; U21-8; Yth

Able to play at right back, or in central defence, and a difficult man to pass, he reads the game well and always appears to have plenty of time on the ball. After making an excellent recovery from a serious ankle injury in 1994-95, Paul faced an even greater battle trying to win back his usual Manchester United right back slot from the Neville brothers in 1995-96. Although he only made five full league appearances all season, his superb goal against Reading in the FA Cup showed that he was back at his best and, while his re-emergence as a major influence at Old Trafford will undoubtedly give Alex Ferguson a few selection problems for the forthcoming season, his adaptability in the United defence gives his manager more options than most. *Stop Press:* Given a free transfer, he was reportedly linked to Derby, QPR and Marseilles.
Fulham (From apprentice on 15/4/82) FL 140+13/2 FLC 16/1 FAC 11 Others 2
Queens Park R (£300,000 on 18/6/87) FL 121+4/1 FLC 14 FAC 16 Others 5
Manchester U (£2,000,000 on 8/8/91) F/PL 100+5/1 FLC 15 FAC 14+1/1 Others 8+3

Paul Parker

PARKIN Brian
Born: Birkenhead, 12 October 1965
Height: 6'3" Weight: 14.7
Club Honours: Div 3 '90

Some inconsistent performances in Bristol Rovers' goal in 1995-96, resulted in Brian losing his position as first choice goalkeeper to Andy Collett after six seasons almost unopposed. Although a proposed loan spell to third division Preston North End in February was surprisingly called off by the club's directors, he was released at the end of the campaign.
Oldham Ath (From juniors on 31/3/83) FL 6 FLC 2
Crewe Alex (Free on 30/11/84) FL 98 FLC 7 FAC 2 Others 6
Crystal Palace (Free on 1/7/88) FL 20 FLC 3 Others 2
Bristol Rov (Free on 11/11/89) FL 241 FLC 15 FAC 12 Others 23

PARKIN Stephen (Steve) John
Born: Mansfield, 7 November 1965
Height: 5'7" Weight: 11.7
International Honours: E: U21-5; Yth; Sch

Not always at ease in Mansfield's midfield, he was dogged by several niggling injuries during 1995-96, eventually missing the last dozen matches. More at home as a full back, where his tackling can be seen to good effect, Steve is Town's club captain. Was added to the coaching staff at the end of the season.
Stoke C (From apprentice on 12/11/83) FL 104+9/5 FLC 9 FAC 9 Others 6
West Bromwich A (£190,000 on 16/6/89) FL 44+4/2 FLC 3 Others 2+1
Mansfield T (Free on 16/7/92) FL 84+3/3 FLC 6 FAC 5+1/1 Others 6+1

PARKINSON Gary Anthony
Born: Thornaby, 10 January 1968
Height: 5"11" Weight: 12.8

It was a disappointing 1995-96 campaign for Gary, whose form seldom approached the level of his early days at Burnley. His right back spot was first taken by Chris Brass and then Gerry Harrison, before injury and suspension, respectively, let him back in to adapt to a new wing/back role as Adrian Heath changed the shape of the side near the end of the season.
Middlesbrough (Free from Everton juniors on 17/1/86) FL 194+8/5 FLC 20/1 FAC 17/1 Others 19
Southend U (Loaned on 10/10/92) FL 6
Bolton W (Free on 2/3/93) FL 1+2 Others 4
Burnley (Signed on 27/1/94) FL 91+1/3 FLC 8 FAC 6 Others 5/1

PARKINSON Joseph (Joe) Simon
Born: Eccles, 11 June 1971
Height: 6'0" Weight: 13.0
Club Honours: FAC '95; CS '95

Lively Everton central midfielder with a competitive streak to go with his undoubted skill. Having become a prominent member of the first team squad in the past two years, turning in classy shows and catching the eye playing in front of the back four, last season he continued to mature at a rapid rate and consolidated his place in the side, displacing Barry Horne as the anchorman. Rarely giving the ball away, and making good use of possession with simple but effective passes, Joe can be a star of the future.
Wigan Ath (From trainee on 1/4/89) FL 115+4/6 FLC 11/1 FAC 9 Others 8
Bournemouth (£35,000 on 1/7/93) FL 30/1 FLC 4/1 FAC 4 Others 1
Everton (£250,000 on 24/3/94) PL 60+2/3 FLC 3 FAC 8/1 Others 3

PARKINSON Philip (Phil) John
Born: Chorley, 1 December 1967
Height: 6'0" Weight: 11.12
Club Honours: Div 2 '94

1995-96 was another season characterised by a series of combative displays in Reading's midfield, though he also played at centre back and as a lone striker in emergencies. Popular with the fans for his commitment and bravery, and runner-up to Mick Gooding in the "Player of the Year" election, Phil has contributed greatly to the club's progress in recent seasons.
Southampton (From apprentice on 7/12/85)
Bury (£12,000 on 8/3/88) FL 133+12/5 FLC 6+1 FAC 4/1 Others 13/1
Reading (£37,500 on 10/7/92) FL 141+13/7 FLC 14/1 FAC 8/1 Others 4+2

PARLOUR Raymond (Ray)
Born: Romford, 7 March 1973
Height: 5'10" Weight: 11.12
Club Honours: FLC '93
International Honours: E: U21-12

Right-sided Arsenal midfield player easily identified by his shock of hair. Having looked set to firmly establish himself as a first team regular last season, being included in the new manager, Bruce Rioch's early selections, a series of injuries ultimately saw him in and out of the side throughout the campaign. An integral part of the club's engine room, and a ball winner with good passing ability, Ray will be undoubtedly looking for an injury free run-in 1996-97.
Arsenal (From trainee on 6/3/91) F/PL 84+22/4 FLC 13+2 FAC 9/1 Others 7+2

Ray Parlour

PARRIS George Michael
Born: Ilford, 11 September 1964
Height: 5'9" Weight: 13.0
International Honours: E: Sch

A competitive, busy midfield player, he joined Brighton on a more permanent basis in September 1995. Likes to get forward and

scored a cheeky goal against Bristol Rovers by hiding behind the goalkeeper and pouncing to gain possession once the 'keeper started to roll the ball out. The incident later featured in the "what happened next" spot on TV's *Question of Sport*.
West Ham U (From apprentice on 9/9/82) FL 211+28/12 FLC 27+3/1 FAC 21/4 Others 7+1/1
Birmingham C (£150,000 on 12/3/93) FL 36+3/1 FLC 2 FAC 1
Brentford (Loaned on 8/8/94) FL 5 FLC 2/1
Bristol C (Loaned on 1/12/94) FL 6
Brighton & Hove A (Loaned on 9/2/95) FL 18/2
Brighton & Hove A (Free on 29/9/95) FL 38/2 FAC 4 Others 4

PARRISH Sean
Born: Wrexham, 14 March 1972
Height: 5'10" Weight: 11.0

Another good season for this hard-working Doncaster all-rounder, who performed with distinction at full back and in midfield during the course of 1995-96. Improved his goalscoring record from the previous term and remains a cornerstone of the side.
Shrewsbury T (From trainee on 12/7/90) FL 1+2 FLC 1 Others 3 (Free to Telford during 1992 close season)
Doncaster Rov (£20,000 on 28/5/94) FL 64+2/8 FLC 3+1 FAC 2/1 Others 3

PARSLEY Neil Robert
Born: Liverpool, 25 April 1966
Height: 5'9" Weight: 10.12

Signed during the 1995 close season from West Bromwich, Neil showed his experience by helping shore up a previously leaky Exeter defence. Considering he was a free transfer, his ability should be even more appreciated. Can play at right back as well as in the centre.
Leeds U (£20,000 from Witton A on 8/11/88)
Chester C (Loaned on 13/12/89) FL 6 Others 1
Huddersfield T (Free on 25/7/90) FL 55+2 FLC 6/1 FAC 6 Others 6
Doncaster Rov (Loaned on 20/2/91) FL 2+1
West Bromwich A (£25,000 on 9/9/93) FL 38+5 FLC 3 FAC 1 Others 1
Exeter C (Free on 10/8/95) FL 29+3 FLC 2 FAC 1 Others 1

PARTRIDGE Scott Malcolm
Born: Leicester, 13 October 1974
Height: 5'9" Weight: 10.9

Potentially Bristol City's best player, unable to get a run-in the team last season, he was loaned out in succession to Torquay, Plymouth and Scarborough. Very quick and very skilful, he scored two goals in five appearances at Torquay, two in seven at Argyle, but, apart from a few flashes, was unable to do himself justice in a Scarborough side struggling at the foot of the third division. However, Scott made a scoring return for City against Rotherham in the penultimate game which, hopefully, will act as a springboard for more this term. Is the son of Malcolm, a former Grimsby star.
Bradford C (From trainee on 10/7/92) FL 0+5 FLC 1+1
Bristol C (Free on 18/2/94) FL 24+27/7 FLC 2+2 FAC 1+3
Torquay U (Loaned on 13/10/95) FL 5/2
Plymouth Arg (Loaned on 22/1/96) FL 6+1/2
Scarborough (Loaned on 8/3/96) FL 5+2

PASCOE Colin James
Born: Port Talbot, 9 April 1965
Height: 5'10" Weight: 12.0
Club Honours: WC '83; AMC '94
International Honours: W: 10; U21-4; Yth; Sch

Suffered for most of last season in Swansea's midfield with ankle ligament injuries and struggled to reproduce his best form. However, it was still a surprise when he was released by the club in February, joining Blackpool on trial a month later.
Swansea C (From apprentice on 12/4/83) FL 167+7/39 FLC 11/3 FAC 9/2 Others 7/1
Sunderland (£70,000 on 25/3/88) FL 116+10/22 FLC 12/3 FAC 4+2 Others 5
Swansea C (Loaned on 24/7/92) FL 15/4 FLC 2
Swansea C (£70,000 on 1/8/93) FL 72+9/11 FLC 7+1/2 FAC 3 Others 13+1/3
Blackpool (Free on 29/3/96) FL 0+1

PASKIN John William
Born: Capetown, South Africa, 1 February 1962
Height: 6'1" Weight: 13.6

Despite his failure to start a game or score a goal in 1995-96 at Bury, the striker appeared as a substitute on 12 occasions, displaying an ability to hold the ball upfield, and was the perfect player to have coming on in the second half to calm things down. Granted a free transfer in May.
West Bromwich A (Free from K.V. Kortrijk on 27/8/88) FL 14+11/5 FLC 1 FAC 0+2
Wolverhampton W (£75,000 on 26/6/89) FL 21+13/3 FLC 2+1 FAC 2 Others 0+1
Stockport Co (Loaned on 11/9/91) FL 3+2/1
Birmingham C (Loaned on 21/11/91) FL 8+2/3 FLC 0+1
Shrewsbury T (Loaned on 13/2/92) FL 1
Wrexham (Signed on 21/2/92) FL 28+23/11 FLC 1+3/3 Others 3+2/2
Bury (Free on 22/7/94) FL 15+23/8 FLC 1 FAC 3/1 Others 3+3/1

PATERSON Jamie Ryan
Born: Dumfries, 26 April 1973
Height: 5'3" Weight: 10.2

Diminutive Scunthorpe left winger, initially at Glanford Park on loan from Falkirk last October, he was happy to make the move permanent a month later. Was an immediate hit with the fans, who admired his speed and ball control, before an ankle injury put him out of the side for five weeks late on in the season.
Falkirk (Signed from Halifax on 11/12/94) SL 1+3
Scunthorpe U (£18,000 on 12/10/95) FL 23+3/2 FAC 3/1 Others 2

PATERSON Scott
Born: Aberdeen, 13 May 1972
Height: 5'11" Weight: 12.0

Following on from the promise shown in 1994-95, this skilful midfield player looked set to have a lengthy run-in the Bristol City side last campaign, making 19 starts, before injury intervened. A composed player, who is good on the ground and in the air, Scott looks ideally suited to a sweeper's role.
Liverpool (£15,000 from Cove R on 19/3/92)
Bristol C (Free on 4/7/94) FL 18+3/1 FLC 2 FAC 1 Others 1

PATTERSON Darren James
Born: Belfast, 15 October 1969
Height: 6'2" Weight: 12.7
International Honours: NI: 10; B-2; U21-1; Yth

Strong-tackling Luton defender or right back who was signed from Crystal Palace in August 1995. Unfortunately, due to a tendon injury, his debut was delayed until November when he lined up against Cesena in the Anglo-Italian Cup in Italy, and, after failing to settle, he was dropped following the 7-1 FA Cup defeat at Grimsby. However, restored to the team at the end of January, he began to show consistent form and won over the Town supporters and gained further international caps for Northern Ireland.

West Bromwich A (From trainee on 5/7/88)
Wigan Ath (Free on 17/4/89) FL 69+28/6 FLC 7+1/3 FAC 5+4/1 Others 7
Crystal Palace (£225,000 on 1/7/92) PL 22/1 FLC 4 FAC 6
Luton T (£100,000 on 21/8/95) FL 21+2 FAC 1 Others 2

PATTERSON Gary
Born: Newcastle, 27 November 1972
Height: 6'1" Weight: 12.5
Club Honours: Div 3 '94

One of Wycombe's most improved players last season, he relished the central midfield role and as a hard tackler and ever willing to run at defences, he will be best remembered for a spectacular 55-yard volley against Gillingham in the FA Cup, live on Sky.

Notts Co (From trainee on 17/7/91)
Shrewsbury T (Free on 2/7/93) FL 52+5/2 FLC 5 FAC 4 Others 3
Wycombe W (£70,000 on 9/12/94) FL 40+10/2 FLC 2 FAC 2/1 Others 0+1

PATTERSON Mark
Born: Leeds, 13 September 1968
Height: 5'10" Weight: 12.4

As the Plymouth's right back, Mark was one of the few members of the 1994-95 relegation squad to stay with the team for last season. Very quick and strong in the tackle, he proved to be a good attacking player, with the ability to supply dangerous crosses, the club turning down a deadline day bid from Burnley to keep his valuable services.

Carlisle U (From trainee on 30/8/86) FL 19+3 FLC 4 Others 1
Derby Co (£60,000 on 10/11/87) FL 41+10/3 FLC 5+2 FAC 4 Others 5+1/2
Plymouth Arg (£85,000 on 23/7/93) FL 120+2/3 FLC 3 FAC 8 Others 9

PATTERSON Mark Andrew
Born: Darwen, 24 May 1965
Height: 5'6" Weight: 11.4
Club Honours: FMC '87

A fiery, gritty midfielder, Mark captained Bolton occasionally in 1995-96 and hit his only Premiership goal when converting a penalty at Liverpool, prior to transferring to Sheffield United last December, as part of the deal that took Nathan Blake to Burnden. An inspired signing, with point-saving goals in his first two appearances, he soon endeared himself to the fans with his no-nonsense tackling and 100 per cent commitment. Took over the captaincy following

injury to Alan Kelly and led the team in its end of season renaissance.

Blackburn Rov (From apprentice on 1/5/83) FL 89+12/20 FLC 4/1 FAC 3+1 Others 2+4/1
Preston NE (£20,000 on 15/6/88) FL 54+1/19 FLC 4 FAC 4 Others 7/2
Bury (Signed on 1/2/90) FL 42/10 FLC 2 FAC 1 Others 4
Bolton W (£65,000 on 10/1/91) P/FL 158+11/11 FLC 16+4/2 FAC 17/1 Others 9
Sheffield U (£300,000 on 22/12/95) FL 21/2 FAC 2

PAUL Martin Leighton
Born: Whalley Common, 2 February 1975
Height: 5'11" Weight: 11.8

As a central striker, Martin found it difficult to hold down a regular place in Bristol Rovers' forward line last season, but did manage to score a league goal in a 2-0 victory over Brentford at Twerton Park. Was subsequently released in the summer.

Bristol Rov (From trainee on 19/7/93) FL 11+11/1 FLC 1 Others 4+2

PAULO Pedro Saraiva Antonio
Born: Portugal, 21 November 1973
Height: 5'8" Weight: 10.5

Another Portuguese signing by David Hodgson for Darlington last season, the young and extremely skilful winger, who could play on both sides, made only eight appearances before returning home to marry his fiancee. Unfortunately, his stay was all too short-lived.

Darlington (Free from Sporting Lisbon on 31/8/95) FL 4+2 FLC 1+1

PAYNE Derek Richard
Born: Edgware, 26 April 1967
Height: 5'6" Weight: 10.8

An aggressive, gritty little Watford midfield player who missed most of 1995-96 through injury, first a groin strain that required surgery, and then a broken toe suffered in a domestic mishap, putting him out of action. More at home in providing for others, he scored his first and only goal for the club on the opening day of the season. Was released during the summer.

Barnet (£12,000 from Hayes on 22/7/91) FL 50+1/6 FLC 2 FAC 2 Others 3+1
Southend U (Free on 15/7/93) FL 32+3 FLC 2 FAC 1 Others 8/1
Watford (Signed on 21/7/94) FL 33+3/1 FLC 3 FAC 0+1 Others 2

PAYNE Ian Neil
Born: Crawley, 19 January 1977
Height: 5'9" Weight: 10.2
International Honours: W: Yth

Having signed professional forms during the 1995 close season, the young Plymouth full back was thought to have a big future. However, he lacked opportunities, being restricted to the AWS competition, and was released during the summer to sign for Vancouver Whitecaps.

Plymouth Arg (From trainee on 10/7/95) FL 1 FLC 1 Others 0+1

PAYTON Andrew (Andy) Paul
Born: Whalley, 23 October 1967
Height: 5'9" Weight: 11.13

Barnsley striker. Although losing his place for a short spell around the Christmas period

last season, he showed what a lethal marksman he could be. Breaking the 20 goal mark, his ability to be in the right position at the right time, allied to his coolness in front of goal, were his major assets. Scored a hat trick in a 4-0 Coca Cola Cup win over Huddersfield and many of his other strikes were either winners or equalisers in vital games. *Stop Press:* Transferred to Huddersfield for £350,000, according to newspaper reports.

Hull C (From apprentice on 29/7/85) FL 116+28/55 FLC 9+2/1 FAC 8 Others 3/1
Middlesbrough (£750,000 on 22/11/91) FL 8+11/3 FAC 1+3
Glasgow Celtic (Signed on 14/8/92) SL 20+16/15 SLC 3+2/5 SC 1+1 Others 3
Barnsley (Signed on 25/11/93) FL 100+8/41 FLC 7/3 FAC 6+1/1

Andy Payton

PEACOCK Darren
Born: Bristol, 3 February 1968
Height: 6'2" Weight: 12.6
Club Honours: WC '90

After a difficult first year in Newcastle's colours, Darren tied back his long flowing hair and applied himself determinedly to such good effect in 1995-96 that he won over his critics, emerging as a centre back of sufficient quality to keep Philippe Albert on the bench. As the season progressed his confidence grew visibly and he became more positive and assertive, improving his use of the ball to convert defence into attack, and scoring in Coca Cola Cup-ties against Stoke and Bristol City, the latter being one of his hometown clubs. Having secured his Newcastle place in the teeth of various challenges, he will be looking forward to the coming season with renewed optimism.

Newport Co (From apprentice on 11/2/86) FL 24+4 FLC 2 FAC 1 Others 1+1

Hereford U (Free on 23/3/89) FL 56+3/4 FLC 6
FAC 6/1 Others 6
Queens Park R (£200,000 on 22/12/90) F/PL
123+3/6 FLC 12/1 FAC 3 Others 2
Newcastle U (£2,700,000 on 24/3/94) PL 77+1/1
FLC 9/2 FAC 7 Others 4

Darren Peacock

PEACOCK Gavin Keith
Born: Eltham, 18 November 1967
Height: 5'8" Weight: 11.8
Club Honours: Div 1 '93
International Honours: E: Yth; Sch

Automatic choice for Chelsea since his
move from Newcastle United in August
1993, a combination of a string of niggling
injuries, and Ruud Gullit's switch into
midfield, cost Gavin his regular place in the
side in 1995-96. A goalscoring left-footed
midfielder, with the ability to ghost unseen
into the penalty area to tuck away half
chances, he had an impact on Blues' season,
nevertheless. In January, he returned to
Newcastle and coolly scored the third
penalty in the FA Cup replay shoot-out, after
coming on as a late substitute. Eighteen days
later he became the first Chelsea player for
nearly six years to score a league hat trick,
since Kerry Dixon in May 1990, during the
Blues' 5-0 televised demolition of
Middlesbrough. Also scored vital FA Cup
goals against QPR and Grimsby Town,
before being pressed into service as an
emergency left back to replace Terry Phelan
during the semi final. Will be hoping for
better luck with injuries in 1996-97, in order
to reclaim that automatic place in the team.
Queens Park R (From apprentice on 19/11/84) FL
7+10/1 FAC 0+1
Gillingham (£40,000 on 5/10/87) FL 69+1/11
FLC 4 FAC 2 Others 5/1
Bournemouth (£250,000 on 16/8/89) FL 56/8
FLC 6 FAC 2 Others 2
Newcastle U (£150,000 on 30/11/90) FL 102+3/35
FLC 6/5 FAC 6/2 Others 3/4
Chelsea (£1,250,000 on 12/8/93) PL 92+11/17
FLC 6/1 FAC 14+4/9 Others 7

PEACOCK Lee Anthony
Born: Paisley, 9 October 1976
Height: 6'0" Weight: 12.8
International Honours: S: Yth

A powerfully built striker who has already
won Scottish youth international recognition, Lee is yet another youngster to have
forced his way into the Carlisle first team
squad in 1995-96. He took special pleasure
in matches against Swansea, netting in both
fixtures against the Vetch Field men.
Carlisle U (From trainee on 10/3/95) FL 14+16/2
FLC 0+1 FAC 0+1 Others 1+3

PEACOCK Richard John
Born: Sheffield, 29 October 1972
Height: 5'10" Weight: 10.9

Struggled to rediscover his outstanding form
of 1994-95 for Hull last season, but added
more strings to his bow when, as a mainly
right-footed winger, he was given an
extended run on the left flank, then a
striking role. The latter development
brought immediate impact, with two
stunning goals in the 3-0 win over Burnley
last February. Shouldered the responsibility
of City's attack when Linton Brown moved
on to Swansea and finished 1995-96 as the
Tigers' top goalscorer.
Hull C (Signed from Sheffield FC on 14/10/93)
FL 71+22/13 FLC 4+1/1 FAC 3 Others 3+1

PEAKE Jason William
Born: Leicester, 29 September 1971
Height: 5'11" Weight: 12.10
International Honours: E: Yth; Sch

The midfield star of Rochdale's early season
promotion challenge in 1995-96, he had a
particularly brilliant game against second
division Rotherham in the cup, scoring
twice. Later, after a temporary lapse in form,
he shone at left back in place of the injured
Kevin Formby.
Leicester C (From trainee on 9/1/90) FL 4+4/1
Others 1+1
Hartlepool U (Loaned on 13/2/92) FL 5+1/1
Halifax T (Free on 26/8/92) FL 32+1/1 FAC 1
Others 2
Rochdale (Signed on 23/3/94) FL 91+4/6 FLC 3
FAC 5/2 Others 7/1

PEAKE Trevor
Born: Nuneaton, 10 February 1957
Height: 6'0" Weight: 12.9
Club Honours: FAC '87
International Honours: E: SP-2

Started last season as Luton's first choice
central defender and club captain, but lost
both roles to Steve Davis within a few
weeks, after a shaky start. Although still
possessing great positional skills, in his 40th
year he was not surprisingly unable to
completely compensate for his lack of speed
in a struggling side, becoming reserve team
coach in January and effectively bringing
his playing career to a close. Before hanging
up his boots, Trevor established the record
as the club's oldest ever league player when
making his last appearance in February at
the age of 39 years and 17 days.
Lincoln C (£27,500 from Nuneaton Borough on
15/6/79) FL 171/7 FLC 16/2 FAC 7
Coventry C (£100,000 on 6/7/83) FL 277+1/6
FLC 30 FAC 17/1 Others 10
Luton T (£100,000 on 27/8/91) FL 175+3 FLC 7
FAC 13 Others 3

PEARCE Andrew (Andy) John
Born: Bradford on Avon, 20 April 1966
Height: 6'4" Weight: 14.6

The tall, lean centre back joined Wimbledon
from Sheffield Wednesday last November in
an effort to solve the club's injury and
suspension crisis. Prior to arriving at
Selhurst Park, Andy had only played four
times during the season, mainly due to the
fact that Peter Atherton, Des Walker, Julian
Watts and himself were vying for just two
places. Strong in the air, and a good
distributor of long passes, although he soon
proved a useful asset for the Dons,
especially at set pieces, he only made eight
appearances. With a multitude of centre
backs available he will face stiff competition
for a place this term.
Coventry C (£15,000 from Halesowen T on
14/5/90) F/PL 68+3/4 FLC 6 FAC 3 Others 1
Sheffield Wed (£500,000 on 24/6/93) PL 66+3/3
FLC 11+1/1 FAC 6+1
Wimbledon (£700,000 on 22/11/95) PL 6+1 FAC
0+1

PEARCE Dennis Anthony
Born: Wolverhampton, 10 September 1974
Height: 5'9" Weight: 11.0

Freed by Aston Villa during the 1995 close
season, he was snapped up by neighbouring
Wolves, making a surprise substitution
against Derby in August and then appearing
in the next three games, only to struggle in
the latter against a classy Norwich side.
Later selected for two of the big cup-ties, he
played in the left back position, but can
perform equally well in midfield. Good in
the air and a strong tackler, Dennis likes to
get involved and packs a powerful shot.
Aston Villa (From trainee on 7/6/93)
Wolverhampton W (Free on 3/7/95) FL 3+2 FLC
1 FAC 1

PEARCE Ian Anthony
Born: Bury St Edmunds, 7 May 1974
Height: 6'1" Weight: 12.4
Club Honours: PL '95
International Honours: E: U21-3; Yth

Blackburn centre back rated by Ray Harford
as potentially the best in England, he has
rare composure for one so young, positions
well, and marks tightly. While his speed on
the turn requires some work, and his
inexperience was shown up in the Champions' Cup, he has the intelligence to limit his
exposure to these situations. An all-rounder,
Ian can play at full back, in midfield, or up
with the attack, where his ability in the air
and his skill on the ground hold him in good
stead. Unfortunately, having played 20
games, a floating piece of bone in his foot
ended last season for him on bonfire night.
Chelsea (From juniors on 1/8/91) F/PL 0+4 Others
0+1
Blackburn Rov (£300,000 on 4/10/93) PL 35+10/2
FLC 3+3/1 FAC 1+2 Others 6+1

PEARCE Stuart
Born: Hammersmith, 24 April 1962
Height: 5'10" Weight: 13.0
Club Honours: FLC '89, '90; FMC '89, '92
International Honours: E: 70; U21-1

The evergreen Nottingham Forest captain
and left back enjoyed an unexpected bonus

in his testimonial season of 1995-96, a recall to the England team following the unfortunate leg break suffered by his rival and Terry Venables' first choice left back, Graham le Saux, and ultimately selection for Euro '96. For Forest he had another excellent campaign, both as a defender and penalty taker, although he was sidelined by injury in February before returning in style during March. Appeared as enduring as ever, his never-say-die tackling, coupled to getting forward whenever the opportunity presented itself, still very much part of his game plan. Had a superb Euro '96 for England, playing in all five games, and well and truly exorcising the memory of his World Cup penalty miss in the shoot-out against Spain, before announcing his retirement from international football at the end of the tournament.

Coventry C (£25,000 from Wealdstone on 20/10/83) FL 52/4 FAC 2
Nottingham F (£200,000 on 3/6/85) F/PL 368/58 FLC 58/10 FAC 35/9 Others 24/6

Stuart Pearce

PEARCEY Jason Kevin
Born: Leamington, 23 July 1971
Height: 6'1" Weight: 13.12

Strong in the box, and with good reflexes, the consistency of Grimsby's first choice goalkeeper, Paul Crichton, limited Jason to just two senior appearances in 1995-96. A reliable and competent 'keeper to have in reserve, he gave a good account of himself in both matches and conceded just one goal.

Mansfield T (From trainee on 18/7/89) FL 77 FLC 5 FAC 2 Others 7
Grimsby T (£10,000 on 15/11/94) FL 5

PEARS Richard James
Born: Exeter, 16 July 1976
Height: 6'0" Weight: 12.6

Forward. Although in and out of the Exeter side due to injury last season, Richard's goal per game ratio was good for a player of his age and experience. Very quick off the mark, he came off the bench to score a superb last minute winner against Barnet.

Exeter C (From trainee on 7/7/94) FL 37+15/7 FLC 1+2 FAC 1 Others 2+1

PEARSON Nigel Graham
Born: Nottingham, 21 August 1963
Height: 6'1" Weight: 14.0
Club Honours: FLC '91; Div 1 '95

Middlesbrough's experienced captain and central defender was a tower of strength and a model of consistency in a topsy-turvy 1995-96 for the Teeside club, missing only two matches due to suspension. A player whose aerial ball-winning qualities and ability to control the midfield areas have an inspirational effect on the rest of the team, he was the lynch pin of the meanest defence in the Premier League until the mid-term collapse. However, his experience and coolness under extreme pressure saw him rally the side to fully earn his sobriquet of "Captain Fantastic".

Shrewsbury T (£5,000 from Heanor T on 12/11/81) FL 153/5 FLC 19 FAC 6 Others 3
Sheffield Wed (£250,000 on 16/10/87) F/PL 176+4/14 FLC 17+2/5 FAC 15/1 Others 10
Middlesbrough (£500,000 on 19/7/94) P/FL 69/3 FLC 5 FAC 5

Nigel Pearson

PEEL Nathan James
Born: Blackburn, 17 May 1972
Height: 6'1" Weight: 13.3

Tall Burnley striker who failed to make the first team last season and had two spells away on loan in an effort to re-establish himself. His first stop was at Mansfield (October), where he made three appearances, while a February trip to Doncaster ended in disaster when he suffered a severe knee injury during his second match, thus forcing an early return to Turf Moor. Was released during the summer.

Preston NE (From trainee on 9/7/90) FL 1+9/1 FLC 1 Others 1+1
Sheffield U (£50,000 on 1/8/91) FL 0+1
Halifax T (Loaned on 3/2/93) FL 3
Burnley (£60,000 on 24/9/93) FL 4+12/2 FLC 1 FAC 0+3 Others 0+2

Rotherham U (Loaned on 23/3/95) FL 9/4
Mansfield T (Loaned on 27/10/95) FL 2 Others 1
Doncaster Rov (Loaned on 23/2/96) FL 2

PEER Dean
Born: Stourbridge, 8 August 1969
Height: 6'2" Weight: 12.4
Club Honours: AMC '91

Released by Walsall at the end of 1994-95, he signed for Northampton at the start of last season and impressed as a midfield player, who covered almost all of the field during a game. Also popped up with a few goals and was at home either attacking or defending from midfield.

Birmingham C (From trainee on 9/7/87) FL 106+14/8 FLC 14+1/3 FAC 3+1 Others 10+1/1
Mansfield T (Loaned on 18/12/92) FL 10 Others 1
Walsall (Free on 16/11/93) FL 41+4/8 FLC 2 FAC 4+2 Others 3
Northampton T (Free on 22/8/95) FL 37+5/1 FLC 2/1 FAC 2 Others 4

PEMBERTON John Matthew
Born: Oldham, 18 November 1964
Height: 5'11" Weight: 12.12

Began last season for Leeds where he left off, forging a solid and consistent partnership with David Wetherall. Unfortunately, the consistency did not last for this pacy, tough-tackling defender, as he suffered the ignominy of suspension after being sent off against Queens Park Rangers in September, before going on to suffer niggling injury problems that saw him miss much of November through to March. Faces a tough battle to maintain a regular place in 1996-97.

Rochdale (Free from Chadderton on 26/9/84) FL 1
Crewe Alex (£1,000 on 29/3/85) FL 116+5/1 FLC 7/1 FAC 3 Others 7
Crystal Palace (£80,000 on 24/3/88) FL 76+2/2 FLC 6+1 FAC 8 Others 12
Sheffield U (£300,000 on 27/7/90) F/PL 67+1 FLC 4 FAC 4 Others 1
Leeds U (£250,000 on 12/11/93) PL 44+9 FLC 3+1 FAC 5+1 Others 4

PEMBERTON Martin Calvin
Born: Bradford, 1 February 1976
Height: 5'11" Weight: 12.6

A second-year professional, Martin became yet another of Oldham's rich vein of youngsters to make his debut last season, having worked his way through the ranks. Blooded from the bench last December at Portsmouth, followed by two further subs' appearances, he impressed as a quick, tricky wide-sided midfielder with deft touches and dribbling qualities, which could trouble a few defences this coming term.

Oldham Ath (From trainee on 22/7/94) FL 0+2 Others 0+1

PEMBRIDGE Mark Anthony
Born: Merthyr Tydfil, 29 November 1970
Height: 5'8" Weight: 11.12
International Honours: W: 16; B-2; U21-1; Sch

Bought from Derby just before the start of last season, the Welsh international midfielder struggled to make a real impact in his early games for Sheffield Wednesday. Small, but combative, and with a neat left foot, he was just beginning to impress when a bad leg injury at Highbury kept him out for 15 matches. However, on his return, Mark seemed determined to make up for lost time and was quickly back into his stride, his linking down the left flank with newly signed, Regi Blinker, towards the end of the campaign, auguring well for the coming one.

Luton T (From trainee on 1/7/89) FL 60/6 FLC 2 FAC 4 Others 4
Derby Co (£1,250,000 on 2/6/92) FL 108+2/28 FLC 9/1 FAC 6/3 Others 15/5
Sheffield Wed (£900,000 on 19/7/95) PL 24+1/2 FLC 3/1

PENDER John Patrick
Born: Luton, 19 November 1963
Height: 6'0" Weight: 13.12
Club Honours: Div 4 '92
International Honours: Ei: U21-5; Yth

A tall, imposing Wigan centre back who hardly ever comes second in the battle for a high ball, John was recruited from Burnley during the early part of last season and went on to form an imposing partnership on the left of the defence alongside Colin Greenall. A former Republic of Ireland U21 international, he brought almost 14 years experience to Latic's cause.

Wolverhampton W (From apprentice on 8/11/81) FL 115+2/3 FLC 5 FAC 7/1
Charlton Ath (£35,000 on 23/7/85) FL 41 FLC 1 FAC 1 Others 2/1
Bristol C (£50,000 on 30/10/87) FL 83/3 FLC 11 FAC 8 Others 12
Burnley (£70,000 on 18/10/90) FL 171/8 FLC 11/1 FAC 17/1 Others 21/1
Wigan Ath (£30,000 on 22/8/95) FL 40+1/1 FAC 4 Others 3

PENNEY David Mark
Born: Wakefield, 17 August 1964
Height: 5'10" Weight: 12.0
Club Honours: WC '91

David's experience in midfield was sorely missed last season by Swansea, following his groin operation the previous summer. A strong hard-working midfielder, capable of scoring from long range, he returned to first team action towards the end of November, making the occasional appearance at right back.

Derby Co (£1,500 from Pontefract on 26/9/85) FL 6+13 FLC 2+3/1 FAC 1/1 Others 1+3/1
Oxford U (£175,000 on 23/6/89) FL 76+34/15 FLC 10+1 FAC 2+2/1 Others 3+1
Swansea C (Loaned on 28/3/91) FL 12/3
Swansea C (£20,000 on 24/3/94) FL 68+7/7 FLC 3+1/2 FAC 5/1 Others 9

PENNOCK Adrian Barry
Born: Ipswich, 27 March 1971
Height: 5'11" Weight: 12.1

Bournemouth's Adrian made a good start to last season before sustaining a serious injury against Brighton at the beginning of December. Hopefully, he will return for the beginning of the 1996-97 season in his preferred position of central midfield, although he can also play in the back four where he will come out of defence and look to pass the ball. Also good in the air.

Norwich C (From trainee on 4/7/89) FL 1
Bournemouth (£30,000 on 14/8/92) FL 130+1/9 FLC 9 FAC 12/1 Others 8

PENRICE Gary Kenneth
Born: Bristol, 23 March 1964
Height: 5'7" Weight: 10.0

Striker. Having made just two substitute appearances for QPR in 1995-96, Gary moved to Watford last November, thus returning to the club he had left in March 1991. To the disappointment of the fans, he sustained a groin injury in his first full game and struggled for fitness thereafter, his skill and vision in the forward line being much missed. An unselfish player, his movement on and off the ball creates chances for team mates.

Bristol Rov (Free from Mangotsfield on 6/11/84) FL 186+2/54 FLC 11/3 FAC 11/7 Others 13+2/2
Watford (£500,000 on 14/11/89) FL 41+2/18 FAC 4/1 Others 1/1
Aston Villa (£1,000,000 on 8/3/91) FL 14+6/1
Queens Park R (£625,000 on 29/10/91) F/PL 55+27/20 FLC 5+2/2 FAC 2+2/1 Others 1
Watford (£300,000 on 15/11/95) FL 4+3/1

PEPPER Colin Nigel
Born: Rotherham, 25 April 1968
Height: 5'10" Weight: 11.13

An experienced and hard-working mid-fielder, Nigel was again an important and regular member of the York side in 1995-96, scoring ten goals, his best tally in a season for the club. Placed on the transfer list at his own request last January, although back in the side, he remains available.

Rotherham U (From apprentice on 26/4/86) FL 35+10/1 FLC 1/1 FAC 1+1 Others 3+3
York C (Free on 18/7/90) FL 197+9/28 FLC 12+1/2 FAC 9/1 Others 14+1

PERKINS Christopher (Chris) Peter
Born: Nottingham, 9 January 1974
Height: 5'11" Weight: 11.0

Having already shown an ability to play in a number of midfield positions, as both a tackler and passer, Chris did not really come on as much as was hoped last season, and usually only occupied one of Chesterfield's full back positions through injury to others. Interestingly, his only substantial run-in the side coincided with Spireites' climb to a play-off place that they slipped out of only after he was left out.

Mansfield T (From trainee on 19/11/92) FL 3+5 Others 0+1
Chesterfield (Free on 15/7/94) FL 35+5 FLC 2/1 FAC 3 Others 6+3

PERKINS Declan Oliver
Born: Ilford, 17 October 1975
Height: 5'11" Weight: 12.4
International Honours: Ei: U21-4

After playing for the Republic of Ireland U21 side against Austria early last September, Southend's Declan was then loaned to Cambridge United a few weeks later, making his debut at Lincoln, and scoring inside 11 minutes before suffering a hamstring strain. Following a sub appear-ance, the hard-running wingman returned to Roots Hall where he surprisingly failed to get a look in and was released during the summer. Is the brother of actress, Louise Lombard.

Southend U (From trainee on 27/5/94) FL 1+5
Cambridge U (Loaned on 22/9/95) FL 1+1/1

PERRETT Darren John
Born: Cardiff, 29 December 1969
Height: 5'8" Weight: 11.6

Striker. A player with enormous potential, Darren was given a free transfer by Swansea last December after having numerous chances to impress. Following a trial with Bristol Rovers, he joined non-league Merthyr Tydfil.

Swansea C (Free from Cheltenham T on 9/7/93) FL 13+17/1 FLC 2+1 FAC 1+2 Others 4+2/4

PERRETT Russell
Born: Barton-on Sea, 18 June 1973
Height: 6'3" Weight: 13.2

Ball-playing Portsmouth central defender. After being released by the club as a youngster back in 1991, Russell returned early last season, following a spell of non-league football. Made his debut in November and, despite being sent off in his second full game, he bounced back with a string of good performances as the injured Guy Butters' replacement during March and April.

Portsmouth (Signed from Lymington on 30/9/95) FL 8+1

PERRY Christopher (Chris) John
Born: Carshalton, 26 April 1975
Height: 5'8" Weight: 11.1

Locally born, and one of the few members of the side to have supported Wimbledon as a lad, Chris had an excellent season in 1995-96, missing just three games and winning the "Most Improved Player of the Year" award. With his impeccable ability in the air, allied to well-timed challenges on the ground, there is every opportunity for him to go far in the game.

Wimbledon (From trainee on 2/7/91) PL 52+9 FLC 4 FAC 10

PERRY Jason
Born: Newport, 2 April 1970
Height: 5'11" Weight: 10.4
Club Honours: WC '92, '93; Div 3 '93
International Honours: W: 1; B-2; U21-3; Yth; Sch

Mr Cardiff City, the third division's Vinny Jones, had a dismal season in 1995-96, wracked by his worst injury crisis since becoming a professional. Not really figuring in the side after October, but always the first name pencilled in before when playing in the number six shirt, Jason is a giant of a player, despite being of small stature.

Cardiff C (From trainee on 21/8/87) FL 243+3/5 FLC 20 FAC 13+1 Others 21+1

PESCHISOLIDO Paolo (Paul) Pasquale
Born: Scarborough, Canada, 25 May 1971
Height: 5'7" Weight: 10.12
International Honours: Canada: 20

A tricky Canadian international striker, Paul had a good season for Stoke before rejoining his wife, Karren Brady, the managing director at Birmingham City, on transfer deadline day, last March. With the deal needed to assist the club's finances, manager, Lou Macari, spoke well of his commitment when questioned on the sale. Despite sustaining an ankle injury when scoring in the 5-0 win against Luton, which kept him out of the side for several games, he proved to be a polished player throughout the campaign.

Birmingham C (£25,000 from Toronto Blizzards on 11/11/92) FL 37+6/16 FLC 2/1 FAC 0+1 Others 1+1
Stoke C (£400,000 on 1/8/94) FL 59+7/19 FLC 6/3 FAC 3 Others 5+1/2
Birmingham C (£400,000 on 29/3/96) FL 7+2/1

Paul Peschisolido

PETERS Mark
Born: St Asaph, 6 July 1972
Height: 6'0" Weight: 11.3
International Honours: W: B-1; U21-3; Yth
Outstanding Mansfield Town central defender who had the misfortune to suffer injury and suspension before a broken leg last March finished his season. Good in the air and on the ground, with his firm tackling ending many an attack, hopefully, he will regain his true form when fully recovered.

Manchester C (From trainee on 5/7/90)
Norwich C (Free on 2/9/92)
Peterborough U (Free on 10/8/93) FL 17+2 FLC 2 Others 2
Mansfield T (Free on 30/9/94) FL 46+1/6 FLC 3 FAC 4 Others 5

PETHICK Robert (Robbie) John
Born: Tavistock, 8 September 1970
Height: 5'10" Weight: 11.7
Not surprisingly, with Portsmouth plumbing the depths of the first division last season, Robbie also had an indifferent time of it. An attacking right back who likes to get forward in wide positions where he can supply crosses into the box, he linked up well with a number of partners, before losses of form saw him first replaced by John Durnin and then by Danny Hinshelwood.

Portsmouth (£30,000 from Weymouth on 1/10/93) FL 83+17/1 FLC 7+2 FAC 3 Others 3+1

PETRESCU Daniel (Dan) Vasile
Born: Bucharest, Romania, 22 December 1967
Height: 5'9" Weight: 11.9
International Honours: Romania: 54
Very talented right-sided wing/back who

signed for Chelsea last November after protracted transfer negotiations with Sheffield Wednesday. Unsettled and unsure of a first team place at Hillsborough, Dan was an inspired signing by Glenn Hoddle as he adapted perfectly to the 3-5-2 strategy. Encouraged to get forward at every opportunity, he is very clever on the ball and finds space intelligently, and, in only his fifth game for the club, scored the only goal at Stamford Bridge to halt Newcastle's runaway start to the season. He scored a screamer from an acute angle in the sixth round FA Cup replay at Selhurst Park against Wimbledon, but was sorely missed through suspension in the semi final against Manchester United. An automatic choice for Romania over the past few years, he was one of four Chelsea players who appeared for three different countries in Euro '96.

Sheffield Wed (£1,250,000 from Genoa on 6/8/94) PL 28+9/3 FLC 2 FAC 0+2
Chelsea (£2,300,000 on 18/11/95) PL 22+2/2 FAC 7/1

PETTERSON Andrew (Andy) Keith
Born: Freemantle, Australia, 26 September 1969
Height: 6'2" Weight: 14.12
Charlton goalkeeper, and an agile shot stopper who kicks long and accurately, Andy only broke into the side last April after being on loan at four different clubs during the season. Made one appearance for Ipswich (a 1-1 draw at Derby), failed to get on the field for Bradford (having gone there on 22 December), impressed in six games at Plymouth, and when arriving at Colchester, as cover for the injured Carl Emberson and Garrett Caldwell's international duty, proved one of the best 'keepers seen at the club in recent years. Back at the Valley, he quickly won the fans over when keeping clean sheets against the division's two top sides, Derby and Sunderland and will be hoping to consolidate his place in 1996-97.

Luton T (Signed on 30/12/88) FL 16+3 FLC 2 Others 2
Ipswich T (Loaned on 26/3/93) PL 1
Charlton Ath (£85,000 on 15/7/94) FL 17+1 FLC 2 Others 2
Bradford C (Loaned on 8/12/94) FL 3
Ipswich T (Loaned on 26/9/95) FL 1
Plymouth Arg (Loaned on 19/1/96) FL 6
Colchester U (Loaned on 8/3/96) FL 5

PETTINGER Paul Allen
Born: Sheffield, 1 October 1975
Height: 6'1" Weight: 13.7
Club Honours: FAYC '93
International Honours: E: Yth; Sch
With Mark Beeney and John Lukic ahead of him at Leeds, the young goalkeeper was loaned to Rotherham at the beginning of last season, his only appearance coming as an outfield substitution in the home draw against Hull City. Smart on crosses, and agile, with good technique, Paul signed for Gillingham in March to understudy Jim Stannard, but was released during the summer without making an appearance.

Leeds U (From trainee on 16/10/92)
Torquay U (Loaned on 23/12/94) FL 3
Rotherham U (Loaned on 11/8/95) FL 0+1
Gillingham (Free on 28/3/96)

PEVERELL Nicholas (Nicky) John
Born: Middlesbrough, 28 April 1973
Height: 5'11" Weight: 11.10
A skilful striker, Nicky had a very good spell early last season, especially when starring in York's second-leg Coca Cola Cup game against Manchester United. However, his form fluctuated after that and he was not able to establish himself in the first team during the second half of the term, resulting in him being released during the summer.

Middlesbrough (From trainee on 3/7/91)
Hartlepool U (Free on 27/11/92) FL 14+21/3 FAC 1+2/1 Others 1+2 (Free to Hong Kong during 1994 close season)
Hartlepool U (Free on 16/12/94) FL 0+1
York C (Free on 3/2/95) FL 13+16/2 FLC 3+1/1 Others 2+2/1

PHELAN Michael (Mike) Christopher
Born: Nelson, 24 September 1962
Height: 5'10" Weight: 12.0
Club Honours: Div 3 '82, Div 2 '86; FAC '90; CS '90; ECWC '91 FLC '92; PL '93
International Honours: E: 1; Yth
An experienced midfield player who never really figured in WBA's plans in 1995-96, struggling for most of the time with a niggling leg injury. Indeed, he only made a handful of first team appearances during the campaign and returned to his former club, Norwich, as the reserve team coach on transfer deadline day.

Burnley (From apprentice on 29/7/80) FL 166+2/9 FLC 16/2 FAC 16 Others 8/2
Norwich C (£60,000 on 13/7/85) FL 155+1/9 FLC 14 FAC 11/1 Others 13
Manchester U (£750,000 on 1/7/89) F/PL 88+14/2 FLC 14+2 FAC 10/1 Others 15+3
West Bromwich A (Free on 11/7/94) FL 18+3 FLC 2

PHELAN Terence (Terry) Michael
Born: Manchester, 16 March 1967
Height: 5'8" Weight: 10.0
Club Honours: FAYC '88
International Honours: Ei: 35; B-1; U23-1; U21-1; Yth
Eyebrows were raised when Chelsea signed yet another left back, but, as with Dan Petrescu on the opposite flank, Terry fitted in perfectly with Glenn Hoddle's wing/back tactics. One of the fastest players in the modern game, the Republic of Ireland international is perfectly suited to an attacking full back role and played 20 matches for Blues, after his move from Maine Road, until the club's left back injury jinx struck again in the FA Cup semi final. With Chelsea leading 1-0 in the second half, he was sprinting clear down the left wing when he pulled up sharply with a torn thigh muscle. Having gamely tried to play on, but little more than a passenger as United exploited his lack of mobility down that flank, he finally hobbled off after the Red's second goal, his season over. Has proven to be a shrewd signing and looks the answer to a problem position that has bothered Chelsea since Tony Dorigo, Clive Wilson, and Tommy Boyd, all left in the early '90s.

Leeds U (From apprentice on 3/8/84) FL 12+2 FLC 3 Others 2
Swansea C (Free on 30/7/86) FL 45 FLC 4 FAC 4 Others 3

Wimbledon (£100,000 on 29/7/87) FL 155+4/1 FLC 13+2 FAC 16/2 Others 8
Manchester C (£2,500,000 on 25/8/92) PL 102+1/2 FLC 11 FAC 8/1
Chelsea (£900,000 on 15/11/95) PL 12 FAC 8

Terry Phelan

PHILLIPS David Owen
Born: Wegburg, Germany, 29 July 1963
Height: 5'10" Weight: 11.2
Club Honours: FAC '87
International Honours: W: 62; U21-4; Yth
Nottingham Forest's Welsh international midfielder lost his regular place in the 1995-96 line-up to Chris Bart-Williams in September, but proved his versatility later in the season when standing in for both full backs, Des Lyttle and Stuart Pearce, and also for Scot Gemmill. Still a regular for Wales, while his defence-splitting passes and coolness on the ball remain, there is every chance he will get a further run-in the Forest side in 1996-97.
Plymouth Arg (From apprentice on 3/8/81) FL 65+8/15 FLC 2+1 FAC 12+1 Others 4/1
Manchester C (£65,000 on 23/8/84) FL 81/13 FLC 8 FAC 5 Others 5/3
Coventry C (£150,000 on 5/6/86) FL 93+7/8 FLC 8 FAC 9/1 Others 5+1/2
Norwich C (£525,000 on 31/7/89) F/PL 152/18 FLC 12 FAC 14/1 Others 8/1
Nottingham F (Signed on 20/8/93) F/PL 86+7/5 FLC 12 FAC 8+2 Others 4

PHILLIPS James (Jimmy) Neil
Born: Bolton, 8 February 1966
Height: 6'0" Weight: 12.7
The Bolton-born left back missed just one game during last season, the last day Premiership defeat at Arsenal. A cool head in Wanderers' defence, he had to face up to some of the best wingers in the game, but came through without being spectacular, producing some of his best performances during February and March when the team switched to a three-man central defensive system. Is a skilful player who often makes good use of a cultured left foot at set plays, especially with inswinging corners, and who links up with the attack well.

Bolton W (From apprentice on 1/8/83) FL 103+5/2 FLC 8 FAC 7 Others 14
Glasgow R (£95,000 on 27/3/87) SL 19+6 SLC 4 Others 4
Oxford U (£110,000 on 26/8/88) FL 79/8 FLC 3 FAC 4 Others 2/1
Middlesbrough (£250,000 on 15/3/90) F/PL 139/6 FLC 16 FAC 10 Others 5/2
Bolton W (£250,000 on 20/7/93) P/FL 124+1/1 FLC 18 FAC 10 Others 9/2

PHILLIPS Kevin
Born: Hitchin, 25 July 1973
Height: 5'7" Weight: 11.0
Watford striker who sustained the promise of his first season with the club, scoring 12 goals, before finishing 1995-96 with a broken foot in plaster. Difficult to mark, he has the ability to be able to get on the blind side of defenders to pick up loose balls around the box. Was also involved in a bizarre clash with the Bournemouth constabulary when mistaken for a fan after the FA Cup-tie at Dean Court.
Watford (£10,000 from Baldock on 19/12/94) FL 41+2/20 FLC 2/1 FAC 2

PHILLIPS Martin John
Born: Exeter, 13 March 1976
Height: 5'11" Weight: 12.8
A ball-playing winger, with a direct style of play in going for goal, Martin joined Manchester City from Exeter last November. Known as "Buster", his move to a higher level had been inevitable, a point merely emphasised when he netted Exeter's goal of the season at home to Fulham in September. Scored on his reserve debut just seven days into his new career at Maine Road and his brief first team appearances have shown that the ability is there. Alan Ball, who discovered Martin at Exeter, has no doubts about his potential, so watch this space.
Exeter C (From trainee on 4/7/94) FL 36+16/5 FLC 1+2 FAC 2+2 Others 1+5
Manchester C (£500,000 on 25/11/95) PL 2+9

PHILLIPS Wayne
Born: Bangor, 15 December 1970
Height: 5'10" Weight: 11.2
International Honours: W: B-1
For many Wrexham fans, Wayne would be their choice as the 1995-96 "Player of the Season", as self belief was added to his game for perhaps the first time. An up-and-down the park midfielder, who is always in the thick of things, he likes to get involved and is always liable to have a crack at goal at any time. He came on so well that the Welsh manager, Bobby Gould, included him on the bench for the friendly against Switzerland in April at Lugano. Is an honest player who deserves to succeed.
Wrexham (From trainee on 23/8/89) FL 144+17/10 FLC 13+1 FAC 10+2/1 Others 18+5/1

PHILLISKIRK Anthony (Tony)
Born: Sunderland, 10 February 1965
Height: 6'1" Weight: 13.3
International Honours: E: Sch
Free at last from injuries, the tall striker partnered Kurt Nogan up front for Burnley during the first six weeks of last season, managing just one goal, before being loaned out to Carlisle in October and playing three

games (one goal). Back at Turf Moor, and unable to displace David Eyres, he transferred to Cardiff in December, where he netted only twice in his first 20 appearances, giving the impression that he was not the sharpest of shots, although holding the ball up well.
Sheffield U (From juniors on 16/8/83) FL 62+18/20 FLC 4+1/1 FAC 5/1 Others 3+2
Rotherham U (Loaned on 16/10/86) FL 6/1
Oldham Ath (£25,000 on 13/7/88) FL 3+7/1 FLC 0+2/1 Others 1
Preston NE (Signed on 10/2/89) FL 13+1/6
Bolton W (£50,000 on 22/6/89) FL 139+2/51 FLC 18/12 FAC 10/7 Others 13/5
Peterborough U (£85,000 on 17/10/92) FL 37+6/15 FLC 2/1 FAC 4/1 Others 2/1
Burnley (£80,000 on 21/1/94) FL 33+7/9 FLC 4+1
Carlisle U (Loaned on 26/10/95) FL 3/1
Cardiff C (£60,000 on 7/12/95) FL 28/4

PHILPOTT Lee
Born: Barnet, 21 February 1970
Height: 5'11" Weight: 12.9
Club Honours: Div 3 '91
Left-sided Leicester City midfielder with a reputation as a good crosser. Appeared only rarely during the first part of last season, before being transferred to Blackpool on deadline day as part of the concerted effort to achieve promotion. Is a good crosser of the ball.
Peterborough U (From trainee on 17/7/86) FL 1+3 FAC 0+1 Others 0+2
Cambridge U (Free on 31/5/89) FL 118+16/17 FLC 10/1 FAC 19/3 Others 15/2
Leicester C (£350,000 on 24/11/92) F/PL 57+18/3 FLC 2+1 FAC 6+2 Others 4+1
Blackpool (£75,000 on 22/3/96) FL 4+6 Others 0+1

PICK Gary Mark
Born: Leicester, 9 July 1971
Height: 5'9" Weight: 11.8
Unable to get a regular game at Hereford in 1995-96, due to heavy competition for midfield places, Gary moved to Cambridge United in March. Although the determined, hard-tackling ball winner made four appearances, he found it difficult to exert any influence over a very young side and was released during the summer.
Stoke C (Signed from Leicester U on 19/8/92)
Hereford U (Free on 28/6/94) FL 33+10/2 FLC 4+1 FAC 2+1/1 Others 5
Cambridge U (Free on 25/3/96) FL 2+2

PICKERING Albert (Ally) Gary
Born: Manchester, 22 June 1967
Height: 5'11" Weight: 11.1
Coventry right back who adds an attacking flair to his defensive game. Played in the majority of games up until the middle of last February and always gave 100 per cent, his greatest assets being his crosses, which were ably demonstrated well in the home win over Blackburn when he made two of the goals. Following a period out of the side, he was recalled at Easter because of injuries and, apart from a skinning received from an irrepressible Ryan Giggs, he played well.
Rotherham U (£18,500 from Buxton on 2/2/90) FL 87+1/2 FLC 6 FAC 9 Others 7
Coventry C (£80,000 on 27/10/93) PL 54+11 FLC 5+1 FAC 4/1

Ally Pickering

PIERCE David Edward
Born: Manchester, 4 October 1975
Height: 6'1" Weight: 12.6
Signed on a monthly contract from Rotherham during the 1995 close season, the former Manchester United trainee made just one appearance between the posts for Chesterfield, at Wycombe. After a shaky start, he made a number of good saves as the team slipped to a 1-0 defeat on the day, prior to being released in January.
Rotherham U (Free from Manchester U juniors on 20/8/94)
Chesterfield (Free on 10/8/95) FL 1

PIKE Martin Russell
Born: South Shields, 21 October 1964
Height: 5'10" Weight: 12.9
Left back Martin made a determined and plucky effort to resurrect his career and when he came on for Rotherham as a substitute at Brighton at the end of March 1996, it was his first appearance since October 1994, following a series of injuries. Earlier, he had looked impressive in the reserves where he assisted the younger players while gradually regaining his own strength. Was released during the summer.
West Bromwich A (From apprentice on 26/10/82)
Peterborough U (Free on 18/8/83) FL 119+7/8 FLC 8 FAC 10 Others 5/1
Sheffield U (£20,000 on 22/8/86) FL 127+2/5 FLC 10 FAC 12 Others 5+1
Tranmere Rov (Loaned on 10/11/89) FL 2 FLC 2 FAC 1
Bolton W (Loaned on 14/12/89) FL 5/1 Others 1
Fulham (£65,000 on 8/2/90) FL 187+3/14 FLC 10 FAC 5/1 Others 12/2
Rotherham U (Free on 3/8/94) FL 7+2

PILKINGTON Kevin William
Born: Hitchin, 8 March 1974
Height: 6'2" Weight: 13.0
Club Honours: FAYC '92
International Honours: E: Sch
Well-built young goalkeeper who commands the area well and makes a

difficult target. After making a promising start to his Manchester United career the previous season, Kevin continued his progress in 1995-96, as Peter Schmeichel's deputy, giving a series of solid displays in back-to-back games against Chelsea and Sheffield Wednesday. However, seemingly assured of a regular place on the bench, the signing of Tony Coton effectively relegated him to third choice, and to keep active he was loaned out to Rochdale in February. Played six matches at Dale, but fared no better than the reserve custodian, Chris Clarke, neither of them figuring in a winning side.
Manchester U (From trainee on 6/7/92) PL 2+2 FLC 1 FAC 1
Rochdale (Loaned on 2/2/96) FL 6

PITCHER Darren Edward
Born: Stepney, 12 October 1969
Height: 5'9" Weight: 12.2
International Honours: E: Yth
A hard-tackling, defensively sound Crystal Palace midfielder, Darren was a regular throughout last season, missing only when injured or suspended. Preferred on the right-hand side of the park, he was a vital, if unspectacular, cog in the Palace formation, and his partnership and understanding with Ray Houghton was a major influence in the club's promotion charge, that was only thwarted in the final minute of the final game of 1995-96.
Charlton Ath (From trainee on 12/1/88) FL 170+3/8 FLC 11 FAC 12/3 Others 8
Crystal Palace (£700,000 on 5/7/94) P/FL 57+4 FLC 5+1/1 FAC 10/1 Others 3

PITCHER Geoffrey (Geoff)
Born: Sutton, 15 August 1975
Height: 5'7" Weight: 11.2
Gutsy and combative Watford midfielder who made a handful of appearances in 1995-96, mainly as a substitute, but was held back by ankle and groin injuries, before being released during the summer.
Millwall (From trainee on 18/3/93)
Watford (Signed on 13/7/94) FL 4+9/2 FLC 1+1 FAC 2

PITMAN Jamie Roy
Born: Trowbridge, 6 January 1976
Height: 5'9" Weight: 10.8
Having failed to attain a regular place in the Swindon squad last season, sitting on the bench just once, Jamie signed for Hereford in February. Playing mainly on the wide left, the little midfield dynamo quickly fitted into the side to give some excellent performances and was retained for the coming season.
Swindon T (From trainee on 8/7/94) FL 2+1
Hereford U (Free on 16/2/96) FL 12+1 Others 2

PLATNAUER Nicholas (Nicky) Robert
Born: Leicester, 10 June 1961
Height: 5'11" Weight: 12.10
Club Honours: WC '88
Started last season as Lincoln's youth team coach, and appeared as a substitute for the last seven minutes of the opening day victory at Preston, before leaving in August to join non-league Bedworth United. More

of a nomad than a long-term servant, the left back played for nine clubs in a 15 year career.
Bristol Rov (Free from Bedford T on 4/8/82) FL 21+3/7 FLC 1/1 FAC 0+1
Coventry C (£50,000 on 26/8/83) FL 38+6/6 FLC 5 FAC 4
Birmingham C (£60,000 on 14/12/84) FL 23+5/2 FLC 3 FAC 5
Reading (Loaned on 30/1/86) FL 7 Others 1
Cardiff C (Free on 26/9/86) FL 110+5/6 FLC 6/2 FAC 9 Others 12
Notts Co (£50,000 on 1/8/89) FL 57/1 FLC 6 FAC 1 Others 10
Port Vale (Loaned on 18/1/91) FL 14 FAC 1
Leicester C (Free on 19/7/91) FL 32+3 FLC 4+1 Others 2
Scunthorpe U (Free on 8/3/93) FL 14/2
Mansfield T (Free on 12/8/93) FL 25 FLC 2 FAC 1 Others 4
Lincoln C (Free on 1/2/94) FL 26+1 FLC 4

PLATT Clive Linton
Born: Wolverhampton, 27 October 1977
Height: 6'4" Weight: 12.7
The exciting young YTS striker made four substitute appearances for Walsall near the end of last season and scored in two of these, the first being a spectacular volley against Burnley in the penultimate home game that had the crowd chanting his name. Just watch him go when he turns professional.
Walsall (Trainee) FL 0+4/2

PLATT David Andrew
Born: Chadderton, 10 June 1966
Height: 5'10" Weight: 11.12
International Honours: E: 62; B-3; U21-3
Returning by popular demand, prior to Euro '96, the England captain signed for Arsenal during the summer of 1995, having spent the previous four years playing for Bari, Juventus, and Sampdoria. A midfield dynamo, who scores more than his fair share of goals, in many ways it was a difficult return. After picking up a knee injury during a pre-season friendly at Wolves, he was sidelined for several periods and eventually required surgery, which meant that he was not fully fit until the latter stages of the campaign. Nevertheless, only Ian Wright and Dennis Bergkamp scored more, and when you bear in mind that he was often playing in an unfamiliar midfield holding role, that was some achievement. Played in four of the five European Championship games that saw England ultimately lose out to Germany in the semi finals, scoring in the penalty shoot-outs against the latter and Spain.
Manchester U (Signed from Chadderton on 24/7/84)
Crewe Alex (Free on 25/1/85) FL 134/55 FLC 8/4 FAC 3/1 Others 7
Aston Villa (£200,000 on 2/2/88) FL 121/50 FLC 14/10 FAC 4/2 Others 6/6 (£5,500,000 to Bari on 20/7/91)
Arsenal (£4,750,000 from Sampdoria, via Juventus, on 14/7/95) PL 27+2/6 FLC 2+1 FAC 1

PLATTS Mark Anthony
Born: Sheffield, 23 May 1979
Height: 5'8" Weight: 10.12
International Honours: E: Yth; Sch
The young Sheffield Wednesday trainee right winger became the youngest outfield

player to appear in the Owls' first team when he came on as substitute against Wimbledon last season. Still obviously learning his trade, he looked to have loads of skill, pace, and confidence, and a bright future is predicted for him if he can be brought on steadily through the Premiership minefield.

Sheffield Wed (Trainee) PL 0+2

PLUMMER Christopher (Chris)
Born: Isleworth, 12 October 1976
Height: 6'3" Weight: 11.6
International Honours: E: U21-5; Yth

A tall, central defender, who looks very accomplished on the ball and likes to get forward for set pieces, Chris made his debut for QPR as a substitute at Nottingham Forest on the final day of last season, after being called onto the bench for three games earlier in the year. As a young player with a future, he was selected for the England U21 squad in April against Croatia, where he made his debut, again from the bench.

Queens Park R (From trainee on 1/7/94) PL 0+1

PLUMMER Dwayne Jermaine
Born: Bristol, 12 May 1978
Height: 5'9" Weight: 11.0

One of the most naturally gifted players at Ashton Gate, this right winger progressed from the Bristol City youth side to make his first team debut in the home Coca Cola Cup match against Newcastle United last September. Although mainly used as a substitute during the season, Dwayne has the refreshing habit of taking players on and it is to be hoped that he will be given plenty of opportunities in the near future.

Bristol C (From trainee on 5/9/95) FL 1+10 FLC 1+2 Others 0+1

POINTON Neil Geoffrey
Born: Church Warsop, 28 November 1964
Height: 5'10" Weight: 11.0
Club Honours: Div 1 '87; CS '87

Neil, or "Nino" as he became affectionately known at Oldham, was one of the most aggressive players the club ever employed, never afraid to throw himself into the tackle, always giving 100 per cent, and capable of scoring vital goals. However, after appearing in four of the opening six games last season, but from thereon not fitting in with manager, Graeme Sharp's plans, he transferred to Hearts for £50,000 early in October and helped them reach the Scottish FA Cup final.

Scunthorpe U (From apprentice on 10/8/82) FL 159/2 FLC 9/1 FAC 13 Others 4
Everton (£75,000 on 8/11/85) FL 95+7/5 FLC 6+2 FAC 16+2 Others 9+3
Manchester C (£600,000 on 17/7/90) FL 74/2 FLC 8 FAC 4 Others 4
Oldham Ath (£600,000 on 10/7/92) P/FL 92+3/3 FLC 5 FAC 7+1/2

POLLITT Michael Francis
Born: Farnworth, 29 February 1972
Height: 6'4" Weight: 14.0

A large but agile, confident, and reliable goalkeeper, Michael transferred to Notts County last November, after giving some superb displays for Darlington, including keeping five clean sheets in his final nine appearances. The most surprising element of the move being that he was merely going to understudy Darren Ward. Although yet to make his debut at County, he quickly impressed that he was more than capable of standing in at any time and given the chance, would be favoured to keep his place.

Manchester U (From trainee on 1/7/90)
Bury (Free on 10/7/91)
Lincoln C (Free on 1/12/92) FL 57 FLC 5 FAC 2 Others 4
Darlington (Free on 11/8/94) FL 55 FLC 4 FAC 3 Others 5
Notts Co (£75,000 on 14/11/95)

POLLOCK Jamie
Born: Stockton, 16 February 1974
Height: 5'11" Weight: 14.0
Club Honours: Div 1 '95
International Honours: E: U21-3; Yth

Middlesbrough's brightest homegrown talent since Gary Pallister, Jamie, a hardworking, bustling central midfielder, proved he could withstand the heat of the Premier League by holding down his place throughout last season. Deployed in a more defensive anchor role than in previous seasons, his goalscoring dried up, apart from one in the league and one to open the scoring in Boro's 2-1 FA Cup victory over Notts County. However, his good play in his new role brought two more England U21 caps and he looks certain to gain many more honours yet.

Middlesbrough (From trainee on 18/12/91) F/PL 144+11/17 FLC 17+2/1 FAC 13+1/1 Others 4+1

Jamie Pollock

POLSTON John David
Born: Walthamstow, 10 June 1968
Height: 5'11" Weight: 11.12
International Honours: E: Yth

A specialist defender and a vital Norwich ever present for six years, under Martin O'Neill's regime last season, he found himself out of the side more often than not, evidenced by the fact that he was on the bench nine times until starting game 18. Although suffering from a mixture of calf injuries, once installed in Gary Megson's side he formed a solid-looking three-man central defensive barrier with Rob Newman and Spencer Prior, making his 200th senior appearance against Birmingham in February. He, along with the rest of the team, must hope for better fortune in 1996-97.

Tottenham H (From apprentice on 16/7/85) FL 17+7/1 FLC 3+1
Norwich C (£250,000 on 24/7/90) F/PL 166+6/6 FLC 16+1/2 FAC 16+1 Others 9/1

POOLE Gary John
Born: Stratford, 11 September 1967
Height: 6'0" Weight: 12.4
Club Honours: GMVC '91; Div 2 '95; AMC '95

Consistent Birmingham right back who was appointed club captain following the departure of Liam Daish last season. Has adapted well to first division football, his tackling ability proving impressive, while his awareness and speed to get forward on the overlap, set up a number of goals, even though he managed only two himself. Unfortunately, Gary became yet another member of the Blues' injured club and was forced to miss a number of games towards the end of the campaign.

Tottenham H (From juniors on 15/7/85)
Cambridge U (Free on 14/8/87) FL 42+1 FLC 2 FAC 2 Others 3
Barnet (£3,000 on 1/3/89) FL 39+1/2 FLC 2 FAC 7 Others 26/1
Plymouth Arg (Free on 5/6/92) FL 39/5 FLC 6/2 FAC 2 Others 0+1
Southend U (£350,000 on 9/7/93) FL 43+1/2 FLC 2 FAC 1 Others 6
Birmingham C (£50,000 on 16/9/94) FL 61+1 FLC 10 FAC 7/1 Others 10/2

POOLE Kevin
Born: Bromsgrove, 21 July 1963
Height: 5'10" Weight: 12.6

Goalkeeper. The 1995 Leicester "Player of the Season" was again "Mr Consistency" in 1995-96. Saved a penalty in the televised win at The Baseball Ground and was outstanding in home defeat at Watford. Briefly displaced by big money signing, Zeljko Kalac, in November, he quickly reestablished himself as first choice. Another penalty save at Ipswich almost turned the game as his immediate clearance led directly to a goal at the other end. Produced a stop of Banks-like proportions in the opening minutes of the play-off semi final to deny Stoke, and made a couple of crucial saves at Wembley, at the end of which, City reached the Premiership following their 2-1 extra-time victory.

Aston Villa (From apprentice on 26/6/81) FL 28 FLC 2 FAC 1 Others 1
Northampton T (Loaned on 8/11/84) FL 3
Middlesbrough (Signed on 27/8/87) FL 34 FLC 4 FAC 2 Others 2
Hartlepool U (Loaned on 27/3/91) FL 12
Leicester C (£40,000 on 30/7/91) F/PL 156 FLC 9 FAC 8 Others 12

POOM Mart
Born: Tallin, Estonia, 3 February 1972
Height: 6'4" Weight: 13.6
International Honours: Estonia: 39

Despite starting in five of the first six matches last season, the big Portsmouth goalkeeper had a dramatic loss of form and gave way to the experienced, long-serving Alan Knight. Unfortunately, having been granted an extension to his work permit at the start of 1995-96, on the proviso that he played in 75 per cent of the games to Christmas, his permit was revoked in the New Year.

Portsmouth (£200,000 from FC Will on 4/8/94) FL 4 FLC 3

POPE Steven Anthony
Born: Stoke, 8 September 1976
Height: 6'1" Weight: 12.3

This young defender came through the Crewe youth ranks to make his debut as a substitute in the 5-2 Coca Cola Cup defeat at Sheffield Wednesday last October and was selected for the squad on a number of occasions since. Could easily develop into a very capable player.

Crewe Alex (From trainee on 3/6/95) FLC 0+1

PORTER Andrew (Andy) Michael
Born: Holmes Chapel, 17 September 1968
Height: 5'9" Weight: 11.2
Club Honours: AMC '93

Having one of his best ever seasons in the Port Vale midfield in 1995-96, the year of his testimonial, he captained the side during the absence of Neil Aspin and led them out at Wembley in the Anglo-Italian Cup final. A tough tackler, he proved to be an adept penalty taker and scored 12 times altogether, by far a personal best.

Port Vale (From trainee on 29/6/87) FL 241+31/17 FLC 16 FAC 17+4/3 Others 26+2/1

Andy Porter

PORTER Gary Michael
Born: Sunderland, 6 March 1966
Height: 5'6" Weight: 11.0
Club Honours: FAYC '82
International Honours: E: U21-12; Yth

A versatile, left-footed player who completed his 13th season as a Watford first teamer in 1995-96 and is now approaching Luther Blissett's all-time club record of 503 appearances. Started the campaign at left back, but missed three months with hip and knee injuries before returning to his favourite left side of midfield and playing a major part in the club's battle against relegation, scoring a crucial winner at Norwich.

Watford (From apprentice on 6/3/84) FL 356+38/47 FLC 28+2/4 FAC 25+2/3 Others 12+1/2

POTTER Graham Stephen
Born: Solihull, 20 May 1975
Height: 6'1" Weight: 11.12
International Honours: E: Yth

Promising left-sided player who broke into the Stoke side last season after switching from left back to left wing. Using his pace and excellent crossing ability to great effect, Graham started to bloom, and at last began to fulfil his early potential. Still only 22, he can only get better.

Birmingham C (From trainee on 1/7/92) FL 23+2/2 FAC 1 Others 6
Wycombe W (Loaned on 17/9/93) FL 2+1 FLC 1 Others 1
Stoke C (£75,000 on 20/12/93) FL 41+4/1 FLC 3+1 FAC 4 Others 5

POTTS Steven (Steve) John
Born: Hartford, USA, 7 May 1967
Height: 5'8" Weight: 10.11
International Honours: E: Yth

The West Ham club captain and central defender, as one has come to expect, had another consistent season in 1995-96. Ever present until being sent off at Newcastle in March, following his ban he temporarily lost his place in the side until regaining it some four games later. Apart from that blip, he went about his work as normal, his positional sense, speed of recovery, and quick tackling more than making up for a distinct lack of inches. After 12 years as a Hammer, Steve can now look forward to his pre-season testimonial game against Crystal Palace.

West Ham U (From apprentice on 11/5/84) F/PL 302+10/1 FLC 30+1 FAC 34 Others 14+1

POUNDER Anthony (Tony) Mark
Born: Yeovil, 11 March 1966
Height: 5'10" Weight: 11.4

Disappointingly, Tony had to settle for irregular Hereford appearances in 1995-96, having earlier been released. Although popular on either wing, where his pace can take him clear of defenders, his ability to win the ball saw him playing equally well in the heart of midfield. Freed during the summer for the second year running.

Bristol Rov (Signed from Weymouth on 24/7/90) FL 102+11/10 FLC 4 FAC 3+1 Others 5/2 (Free to Weymouth during 1994 close season)
Hereford U (Free on 2/9/94) FL 54+8/4 FLC 3 FAC 4+2 Others 5+3

POVEY Neil Andrew
Born: Birmingham, 26 June 1977
Height: 5'8" Weight: 10.0

Signing professional forms for Torquay during the summer of 1995, having made his debut the previous season, Neil was fully expected to go from strength to strength as an attacking midfielder who could play on both flanks and get in good crosses. Unfortunately, for some reason, he never came up to the manager's expectations and after just three games was released in March.

Torquay U (From trainee on 4/7/95) FL 8+3

POWELL Christopher (Chris) George Robin
Born: Lambeth, 8 September 1969
Height: 5'8" Weight: 11.7

Was Southend's skipper, having played 34 games for them in 1995-96, when Derby moved for him last January, in order for him to take over the left back role at the Baseball Ground. Quickly established himself as a member of a side that ultimately won promotion, showing excellent ball control with either foot, and good distribution, qualities which will be valued in the Premiership. He was yet another excellent Jim Smith signing.

Crystal Palace (From trainee on 24/12/87) FL 2+1 FLC 0+1 Others 0+1
Aldershot (Loaned on 11/1/90) FL 11
Southend U (Free on 30/8/90) FL 246+2/3 FLC 13 FAC 8 Others 21
Derby Co (£750,000 on 31/1/96) FL 19

POWELL Darryl Anthony
Born: Lambeth, 15 November 1971
Height: 6'0" Weight: 12.3

Held in high regard by the Derby manager, Jim Smith, Darryl moved from Portsmouth to Derby during the 1995 close season. A versatile player, at home anywhere on the field, he made the central midfield role his own with a series of performances which emphasised his strength and explosive pace. Suffered a knee injury early on, but came back to appear in almost all the subsequent games.

Portsmouth (From trainee on 22/12/88) FL 83+49/16 FLC 11+3/3 FAC 10 Others 9+5/4
Derby Co (£750,000 on 27/7/95) FL 37/5 FLC 1+1

POWELL Francis (Franny) Michael
Born: Burnley, 17 June 1977
Height: 6'2" Weight: 12.0

The former Burnley youth team forward signed for Rochdale last September after a trial with the reserve and "A" sides. Figured both in the centre and on the flank in the reserves and made his first team debut in an injury crisis in April, coming on as substitute against Colchester, prior to being released during the summer.

Rochdale (Free from Burnley juniors on 19/9/95) FL 0+2

POWELL Paul
Born: Wallingford, 30 June 1978
Height: 5'8" Weight: 11.0

As Oxford's youth team "Player of the Year", Paul made his first team debut as a full back at Chesterfield in 1995-96, when Mike Ford and Simon Marsh were both injured. A few games from the bench followed and he proved to be equally at home on the left wing. Has a good long throw for a small player.

Oxford U (Trainee) FL 1+2 Others 0+2

POWER Lee Michael
Born: Lewisham, 30 June 1972
Height: 6'0" Weight: 11.10
International Honours: Ei: B-1; U21-13; Yth

Signed from Bradford during the summer of 1995, although occasionally impressing, Lee had a rather inconsistent start to his Peterborough career, 17 of his 46 appearances coming from the bench. Not an out-and-out striker, with just seven goals to his credit, but one who shields the ball well and brings his team mates into the play.

Norwich C (From trainee on 6/7/90) F/PL 28+16/10 FLC 1 FAC 0+1 Others 0+2
Charlton Ath (Loaned on 4/12/92) FL 5
Sunderland (Loaned on 13/8/93) FL 1+2 FLC 2/1
Portsmouth (Loaned on 15/10/93) FL 1+1 Others 1
Bradford C (£200,000 on 8/3/94) FL 14+16/5 FLC 0+2 FAC 0+1 Others 1+1/1
Peterborough U (£80,000 on 26/7/95) FL 25+13/6 FLC 2+2 FAC 1+2 Others 1/1

Andy Preece

PREECE Andrew (Andy) Paul
Born: Evesham, 27 March 1967
Height: 6'1" Weight: 12.0

Blackpool striker who joined the club from Crystal Palace in the summer of 1995. Failed to score in his first five starts, but then opened his account with eight from the next 11 games, before having a lean spell and being dropped and listed at his own request. Subsequently regained his place in the side, and came off the transfer list, as the 'Pool chased hard for promotion. Finished the season as top scorer.

Northampton T (Free from Evesham on 31/8/88) FL 0+1 FLC 0+1 Others 0+1 (Free to Worcester C during 1989 close season)

Wrexham (Free on 22/3/90) FL 44+7/7 FLC 5+1/1 FAC 1/2 Others 5/1
Stockport Co (£10,000 on 18/12/91) FL 89+8/42 FLC 2+1 FAC 7/3 Others 12+2/9
Crystal Palace (£350,000 on 23/6/94) PL 17+3/4 FLC 4+2/1 FAC 2+3
Blackpool (£200,000 on 5/7/95) FL 37+4/14 FLC 2 FAC 1+2/1 Others 6

PREECE David William
Born: Bridgnorth, 28 May, 1963
Height: 5'6" Weight: 11.6
Club Honours: FLC '88
International Honours: E: B-3

A small, but combative midfield playmaker who signed on a two year contract to lend experience to Derby's new look midfield, having been released by Luton during the 1995 close season, he started as a first choice, before losing his place in October following the arrival of new players. Unable to get back into the side, David subsequently went on loan to Birmingham, and then on to Swindon, playing seven games in their promotion march.

Walsall (From apprentice on 22/7/80) FL 107+4/5 FLC 18/5 FAC 6/1 Others 1
Luton T (£150,000 on 6/12/84) FL 328+8/21 FLC 23/3 FAC 27/2 Others 8+1/1
Derby Co (Free on 11/8/95) FL 10+3/1 FLC 2
Birmingham C (Loaned on 24/11/95) FL 6 Others 1
Swindon T (Loaned on 21/3/96) FL 7/1

PREECE Roger
Born: Much Wenlock, 9 June 1969
Height: 5'8" Weight: 10.11

Roger, a tenacious and enthusiastic Chester midfielder, who beavers away endlessly for the team, will be remembered as one of last season's unluckiest players. Unfortunate to sustain an injury in the opening game, he was unable to get another opportunity, following a number of set backs, and can only hope for better luck this time round.

Wrexham (Free from Coventry C juniors on 15/8/86) FL 89+21/12 FLC 2+1 FAC 5 Others 8+1/1
Chester C (Free on 14/8/90) FL 165+5/4 FLC 10 FAC 8/1 Others 11

PREEDY Philip (Phil)
Born: Hereford, 20 November 1975
Height: 5'10" Weight: 10.8

Again limited to a handful of games for Hereford last season, Phil, now considered to be a left back, can perform equally well anywhere in a left-sided position. Is especially effective moving forward on the overlap, where his pace can take him past defenders to get the cross in.

Hereford U (From trainee on 13/7/94) FL 29+13/2 FLC 4 FAC 3 Others 1+1/1

PRESSMAN Kevin Paul
Born: Fareham, 6 November 1967
Height: 6'1" Weight: 14.2
International Honours: E: B-2; U21-1; Yth; Sch

Continuing his battle with Chris Woods for the Sheffield Wednesday goalkeeper's jersey, Kevin started last season in fine fettle, before a little dip in form, followed by injury, let in his rival. Regained his place, but another injury saw Woods again re-

instated. Still a fine goalkeeper, especially in one-to-one situations, and possessing a tremendous left foot kick, like most 'keepers he fancies his chances as a striker, having scored in the penalty shoot-out against Wolves in 1994-95. Came back towards the end of the campaign and played very well during difficult times for the club.

Sheffield Wed (From apprentice on 7/11/85) F/PL 158 FLC 25 FAC 8 Others 4
Stoke C (Loaned on 10/3/92) FL 4 Others 2

PRESTON Michael John
Born: Plymouth, 22 November 1977
Height: 5'7" Weight: 11.0

Given eight games, four of them from the bench, the young Torquay YTS winger showed enough promise down the right-hand side of the pitch in 1995-96 to convince the fans that he has a promising future ahead of him.

Torquay U (Trainee) FL 4+4

PRICE James Richard
Born: Preston, 1 February 1978
Height: 5'9" Weight: 11.0

Rochdale YTS defender who recovered from a broken leg to earn his league baptism in three games at left back last February. Unfortunately, he suffered yet another fracture in a reserve game shortly afterwards, but, nevertheless, is still considered to be a long-term acquisition.

Rochdale (Trainee) FL 3

PRIDMORE Lee Craig
Born: Rotherham, 23 April 1978
Height: 5'9" Weight: 10.7

A shock inclusion for the first round tie against Wrexham last season, Lee became the first Hull City player to make his club debut in the FA Cup for nearly 40 years. The nippy left back, also used as a sweeper in the junior ranks, had still to play in the league before being released at the end of his YTS period.

Hull C (Trainee) FAC 1

PRIEST Christopher (Chris)
Born: Leigh, 18 October 1973
Height: 5'10" Weight: 10.10

Producing some tremendous performances in Chester's midfield last season, Chris proved to have both skill and engine power. On top of that, he finished as the club's joint leading scorer, starting with a goal on the opening day, followed by another 12, four of them coming in successive games early in March.

Everton (From trainee on 1/6/92)
Chester C (Loaned on 9/9/94) FL 11/1 Others 2
Chester C (Free on 11/1/94) FL 49+3/13 FLC 3 FAC 1 Others 2

PRIMUS Linvoy Stephen
Born: Forest Gate, 14 September 1973
Height: 6'0" Weight: 14.0

A classy Barnet centre half destined for bigger things, Linvoy is quick, good in the air, and always a threat from set pieces. Missing just four league games throughout

197

last season, he impressed alongside Lee Howarth, scoring four goals for good measure.

Charlton Ath (From trainee on 14/8/92) FL 4 FLC 0+1 Others 0+1
Barnet (Free on 18/7/94) FL 81/4 FLC 5+1 FAC 4/1 Others 3

PRIOR Spencer Justin
Born: Southend, 22 April 1971
Height: 6'3" Weight: 12.10
Eventually becoming Norwich City's "Player of the Year", he made more senior appearances during last season than any other member of the side, finding favour with both managers. He even celebrated the 200th league game of his career with a powerful downward header from a corner to score against Reading, his only goal of the campaign. And, at a time when heads were down, his ability to attack the ball positively, both in the air and on the ground, proved him to be a formidable opponent for even the most talented of strikers. Is very mobile for a big man and has an excellent recovery rate.

Southend U (From trainee on 22/5/89) FL 135/3 FLC 5 FAC 5 Others 7/1
Norwich C (£200,000 on 24/6/93) P/FL 67+6/1 FLC 10+1/1 FAC 0+2 Others 2

PRITCHARD David Michael
Born: Wolverhampton, 27 May 1972
Height: 5'8" Weight: 11.4
Hard-tackling full back whose absence from Bristol Rovers' defence was sorely missed for a large chunk of 1995-96. A serious knee injury, sustained in November, resulted in surgery and he took no further part in Rovers' season. It is only to be hoped that David will resume his place once full fitness is restored and that his reliable defending and positive attacking play will feature once again.

Bristol Rov (£15,000 from Telford on 25/2/94) FL 66 FLC 6 FAC 4 Others 6

PROCTOR James Anthony
Born: Doncaster, 25 October 1976
Height: 5'8" Weight: 10.5
James joined Rochdale on trial early last season, having been a trainee at Bradford, and was quickly signed on after giving some outstanding appearances on the left wing for the reserves. Made his FL debut, coming on as substitute at Colchester, and played from the start in the following match, before being released in the summer.

Rochdale (Free from Bradford C juniors on 2/10/95) FL 1+2

PROKAS Richard
Born: Penrith, 22 January 1976
Height: 5'9" Weight: 11.4
Club Honours: Div 3 '95
Another product of the Carlisle youth squad, and one of several Cumbrians in the team, Richard missed much of last season with injury problems. Nevertheless, his quietly effective work as a defensive midfielder provided the platform for the team's more creative talents and at 20 he looks to have plenty of years ahead of him in the game.

Carlisle U (From trainee on 18/7/94) FL 54+5/1 FLC 3 FAC 4 Others 12+1

PRUDHOE Mark
Born: Washington, 8 November 1963
Height: 6'0" Weight: 13.0
Club Honours: GMVC '90; Div 4 '91
Goalkeeper with great shot-stopping skills who had a fine season for Stoke City after regaining and keeping first team spot last September. Prone to the occasional "howler", yet a firm favourite with supporters, Mark performed heroics around Easter time, first against Wolves and then Luton Town. His excellent form saw Ron Sinclair play just a couple of games and Carl Muggleton loaned out to Rotherham and Sheffield United.

Sunderland (From apprentice on 11/9/81) FL 7
Hartlepool U (Loaned on 4/11/83) FL 3
Birmingham C (£22,000 on 24/9/84) FL 1 FLC 4
Walsall (£22,000 on 27/2/86) FL 26 FLC 4 FAC 1
Doncaster Rov (Loaned on 11/12/86) FL 5
Grimsby T (Loaned on 26/3/87) FL 8
Hartlepool U (Loaned on 29/8/87) FL 13
Bristol C (Loaned on 6/11/87) FL 3 Others 2
Carlisle U (£10,000 on 11/12/87) FL 34 FLC 2
Darlington (£10,000 on 16/3/89) FL 146 FLC 8 FAC 9 Others 6
Stoke C (£120,000 on 24/6/93) FL 69 FLC 6 FAC 4 Others 37
Peterborough U (Loaned on 30/9/94) FL 6

Mark Prudhoe

PRUNIER William
Born: France, 14 August 1967
Height: 5'11" Weight: 12.7
International Honours: France: 1
Excellent central defender who possesses super ball skills, is cool and collective, and likes to play his way out of trouble. William's arrival at Manchester United on loan from Bordeaux last December, as a possible long-term replacement for Steve Bruce, showed much promise when the Frenchman gave polished performances in

successive PL games against Newcastle (as a sub), Queens Park Rangers and Tottenham. However, when Alex Ferguson offered him another month's trial, William wanted a longer-term contract and after much deliberation decided to return to the French first division.

Manchester U (Loaned from Bordeaux on 29/12/94) PL 2

PUGH David
Born: Liverpool, 19 September 1964
Height: 6'1" Weight: 13.0
An excellent season's work by the Bury captain who managed to score ten goals from his left wing position in 1995-96. An exciting attacking player, his enthusiasm is undoubted and his contribution to the team, whether in midfield or dropping back to play a deeper, more defensive role, is vitally important.

Chester C (£35,000 from Runcorn on 21/7/89) FL 168+11/23 FLC 13 FAC 11+1 Others 9
Bury (£22,500 on 3/8/94) FL 84/26 FLC 6 FAC 5 Others 8/2

PUGH Michael Sutherland
Born: Stockton, 27 March 1977
Height: 5'7" Weight: 10.5
Tenacious Darlington midfielder who progressed through the youth team to come off the bench during the home AWS game against Lincoln last November. A regular on the left flank for the reserves, he showed a penchant for scoring spectacular goals, prior to his release during the summer.

Darlington (From trainee on 5/7/95) Others 0+1

PURSE Darren John
Born: London, 14 February 1977
Height: 6'2" Weight: 12.8
Another young man who has progressed through Leyton Orient's ranks, Darren looks far more comfortable in the centre of defence, where he can take full advantage of his height, although he also appeared in the right back position last season. Continuing to show all the signs that he will fulfill his promise, he was confident enough to save a penalty at Torquay after Ron Fearon was sent off.

Leyton Orient (From trainee on 22/2/94) FL 48+7/3 FLC 2 FAC 1 Others 7+1/2

PUTTNAM David Paul
Born: Leicester, 3 February 1967
Height: 5'10" Weight: 11.9
Began last season at Lincoln, scoring in the opening two games, until losing his place in the side due to first a hamstring and then a hernia operation, before being transferred to Gillingham early in October. A skilful left-sided winger or midfielder, although most of his appearances came as a substitute, he scored the important winning goal against Exeter in April, a strike that kept the Gills in second place.

Leicester C (£8,000 from Leicester U on 9/2/89) FL 4+3 FLC 0+1
Lincoln C (£35,000 on 21/1/90) FL 160+17/21 FLC 13+1/1 FAC 4 Others 8+1
Gillingham (£50,000 on 6/10/95) FL 10+16/1 FAC 0+3 Others 1

QUASHIE Nigel Francis
Born: London, 20 July 1978
Height: 5'9" Weight: 11.0
International Honours: E: Yth

Young central midfielder, very good at getting forward, and very stylish when in possession of the ball, Nigel was the find of last season in the eyes of QPR supporters, making his league debut as a 17 year old against Manchester United at Old Trafford on 30 December and having an outstanding game. Plucked from the youth team after just a handful of reserve games, he handled the pressure really well and seemed to enjoy the FA Cup games, scoring his first QPR goal at Tranmere in the third round, followed by a superb strike against Chelsea in the fourth round. Unfortunately, he was struck down by illness at the end of March and missed the rest of the campaign.
Queens Park R (From trainee on 1/8/95) PL 11 Others 2/2

QUIGLEY Michael (Mike) Anthony
Born: Manchester, 2 October 1970
Height: 5'7" Weight: 9.13

As a free-transfer signing for Hull in the summer of 1995, having been released by Manchester City, he soon impressed his new Boothferry audience, before his season was cruelly stopped in its tracks when breaking his left fibula in City's first away game at Rotherham. Did not return until the end of February, then had to work hard to rediscover his form. Mike is intelligent, a gritty competitor, and mainly right-footed passer, who is likely to play a vital part of City's 1996-97 plans.
Manchester C (From trainee on 1/7/89) F/PL 3+9 Others 1
Wrexham (Loaned on 17/2/95) FL 4
Hull C (Free on 5/7/95) FL 9+4/1 FLC 1

QUINN James (Jimmy) Martin
Born: Belfast, 18 November 1959
Height: 6'0" Weight: 11.6
Club Honours: Div 2 '94
International Honours: NI: 46; B-1

Like Mick Gooding, he combines the roles of Reading first team regular and joint manager with success and great enthusiasm. Retaining his place in the Northern Ireland side, Jimmy ended 1995-96 as leading goalscorer for Royals' first and reserve teams, and even managed a second half appearance as emergency goalkeeper against WBA, keeping a clean sheet. Also scored two of the most memorable goals of recent years at Elm Park, against Sunderland and Wolves.
Swindon T (£10,000 from Oswestry on 31/12/81) FL 34+15/10 FLC 1+1 FAC 5+3/6 Others 1/2
Blackburn Rov (£32,000 on 15/8/84) FL 58+13/17 FLC 6+1/2 FAC 4/3 Others 2/1
Swindon T (£50,000 on 19/12/86) FL 61+3/30 FLC 6/8 FAC 5 Others 10+1/5

Leicester C (£210,000 on 20/6/88) FL 13+18/6 FLC 2+1 FAC 0+1 Others 0+1
Bradford C (Signed on 17/3/89) FL 35/14 FLC 2/1 Others 1
West Ham U (£320,000 on 30/12/89) FL 34+13/19 FLC 3/1 FAC 4+2/2 Others 1
Bournemouth (£40,000 on 5/8/91) FL 43/19 FLC 4/2 FAC 5/2 Others 2/1
Reading (£55,000 on 27/7/92) FL 139+19/68 FLC 11+3/11 FAC 9/5 Others 7+3/6

QUINN Stephen James (Jimmy)
Born: Coventry, 15 December 1974
Height: 6'1" Weight: 12.10
International Honours: NI: 1; B-1; U21-1; Yth

Young Blackpool striker who continued to sharpen up his goalscoring attributes last season, netting in five consecutive games during a purple patch in October and November. Also called up for Northern Ireland's full squad, having scored for the "B" side against the Norwegian Olympic XI. Pacy enough to rattle the best of defences.
Birmingham C (Trainee) FL 1+3
Blackpool (£25,000 on 5/7/93) FL 80+19/20 FLC 4+4/2 FAC 3+2/3 Others 3+3/2
Stockport Co (Loaned on 4/3/94) FL 0+1

Niall Quinn

QUINN Niall John
Born: Dublin, 6 October 1966
Height: 6'4" Weight: 13.10
Club Honours: FLC '87
International Honours: Ei: 60; B-1; U23-1; U21-5; Yth; Sch

The seasoned Manchester City striker, with clever shielding and ball control, had another good season in 1995-96, although starting as a substitute for the first three games. Although playing well, unfortunately, the goals dried up as his partnership with Uwe Rosler never really came to fruition, the lack of service from midfield having a lot to do with this. However, the "big man" certainly benefited from the skill and support of Georgiou Kinkladze and, at international level, continued to be a regular for the Republic of Ireland. His great attribute is still in receiving the ball from all directions, whether it be on the ground or in the air, and bringing it immediately under control.
Arsenal (From juniors on 30/11/83) FL 59+8/14 FLC 14+2/4 FAC 8+2/2 Others 0+1
Manchester C (£800,000 on 21/3/90) F/PL 183+20/66 FLC 20+2/7 FAC 13+3/4 Others 3/1

QUINN Philip
Born: Wallasey, 5 October 1978
Height: 6'0" Weight: 12.6

Striker. A first year YTS, Philip was given an early first team chance for Chester last October, spending the final 21 minutes of the Coca Cola home game against Spurs filling in for Leroy Chambers. The experience would have done him no harm.
Chester C (Trainee) FLC 0+1

QUINN Robert John
Born: Sidcup, 8 November 1976
Height: 5'11" Weight: 11.2

A Crystal Palace central defender who made his debut, along with Danny Boxall, in the final league match against Norwich in May, astonishingly, he was then selected by Dave Bassett for the play-off games, ahead of more experienced players. He did not let the side down. Indeed, he performed heroically in Palace's backs to the wall resistance under extreme pressure and it was a tragedy both for him and the team that their efforts should end in defeat in the last minute of extra time.
Crystal Palace (From trainee on 11/3/95) FL 1 Others 2+1

QUITONGO Jose Manuel
Born: Angola, 18 November 1974
Height: 5'8" Weight: 11.5

Fast and direct right winger from the African continent who joined Darlington on trial last September from Benfica, via the Swedish side, Norkoping. Made his debut at Barnet a day later, his only game for the club, before continuing his cosmopoltan travels to link up with Hamilton Academicals.
Darlington (Free from Benfica on 29/9/95) FL 1

PANINI

OFFICIAL LICENSEE

 **NUMBER 1 FOR FOOTBALL CARDS & STICKERS**

R

RADEBE Lucas
Born: Johannesburg, South Africa, 12 April 1969
Height: 6'0" Weight: 11.8
International Honours: South Africa: 19

After suffering some ten months being out injured, Leeds United's speedy South African defender, made a successful and victorious return in the African Cup with his country last season. On his return to Elland Road, he became a regular member of the side in a three-man central defence, where, although technically good on the ball, he sometimes appeared to struggle with the defensive duties of the system. Turned in a tremendous second half performance as a goalkeeper, following an injury to John Lukic against Middlesbrough, keeping a clean sheet in the process.
Leeds U (£250,000 from Kaizer Chiefs on 5/9/94) PL 19+6 FLC 1+3 FAC 4+2

RAE Alexander (Alex) Scott
Born: Glasgow, 30 September 1969
Height: 5'9" Weight: 11.8
International Honours: S: B-2; U21-8

Millwall's idea of a role model for a midfield footballer. His tireless energy, great ball control, and a devasting shot, winning him a further Scotland "B" cap against Sweden in 1995-96. Once again the Lions' leading goalscorer and penalty taker, he also took over the captaincy while Keith Stevens was out of action. Elected by his fellow professionals to the PFA award winning first division side. *Stop Press:* Signed for Sunderland in a £750,000 transfer deal.
Falkirk (Free from Bishopbriggs in 1987) SL 71+12/20 SLC 5/1 SC 2+1
Millwall (£100,000 on 20/8/90) FL 205+13/63 FLC 13+2/1 FAC 13/6 Others 10/1

Craig Ramage

RAMAGE Craig Darren
Born: Derby, 30 March 1970
Height: 5'9" Weight: 11.8
International Honours: E: U21-3

It was a season of two halves for this Watford midfield player, cum striker, who possesses outstanding skill and potential. Having started sluggishly, he was dropped for a time, before Graham Taylor restored him to the first team in his favoured position, just behind the front two. He then responded by tucking in his shirt and notching 15 goals, his best-ever total, putting him on top of the charts for the second consecutive season.
Derby Co (From trainee on 20/7/88) FL 33+9/4 FLC 6+1/2 FAC 3+1/1 Others 0+3
Wigan Ath (Loaned on 16/2/89) FL 10/2 Others 0+1
Watford (£90,000 on 21/2/94) FL 89+4/24 FLC 7/2 FAC 7

RAMMELL Andrew (Andy) Victor
Born: Nuneaton, 10 February 1967
Height: 6'0" Weight: 13.5

Signed in an exchange deal involving Dave Regis in February, Andy's strong front running was seen as the thing that had been missing from the Southend side, until a cartilage injury almost ended his season. A good player in the air and equally strong on the ground, he is a defender's nightmare, and his goal against his previous club, Barnsley, where he had scored only five times in 1995-96, was a most enjoyable moment for him.
Manchester U (£40,000 from Atherstone U on 26/9/89)
Barnsley (£100,000 on 14/9/90) FL 149+36/44 FLC 11+3/1 FAC 12+1/4 Others 8/1
Southend U (Signed on 22/2/96) FL 6+1/2

RAMSEY Paul Christopher
Born: Londonderry, 3 September 1962
Height: 5'11" Weight: 13.0
Club Honours: Div 3 '93; WC '92, '93
International Honours: NI: 14; Sch

On loan at Cardiff in 1994-95, Paul arrived at Torquay last November, via a spell with non-league, Telford, and quickly impressed with his midfield skills. As manager, Eddie May's first signing, the former Northern Ireland international was felt to be the perfect foil for Charlie Oatway, until a broken toe put him out of action at a vital stage of the season. Was released during the summer clear out.
Leicester C (From apprentice on 11/4/80) FL 278+12/13 FLC 19/1 FAC 9+1/1 Others 2+1
Cardiff C (£100,000 on 23/8/91) FL 69/7 FLC 2 FAC 2 Others 7/1
St Johnstone (Signed on 8/10/93) SL 31+2 SLC 5 SC 5 Others 1+1/1 (Freed during 1995 close season)
Cardiff C (Loaned on 4/11/94) FL 11 FAC 1 Others 3
Torquay U (Free from Telford U on 17/11/95) FL 18

RANDALL Adrian John
Born: Amesbury, 10 November 1968
Height: 5'11" Weight: 12.4
Club Honours: Div 4 '92
International Honours: E: Yth

The form which had earned Adrian several "Player of the Year" awards in 1994-95 was

rarely seen in the early stages of last season, so much so that he even lost his Burnley place for a spell. Nevertheless, the departure for York, in December, of a player whose creative skills could be Premiership standard when seen at their best, came as a shock to most Clarets' supporters. Unfortunately, the strong, attacking midfielder was troubled by both injury and illness during his first four months at Bootham Crescent.
Bournemouth (From apprentice on 2/9/86) FL 3 Others 1+2
Aldershot (Signed on 15/9/88) FL 102+5/12 FLC 3 FAC 11/3 Others 10/2
Burnley (£40,000 on 12/12/91) FL 105+20/8 FLC 6/1 FAC 8+3 Others 3
York C (£140,000 on 28/12/95) FL 13+3

RANKINE Simon Mark
Born: Doncaster, 30 September 1969
Height: 5'10" Weight: 12.3

Having eventually got into Wolves' midfield in 1994-95, he missed the first two games of 1995-96, then found himself as right back again. Harshly sent off at Port Vale for a handball offence, Mark was still involved in 34 of the next 35 games, up until the FA Cup exit at the hands of Spurs. A hard-working player and a fetcher and carrier for others, he came back for the last eight matches.
Doncaster Rov (From trainee on 4/7/88) FL 160+4/20 FLC 8+1/1 FAC 8/2 Others 14/2
Wolverhampton W (£70,000 on 31/1/92) FL 112+20/1 FLC 9+1 FAC 14+2 Others 7+2

Mark Rankine

RATCLIFFE Simon
Born: Urmston, 8 February 1967
Height: 5'11" Weight: 11.9
Club Honours: Div 3 '92
International Honours: E: Yth; Sch

Yet another of Gillingham's many new players, he signed from Brentford prior to the start of last season, Simon is a midfielder who plays the simple game and has a strong finish with his right foot. Captaining the side in the absence of Dave Martin, and missing only five league games in what was another steady season for him, he achieved what he had failed to do in 1994-95 – win promotion.

Manchester U (From apprentice on 13/2/85)
Norwich C (£40,000 on 16/6/87) FL 6+3 FLC 2
Brentford (£100,000 on 13/1/89) FL 197+17/14 FLC 13+3 FAC 9+1 Others 26+2/2
Gillingham (Free on 4/8/95) FL 41/3 FLC 2 FAC 3/1

RATTLE Jonathan (Jon) Paul
Born: Melton, 22 July 1976
Height: 5'9" Weight: 12.6

Left-footed Cambridge United utility player who had a run-in the side last season but struggled to match his early promise. With a view to getting match fit for the new season, Jon was spending the summer playing in Australia.

Cambridge U (From trainee on 24/5/94) FL 13+2 FLC 1 FAC 1 Others 1

RATTRAY Kevin Winston
Born: Tottenham, 6 October 1968
Height: 5'10" Weight: 11.11
Club Honours: FAT '95

A never-say-die midfielder, who joined Gillingham from non-league, Woking, in June 1995, he proved to have bundles of enthusiasm and energy and a liking to get forward for those half chances in the area. And, having been a member of the Woking squad that won the FA Trophy in 1995, promotion to the second division with his new club was a further bonus.

Gillingham (£5,000 from Woking on 23/6/95) FL 18+8/3 FLC 1 FAC 2 Others 2

RAVEN Paul Duncan
Born: Salisbury, 28 July 1970
Height: 6'1" Weight: 12.1
International Honours: E: Sch

Paul had a marvellous season in WBA's defence, performing admirably throughout the 1995-96 campaign. Strong in the air, resilient on the ground, he was the king-pin of the back division, where he played alongside Daryl Burgess and Paul Mardon, finding time to get forward at set pieces to both score and lay on some important goals. He was voted runner up in "Player of the Year" awards.

Doncaster Rov (From juniors on 6/6/88) FL 52/4 FLC 2 FAC 5 Others 2
West Bromwich A (£100,000 on 23/3/89) FL 175+4/13 FLC 11 FAC 7/3 Others 15/1
Doncaster Rov (Loaned on 27/11/91) FL 7

RAVENSCROFT Craig Anthony
Born: Hammersmith, 20 December 1974
Height: 5'6" Weight: 9.7

Small, with plenty of pace, in the past, Craig has been deployed by Brentford down the middle, but would be better recognised as a wingman. Although little used for the first team in 1995-96, he was an ever present for the reserves, before being released during the summer.

Brentford (From trainee on 27/7/93) FL 6+3/1 Others 1+2

RAWLINSON Mark David
Born: Bolton, 9 June 1975
Height: 5'10" Weight: 11.0

After joining Bournemouth from Manchester United in the summer of 1995, Mark had limited opportunities to make his mark in the first team, normally playing in the centre of midfield. A good tackler and man-to-man marker, he started five games and made 17 substitute appearances. Is still only 20, with a bright future ahead.

Manchester U (From trainee on 5/7/93)
Bournemouth (Free on 1/7/95) FL 3+16 FLC 0+1 FAC 1 Others 1

RAYNOR Paul James
Born: Nottingham, 29 April 1966
Height: 6'0" Weight: 12.11
Club Honours: WC '89, '91

Experienced midfield player who rejoined Cambridge United last September in a straight swap for Dean Barrick, having been unable to command a regular place in the Preston starting line up. Adding width and experience to a young team, until an early end to his season for knee surgery, he proved skilful with either foot, and was always guaranteed to give 100 per cent.

Nottingham F (From apprentice on 2/4/84) FL 3 FLC 1
Bristol Rov (Loaned on 28/3/85) FL 7+1
Huddersfield T (Free on 15/8/85) FL 38+12/9 FLC 3 FAC 2+1 Others 1
Swansea C (Free on 27/3/87) FL 170+21/27 FLC 11+1/3 FAC 8+1/1 Others 15+1/3
Wrexham (Loaned on 17/10/88) FL 6
Cambridge U (Free on 10/3/92) FL 46+3/2 FLC 5 FAC 1 Others 2+1/1
Preston NE (£36,000 on 23/7/93) FL 72+8/9 FLC 4+1 FAC 7/1 Others 10/2
Cambridge U (Signed on 12/9/95) FL 35/3 FAC 1

REA Simon
Born: Coventry, 20 September 1976
Height: 6'1" Weight: 13.0

A young Birmingham defender who was given a couple of first team opportunities from the subs' bench in 1995-96, after performing impressively in the reserve side, Simon showed up well during the brief time he was on the pitch. Having also had a spell on loan at non-league, Kettering, last season, expect him to be given further opportunities this season.

Birmingham C (From trainee on 27/1/95) FL 0+1 Others 1+1

READ Paul Colin
Born: Harlow, 25 September 1973
Height: 5'11" Weight: 12.6
International Honours: E: Sch

Striker. Paul joined Southend on loan from Arsenal last October in an attempt to solve a goalscoring crisis, but a serious ankle injury in his first game severely hampered his chances of making the move permanent. A mobile and fast player, he scored at Watford in a 2-2 draw, but was unable to convince Ronnie Whelan to pay the £500,000 that the Gunners wanted.

Arsenal (From trainee on 11/10/91)
Leyton Orient (Loaned on 10/3/95) FL 11 Others 1
Southend U (Loaned on 6/10/95) FL 3+1/1 Others 1

READY Karl
Born: Neath, 14 August 1972
Height: 6'1" Weight: 12.2
International Honours: W: B-2; U21-5; Sch

Solid QPR centre back who is very good in the air. Started last season as a substitute, but was in the starting line up at Leeds as Ray Wilkins changed the team formation, before moving to right back in place of the injured David Bardsley, and scoring only his second ever goal, in the Coca Cola Cup versus Oxford, to keep Rangers in the game. Unlucky to be sent off at West Ham in November, after his suspension he found himself back on the bench, until being brought into the side in March (to replace the injured Danny Maddix) for three games. He then appeared at right back against West Ham and scored the first goal in a 3-0 win in the last home game of the season.

Queens Park R (From trainee on 13/8/90) F/PL 49+12/3 FLC 4+2/1 FAC 1

REDDISH Shane
Born: Bolsover, 5 May 1971
Height: 5'10" Weight: 11.10

Attacking right back who had a disappointing time at Hartlepool in 1995-96. His season was ruined by a sequence of injuries, which culminated in him being hospitalised for a hernia operation early in the New Year and somewhat bitter when released by the club in March, feeling he had not been given the chance to prove himself. Not too disheartened, though, he lost no time in setting up a move to Norwegian club, Harstad.

Mansfield T (From trainee on 25/7/89)
Doncaster Rov (Free on 7/2/90) FL 51+9/3 FLC 1 FAC 2 Others 2
Carlisle U (Free on 7/7/93) FL 35+2/1 FLC 3 FAC 3+1 Others 7+2
Chesterfield (Loaned on 30/9/94) FL 2+1
Hartlepool U (Free on 18/11/94) FL 41+2 FLC 1

REDFEARN Neil David
Born: Dewsbury, 20 June 1965
Height: 5'10" Weight: 12.8
Club Honours: Div 2 '91

Day in day out one of the games real pro's, Neil had another hard-working season in 1995-96 at the heart of Barnsley's midfield. Again he netted more than his fair share of goals, mostly from long-range drives, scoring winners against Millwall, Wolves, and Luton, among others. It is difficult to imagine him out of the side for a long period.

Bolton W (Free from Nottingham F juniors on 23/6/82) FL 35/1 FLC 2 FAC 4
Lincoln C (£8,250 on 23/3/84) FL 96+4/13 FLC 4 FAC 3/1 Others 7
Doncaster Rov (Signed on 22/8/86) FL 46/14 FLC 2 FAC 3/1 Others 2
Crystal Palace (£100,000 on 31/7/87) FL 57/10 FLC 6 FAC 1 Others 1
Watford (£150,000 on 21/11/88) FL 22+2/3 FLC 1 FAC 6/3 Others 5/1
Oldham Ath (£150,000 on 12/1/90) FL 56+6/16 FLC 3/1 FAC 7+1/3 Others 1
Barnsley (£150,000 on 5/9/91) FL 209+3/44 FLC 14/3 FAC 12/3 Others 5

Jamie Redknapp

REDKNAPP Jamie Frank
Born: Barton on Sea, 25 June 1973
Height: 6'0" Weight: 12.0
Club Honours: FLC '95
International Honours: E: 5; B-1; U21-18;
Yth; Sch

In the first three months of 1995-96, Jamie was playing to the peak of his ability in Liverpool's midfield, displaying super control and passing skills, scoring outstanding goals against Vladikavkaz in the UEFA Cup and Blackburn Rovers, and seemed a certainty to establish himself in the England team until a serious injury, suffered in the early stages of the England v Switzerland match in November, totally disrupted his season. By the time he was fit again in February, Liverpool were in top gear and manager, Roy Evans, chose not to disturb a winning team. However, after several weeks on the bench he was restored to first team duty for the FA Cup semi final against Aston Villa and retained his place to the end of the season, without ever recapturing his early form. Came back for England in Euro '96, coming on as a substitute in the Scotland game, and looks to make giant strides at international level. Is the son of West Ham's manager, Harry, who also played for the club as well as appearing for Bournemouth and Brentford.
Bournemouth (From trainee on 27/6/90) FL 6+7 FLC 3 FAC 3 Others 2
Liverpool (£350,000 on 15/1/91) F/PL 116+18/13 FLC 21/3 FAC 13+1/1 Others 9+1/1

REDMILE Matthew Ian
Born: Nottingham, 12 November 1976
Height: 6'3" Weight: 12.0

A former trainee with Notts County who signed professional forms in the summer of 1995, the young central defender made his first team bow in the Auto Windscreen Shield game at Chesterfield in October, which remained his sole appearance of last season. Tall and commanding, County expect him to develop further in 1996-97.
Notts Co (From trainee on 4/7/95) Others 1

REDMOND Stephen (Steve)
Born: Liverpool, 2 November 1967
Height: 5'11" Weight: 12.13
Club Honours: FAYC '86
International Honours: E: U21-14; Yth

The experienced former Manchester City player continued to pass on his knowledge to Oldham's youngsters in 1995-96, missing very few games and proving invaluable in the centre of defence. Starting alongside Richard Jobson, following the latter's move to Leeds, Richard Graham came in and Steve was instrumental in helping him find his feet as the pair gradually forged a reliable partnership. A great organiser, who reads the game well and is comfortable on the ball, the Latics would find it difficult managing without him.
Manchester C (From apprentice on 3/12/84) FL 231+4/7 FLC 24 FAC 17 Others 11
Oldham Ath (£300,000 on 10/7/92) P/FL 139+8/2 FLC 13 FAC 7+2 Others 1+1

REECE Andrew (Andy) John
Born: Shrewsbury, 5 September 1962
Height: 5'11" Weight: 12.0
Club Honours: Div 3 '90

A battling midfielder who preferred a central role, Andy was a regular for Hereford last season before leaving to join the West Midlands Police Force in October. Another 100 per center, his speciality was most definitely at free kicks.
Bristol Rov (Signed from Dudley T on 11/8/87) FL 230+9/17 FLC 11+1 FAC 10+2/3 Others 21/3
Walsall (Loaned on 20/11/92) FL 9/1 Others 3
Walsall (Loaned on 12/8/93) FL 6 FLC 2
Hereford U (Signed on 5/11/93) FL 69+2/5 FLC 5/1 FAC 4 Others 6/2

REECE Paul John
Born: Nottingham, 16 July 1968
Height: 5'10" Weight: 12.7
Club Honours: AIC '95

Signed from Notts County prior to the start of 1995-96, as a deputy to Stuart Naylor, Paul was called upon just once by WBA manager, Alan Buckley, spending most of his time languishing in the reserves, who finished bottom of the Pontins League division one. An alert and courageous goalkeeper, he later found himself out in the cold following the acquisition of the veteran, Nigel Spink. Had a spell on loan at non-league, Ilkeston, in March.
Stoke C (From apprentice on 18/7/86) FL 2 (Free to Kettering T during 1987 close season)
Grimsby T (£10,000 on 18/7/88) FL 54 FLC 3 FAC 5 Others 4
Doncaster Rov (Free on 25/9/92) FL 1
Oxford U (Free on 2/10/92) FL 39 FLC 3 FAC 2 Others 1
Notts Co (Free on 2/8/94) FL 11 FLC 1 Others 2+1
West Bromwich A (Free on 11/8/95) FL 1

REED Ian Paul
Born: Lichfield, 4 September 1975
Height: 5'9" Weight: 10.10

Young Shrewsbury midfielder who is on the verge of establishing a first team place. Displayed maturity beyond his years with a fine performance in the Auto Windscreens regional final in 1995-96, scoring two early season goals with fine shots. Was quite a regular on the bench.
Shrewsbury T (From trainee on 4/7/94) FL 10+5/2 FLC 2 FAC 0+1 Others 1

REED John Paul
Born: Rotherham, 27 August 1972
Height: 5'10" Weight: 10.11

The Sheffield United midfielder spent most of 1995-96 recovering from his injury of the previous season, only returning to the first team squad at the end of the campaign and making two subs' appearances. A right-sided player who gets forward well to provide accurate crosses to the front men, John also has good ball skills.
Sheffield U (From trainee on 3/7/90) FL 11+4/2 FLC 1 Others 1/1
Scarborough (Loaned on 10/1/91) FL 14/6
Scarborough (Loaned on 26/9/91) FL 5+1 FLC 1
Darlington (Loaned on 19/3/93) FL 8+2/2
Mansfield T (Loaned on 23/9/93) FL 12+1/2 FAC 1 Others 3/2

REES Anthony (Tony) Andrew
Born: Merthyr Tydfil, 1 August 1964
Height: 5'9" Weight: 11.13
Club Honours: FAYC '80
International Honours: W: 1; B-1; U21-1; Yth; Sch

Striker. Alan Buckley's first signing for WBA (in 1994), Tony struggled throughout 1995-96 to get regular first team football, appearing in only a handful of senior matches owing to the form of Bob Taylor and Andy Hunt. He received one or two niggling knee and ankle injuries which didn't help matters, but was mainly confined to the reserves, prior to being released in the summer.
Aston Villa (From apprentice on 1/8/82)
Birmingham C (Free on 1/7/83) FL 75+20/12 FLC 7+1/2 FAC 5/2 Others 1+2
Peterborough U (Loaned on 1/10/85) FLC 5/2
Shrewsbury T (Loaned on 1/3/86) FL 1+1
Barnsley (Signed on 1/3/88) FL 27+4/3 FLC 2 FAC 0+1 Others 1
Grimsby T (Signed on 17/8/89) FL 124+17/33 FLC 11+2/1 FAC 8+1 Others 5/3
West Bromwich A (£30,000 on 25/11/94) FL 11+12/2 FLC 0+2 FAC 2 Others 2+1/1

REES Jason Mark
Born: Aberdare, 22 December 1969
Height: 5'5" Weight: 10.2
International Honours: W: 1; U21-3; B-1; Yth; Sch

Started last season in Portsmouth's midfield, scoring on the opening day at home to Southend, before the arrival of Martin Allen relegated him to the subs' bench for the remainder of the campaign. A tenacious, hard-working ball winner, Jason will not want to settle for anything less than first team football.
Luton T (From trainee on 1/7/88) FL 59+23 FLC 3+2 FAC 2+1 Others 5+1/2
Mansfield T (Loaned on 23/12/93) FL 15/1 Others 1
Portsmouth (Free on 18/7/94) FL 29+11/2 FLC 2+1 FAC 0+1

REEVES Alan
Born: Birkenhead, 19 November 1967
Height: 6'0" Weight: 12.0

A thoroughly committed Wimbledon centre back, who came to the club as an immediate replacement for John Scales in the autumn of 1994, the signing and return to fitness of other defenders meant that he had to fight hard for his place in 1995-96. Suffered the odd injury earlier in the season, but, following a spectacular own goal in the match against Aston Villa in February, he was out until the final three games. Good in the air, with sound distribution, and a strong tackler, he will not give his place up easily in 1996-97.

Norwich C (Signed from Heswall on 20/9/88)
Gillingham (Loaned on 9/2/89) FL 18
Chester C (£10,000 on 18/8/89) FL 31+9/2 FLC 1+1 FAC 3 Others 3
Rochdale (Free on 2/7/91) FL 119+2/9 FLC 12/1 FAC 6 Others 5
Wimbledon (£300,000 on 6/9/94) PL 52+3/4 FLC 1 FAC 8

REEVES David Edward
Born: Birkenhead, 19 November 1967
Height: 6'0" Weight: 11.7
Club Honours: Div 3 '95

Once again Carlisle's record signing finished as the club's top scorer in 1995-96. His hat trick against Burnley in the AWS was the first by any Carlisle player for seven years and the first at Brunton Park in a decade. A wholehearted player with an exceptional workrate, he performed in similar vein to last term and, as team captain, continued to lead by example.

Sheffield Wed (Free from Heswall on 6/8/88) FL 8+9/2 FLC 1+1/1 FAC 1+1 Others 0+1
Scunthorpe U (Loaned on 17/12/86) FL 3+1/2
Scunthorpe U (Loaned on 1/10/87) FL 6/4
Burnley (Loaned on 20/11/87) FL 16/8 Others 2/1
Bolton W (£80,000 on 17/8/89) FL 111+23/29 FLC 14+1/1 FAC 8+5/5 Others 9+2/7
Notts Co (£80,000 on 25/3/93) FL 9+4/2 FLC 1+1
Carlisle U (Signed on 1/10/93) FL 119/45 FLC 6/4 FAC 9/4 Others 23/7

David Reeves

Cyrille Regis

REGIS Cyrille
Born: French Guyana, 9 February 1958
Height: 6'0" Weight: 13.7
Club Honours: FAC '87
International Honours: E: 5; B-3; U21-6

The former England centre forward soon became a firm favourite with the Chester fans after signing from Wycombe, prior to 1995-96 getting underway. A shining example to the younger players, Cyrille led the line to good effect, scoring seven goals in the process, before missing the last month due to injury.

West Bromwich A (£5,000 from Hayes on 1/5/77) FL 233+4/82 FLC 27+1/16 FAC 25/10 Others 10/4
Coventry C (£250,000 on 11/10/84) FL 231+7/47 FLC 24/12 FAC 15+1/3 Others 4
Aston Villa (Free on 2/7/91) F/PL 46+6/12 FLC 3+1 FAC 5+2
Wolverhampton W (Free on 3/8/93) FL 8+11/2 FAC 1+2 Others 1
Wycombe W (Free on 12/8/94) FL 30+5/9 FLC 2/1 FAC 1
Chester C (Free on 2/8/95) FL 29/7 FLC 3 FAC 1

REGIS David (Dave)
Born: Paddington, 3 March 1964
Height: 6'1" Weight: 13.8
Club Honours: Div 2 '93

Despite transferring to Barnsley last February, in an exchange deal involving Andy Rammell, Dave still finished the campaign as Southend's leading scorer with nine goals. However, with the two Andys, Payton and Liddell, in excellent form he was forced to sit out most of his time on the subs' bench, although when called upon, his strong running and aerial strength often gave the side a different dimension.

Notts Co (£25,000 from Barnet on 28/9/90) FL 31+15/15 FLC 0+2 Others 6/2
Plymouth Arg (£200,000 on 7/11/91) FL 28+3/4 FLC 2/3 FAC 1

Bournemouth (Loaned on 13/8/92) FL 6/2
Stoke C (£100,000 on 23/10/92) FL 49+14/15 FLC 2/1 FAC 4+1/2 Others 7+1/2
Birmingham C (£200,00 on 1/8/94) FL 4+2/2 FLC 1
Southend U (Signed on 16/9/94) FL 34+4/9 FLC 1 FAC 1 Others 1+2/1
Barnsley (Signed on 21/2/96) FL 4+8/1

REID Nicholas (Nicky) Scott
Born: Davyhulme, 30 October 1960
Height: 5'10" Weight: 12.5
International Honours: E: U21-6

An inspired signing by manager, Stan Ternent, the 35 year old joined Bury last December, having been playing for non-league Witton Albion, after being released by Woking. Relishing the chance of returning to the Football League, Nicky made the left back spot his own in the closing two months of the season, his passing skill a revelation.

Manchester C (From apprentice on 4/11/78) FL 211+6/2 FLC 20 FAC 17 Others 8 (Signed for Seattle Sounders on 9/5/82. Transferred back on 24/9/82)
Blackburn Rov (Free on 10/7/87) FL 160+14/9 FLC 13 FAC 6+2 Others 13+1/1
Bristol C (Loaned on 17/9/92) FL 3+1 Others 1
West Bromwich A (Free on 7/11/92) FL 13+7 FAC 2+1 Others 2+1/1
Wycombe W (Free on 4/3/94) FL 6+2 FAC 0+1 Others 5 (Free to Woking during 1995 close season)
Bury (Free from Witton A on 15/12/95) FL 13+5

REID Paul Robert
Born: Oldbury, 19 January 1968
Height: 5'9" Weight: 10.8

After missing out on the play-off run-in at the end of 1994-95 due to injury, Paul found it difficult to re-establish himself at Huddersfield last season. Generally at home on the wing, he found himself being asked to play a more central midfield role when selected, where he performed well with his hard running and tackling.

Leicester C (From apprentice on 9/1/86) FL 140+22/21 FLC 13/4 FAC 5+1 Others 6+2
Bradford C (Loaned on 19/3/92) FL 7
Bradford C (£25,000 on 27/7/92) FL 80+2/15 FLC 3/2 FAC 3 Others 5/1
Huddersfield T (Signed on 20/5/94) FL 50+5/6 FLC 5/1 FAC 4 Others 1

REID Shaun
Born: Huyton, 13 October 1965
Height: 5'8" Weight: 11.10

A 1995 close-season signing from Rochdale, tough-tackling midfielder, Shaun, brother of Peter, experienced a frustrating first season at Bury. He was dismissed in only his second outing for the club and then, after establishing himself in the side, suffered a calf strain in December and was replaced by Nick Daws for the remainder of the campaign.

Rochdale (From apprentice on 20/9/83) FL 126+7/4 FLC 10/2 FAC 5/1 Others 11
Preston NE (Loaned on 12/12/85) FL 3
York C (£32,500 on 23/12/88) FL 104+2/7 FLC 7 FAC 4 Others 5/1
Rochdale (Free on 16/8/92) FL 106+1/10 FLC 8 FAC 5/1 Others 8+1/2
Bury (£25,000 on 5/7/95) FL 20+1 FLC 5 FAC 1 Others 2

REINELT Robert (Robbie) Squire
Born: Loughton, 11 March 1974
Height: 5'10" Weight: 11.13
The young Colchester striker took his chance eagerly following Steve Whitton's injury last season, with five goals in his first six games, before himself getting injured and missing several months action. Returned with a vital winner against Rochdale and formed an exciting partnership with Scott McGleish.
Aldershot (Trainee) FL 3+2
Gillingham (Free from Wivenhoe T on 19/3/93) FL 34+18/5 FLC 3/1 FAC 5+2/2 Others 5
Colchester U (Signed on 22/3/95) FL 14+13/7 FLC 0+1 Others 3/1

RENNIE David
Born: Edinburgh, 29 August 1964
Height: 6'0" Weight: 12.0
International Honours: S: Yth;
Coventry central defender who had an achilles tendon injury which kept him out of the squad for most of 1995-96. Despite his undoubted strengths, excellent timing, being good in the air, and tigerish in the tackle, he was unfortunate to be playing in central defence during the blackest spell of the club's season in October and November. Recalled for the crucial home game with QPR, he injured an ankle and missed the rest of the season, prior to being released during the summer.
Leicester C (From apprentice on 18/5/82) FL 21/1 FLC 2
Leeds U (£50,000 on 17/1/86) FL 95+6/5 FLC 7 FAC 7/1 Others 4/1
Bristol C (£175,000 on 31/7/89) FL 101+3/8 FLC 8 FAC 9 Others 5
Birmingham C (£120,000 on 20/2/92) FL 32+3/4 FLC 1 Others 1
Coventry C (£100,000 on 11/3/93) PL 80+2/3 FLC 6 FAC 3+1

RICE Gary James
Born: Zambia, 25 September 1975
Height: 5'9" Weight: 11.6
Left-footed defender. Given a free transfer at the end of 1994-95, due to Exeter's dire financial straits, he was re-signed after Peter Fox took over as the manager. Was a regular until the arrival of Darren Hughes, but still has time on his side to make a big impact in the team. Came up through the youth ranks.
Exeter C (From trainee on 7/7/94) FL 22+7 FLC 3 Others 2

RICHARDS David Simon
Born: Birmingham, 12 December 1976
Height: 6'1" Weight: 12.7
After doing well at reserve and youth level, the young Walsall forward came off the bench to make his first team debut against Wycombe in the AWS competition last November. Following that, he had a spell on loan at Leicester United in January, prior to being released at the end of the season.
Walsall (From trainee on 24/4/95) Others 0+1

RICHARDS Dean Ivor
Born: Bradford, 9 June 1974
Height: 6'2" Weight: 13.5
International Honours: E: U21-4
On loan from Bradford the previous season, the classy central defender captained the

England U21 side three times during the summer, eventually signing for a potential £1.85m, easily a Wolves' club record. Did well in the first 17 games, apart from a spectacular own goal at Port Vale, until a fractured cheekbone checked his progress. Was outstanding at Tottenham, but his car hit a patch of black ice and smashed into a lamp post on the way home, causing a lingering knee injury. Missed six games and still did not look up to it at Millwall, being rested, before coming back for the last 13 matches, although not being as sharp as he would have liked. Had earlier been elected by his fellow professionals to the PFA award winning first division side.
Bradford C (From trainee on 10/7/92) FL 82+4/4 FLC 7/1 FAC 4/1 Others 3+2
Wolverhampton W (£1,850,000 on 25/3/95) FL 46+1/3 FLC 5 FAC 2 Others 2

Dean Richards

RICHARDS Tony Spencer
Born: Newham, 17 September 1973
Height: 6'0" Weight: 13.1
The bustling Cambridge United forward made an impressive start to 1995-96, having been signed from Sudbury Town during the summer, until suffering a collarbone injury in mid-season. Returned to first team action in the latter part of the campaign to replace Carlo Corazzin.
West Ham U (From trainee on 14/8/92. Free to Hong Kong R during 1993 close season)
Cambridge U (Signed from Sudbury T on 10/8/95) FL 15+4/1 Others 2

RICHARDSON Barry
Born: Wallsend, 5 August 1969
Height: 6'1" Weight: 12.1
Experienced goalkeeper who was John Beck's first signing for Lincoln last October, after being relegated to second choice at Preston behind John Vaughan. An excellent shot stopper, he saved City on numerous occasions, and was extremely popular with

the fans who voted him runner up in the club's "Player of the Season" award.
Sunderland (From trainee on 20/5/88)
Scarborough (Free on 21/3/89)
Scarborough (Free from Seaham Red Star on 3/8/89) FL 30 FLC 1 Others 1
Stockport Co (Free on 16/8/91)
Northampton T (Free on 10/9/91) FL 96 FLC 4 FAC 5 Others 8
Preston NE (£20,000 on 25/7/94) FL 20 FLC 2 FAC 3 Others 2
Lincoln C (£20,000 on 20/10/95) FL 34 FAC 1

RICHARDSON Dominic Kevin
Born: Plymouth, 19 March 1978
Height: 5'11" Weight: 11.6
Lively Plymouth centre forward. A product of the youth scheme, and still a trainee, Dominic scored plenty of goals at youth and reserve level, before being introduced to the first team as a substitute against Peterborough in the Auto Windscreen competition last season. One to look out for.
Plymouth Arg (Trainee) Others 0+2

RICHARDSON Ian George
Born: Bolton, 22 October 1970
Height: 5'10" Weight: 11.1
International Honours: E: SP-1
Another Birmingham signing from non-league football last season, Ian featured spasmodically in midfield early on and impressed with his battling qualities, especially during the Coca Cola Cup run. However, with opportunities few and far between at St Andrews, he was loaned to Notts County in January, a move that would later become permanent, and went straight into the team. Makes good use of the ball when in possession.
Birmingham C (Free from Dagenham & Redbridge on 23/8/95) FL 3+4 FLC 3+1 FAC 2 Others 1+2
Notts Co (£200,000 on 19/1/96) FL 15 Others 3

RICHARDSON Jonathan (Jon) Derek
Born: Nottingham, 29 August 1975
Height: 6'0" Weight: 12.0
Came on in leaps and bounds for Exeter last season, which alerted Crystal Palace, who invited him for a trial. Jon was magnificent in defence and was no doubt aided by the experience of Noel Blake and Mark Came in the centre of defence. Good in the air, he certainly has no lack of pace on the ground.
Exeter C (From trainee on 7/7/94) FL 85+3/2 FLC 3/1 FAC 3 Others 5

RICHARDSON Kevin
Born: Newcastle, 4 December 1962
Height: 5'7" Weight: 11.7
Club Honours: FAC '84; CS '84, '86; Div 1 '85, '89; ECWC '85; FLC '94
International Honours: E: 1
Covered miles in the Coventry midfield during last season and never let the side down. His ball-winning abilities were still excellent and he retained a high level of fitness. He also created a number of good goals with his delicate chips behind the defence, most notably Noel Whelan's winner against Chelsea. Although towards the end of a long, hard campaign there were a few tell-tale signs that he might have lost a

little pace, his workrate was as intense as ever. Always makes himself available at set pieces.

Everton (From apprentice on 8/12/80) FL 95+14/16 FLC 10+3/3 FAC 13/1 Others 7+2
Watford (£225,000 on 4/9/86) FL 39/2 FLC 3 FAC 7 Others 1
Arsenal (£200,000 on 26/8/87) FL 88+8/5 FLC 13+3/2 FAC 9/1 Others 3 (£750,000 to Real Sociedad on 1/7/90)
Aston Villa (£450,000 on 6/8/91) F/PL 142+1/13 FLC 15/3 FAC 12 Others 10
Coventry C (£300,000 on 16/2/95) PL 51 FLC 4/1 FAC 3

RICHARDSON Lee James
Born: Halifax, 12 March 1969
Height: 5'11" Weight: 11.0

What can be said about Lee that has not already been chronicled elsewhere! Voted Oldham's "Player of the Year" last season by the fans, he then picked up the press' award of "First Division Player of the Season", even though he had missed a fair chunk of the campaign due to a groin injury. Playing with great flair and trickery, and possessing a shot like a cruise missile, the Latics' midfielder was a joy to watch.

Halifax T (From trainee on 6/7/87) FL 43+13/2 FLC 4 FAC 4+2 Others 6
Watford (£175,000 on 9/2/89) FL 40+1/1 FLC 1+1 FAC 1
Blackburn Rov (£250,000 on 15/8/90) FL 50+12/3 FLC 1 Others 2+2
Aberdeen (Signed on 16/9/92) SL 59+5/6 SLC 2/1 SC 8/2 Others 3/1
Oldham Ath (£300,000 on 12/8/94) FL 55+2/17 FLC 2/1 FAC 2 Others 4

RICHARDSON Neil Thomas
Born: Sunderland, 3 March 1968
Height: 6'0" Weight: 13.9
Club Honours: AMC '96

At the start of last season Neil was not considered to be a Rotherham first team regular, but when he came into the side in early December he went on to be one of the main successes of the campaign, his versatility enabling him to fulfil more than one role. Considered to be the most accurate passer of a ball in the club, he was able to show that from the heart of the defence, although he also played in midfield. He also took over the mantle of penalty taker and cooly displayed the reason for him being known as "Mr Reliable". Was a member of the side that beat Shrewsbury 2-1 to win the AWS final at Wembley.

Rotherham U (Signed from Brandon U on 18/8/89) FL 117+10/6 FLC 10+1 FAC 4+1 Others 10+2/1

RICHARDSON Nicholas (Nick) John
Born: Halifax, 11 April 1967
Height: 6'1" Weight: 12.6
Club Honours: Div 3 '93; WC '93

Having started last season at Bury, after being signed from Cardiff during the 1995 close season, Nick only appeared six times before moving on again, this time to Chester. At City, in 40 games on the right hand side of midfield, he proved to be a skilful, attacking player, who will be long remembered for his tremendous goal in the home game against Preston.

Halifax T (Free from Emley on 15/11/88) FL 89+12/17 FLC 6+4/2 FAC 2+1/1 Others 6/1
Cardiff C (£35,000 on 13/8/92) FL 106+5/13 FLC 4 FAC 6 Others 12+2/2
Wrexham (Loaned on 21/10/94) FL 4/2
Chester C (Loaned on 16/12/94) FL 6/1
Bury (Signed on 8/8/95) FL 3+2 FLC 1
Chester C (£40,000 on 7/9/95) FL 36+1/4 FAC 1 Others 2/1

RICKERS Paul Steven
Born: Leeds, 9 May 1975
Height: 5'10" Weight: 11.0

Paul burst into the Oldham first team last season, making the number seven shirt his own for the last eight games, his quick-footed, cheeky ball play showing to excellent effect. Although it seems fair to assume that the experience of Gunnar Halle played no little part in his improving status, his stamina and ease on the ball demanded that he be given the opportunity and if his improvement continues he will become a key player.

Oldham Ath (From trainee on 16/7/93) FL 27/1 FAC 1+1 Others 1+1

RICKETTS Michael Barrington
Born: Birmingham, 4 December 1978
Height: 6'2" Weight: 11.12

Walsall YTS striker who made a sensational entrance on the Football League stage when, in the final game last season, he calmly chipped the Brighton 'keeper within three minutes of coming on as a sub. It is therefore hardly surprising that the club have such high hopes of their promising youngster.

Walsall (Trainee) FL 0+1/1

Paul Rideout

RIDEOUT Paul David
Born: Bournemouth, 14 August 1964
Height: 5'11" Weight: 12.2
Club Honours: FAC '95; CS '95
International Honours: E: U21-5; Yth; Sch

Much travelled and experienced Everton striker, who is unselfish and holds the ball up well with his back to goal before passing and moving into space. Excellent in the air, with good chest control, Paul can generate tremendous power to send bullet-like headers goalwards and is always looking to flick the ball on for colleagues. Playing consistently well, he began all games up until early last December, prior to being injured against Sheffield Wednesday, and thereafter struggling to find the net regularly, possibly due to having several different strike partners. Eventually had to settle for the subs' bench when Duncan Ferguson returned and will have to fight hard to get his place back.

Swindon T (From apprentice on 15/8/81) FL 90+5/38 FLC 3/2 FAC 7/1
Aston Villa (£200,000 on 1/6/83) FL 50+4/19 FLC 4+2/3 FAC 1+1 Others 1 (£400,000 to Bari on 1/7/85)
Southampton (£430,000 on 5/7/88) FL 68+7/19 FLC 13/2 FAC 5+2 Others 1
Swindon T (Loaned on 28/3/91) FL 9/1
Notts Co (£250,000 on 16/9/91) FL 9+2/3 FLC 2 FAC 1 Others 2
Glasgow R (£500,000 on 10/1/92) FL 7+5/1 FLC 0+1 FAC 1
Everton (£500,000 on 14/8/92) PL 82+20/29 FLC 10+1/2 FAC 8+1/3 Others 5/1

RIDINGS David
Born: Farnworth, 27 February 1970
Height: 6'0" Weight: 12.0

Forward. Came to Crewe from non-league side, Ashton United, during the 1995 close season, having previously played at league level with Lincoln City. Made just one league outing, at home to Hull City before being sent out to Hednesford on loan and being released during the summer.

Halifax T (Signed from Curzon Ashton on 8/1/93)
Lincoln C (£10,000 on 22/2/94)
Crewe Alex (From Ashton U on 13/7/95) FL 1 Others 1

RIEPER Marc
Born: Rodoure, Denmark, 5 June 1968
Height: 6'4" Weight: 14.2
International Honours: Denmark: 40

Tall Danish international defender who remained a fixture in the centre of the West Ham defence in 1995-96, his aerial ability outstanding, and his tackling supreme. Also cool and collected under pressure, he eventually formed an excellent partnership with Croatian, Slaven Bilic, a man he had played against in the European Championships. Such height makes him a threat at set pieces, especially corners, and both his goals last season were identical ten-yard volleys in games against Coventry. The Rieper-Bilic combination could lead the way in the Premiership in 1996-97. Was one of 12 players from the continent, who regularly appeared in the English leagues last season, participating in Euro '96.

West Ham U (£500,000 from Brondby on 8/12/94) PL 52+5/3 FLC 2+1 FAC 3

RIGBY Anthony (Tony) Angelo
Born: Ormskirk, 10 August 1972
Height: 5'10" Weight: 12.12
The most naturally skilful player on Bury's books, the midfield man has the eye for a spectacular goal and has the knack of doing the unexpected. In what was undoubtedly his best season at Gigg Lane, Tony notched eight league and cup goals in 1995-96, his spectacular free kick in the Coca Cola Cup at Reading being voted by the supporters as Bury's "Goal of the Season".
Crewe Alex (From trainee on 16/5/90)
Bury (Free from Burscough, via Lancaster C, on 6/1/93) FL 111+14/18 FLC 4+2/2 FAC 5+2/1 Others 13+1/2

RIMMER Neil
Born: Liverpool, 13 November 1967
Height: 5'6" Weight: 10.3
International Honours: E: Yth; Sch
A strong and willing worker in Wigan's midfield, who enjoys the tackling side of the game, Neil was back to his very best in the second half of last season. And as the longest serving player at the club, he celebrated his 200th game during the campaign, prior to being freed during the summer.
Everton (From apprentice on 14/4/84) FL 0+1
Ipswich T (Free on 13/8/85) FL 19+3/3 FLC 3 Others 1+1
Wigan Ath (Free on 4/7/88) FL 184+6/10 FLC 14/1 FAC 10/2 Others 14/2

RIMMER Stuart Alan
Born: Southport, 12 October 1964
Height: 5'7" Weight: 11.0
International Honours: E: Yth
Joint top goalscorer for Chester with 13 last season, Stuart is also the club's all-time record holder. A skilful forward, whose speed is a great asset, he scored City's only hat trick in a 4-3 AWS win at Mansfield in November and went on to make his 300th league appearance for them against Northampton in March.
Everton (From apprentice on 15/10/82) FL 3
Chester C (£10,000 on 17/1/85) FL 110+4/67 FLC 6/6 FAC 4+3 Others 11+1/3
Watford (£205,000 on 18/3/88) FL 10/1 FLC 0+1/1
Notts Co (£200,000 on 10/11/88) FL 3+1/2 FAC 2 Others 3
Walsall (£150,000 on 2/2/89) FL 85+3/31 FLC 6/4 FAC 5/2 Others 7/7
Barnsley (£150,000 on 5/3/91) FL 10+5/1 Others 1
Chester C (£150,000 on 15/8/91) FL 165+23/56 FLC 11+2/3 FAC 6+2 Others 8+2/1
Rochdale (Loaned on 2/9/94) FL 3
Preston NE (Loaned on 5/12/94) FL 0+2

RIOCH Gregor (Greg) James
Born: Sutton Coldfield, 24 June 1975
Height: 5'11" Weight: 10.9
Having failed to make an appearance for Luton in 1994-95, Greg moved to Peterborough, where he started in the left back position, four games into last season. A wholehearted player, the son of Bruce, the current Arsenal manager, played 11 consecutive games before becoming an in and outer, only being in the starting line-up three times after November. Was released during the summer.

Luton T (From trainee on 19/7/93)
Barnet (Loaned on 17/9/93) FL 3 FLC 2 Others 1
Peterborough U (Free on 11/8/95) FL 13+5 FLC 2 FAC 2+1 Others 2+1

RIPLEY Stuart Edward
Born: Middlesbrough, 20 November 1967
Height: 5'11" Weight: 12.6
Club Honours: PL '95
International Honours: E: 1; U21-8; Yth
A modern day wide player, Stuart's great value to the Blackburn side in 1995-96, as in previous seasons, was his ability to receive the outlet ball from defence and hold up play while others pushed forward into scoring positions. Appearing mainly on the right, he also dropped back to cover in defence, but troubled by sporadic injuries and fitful throughout the campaign, there is no doubt his game suffered, despite the fact that he was absent only 11 times. Enigmatic with his crossing and once a danger near goal, with the licence to roam inside, he has now gone two years without scoring and will be looking to put that right before too long.
Middlesbrough (From apprentice on 23/12/85) FL 210+39/26 FLC 21+2/3 FAC 17+1/1 Others 20+1/1
Bolton W (Loaned on 18/2/86) FL 5/1 Others 0+1
Blackburn Rov (£1,300,000 on 20/7/92) PL 142+3/11 FLC 18 FAC 11/2 Others 8+1

RISETH Vidar
Born: Levanger, Norway, 21 April 1972
Height: 6'2" Weight: 12.7
An enthusiastic, but rather raw and awkward striker signed by Luton from Kongsvinger, Norway, last September, Vidar made his debut in the 5-0 away defeat at Stoke in November, but made little impact in that or any of the other games in which he appeared. Hampered by a back injury in January, by the end of the season he was back on loan to Kongsvinger, although still young enough to adapt to the English game.
Luton T (£110,000 from Kongsvinger on 26/10/95) FL 6+5 Others 1

RITCHIE Andrew (Andy) Timothy
Born: Manchester, 28 November 1960
Height: 5'10" Weight: 11.10
Club Honours: Div 2 '91
International Honours: E: U21-1; Yth; Sch
Freed by Oldham during the 1995 close season, the veteran striker with excellent ball skills was the big name signing that Scarborough fans had wanted for some time. Although showing flashes of his undoubted class, Andy found it difficult to adapt to the level of play in division three at times, but still finished top scorer with eight goals to his name.
Manchester U (From apprentice on 5/12/77) FL 26+7/13 FLC 3+2 FAC 3+1
Brighton & Hove A (£500,000 on 17/10/80) FL 82+7/23 FLC 3+1/1 FAC 9/2
Leeds U (£150,000 on 25/3/83) FL 127+9/40 FLC 11/3 FAC 9/1 Others 2+1
Oldham Ath (£50,000 on 14/8/87) F/PL 187+30/82 FLC 18+2/18 FAC 8+2/4 Others 3
Scarborough (Free on 3/8/95) FL 33+4/8 FLC 2 FAC 1

RIVERS Mark Alan
Born: Crewe, 26 November 1975
Height: 6'0" Weight: 11.2
Forward. The only Crewe-born player in the side in 1995-96. Having shown much improvement, his attacking style saw him get into double figures, in what was his first league season, with the promise of more to come. Looks to be a natural goalscorer.
Crewe Alex (From trainee on 6/5/94) FL 24+9/10 FLC 0+1 FAC 5/2 Others 2+2/2

ROBBINS Terence (Terry) John
Born: Southwark, 14 January 1965
Height: 5'7" Weight: 10.8
International Honours: E: SP-5
After 12 years of non-league football, the England semi-professional international striker found the step up to league status just a little too much when joining Barnet in the summer of 1995. Playing in a number of forward positions, Terry scored just two goals in 18 appearances before being released at the end of the season.
Barnet (Free from Welling U on 17/7/95) FL 9+6/1 FLC 2 Others 0+1/1

Andy Roberts

ROBERTS Andrew (Andy) James
Born: Dartford, 20 March 1974
Height: 5'10" Weight: 13.0
Club Honours: FAYC '91
International Honours: E: U21-5
Crystal Palace's record signing from Millwall in the summer of 1995, Andy proved a defensively sound midfielder who could also play sweeper. After missing the opening weeks of the season through injury, he made his first full appearance in October against Sunderland and played in every game, bar one, thereafter. Voted "Player of the Year" by Palace fans, he went through the whole campaign without an "official" goal until scoring the opener in the

Wembley play-off final against Leicester, which for a long time seemed likely to be the winner. A few weeks earlier he thought he had scored a last minute winner against Portsmouth, only to find that the referee had blown for full time whilst the ball was on its way into the net!

Millwall (From trainee on 29/10/91) FL 132+6/5 FLC 12/2 FAC 7 Others 4/1
Crystal Palace (£2,520,000 on 29/7/95) FL 36+2 FLC 3+1 FAC 2 Others 3/1

ROBERTS Anthony (Tony) Mark
Born: Holyhead, 4 August 1969
Height: 6'0" Weight: 12.0
International Honours: W: 1; B-2; U21-2; Yth

A good shot stopper who continually gives instructions to his defenders, and an accurate long kicker from his hands, Tony started last season as QPR's first choice goalkeeper, but, after just five league games, lost out to new signing, Juergen Sommer. Although he returned to the starting line-up for the four Coca Cola Cup games, due to Sommer being cup-tied, he could not regain his place and will be hoping for further opportunities this time round.

Queens Park R (From trainee on 24/7/87) F/PL 99 FLC 10 FAC 6+1 Others 2

ROBERTS Benjamin (Ben) James
Born: Bishop Auckland, 22 June 1975
Height: 6'0" Weight: 12.6

Unable to further his opportunities at Middlesbrough last season, with Gary Walsh and Alan Miller in outstanding form, Ben had two spells away from the Riverside on loan. After impressing at Hartlepool in October, he moved on to Wycombe in December, proving to be a tremendously popular signing, visibly growing in confidence during the three months he spent there. Good in all departments, he will be remembered for many spectacular saves, some defying belief, and it was a great disappointment to the fans when Middlesbrough offered him a new three year contract whilst still on loan to them.

Middlesbrough (From trainee on 24/3/93) Others 1
Hartlepool U (Loaned on 19/10/95) FL 4 Others 1
Wycombe W (Loaned on 8/12/95) FL 15

ROBERTS Darren Anthony
Born: Birmingham, 12 October 1969
Height: 6'0" Weight: 12.4

Despite scoring freely for the reserves, the hard-running front man was given only six league starts with Chesterfield last season. As they struggled to replace injured forwards, it seemed the best that Darren could hope for was a place on the bench, before slipping out of John Duncan's consideration completely in April. Was released during the summer.

Wolverhampton W (£20,000 from Burton A on 23/4/92) FL 12+9/5 FLC 0+1 Others 1+1
Hereford U (Loaned on 18/3/94) FL 5+1/5
Doncaster Rov (Free on 6/7/94)
Chesterfield (Free on 18/7/94) FL 10+15/1 FLC 3/1 FAC 1+1 Others 2+5/3

ROBERTS Iwan Wyn
Born: Bangor, 26 June 1968
Height: 6'3" Weight: 14.2
International Honours: W: 7; B-1; Yth; Sch

Striker. Scored a first half hat trick for Leicester in the home win over Portsmouth, lobbed the 'keeper from 25 yards at West Bromwich, and netted in five successive games just before Christmas, to eventually become the first City player to score 20 goals in a season since Alan Smith in 1987. His powerful, bustling style regularly proved a handful for opposition defences, before he was carried off with a cracked rib after just seven seconds on Easter Tuesday and sidelined for the rest of the season.

Watford (From trainee on 4/7/88) FL 40+23/9 FLC 6+2/3 FAC 1+6 Others 5
Huddersfield T (£275,000 on 2/8/90) FL 141+1/50 FLC 13+1/6 FAC 12/4 Others 14/8
Leicester C (£100,000 on 25/11/93) F/PL 92+8/41 FLC 5/1 FAC 5/2 Others 1

ROBERTSON John Nicholas
Born: Liverpool, 8 January 1974
Height: 6'2" Weight: 13.2

Having celebrated 100 league games for Wigan, following the signings of Colin Greenall and John Pender, John was allowed to move to Lincoln last December. At Sincil Bank, the solid central defender partnered Grant Brown in the back four until losing his place in the final weeks of the season. Recognised as an old-style centre back who is strong in the air.

Wigan Ath (From trainee on 6/7/92) FL 108+4/4 FLC 12 FAC 8+1 Others 8+1
Lincoln C (£15,000 on 5/12/95) FL 21+1 Others 1

ROBERTSON Paul
Born: Manchester, 5 February 1972
Height: 5'7" Weight: 11.6

A pacy defender with earlier FL experience, he came out of non-league soccer to sign for Doncaster early in 1995-96, but lost his place through injury and found it hard to get back into the first team. Was another victim of the massive pool of players at Belle Vue.

Stockport Co (Free from York C juniors on 29/8/89) FL 7+3 FLC 3 Others 3
Bury (Free on 18/7/91) FL 8 FLC 3 (Free to Runcorn on 15/12/92)
Doncaster Rov (Free on 30/10/95) FL 12+4 Others 2

ROBINS Mark Gordon
Born: Ashton under Lyme, 22 December 1969
Height: 5'8" Weight: 11.8
Club Honours: FAC '90; ECWC '91; ESC '91
International Honours: E: U21-6

Right-footed striker. Scored a classy winner for Leicester on the opening day of last season and chipped in with useful strikes throughout. Often the one to miss out if the team operated with only a lone striker, he regularly found himself on the bench once Martin O'Neill took charge, even when City operated with a front three. Scored with a magnificent volley against West Bromwich on Easter Tuesday and still managed a double figure goal tally from limited opportunities. Appeared as a late substitute

in the Wembley play-off final and went close to sneaking a winner, before Steve Claridge struck the goal that took the Foxes into the Premiership.

Manchester U (From apprentice on 23/12/86) FL 19+29/11 FLC 0+7/2 FAC 4+4/3 Others 4+3/1
Norwich C (£800,000 on 14/8/92) PL 57+10/20 FLC 6+3/1 Others 1+1
Leicester C (£1,000,000 on 16/1/95) P/FL 35+13/11 FLC 2+1/4 FAC 3+1 Others 1+1

Mark Robins

ROBINSON Carl Phillip
Born: Llandrudod, 13 October 1976
Height: 5'10" Weight: 12.10
International Honours: W: U21-1; Yth

Midfielder. Signed on deadline day last March on loan from Wolves, having yet to play in their first team, and soon made his league debut. A good passer of the ball, his move earned him an appearance in the Auto Windscreens final. Not a bad transformation in three weeks from reserve football to Wembley.

Wolverhampton W (From trainee on 3/7/95)
Shrewsbury T (Loaned on 28/3/96) FL 2+2 Others 1

ROBINSON David John
Born: Newcastle, 27 November 1969
Height: 6'0" Weight: 13.2

Signed from Gateshead last December, he joined Cambridge United on a non-contract basis as cover for the forwards, making most of his appearances as a substitute, prior to being released at the end of the season.

Newcastle U (From trainee on 27/6/88) FL 0+8 FLC 0+1 FAC 0+1/1
Peterborough U (Loaned on 25/2/91) FL 7/3
Reading (Free on 26/3/92) FL 8
Blackpool (Free on 20/7/92) FL 21+5/4 FLC 3+1/1 FAC 0+1 Others 0+2 (Free to Gateshead on 20/8/94)
Cambridge U (Free on 1/12/95) FL 4+13/1

ROBINSON Ian Brendan
Born: Gedling, 25 August 1978
Height: 5'9" Weight: 10.8

Young Mansfield midfield apprentice who was thrown in at the deep end early in 1995-96, when he was used as a substitute ten days before his 17th birthday. Made several other senior appearances before the season's end and showed much promise.

Mansfield T (Trainee) FL 4+5/1 FLC 0+1

ROBINSON Jamie
Born: Liverpool, 26 February 1972
Height: 6'1" Weight: 12.3
Club Honours: Div 3 '95
A left-sided Carlisle utility player, Jamie made most of his appearances last season in the back four. Despite his defensive brief, he was not afraid to venture upfield, particularly at set pieces, where he made his presence felt.
Liverpool (From trainee on 4/6/90)
Barnsley (Free on 17/7/92) FL 8+1 Others 3
Carlisle U (Signed on 28/1/94) FL 40+10/4 FLC 0+1 FAC 2 Others 7+6/1

ROBINSON John Robert Campbell
Born: Bulawayo, Rhodesia, 29 August 1971
Height: 5'10" Weight: 11.2
International Honours: W: 3; U21-5
Charlton winger, cum full back, who can play on either flank. Appearing mainly down the left in 1995-96, although wearing the number nine shirt, he had his best ever season at the club, his good form being recognised by the Welsh selectors in the shape of three full caps. Able to perform equally well at right back, it was in this position that he made an encouraging start for his country. Impressive when attacking defenders, his speed often leaving them in his wake, John is a good crosser and possesses a strong shot, scoring several valuable goals, including two in the home game against WBA. Voted "Player of the Year" by the supporters' club.
Brighton & Hove A (From trainee on 21/4/89) FL 57+5/6 FLC 5/1 FAC 2+1 Others 1+2/2
Charlton Ath (£75,000 on 15/9/92) FL 101+6/12 FLC 6+2/2 FAC 7+1/1 Others 4

ROBINSON Leslie (Les)
Born: Shirebrook, 1 March 1967
Height: 5'8" Weight: 11.1
No frills, Les continued to be a virtual ever present in the Oxford right back berth in 1995-96, apart from missing eight games with a hamstring injury. Always gave honest, hard-working performances, scoring just once in a Coca Cola Cup-tie at QPR, when he finished with the aplomb of a seasoned striker. Since joining United in 1990, only injury has kept him out of the side.
Mansfield T (Free from Chesterfield juniors on 6/10/84) FL 11+4 Others 1
Stockport Co (£10,000 on 27/11/86) FL 67/3 FLC 2 FAC 4 Others 4
Doncaster Rov (£20,000 on 24/3/88) FL 82/12 FLC 4 FAC 5 Others 5/1
Oxford U (£150,000 on 19/3/90) FL 207+3/2 FLC 18/2 FAC 12+1 Others 10

ROBINSON Spencer Liam
Born: Bradford, 29 December 1965
Height: 5'7" Weight: 12.7
Burnley's one time record signing barely got a look in during 1995-96, until after the departure of the manager who brought him to Turf Moor, Jimmy Mullen. Always a competitor, and the possessor of a fierce shot, he was employed in a wider role by Adrian Heath and often looked as likely to any to make the scoring breakthrough that seemed elusive late in the season.

Huddersfield T (Free from Nottingham F juniors on 5/1/84) FL 17+4/2
Tranmere Rov (Loaned on 18/12/85) FL 4/3
Bury (£60,000 on 8/7/86) FL 248+14/89 FLC 17+3/6 FAC 9/1 Others 24/4
Bristol C (£130,000 on 14/7/93) FL 31+10/4 FLC 2/1 FAC 5 Others 1
Burnley (£250,000 on 26/7/94) FL 40+15/9 FLC 4/2 FAC 5/1 Others 0+1

ROBINSON Mark James
Born: Rochdale, 21 November 1968
Height: 5'9" Weight: 11.8
Club Honours: Div 2 '96
Enjoyed his most consistent spell since arriving at the County Ground, ever present in the league and featuring in 58 out of 59 games for Swindon last season. Performed mainly as an attacking right back, but when the occasion arose he looked comfortable as a central defender, being quite strong in the air for a man who is not particularly tall. A key player in the run to the first division, a second division championship medal was a just return.
West Bromwich A (From apprentice on 10/1/87) FL 2 FLC 0+1
Barnsley (Free on 23/6/87) FL 117+20/6 FLC 7+2 FAC 7+1 Others 3+2/1
Newcastle U (£450,000 on 9/3/93) F/PL 14+11 FAC 1
Swindon T (£600,000 on 22/7/94) FL 86/1 FLC 10 FAC 8 Others 6+1

ROBINSON Matthew Richard
Born: Exeter, 23 December 1974
Height: 5'11" Weight: 11.2
Promising Southampton left-sided midfielder. Brought on as a sub six times last season, he proved confident, showing a good touch, and often got into good attacking positions. Definitely looks to be one for the future.
Southampton (From trainee on 1/7/93) PL 0+6 FAC 0+2

ROBINSON Paul Derrick
Born: Sunderland, 20 November 1978
Height: 5'11" Weight: 11.0
The young Darlington youth team player made five subs' appearances for the seniors last season and showed much promise as a tricky forward. Only a first year YTS, he has a long way to go yet.
Darlington (Trainee) FL 0+4 FAC 0+1

ROBINSON Phillip (Phil) John
Born: Stafford, 6 January 1967
Height: 5'10" Weight: 11.7
Club Honours: Div 4 '88, Div 3 '89; AMC '88, '91
Much of Chesterfield's more patient attacking play revolved around this busy, creative midfielder in 1995-96. With him in the side, they seemed to have many more options and when injury robbed the club of his talent, they resorted more to straight-forwardly humping the ball up in the air. With a fit Phil Robinson, Chesterfield can pose a threat to any other side, as much for his ability to come through and score, as his playmaking.
Aston Villa (From apprentice on 8/1/85) FL 2+1/1

Wolverhampton W (£5,000 on 3/7/87) FL 63+8/8 FLC 6 FAC 3/1 Others 8+2
Notts Co (£67,500 on 18/8/89) FL 65+1/5 FLC 6/1 FAC 1+1 Others 9+1
Birmingham C (Loaned on 18/3/91) FL 9 Others 2+1
Huddersfield T (Signed on 1/9/92) FL 74+1/5 FLC 4 FAC 8/1 Others 8
Northampton T (Loaned on 2/9/94) FL 14 FLC 1 FAC 1 Others 2
Chesterfield (Signed on 9/12/94) FL 60+1/17 FLC 1 FAC 2 Others 8/4

ROBINSON Ronald (Ronnie)
Born: Sunderland, 22 October 1966
Height: 5'9" Weight: 11.5
A solid and dependable full back who joined Scarborough in the summer of 1995 from Exeter and impressed in the pre-season matches, before being injured in a car crash on the eve of 1995-96. Unfortunately, when he resumed playing, Richard Lucas had filled the left back berth and, unable to get back in the team, he was released in November.
Ipswich T (Free from SC Vaux on 6/11/84)
Leeds U (Free on 22/11/85) FL 27
Doncaster Rov (£5,000 on 25/2/87) FL 76+2/5 FLC 6 FAC 5 Others 3
West Bromwich A (£80,000 on 22/3/89) FL 1
Rotherham U (£40,000 on 18/8/89) FL 86/2 FLC 9/1 FAC 6 Others 7/1
Peterborough U (Free on 10/12/91) FL 44+3 FLC 3 FAC 3 Others 10
Exeter C (£25,000 on 24/7/93) FL 37+2/1 FLC 4 FAC 2+1 Others 3+1
Huddersfield T (Loaned on 13/1/94) FL 2
Scarborough (Free on 4/8/95) FL 1 Others 1

ROBINSON Stephen (Steve)
Born: Lisburn, 10 December 1974
Height: 5'8" Weight: 10.7
International Honours: NI: B-2; U21-1; Yth; Sch
After playing in Bournemouth's midfield for most of the early part of 1995-96, Steve spent the rest of the season alternating between midfield and acting as a partner for Steve Jones, looking comfortable in both positions. However, he preferred the striking role, finishing with nine goals, and was always full of running, his workrate being excellent. Also called up for the Northern Ireland "B" squad.
Tottenham H (From trainee on 27/1/93) PL 1+1
Bournemouth (Free on 20/10/94) FL 66+7/12 FLC 3 FAC 4+1/1 Others 4/1

ROBINSON Steven (Steve) Eli
Born: Nottingham, 17 January 1975
Height: 5'4" Weight: 10.11
Having shown early promise in Birmingham's midfield in 1994-95, it was expected he would be given further opportunities last season. However, unable to get on the team sheet, even though 46 other players did, Steve was loaned to Kidderminster (December), before going to Peterborough in March and replacing his former Brum team mate, Ben Sedgemore, on the right-hand side of the pitch for five games. Looks to be a ball winner.
Birmingham C (From trainee on 9/6/93) FL 5+1 Others 1
Peterborough U (Loaned on 15/3/96) FL 5

ROBSON Bryan

Born: Witton Gilbert, 11 January 1957
Height: 5'11" Weight: 12.6
Club Honours: CS '83, '93; FAC '83, '85, '90; ECWC '91; PL '93, '94; Div 1 '95
International Honours: E: 90; B-3; U21-7; Yth

Middlesbrough's veteran player/manager, and former Manchester United and England captain, made only three starts as a player in 1995-96, against Crystal Palace in the Coca-Cola Cup in November, versus West Ham in December in what was arguably Boro's best performance of the season, and in the 2-1 FA Cup win at Notts County (January). Although he has not formally announced his retirement as a player, he seems unlikely to turn out again, except in a dire emergency. He was widely tipped as a successor to Terry Venables as England manager but, perhaps wisely, declared his ineligibility, claiming insufficient experience as a club manager and a greater commitment to Boro. Such esteem is he held in by world class players that Brazilian superstars, Juninho and Branco, were willing to sign on for the club during the campaign and it is unlikely that he will stop there.

West Bromwich A (From apprentice on 1/8/74) FL 194+4/39 FLC 17+1/2 FAC 10+2/2 Others 12/3
Manchester U (£1,500,000 on 5/10/81) F/PL 326+19/74 FLC 50+1/5 FAC 33+2/10 Others 32+2/11
Middlesbrough (Free on 1/5/94) P/FL 22+2/1 FLC 1 FAC 1

ROBSON Gary

Born: Chester le Street, 6 July 1965
Height: 5'8" Weight: 11.6

The younger brother of Middlesbrough's Bryan, and a hard-tackling midfielder in his own right, Gary was unfortunate to damage his knee in Bradford's opening game of last season, an injury that forced him out of action until mid-October. Back in the side, but having broken down again, he was released in December, signing for the Conference's Gateshead.

West Bromwich A (From apprentice on 5/5/83) FL 184+34/28 FLC 12+2 FAC 10+2/3 Others 7+5/3
Bradford C (Free on 16/7/93) FL 72+3/3 FLC 7+1 FAC 3/1 Others 2

ROBSON Mark Andrew

Born: Newham, 22 May 1969
Height: 5'7" Weight: 10.2

Charlton winger with great skill and balance who, more often than not, beats defenders with ease. Unable to command a regular place last season, due to the consistent form of Shaun Newton and John Robinson, Mark still did well when called upon, being at his most dangerous when getting to the byline and cutting the ball back for the oncoming strikers. Has two good feet and can score goals, but his main strength is in creating chances for others.

Exeter C (From apprentice on 17/12/86) FL 26/7 FAC 2 Others 2
Tottenham H (£50,000 on 17/7/87) FL 3+5 FLC 1
Reading (Loaned on 24/3/88) FL 5+2
Watford (Loaned on 5/10/89) FL 1
Plymouth Arg (Loaned on 22/12/89) FL 7

Exeter C (Loaned on 3/1/92) FL 7+1/1 Others 3/1
West Ham U (Free on 14/8/92) F/PL 42+5/8 FLC 2 FAC 2/1 Others 4+1
Charlton Ath (£125,000 on 17/11/93) FL 71+19/6 FLC 4+2 FAC 8/1 Others 2

ROCASTLE David Carlyle

Born: Lewisham, 2 May 1967
Height: 5'9" Weight: 11.12
Club Honours: FLC '87; Div 1 '89, '91
International Honours: E: 14; B-2; U21-14

Skilful ex-international right-sided midfield player who was yet another to be struck down by the Chelsea injury curse. David played just one league match, a 3-0 defeat at Ewood Park last October, before sustaining a broken toe which finished his season. Injuries have restricted him to just 40 matches in his two seasons at Stamford Bridge, which is a great pity, because fully fit he is one of the most attractive players to watch in the Premiership.

Arsenal (From apprentice on 31/12/84) FL 204+14/24 FLC 32+1/6 FAC 18+2/4 Others 9
Leeds U (£2,000,000 on 4/8/92) PL 17+8/2 FLC 0+3 FAC 0+3 Others 2+1
Manchester C (£2,000,000 on 22/12/93) PL 21/2 FAC 2
Chelsea (£1,250,000 on 12/8/94) PL 27+2 FLC 3/1 Others 7+1/1

ROCKETT Jason

Born: London, 26 September 1969
Height: 6'1" Weight: 13.0

A commanding centre back, and the main-stay of the Scarborough defence, Jason impressed once again as a powerful header of the ball, with good distribution. Despite the club having a poor campaign in 1995-96, he remained as consistent as ever, although a knee injury late in the season caused him to miss several matches.

Rotherham U (Signed on 25/3/92)
Scarborough (Free on 4/8/93) FL 99+1/4 FLC 6 FAC 5 Others 4

RODGER Graham

Born: Glasgow, 1 April 1967
Height: 6'2" Weight: 11.13
Club Honours: FAC '87
International Honours: E: U21-4

The plethora of fine central defenders at Grimsby, limited Graham's appearance to just 15 starts and two from the bench in 1995-96, having been in the side for the first three matches. However, with his aerial strengths, both in defence and at set pieces at the club's disposal, he deputised competently at various stages of the season without frills.

Wolverhampton W (Apprentice) FL 1
Coventry C (From apprentice on 18/2/85) FL 31+5/2 FLC 3+1 FAC 1+1 Others 0+1
Luton T (£150,000 on 1/8/89) FL 27+1/2 FLC 2 Others 3
Grimsby T (£135,000 on 8/1/92) FL 97+10/9 FLC 3 FAC 6 Others 2

RODGER Simon Lee

Born: Shoreham, 3 October 1971
Height: 5'9" Weight: 10.13
Club Honours: Div 1 '94

A left-sided midfield player with Crystal Palace, who missed most of the previous campaign with a back injury, Simon found

difficulty in winning back a regular place in the team in 1995-96. However, he was a vital squad member, frequently standing in to cover the absence of first choice midfield players, his strong tackling, coupled to an ability to place deep crosses into the penalty area, being a healthy asset during the club's ultimately unsuccessful drive for promotion, via the play offs.

Crystal Palace (£1,000 from Bognor Regis T on 2/7/90) F/PL 97+18/5 FLC 15 FAC 2+3 Others 2+2

RODGERSON Ian

Born: Hereford, 9 April 1966
Height: 5'8" Weight: 11.6

Ended last season at full back after spells up front and in midfield as the management strived to halt Cardiff's unsuccessful run. In his second term at Ninian, after arriving back from Sunderland during the summer of 1995, Ian proved competent and assured as an attacking full back, having earlier struggled in a weak midfield.

Hereford U (From juniors on 3/7/85) FL 95+5/6 FLC 7 FAC 4 Others 7+1
Cardiff C (£35,000 on 3/8/88) FL 98+1/4 FAC 10 Others 6+1
Birmingham C (£50,000 on 4/12/90) FL 87+8/13 FLC 7+1/2 FAC 2 Others 11/1
Sunderland (£140,000 on 23/7/93) FL 5+5
Cardiff C (Free on 31/7/95) FL 28+6 FLC 3+1/1 FAC 2 Others 2

Ian Rodgerson

ROGAN Anthony (Anton) Gerard Patrick

Born: Belfast, 25 March 1966
Height: 5'11" Weight: 12.6
Club Honours: SPD '88; SC '88, '89
International Honours: NI: 17

Released by Oxford, he signed for Millwall last August, but his appearances were curtailed due to tough competition for first team places. Making eight in all, including substitutions, Anton stood in for Tony Witter and Keith Stevens when required and never let the side down. Is a resolute defender who is good in the air.

Glasgow Celtic (Signed from Distillery on 9/5/86) SL 115+12/4 SLC 12+1 SC 18/1 Others 8
Sunderland (£350,000 on 4/10/91) FL 45+1/1 FLC 1 FAC 8 Others 2
Oxford U (Signed on 9/8/93) FL 56+2/3 FLC 4 FAC 4 Others 2
Millwall (Free on 11/8/95) FL 4+4

ROGERS Alan
Born: Liverpool, 3 January 1977
Height: 5'10" Weight: 11.8
Exciting young Tranmere left back who burst on to the scene last December and earned himself a place in the side on merit with a series of mature performances, allied to a willingness to support the attack down the left flank. He also scored twice himself. Just 19, he is regarded as a tremendous prospect and, if he continues to progress at his present rate, could be a future England left back.
Tranmere Rov (From trainee on 1/7/95) FL 25+1/2 FAC 1

ROGERS Darren John
Born: Birmingham, 9 April 1970
Height: 6'0" Weight: 13.0
Not a regular in the starting line-up for Walsall at the beginning of last season, Darren was only called up when Ray Daniel was injured in October. However, when the latter was fit again, he had the better of the tussle for the left back slot, his speed and overlapping making him a real crowd pleaser.
West Bromwich A (From trainee on 5/7/88) FL 7+7/1 FAC 0+1 Others 1/1
Birmingham C (Free on 1/7/92) FL 15+3 FLC 2 FAC 0+1 Others 5
Wycombe W (Loaned on 5/11/93) FL 0+1 Others 1
Walsall (Free on 19/7/94) FL 43+9 FLC 4 FAC 5+2 Others 5

ROGERS David (Dave) Raymond
Born: Liverpool, 25 August 1975
Height: 6'1" Weight: 12.0
A Chester defender who arrived from Tranmere during the 1995 close season, Dave made his debut in league football from the bench against Gillingham in September. Was given an extended run later on, playing in the number three shirt, and impressed.
Tranmere Rov (From trainee on 6/7/94)
Chester C (Free on 7/8/95) FL 14+6/1 FLC 0+2 Others 1

ROGERS Lee Julian
Born: Doncaster, 28 October 1966
Height: 5'11" Weight: 12.1
In his testimonial season, Lee was a Chesterfield regular in defence until last Christmas, when injury and illness sidelined him for most of the rest of the season. A hugely popular, determined and capable figure, he seems to improve as every season passes, and his July testimonial against Nottingham Forest was just reward for his contribution to Chesterfield FC. Can play equally well in either full back positions, with a penchant for getting down the flank.
Doncaster Rov (From trainee on 27/7/84) Others 1
Chesterfield (Free on 29/8/86) FL 294+20/1 FLC 16+1 FAC 11+1 Others 27+1

ROGERS Paul Anthony
Born: Portsmouth, 21 March 1965
Height: 6'0" Weight: 12.0
International Honours: E: SP-6
A hard-working, gritty midfielder, Paul lost his Sheffield United place following the Coca Cola Cup defeat at Bury last October, until a change of management saw him filling in at full back for three games, prior to being transferred to Notts County in December. Scored in his first two matches – in the FA Cup against Middlesbrough and at Wycombe in the league – and maintained his place all the way to the losing division two Wembley play-off final against Bradford.
Sheffield U (£35,000 from Sutton U on 29/1/92) F/PL 120+5/10 FLC 8+1/1 FAC 4 Others 1
Notts Co (Signed on 29/12/95) FL 21/2 FAC 1 Others 4/1

ROGET Leo Thomas Earl
Born: Ilford, 1 August 1977
Height: 6'1" Weight: 12.2
Tall and strong, and with an unmistakable hairstyle, Leo came into the Southend team near the end of last season when an injury crisis robbed the team of many players and, almost instantly, became a cult figure with the fans. His cool and competent displays at centre half meant that Mick Bodley could not displace him and the new season bodes well. A product of the Southend youth system, his greatest moment came in the home game against Watford when he came off the subs' bench in the 86th minute to grab an equaliser for the Blues. Had a spell on loan at non-league Dover in December.
Southend U (From trainee on 5/7/95) FL 4+4/1

ROLLING Franck Jacques
Born: Colmar, France, 23 August 1968
Height: 6'2" Weight: 13.0
A right-footed central defender, Franck was Mark McGhee's final signing for Leicester, the Frenchman joining from Ayr United last October, having been at the club on loan since the previous month. Enjoyed an outstanding debut at Carrow Road. Comfortable on the ball, and occasionally thrust into midfield very effectively, he is only an intermittent selection under Martin O'Neill, usually in a three-man central defence.
Ayr U (Signed from FC Pau on 8/8/94) SL 35/2 SLC 2 SC 1 Others 4
Leicester C (£100,000 on 4/9/95) FL 17 FLC 3 FAC 0+1

ROLLO James Stuart
Born: Birmingham, 22 May 1976
Height: 5'11" Weight: 11.5
Young Walsall defender and a first-year professional. James made just one subs' appearance, along with David Richards, in last November's AWS win over Wycombe, before being released in the summer.
Walsall (From trainee on 26/5/95) Others 0+1

ROPER Ian Robert
Born: Nuneaton, 20 June 1977
Height: 6'4" Weight: 14.0
The tall, powerful Walsall defender made his first team debut in last season's 5-2 AWS

win at Fulham, before impressing in two further matches, the one in the league, the other in the FA Cup. Is one of the rapidly developing players the club has high hopes of.
Walsall (From trainee on 15/5/95) FL 3+2 FAC 1 Others 1

ROSCOE Andrew (Andy) Ronald
Born: Liverpool, 4 June 1973
Height: 5'11" Weight: 12.0
Club Honours: AMC '96
Andy was a virtual ever present for Rotherham last season, playing wide on the left from where he produced the openings for many of the side's goals. He also played a major role in helping the Millers to reach Wembley in the Auto Windscreens Shield, starting them off on the trail with a blistering free kick, which proved to be the match winner in the opening game of that competition at Chester. In fact, he became quite an expert with free kicks from the edge of the penalty area.
Bolton W (Free from Liverpool juniors on 17/7/91) FL 2+1 Others 1+1
Rotherham U (£70,000 on 27/10/94) FL 75+1/6 FLC 4 FAC 1 Others 7/2

ROSE Matthew
Born: Dartford, 24 September 1975
Height: 5'11" Weight: 11.1
A young Arsenal central defender and captain of their 1994 FA Youth Cup winning side. Having already been blooded as a sub, when coming on for Steve Morrow last March, Matthew made his full debut three days later as the Irishman's replacement in the 3-1 win over Manchester City. Looks a good prospect.
Arsenal (From trainee on 19/7/94) PL 1+3

Ronny Rosenthal

ROSENTHAL Ronny
Born: Haifa, Israel, 11 October 1963
Height: 5'10" Weight: 12.13
Club Honours: CS '90
International Honours: Israel: 54

Usually a striker, Spurs' Israeli international was redeployed by Gerry Francis to play behind Teddy Sheringham and Chris Armstrong on the wing last October. An enthusiastic competitor, who loves to pick the ball up and run at opponents, he continued to get into some glorious goalscoring positions, although only scoring four goals, including two in the FA Cup against Hereford and Wolves, respectively. Often able to create something from nothing, he remained a key player in the Tottenham squad, even though his first team appearances became less frequent following the arrival of Andy Sinton in February.

Liverpool (Loaned from Standard Liege on 22/3/90) FL 5+3/7
Liverpool (£1,000,000 on 29/6/90) F/PL 27+39/14 FLC 2+7/1 FAC 5+3 Others 2+4
Tottenham H (£250,000 on 26/1/94) PL 51+17/3 FLC 3/1 FAC 7+2/6

ROSLER Uwe

Born: Attenburg, Germany, 15 November 1968
Height: 6'0" Weight: 12.4
International Honours: East Germany: 5

Following a superb 1994-95, his first full season in Manchester City's colours, the exuberant striker signed a new four year contract. Unfortunately, in 1995-96, Uwe was unable to show the same levels of consistency, his dual striking role with Niall Quinn being disappointing. That apart, he remained a firm favourite with the crowd, always giving 100 per cent and always chasing supposed lost causes in an effort to get on the score sheet. His ability to create something out of nothing was further underlined when he scored two snap goals in games against Manchester United and Sheffield Wednesday. Will be looking to pick up on his goals per games ratio this coming term.

Manchester C (£750,000 from Dynamo Dresden on 2/3/94) PL 75+4/29 FLC 6+1/4 FAC 9/7

ROSS Michael (Mickey) Patrick

Born: Southampton, 2 September 1971
Height: 5'7" Weight: 9.13
International Honours: E: Sch

A quick centre forward who was reduced to a bit part role for Plymouth in 1995-96, he rejoined Exeter on loan in November, playing seven times and scoring two goals, before returning to Home Park. Deemed as surplus to requirements, Mickey was released in the summer and joined Vancouver Whitecaps.

Portsmouth (From trainee on 30/12/88) FL 0+4 FAC 0+1 Others 2+3
Exeter C (£60,000 on 1/8/93) FL 27+1/9 FLC 4 FAC 3/1 Others 2+1
Plymouth Arg (Free on 22/11/94) FL 11+6 FAC 1/2 Others 2
Exeter C (Loaned on 17/11/95) FL 7/2

ROWBOTHAM Darren

Born: Cardiff, 22 October 1966
Height: 5'10" Weight: 11.5
Club Honours: Div 4 '90
International Honours: W: Yth

Striker. Signed by Shrewsbury on a free transfer from Crewe during the 1995 close season, Darren proved to be a keen, busy forward, always looking for the chance. A consistent scorer, especially early on, the best of him was never seen due to injury absences, culminating at the end of March with ligament trouble likely to keep him out for some time.

Plymouth Arg (From juniors on 7/11/84) FL 22+24/2 FLC 1 FAC 0+3/1 Others 1+1
Exeter C (Signed on 31/10/87) FL 110+8/47 FLC 11/6 FAC 8/5 Others 5/1
Torquay U (£25,000 on 13/9/91) FL 14/3 FAC 3/1 Others 2
Birmingham C (£20,000 on 2/1/92) FL 31+5/6 FLC 0+1 Others 3+1
Mansfield T (Loaned on 18/12/92) FL 4
Hereford U (Loaned on 25/3/93) FL 8/2
Crewe Alex (Free on 6/7/93) FL 59+2/21 FLC 1/1 FAC 4/3 Others 6+2/1
Shrewsbury T (Free on 28/7/95) FL 20+6/8 FLC 2+1/1 FAC 4/1 Others 1+3

ROWBOTHAM Jason

Born: Cardiff, 3 January 1969
Height: 5'9" Weight: 11.0
Club Honours: S Div 1 '95; SLC '95

Signed last September from Raith Rovers, he proved a dependable and hard-working right back for Wycombe in 1995-96, always willing to support the attack. Although losing form in February and being dropped until the end of the season, Jason was still offered a new contract.

Plymouth Arg (From trainee on 20/7/87) FL 8+1 FLC 0+1
Shrewsbury T (Free on 26/3/92)
Hereford U (Free on 17/10/92) FL 3+2/1 FAC 1
Raith Rov (Free on 31/7/93) SL 47+9/1 SLC 3+2 SC 2+1 Others 1
Wycombe W (£40,000 on 14/9/95) FL 27 FLC 2 FAC 2 Others 2

ROWE Ezekiel (Zeke) Bartholomew

Born: Stoke Newington, 30 October 1973
Height: 6'0" Weight: 12.8

Yet to play first team football for Chelsea, Zeke, a striker, joined Brighton on loan, making his debut on 30 March 1996 against Rotherham at the Goldstone. Created an immediate impression with his pace, which unsettled opposing defences, and was soon finding the net with cool finishing. A willing runner into the channels, he puts defenders under pressure and picks up the pieces. *Stop Press:* Released during the summer, he was reported to have signed for Peterborough.

Chelsea (From trainee on 12/6/92)
Barnet (Loaned on 12/11/93) FL 9+1/2 FAC 2/1
Brighton & Hove A (Loaned on 28/3/96) FL 9/3

ROWE Rodney Carl

Born: Huddersfield, 30 July 1975
Height: 5'8" Weight: 12.8

Huddersfield midfielder who has also played as a central striker. Was finally given an extended run-in the side in 1995-96, but found it difficult to establish himself and thus found himself back out in the cold at the end of the season. More comfortable on the right side, he has the pace to take on defenders.

Huddersfield T (From trainee on 12/7/93) FL 13+14/2 FLC 0+1 FAC 6+1/2 Others 3/1
Scarborough (Loaned on 11/8/94) FL 10+4/1 FLC 4/1
Bury (Loaned on 20/3/95) FL 1+2

ROWETT Gary

Born: Bromsgrove, 6 March 1974
Height: 6'0" Weight: 12.10

A 1995 close season signing for Derby, as part of the deal which took Craig Short to Everton, Gary was valued at £300,000 which soon proved to be a bargain as Jim Smith gave him a sweeper role in a five-man back line. Having undergone a cartilage operation, he moved to a more right-sided role in the second half of the season, and continued to show excellent vision and the ability to read the game. Represented the Football League U21 side that drew 1-1 with the Italian Serie "B" XI at Huddersfield in November.

Cambridge U (From trainee on 10/9/91) FL 51+12/9 FLC 7/1 FAC 5+2 Others 5/3
Everton (£200,000 on 21/5/94) PL 2+2
Blackpool (Loaned on 23/1/95) FL 17
Derby Co (£300,000 on 20/7/95) FL 34+1 FLC 2 FAC 1

ROWLAND Keith

Born: Portadown, 1 September 1971
Height: 5'10" Weight: 10.0
International Honours: NI: 9; B-1; Yth

West Ham and Northern Ireland left-sided midfielder. In adding to his international appearances last season, Keith also discovered a newly found confidence, helping him to establish himself with the Hammers, where he came into his own, firstly as cover for Julian Dicks and then when playing alongside him. To allow the partnership with Dicks to bloom, Michael Hughes switched flanks, the move being complimentary. Yet to score for the club, he is more of a provider than taker of chances, able to go past defenders to deliver excellent crosses from a sweet left foot, or whip the early ball in if required.

Bournemouth (From trainee on 2/10/89) FL 65+7/2 FLC 5 FAC 8 Others 3
Coventry C (Loaned on 8/1/93) PL 0+2
West Ham U (£110,000 on 6/8/93) PL 46+12 FLC 3 FAC 5+1

ROY Bryan Edward

Born: Amsterdam, Holland, 12 February 1970
Height: 5'10" Weight: 10.8
International Honours: Holland: 33

Perhaps the biggest disappointment of 1995-96 for both Frank Clark and Nottingham Forest supporters was the failure of the immensely talented Dutch forward to recapture the outstanding form he shared in 1994-95, when in partnership with Stan Collymore. Whether this was due to the loss of his partner and the lack of an effective replacement, or Bryan's problems with a cartilage injury is unclear, but he started in good form with two goals in Forest's opening day 4-3 victory at Southampton. As the season advanced, however, his form dipped and he was frequently dropped, his ability to run at defenders and pass them having deserted him. Obviously too good a player to be sidelined for long, the summer's rest will hopefully clear up any injury problems and leave him refreshed for the new season.

Nottingham F (£2,500,000 from Foggia on 4/8/94) PL 62+3/21 FLC 5/1 FAC 8/1 Others 6/1

Bryan Roy

ROYCE Simon Ernest
Born: Forest Gate, 9 September 1971
Height: 6'2" Weight: 12.8
Simon had a fairytale ending for Southend United in 1995-96, not only holding the first choice goalkeeper's position for the complete season, but earning the accolade of "Player of the Year" from the fans. His reflex saves and general handling were excellent and he inspired those in front of him with his ability and confidence. Premiership clubs have already begun to show an interest in him, and it may not be long before his skills grace a greater stage.
Southend U (£10,000 from Heybridge Swifts on 15/10/91) FL 67+2 FLC 4 FAC 2 Others 5

RUDDOCK Neil
Born: Wandsworth, 9 May 1968
Height: 6'2" Weight: 12.12
Club Honours: FLC '95
International Honours: E: 1; B-1; U21-4; Yth
Unable to get a consistent run at Liverpool in 1995-96 as manager, Roy Evans, experimented with the three central defender system, the burly centre back's season was disrupted by injuries and suspensions. Although his strong tackling and fierce leadership qualities continued to mark him out as a defender of great presence and ability, when fit, Neil found it difficult to dislodge the born-again Mark Wright. A comeback in mid-term lasted only three games, despite scoring twice in a 5-0 victory over Leeds, and it was not until towards the end of the campaign that he was back in contention, this time as a stand in for the injured Phil Babb.
Millwall (From apprentice on 3/3/86) Others 3+1/1
Tottenham H (£50,000 on 14/4/86) FL 7+2 FAC 1+1/1
Millwall (£300,000 on 29/6/88) FL 0+2/1 FLC 2/3 Others 1+1
Southampton (£250,000 on 13/2/89) FL 100+7/9 FLC 14+1/1 FAC 10/3 Others 6

Tottenham H (£750,000 on 29/7/92) PL 38/3 FLC 4 FAC 5
Liverpool (£2,500,000 on 22/7/93) PL 94+2/10 FLC 16+1/1 FAC 11 Others 2

RUFUS Richard Raymond
Born: Lewisham, 12 January 1975
Height: 6'1" Weight: 11.2
International Honours: E: U21-5
The young Charlton central defender continued his improvement last season, being rewarded for his outstanding form with an England U21 call up for the game against Croatia in April, the first of five caps, having earlier represented the Football League U21 side against an Italian Serie "B" XI. And, without a league goal to his name, he came the closest to scoring in a 1-0 defeat, when hitting the bar with a powerful header. Very calm under pressure, good in the air, a firm tackler, with excellent powers of recovery. Richard was a regular in a side that was pushing hard for promotion and was one of two Athletic players elected by his fellow professionals to the PFA first division side on awards night.
Charlton Ath (From trainee on 1/7/93) FL 67+2 FLC 5 FAC 2 Others 2

RUSH David
Born: Sunderland, 15 May 1971
Height: 5'11" Weight: 10.10
Popular with the Oxford fans, "Rushie" is an effervescent striker. He had his best season for appearances and goals in 1995-96 – his final day strike against Peterborough, being his 14th. Also dropped back to a wide right midfield role, and formed good partnerships with Matt Murphy, Martin Aldridge and Paul Moody. Makes up for his lack of inches with 110 per cent effort.
Sunderland (Free from Notts Co juniors on 21/7/89) FL 40+19/12 FLC 1+1 FAC 9/1 Others 1+1
Hartlepool U (Loaned on 15/8/91) FL 8/2
Peterborough U (Loaned on 27/10/93) FL 2+2/1 FLC 1/1
Cambridge U (Loaned on 12/9/94) FL 2
Oxford U (£100,000 on 23/9/94) FL 63+14/20 FLC 3+1 FAC 2+3/1 Others 6+1/2

RUSH Ian James
Born: St Asaph, 20 October 1961
Height: 6'0" Weight: 12.6
Club Honours: Div 1 '82, '83, '84, '86, '90; FLC '81, '82, '83, '84, '95; FAC '86, '89, '92; EC '84
International Honours: W: 73; U21-2; Sch
A model professional and one of Liverpool's finest ever players, it was a sad day when the Welsh international striker announced in March that he would be seeking a new club for 1996-97, to see out his career. Although the writing was on the wall when Liverpool signed Stan Collymore, Ian won his first team place back following Collymore's indifferent early season performances and only lost it in November through injury. By the time he regained fitness in January, the Collymore/Robbie Fowler partnership was in full swing and he spent the rest of the season on the bench. Happily, he signed off his Anfield career with a goal in his last Premiership match for the club at

Manchester City, bringing his total of league goals for Liverpool to 229, second only to Roger Hunt's 245. *Stop Press:* Signed for Leeds at the end of May.
Chester C (From apprentice on 25/9/79) FL 33+1/14 FAC 5/3
Liverpool (£300,000 on 1/5/80) FL 182/109 FLC 38/21 FAC 22/20 Others 31+1/17 (£3,200,000 to Juventus on 1/7/86)
Liverpool (Loaned on 1/7/86) FL 42/30 FLC 9/4 FAC 3 Others 3/6
Liverpool (£2,800,000 on 23/8/88) F/PL 223+22/90 FLC 30/23 FAC 30+6/19 Others 16+1/7

RUSH Matthew James
Born: Hackney, 6 August 1971
Height: 5'11" Weight: 12.10
International Honours: Ei: U21-4
Ten years at West Ham saw him want a new challenge, hence a transfer to Norwich at the beginning of 1995-96, but the season was a personal disaster for him. Injured in his only appearance against Sunderland, Matthew tried to play on in a following reserve match against his former side, before being stretchered off, leading to a knee ligament operation in October. A winger, with terrific pace and two good feet, he started full training in April and looks to be fully fit by the time you read this.
West Ham U (From trainee on 24/3/90) F/PL 29+19/5 FLC 4 Others 2+1
Cambridge U (Loaned on 12/3/93) FL 4+6
Swansea C (Loaned on 10/1/94) FL 13 Others 4
Norwich C (£500,000 on 18/8/95) FL 0+1

RUSHFELDT Sigurd (Siggi)
Born: Tromso, Norway, 11 December 1972
Height: 6'2" Weight: 12.10
On trial from Sweden, Siggi's first touch in English football for Birmingham last October, a miskick, was hardly memorable, but bearing in mind he had arrived just 48 hours earlier it was understandable. Although the striker managed to find the net on one occasion in nine outings, he found the pace of the English game too fast for his liking and returned home at the end of November.
Birmingham C (Loaned from Tromso on 27/10/95) FL 3+4 FLC 1/1 Others 1

RUSSELL Alexander (Alex) John
Born: Crosby, 17 March 1973
Height: 5'8" Weight: 11.7
Alex gained an unexpected place at right back for Rochdale in 1995-96, when skipper, Andy Thackeray, was injured pre-season, and impressed greatly in his new role. Spent a short loan period at Glenavon for further experience and reverted to midfield in some games near the end of the season, before being incapacitated. Is the son of Alex, the old Southport favourite.
Rochdale (£4,000 from Burscough on 11/7/94) FL 22+10/1 FLC 2 FAC 0+1 Others 1+2

RUSSELL Craig Stewart
Born: South Shields, 4 February 1974
Height: 5'10" Weight: 12.6
Club Honours: Div 1 '96
A life-long Sunderland fan, the young centre forward had the added pleasure of finishing the 1995-96 first division championship

winning campaign as the club's leading scorer for the first time, with 13 goals in 35 games. His tremendous pace and strength troubled defences all season and amongst many high spots, his four goal haul against Millwall in December at Roker, and the goal that put the Rokerites ahead in the FA Cuptie against Manchester United at Old Trafford, were particularly memorable. Popular with the fans, 1996-97 will hopefully see Craig establish himself as a top class striker in the Premiership.

Sunderland (From trainee on 1/7/92) FL 93+25/27 FLC 4+3/1 FAC 5+2/2 Others 2

Craig Russell

RUSSELL Kevin John
Born: Portsmouth, 6 December 1966
Height: 5'9" Weight: 10.12
Club Honours: Div 2 '93
International Honours: E: Yth

Transferred from Notts County to Wrexham during the 1995 close season, Kevin returned his old club to add weight to the striker's department, where he had been so successful in his earlier spell at the Racecourse. However, the majority of the clubs where he has been deployed since, had utilised him more in an attacking midfield role, which was soon apparent early in the season, after he struggled to find any form up front. Having got the message, manager, Brian Flynn, withdrew "Rooster" into left midfield, where he enjoyed a good run with fine workrate and industry, and the ability to be able to add to his goal tally on occasion, a feature of his play.

Portsmouth (Free from Brighton & Hove A juniors on 9/10/84) FL 3+1/1 FLC 0+1 FAC 0+1 Others 1+1

Wrexham (£10,000 on 17/7/87) FL 84/43 FLC 4/1 FAC 4 Others 8/3
Leicester C (£175,000 on 20/6/89) FL 24+19/10 FLC 0+1 FAC 1 Others 5/2
Peterborough U (Loaned on 6/9/90) FL 7/3
Cardiff C (Loaned on 17/1/91) FL 3
Hereford U (Loaned on 7/11/91) FL 3/1 Others 1/1
Stoke C (Loaned on 2/1/92) FL 5/1
Stoke C (£95,000 on 16/7/92) FL 30+10/5 FLC 3 FAC 2 Others 4+1/1
Burnley (£150,000 on 28/6/93) FL 26+2/6 FLC 4/1 FAC 4 Others 1/1
Bournemouth (£125,000 on 3/3/94) FL 30/1 FLC 3/1 FAC 2/1
Notts Co (£60,000 on 24/2/95) FL 9+2
Wrexham (£60,000 on 21/7/95) FL 37+3/7 FLC 2/1 FAC 3 Others 2

RUSSELL Lee Edward
Born: Southampton, 3 September 1969
Height: 5'11" Weight: 12.0

Started the first 12 games for Portsmouth last season at left back, before giving way to Tony Dobson and later moving to the other flank to deputise for Robbie Pethick. Also capable of playing in midfield and central defence, where he has good aerial ability, Lee would have made far more appearances for Pompey in the past had it not been for injuries.

Portsmouth (From trainee on 12/7/88) FL 77+18/1 FLC 4+1 FAC 3+2 Others 5+2
Bournemouth (Loaned on 9/9/94) FL 3

Lee Russell

RUSSELL Wayne Leonard
Born: Cardiff, 29 November 1967
Height: 6'2" Weight: 13.7
Burnley's stand-in goalkeeper during Marlon

Beresford's enforced absences in 1995-96, Wayne proved adept at spectacular saves, but his occasional tendency to error ensured that the former remained the first choice.

Burnley (Signed from Ebbw Vale on 28/10/93) FL 16+2 FAC 1

RUST Nicholas (Nicky) Charles Irwin
Born: Cambridge, 25 September 1974
Height: 6'0" Weight: 13.1
International Honours: E: Yth

A young goalkeeper who, despite the odd blemish, had a good 1995-96 in the Brighton goal. Brave, and a sure shot stopper, he was the only Albion player to appear in every match.

Brighton & Hove A (Free from Arsenal juniors on 9/7/93) FL 136 FLC 12 FAC 6 Others 8

RYAN Darren Thomas
Born: Oswestry, 3 July 1972
Height: 5'10" Weight: 11.0

Having started last season on the Rochdale subs' bench, the speedy forward was recalled for first team duty in November after scoring five goals for the reserves the previous week. However, the front line failed to click and he joined Chester on noncontract forms in March, making less than a handful of appearances before trying his luck in Norway.

Shrewsbury T (From trainee on 23/10/90) FL 3+1 Others 0+1
Chester C (Free on 14/8/92) FL 5+12/2 FLC 2 FAC 1+1/1 Others 1+1
Stockport Co (Signed on 25/1/93) FL 29+7/6 FLC 2/1 FAC 1+1 Others 5+1
Rochdale (Free on 21/7/94) FL 19+13/2 FLC 1+2 FAC 1+3 Others 1+5
Chester C (Free on 18/3/96) FL 2+2/1

RYAN Keith James
Born: Northampton, 25 June 1970
Height: 5'11" Weight: 12.8
Club Honours: FAT '91, '93; GMVC '93

Absent for a year with a cruciate ligament injury, he made a welcome return to his Wycombe central midfield role last January, and having regained his match fitness, put in some memorable performances and underlined his goal scoring ability with four goals. A natural athlete with great strength and stamina, he wins balls he has no right to and delights in surging runs into the penalty area.

Wycombe W (Signed from Berkhamstead in 1989-90) FL 84+5/9 FLC 6/1 FAC 6+3/3 Others 10+1

RYDER Stuart Henry
Born: Sutton Coldfield, 6 November 1973
Height: 6'0" Weight: 12.1
International Honours: E: U21-3

Following on from his highly successful 1994-95, this talented central defender was expected to be one of Walsall's stars last season. However, after playing just four times, a crude tackle in a September reserve fixture forced him out of action with severe knee ligament damage and that was it. Hopefully, Stuart will be ready for 1996-97.

Walsall (From trainee on 16/7/92) FL 75+12/5 FLC 4+1 FAC 8 Others 4+1

SAHLIN Dan
Born: Falum, Sweden, 18 April 1967
Height: 5'10" Weight: 11.6
The Swedish striker remains much of a mystery man for most Birmingham fans. Arriving on trial last November, and following in the footsteps of another Swede, Siggi Rushfeldt, he made a 20-minute subs' appearance against Leicester in the league, before returning home in December.
Birmingham C (Loaned from Hammarby IF on 16/11/95) FL 0+1

John Salako

SALAKO John Akin
Born: Nigeria, 11 February 1969
Height: 5'10" Weight: 12.8
Club Honours: FMC '91; Div '94
International Honours: E: 5
Enigmatic winger purchased by Coventry in the summer of 1995 from Crystal Palace. With excellent ball control, two good feet, and probably the best crosser of the ball in the squad, he showed this to good effect at QPR when making Dion Dublin's equaliser. He also scored a handful of goals himself, including the winner in the classic Coca Cola Cup win over Tottenham and a superb fifth in the 5-0 drubbing of Blackburn. At times, John frustrated the fans by seemingly not getting involved in the game, but he was good enough to be recalled to the England squad after some good early season displays. As his form dipped in the spring, however, he lost his place, only to be called in as a left back because of injury, and was sadly involved with Steve Harkness' broken leg injury in the Easter game at Coventry.
Crystal Palace (From apprentice on 3/11/86) F/PL 172+43/22 FLC 19+5/5 FAC 20/4 Others 11+3/2
Swansea C (Loaned on 14/8/89) FL 13/3 Others 2/1
Coventry C (£1,500,000 on 7/8/95) PL 34+3/3 FLC 3/1 FAC 3/1

SALE Mark David
Born: Burton on Trent, 27 February 1972
Height: 6'5" Weight: 13.8
Striker. Signed from Preston during the 1995 close season, with his height – he is one of the tallest players in the league – Mark soon became a target man for Mansfield and was less effective than he may have been otherwise. Played for the last few months of the season with a broken nose. Has good on the ground skills.
Stoke C (From trainee on 10/7/90) FL 0+2
Cambridge U (Free on 31/7/91. Free to Rocester in December 1991)
Birmingham C (Free on 26/3/92) FL 11+10 FLC 2/1 Others 3+1/2
Torquay U (£10,000 on 5/3/93) FL 30+14/8 FLC 1 FAC 2/1 Others 3+1
Preston NE (£20,000 on 26/7/94) FL 10+3/7 FLC 1+1 FAC 0+1 Others 4
Mansfield T (£50,000 on 31/7/95) FL 24+3/7 FLC 2/1 FAC 1 Others 1

SALMON Michael (Mike) Bernard
Born: Leyland, 14 July 1964
Height: 6'2" Weight: 12.12
Tried and tested Charlton goalkeeper who was first choice for most of last season, other than missing several games through injury, as the team maintained a promotion drive. On one such occasion, he was fortunate to regain his place after Mike Ammann's match winning display at Barnsley, but then kept it by giving some sterling performances. Although his laid back approach sometimes disguised his ability, it was Mike's best campaign to date.
Blackburn Rov (From juniors on 16/10/81) FL 1
Chester C (Loaned on 18/10/82) FL 16 FAC 2
Stockport Co (Free on 3/8/83) FL 118 FLC 10 FAC 3 Others 3
Bolton W (Free on 31/7/86) FL 26 FLC 2 FAC 4 Others 4
Wrexham (£18,000 on 7/3/87) FL 100 FLC 4 FAC 4 Others 9
Charlton Ath (£100,000 on 6/7/89) FL 114 FLC 8 FAC 8 Others 6

SAMPSON Ian
Born: Wakefield, 14 November 1968
Height: 6'2" Weight: 12.8
A solid, dependable Northampton Town central defender. With a penchant to move upfield on set pieces, netting a few goals via free kicks in the process, suspension blighted his appearances last season. Assisted Spurs in the 1995 Inter-Toto Cup.
Sunderland (Signed from Goole T on 13/11/90) FL 13+4/1 FLC 1 FAC 0+2 Others 0+1
Northampton T (Loaned on 8/12/93) FL 8
Northampton T (Free on 5/8/94) FL 72+3/6 FLC 4 FAC 1 Others 5

SAMUEL Randolf (Randy) Fitzgerald
Born: Trinidad, W.I., 23 December 1963
Height: 6'2" Weight: 13.3
International Honours: Canada: 63
Central defender who operated all across the back four for Port Vale in 1995-96 with equal aplomb. Captain of the Canadian national team, he joined the Vale on an extended loan from Dutch team, Fortuna Sittard, after impressing in the reserves. Scored a vital equaliser on his debut against Watford, but, after suffering a leg injury at Southend in December, he hardly appeared again as the club embarked on a long unbeaten run.
Port Vale (Loaned from Fortuna Sittard on 9/11/95) FL 9/1 Others 1

SAMWAYS Mark
Born: Doncaster, 11 November 1968
Height: 6'2" Weight: 14.0
Scunthorpe goalkeeper. Once again gave consistently good performances in 1995-96, before losing form and his place in the side, last March. At his best, is a shot stopper who can keep his side in the game with point-blank saves, his speciality.
Doncaster Rov (From trainee on 20/8/87) FL 121 FLC 3 FAC 4 Others 10
Scunthorpe U (Signed on 26/3/92) FL 155 FLC 8 FAC 13 Others 16

SAMWAYS Vincent (Vinny)
Born: Bethnal Green, 27 October 1968
Height: 5'8" Weight: 11.0
Club Honours: FAC '91; CS '91, '95
International Honours: E: U21-5; Yth
Versatile Everton midfielder with stamina and skill. Began last season in the best possible fashion, performing admirably in the Charity Shield and rounding off a fine performance with the winner. Despite that, however, Vinny did not figure in the manager's plans, although making the odd appearance, and he was loaned out first to Wolves (December), where he played three games, and then to Birmingham (February) for an extended period. Standing in for the injured Paul Tait, and playing mainly in the centre or left-hand side of midfield, he failed to influence Barry Fry enough to make the move permanent and returned to Goodison early.
Tottenham H (From apprentice on 9/11/85) F/PL 165+28/11 FLC 27+4/4 FAC 15+1/2 Others 7+1
Everton (£2,200,000 on 2/8/94) PL 17+5/2 FLC 3/1 Others 2/1
Wolverhampton W (Loaned on 21/12/95) FL 3
Birmingham C (Loaned on 9/2/96) FL 12

SANDEMAN Bradley Robert
Born: Northampton, 24 February 1970
Height: 5'10" Weight: 10.8
Right-sided Port Vale defender who loves to attack. Limited to being a squad member, with only two first team appearances to his credit in 1995-96, one in the Coca Cola Cup and one in the Endsleigh League. Regularly appeared for the reserve side, but was unable to force himself back into first team contention, before being released in the summer.
Northampton T (From trainee on 14/7/88) FL 28+30/3 FLC 2+3 FAC 2 Others 6+1
Maidstone U (£10,000 on 22/2/91) FL 55+2/8 FLC 1 FAC 2 Others 2
Port Vale (Free on 14/8/92) FL 62+7/1 FLC 6+1 FAC 3+1 Others 2

SANDFORD Lee Robert
Born: Basingstoke, 22 April 1968
Height: 6'1" Weight: 12.12
Club Honours: AMC '92; Div 2 '93
International Honours: E: Yth

Defensive left-sided Stoke City centre back who formed a sound partnership with Graham Potter down the flank last season, proving to be a strong tackler and reliable performer. Another virtually ever-present member of the side, and a fully committed defender, there was great concern in the supporters ranks when Sheffield United tried to tease Lee away prior to the deadline.
Portsmouth (From apprentice on 4/12/85) FL 66+6/1 FLC 11 FAC 4 Others 2+1
Stoke C (£140,000 on 22/12/89) FL 255+3/8 FLC 19 FAC 16/2 Others 31/4

SANSAM Christian (Chris)
Born: Hull, 26 December 1975
Height: 5'11" Weight: 11.7

A nippy attacker who failed to achieve his earlier potential, Chris was released by Scunthorpe last February and put in a few appearances for non-league, Halifax, before joining Scarborough a month later on non-contract forms. Impressed when making his debut at Leyton Orient, he remained in the first team squad for the remainder of the season, prior to being released.
Scunthorpe U (From trainee on 23/12/93) FL 10+11/1 FAC 2+1 Others 1+4 (Free to Halifax on 16/2/96)
Scarborough (Free on 15/3/96) FL 5+1

SANSOME Paul Eric
Born: New Addington, 6 October 1961
Height: 6'0" Weight: 13.8
Club Honours: FLT '83

With Simon Royce an ever present in the Southend goal last season, apart from odd appearances on the bench, Paul was consigned to the reserves, until having a spell on loan at Birmingham in January. Summoned to St Andrews during a goalkeeping injury crisis, he played twice, before departing after the 4-3 home defeat at the hands of Charlton in the league. An experienced shot stopper, he is bound to be called upon again.
Millwall (Free from Crystal Palace juniors on 18/4/80) FL 156 FLC 12 FAC 13 Others 9
Southend U (£40,000 on 24/3/88) FL 305 FLC 18 FAC 8 Others 16
Birmingham C (Loaned on 9/1/96) FL 1 FLC 1

SANTOS Yazalde (Ali) Damas
Born: Jersey, 30 July 1975
Height: 5'5" Weight: 10.5

Striker. Joined Bournemouth last November after writing to the club asking for a trial. Having previously played in the Channel Islands, and very quick, Ali made his debut as a substitute in the Auto Windscreen Shield defeat at Bristol Rovers. Received three more opportunities, all of them from the bench, prior to being released in the summer.
Bournemouth (Free from Jersey Scots on 27/11/95) FL 0+3 Others 0+1

SAUNDERS Mark Philip
Born: Reading, 23 July 1971
Height: 5'11" Weight: 10.8

A Plymouth signing from local non-league football, Mark is a combative midfielder with a good eye for goal. Just maturing into the task of professional football when he became a long-term injury casualty, he had already showed enough to prove he has a future at this level. Scored his first league goal away at eventual champions, Preston North End.
Plymouth Arg (Signed from Tiverton T on 22/8/95) FL 4+6/1 FLC 0+1 FAC 0+1

SAVAGE David (Dave) Thomas Patrick
Born: Dublin, 30 July 1973
Height: 6'1" Weight: 12.7
International Honours: Ei: 5; U21-5

Attacking right-sided Millwall midfielder. In and out of the side last season, with a recurring back problem, he has exciting dribbling skills that were highlighted in the Coca Cola Cup-tie at Everton. It was there that he scored a lovely goal, following a mazy run, having sent experienced defenders all over the place in the last minute of Millwall's 4-2 win. His continuing good form saw him remain a fixture in the Eire U21 side, while stepping up to full international status with five caps.
Millwall (£15,000 from Longford T on 27/5/94) FL 48+16/2 FLC 7/1 FAC 3+2/1

SAVAGE Robert (Rob) William
Born: Wrexham, 18 October 1974
Height: 5'11" Weight: 10.7
Club Honours: FAYC '92
International Honours: W: 3; U21-5; Yth; Sch

Rob made the international breakthrough in 1995-96, when earning his first full caps for Wales. Prior to last season, he had mainly played up front for Crewe, but quickly settled down in a new midfield role, his good form influencing the Welsh selectors. All part of the learning process, he will undoubtedly continue to improve.
Manchester U (From trainee on 5/7/93)
Crewe Alex (Free on 22/7/94) FL 33+3/9 FLC 3 FAC 1 Others 5/1

SAVILLE Andrew (Andy) Victor
Born: Hull, 12 December 1964
Height: 6'0" Weight: 12.6
Club Honours: Div 3 '96

Signed by Preston from Birmingham during the 1995 close season to provide chances for his strike partners, Andy completely misread the script and ended 1995-96 as leading scorer, winning a third division championship medal into the bargain. His rugged, shaven-headed appearance hides a skilful touch on the ball, as well as strength in the air and on the ground. The scorer of two hat tricks in the league, he was honoured by selection for the third division team at the PFA Awards Night.
Hull C (Signed on 23/9/83) FL 74+27/18 FLC 6/1 FAC 3+2/1 Others 4+2
Walsall (£100,000 on 23/3/89) FL 28+10/5 FLC 2 Others 1+1
Barnsley (£80,000 on 9/3/90) FL 71+11/21 FLC 5+1 FAC 4 Others 4/1
Hartlepool U (£60,000 on 13/3/92) FL 37/14 FLC 4/1 FAC 4/5 Others 3/1
Birmingham C (£155,000 on 22/3/93) FL 51+8/17 FLC 4/1 FAC 1 Others 1
Burnley (Loaned on 30/12/94) FL 3+1/1 FAC 1
Preston NE (£100,000 on 29/7/95) FL 44/29 FLC 2 FAC 2 Others 2/1

Andy Saville

SCAIFE Nicholas (Nick)
Born: Middlesbrough, 14 May 1975
Height: 6'2" Weight: 11.13

Having made one substitute appearance for York early last season, the hard-tackling central midfielder was unable to establish himself and was released early in February. Two weeks later, he joined Darlington on a non-contract basis, before moving on in April after failing to make an appearance.
York C (Signed from Whitby T on 4/3/95) FL 0+2
Darlington (Free on 2/2/96)

SCALES John Robert
Born: Harrogate, 4 July 1966
Height: 6'2" Weight: 13.5
Club Honours: FAC '88; FLC '95
International Honours: E: 3; B-2

After missing the first nine games of last season through a groin strain, John re-established himself at Liverpool as one of the three first choice central defenders, his perfectly timed tackles, pin-point distribution, and cool head, making him an integral part of the defensive formation that manager, Roy Evans, was trying to perfect. Once back in the side, he missed just six more games, looking to be a defender very much out of the Alan Hansen mould and a possible future captain. And, although surely disappointed after the 1-0 FA Cup final defeat at the hands of Manchester United, by most peoples' reckoning, he was the outstanding Liverpool player on the day, giving a performance to be built on.
Bristol Rov (Free from Leeds U juniors on 11/7/85) FL 68+4/2 FLC 3 FAC 6 Others 3+1
Wimbledon (£70,000 on 16/7/87) F/PL 235+5/11 FLC 18+1 FAC 20+1 Others 7+1/4
Liverpool (£3,500,000 on 2/9/94) PL 62 FLC 9/2 FAC 14 Others 2

SCHMEICHEL Peter Boleslaw
Born: Gladsaxe, Denmark, 18 November 1963
Height: 6'4" Weight: 16.0
Club Honours: ESC '91; FLC '92; PL '93, '94, '96; FAC '94, '96; CS '93, '94
International Honours: Denmark (UEFAC '92): 87

Manchester United goalkeeper with great presence who is quick off his line and is excellent at narrowing the angles. A regular for Denmark, and recognised as one of the world's leading exponents of the art, his distribution is also first class. Once again his influence on the United team was beyond reproach, as the club mounted its perennial quest for major honours in 1995-96, becoming the first goalie since Alex Stepney to get his name on the scoring sheets, when heading home a last minute equaliser against Rotor Volgograd in the UEFA Cup in September. Despite the Reds premature exit from that competition, Peter continued to lead from the back, his magnificent achievement of 22 clean sheets instrumental in United's league and FA Cup double success. Won the "Man of the Match" award against Portugal, playing in all three Euro '96 group matches, before the Danes were eliminated.
Manchester U (£550,000 from Brondby on 12/8/91) F/PL 190 FLC 17 FAC 26 Others 16/1

SCHOFIELD John David
Born: Barnsley, 16 May 1965
Height: 5'11" Weight: 11.3
Solid and reliable Doncaster defender, cum midfielder. Spent much of last season as an integral part of the Rovers' midfield, although he also featured in the back four as a central defender, where he did well. Captained the side occasionally in the absence of Gary Brabin.
Lincoln C (Free from Gainsborough Trinity on 10/11/88) FL 221+10/11 FLC 15/4 FAC 5+2 Others 13+1
Doncaster Rov (Free on 18/11/94) FL 65+3/5 FLC 2 FAC 1 Others 2

SCHOLES Paul
Born: Salford, 16 November 1974
Height: 5'7" Weight: 11.0
Club Honours: PL '96; FAC '96
International Honours: E: Yth (UEFAC '93)
The meteoric rise of Paul delighted Alex Ferguson to such an extent that he likened his young Manchester United star to a younger version of Kenny Dalglish and, at the same time, stated: "You only see a player like you in once in a lifetime". Equally at home playing up front, or in central midfield, Paul notched 11 goals in his first 23 outings for 1995-96 – an amazing fact when one considers that he only completed five of those games. As the season reached its exciting climax, he was seriously challenging Andy Cole for the regular centre forward slot, coming on for the latter in the FA Cup final win over Liverpool to collect another medal, having already received one following the championship success.
Manchester U (From trainee on 29/1/93) PL 22+21/15 FLC 4/4 FAC 1+3/1 Others 1+3/1

SCIMECA Riccardo
Born: Leamington Spa, 13 June 1975
Height: 6'1" Weight: 12.9
Club Honours: FLC '96
International Honours: E: U21-1
An extremely versatile player, Riccardo, top scorer for Aston Villa reserves in 1994-95 while playing in midfield, was added to the first team squad last season as a central defender, making his Premiership debut as a sub against Manchester United. His first full game came against Nottingham Forest in December and thereafter he made several more appearances, both from the bench and as first choice. Recognised by England at U21 level against Portugal, he was also selected as Villa's "Young Player of the Year" by the supporters.
Aston Villa (From trainee on 7/7/93) PL 7+10 FLC 1+2 FAC 2

SCOTT Andrew (Andy)
Born: Epsom, 2 August 1972
Height: 6'1" Weight: 11.5
A utility speedy Sheffield United player, he suffered a serious knee injury in a reserve game and was out for eight weeks, after which he spent the remainder of last season regaining full fitness. Once fully fit, his terrific pace will almost certainly be an asset to the Blades in any number of roles, preferably down the left side, in 1996-97.
Sheffield U (£50,000 from Sutton U on 1/12/92) P/FL 34+27/5 FLC 3/1 FAC 1+1 Others 3+1/3

SCOTT Andrew (Andy) Michael
Born: Manchester, 27 June 1975
Height: 6'0" Weight: 12.11
Injured for so long the ex-Blackburn left back made a lot of trips with the Cardiff first team last season, but was limited to four appearances on the bench and only got involved once – the home game against Fulham. Will be hoping for a change of fortune in 1996-97.
Blackburn Rov (From trainee on 4/1/93)
Cardiff C (Free on 9/8/94) FL 13+1/1 FAC 1 Others 1

SCOTT Keith
Born: London, 9 June 1967
Height: 6'3" Weight: 14.3
Club Honours: GMVC '93; FAT '93
Signed by Norwich from Stoke last November, in a move that saw Mike Sheron go in the opposite direction, Keith made an excellent start with his new club, scoring in each of his first two games, an achievement that was swiftly followed by Martin O'Neill dropping him. Apart from an occasional appearance, five goals in seven reserve matches encouraged Bournemouth to take him on loan in February, but he returned to Carrow Road after just one strike in eight starts. Disappointingly, with Gary Megson operating a 4-4-2 system, following the transfer of Ashley Ward to Derby, it was Ade Akinbiyi who partnered Robert Fleck up front.
Lincoln C (Free from Leicester U on 22/3/90) FL 7+9/2 FLC 0+1 Others 1+1
Wycombe W (£30,000 during 1991 close season) FL 15/10 FLC 4/2 FAC 8/1 Others 10/2

Swindon T (£300,000 on 18/11/93) P/FL 43+8/12 FLC 5/3 Others 3/1
Stoke C (£300,000 on 30/12/94) FL 22+3/3 FAC 2/1 Others 0+1
Norwich C (Signed on 11/11/95) FL 5+7/2 FLC 0+2
Bournemouth (Loaned on 16/2/96) FL 8/1

SCOTT Kevin Watson
Born: Easington, 17 December 1966
Height: 6'4" Weight: 14.0
Club Honours: FAYC '85; Div 1 '93
Tottenham centre back who combines aerial strength at both ends of the field with solid defending and the ability to come out with the ball to get up an attack. Having injured his knee in the 1994-95 end of season tour of Hong Kong, Kevin gamely persevered, making three subs' appearances, before finally giving in to the demands of an operation last December. Unfortunately, it was not a success and had to be followed up by further surgery in order to clear the problem. Hopes to be fit in time for the new campaign, after spending the summer months on a fitness regime.
Newcastle U (From apprentice on 19/12/84) F/PL 227/8 FLC 18 FAC 15+1/1 Others 12+1/2
Tottenham H (£850,000 on 1/2/94) PL 16+2/1 FLC 0+1
Port Vale (Loaned on 13/1/95) FL 17/1

Martin Scott

SCOTT Martin
Born: Sheffield, 7 January 1968
Height: 5'9" Weight: 11.7
Club Honours: Div 4 '89; Div 1 '96
In 1995-96, the left back firmly established himself as the best Sunderland player in that position since the days of Joe Bolton. Always willing to get forward and link up with the attack, "Scotty" is also dangerous from free kicks and was the club's penalty taker. Scored six goals in the promotion campaign, including a brilliant solo effort against Oldham at Roker in March. Missed just three league games in winning a first division championship medal.
Rotherham U (From apprentice on 10/1/86) FL 93+1/3 FLC 11/2 FAC 7+2 Others 7/2
Bristol C (£200,000 on 5/12/90) FL 171/14 FLC 10/1 FAC 10 Others 8/1
Sunderland (£750,000 on 23/12/94) FL 67/6 FLC 3 FAC 5

SCOTT Peter Reginald
Born: Notting Hill, 1 October 1963
Height: 5'9" Weight: 11.12
Barnet club captain at the start of 1995-96, he lost his place in the heart of midfield to Phil Simpson during the season. An experienced pro with 15 years in the game, Peter was released this summer.
Fulham (From apprentice on 2/10/81) FL 268+9/27 FLC 18+2/6 FAC 9/1 Others 15
Bournemouth (Free on 14/8/92) FL 9+1 FLC 2 FAC 1 Others 0+1
Barnet (Free on 4/11/93) FL 72+6/3 FLC 4+2 FAC 8 Others 4

SCOTT Richard Paul
Born: Dudley, 29 September 1974
Height: 5'9" Weight: 10.10
Right-sided Shrewsbury midfielder who can also play at full back. His first full season at Shrewsbury in 1995-96 saw his influence grow, scoring a number of vital point-winning goals with some fine strikes, after arriving in the box with excellent timing. Without a knee injury he would have been ever present.
Birmingham C (From trainee on 17/5/93) FL 11+1 FLC 3+1 Others 3
Shrewsbury T (Signed on 22/3/95) FL 43+1/7 FLC 3 FAC 5/3 Others 6/1

SCOTT Robert (Rob)
Born: Epsom, 15 August 1973
Height: 6'1" Weight: 11.10
Following his move to Fulham from Sheffield United last January, Rob was voted "Man of the Match" on his debut against Scarborough. With great pace and crossing the ball superbly, he appeared mostly as a striker, where his centres, when in a wide right position, brought several goals. Played six games on loan at Northampton, prior to arriving at Craven Cottage.
Sheffield U (£20,000 from Sutton U on 1/8/93) FL 2+4/1 FLC 0+1 Others 2+1
Scarborough (Loaned on 22/3/95) FL 8/3
Northampton T (Loaned on 24/11/95) FL 5 Others 1
Fulham (£30,000 on 10/1/96) FL 21/5

SCOWCROFT James Benjamin
Born: Bury St Edmunds, 15 November 1975
Height: 6'1" Weight: 12.2
An excellent debut season for the young Ipswich striker in 1995-96. First called up to deputise for the injured Ian Marshall at home to Wolves in October, he made good use of his height to win more than his fair share of high balls, in 16 starts and 13 calls from the bench, while scoring two goals. Always gave 100 per cent and looked particularly impressive when leading the line at Derby, a side that eventually made it to the Premier League.
Ipswich T (From trainee on 1/7/94) FL 13+10/2 FLC 0+1 FAC 2 Others 1+2

SCULLY Anthony (Tony) Derek Thomas
Born: Dublin, 12 June 1976
Height: 5'7" Weight: 11.12
International Honours: Ei: U21-7; Yth; Sch
The young Crystal Palace and Eire U21 international finally made his league debut

for the club in 1995-96, as a substitute on the left wing against Charlton, and added another from the bench before going on loan to Cardiff in January. Proving to be a busy ball-winning midfielder in the two months spent at Ninian, and with Phil Neal interested in keeping him, but to no avail, he was recalled to Selhurst Park.
Crystal Palace (From trainee on 2/12/93) FL 0+2
Bournemouth (Loaned on 14/10/94) FL 6+4 Others 2
Cardiff C (Loaned on 5/1/96) FL 13+1

SCULLY Patrick (Pat) Joseph
Born: Dublin, 23 June 1970
Height: 6'1" Weight: 12.7
International Honours: Ei: 1; B-2; U23-1; U21-9; Yth; Sch
Central defender. Established himself as first choice for Huddersfield in 1994-95, last season he found his appearances restricted by the emergence of Kevin Gray. As a result he was placed on the transfer list, but turned down a move to York City in favour of trying to regain his place, something he did at the end of the campaign. Strong in the air and reads the game well.
Arsenal (From trainee on 16/9/87)
Preston NE (Loaned on 7/9/89) FL 13/1 Others 1
Northampton T (Loaned on 23/8/90) FL 15 Others 1
Southend U (£100,000 on 8/1/91) FL 114+1/6 FLC 3 FAC 4 Others 5
Huddersfield T (Free on 24/3/94) FL 74/2 FLC 7/1 FAC 2 Others 6

SEABURY Kevin
Born: Shrewsbury, 24 November 1973
Height: 5'9" Weight: 11.6
Shrewsbury right back. A favourite with the crowd, he consolidated his place in the side in 1995-96, although being absent towards the season's end. As a solid defender, Kevin used the ball sensibly, also playing in central defence and midfield, and always fully committed to the cause. Scored the goal which ensured progress to round two of the Coca Cola Cup.
Shrewsbury T (From trainee on 6/7/92) FL 53+12 FLC 4/1 FAC 4 Others 6+2

SEAGRAVES Mark
Born: Bootle, 22 October 1966
Height: 6'0" Weight: 13.4
Club Honours: Div 2 '96
International Honours: E: Yth
Signed from Bolton during the summer of 1995, Mark proved to be a strong, solid central defender for Swindon last season, playing neat and uncomplicated football in a steady, rather than spectacular fashion, and forged an excellent understanding with Shaun Taylor, a partnership which would have undoubtedly blossomed longer had injuries not kept him sidelined for several weeks. And, with a second division championship medal safely wrapped up, his experience at a higher level should stand him in good stead for the club's return to the Football League elite.
Liverpool (From apprentice on 4/11/83) FLC 1 FAC 1
Norwich C (Loaned on 21/11/86) FL 3
Manchester C (£100,000 on 25/9/87) FL 36+6 FLC 3 FAC 3 Others 2

Bolton W (£100,000 on 24/9/90) FL 152+5/7 FLC 8 FAC 17/1 Others 13/1
Swindon T (£100,000 on 6/6/95) FL 25+3 FLC 4 FAC 3+1 Others 2

SEAL David
Born: Penrith, Australia, 26 January 1972
Height: 5'11" Weight: 12.4
Although coming to Bristol City in 1994-95 with the reputation of being a prolific goalscorer, it was not until last season that he demonstrated this ability in the Robins' first team, notching five goals in the opening five games of the season and finishing up as top scorer with 14 from 26 starts. All at Ashton Gate are hopeful that the necessary awareness required to be successful in the English game will be ably demonstrated in 1996-97, when he should become a real force in the side.
Bristol C (£80,000 from Eendracht Aalst on 7/10/94) FL 24+15/10 FLC 4/3 FAC 1+1 Others 2+1/1

SEALEY Leslie (Les) Jesse
Born: Bethnal Green, 29 September 1957
Height: 6'1" Weight: 13.6
Club Honours: FAC '90; ECWC '91; CS '90
Having joined West Ham in 1994-95 as cover for Ludek Miklosko, Les made an unusual debut for the club at Arsenal last September, when, with two substitutes already on the field of play, he came on as a forward for the concussed John Moncur. Eventually making his full debut at Newcastle, the experienced, brave shot stopper will be remembered for a host of brilliant saves as the Hammers were run ragged in a 3-0 defeat. Freed at the end of the season to join Leyton Orient.
Coventry C (From apprentice on 1/3/76) FL 158 FLC 11 FAC 9
Luton T (£100,000 on 3/8/83) FL 207 FLC 21 FAC 28 Others 3
Plymouth Arg (Loaned on 5/10/84) FL 6
Manchester U (Loaned on 21/3/90) FL 2 FAC 1
Manchester U (Free on 6/6/90) FL 31 FLC 8 FAC 3 Others 9
Aston Villa (Free on 19/7/91) FL 18 FAC 4 Others 2
Coventry C (Loaned on 25/3/92) FL 2
Birmingham C (Loaned on 2/10/92) FL 12 Others 3
Manchester U (Free on 6/1/93) FLC 1 FAC 0+1
Blackpool (Free on 18/7/94) FL 7 FLC 2
West Ham U (Free on 28/11/94) PL 1+1

SEAMAN David Andrew
Born: Rotherham, 19 September 1963
Height: 6'4" Weight: 14.10
Club Honours: Div 1 '91; FAC '93; FLC '93; ECWC '94
International Honours: E: 29; B-6; U21-10
Arsenal goalkeeper who is also firmly entrenched as England's number one. An ever present in 1995-96, David's great presence and calmness instilled confidence in all those around him and greatly helped youngsters like Scott Marshall and Matthew Rose establish themselves as first team squad members. That the Gunners made such a smooth transition to a three-man defence owed much to his control of the area and he continued to add to his game, always trying to find his own players with well-judged, quick throws, his kicking excellent. Enhanced his reputation even more in Euro '96 with two superb penalty saves, one

against Scotland in the group match and the other in a quarter final shoot-out versus Spain, that were instrumental in England reaching the semi-final stage. Is now recognised by many as the best 'keeper in the world.

Leeds U (From apprentice on 22/9/81)
Peterborough U (£4,000 on 13/8/82) FL 91 FLC 10 FAC 5
Birmingham C (£100,000 on 5/10/84) FL 75 FLC 4 FAC 5
Queens Park R (£225,000 on 7/8/86) FL 141 FLC 13 FAC 17 Others 4
Arsenal (£1,300,000 on 18/5/90) F/PL 227 FLC 28 FAC 30 Others 26

SEARLE Damon Peter
Born: Cardiff, 26 October 1971
Height: 5'11" Weight: 10.4
Club Honours: WC '92, '93; Div 3 '93
International Honours: W: B-1; U21-6; Yth
After representing Wales at various levels, and hoping to progress to the senior side, Cardiff's Damon fell victim to loss of form and weight gain in the two seasons leading up 1995-96. Now almost back to his overlapping, attacking best at full back and captaining the side in the absence of Paul Harding, he is currently being monitored by the new Welsh boss, Bobby Gould. *Stop Press:* Signed by Stockport County on 21 May.

Cardiff C (From trainee on 20/8/90) FL 232+2/3 FLC 9/1 FAC 13 Others 29

SEBA Jesus
Born: Zaragoza, Spain, 11 April 1974
Height: 5'7" Weight: 10.3
International Honours: Spain: U21
The third of Wigan Athletic's three Spanish players, Jesus, a small, compact striker with good control and the ability to turn defenders, who signed from Real Zaragoza prior to the start of 1995-96, scored with his first touch in England during a pre-season friendly. Disappointingly, after an impressive start, his appearances were limited to mainly substitute roles.

Wigan Ath (Free from Real Zaragoza on 10/8/95) FL 8+12/3 FLC 2 FAC 0+2 Others 1

SEDGEMORE Benjamin (Ben) Redwood
Born: Wolverhampton, 5 August 1975
Height: 5'10" Weight: 13.11
International Honours: E: Sch
On Birmingham's books as a professional for two years without a first team opportunity, the talented young midfielder went on loan to Mansfield last August, where, after a moderate start, he improved with every game before returning to St Andrews. Still without recognition at City, Ben was snapped up on a free by Peterborough in January, right from under Town's nose, and appeared in 18 of the remaining 26 matches.

Birmingham C (From trainee on 17/5/93)
Northampton T (Loaned on 22/12/94) FL 1
Mansfield T (Loaned on 25/8/95) FL 4+5 Others 1
Peterborough U (Free on 10/1/96) FL 13+4 FAC 1

SEDGLEY Stephen (Steve) Philip
Born: Enfield, 26 May 1968
Height: 6'1" Weight: 13.13
Club Honours: FAC '91; CS '91
International Honours: E: U21-11

Having sorted out his differences with Ipswich during the 1995 close season, Steve finally came good to produce the consistent performances that had been expected of him. A true competitor who is aggressive and makes decisive tackles, he played equally well, whether it was in central defence, in midfield, or even as a sweeper. Although a foot injury forced him to miss the whole of November, he came back without any loss of form to eventually take over the captaincy on Tony Mowbray's enforced absence. Also took over penalty kick duties.

Coventry C (From apprentice on 2/6/86) FL 81+3/3 FLC 9/2 FAC 2+2 Others 5+1
Tottenham H (£750,000 on 28/7/89) F/PL 147+17/8 FLC 24+3/1 FAC 22+1/1 Others 5+3
Ipswich T (£1,000,000 on 15/6/94) P/FL 66/8 FLC 4/1 FAC 5 Others 3/1

Steve Sedgley

SEGERS Johannes (Hans)
Born: Eindhoven, Holland, 30 October 1961
Height: 5'11" Weight: 12.12
Wimbledon goalkeeper. 1995-96 was one which was more about off-field than on-field concerns for the well-travelled Dutchman. In the four league games he did appear, the Dons picked up two vital wins against Chelsea and Arsenal and scraped a draw against Blackburn. In that brief period it was clear to see that Hans had lost none of his acrobatic ability, but, perhaps more important than that, his command over the back four was still a crucial factor. However, at 34 years of age and with match-rigging charges still in the offing, he was released during the summer.

Nottingham F (£50,000 from PSV Eindhoven on 14/8/84) FL 58 FLC 4 FAC 5
Stoke C (Loaned on 13/2/87) FL 1
Sheffield U (Loaned on 19/11/87) FL 10 Others 1
Dunfermline Ath (Loaned on 1/3/88) SL 4
Wimbledon (£180,000 on 28/9/88) F/PL 265+2 FLC 26 FAC 22 Others 7

Scott Sellars

SELLARS Scott
Born: Sheffield, 27 November 1965
Height: 5'8" Weight: 10.0
Club Honours: FMC '87; Div 1 '93
International Honours: E: U21-3
A skilful wide or central left-sided midfield player, who is deadly at free kicks, he settled into the side well, following his transfer from Newcastle last December, and was a part of Bolton's mini-revival towards the latter stages of the campaign. His first goal for the club came at Queens Park Rangers, a powerful long-range drive that became a contender for December's "Goal of the Month" on BBC's *Match Of The Day*. Another feature of his play was the ability to cover back whenever attacks broke down.

Leeds U (From apprentice on 25/7/83) FL 72+4/12 FLC 4/1 FAC 4 Others 2/1
Blackburn Rov (£20,000 on 28/7/86) FL 194+8/35 FLC 12/3 FAC 11/1 Others 20/2
Leeds U (£800,000 on 1/7/92) PL 6+1 FLC 1+1 Others 1
Newcastle U (£700,000 on 9/3/93) F/PL 56+5/5 FLC 6+1/2 FAC 3 Others 4/1
Bolton W (£750,000 on 7/12/95) PL 22/3 FAC 1

SERRANT Carl
Born: Bradford, 12 September 1975
Height: 5'11" Weight: 12.1
International Honours: E: Yth
Another Oldham youngster to make his mark in 1995-96, Carl made his first team debut against Cesena in the Anglo-Italian Cup in the left back position last October. He was soon staking a claim for a regular place and towards the end of January, Chris Makin moved over to the other flank, allowing him to play in 22 of the last 23 games. Strong, with lightening pace, and good in the air, the young defender has quickly become an asset and is one to watch out for.

Oldham Ath (From trainee on 22/7/94) FL 20/1 FAC 2 Others 3

SERTORI Mark Anthony
Born: Manchester, 1 September 1967
Height: 6'3" Weight: 14.2
Club Honours: GMVC '88

A squad player, able to perform both in defence and attack, Mark started four league games for Bury in 1995-96, playing twice as a full back and twice as centre forward. When chosen for the home game against Fulham in April (ahead of fans' choice Phil Stant) he silenced his critics with the opening goal in a 3-0 win – his only ever goal for the club, prior to being freed at the end of the campaign. Had earlier spent a period on loan at non-league Witton Albion.

Stockport Co (Signed on 7/2/87) FL 3+1 FLC 1
Lincoln C (Free on 1/7/88) FL 43+7/9 FLC 6 FAC 4/1 Others 5/2
Wrexham (£30,000 on 9/2/90) FL 106+4/3 FLC 8+1 FAC 6 Others 9+1
Bury (Free on 22/7/94) FL 4+9/1 FLC 1 FAC 2+1 Others 1+2/1

SHAIL Mark Edward David
Born: Sandviken, Sweden, 15 October 1966
Height: 6'1" Weight: 13.3
International Honours: E: SP-1

The Bristol City central defender had a wretched season in 1995-96, due to injury problems which saw him miss the second half of the campaign after just 13 starts. However, as a cool, composed player, good in the air, and more than capable on the ground, he has proved to have been a good purchase from non-league Yeovil Town just over three years ago.

Bristol C (£45,000 from Yeovil on 25/3/93) FL 84+6/4 FLC 5+1 FAC 10/1 Others 2

SHAKESPEARE Craig Robert
Born: Birmingham, 26 October 1963
Height: 5'10" Weight: 12.5

Grimsby midfield ball winner. Having played in the opening eight matches of 1995-96 before being dropped, changes during the club's indifferent mid-season run, enabled him to re-establish himself in the number eight shirt, his ability to carry the ball, giving Town further options. Is equally at home in central midfield or wide on the flanks.

Walsall (From apprentice on 5/11/81) FL 276+8/45 FLC 31/6 FAC 22/6 Others 18/2
Sheffield Wed (£300,000 on 19/6/89) FL 15+2 FLC 3/1 Others 0+1
West Bromwich A (£275,000 on 8/2/90) FL 104+8/3 FLC 6/1 FAC 5/2 Others 5/1
Grimsby T (£115,000 on 14/7/93) FL 61+19/8 FLC 4+1 FAC 5+2 Others 0+1

SHARP Kevin Phillip
Born: Canada, 19 September 1974
Height: 5'9" Weight: 11.11
Club Honours: FAYC '93
International Honours: E: Yth (UEFAYC '93); Sch

Having made just one subs' appearance for Leeds in 1995-96, Kevin became Wigan Athletic's first £100,000 signing last November. A skilful, left-sided midfielder with vision, who is also a good tackler, he scored the club's "Goal of the Season", his second in an impressive home victory over

Cardiff City. Out of action due to injury, his strong running and passing skills were sorely missed in Latic's push for promotion in the final months of the season.

Leeds U (£60,000 from Auxerre on 20/10/92) PL 11+6 Others 0+1
Wigan Ath (£100,000 on 30/11/95) FL 20/6 FAC 1

SHARP Raymond (Ray)
Born: Stirling, 16 November 1969
Height: 5'11" Weight: 12.5
Club Honours: S Div 1 '89
International Honours: S: U21-4

Left back Ray was relegated to the role of squad player at Preston last season, but his limited appearances for the first team confirmed he is still a good defensive player, who is sound in the tackle, with good heading ability. In short, a very experienced defender.

Dunfermline Ath (Signed from Gairdoch U on 18/8/86) SL 144+7/1 SLC 4+3 SC 7 Others 2+1/1
Stenhousemuir (Loaned in February 1989) SL 5
Preston NE (Signed on 5/10/94) FL 22 FLC 2 FAC 3 Others 2

SHARPE John James
Born: Birmingham, 9 August 1975
Height: 5'11" Weight: 11.6

The brother of Manchester United's Lee, and a Manchester City professional since 1993, in order to have a taste of first team football, John went to Exeter on loan last February, appearing 14 times and scoring his first ever goal at Lincoln, before arriving back at Maine Road. The experience should have benefited him greatly. Released at the end of the season, just like his brother, he is a left-sided midfielder who goes past defenders to cross examining balls into dangerous areas and should have no difficulty in finding another club.

Manchester C (From trainee on 9/7/93)
Exeter C (Loaned on 1/2/96) FL 9+5/1

SHARPE Lee Stuart
Born: Halesowen, 27 May 1971
Height: 6'0" Weight: 12.7
Club Honours: ECWC '91; FLC '92; PL '93, '94, '96; FAC '94, '96; CS '94
International Honours: E: 8; B-1; U21-8

Very skilful Manchester United left-sided player who loves running at defenders to give himself the option of shooting or crossing. Very strong in possession, and highly competitive, although his form suffered badly in 1995-96 due to a succession of serious back injuries suffered during the early part of the season, he came back well to lead United through their successful FA Cup campaign, with goals against Manchester City, and Southampton in successive rounds. And, at the end of another great season, his 41 games, including 12 from the subs' bench, were more than enough for him to collect both the championship and FA Cup winners' medal double for the second time in his career.

Torquay U (From trainee on 31/5/88) FL 9+5/3 Others 2+3
Manchester U (£185,000 on 10/6/88) F/PL 160+33/21 FLC 15+8/9 FAC 22+7/3 Others 18+2/3

SHARPLES John Benjamin
Born: Bury, 26 January 1973
Height: 6'1" Weight: 12.8

Signed from Ayr United, whom he captained, just before the transfer deadline, he figured in York's defence during the closing weeks of last season. A tall central defender, John quietly impressed with his passing skills and could become a leading light at Bootham Crescent. Also, a good tackler.

Heart of Midlothian (Free from Manchester U juniors on 26/7/91)
Ayr U (Signed on 13/7/94) SL 53/4 SLC 2 SC 2 Others 2
York C (£75,000 on 28/3/96) FL 10

SHAW Graham Paul
Born: Stoke, 7 June 1967
Height: 5'9" Weight: 11.5
Club Honours: Div 2 '93

Rochdale's initial choice at centre forward in 1995-96, he had a long spell alternating between the starting line-up and the substitute's bench. Sadly, he was unable to get on the score sheet in league games and disappeared from the scene after the end of January, before being released at the end of the season.

Stoke C (From apprentice on 10/6/85) FL 83+16/18 FLC 7/2 FAC 2+4/1 Others 3+2/2
Preston NE (£70,000 on 24/7/89) FL 113+8/29 FLC 5/6 FAC 5/1 Others 13/6
Stoke C (£70,000 on 12/8/92) FL 23+13/5 FLC 2+1/1 FAC 2+1 Others 2+4
Plymouth Arg (Loaned on 26/8/94) FL 6
Rochdale (Free on 23/3/95) FL 13+9/1 FLC 1/1 FAC 0+3 Others 1+1

SHAW Paul
Born: Burnham, 4 September 1973
Height: 5'11" Weight: 12.4
International Honours: E: Yth

Free-scoring Arsenal fringe player who, unable to get a chance at Highbury, was again loaned out in 1995-96. Beginning the season at Cardiff, Paul failed to find the net in six games, before spending a three month spell at Peterborough, which proved more fruitful. There, he not only added skill and craft in 14 games, but scored five goals, two of them on his last appearance for the club. Much to the disappointment of the fans, Posh were quoted a ridiculous fee to take him permanently. Able to play up front or in midfield, he came off the bench three times for the Gunners at the end of the campaign.

Arsenal (From trainee on 18/9/91) PL 0+4
Burnley (Loaned on 23/3/95) FL 8+1/4
Cardiff C (Loaned on 11/8/95) FL 6
Peterborough U (Loaned on 20/10/95) FL 12/5 Others 2

SHAW Richard Edward
Born: Brentford, 11 September 1968
Height: 5'9" Weight: 12.8
Club Honours: FMC '91; Div 1 '94

A highly-rated Coventry defender, who can play in the centre of defence or at full back, Richard was signed from Crystal Palace last November. Unfortunately, it was during City's worst spell of the season and they conceded 16 goals in his first five games. Settling down, however, and seemingly developing a good understanding with

David Busst, when Liam Daish arrived his form seemed to suffer. Had an outstanding game at full back at Everton when asked to do a man-to-man marking job on Andrei Kanchelskis, but suffered a fractured cheek-bone at White Hart Lane and missed the Easter games, before returning for the run-in, playing with a special mask to protect his cheek. Comfortable with ball at his feet and an excellent passer.

Crystal Palace (From apprentice on 4/9/86) F/PL 193+14/3 FLC 28+2 FAC 18 Others 12+1
Hull C (Loaned on 14/12/89) FL 4
Coventry C (£1,000,000 on 17/11/95) PL 21 FAC 3

SHAW Simon Robert
Born: Middlesbrough, 21 September 1973
Height: 6'0" Weight: 12.0

After playing in Darlington's midfield for three seasons, Simon made the right back spot his own in 1995-96, where his skill and strength were seen to good effect. Sadly, an excellent season was marred when he received a broken jaw, causing him to miss the play offs and a Wembley selection.

Darlington (From trainee on 14/8/92) FL 82+25/7 FLC 4+1 FAC 4/1 Others 4+1

SHEARER Alan
Born: Newcastle, 13 August 1970
Height: 6'0" Weight: 12.1
Club Honours: PL '95
International Honours: E: 28; B-1; U21-11; Yth

Blackburn and England striker who is simply the best. What can be said of a man who scored five Premier League hat tricks in 1995-96, with a side that were often struggling with enforced changes every week. Yet it is not just as a goalscorer that Alan ranks supreme. He lifts his team mates by working harder than anyone, acting as target man, running unselfishly, and when he has to, tackling back with great vigour and commitment. Added to an ideal temperament and a perfect attitude, this is a man who already has achieved sufficient in his Rovers' career to be ranked as one of their four greatest players of all time. There is probably no other player in the Premier League who exerts as great an influence on the team as Alan Shearer at Blackburn. Handicapped by a groin injury that necessitated surgery, so that he could be fit for European Championship, this forced him to miss the final two games of the season and gave him just one opportunity to obtain the goal that would make him the first top flight player to score 30 goals in three successive seasons. He took just 13 minutes against Wimbledon and, for good measure, added another to leave the campaign with an ovation from the entire crowd, who stood at the end to salute his contribution to football in general. Once again elected by his fellow professionals to the Premiership award winning team, the best centre forward to be found had a brilliant Euro '96, scoring in four out of five games, and heading the competition with five goals.

Southampton (From trainee on 14/4/88) FL 105+13/23 FLC 16+2/11 FAC 11+3/4 Others 8/5
Blackburn Rov (£3,600,000 on 24/7/92) PL 132+6/112 FLC 16/14 FAC 8/2 Others 9/2

Alan Shearer

SHEARER Lee Sean
Born: Southend, 23 October 1977
Height: 6'3" Weight: 12.0

Having signed professional forms for Leyton Orient during the 1995 close season, the tall central defender made only a handful of appearances in 1995-96 – all part of the plan not to rush him. However, he continued to show great promise and is set to become an Orient star.

Leyton Orient (From trainee on 6/7/95) FL 7+3/1 FLC 1+1

SHEFFIELD Jonathan (Jon)
Born: Bedworth, 1 February 1969
Height: 5'11" Weight: 12.10

As Cambridge's only experienced goal-keeper, the club somewhat surprisingly transferred him to Peterborough during the 1995 close season. Ever present at Posh in 1995-96, his displays in a team that struggled were often the difference between victory and defeat, just as they had been at City a year earlier. Is extremely agile and an excellent shot stopper.

Norwich C (From apprentice on 16/2/87) FL 1
Aldershot (Loaned on 22/9/89) FL 11 Others 1
Aldershot (Loaned on 21/8/90) FL 15 Others 1
Cambridge U (Free on 18/3/91) FL 56 FLC 3 FAC 4 Others 6
Colchester U (Loaned on 23/12/93) FL 6
Swindon T (Loaned on 28/1/94) PL 2
Hereford U (Loaned on 15/9/94) FL 8 FLC 2
Peterborough U (£150,000 on 20/7/95) FL 46 FLC 4 FAC 4 Others 5

SHELTON Gary
Born: Nottingham, 21 March 1958
Height: 5'7" Weight: 11.2
International Honours: E: U21-1

Although the vastly experienced Chester midfielder was appointed player/coach during the 1995 close season, working under new manager, Kevin Ratcliffe, he was still considered a skilful playmaker and, to that end, made 11 appearances in the league in 1995-96. Looked a cut above most, even at the age of 38.

Walsall (From apprentice on 1/3/76) FL 12+12 FLC 0+1 FAC 2+2/1
Aston Villa (£80,000 on 18/1/78) FL 24/7 FLC 2+1/1
Notts Co (Loaned on 13/3/80) FL 8
Sheffield Wed (£50,000 on 25/3/82) FL 195+3/18 FLC 19/3 FAC 23+1/3 Others 1
Oxford U (£150,000 on 24/7/87) FL 60+5/1 FLC 7+1/2 FAC 5 Others 1
Bristol C (Signed on 24/8/89) FL 149+1/24 FLC 12 FAC 9 Others 9/3
Rochdale (Loaned on 11/2/94) FL 3
Chester C (Free on 22/7/94) FL 41+3/3 FLC 2+1 FAC 2 Others 2/2

SHEPPARD Simon
Born: Clevedon, 7 August 1973
Height: 6'4" Weight: 14.12
International Honours: E: Yth; Sch

Transferred from Watford last September, it was always going to be difficult for him to replace the cult figure of Shaka Hislop in the Reading fans' minds, and he was never certain of a regular spot between the posts. He contributed to his own downfall with some erratic displays, but showed great courage in continuing to play, whilst knowing that he was never first choice and that he would be given a free transfer at the end of the season.

Watford (From trainee on 30/4/91) FL 23 FLC 4 FAC 1 Others 2
Scarborough (Loaned on 17/3/94) FL 9
Reading (Signed on 9/9/94) FL 18 FLC 4

SHERIDAN Darren Stephen
Born: Manchester, 8 December 1967
Height: 5'6" Weight: 10.12

Showed his versatility during last season by being equally at home for Barnsley in either the left wing/back or central midfield position. The experience he gained in 1994-95 was put to great effect, as he mixed hard tackling with delicate passing in whatever position he occupied.

Barnsley (£10,000 from Winsford U on 12/8/93) FL 75+4/2 FLC 3 FAC 3 Others 1+1

SHERIDAN John Joseph
Born: Stretford, 1 October 1964
Height: 5'9" Weight: 12.0
Club Honours: FLC '91
International Honours: Ei: 34; B-1; U23-2; U21-2; Yth

This polished Irish international midfield playmaker seemed to spend most of 1995-96 out of favour with Sheffield Wednesday boss, David Pleat and was farmed out to Birmingham on loan in February, with talk of a full transfer. However, John came back to Hillsborough to regain his spot in the side and the reception he got from the fans and the difference he made showed that he still had a vital contribution to make to Owls' future. He may be nearing the veteran stage, but he is still a great passer of the ball and despite an in-and-out season, continued to be selected for the Republic.

Leeds U (Free from Manchester C juniors on 2/3/82) FL 225+5/47 FLC 14/3 FAC 11+1/1 Others 11/1
Nottingham F (£650,000 on 3/8/89) FLC 1
Sheffield Wed (£500,000 on 3/11/89) F/PL 187+8/25 FLC 24/3 FAC 17+1/3 Others 4/2
Birmingham C (Loaned on 9/2/96) FL 1+1 FLC 2

221

SHERINGHAM Edward (Teddy) Paul
Born: Highams Park, 2 April 1966
Height: 5'11" Weight: 12.5
Club Honours: Div 2 '88; FMC '92
International Honours: E: 20; U21-1; Yth

A natural goalscorer, and thought by many to be at the peak of his career in 1995-96, Teddy was once again among the top five sharpshooters in the Premiership, with 24 goals for Tottenham, and earned himself an England recall as a reward. Continuing to demonstrate his intelligence, quick thinking, and unselfishness, both for club and country, Les Ferdinand was one who benefited from his skills during a superb performance against Bulgaria in the run up to Euro '96, and it was no coincidence that Chris Armstrong had such a terrific season, scoring 22 goals, after replacing Jurgen Klinsmann as his strike partner at Spurs. Apart from being ever present, a hat trick in the FA Cup third round replay against Hereford, an exquisite chip to earn him "Goal of the Month" at Coventry, and the opener in the 4-1 defeat of Manchester United, were the highlights of his club season. An automatic choice for Terry Venables' England squad for the European Championship '96, Teddy played in all five matches that ended in the semi finals at the hands of Germany.
Millwall (From apprentice on 19/1/84) FL 205+15/93 FLC 16+1/8 FAC 12/5 Others 11+2/5
Aldershot (Loaned on 1/2/85) FL 4+1 Others 1
Nottingham F (£2,000,000 on 23/7/91) FL 42/14 FLC 10/5 FAC 4/2 Others 6/2
Tottenham H (£2,100,000 on 28/8/92) PL 134+3/69 FLC 11/6 FAC 17/13

SHERLOCK Paul Graeme
Born: Wigan, 17 November 1973
Height: 5'10" Weight: 11.5
Signed by Mansfield as defensive cover during the play-off challenge in 1994-95, he had a mixed season in 1995-96 being in and out of the team at various times, sometimes due to injury. Predominately a left-sided player.
Notts Co (From trainee on 1/7/92) FL 8+4/1 FLC 1 FAC 2 Others 2+1
Mansfield T (£15,000 on 23/3/95) FL 15+5/2 FLC 1 FAC 2/1 Others 0+1

SHERON Michael (Mike) Nigel
Born: Liverpool, 11 January 1972
Height: 5'9" Weight: 11.7
International Honours: E: U21-16
Joined Stoke from Norwich last season, in a swap deal involving Keith Scott going in the reverse direction, with Stoke agreeing to pay £150,000 after 30 appearances. Regarded by many as a great prospect, his goals per game average was certainly first class and all Potters' fans surely believe the club had the best end of the transfer swop. Injury had disrupted his spell at Norwich, but the future for Mike is now brighter than at any time since his peak Manchester City spell.
Manchester C (From trainee on 5/7/90) F/PL 82+18/24 FLC 9+1/1 FAC 5+3/3 Others 1
Bury (Loaned on 28/3/91) FL 1+4/1 Others 2
Norwich C (£1,000,000 on 26/8/94) P/FL 19+9/2 FLC 6/3 FAC 4/2
Stoke C (£450,000 on 13/11/95) FL 23+5/15 Others 2

SHERWOOD Timothy (Tim) Alan
Born: St Albans, 6 February 1969
Height: 6'0" Weight: 11.6
Club Honours: PL '95
International Honours: E: B-1; U21-4
A mobile Blackburn midfielder, who relishes work, keeps on his feet and never shirks a contest. It was forecast that Tim would return to London during the 1995 close season, but he stayed and battled on, profiting from David Batty's split with Ray Harford, to keep his place and the captaincy, while missing just five games.
Watford (From trainee on 7/2/87) FL 23+9/2 FLC 4+1 FAC 9 Others 4+1
Norwich C (£175,000 on 18/7/89) FL 66+5/10 FLC 7/1 FAC 4 Others 5+1/2
Blackburn Rov (£500,000 on 12/2/92) F/PL 154+5/14 FLC 18 FAC 9+2/1 Others 10

SHILTON Samuel (Sam) Roger
Born: Nottingham, 21 July 1978
Height: 5'10" Weight: 10.0
A useful left winger, Sam was sold to Coventry early last season, having played just one match for Plymouth in 1995-96 as a substitute and yet to turn professional. The son of Peter, the former England goalkeeper, he is very much one for the future and has yet to make his debut for City.
Plymouth Arg (Trainee) FL 1+2 FAC 0+1
Coventry C (£12,500 on 31/10/95)

SHIPPERLEY Neil Jason
Born: Chatham, 30 October 1974
Height: 6'1" Weight: 13.12
International Honours: E: U21-7
Southampton centre forward who is good on the ball, with distribution to match, and who packs a shot in both feet. He also has good workrate, being prepared to chase lost causes and to pressure defenders into errors. The leading scorer last season with 11 goals, he was perhaps unfortunate not to have hit the net more often, his televised disallowed goal at Manchester United in the FA Cup being just one that he could have added to his final total. Still the club's record signing, and a current England U21 international, Neil promises to be right up there among the leading Premiership strikers.
Chelsea (From trainee on 24/9/92) PL 26+11/7 FLC 4+2/1 FAC 3/1 Others 2
Watford ((Loaned on 7/12/94) FL 5+1/1
Southampton (£1,250,000 on 6/1/95) PL 56/10 FLC 4/2 FAC 10/5

SHIRTLIFF Peter Andrew
Born: Hoyland, 6 April 1961
Height: 6'2" Weight: 13.3
Club Honours: FLC '91
Experienced Barnsley central defender. Signed from Wolves at the beginning of 1995-96, having suffered with injuries throughout the previous season, another injury early into the campaign forced him to miss a number of games. However, his organisational value to the team came through as 1995-96 unfolded. Big and brave, rarely losing out in the air, and a strong tackler, Peter could still have a say this coming term.
Sheffield Wed (From apprentice on 31/10/78) FL 188/4 FLC 17+1 FAC 17+1/1

Charlton Ath (£125,000 on 6/8/86) FL 102+1/7 FLC 10 FAC 5 Others 7/2
Sheffield Wed (£500,000 on 26/7/89) F/PL 104/4 FLC 18/1 FAC 9/2 Others 4
Wolverhampton W (£250,000 on 18/8/93) FL 67+2 FLC 4 FAC 7 Others 5
Barnsley (£125,000 on 25/8/95) FL 32 FAC 1

SHORT Christian (Chris) Mark
Born: Munster, Germany, 9 May 1970
Height: 5'10" Weight: 12.2
Club Honours: AIC '95
Having languished in Notts County's reserves for most of the first half of 1995-96, apart from making just three subs' appearances for the first team, Chris signed for Sheffield United last December in a deal which took Paul Rogers in the opposite direction, plus a cash adjustment in favour of the Blades. The brother of Everton's Craig, he soon made the right back spot his own with some fine attacking displays and quality crossing. Is a strong tackler who can be used in the centre of the defence if required.
Scarborough (Free from Pickering T on 11/7/88) FL 42+1/1 FLC 5 FAC 1 Others 3+1
Notts Co (£100,000 on 5/9/90) FL 77+17/2 FLC 4+1 Others 8+1/1
Huddersfield T (Loaned on 23/12/94) FL 6 Others 1
Sheffield U (Signed on 29/12/95) FL 13+2 FAC 3

Craig Short

SHORT Craig Jonathan
Born: Bridlington, 25 June 1968
Height: 6'2" Weight: 13.2
A strong, tall and imposing centre back, Craig joined Everton from Derby during the 1995 close season and, despite an unconvincing debut against Nottingham Forest, soon began to find the accomplished form that had alerted Joe Royle in the first place. After settling in, and striking up a good understanding with fellow defender, Dave

Watson, it was easy for the supporters to see why a relatively large fee had been involved to warrant his signature. Continuing to grow in confidence, and providing a constant threat from set pieces with his heading ability, his long awaited first goal arrived in the 4-0 Boxing Day success over Middlesbrough.

Scarborough (Free from Pickering T on 15/10/87) FL 61+2/7 FLC 6 FAC 2 Others 7/1
Notts Co (£100,000 on 27/7/89) FL 128/6 FLC 6/1 FAC 8/1 Others 16/2
Derby Co (£2,500,000 on 18/9/82) FL 118/9 FLC 11 FAC 7/4 Others 7
Everton (£2,700,000 on 18/7/95) PL 22+1/2 FLC 2 FAC 3 Others 3

SHOTTON Malcolm
Born: Newcastle, 16 February 1957
Height: 6'3" Weight: 13.12
Club Honours: Div 3 '84, Div 2 '85; FLC '88

Was again brought out of retirement in 1995-96 when Barnsley suffered suspension and injuries to the central defence in mid-September, his never-say-die attitude coming to the fore. Later in the season it was announced there would be no more come-backs and that he would concentrate on his duties as Danny Wilson's assistant.

Leicester C (From apprentice on 1/2/75)
Oxford U (£15,000 from Nuneaton Borough on 19/5/80) FL 262+1/12 FLC 41+1/2 FAC 21/1 Others 6
Portsmouth (£70,000 on 28/8/87) FL 10 FLC 2
Huddersfield T (£20,000 on 16/2/88) FL 16/1 FLC 2
Barnsley (Signed on 9/9/88) FL 64+2/6 FLC 2 FAC 3+1 Others 2
Hull C (£35,000 on 28/2/90) FL 58+1/2 FLC 2 FAC 4 Others 3
Ayr U (Free on 4/9/92) SL 73/3 SLC 1 SC 3 Others 6
Barnsley (Free on 20/7/94) FL 10/1 FLC 1

SHOWLER Paul
Born: Doncaster, 10 October 1966
Height: 5'10" Weight: 11.6
International Honours: E: SP-2

Playing in midfield, although occasionally at centre forward for Bradford last season, the former PC appeared in 43 of the opening 48 games, prior to being forced out of action, firstly with a groin strain and then the need for a cartilage operation. Mainly left sided, and capable of attacking the full back to get his crosses in, Paul remained City's leading scorer with 14 to his credit.

Barnet (Free from Altrincham T on 15/8/91) FL 69+2/12 FLC 2 FAC 3+1/1 Others 7
Bradford C (Free on 4/8/93) FL 72+16/15 FLC 8+1/5 FAC 6/2 Others 4+1

SHUTT Carl Steven
Born: Sheffield, 10 October 1961
Height: 5'10" Weight: 11.13
Club Honours: Div 2 '90; Div 1 '92

A hard-working midfielder, cum forward, Carl played in most of Bradford's games prior to last January, following which he was used mainly as a substitute. Put on the transfer list in March, but only offered loan spells, he continued to fight for his place, before coming back into the side and scoring the goal that took City into the play offs and, ultimately, the first division.

Sheffield Wed (Free from Spalding on 13/5/85) FL 36+4/16 FLC 3/1 FAC 4+1/4
Bristol C (£55,000 on 30/10/87) FL 39+7/10 FLC 5+2/4 FAC 7+1/4 Others 10+1/4
Leeds U (£50,000 on 23/3/89) F/PL 46+33/17 FLC 6+2/2 FAC 10/1 Others 4+5/4
Birmingham C (£50,000 on 23/8/93) FL 18+8/4 FLC 3
Manchester C (Loaned on 31/12/93) PL 5+1
Bradford C (£75,000 on 11/8/94) FL 50+16/12 FLC 7+1/1 FAC 2+2 Others 5+2/1

SIGURDSSON Larus Orri
Born: Akureyri, Iceland, 4 June 1973
Height: 6'0" Weight: 12.8
International Honours: Iceland: U21; Yth

Icelandic U21 international centre half prospect who had another good season for Stoke in 1995-96. An excellent stopper and reliable tackler, occasionally let down somewhat by erratic distribution, he is a cousin of former City midfielder, Toddy Orlygsson, now with Oldham. For what he cost, the club have one of the best bargains secured in a long time. Still an improving player. Ever present in the league, Larus missed just one match throughout the campaign.

Stoke C (£150,000 on 21/10/94) FL 68+2/1 FLC 3 FAC 2+1 Others 4

SILENZI Andrea
Born: Rome, Italy, 10 February 1966
Height: 6'3" Weight: 11.13
International Honours: Italy: 1

The first Italian player to move from the Serie "A" to the Premiership, his signing by Nottingham Forest from Torino, prior to 1995-96 getting underway, was cited as evidence that English football could at last compete on equal terms with anyone in terms of money. However, the highly-rated former Italian international, with over 30 goals to his name during the past two seasons, did not fit into Forest's style of play, starting just seven games, plus 11 from the bench, and scoring a meagre couple of goals. A tall, gangling forward, Andrea was bought specifically to lend his aerial skills to Forest's assault on the championship and their European quest, but plagued by injury and illness throughout the campaign, the plan backfired.

Nottingham F (£1,800,000 from Torino on 16/8/95) PL 3+7 FLC 1/1 FAC 2+1/1 Others 1+3

SIMPSON Colin Robertson
Born: Oxford, 30 April 1976
Height: 6'1" Weight: 11.5

Leggy, coltish Watford winger who was given a first team chance late last season, making his debut as a second half substitute against Portsmouth. A regular reserve, he normally plays on the right flank.

Watford (From trainee on 6/7/94) FL 0+1

SIMPSON Fitzroy
Born: Bradford on Avon, 26 February 1970
Height: 5'8" Weight: 10.7

Signed by Portsmouth from Manchester City early in 1995-96, as a makeweight in the deal that saw Kit Symons travel in the opposite direction, "Fitz" immediately fitted into the team as a tough-tackling midfielder,

contributing with a handful of goals into the bargain. Ruled out by injury and suspension for the mid-part of the season, he returned for the relegation dog-fight. Not afraid to take defenders on and has good stamina.

Swindon T (From trainee on 6/7/88) FL 78+27/9 FLC 15+2/1 FAC 2+1 Others 3+2
Manchester C (£500,000 on 6/3/92) F/PL 58+13/4 FLC 5+1 FAC 4+1
Bristol C (Loaned on 16/9/94) FL 4
Portsmouth (£200,000 on 17/8/95) FL 27+3/5 FLC 1 FAC 1

SIMPSON Gary John
Born: Ashford, 14 February 1976
Height: 6'2" Weight: 14.0

Made a promising debut for Luton as a substitute in the Anglo-Italian Cup last November away to Cesena, prior to being loaned to Fulham just before the transfer deadline in March. As a tall central defender, Gary showed up well in seven games, being used as the third centre back in a new formation and, back at Kenilworth Road, can be expected to challenge for a place in 1996-97. Had actually started 1995-96 on loan at non-leaguers, Aylesbury.

Luton T (From trainee on 1/7/94) Others 0+1
Fulham (Loaned on 28/3/96) FL 5+2

SIMPSON Karl Edward
Born: Newmarket, 14 October 1976
Height: 5'11" Weight: 11.9

Having studied for his "A" levels, it was not until July 1995, when Karl joined Norwich's pro ranks, had he ever trained on a full-time basis. Well built, with a competitive attitude and good pace, he was unfortunate to be sent off after 78 minutes of his first team debut against Torquay in the Coca Cola Cup, prior to making his only appearance in the league at home to Barnsley. A versatile player, who can be utilised as an out-and-out striker on occasions, Karl has an arrow-like long throw which will serve him well, as will his enthusiasm.

Norwich C (From juniors on 4/7/95) FL 1 FLC 1

SIMPSON Michael
Born: Nottingham, 28 February 1974
Height: 5'9" Weight: 10.8
Club Honours: AIC '95

The young homegrown Notts County midfielder was a regular first team selection in the first half of last season, before finding himself squeezed out of contention in the latter stages, following the arrival of Paul Rogers and Ian Richardson. A useful dead ball kicker with free kicks and corners, who can also pass long balls with accuracy, County will be looking for him to come again.

Notts Co (From trainee on 1/7/92) FL 38+10/3 FLC 4+1 FAC 2+1 Others 7+3

SIMPSON Paul David
Born: Carlisle, 26 July 1966
Height: 5'7" Weight: 11.12
International Honours: E: U21-5; Yth

Left-sided winger, cum striker, Paul is Derby's dead ball specialist who, in 1995-96, again had a most consistent campaign. Still very quick, and possessing the ability to swing over telling crosses, he was behind much of the success that Dean Sturridge achieved. Proved he was a constant goal threat when hitting a 15 minute hat trick against Tranmere in the promotion run-in. There was talk of a move to Leicester last autumn, before County pulled the plug.

Manchester C (From apprentice on 4/8/83) FL 99+22/18 FLC 10+1/2 FAC 10+2/4 Others 8+3
Oxford U (£200,000 on 31/10/88) FL 138+6/43 FLC 10/3 FAC 9/2 Others 5/2
Derby Co (£500,000 on 20/2/92) FL 133+33/46 FLC 10+1/5 FAC 4+1/1 Others 14+2/2

Paul Simpson

SIMPSON Phillip (Phil) Mark
Born: Lambeth, 19 October 1969
Height: 5'8" Weight: 11.1

Spotted by Barnet's chairman while playing for Stevenage Borough last October, he proved a shrewd buy. A tough-tackling midfielder, with a silky touch, and able to beat men with ease, Phil took over Peter Scott's role as the provider in chief.

Barnet (Signed from Stevenage Borough on 27/10/95) FL 24/1

SINCLAIR Frank Mohammed
Born: Lambeth, 3 December 1971
Height: 5'8" Weight: 11.2

This enthusiastic young Chelsea defender was playing some of the best football of his career until a disastrous eight-day period last October saw him sent off at home to Manchester United and the following week pick up a shin splints injury, which necessitated an operation and a 16-match lay off. Replaced the suspended Michael Duberry for the 5-0 defeat at Middlesbrough and the following week's 1-0 defeat at Coventry but, apart from a substitute appearance, that was the end of his season. Looking more comfortable on the ball, and appearing to cut out unneccessary mistakes, it will be interesting to see if this likeable young man can force his way back into the new defensive set up at Stamford Bridge.

Chelsea (From trainee on 17/5/90) F/PL 126+1/5 FLC 13/1 FAC 12/1 Others 7/2
West Bromwich A (Loaned on 12/12/91) FL 6/1

SINCLAIR Ronald (Ronnie) McDonald
Born: Stirling, 19 November 1964
Height: 5'10" Weight: 12.3
Club Honours: Div 2 '93
International Honours: S: Yth; Sch

The out of favour Stoke City goalkeeper played only twice during 1995-96 due to strong form of Mark Prudhoe. And this after his excellent form of the previous season. Released during the summer, he is both brave and an excellent shot stopper and, although in his early 30s, is sure to come again.

Nottingham F (From apprentice on 30/10/82)
Wrexham (Loaned on 1/3/84) FL 11 Others 1
Leeds U (£10,000 on 27/6/86) FL 8 FLC 1
Halifax T (Loaned on 1/3/87) FL 4
Halifax T (Loaned on 23/12/88) FL 10 Others 1
Bristol C (Free on 1/9/89) FL 44 FLC 3 FAC 5 Others 3
Walsall (Loaned on 5/9/91) FL 10 Others 1
Stoke C (£25,000 on 21/11/91) FL 78+2 FLC 2 FAC 4 Others 10

SINCLAIR Trevor Lloyd
Born: Dulwich, 2 March 1973
Height: 5'10" Weight: 11.2
International Honours: E: U21-13; Yth

Very fast, skilful wide player, difficult to dispossess when in full flow, who is also effective as an out-and-out striker. Seen by many as the one person who could save QPR from the drop in 1995-96, he turned in some excellent performances throughout the season, scoring four goals, all in games Rangers did not lose, and was a constant source of inquiries, regarding a big money transfer. Altouth he did not score in the latter part of the season, his "assists" were invaluable in the club's ultimately vain battle to avoid relegation. Continued to play for the England U21s and cannot be far away from a call up for the full side.

Blackpool (From trainee on 21/8/90) FL 84+28/15 FLC 8 FAC 6+1 Others 8+5/1
Queens Park R (£600,000 on 12/8/93) PL 99+3/10 FLC 9/3 FAC 4/1

Trevor Sinclair

SINNOTT Lee
Born: Pelsall, 12 July 1965
Height: 6'1" Weight: 12.13
International Honours: E: U21-1; Yth

After a tug of war with Pat Scully, he initially established himself as the central defensive partner for Kevin Gray at Huddersfield in 1995-96. And his assured performances saw him become the club, as well as team, captain. A very experienced player, he proved more than capable of playing at first division level, but lost out at the end of the season to Scully.

Walsall (From apprentice on 16/11/82) FL 40/2 FLC 3 FAC 4
Watford (£100,000 on 15/9/83) FL 71+7/2 FLC 6 FAC 11
Bradford C (£130,000 on 23/7/87) FL 173/6 FLC 19 FAC 9 Others 12/1
Crystal Palace (£300,000 on 8/8/91) F/PL 53+4 FLC 9+1 FAC 1 Others 4
Bradford C (Signed on 9/12/93) FL 34/1 FLC 2 FAC 2 Others 2
Huddersfield T (£105,000 on 23/12/94) FL 57/1 FLC 4 FAC 4 Others 3

SINTON Andrew (Andy)
Born: Newcastle, 19 March 1966
Height: 5'8" Weight: 11.0
International Honours: E: 12; B-3; Sch

Plagued by injuries, the left-sided midfielder never got going at Sheffield Wednesday under David Pleat in 1995-96, despite his enthusiasm to make things happen, and his career was rescued by his former QPR manager, Gerry Francis, who signed him for Spurs in January. An early ball specialist, who places accurate crosses into the heart of the penalty area, Andy added width to a side which was missing Darren Anderton for much of the season. Disappointingly, niggling injuries made it difficult to put a run of good performances together, but he made a promising start and the best is yet to come.

Cambridge U (From apprentice on 13/4/83) FL 90+3/13 FLC 6/1 FAC 3 Others 2/1
Brentford (£25,000 on 13/12/85) FL 149/28 FLC 8/3 FAC 11/1 Others 14/2
Queens Park R (£350,000 on 23/3/89) F/PL 160/22 FLC 14 FAC 13/2 Others 3/1
Sheffield Wed (£2,750,000 on 19/8/93) PL 54+6/3 FLC 13 FAC 5
Tottenham H (£1,500,000 on 23/1/96) PL 8+1

SKELTON Aaron Matthew
Born: Welwyn Garden City, 22 November 1974
Height: 5'10" Weight: 11.5

Young defensive, left-sided Luton midfielder who debuted in 1994-95. Played in an Anglo-Italian Cup match for the club early last season and appeared to be about to win promotion to the league side when he was diagnosed as being out for the season in October with cruciate ligament damage. This was a particularly harsh blow for someone who lost the whole of 1993-94 due to injury and was playing well in an attempt to re-establish a shattered career.

Luton T (From trainee on 16/12/92) FL 3+2 FLC 0+1 Others 1

SKINNER Craig Richard
Born: Heywood, 21 October 1970
Height: 5'10" Weight: 11.6

Bought from Plymouth Argyle in the 1995

close season to add some width down the Wrexham right side of midfield, which had been previously lacking. After a slow start, Craig proved to be an obvious asset, his clever wing play and pace, together with the capability of funnelling back to help out the defence and making himself available to his team mates, being of great benefit. Following the signing of Martyn Chalk there is sure to be keen competition for the number seven shirt in 1996-97.

Blackburn Rov (From trainee on 13/6/89) FL 11+5 FLC 0+1 FAC 1 Others 3/1
Plymouth Arg (Signed on 21/8/92) FL 42+11/4 FLC 4 FAC 5+2/1 Others 3+1
Wrexham (£50,000 on 21/7/95) FL 21+2/3 FLC 1 FAC 3 Others 3

SKINNER Justin

Born: Hounslow, 30 January 1969
Height: 6'0" Weight: 12.0

Is a creative central midfielder whose accurate free kicks and corners were an important source of goalscoring opportunities for Bristol Rovers in 1995-96. Unfortunately, in January, Justin broke his leg in an Auto Windscreen Shield-tie at Fulham, his former club, although recovering to play again in the last six weeks of the season. When he is on song, Rovers certainly are.

Fulham (From apprentice on 17/11/86) FL 111+24/23 FLC 10+1/4 FAC 5+1 Others 10+1/1
Bristol Rov (£130,000 on 27/8/91) FL 141+8/10 FLC 11 FAC 8 Others 14+1/2

SKINNER Justin James

Born: Dorking, 17 September 1972
Height: 5'8" Weight: 10.12

Skilful Wimbledon left back who is good in the air and capable of turning in battling, strong-tackling performances. Made just one first team start last season, in deputising for Gary Elkins, but showed up as a dominating defender in 31 reserve matches, prior to being released in the summer.

Wimbledon (From trainee on 2/7/91) PL 2
Bournemouth (Loaned on 7/3/94) FL 16
Wycombe W (Loaned on 26/8/94) FL 4+1

SKIVERTON Terence (Terry) John

Born: Mile End, 26 June 1975
Height: 6'0" Weight: 12.6

Making a welcome return to Wycombe on a free from Chelsea last March, after a loan period the previous season, Terry celebrated by scoring his debut Football League goal on his first full appearance, at York. Wins most of the balls in the air, either as a right back or central defender, and shows good commitment.

Chelsea (From trainee on 19/5/93)
Wycombe W (Loaned on 17/2/95) FL 8+2
Wycombe W (Free on 26/3/96) FL 3+1/1

SLADE Steven (Steve) Anthony

Born: Romford, 6 October 1975
Height: 5'11" Weight: 10.10
International Honours: E: U21-4

A highly promising Tottenham reserve forward, Steve made his first team bow as a substitute in the Coca Cola Cup at Chester last October and his Premier League debut, also from the bench, at Wimbledon in

December, prior to starting against Southampton 12 games from the end of the season. Definitely a player for the future, despite his lack of weight, he impressed with his aerial technique and general toughness, while displaying good running, both on and off the ball. Also showed fine control.

Tottenham H (From trainee on 1/7/94) PL 1+4 FLC 0+1 FAC 0+2

SLATER Darren

Born: Bishop Auckland, 4 January 1979
Height: 5'7" Weight: 11.0

A first-year trainee with Hartlepool, and one of the latest batch of juniors rated highly by youth team coaches, Billy Horner and Brian Honour, the right-sided midfielder, made his debut late last season, coming on to play just 14 minutes as substitute. Hopefully, this experience will stand him in good stead as he attempts to win a professional contract.

Hartlepool U (Trainee) FL 0+1

SLATER Robert (Robbie) David

Born: Skelmersdale, 22 November 1964
Height: 5'11" Weight: 13.0
Club Honours: PL '95
International Honours: Australia: 17

Having joined West Ham from Blackburn at the start of 1995-96, as part of the deal that saw Matty Holmes travelling in the opposite direction, the fast-running winger made his debut on the wide left at Nottingham Forest, before switching to the other flank some three games later. Desperately looking for consistency, a blinding goal at Ewood and the winner against Forest, was scant reward for the number of times he was substituted. Very competitive, Robbie is bound to find a role within the Hammers' framework that suits him.

Blackburn Rov (£300,000 from Lens on 4/8/94) PL 12+6 FLC 1 FAC 1 Others 2
West Ham U (£600,000 on 15/8/95) PL 16+6/2 FLC 3 FAC 1

SLATER Stuart Ian

Born: Sudbury, 27 March 1969
Height: 5'9" Weight: 11.6
International Honours: E: B-2; U21-3

An adaptable player, who can perform in midfield or as a striker, Stuart was forced to miss Ipswich's start to 1995-96, after twisting an ankle in training. On recovering, two games into the season, he gave an outstanding display at home to Stoke, scoring two goals, and went on to play a further 15 times before breaking down with an achilles tendon injury in November. Back again, he made few appearances, despite impressing against WBA, but remains at the club, having turned down a move to Stoke immediately prior to the transfer deadline. Always looking to take defenders on.

West Ham U (From apprentice on 2/4/87) FL 134+7/11 FLC 16+1/2 FAC 16/3 Others 5/2
Glasgow Celtic (£1,500,000 on 14/8/92) SL 40+3/3 SLC 3+2 SC 3 Others 4
Ipswich T (£750,000 on 30/9/93) P/FL 61+11/4 FLC 6 FAC 6 Others 2+2

SLAWSON Stephen Michael

Born: Nottingham, 13 November 1972
Height: 6'2" Weight: 12.6

Left-sided forward. Released by Shrewsbury Town during the summer of 1995, he signed for Mansfield and after starting in the senior squad at the beginning of the season, fell out of favour, only regaining his place due to injuries. When he returned, was played as a striker, being far more effective, and scored several spectacular goals. *Stop Press:* Signed by Rotherham after being freed by Town in May.

Notts Co (From trainee on 9/7/91) FL 16+22/4 FLC 1+1 FAC 0+3 Others 3+1
Burnley (Loaned on 12/2/93) FL 5/2
Shrewsbury T (Loaned on 31/10/94) FL 6 Others 0+1
Mansfield T (Free on 4/7/95) FL 21+8/5 FLC 2 Others 1+1

SLOAN Scott

Born: Wallsend, 14 December 1967
Height: 5'10" Weight: 11.13

Hartlepool striker. Suffering a broken collar bone, early in 1995-96, his season never really got going and a goal in the FA Cup-tie against Darlington was the only bright spot. Released in February 1996, he may now try his luck playing overseas.

Berwick R (Signed from Ponteland in 1988) SL 58+3/20 SLC 2/2 SC 4/1
Newcastle U (£75,000 on 31/7/90) FL 11+5/1 FAC 1 Others 1
Falkirk (£50,000 on 8/11/91) SL 49+15/11 SLC 6/2 SC 3+1/4 Others 3+1/2
Cambridge U (Loaned on 25/2/94) FL 4/1
Hartlepool U (Free on 12/8/94) FL 27+8/2 FLC 2+1 FAC 1+1/1 Others 1+1

SMALL Bryan

Born: Birmingham, 15 November 1971
Height: 5'9" Weight: 11.9
International Honours: E: U21-12; Yth

A speedy left back who joined Bolton on a free transfer from Aston Villa last March, having been unable to get a first team game all season, his only appearance came in the final day defeat at Arsenal where he produced an eye-catching performance in a Wanderers side that only lost the game thanks to two late goals. Very strong on the ball, and difficult to dispossess, Bryan is capable of getting forward and lending his pace in an attacking role. Can also play in midfield.

Aston Villa (From trainee on 9/7/90) F/PL 31+5 FLC 2 FAC 2+1 Others 4
Birmingham C (Loaned on 9/9/94) FL 3
Bolton W (Free on 20/3/96) PL 1

SMART Allan Andrew Colin

Born: Perth, 8 July 1974
Height: 6'2" Weight: 12.7

Strong-running young Preston centre forward who only featured occasionally in 1995-96, due to the form of Andy Saville. As a player who is still learning the game, he enjoyed a successful loan spell at Carlisle in mid-season, showing good ball skills for a big man.

Preston NE (£15,000 from Caledonian Thistle on 22/11/94) FL 17+4/6 FAC 2/1 Others 1+1
Carlisle U (Loaned on 24/11/95) FL 3+1

SMITH Alexander (Alex) Philip
Born: Liverpool, 15 February 1976
Height: 5'7" Weight: 9.0

A skilful, but lightweight left back signed on a free transfer from Everton last March, Alex was given a couple of first team outings in the closing Swindon fixtures of the season. Following the departure of Paul Bodin, the way ahead looks promising for this youngster.

Everton (From trainee on 1/7/94)
Swindon T (Free on 12/1/96) FL 2+6

SMITH Anthony (Tony)
Born: Sunderland, 21 September 1971
Height: 5'10" Weight: 11.9
International Honours: E: Yth

Released by Sunderland during the summer of 1995, Tony arrived at Northampton on a non-contract basis, prior to the start of last season, in a bid to establish himself in the club's problem left back spot. Also able to fill in as a central defender, he played four games before returning to the north east, having not been offered terms.

Sunderland (From trainee on 31/7/90) FL 19+1 FLC 5
Hartlepool U (Loaned on 6/1/92) FL 4+1 Others 2
Northampton T (Free on 14/8/95) FL 2 FLC 2

SMITH Christopher (Chris) Gerald
Born: Birmingham, 3 January 1977
Height: 5'8" Weight: 11.4

A professional signing for Walsall right at the end of 1994-95, the young midfielder made substitute appearances last season against Wycombe (AWS) and Brentford (FL) and played regularly in the reserves, prior to being released during the summer.

Walsall (From trainee on 15/5/95) FL 0+1 Others 0+1

SMITH David
Born: Stonehouse, 29 March 1968
Height: 5'8" Weight: 10.7
International Honours: E: U21-10

David had a disappointing season in 1995-96 for WBA, in as much that he was never a regular in the first team and when called upon by his manager he was asked to fill a variety of roles, lining up at left back, in midfield, and on the wing. He always gave a good account of himself and it was his penalty in the shoot-out against his former club, Birmingham (at St. Andrew's), which sent Albion through to the English final of the Anglo-Italian Cup. At home on the left flank, he likes nothing better than taking opponents on to get in telling crosses.

Coventry C (From apprentice on 7/7/86) F/PL 144+10/19 FLC 17 FAC 6 Others 4+1
Bournemouth (Loaned on 8/1/93) FL 1
Birmingham C (Signed on 12/3/93) FL 35+3/3 FLC 4 FAC 0+1 Others 1
West Bromwich A (£90,000 on 31/1/94) FL 43+13 FLC 1+2 FAC 0+3 Others 4+1

SMITH David (Dave) Christopher
Born: Liverpool, 26 December 1970
Height: 5'10" Weight: 11.12

Again a regular in the Oxford side, the midfielder was a vital cog in the team's promotion campaign in 1995-96. Scored the first goal of his career, although his strike

against Wycombe will be remembered for other reasons (a 1-4 home defeat). Employed initially as the holding player, Dave has come forward more, following the injury to Bobby Ford and latterly the signing of Martin Gray, and continues to look a good player.

Norwich C (From trainee on 4/7/89) F/PL 13+5 FAC 2+1 Others 1+1
Oxford U (£100,000 on 5/7/94) FL 86+1/1 FLC 8/1 FAC 7 Others 7

SMITH Dean
Born: West Bromwich, 19 March 1971
Height: 6'1" Weight: 12.10

Virtually an ever present in the centre of Hereford's defence in 1995-96, and dominating the aerial play, Dean rarely put a foot wrong. Even when suffering from a bruised foot and ribs, the club's specialist for penalties and set pieces always gave 100 per cent and more. Once seen, you would need no reminding that he is United's captain.

Walsall (From trainee on 1/7/89) FL 137+5/2 FLC 10 FAC 4 Others 10
Hereford U (£75,000 on 17/6/94) FL 74+1/11 FLC 6/1 FAC 6 Others 10+1/4

Dean Smith

SMITH James (Jamie) Jade Anthony
Born: Birmingham, 17 September 1974
Height: 5'6" Weight: 10.1

The right back began two games last September for Wolves, but was then out of contention for a while. In November, he came on for nine minutes when a Football League U21 side played the Italian Serie "B" XI and drew 1-1, but had to wait until March before starting another club fixture, although usually in the side from thereon. A player not afraid to take his opposite number on, especially on the overlap, to get in good early crosses.

Wolverhampton W (From trainee on 7/6/93) FL 34+4 FLC 4 FAC 1 Others 2

SMITH Martin Geoffrey
Born: Sunderland, 13 November 1974
Height: 5'11" Weight: 12.6
Club Honours: Div 1 '96
International Honours: E: U21-1; Sch

Although Martin struggled for most of last season with a groin injury, only managing nine first team starts for Sunderland in the league, his 11 substitute appearances were enough to give him a first division championship medal. One of the most promising young players at Roker, possessing tremendous ability on the ball and a keen eye for goal, he scored one that proved to be one of the most important goals of the campaign, when coming off the bench away at Millwall in September to secure three points. Fully fit and back to his best, the left-sided midfielder, cum striker, will be a great asset to the club's Premiership hopes. Represented the Endsleigh League U21 side against an Italian Serie "B" XI in November.

Sunderland (From trainee on 9/9/92) FL 69+15/20 FLC 4+3 FAC 7+1/1

SMITH Michael
Born: Liverpool, 28 September 1973
Height: 5'11" Weight: 11.7

An attacking winger who featured in the Doncaster Rovers' first team occasionally, following his move from non-league football in January 1996, the experience should stand him in good stead for the future.

Doncaster Rov (Signed from Runcorn on 5/1/96) FL 12+1

SMITH Neil James
Born: Lambeth, 30 September 1971
Height: 5'9" Weight: 12.0
Club Honours: FAYC '90

Gillingham midfielder. Starting last season on weekly contracts, he improved no end under manager, Tony Pulis, and now looks twice the player he was. A key member of the successful promotion winning side, despite suffering from suspensions and missing crucial games, his ball-winning ability and enthusiasm were vital to the cause. Has one of the longest throws in the Endsleigh League.

Tottenham H (From trainee on 24/7/90)
Gillingham (£40,000 on 17/10/91) FL 162+9/9 FLC 8 FAC 16/2 Others 7+1/2

SMITH Ian Paul
Born: Easington, 22 January 1976
Height: 6'0" Weight: 12.8

A left winger who had starred in Burnley's 1994 youth side, Paul had only one first team appearance to his name before Adrian Heath's arrival as manager last March brought belated recognition. Yet to make a major impact in the side, his time will surely come.

Burnley (From trainee on 10/7/94) FL 3+8

SMITH Paul Elton
Born: Lewisham, 2 November 1971
Height: 6'1" Weight: 11.12

Midfielder. Signed from non-league Horsham during the 1995 close season, Paul overcame a broken leg to make his debut from Barnet's bench at Bury last September. That would be his only opportunity of first team football and he was released in March.

Barnet (Signed from Horsham on 15/5/95) FL 0+1

SMITH Paul William
Born: East Ham, 18 September 1971
Height: 5'11" Weight: 14.0

Brentford central midfielder. A good passer and ball winner, he is also noted for his runs from deep into the penalty area. As an ever present it was another impressive campaign for Paul in 1995-96 and he would probably have done even better had he been blessed with a regular partner in midfield.

Southend U (From trainee on 16/3/90) FL 18+2/1 Others 0+1
Brentford (Free on 6/8/93) FL 113/10 FLC 8/1 FAC 9/2 Others 10/1

SMITH Peter John
Born: Stone, 12 July 1969
Height: 6'1" Weight: 12.7

Brighton's right back, who was the club's "Player of the Year" in 1994-95, made a disappointing start to the 1995-96 season, losing his place, before fighting back into contention. A firm tackler, he shows great pace when bursting forward down the right flank. Unfortunately, a hamstring injury in early March 1996, ruled him out of some vital relegation battles.

Brighton & Hove A (Free from Alma Swanley on 8/8/94) FL 63+6/2 FLC 6+1 FAC 5/1 Others 4+1

SMITH Richard Geoffrey
Born: Lutterworth, 3 October 1970
Height: 6'0" Weight: 13.13

A right-footed Leicester central defender with a prodigious long throw, he was loaned to Grimsby early last season. On his return, he only got as far as the Foxes' bench during the first half of the campaign, but was recalled to the fray for the FA Cup-tie with Manchester City. Transferred to Grimsby in March, where he was a regular in the club's ultimately successful rearguard action close to the foot of the first division.

Leicester C (From trainee on 15/12/88) F/PL 82+16/1 FLC 4 FAC 6/1 Others 12
Cambridge U (Loaned on 6/9/89) FL 4 FLC 1
Grimsby T (Loaned on 8/9/95) FL 8
Grimsby T (£50,000 on 11/3/96) FL 10

SMITH Scott David
Born: Christchurch, New Zealand, 6 March 1975
Height: 5'8" Weight: 11.6
Club Honours: AMC '96

One of two New Zealanders at Rotherham, Scott is a right back who was unable to create a regular first team place for himself last season, but never let the side down when called into action, invariably because of injuries to other players. Is accomplished enough to be able to make a good career as a professional footballer.

Rotherham U (From trainee on 1/10/93) FL 21+4 FAC 2 Others 2+1

SMITH Gareth Shaun
Born: Leeds, 9 April 1971
Height: 5'10" Weight: 11.0

Crewe's expert in dead ball situations, as his

goal tally over the seasons has proved. A naturally left-footed player, who normally appears in the left back position, sharing with Martyn Booty in 1995-96, Shaun also enjoys his surging runs up the flank.

Halifax T (From trainee on 1/7/89) FL 6+1 Others 1 (Free to Emley in May 1991)
Crewe Alex (Free on 31/12/91) FL 142+15/20 FLC 3+1 FAC 7+2/2 Others 15+1/1

SNEEKES Richard
Born: Amsterdam, Holland, 30 October 1968
Height: 5'11" Weight: 12.2

Arriving at WBA from Bolton last March, the former Ajax star, Richard, proved an inspired signing by manager, Alan Buckley, at a time when nothing was going right for the club. The introduction of the Dutch midfielder changed things dramatically at The Hawthorns, and his record of goals per games from his debut against Watford until the last match of the season against Derby, was quite outstanding. He quickly became a cult hero with the Baggies' fans with his powerful shooting, while his presence in the side certainly boosted morale and went a long way towards securing Albion's first division status. As a 16 year old, Richard became the youngest-ever player to appear in league football for Ajax – a record since beaten by Clarence Seedorf.

Bolton W (£200,000 from Fortuna Sittard on 12/8/94) P/FL 51+4/7 FLC 11+1/3 FAC 2/1
West Bromwich A (£385,000 on 11/3/96) FL 13/10

SNODIN Ian
Born: Rotherham, 15 August 1963
Height: 5'7" Weight: 11.0
Club Honours: Div 1 '87
International Honours: E: B-2; U21-4; Yth

The brother of Glyn, who failed to make a league appearance last season, Ian again proved solid and reliable at the back for Oldham, his uncompromising play being mainly seen to good effect in the right back position. While very much the instigator of the injection of steel in Latics' back four, he is also an accomplished passer of the ball, who is equally at home in midfield, or when springing an attack down the flank. Towards the end of the campaign, he shared the number two shirt with Chris Makin.

Doncaster Rov (From apprentice on 18/8/80) FL 181+7/25 FLC 9/1 FAC 11+1/1 Others 3
Leeds U (£200,000 on 22/5/85) FL 51/6 FLC 3/2 FAC 1
Everton (£840,000 on 16/1/87) F/PL 142+6/3 FLC 19+4/2 FAC 26/2 Others 3
Sunderland (Loaned on 13/10/94) FL 6
Oldham Ath (Free on 9/1/95) FL 41+2 FAC 1 Others 1

SOLOMAN Jason Rafael
Born: Welwyn Garden City, 6 October 1970
Height: 6'0" Weight: 12.2
Club Honours: FAYC '89
International Honours: E: Yth

Began 1995-96 as Wycombe's first choice left-sided midfield player, but by September was mostly confined to the substitute's bench and was released at the end of the season. He is certainly not lacking in either skill or strength.

Watford (From trainee on 9/12/88) FL 79+21/5 FLC 9/1 FAC 1 Others 5+1
Peterborough U (Loaned on 13/1/95) FL 4
Wycombe W (Free on 17/3/95) FL 11+2/1 FLC 1

SOMMER Juergen Petersen
Born: New York, USA, 27 February 1969
Height: 6'4" Weight: 15.12
International Honours: USA: 5

A tall, commanding goalkeeper, and an excellent shot stopper, Juergen left Luton Town bound for QPR just after last season had started. Made his Premiership debut for Rangers at Leeds in a 3-1 win and kept his place in the side throughout the campaign, though cup-tied in the Coca Cola Cup. Had an outstanding game against Aston Villa in December, keeping everything out, enabling Rangers to win 1-0 and earned the club further points with superb performances against Arsenal, Chelsea, and especially, Manchester United. Could not be blamed for the losing relegation battle and is a prime candidate for the number one jersey in the US national Olympic squad.

Luton T (Signed on 5/9/91) FL 82 FLC 6 FAC 11 Others 2
Brighton & Hove A (Loaned on 13/11/91) FL 1
Torquay U (Loaned on 31/10/92) FL 10 Others 1
Queens Park R (£600,000 on 29/8/95) PL 33 FLC 1 FAC 2

Neville Southall

SOUTHALL Neville
Born: Llandudno, 16 September 1958
Height: 6'1" Weight: 13.0
Club Honours: FAC '84, '95; CS '84, '85, '95; Div 1 '85, '87; ECW '85
International Honours: W: 86

Still one of the best goalkeepers in the Premiership, Neville's main qualities are positional sense, excellent reflexes, the ability to impose himself on challenging strikers, and, of course, his great consistency. Yet again first choice Everton 'keeper in 1995-96, no doubt the first name on the team sheet, he continued to provide a solid and reliable rearguard as an ever present and was one of the main reasons for the club being able to attain sixth place in the table. Relentlessly serving his country at the age of 37, he remains an example to fellow goalies and youngsters alike. And like "Old Father Time", he just goes rolling along.

Bury (£6,000 from Winsford U on 14/6/80) FL 39 FAC 5
Everton (£150,000 on 13/7/81) F/PL 532 FLC 62 FAC 68 Others 37
Port Vale (Loaned on 27/1/83) FL 9

SOUTHALL Leslie Nicholas (Nicky)
Born: Stockton, 28 January 1972
Height: 5'10" Weight: 12.12

Transferred from Hartlepool during the 1995 close season, Nicky quickly established himself in Grimsby's starting line up on the left wing, where his fast raiding and telling crosses contributed well to the Mariner's attack. Although making way for Ivano Bonetti, following the Italian's arrival from Serie "A", he soon re-adjusted to first division football during the latter's enforced absence, to become a valued member of the side. Also proved he could get among the goals.

Hartlepool U (Free from Darlington juniors on 21/2/91) FL118+20/24 FLC 6+1/3 FAC 4+4 Others 6+2
Grimsby T (£40,000 on 12/7/95) FL 28+5/2 FLC 2/1 FAC 3+2/1

SOUTHGATE Gareth
Born: Watford, 3 September 1970
Height: 5'10" Weight: 12.3
Club Honours: Div 1 '94; FLC '96
International Honours: E: 9

Signed from Crystal Palace as a midfielder during the summer of 1995, Gareth was one of the discoveries of last season as part of Villa's three-man defensive system, alongside Ugo Ehiogu and Paul McGrath. A two-footed player who could carry the ball out of defence, he was rarely flustered, very effective in aerial challenges, and this good form saw him called up to the England squad, where he won his first cap as a substitute versus Portugal in December, before making his full international debut in March against Bulgaria. Having suffered from an ankle injury in early March, he returned in time to assist Villa to victory in the Coca Cola Cup final, only to be laid low by a knee injury in the FA Cup semi final versus Liverpool. Happily, he regained fitness in time to be included in the England squad for Euro '96, and was one of the stars, despite his penalty shoot-out miss, of a side that reached the semi finals before losing to the eventual tournament winners, Germany.

Crystal Palace (From trainee on 17/1/89) F/PL 148+4/15 FLC 23+1/7 FAC 9 Others 6
Aston Villa (£2,500,000 on 1/7/95) PL 31/1 FLC 8/1 FAC 4

SPACKMAN Nigel James
Born: Romsey, 2 December 1960
Height: 6'1" Weight: 13.2
Club Honours: Div 2 '84; Div 1 '88; FMC '86; SPD '90, '91, '92; SLC '91; SC '92

Great Chelsea servant, now in his second spell at the club, he again proved to be a dependable midfield deputy whenever called upon to replace injured regulars in 1995-96. One of the gentlemen of the game, it was a shock when he was sent off against Arsenal in September for throwing a retaliatory punch at an Arsenal player – the first dismissal of a long and distinguished career. *Stop Press:* An unsung performer in the essential midfield anchor role, having expressed an ambition to move into player/managership when his current contract ends, according to newspaper reports, he was due to join up with Howard Kendall at Sheffield United in the summer.

Bournemouth (Free from Andover on 8/5/80) FL 118+1/10 FLC 5 FAC 7
Chelsea (£40,000 on 20/6/83) FL 139+2/12 FLC 22+1 FAC 8/1 Others 7/1
Liverpool (£400,000 on 24/2/87) FL 39+12 FLC 6+1 FAC 5
Queens Park R (£500,000 on 2/2/89) FL 27+2/1 FLC 2/1 Others 2
Glasgow R (£500,000 on 30/11/89) SL 100/1 SLC 10 SC 9 Others 5
Chelsea (£485,000 on 8/9/92) PL 60+7 FLC 5 FAC 6+3 Others 7

SPARROW Paul
Born: Wandsworth, 24 March 1975
Height: 6'1" Weight: 11.6
Club Honours: Div 3 '96

Having made his debut for Crystal Palace, when coming on for Richard Shaw at Middlesbrough in a Coca Cola Cup-tie, and with opportunities limited, he was loaned to Preston last March, signing permanently two games later. Calm and steady at right back, with a good turn of speed and accurate distribution, Paul looks set to develop into a bargain buy. To cap an excellent start, he won a third division championship medal as North End re-asserted themselves.

Crystal Palace (From trainee on 13/7/93) FL 1 FLC 0+1
Preston NE (Signed on 8/3/96) FL 13

SPEARING Anthony (Tony)
Born: Romford, 7 October 1964
Height: 5'6" Weight: 11.10
International Honours: E: Yth

Started last season as the left back in possession at Peterborough, before giving way to Greg Rioch after just three games and from then on only playing sporadically. An enthusiastic clubman, who always gives nothing less than his best, Tony can still tackle with the best of them.

Norwich C (From apprentice on 11/10/82) FL 67+2 FLC 5 FAC 4 Others 4
Stoke C (Loaned on 1/11/84) FL 9
Oxford U (Loaned on 1/2/85) FL 5
Leicester C (£100,000 on 12/7/88) FL 71+2/1 FLC 2+1 FAC 1 Others 2
Plymouth Arg (Free on 1/7/91) FL 35 FLC 6 FAC 1 Others 2+1
Peterborough U (Free on 21/1/93) FL 94+4/2 FLC 5 FAC 3+2 Others 6

SPEED Gary Andrew
Born: Mancot, 8 September 1969
Height: 5'11" Weight: 12.10
Club Honours: Div 2 '90, Div 1 '92; CS '92
International Honours: W: 35; U21-3; Yth

Highly-rated Leeds' Welsh International, Gary has now become one of the more influential figures at Elland Road, apart from being one of the more senior players at the club. Although operating in many positions, he began last season in the more customary role on the left-hand side of midfield and looked to have regained all his old consistency and goalscoring adeptness, weighing in with some important strikes, particularly in the cups. Unfortunately, he suffered a fractured cheek bone against Port Vale, but such was his commitment to the club, that he returned to action only five weeks later. *Stop Press:* Signed for Everton in a five year deal at the beginning of June.

Leeds U (From trainee on 13/6/88) F/PL 231+17/39 FLC 25+1/11 FAC 21/5 Others 14+3/2

Gary Speed

SPEIGHT Martyn Stephen
Born: Stockton, 26 July 1978
Height: 5'9" Weight: 10.10

With Doncaster virtually free of any relegation fears, two young defenders, Martyn and Darren Utley, were blooded in the 2-2 draw at Cambridge last April. Still a trainee, he showed up well until being withdrawn in the latter stages.

Doncaster Rov (Trainee) FL 1

SPENCER John
Born: Glasgow, 11 September 1970
Height: 5'6" Weight: 9.10
International Honours: S: 12; U21-3; Yth; Sch

1995-96 was a great season for this small, livewire striker who ended up as Chelsea's top scorer with 13 league goals from 23 starts, after beginning the season on the subs' bench for the second successive time, and forced his way into the Scotland set up for Euro '96. Chelsea had failed to find the net in their first three league matches until "Spenny" came into the side to partner Mark Hughes for the fourth match – at home to Coventry City. Two first half goals ended the barren spell, and although sloppy defending let Coventry back for a draw, it looked as if Blues had found the right combination up front. The following league match at Upton Park saw John score twice in the 3-1 victory before his head came into contact with the sole of Julian Dicks' boot! This nasty injury did not deter the brave Scot, who continued to score consistently, including two crackers against Liverpool at the Bridge on 30 December. A clever striker with an uncanny ability to lose defenders, he was a vital part of Craig Brown's plans for Scotland's assault on Euro '96 which ended at the group stage.

Glasgow R (From juniors in 1986) SL 7+6/2 SLC 2 Others 1+1/1
Morton (Loaned on 4/3/89) FL 4/1
Chelsea (£450,000 on 1/8/92) PL 75+24/36 FLC 2+4 FAC16+4/4 Others 4+1/1

SPINK Dean Peter

Born: Birmingham, 22 January 1967
Height: 5'11" Weight: 13.8
Club Honours: Div 3 '94

Shrewsbury Town striker or central defender. Began last season up front, but spent much of it filling in for central defenders and looking very comfortable. Always fully committed, by his standards the goals did not come so freely in 1995-96, due to his defensive duties. Strong in the air, difficult to knock off the ball, with good control, Dean is a fine player to have in your club.

Aston Villa (£30,000 from Halesowen T on 1/7/89)
Scarborough (Loaned on 20/11/89) FL 3/2 Others 1
Bury (Loaned on 1/2/90) FL 6/1
Shrewsbury T (£75,000 on 15/3/90) FL 205+27/49 FLC 20+2/1 FAC 16+2/6 Others 17+2/3

SPINK Nigel Philip

Born: Chelmsford, 8 August 1958
Height: 6'2" Weight: 14.6
Club Honours: EC '82; ESC '82; FLC '94
International Honours: E: 1; B-2

Goalkeeper. Well and truly in the shadows of Mark Bosnich at Aston Villa, Nigel became the oldest player ever to join the WBA ranks when he arrived last January, his vast experience and know-how certainly boosting the club's flagging defence which, prior to his arrival, had conceded 20 goals in seven games. His huge presence between the posts was a confidence booster of the highest calibre and Albion certainly played with great spirit after he had joined.

Aston Villa (£4,000 from Chelmsford C on 1/1/77) F/PL 357+4 FLC 45 FAC 28 Others 25+1
West Bromwich A (Free on 31/1/96) FL 15 Others 2

SQUIRES James (Jamie) Alexander

Born: Preston, 15 November 1975
Height: 6'1" Weight: 12.3

Young Preston defender who regained his confidence in 1995-96 after setbacks early in his career. Jamie is undoubtedly a class player, who could have a tremendous future in the game, with his coolness under pressure and strong defensive qualities.

Preston NE (From trainee on 26/4/94) FL 18+4 Others 2+1

SRNICEK Pavel

Born: Ostrava, Czechoslovakia, 10 March 1968
Height: 6'2" Weight: 14.9
Club Honours: Div 1 '93
International Honours: Czechoslovakia: 4

A goalkeeper who has become a cult figure at Newcastle, "Pav" is an athletic shot stopper who initially found the physical contact of English football difficult when dealing with crosses, but worked to improve this element of his game. Began last season suspended, giving Shaka Hislop the opportunity to keep him on the bench until December, when he came on for the latter at Chelsea, his first touch being to retrieve the ball from the net! He played brilliantly in the following game against Everton, and maintained his place with a series of fine performances before being dropped, following the defeat at Liverpool, as United stuck to their dream of landing the Premiership.

Newcastle U (£350,000 from Banik Ostrava on 5/2/91) F/PL 125+1 FLC 9+1 FAC 11 Others 10

STALLARD Mark

Born: Derby, 24 October 1974
Height: 6'0" Weight: 12.6

Unable to force his way into the Derby side on a regular basis, playing the odd match here and there, Mark was transferred to Bradford last January to assist the promotion challenge. A bustling centre forward, but skilful with it, he quickly got down to business, despite having five different partners at varying times. Instrumental in City reaching the play offs, he scored the deciding goal that took them to Wembley and the second in a 2-0 win over Notts County that booked first division football for 1996-97. Already a great favourite with the crowd.

Derby Co (From trainee on 6/11/91) FL 19+8/2 FLC 2+1/2 FAC 2+1 Others 3/2
Fulham (Loaned on 23/9/94) FL 4/3
Bradford C (£110,000 on 12/1/96) FL 20+1/9 Others 3/2

Philip Stamp

STAMP Philip Lawrence

Born: Middlesbrough, 12 December 1975
Height: 5'10" Weight: 12.3
International Honours: E: Yth

Another product of Middlesbrough's thriving youth policy, the strong-tackling and aggressive midfielder enjoyed two short spells of Premier League football in 1995-96, scoring twice, first against Manchester City in a 4-1 victory, and the second to secure a 2-1 lead over Arsenal in January, only for Boro to lose the match in the next six minutes. An exciting young prospect, who also produces intelligent running off the ball, he seems certain to stake a claim to a regular berth in midfield during the coming season.

Middlesbrough (From trainee on 4/2/93) P/FL 20+5/2 FLC 4 FAC 1+1 Others 5+1

STAMPS Scott

Born: Birmingham, 20 March 1975
Height: 5'11" Weight: 11.0

The talented Torquay left back who, on the face of it, appears to be far too good for the third division, once again failed to live up to expectation in 1995-96, his excellent distribution and control being sadly wasted in a struggling side.

Torquay U (From trainee on 6/7/93) FL 50+6/2 FLC 5 FAC 1 Others 1+1/1

STANISLAUS Roger Edmund Philbert

Born: Hammersmith, 2 November 1968
Height: 5'11" Weight: 13.2

Signed from Bury, he came back to London during the 1995 close season with Leyton Orient and after appearing wide on the left flank in the opening two games, soon settled down at left back, where his ability to get forward took the eye. Regrettably, he brought disgrace on the game when failing a drug test and was fired in February by the chairman, Barry Hearn, who had vowed to take a hard line, regardless.

Arsenal (From apprentice on 31/7/86)
Brentford (Free on 18/9/87) FL 109+2/4 FLC 8/1 FAC 7 Others 9
Bury (£90,000 on 30/7/90) FL 167+9/5 FLC 9/1 FAC 10/1 Others 21
Leyton Orient (£50,000 on 11/7/95) FL 20+1 FLC 1 FAC 1 Others 1

STANNARD James (Jim) David

Born: Harold Hill, 6 October 1962
Height: 6'2" Weight: 16.6

Freed by Fulham during the summer of 1995, Jim signed for Gillingham immediately prior to the start of 1995-96 and went straight into the side as first choice goalkeeper. Tagged by the Priestfield patrons as "Big Jim", due to his bulk, he remained surprisingly agile, his shot stopping and bravery always to the fore, and was ever present throughout a campaign where records fell as the club were runners up for the third division title. Voted "Player of the Year", and elected to the PFA divisional team, he conceded just 20 league goals (beating Port Vale's 21 set in 1953-54) and broke the club record in keeping 29 clean sheets, with 14 away from home setting a new FL record. Not bad for a player who made his 500th league appearance on the opening day.

Fulham (Signed from Ford U on 5/6/80) FL 41 FLC 3 FAC 1
Southend U (Loaned on 17/9/84) FL 6
Charlton Ath (Loaned on 1/2/85) FL 1
Southend U (£12,000 on 28/3/85) FL 103 FLC 6 FAC 4 Others 5
Fulham (£50,000 on 14/8/87) FL 348/1 FLC 22 FAC 13 Others 18
Gillingham (Free on 4/8/95) FL 46 FLC 2 FAC 4 Others 1

STANT Phillip (Phil) Richard
Born: Bolton, 13 October 1962
Height: 6'1" Weight: 12.7
Club Honours: Div 3 '93; WC '93

A roller-coaster season of mixed emotions for Bury's popular front man in 1995-96. The regular choice for the opening six months, his undoubted high was a four goal haul in the Shakers' 5-1 away win against his old club Mansfield, before a drop in form, a rare goal drought, and subsequent loss of his place in the team followed. However, one must not forget he still scored 13 league and cup goals and played a big part in the club's promotion success.
Reading (Signed from Camberley on 19/8/82) FL 3+1/2
Hereford U (Free from Army on 25/11/86) FL 83+6/38 FLC 3/2 FAC 3/2 Others 11/7
Notts Co (£175,000 on 18/7/89) FL 14+8/6 FLC 2/1 FAC 0+1 Others 3+2
Blackpool (Loaned on 5/9/90) FL 12/5
Huddersfield T (Loaned on 3/1/91) FL 5/1
Lincoln C (Loaned on 22/11/90) FL 4
Fulham (£60,000 on 8/2/91) FL 19/5 Others 1
Mansfield T (£50,000 on 1/8/91) FL 56+1/32 FLC 4/1 FAC 2 Others 2
Cardiff C (£100,000 on 4/12/92) FL 77+2/34 FLC 2/2 FAC 6+1/4 Others 10/3
Mansfield T (Loaned on 12/8/93) FL 4/1 FLC 1/1
Bury (£90,000 on 27/1/95) FL 46+8/22 FLC 5/4 FAC 1 Others 5

STAPLETON Simon John
Born: Oxford, 10 December 1968
Height: 6'0" Weight: 13.0
Club Honours: FAT '91; GMVC '93
International Honours: E: SP-1

Out of action since February 1995 with a recurring knee injury, Simon was given just one opportunity to prove himself in 1995-96, before being released at the end of the season after seven years at Wycombe, playing in nearly every position. Best remembered as a forceful, two-footed central midfielder.
Portsmouth (From apprentice on 16/12/86)
Bristol Rov (Free on 19/7/88) FL 4+1 FLC 1 FAC 1 Others 1
Wycombe W (Free on 1/8/89) FL 46+3/3 FLC 3 FAC 12+1/3 Others 4

STARBUCK Philip (Phil) Michael
Born: Nottingham, 24 November 1968
Height: 5'10" Weight: 10.13

Sheffield United striker. Selected as substitute for the first match of 1995-96, he was then allowed to go on loan to Bristol City in September, where he proved an instant hit with his all-action style of play in six games before signing off with a goal against Hull. Back at Bramall Lane and transfer listed, he found a resurgence of form when replacing Nathan Blake in the first match under Howard Kendall, and the offer of a new contract followed in April, despite his season being cut short by injury.

Nottingham F (From apprentice on 19/8/86) FL 9+27/2 FLC 1+3 FAC 2+5 Others 0+4
Birmingham C (Loaned on 7/3/88) FL 3
Hereford U (Loaned on 19/2/90) FL 6 Others 1
Blackburn Rov (Loaned on 6/9/90) FL 5+1/1
Huddersfield T (Free on 17/8/91) FL 120+17/36 FLC 13+2/4 FAC 5+1 Others 16+3/7
Sheffield U (£150,000 on 28/10/94) FL 25+9/2 FAC 1+1
Bristol C (Loaned on 15/9/95) FL 5/1 Others 1

STATHAM Brian
Born: Zimbabwe, 21 May 1969
Height: 5'8" Weight: 11.0
Club Honours: Div 3 '92
International Honours: E: U21-3

Fast, right-footed Brentford defender, or central midfielder. Another consistently impressive campaign for Brian until he suffered a badly broken leg in the FA Cup-tie at Bournemouth last December, an injury that saw him miss the rest of the season. Good in the air.
Tottenham H (From trainee on 3/8/87) FL 20+4 FLC 2 FAC 0+1
Reading (Loaned on 28/3/91) FL 8
Bournemouth (Loaned on 20/11/91) FL 2 Others 1
Brentford (£70,000 on 16/1/92) FL 137+10/1 FLC 12 FAC 5 Others 17

STAUNTON Stephen (Steve)
Born: Dundalk, 19 January 1969
Height: 6'0" Weight: 12.4
Club Honours: FAC '89; CS '89; Div 1 '90; FLC '94, '96
International Honours: Ei: 62; U21-4; Yth
1995-96 was a desperately disappointing season for the Irish Republic international, who was laid low by a catalogue of different injuries, including achilles heel, double hamstring and thigh strain. When fit, his normal Aston Villa left back slot was held down by Alan Wright and he was forced to play in an unfamiliar central defensive position in place of Paul McGrath, where he often looked uncomfortable. A non-playing substitute in the Coca Cola Cup final side, at his best, Steve always seems to have plenty of time on the ball and likes to drive forward to get in telling, swirling crosses.
Liverpool (£20,000 from Dundalk on 2/9/86) FL 55+10 FLC 6+2/4 FAC 14+2/1 Others 1/1
Bradford C (Loaned on 13/11/87) FL 7+1 FLC 2 Others 1
Aston Villa (£1,100,000 on 7/8/91) F/PL 148+3/13 FLC 16+2/1 FAC 13+1 Others 6

STEELE Timothy (Tim) Wesley
Born: Coventry, 1 December 1967
Height: 5'9" Weight: 11.7

As in the case of Tony James at Hereford, Tim was out for a long time in 1995-96 with injuries that required surgery, thus making him unavailable for selection until later in the season. A determined midfielder, and a good crosser, he eventually showed, mainly as a substitute, prior to being released in the summer.
Shrewsbury T (From apprentice on 7/12/85) FL 41+20/5 FLC 3+1/1 Others 1+1
Wolverhampton W (£80,000 on 22/2/89) FL 53+22/7 FLC 5/3 FAC 1 Others 4
Stoke C (Loaned on 20/2/92) FL 7/1
Bradford C (Free on 16/7/93) FL 8+3 FLC 2+1/1
Hereford U (Free on 14/1/94) FL 24+8/2 FLC 2 FAC 1+1 Others 1+2

STEFANOVIC Dejan
Born: Yugoslavia, 28 October 1974
Height: 6'2" Weight: 12.2
International Honours: Yugoslavia: 7

Signed from Red Star Belgrade, along with Darko Kovacevic last December, this elegant, left-sided player has so far not adjusted to the extra speed of the English game with Sheffield Wednesday. Although classy when on the ball, too often the game seemed to pass him by, and like Kovacevic, he was not given too many chances with the Owls' desperate need for points. However, this season should see him make more of an impact.
Sheffield Wed (£2,000,000 from Red Star Belgrade on 22/12/95) PL 5+1 FAC 1

STEIN Mark Earl Sean
Born: Capetown, South Africa, 28 January 1966
Height: 5'6" Weight: 11.2
Club Honours: FLC '88; AMC '92; Div 2 '93
International Honours: E: Yth

Yet another Chelsea player to have had an injury wrecked season in 1995-96. In Mark's case this was his third in a row, only managing seven league starts and having a desperate time since picking up a broken ankle at Old Trafford in March 1994, just as he was enjoying a hot streak in front of goal. A nimble opportunist striker, his latest setback was a knee ligament injury which kept him away from first team action after the home fixture with Bolton Wanderers on 22 November 1995.
Luton T (From juniors on 31/1/84) FL 41+13/19 FLC 4+1 FAC 9/3 Others 3/1
Aldershot (Loaned on 29/1/86) FL 2/1
Queens Park R (£300,000 on 26/8/88) FL 20+13/4 FLC 4/2 FAC 2+1/1 Others 4
Oxford U (Signed on 15/9/89) FL 72+10/18 FLC 4 FAC 2+1 Others 3
Stoke C (£100,000 on 15/9/91) FL 94/50 FLC 8/8 FAC 4 Others 17/10
Chelsea (£1,500,000 on 28/10/93) PL 46+4/21 FLC 0+1 FAC 9/2 Others 2+1/2

STEPHENS Anthony (Tony) John
Born: Portsmouth, 12 January 1977
Height: 5'10" Weight: 11.0

Tony, a young Bournemouth trainee midfielder, made just one substitute appearance last season when coming on at Bristol Rovers in the AWS competition. Contracted until January, he was not offered professional terms and released.
Bournemouth (Trainee) Others 0+1

STEPHENSON Ashlyn
Born: South Africa, 6 July 1974
Height: 6'2" Weight: 12.0
International Honours: E: Yth

A former England youth team goalkeeper from his days as a Crewe Alexandra trainee, Ashlyn trialed with Darlington last September, playing in a 2-2 home draw against Colchester, before trying his luck at Birmingham a few weeks later. With no opportunities forthcoming, he moved on within a month.
Darlington (Free from Waterford on 11/9/95) FL 1

STEPHENSON Paul
Born: Wallsend, 2 January 1968
Height: 5'10" Weight: 12.12
International Honours: E: Yth

Signed from Brentford prior to the start of 1995-96, Paul proved to be a very skilful and talented left winger. Fought back from two serious injuries (broken arm and a hairline fracture of a leg) to play a vital role in York's late season rally, which avoided relegation to division three. His ball-playing abilities and experience were great assets to the club.
Newcastle U (From apprentice on 2/1/86) FL 58+3/1 FLC 3+1 FAC 2 Others 2
Millwall (£300,000 on 10/11/88) FL 81+17/6 FLC 3/1 FAC 9/2 Others 8/1
Gillingham (Loaned on 21/11/92) FL 12/2 Others 2
Brentford (£30,000 on 4/3/93) FL 70/2 FLC 6/1 FAC 1+1 Others 5
York C (Signed on 7/8/95) FL 24+3/2 FLC 2 Others 1+1/1

STERLING Worrell Ricardo
Born: Bethnal Green, 8 June 1965
Height: 5'7" Weight: 11.0
Club Honours: FAYC '82

An experienced and hard-working Bristol Rovers' winger, and usually a consistent provider of accurate crosses, Worrell did not enjoy the best of fortunes in 1995-96, culminating in him asking for a transfer and being released during the summer. In what was also the first time in over 13 seasons that he had failed to score, he completed over 400 appearances in the Football League.
Watford (From apprentice on 10/6/83) FL 82+12/14 FLC 7+2/1 FAC 18/2 Others 0+1
Peterborough U (£70,000 on 23/3/89) FL 190+3/28 FLC 15/3 FAC 14/5 Others 14/2
Bristol Rov (£140,000 on 29/7/93) FL 117+2/6 FLC 7/1 FAC 6 Others 15

Gary Stevens

STEVENS Michael Gary
Born: Barrow, 27 March 1963
Height: 5'11" Weight: 12.7
Club Honours: FAC '84; Div 1 '85, '87; ECWC '85; CS '84, '85; SPD '89, '90, '91, '92, '93, '94; SLC '89, '91, '94; SC '92
International Honours: E: 46; B-1

In what has proved a difficult last season for Tranmere, Gary's experience and versatility proved an invaluable asset. Despite missing 14 games through injury, the former Glasgow Rangers and England defender produced some sterling displays at either right back, left back, or as one of three central defenders, where he acted as a cover player. When Tranmere needed a steadying influence he was there, calming everyone down and doing the simple things well.
Everton (From apprentice on 8/4/81) FL 207+1/8 FLC 30/1 FAC 39/3 Others 10
Glasgow R (£1,000,000 on 19/7/88) SL 186+1/8 SLC 22 SC 22/1 Others 14
Tranmere Rov (£350,000 on 22/9/94) FL 70+1/1 FLC 7 FAC 3 Others 4

STEVENS Ian David
Born: Malta, 21 October 1966
Height: 5'9" Weight: 12.0
Club Honours: AMC '89

Shrewsbury striker. A firm favourite, who struggled to establish himself early last season, something that made his strike rate even more creditable after becoming a regular in the New Year, his goals being instrumental in enabling the club to reach Wembley in the Auto Windscreens Shield. Can turn sharply to snap up chances and is also useful with his head.
Preston NE (From apprentice on 22/11/84) FL 9+2/2 Others 1
Stockport Co (Free on 27/10/86) FL 1+1 FAC 0+1 Others 0+1 (Free to Lancaster C on 27/11/86)
Bolton W (Free on 25/3/87) FL 26+21/7 FLC 1+2 FAC 4/2 Others 3+1
Bury (Free on 3/7/91) FL 100+10/38 FLC 3+1 FAC 2+2 Others 7+1/2
Shrewsbury T (£20,000 on 11/8/94) FL 53+17/20 FLC 0+1 FAC 2+2/1 Others 8+2/11

STEVENS Keith Henry
Born: Merton, 21 June 1964
Height: 6'0" Weight: 12.12
Club Honours: FLT '83; Div 2 '88

As Millwall's longest-serving player and captain, Keith continues to be a tough-tackling central defender with a never-say-die attitude. Once again, he had a consistently good season in 1995-96, giving many faultless displays, and has now overtaken old favourite, Henry Cripps, in the all-competition appearance stakes, lying second only to Barry Kitchener.
Millwall (From apprentice on 23/6/81) FL 442+7/9 FLC 34/1 FAC 28 Others 29

STEWART William Paul Marcus
Born: Bristol, 8 November 1972
Height: 5'10" Weight: 11.0
International Honours: E: Sch

One of the hottest strikers outside of the Premiership, he was Bristol Rovers' top goalscorer with 30 goals in 1995-96, including Pirates' quickest league goal in their history – just 28 seconds against Hull City on 6 January. Marcus, who also

managed the club's only hat trick in a Coca Cola Cup-tie victory over Gillingham, was hardly surprisingly selected by his PFA colleagues for the award winning second division team. *Stop Press:* Reported to have signed for Huddersfield as the replacement for Andy Booth, a sum of £1.2m changing hands.
Bristol Rov (From trainee on 18/7/91) FL 137+34/57 FLC 11/5 FAC 7+1/3 Others 16+1/14

STEWART Paul Andrew
Born: Manchester, 7 October 1964
Height: 5'11" Weight: 12.4
Club Honours: FAC '91; CS '91; Div 1 '94, '96
International Honours: E: 3; B-5; U21-1; Yth

The signing of the ex-England striker, or midfielder, on a free transfer from Liverpool last March, proved to be an inspired piece of business by Sunderland's Peter Reid. Paul had originally arrived at Roker on loan in August, but, after only two appearances, sustained an injury at Ipswich that saw him return to Anfield. Having signed permanently, his experience and ability to hold the ball up in attack proved crucial in the promotion run-in. Opened his goalscoring account in the 3-0 victory over Birmingham in April, before missing the last three games through suspension, which, significantly, saw the club's goal tally dry up at the same time. Happily, his 12 appearances saw him qualify for a first division championship medal.
Blackpool (From apprentice on 13/10/81) FL 188+13/56 FLC 11/3 FAC 7/2 Others 6/1
Manchester C (£200,000 on 19/3/87) FL 51+26 FLC 4/2 FAC 6/1 Others 2/1
Tottenham H (£1,700,000 on 21/6/88) FL 126+5/28 FLC 23/7 FAC 9/2 Others 9
Liverpool (£2,300,000 on 29/7/92) PL 28+4/1 FLC 6 FAC 1 Others 3/2
Crystal Palace (Loaned on 24/1/94) FL 18/3
Wolverhampton W (Loaned on 2/9/94) FL 5+3/2 Others 2
Burnley (Loaned on 8/2/95) FL 6
Sunderland (Loaned on 29/8/95) FL 1+1
Sunderland (Free on 5/3/96) FL 10/1

STEWART Simon Andrew
Born: Leeds, 1 November 1973
Height: 6'1" Weight: 12.8

Unable to impose himself at Sheffield Wednesday in 1995-96, the young central defender was loaned out to Shrewsbury in time for the start of the season and played just four games with varying partners before going back to Hillsborough. Having previously impressed Wednesday fans as a positive youngster who attacked the ball and defended well, he was deemed surplus to requirements and given a free transfer in the summer.
Sheffield Wed (From trainee on 16/7/92) PL 6 FLC 0+1
Shrewsbury T (Loaned on 11/8/95) FL 4

STEWART William (Billy) Ian
Born: Liverpool, 1 January 1965
Height: 6'2" Weight: 14.7

Recognised as one of the leading shot stoppers in the lower divisions, the experienced goalkeeper rejoined Chester during the 1995 close season, having spent the previous 12 months with Northampton. Apart from two games, an ever present, Billy quickly re-established himself with breathtaking saves and has now passed 300 league appearances for the club. Was surprisingly released during the summer.

Liverpool (From apprentice on 5/1/83)
Wigan Ath (Free on 2/7/84) FL 14 Others 1
Chester C (Free on 11/8/86) FL 272 FLC 21 FAC 19 Others 20
Northampton T (Free on 4/7/94) FL 26+1 FLC 2 FAC 1 Others 1
Chesterfield (Loaned on 17/3/95) FL 1 Others 1+1
Chester C (Free on 6/7/95) FL 45 FLC 4 FAC 1 Others 1

STIMAC Igor
Born: Croatia, 6 September 1967
Height: 6'2" Weight: 12.8
International Honours: Croatia: 18

Derby centre back and Croatian international captain whose transfer from Hajduk Split last October was the catalyst for the club's long unbeaten run, culminating in promotion. Invariably calm under pressure, Igor took no time at all to settle successfully into English football. With good vision and ball control – as is typical of the continental sweeper – he quickly became the fan's favourite and was eagerly watched in Euro '96 as a key player for Croatia.

Derby Co (£1,570,000 from Hadjuk Split on 31/10/95) FL 27/1 FAC 1

STIMSON Mark
Born: Plaistow, 27 December 1967
Height: 5'11" Weight: 11.0

Mark started last season by going on loan to Barnet, where he produced a number of fine performances, before returning to the left back position at Portsmouth. After losing his place to Andy Awford, he joined Southend on transfer deadline day as a replacement for Chris Powell, a move that was greeted by the fans with wonderment, as his abilities soon became apparent. A strong tackler and excellent distributor of the ball, his reading of the game is exceptional, and he immediately became a firm favourite.

Tottenham H (From apprentice on 15/7/85) FL 1+1
Leyton Orient (Loaned on 15/3/88) FL 10
Gillingham (Loaned on 19/1/89) FL 18
Newcastle U (£200,000 on 16/6/89) FL 82+4/2 FLC 5 FAC 7/1 Others 6
Portsmouth (Loaned on 10/12/92) FL 3+1
Portsmouth (£100,000 on 23/7/93) FL 57+1/2 FLC 9/1 FAC 3 Others 3
Barnet (Loaned on 21/9/95) FL 5 Others 1
Southend U (£25,000 on 15/3/96) FL 10

STOCK Russell John
Born: Great Yarmouth, 25 June 1977
Height: 6'2" Weight: 13.5

Strong young Cambridge United midfielder who impressed in pre-1995-96 friendlies and played in nine of the first 13 games of the season. Never gaining a regular place, after an injury suffered when attacked socially, Russell was released at the end of the season.

Cambridge U (From trainee on 20/7/95) FL 15+2/1 FLC 1 Others 1

STOCKWELL Michael (Micky) Thomas
Born: Chelmsford, 14 February 1965
Height: 5'9" Weight: 11.4
Club Honours: Div 2 '92

A one club man who has proved that he can play almost anywhere Ipswich need him, he was honoured to be handed the captaincy at the start of last season, but, with his game suffering, it was eventually passed on to new signing, Tony Mowbray. After making the majority of his appearances at right back, where he combined well with Gus Uhlenbeek, towards the end of the campaign, Micky took on a right-sided midfield role. Is a quick tackler who is never easily beaten, and passes and moves well.

Ipswich T (From apprentice on 17/12/82) F/PL 332+20/21 FLC 24+3/2 FAC 21+3/1 Others 18+2/1

STOKER Gareth
Born: Bishop Auckland, 22 February 1973
Height: 5'9" Weight: 10.10

Gareth made fairly regular appearances for Hereford last season, despite having to battle hard for places. Chasing everything, he is a solid, terrier-like type of player, who always gave 100 per cent, and his tremendous goal at Tottenham in the 5-1 FA Cup replay defeat will long be remembered by Bulls' fans.

Hull C (Free from Leeds U juniors on 13/9/91) FL 24+6/2 FLC 3 FAC 2+1 Others 0+2 (Released during 1993 close season)
Hereford U (Signed on 16/3/95) FL 40+3/3 FLC 2 FAC 2+1/1 Others 5+1/1

STOKES Dean Anthony
Born: Birmingham, 23 May 1970
Height: 5'9" Weight: 10.5

Port Vale left back who is a particularly strong tackler. Limited first team opportunities in 1995-96 prompted a transfer request, but injury to Allen Tankard gave him his chance and he held on for an extended run-in the team from March onwards. This coincided with six successive league wins and an appearance in the Anglo-Italian Cup final at Wembley.

Port Vale (Signed from Halesowen T on 15/1/93) FL 40+2 FLC 0+1 FAC 3 Others 5+3

STOKOE Graham
Born: Newcastle under Lyme, 17 December 1975
Height: 6'0" Weight: 11.11

The promising Stoke midfielder joined Hartlepool on loan to get some first team experience last February. He looked a useful player in the games he played, but admitted that he struggled with the faster pace in division three and after barely a month he was recalled by City to strengthen their squad in their push for promotion. However, he has yet to play for the Potters.

Stoke C (Free from Newcastle U juniors on 7/7/94)
Hartlepool U (Loaned on 23/2/96) FL 8

STONE Steven (Steve) Brian
Born: Gateshead, 20 August 1971
Height: 5'9" Weight: 12.7
International Honours: E: 9

Without doubt Nottingham Forest's player

of last season, and one of the leading performers in the Premier League, the right flank midfielder carried on improving on the excellent form he had shown the previous season and by the end of 1995-96 had established himself as a near automatic choice in the England team. A prodigiously hard-working player, with great skill and confidence on the ball, and a rare talent for shooting with accuracy and power, he was fortunate to play almost a full game as substitute on his England debut against Switzerland in November, replacing Jamie Redknapp after only seven minutes, and capped a virtuoso display with the third goal in a 3-1 victory. He went on to prove that was no fluke when scoring the only goal in his second international against Portugal. Whilst many players take years to establish themselves as true international class, Steve acclimatised himself in the national team almost immediately and was an automatic Euro '96 squad selection.

Nottingham F (From trainee on 20/5/89) F/PL 131+2/18 FLC 11+1 FAC 8 Others 12/2

Steve Stone

STORER Stuart John
Born: Rugby, 16 January 1967
Height: 5'11" Weight: 12.13
Club Honours: AMC '89

An industrious forward who played down both flanks for Brighton in 1995-96, Stuart is full of running and a supplier of good crosses, his excellent pace often leaving defenders trailing in his wake.

Mansfield T (Juniors) FL 0+1 (Freed in March 1984)
Birmingham C (Free from VS Rugby on 18/7/84) FL 5+3 FLC 1
Everton (Signed on 6/3/87)
Wigan Ath (Loaned on 23/7/87) FL 9+3 FLC 4
Bolton W (£25,000 on 24/12/87) FL 95+28/12 FLC 9+2 FAC 7+3/2 Others 16+5/1
Exeter C (£25,000 on 25/3/93) FL 75+2/8 FLC 4/1 FAC 4+1/1 Others 6
Brighton & Hove A (£15,000 on 2/3/95) FL 30+10/3 FLC 2 FAC 1+1 Others 3/1

STOREY Brett Barry
Born: Sheffield, 7 July 1977
Height: 5'11" Weight: 12.0
A left-footed Lincoln midfield player who was signed on a non-contract basis last March, after being released by Sheffield United, he did well enough in reserve games to earn a couple of FL outings as substitute and netted with a spectacular volley in the final day victory over Torquay.
Lincoln C (Free from Sheffield U juniors on 27/3/96) FL 0+2/1

STOWELL Michael (Mike)
Born: Portsmouth, 19 April 1965
Height: 6'2" Weight: 14.2
The Wolves' goalkeeper was unavailable for the opener in 1995-96, but was then a regular until suffering a depressed fracture of the cheekbone, after colliding with a team mate in October. Typical of his luck was the last-minute equaliser by Ipswich, when Darren Ferguson headed off the line only for it to go in off the 'keeper's back. Gave some fine shot-stopping displays, even saving penalties in successive January games.
Preston NE (Free from Leyland Motors on 14/2/85)
Everton (Free on 12/12/85) Others 1
Chester C (Loaned on 3/9/87) FL 14 Others 2
York C (Loaned on 24/12/87) FL 6
Manchester C (Loaned on 2/2/88) FL 14 FAC 1
Port Vale (Loaned on 21/10/88) FL 7 Others 1
Wolverhampton W (Loaned on 17/3/89) FL 7
Preston NE (Loaned on 8/2/90) FL 2
Wolverhampton W (£250,000 on 28/6/90) FL 232 FLC 16 FAC 13 Others 9

STRACHAN Gordon David
Born: Edinburgh, 9 February 1957
Height: 5'6" Weight: 10.8
Club Honours: SPD '80, '84; SC '82, '83, '84; ECWC '83; ESC '83; FAC '85; Div 2 '90, Div 1 '92; CS '92
International Honours: S: 50; U21-1; Yth; Sch
Assistant Coventry manager, and still called up for service from time to time. In the first half of last season he played when Paul Telfer was injured and after Christmas he appeared in vital games, never letting the side down. Always influenced everybody with his non-stop running and fighting spirit, not to mention his immense skill and incredible fitness at the age of 39. Outstanding in the Manchester City home FA Cup-tie, when he set up the late equaliser, and in the home win over QPR, he suffered a hamstring injury which kept him out of the vital last two games. Is booked to become Coventry manager in the summer of 1997 when Big Ron moves upstairs.
Dundee (From juniors in 1971) SL 56+13/13 SLC 11+2/1 SC 7/1 Others 1+1
Aberdeen (£50,000 on 1/11/77) SL 175+8/55 SLC 43+3/20 SC 25/7 Others 30+4/7
Manchester U (£500,000 on 13/8/84) FL 155+5/33 FLC 12+1/1 FAC 22/2 Others 10+2/3
Leeds U (£300,000 on 23/3/89) F/PL 188+9/37 FLC 19/3 FAC 14/2 Others 14+1/3
Coventry C (Free on 22/3/95) PL 10+7 FLC 3 FAC 2

STRODDER Gary John
Born: Cleckheaton, 1 April 1965
Height: 6'1" Weight: 13.3

Notts County central defender and captain. Signed from West Bromwich in the summer of 1995, Gary enjoyed an excellent first season at Meadow Lane, missing only three league games and forming a highly effective partnership with Shaun Murphy. Very powerful in the air, both in defence and attack, knocking in three goals from set pieces, his dour and solid performances kept Graeme Hogg on the bench throughout the campaign.
Lincoln C (From apprentice on 8/4/83) FL 122+10/6 FLC 7+1 FAC 2+1 Others 5+1
West Ham U (Signed on 20/3/87) FL 59+6/2 FLC 8 FAC 4+2 Others 2
West Bromwich A (£190,000 on 22/8/90) FL 123+17/8 FLC 8+1 FAC 7/1 Others 10
Notts Co (£145,000 on 14/7/95) FL 43/3 FLC 3 FAC 3 Others 6

STRONG Gregory (Greg)
Born: Bolton, 5 September 1975
Height: 6'2" Weight: 11.12
International Honours: E: Yth; Sch
Strong by name and strong by nature for the centre half who joined Bolton last August from Wigan Athletic. A regular in the club's reserve side, he made just one appearance during the season when he came on as a substitute against Sheffield Wednesday at Hillsborough on New Year's Day. Also capable of playing at left back, Greg has good ability on the ball for one so tall and is definitely one for the future.
Wigan Ath (From trainee on 1/10/92) FL 28+7/3 FLC 5 FAC 1 Others 3+1
Bolton W (Signed on 10/8/95) PL 0+1

STRONG Steven (Steve) George
Born: Watford, 15 March 1978
Height: 5'7" Weight: 11.2
As an extremely quick left back who made two appearances as a substitute for Bournemouth in 1995-96, he will certainly be looking for more first team opportunities in the coming season. Still a trainee, Steve can also play on the left side of midfield, or up with the attack, and has very good ball skills.
Bournemouth (Trainee) FL 0+2 FAC 0+1

STUART Graham Charles
Born: Tooting, 24 October 1970
Height: 5'9" Weight: 11.6
Club Honours: FAC '95
International Honours: E: U21-5; Yth
Everton forward who can play on either wing or in a more advanced striking role. Encompassing a tremendous turn of pace with excellent control, and proficient with either foot, Graham is a good linking player who feeds from defenders well and distributes in style. Having been assigned to a right wing role when first joining the club, in 1995-96 he moved to the left, following Andrei Kanchelskis' arrival and, although injury prevented him from starting until October, he soon topped Blues' mid-season scoring charts, most notably, netting twice in the 4-0 drubbing of Middlesbrough. Continued to frustrate full backs throughout the campaign with jinking runs and proved an important cog in the team's make-up.

Chelsea (From trainee on 15/6/89) F/PL 70+17/14 FLC 11/2 FAC 5+2/1 Others 3+2/1
Everton (£850,000 on 19/8/93) PL 73+14/16 FLC 5/2 FAC 8+3/5 Others 2+1/1

STUART Jamie Christopher
Born: Southwark, 15 October 1976
Height: 5'10" Weight: 11.0
International Honours: E: U21-4; Yth
As Charlton's regular left back throughout 1995-96, Jamie looked a most assured youngster, impressing with both his tackling and passing games. He also showed a liking for getting down the flank in order to produce good early crosses. Scored his first goal for the club, the second in a 2-1 home win against Huddersfield in September, and got another in a 4-1 victory over WBA. His good form was recognised when selected for the England U21 squad in April and making four appearances.
Charlton Ath (From trainee on 18/1/95) FL 39 FLC 5 FAC 3 Others 0+1

STUART Mark Richard
Born: Chiswick, 15 December 1966
Height: 5'10" Weight: 11.3
International Honours: E: Sch
After a spell on loan at Chesterfield early last season, when he failed to get on the team sheet, Mark was thrust into the Rochdale's number nine shirt and responded with a return to his form of 1993-94, seven goals in seven games being the end product. His sparkling wide play was so badly missed when he suffered a broken jaw, that Dale, previously the top scorers in the country, managed only one (penalty) goal in their next six league games. Also the club's dead ball specialist.
Charlton Ath (From juniors on 3/7/84) FL 89+18/28 FLC 7+3/2 FAC 1/1 Others 9+1
Plymouth Arg (£150,000 on 4/11/88) FL 55+2/11 FLC 4 FAC 3 Others 2/1
Ipswich T (Loaned on 22/3/90) FL 5/2
Bradford C (£80,000 on 3/8/90) FL 22+7/5 FLC 6/1 FAC 0+1 Others 1+1
Huddersfield T (Free on 30/10/92) FL 9+6/3 FAC 2 Others 4/1
Rochdale (Free on 5/7/93) FL 99+8/28 FLC 5+1/1 FAC 4/1 Others 5+3/1

STUBBS Alan
Born: Liverpool, 6 October 1971
Height: 6'2" Weight: 13.10
International Honours: E: B-1
Bolton's club captain during 1995-96, Alan is capable of playing in either a central defensive role, as a sweeper, or in midfield. A regular in the side except when he was injured, disappointingly, the season did not get off to a good start for him when a move to Blackburn, along with former team mate, Jason McAteer, fell through. He came through that setback, but it was not until the New Year that he produced his best form, which included scoring two goals in a game for the first time against Coventry City at Highfield Road. Four days after the end of the campaign, with Wanderers' already on their way back to the first division, he got his move to a big club, when Celtic paid £3,500,000 for his services.
Bolton W (From trainee on 24/7/90) P/FL 181+21/9 FLC 23/4 FAC 16+3/2 Others 12+1

STURGESS Paul Christopher
Born: Dartford, 4 August 1975
Height: 5'11" Weight: 12.5

Charlton left back whose appearances in 1995-96 were limited by injuries and the excellent form of Jamie Stuart. Comfortable on the ball, and a good crosser, despite a distinct lack of goals, he likes to get forward into shooting positions. Hopefully, his problems are now fully behind him and he can mount a sustained challenge for a first team place this coming season.

Charlton Ath (From trainee on 1/7/93) FL 42+6 FLC 3 Others 5

STURRIDGE Dean Constantine
Born: Birmingham, 26 July 1973
Height: 5'8" Weight: 12.1

Dean's form was the revelation of last season and his goals were paramount to Derby gaining promotion. Playing more of a central role, he finally showed the consistency which a long run-in the side allowed. Confidence and self belief brought a deluge of goals, including four in his first five appearances and, though his scoring rate slowed slightly in the second half of the campaign, his contribution had already put County amongst the promotion favourites. A striker more than useful on the ground, as well as in the air, his sharp reflexes and speed brought him the opening goal in the crucial game against Crystal Palace, a win that guaranteed promotion to the Premiership. Was one of two Derby players to be selected for the Endsleigh League U21 side that drew 1-1 with an Italian Serie "B" XI in November. Also elected by his fellow professionals to the PFA first division award winning team.

Derby Co (From trainee on 1/7/91) FL 49+13/21 FLC 0+1 Others 2+1
Torquay U (Loaned on 16/12/94) FL 10/5

Dean Sturridge

STURRIDGE Simon Andrew
Born: Birmingham, 9 December 1969
Height: 5'5" Weight: 10.13
Club Honours: AMC '91

Diminutive striker who burst explosively into the Stoke City team last November and was a key factor in the side's rise up the first division table. A very tricky player, with the ability to dribble in dangerous areas, he had his best season since arriving as a cut price signing from Birmingham. Many knowledgeable followers had long thought that Simon needed the confidence that a long run-in the side would bring and so it turned out. Brother Dean currently plays for Derby.

Birmingham C (From trainee on 8/7/88) FL 129+21/30 FLC 10+4/1 FAC 8/2 Others 14/5
Stoke C (£75,000 on 24/9/93) FL 37+25/14 FLC 2 FAC 3+3/1 Others 7+3

SUCKLING Perry John
Born: Leyton, 12 October 1965
Height: 6'1" Weight: 13.2
International Honours: E: U21-10; Yth

First choice Doncaster goalkeeper for much of last season, with eight clean sheets in 20 games at one point, until a severe back injury cost him his place. Left Belle Vue in March to pursue a playing/coaching career in South Africa.

Coventry C (From apprentice on 19/10/83) FL 27 FLC 2
Manchester C (Signed on 5/6/86) FL 39 FLC 3 FAC 1 Others 3
Crystal Palace (£100,000 on 14/1/88) FL 59 FLC 4 FAC 1 Others 7
West Ham U (Loaned on 15/12/89) FL 6
Brentford (Loaned on 11/10/91) FL 8 Others 1
Watford (Free on 13/7/92) FL 39 FLC 4 FAC 1 Others 2
Doncaster Rov (Free on 8/7/94) FL 30 FLC 3 FAC 1 Others 1

SULLIVAN Neil
Born: Sutton, 24 February 1970
Height: 6'0" Weight: 12.1

Contrary to popular opinion, Neil gained his goalkeeping place in the Wimbledon first team for 1995-96 on merit, and not due to Hans Seger's off field problems. After a broken leg suffered at the end of 1994-95, he was forced to wait until January to regain his place and was ever present from then on. His main strengths were in his reflexes, allied to shot stopping, and, in a difficult season for Dons, the youngster did well, often emerging with credit.

Wimbledon (From trainee on 26/7/88) F/PL 31+1 FAC 8
Crystal Palace (Loaned on 1/5/92) FL 1

SUMMERBEE Nicholas (Nicky) John
Born: Altrincham, 26 August 1971
Height: 5'11" Weight: 11.8
International Honours: E: B-1; U21-3

Stylish and deceptive Manchester City right back, cum winger, who has the knack of drifting past defenders, particularly in tight areas out on the touchline. Completed his second full season at Maine Road in 1995-96, the quality and accuracy of his crosses being a rare feature in today's game. He is equally adept at bringing the ball out of defence to set up the front men. Not recognised as a taker of chances, Nicky

scored just one league goal, against Bolton, earning the club their first win of the season after 12 games. Is one of the few players to have followed both his father and grandfather into league soccer. Mike, his father, also played for Manchester City.

Swindon T (From trainee on 20/7/89) F/PL 89+23/6 FLC 9+1/3 FAC 2+4 Others 7/1
Manchester C (£1,500,000 on 24/6/94) PL 72+6/2 FLC 7+2/2 FAC 9

SUMMERBELL Mark
Born: Durham, 30 October 1976
Height: 5'9" Weight: 10.7

A former Middlesbrough trainee, who only turned professional during the 1995 close season, the young midfield prospect was surprisingly elevated from the juniors to the first team bench for the Spurs' match last April, having very little reserve experience behind him. Replaced the injured Robbie Mustoe for the last 50 minutes, and, although receiving no further action, his early introduction to PL football indicates he is highly regarded by Bryan Robson.

Middlesbrough (From trainee on 1/7/95) PL 0+1

SUMMERFIELD Kevin
Born: Walsall, 7 January 1959
Height: 5'11" Weight: 11.0
Club Honours: FAYC '76; Div 3 '94
International Honours: E: Yth

At his best, Kevin showed good ball skills, both in midfield or further forward, but in 1995-96 concentrated more on the coaching side at Shrewsbury. Vastly experienced, having played well over 400 first team games since 1978-79, he was limited to just two appearances as a substitute, prior to being released in the summer.

West Bromwich A (From apprentice on 1/1/77) FL 5+4/4 FLC 2
Birmingham C (Free on 31/5/82) FL 2+3/1 FLC 1 FAC 1+1/1
Walsall (Free on 14/12/82) FL 42+12/17 FLC 5+2/2 FAC 1
Cardiff C (Free on 6/7/84) FL 10/1 FLC 2
Plymouth Arg (Free on 21/12/84) FL 118+21/26 FLC 6+1/3 FAC 13/4 Others 4/1
Exeter C (Loaned on 22/3/90) FL 4
Shrewsbury T (Free on 10/10/90) FL 140+23/21 FLC 13+1/7 FAC 11+1/1 Others 8+1

SUNDERLAND Jonathan (Jon) Paul
Born: Newcastle, 2 November 1975
Height: 5'11" Weight: 11.9

Having been at non-league Northwich Victoria on loan last October, the young winger was allowed to leave Blackpool in March, becoming the new Scarborough boss, Mitch Cook's first signing, and making his debut in the 1-2 home defeat by Preston on 30 March. Looks to be a bright prospect for the future, with the added advantage of being able to adapt to a midfield role.

Blackpool (From trainee on 18/7/94) FL 0+2 Others 0+1
Scarborough (Free on 28/3/96) FL 3+3

SUSSEX Andrew (Andy) Robert
Born: Enfield, 23 November 1964
Height: 6'3" Weight: 13.8

Although a player possessing a great deal of natural talent, Andy struggled to make an impact in a Southend team already full of good midfield skills in 1995-96. Injury also greatly hampered his season and he was loaned out to Brentford for three games in December, before returning to Roots Hall. Will be hoping for a chance this coming season to show his passing abilities to greater effect.

Leyton Orient (From apprentice on 25/11/82) FL 126+18/17 FLC 7+1/2 FAC 8/1 Others 5+3
Crewe Alex (£16,000 on 23/6/88) FL 86+16/24 FLC 10/6 FAC 7+1/4 Others 5/2
Southend U (£100,000 on 4/7/91) FL 63+13/14 FLC 7 FAC 2+1 Others 3+1/1
Brentford (Loaned on 12/12/95) FL 3

SUTCH Daryl
Born: Beccles, 11 September 1971
Height: 6'0" Weight: 12.0
International Honours: E: U21-4; Yth

A Norwich midfielder who likes to join in the play in order to create chances for others, Daryl suffered a groin strain prior to the start of last season in Ireland and when coming on as sub in the opening match at Luton, without touching the ball, a clash of heads necessitated him having five stitches. His luck did not change, being sent off on his comeback (a reserve game) and, following a suspension, going down with a knee ligament strain. His best moment came when he strode half the length of the field to make Ashley Ward's goal in the 4-1 win at WBA. Is an excellent passer of the ball.

Norwich C (From trainee on 6/7/90) F/PL 49+32/3 FLC 8+3 FAC 4+2 Others 2+3

Chris Sutton

SUTTON Christopher (Chris) Roy
Born: Nottingham, 10 March 1973
Height: 6'3" Weight: 13.5
Club Honours: PL '95
International Honours: E: B-2; U21-13

The young Blackburn striker with a goal flair and good positional sense, plus the ability to get free in the penalty area, started last season under pressure for his place, alongside Alan Shearer, from a returning Mike Newell. Although Chris had a better goalscoring record there was a belief that Shearer responded better to the presence of Newell and his early inability to strike form resulted in his demotion. Unluckily, after a brief trial in defence, when the side played three at the back, he injured tendons and ligaments at Coventry in early December. The injury has been slow to clear up and it is possible that surgery will be needed before we see him back on the field of play. Is the son of Mike, who played for Norwich, Chester, and Carlisle, between 1962-1971.

Norwich C (From trainee on 2/7/91) F/PL 89+13/35 FLC 8+1/3 FAC 10/5 Others 6
Blackburn Rov (£5,000,000 on 13/7/94) PL 49+4/15 FLC 6+1/4 FAC 2/2 Others 6+3/1

SUTTON Stephen (Steve) John
Born: Hartington, 16 April 1961
Height: 6'1" Weight: 14.11
Club Honours: FLC '89, '90; FMC '89

Appointed Derby club captain, he started off last season as the first choice goalkeeper, before being replaced in a tactical ploy at Sheffield United in October, losing out to Russell Hoult. From thereon, the latter's excellent form kept him on the bench for the rest of the campaign and in January he was loaned to Reading, becoming one of seven goalies used by the club during 1995-96.

Nottingham F (From apprentice on 16/4/79) FL 199 FLC 33 FAC 14 Others 11
Mansfield T (Loaned on 10/3/81) FL 8
Derby Co (Loaned on 25/1/85) FL 14
Coventry C (Loaned on 1/2/91) FL 1
Luton T (Loaned on 28/11/91) FL 14
Derby Co (£300,000 on 6/3/92) FL 60+1 FLC 7 FAC 3 Others 11
Reading (Loaned on 19/1/96) FL 2

SUTTON Wayne Frank
Born: Derby, 1 October 1975
Height: 6'0" Weight: 13.2

Talented young Derby defender whose chances of first team action in 1995-96 were limited with so much transfer activity. Predominately right footed, and from County's prolific youth set up, Wayne will hopefully continue his progress towards the first team squad in 1996-97. Is an excellent tackler and ball winner.

Derby Co (From trainee on 27/10/92) FL 4+3 FAC 1

SWAILES Christopher (Chris) William
Born: Gateshead, 19 October 1970
Height: 6'2" Weight: 12.11

The tall Ipswich central defender was unfortunately restricted in terms of appearances last season by the number of quality players in the squad, making just five in all. His cause was further undermined when undergoing a hernia operation in December, but he came back strongly to give his best performance in the home match against Derby in April. Should be well placed to challenge for a regular slot this coming term.

Ipswich T (From trainee on 23/5/89)
Peterborough U (£10,000 on 28/3/91)
Birmingham C (Free from Boston U on 26/3/92)
Doncaster Rov (Free from Guisborough on 27/10/93) FL 49 FLC 2/1 FAC 1 Others 2
Ipswich T (£225,000 on 23/3/95) P/FL 8+1

SWALES Stephen (Steve) Colin
Born: Whitby, 26 December 1973
Height: 5'8" Weight: 10.6

A 1995 close season signing from division three side, Scarborough, although he only made intermittent appearances in defence for Reading, he showed that he is a young player with enough pace and strength in the tackle to become a more than competent defender. Most effective at full back, though he did well as an emergency central defender in the final game at Birmingham.

Scarborough (From trainee on 3/8/92) FL 51+3/1 FAC 5 Others 3
Reading (£70,000 on 13/7/95) FL 4+5 FLC 0+1 FAC 1

SWAN Peter Harold
Born: Leeds, 28 September 1966
Height: 6'2" Weight: 14.12
Club Honours: AMC '93

The type of defender to instil fear into all but the bravest of strikers, he had a highly effective start to his Burnley career, having been signed from Plymouth during the 1995 close season, but suffered from the malaise that seemed to affect the rest of the defence when the team's fortunes declined. He was occasionally used up front, but his old striker's instincts were best seen at set pieces.

Leeds U (From trainee on 6/8/84) FL 43+6/11 FLC 3/2 FAC 3 Others 1+2
Hull C (£200,000 on 23/3/89) FL 76+4/24 FLC 2+3/1 FAC 2 Others 1
Port Vale (£300,000 on 16/8/91) FL 105+6/5 FLC 6 FAC 9/1 Others 12/1
Plymouth Arg (£300,000 on 22/7/94) FL 24+3/2 FLC 2/1 FAC 2
Burnley (£200,000 on 4/8/95) FL 31+1/5 FLC 2 FAC 1 Others 4

SYMONS Christopher (Kit) Jeremiah
Born: Basingstoke, 8 March 1971
Height: 6'2" Weight: 13.0
International Honours: W: 22; B-1; U21-2; Yth

One of the best deals that Manchester City manager, Alan Ball, has concluded was the one that brought Portsmouth's Kit to Maine Road at the beginning of last season in exchange for Fitzroy Simpson and Carl Griffiths, plus a cash adjustment. An experienced central defender who, without frills, appeared in every game, showing a positive and constructive side to his play, particularly when City were under pressure, he formed a reliable partnership with Keith Curle. As a seasoned international, having played over 20 times for Wales, his strength is that not only can he stop strikers running at him, but he also has the skill and foresight to play the ball forward sensibly in order to create an attack.

Portsmouth (From trainee on 30/12/88) FL 161/10 FLC 19 FAC 10 Others 13+1/1
Manchester C (£1,600,000 on 17/8/95) PL 38/2 FLC 3 FAC 5

GEORGE DAVIES & CO

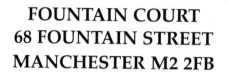

SOLICITORS

FOUNTAIN COURT
68 FOUNTAIN STREET
MANCHESTER M2 2FB

Solicitors to the PFA

COMPANY

COMPANY FORMATION
COMPANY DISPUTES
INSOLVENCY

COMMERCIAL

SPONSORSHIP CONTRACTS
TERMS OF BUSINESS
TAXATION

EMPLOYMENT

SERVICE CONTRACTS
INDUSTRIAL TRIBUNALS
DISCRIMINATION CLAIMS

PROPERTY

HOUSE PURCHASE
WILLS AND TRUSTS
INHERITANCE AND INVESTMENT

LITIGATION

PERSONAL INJURY
CRIME

FAMILY

CUSTODY AND DIVORCE
CARE PROCEEDINGS

*George Davies & Co are proud
to have been solicitors to the PFA for over 25 years.*

*Whatever your legal problem telephone us
and we will explain how we can help you.*

INVESTOR IN PEOPLE

0161-236-8992

TAGGART Gerald (Gerry) Paul
Born: Belfast, 18 October 1970
Height: 6'1" Weight: 13.12
International Honours: NI: 35; U23-2; Yth; Sch

Commanding Northern Ireland international centre half who joined Bolton for a club record fee from Barnsley at the start of last season. Troubled throughout by injury and suspension, receiving eight yellow cards in his 15 first class appearances, when playing he proved strong in the air, with a good left foot. Always a danger at set pieces, Gerry scored one goal last season, a powerful header at Sheffield Wednesday. Wanderers should see the best of him next season when he should be fully fit.

Manchester C (From trainee on 1/7/89) FL 10+2/1 Others 1
Barnsley (£75,000 on 10/1/90) FL 209+3/16 FLC 15/1 FAC 14/2 Others 6/1
Bolton W (£1,500,000 on 1/8/95) PL 11/1 FLC 2 FAC 2

Gerry Taggart

TAIT Michael (Mick) Paul
Born: Wallsend, 30 September 1956
Height: 5'11" Weight: 12.5
Club Honours: Div 3 '83, Div 4 '91; FMC '88

Hartlepool player/coach who had a successful season in 1995-96 playing a stopper role just in front of the defence. It was expected that he would appear in few first team games, but he justified his place with the same total commitment he has shown throughout his career. Assumedly, Mick is

---

contemplating retirement, but there is every chance he will become the first ever 40 year old to play league football for Hartlepool.

Oxford U (From apprentice on 8/10/74) FL 61+3/23 FLC 2+1/1 FAC 2
Carlisle U (£65,000 on 3/2/77) FL 101+5/20 FLC 7 FAC 7/2
Hull C (£150,000 on 6/9/79) FL 29+4/3 FAC 1/1
Portsmouth (£100,000 on 11/6/80) FL 228+12/30 FLC 23+1/1 FAC 13/1 Others 2+1
Reading (£50,000 on 1/9/87) FL 98+1/9 FLC 9/2 FAC 16 Others 9/3
Darlington (Free on 3/8/90) FL 79/2 FLC 5 FAC 4 Others 3
Hartlepool U (Free on 31/7/92) FL 60+1/1 FLC 5/1 FAC 2 (Free to Gretna during 1994 close season)
Hartlepool U (Free on 9/9/94) FL 58+1/2 FLC 5 FAC 1 Others 1

TAIT Paul Ronald
Born: Sutton Coldfield, 31 July 1971
Height: 6'1" Weight: 10.10
Club Honours: Div 2 '95; AMC '95

The scorer of Birmingham's first goal in 1995-96, this combative midfielder again suffered from injuries, his appearances being reduced accordingly. At one stage it seemed as though Paul was on his way to Coventry, but the move fell through and he fought his way back into the first team, displaying all his usual skill and aggression. Formerly a striker, and always likely to pop up with valuable goals, everyone associated with the club must be praying that he remains injury free in 1996-97.

Birmingham C (From trainee on 2/8/88) FL 118+26/14 FLC 13+1 FAC 5+2 Others 13+5/4

TALBOT Stuart
Born: Birmingham, 14 June 1973
Height: 5'10" Weight: 11.0

Hard-working midfield player with Port Vale. After an impressive pre-season in which he scored four times in one game, he became a regular member of the first team in 1995-96, albeit being mainly on the bench. Scored a very good goal in the Anglo-Italian Cup-tie against Ancona.

Port Vale (Signed from Moor Green on 10/8/94) FL 10+12 FAC 2+1 Others 2+3/1

TALBOYS Steven (Steve) John
Born: Bristol, 18 September 1966
Height: 5'10" Weight: 11.10

An enthusiastic Wimbledon man who plays on the left wing, but regularly pops up in the box looking to get into shooting positions, Steve is full of industry and determination and, above all, team spirit. Initially signed by Peter Withe, he has become a very useful squad player, making five starts, spread over three competitions last season, and appearing regularly for the reserves. Also good in the air.

Wimbledon (£10,000 from Gloucester C on 10/1/92) PL 19+7/1 FLC 2+1 FAC 1+1

TALIA Francesco (Frank)
Born: Melbourne, Australia, 20 July 1972
Height: 6'1" Weight: 13.6
Club Honours: Div 2 '96

The extrovert Aussie goalkeeper, first signed from Blackburn on loan last September, was recalled to Rovers and actually sat on the

---

bench against Swindon for the Coca Cola second round, second-leg tie! However, after making the move permanent in November, following his return, he had to wait until March to oust Fraser Digby, and then missed the championship run in through injury.

Blackburn Rov (Free from Sunshine George Cross on 28/8/92)
Hartlepool U (Loaned on 29/12/92) FL 14 Others 1
Swindon T (£150,000 on 8/9/95) FL 16

TANKARD Allen John
Born: Fleet, 21 May 1969
Height: 5'10" Weight: 11.7

An attacking Port Vale full back, who has a sharp turn of pace, he was the club's first choice for the majority of last season until a controversial sending off at West Bromwich, and then a hamstring injury, meant that he lost his place to Dean Stokes. His best games came during the FA Cup run to the fifth round, starring against both Everton and Leeds United.

Southampton (From apprentice on 27/5/87) FL 5 Others 2
Wigan Ath (Free on 4/7/88) FL 205+4/4 FLC 15/1 FAC 13 Others 20
Port Vale (£87,500 on 26/7/93) FL 89+5/1 FLC 8 FAC 10/1 Others 8+1

TANNER Adam David
Born: Maldon, 25 October 1973
Height: 6'0" Weight: 12.1

A right-sided Ipswich midfield player with good vision and a strong shot, Adam received limited opportunities last season, due to heavy competition for places. However, he remains one to watch out for, his speciality being his ability to hit long passes from deep positions to the front men.

Ipswich T (From trainee on 13/7/92) P/FL 12+8/2 FAC 1 Others 3+1/1

TARICCO Mauricio Ricardo
Born: Buenos Aires, Argentine, 10 March 1973
Height: 5'9" Weight: 11.7
International Honours: Argentine: U23

Did not figure in the Ipswich team at the beginning of last season, but was brought in at left back following Neil Thompson's opening day injury. Although making the occasional appearance on the right, he was far more comfortable in the number three spot, despite being naturally right footed. Became more influential as the campaign wore on, combining well with Stuart Slater, and looked the part in an attacking role, especially when the side played with three central defenders. Now established as a first team regular, it is difficult to imagine why he was allowed to languish in the reserves for most of 1994-95.

Ipswich T (£175,000 from Argentinos on 9/9/94) FL 36+3 FLC 3 FAC 3 Others 3

TAYLOR Gareth Keith
Born: Weston super Mare, 25 February 1973
Height: 6'2" Weight: 12.5
International Honours: W: 3; U21-7

Having scored four goals in seven league games for Bristol Rovers in 1995-96, the tall striker was snapped up by Crystal Palace early in September. However, after netting just twice in 22 appearances, he transferred to Sheffield United in the March deal that saw Dave Tuttle and Carl Veart move in the opposite direction. Despite having to wait for his first goal, he struck up an immediate understanding with Andy Walker which bodes well for the coming season. Capped at U21 level for Wales, Gareth stepped up to full international status against Albania in November and went on to play twice more.

Bristol Rov (Free from Southampton juniors on 29/7/91) FL 31+16/16 FLC 3+1 FAC 1+1 Others 5
Crystal Palace (£750,000 on 27/9/95) FL 18+2/1 FAC 2/1
Sheffield U (Signed on 8/3/96) FL 10/2

TAYLOR Ian Kenneth

Born: Birmingham, 4 June 1968
Height: 6'1" Weight: 12.4
Club Honours: AMC '93; FLC '96

A regular performer for Aston Villa in midfield in the opening months of 1995-96, Ian suffered from hamstring and ankle injuries in November and December and thereafter was in and out of the team, occasionally playing as a defender. He returned in triumph for the Coca Cola Cup final, scoring Villa's second and decisive goal from 20 yards in their emphatic 3-0 victory over Leeds. Composed on the ball and a willing tackler, he is always looking to get forward as his five goals last season would suggest.

Port Vale (£15,000 from Moor Green on 13/7/92) FL 83/28 FLC 4/2 FAC 6/1 Others 13/4
Sheffield Wed (£1,000,000 on 12/7/94) PL 9+5/1 FLC 2+2/1
Aston Villa (£1,000,000 on 21/12/94) PL 46+1/4 FLC 5+1/1 FAC 4+1/1

TAYLOR Jamie Lee

Born: Bury, 11 January 1977
Height: 5'6" Weight: 9.12

Jamie, still only 18, became Rochdale's youngest ever hat trick hero when he grabbed three out of four against Hartlepool last September. Even so, he spent most of the season back in the reserves, where he was transformed from striker to midfielder to make use of his non-stop running ability.

Rochdale (From trainee on 12/1/94) FL 10+25/4 FLC 0+1 Others 1+2/1

TAYLOR John Patrick

Born: Norwich, 24 October 1964
Height: 6'3" Weight: 13.6
Club Honours: Div 3 '91

Tall Luton striker who failed in 1995-96, largely due to injury, to deliver the promise that his transfer from Bradford towards the end of the previous term had suggested. His aerial power and finishing ability was sorely needed in a goal-shy attack, but injuries, including a three month lay off with back problems, sapped his confidence and he rarely played to his potential, despite his obvious efforts. Unlucky not to find the net more often at a time when he needed a boost, he managed to score just once in 21 starts and ten substitute appearances and was omitted from the side at the end of the season.

Colchester U (From juniors on 17/12/82)
Cambridge U (Signed from Sudbury T on 24/8/88) FL 139+21/46 FLC 9+2/2 FAC 21/10 Others 12+2/2
Bristol Rov (Signed on 28/3/92) FL 91+4/44 FLC 4/1 FAC 3 Others 5
Bradford C (£300,000 on 5/7/94) FL 35+1/11 FLC 4/2 FAC 2 Others 3
Luton T (£200,000 on 23/3/95) FL 27+10/3 FLC 2 Others 1/1

TAYLOR Maik Stefan

Born: Germany, 4 September 1971
Height: 6'5" Weight: 13.8

Having signed from non-league circles in the summer of 1995, Maik started last season as Barnet's first choice goalkeeper, missing just one match all season and creating an excellent impression, so much so that his manager, Ray Clemence, now reckons him to be the best in the third division. All that after conceding a dropped-kick goal from his opposite number on his debut at Hereford.

Barnet (Free from Farnborough on 7/6/95) FL 45 FLC 2 FAC 2 Others 2

TAYLOR Mark Simon

Born: Saltburn, 8 November 1974
Height: 6'2" Weight: 13.10

A left-sided central defender, or left back, Mark came for a trial at Fulham during the 1995 close season, having been released by Middlesbrough, and proved a more than adequate stand in when injuries piled up. He even did well in a three game stint in central midfield, but was allowed to move on when the injury situation eased, joining Northampton as cover for the injured Lee Maddison. Sadly, his one and only game for the club saw him carried off against Exeter.

Middlesbrough (From trainee on 29/3/93) Others 3+1
Darlington (Loaned on 28/10/94) FL 8 Others 2
Fulham (Free on 7/9/95) FL 7 FAC 1 Others 2
Northampton T (Free on 26/2/96) FL 1

TAYLOR Robert Mark

Born: Birmingham, 22 February 1966
Height: 5'8" Weight: 11.8
Club Honours: Div 3 '94

1995-96 was another excellent season for the midfielder who can also play at full back. When he performed well his influence usually meant Shrewsbury did also. Equally at home creating, with some superb crosses from tight touchline positions, or defending, he captained the side for part of the campaign and scored at Wembley in the Auto Windscreen final.

Walsall (From trainee on 24/7/84) FL 100+13/4 FLC 7+1 FAC 3+4 Others 10
Sheffield Wed (£50,000 on 22/6/89) FL 8+1 FLC 2
Shrewsbury T (£70,000 on 13/9/91) FL 213/36 FLC 15 FAC 14 Others 15+1/3

TAYLOR Robert (Bob)

Born: Horden, 3 February 1967
Height: 5'10" Weight: 12.0

WBA appointed Bob as team captain halfway through last season and immediately his form improved ten-fold! He regained his goalscoring touch, which had eluded him prior to Christmas, and thereafter went from strength to strength, finishing up as the leading marksman with 23 goals, including his 100th strike for the club. Physically strong, he holds up play well and feeds in his fellow strikers with deft touches and smart headers, working exceedingly well with Richard Sneekes and Andy Hunt during the last eight weeks of the campaign.

Leeds U (Free from Horden Colliery on 27/3/86) FL 33+9/9 FLC 5+1/3 FAC 1 Others 4+1/1
Bristol C (£175,000 on 23/3/89) FL 96+10/50 FLC 6+1/2 FAC 9+1/5 Others 3/1
West Bromwich A (£300,000 on 31/1/92) FL 184+7/84 FLC 11/5 FAC 6+1/3 Others 16+3/8

Mark Taylor (Shrewsbury T)

Bob Taylor

TAYLOR Robert Anthony
Born: Norwich, 30 April 1971
Height: 6'1" Weight: 13.8
Although his goals tally last season was down on 1994-95 he still finished as Brentford's top scorer and played well up front, often with little support, as the side struggled. Despite missing a month of the season with a facial injury, Robert was good value for the "Player of the Year" award.
Norwich C (From trainee on 26/3/90)
Leyton Orient (Loaned on 28/3/91) FL 0+3/1
Birmingham C (Signed on 31/8/91)
Leyton Orient (Free on 21/10/91) FL 54+19/20 FLC 1+1 FAC 2+1 Others 2+1
Brentford (£100,000 on 24/3/94) FL 90/36 FLC 8/2 FAC 6/4 Others 7/1

Robert Taylor

TAYLOR Scott Dean
Born: Portsmouth, 28 November 1970
Height: 5'9" Weight: 12.0
Club Honours: Div 2 '94
Right-footed Leicester midfielder with boundless energy. Signed from Reading during July 1995, he scored fine goals at Bramall Lane and The Hawthorns through breaking into the box from midfield. Suffered a heavy dose of flu in November, which took its toll for several weeks thereafter. A persistent knee injury also curtailed his effectiveness, resulting in an operation in January, before he could return in February, scoring with a spectacular long-range effort against Port Vale. His hard-running style made him a popular figure on the terraces and one of City's key players in the Wembley play-off victory over Crystal Palace.
Reading (From trainee on 22/6/89) FL 164+43/24 FLC 7+5/1 FAC 11+2/3 Others 12+4/1
Leicester C (£500,000 on 12/7/95) FL 39/6 FLC 3 FAC 1 Others 3

TAYLOR Scott James
Born: Chertsey, 5 May 1976
Height: 5'10" Weight: 11.4
Purchased by Bolton just prior to the transfer deadline, as a player for the future, he did, however, make a brief Premiership appearance when coming on as a substitute in the Wanderers' last win of the season against Chelsea at Burnden. More should be heard of this youngster. A tall, pacy striker, with clever ball control, Scott first hit the headlines last October with a great Coca Cola Cup performance at Everton, who were 2-0 up at the time, scoring two fine goals to set up a 4-2 victory for the Londoners.
Millwall (£15,000 from Staines on 8/2/95) FL 13+15 FLC 0+2/2 FAC 1+1
Bolton W (£150,000 on 29/3/96) PL 0+1

TAYLOR Shaun
Born: Plymouth, 26 March 1963
Height: 6'1" Weight: 13.0
Club Honours: Div 4 '90; Div 2 '96
Another splendid season for the Swindon captain, the only man ever to be voted the club's "Player of the Year" on three occasions, having earlier been elected to the PFA award winning second division team by his fellow professionals. A lion-hearted defender, he always gave the proverbial 110 per cent and, although often battle scarred, he led by example, pushing himself and his colleagues on, regardless of the task ahead, missing just three league games as Town stormed to the second division championship.
Exeter C (Free from Bideford T on 10/12/86) FL 200/16 FLC 12 FAC 9 Others 12
Swindon T (£200,000 on 26/7/91) F/PL 210/30 FLC 21/2 FAC 14 Others 10/1

TAYLOR Stephen (Steve) Christopher Edward
Born: Stone, 7 January 1970
Height: 6'0" Weight: 12.8
International Honours: E: SP-1
Picked up by Crystal Palace from Vauxhall Conference side, Bromsgrove Rovers, during the 1995 close season, after scoring nine goals in 31 appearances in 1994-95, the tall, well-built striker was unable to break into contention with the first division side and was loaned out to Northampton in October. Returning after just two matches, he later had another spell on loan, this time at Rushden, and, unable to progress there either, he went back to Selhurst Park where his registration was cancelled by mutual consent in April, less than ten months into a two year contract. A player with good aerial power and the ability to hold the ball up, he is currently with Hednesford.
Crystal Palace (£90,000 from Bromsgrove on 24/6/95)
Northampton T (Loaned on 27/10/95) FL 1+1

TEALE Shaun
Born: Southport, 10 March 1964
Height: 6'0" Weight: 13.10
Club Honours: FLC '94
International Honours: E: SP-1
Shaun became Tranmere Rovers' record buy in August 1995 when purchased from Aston Villa. A tough, combative central defender, and a natural leader on the park, his season was dogged by a long-standing injury problem and a series of suspensions, resulting from accumulated cautions. Despite that, he picked up more "Man of the Match" awards from the local radio station than any other player, a measure of his importance to the side.
Bournemouth (£50,000 from Weymouth on 22/1/89) FL 99+1/4 FLC 8 FAC 5/1 Others 3
Aston Villa (£300,000 on 25/7/91) F/PL 146+1/2 FLC 15/3 FAC 13 Others 6
Tranmere Rov (£450,000 on 14/8/95) FL 29 FLC 4

TELFER Paul Norman
Born: Edinburgh, 21 October 1971
Height: 5'9" Weight: 11.6
International Honours: S: B-2; U21-3
Right-sided midfielder who Coventry signed from Luton during the summer of 1995. Started the season well and scored a good headed goal on his home debut against Manchester City, but a run of poor results seemed to affect his confidence, although he never gave less than 100 per cent, despite not achieving the expectations of his manager. Called up for the Scotland "B" team, and tipped for full honours, his lack of form saw him dropped from the squad and, after being linked with a £3m move to Blackburn, which City allegedly rejected, Paul lost his place on the run-in. Hopefully, this coming season, he can get back to his ball-winning and distributive skills that everyone at the club knows he is capable of.
Luton T (From trainee on 7/11/88) FL 136+8/19 FLC 5 FAC 14/2 Others 2/1
Coventry C (£1,500,000 on 11/7/95) PL 31/1 FLC 4 FAC 3/1

Paul Telfer

TEN HEUVEL Laurens
Born: Amsterdam, Holland, 6 June 1976
Height: 6'0" Weight: 12.3
Signed from the Dutch side FC Den Bosch last March, the 19-year-old striker was given a couple of subs' opportunities for Barnsley, before making his full debut on the final day of the season, a 1-1 draw at home to Grimsby. Retained for the coming season, Laurens looks to be a typical continental player who likes the ball to feet and the passing game.
Barnsley (Signed from FC Den Bosch on 12/3/96) FL 1+2

THACKERAY Andrew (Andy) John
Born: Huddersfield, 13 February 1968
Height: 5'9" Weight: 11.0
Club Honours: FAYC '86
The Rochdale skipper suffered his worst ever season in 1995-96 with injuries, including ligament damage, a knee problem, and a dislocated shoulder, all causing long lay offs. Experienced, consistent, and defensively sound, he was still the automatic choice at right back when fit, however.
Manchester C (From juniors on 15/2/86)
Huddersfield T (Free on 1/8/86) FL 2 Others 0+1
Newport Co (£5,000 on 27/3/87) FL 53+1/4 FLC 3+1 FAC 1 Others 2+1/1
Wrexham (£5,000 on 20/7/88) FL 139+13/14 FLC 10/1 FAC 6 Others 13+2
Rochdale (£15,000 on 15/7/92) FL 144+4/13 FLC 8 FAC 7 Others 10+2/2

THATCHER Benjamin (Ben) David
Born: Swindon, 30 November 1975
Height: 5'10" Weight: 12.7
International Honours: E: U21-1; Yth
Talented Millwall central defender and left back, his sound performances earned him England U21 recognition and an opportunity to represent the Endsleigh League U21 side against an Italian Serie "B" XI in 1995-96. Very good in the air, with tackles timed to perfection, while supporting the attack along the left flank, Ben was both the supporters and junior Lions' choice as "Player of the Year". *Stop Press:* Reported to be joining Leicester in a £1.8m move at the end of June, he eventually signed for Wimbledon.
Millwall (From trainee on 8/6/92) FL 87+3/1 FLC 6 FAC 7 Others 1

THEW Lee
Born: Sunderland, 23 October 1974
Height: 5'10" Weight: 11.5
Hard-working midfielder who joined Scarborough at the start of last season on a short-term contract, having been released by Doncaster, and gave some good early performances. However, financial constraints at the club led to a high turnover of players, as the team battled to avoid relegation, and he moved on for spells with non-league sides, Guiseley and Gateshead.
Doncaster Rov (From trainee on 3/8/93) FL 21+11/2 FLC 1 FAC 0+2 Others 2/1
Scarborough (Free on 3/8/95) FL 9+5 FLC 2 Others 2

THIRLBY Anthony Dennis
Born: Berlin, Germany, 4 March 1976
Height: 5'10" Weight: 11.5
International Honours: NI: Yth
Exeter's Anthony found himself out of favour last season, his only appearance being as substitute against Torquay in the Coca Cola Cup, prior to being released during the summer. A constructive midfielder, he had earlier been sidelined with a thigh injury.
Exeter C (From trainee on 4/7/94) FL 27+12/2 FLC 2+2 Others 1

THOMAS Andrew (Andy) Paul
Born: Chester, 14 December 1977
Height: 5'10" Weight: 10.7
Defender. Andy gave a very promising

display for Wrexham in the ECWC second-leg match in Romania against Petrolul Ploiesti last season and continued to impress the Wrexham coaching staff who rate him highly.
Wrexham (Trainee) Others 1

THOMAS Anthony (Tony)
Born: Liverpool, 12 July 1971
Height: 5'11" Weight: 12.5
Club Honours: AMC '90
Officially still on the Tranmere transfer list, Tony had enjoyed a relatively injury-free season in 1995-96 and was consequently back to his "Thomas the Tank" best in several games, before missing the last month of the campaign. A strong-running right back, who can whip over dangerous crosses and defend competently as well, he has lost his way a little from the days when top clubs were chasing him and Rovers were quoting £1.5m for him, but he will come good in time, rest assured.
Tranmere Rov (From trainee on 1/2/89) FL 226+1/12 FLC 22+1/1 FAC 6 Others 26/1

THOMAS David John
Born: Caerphilly, 26 September 1975
Height: 5'10" Weight: 11.7
Striker. Despite regular appearances in the first team squad last season, David found it difficult to get on the goalscoring sheet at league level for Swansea and was offered a free transfer in November. However, he remained a regular member of the Swans' first team squad and finally scored his first goal for the club, against Crewe, in the last game of 1995-96.
Swansea C (From trainee on 25/7/94) FL 5+15/1 Others 0+3/1

THOMAS Geoffrey (Geoff) Robert
Born: Manchester, 5 August 1964
Height: 6'1" Weight: 13.2
Club Honours: FMC '91
International Honours: E: 9; B-3
The former England midfielder came on as substitute in two early games for Wolves in 1995-96, being summarily dismissed in the former at Sunderland. His knee was still poorly though and this 59 minutes of action proved to be it for the season. His series of operations since joining the club despairingly continued, the reconstructed cruciate ligament being removed completely.
Rochdale (Free from Littleborough on 13/8/82) FL 10+1/1 Others 0+1
Crewe Alex (Free on 22/3/84) FL 120+5/20 FLC 8 FAC 2 Others 2+1
Crystal Palace (£50,000 on 8/6/87) F/PL 192+3/26 FLC 24/3 FAC 13+1/2 Others 15+1/4
Wolverhampton W (£800,000 on 18/6/93) FL 21+3/5 FLC 1 Others 4

THOMAS Glen Andrew
Born: Hackney, 6 October 1967
Height: 6'1" Weight: 12.7
Equally at home in a central defensive position or at left back, Glen was ever present for Barnet until the end of last October, before being out of the side until the beginning of January. Back in full stride, he signed for Gillingham, his experience telling in the last few weeks of the season as

the club stormed to the second division as runners up.
Fulham (From apprentice on 9/10/85) FL 246+5/6 FLC 21 FAC 8 Others 14+1
Peterborough U (Free on 4/11/94) FL 6+2 FAC 0+1 Others 2
Barnet (Free on 23/3/95) FL 22+1 FLC 2 Others 1
Gillingham (£30,000 on 15/1/96) FL 14+1

THOMAS Martin Russell
Born: Lymington, 12 September 1973
Height: 5'8" Weight: 10.8
Playing on the right side or in central midfield, with pace and an eye for goal, Martin is a very committed player and is always liable to grab a goal out of nothing as his six last season for Fulham would suggest. Is also an excellent crosser of the ball.
Southampton (From trainee on 19/6/92)
Leyton Orient (Free on 24/3/94) FL 5/2
Fulham (Free on 21/7/94) FL 53+7/8 FLC 5 FAC 4/1 Others 4

THOMAS Michael Lauriston
Born: Lambeth, 24 August 1967
Height: 5'10" Weight: 12.4
Club Honours: FLC '87, 95; Div 1 '89, '91; CS '91; FAC '92
International Honours: E: 2; B-5; U21-12; Yth; Sch
A midfield player with great stamina who can make excellent runs, both on and off the ball, Michael has been beset by persistent injury problems, which have prevented him from winning a regular place in the Liverpool team since his arrival four years ago. Although the first half of 1995-96 seemed to be no different, being employed as a substitute until December, an excellent performance against Manchester United led to a run of 19 consecutive games, his longest ever spell in the side. However, by the end of the season he had been displaced by Jamie Redknapp and, after refusing the offer of a new contract, at the time of going to press, is expected to join a continental club.
Arsenal (From apprentice on 31/12/84) FL 149+14/24 FLC 21+2/5 FAC 14+3/1 Others 5+2/1
Portsmouth (Loaned on 30/12/86) FL 3
Liverpool (£1,500,000 on 16/12/91) F/PL 57+25/5 FLC 2+3/1 FAC 14+2/2 Others 4+1

Mitchell Thomas

THOMAS Mitchell Anthony
Born: Luton, 2 October 1964
Height: 6'0" Weight: 12.0
International Honours: E: B-1; U21-3; Yth
Mainly used in a left-sided defensive role by Luton in 1995-96, Mitchell remains an adventurous player who makes a virtue out of being awkward and strong. Unfortunately, in a team that found it both difficult to score and had an unsteady defence he failed to shine. Although lacking some of the pace of yesteryear, his attitude and never-say-die spirit saw him holding down a fairly regular place in the side, his aerial ability and will to drive forward down the flank, continuing to make him an asset.
Luton T (From apprentice on 27/8/82) FL 106+1/1 FLC 5 FAC 18
Tottenham H (£233,000 on 7/7/86) FL 136+21/6 FLC 28+1/1 FAC 12/1
West Ham U (£525,000 on 7/8/91) FL 37+1/3 FLC 5 FAC 4 Others 2
Luton T (Free on 12/11/93) FL 75+8/1 FLC 1+1 FAC 5 Others 0+1

THOMAS Roderick (Rod) Clive
Born: Brent, 10 October 1970
Height: 5'6" Weight: 11.0
Club Honours: FAYC '89; Div 3 '95
International Honours: E: U21-1; Yth; Sch
On his day, probably the most exciting player at Carlisle, with an ability to take on defenders and deliver dangerous crosses from either flank. Disappointingly, he was another United player whose 1995-96 season was disrupted by injury problems, but gave some fine displays in the latter part of the campaign in setting up a number of goals for his colleagues.
Watford (From trainee on 3/5/88) FL 63+21/9 FLC 3+2 FAC 0+1 Others 3+1
Gillingham (Loaned on 27/3/92) FL 8/1 Others 1
Carlisle U (Free on 12/7/93) FL 101+9/16 FLC 7+1/1 FAC 9 Others 20/8

THOMAS Wayne
Born: Walsall, 28 August 1978
Height: 5'11" Weight: 11.12
One of seven Torquay trainees to make their first team debuts in 1995-96, the young midfielder was given his opportunity late in the season, with five subs' appearances and a start at Colchester. Although withdrawn late in the game, he is sure to figure again.
Torquay U (Trainee) FL 1+5

THOMPSON Alan
Born: Newcastle, 22 December 1973
Height: 6'0" Weight: 12.8
International Honours: E: U21-2; Yth
The speedy, skilful left-sided midfield player scored Bolton's first ever Premiership goal when he converted a penalty on the opening day at Wimbledon last season. Surprisingly, that was to be his only league strike of the campaign. The following month, Alan added an England U21 cap to his collection, but was sent off in the process, and later was unfortunate to miss two months of the term with a hernia problem as Wanderers floundered at the foot of the table. Although he eventually managed to get back into the side for the relegation dog-fight it was to no avail and he

will be looking for a more comfortable ride this season.
Newcastle U (From trainee on 11/3/91) FL 13+3 FAC 1 Others 3
Bolton W (£250,000 on 22/7/93) P/FL 76+14/14 FLC 16+1/3 FAC 4+1/1 Others 7+1/1

Alan Thompson

THOMPSON Andrew (Andy) Richard
Born: Cannock, 9 November 1967
Height: 5'4" Weight: 10.11
Club Honours: Div 4 '88, Div 3 '89; AMC '88
Determined little Wolves' full back who played on both the right and left side in 1995-96. Scored four more penalties, though he did miss one at Birmingham, and continued to show his defensive qualities, tackling being his forte. An ever present until Easter Monday, Andy had a testimonial match against Chelsea arranged for July.
West Bromwich A (From apprentice on 16/11/85) FL 18+6/1 FLC 0+1 FAC 2 Others 1+1
Wolverhampton W (£35,000 on 21/11/86) FL 330+14/41 FLC 20 FAC 20/1 Others 32/1

THOMPSON David (Dave) George
Born: Ashington, 20 November 1968
Height: 6'3" Weight: 12.7
Tall central defender who was a mainstay in Cambridge United's defence for the first three months of last season until damaging his knee ligaments in November. A player with good aerial ability, he battled back to fitness and made a brief substitute appearance in the last game of the season.
Millwall (From apprentice on 26/11/86) FL 88+9/6 FLC 4 FAC 4/1 Others 6
Bristol C (Signed on 18/6/92) FL 17 FLC 4 Others 5+1
Brentford (Free on 1/2/94) FL 9+1/1
Blackpool (Signed on 9/9/94) FL 17 FAC 1 Others 2
Cambridge U (Free on 23/3/95) FL 21+1 FLC 2

THOMPSON David (Dave) Stephen
Born: Manchester, 27 May 1962
Height: 5'11" Weight: 12.10

Another Rochdale player back to his best in 1995-96, after losing form slightly at the tail-end of the previous season, right winger, "Tommo", terrorised third division full backs, laying on chances for scorer-in-chief, Steve Whitehall, before having to turn full back himself in an injury crisis. Has passed 270 senior appearances for the club and is currently lying fifth in the all-time listing.
Rochdale (Free from North Withington on 26/9/81) FL 147+8/13 FLC 7 FAC 7+1 Others 6
Notts Co (Signed on 22/8/86) FL 52+3/8 FLC 3+1 FAC 3 Others 2
Wigan Ath (£35,000 on 20/10/87) FL 107+1/14 FLC 5/2 FAC 3+1 Others 6/1
Preston NE (£77,500 on 1/8/90) FL 39+7/4 FLC 1+1 Others 3+1
Chester C (Free on 14/8/92) FL 70+10/9 FLC 4 FAC 5 Others 4
Rochdale (£6,000 on 8/8/94) FL 81+2/10 FLC 4 FAC 4 Others 10

THOMPSON Garry Linsey
Born: Birmingham, 7 October 1959
Height: 6'2" Weight: 14.0
Club Honours: FMC '91
International Honours: E: U21-6
Northampton Town striker. This old warhorse kept going, his aerial power and ability to hold up a ball, having a lot to do with Jason White's goal tally last season. After almost 20 years in league football, his experience is invaluable.
Coventry C (From apprentice on 29/6/77) FL 127+7/38 FLC 12+1/7 FAC 11/4
West Bromwich A (£225,000 on 17/2/83) FL 91/39 FLC 9/5 FAC 5/1
Sheffield Wed (£450,000 on 12/8/85) FL 35+1/7 FLC 2+1/1 FAC 5/1
Aston Villa (£450,000 on 5/6/86) FL 56+4/17 FLC 6/2 FAC 4 Others 3
Watford (£325,000 on 24/12/88) FL 24+10/8 FLC 0+1 FAC 7+1
Crystal Palace (£200,000 on 24/3/90) FL 17+3/3 FLC 0+1/1 Others 0+1
Queens Park R (£125,000 on 19/8/91) F/PL 10+9/1 FLC 3+2/3 Others 1
Cardiff C (Free on 15/7/93) FL 39+4/5 FLC 2 FAC 5+2/1 Others 6+3/3
Northampton T (Signed on 10/2/95) FL 36+13/6 FLC 0+2 Others 0+1

Garry Thompson

THOMPSON Neil
Born: Beverley, 2 October 1963
Height: 5'11" Weight: 13.7
Club Honours: GMVC '87; Div 2 '92
International Honours: E: SP-4

As in the previous season, Neil's Ipswich appearances were again decimated by injury, when, after just 13 minutes of the opening game of 1995-96, he badly damaged his left knee and was out of action until the middle of November. Making his comeback in the home match against Portsmouth, the stylish, attacking left back scored with a stunning free kick to secure a 3-2 win in injury time, but three games later was struck down with an achilles tendon injury, which eventually required an operation. Taking into account the above and his age, although still a good player, he was given a free transfer during the summer.

Hull C (Free from Nottingham F. juniors on 28/11/81) FL 29+2
Scarborough (Free on 1/8/87) FL 87/15 FLC 8/1 FAC 4 Others 9/1
Ipswich T (£100,000 on 9/6/89) F/PL 199+7/19 FLC 14+1/1 FAC 17/1 Others 8/2

THOMPSON Neil Philip
Born: Hackney, 30 April 1978
Height: 5'11" Weight: 11.6

A young wide midfielder, and still a trainee, Neil was given his Barnet debut when coming off the bench at Scarborough last January. Realistically, it will probably be 1997-98 before he claims a regular first team place.

Barnet (Trainee) FL 1+1

THOMPSON Steven (Steve) James
Born: Oldham, 2 November 1964
Height: 5'10" Weight: 13.0
Club Honours: AMC '89

Burnley midfielder. An injury from the previous season kept Steve out until last February, but on his return the side immediately benefited from his inch-perfect passing and battling approach, which made him the ideal choice for captain following Jamie Hoyland's injury. His return was a major factor in the club ultimately avoiding relegation to the third division.

Bolton W (From apprentice on 4/11/82) FL 329+6/49 FLC 27/2 FAC 21/4 Others 39/2
Luton T (£180,000 on 13/8/91) FL 5 FLC 2
Leicester C (Signed on 22/10/91) F/PL 121+6/18 FLC 6/2 FAC 8/1 Others 11+3/4
Burnley (£200,000 on 24/2/95) FL 30

THOMPSTONE Ian Philip
Born: Bury, 17 January 1971
Height: 6'0" Weight: 13.0

Rochdale's only new player in the 1995 close season, having been freed by Scunthorpe, Ian proved his worth as a utility man, appearing in midfield, at full back, centre half, and even at centre forward. Apart from a couple of short absences' he was almost always in the squad, often as substitute, until suffering a head injury near the end of the campaign and being freed in the summer.

Manchester C (From trainee on 1/9/89) FL 0+1/1
Oldham Ath (Free on 25/5/90)
Exeter C (Free on 23/1/92) FL 15/3

Halifax T (Free on 14/7/92) FL 31/9 FLC 1+1 FAC 1 Others 2
Scunthorpe U (£15,000 on 25/3/93) FL 47+13/8 FLC 2 FAC 4+2/1 Others 2
Rochdale (Free on 28/7/95) FL 11+14/1 FLC 1/1 FAC 2+2 Others 1+1

THOMSEN Claus
Born: Aarhus, Denmark, 31 May 1970
Height: 6'3" Weight: 13.6
International Honours: Denmark: 5

Having missed the pre-season games in 1995-96 after picking up a groin strain while playing for Denmark, Claus came back into the Ipswich side, initially in his favoured central midfield role. However, he seemed ill at ease in that position and, following another period on the sidelines due to a broken toe, he returned again, this time as a central defender. Benefiting from playing alongside the experienced Tony Mowbray, he was seen at his best, using his undoubted class to keep the most dangerous of forwards at bay and being a problem at set pieces. When this partnership was in harness, Town produced their best defensive displays of the campaign. Selected for the Danish Euro '96 squad, he played in two of the three group games before the team was eliminated.

Ipswich T (£250,000 from Aarhus on 15/6/94) P/FL 67+3/7 FLC 4/1 FAC 4 Others 2+1

THOMSON Andrew (Andy)
Born: Motherwell, 1 April 1971
Height: 5'10" Weight: 10.7

Although a favourite with the Southend fans, Andy didn't manage to hold down a regular first team spot up front last season. Very lively, with good ball control and an awareness of his team mates, his style did not seem to suit that required by manager, Ronnie Whelan. However, he always gave 100 per cent for the team when called upon, until an injury forced him out completely.

Queen of the South (Free from Jerviston BC on 28/7/89) SL 163+12/93 SLC 8/3 SC 7+2/5 Others 9/8
Southend U (£250,000 on 4/7/94) FL 57+15/17 FLC 2+1 FAC 1+1 Others 1+1

THOMSON Andrew (Andy) John
Born: Swindon, 28 March 1974
Height: 6'3" Weight: 14.12

Not part of Swindon's selection plans last season, Andy moved to Portsmouth in December, where he waited in the wings for a month before making his debut as a sub at Millwall. Following that, the strong central defender forced his way into the side to form impressive partnerships with both Guy Butters and Russell Perrett. Producing a string of good performances, was all the more admirable for the fact that the side was constantly struggling in the face of relegation, eventually escaping the drop to the second division on goal difference.

Swindon T (From trainee on 1/5/93) P/FL 21+1 FLC 5/1 Others 3
Portsmouth (£75,000 on 29/12/95) FL 15+1

THORN Andrew (Andy) Charles
Born: Carshalton, 12 November 1966
Height: 6'0" Weight: 11.5
Club Honours: FAC '88
International Honours: E: U21-5

A well travelled and experienced Wimbledon centre back, Andy lets his quick-thinking football mind compensate for any loss of pace. Starting in 11 of the first 15 matches last season, he showed himself to be an excellent marshal of his defence, and one who imparted valuable wisdom to the young members of the team, while his well-timed tackles continued to be an exemplary aspect of his game. When not playing he can be regularly seen barking orders and encouragement from the touchline.

Wimbledon (From apprentice on 13/11/84) FL 106+1/2 FLC 7 FAC 9 Others 1
Newcastle U (£850,000 on 1/8/88) FL 36/2 FLC 4/1 Others 3
Crystal Palace (£650,000 on 5/12/89) F/PL 128/3 FLC 19/4 FAC 10 Others 11
Wimbledon (Free on 5/10/94) PL 33+4/1 FLC 2 FAC 3

THORNBER Stephen (Steve) John
Born: Dewsbury, 11 October 1965
Height: 5'10" Weight: 11.8
Club Honours: WC '89

Hard-working midfielder, who can both attack and defend. Having started the first nine games on the right side of Scunthorpe's midfield in 1995-96, he suffered an injury and, on coming back, was unable to hold down a regular place, playing in a variety of positions, before being released to join Halifax in February.

Halifax T (From juniors on 24/1/83) FL 94+10/4 FLC 3+1/1 FAC 9/1 Others 11
Swansea C (£10,000 on 23/8/88) FL 98+19/6 FLC 7/3 FAC 9+2/1 Others 8+3
Blackpool (Free on 13/8/92) FL 21+3 FLC 3 Others 1
Scunthorpe U (Free on 12/7/93) FL 71+6/7 FLC 4 FAC 4+1 Others 5

THORNE Gary Robert
Born: Reading, 22 March 1977
Height: 5'9" Weight: 11.9

After signing professional forms during the summer, Gary was given a run out in Swindon's AWS games last season, coming off the bench at Torquay and starting against Colchester. Looked quite promising in the centre of defence, although on the small side, but, later deemed to be surplus to requirements, he moved to non-league, Gloucester City, in March.

Swindon T (From trainee on 6/7/95) Others 1+1

THORNE Peter Lee
Born: Manchester, 21 June 1973
Height: 6'0" Weight: 12.10
Club Honours: Div 2 '96

Missed Swindon's opening games of last season with a hamstring injury and then had to battle for his place back, due to the impressive striking partnership of Wayne Allison and Steve Finney. Injured again on his comeback at Wrexham, he did not fully recover until December, but still averaged almost a goal every other game and did well to finish with 11 on his way to a second division championship medal.

Blackburn Rov (From trainee on 20/6/91) Others 0+1
Wigan Ath (Loaned on 11/3/94) FL 10+1
Swindon T (£225,000 on 18/1/95) FL 42+4/19 FLC 3/2 FAC 4+2 Others 1+1/1

THORNLEY Benjamin (Ben) Lindsay
Born: Bury, 21 April 1975
Height: 5'9" Weight: 11.12
Club Honours: FAYC '92
International Honours: E: U21-3; Sch

Manchester United left winger who is essentially right footed. Besides being a great crosser of the ball, he possesses good passing ability, coupled to control, and relishes taking defenders on. Since making his PL debut in 1994, Ben's career has been hit by a series of niggling injuries and much of his rehabilitation has taken place away from Old Trafford. After making just one appearance as a sub in the second game of last season against West Ham, he went on loan to Stockport in November, becoming a huge favourite and scoring his first league goal in the process, before stopping off at Huddersfield in February and, again proving a class act. Having won three England U21 caps during 1995-96, he is now back in Manchester and looking for a run-in the side.
Manchester U (From trainee on 29/1/93) PL 0+2
Stockport Co (Loaned on 6/11/95) FL 8+2/1 Others 1
Huddersfield T (Loaned on 22/2/96) FL 12/2

THORP Michael Stephen
Born: Wallington, 5 December 1975
Height: 6'0" Weight: 12.0

Another product of Reading's youth scheme who finally made the breakthrough into the first team with a handful of mid-season appearances in 1995-96. Undoubtedly a centre back of great promise, he played with great composure, though his greatest asset was the perception with which he sent long, penetrating passes out of defence, even when under pressure.
Reading (From trainee on 12/1/95) FL 2 FLC 2 FAC 1

Tony Thorpe

THORPE Anthony (Tony) Lee
Born: Leicester, 10 April 1974
Height: 5'9" Weight: 12.0

Enthusiastic Luton midfielder who established a regular place in the second half of last season and looks set for a fine future. Able to control his aggression to positive effect, he injected pace and urgency to an uninspiring Town and showed himself to be a good all-round player, particularly willing and able to back up the attack. Scored eight goals to finish third in the club charts, including four in April – the best being a 25-yard chip, after running on to a through pass against Barnsley.
Luton T (Free from Leicester C juniors on 18/8/92) FL 27+24/8 FLC 0+2 FAC 1+3/1 Others 1+2/1

THORPE Jeffrey (Jeff) Roger
Born: Cockermouth, 17 November 1972
Height: 5'10" Weight: 12.8
Club Honours: Div 3 '95

Jeff is a left-sided player who can operate either in defence or down the flank where his pace is a principal asset. Another of the locally born members of the Carlisle side, he has recovered well after missing the whole of the 1993-94 season through injury. An enthusiastic performer in whatever role he was asked to fulfil last season, he made many of his appearances as a substitute, but was also in the starting line-up on occasions.
Carlisle U (From trainee on 2/7/91) FL 80+51/6 FLC 6+3 FAC 4+2 Others 7+8/1

THORPE Lee Anthony
Born: Wolverhampton, 14 December 1975
Height: 6'1" Weight: 12.4

Still an improving youngster, the Blackpool striker made only one first team appearance last season, from the bench, but continued to learn his trade in the reserves, where he scored ten goals. Retained for 1996-97, Lee will be looking for a run-in the side, despite the club being well stocked with forwards.
Blackpool (From trainee on 18/7/94) FL 0+3

TIERNEY Francis
Born: Liverpool, 10 September 1975
Height: 5'10" Weight: 11.0
International Honours: E: Yth

Capped at youth level by England, prior to 1995-96 he had been used by Crewe in a wide attacking role, but like Rob Savage he too has been working on the change into a midfield role that the club sees as being his future spot. His good ball control and excellent temperament saw him continuing to be tracked by Premier League sides.
Crewe Alex (From trainee on 22/3/93) FL 38+13/7 FLC 4 FAC 0+3 Others 4+4/2

TILER Carl
Born: Sheffield, 11 February 1970
Height: 6'4" Weight: 13.0
International Honours: E: U21-13

After three seasons in the shadows at Nottingham Forest, Brian Little gave the experienced central defender a chance to reactivate his career in the Premier League by signing him for Aston Villa last October and putting him straight into first team

action at home to Everton. Tragically, he suffered a hamstring injury on his Villa debut which put him out of action for the remainder of the campaign. Still a young man, Carl has plenty of time left to prove his value and once back, his added height at both ends of the park will be put to the club's advantage.
Barnsley (From trainee on 2/8/88) FL 67+4/3 FLC 4 FAC 4+1 Others 3+1
Nottingham F (£1,400,000 on 30/5/91) F/PL 67+2/1 FLC 10+1 FAC 6 Others 1
Swindon T (Loaned on 18/11/94) FL 2
Aston Villa (£750,000 on 28/10/95) PL 1

TILLSON Andrew (Andy)
Born: Huntingdon, 30 June 1966
Height: 6'2" Weight: 12.10

Centre back and captain, Andy enjoyed another good season at the heart of Bristol Rovers' defence in 1995-96. His dependability and inspiration did much to help the club reach the southern area final of the Auto Windscreen Shield and to be within distance of a division two play-off place after a good second half run-in. Is comfortable in possession and dominant in the air.
Grimsby T (Free from Kettering T on 14/7/88) FL 104+1/5 FLC 8 FAC 10 Others 5
Queens Park R (£400,000 on 21/12/90) FL 27+2/2 FLC 2 Others 1
Grimsby T (Loaned on 15/9/92) FL 4 Others 1
Bristol Rov (£370,000 on 7/11/92) FL 119+1/3 FLC 8/1 FAC 6 Others 14/1

TILSON Stephen (Steve) Brian
Born: Wickford, 27 July 1966
Height: 5'11" Weight: 12.6

Added a biting tackle and more ability with his right foot to his left foot skills last season, even though he could not gain a regular berth in the Southend first team. Always more comfortable in a left-sided role, Steve played in midfield and defence, never letting the team down, and as one of the longest serving members of the club and a useful squad member, he has the ability to force himself back into the team before too long.
Southend U (Signed from Witham T on 7/2/89) FL 172+38/25 FLC 7+1 FAC 3 Others 12+1/4
Brentford (Loaned on 16/9/93) FL 2

TIMONS Christopher (Chris) Bryan
Born: Old Langwith, 8 December 1974
Height: 6'1" Weight: 12.6

This young Mansfield central defender failed to get an outing in 1995-96 until a crop of injuries struck the team, but acquitted himself very well from March onwards and gave some sterling performances, prior to being released in the summer. More at home on the right side of the park, he started the season on loan at non-league, Halifax.
Mansfield T (Signed from Clipstone Colliery on 1/2/94) FL 35+4/2 Others 2+1

TINKLER Mark Roland
Born: Bishop Auckland, 24 October 1974
Height: 6'0" Weight: 13.3
Club Honours: FAYC '93
International Honours: E: Yth (UEFAC '93); Sch

Although a mainstay of Leeds' reserve side, the young midfielder once again struggled to make a regular breakthrough into the first XI last season. However, with his skill, confidence and vision on the ball, he should remain optimistic of his long-term chances at Elland Road, where he is most highly rated.

Leeds U (From trainee on 29/11/91) PL 13+9 FLC 1 Others 0+1

TINNION Brian

Born: Stanley, 23 February 1968
Height: 5'11" Weight: 11.5

The left-sided player really came back to form with a vengeance last season after a dismal time in 1994-95, when much barracking had caused him to request a transfer from Bristol City. Restored to the Robins' first team at Crewe in December, his skill on the left, plus a passion that had seemed absent before, meant that he soon regained a permanent place in the side and went on to form a good partnership with Darren Barnard. Created many opportunities for the strikers as well as being able to score on occasions himself, including notable strikes at Wycombe and at home to Wrexham.

Newcastle U (From apprentice on 26/2/86) FL 30+2/2 FLC 5 Others 1+1
Bradford C (£150,000 on 9/3/89) FL 137+8/22 FLC 12/1 FAC 9/4 Others 7+1/2
Bristol C (£180,000 on 23/3/93) FL 111+6/12 FLC 4 FAC 8+1/3 Others 1+1

TISDALE Paul Robert

Born: Malta, 14 January 1973
Height: 5'9" Weight: 11.9
International Honours: E: Sch

Currently a regular member of Southampton's first team squad, having been in the starting line up five times last season, he proved a versatile and mobile midfielder who likes to pass the ball around. Also able to play at right back if required, Paul scored his first goal for the club at Manchester City in March.

Southampton (From juniors on 5/6/91) PL 5+11/1 FLC 0+1 FAC 0+1
Northampton T (Loaned on 12/3/92) FL 5

TODD Andrew (Andy) John James

Born: Derby, 21 September 1974
Height: 5'9" Weight: 12.3

Son of the Bolton manager, Colin, Andy came to Burnden at the start of last season from Middlesbrough. Capable of playing in a central defensive role, or in a midfield holding position, he made his Premiership debut when coming on as a substitute at Liverpool and found the net. Yet another Wanderers' player to suffer from a long injury problem he did, however, manage to regain fitness to play in the last game of the season at Arsenal, where he again scored. Good in the air, and on the ground, and an excellent passer.

Middlesbrough (From trainee on 6/3/92) FL 7+1 FLC 1+1 Others 5
Swindon T (Loaned on 27/2/95) FL 13
Bolton W (£250,000 on 1/8/95) PL 9+3/2 FLC 2+2

TODD Lee

Born: Hartlepool, 7 March 1972
Height: 5'5" Weight: 10.3

Stockport's diminutive left back continued to mature in his role as a raiding wing/back and was a steady regular throughout last season. A bubbly character with an all-action style, he is a real crowd pleaser.

Stockport Co (Free from Hartlepool U juniors on 23/7/90) FL 175+9/2 FLC 15+1 FAC 13/2 Others 26+1

TODD Mark Kenneth

Born: Belfast, 4 December 1967
Height: 5'9" Weight: 10.2
International Honours: NI: U23-1; Yth; Sch

Rejected by Mansfield after a trial last August, midfielder Mark linked up with Scarborough until February, when they had to release him on financial grounds. Having a change of heart, Andy King brought him back to the Field Mill Ground and his displays were such that it was difficult to understand why he had not been kept in the first place. Suffered a knee injury in March which kept him out of action for several weeks.

Manchester U (From apprentice on 7/8/85)
Sheffield U (Free on 1/7/87) FL 62+8/5 FLC 5+1 FAC 10+1/1 Others 5+1
Wolverhampton W (Loaned on 14/3/91) FL 6+1
Rotherham U (£35,000 on 11/9/91) FL 60+4/7 FLC 5/2 FAC 3 Others 2/1
Scarborough (Free on 8/8/95) FL 23/1 FLC 2 FAC 1 Others 0+1
Mansfield T (Free on 2/2/96) FL 10+2

TOLSON Neil

Born: Walsall, 25 October 1973
Height: 6'2" Weight: 12.4

Bradford's promising centre forward who was the club's second top scorer in 1995-96 with ten goals, despite playing the majority of his games as a sub, Neil actually came off the bench in the opening game to net City's first goal. Good in the air, aggressive, and extremely quick off the mark, he will benefit from experience.

Walsall (From trainee on 17/12/91) FL 3+6/1 FAC 0+1/1 Others 1+2
Oldham Ath (£150,000 on 24/3/92) PL 0+3
Bradford C (Signed on 2/12/93) FL 32+31/12 FLC 1+4/1 FAC 3+1/1 Others 2+2/3
Chester C (Loaned on 6/1/95) FL 3+1

TOMAN James Andrew (Andy)

Born: Northallerton, 7 March 1962
Height: 5'10" Weight: 11.7
Club Honours: GMVC '90; Div 4 '91

Experienced Scarborough midfielder, who, at his best, was one of the most accurate passers of the ball in the lower divisions. Unfortunately, illness and injury blighted his career over the past couple of seasons, and he struggled to maintain a first team place, being released at the end of 1995-96. Always gave 100 per cent commitment and was well thought of by the supporters.

Lincoln C (£10,000 from Bishop Auckland on 16/8/85) FL 21+3/4 FLC 2 Others 0+1 (Free to Bishop Auckland during 1986 close season)
Hartlepool U (£6,000 on 23/1/87) FL 112/28 FLC 4 FAC 9/4 Others 7
Darlington (£40,000 on 1/8/89) FL 108+7/10 FLC 8 FAC 8/2 Others 6/3

Scarborough (Loaned on 25/2/93) FL 6
Scunthorpe U (Free on 20/8/93) FL 15/5 FLC 1 FAC 2/1 Others 1
Scarborough (Free on 10/12/93) FL 33+12/3 FLC 1 FAC 3/1 Others 2

TOMLINSON Graeme Murdoch

Born: Watford, 10 December 1975
Height: 5'9" Weight: 11.7

Yet to make his Premiership debut, the young Manchester United striker was loaned to relegation threatened Luton just before last March's transfer deadline. However, having added aerial power to Town's impotent attack during six subs' appearances, he was given his full debut at Port Vale in April, but tragically broke his right leg in two places just before half time. Hopefully, Graeme is young enough to come back as good as new, his awareness, touch, ability in the air, and goalscoring prowess, giving him a crack at the highest level.

Bradford C (Trainee) FL 12+5/6 FAC 0+1
Manchester U (£100,000 on 12/7/94) FLC 0+2
Luton T (Loaned on 22/3/96) FL 1+6

TOMLINSON Michael (Micky) Lloyd

Born: Lambeth, 15 September 1972
Height: 5'9" Weight: 11.0

Fought back well from an early season loss of form in 1995-96, to become an important starter as Barnet went for promotion. Quick and tricky, with the ability to beat his man from the right wing, it is often the "out" ball for under pressure defenders.

Leyton Orient (From trainee on 5/7/91) FL 7+7/1 FLC 4/1 FAC 1 Others 0+1
Barnet (Free on 21/3/94) FL 48+15/3 FLC 3+2 FAC 0+4 Others 1+2

Micky Tomlinson

TORPEY Stephen David James
Born: Islington, 8 December 1970
Height: 6'3" Weight: 14.13
Club Honours: AMC '94

Striker. Stephen yet again answered his critics at the Vetch Field in 1995-96 by ending up top goalscorer for Swansea for the second successive season. Despite a poor and inconsistent supply line, he battled hard throughout the campaign, showing 100 per cent commitment and an all-round improvement in his game.

Millwall (From trainee on 14/2/89) FL 3+4 FLC 0+1
Bradford C (£70,000 on 21/11/90) FL 86+10/22 FLC 6 FAC 2+1 Others 8/6
Swansea C (£80,000 on 3/8/93) FL 114+9/35 FLC 8+1/2 FAC 8/4 Others 13+3/5

TOVEY Paul William
Born: Wokingham, 5 December 1973
Height: 5'8" Weight: 11.7

A ball-winning midfielder, Paul finally made his full league debut for Bristol Rovers in 1995-96, following a successful one month loan spell with Irish club, Bangor City. The highlight of his season came when appearing in both legs of the Southern Area Auto Windscreen Shield Final against Shrewsbury Town, before being released in the summer.

Bristol Rov (From trainee on 24/7/92) FL 8+1 Others 2+1

TOWN David Edward
Born: Bournemouth, 9 December 1976
Height: 5'8" Weight: 11.7

Striker. A prolific scorer for Bournemouth's reserves last season, David failed to make his mark in the first team, with just ten appearances, nine of them as a substitute. Still at the learning stage, however, his quickness around the box will hold him in good stead.

Bournemouth (From trainee on 11/4/95) FL 1+12 FLC 0+3 Others 0+1

TOWNSEND Andrew (Andy) David
Born: Maidstone, 23 July 1963
Height: 5'11" Weight: 12.7
Club Honours: FLC '94, '96
International Honours: Ei: 60; B-1

One of the few Ron Atkinson signings to survive Brian Little's purge of the old guard last season, the classy left-sided midfielder responded to the honour of the Aston Villa captaincy by showing his best form since arriving at Villa Park three years ago. A tremendous competitor, who covers every blade of grass, he led by example and was voted "Man of the Match" following the Coca Cola Cup victory over Leeds, in preference to the goalscorers. Unfortunate to be sent off for a second offence in an early match against Nottingham Forest – the first being an over exuberant celebration of a rare goal. Won his 60th Republic of Ireland cap against Portugal in May.

Southampton (£35,000 from Weymouth on 15/1/85) FL 77+6/5 FLC 7+1 FAC 2+3 Others 3+2
Norwich C (£300,000 on 31/8/88) FL 66+5/8 FLC 3+1 FAC 10/2 Others 3

Chelsea (£1,200,000 on 5/7/90) F/PL 110/12 FLC 17/7 FAC 7 Others 4
Aston Villa (£2,100,000 on 26/7/93) PL 96+1/6 FLC 18/2 FAC 9 Others 8/1

Andy Townsend

TRACEY Simon Peter
Born: Woolwich, 9 December 1967
Height: 6'0" Weight: 13.0

Starting 1995-96 as third choice Sheffield United goalkeeper behind Alan Kelly and Billy Mercer, Simon took in loan spells at Nottingham Forest and Wimbledon, where he played one match before being recalled. After signing a new two and a half year contract in January, a back injury to Kelly led to his return to the first team, where a run of fine form saw the defence concede only two goals in eight games. Will be challenging hard for the jersey in 1996-97 if he can stay free of injury.

Wimbledon (From apprentice on 3/2/86) FL 1 Others 1
Sheffield U (£7,500 on 19/10/88) F/PL 152+2 FLC 7 FAC 10 Others 7
Manchester C (Loaned on 27/10/94) PL 3
Norwich C (Loaned on 31/12/94) PL 1 FAC 2
Wimbledon (Loaned on 2/11/95) PL 1

TRAVIS Simon Christopher
Born: Preston, 22 March 1977
Height: 5'10" Weight: 11.0

While still a trainee, Simon was thrust into first team service with Torquay last season, making his debut in the opening match at right back, before succumbing to injury after ten appearances. Very skilful, and extremely quick (being able to do the 100 metres in evens), especially on the overlap, he was surprisingly released in January. Is good enough to come back strongly with another team.

Torquay U (Trainee) FL 4+4 FLC 1 FAC 1

TREBBLE Neil David
Born: Hitchin, 16 February 1969
Height: 6'3" Weight: 12.10

An ideal target man, with physical presence and mobility, the tall striker was always willing to battle for the ball, but suffered from poor service as Scarborough struggled for most of last season, finding goals difficult to come by. The upshot being his release to join one of his former clubs, Stevenage Borough, in March.

Scunthorpe U (Free from Stevenage Borough on 8/7/93) FL 8+6/2 FLC 0+1 FAC 1 Others 1+1
Preston NE (Free on 18/7/94) FL 8+11/4 FLC 1 FAC 2+1 Others 2/1
Scarborough (Signed on 20/2/95) FL 40+7/3 FAC 0+1 Others 2

TREVITT Simon
Born: Dewsbury, 20 December 1967
Height: 5'11" Weight: 11.10

Surprisingly, last November, Simon left Huddersfield Town in his testimonial season to add vital experience to Hull City's struggling squad. A fine, overlapping right back, especially suited to the Tigers' preferred five-man defence, he has the ability to go past his opponent and supply a quality cross. His know-how was also utilised in the absence of regular central defenders. Currently vice captain to Greg Abbott.

Huddersfield T (From apprentice on 16/6/86) FL 216+13/3 FLC 23/1 FAC 13 Others 19+1
Hull C (Free on 24/11/95) FL 25 Others 1

TRINDER Jason Lee
Born: Leicester, 3 March 1970
Height: 5'11" Weight: 14.2

Given an opportunity to take over the goalie's jersey from Ian Bowling last November, sadly, he made a series of mistakes which cost Mansfield the match after the forwards had managed to score three goals for the only time during the season. Released the following month, he joined non-league, Matlock Town, and later, VS Rugby.

Mansfield T (Free from Oadby T on 18/11/94) FL 5+3 Others 1

TROLLOPE Paul Jonathan
Born: Swindon, 3 June 1972
Height: 6'0" Weight: 12.6

A ball-playing Derby midfielder whose ability to link defence and attack makes him a key squad member, Paul started and finished last season in the first team, although restricted to mostly subs' appearances in between. From a footballing family, his father, John, holds the Swindon appearance record, he can also be relied upon to win the ball when the occasion demands.

Swindon T (From trainee on 23/12/89)
Torquay U (Free on 26/3/92) FL 103+3/16 FLC 9+1/1 FAC 7 Others 8+1
Derby Co (£100,000 on 16/12/94) FL 30+11/4 FLC 1+1 FAC 0+1

TUCK Stuart Gary
Born: Brighton, 1 October 1974
Height: 5'11" Weight: 11.7

Unfortunately, his appearances for Brighton in 1995-96 were restricted due to a hernia operation. A promising left-footed full back, or central defender, he looks to get back in the swing of things this coming season.

Brighton & Hove A (From trainee on 9/7/93) FL 30+12 FLC 5 FAC 1 Others 4+1

TURLEY William (Billy) Lee
Born: Wolverhampton, 15 July 1973
Height: 6'4" Weight: 14.10
Goalkeeper. Signed from non-league football during the 1995 close season, he could be another name for the future, impressing in the few appearances he made for the Northampton first team in 1995-96.

Northampton T (Free from Evesham on 10/7/95) FL 2

TURNBULL Lee Mark
Born: Stockton, 27 September 1967
Height: 6'0" Weight: 13.0
Central midfielder. Firming up his loan period of the final two months of 1994-95, he signed for Scunthorpe on a more permanent basis during the 1995 close season. Played in the first four games of 1995-96, scoring a goal, before being out of action for the next 19. A solid tackler, who is effective in the air, Lee can also be used up front and as an emergency central defender.

Middlesbrough (From trainee on 7/9/85) FL 8+8/4 FLC 0+1 Others 1+1/1
Aston Villa (Signed on 24/8/87)
Doncaster Rov (£17,500 on 3/11/87) FL 108+15/21 FLC 3+1/2 FAC 5+1 Others 9+1/2
Chesterfield (£35,000 on 14/2/91) FL 80+7/26 FLC 2+3/1 FAC 3/1 Others 5
Doncaster Rov (Signed on 8/10/93) FL 10+1/1 FAC 2 Others 1
Wycombe W (£20,000 on 21/1/94) FL 8+3/1 FLC 0+1/1 FAC 1 Others 1
Scunthorpe U (£12,000 on 6/3/95) FL 26+7/6 FLC 2 FAC 2 Others 1

TURNER Andrew (Andy) Peter
Born: Woolwich, 23 March 1975
Height: 5'10" Weight: 11.7
International Honours: Ei: U21-7. E: Yth; Sch

Signed on loan from Spurs last November, the pacy Republic of Ireland U21 international left winger will long be remembered by Huddersfield fans for his stunning goal against WBA, after coming on as a substitute. However, unable to meet the Spurs' price tag of £1m plus, Town were forced to say goodbye. Later, in March, on a similar basis, Andy arrived at Southend, where he showed an ability to get the ball across from seemingly impossible positions. Disappointingly, his arrival at Southend coincided with the loss through injury of the Blues' two tall centre forwards, thus hampering the effectiveness of his play.

Tottenham H (From trainee on 8/4/92) PL 8+12/3 FLC 0+2/1 FAC 0+1
Wycombe W (Loaned on 26/8/94) FL 3+1
Doncaster Rov (Loaned on 10/10/94) FL 4/1 Others 1
Huddersfield T (Loaned on 28/11/95) FL 2+3/1
Southend U (Loaned on 28/3/96) FL 4+2

TURNER Philip (Phil)
Born: Sheffield, 12 February 1962
Height: 5'8" Weight: 11.0
Club Honours: AIC '95
A veteran midfielder now in his eighth full season at Notts County, Phil played in the first 11 games last season before dropping out with injury. Returned for six matches in November and December until being ruled out for the remainder of the season, forcing him to hand over the club captaincy to Gary Strodder as a result. An outstanding club servant, and corner kick specialist, who has played a defensive midfield anchor role in recent seasons, hopefully, he will come back restored.

Lincoln C (From apprentice on 5/2/80) FL 239+2/19 FLC 19 FAC 12/1 Others 5
Grimsby T (Signed on 22/8/86) FL 62/8 FLC 6 FAC 6 Others 3/1
Leicester C (£42,000 on 19/2/88) FL 18+6/2 FLC 1+1 FAC 1
Notts Co (£125,000 on 3/3/89) FL 223+14/16 FLC 17+3 FAC 15/3 Others 33+1/3

Robbie Turner

TURNER Robert (Robbie) Peter
Born: Ripon, 18 September 1966
Height: 6'3" Weight: 14.1
Robbie, a no-nonsense Cambridge United forward, was initially signed on loan from Exeter last December, before making the move permanent in February. However, having become an instant hit with the fans, after scoring three times in ten games, his season came to an end in late February when he was forced onto the sidelines by the demands of a hernia operation.

Huddersfield T (From apprentice on 19/9/84) FL 0+1 FLC 1
Cardiff C (Free on 19/7/85) FL 34+5/8 FLC 3/1 FAC 1 Others 1
Hartlepool U (Loaned on 2/10/86) FL 7/1
Bristol Rov (Free on 31/12/86) FL 19+7/2 FLC 2 Others 0+1
Wimbledon (£15,000 on 17/12/87) FL 2+8 FLC 1+1 FAC 0+1/1 Others 3+1/1
Bristol C (£45,000 on 27/1/89) FL 45+7/12 FAC 7/3 Others 2

Plymouth Arg (£150,000 on 23/7/90) FL 66/17 FLC 5/1 FAC 3 Others 3/1
Notts Co (£90,000 on 21/11/92) FL 7+1/1 FAC 1
Shrewsbury T (Loaned on 25/3/93) FL 9
Exeter C (Free on 4/2/94) FL 38+7/7 FLC 2/1 FAC 1+1 Others 2/1
Cambridge U (Signed on 19/12/95) FL 10/3

TUTILL Stephen (Steve) Alan
Born: York, 1 October 1969
Height: 6'1" Weight: 12.6
International Honours: E: Sch
As York City's club captain it was a huge blow for him to miss the final three months of last season owing to injury, especially with the club fighting hard to avoid relegation. A totally committed central defender, local lad Steve has recently been awarded a testimonial after ten seasons of outstanding service at Bootham Crescent.

York C (From trainee on 27/1/88) FL 278+6/6 FLC 19 FAC 15 Others 21+3/1

TUTTLE David Philip
Born: Reading, 6 February 1972
Height: 6'1" Weight: 12.10
Club Honours: FAYC '90
International Honours: E: Yth
The Sheffield United centre back missed several games at the start of last season due to niggling injuries and illness, plus an operation to remove a screw from his knee, but still became a dominant member of the defence, scoring his first goal for the club in the draw against Watford. Despite being a regular under the new management team, in March he followed Dave Bassett to Crystal Palace in the deal which took Gareth Taylor to Bramall Lane, being credited with the goal at Grimsby, as the Londoners fought tooth and nail to reach the play offs.

Tottenham H (From trainee on 8/2/90) F/PL 10+3 FLC 3+1 Others 1/1
Peterborough U (Loaned on 21/1/93) FL 7
Sheffield U (£350,000 on 1/8/93) P/FL 63/1 FLC 2 FAC 3
Crystal Palace (Signed on 8/3/96) FL 9+1/1 Others 3

TWIDDY Christopher (Chris)
Born: Pontypridd, 19 January 1976
Height: 5'10" Weight: 11.2
International Honours: W: U21-3; Yth
Young Plymouth winger who started only three games last term. Has already proved that he has the pace and ability to play at this level, and was again recognised by the Welsh selectors at U21 level, but despite that, he was released during the summer.

Plymouth Arg (From trainee on 29/6/94) FL 14+3/1 FLC 1+1 FAC 1+1 Others 3+1

TWYNHAM Gary Steven
Born: Manchester, 8 February 1976
Height: 6'0" Weight: 12.1
A former Manchester United youngster who was released by the club in December 1994, having run foul of the law, Gary came back into league football, playing two games in Darlington's midfield late last season, and impressed enough to be a named sub for the Wembley play-off final.

Manchester U (From trainee on 1/7/94)
Darlington (Free on 28/3/96) FL 2

UV

UHLENBEEK Gustav (Gus) Reinier
Born: Paramaribo, 20 August 1970
Height: 5'8" Weight: 11.1

Gus joined Ipswich on a permanent basis from the Dutch side, Tops SV, on the eve of last season, having impressed during summer trials as a fast and direct winger with a powerful shot. Quickly becoming a great favourite, in an astute tactical gamble by manager, George Burley, he was later switched to right back against Brescia in the Anglo-Italian Cup and looked like he had played there for years, his attacking strengths far outweighing any defensive deficiencies. Particularly effective away from home, where his pace was an excellent counter attack weapon on the break, he was unfortunate to miss the last few matches because of a blood clot on the thigh.
Ipswich T (£100,000 from Tops SV on 11/8/95) FL 37+3/4 FLC 2 FAC 1+3 Others 4

ULLATHORNE Robert
Born: Wakefield, 11 October 1971
Height: 5'8" Weight: 10.10
International Honours: E: Yth

A sharp challenger from the left back spot, and keen to get to the byline to produce crosses with his accurate left foot, Robert enjoyed his best season yet for Norwich in 1995-96, despite only being on a weekly contract. Made his 100th senior appearance for the club during the year, before injured knee ligaments kept him out for nine weeks. An enthusiastic performer who always gives off his best, most supporters will forever remember his back pass that goalkeeper, Bryan Gunn, completely missed in the East Anglian derby match at Ipswich.
Norwich C (From trainee on 6/7/90) F/PL 86+8/7 FLC 10+2/1 FAC 7+1 Others 1

UNSWORTH David Gerald
Born: Chorley, 16 October 1973
Height: 6'2" Weight: 14.7
Club Honours: FAC '95; CS '95
International Honours: E: 1; U21-7; Yth

An Everton left-footed defender, who can play equally well at full back or as a centre back, he is both strong in the air and fast across the ground, with great first touch and balance. Technically an excellent all-rounder, David continued to improve in 1995-96, even if he did fail to add to his full England cap, beginning the campaign in a central position before switching to the left back spot and showing great maturity along the way. He now appears to have settled in that position, having displaced Andy Hinchcliffe, but with such adaptability, who knows where he might turn up in 1996-97. Continued to win England U21 caps, adding two more to his collection.
Everton (From trainee on 25/6/92) F/PL 76+6/6 FLC 3+2 FAC 7 Others 4/1

David Unsworth

UNSWORTH Lee Peter
Born: Eccles, 25 February 1973
Height: 5'11" Weight: 11.8

Although recruited by Crewe towards the end of 1994-95, it was on the opening day of the 1995-96 campaign that Lee got his league baptism at Wycombe. A full back who can play on either flank, and shows a fine turn of speed, he made good progress in his first full season.
Crewe Alex (Signed from Ashton U on 20/2/95) FL 16+13 FLC 2+1/1 FAC 3+1/1 Others 3+2

UPSON Matthew James
Born: Hartismere, 18 April 1979
Height: 6'1" Weight: 11.4

As a regular for Luton's youth team, Matthew made a surprise debut at left back in the Anglo-Italian Cup against Cesena last November and, in doing so, became the second youngest first team player in the club's history. A trainee at the time, he turned professional in April and hopes to build on that confident performance.
Luton T (From trainee on 24/4/96) Others 1

UTLEY Darren
Born: Barnsley, 28 September 1977
Height: 6'0" Weight: 11.7

Another graduate from Doncaster's trainee ranks, Darren turned professional last December and made his first team debut from the subs' bench at Cambridge in April. Sure to be given further opportunities, the young central defender shows much promise for the future.
Doncaster Rov (From trainee on 9/12/95) FL 1

VALENTINE Peter
Born: Huddersfield, 16 April 1963
Height: 5'10" Weight: 12.0

Though still a force at centre half for Rochdale when fit, Peter missed a large fraction of last season through injury. A

qualified FA coach, he decided to give up league football at the end of 1995-96 in order to look for a coaching job.
Huddersfield T (From apprentice on 16/4/81) FL 19/1 FLC 2 FAC 1
Bolton W (Free on 18/7/83) FL 66+2/1 FLC 4 FAC 4 Others 5
Bury (Free on 23/7/85) FL 314+5/16 FLC 28/3 FAC 17/1 Others 23+1
Carlisle U (£10,000 on 18/8/93) FL 27+2/2 FLC 3 Others 4/1
Rochdale (£15,000 on 18/11/94) FL 49+1/2 FLC 2 FAC 4 Others 1

VAN BLERK Jason
Born: Sydney, Australia, 16 March 1968
Height: 6'1" Weight: 13.0
International Honours: Australia: 22

Left-sided Millwall defender who is also comfortable in midfield. Played in five different shirts last season, including those of a central defender, left back and left winger, with his exciting turn of pace, deft ball control, and well judged crosses, there for all to see. Currently a first team regular, he also added to his list of Australian caps when playing at Hampden Park in the centre of the defence.
Millwall (£300,000 from Go Ahead on 8/9/94) FL 66+3/2 FLC 5 FAC 6

VAN DER LAAN Robertus (Robin) Petrus
Born: Schiedam, Holland, 5 September 1968
Height: 5'10" Weight: 12.5
Club Honours: AMC '93

Purchased in the 1995 close season from Port Vale, he made an immediate impact at Derby, being appointed team captain within a few days. Robust in the tackle and excellent at set pieces, Robin appeared in virtually every game, and having led from the front, it was apt that he scored the goal which guaranteed promotion against Crystal Palace.
Port Vale (£80,000 from Wageningen on 21/2/91) FL 154+22/24 FLC 11+1/1 FAC 9+1/1 Others 11+1/1
Derby Co (£475,000 on 2/8/95) FL 39/6 FLC 3 FAC 1

VAN DER VELDEN Carel
Born: Arnhem, Holland, 3 August 1972
Height: 5'8" Weight: 13.7

Signed last March from the Dutch side, FC Den Bosch, he broke into the Barnsley first team by the end of the month. Although it is early days, this midfielder is seen as an eventual replacement on the field for Danny Wilson. Has all the attributes, being a good passer and an organiser, and his ability to beat men makes him a difficult opponent.
Barnsley (Signed from FC Den Bosch on 12/3/96) FL 6+1

VAN HEUSDEN Arjan
Born: Alphen, Holland, 11 December 1972
Height: 6'4" Weight: 12.0

Second choice goalkeeper at Port Vale, who had a six-game run in the first team last October, he is tall and confident and appears to have a bright future in the game. However, once again had to continue his learning curve in the Pontins League until being recalled just before the end of the season.

Port Vale (£4,500 from Noordwijk on 15/8/94) FL 9 Others 2

VARADI Imre
Born: Paddington, 8 July 1959
Height: 5'10" Weight: 12.3
Club Honours: Div 2 '90

Signed by Mansfield during the 1995 close season, after being freed by Rotherham, the vastly experienced forward started just one game and was on the bench for another before being released. Had a short spell at Boston before joining Scunthorpe, where he made two subs' appearances on a non-contract basis in October, prior to becoming player/manager of Matlock Town.

Sheffield U (Free from Letchworth on 1/4/78) FL 6+4/4 FAC 2
Everton (£80,000 on 1/3/79) FL 22+4/6 FAC 6+1/1 Others 0+2
Newcastle U (£100,000 on 27/8/81) FL 81/39 FLC 4/1 FAC 5/2
Sheffield Wed (£150,000 on 26/8/83) FL 72+4/33 FLC 11/2 FAC 7/5
West Bromwich A (£285,000 on 19/7/85) FL 30+2/9 FLC 5/4 FAC 2 Others 2
Manchester C (£50,000 on 17/10/86) FL 56+9/26 FLC 4+2/2 FAC 6+1/1 Others 2+1/2
Sheffield Wed (£50,000 on 30/9/88) FL 14+8/3 FLC 1+1/1 FAC 2/2 Others 1
Leeds U (£50,000 on 8/2/90) F/PL 21+5/5 FLC 1 Others 1+1/1
Luton T (Loaned on 26/3/92) FL 5+1/1
Oxford U (Loaned on 21/1/93) FL 3+2
Rotherham U (Free on 5/3/93) FL 55+12/25 FLC 5/2 FAC 2+1 Others 2+2/1
Mansfield T (Free on 11/8/95) FL 1 (Free to Boston U in August 1995)
Scunthorpe U (Free on 29/9/95 FL 0+2

Tony Vaughan

VAUGHAN Anthony (Tony) John
Born: Manchester, 11 October 1975
Height: 6'1" Weight: 11.2
International Honours: E: Sch; Yth

Tony experienced a mixed season for Ipswich in 1995-96, playing well one moment, but getting booked the next, and serving three suspensions, mainly due to arriving slightly late for challenges which he put down to a lack of timing and pace following injuries. As a left-sided defender who can play at full back and in central defence with equal ability, and a young man who many feel is bound to go to the top, the highlight of his campaign came when he soared to head home the winner from a corner against Derby at Portman Road. Hopefully, the injuries and suspensions are now behind him.

Ipswich T (From trainee on 1/7/94) P/FL 29+6/1 FAC 2 Others 2

VAUGHAN John
Born: Isleworth, 26 June 1964
Height: 5'10" Weight: 13.1
Club Honours: Div 3 '91, '96

Having seen off the challenge of Barry Richardson, 1995-96 proved to be a sound season for Preston's experienced number one goalkeeper, although his lack of height did cause him occasional problems. Calm and decisive, and an excellent shot stopper, John, who kept 19 clean sheets, was good value for his third division championship medal as North End swept to the league title. However, out of contract at the end of June, both club and player decided it was time for a change.

West Ham U (From apprentice on 30/6/82)
Charlton Ath (Loaned on 11/3/85) FL 6
Bristol Rov (Loaned on 5/9/85) FL 6
Wrexham (Loaned on 23/10/85) FL 4
Bristol C (Loaned on 4/3/86) FL 2
Fulham (£12,500 on 21/8/86) FL 44 FLC 4 FAC 4 Others 3
Bristol C (Loaned on 21/1/88) FL 3
Cambridge U (Free on 6/6/88) FL 178 FLC 13 FAC 24 Others 16
Charlton Ath (Free on 5/8/93) FL 5+1 FAC 2 Others 1+1
Preston NE (Free on 26/7/94) FL 65+1 FLC 2 FAC 2 Others 5

VEART Thomas Carl
Born: Whyalla, Australia, 21 May 1970
Height: 5'11" Weight: 12.8
International Honours: Australia: 20

An Australian striker who never failed to give 100 per cent for Sheffield United in 1995-96, despite often being used as a substitute, or in the unfamiliar position of midfield. Transfer listed by Howard Kendall, a decision which surprised many fans, having scored a memorable winner against Arsenal in the FA Cup replay, he left for Crystal Palace, along with David Tuttle, in the deal which brought Gareth Taylor to Bramall Lane in March. Used more as a sub, and unable to score in the Londoner's promotion run, he got the winner at Charlton in the first leg of the play-off semi final, a goal that took the club to Wembley, but, unfortunately for him, not ultimately to the Premiership.

Sheffield U (£250,000 from Adelaide C on 22/7/94) FL 47+19/15 FLC 2+1/1 FAC 2+1/1 Others 2
Crystal Palace (Signed on 8/3/96) FL 5+7 Others 2+1/1

VENISON Barry
Born: Consett, 16 August 1964
Height: 5'10" Weight: 11.12
Club Honours: CS '86, '88, '89, '90; ESC '86; Div 1 '88, '90, '93; FAC '89
International Honours: E :2; U21-10; Yth

Experienced Southampton player who joined the club from Turkish side, Galatasaray, last October, having left Newcastle to join his former boss, Graham Souness, the previous summer. Versatile in defence or midfield, where his ability to pass the ball and link play was at force, Barry gave Saints' young side valuable experience and stability, and was made captain when Matt le Tissier decided to step down. He is also well known as a TV football commentator and for his distinctive sartorial appearance.

Sunderland (From apprentice on 20/1/82) FL 169+4/2 FLC 21 FAC 7+1 Others 3/1
Liverpool (£200,000 on 31/7/86) FL 103+7/1 FLC 14+3 FAC 16+5 Others 6+4/2
Newcastle U (£250,000 on 31/7/92) F/PL 108+1/1 FLC 9 FAC 11 Others 4 (£750,000 to Galatasaray during 1995 close season)
Southampton (£850,000 on 25/10/95) PL 21+1 FLC 2 FAC 3

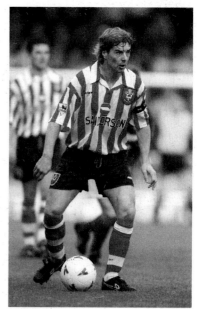

Barry Venison

VENUS Mark
Born: Hartlepool, 6 April 1967
Height: 6'0" Weight: 13.11
Club Honours: Div 3 '89

His 1995-96 season did not get going properly until late November, when he rocketed in a free kick for Wolves that the Coventry goalkeeper hardly saw. Generally involved in a number of positions, even tidying up at the back as a sweeper, until the fateful March night in Grimsby, he clawed his way back into the starting line up for the last four games. A wholehearted player, whether turning out at full back, in the centre of defence, or in midfield, Mark gives everything.

Hartlepool U (From juniors on 22/3/85) FL 4 Others 0+1
Leicester C (Free on 6/9/85) FL 58+3/1 FLC 3 FAC 2 Others 2+1
Wolverhampton W (£40,000 on 23/3/88) FL 235+12/7 FLC 15+1/1 FAC 14+1 Others 17/2

VICK Lee
Born: Cardiff, 8 January 1978
Height: 5'9" Weight: 10.3
Midfielder. Another YTS boy called upon late in 1994-95 to try and keep Cardiff out of division three, and mercifully only required at the end of last term for a couple of games, before City's season finally petered out to a non-event.

Cardiff C (Trainee) FL 2+2

VICKERS Stephen (Steve)
Born: Bishop Auckland, 13 October 1967
Height: 6'1" Weight: 12.12
Club Honours: AMC '90; Div 1 '95
A solid central defender for Middlesbrough with excellent ball skills. After 380 games, all in the lower divisions, doubts were expressed about his ability to survive in the Premier League. Three months into 1995-96, and Boro having established the meanest defence in the Premier League with only nine goals conceded in 15 games, such doubts were proved groundless. His partnership with Nigel Pearson and Derek Whyte in a three-man central defence seemed almost impregnable, although he suffered from the collective collapse of confidence in the dreadful mid-season run, perhaps his greatest accolade was being voted the supporters' "Player of the Year", ahead of the obvious favourite, Juninho, an acknowledgement of his contribution over the whole season.

Tranmere Rov (Signed from Spennymoor U on 11/9/85) FL 310+1/11 FLC 20+1/5 FAC 19/3 Others 36/1
Middlesbrough (£700,000 on 3/12/93) P/FL 101+1/7 FLC 9/1 FAC 7 Others 2

Steve Vickers

249

VICTORY Jamie Charles
Born: Hackney, 14 November 1975
Height: 5'10" Weight: 12.0
Defender. Signed from West Ham in the summer of 1995, Jamie was unable to secure himself a regular place in the Bournemouth first team and was released during the summer. Able to play as a centre back, or left back, he made seven starts, and 13 substitute appearances in the 1995-96 season, scoring the winner against Brentford in the home League game. Two footed and fairly quick, he is also capable of playing in midfield.
West Ham U (From trainee on 1/7/94)
Bournemouth (Free on 1/7/95) FL 5+11/1 FLC 1+1 Others 1+1

VILJOEN Nicholas (Nik) Luke
Born: New Zealand, 3 December 1976
Height: 5'10" Weight: 12.0
Club Honours: AMC '96
A New Zealander who has been a prolific scorer with the reserves and juniors during his time at Rotherham, he forced his way into the first team last season for a handful of games and netted one of the goals in the elusive first away win of the season at Hull in January 1996. He bettered that by hitting the only goal of the game against Oxford four weeks later.
Rotherham U (From trainee on 17/6/95) FL 5+3/2 Others 0+2

VILSTRUP Johnny Pedersen
Born: Copenhagen, Denmark, 27 February 1967
Height: 6'0" Weight: 13.2
An attacking midfielder who came to Luton last September from Lyngby (Denmark) with a fine reputation, including that of possessing the hardest left-foot shot in his country. Having cost the Hatters' dearly, sadly he was never able to live up to his promise and, although unlucky not to score with one or two long-range shots, he generally appeared unable to sustain the pace of English football. While making a promising debut against Millwall, injuries and form restricted him to just nine first team outings and he failed to find the net in any of them. By the end of the season he was back in Denmark, on loan to Aarhus – the country's top team – and after scoring in their cup final victory and helping them to the league and cup double, Town were able to recover £100,000, as Aarhus made the move permanent.
Luton T (£205,000 from Lyngby on 13/9/95) FL 6+1 Others 2

VINCENT Jamie Roy
Born: London, 18 June 1975
Height: 5'10" Weight: 11.8
Having made his Football League debut on loan at Bournemouth in 1994-95, the experience held the young blond left back in good stead last season when he was called upon by Crystal Palace to deputise for Dean Gordon, and make occasional appearances in midfield. Although not required for the play offs, as Palace vainly tried to reach the

Premiership, he scored his first ever goal in the 2-0 home Coca Cola Cup win over Southend.
Crystal Palace (From trainee on 13/7/93) FL 19+6 FLC 2+1/1 FAC 1
Bournemouth (Loaned on 18/11/94) FL 8

VINNICOMBE Christopher (Chris)
Born: Exeter, 20 October 1970
Height: 5'9" Weight: 10.4
Club Honours: SPD '91
International Honours: E: U21-12
Although his form suffered as Burnley struggled last season, Chris' position at left-back was never threatened and he was a virtual ever present until being sidelined by an ankle break at Wycombe, which is likely to keep him out well into 1996-97. Always a defender who relies on speed and skill, rather than the more old-fashioned virtues, he will be sorely missed.
Exeter C (From trainee on 1/7/89) FL 35+4/1 FLC 5/1 Others 2
Glasgow R (£150,000 on 3/11/89) SL 14+9/1 SLC 1+2 Others 1
Burnley (£200,000 on 30/6/94) FL 64/3 FLC 7 FAC 1 Others 4

VIRGO James Robert
Born: Brighton, 21 December 1976
Height: 5'11" Weight: 11.4
From Ardingley College and a product of Brighton's youth scheme, James turned professional during the 1995 close season and made his first team debut from the bench in the home Coca Cola Cup-tie against Fulham, playing the last five minutes. Highly rated, the young left-sided defender will be looking for further opportunities in 1996-97.
Brighton & Hove A (From juniors on 10/7/95) FLC 0+1

VIVEASH Adrian Lee
Born: Swindon, 30 September 1969
Height: 6'1" Weight: 11.9
Loaned to Barnsley at the start of last season, the strong, commanding central defender made two appearances and scored on his debut before returning to Swindon. However, unable to find his way past newcomer, Mark Seagraves, Adrian signed for Walsall in October, initially on trial, and quickly proved outstanding in forming a solid and reliable partnership with Derek Mountfield. Apart from defensive duties, he makes good use of the ball with long passes from the back third.
Swindon T (From trainee on 14/7/88) FL 51+3/2 FLC 6+1 FAC 0+1 Others 2
Reading (Loaned on 4/1/93) FL 5 Others 1/1
Reading (Loaned on 20/1/95) FL 6
Barnsley (Loaned on 10/8/95) FL 2/1
Walsall (Free on 16/10/95) FL 31 FAC 5 Others 3/1

VONK Michel Christian
Born: Alkmaar, Holland, 28 October 1968
Height: 6'3" Weight: 13.3
A classy central defender who was one of Howard Kendall's first bargain signings from Manchester City last December, following his loan spell at Oldham, Michel proved to be a dominant defender who

missed little in the air and showed classy distribution of the ball out of defence. Unluckily sent off at Tranmere after two bookable offences, the second in the final minute of the game, he later formed a formidable partnership with Everton's Gary Ablett which made Kendall very keen to sign the latter on a permanent basis to aid the promotion push in the coming season.
Manchester C (£500,000 from SVV Dordrecht on 11/3/92) F/PL 87+4/3 FLC 3+2/1 FAC 6+1/1
Oldham Ath (Loaned on 17/11/95) FL 5/1
Sheffield U (£350,000 on 21/12/95) FL 17 FAC 2

Michel Vonk

VOWDEN Colin Dean
Born: Newmarket, 13 September 1971
Height: 6'0" Weight: 13.0
Signed from Cambridge City during the summer of 1995, he was put straight into the centre of near neighbours, Cambridge United's defence, and made a solid start to his first season of league football. Can also play as full back on either side.
Cambridge U (£15,000 from Cambridge C on 19/5/95) FL 22+2 FLC 2 Others 2

WADDLE Christopher (Chris) Roland
Born: Felling, 14 December 1960
Height: 6'2" Weight: 12.13
International Honours: E: 62; U21-1

1995-96 was a most frustrating time for the wonderfully gifted Sheffield Wednesday player. At the start of the campaign, he negotiated for a new two year contract, but was only offered a 12 month one, while Owls' fans wanted him to be given the assistant manager's job. His performances, though, lacked the spark of previous seasons and, subsequently, he was left out on many occasions. Hopefully, he will stay with the club, but whatever happens, Chris will be fondly remembered by the Wednesday supporters for his wonderful skill, certain marvellous, magic moments and, of course, his goals.
Newcastle U (£1,000 from Tow Law on 28/7/80) FL 169+1/46 FLC 8/2 FAC 12/4
Tottenham H (£590,000 on 1/7/85) FL 137+1/33 FLC 21/4 FAC 14/5 Others 4 (£4,250,000 to Marseilles on 1/7/89)
Sheffield Wed (£1,000,000 on 1/7/92) PL 94+15/10 FLC 19 FAC 12+1/3 Others 3+1/1

Chris Waddle

WADDOCK Gary Patrick
Born: Kingsbury, 17 March 1962
Height: 5'10" Weight: 11.12
Club Honours: Div 2 '83
International Honours: Ei: 21; B-1; U23-1; U21-1

Still a tenacious, hard-tackling, defensive Luton midfielder, Gary was not a regular in the side at the start of 1995-96, but won back his place to become one of the few Town players to be able to claim a good season. Although battling hard to keep the team out of the relegation zone, unfortunately injury and suspension kept him out at crucial times towards the end of the campaign. However, his trojan efforts in midfield, winning the ball and breaking up opposing attacks, was recognised by his team mates who elected him their "Player of the Year".
Queens Park R (From apprentice on 26/7/79) FL 191+12/8 FLC 21+1/2 FAC 14 Others 1 (Free to Charleroi in December 1987)
Millwall (£130,000 on 16/8/89) FL 51+7/2 FLC 5+1 FAC 5 Others 3/1
Queens Park R (Free on 20/12/91)
Swindon T (Loaned on 19/3/92) FL 5+1
Bristol Rov (£100,000 on 7/11/92) FL 71/1 FLC 2 FAC 2 Others 2
Luton T (Free on 9/9/94) FL 62+4/1 FLC 1 FAC 2 Others 1+1

WALKER Andrew (Andy) Francis
Born: Glasgow, 6 April 1965
Height: 5'8" Weight: 10.7
Club Honours: S Div 1 '85; SPD '88; SFAC '88
International Honours: S: 3; U21-1

A top class striker signed from Celtic last February, in an attempt to solve the Sheffield United scoring problem which Howard Kendall inherited, he appeared not to be fully match-fit following a long spell on the Bhoys' bench. However, his pairing with the new acquisition, Gareth Taylor, showed all the makings of a formidable partnership and he finished the season in fine style with some important goals for the club.
Motherwell (From Baillieston Juniors on 31/7/84) SL 65+12/17 SLC 2+4/1 SC 8+2/2
Glasgow Celtic (£350,000 on 1/7/87) SL 85+21/40 SLC 9+6/7 SC 8+3/6 Others 4+2/2
Newcastle U (Loaned on 1/9/91) FL 2 FLC 1
Bolton W (£160,000 on 9/1/92) FL 61+6/44 FLC 3/1 FAC 9+3/8 Others 5/2
Glasgow Celtic (Signed on 1/7/94) SL 26+16/10 SLC 6+1/2 SC 3+2 Others 2+1/1
Sheffield U (£500,000 on 23/2/96) FL 12+2/8

WALKER Desmond (Des) Sinclair
Born: Hackney, 26 November 1965
Height: 5'11" Weight: 11.9
Club Honours: FLC '89, '90; FMC '89, '92
International Honours: E: 59; U21-7

1995-96 was another consistently brilliant season for the Sheffield Wednesday defender, who continued in his usual undemonstrative way. Still overlooked by Terry Venables, his England career seems to be over, but the Owls' fans readily acknowledge his value to the side as an outstanding sweeper. Relieved of the captaincy near the end of the campaign, primarily because David Pleat wanted more of a motivator as the team struggled, Des is still awaiting his first goal for the club. However, as he is the one player who stays back as cover when corners and free kicks are taken, it is hardly surprising that he has failed to find the net in three years at Hillsborough. Is still noted for his terrific recovery rate.
Nottingham F (From apprentice on 2/12/83) FL 259+5/1 FLC 40 FAC 27 Others 14 (£1,500,000 to Sampodoria on 1/8/92)
Sheffield Wed (£2,700,000 on 22/7/93) PL 116 FLC 14 FAC 8

WALKER Ian Michael
Born: Watford, 31 October 1971
Height: 6'2" Weight: 11.9
Club Honours: FAYC '90; CS '91
International Honours: E: 2; U21-9; Yth

Spurs' first choice goalkeeper whose consistency has helped him become a regular choice for the England first team squad, while winning two caps, Ian's best form last season was demonstrated with five consecutive clean sheets, beginning at Middlesbrough in November and continuing until the 1-0 defeat of Wimbledon in December. A cool temperament and great anticipation are amongst his main attributes, plus his ability to perform in the big pressure games, his displays away to Liverpool, Manchester United and Newcastle, established Tottenham's reputation as a defence extremely difficult to break down. Ever present for Spurs in a 47 match programme.
Tottenham H (From trainee on 4/12/89) F/PL 125+1 FLC 9 FAC 14 Others 2
Oxford U (Loaned on 31/8/90) FL 2 FLC 1

Ian Walker

WALKER James Barry
Born: Nottingham, 9 July 1973
Height: 5'11" Weight: 13.0

After returning to the Walsall side for the final game of 1994-95, James began last season as first choice goalkeeper and ended up as the man in possession, despite twice losing his place to Trevor Wood. His finest hour came in the Swindon game last December, when he carried on regardless of the serious shoulder injury that was to keep him out of action for several weeks, to earn the Saddlers a point. Nicknamed "Whacker" due to his powerful kicking.
Notts Co (From trainee on 9/7/91)
Walsall (Free on 4/8/93) FL 60+1 FLC 2 FAC 7 Others 3

WALKER John
Born: Glasgow, 12 December 1973
Height: 5'9" Weight: 11.6
International Honours: S: Yth

Transferred from Clydebank to Grimsby last September, it took John until the last three games of 1995-96 to make his mark in first team football, having impressed in the reserves throughout the season. After making his debut, when coming off the bench to score at Watford, the former Glasgow Rangers' midfielder started the final game and will be looking for a regular spot in 1996-97.

Glasgow R (From Clydebank BC on 29/8/90)
Clydebank (Signed on 31/7/93) SL 18+9/2 Others 4+3
Grimsby T (Signed on 19/9/95) FL 1+1/1

WALKER Keith Cameron
Born: Edinburgh, 17 April 1966
Height: 6'0" Weight: 12.8

A popular player with the Swansea supporters, Keith again turned out consistent performances last season, despite having different partners in central defence. A strong-tackling defender, distribution is a feature of his game.

Stirling A (Signed from ICI in 1984) SL 82+9/17 SLC 5/3 SC 5/2
St Mirren (Signed during 1987 close season) SL 41+2/6 SLC 3 SC 1 Others 3
Swansea C (£80,000 on 23/11/89) FL 191+8/5 FLC 8 FAC 16/1 Others 21

WALKER Raymond (Ray)
Born: North Shields, 28 September 1963
Height: 5'10" Weight: 12.0
Club Honours: FAYC '80
International Honours: E: Yth

Skilful Port Vale midfield player with excellent passing skills. Spent last season in and out of the team, competing with Ian Bogie for the role of the central playmaker. Scored his only goals of the campaign from the substitutes' bench against Crystal Palace in an FA Cup replay and also came on during the Anglo-Italian Cup final at Wembley. Completed the 400th senior appearance of his career in 1995-96.

Aston Villa (From apprentice on 26/9/81) FL 15+8 FLC 2+1 FAC 2
Port Vale (Loaned on 7/9/84) FL 15/1
Port Vale (£12,000 on 5/8/86) FL 313+21/33 FLC 17+1/1 FAC 25+3/5 Others 22+3/3
Cambridge U (Loaned on 23/9/94) FL 5 Others 2

WALKER Richard Neil
Born: Derby, 9 November 1971
Height: 6'0" Weight: 12.0

One of many homegrown players in Notts County's squad, he seemed to have established a regular place at left back, until a fractured collar bone injury last October ruled him out for the remainder of the season and forced the manager to sign Ian Baraclough as a replacement. Sound in the tackle, with an aerial presence at both ends of the park, he will thus face some fierce competition to win back his place in 1996-97.

Notts Co (From trainee on 3/7/90) FL 50+1/4 FLC 10 Others 6+1
Mansfield T (Loaned on 23/3/95) FL 4

WALLACE Raymond (Ray) George
Born: Greenwich, 2 October 1969
Height: 5'6" Weight: 10.2
International Honours: E: U21-4

As an energetic midfielder, Ray covered every inch of the pitch for Stoke during the 1995-96 season. Although the least known of the three Wallace brothers, he had a good season as the perfect foil for midfield partner Nigel Gleghorn's experience and playmaking skills. Can also play at full back if required.

Southampton (From trainee on 21/4/88) FL 33+2 FLC 8 FAC 2 Others 2
Leeds U (£100,000 on 8/7/91) F/PL 5+2
Swansea C (Loaned on 20/3/92) FL 2
Reading (Loaned on 11/3/94) FL 3
Stoke C (Free on 11/8/94) FL 60+4/7 FLC 4 FAC 3 Others 11/1
Hull C (Loaned on 16/12/94) FL 7

WALLACE Rodney (Rod) Seymour
Born: Greenwich, 2 October 1969
Height: 5'7" Weight: 11.3
Club Honours: Div 1 '92; CS '92
International Honours: E: B-2; U21-11

Although he began 1995-96 in the Leeds' side, it was a very poor season for Rod, with first team chances limited, especially following the arrival of Tomas Brolin. Indeed, he twice turned down a return to his previous club, Southampton, after a fee had been agreed between the two clubs. Past performances have proved him to be one of the most skilful and direct players in the Premier League, but he needs a change of fortune. Has tremendous pace over the initial vital ten yards, which take him away from defenders and gets him into shooting or crossing positions.

Southampton (From trainee on 19/4/88) FL 111+17/45 FLC 18+1/6 FAC 10/3 Others 3+1/2
Leeds U (£1,600,000 on 7/6/91) F/PL 141+18/40 FLC 11+1/3 FAC 8+5/1 Others 1+4/1

WALLING Dean Anthony
Born: Leeds, 17 April 1969
Height: 6'0" Weight: 11.4
Club Honours: Div 3 '95

A wholehearted central defender who was Carlisle's "Player of the Year" in the club's record breaking 1994-95 campaign, "Deano" found the going harder last season, but he was still almost ever present at the heart of the defence. As a converted striker blessed with aerial ability, his frequent sorties upfield at corners and free kicks posed problems for opposing defences.

Rochdale (Free from Leeds U juniors on 30/7/87) FL 43+22/8 FAC 3 FLC 0+1 Others 1+1 (Free to Kitchener (Toronto), during 1990 close season)
Carlisle U (Free from Guiseley, via Franklin (Toronto), on 1/7/91) FL 178+6/19 FLC 13/2 FAC 10+1/1 Others 28/3

WALSH Colin David
Born: Hamilton, 22 July 1962
Height: 5'9" Weight: 11.0
International Honours: S: U21-5; Yth; Sch

Sadly, for Charlton's longest serving player, a knee injury limited his appearances during 1995-96 and he was forced to announce his retirement on medical grounds in March. At his best, Colin was a quality midfielder who was able to turn defence into attack with accurate long passes, allied to the ability to power in goals from set pieces or long range.

Nottingham F (From apprentice on 16/8/79) FL 115+24/32 FLC 8+5 FAC 9+2/2 Others 12/3
Charlton Ath (£125,000 on 11/9/86) FL 223+19/21 FLC 18+1/4 FAC 11+2 Others 17/5

Peterborough U (Loaned on 2/2/89) FL 5/1
Middlesbrough (Loaned on 17/1/91) FL 10+3/1 FAC 1

WALSH Gary
Born: Wigan, 21 March 1968
Height: 6'3" Weight: 15.10
Club Honours: ECWC '91; ESC '91; FAC '94
International Honours: E: U21-2

After ten years in the wings with Manchester United, as understudy to Jim Leighton and then Peter Schmeichel, Gary was rescued from obscurity by former club colleague, Bryan Robson, immediately prior to the start of 1995-96, to provide Middlesbrough with some competition for the goalkeeping position. His chance came early in the season when Alan Miller was injured after just three games and so well did he grasp the opportunity that he remained first choice 'keeper even when Miller was available again, playing 41 consecutive games before being rested for a virus complaint late in the campaign.

Manchester U (From juniors on 25/4/85) F/PL 49+1 FLC 7 Others 6
Airdrie (Loaned on 11/8/88) SL 3 SLC 1
Oldham Ath (Loaned on 19/11/93) PL 6
Middlesbrough (£500,000 on 11/8/95) PL 32 FLC 6 FAC 3

Gary Walsh

WALSH Michael Shane
Born: Rotherham, 5 August 1977
Height: 6'0" Weight: 12.8

Following his Scunthorpe debut in 1994-95 while still a trainee, he signed professional forms for the club during the 1995 close season. Proved he could play in either full back position, though probably favouring the right side. Highly regarded, having attracted attention from the bigger clubs, an added benefit is his long throw.

Scunthorpe U (From trainee on 3/7/95) FL 25+3 FLC 2 FAC 2 Others 1

WALSH Paul Anthony
Born: Plumstead, 1 October 1962
Height: 5'8" Weight: 10.8
Club Honours: Div 1 '86; FAC '91; CS '91
International Honours: E: 5; U21-4; Yth

A tricky, ball-playing forward, Paul was surprisingly allowed to leave Manchester City, having started just three matches in 1995-96, as part of the deal that saw Portsmouth's Gerry Creaney move in the opposite direction. Highly popular, with an excellent workrate and 100 per cent committed, throughout his career he has proved that he is more than capable of creating chances out of nothing. Unfortunately, after making an excellent start at Fratton Park, in giving the team more edge up front, his season was cruelly cut short by a knee ligament injury which looks like keeping him out of the game until the end of 1996.
Charlton Ath (From apprentice on 2/10/79) FL 85+2/24 FLC 9/6 FAC 4/1
Luton T (£400,000 on 26/7/82) FL 80/24 FLC 5/1 FAC 4/3
Liverpool (£700,000 on 21/5/84) FL 63+14/25 FLC 10+2/4 FAC 6+2/3 Others 13+2/5
Tottenham H (£500,000 on 16/2/88) FL 84+44/19 FLC 9+6/2 FAC 4+4 Others 1+3
Queens Park R (Loaned on 16/9/91) FL 2
Portsmouth (£400,000 on 3/6/92) FL 67+6/14 FLC 7+1/4 FAC 3 Others 6+1/3
Manchester C (£750,000 on 10/3/94) PL 53/16 FLC 6/2 FAC 3/1
Portsmouth (£500,000 on 14/9/95) FL 21/5 FAC 1

Steve Walsh

WALSH Steven (Steve)
Born: Preston, 3 November 1964
Height: 6'3" Weight: 14.6
Club Honours: AMC '85

Left-footed central defender. Reached 300 appearances and 50 goals for Leicester City during last season, even though he suffered with yet another knee injury. Helped to take charge of team affairs between Mark McGhee's departure and Martin O'Neill's arrival, before scoring a dramatic last gasp equaliser at Grimsby in the latter's first game as the new manager. Took over as club captain in March and led City to victory in the first division play-off final at the expense of Crystal Palace, even having a late header cleared off the line that denied him a repeat of his 1994 glory. Is due a testimonial in 1996.
Wigan Ath (From juniors on 11/9/82) FL 123+3/4 FLC 7 FAC 6 Others 10+2
Leicester C (£100,000 on 24/6/86) F/PL 285+2/45 FLC 23/3 FAC 9 Others 22/4

WALTERS Mark Everton
Born: Birmingham, 2 June 1964
Height: 5'9" Weight: 11.8
Club Honours: FAYC '80; ESC '82; SPD '89, '90, '91; SLC '89, '91; FAC '92
International Honours: E: 1; B-1; U21-9; Yth; Sch

Having failed to make a first team appearance at Liverpool last season, the skilful and fast-raiding left winger signed for Southampton on a free in January after spending much of his time at Anfield in the reserves or on the bench. However, limited to just eight starts, due to team tactics and competition from Neil Heaney, he will be looking to put down a stronger challenge this season.
Aston Villa (From apprentice on 18/5/82) FL 168+13/39 FLC 20+1/6 FAC 11+1/1 Others 7+3/2
Glasgow R (£500,000 on 31/12/87) SL 101+5/32 SLC 13/11 SC 14/6 Others 10/2
Liverpool (£1,250,000 on 13/8/91) F/PL 58+36/14 FLC 10+2/4 FAC 6+3 Others 8+1/1
Stoke C (Loaned on 24/3/94) FL 9/2
Wolverhampton W (Loaned on 9/9/94) FL 11/3
Southampton (Free on 18/1/96) PL 4+1 FAC 4

WALTON David (Dave) Lee
Born: Bedlington, 10 April 1973
Height: 6'2" Weight: 13.4
Club Honours: Div 3 '94

Thoroughly committed, strong central defender who is happy in the air or on the ground. Gaining experience all the time, having disappointed himself in two of last season's bigger games, his character saw him bounce back immediately. Is one of the first names on the Shrewsbury team sheet.
Sheffield U (Free from Ashington on 15/5/91)
Shrewsbury T (Signed on 5/11/93) FL 98/8 FLC 5 FAC 9/1 Others 8/1

WALTON Paul Anthony
Born: Sunderland, 2 July 1979
Height: 5'9" Weight: 11.0

Speedy, left-sided forward tipped for future stardom by Hartlepool youth team coach, Billy Horner. Although only a first year trainee in 1995-96, he showed great enthusiasm as the leading goalscorer for the juniors and on several occasions was included in the first team squad, eventually making six brief appearances in the Endsleigh League.
Hartlepool U (Trainee) FL 1+5

WANLESS Paul Steven
Born: Banbury, 14 December 1973
Height: 6'1" Weight: 13.4

Signed from Oxford during the 1995 close season, Paul was injured before 1995-96 got underway and found it difficult to win a first team place at Lincoln. Had loan spells first at Woking (January) and then at Cambridge (March), where he showed as a player who could perform equally well in defence or midfield. Also proved to be a capable stand in goalie for much of the last match of the campaign, helping United to a 2-0 win over Leyton Orient.
Oxford U (From trainee on 3/12/91) FL 12+20 FLC 0+3/1 Others 2+2
Lincoln C (Free on 7/7/95) FL 7+1 Others 2
Cambridge U (Loaned on 8/3/96) FL 14/1

WARBURTON Raymond (Ray)
Born: Rotherham, 7 October 1967
Height: 6'0" Weight: 12.9

Northampton central defender and club captain who is both solid and dependable at the heart of the defence. Also likes to come forward on set pieces and scored a few goals, via free kicks last season. His all-round ability was vital in Town's cause.
Rotherham U (From apprentice on 5/10/85) FL 3+1 FAC 2 Others 1
York C (Free on 8/8/89) FL 86+4/9 FLC 8/1 FAC 6/1 Others 7
Northampton T (£35,000 on 4/2/94) FL 100/7 FLC 4 FAC 3/1 Others 7/1

WARD Ashley Stuart
Born: Manchester, 24 November 1970
Height: 6'1" Weight: 12.4

Ashley finished as Norwich's top scorer for 1995-96, despite being controversially sold to Derby County with 11 games still to play. A hamstring injury against Millwall in September, saw him miss five matches, before returning to confirm his reputation as probably the best target man outside the Premiership. His first nine goals were scored on opponents' grounds, including a fine hat trick at Bradford City, as part of a run of eight goals in nine games. Having named his first child Darby, he co-incidentally joined the promotion seeking side as City's 10th million pound sale of the 1990s.
Manchester C (From trainee on 5/8/89) FL 0+1 FAC 0+2
Wrexham (Loaned on 10/1/91) FL 4/2 Others 1
Leicester C (£80,000 on 30/7/91) FL 2+8 FLC 2+1 FAC 0+1 Others 0+1
Blackpool (Loaned on 21/11/92) FL 2/1
Crewe Alex (£80,000 on 1/12/92) FL 58+3/25 FLC 4/2 FAC 2/4 Others 7/5
Norwich C (£500,000 on 8/12/94) P/FL 53/18 FLC 6/3 FAC 1
Derby Co (£1,000,000 on 19/3/96) FL 5+2/1

WARD Darren
Born: Worksop, 11 May 1974
Height: 5'11" Weight: 12.9
International Honours: W: U21-2

An outstanding young goalkeeper signed by Notts County from Mansfield during the summer of 1995. Darren enjoyed an excellent first season at Meadow Lane, playing in all 60 games of his club's programme and making many remarkable saves along the way. Rewarded with a call up to the Welsh U21 team, he may yet prove to be Neville Southall's natural successor and will undoubtedly come under close scrutiny from many higher placed clubs this coming season.

Mansfield T (From trainee on 27/7/92) FL 81 FLC 5 FAC 5 Others 6
Notts Co (£160,000 on 11/7/95) FL 46 FLC 4 FAC 3 Others 7

WARD Darren Philip
Born: Kenton, 13 September 1978
Height: 5'11" Weight: 11.4
First year Watford YTS central defender who made a confident first team debut in 1995-96 at the age of 17 at Luton, of all places. Is a tackler who keeps his passing simple.
Watford (Trainee) FL 1

WARD Gavin John
Born: Sutton Coldfield, 30 June 1970
Height: 6'4" Weight: 14.12
Club Honours: Div 3 '93; WC '93
Safe and commanding goalkeeper. Unable to displace Kevin Poole at Leicester, Gavin signed for Bradford during the 1995 close season and quickly became one of the most popular players to have graced Valley Parade in recent years, missing just one game due to injury, before moving to Bolton as cover for the injured Keith Branagan in March. Going straight into the side that faced Manchester City, dejectedly, his first job was to pick the ball out of the net, City scoring inside 90 seconds. Played in five of the last six Premiership games.
Shrewsbury T (Free from Aston Villa juniors on 26/9/88)
West Bromwich A (Free on 18/9/89)
Cardiff C (Free on 5/10/89) FL 58+1 FAC 1 Others 7
Leicester C (£175,000 on 16/7/93) F/PL 38 FLC 3 FAC 0+1 Others 4
Bradford C (£175,000 on 13/7/95) FL 36 FLC 6 FAC 3 Others 2
Bolton W (£300,000 on 29/3/96) PL 5

Gavin Ward

WARD Mark William
Born: Huyton, 10 October 1962
Height: 5'5" Weight: 10.0
Club Honours: Div 2 '95; AMC '95
International Honours: E: SP-1
Started 1995-96 as Birmingham's player/coach, and looking to play a major part in the club's future, he suffered a back injury early on and failed to gain a regular place on recovering fitness. Desperate to get a game, Huddersfield took over the remaining three months of his contract and, playing in a central midfield role, he used his skill and experience to good effect in eight appearances. Released at the end of June, Mark is still a tenacious ball winner, despite his 34 years, and a continuing danger at set pieces.
Everton (From apprentice on 5/9/80)
Oldham Ath (£10,000 from Northwich Victoria on 19/7/83) FL 84/12 FLC 5 FAC 3
West Ham U (£250,000 on 15/8/85) FL 163+2/12 FLC 20+1/2 FAC 17 Others 6
Manchester C (£1,000,000 on 29/12/89) FL 55/14 FLC 3 FAC 6 Others 3/2
Everton (£1,100,000 on 12/8/91) F/PL 82+1/6 FLC 6/1 FAC 4 Others 1
Birmingham C (£500,000 on 24/3/94) FL 63/7 FLC 6+1 FAC 4 Others 8/1
Huddersfield T (Free on 22/3/96) FL 7+1

WARD Mitchum (Mitch) David
Born: Sheffield, 19 June 1971
Height: 5'8" Weight: 10.12
Versatile homegrown player who began last season in the Sheffield United side, but was placed on the transfer list in October by Dave Bassett who considered he would only ever be a squad member. However, the arrival of Howard Kendall saw him back in the first team picture, and strong performances in both full back slots, as well as left and right-sided midfield positions, led to him signing a new two and a half year contract. Probably the most improved player of 1995-96, Mitch also proved to be an admirable penalty taker when called upon.
Sheffield U (From trainee on 1/7/89) F/PL 98+16/6 FLC 4+3/1 FAC 7+2/2 Others 2+1/1
Crewe Alex (Loaned on 1/11/90) FL 4/1 FAC 1/1 Others 2

WARD Peter
Born: Durham, 15 October 1964
Height: 6'0" Weight: 11.10
A very good signing from Stockport County during the 1995 close season, Peter proved to be an important member of the Wrexham team in 1995-96, as an excellent passer of the ball who liked to be involved in the hurly-burly of central midfield. His real forte, however, were free kicks on the edge of an opponent's penalty area, which brought him a number of crackers during the campaign, including one against his former club at Edgeley Park in February, and a last minute equaliser at Saltergate in March.
Huddersfield T (Signed from Chester le Street on 7/1/87) FL 24+13/2 FLC 1+1 FAC 2 Others 1
Rochdale (Free on 20/7/89) FL 83+1/10 FLC 5 FAC 7/1 Others 5
Stockport Co (Signed on 6/6/91) FL 140+2/10 FLC 8/1 FAC 7 Others 26/6
Wrexham (£50,000 on 19/7/95) FL 33+1/6 FLC 1 FAC 4 Others 1/1

WARE Paul David
Born: Congleton, 7 November 1970
Height: 5'9" Weight: 11.5
Club Honours: Div 2 '93
Industrious Stockport midfielder. Even with first team chances limited, amid fierce competition for midfield places at Stockport in 1995-96, he was always a committed and effective player, the highlight of his season being a brilliant 25-yard "banana" goal to win an important league game at Carlisle.
Stoke C (From trainee on 15/11/88) FL 92+23/10 FLC 7+1 FAC 4+1 Others 12+2/4
Stockport Co (Signed on 8/9/94) FL 38+8/4 FLC 5+1 FAC 2 Others 2/1

WARHURST Paul
Born: Stockport, 26 September 1969
Height: 6'1" Weight: 12.10
Club Honours: PL '95
International Honours: E: U21-8
Blackburn utility player who is capable of playing in almost any position, having great instant control, composure, and the ability to look up and pass the crucial ball. Recovered after breaking both legs within a year, but not ready until the end of last September, he was then struck down by a succession of minor injuries and illnesses. When back, Paul was mainly used in Europe, where the club had not sufficient eligible players, before getting sent off in Rovers' one Champions' Cup victory. It was no surprise, given his luck, that on his first start in the Premier League he broke his ribs. Is the son of Roy, who played for Sheffield United, Birmingham, Manchester City, Crewe and Oldham between 1944 and 1960.
Manchester C (From trainee on 1/7/88)
Oldham Ath (£10,000 on 27/10/88) FL 60+7/2 FLC 8 FAC 5+4 Others 2
Sheffield Wed (£750,000 on 17/7/91) F/PL 60+6/6 FLC 9/4 FAC 7+1/5 Others 5/3
Blackburn Rov (£2,700,000 on 17/8/93) PL 25+21/2 FLC 6+2 FAC 2 Others 4+2

WARK John
Born: Glasgow, 4 August 1957
Height: 5'10" Weight: 12.10
Club Honours: FAYC '75; FAC '78; UEFAC '81; SC '86; Div 2 '92
International Honours: S: 29; U21-8; Yth
Although troubled throughout 1995-96 with back and achilles tendon problems, and despite making less outings than in any previous seasons, the Ipswich player/coach still made useful contributions, his experience often proving vital. Now playing in the centre of defence, the game at Norwich last November saw him break the derby appearance record held jointly by Mick Mills and Kevin Keelan, and when he scored from the spot he broke the goalscoring record as well. Has stated that he does not intend to play this coming term, and will combine coaching with work in the club's commercial department, even though registered in case of an emergency.
Ipswich T (From apprentice on 1/8/74) FL 295+1/94 FLC 24+1/12 FAC 36+1/12 Others 25/18
Liverpool (£450,000 on 10/3/84) FL 64+6/28 FLC 6+4/3 FAC 11+2/6 Others 13+2/5
Ipswich T (£100,000 on 4/1/88) FL 87+2/23 FLC 4 FAC 3 Others 9/2

Middlesbrough (£50,000 on 23/8/90) FL 31+1/2 FLC 5 FAC 2 Others 1
Ipswich T (Free on 21/9/91) F/PL 149+3/18 FLC 13+1 FAC 16/2 Others 5

WARNER Vance

Born: Leeds, 3 September 1974
Height: 6'0" Weight: 11.12
International Honours: E: Yth

With Nottingham Forest's back four rarely absent last season, first team opportunities were non-existent for the big central defender and in February he had a brief spell on loan at Grimsby, making just three appearances. Normally a sound tackler and firm under pressure, Vance needs regular work if he is to climb the Premiership ladder.
Nottingham F (From trainee on 14/9/91) FL 2 FLC 1
Grimsby T (Loaned on 2/2/96) FL 3

WARREN Christer

Born: Bournemouth, 10 October 1974
Height: 5'10" Weight: 11.3

Signed from non-league football towards the end of 1994-95, the young Southampton winger made his debut when coming off the bench during a 4-2 defeat at Arsenal last September. Promising enough to be given further chances, Christer showed himself to be capable of playing on either flank in an attacking capacity and not afraid to have a shot.
Southampton (£40,000 from Cheltenham T on 31/3/95) PL 1+6 FLC 1

WARREN Lee Anthony

Born: Manchester, 28 February 1969
Height: 6'0" Weight: 11.10

A skilful, if lightweight Doncaster Rovers' midfielder, he also played in the club's back four during the 1995-96 season. Neat and tidy, Lee makes up for his lack of physical presence with plenty of skill on the ball.
Leeds U (From trainee on 27/7/87)
Rochdale (Free on 28/10/87) FL 31/1 FAC 1 Others 2
Hull C (£40,000 on 25/8/88) FL 141+12/1 FLC 2 FAC 5+1 Others 1
Lincoln C (Loaned on 20/9/90) FL 2+1/1
Doncaster Rov (Free on 21/7/94) FL 50+6/2 FLC 2 FAC 1 Others 3+1

WARREN Mark Wayne

Born: Clapton, 12 November 1974
Height: 5'9" Weight: 10.5
International Honours: E: Yth

After starting last season for Leyton Orient at right back, he also appeared as a striker and in midfield, his hard tackling and liking for moving out of defence to send in the occasional long-range effort, giving the manager plenty of options. Hopefully, 1996-97 will see him settling into the side on a more regular basis.
Leyton Orient (From trainee on 6/7/92) FL 58+16/4 FLC 4 Others 7+4/1

WARRINGTON Andrew (Andy) Clifford

Born: Sheffield, 10 June 1976
Height: 6'3" Weight: 12.13

As York's reserve goalkeeper, he made his first team debut in last season's Coca Cola second-leg tie against Manchester United.

Continuing to deputise for the injured Dean Kiely, Andy also played in the next round at Queens Park Rangers, while a run of 11 senior games was all valuable experience for the tall, well-built custodian.
York C (From trainee on 11/6/94) FL 6 FLC 2 FAC 1 Others 2

WASSALL Darren Paul

Born: Birmingham, 27 June 1968
Height: 5'11" Weight: 12.10
Club Honours: FMC '92

The ex-Forest centre back and specialist marker had a difficult season in 1995-96, as first injury and then further speculation about his future at Derby, limited his appearances. However, having signed a two year contract in September to quash any rumours, he found it difficult to regain his place upon the arrival of Igor Stimac. Still one of the paciest defenders at the club though.
Nottingham F (From apprentice on 1/6/86) FL 17+10 FLC 6+2 FAC 3+1 Others 4+2/1
Hereford U (Loaned on 23/10/87) FL 5 FAC 2 Others 1
Bury (Loaned on 2/3/89) FL 7/1
Derby Co (£600,000 on 15/6/92) FL 90+8 FLC 9 FAC 4 Others 11

WATKIN Stephen (Steve)

Born: Wrexham, 16 June 1971
Height: 5'10" Weight: 11.10
Club Honours: WC '95
International Honours: W: B-2; Sch

Striker. By his own admission, Steve would be honest enough to say that 1995-96 was not one of his best seasons. Although still an important member of the Wrexham squad, he did not look match-fit in many games and was on the bench on several occasions. A fit Steve Watkin always adds to the side, a feature of his play being fine lay offs for team mates and a fair share of goals.
Wrexham (From juniors on 24/7/89) FL 144+28/47 FLC 9+2/4 FAC 11+3/9 Others 17+5/4

WATKISS Stuart Paul

Born: Wolverhampton, 8 May 1966
Height: 6'2" Weight: 13.7

Tall, brave defender who gave some outstanding early season displays for Walsall in 1995-96, before being displaced following the arrival of Adrian Viveash and Derek Mountfield. Moving to Hereford in February, Stuart brought a more solid look to the Bull's defence, his experience and versatility proving invaluable, while making the left back position his own. Was surprisingly released during the summer.
Wolverhampton W (From trainee on 13/7/84) FL 2
Crewe Alex (Free on 28/2/86) FL 3
Walsall (Free from Rushall Olympic on 5/8/93) FL 60+2/2 FLC 8/1 FAC 5 Others 2
Hereford U (Free on 16/2/96) FL 19 Others 2

WATSON Alexander (Alex) Francis

Born: Liverpool, 5 April 1968
Height: 6'0" Weight: 11.9
Club Honours: CS '88
International Honours: E: Yth

Having failed to regain his position at the heart of the Bournemouth defence, Alex transferred to Torquay last November after a spell on loan at Gillingham, where he stood

in for Tony Butler. Strong in the air, good in the tackle, and ever present, his performances were solid and reliable, and at least gave United something to build on in difficult times. Is the brother of Everton's Dave.
Liverpool (From apprentice on 18/5/85) FL 3+1 FLC 1+1 FAC 1+1 Others 1
Derby Co (Loaned on 30/8/90) FL 5
Bournemouth (£150,000 on 18/1/91) FL 145+6/5 FLC 14/1 FAC 12/1 Others 5
Gillingham (Loaned on 11/9/95) FL 10/1
Torquay U (£50,000 on 23/11/95) FL 29/2 FAC 2

WATSON Andrew (Andy) Anthony

Born: Leeds, 1 April 1967
Height: 5'9" Weight: 11.2
Club Honours: WC '91

Striker. Started last season at Blackpool in dispute with the club, before eventually signing a weekly contract and getting on the team sheet. A consistent scorer at Bloomfield Road over the past three years, in October he netted five goals in three games for the reserves, before opening his first team account in December.
Halifax T (Free from Harrogate T on 23/8/88) FL 75+6/12 FLC 5+1/2 FAC 6/1 Others 7/1
Swansea C (£40,000 on 31/7/90) FL 9+5/1 FLC 0+1 Others 1+1
Carlisle U (£30,000 on 19/9/91) FL 55+1/22 FLC 4/5 FAC 3 Others 1/1
Blackpool (£55,000 on 5/2/93) FL 88+27/43 FLC 6/5 FAC 3+2 Others 7+1/1

WATSON David (Dave)

Born: Liverpool, 20 November 1961
Height: 6'0" Weight: 13.7
Club Honours: FLC '85; Div 2 '86; Div 1 '87, CS '87, '95; FAC '95
International Honours: E: 12; U21-7 (UEFAC '84)

An Everton central defender who is strong in the air and aggressive in the tackle, Dave uses his height to great effect at both ends of the park and remains vital to the club's cause, sticking to the task regardless. Began 1995-96 carrying a back problem, but that did not stop him continuing his influential job at the heart of the defence, and although missing the occasional match, his performances were kept up to their normal impeccably high standard. Along with Neville Southall, probably the main reason for the club's climb into sixth place in the table, this was achieved partnering a number of players as injuries took their toll on the squad, before he finally settled down with Craig Short to form a tight defensive unit.
Liverpool (From juniors on 25/5/79)
Norwich C (£100,000 on 29/11/80) FL 212/11 FLC 21/3 FAC 18/1
Everton (£900,000 on 22/8/86) F/PL 338+2/22 FLC 35/6 FAC 42/5 Others 16+1/3

WATSON David Neil

Born: Barnsley, 10 November 1973
Height: 6'0" Weight: 12.3
International Honours: E: U21-5; Yth

Again Barnsley's number one goalkeeper, representing England U21s and the Endsleigh League early last season, his shot stopping throughout 1995-96 was second to none. However, disruption to the centre of the Tykes' defence caused problems with communication and his confidence ebbed a little as the campaign wore on, but he still kept several clean sheets, including three in a row in November.

Barnsley (From trainee on 4/7/92) FL 96 FLC 9 FAC 3 Others 1

David Watson (Barnsley)

WATSON Gordon William George
Born: Sidcup, 20 March 1971
Height: 6'0" Weight: 12.9
International Honours: E: U21-2
A Southampton forward signed from Sheffield Wednesday in early 1995, he developed a good partnership up front with Neil Shipperley in 1995-96, where his energetic and enthusiastic style produced six goals, plus many opportunities for others. Sometimes missed out when Saints played with only one man up front, but was always a favourite with the fans for his total commitment.
Charlton Ath (From trainee on 5/4/89) FL 20+11/7 FLC 2/1 FAC 0+1 Others 1+1
Sheffield Wed (£250,000 on 20/2/91) F/PL 29+37/15 FLC 6+5/3 FAC 5+2/2 Others 2+2/1
Southampton (£1,200,000 on 17/3/95) PL 30+7/6 FLC 2+1/2 FAC 5/1

WATSON Mark Leon
Born: Birmingham, 28 December 1973
Height: 6'3" Weight: 13.11
Signed from non-league, Sutton United, at the end of 1994-95, in order to give the young striker experience, West Ham loaned him out several times last season. Came on at Plymouth for Leyton Orient (September), equalising in a 1-1 draw with an overhead kick, and then scored for Cambridge (October) in the 2-1 defeat at Doncaster, while playing in his first full game, before making one appearance for Shrewsbury in February. Back at Upton Park, and having made his Premiership debut in the penultimate game of the campaign, he joined Bournemouth as part of the deal that took Steve Jones in the opposite direction.

West Ham U (Signed from Sutton U on 9/5/95) PL 0+1
Leyton Orient (Loaned on 4/9/95) FL 0+1/1
Cambridge U (Loaned on 27/10/95) FL 1+3/1 Others 1
Shrewsbury T (Loaned on 2/2/96) FL 1
Bournemouth (Signed on 17/5/96)

WATSON Paul Douglas
Born: Hastings, 4 January 1975
Height: 5'8" Weight: 10.10
Equally at home at left back or in midfield for Gillingham, he made only a handful of appearances in 1995-96, after being a permanent fixture the season before. Still highly thought of at the club, Paul was unfortunate to be in the slipstream of the excellent newcomer, Dominic Naylor, but was a regular in the reserves, where he continued to impress at dead ball situations.
Gillingham (From trainee on 8/12/92) FL 57+5/2 FLC 4 FAC 6 Others 5+3

WATSON Stephen (Steve) Craig
Born: North Shields, 1 April 1974
Height: 6'0" Weight: 12.7
International Honours: E: U21-12; Yth
Steve is very versatile and can play in any position, as he demonstrated during last season, even being the nominated replacement goalkeeper, although yet to perform in that role. Unable to gain an established place in the Newcastle side until April, when he came in at right-back against Liverpool, many believed this to be his best position, supported in the knowledge that right back is where he continued to play for the England U21 side. Wholehearted and skilful, he scored a stunning goal to eliminate holders, Liverpool, from the Coca Cola Cup, just three weeks after scoring a late winner against them in the Premiership.
Newcastle U (From trainee on 6/4/91) F/PL 112+24/10 FLC 8+4/1 FAC 8+2 Others 4+3/1

WATSON Thomas (Tommy) Robert
Born: Liverpool, 29 September 1969
Height: 5'8" Weight: 11.6
The right-sided Grimsby midfield ball winner was unable to command a place in the senior squad last season, his only full appearance coming in the Coca Cola Cup match at Birmingham. With that in mind, he took the opportunity to get back into first team action during a loan spell at Hull in October, being used in the unfamiliar right back berth for five games, before returning to Blundell Park. Still not part of Brian Laws' plans, he was released during the summer.
Grimsby T (From trainee on 12/7/88) FL 134+38/24 FLC 10+5/4 FAC 3 Others 8+2
Hull C (Loaned on 13/10/95) FL 4 Others 1

WATTS Julian
Born: Sheffield, 17 March 1971
Height: 6'3" Weight: 12.8
A young, tall centre back with a calmness befitting someone with more maturity, Julian never had an extended run-in the Sheffield Wednesday team and following the signing of John Newsome, he opted for a transfer to Leicester City last March. Made his debut against Sheffield United when City were decidedly off-key, but soon

played a vital role in successive wins at Charlton and Palace to keep the Foxes in the hunt for a play-off place. Established a solid partnership with Steve Walsh at the heart of a defence that kept several clean sheets on their way back to Premiership football, following the 2-1 Wembley win over Crystal Palace.
Rotherham U (From trainee on 10/7/90) FL 17+3/1 FLC 1 FAC 4 Others 2
Sheffield Wed (£80,000 on 13/3/92) PL 11+5/1 FLC 1 Others 1
Shrewsbury T (Loaned on 18/12/92) FL 9 Others 1
Leicester C (£210,000 on 29/3/96) FL 9 Others 3

WDOWCZYK Dariusz
Born: Warsaw, Poland, 21 September 1962
Height: 5'11" Weight: 11.11
International Honours: Poland : 51
Although worried by a string of niggling injuries in 1995-96, the Reading defence still looked far more solid and composed when he was at its heart. Despite his age, he is clearly a player of consummate ability, and signed a new two year contract for Royals during the summer of 1996, having played outstandingly in the 3-0 win over Wolves, a result which ensured the club's survival in division one.
Glasgow Celtic (£400,000 from Legia on 17/11/89) SL 112+4/4 SLC 11 SC 13/2 Others 6+1
Reading (Free on 12/8/94) FL 66+2 FLC 4 FAC 1 Others 3

WEAVER Nicholas (Nicky) James
Born: Sheffield, 2 March 1979
Height: 6'3" Weight: 13.6
The Mansfield goalkeeper made his debut when Ian Bowling was unfit for the match at Cambridge on 23 March, 1996, whilst still a first year apprentice and gave an excellent performance in keeping a clean sheet. Trained with the England Youth squad during the season and could be one to watch for the future.
Mansfield T (Trainee) FL 1

WEBBER Damien John
Born: Rustington, 8 October 1968
Height: 6'4" Weight: 14.0
Tall Millwall defender who clears his lines with towering headers. Tough competition coupled to injuries, saw the big man suffer a frustrating time of it in 1995-96, a broken jaw received in the home Birmingham match in April, terminating his season.
Millwall (Signed from Bognor Regis on 27/10/94) FL 27+11/2 FLC 1+2 FAC 2+2

WEBSTER Simon Paul
Born: Hinckley, 20 January 1964
Height: 6'0" Weight: 12.0
Never really recovering from the horrific broken leg suffered three years ago, Simon had a spell on loan with Derby at the beginning of last season, before coming back to West Ham and announcing his retirement from the game in November. A central defender, who could also perform admirably at full back, he is now studying physiotherapy at the University of East London.
Tottenham H (From apprentice on 1/12/81) FL 2+1

Exeter C (Loaned on 10/11/83) FL 26 Others 3
Huddersfield T (£15,000 on 21/2/85) FL 118/4 FLC 7 FAC 7 Others 2
Sheffield U (£35,000 on 18/3/88) FL 26+11/3 FLC 5 FAC 5+1 Others 3+1
Charlton Ath (£50,000 on 16/8/90) FL 127/7 FLC 7 FAC 6 Others 3
West Ham U (£525,000 on 30/6/93) PL 0+5
Oldham Ath (Loaned on 24/3/95) FL 7
Derby Co (Loaned on 29/8/95) FL 3

WEIR Michael (Micky) Graham
Born: Edinburgh, 16 January 1966
Height: 5'4" Weight: 10.5
Club Honours: SLC '91

An experienced transfer deadline loan signing from Hibernian last March, Micky arrived to help bolster Millwall's flagging fortunes. Playing on the wide left, he showed all the trickery one normally associates with Scottish midfielders, mixing early crosses with getting to the byline and fighting hard for possession. Also delivered excellent near post in-swinging corners.
Hibernian (Free from Portobello Thistle on 23/11/82) SL 19+5 SLC 4+1 SC 1
Luton T (Signed on 11/9/87) FL 7+1
Hibernian (Signed on 14/1/88) SL 140+34/28 SLC 13+1 SC 13/4 Others 3
Millwall (Loaned on 28/3/96) FL 8

WELCH Keith James
Born: Bolton, 3 October 1968
Height: 6'2" Weight: 12.5

Goalkeeper. A serious back injury, suffered at Peterborough last September, brought about an absence from the Bristol City side for just over two months. Many expected that the injury would have kept him out for longer, but he came back and demonstrated that he had lost none of his ability as a shot stopper, and was still confident in claiming crosses. A cool, seemingly unflappable 'keeper, Keith has performed well for City since being signed from Rochdale in the close season of 1991 and has now played in over 200 first team games for the Robins.
Rochdale (Free from Bolton W juniors on 3/3/87) FL 205 FLC 12 FAC 10 Others 12
Bristol C (£200,000 on 25/7/91) FL 195 FLC 12 FAC 11 Others 9

WELLER Paul Anthony
Born: Brighton, 6 March 1975
Height: 5'8" Weight: 11.0

After an impressive performance in an Auto Windscreens Shield game at Crewe last November, Paul became a regular on the right side of Burnley's midfield. A skilful player, who can create good opportunities for himself and others, he perhaps needs a touch more aggression to really impose himself at second division level.
Burnley (From trainee on 30/11/93) FL 24+1/1 FLC 1 Others 2

WELLS Mark Anthony
Born: Leicester, 15 October 1971
Height: 5'9" Weight: 10.10

A no-nonsense left back, he spent much of last season in the Scarborough reserve side, apart from a spell at non-league, Dagenham, on loan, due to the fine form of Richard Lucas, although when he did get a chance in the team he always looked impressive.

Having been blighted by injury for much of his time at Boro, he was released on a free transfer during the summer.
Notts Co (From trainee on 3/7/90) FL 0+2 Others 0+1
Huddersfield T (Free on 9/8/93) FL 21+1/4 FLC 4 FAC 3 Others 2+1
Scarborough (Free on 21/7/94) FL 26+6/1 FAC 4 Others 2

Mark Wells

WEST Colin
Born: Wallsend, 13 November 1962
Height: 6'1" Weight: 13.11

Much travelled Leyton Orient striker, now in his fourth season with the club, his 17 goals in 1995-96 saw him finish top scorer yet again. Particularly good in the air, and possessing a fierce long-range shot, Colin, now in the twilight of his career, could be seen actively encouraging his team mates, this despite playing in a side that finished only three places away from re-election.
Sunderland (From apprentice on 9/7/80) FL 88+14/21 FLC 13+4/5 FAC 3+1/2
Watford (£115,000 on 28/3/85) FL 45/20 FLC 2+1 FAC 8/3
Glasgow R (£180,000 on 23/5/86) SL 4+6/2 SLC 2/1 SC 0+1 Others 0+2
Sheffield Wed (£150,000 on 7/9/87) FL 40+5/8 FLC 6/3 FAC 6 Others 3/1
West Bromwich A (Signed on 24/2/89) FL 64+9/22 FLC 2 FAC 4/1 Others 2/1
Port Vale (Loaned on 1/11/91) FL 5/1
Swansea C (Free on 5/8/92) FL 29+4/12 FLC 0+1 FAC 5/2 Others 3+2/1
Leyton Orient (Free on 26/7/93) FL 108+4/39 FLC 3/1 FAC 5/1 Others 8/4

WEST Dean
Born: Morley, 5 December 1972
Height: 5'10" Weight: 11.7

As Bury boss Stan Ternent's first signing last September from Lincoln City, Dean was initially tried on the wide right of midfield,

but failed to impress. It was when he switched to right back in November that he found his true position and remained ever present, showing superb form and displaying a willingness to attack, which made him a popular Shaker.
Lincoln C (From trainee on 17/8/91) FL 93+26/20 FLC 11/1 FAC 5/1 Others 5+2/1
Bury (Signed on 29/9/95) FL 32+5/1 FAC 1 Others 1+1

WESTLEY Shane Lee Mark
Born: Canterbury, 16 June 1965
Height: 6'2" Weight: 13.8

Solid central defender signed by Cambridge United immediately prior to 1995-96 getting underway, having been released by Brentford. After just three games, Shane was transferred to Lincoln, where he was appointed team captain, but was eventually dropped following the arrival of new manager, John Beck.
Charlton Ath (From apprentice on 8/6/83) FL 8 FAC 1
Southend U (£15,000 on 1/3/85) FL 142+2/10 FLC 10+1/1 FAC 5 Others 7/1
Wolverhampton W (£150,000 on 19/6/89) FL 48+2/2 FLC 5/1 Others 2
Brentford (£100,000 on 30/10//92) FL 61+3/1 FLC 5/2 FAC 5 Others 6
Southend U (Loaned on 3/2/95) FL 4+1
Cambridge U (Free on 10/8/95) FL 3 FLC 1
Lincoln C (£7,500 on 6/10/95) FL 9/1 FAC 1 Others 1

WESTWOOD Ashley Michael
Born: Bridgnorth, 31 August 1976
Height: 6'0" Weight: 11.3
Club Honours: FAYC '95
International Honours: E: Yth

Signed during the 1995 close season from Manchester United, Crewe could rightly claim this as a real coup. Making his debut on the opening day of 1995-96, Ashley was a regular until having to receive remedial surgery late in the campaign. A natural athlete, who reads the game well and, despite his height, is very good in the air, he shared a fine centre back pairing with Steve Macauley.
Manchester U (From trainee on 1/7/94)
Crewe Alex (£40,000 on 26/7/95) FL 31+2/4 FLC 4 FAC 5/1 Others 4

WETHERALL David
Born: Sheffield, 14 March 1971
Height: 6'3" Weight: 13.12
International Honours: E: Sch

Good young Leeds' central defender who, along with a number of others in 1995-96, struggled to maintain the consistency of performance of the previous season. Although there were many signs of a promising partnership with Richard Jobson, before the latter's season was curtailed by injury, David still seems more at home when up against big strikers, rather than the smaller, speedier types. Again weighed in with some goals and remains very much a threat in set piece situations. Is a good professional with a big future in the game.
Sheffield Wed (From trainee on 1/7/89)
Leeds U (£125,000 on 15/7/91) F/PL 116+2/9 FLC 13 FAC 13+2/3 Others 4

WHALLEY Gareth
Born: Manchester, 19 December 1973
Height: 5'10" Weight: 11.6
As the captain of the Crewe side, this talented midfielder continued to impress in 1995-96 with his natural talent and was selected for the Endsleigh League U21 side against an Italian Serie "B" XI at Huddersfield. Seems destined to play at a higher level before too long.
Crewe Alex (From trainee on 29/7/92) FL 118+6/5 FLC 8+1/1 FAC 11+1/4 Others 18/3

WHARTON Paul William
Born: Newcastle, 26 July 1977
Height: 5'4" Weight: 9'9"
International Honours: E: Yth
The shortest player to have represented Hull City since Alan Shaw in 1964, Paul has already made a big impression with the Boothferry faithful. Enjoyed a tremendous debut against Bournemouth (one of four 18 year olds in the City XI) just a month after being released by Leeds United last February. Right footed, and a confident performer, he has good vision which enables considered distribution.
Leeds U (From trainee on 27/6/94)
Hull C (Free on 13/2/96) FL 7+2

WHELAN Noel
Born: Leeds, 30 December 1974
Height: 6'2" Weight: 12.3
Club Honours: FAYC '93
International Honours: E: U21-2; Yth (UEFAC '93)
Purchased from Leeds last December for a club record, Noel made an impressive start to his Coventry career, scoring seven goals in his first 11 games, including spectacular strikes at home to Southampton and at West Ham. Has a high level of skill, especially when dribbling, his first touch is excellent and he holds the ball up well. Scored several goals in one-to-one situations by keeping the ball long enough for the goalies to commit themselves, before chipping over them. After four games without a goal, in March he scored a superb winner against Liverpool and has undoubtedly been a superb acquisition for the Sky Blues.
Leeds U (From trainee on 5/3/93) PL 28+20/7 FLC 3+2/1 FAC 2 Others 3
Coventry C (£2,000,000 on 16/12/95) PL 21/8 FAC 3/1

WHELAN Philip (Phil) James
Born: Stockport, 7 March 1972
Height: 6'4" Weight: 14.1
International Honours: E: U21-3
The towering central defender signed by Middlesbrough from Ipswich too late to take part in Boro's division one championship run-in 1994-95, made his debut as substitute in the club's opening Premier League game at Arsenal. Following that, however, he remained on the bench until October, when introduced for his full debut against Manchester United, after which he was unlucky to be sidelined with a jaw injury. He came back into contention in the New Year, only to be sent off at Southampton in January, before his stop-start season was climaxed by a vital equalising goal at

Tottenham, five minutes from time in April. Having overcome all the setbacks, Phil is expected to be right up there in 1996-97.
Ipswich T (From juniors on 2/7/90) F/PL 76+6/2 FLC 6+1 FAC 3+1 Others 1
Middlesbrough (£300,000 on 3/3/95) PL 9+4/1 FLC 3 FAC 3

WHELAN Ronald (Ronnie) Andrew
Born: Dublin, 25 September 1961
Height: 5'9" Weight: 11.0
Club Honours: Div 1 '82, '83, '84, '86, '88, '90; FLC '82, '83, '84; EC '84; FAC '86, '89
International Honours: Ei: 53; U21-1; B-1; Yth; Sch
A serious knee injury, which now threatens to end his career, meant that the player/manager only appeared in one game in Southend's midfield last season. However, with the signing of players, such as Mike Marsh, Paul Byrne and Mark McNally, Ronnie proved that his ability on the field will stand him in good stead as a manager, especially with the club playing good, Liverpool-style passing football.
Liverpool (Free from Home Farm on 1/10/79) F/PL 351+11/46 FLC 46+4/14 FAC 40+1/7 Others 38+2/6
Southend U (Free on 9/9/94) FL 34/1 FAC 1

WHELAN Spencer Randall
Born: Liverpool, 17 September 1971
Height: 6'2" Weight: 13.0
A pacy Chester central defender, now in his sixth year at the club, Spencer well and truly put his broken leg experience behind him in 1995-96, producing many eye-catching performances and continuing to attract the scouts. Has now made over 150 FL appearances for City.
Chester C (Free from Liverpool juniors on 3/4/90) FL 143+12/3 FLC 9+1/2 FAC 6+1 Others 3+1

WHISTON Peter Michael
Born: Widnes, 4 January 1968
Height: 6'1" Weight: 12.4
Shrewsbury Town central defender. Signed in the autumn of 1995 from Southampton, initially on loan, his form soon persuaded the club to make it permanent. Forged an almost instant partnership with Dave Walton, showing skill to go with his distribution and strong head work, and brought some much needed organisation to the defence. This has already proved to be a good signing and there are high hopes for Peter in the coming season.
Plymouth Arg (Signed on 17/12/87) FL 4+6 FAC 1 Others 1
Torquay U (Free on 21/3/90) FL 39+1/1 FLC 5/1 FAC 1 Others 6
Exeter C (£25,000 on 13/9/91) FL 85/7 FLC 7 FAC 10 Others 10/1
Southampton (£30,000 on 10/8/94) PL 0+1
Shrewsbury T (Signed on 11/9/95) FL 28/2 FAC 5/2 Others 6

WHITBREAD Adrian Richard
Born: Epping, 22 October 1971
Height: 6'2" Weight: 11.13
The young West Ham centre half failed to establish himself at Upton Park in 1995-96, mainly due to the outstanding presence of Marc Rieper and Slaven Bilic, making just two appearances from the bench. However,

earlier, in November, Adrian had spent an extended loan period at Portsmouth, during which time he forged an impressive partnership with Guy Butters. Strong and uncompromising, his height was used to good advantage with Pompey.
Leyton Orient (From trainee on 13/11/89) FL 125/2 FLC 10+1 FAC 11/1 Others 8
Swindon T (£500,000 on 29/7/93) P/FL 35+1/1 FAC 2
West Ham U (£650,000 on 17/8/94) PL 3+7 FLC 2+1 FAC 1
Portsmouth (Loaned on 9/11/95) FL 13

WHITE David
Born: Manchester, 30 October 1967
Height: 6'1" Weight: 12.9
International Honours: E: 1; B-2; U21-6; Yth
Following just three starts from seven appearances for Leeds in 1995-96, the former England striker arrived at Sheffield United on loan last November in order to play some first team football and regain his fitness. Although his early performances were unconvincing, the change of management convinced him to make the move permanent a month later and he played a strong part in the resurgence of the club. His commitment to the cause was proved by the postponement of an operation for a persistent groin problem, and playing while not fully fit, until the Blades were mathematically safe from relegation. Hopefully, he should start this season fully fit and be a threat to any defence from his wide-right raiding.
Manchester C (From apprentice on 7/11/85) F/PL 273+12/79 FLC 24+2/11 FAC 22/4 Others 9/2
Leeds U (£2,000,000 on 22/12/93) PL 28+14/9 FLC 1 FAC 6/1 Others 1+1
Sheffield U (Signed on 17/11/95) FL 24+4/7 FAC 3

Devon White

WHITE Devon Winston
Born: Nottingham, 2 March 1964
Height: 6'3" Weight: 14.0
Club Honours: Div 3 '90; AIC '95

Beanpole Watford striker who was signed from Notts County last February, following a burst of 15 goals in 18 games earlier in the season. Looked ungainly at times, but was a willing target man, dominating in the air, and difficult to dispossess or police in the penalty area. Towards the end of the campaign, Devon struck up a promising partnership with David Connolly and scored some important goals.

Lincoln C (From Arnold Kingswell on 14/12/84) FL 21+8/4 Others 2+1/2 (Free to Boston U in October 1986)
Bristol Rov (Free on 21/8/87) FL 190+12/53 FLC 9/2 FAC 10/3 Others 19/2
Cambridge U (£100,000 on 28/3/92) FL 15+7/4 FLC 4/1 FAC 1 Others 1/1
Queens Park R (£100,000 on 26/1/93) PL 16+10/9 FLC 1+1
Notts Co (£110,000 on 23/12/94) FL 34+6/15 FLC 4/6 FAC 2+1/2 Others 4/1
Watford (£100,000 on 16/2/96) FL 9+7/4

WHITE Jason Gregory
Born: Meriden, 19 October 1971
Height: 6'2" Weight: 12.10

Striker. Having had a great season for Scarborough in 1994-95, he joined Northampton at the beginning of 1995-96. Although making a slow start, he soon established himself with his juggling and pace, becoming a great favourite with the crowd. His ability to ruffle a defence is ably complimented by his ball skills.

Derby Co (From trainee on 4/7/90)
Scunthorpe U (Free on 6/9/91) FL 44+24/16 FLC 2 FAC 3+3/1 Others 4+4/1
Darlington (Loaned on 20/8/93) FL 4/1
Scarborough (Free on 10/12/93) FL 60+3/20 FLC 2+1 FAC 5/1 Others 1
Northampton T (£35,000 on 15/6/95) FL 40+5/16 FLC 0+1 FAC 2 Others 3

WHITE Stephen (Steve) James
Born: Chipping Sodbury, 2 January 1959
Height: 5'10" Weight: 11.4
Club Honours: Div 2 '82

Steve again showed himself to be the classic centre forward last season. Cool, calm and deadly, he became the first Hereford player to score more than 30 in a season and four in one game, during a 5-2 home win over Cambridge, since Dixie McNeill. A class act, despite having to tolerate an array of niggling injuries throughout the campaign, and one of the main reasons for the club reaching the third division play offs.

Bristol Rov (Free from Mangotsfield on 11/7/77) FL 46+4/20 FLC 2/1 FAC 3/3
Luton T (£200,000 on 24/12/79) FL 63+9/25 FLC 3+1/1 FAC 2+1
Charlton Ath (£150,000 on 30/7/82) FL 29/12 FLC 2
Lincoln C (Loaned on 28/1/83) FL 2+1
Luton T (Loaned on 24/2/83) FL 4
Bristol Rov (£45,000 on 26/8/83) FL 89+12/24 FLC 8/2 FAC 7+1/2 Others 5+2/1
Swindon T (Free on 8/7/86) F/PL 200+44/83 FLC 21+8/11 FAC 9+2/2 Others 22+6/15
Hereford U (Free on 26/8/94) FL 70+6/44 FLC 6/4 FAC 6/4 Others 9+2/3

WHITE Thomas (Tom) Matthew
Born: Bristol, 26 January 1976
Height: 6'1" Weight: 13.6

A persistent thigh injury hampered the young central defender's progress to challenge for regular football with Bristol Rovers in 1995-96. However, following an operation, Tom is expected to be in serious contention for a first team place in the future.

Bristol Rov (From trainee on 13/7/94) FL 4+2 Others 0+1

WHITEHALL Steven (Steve) Christopher
Born: Bromborough, 8 December 1966
Height: 5'9" Weight: 10.11

Rochdale's top scorer for the fourth time in 1995-96, Steve again proved himself to be one of the best front runners in division three, in one purple patch scoring ten goals in 11 games. An ever present, he has now passed 200 league games for Rochdale and is currently third in the all-time scoring chart.

Rochdale (£20,000 from Southport on 23/7/91) FL 185+18/66 FLC 9+3/3 FAC 11+2/3 Others 14+1/10

Steve Whitehall

WHITEHEAD Philip Matthew
Born: Halifax, 17 December 1969
Height: 6'3" Weight: 13.7

Injury cost Phil his place in Oxford's goal in the opening few games of 1995-96, and with Tim Carter in good form, he had to wait on the bench before regaining the number one jersey he had held for the past two seasons. Keeping 11 clean sheets in the last 16 matches, he is a big, solid 'keeper who commands his area well and has a good kick.

Halifax T (From trainee on 1/7/88) FL 42 FLC 2 FAC 4 Others 4
Barnsley (£60,000 on 9/3/90) FL 16
Halifax T (Loaned on 7/3/91) FL 9
Scunthorpe U (Loaned on 29/11/91) FL 8 Others 2
Scunthorpe U (Loaned on 4/9/92) FL 8 FLC 2

Bradford C (Loaned on 19/11/92) FL 6 Others 4
Oxford U (£75,000 on 1/11/93) FL 111 FLC 4 FAC 11 Others 3

WHITEHOUSE Dane Lee
Born: Sheffield, 14 October 1970
Height: 5'9" Weight: 10.12

Local-born Sheffield United midfielder who survived the Howard Kendall revolution, despite an up and downer in 1995-96. Somehow managing to score against Ipswich, before being sent off following a controversial clash with Town defender, Maurico Taricco, which proved a costly loss, he also suffered a fractured rib against Huddersfield, which again disrupted his season. Was yet another United player to disappoint in his goals output, including missed penalties.

Sheffield U (From trainee on 1/7/89) F/PL 157+27/30 FLC 11+1/5 FAC 14+3/2 Others 3/2

WHITLOW Michael (Mike) William
Born: Northwich, 13 January 1968
Height: 6'0" Weight: 13.3
Club Honours: Div 2 '90, Div 1 '92

Trusty Leicester City left back. Scored winning goals last season, at home to Wolves and Norwich, courtesy of a rasping free kick in the televised home victory, while another fierce free kick pierced the Oldham rearguard in March. Avoided the injury and illness problems that have beset him in the past to turn in consistent performances, culminating in the Wembley first division play-off victory over Crystal Palace.

Leeds U (£10,000 from Witton A on 11/11/88) FL 62+15/4 FLC 4+1 FAC 14+4 Others 9
Leicester C (£250,000 on 27/3/92) F/PL 127+3/8 FLC 8/1 FAC 6 Others 14

WHITNEY Jonathan (Jon) David
Born: Nantwich, 23 December 1970
Height: 5'10" Weight: 12.3

Finding it difficult to establish himself at Huddersfield in 1995-96, despite being involved in the first team squad, Jon made just three starts before signing for Lincoln in October. At Sincil Bank, however, he proved to be a hard-tackling and enthusiastic left back, who also played a few games on the left side of midfield and looked effective going forward, scoring spectacular long-range goals against Fulham and Hereford.

Huddersfield T (£10,000 from Winsford, via Wigan Ath YTS and Skelmersdale, on 21/10/93) FL 17+1 FLC 0+1 Others 4/1
Wigan Ath (Loaned on 17/3/95) FL 12
Lincoln C (£20,000 on 31/10/95) FL 25+1/2 FAC 1 Others 3

WHITTAKER Stuart
Born: Liverpool, 2 January 1975
Height: 5'7" Weight: 9.6

A regular in the Bolton reserve side as on out-and-out winger, Stuart managed to make only one senior appearance last term, when coming on as a substitute in the Coca Cola Cup penalty defeat by Norwich at Burnden. Is sure to get more opportunities in the first division.

Bolton W (Free from Liverpool juniors on 14/5/93) FL 2+1 FLC 0+1

WHITTINGHAM Guy
Born: Evesham, 10 November 1964
Height: 5'10" Weight: 11.12

Despite not being in the Sheffield Wednesday team at the start of last season, and seemingly on his way out of Hillsborough, Guy had a very satisfying year. A well respected striker for all of his career, he took the switch to that of a hard-working midfielder in his stride, continuing to score at a useful rate. With age starting to tell against him, in the most competitive part of the pitch, he always gave of his best for the team, as one of the quieter members of the squad.

Portsmouth (Free from Yeovil on 9/6/89) FL 149+11/88 FLC 7+2/3 FAC 7+3/10 Others 9/3
Aston Villa (£1,200,000 on 1/8/93) PL 17+8/5 FLC 4+1/1 Others 2+1
Wolverhampton W (Loaned on 28/2/94) FL 13/8 FAC 1
Sheffield Wed (£700,000 on 21/12/94) PL 43+7/15 FLC 3+1/1 FAC 3+1

Guy Whittingham

WHITTLE Justin Phillip
Born: Derby, 18 March 1971
Height: 6'1" Weight: 12.12

The tall central defender featured a number of times on the substitutes' bench for Stoke in the 1995-96 season, before making his full debut in the great win at Luton Town during Easter week. Part of the squad on several occasions, and a committed defender who deserves to progress in the game, Justin was signed from Celtic by Lou Macari, the manager who had earlier taken him to the Glasgow club after buying him out of the army.

Glasgow Celtic (Free from Army during 1994 close season)
Stoke C (Free on 20/10/94) FL 7+1 Others 2

WHITTON Stephen (Steve) Paul
Born: East Ham, 4 December 1960
Height: 6'1" Weight: 13.7
Club Honours: Div 2 '92

Colchester's assistant manager, who, on the playing front, is an experienced striker and Layer Road crowd favourite. Had a nightmare season in 1995-96 with injuries, initially suffering cruciate and medial ligament damage in September, just as the goals had started to come. A remarkable recovery, and miraculous return to the first team in March, was quickly followed by a calf injury, taking him out of contention yet again.

Coventry C (From apprentice on 15/9/78) FL 64+10/21 FLC 3+2 FAC 3/2
West Ham U (£175,000 on 11/7/83) FL 35+4/6 FLC 6/2 FAC 1
Birmingham C (Loaned on 31/1/86) FL 8/2
Birmingham C (£60,000 on 28/8/86) FL 94+1/28 FLC 7+1/4 FAC 5 Others 3/1
Sheffield Wed (£275,000 on 3/3/89) FL 22+10/4 FLC 3/4 FAC 0+1 Others 0+1
Ipswich T (£150,000 on 11/1/91) F/PL 80+8/15 FLC 7+1/4 FAC 8+1/2 Others 4
Colchester U (£10,000 on 24/3/94) FL 54+2/14 FLC 4 FAC 4/2 Others 2+2

WHYTE Christopher (Chris) Anderson
Born: Islington, 2 September 1961
Height: 6'1" Weight: 13.0
Club Honours: Div 1 '92, Div 2 '95
International Honours: E: U21-4

Experienced central defender who can also play at left back. Unable to hold down a regular place at Birmingham last season, Chris was loaned out to struggling Premiership side, Coventry, keeping the England centre forward, Alan Shearer, under wraps in the club's 5-0 win over the champions, Blackburn, before returning to St Andrews. Released in March, and signed by Charlton on a 15 week short-term contract, he sat alongside Stuart Balmer in the centre of the defence as the club pushed for promotion, only to lose out at the play-off semi final stage to neighbouring Crystal Palace. Continues to be dangerous at corners and set pieces.

Arsenal (From apprentice on 24/12/79) FL 86+4/8 FLC 14 FAC 5 Others 3+1 (Free to Los Angeles Lazers during 1986 close season)
Crystal Palace (Loaned on 23/8/84) FL 13 FLC 4
West Bromwich A (Free on 25/8/88) FL 83+1/7 FLC 5/2 FAC 5 Others 2
Leeds U (£400,000 on 18/6/90) F/PL 113/5 FLC 14+1/1 FAC 8 Others 11
Birmingham C (£250,000 on 12/8/93) FL 68/1 FLC 12 FAC 4 Others 5+1
Coventry C (Loaned on 9/12/95) PL 1
Charlton Ath (Free on 11/3/96) FL 10+1 Others 2

WHYTE David Antony
Born: Greenwich, 20 April 1971
Height: 5'9" Weight: 10.7
Club Honours: Div 1 '94

Charlton striker who failed to recapture his devastating form of 1994-95. Lost his place through injury after the first six games last season and never picked up momentum, scoring only two goals, one of which was from the penalty spot. Quick off the mark, with a powerful shot, especially in the right foot, the Addicks will be looking for him to come good in 1996-97.

Crystal Palace (Free from Greenwich Borough on 15/2/89) FL 17+10/4 FLC 5+2/2 FAC 0+1 Others 0+3/1
Charlton Ath (Loaned on 26/3/92) FL 7+1/2
Charlton Ath (£450,000 on 5/7/94) FL 47+16/21 FLC 4/2 FAC 1+1/1 Others 0+2

WHYTE Derek
Born: Glasgow, 31 August 1968
Height: 5'11" Weight: 12.12
Club Honours: SPD '88; SC '88, '89; Div 1 '95
International Honours: S: 9; B-3; SU21-9; Yth; Sch

Excellent central defender whose partnership with Nigel Pearson and Steve Vickers made the Middlesbrough defence virtually water tight in the opening weeks of last season. Unfortunately, his appearances were reduced by two fairly long-term injuries, from October to December and again in January and February, his absence from the defence being a major factor in Boro's alarming collapse of confidence. Happily, fully recovered for the closing weeks, his polished displays helped to steer the side to safety and he was justly rewarded by a last minute inclusion in Scotland's team for the match against the USA and a place in the squad for the European Championships.

Glasgow Celtic (From juniors in 1985) SL 211+5/7 SLC 18+1 SC 26 Others 15/1
Middlesbrough (Signed on 1/8/92) F/PL 134+2/2 FLC 11 FAC 1+1 Others 6

WIDDRINGTON Thomas (Tommy)
Born: Newcastle, 1 October 1971
Height: 5'10" Weight: 11.12

The versatile Southampton player can always be relied upon to produce whole-hearted performances whether he is in midfield, at full back, or performing in the sweeper roll, which is perhaps his best position. Managed to get forward on enough occasions to score two goals last season, including the equaliser that preserved a home point against Leeds. A battler, Tommy does not give the ball away without a fight.

Southampton (From trainee on 10/5/90) F/PL 67+8/3 FLC 3+1 FAC 11
Wigan Ath (Loaned on 12/9/91) FL 5+1 FLC 2

WIGG Nathan Marlow
Born: Newport, 27 September 1974
Height: 5'9" Weight: 10.5

Very enthusiastic Cardiff midfielder with a biting tackle and competitive tendencies. Sadly, Nathan did not make the progress that was expected of him in 1995-96 and thus failed to command a regular place in the club's engine room.

Cardiff C (From trainee on 4/8/93) FL 40+18/1 FLC 3 FAC 1+2 Others 9+3

WILCOX Jason Malcolm
Born: Farnworth, 15 July 1971
Height: 5'10" Weight: 11.10
Club Honours: PL '95
International Honours: E: 1; B-1

Blackburn left-sided wide player with pace and the ability to raking angled cross. A hard worker, who tackles back, and a natural footballer who contributes to flowing movement, after cruciate ligament repairs he had to have further surgery for the removal of cysts, which delayed his re-appearance until last February. Within two weeks he damaged his left foot, before finally returning to remedy the club's problem that arose when he disappeared ten months earlier. Scored a superb headed goal against

Liverpool and two more at Nottingham Forest, prior to being called into the England squad for the game against Croatia after little first team football in 1995-96. The best was still to come as Jason won his first cap in the Hungary match, making an outstanding contribution to the 3-0 success.
Blackburn Rov (From trainee on 13/6/89) F/PL 148+12/22 FLC 13+1/1 FAC 11/1 Others 5

Jason Wilcox

WILCOX Russell (Russ)
Born: Hemsworth, 25 March 1964
Height: 6'0" Weight: 11.10
Club Honours: Div 4 '87; Div 3 '96
International Honours: E: SP-3
A central defender who was allowed to leave Doncaster after just four games last season, much to the disgust of their supporters, he brought a wealth of experience to the centre of Preston's defence, and also contributed one of the goals of the season with a match-winning chip over the Carlisle 'keeper in injury time of the first round FA Cup-tie. Always one to lead by example, he was elected to the award winning PFA divisional team for the second year in succession and also won a third division championship medal as North End swept to the title.
Doncaster Rov (Apprentice) FL 1
Northampton T (£15,000 from Frickley Ath on 30/6/86) FL 137+1/9 FLC 6 FAC 10 Others 8/1
Hull C (£120,000 on 6/8/90) FL 92+8/7 FLC 5 FAC 5/1 Others 5+1
Doncaster Rov (£60,000 on 30/7/93) FL 81/6 FLC 5/2 FAC 3 Others 3
Preston NE (Signed on 22/9/95) FL 27/1 FAC 1/1 Others 1

WILDER Christopher (Chris) John
Born: Stocksbridge, 23 September 1967
Height: 5'11" Weight: 12.8
The Rotherham skipper, until joining Notts County last January, during his stay at Millmoor, Chris not only proved what a fine right back he is, but also showed he could fill in as a sweeper and in midfield when required. Disappointingly, having been signed by County to replace the injured

Gary Mills, he himself was forced out by injury after just seven games, while a comeback in April was quickly aborted, forcing him to miss the play offs. Is a long throw expert and free kick specialist.
Southampton (From apprentice on 26/9/85)
Sheffield U (Free on 20/8/86) FL 89+4/1 FLC 8+1 FAC 7 Others 3
Walsall (Loaned on 2/11/89) FL 4 FAC 1 Others 2
Charlton Ath (Loaned on 12/10/90) FL 1
Charlton Ath (Loaned on 28/11/91) FL 2
Leyton Orient (Loaned on 27/2/92) FL 16/1 Others 1
Rotherham U (£50,000 on 30/7/92) FL 129+3/11 FLC 11 FAC 6+1/1 Others 6+1
Notts Co (£150,000 on 2/1/96) FL 9

WILKINS Dean Mark
Born: Hillingdon, 12 July 1962
Height: 5'10" Weight: 12.8
As a creative midfield player with Brighton, Dean had a well deserved pre-1995-96 benefit match when brother, Ray, brought Queens Park Rangers to the Goldstone. Is a stylish player who passes the ball well and dangerous from free kicks just outside the penalty area. Having come back from an enforced seven-match lay off during the season with knee ligament damage, he was released during the summer.
Queens Park R (From apprentice on 17/5/80) FL 1+5 FLC 1
Brighton & Hove A (Free on 4/8/83) FL 2 FAC 1 (Freed during 1984 close season)
Leyton Orient (Loaned on 22/3/84) FL 10
Brighton & Hove A (Free from PEC Zwolle on 28/7/87) FL 295+15/25 FLC 22/3 FAC 17+2 Others 21/3

WILKINS Raymond (Ray) Colin
Born: Hillingdon, 14 September 1956
Height: 5'8" Weight: 11.2
Club Honours: FAC '83; SPD '90
International Honours: E: 84; U23-2; U21-1; Yth; Sch
Into his second season as player/manager of QPR his performances on the pitch in 1995-96 were again invaluable, as he had a calming influence on those around him. Although restricting his appearances as the relegation battle gained momentum, he returned to the side over the Easter period, replacing the suspended Simon Barker, and played superbly. Despairingly, Rangers were ultimately relegated but the fans still feel Ray is the ideal man to manage the club. At the age of 39, is still a very stylish and experienced midfielder, equally adept at passing short or long.
Chelsea (From apprentice on 1/10/73) FL 176+3/30 FLC 6+1/2 FAC 10+1/2
Manchester U (£825,000 on 1/8/79) FL 158+2/7 FLC 14+1/1 FAC 10/1 Others 9/1 (£1,500,000 to AC Milan on 1/7/84)
Glasgow R (£250,000 from Paris St Germain on 1/11/87) SL 69+1/2 SLC 10/1 SC 8+1 Others 7
Queens Park R (Free on 30/11/89) F/PL 153+1/7 FLC 13 FAC 13/2 Others 2/1
Crystal Palace (Free on 26/5/94) PL 1
Queens Park R (Free on 17/11/94) PL 12+5 FLC 2+1 FAC 1

WILKINS Richard John
Born: Lambeth, 28 May 1965
Height: 6'0" Weight: 12.3
Club Honours: Div 3 '91
Leading by example, Richard impressed in

the middle of Hereford's midfield last season with his solid, reliable and hard-working displays, his pace often acting as the springboard for the attack. Sadly, he suffered a broken arm which put a stop to his spectacular long throws.
Colchester U (Free from Haverhill Rov on 20/11/86) FL 150+2/2 FLC 6 FAC 7+2/4 Others 9+3/3
Cambridge U (£65,000 on 25/7/90) FL 79+2/7 FLC 6 FAC 8+1 Others 9
Hereford U (Free on 20/7/94) FL 76+1/5 FLC 6 FAC 6 Others 8/2

WILKINSON Ian James
Born: Hull, 19 September 1977
Height: 6'2" Weight: 13.0
Ian, a tall, somewhat gangly centre back, who had also regularly been used in the centre forward role, and still a second year trainee, was one of five 18 year olds in the Hull City team when he made his debut in the vital relegation clash at Brighton last March and established his place when Gary Hobson moved to Brighton later that month. Genuinely impressive at a difficult time, he was awarded a full pro contract in April.
Hull C (Trainee) FL 8/1

WILKINSON Paul
Born: Louth, 30 October 1964
Height: 6'1" Weight: 12.4
Club Honours: CS '86; Div 1 '87, '95
International Honours: E: U21-4
Fearless Middlesbrough front runner, with 200 first team games behind him, his appearances in 1995-96 were curtailed by injuries and loan transfers to just five starts. His first spell on loan at Oldham in October saw him score twice in five games, although still recovering from a bad knee injury, while his next temporary transfers at Watford (December) and Luton (March) produced nothing other than further problems. Playing for Luton, after Watford had failed to sign their former player on a permanent basis, he broke a big toe in his third outing, thus bringing his season to an end. Adept at winning aerial battles to create chances for others.
Grimsby T (From apprentice on 8/11/82) FL 69+2/27 FLC 10/5 FAC 4+2/1
Everton (£250,000 on 23/3/85) FL 19+12/7 FLC 4+1/7 FAC 3/1 Others 6+2/1
Nottingham F (£200,000 on 26/3/87) FL 32+2/5 FLC 3/1 FAC 4+1/1/2 Others 1
Watford (£300,000 on 16/8/88) FL 133+1/52 FLC 4/1 FAC 8+1 Others 8/3
Middlesbrough (£550,000 on 16/8/91) F/PL 161+3/52 FLC 16/8 FAC 14/5 Others 5+1/4
Oldham Ath (Loaned on 26/10/95) FL 4/1 Others 1/1
Watford (Loaned on 1/12/95) FL 4
Luton T (Loaned on 28/3/96) FL 3

WILKINSON Stephen (Steve) John
Born: Lincoln, 1 September 1968
Height: 6'0" Weight: 11.6
Club Honours: Div 3 '96
Transferred from Mansfield during the 1995 close season, instead of scoring goals for Preston from Andy Saville's knockdowns, Steve performed more of a linking role between midfield and attack. Much of his running off the ball went unnoticed, but the space he created benefited the team's

attacking moves. His personal highlight, apart from winning a third division championship medal as North End swept to the title, was undoubtedly his hat trick against his former club. Proved to be a pacy, two-footed all-rounder.

Leicester C (From apprentice on 6/9/86) FL 5+4/1 FAC 1
Crewe Alex (Loaned on 8/9/88) FL 3+2/2
Mansfield T (£80,000 on 2/10/89) FL 214+18/83 FLC 13+1/4 FAC 10/2 Others 17/1
Preston NE (£90,000 on 15/6/95) FL 36+6/10 FLC 2 FAC 2/1 Others 2

WILLEMS Ron
Born: Epe, Holland, 20 September 1966
Height: 6'0" Weight: 11.13
Signed by Derby from Grasshoppers of Zurich during the 1995 close season, the former Ajax striker was brought to the Baseball Ground to play an attacking role just behind the front two strikers. Although suffering an achilles tendon injury after just two appearances, Ron came back to score three goals in as many games on his return and took over from Paul Simpson as the team's penalty taker. Played a slightly more withdrawn role as 1995-96 progressed, but proved to be a real bargain, despite having problems in dealing with the English language.

Derby Co (£300,000 from Grasshoppers, Zurich on 28/7/95) FL 31+2/11 FLC 2/1 FAC 1

WILLGRASS Alexandre (Alex) Paul
Born: Scarborough, 8 April 1976
Height: 5'10" Weight: 11.12
Alex, a combative midfielder now entering his third season as a professional with Scarborough, having originally started training with his hometown club at the age of 14, progressed, via youth and reserve sides, to finally make the breakthrough to first team football last season. Highly rated at the club, he was voted Scarborough's "Young Player of the Year".

Scarborough (From juniors on 4/7/94) FL 2+5 FLC 0+1 Others 0+2

WILLIAMS Adrian
Born: Reading, 16 August 1971
Height: 6'2" Weight: 12.6
Club Honours: Div 2 '94
International Honours: W: 7
A Welsh international and Reading club skipper, and a lynchpin in the Royals' defence in 1995-96, he continued to score goals from his centre back position and was unfortunate to miss the last seven games of the season with ligament damage to the left knee. Equally effective in midfield or up front, and regularly watched by Premier League clubs, Adrian is a player who would benefit from a higher grade of football. *Stop Press:* Reportedly signed for his former manager, Mark McGhee, a fee of £750,000 tempting him to Wolves at the end of June.

Reading (From trainee on 4/3/89) FL 191+5/14 FLC 16/1 FAC 16/2 Others 14/2

WILLIAMS Andrew (Andy)
Born: Birmingham, 29 July 1962
Height: 6'2" Weight: 12.0
Club Honours: Div 2 '90
Seven years after turning down a move to

Boothferry Park, Andy finally became a Hull City player following his surprise release by Rotherham during the 1994 close season. Initially sidelined by a troublesome calf strain, he moved into defence to become a genuine, and very impressive sweeper, as City employed a five-man rearguard. Cool, calm, and collected, he was astonishingly freed during the summer.

Coventry C (£20,000 from Solihull Borough on 24/7/85) FL 3+6 Others 0+1
Rotherham U (Signed on 16/10/86) FL 87/13 FLC 8 FAC 6 Others 5/2
Leeds U (£175,000 on 11/11/88) FL 25+21/3 FLC 3+3 FAC 2 Others 5+2/2
Port Vale (Loaned on 11/12/91) FL 5
Notts Co (£115,000 on 4/2/92) FL 32+7/2 FLC 3 FAC 1
Huddersfield T (Loaned on 13/9/93) FL 4+2
Rotherham U (Signed on 21/10/93) FL 51/2 FLC 2 FAC 3 Others 4
Hull C (Free on 19/7/95) FL 33+1 FLC 2 FAC 1 Others 2

WILLIAMS Carl Junior
Born: Cambridge, 14 January 1977
Height: 5'8" Weight: 12.10
A right-sided or central midfielder, who frequently played up front, Carl's first team appearances for Fulham in 1995-96 were mostly restricted to late substitutions and he was freed at the end of the season.

Fulham (From trainee on 1/7/95) FL 2+11 FAC 0+1 Others 0+1

WILLIAMS Darren
Born: Middlesbrough, 28 April 1977
Height: 5'10" Weight: 10.10
As a highly promising young York midfielder, Darren gained a lot of first team experience in 1995-96 and created a big impression during the first half of the season. It should hardly be surprising that a bright future is predicted for a lad who played his part in the downfall of Manchester United. Is an all-rounder who can play on either side, with good skills and vision.

York C (From trainee on 21/6/95) FL 16+3 FLC 4+1 FAC 1 Others 3/1

WILLIAMS David Peter
Born: Liverpool, 18 September 1968
Height: 6'0" Weight: 12.0
Cardiff City goalkeeper. Ever present in 1995-96, until losing his place to namesake Steve Williams, at Scunthorpe in mid-April, the ex-Burnley man proved to be a great favourite with the fans, before being released during the summer.

Oldham Ath (From trainee on 15/8/87)
Burnley (Signed on 23/3/88) FL 24 FLC 2 Others 2
Rochdale (Loaned on 2/9/91) FL 6 FLC 1
Cardiff C (Free on 12/8/94) FL 82 FLC 6 FAC 3 Others 11

WILLIAMS Dean Paul
Born: Lichfield, 5 January 1972
Height: 6'0" Weight: 12.8
Second choice Doncaster Rovers' goalkeeper to Perry Suckling for much of 1995-96, he was on a weekly contract for quite a long time. Eventually regained the first team jersey on Suckling's departure to South Africa, but now faces a battle from Gary O'Connor to retain it. Very agile and a good shot stopper.

Birmingham C (From trainee on 11/7/90) FL 4 FAC 1 (Free to Tamworth in March 1992)
Brentford (£2,000 on 8/8/93) FL 6+1
Doncaster Rov (Free on 12/8/94) FL 50+2 FLC 1 FAC 1 Others 5

WILLIAMS Gareth James
Born: Isle of Wight, 12 March 1967
Height: 5'10" Weight: 11.8
Having initially come to Northampton as a striker, he was moved to midfield and finished last season as an emergency left back, prior to being released in the summer. Dependable in whatever position he is selected for, Gareth can justifiably be termed a utility player.

Aston Villa (£30,000 from Gosport Borough on 9/1/88) FL 6+6 FLC 0+1 FAC 2 Others 0+1
Barnsley (£200,000 on 6/8/91) FL 23+11/6 FLC 1 FAC 1+1 Others 1+1
Hull C (Loaned on 17/9/92) FL 4
Hull C (Loaned on 6/1/94) FL 16/2
Wolverhampton W (Free on 23/8/94)
Bournemouth (Free on 16/9/94) FL 0+1
Northampton T (Free on 27/9/94) FL 38+12/1 FLC 2 FAC 2 Others 5+1

WILLIAMS David Geraint
Born: Treorchy, 5 January 1962
Height: 5'7" Weight: 12.6
Club Honours: Div 2 '87
International Honours: W: 13; U21-2; Yth
A hard-tackling, competitive Ipswich and Welsh international midfielder, who is always in the thick of things, breaking up attacks as well as setting them up with simple passing movements, Geraint enhanced his reputation even further last season, missing just six games. He was never happier than when battling for midfield supremacy, especially in the derby games against his old team, Norwich, and when scoring only his second goal for the club, after running half the length of the pitch at Reading.

Bristol Rov (From apprentice on 12/1/80) FL 138+3/8 FLC 14 FAC 9+2/2 Others 5
Derby Co (£40,000 on 29/3/85) FL 276+1/9 FLC 26+1/1 FAC 17 Others 11
Ipswich T (£650,000 on 1/7/92) P/FL 151/2 FLC 11+1 FAC 13 Others 2

WILLIAMS John Nelson
Born: Birmingham, 11 May 1968
Height: 6'2" Weight: 12.4
As Wycombe's record signing from Coventry last September, he struggled initially as a striker, with just one goal in his first 14 starts. However, after a period on the bench, he returned to the first team as a much improved player, scoring a spectacular hat trick against Stockport and proving a real handful to every defence, before an ankle injury in March saw him miss more games, prior to ending the season on good form. Blessed with great speed, and a thumping shot, the supporters especially relished his exciting runs.

Swansea C (£5,000 from Cradley T on 19/8/91) FL 36+3/11 FLC 2/1 FAC 3 Others 1
Coventry C (£250,000 on 1/7/92) PL 66+14/11 FLC 4 FAC 2
Swansea C (Loaned on 2/7/94) FL 6+1/2
Notts Co (Loaned on 7/10/94) FL 3+2/2
Stoke C (Loaned on 23/12/94) FL 1+3
Wycombe W (£150,000 on 15/9/95) FL 23+6/7 FLC 2 FAC 1 Others 2

WILLIAMS Lee
Born: Birmingham, 3 February 1973
Height: 5'7" Weight: 11.13
International Honours: E: Yth
Capable of playing in midfield or at right back, Lee had a disappointing season for Peterborough in 1995-96. A very useful passer, and able to use both feet to advantage, he started well enough but was dropped after a 5-1 defeat at Rotherham and, although coming back and working hard, with the side struggling, his composure naturally suffered. Released during the summer, he is too good a player to languish for long.
Aston Villa (From trainee on 26/1/91)
Shrewsbury T (Loaned on 8/11/92) FL 2+1 FAC 1+1/1 Others 2
Peterborough U (Signed on 23/3/94) FL 83+8/1 FLC 4+1 FAC 5+1/1 Others 7

Lee Williams (Peterborough U)

WILLIAMS Lee
Born: Harold Wood, 13 March 1977
Height: 5'10" Weight: 10.10
Picked up by Leyton Orient from non-league football during the 1995 close season, Lee proved to be a pacy forward, who could operate on either flank with no little skill. Given his first team debut in the AWS competition against Shrewsbury in November, he appeared on four more occasions before being released, although the club still hold his registration.
Leyton Orient (Signed from Purfleet on 3/7/95) FL 1+2 FAC 1 Others 1

WILLIAMS Marc Lloyd
Born: Bangor, 8 February 1973
Height: 5'11" Weight: 12.0
Bought as a goalscorer, the young Welshman failed to break into the Stockport attack last season, largely because his inexperience failed to match his undoubted pace and directness. He finally became the latest in a long line of Stockport wingers

who ended up as a left back, although only as a stand in for the injured Lee Todd.
Stockport Co (£10,000 from Bangor on 23/3/95) FL 12+6/1 FLC 1+2 Others 0+1

WILLIAMS Mark Frank
Born: Johannesburg, South Africa, 11 August 1966
Height: 5'10" Weight: 11.3
International Honours: South Africa: 12
Signing from RWD Molenbeck last September, the striker got two early goals for Wolves, but often played wider than he would have liked and after being involved in six successive games, he was then used only occasionally. Representing South Africa in the African Nations Cup, scoring in the 1-0 win over Angola, playing in another game, and being a substitute for the final against Tunisia, Mark was the hero, coming on after 65 minutes, then scoring with a header and a left-foot shot, as his country won 2-0. Excellent as a target man, with timely lay offs, he came back into the side after being in the wilderness for 22 matches, lasting just 26 minutes of a physical encounter against Crystal Palace. However, to earn a work permit he had to appear in 75 per cent of the games he was available for, something he was unable to do.
Wolverhampton W (£300,000 from RWD Molenbeek on 20/9/95) FL 5+7/1 FLC 2+1/1 FAC 1

WILLIAMS Mark Stuart
Born: Hyde, 28 September 1970
Height: 6'0" Weight: 13.0
Club Honours: Div 3 '94
This commanding centre half was John Duncan's only 1995 close season Chesterfield signing and turned out to be a steal. Mark got on with it in an unostentatious way, but was no less effective for that, being the best defender at a club which places much emphasis on defending. The warm welcome he got from Shrewsbury fans on returning to the Gay Meadow was particularly pleasing to hear. Dangerous at set pieces with his heading ability.
Shrewsbury T (Free from Newtown on 27/3/92) FL 96+6/3 FLC 7+1 FAC 6 Others 6/1
Chesterfield (£50,000 on 7/8/95) FL 42/3 FLC FAC 2 Others 5

WILLIAMS Martin Keith
Born: Luton, 12 July 1973
Height: 5'9" Weight: 11.12
Nippy Reading front player signed on a free transfer from Luton during the 1995-96 close season. Had extended spells in the Royals' first team, both early and late on in the campaign, but never really showed until a proposed transfer to Peterborough fell through, coming back to perform brilliantly and scoring a vital goal against Wolves. Signed a new two year contract with the club during the summer of 1996.
Luton T (Free from Leicester C juniors on 13/9/91) FL 12+28/2 FLC 1 FAC 0+1 Others 2+1
Colchester U (Loaned on 9/3/95) FL 3
Reading (Free on 13/7/95) FL 11+4/1 FLC 0+1

WILLIAMS Michael (Mike) Anthony
Born: Bradford, 21 November 1969
Height: 5'10" Weight: 11.6

A young Sheffield Wednesday utility player, who started on the wing as a junior but now seems to be regarded as a midfielder, Mike has yet to make the big breakthrough and be considered a first team squad regular. Last season should have given him his big chance under a new manager, but, sadly, a broken leg after a few substitute and full appearances early on, left him having to start up again. Although back to fitness, he must be hoping he can make up for lost time in 1996-97.
Sheffield Wed (Free from Maltby Colliery on 13/2/91) F/PL 16+6/1 FLC 2+2 Others 1
Halifax T (Loaned on 18/12/92) FL 9/1

WILLIAMS Paul Andrew
Born: Sheffield, 8 September 1963
Height: 6'3" Weight: 14.6
International Honours: NI: 1; Yth
The big, veteran centre forward never really figured in Rochdale manager, Mick Docherty's starting plans in 1995-96, though he did appear quite frequently from the bench, until being loaned to Doncaster in March. Scored on his debut two days later, and played twice more, prior to returning to Spotland and being released during the summer.
Preston NE (Free from Nuneaton Borough on 18/12/86) FL 1 Others 1
Carlisle U (Free on 17/7/87)
Newport Co (Free on 12/8/87) FL 26/3 FLC 2 Others 2
Sheffield U (£17,000 on 7/3/88) FL 6+2 Others 2+1
Hartlepool U (Free on 10/10/89) FL 7+1 FAC 1 Others 1
Stockport Co (Free on 23/8/90) FL 24/14 FLC 2/1 Others 3/1
West Bromwich A (£250,000 on 28/3/91) FL 26+18/5 FLC 1+1 FAC 1+2/1 Others 1+2/1
Coventry C (Loaned on 23/10/92) PL 1+1
Stockport Co (£25,000 on 12/1/93) FL 6+10/3 Others 5/1
Rochdale (Free on 5/11/93) FL 22+15/7 FLC 2 FAC 1 Others 2+1
Doncaster Rov (Loaned on 28/3/96) FL 2+1/1

WILLIAMS Paul Anthony
Born: Stratford, 16 August 1965
Height: 5'7" Weight: 10.9
Club Honours: FLC '91; Div 1 '94
International Honours: E: B-3; U21-4
Unable to make a mark at Crystal Palace, Paul returned to Charlton on a free transfer last September, having been away for five years. A striker, whose main asset has been his speed and shooting power, he only made spasmodic appearances, never showing the kind of form that had made him so popular in his previous spell at the club, and was allowed to go on loan to Torquay in March. Played out the final weeks of the campaign with United, before returning and being released during the summer.
Charlton Ath (£12,000 from Woodford T on 23/2/87) FL 74+8/23 FLC 6/3 FAC 6+1/3
Brentford (Loaned on 20/10/87) FL 7/3 Others 1/3
Sheffield Wed (£700,000 on 15/8/90) F/PL 78+15/25 FLC 10+3/3 FAC 3+2 Others 3
Crystal Palace (Signed on 11/9/92) F/PL 38+8/7 FLC 4+1 Others 2/2
Sunderland (Loaned on 19/1/95) FL 3
Birmingham C (Loaned on 13/3/95) FL 8+3 Others 1/1
Charlton Ath (Free on 29/9/95) FL 2+7
Torquay U (Loaned on 28/3/96) FL 9

WILLIAMS Paul Darren
Born: Burton, 26 March 1971
Height: 6'0" Weight: 14.3
International Honours: E: U21-6

Hard-tackling Coventry midfield player who can also play in the centre of the back four. Signed in the 1995 close season from Derby County, in a deal which took Sean Flynn in the opposite direction, he played in the centre of the defence for the first half of the campaign and after looking an excellent buy early on he lost his form. Sent off for handball in the 3-3 home draw against Wimbledon, on his return to the side, Paul moved to midfield. He performed well and City's midfield always looked tighter when he was present. Possesses a fierce shot and, although he only scored twice, he threatened more. Endeared himself to the fans with his wholehearted, never-say-die approach and was voted "Player of the Year".

Derby Co (From trainee on 13/7/89) FL 153+7/26 FLC 10+2/2 FAC 8/3 Others 14+1/2
Lincoln C (Loaned on 9/11/89) FL 3 FAC 2 Others 1
Coventry C (£975,000 on 6/8/95) PL 30+2/2 FLC 4/1 FAC 1

WILLIAMS Paul Richard Curtis
Born: Leicester, 11 September 1969
Height: 5'7" Weight: 10.7

A speedy left back signed from Coventry in the 1995 close season, Paul proved a valuable asset for Plymouth, especially as an ever present, with his ability to attack as well as defend. Performed exceptionally well against his old club in the FA Cup when he was made captain for the day and was later voted into the PFA third division team, a well deserved honour.

Leicester C (From trainee on 1/7/88)
Stockport Co (Free on 5/7/89) FL 61+9/4 FLC 3 FAC 4 Others 7+5/1
Coventry C (£150,000 on 12/8/93) PL 8+6 FLC 1+1 FAC 3
West Bromwich A (Loaned on 19/11/93) FL 5
Huddersfield T (Loaned on 17/11/94) FL 2 Others 1
Huddersfield T (Loaned on 17/3/95) FL 7
Plymouth Arg (£50,000 on 10/8/95) FL 46/2 FLC 2 FAC 3 Others 4/1

Paul Williams (Plymouth Arg)

WILLIAMS Ryan Neill
Born: Mansfield, 31 August 1978
Height: 5'5" Weight: 9.6
International Honours: E: Yth

This striker is probably the smallest player currently playing and is still a first year apprentice. On his full debut for Mansfield last season versus the league leaders, he won the "Man of the Match" award for his skilful and courageous performance against very physical odds. A tricky goalscoring type, he was drafted into the England U17 team in April and may develop better as an attacking midfielder as time goes on.

Mansfield T (Trainee) FL 5+5/3

WILLIAMS Steven (Steve) David
Born: Aberystwyth, 16 October 1974
Height: 6'3" Weight: 12.12
International Honours: W: Yth

Goalkeeper. In his third season at Cardiff after being released by Coventry, ironically he is now re-united with ex-boss, Phil Neal. Made only four appearances for the senior side in 1995-96, having displaced his namesake, David Williams (no relation), at Scunthorpe, and, in giving a solid display, continued for the remainder of the league programme.

Cardiff C (Free from Coventry C juniors on 13/8/93) FL 28 FAC 1 Others 5+1

WILLIAMS Steven (Steve) Robert
Born: Sheffield, 3 November 1975
Height: 6'1" Weight: 12.0

The young striker began last season as part of the Lincoln first team squad, but was one of a number of inexperienced players dropped when John Beck became manager. Had a two month loan spell at Spalding before joining Peterborough, who took over the remaining four months of his contract. Ended 1995-96 on loan at Cambridge City, prior to being released.

Lincoln C (From trainee on 11/6/94) FL 8+9/2 FAC 0+1 Others 0+2
Peterborough U (Free on 26/2/96) FL 0+3

WILLIAMSON Daniel (Danny) Alan
Born: West Ham, 5 December 1973
Height: 5'11" Weight: 12.3

Danny had an outstanding season for West Ham in 1995-96, scoring against Leeds on the opening day and his influence on the team from central midfield growing stronger with each game played. Was the most improved player on the staff, his run from the Hammers' penalty area to thread the ball home at Bolton could possibly have been acclaimed as one of the goals of the season. With a real football brain to go with good engines and enjoying the passing game, he is a real comer.

West Ham U (From trainee on 3/7/92) PL 34+2/5 FLC 0+1 FAC 3
Doncaster Rov (Loaned on 8/10/93) FL 10+3/1 FAC 2/2 Others 1

WILLIS James (Jimmy) Anthony
Born: Liverpool, 12 July 1968
Height: 6'2" Weight: 12.4
Club Honours: GMVC '90

The popular right-footed central defender was a regular choice for Leicester at the start

of last season, before suffering a groin injury which kept him out from October onwards. Asked for a transfer, due to the desire of his family to return to Merseyside area, before briefly re-appearing during March. Looked set to join Burnley, but the deal fell through on transfer deadline day.

Halifax T (Free from Blackburn Rov juniors on 21/8/86)
Stockport Co (Free on 30/12/87) FL 10
Darlington (£12,000 on 24/3/88) FL 90/6 FLC 5 FAC 5 Others 6/1
Leicester C (£100,000 on 20/12/91) F/PL 58+2/3 FLC 4+1 FAC 4 Others 5+1
Bradford C (Loaned on 26/3/92) FL 9/1

WILLIS Roger Christopher
Born: Sheffield, 17 June 1967
Height: 6'2" Weight: 12.0
Club Honours: GMVC '91
International Honours: E: SP-1

Injury reduced the 1995-96 season for "Harry", with his Southend appearances limited to a short run up front in a team that was severely weakened by injury. Released during the summer, his aerial ability was excellent, but he was let down on occasions by his control, something which will improve with better match fitness and an obvious change of club.

Grimsby T (Signed on 20/7/89) FL 1+8 FLC 0+1
Barnet (£10,000 on 1/8/90) FL 39+5/13 FLC 2 FAC 5+1/3 Others 1+4/1
Watford (£175,000 on 6/10/92) FL 30+6/2 FAC 1
Birmingham C (£150,000 on 31/12/93) FL 12+7/5 FAC 0+1
Southend U (Signed on 16/9/94) FL 30+1/7 FAC 1 Others 1

Clive Wilson

WILSON Clive Euclid Aklana
Born: Manchester, 13 November 1961
Height: 5'7" Weight: 10.0
Club Honours: Div 2 '89

Signed by Spurs on a free transfer from QPR in the summer of 1995, apparently as cover for the full back positions, Clive established himself as a regular first choice on either flank and played in over half of the available games in 1995-96. An accurate crosser of the ball, who enjoys taking on players, he demonstrated great confidence on the ball and an eagerness to join the attack, scoring an impressive individual goal against Wolves in the fourth round of the FA Cup, bringing the ball from deep in his own half and finishing with a low, powerful drive to open his account for Tottenham. Always aware of his team mates' positioning, and consistent to a fault, his move to White Hart Lane has merely confirmed Gerry Francis' good judgement.

Manchester C (From juniors on 8/12/79) FL 96+2/9 FLC 10/2 FAC 2 Others 5
Chester C (Loaned on 16/9/82) FL 21/2
Chelsea (£250,000 on 19/3/87) FL 68+13/5 FLC 3+3 FAC 4 Others 10+2
Manchester C (Loaned on 19/3/87) FL 11
Queens Park R (£450,000 on 4/7/90) F/PL 170+2/12 FLC 16/1 FAC 8/1 Others 2+1
Tottenham H (Free on 12/6/95) PL 28 FLC 3 FAC 4+1/1

WILSON Kevin James
Born: Banbury, 18 April 1961
Height: 5'7" Weight: 11.4
Club Honours: Div 2 '89; FMC '90
International Honours: NI: 42

Even at the age of 35, Kevin incredibly played in all 56 league and cup matches for Walsall last season, having yet to miss a game since joining the club as player/coach two years earlier. A skilful, brave and opportunist striker, he is now just three short of 200 goals in a career that began with Derby in 1979. Also continued to be selected for Northern Ireland.

Derby Co (£20,000 from Banbury U on 21/12/79) FL 106+16/30 FLC 8+3/8 FAC 8/3
Ipswich T (£100,000 on 5/1/85) FL 94+4/34 FLC 8/8 FAC 10/3 Others 7/4
Chelsea (£335,000 on 25/6/87) FL 124+28/42 FLC 10+2/4 FAC 7+1/1 Others 14+5/8
Notts Co (£225,000 on 27/3/92) FL 58+11/3 FLC 3+1 FAC 2 Others 5+1
Bradford C (Loaned on 13/1/94) FL 5
Walsall (Free on 4/8/94) FL 88/31 FLC 6/3 FAC 9/5 Others 5/1

WILSON Paul Anthony
Born: Bradford, 2 August 1968
Height: 5'11" Weight: 11.10

Transferred to Scunthorpe during the 1995 close season, having lost his place in the York City side the previous season, Paul quickly settled down at left back, showing improved form throughout 1995-96. The provider of deep crosses and an occasional long-range effort on goal, he also showed sound defensive qualities, his tackling often catching the eye.

Huddersfield T (From apprentice on 12/6/86) FL 15 FLC 1
Norwich C (£30,000 on 23/7/87)
Northampton T (£30,000 on 12/2/88) FL 132+9/6 FLC 10/1 FAC 7 Others 6+3
Halifax T (£30,000 on 19/12/91) FL 45/7 FLC 2 FAC 1 Others 2
Burnley (Signed on 1/2/93) FL 31 FAC 0+1
York C (Signed on 6/10/94) FL 21+1 FAC 2 Others 1
Scunthorpe U (Signed on 9/8/95) FL 40/1 FLC 2 FAC 3 Others 2

WILSON Paul Robert
Born: Forest Gate, 26 September 1964
Height: 5'9" Weight: 11.4
Club Honours: GMVC '91

An uncompromising midfielder, he went goal crazy last term when scoring Barnet's winners against champions elect, Preston, both home and away, to earn the club six points. Unfortunately, lost his place at the end of the season due to injury, but is bound to return shortly.

Barnet (Signed from Barking on 1/3/88) FL 130+7/11 FLC 6 FAC 16+1 Others 8+2

WILSON Stephen (Steve) Lee
Born: Hull, 24 April 1974
Height: 5'10" Weight: 10.7

Became Hull City's first choice goalkeeper last season after Alan Fettis became embroiled in a summer contract wrangle. Responded in magnificent fashion, with a string of fine displays, including a vital penalty save in the win against Blackpool. The team's continuing struggles led to a loss of confidence and he was replaced by young Roy Carroll, but still a youngster himself, he has the spirit and ability to bounce back.

Hull C (From trainee on 13/7/92) FL 79 FLC 7 FAC 5 Others 7

WINDASS Dean
Born: Hull, 1 April 1969
Height: 5'10" Weight: 12.3

Resumed 1995-96 in the strikers role and began in sparkling form, notably with two goals in Hull's Coca Cola Cup win at Carlisle. A knee ligament problem curtailed his involvement, then his form suffered dramatically with the on-off saga of his proposed switch to Norwich City. Once that was officially off, "Deano" returned to his irresistible best before earning a £700,000 move north of the border to Aberdeen.

Hull C (Free from North Ferriby U on 24/10/91) FL 173+3/57 FLC 11/4 FAC 7 Others 12/3

WINSTANLEY Mark Andrew
Born: St Helens, 22 January 1968
Height: 6'1" Weight: 12.7
Club Honours: AMC '89

Much experienced centre back. Often the most reliable unit of a sometimes shaky defence, Mark's speed and sureness in the tackle rescued Burnley on numerous occasions during 1995-96. His lapses tend to be spectacular, but they were rare, and his place in the Claret's line up seems as safe as ever.

Bolton W (From trainee on 22/7/86) FL 215+5/3 FLC 19+1 FAC 19 Others 26/3
Burnley (Signed on 5/8/94) FL 89/5 FLC 7 FAC 6 Others 4

WINTER Steven (Steve) David
Born: Bristol, 26 October 1973
Height: 5'7" Weight: 10.3

A bargain buy from non-league, Taunton Town, early last season, Steve almost immediately came into the Torquay side at right back and showed enough to suggest that he still has a bright future in the game, despite being released by Walsall two years earlier. Is equally at home on either flank.

Walsall (From trainee on 13/3/92) FL 14+4 Others 3 (Free to Newport, IoW on 30/6/93)
Torquay U (£10,000 from Taunton T on 25/8/95) FL 36 FLC 1 FAC 1 Others 1

WINTERBURN Nigel
Born: Nuneaton, 11 December 1963
Height: 5'10" Weight: 11.4
Club Honours: Div 1 '89, '91; FAC '93; FLC '93; ECWC '94
International Honours: E: 2; B-3; U21-1; Yth

Fierce-tackling Arsenal left back who, for once, had an injury-free season in 1995-96, missing just three games. Extremely competititve, and just like his full back partner, Lee Dixon, a fixture in the Gunners' defence for nearly a decade, his experience enabled him to revel in his new wing/back role later on in the campaign. He even scored twice from open play against Wimbledon, his former club, and Sheffield Wednesday, and looks good for a few more years yet.

Birmingham C (From apprentice on 14/8/81)
Wimbledon (Free on 22/9/83) FL 164+1/8 FLC 13 FAC 12 Others 2
Arsenal (£407,000 on 26/5/87) F/PL 307+1/7 FLC 42/3 FAC 31 Others 30

Dennis Wise

WISE Dennis Frank
Born: Kensington, 15 December 1966
Height: 5'6" Weight: 9.5
Club Honours: FAC '88
International Honours: E: 12; B-3; U21-1

Inspirational skipper who covers every blade of grass in Chelsea's cause. An effervescent, hard-tackling character, who can spray the ball around accurately in midfield, he is comfortable dribbling down either flank where he can cross the ball on to a sixpence with either foot. A penalty and free kick expert, who packs a great right-footed shot, he scored an absolute belter against Southampton at the Dell from 30 yards. Has been a regular in Terry Venables' England squads over the past two years, his versatility making him a very handy player to have around, but, despite that, Dennis failed to make the final 22 for Euro '96.

Wimbledon (Free from Southampton juniors on 28/3/85) FL 127+8/27 FLC 14 FAC 11/3 Others 5
Chelsea (£1,600,000 on 3/7/90) F/PL 184+3/40 FLC 21/6 FAC 18/3 Others 10/3

WITHE Christopher (Chris)

Born: Liverpool, 25 September 1962
Height: 5'10" Weight: 11.12
Club Honours: Div 3 '85, '94

A Shrewsbury left back, whose commitment and enjoyment from the game is always evident, Chris continued to get forward in 1995-96 and, as always, was an effective creator from midfield forrays. Released during the summer, the fans will be disappointed not to be able to enjoy his celebratory crow dance in the future.

Newcastle U (From apprentice on 10/10/80) FL 2
Bradford C (Free on 1/6/83) FL 141+2/2 FLC 14 FAC 7 Others 6
Notts Co (£50,000 on 2/10/87) FL 80/3 FLC 4 FAC 5 Others 12/1
Bury (£40,000 on 31/7/89) FL 22+9/1 FLC 2+2 Others 0+3
Chester C (Loaned on 18/10/90) FL 2
Mansfield T (Signed on 24/1/91) FL 75+1/5 FLC 4 FAC 2 Others 2
Shrewsbury T (Free on 11/8/93) FL 80+9/2 FLC 7+2 FAC 8/1 Others 9+1

WITTER Anthony (Tony) Junior

Born: London, 12 August 1965
Height: 6'1" Weight: 13.0

An extremely fast Millwall central defender, whose quick turn of pace again came to the rescue when all seemed lost on occasion in 1995-96. Not one for scoring many goals, he should get more with his ability in the air, especially at set pieces, Tony volleyed a cracker against Ipswich in November. A regular up to January, but then in and out of the side due to injuries and suspensions, at the end of the campaign he was surprisingly out of favour with the new manager, Jimmy Nicholl.

Crystal Palace (£10,000 from Grays Ath on 24/10/90)
Queens Park R (£125,000 on 19/8/91) PL 1
Plymouth Arg (Loaned on 9/1/92) FL 3/1
Reading (Loaned on 11/2/94) FL 4
Millwall (£100,000 on 14/10/94) FL 56+2/2 FLC 4 FAC 7

WOAN Ian Simon

Born: Heswall, 14 December 1967
Height: 5'10" Weight: 12.4

The left winger enjoyed his best ever season for Nottingham Forest in 1995-96, missing only five games and finishing as the club's leading scorer with 12 goals, of which the highlights were two brilliant free kicks against Tottenham in the FA Cup fifth round-tie at the City Ground, which ended 2-2, and a sole strike from 30 yards in the penultimate game at home to Newcastle, that effectively put paid to the Geordies' hopes of winning the championship. The season was slightly marred by an admission to a journalist that Forest were not "good enough to win anything", for which he was dropped as a disciplinary measure, but

Frank Clark was clearly determined to hang on to his star by turning down an offer of £3m from Everton late in the season.

Nottingham F (£80,000 from Runcorn on 14/3/90) F/PL 147+8/29 FLC 12+2/1 FAC 17+1/4 Others 13/2

WOOD Paul Anthony

Born: Saltburn, 1 November 1964
Height: 5'9" Weight: 11.3

Playing as a wide, attacking midfielder, predominately on the right, Paul served up some useful displays for Portsmouth last season, culminating in his best run for the team since arriving from Bournemouth some four years earlier. Unlucky to suffer an ankle injury, he missed the last third of the campaign.

Portsmouth (From apprentice on 3/11/82) FL 25+22/6 FLC 5+3/1 FAC 2 Others 2+2/3
Brighton & Hove A (£40,000 on 28/8/87) FL 77+15/8 FLC 4 FAC 2+2 Others 5
Sheffield U (£90,000 on 9/2/90) FL 19+9/3 FLC 1 Others 1
Bournemouth (Loaned on 31/1/91) FL 20+1
Bournemouth (£40,000 on 3/10/91) FL 73+5/18 FLC 1+1 FAC 13/2 Others 5/2
Portsmouth (Signed on 18/2/94) FL 25+7/3 FAC 2

WOOD Simon Onward

Born: Hull, 24 September 1976
Height: 5'9" Weight: 11.8

Following his transfer from Coventry, following a spell on loan at non-league, VS Rugby, he became the seventh central defender to be used by Mansfield, during last season, five still being on the books at the end of the campaign. Made an impressive debut, showing excellent defensive and distributive skills and should be very much in the club's reckoning in the future. Surprisingly dropped for the game at Lincoln on 13 April, after he had helped the defence to concede only one goal in six games, the team proceeded to give away two without him!

Coventry C (From trainee on 11/11/93)
Mansfield T (Free on 15/3/96) FL 9+1/1

WOOD Stephen (Steve) Alan

Born: Bracknell, 2 February 1963
Height: 6'0" Weight: 12.7
Club Honours: Div 3 '86, Div 2 '88

Prior to being released during the summer, Steve completed a second frustrating season at Oxford, having been injured for most of 1994-95. Usually a centre back, he made most of his appearances during 1995-96 in the right back spot, being relegated as experienced back up for the United back four, which stayed largely unchanged throughout the campaign.

Reading (From apprentice on 19/2/81) FL 216+3/9 FLC 10 FAC 15 Others 4
Millwall (£80,000 on 17/6/87) FL 108+2 FLC 10 FAC 10 Others 3+1
Southampton (£400,000 on 9/10/91) F/PL 46 FLC 1+1 FAC 3/1 Others 4
Oxford U (Free on 20/7/94) FL 12+1 FAC 3/2 Others 3

WOOD Trevor John

Born: Jersey, 3 November 1968
Height: 6'0" Weight: 13.7
International Honours: NI: 1; B-1

After a minor operation in the summer of

1995, Trevor was initially kept out of the Walsall side by James Walker, before regaining the goalkeeper's jersey at the end of September. Although temporarily losing the job and going on the transfer list, he came back impressively to keep four clean sheets at the end of the year, his good form seeing him called into the Northern Ireland squad and winning his first cap when coming on as a 76th minute sub for Alan Fettes in the Euro '96 qualifier against Liechtenstein in October. Finished the season out of the side, but is still a great shot stopper.

Brighton & Hove A (From apprentice on 7/11/86)
Port Vale (Free on 8/7/88) FL 42 FLC 4 FAC 2 Others 2
Walsall (Free on 18/7/94) FL 59 FLC 4 FAC 7 Others 3

WOODMAN Andrew (Andy) John

Born: Camberwell, 11 August 1971
Height: 6'1" Weight: 12.4

Northampton goalkeeper and another favourite with the crowd, Andy saw it all last season, having been sent off, saved two penalties, and pulled off many fine point-blank saves when the side were all at sea. Comfortable on crosses, he gives the defence added stability.

Crystal Palace (From trainee on 1/7/89)
Exeter C (Free on 4/7/94) FL 6 FLC 1 FAC 1 Others 2
Northampton T (Free on 10/3/95) FL 54 FLC 2 FAC 2 Others 4

WOODS Christopher (Chris) Charles Eric

Born: Boston, 14 November 1959
Height: 6'2" Weight: 14.5
Club Honours: Div 2 '86; FLC '78, '85; SPD '87, '89, '90, '91; SLC '87, '89, '91
International Honours: E: 43; B-2; U21-6; Yth

Started last season in the Sheffield Wednesday reserve side understudying Kevin Pressman, before a loan spell at Reading in October, afforded him some first team experience. Back at Hillsborough five games later, with the latter injured, he stepped up to play well, showing flashes of his old brilliance and looking generally sound and composed under pressure, before injury forced him out.

Nottingham F (From apprentice on 1/12/76) FLC 7
Queens Park R (£250,000 on 4/7/79) FL 63 FLC 8 FAC 1
Norwich C (£225,000 on 12/3/81) FL 216 FLC 26 FAC 19 Others 6
Glasgow R (£600,000 on 2/7/86) SL 173 SLC 21 SC 15 Others 21
Sheffield Wed (£1,200,000 on 15/8/91) F/PL 106+1 FLC 13 FAC 10 Others 5
Reading (Loaned on 27/10/95) FL 5

WOODS Neil Stephen

Born: York, 30 July 1966
Height: 6'0" Weight: 12.11

Although starting in 16 of Grimsby's opening 18 matches last season, and scoring four goals, Neil gave way to Jamie Forrester following the latter's arrival from Leeds. Continuing to struggle for a first team place, he was eventually re-introduced in an attempt to stem the slump and showed up well alongside Clive Mendonca. Is not an out-and-out scorer, but more of a target man who creates chances for others.

Doncaster Rov (From apprentice on 31/8/83) FL 55+10/16 FLC 4/1 FAC 5/2 Others 5+2/3
Glasgow R (£120,000 on 22/12/86) SL 0+3
Ipswich T (£120,000 on 3/8/87) FL 15+12/5 Others 4/1
Bradford C (Signed on 1/3/90) FL 13+1/2
Grimsby T (£82,000 on 23/8/90) FL 153+39/42 FLC 10+1/2 FAC 7+1/2 Others 7/1

WOODS Raymond (Ray) Guy
Born: Birkenhead, 7 June 1965
Height: 5'11" Weight: 11.9

On his day one of the best right wingers in the second division, his efforts in mid-1995-96 were no small contribution to Shrewsbury's successful run of eight wins in nine games. His pace and ability to take defenders on made him very effective, although minor injuries, and being out of favour in late season, restricted him somewhat. Was released during the summer.

Tranmere Rov (From apprentice on 8/6/83) FL 9+5/2 FLC 1 Others 0+1 (Free to Bangor C in November 1984)
Wigan Ath (Free from Colne Dynamoes, via Northwich Victoria, Runcorn and Caernarfon, on 1/3/89) FL 25+3/3 FLC 2 FAC 4/1 Others 2
Coventry C (£200,000 on 30/1/91) FL 21/1 FLC 1 FAC 0+1
Wigan Ath (Loaned on 8/1/93) FL 12+1 Others 4/3
Shrewsbury T (Free on 23/3/94) FL 40+15/1 FLC 2 FAC 5 Others 6+1/1

Ray Woods

WOODSFORD Jamie Marcus
Born: Ipswich, 9 November 1976
Height: 5'11" Weight: 11.10
International Honours: E: Yth

Young Luton striker who, following his debut the previous season, might have expected more chances in 1995-96. Unfortunately, due to Town's perilous position his opportunities were restricted and, although he showed promise in his rare appearances and continued to score for the reserves, towards the end of the campaign he was loaned to Portadown to gain experience.

Luton T (From trainee on 3/3/95) FL 2+8 Others 0+2

WOODWARD Andrew (Andy) Stephen
Born: Stockport, 23 September 1973
Height: 5'11" Weight: 11.0

What a frustrating season 1995-96 was for Bury's talented right back. Having played in the opening day fixture at Northampton, he damaged ankle ligaments a few days later, subsequently caught chicken-pox from his son, and then pulled his hamstring, making no further appearances.

Crewe Alex (From trainee on 29/7/92) FL 9+11 FLC 2 Others 0+3
Bury (Signed on 13/3/95) FL 9 Others 3

WORBOYS Gavin Anthony
Born: Doncaster, 14 July 1974
Height: 6'2" Weight: 12.0

Young striker who was Darlington's top scorer in 1994-95, never really established himself last season, making more subs' appearances than starts and scoring just two goals, before being transferred to Northampton in January. Although proving dangerous around the box, especially in the air, during the few games he played for Town, opportunities were again limited, due to the form of the men in possession and he was freed during the summer.

Doncaster Rov (From trainee on 1/4/92) FL 6+1/2
Notts Co (£100,000 on 1/5/92)
Exeter C (Loaned on 6/12/93) FL 4/1 Others 1/1
Darlington (Free on 1/11/94) FL 30+11/8 FLC 1+1 FAC 3/2 Others 3+1/3
Northampton T (Free on 18/1/96) FL 4+9/1

WORTHINGTON Nigel
Born: Ballymena, 4 November 1961
Height: 5'10" Weight: 12.6
Club Honours: FLC '91
International Honours: NI: 64; Yth

The vastly experienced Northern Ireland left back, who can also play in midfield, was a firm squad member at Leeds in 1995-96, filling in on the left-hand side of the park when there were injuries to either Tony Dorigo or Gary Speed. Although a target for the "Boo-Boys" at Elland Road, he never gave less than 100 per cent for the club, continuing as a corner kick specialist and a player capable of supplying quality crosses to the front men when he got forward. *Stop Press:* Out of contract, Nigel left United during the summer.

Notts Co (£100,000 from Ballymena on 1/7/81) FL 62+5/4 FLC 11 FAC 4
Sheffield Wed (£125,000 on 6/2/84) F/PL 334+4/12 FLC 41/1 FAC 29 Others 9/1
Leeds U (£325,000 on 4/7/94) PL 33+10/1 FLC 4+1 FAC 6+1

WOSAHLO Bradley Edward
Born: Ipswich, 14 February 1975
Height: 5'10" Weight: 10.6

Bradley, the son of the former Chelsea and Ipswich player, Roger, joined Cambridge United on non-contract terms last December, making four subs' appearances. A left winger who needs time to adjust to the tempo of league football, he spent the summer months in Finland.

Brighton & Hove A (From trainee on 22/7/93) FL 1 FLC 0+1 Others 0+1 (Freed during 1994 close season)
Cambridge U (Signed from Sudbury T on 8/12/95) FL 0+4

WOTTON Paul Anthony
Born: Plymouth, 17 August 1977
Height: 5'11" Weight: 11.1

A strong Plymouth midfielder, with a very useful shot on him, Paul had already shown that he was a player with a sound future, having appeared as a trainee in 1994-95. Continuing his progress last season, after signing professional forms during the summer, he made two starts in the Auto Windscreen Shield and impressed. His passing ability will ensure that he is a regular before too long.

Plymouth Arg (From trainee on 10/7/95) FL 5+3 Others 2

WRACK Darren
Born: Cleethorpes, 5 May 1976
Height: 5'9" Weight: 11.10

Another of Derby's younger players who, though still making progress, had to be content with a place in the reserves for most of last season, having been squeezed out by the club's prolific dealings in the transfer market. A right-footed winger, who specialises in accurate crossing, Darren is little more than 12 months into a three year contract.

Derby Co (From trainee on 12/7/94) FL 4+22/1 FLC 0+3 FAC 0+2

WRAY Shaun Warren
Born: Birmingham, 14 March 1978
Height: 6'1" Weight: 12.11

Shrewsbury right winger. A product of the youth team just setting out on his first team career, he made his debut as a substitute in a 6-0 defeat at Oxford last season, so it can only get better for him.

Shrewsbury T (From trainee on 1/7/95) FL 0+3

WRIGHT Alan Geoffrey
Born: Ashton under Lyme, 28 September 1971
Height: 5'4" Weight: 9.4
Club Honours: FLC '96
International Honours: E: U21-2; Yth; Sch

Squeezed out by Graham le Saux at Ewood Park, it seemed likely that the left back would play second fiddle to Steve Staunton at Aston Villa in 1995-96. Instead, Staunton's injury problems opened the way for him to become Villa's first choice left wing/back, an opportunity he seized gratefully, as the only ever-present outfield player. He also revelled in the freedom to attack in the new Villa formation, scoring two excellent goals against Middlesbrough and Leeds and deserved more with other long-range shots that hit the woodwork or were kept out by acrobatic goalkeepers. A player with great skill and pace, which was seen to good advantage throughout the campaign, he won his first medal following the Coca Cola Cup final victory over Leeds and was called up to the England squad on two occasions, indicating that he could become an international of the future. Also elected by his fellow professionals to the PFA award winning Premiership side.

Blackpool (From trainee on 13/4/89) FL 91+7 FLC 10+2 FAC 8 Others 11+2
Blackburn Rov (£400,000 on 25/10/91) F/PL 67+7/1 FLC 8 FAC 5+1 Others 3
Aston Villa (£1,000,000 on 10/3/95) PL 46/2 FLC 8 FAC 5

Alan Wright

WRIGHT Ian Edward
Born: Woolwich, 3 November 1963
Height: 5'10" Weight: 11.8
Club Honours: FMC '91; FLC '93; FAC '93
International Honours: E: 20; B-3

1995-96 was yet another prolific season for Ian, who was once again Arsenal's leading scorer, notching 23 in 40 appearances. Still retaining his amazing speed, with the joy of running at defenders and capable of scoring spectacularly or just simple bread-and-butter goals, he is undoubtedly in the top rung of strikers who have played for the club down the years. His performances this time round were even more meritorious in many respects, considering he was troubled with a recurring groin problem for most of the campaign. The fans were mortified when it was rumoured that he wished to leave the club, something that appears to have now been sorted out and, at the age of 32, he still has plenty in the tank.

Crystal Palace (Free from Greenwich Borough on 2/8/85) FL 206+19/89 FLC 19/9 FAC 9+2/3 Others 19+3/16
Arsenal (£2,500,000 on 24/9/91) F/PL 160+2/95 FLC 25/23 FAC 14/12 Others 18/14

WRIGHT Ian Matthew
Born: Lichfield, 10 March 1972
Height: 6'1" Weight: 12.8

Central defender. Although featuring in the Bristol Rovers' first team squad for most of last season, the majority of the time he had to be content with a place on the substitutes' bench, due to the excellent form of Andy Tillson and Billy Clark, and was released during the summer. Is a good passer for a defender.

Stoke C (From trainee on 11/7/90) FL 6 FLC 1+1 Others 1
Bristol Rov (Signed on 23/9/93) FL 50+4/1 FLC 2 FAC 2 Others 5+1

WRIGHT Jermaine Malaki
Born: Greenwich, 21 October 1975
Height: 5'9" Weight: 11.9
International Honours: E: Yth

The exciting young winger crowned his full debut for Wolves in 1995-96, with a neat

goal against Fulham and was involved in nine games up to 22 November, before fading from the picture and eventually going out on an extended loan to Doncaster. At Belle Vue, Jermaine proved to be very much a winger in the old style, sticking to the line and running at defenders. Able to play on either flank, although favouring the right, he often turns up in dangerous positions.

Millwall (From trainee on 27/11/92)
Wolverhampton W (£60,000 on 29/12/94) FL 4+9 FLC 1+1/1 Others 0+1
Doncaster Rov (Loaned on 1/3/96) FL 13

WRIGHT Jonathan (Jon)
Born: Belfast, 24 November 1975
Height: 5'8" Weight: 11.4
International Honours: NI: B-2; Yth

Jon became Norwich's 29th first team appearance maker in 1995-96, when playing in the final game of the season, a 1-0 victory at Selhurst Park. Unfortunately injured after ten minutes play in a pre-season friendly versus Coleraine, it took until November before he fully recovered. From then on, playing consistently well in both full back positions as well as at centre half for the reserves, he was deservedly awarded his second Northern Ireland "B" cap versus Norway in March.

Norwich C (From trainee on 1/7/94) P/FL 2+1

Mark Wright

WRIGHT Mark
Born: Dorchester, 1 August 1963
Height: 6'3" Weight: 13.3
Club Honours: FAC '92
International Honours: E: 45; U21-4

After making only six Premiership appearances in 1994-95, Mark apparently had no future at Liverpool. However, an injury to John Scales at the start of 1995-96 gave him another chance to impress and so well did he perform that he held his place until the end of the season, mainly at the expense of Neil Ruddock. Indeed, he was the most consistent of the four centre backs at Roy Evans' disposal and he capped his remarkable comeback with a recall to the England team after four years absence, when selected for the match with Croatia in April. Never seemingly hurried and always

appearing to have plenty of time, he attacks the ball well at both ends of the park and is a constructive passer when in possession. Sadly, as in earlier major international tournaments, just when he seemed assured of a Euro '96 squad place, injury once again sidelined him.

Oxford U (From juniors on 26/8/80) FL 8+2 FAC 1
Southampton (£80,000 on 25/3/82) FL 170/7 FLC 25/2 FAC 17/1 Others 10/1
Derby Co (£760,000 on 27/8/87) FL 144/10 FLC 15 FAC 5 Others 7
Liverpool (£2,200,000 on 15/7/91) F/PL 117+2/5 FLC 11+2 FAC 16 Others 12

WRIGHT Richard Ian
Born: Ipswich, 5 November 1977
Height: 6'2" Weight: 13.0
International Honours: E: Sch; Yth

Described by his manager as the best young goalkeeper in the country, Richard did not start last season as Ipswich's first choice, but took his chance with Craig Forrest injured and then away on international duty. Unflappable, with a physique that belies his age, his brilliant performances, especially the one at Blackburn in the FA Cup, saw him play in 26 of the final 27 games. Not yet 20, and having come through the international ranks at the schoolboy and youth level, his excellent form was rewarded when he was asked to join the full England squad in training for the Croatia game.

Ipswich T (From trainee on 2/1/95) P/FL 26 FLC 1 FAC 3 Others 2

WRIGHT Thomas (Tommy) Elliott
Born: Dunfermline, 10 January 1966
Height: 5'7" Weight: 11.4
International Honours: S: U21-1; Yth

A free transfer signing from Middlesbrough during the 1995 close season, Tommy proved to be an effective wide player for Bradford in 1995-96. Although hampered by back and hamstring injuries, he missed very few matches and soon settled down, mainly on the right, to create opportunities for others with an accurate supply of crosses.

Leeds U (From apprentice on 15/1/83) FL 73+8/24 FLC 3+2/1 FAC 4/3
Oldham Ath (£80,000 on 24/10/86) FL 110+2/23 FLC 7+1/2 FAC 3/2 Others 3
Leicester C (£350,000 on 14/8/89) FL 122+7/22 FLC 7+1 FAC 4 Others 10/7
Middlesbrough (£650,000 on 1/7/92) F/PL 44+9/5 FLC 3+1 FAC 3/1 Others 5+1
Bradford C (Free on 4/7/95) FL 28+6/4 FLC 6/2 FAC 1 Others 2+1

WYATT Michael (Mike) James
Born: Bristol, 12 September 1974
Height: 5'10" Weight: 11.3

Mike, a tall, ball-playing winger, was involved in one of the rare instances where players have crossed the City of Bristol to join their arch-rivals. Included in Bristol Rovers early team line-ups, having been freed by City during the 1995 close season, his form dipped and he failed to add many further league appearances before being released during the summer.

Bristol C (From trainee on 7/7/93) FL 9+4 FLC 2 Others 1
Bristol Rov (Free on 4/7/95) FL 3+1 FLC 0+1

YALLOP Frank Walter
Born: Watford, 4 April 1964
Height: 5'11" Weight: 12.0
International Honours: E: Yth. Canada: 34

Although still regarded as an international defender by Canada, Frank made very few appearances for Ipswich last season and even had a spell on loan at Blackpool in November. A few months later, in February, in a bid to cut the club wage bill, the experienced right back was released on a free transfer to join Tampa Bay of the new American League, having spent 14 years at Portman Road.

Ipswich T (From apprentice on 5/1/82) F/PL 289+27/7 FLC 23+2/1 FAC 15+2 Others 22+3
Blackpool (Loaned on 3/11/95) FL 3 Others 1

YATES Dean Richard
Born: Leicester, 26 October 1967
Height: 6'1" Weight: 12.0
Club Honours: AIC '95
International Honours: E: U21-5

Dean, a tall and imposing Derby centre back, having recuperated from a summer cartilage operation, at last managed an injury free season in 1995-96, teaming up in defence with Croatian, Igor Stimac – the partnership which set County on the road to promotion. Useful in the air at set pieces at both ends of the park, his coolness under pressure and distribution ability did not go unrewarded when voted the supporter's "Player of the Year".

Notts Co (From apprentice on 14/6/85) FL 312+2/33 FLC 24 FAC 20 Others 36/4
Derby Co (£350,000 on 26/1/95) FL 49/3 FLC 3 FAC 1

YATES Stephen (Steve)
Born: Bristol, 29 January 1970
Height: 5'11" Weight: 11.0
Club Honours: Div 3 '90

Tough-tackling QPR central defender who can also be effective in either full back position. Came into the side last October for the injured Alan McDonald, and although the captain eventually returned, he kept his place with some excellent defensive displays, ultimately making 34 appearances. A player with a very good disciplinary record, while those around him suffered suspensions, Steve received just three yellow cards all season and was voted the supporters and players' "Player of the Season".

Bristol Rov (From trainee on 1/7/88) FL 196+1 FLC 9 FAC 11 Others 21
Queens Park R (£650,000 on 16/8/93) PL 79+3/1 FLC 5 FAC 4

YEBOAH Anthony (Tony)
Born: Ghana, 6 June 1966
Height: 5'10" Weight: 13.11
International Honours: Ghana: 25

Ghanaian International striker who began last season for Leeds in explosive fashion, after completing his permanent transfer from Eintracht, Frankfurt during the summer. Opened his 1995-96 account with two superbly taken efforts at West Ham, and followed that up two days later, with a much publicised volley against Liverpool. A goal to be shown over and over again on television and, arguably, taken with his weaker foot. Went on to score two unforgettable hat tricks in September, firstly with opportunist strikes in the UEFA Cup at Monaco, and then in the Premier League at Wimbledon, where his second goal, another glorious right-foot volley, matched his earlier effort against Liverpool. Indeed, most of Tony's goals verge on the spectacular, but, unfortunately for the club, he missed two large periods of the campaign, after picking up injuries when representing Ghana. Superbly strong and excessively quick, this brilliant striker was voted "Player of the Year" by the Leeds supporters.

Leeds U (£3,400,000 from Eintracht Frankfurt on 5/1/95) PL 38+2/24 FLC 7/3 FAC 6+2/2 Others 4/3

YORKE Dwight
Born: Canaan, Tobago, 3 November 1971
Height: 5'10" Weight: 11.12
Club Honours: FLC '96
International Honours: Trinidad & Tobago: 10

The revelation of 1995-96 at Aston Villa and deservedly voted the club's "Player of the Year" by supporters, even though there were so many outstanding candidates available. For many years, Dwight had never quite established himself as an automatic first choice, and was frequently used as cover for both wing and striking positions. However, at the beginning of the season, Brian Little gave him the opportunity to prove himself as a central striker, in which role he justified his manager's confidence to such an extent that by the final whistle he could be considered to be in the same bracket as Les Ferdinand and Ian Wright. As Villa's top scorer with 19 PL goals (and 27 in all competitions), he proved himself to be a player for the big occasion. Highlights of the season, to mention only a few, were a 13-

Tony Yeboah

Dwight Yorke

second goal at Coventry – the quickest to date in the Premier League – two in the Coca Cola Cup semi final against Arsenal at Highbury, and the third in the Coca Cola Cup final victory over Leeds. But for his previous qualification for Trinidad and Tobago, he would surely be a candidate for England international selection.

Aston Villa (£120,000 from Signal Hill on 19/12/89) F/PL 127+36/46 FLC 17+2/7 FAC 18+2/9 Others 1/1

YOUDS Edward (Eddie) Paul
Born: Liverpool, 3 May 1970
Height: 6'1" Weight: 13.0

As the Bradford captain, Eddie is a strong and dominating player who is equally at home in midfield or in the centre of the defence, could be justifiably proud of his achievement last season, when leading his team to the first division. Disappointed to miss 18 games through injury and suspension, with a hernia operation thrown in, the play-off victory over Notts County was the perfect tonic.

Everton (From trainee on 10/6/88) FL 5+3 FLC 0+1 Others 1
Cardiff C (Loaned on 29/12/89) FL 0+1 FAC 0+1
Wrexham (Loaned on 8/2/90) FL 20/2
Ipswich T (£250,000 on 15/11/91) F/PL 38+12/1 FLC 1+2 FAC 5+1
Bradford C (£175,000 on 2/1/95) FL 47/7 FLC 5/2 FAC 2 Others 4

YOUNG Eric
Born: Singapore, 25 March 1960
Height: 6'3" Weight: 13.5
Club Honours: FAC '88; FMC '91; Div 1 '94
International Honours: W: 21

Released by Crystal Palace last September, the central defender was a surprise Wolves' signing as, the man he would replace, Peter Shirtliff, had left the club partly because of his age, Eric being older and having actually retired! He found life hard during a 15-game spell and when he was dropped it seemed permanent. However, in January, after he was given a man-marking job to do in the FA Cup at Birmingham, his season quickly improved and he was called back into the Welsh squad, while continuing to give Wolves some steel at the back.

Brighton & Hove A (£10,000 from Slough T on 1/11/82) FL 126/10 FLC 8 FAC 11/1 Others 2
Wimbledon (£70,000 on 29/7/87) FL 96+3/9 FLC 12 FAC 6+1/1 Others 7
Crystal Palace (£850,000 on 15/8/90) F/PL 161/15 FLC 25/1 FAC 10 Others 8/1
Wolverhampton W (Free on 13/9/95) FL 30/2 FLC 5 FAC 4

YOUNG Neil Anthony
Born: Harlow, 31 August 1973
Height: 5'8" Weight: 11.3

Neil played at either right back or in the centre of the Bournemouth defence, whenever a five-man defence was used in 1995-96, and looked equally comfortable in both positions. Had another solid season with consistently good performances making him one of the most established players in the first team. Although he can tackle with the best of them, he is just as capable at getting forward in support of the attack.

Tottenham H (From trainee on 17/8/91)
Bournemouth (Free on 11/10/94) FL 72+1 FLC 3 FAC 5 Others 4

YOUNG Scott
Born: Pontypridd, 14 January 1976
Height: 6'1" Weight: 12.0
International Honours: W: U21-1

A Cardiff defender who can truly hold his head up with his performances whenever he played in 1995-96, having matured into a seasoned Endsleigh League player. Reliable and solid, Scott relished linking up with the equally promising Lee Jarman, both men being capped at Welsh U21 level during the season.

Cardiff C (From trainee on 4/7/94) FL 55+14 FLC 3+1 FAC 2 Others 7+3/1

YOUNG Stuart Rodney
Born: Hull, 16 December 1972
Height: 5'11" Weight: 13.0

Lively forward whose strong running can create space for others. Began last season for Scunthorpe on a short-term contract but, apart from a spell of six games early on, he was mainly consigned to the subs' bench and was eventually released.

Hull C (Free from Arsenal juniors on 11/7/91) FL 11+8/2 FLC 1/1 FAC 2 Others 1+1
Northampton T (Free on 5/2/93) FL 7+1/2
Scarborough (Free on 4/8/93) FL 28+13/10 FLC 3+2/1 FAC 3+1/1 Others 3
Scunthorpe U (Free on 23/12/94) FL 19+9/3 FLC 0+2 FAC 1 Others 1+2

ZELIC Nedjeljko (Ned)
Born: Australia, 4 July 1971
Height: 6'2" Weight: 13.8
International Honours: Australia: 25

The Australian captain signed for QPR immediately prior to the start of last season, having been playing in Germany for Borussia Dortmund. Although making his debut as a sub at home to Wimbledon in the second match, the big, strong midfielder then had to undergo a knee operation, which was followed by a virus, before being able to come back in November. However, three full appearances later, Ned returned to Germany with Eintracht Frankfurt for £1m in mid-December, following a loan spell, after failing to make his mark in the Premiership.

Queens Park R (£1,250,000 from Borussia Dortmund on 17/8/95) PL 3+1

ZUMRUTEL Soner
Born: Islington, 6 October 1974
Height: 5'6" Weight: 11.0

A right winger who is very quick and always on the go, and able to defend if he has to, Soner was freed by Arsenal during the 1995 close season. Looking for the opportunity of first team football, he trialed at Cambridge in September on a non-contract basis, but, after just one AWS game, moved on.

Arsenal (From trainee on 6/7/93)
Cambridge U (Free on 25/9/95) Others 1

FA Carling Premiership and Endsleigh League Clubs : Summary of Appearances and Goals for 1995-96.

KEY TO TABLES: P/FL = Premier/Football League. FLC = Football League Cup. FAC = FA Cup. Others = Other first team appearances.
Left hand figures in each column list number of full appearances + appearances as substitute. Right hand figures list number of goals scored.

ARSENAL (PREM: 5th)

	P/FL App	Goals	FLC App	Goals	FAC App	Goals	Others App	Goals
Adams	21	1	5	2	2			
Bergkamp	33	11	7	5	1			
Bould	19		5	1				
Clarke	4+2				1+1			
Dickov	1+6	1						
Dixon	38	2	7		2			
Hartson	15+4	4	1+2	1	1			
Helder	15+9	1	4+2		2			
Hillier	3+2		2					
Hughes	0+1		0+1					
Jensen	13+2		5+1		2			
Keown	34		5	1	2			
Linighan	17+1		2		0+1			
Marshall	10+1	1						
McGoldrick	0+1							
McGowan	1				1			
Merson	38	5	7		2			
Morrow	3+1		1					
Parlour	20+2		3+1					
Platt	27+2	6	2+1		1			
Rose	1+3							
Seaman	38		7		2			
Shaw	0+3							
Winterburn	36	2	7		1			
Wright	31	15	7	7	2	1		

ASTON VILLA (PREM: 4th)

	P/FL App	Goals	FLC App	Goals	FAC App	Goals	Others App	Goals
Bosnich	38		8		5			
Browne	2							
Carr	1				1	1		
Charles	34	1	8		5			
Davis	0+2				0+1			
Draper	36	2	8	1	5	2		
Ehiogu	36	1	8	1	5			
Farrelly	1+4		0+1					
Fenton	0+3		0+2					
Hendrie	2+1							
Joachim	4+7	2						
Johnson	17+6	5	4	2	3+1	1		
McGrath	29+1	2	5+1		3+1			
Milosevic	36+1	10	7	1	5	1		
Murray	3							
Scimeca	7+10		1+2		2			
Southgate	31	1	8	1	4			
Spink	0+2							
Staunton	11+2		2+2	1	1+1			
Taylor	24+1	3	5+1	1	2+1	1		
Tiler	1							
Townsend	32+1	2	8	1	4			
Wright	38	2	8		5			
Yorke	35	19	8	6	5	2		

BARNET (DIV 4: 9th)

	P/FL App	Goals	FLC App	Goals	FAC App	Goals	Others App	Goals
Adams	1							
Brady	1+1							
Campbell	14+10	1	2		2			
Charles	2+3				0+1			
Codner	8							
Cooper	26+7	8	0+2		2		2	1
Devine	35	19			2	1	2	
Dunwell	3+10	1						
Dyer	30+5	2					1	
Freedman	5	3	2					
Gale	44	1	2		2		2	
Hodges	34+6	17	2		1+1	1	1+1	

BARNET cont.

	P/FL App	Goals	FLC App	Goals	FAC App	Goals	Others App	Goals
Howarth	19							
McDonald	30+2				2		2	
Mills	5+14				1+1		0+1	
Newell	1							
Pardew	41		2		2		2	
Primus	42	4	2		2	1	1	
Robbins	9+6	1	2				0+1	1
Scott	19+1		2		2		2	
Simpson	24	1						
Smith	0+1							
Stimson	5						1	
Taylor	45		2		2		2	
Thomas	16		2				1	
Thompson	1+1							
Tomlinson	17+8	2	0+2		0+2		1	
Wilson	29+4	4			2		2	

BARNSLEY (DIV 1: 10th)

	P/FL App	Goals	FLC App	Goals	FAC App	Goals	Others App	Goals
Archdeacon	36+2	3	3		2			
Bishop	12+1		3					
Bochenski	0+1				0+1			
Bullock	25+16	1	2+1		0+2			
Butler	1+2							
Davis	27	5	3		2			
De Zeeuw	31	1			2			
Eaden	46	2	3		2			
Fleming	2+1							
Hurst	0+5							
Jackson	6+2		1					
Jones	4							
Kane	4							
Liddell	43	9	2		2			
Molby	5							
Moses	21+3	1	2		1			
O'Connell	20+5	1			2			
Payton	37+3	17	3	3	1+1			
Rammell	11+9	4	1+1	1	1			
Redfearn	45	14	3		2	1		
Regis	4+8	1						
Sheridan	38+3		3		2			
Shirtliff	32				1			
Shotton	2		1					
Ten Heuval	1+2							
Van der Velden	6+1							
Viveash	2							
Watson	45		3		2			

BIRMINGHAM CITY (DIV 1: 15th)

	P/FL App	Goals	FLC App	Goals	FAC App	Goals	Others App	Goals
Bass	5		1					
Barber	1							
Barnes P	15	7						
Barnes S	0+3		0+1				0+1	
Bennett	24		8	1	4			
Bowen	16+7	4	3+5	2	0+2		2	2
Breen	17+1	1						
Bull	3+3		0+1		0+2		1	1
Castle	12+3	1	7		1		3	1
Charlery	8+9	4	3+1	2			2+1	
Claridge	28	8	11+1	1			2+1	1
Cooper	16+2		5+1				2+1	
Cornforth	8							
Daish	16+1		7	2	2			
Devlin	16	7						
Doherty	0+2	1	1+1				0+1	
Donowa	5+8		2+5		1			

BIRMINGHAM CITY cont.

	P/FL App	Goals	FLC App	Goals	FAC App	Goals	Others App	Goals
Edwards	36+1	1	11	1	2		5	1
Finnan	6+6	1	2+2				2+1	
Forsyth	12+14	2	7+2		2		3+1	
Frain	22+1		6		2		2	
Francis	11+8	3	6	4	2		1	
Grainger	8							
Griemink	20		3		1		1+1	
Hiley	5		1				1	
Hill	5		2					
Hunt	43+2	11	9+3	2	1+1	1	5	1
Johnson	31+2		5		1		4	
Legg	9+3	1						
Lowe	0+2							
Martin	1+6						0+2	
Muir	1		0+1					
Otto	6+12	2	3+3				3	
Peschisolido	7+2	1						
Poole	27+1		10		2	1	3	1
Preece	6							
Rea	0+1						1+1	
Richardson	3+4		3+1		2		1+2	
Rushfeldt	3+4		1	1			1	
Sahlin	0+1							
Samways	12							
Sansome	1		1					
Sheridan	1+1		2					
Tait	23+4	3	4+1				1+2	
Ward	13	3	3+1				1	
Whyte	4		5				1	

BLACKBURN ROVERS (PREM: 7th)

	P/FL App	Goals	FLC App	Goals	FAC App	Goals	Others App	Goals
Atkins	0+4						1+1	
Batty	23	1	4		1		6	
Berg	38		4		2		6	
Bohinen	17+2	4			1			
Coleman	19+1				2			
Fenton	4+10	6						
Flitcroft	3							
Flowers	37		3		2		7	
Gallagher	14+2	2			2		1+1	
Gudmundsson	1+3							
Hendry	33	1	4		2		5	
Holmes	8+1	1					2+1	
Kenna	32		4		2		6	
Le Saux	13+1	1	2				3+1	
McKinlay	13+6	2	1		1+1			
Makel	0+3						1+2	
Marker	8+1	1					1+1	
Mimms	1+1		1					
Newell	26+4	3	4	1	2		6+1	4
Pearce	12	1	3				5	
Ripley	28		3		2		5+1	
Shearer	35	31	4	5	2		7	1
Sherwood	33	3	4		1+1		7	
Sutton	9+4		2+1	1			4+3	
Warhurst	1+9		1+2				4+1	
Wilcox	10	3						

BLACKPOOL (DIV 2: 3rd)

	P/FL App	Goals	FLC App	Goals	FAC App	Goals	Others App	Goals
Allardyce	0+1							
Banks	24		1		3		4	
Barber	1							
Barlow	34	1	2		2		3	
Beech	3+15		1+1				1+3	2
Bonner	41+1	3	1+1		3		5	1

BLACKPOOL cont.

	P/FL App	P/FL Goals	FLC App	FLC Goals	FAC App	FAC Goals	Others App	Others Goals
Bradshaw	25		2		2		4	
Brown P	5+8				1+2		0+1	
Brown R	2+1		2					
Bryan	44+2	1	0+2		3		6	
Capleton	1		1					
Charnock	0+4							
Darton	5+4						0+1	
Ellis	41+2	14	2	2	3		5	1
Gouck	8+8	1	2		1+1		4+1	
Holden	19+3	2			2		2+1	
Linighan	29	4					4	
Lydiate	30+2	1	2		3	1	3	
Mellon	45	6	2	1	3		5	1
Morrison	29	3			2		4	
Nixon	20						2	
Pascoe	0+1							
Philpott	4+6						0+1	
Preece	37+4	14	2		1+2	1	6	
Quinn	42+2	9	2		3	3	3+2	2
Thorpe	0+1							
Watson	14+13	6			1+2		4+1	
Yallop	3						1	

BOLTON WANDERERS (PREM: 20th)

	P/FL App	P/FL Goals	FLC App	FLC Goals	FAC App	FAC Goals	Others App	Others Goals
Bergsson	34	4	6					
Blake	14+4	1			2			
Branagan	31		6		2			
Burnett	0+1							
Coleman	12	1						
Coyle	2+3		0+1					
Curcic	28	4	3	1	2	2		
Davison	2							
De Freitas	17+10	5	2+1		1			
Fairclough	33				2			
Green	26+5	3	3+2		2			
Lee	9+9	1	3+1		1			
McAnespie	7+2		3					
McAteer	4							
McGinlay	29+3	6	6	2	1+1	1	1	
Paatelainen	12+3	1	1		0+1			
Patterson	12+4	1	5+1	1				
Phillips	37		6		2			
Sellars	22	3			1			
Small	1							
Sneekes	14+3	1	4		2	1		
Strong	0+1							
Stubbs	24+1	4	3		2			
Taggart	11	1	2		2			
Taylor	0+1							
Thompson	23+3	1	5	1	1			
Todd	9+3	2	2+2					
Ward	5							
Whittaker			0+1					

BOURNEMOUTH (DIV 2:14th)

	P/FL App	P/FL Goals	FLC App	FLC Goals	FAC App	FAC Goals	Others App	Others Goals
Andrews	26		4				1	
Bailey	36+8	4	2+1		3		2+1	
Beardsmore	44		4		3		3	
Brissett	43	3	4		3		3	2
Casper	16	1						
Coll	8							
Cox	8							
Cureton	0+5						0+1	
Dean	4+1							
Duberry	7							
Fletcher	3+4	1	1		2		1	
Glass	13							
Holland	43	10	4		2		2	
Howe	4+1							
Jones	44	17	4	3	2		2	
McElhatton	2+2		0+1		1		1	
Mean	13+1	1	3				0+1	

BOURNEMOUTH cont.

	P/FL App	P/FL Goals	FLC App	FLC Goals	FAC App	FAC Goals	Others App	Others Goals
Mitchell	2+2							
Morris	28+3	1	4	1	3		2	
Moss	7				3		2	
Murray	30+5	2	4		2		1	
Ndah	12	2					1	
Oldbury	2+11		0+1	1	0+1		1	
O'Neill	2+4						1	
Pennock	16+1		3		3		3	
Rawlinson	3+16		0+1		1		1	
Robinson	36+5	7	3		2+1	1	3	1
Santos	0+3						0+1	
Scott	8		1					
Stephens							0+1	
Strong	0+1				0+1			
Town	1+6		0+2				0+1	
Victory	5+11	1	1+1				1+1	
Young	40+1	1	3		3		2	

BRADFORD CITY (DIV 2: 6th)

	P/FL App	P/FL Goals	FLC App	FLC Goals	FAC App	FAC Goals	Others App	Others Goals
Brightwell	21+1				1		2	
Bullimore	1+1							
Duxbury	30	4			2		3	
Foley	0+1							
Ford	18+1		4		2			
Gould	9						3	
Grayston	2							
Hamilton	18+6	3	4	1	2		3+1	2
Harper								
Huxford	21+5	1	5		1+1		4+1	
Jacobs	28		4		3	2	4	
Jewell	7+11	3			1			
Kiwomya	7+9	2	0+2				2+1	
Kernaghan	5							
Liburd	33	1	3+2		1		2	
Midgley	0+5	1			0+2			
Mitchell	32+1	1	6		2		4	
Mohan	39	4	6		2		5	
Murray	25+9	2	2+2		1+2		2	1
Ormondroyd	28+9	6	6	3	2+1	1	2+2	
Robson	4+2		0+1		1		1	
Showler	29+4	8	5	4	3	2	2	
Shutt	22+12	8	3+1		1+1		3+2	1
Stallard	20+1	9					3	2
Tolson	12+19	8	1+1	1	2+1		1+1	1
Ward	36		6		3		2	
Wright	28+4	6	6	2	1		2+1	
Youds	30	4	5	2	2		4	

BRENTFORD (DIV 2: 15th)

	P/FL App	P/FL Goals	FLC App	FLC Goals	FAC App	FAC Goals	Others App	Others Goals
Abrahams	14+3	3						
Anderson	25	2	2	1	1+2		0+1	
Annon	0+1							
Ansah	6	1						
Asaba	5+5	2	1					
Ashby	31+2	1	4		4	1	3	
Bates	36	4	4		5		3	
Bent	8+4	1			4	3	1	
Canham	14							
Davis	5		2				1	
Dearden	41		4		3		2	
Fernandes	5				2		1	
Forster	37+1	5	4	2	3		2	1
Grainger	33	3	4	1	5		3	
Greene	11							
Harvey	38+2		2+1	1	4+1		1	
Hooker	4		1		0+2			
Hurdle	11+3		2					
Hutchings	20+3				5		1+1	
McGhee	31+5	5	1+1	1	4		2+1	
Martin	14+5	1			4+1		1	
Mundee	5+1		1+1					
Omigie	3+7							

BRENTFORD cont.

	P/FL App	P/FL Goals	FLC App	FLC Goals	FAC App	FAC Goals	Others App	Others Goals
Ravenscroft	1							
Smith	46	4	4		5	2	3	
Statham	17		4		1		3	
Sussex	3							
Taylor	42	11	4	1	4	3	3	1

BRIGHTON & HOVE ALBION (DIV 2: 23rd)

	P/FL App	P/FL Goals	FLC App	FLC Goals	FAC App	FAC Goals	Others App	Others Goals
Allan	8							
Andrews	0+8		1+1		1+1		1+1	
Berry	6	2						
Bull	10				1		2	
Byrne	15+10	2	1+1		3	2	0+1	
Case	0+2							
Chapman	36	3	1+1		2		4	
Coughlan	1							
Foster	8	1						
Fox M	0+2							
Fox S	0+6		0+1				0+1	
Hobson	9							
Johnson	19+1				2		2	
McCarthy	33	1	2		4		2	1
McDonald	3							
McDougald	34+3	4	1		3	3	4	2
McGarrigle	8+6	1	2				1+1	
Maskell	15	4						
Minton	37+2	8	1		4		3	
Munday	6+3				0+2		1	
Mundee	31+1	3			4		2	1
Myall	27+6	2	2		4		2+1	
Osman	11+1				2		3	
Parris	38				4		4	
Rowe	9	3						
Rust	46		2		4		4	
Smith	28+3	1	2		4	1	3+1	
Storer	28+10	2	2		1+1		3	1
Tuck	7+1		2				1	
Virgo			0+1					
Wilkins	31+4	3	2		2+1		3	

BRISTOL CITY (DIV 2 : 13th)

	P/FL App	P/FL Goals	FLC App	FLC Goals	FAC App	FAC Goals	Others App	Others Goals
Agostino	29+11	10	4	1			2+1	
Armstrong	6							
Baird	1				1			
Barber	3		2					
Barclay	0+2							
Barnard	33+1	4			2		2	
Bent	33+7	2			2		3	
Bryant	31+1		2+1		1		3	
Carey	22+1				2		1	
Dryden	17+1	1	4		1		2	
Dykstra	8						2	
Edwards	18+1		2		2		3	1
Fowler	6+4		1+1				1	
Hansen	7+1		4				1	
Hewlett	27	2			0+1		1	
Kite	3+1		2					
Kuhl	46	6	4		2		3	
McLeary	30+1		2					
Maskell	5	1						
Munro	3		2				0+1	
Nugent	29+5	8			2			
Owers	34+3	2	1		2		3	
Partridge	3+6	1	1+2		0+1			
Paterson	16+2	1	1		1		1	
Plummer	1+10		1+2				0+1	
Seal	19+11	10	4	3	1		2+1	1
Shail	9+3		1+1		2		1	
Starbuck	5	1					1	
Tinnion	27+3	3			0+1		1+1	
Welch	35		2		2		1	

BRISTOL ROVERS (DIV 2: 10th)

	P/FL App	P/FL Goals	FLC App	FLC Goals	FAC App	FAC Goals	Others App	Others Goals
Archer	13+6	1			1	1	2	1
Armstrong	13+1							
Beadle	26+1	12					3	
Browning	45	4	4				6	1
Channing	35+1		2		0+1		5	
Clark	38+1	2	2				5	
Collett	26				1		5	
Davis	1+3		0+1				0+1	1
French	3+7	1					2+1	1
Gurney	42+1	6	4		1		7	
Hayfield	3+3				1		1+1	
Hope							0+1	
Low	0+1							
McLean	4+3		0+1		1		1	
Matthew	8						2	1
Miller	37+1	4	3		1		5	
Morgan	5						2	
Parkin	20		4				2	
Paul	9+4	1	1				2+1	
Pritchard	12		4		1			
Skinner	23+5		4		1		3	
Sterling	28+2		3		1		6	
Stewart	44	21	4	4	1		7	5
Taylor	7	4	3					
Tillson	38	1	4		1		7	1
Tovey	8						2+1	
White	0+2						0+1	
Wyatt	3+1		0+1					
Wright	15+3		2		1		2+1	

BURNLEY (DIV 2: 17th)

	P/FL App	P/FL Goals	FLC App	FLC Goals	FAC App	FAC Goals	Others App	Others Goals
Adams	0+2							
Beresford	36		4		1		4	
Bishop	9							
Borland	1		2		0+1			
Brass	7+2						2	
Cooke	10+13	5			0+1		2+2	
Dowell	1							
Eyres	39+3	6	3		1	1	0+3	
Francis	4+18	2	0+3		0+1		0+3	
Harper	3+1		2					
Harrison	35	1	2		1		4	
Heath	5+2		1				1	
Helliwell	3+1							
Hoyland	21+2		1		1		3	
Joyce	42+1	5	4				3	
McDonald	8+1	1					2	
McMinn	7+3		1		1		0+1	
Mahorn	3+5	1						
Nogan	46	20	4	3	4		4	3
Parkinson	29		4		1		2	
Pender	1		1					
Philliskirk	7+1	1	3					
Randall	12+3		2		1	1	1	
Robinson	11+5	2			0+1		0+1	
Russell	10							
Smith	3+7							
Swan	31+1	5	2		1		4	
Thompson	18							
Vinnicombe	35	2	4		1		4	
Weller	24+1	1	1		1		2	
Winstanley	45	3	3		1		4	

BURY (DIV 3: 3rd)

	P/FL App	P/FL Goals	FLC App	FLC Goals	FAC App	FAC Goals	Others App	Others Goals
Bimson	16		4				1	
Brabin	5							
Bracey	21		3					
Carter	28+4	16	4+1	2	1		1	
Cross	13		4		1		2	
Daws	33+4	1	2+2	1				
Edwards	4							
Harle	0+1							

BURY cont.

	P/FL App	P/FL Goals	FLC App	FLC Goals	FAC App	FAC Goals	Others App	Others Goals
Hughes	30+2		2+1		1		2	
Hulme	0+1		1					
Jackson	31	4	1					
Johnrose	34	7	3				1	
Johnson	21+15	4	1+2	1	0+1		1+1	
Kelly	25		2		1		2	
Lancaster	1+4		0+1				0+1	
Lucketti	42	1	5		1		2	
Matthews	11+5	4						
Matthewson	16		4		1		2	
Mulligan	0+2							
Paskin	0+12							
Pugh	42	10	5		1		1	
Reid N	13+5							
Reid S	20+1		5		1		2	
Richardson	3+2		1					
Rigby	33+8	7	2+2	1	1		2	
Sertori	4+7	1	1		0+1		0+1	
Stant	27+7	9	5	4	1		2	
West	32+5	1			1		1+1	
Woodward	1							

CAMBRIDGE UNITED (DIV 3: 16th)

	P/FL App	P/FL Goals	FLC App	FLC Goals	FAC App	FAC Goals	Others App	Others Goals
Adekola	1+4	1	2				1+1	1
Barnwell-Edinboro	7	2						
Barrett	31		2		1		1	
Barrick	2+1	1	1					
Beall	15	5					0+1	
Benjamin	0+5							
Butler	16	10			1	1	1	
Clark	2							
Corazzin	31	10	2	2	1			
Craddock	44+2	3	1		1		1	
Davies	15						1	
Fowler	0+2		0+1				1	
Granville	31+4		0+2		0+1		2	
Gutzmore	0+2							
Hayes	1							
Howes	0+1							
Hyde	20+4	4			1		1	
Illman	1+4							
Jeffrey	20+7		1		1		1	
Joseph M E	10+2						1	
Joseph M N	42	2	2		1			
Kyd	3+6	1	1+1		0+1		1+1	
Middleton C	38+2	9	2		1		1	
Middleton L	1+2							
Pack	2+9		1+1				1	
Palmer	30	1	1		1		1	
Perkins	1+1	1						
Pick	2+2							
Rattle	7+2				1		1	
Raynor	35	3			1			
Richards	15+4	1					2	
Robinson	4+13	1						
Stock	15+2	1	1					
Thompson	14+1		2					
Turner	10	3						
Vowden	22+2		2				2	
Wanless	14		1					
Watson	1+3	1						
Westley	3							
Wosahlo	0+4							
Zumrutel	1							

CARDIFF CITY (DIV 3: 22nd)

	P/FL App	P/FL Goals	FLC App	FLC Goals	FAC App	FAC Goals	Others App	Others Goals
Adams	8+6	3	1+1		2		2+1	2
Baddeley	27+1	3	4		1		3	
Bird	9+3	3	3		0+1		1+1	
Bolesan	0+1							
Brazil	19+1		2		1		1	

CARDIFF CITY cont.

	P/FL App	P/FL Goals	FLC App	FLC Goals	FAC App	FAC Goals	Others App	Others Goals
Dale	44	21	4	2	2	2	3	5
Dobbs	3		1					
Downing	3+1		0+1					
Evans D A	1+1		0+2		0+1		0+1	
Evans T	1+1		0+1				0+1	
Flack	5+5	1						
Fleming	20+2		2				1	
Gardner	32+3	4	2				2	
Harding	36		4		1		2	
Harper	5						1	
Haworth	7+6		4				2	
Ingram	4+4	1	1				1+1	
Jarman	31+1				2		1+1	
Johnson	1+4							
Jones	1							
McGorry	7							
Oatway	2				0+1			
Osman	14+1							
Perry	13+1		4				1	
Philliskirk	28+4							
Rodgerson	28+6		3+1	1	2		2	
Scott	0+1							
Scully	13+1							
Searle	41	1	4		2		3	
Shaw	6							
Vick	0+2							
Wigg	14+6		3		1+1		1	
Williams D	42		4		2		3	
Williams S	4							
Young	37+4		2+1		2		2	

CARLISLE UNITED (DIV 2: 21st)

	P/FL App	P/FL Goals	FLC App	FLC Goals	FAC App	FAC Goals	Others App	Others Goals
Allen	3							
Aspinall	36+6	6	2	1			4+1	1
Atkinson	2						1	
Bennett	26	5					5	1
Caig	33		2		1		4	
Conway	13+9	3	1+1		0+1		0+3	
Currie	41+1	9	2		1		6+1	1
Delap	5+14	3					3+1	
Donachie	0+1							
Dowell	2+5							
Edmondson	40+2	1	2				3	2
Elliott	13						3	
Gallimore	36	2	2		1		7	
Hayward	36+2	4	2				6	1
Hopper	1+4						1	
Joyce	0+3		1					
McAlindon	0+3							
Moore	13						2	
Mountfield			1					
Murray	23+5	1	2				4	
Peacock	12+10	2	0+1		0+1		1+3	
Philliskirk	3		1					
Prokas	17+3				1		5+1	
Reeves	43	13	2	2	1	1	7	3
Robinson	18+2	2	0+1		1		2+2	
Smart	3+1							
Thomas	28+8	1	1+1		1		4	1
Thorpe	16+18	1			1		2+2	
Walling	43		2		1	1	7	

CHARLTON ATHLETIC (DIV 1: 6th)

	P/FL App	P/FL Goals	FLC App	FLC Goals	FAC App	FAC Goals	Others App	Others Goals
Allen	10	3					1+1	
Ammann	10+1	1						
Balmer	30+2	1	4		3		2	
Bowyer	41	8	6	5	3	1	2	
Brown	17+2		1		2		1	
Chandler	0+1							
Chapple	13+3	2	3					
Garland	3		2	1				
Grant	20+10	7	1+4	1	2+1	2		

CHARLTON ATHLETIC cont.

	P/FL App	P/FL Goals	FLC App	FLC Goals	FAC App	FAC Goals	Others App	Others Goals
Humphrey	28		6		2			
Jackson	8						2	
Jones	24+1		2+1		1			
Leaburn	38+2	9	4	1	3		2	
Linger	2+6	1	0+1					
Mortimer	13+6	5			2	1		
Nelson	12+18	3	5		1+2		1+1	
Newton	39+2	5	4	1	2+1		2	1
Petterson	9						2	
Robinson	43+1	6	5+1	2	3	1	1	
Robson	11+16	1	2+2		1		1	
Rufus	40+1		5		2		2	
Salmon	27		5		3			
Stuart	27	2	5		3		0+1	
Sturgess	13		1					
Walsh	5+1		2+1					
Whyte C	10+1						2	
Whyte D	11+14	2	2		0+1	1	0+2	
Williams	2+7							

CHELSEA (PREM: 11th)

	P/FL App	P/FL Goals	FLC App	FLC Goals	FAC App	FAC Goals	Others App	Others Goals
Barness					1			
Burley	16+6		2		2			
Clarke	21+1	1	1		6+2			
Dow	1							
Duberry	22				8	2		
Furlong	14+14	3	1+1		4+4	1		
Gullit	31	3	2		7	3		
Hall	5	1						
Hitchcock	12				7			
Hughes	31	8	2		6	4		
Johnsen	18+4		2		1+1			
Kharine	26		2		1			
Lee	29+2	1	0+1		7			
Minto	10		1					
Morris	0+1							
Myers	20				3			
Newton	21+3	1	1		3			
Peacock	17+11	5	1		3+4	2		
Petrescu	22+2	2			7	1		
Phelan	12				8			
Rocastle								
Sinclair	12+1	1	2					
Spackman	13+3	1			0+3			
Spencer	23+5	13	1		8	1		
Stein	7+1	1	0+1					
Wise	34+1	7	2		7	1		

CHESTER CITY (DIV 3: 8th)

	P/FL App	P/FL Goals	FLC App	FLC Goals	FAC App	FAC Goals	Others App	Others Goals
Alsford	22+2		3+1		1		2	
Barlow			0+1					
Bishop	7+2	5	4	2			1	
Brenchley			0+1					
Brien	8							
Brown	1+2						0+1	
Burnham	40	1	4		1		2	
Chambers	2+6	1	1				0+1	
Cutler								
Davidson	19	1						
Fisher	43+1	2	4		1		1	
Flitcroft	7+2	1	3				1	
Jackson	36	1	3		1		1	
Jenkins	12+1		2		0+1		1	
Jones							0+1	
Kenworthy	5+2	1						
Milner	35+7	4	2	3	1	1	1	
Murphy	1+17	3	1+2	1			1	
Newland							1	
Noteman	27+6	9			1		1+1	
Preece	1							
Priest	38+1	13	3		1		2	
Quinn			0+1					

CHESTER CITY cont.

	P/FL App	P/FL Goals	FLC App	FLC Goals	FAC App	FAC Goals	Others App	Others Goals
Regis	29	7	3		1			
Richardson	36+1	4	1				2	
Rimmer	30+11	13	2+2				2	
Rogers	14+6	1	0+2				1	
Ryan	2+2	1						
Shelton	10+1	1	2+1					
Stewart	45		4		1		1	
Whelan	35+4	2	3	1	1		1	

CHESTERFIELD (DIV 2: 7th)

	P/FL App	P/FL Goals	FLC App	FLC Goals	FAC App	FAC Goals	Others App	Others Goals
Beasley	11		2		2		1	
Carr	1		1					
Curtis	46		2		2		5	
Davies	28+2	4	2		2	2	4	
Dyche	39+2		2		2		3	
Fairclough	0+2						0+1	
Hazel	16+5		1		0+1		1	
Hewitt	23+5	2	2				1	
Holland	16+1	2					1	
Howard	16+14	2	1		1+1		3+2	
Jules	28+4	2					3	
Law	38	7	1		2		4	1
Lormor	38+3	13	2		2	2	3+1	1
Lund	6+2	1					1	
McDougald	9	3						
Madden	1							
Mercer	34						4	
Morris	14+2	5	0+1		1		3	
Moss	6+7							
Narbett	11+6	1	1+1		1		2+3	
Perkins	18+4		1				3+1	
Pierce	1							
Roberts	6+8	1	1	1	1+1		1+4	2
Robinson	38+1	9	1		2		5	2
Rogers	20+1	1	1		1		2	
Williams	42	3	1		2		5	

COLCHESTER UNITED (DIV 3: 7th)

	P/FL App	P/FL Goals	FLC App	FLC Goals	FAC App	FAC Goals	Others App	Others Goals
Abrahams	8	2					1	
Adcock	41	12	2	1	1		3+1	4
Ball	6+2	1					1+1	
Betts	45	5	2		1		6	2
Boyce	0+2							
Caesar	23	2	2		1		3	
Caldwell							1	
Cawley	42	1	2		1		5	1
Cheetham	25+3	2	2		1	1	3	
Dennis	24+8	3					3+1	
Duguid	7+9	1					0+1	
Dunne	2+3	1						
Emberson	41		2		1		5	
English	20+1		2		1		3+1	
Fry	35+3	2	0+1		1		6	
Gibbs	13+11	3			0+1		3	
Greene	14	1			1		2	
Gregory	7+3							
Kinsella	45	5	2	1	1		6	3
Lewis	1+1				1			
Locke	22+3	3	2				2+2	
McCarthy	44		2		1		6	
McGleish	10+5	6					2	
Mardenborough	4+8	2			1		1	
Petterson	5							
Reinelt	12+10	7	0+1				3	1
Whitton	10+2	2	2				0+2	

COVENTRY CITY (PREM: 16th)

	P/FL App	P/FL Goals	FLC App	FLC Goals	FAC App	FAC Goals	Others App	Others Goals
Barnwell-Edinboro	0+1							
Boland	2+1							
Borrows	21		3		1			
Burrows	11				1			

COVENTRY CITY cont.

	P/FL App	P/FL Goals	FLC App	FLC Goals	FAC App	FAC Goals	Others App	Others Goals
Busst	16+1	2	2	1	3			
Christie	0+1		0+1					
Cook	2+1							
Daish	11	1						
Dublin	34	14	1+1		3	2		
Filan	13		2					
Gould			1+1					
Hall	24+1		4		2			
Isaias	9+2	2	2					
Jess	9+3	1						
Lamptey	3+3		3+1	2	0+1			
Ndlovu	27+5	5	4	1	0+1			
Ogrizovic	25		1		3			
Pickering	26+4		2+1		2	1		
Rennie	9+2	2	1					
Richardson	33		4	1	3			
Salako	34+3	3	3	1	3	1		
Shaw	21				3			
Strachan	5+7		3		2			
Telfer	31	1	4		3	1		
Whelan	21	8	4		3	1		
Whyte	1							
Williams	30+2	2	4		1	1	1	

CREWE ALEXANDRA (DIV 2: 5th)

	P/FL App	P/FL Goals	FLC App	FLC Goals	FAC App	FAC Goals	Others App	Others Goals
Adebola	20+9	8	1+1	1	4+1	2	2+1	
Barr	15+2		2				0+1	
Blissett	10	1					1+1	
Booty	21	2	4		3		2	
Clarkson	1+4		0+1		0+1		1	
Collier	2+4		1					
Collins	37+5	1	3		4		4+1	1
Edwards	29+3	15	3	4	5	2	2	
Ellison	0+1						0+1	
Garvey	18+11	2	2		0+2		2+1	1
Gayle	46		2		5		5	
Lennon	25		4		5		3	
Lightfoot	5+1						2	
Little	7+5	1			1		1	
McAllister	13	1			2			
Macauley	27+2	7	4		3		5	1
Murphy	41+1	10	4		3	1	3+1	1
Pope			0+1					
Ridings	1						1	
Rivers	24+9	10	0+1		5	2	2+2	2
Savage	28+2	7	3		1		5	1
Smith	24+5	1			2+2		1	
Tierney	21+1	2	2		0+1		0+2	
Unsworth	16+13		2+1	1	3+1	1	3+2	
Westwood	31+2	4	4		5	1	4	
Whalley	44	2	4		4	1	4	

CRYSTAL PALACE (DIV 1: 3rd)

	P/FL App	P/FL Goals	FLC App	FLC Goals	FAC App	FAC Goals	Others App	Others Goals
Andersen	12+4						1	
Boere	0+8	1						
Boxall	1							
Brown	5+1	2			3	1		
Coleman	17		4					
Cox	1+3				0+1	1		
Cundy	4							
Davies	17+3	2			2			
Dowie	4	2						
Dyer	21+14	13	4		0+1	1	0+2	
Edworthy	44		4		2		3	
Freedman	37+2	20	2		2		3	
Gale	2				1			
Gordon	34	8	4		2			
Hopkin	41+1	8	4	4	1		1	
Houghton	41	4	4		3		2	
Launders	0+2		0+1					
McKenzie	4+8		3	1	1+1			
Martyn	46		4		2		3	

CRYSTAL PALACE cont.

	P/FL App	Goals	FLC App	Goals	FAC App	Goals	Others App	Goals
Matthew	4+4		1+1					
Ndah	17+6	4	0+1				3	
Pitcher	36		2+1		2		3	
Quinn	1						2+1	
Roberts	36+2		3+1		2		3	1
Rodger	14+10		1		0+2		0+1	
Scully	0+2							
Shaw	15		4					
Sparrow	1		0+1					
Taylor	18+2	1			2		1	
Tuttle	9+1	1					3	
Veart	5+7						2+1	1
Vincent	19+6		2+1	1	1			

Dougie Freedman (Crystal Palace)

DARLINGTON (DIV 3: 5th)

	P/FL App	Goals	FLC App	Goals	FAC App	Goals	Others App	Goals
Andersson							0+1	
Appleby	42+1	6			3		5	2
Bannister	39+2	10	2		3		4+1	
Barnard	37	3	1				3	
Blake	23+6	11	0+2		1+1		3	1
Brumwell	16+12		1+1		3		3+2	
Burridge	3							
Carmichael	11+2	2					2+1	
Carss	13+15	2	2	1	1+1		3	
Crosby	45		1		3		5	
Gaughan	34+7	3	2		2	1	5	
Gregan	38		1		2		5	1
Guinan	3							
Himsworth	26+2	3	2		3		1	
Lucas	6							
McMahon	6+4	1					0+1	
Mattison	1+6							
Muir	4	1						
Naylor	3+1	1					1+1	
Neves	3+2		2				2	
Newell	21						3	
Olsson	34	4	1		3	1	1	1
Painter	33+2	8			2+1	1	4	1
Paulo	4+2		1+1					
Pollitt	15		2		1		2	
Pugh							0+1	
Quitongo	1							

DARLINGTON cont.

	P/FL App	Goals	FLC App	Goals	FAC App	Goals	Others App	Goals
Robinson	0+4				0+1			
Shaw	36+5	1	2		3	1	2	
Stephenson	1							
Twynham	2							
Worboys	6+8	2	1+1		1		1+1	

DERBY COUNTY (DIV 1: 2nd)

	P/FL App	Goals	FLC App	Goals	FAC App	Goals	Others App	Goals
Boden	4							
Carbon	2+4							
Carsley	31+4	1	2					
Cooper	0+1							
Flynn	29+13	2	3		1			
Gabbiadini	33+6	11	3	1	1	1		
Harkes	7+1							
Hodges	1+8							
Hoult	40+1		2		1			
Kavanagh	8+1	1						
Nicholson	19+1		3		1			
Powell C	19							
Powell D	37	5	1+1					
Preece	10+3	1	2					
Rowett	34+1		2		1			
Simpson	21+18	10	2	1	1	1		
Stallard	3		1	1				
Stimac	27	1						
Sturridge	33+6	20						
Sutton S	6		1					
Sutton W	1							
Trollope	7+10		1+1		0+1			
Van der Laan	39	6	3		1			
Ward	5+2	1						
Wassall	16+1	1						
Webster	3							
Willems	31+2	11	2	1	1			
Wrack	2+8		0+3		0+1			
Yates	38	2	1					

DONCASTER ROVERS (DIV 3: 13th)

	P/FL App	Goals	FLC App	Goals	FAC App	Goals	Others App	Goals
Ashley	3							
Barker	5+1						0+1	
Brabin	31	3			1		2	
Brodie	5	1						
Carmichael	19+8	4	0+1		0+1	1	2+1	
Clark	14+9	1	0+2		1		3	1
Cramb	20+1	7						
Colcombe	21+9	3			1		2	1
Darby	8+9	4	2		0+1		1+1	
Doling	0+1							
Gore	5							
Hackett	7		2				1	
Harper	0+1		0+1					
Jones	31+1	10	2		1		2	
Kirby	32+4				1		2	
Knight	1+3							
Marquis	15	1						
Maxfield	12+7	1					1	
Meara	0+1							
Measham	7+3		2		1		2	
Moore	35	2	2		1		2	1
Murphy	17+6						2	
Norbury	2+3		0+1				0+1	
Noteman	4		1	2				
O'Connor	8							
Parrish	39+2	5	2		1	1	1	
Peel	2							
Robertson	12+4						2	
Schofield	40+1	4	2		1		2	
Smith	12+1							
Speight	1							
Suckling	21		2		1		1	
Utley	1							
Warren	40+2		2		1		3	

DONCASTER ROVERS cont.

	P/FL App	Goals	FLC App	Goals	FAC App	Goals	Others App	Goals
Wilcox	4		2	1				
Williams D	17						2	
Williams P	2+1	1						
Wright	13							

EVERTON (PREM: 6th)

	P/FL App	Goals	FLC App	Goals	FAC App	Goals	Others App	Goals
Ablett	13		1		3	1	4	
Amokachi	17+8	6	1		2+1	1	3	1
Barlow	0+3		0+1				0+2	
Barrett	8		2				3	
Branch	1+2							
Ebbrell	24+1	4			4	1	3	1
Ferguson	16+2	5			2	2		
Grant	11+2	1	2		0+1		2+2	1
Hinchcliffe	23+5	1	2	1	1+2		4	
Holmes	1						0+2	
Horne	25+1	1	2		4		3	
Hottiger	9	1						
Jackson	14		1		2		3	
Kanchelskis	32	17			4			
Limpar	22+6	3	1		2+2		4	
O'Connor	3+1							
Parkinson	28		3		2		3	
Rideout	19+6	6	2		1+1		5	1
Samways	3	1	1		2		2	1
Short	22+1	2	2		3		3	
Southall	38		2		4		5	
Stuart	27+2	10	1	1	4	3	2+1	1
Unsworth	28+3	2	0+1		2		4	1
Watson	34	1	1		4		2+1	

EXETER CITY (DIV 3: 14th)

	P/FL App	Goals	FLC App	Goals	FAC App	Goals	Others App	Goals
Anderson	5+8				0+1		1	
Bailey	41+1	1	2		1		2	
Blake	44	2	2		1			
Bradbury	14	5						
Braithwaite	14+9	3						
Buckle	22	2			1		2	
Came	38	4	2		1		2	1
Cecere	5+8	1	1				0+1	
Chamberlain	29+4	1	2				1	
Cooper	26+1	6	2					
Coughlin	6+2	1						
Foster	4+3							
Fox	46		2		1		2	
Gavin	24+4	2	1				2	
Hare	10+3				0+1		2	
Hughes	25+1				1			
McConnell	1+7							
Medlin	2+4						1	
Morgan	2+4						0+1	
Myers	7+1							
Parsley	29+3				1		1	
Pears	19+3	5	0+1		1		1	
Phillips	11+2	3	0+1		1		1	
Rice	17+2		2				1	
Richardson	43	1	2	1	1		2	
Ross	7	2						
Sharpe	9+5	1						
Thirlby	0+2		0+1					
Turner	6+6	3			0+1			

FULHAM (DIV 3: 17th)

	P/FL App	Goals	FLC App	Goals	FAC App	Goals	Others App	Goals
Adams	5	1	2					
Angus	30+1	2	4		5	1	4	
Barber	13							
Barkus	3+6	1	1+1	1	2+1		2	
Bartley							0+1	
Blake	35+3	5	4		2		3	
Bolt	7+4	2			4+1		2+1	
Bower	4						2	
Brazil	17+1	2	3+1	1	2		3	

FULHAM cont.

	P/FL App Goals	FLC App Goals	FAC App Goals	Others App Goals
Brooker	9+11 2		1+2 1	0+1
Conroy	38+ 2 9	4 2	4+1 3	3 1
Cusack	38+ 4 5	1+3 1	4+1 1	2+2 1
Finnigan	1+ 1	1		2
Gray	6			1
Hamill	6+19 2	2	2+2 1	1+2
Hamsher	0+ 3			
Harrison	5			2
Herrera	42+ 1	4	5	2+1
Jupp	35+ 1	3+1	5 1	2 1
Lange	41	4	5	2
McAree	16+ 1 2			0+1
Marshall	14+ 2		2	1
Mison	16+ 7 4	4 1	1+1	2
Moore	17+ 3 1		3+2	1
Morgan	41 6	3	3	4 2
Scott	21 5			
Simpson	5+ 2			
Taylor	7		1	2
Thomas	32+ 5 5	4	4 1	3
Williams	2+11		0+1	

GILLINGHAM (DIV 3: 2nd)

	P/FL App Goals	FLC App Goals	FAC App Goals	Others App Goals
Ansah	0+ 2			
Arnott	0+ 1			0+1
Bailey	40+ 5 8	2 1	4 1	
Bremner				0+1
Brown	0+ 1			
Butler P	34+ 2 2	2	1+1	2
Butler S	14+ 6 5			2
Carpenter	7+ 5		0+1	2
Castle	5+ 1 1			
Dunne	1+ 1	1	0+1	1+1
Fortune-West	36+ 4 12	2 1	.3 2	
Foster	1+10 1	0+2		2 2
Freeman	4+ 6		0+1	2 1
Gayle	9 3			
Green	35 2	2	4	2
Harris	44 2	2	4	
Manuel	6+ 4			
Martin	27+ 4 1		4 1	1
Micklewhite	17+14		4	2
Naylor	30+ 1 1	2 1	3	1
Nicholls				1
O'Connor	18	2	2	
Puttnam	10+16 1		0+3	1
Ratcliffe	41 3	2	2	
Rattray	18+ 8 3	1	2	2
Smith	36+ 1 1	1	4	0+1
Stannard	46	2	4	1
Thomas	14+ 1			
Watson A	10 1			
Watson P	3+ 5		2	2

GRIMSBY TOWN (DIV 1: 17th)

	P/FL App Goals	FLC App Goals	FAC App Goals	Others App Goals
Bonetti	19 3	1	2 1	
Butler	3			
Childs	33+ 2 3	1	5 1	
Clare	0+ 1	0+1		
Crichton	44	2	5	
Croft	36 1	2	5	
Dobbin	21+ 5 3	2	1+1	
Fickling	5+ 6	2	1+1	
Flatts	4+ 1			
Forrester	23+ 5 5		3+1 3	
Gallimore	10 1			
Gambaro	0+ 1			
Groves	46 9	2	5 1	
Handyside	30	2	1	
Jewell	2+ 3 1	1		
Jobling	3			
Laws	21+ 6 1	2	4 1	

GRIMSBY TOWN cont.

	P/FL App Goals	FLC App Goals	FAC App Goals	Others App Goals
Lester	0+ 5	0+1		
Lever	23+ 1 1		4	
Livingstone	33+ 5 11	1	3+2 2	
McDermott	27+ 1 1		4	
Mendonca	8 4			
Neill	1			
Pearcey	2			
Rodger	14+ 2		1	
Shakespeare	24+ 4 2		4	
Smith	18			
Southall	28+ 5 2	2 1	3+2 1	
Walker	1+ 1 1			
Warner	3			
Watson	0+ 2	1		
Woods	24+ 9 4	1 1	4+1 2	

HARTLEPOOL UNITED (DIV 3: 20th)

	P/FL App Goals	FLC App Goals	FAC App Goals	Others App Goals
Allinson	3+ 1		1	1
Allon	22 8			2 1
Billing	35+ 1	4	1	2
Canham	25+ 4 1	3		1
Conlon	11+ 4 4			
Debont	1			
Dixon	3			
Ford	2+ 1	0+1		
Foster	0+ 1			
Gallagher	1			
Halliday	36+ 3 7	4	1 1	2
Henderson	33+ 3 3	3+1	1	2
Homer	1+ 4	0+1		0+1
Horne	32	2		0+1
Houchen	36+ 2 6	3		
Howard	32+ 7 7	3	1	2 2
Hutt	0+ 1			
Ingram	32+ 1 2	3	1	2
Jones	7+ 2	2		1
Key	1			
Lee	3+ 3	0+1		0+1
Lowe	13 3	2		
Lynch	13+ 6 1	1+3	0+1	1
McAuley	46	4	1	2
McGuckin	40 2	4	1 1	1
O'Connor	1			
Oliver	7+ 6	1+3	0+1	1
Reddish	18+ 2	1		
Roberts	4		1	
Slater	0+ 1			
Sloan	1+ 5		1 1	0+1
Stokoe	8			
Tait	38+ 1 2	4	1	1
Walton	1+ 5			

HEREFORD UNITED (DIV 3: 6th)

	P/FL App Goals	FLC App Goals	FAC App Goals	Others App Goals
Blatherwick	10 1			2
Brough	22 1	1	3 1	3+1
Clarke	5			
Cross	32+ 5 8	0+2	4 1	7 2
Debont	8			
Downing	29		3	4
Evans	24		4	5
Fishlock	26+ 1 3	2	3	4
Hall	0+ 1			
Hargreaves	15+ 2 2			1
James	17 2			2
Lloyd	25+ 2	2	1	3
Lyne	22+10 1	2	3	5+1
MacKenzie	38 1	2	4	7
Pick	10+ 4	1	1	2
Pitman	12+ 1			2
Pounder	31+ 3 2	2	3+1	4+2
Preedy	5+ 8 1		1	0+1
Reece	6	2 1		

HEREFORD UNITED cont.

	P/FL App Goals	FLC App Goals	FAC App Goals	Others App Goals
Smith	39+ 1 8	2 1	4	7 3
Steele	0+ 7		0+1	0+2
Stoker	30+ 3 3	2	2+1 1	5+1 1
Watkiss	19			2
White	39+ 1 29	2	4 3	6+1 2
Wilkins	42 3	2	4	6 2

HUDDERSFIELD TOWN (DIV 1: 8th)

	P/FL App Goals	FLC App Goals	FAC App Goals	Others App Goals
Baldry	3+11	0+1		
Booth	43 16	4 3	4 2	
Brown	5			
Bullock	42 6	4 1	4 1	
Collins	18+12 3	4 1	1+2	
Cowan	43 2	4	4 1	
Crosby	0+ 1	1		
Dalton	29 5	4 1	3+1	
Dunn	3+11	1+2	1+1	
Duxbury	3	1		
Dyson	15+ 2	2		
Edwards	13 7			
Francis	43	3	4	
Gray	38	4	4	
Jenkins	31 1		4	
Jepson	40+ 3 12	3	2 2	
Logan	2			
Makel	33 2		4	
Norman	3	1		
Reid	8+ 5	2	2	
Rowe	6+ 8 1	0+1	3+1 1	
Scully	25 1	3		
Sinnott	32	4	4	
Thornley	12 2			
Trevitt	4	2		
Turner	2+ 3 1			
Ward	7+ 1			
Whitney	3+ 1	0+1		

HULL CITY (DIV 2: 24th)

	P/FL App Goals	FLC App Goals	FAC App Goals	Others App Goals
Abbott	31 6	2	1	2
Allison	33+ 2 2	1 1	1	3
Brown	21+ 2 1	2	1+1	2
Carroll	23			
Dakin	2+ 4		0+1	1
Darby	8 1			
Davison	11 4			1
Dewhurst	16	3	2	1
Fettis	4+ 3	0+1		1
Fewings	16+ 9 2	3+1 1	2	0+1 1
Fidler	0+ 1			
Gilbert	6+ 7			
Gordon	3+10 3	0+2		0+1
Graham	24 1	2		
Hobson	28+ 1	3+1	1+1	2
Humphries	9+ 3	2	1	1
Lawford	20+11	3+1	0+1	3
Lee	25+ 3 1	2	2	2
Lowthorpe	15+ 4	3	2	1
Mann	34+ 4 1	4	2	2+1 1
Marks	4			
Mason	10+10 1	1+3		1+1
Maxfield	3+ 1			
Peacock	39+ 6 7	2+1	2	1+1
Pridmore			1	
Quigley	9+ 4 1	1		
Trevitt	25			
Watson	4			1
Wharton	7+ 2			
Wilkinson	8 1			
Williams	33+ 1	2	1	2
Wilson	19	4	2	2
Windass	16 4	4 3	1	3 1

IPSWICH TOWN (DIV 1: 7th)

	P/FL App	Goals	FLC App	Goals	FAC App	Goals	Others App	Goals
Appleby	0+3						1	
Barber	1							
Chapman	2+4		1				2	
Durrant							0+1	
Forrest	21		1		1		3	
Gregory	5+12	2	2		0+1		3+2	2
Linighan	2		1				1	
Marshall	35	19			4			
Mason	24+2	7			2+1	3	3	3
Mathie	39	18	1		2		4	1
Milton	34+3	9	0+2		4		4+1	
Mowbray	19	2			4		3	1
Norfolk							1	
Palmer	5						1	
Petterson	1							
Scowcroft	13+10	2	0+1		2		1+2	
Sedgley	40	4	2		4		3	1
Slater	11+6	2	2				2+2	
Stockwell	33+4	1	1		3		2	
Swailes	4+1							
Tanner	3+7						3+1	1
Taricco	36+3		2		3		3	
Thompson	5	1						
Thomsen	36+1	2	2	1	3		2+1	
Uhlenbeek	37+3	4	2		1+3		4	
Vaughan	19+6	1			1		2	
Wark	13+1	2	1		2		2	
Williams	42	1	2		4		2	
Wright	23		1		3		2	
Yallop	3+4		1		1		1+1	

LEEDS UNITED (PREM: 13th)

	P/FL App	Goals	FLC App	Goals	FAC App	Goals	Others App	Goals
Beeney	10		1		1			
Beesley	8+2		4+1		4		2+2	
Blunt	2+1							
Bowman	1+2		0+1				1	
Brolin	17+2	4	2+2		1+1			
Chapman	2							
Couzens	8+6		1+1	1			0+2	
Deane	30+4	7	5+2	2	3+3	1	3	
Dorigo	17		4		3		2	
Ford	12		4		5		0+1	
Gray	12+3		1+1		0+2			
Harte	2+2		0+1					
Jackson	0+1							
Jobson	12	1			1			
Kelly	34		8		5		4	
Kewell	2							
Lukic	28		7		5		4	
McAllister	36	5	8	2	6	3	4	1
Masinga	5+4		2	1	1			
Maybury	1							
Palmer	35	2	8		6		4	1
Pemberton	16+1		3		1+1		4	
Radebe	10+3		1+2		3+1			
Sharp	0+1						0+1	
Speed	29	2	7	3	4	1	4	1
Tinkler	5+4		1				0+1	
Wallace	12+12	1	3+1		3+1	1	0+1	
Wetherall	34	4	8		5		4	
Whelan	3+5		0+2				3	
White	1+3	1	1				1+1	
Worthington	12+4		2+1		3			
Yeboah	22	12	7	3	6	1	4	3

LEICESTER CITY (DIV 1: 5th)

	P/FL App	Goals	FLC App	Goals	FAC App	Goals	Others App	Goals
Blake	6+2		2					
Carey	16+3	1	2					
Claridge	14	5					3	1
Corica	16	2			2			
Gee	1+1							
Grayson	39+2	2	3+1		2		3	

LEICESTER CITY cont.

	P/FL App	Goals	FLC App	Goals	FAC App	Goals	Others App	Goals
Heskey	20+10	7	1+1				3	
Hill	24+3		3+1		2		0+1	
Izzett	8+1	1					3	
Joachim	14+8	1	2+1	1	1+1			
Kaamark	1		1					
Kalac	1		1				0+1	
Lawrence	10+5							
Lennon	14+1	1					3	
Lewis	10+4	1	0+1					
Lowe	21+7	3	4		1			
McMahon	1+2	1	0+1					
Parker	36+4	3	4		2		2+1	2
Philpott	1+5				2			
Poole	45		3		2		3	
Roberts	34+3	19	3	1	2			
Robins	19+12	6	2+1	4	1+1		1+1	
Rolling	17		3		0+1			
Smith	1							
Taylor	39	6	3		1		3	
Walsh	37	4	2		2		3	
Watts	9						3	
Whitlow	41+1	3	4		1		3	
Willis	11+1		1+1					

LEYTON ORIENT (DIV 3: 21st)

	P/FL App	Goals	FLC App	Goals	FAC App	Goals	Others App	Goals
Arnott	19	3						
Austin	32+8	1	2	1	1		1	
Ayorinde	1							
Baker	4+16		0+2		0+1		0+2	
Bellamy	32	1	1		1		2	
Berry	4+3							
Brooks	34+7	2	2		1		1	
Caldwell	28		2				1	
Chapman	38	2	2		1		2	
Cockerill	38	1	2		1		1	
Currie	9+1							
Fearon	18				1		1	
Gray	3+4							
Hanson	7+4	1					2	
Hendon	38	2	2		1		2	1
Inglethorpe	30	9	2				1	
Kelly N A	32+2	3	1		1		2	
Kelly R	5+1							
Lakin	5+3						1	
McCarthy	40+3		1				2	
Purse	9+3						0+1	
Shearer	5+3	1	1+1					
Stanislaus	20+1		1		1		1	
Warren	15+7	1	2				1	
Watson	0+1	1						
West	39	16	1	1	1			
Williams	1+2				1			

LINCOLN CITY (DIV 3: 18th)

	P/FL App	Goals	FLC App	Goals	FAC App	Goals	Others App	Goals
Ainsworth	31	12			1		3	1
Alcide	22+5	6					1	
Allon	3+1		1					
Appleton	4							
Barnett	27+5	2			1		3	
Bos	10+1	5						
Bound	3+1						1	
Brightwell	5		2					
Brown G	34				1		2	
Brown S	22+4	3			1		3	1
Carbon	26	3	1				2+1	
Daley	6+6	1			0+1		0+1	
Davis	3						1	
Daws	8+3	3						
Dixon	10+2		2					
Dyer	1		1					
Fleming	17+5							
Greenall	4		2					

LINCOLN CITY cont.

	P/FL App	Goals	FLC App	Goals	FAC App	Goals	Others App	Goals
Holmes	23	2					2	
Huckerby	16	2	2				1	2
Hulme	4+1				1		1+1	
Johnson A	17+5				1		1	
Johnson D	14+10	1			1		2	2
Key	5							
Leaning	7		2				4	
Megson	2		2					
Minett	39+3	5	2		1		4	
Mudd	2+2						1	
Onwere	33+2	4	2		1		3	1
Platnauer	0+1							
Puttnam	4+1	1	1					
Richardson	34				1			
Robertson	21+1						1	
Storey	0+2	1						
Wanless	7+1						2	
West	7+1	1	2					
Westley	9	1			1		1	
Whitney	25+1	2			1		3	
Williams	1+2							

LIVERPOOL (PREM: 3rd)

	P/FL App	Goals	FLC App	Goals	FAC App	Goals	Others App	Goals
Babb	28		4		4		4	
Barnes	36	3	3		7		4	
Bjornebye	2							
Clough	1+1							
Collymore	30+1	14	2+2		7	5	1+1	
Fowler	36+2	28	4	2	7	6	3+1	
Harkness	23+1	1	4	1	4		4	
James	38		4		7		4	
Jones	33		3		7		4	
Kennedy	1+3		0+1				0+1	
McAteer	27+2		3+1		7	3		
McManaman	38	6	4		7	2	4	1
Matteo	5				0+1			
Redknapp	19+4	3	3		2+1		4	
Ruddock	18+2	5	3+1		2		2	
Rush	10+10	5	2	1	0+4	1	2+1	
Scales	27		2		7		2	
Thomas	18+9	1	0+1	1	5+1		2+1	
Wright	28	2	3		7		4	

LUTON TOWN (DIV 1: 24th)

	P/FL App	Goals	FLC App	Goals	FAC App	Goals	Others App	Goals
Alexander	35+2	1	2		0+1		1+1	
Chenery	2							
Davis K	6				4			
Davis S	36	2	2				4	
Douglas	3+5	1					0+1	
Evers	1						1	
Feuer	38				1			
Grant	10	3						
Guentchev	25+10	9	2		1		2+1	2
Harvey	28+8	1	2				4	
Hughes	21+2	1	1				1	
James	23+4		1		1		2	
Johnson G	4+1							
Johnson M	34+2		2	1	1		2	
Linton	6+4						3	
McLaren	9+3	1			1		3	
Marshall	23+3	9	2	1	1	1	2+1	2
Matthews			0+1					
Oakes	26+3	3			1		3	1
Oldfield	23+11	2	2		1		2	
Patterson	21+2				1		2	
Peake	15+3							
Riseth	6+5							
Simpson							0+1	
Skelton							1	
Sommer	2		2					
Taylor	18+10		2				1	1
Thomas	25+2		1+1		1		0+1	

LUTON TOWN cont.

	P/FL App	Goals	FLC App	Goals	FAC App	Goals	Others App	Goals
Thorpe	23+10	7	0+2		0+1		1+2	1
Tomlinson	1+6							
Upson							1	
Vilstrup	6+1						2	
Waddock	32+4		1		1		1+1	
Wilkinson	3							
Woodsford	1+2						0+2	

MANCHESTER CITY (PREM: 18th)

	P/FL App	Goals	FLC App	Goals	FAC App	Goals	Others App	Goals
Beagrie	4+1		2					
Brightwell	26+3		3		2			
Brown	16+5		0+2		5			
Clough	15	2			3	1		
Creaney	6+9	3			0+3	1		
Curle	32		3	1	5			
Edghill	13		3					
Ekelund	2+2				1+1			
Flitcroft	25		1		4	1		
Foster	4		1					
Frontzeck	11+1				1			
Hiley	2+4							
Immel	38		3		5			
Ingram	5				1			
Kavelashvili	3+1	1						
Kernaghan	4+2							
Kerr	0+1							
Kinkladze	37	4	3		4	1		
Lomas	32+1	3	3		5	1		
Margetson			0+1					
Mazzarelli	0+2							
Phelan	9		1					
Phillips	2+9							
Quinn	24+8	8	3	1	4	2		
Rosler	34+2	9	3	2	5	2		
Summerbee	33+4	1	1+2		5			
Symons	38	2	3		5			
Walsh	3							

MANCHESTER UNITED (PREM: 1st)

	P/FL App	Goals	FLC App	Goals	FAC App	Goals	Others App	Goals
Beckham	26+7	7	2		3	1	2	
Bruce	30	1	1+1		5		2	
Butt	31+1	2	1		7	1	2	
Cantona	30	14	1		7	5		
Cole	32+2	11	1		7	2	1	
Cooke	1+3		1+1	1			0+1	
Davies	1+5		1				0+1	
Giggs	30+3	11	2		7	1	2	
Irwin	31	1	1		6		1	
Keane	29	6	0+1	1	7		2	
McClair	12+10	3	1					
McGibbon			1					
May	11+5	1			2			
Neville G	30+1				5+1		1	
Neville P	21+3		1+1		6+1		1	
O'Kane	0+1						1	
Pallister	21	1	2		3		2	
Parker	5+1		1		1+1	1	0+1	
Pilkington	2+1		1		1			
Prunier	2							
Schmeichel	36		1		6		2	1
Scholes	16+10	10	1	2	0+2	1	1+1	1
Sharpe	21+10	4	2		4+2	2	2	
Thornley	0+1							

MANSFIELD TOWN (DIV 3: 19th)

	P/FL App	Goals	FLC App	Goals	FAC App	Goals	Others App	Goals
Alexander	0+1		0+1					
Baraclough	11	2	2				1	
Barber	4	1					1	
Boothroyd	42+1	2	2		2		2	
Bowling	44		2		2		1	
Brien	4							
Carmichael	1	1						

MANSFIELD TOWN cont.

	P/FL App	Goals	FLC App	Goals	FAC App	Goals	Others App	Goals
Clarke	1+2							
Doolan	42	2	2		1	1	2	1
Eustace	25+2	1			1		2	
Hackett	32	3			2			
Hadley	27+6	7	2		2		1+1	1
Harper	29	5			2	1	2	
Howarth	17		2		1		1	
Ireland	38+1	6	2		2		1+1	
Kerr	4+1						1	
Kilcline	18+1							
Lampkin	2+4		0+1					
Onuora	7+7	1			0+1			
Parkin	15+1	1	2		2	1	1	
Peel	2						1	
Peters	21	2	1		2		1	
Robinson	4+5	1	0+1					
Sale	24+3	7	2	1	1		1	
Sedgemore	4+5						1	
Sherlock	14+4	2	1		2	1		
Slawson	21+8	5	2				1+1	
Timons	16+1	1						
Todd	10+2							
Trinder	1						1	
Varadi	1							
Weaver	1							
Williams	5+5	3						
Wood	9+1	1						

MIDDLESBROUGH (PREM: 12th)

	P/FL App	Goals	FLC App	Goals	FAC App	Goals	Others App	Goals
Barmby	32	7	4	1	3	1		
Barron	1							
Blackmore	4+1		0+1					
Branco	5+2							
Campbell	1+1							
Cox	35	2	5		2			
Fjortoft	27+1	6	6	2				
Fleming	13	1	1		1			
Freestone	2+1	1			0+1			
Hendrie	7+6	1	1+1					
Hignett	17+5	5	3+1	2	0+1			
Juninho	20+1	2	2		3			
Kavanagh	6+1							
Liddle	12+1		2+1		1			
Miller	6							
Moore	5+7		1+2					
Moreno	2+5		2		0+1			
Morris	22+1	2	4		2			
Mustoe	21	1	3	1	1			
O'Halloran	2+1				2			
Pearson	36		5		3			
Pollock	31	1	6		3	1		
Robson	1+1		1		1			
Stamp	11+1	2	2		0+1			
Summerbell	0+1							
Vickers	32		6	1	3			
Walsh	32		6		3			
Whelan	9+4	1	3		3			
Whyte	24+1		3					
Wilkinson	2+1				3			

MILLWALL (DIV 1: 22nd)

	P/FL App	Goals	FLC App	Goals	FAC App	Goals	Others App	Goals
Bennett	1+1							
Berry	1				1			
Black	1+2	1	0+1					
Bowry	33+5	2	3		2			
Cadette	0+1							
Carter	4				1			
Connor	7+1							
Dixon	15+7	5	1+2		1			
Dolby	6+4							
Doyle	15+3		2					
Forbes	0+4		0+1		0+1			

MILLWALL cont.

	P/FL App	Goals	FLC App	Goals	FAC App	Goals	Others App	Goals
Fuchs	21+11	5	2+1		0+1			
Gordon	6							
Iouran	13	1						
Keller	42		3		1			
Keown					0+1			
Kulkov	6							
Lavin	18+2				1			
McRobert	1+6		1		1			
Malkin	39+4	11	3		2	1		
Neill	5+8							
Newman	34+2	1	3		2			
Rae	37	13	2	1	2	2		
Rogan	4+4							
Savage	17+10		2	1	1			
Stevens	39	2	3					
Taylor	12+10		0+2	2	1+1			
Thatcher	41+1		2		2			
Van Blerk	42	1	3		1			
Webber	8+8		0+1					
Weir	8							
Witter	30+1	1	3		2			

NEWCASTLE UNITED (PREM: 2nd)

	P/FL App	Goals	FLC App	Goals	FAC App	Goals	Others App	Goals
Albert	19+4	4	2+1	1	2	1		
Asprilla	11+3	2						
Barton	30+1		5		2			
Batty	11		1					
Beardsley	35	9	3	2	2	1		
Beresford	32+1		2		1			
Brayson			1					
Clark	22+6	2	3		1+1			
Crawford			0+1					
Elliott	5+1		2		1+1			
Ferdinand	37	25	5	3	2	1		
Fox	2+2		1					
Gillespie	26+2	4	4		1			
Ginola	34	5	4		2			
Hislop	24		4					
Holland			0+1					
Hottiger	0+1		1+1					
Howey	28	1	4		1			
Huckerby	0+1				0+1			
Kitson	2+5	2			2			
Lee	36	8	4	1	1			
Peacock	33+1		5	2	2			
Sellars	2+4		2	1				
Srnicek	14+1		1+1		2			
Watson	15+8	3	2+3	1	1			

NORTHAMPTON TOWN (DIV 3: 11th)

	P/FL App	Goals	FLC App	Goals	FAC App	Goals	Others App	Goals
Aldridge							0+2	
Armstrong	4	1					1	
Beckford	0+1				0+1		0+2	
Burns	40+3	7	2	1	2		3	1
Cahill	2+1				0+1			
Colkin	14+10	1	2		1+1		2	
Doherty	3+6	1						
Gibb	12+11	2					2	
Grayson	37+5	11	2		1		2	1
Hughes	7+1						1	
Hunter	26+8				2		4	1
Lee	1+4				1+1		2	
Maddison	21				2		2	
Mountfield	4							
Norton	42+2		2		2		3	
O'Shea	37+1		2		2		2+1	
Peer	37+5	1	2	1	2		4	
Sampson	30+3	4	2				2	
Scott	5						1	
Smith	2		2					
Taylor M	1							
Taylor S	1+1							

NORTHAMPTON TOWN cont.

	P/FL		FLC		FAC		Others	
	App	Goals	App	Goals	App	Goals	App	Goals
Thompson	21+13	2	0+2				0+1	
Turley	2							
Warburton	44	3	2		2	1	4	
White	40+ 5	16	0+1		2		3	
Williams	25+10	1	2		1		2+1	
Woodman	44		2		2		4	
Worboys	4+ 9	1						

NORWICH CITY (DIV 1: 16th)

	P/FL		FLC		FAC		Others	
	App	Goals	App	Goals	App	Goals	App	Goals
Adams	40+ 2	2	4+1		1			
Akinbiyi	13+ 9	3	2+1	2				
Bowen	30+ 1	2	6		1			
Bradshaw	18+ 3	1	3		1			
Carey	6+ 3		2+1					
Crook	27+ 1	2	4	1				
Cureton	4+ 8	2						
Eadie	29+ 2	6	6+1	1	0+1			
Fleck	37+ 4	10	5+2	2	1			
Goss	9+ 7	1			1			
Gunn	43		7		1			
Johnson	23+ 3	7	3+1	1				
Marshall	3		1					
Milligan	21+ 7	2	4					
Mills	8+ 6		1+2	1				
Molby	3		2	1				
Newman	15+ 8	1	2					
Newsome	26+ 1	4	5		1	1		
O'Neill	12+ 7	1	4+1		1			
Polston	27+ 3		5		1			
Prior	42+ 2	1	6+1		0+1			
Rush	0+ 1							
Scott	5+ 7	2	0+2					
Sheron	2+ 5	1	2	2				
Simpson	1		1					
Sutch	7+ 6		2		0+1			
Ullathorne	26+ 3		5+1	1	1			
Ward	28	10	6	3	1			
Wright	1							

NOTTINGHAM FOREST (PREM: 9th)

	P/FL		FLC		FAC		Others	
	App	Goals	App	Goals	App	Goals	App	Goals
Allen	1+ 2	1						
Bart-Williams	33		2		7		7+1	
Black	1+ 1							
Bohinen	7		1	2			1	
Campbell	21	3			7	3	3	
Chettle	37		2		7		8	1
Cooper	37	5	2		5		7	
Crossley	38		2		7		8	
Gemmill	26+ 5	1	1		7		6+1	
Guinan	1+ 1							
Haaland	12+ 5				1+1		2+3	
Howe	4+ 5	2					1+1	
Irving	0+ 1							
Lee	21+ 7	8	2		0+4		4+2	
Lyttle	32+ 1	1	2		7		7	
McGregor	7+ 7	2			0+2		0+3	1
Pearce	31	3	1		4	2	8	
Phillips	14+ 4				4+2		3	
Roy	25+ 3	8	1		6	1	6	1
Silenzi	3+ 7			1	2+1	1	1+3	
Stone	34	7	2		6		8	2
Woan	33	8	2		7	3	8	1

NOTTS COUNTY (DIV 2: 4th)

	P/FL		FLC		FAC		Others	
	App	Goals	App	Goals	App	Goals	App	Goals
Agana	20+ 9	2	3		0+2	1	6	
Arkins	17+ 6	7	1+1		3		4	
Ashcroft	4+ 2							
Baraclough	35		2		3			
Battersby	14+ 7	7					4	
Derry	12						3	
Devlin	26	6	2		3	2	3+1	
Finnan	14+ 3	2					3	1

NOTTS COUNTY cont.

	P/FL		FLC		FAC		Others	
	App	Goals	App	Goals	App	Goals	App	Goals
Gallagher	21+ 1	2	1		3		3	1
Galloway	7+ 2		2				3	
Hogg	10		2		1		2	
Hoyle	2							
Hunt	10	1						
Jemson	2+ 1		1+1					
Jones	16+ 2	5					1+1	
Legg	24+ 1	4	4		3		6+1	2
McSwegan	0+ 3		0+1					
Marsden	3		1					
Martindale	13+ 3	6					2+1	2
Mills	11+ 2				2		3	
Murphy	39	3	2		3	1	6	
Nicol	13	2	1		1		1	
Redmile							1	
Richardson	15						3	
Rogers	21	2			1		4	1
Short	0+ 2		2				1+1	
Simpson	18+ 5		2		2+1		3	
Strodder	43	3	2		3		6	
Turner	12	1	3		2			
Walker	11		4				1	
Ward	46		2		3		7	
White	18+ 2	8		6	0+1	1	1	
Wilder	9							

OLDHAM ATHLETIC (DIV 1: 18th)

	P/FL		FLC		FAC		Others	
	App	Goals	App	Goals	App	Goals	App	Goals
Banger	8+ 5	2			0+1		0+1	
Barlow	21+ 5	7	3		1		1	
Beckford	12+ 8	2			1	2	1+1	
Beresford	8+20	2	1+1				3	
Bernard	7	1	1				1	
Brennan	23+ 2	3	2		2		2	
Creaney	8+ 1	2						
Fleming	21+ 1		1				3	
Gannon	5							
Gerrard	36		2		3		2+1	
Graham	31+ 1	1	2		3		2	
Halle	37	3	2	1	3		4	
Hallworth	10+ 1						2	
Henry	14						1	
Hughes	10+ 5	1			3		0+2	
Jobson	12		2				2	
Lonergan	1+ 1							
McCarthy	30+ 5	10	2		2		3	1
McNiven	14+ 1		2		1		4	
Makin	39	2	2		2		1+1	
Olney	1		0+1				1	
Orlygsson	15+ 1				3			
Pemberton	0+ 2						0+1	
Pointon	3+ 1							
Redmond	37+ 3	1	1		3		1+1	
Richardson	27	11					4	
Rickers	23				1+1		1+1	
Serrant	20	1			2		3	
Snodin	24+ 2				1		1	
Vonk	5	1						
Wilkinson	4		1				1	1

OXFORD UNITED (DIV 2: 2nd)

	P/FL		FLC		FAC		Others	
	App	Goals	App	Goals	App	Goals	App	Goals
Aldridge	15+ 3	9			1+2			
Allen	13+11	3	4	2	1+2		1	
Angel	16+11	1	0+1		4+1		2+1	1
Beauchamp	25+ 7	7			2+2	1	0+2	
Biggins	8+ 2	1	3+1	1			0+1	
Carter	12		4				1	
Druce	1+ 7							
Elliott	45	8	4		6		3	
Ford M	43+ 1	2	4		5	1	3	
Ford R	26+ 2	3	3		6	2	3	
Gilchrist	42	3	4		5		3	
Gray	6+ 1							

OXFORD UNITED cont.

	P/FL		FLC		FAC		Others	
	App	Goals	App	Goals	App	Goals	App	Goals
Lewis	5+14				1			
Marsh	2+ 3		0+2					
Massey	33+ 2	4	2		6	4	2	
Milsom							0+1	
Moody	30+12	17	3	1	6	5	2	1
Murphy	13+21	5	2+2	1	2+2		2+1	2
Powell	1+ 2						0+2	
Robinson	40+ 1		4		4		1	
Rush	41+ 2	11	3		2+2	1	3	2
Smith	45	1	4		6		3	
Whitehead	34				6		2	
Wood	10+ 1				3	2	2	

Stuart Massey (Oxford U)

PETERBOROUGH UNITED (DIV 2: 19th)

	P/FL		FLC		FAC		Others	
	App	Goals	App	Goals	App	Goals	App	Goals
Ansah	0+ 2	1						
Ashley	9		1		2		2	
Basham	13+ 1	1						
Blount	4+ 1							
Breen	25		4		4		3	
Carter	30+ 7	1	3		2		3	
Charlery	19	7					1	
Clark	39+ 1	1	3		4		4	1
Codner	1+ 1							
Dobson	4							
Drury	0+ 1							
Ebdon	39	2	3		4	1	2	
Farrell	20+ 6	9	1+1		3+1	3	2+1	1
Foran	17						1	
Furnell	0+ 1				0+1		0+1	
Grazioli	2+ 1	1						
Gregory	0+ 3		1		1		2	
Griffiths	4						1	
Heald	40	4	3		3		5	
Hooper	4							
Inman	1							
Le Bihan	16+ 9		2+1	1	2+1	2	3+1	
McGleish	3+ 9		0+1		1		3+1	2
Manuel	13		4	3	1+1		2	
Martindale	26+ 5	15	4	1	4		4	2
Meredith	1+ 1							
Morrison	21+ 3	2	3+1		2		2+1	
Power	25+13	6	2+2		1+2		1	1
Rioch	13+ 5		2		2+1		2+1	
Robinson	5							
Sedgemore	13+ 4				1			
Shaw	12	5					2	

PETERBOROUGH UNITED cont.

	P/FL App	P/FL Goals	FLC App	FLC Goals	FAC App	FAC Goals	Others App	Others Goals
Sheffield	46		4		4		5	
Spearing	9	1	1		1+1		1	
Williams L	32+1		3		3+1		5	
Williams S	0+3							

PLYMOUTH ARGYLE (DIV 3: 4th)

	P/FL App	P/FL Goals	FLC App	FLC Goals	FAC App	FAC Goals	Others App	Others Goals
Baird	24+3	6			1+1	1		
Barlow	25+3	5					4	
Billy	22+10	4	2		3		2	
Blackwell	20				3			
Burnett	6		2					
Cherry	16						3	
Clayton	32+4	2	2		2		1	
Corazzin	1+5	1					0+1	
Curran	6+2						3	
Dawe							0+1	
Dungey							1	
Evans	41+4	12	0+1		3		5	1
Hammond	4		2				1	
Heathcote	44	4	2	1	3	1	4	
Hill	21+3		2		3		2	
Hodgson	3+2							
Leadbitter	29+4	1			3	1	4+1	1
Littlejohn	40+2	17	2		3	1	3	
Logan	25+6	4			1+2		4	
McCall	2+2							
Magee	0+4				0+1			
Mauge	36+1	6	2		3		3+1	1
Nugent	4+2		2				1	
O'Hagan	0+6		0+1					
Partridge	6+1	2						
Patterson	42+1		1		2		4	
Payne							0+1	
Petterson	6							
Richardson							0+2	
Ross							2	
Saunders	4+6	1	0+1		0+1			
Shilton	0+1							
Twiddy	1+1		1		0+1		1+1	
Williams	46	2	2		3		4	1
Wotton	0+1						2	

PORTSMOUTH (DIV 1: 21st)

	P/FL App	P/FL Goals	FLC App	FLC Goals	FAC App	FAC Goals	Others App	Others Goals
Awford	17+1	1	2					
Allen	27	4						
Bradbury	3+9							
Burton	24+8	7	1+1		0+1			
Butters	37	2	2		1			
Carter	31+4	4	1+1		0+1			
Creaney	3	3	2					
Dobson	7+2							
Durnin	30+11	3	2		1			
Gittens	14+1	1			1			
Griffiths	2+12	2	0+1		1			
Hall	44+2	10	2		1			
Hinshelwood	5							
Igoe	4+18		0+2					
Knight	42		1		1			
McLoughlin	38+2	10	1		1			
Perrett	8+1							
Pethick	30+8		2		1			
Poom	4		1					
Rees	15+6	1	2					
Russell	17+2		2					
Simpson	27+3	5	1		1			
Stimson	14	1			1			
Symons	1							
Thomson	15+1							
Walsh	21	5			1			
Whitbread	13							
Wood	13+2	1			1			

PORT VALE (DIV 1: 12th)

	P/FL App	P/FL Goals	FLC App	FLC Goals	FAC App	FAC Goals	Others App	Others Goals
Aspin	22	1	1		4		3	
Bogie	27+5	3	2		5+1	2	8	
Corden	2							
Foyle	24+1	7	1		4	2	2+2	4
Glover D	27+2		2	1	2		2	
Glover L	17+7	3	1+1	1			3+2	2
Griffiths	40+1	2	1		4		7	
Guppy	43+1	4	2		6		7+1	1
Hill	35				6		6	
Kent	0+1							
Lawton	2						1+1	
McCarthy	44+1	8	2		6	1	8	2
Mills	20+12	8	2	1	0+2		6	4
Musselwhite	39		2		6		6	
Naylor	30+9	11			6	1	5+1	3
Porter	44+1	10	2		6	1	7+1	1
Samuel	9	1						
Sandeman	1		1					
Stokes	16+2		0+1				4+3	
Talbot	8+12				2+1		2+3	1
Tankard	28+1		2		6		5+1	
Van Heusden	7						2	
Walker	21+14				3+3	2	3+3	

PRESTON NORTH END (DIV 3: 1st)

	P/FL App	P/FL Goals	FLC App	FLC Goals	FAC App	FAC Goals	Others App	Others Goals
Ainsworth	0+2		0+2					
Atkinson	42+2	5	2		2		3	1
Barrick	39+1				2		2	
Bennett	5+3	1						
Birch	11		2					
Bishop	4							
Brown	6+4	1					1	
Bryson	44	9	2	1	2		3	
Cartwright	22+4	3	1		1+1	1	1+2	
Davey	37+1	10			2		3	
Fensome	20		1		2		2	
Fleming	5		2				0+1	
Gage	4+3							
Grant	0+1							
Holmes	8							
Johnson	2							
Kidd	23+7		2		1		2+1	1
Kilbane	7+4	1					1+1	
Lancashire	2+4	2					0+1	
Lucas	1							
McDonald	8+3				1		2	
Magee	4+1		1+1					
Moilanen	2							
Moyes	41	3	2		2		3	
Raynor	2+1	1	1					
Richardson	3						1	
Saville	44	29	2		2		2	1
Sharp	1		2				1	
Smart	0+2						0+1	
Sparrow	13							
Squires	3+4						1+1	
Vaughan	40		2		2		2	
Wilcox	27	1			1	1	1	
Wilkinson	36+6	10	2		2	1	2	

QUEENS PARK RANGERS (PREM: 19th)

	P/FL App	P/FL Goals	FLC App	FLC Goals	FAC App	FAC Goals	Others App	Others Goals
Allen	5+3	1			2			
Bardsley	28+1		2		1			
Barker	33	5	4					
Brazier	6+5		1+1		1			
Brevett	27		3					
Challis	10+1				2			
Charles	0+4							
Dichio	21+8	11	3	1	0+1			
Gallen	26+4	8	2	1				
Goodridge	0+7	1	0+1		0+1			
Hateley	10+4	2	0+1		1			

QUEENS PARK RANGERS cont.

	P/FL App	P/FL Goals	FLC App	FLC Goals	FAC App	FAC Goals	Others App	Others Goals
Holloway	26+1	1	2		1			
Impey	28+1	3	4	1	2			
McDonald	25+1	1	3					
Maddix	20+2		3		0+2			
Murray	1							
Osborn	6+3	1	2					
Penrice	0+3							
Plummer	0+1							
Quashie	11				2	2		
Ready	16+6	1	4	1	2			
Roberts	5		3					
Sinclair	37	2	3	1	2			
Sommer	33				2			
Wilkins	11+4		2+1		2			
Yates	30		2		2			
Zelic	3+1							

READING (DIV 1: 19th)

	P/FL App	P/FL Goals	FLC App	FLC Goals	FAC App	FAC Goals	Others App	Others Goals
Bernal	34	2	4		1			
Booty	17	1						
Brown	12	1	3					
Caskey	15	2						
Codner	3+1		1					
Freeman	0+1							
Gilkes	36+8		3+2		1			
Gooding	37+3	3	4		2			
Gordon	0+1							
Hammond	5				1			
Holsgrove	27+3	1	5		2			
Hopkins	14							
Jones	13+8		3		2			
Kerr	4+4	2	0+1					
Lambert	10+5	4	2+2	1	0+2			
Lovell	28+7	8	3	2	0+2			
McPherson	16		3					
Meaker	15+6				0+1			
Mihailov	16				1			
Morley	14+3	4	2	1	2	1		
Nixon	1							
Nogan	32+7	10	4	1	2			
Parkinson	36+6		5		2			
Quinn	20+15	11	2+3	4	2	2		
Sheppard	18		4					
Sutton	2							
Swales	4+5		0+1		1			
Thorp	2		2					
Wdowczyk	29+1		2					
Williams A	31		3		2		2	
Williams M	11+4	1	0+1					
Woods	5							

ROCHDALE (DIV 3: 15th)

	P/FL App	P/FL Goals	FLC App	FLC Goals	FAC App	FAC Goals	Others App	Others Goals
Barlow	1+1							
Bayliss	25+3		2		1+1		2	
Butler	38	3	2		3		3	
Clarke	6				1			
Deary	36	4	1		3	2	3	1
Formby	18		2		4		3	
Gray	20		2		3		3	
Hall	9+5	1						
Hardy	5+2							
Key	14							
Lancaster	13+1	2						
Lyons	1+2							
Martin	33+4		0+1		4	1	2+1	
Mitchell	3+1							
Moulden	6+10	1			3	2	2	3
Peake	45+1	4	2		4	2	2	1
Pilkington	1							
Powell	0+2							
Price	3							
Proctor	1+2							

ROCHDALE cont.

	P/FL App	Goals	FLC App	Goals	FAC App	Goals	Others App	Goals
Russell	20+5		2				0+1	
Ryan	4+3		0+1		1+2		0+1	
Shaw	9+9	1	1	1	0+3		1+1	
Stuart	32+2	13			1		2	
Taylor	8+8	3						
Thackeray	27+2				2		2	
Thompson	43	4	2		4		3	
Thompstone	11+14	1	1	1	2+2		1+1	
Valentine	22+1		2		4		1	
Whitehall	46	20	2		4	1	3	3
Williams	1+11		1				0+1	

ROTHERHAM UNITED (DIV 2: 16th)

	P/FL App	Goals	FLC App	Goals	FAC App	Goals	Others App	Goals
Berry	33+3	7			1		7	1
Blades	34	1	3		1		7	
Bowyer	23+4		3				5	
Breckin	37+2	1	3		1		7	
Clarke	40		4				7	
Davis					1			
Davison	1		1					
Garner	31	1	3		1		6	1
Goater	44	18	4	3	1	2	8	1
Goodwin	25+1	4	3				5	3
Hayward	22+14	2	2	2	0+1		4+3	2
Hurst	32+8	1	1		1		6+1	
James	0+1							
Jeffrey	22	5	3	1	1		3	
Jemson	16	5					3	4
McGlashan	13+3	2	2		1	1	1	
McLean	9							
Monington	7+4		2				2	
Moore	10+1							
Muggleton	6						1	
Pettinger	0+1							
Pike	0+2							
Richardson	23+2	2	2				6+1	1
Roscoe	44+1	2	4		1		7	2
Smith	11+3						2	
Viljoen	5+3	2					0+2	
Wilder	18		4		1		1	

Andy Hayward (Rotherham U)

SCARBOROUGH (DIV 3: 23rd)

	P/FL App	Goals	FLC App	Goals	FAC App	Goals	Others App	Goals
Anthony	2							
Boardman	6+3				1		1+1	
Charles	41	5	2		1		1	
Cook	2							
Curtis	3+2							
D'Auria	18	1	2	1	1		1	
Fairclough	7							
Foreman	1+3							
Gardner	5+1	1						
Heald	1+8	1	0+2		0+1		2	1
Hicks	39+2	1	2		1		2	
Ironside	40				1		2	
Kelly	6		2					
Kinnaird	3				1			
Knowles	46		2		1		2	
Lee							1	
Lucas	44		2		1		1	
Magee	26+2	1						
Midgley	14+2	1						
Myers	8+1							
O'Riordan	1							
Page	26+11	5	2		1		2	
Partridge	5+2							
Ritchie	33+4	8	2		1			
Robinson	1						1	
Rockett	39	4	2				1	
Sansam	5+1							
Sunderland	3+3							
Thew	9+5		2				2	
Todd	23	1	2		1		0+1	
Toman	12+4	2					1	
Trebble	25+7	5			0+1		2	
Wells	10+4	1					1	
Willgrass	2+5		0+1				0+2	

SCUNTHORPE UNITED (DIV 3: 12th)

	P/FL App	Goals	FLC App	Goals	FAC App	Goals	Others App	Goals
Bradley	36+2	1	2		3		3	
Bullimore	11+3	1	0+2		2		2	
Butler	2							
Clarkson	21+3	6						
D'Auria	27	5						
Eyre	36+3	10	2	2	3	1	2	1
Ford	35+3	7	2	1	3	1	3	
Germaine	11							
Graham	1+2	1						
Hope	38+2	3	1+1		2		3	
Housham	21+7				1		2	1
Jones	11	3						
Knill	38	3	1		1		2	
McFarlane	41+5	16	2	1	2	2	3	2
Murfin	1							
Nicholson	13+23		2		1+2		0+3	
O'Halloran	6+1							
Paterson	23+3	2			3	1	2	
Samways	33		2		3		3	
Sansam	2+3	1					1+1	
Thornber	14+2		2		1		2	
Turnbull	16+7	3	2		2		1	
Varadi	0+2							
Walsh	22+3		2		2		1	
Wilson	40	1	2		3		2	
Young	7+7	1	0+2		1		1+2	

SHEFFIELD UNITED (DIV 1: 9th)

	P/FL App	Goals	FLC App	Goals	FAC App	Goals	Others App	Goals
Ablett	12							
Angell	6	2						
Anthony			1					
Battersby	3+7	1	1+1					
Beard	13+7		2					
Blake	20+2	12	1					
Blount	7+1		2					
Cowans	18+2				3			

SHEFFIELD UNITED cont.

	P/FL App	Goals	FLC App	Goals	FAC App	Goals	Others App	Goals
Davidson	1							
Fitzgerald	6							
Flo	17+2	4	1		1			
Foran	6+1							
Gage	2							
Gannon	12				1			
Gayle	3+2							
Hawes	1+1							
Heath	0+4				0+1			
Hodges	15+7	3	0+2		1+2			
Hodgson	12+4		1		1+1			
Holland	11+7	1			1			
Hutchison	18+1	2			1			
Kelly	34+1		2		3			
Mercer	1							
Muggleton	0+1							
Nilsen	39		2		3			
Patterson	21	2			2			
Reed	0+2							
Rogers	13+3		1+1					
Scott A	3+4		1					
Scott R	2+3	1						
Short	13+2				3			
Starbuck	5+6	1			1			
Taylor	10	2						
Tracey	11							
Tuttle	26	1	1		2			
Veart	17+10	5	1+1	1	1+1	1		
Vonk	17							
Walker	12+2	8						
Ward	39+3	1	1		3			
White	24+4	7			3			
Whitehouse	36+2	4	2	1	3	1		

SHEFFIELD WEDNESDAY (PREM: 15th)

	P/FL App	Goals	FLC App	Goals	FAC App	Goals	Others App	Goals
Atherton	36		4		1			
Blinker	9	2						
Bright	15+10	7	3+1	3	1			
Briscoe	22+4		1					
Degryse	30+4	8	3		4	1		
Donaldson	1+2	1						
Hirst	29+1	13	2+1	1	1			
Humphreys	1+4							
Hyde	14+12	1	2+1					
Ingesson	3+2		1					
Kovacevic	8+8	4			1			
Newsome	8	1						
Nicol	18+1							
Nolan	29		4		1			
Pearce	3		1					
Pembridge	24+1	2	3		1			
Petrescu	8							
Platts	0+2							
Pressman	30		4					
Sheridan	13+4							
Sinton	7+3		3		1			
Stefanovic	5+1				1			
Waddle	23+9	2	4		1			
Walker	36		4		1			
Watts	9+2	1	1					
Whittingham	27+2	6	3+1	1	1			
Williams	2+3		1+1					
Woods	8							

SHREWSBURY TOWN (DIV 2: 18th)

	P/FL App	Goals	FLC App	Goals	FAC App	Goals	Others App	Goals
Anthrobus	27+12	10	2+1		3+3	1	5+1	
Berkley	36+2	1	3		5		6	
Boden	5							
Clarke	15		3				1	
Cope	0+1							
Currie	11+2	2						
Dempsey	17+11	2	2+2		3+3	2	4+1	1

SHREWSBURY TOWN cont.

	P/FL App	P/FL Goals	FLC App	FLC Goals	FAC App	FAC Goals	Others App	Others Goals
Edwards	31		1		6		7	
Evans	25+9	3	2+1		6	2	5	1
Hughes	2		3					
Jackson	0+1							
Kay	7						1	
King			1					
Lynch	22+3	3	2	1			3+1	
Martin			0+1					
Megson	2							
Reed	9+2	2	2		0+1		1	
Robinson	2+2		2					
Rowbotham	20+6	8	2+1	1	4	1	1+3	
Scott	36	6	3		5	3	6	1
Seabury	26+8		4	1	4		4+1	
Spink	32+2	6	4		3+1	3	7+1	
Stevens	27+5	12			1+2	1	6+1	7
Stewart	4							
Summerfield	0+1						0+1	
Taylor	38	1	4		5		6+1	2
Walton	35		3		6		7	1
Watson	1							
Whiston	28	2			5	2	6	
Withe	30+2		2		6	1	7	
Woods	18+5		1		4		4+1	1
Wray	0+3							

SOUTHAMPTON (PREM: 17th)

	P/FL App	P/FL Goals	FLC App	FLC Goals	FAC App	FAC Goals	Others App	Others Goals
Beasant	36		4		6			
Benali	28+1		4		1			
Bennett	5+6		0+1					
Charlton	24+2		0+1		6			
Dodd	37	2	4		5	1		
Grobbelaar	2							
Hall	30	1	4	1	5	1		
Heaney	15+2	2	2+1		1			
Hughes	6+5	1	2		0+1			
Le Tissier	34	7	4	2	5	1		
McDonald	0+1				0+1			
Maddison	13+2	1	2+1		0+2			
Magilton	31	3	3		6	2		
Maskell	0+1				0+1			
Monkou	31+1	2	4	1	6			
Neilson	15+3				1+1			
Oakley	5+5	1			2+1	1		
Robinson	0+5				0+2			
Shipperley	37	6	4	2	6	3		
Tisdale	5+4	1						
Venison	21+1		2		3			
Walters	4+1				4			
Warren	1+6		1					
Watson	18+7	3	2+1	2	5	1		
Widdrington	20+1	2	2		4			

SOUTHEND UNITED (DIV 1: 14th)

	P/FL App	P/FL Goals	FLC App	FLC Goals	FAC App	FAC Goals	Others App	Others Goals
Ansah	0+4						1+1	
Barness	5							
Belsvik	3	1			1			
Bodley	38+1	1	2		1		4	
Boere	6	2						
Brown	6							
Byrne	38+3	5	2	1	1		4	
Charlery	2+1							
Dublin	42+1	3	2		1		2	
Gridelet	37+3	2	1		1		3	
Hails	39+3	4	1+1		1		3	
Hayes							1	
Hone	11+5		0+2				2	
Iorfa	1+1						0+3	
Jones	14+9	2	2	1	1		2	
Lapper	23+1		2				4	
McNally	20	2			1			
Marsh	40	5	2		1		3	1

SOUTHEND UNITED cont.

	P/FL App	P/FL Goals	FLC App	FLC Goals	FAC App	FAC Goals	Others App	Others Goals
Powell	27		2		1		4	
Rammell	6+1	2						
Read	3+1	1					1	
Regis	25+4	8	1		1		1+2	1
Roget	4+4	1						
Royce	46		2		1		4	
Stimson	10		·					
Sussex	1+1		1					
Thomson	22+11	6	1+1		0+1		1+1	
Tilson	23+5	3	1				2	1
Turner	4+2							
Whelan	1							
Willis	9+1	3					1	

STOCKPORT COUNTY (DIV 2: 9th)

	P/FL App	P/FL Goals	FLC App	FLC Goals	FAC App	FAC Goals	Others App	Others Goals
Allen			0+1					
Armstrong	44+2	13	5	2	4	3	2	
Beaumont	38+5		5		4		2	
Bennett	24	1	5		3		2	
Bound	26	5			2	1		
Chalk	5+5		4+1	1	1+3		1+1	
Connelly	42+1		5		4		2	
Croft	0+3							
Dickins	1							
Dinning	1+9	1	0+2		0+2			
Durkan	11+5							
Eckhardt	30+5	6	2+2	1	4	4	1	
Edwards	45		5		4		2	
Flynn	46	6	5		4		2	
Gannon	22+1	1	5	1	2		2	
Helliwell	18+4	9	4	1	2	1	1	
Jeffers	21+2	3			3			
Landon	7+4	4	0+1					
Marsden	19+1	1						
Mike	4+4				0+1			
Mutch	11	4						
Oliver	7+2	1	0+2		2		1	
Thornley	8+2	1						
Todd	42		5		4		2	
Ware	22+5	3	4		1		1	1
Williams	12+5	1	1+2				0+1	

STOKE CITY (DIV 1: 4th)

	P/FL App	P/FL Goals	FLC App	FLC Goals	FAC App	FAC Goals	Others App	Others Goals
Beeston	13+3							
Brightwell	0+1						1	
Carruthers	10+14	3	3		1		2+1	
Clarkson	43		3		2		4	
Cranson	23+1	1	0+1		1		1	
Devlin	5+5						2+2	
Dreyer	4+15				1		1+1	
Gayle	5+5	3			0+1		1+1	
Gleghorn	46+9		3		2		5	
Keen	27+6	3	2		2		2	
Muggleton	6							
Orlygsson	6+1						1	
Overson	18		3				2	
Peschisolido	20+6	6	3	1	1		2	2
Potter	38+3	1	3		2		5	
Prudhoe	39		3		2		4	
Sandford	46		3		2		4	
Scott	6+1						0+1	
Sheron	23+5	15					2	
Sigurdsson	46		3		2		4	
Sinclair	1						1	
Sturridge	30+11	13	1		2	1	4	
Wallace	44	6	3		2		5	1
Whittle	7+1						2	

SUNDERLAND (DIV 1: 1st)

	P/FL App	P/FL Goals	FLC App	FLC Goals	FAC App	FAC Goals	Others App	Others Goals
Agnew	26+3	5	1		1+1	1		
Aiston	4+10		0+1					
Angell	2		1		1			

SUNDERLAND cont.

	P/FL App	P/FL Goals	FLC App	FLC Goals	FAC App	FAC Goals	Others App	Others Goals
Armstrong	0+1		0+1					
Atkinson	5+2		3					
Ball	35+1	4	4		1			
Bracewell	38		4		2			
Bridges	2+13	4						
Chamberlain	29		4		2			
Cooke	6							
Given	17							
Gray Martin	4+3		1+1		0+1			
Gray Michael	46		4		2			
Gray P	28+4	8	4		2	1		
Hall	8+6							
Howey	17+10	3	1	2	0+2			
Kelly	9+2	1	1		1			
Kubicki	46		4		2			
Melville	40	4	2+1		2			
Mullin	5+5	1	1		0+1			
Ord	41+1	1	3		2			
Russell	35+6	13	1+3		2			
Scott	43	6	3		2			
Smith	9+11	2	2+2		1+1			
Stewart	11+1	1						

SWANSEA CITY (DIV 2: 22nd)

	P/FL App	P/FL Goals	FLC App	FLC Goals	FAC App	FAC Goals	Others App	Others Goals
Ampadu	40+3	2	2		1		3	
Barnhouse	12+3		2		1		3	
Barnwell-Edinboro	2+2							
Basham	9+2	1			1		0+2	
Beresford	4+2							
Brown	3+1							
Chapman	7	4						
Chapple	15+7	2	1		1			
Clode	25+5		0+2				1	
Coates	7+11		1+1	1	1		2	
Cook	30+3				1		2	
Cornforth	17	2	2					
Dennison	9						2	
Edwards	36+2	2	2		1		3	
Freestone	45	2	2		1		3	
Garnett	9							
Heggs	28+4	5	2		1		2	
Hodge	34+7	1	2	2	1		2+1	
Hurst	2	1						
Jenkins	15		2				1	
Jones L	16+1							
Jones S	16+1							
Lampard	8+1	1					1+1	
McDonald	3+5							
Mardenborough	1							
Molby	12	2						
O'Leary	1							
Pascoe	9+4	1			1		1+1	
Penney	28+1						1	
Perrett	2+2		0+1		0+1		0+1	
Thomas	3+13	1						
Torpey	41+1	15	2	1	1		3	1
Walker	32+1		2				3	

SWINDON TOWN (DIV 2: 1st)

	P/FL App	P/FL Goals	FLC App	FLC Goals	FAC App	FAC Goals	Others App	Others Goals
Allen	25+2				5	1	1	
Allison	43+1	17	3		6	2	3	
Beauchamp	1+2		0+1	1				
Bodin	32+1	2	4		4	1	1	
Collins	2+3				1		1	
Cowe	4+7	1						
Culverhouse	46		4		6		1	
Digby	25		2		6		3	
Drysdale	10+3				2+2		2	
Finney	22+8	12	4		2+4	2	2+1	1
Given	5							
Gooden	14+12	3	1+1	1	3+1		3	

SWINDON TOWN cont.

Player	P/FL App	Goals	FLC App	Goals	FAC App	Goals	Others App	Goals
Grant	3	1						
Hooper	0+1						2	
Horlock	44+1	12	3+1	1	6	3	1+2	
Leitch	7							
Ling	12+4				2+1	1	3	1
McMahon	20+1		4		3+1		0+1	
Mildenhall			2					
Murray	3+2	1	1				1	
Nijholt			0+1					
O'Sullivan	27+7	3	4		1		0+2	
Preece	7	1						
Robinson	46	1	3		6		2+1	
Seagraves	25+3		4		3+1		2	
Smith	2+6							
Talia	16							
Taylor	43	7	4		6		3	
Thorne G							1+1	
Thorne P	22+4	10	1		4+1		1+1	1

TORQUAY UNITED (DIV 3: 24th)

Player	P/FL App	Goals	FLC App	Goals	FAC App	Goals	Others App	Goals
Baker	20	4						
Barnes	0+1							
Barrow	35+6		4	2	3	1	2	
Bayes	28		4		3		2	
Bedeau	1+3				0+1			
Buckle	11	4	4					
Byng	4+10		1+2		1+1	1	1	
Canham	3							
Cooke	1						0+1	
Coughlin	22+3				3		1	
Croft	0+1		0+1					
Curran	17+2	1	3		3		2	1
Garner	10+1	1						
Gore	25	2	4		1	1	2	
Gregg	1							
Haddoui	0+2							
Hall	22+7		3		2+1		0+1	
Hancox	15+10	1	2+1		1	1	1	1
Hathaway	22+4	1	4	1	3	1	1	
Hawthorne	17+5		3	1	2		2	
Hodges	1+1				0+1			
Jack	12+2	2			3		1	
Kaasikmae							1	
Kelly	26+5		4		1		1	
Laight	8+12	2	0+2		1+1		0+2	
Mateu	5+5	1	0+1		0+2	1	2	
Monk	4+1							
Moors	0+1				1			
Ndah	16	3	2+1		1			
Newhouse	4	2						
Newland	17							
Oatway	24							
O'Riordan	6+2		1+1				2	
Partridge	5	2						
Povey	3							
Preston	4+4							
Ramsey	18							
Stamps	20+3	1	3				0+1	1
Thomas	1+5							
Travis	4+4		1		1			
Watson	29	2			2			
Williams	9							
Winter	36		1				1	

TOTTENHAM HOTSPUR (PREM: 8th)

Player	P/FL App	Goals	FLC App	Goals	FAC App	Goals	Others App	Goals
Anderton	6+2	2	1					
Armstrong	36	15	3	3	6	4		
Austin	28		3		4			
Calderwood	26+3	1	2		4			
Campbell	31	1	2		6			
Caskey	3				3			
Cundy	0+1							

TOTTENHAM HOTSPUR cont.

Player	P/FL App	Goals	FLC App	Goals	FAC App	Goals	Others App	Goals
Dozzell	24+4	3	1+2		2+1			
Dumitrescu	5							
Edinburgh	15+7		1+1		4			
Fox	26	6			6			
Howells	29	3	2		2			
Kerslake	2							
Mabbutt	32		3		6			
McMahon	7+7	3			0+1			
Nethercott	9+4				2+1			
Rosenthal	26+7	1	2	1	5	2		
Scott	0+2		0+1					
Sheringham	38	16	3	3	6	5		
Sinton	8+1							
Slade	1+4		0+1		0+2			
Walker	38		3		6			
Wilson	28		3		4+1	1		

TRANMERE ROVERS (DIV 1: 13th)

Player	P/FL App	Goals	FLC App	Goals	FAC App	Goals	Others App	Goals
Aldridge	45	27	3	2	1			
Bennett	26+3	9	4					
Branch	11+10	2	0+2					
Brannan	44		4	1	1			
Cook	15	1						
Coyne	46		4		1			
Garnett	17+1		1		1			
Higgins	16+1							
Irons	25+7	3	2		1			
Jones	17+6	1	3	2	1			
Kenworthy	0+4							
McGreal	32		4					
Mahon	0+2							
Moore	27+9	9	3+1	1	1			
Morgan	0+4	1						
Morrissey	8+8		1		1			
Mungall	2+4							
Nevin	39+1	3	3		1			
O'Brien	18+4	4			0+1			
Rogers	25+1	2			1			
Stevens	33+1		4					
Teale	29		4					
Thomas	31		4					

WALSALL (DIV 2: 11th)

Player	P/FL App	Goals	FLC App	Goals	FAC App	Goals	Others App	Goals
Bradley	45	1	2		5	2	2	
Butler	13+15	4			1+3		1+2	2
Daniel	23+2		2		1			
Evans	20+4	1	2	1			1	
Houghton	38+2	6	0+1	1	5	2	2	
Keister	9+12				1+2		2+1	
Kerr	0+1				0+1		0+1	
Lightbourne	37+6	15	2		3+2	3	3	5
Marsh	39+2	2	2		5	2	3	
Mountfield	28	1			3		2	
Ntamark	34+8		2		5		2+1	
O'Connor	41	9	2	1	5	1	2	1
Palmer	15		1				0+1	
Platt	0+4	2						
Richards							0+1	
Ricketts	0+1	1						
Rogers	23+2				4		3	
Rollo					0+1			
Roper	3+2				1		1	
Ryder	1+2		1					
Smith	0+1						0+1	
Viveash	31				5		3	2
Walker	26				3		2	
Watkiss	14+1		2		1			
Wilson	46	15	2	1	5	2	3	1
Wood	20				2			

WATFORD (DIV 1: 23rd)

Player	P/FL App	Goals	FLC App	Goals	FAC App	Goals	Others App	Goals
Andrews	0+1							
Barnes	10							
Bazeley	35+6	1	2+1	1	2			
Beadle	3		1					
Caskey	6	1						
Cherry	4							
Connolly	7+4	8			0+1			
Dixon	8+3							
Foster	26	4	3		1			
Gibbs	8+1							
Hessenthaler	30							
Hill	1							
Hodge	2							
Holdsworth	26+1	1	2		2			
Johnson	17+3	1	2	1	2			
Lavin	16		2					
Ludden	9+3				1+1			
Millen	32+1	1	3		2			
Miller	42		3		2			
Mooney	38+4	6	3		1	1		
Moralee	17+8	3	2+1		2			
Neill	1							
Page	16+3				1			
Palmer	35		2					
Payne	9+3	1			0+1			
Penrice	4+3	1						
Phillips	26+1	11	2	1	2			
Pitcher	2+7	1	1+1		2			
Porter	28+1	1	2					
Ramage	34+2	15	3		2			
Simpson	0+1							
Ward	1							
White	9+7	4						
Wilkinson	4							

WEST BROMWICH ALBION (DIV 1: 11th)

Player	P/FL App	Goals	FLC App	Goals	FAC App	Goals	Others App	Goals
Agnew	3		1					
Angell	0+3							
Ashcroft	11+15	4	0+1		0+1		3+2	
Brien	2		1					
Burgess	45	2	4	2	1		6	
Butler	9							
Coldicott	20+12		4		1	1	3+2	
Comyn	3							
Cunnington	8+1		1				2	
Darby	19+3	1			1		4	
Donovan	28+6		4	2	1		6	
Edwards	13+3		3		1		2	
Fettis	3							
Gilbert	35+5	5	4		1		7	
Hamilton	39+2	3	2		0+1		5	
Hargreaves	0+1						0+1	
Herbert					1		1	
Holmes	18						3	
Hunt	44+1	14	4	1	1		5+1	1
King	4						1	
Mardon	35+4		4		1		2	
Naylor	27		4		1		5	
Nicholson	18						2	
Phelan	1							
Raven	40	4	4		1	1	6	1
Reece	1							
Rees	3+6		0+2				2+1	1
Smith	9+7		0+2		0+1		4+1	
Sneekes	13	10						
Spink	15						2	
Taylor	39+3	17	4		3	1	5+2	3

WEST HAM UNITED (PREM: 10th)

Player	P/FL App	Goals	FLC App	Goals	FAC App	Goals	Others App	Goals
Allen	3	1						
Bilic	13							
Bishop	35	1	3	1	3			

WEST HAM UNITED cont.

	P/FL App	P/FL Goals	FLC App	FLC Goals	FAC App	FAC Goals	Others App	Others Goals
Boere	0+1							
Boogers	0+4							
Breacker	19+3		2					
Brown	3							
Cottee	30+3	10	3	2	3			
Dani	3+6	2						
Dicks	34	10	3	1	3			
Dowie	33	8	3		3	1		
Dumitrescu	2+1							
Ferdinand	0+1							
Finn	1							
Gordon	0+1				0+1			
Harkes	6+5				1+1			
Hughes	28		2		3	1		
Hutchison	8+4	2						
Lampard	0+2							
Lazaridis	2+2		1		0+1			
Martin	10+4		2		1			
Miklosko	36		3		3			
Moncur	19+1		3	1	1	1		
Potts	34		3		3			
Rieper	35+1	2	2+1		3			
Rowland	19+4				1+1			
Sealey	1+1							
Slater	16+6	2	3		1			
Watson	0+1							
Whitbread	0+2				1			
Williamson	28+1	4	0+1		3			

WIGAN ATHLETIC (DIV 3: 10th)

	P/FL App	P/FL Goals	FLC App	FLC Goals	FAC App	FAC Goals	Others App	Others Goals
Barnwell-Edinboro	2+8	1						
Benjamin	1+2						1	1
Biggins	15+3	2						
Black	8+13	2			2	2	0+1	
Butler	33		1		3		3	
Carragher	22+6		1+1		4		2	
Diaz	31+6	10	2		4	2	3	
Doolan	2+1		1					
Farnworth	43				4		3	
Farrell	21+2	1	2		2+1		1	
Felgate	3		2					
Greenall	37		2		3		2+1	
Johnson	27	3						
Kelly	2						1	
Kilford	18+7	3			1+1		2	
Lancashire	5	3						
Leonard	32+3	7	2		4	1	2	
Lightfoot	11+3	1	2		2		3	
Lowe	7	3						
Lyons	14+8	1	1+1	1	3+1		3	
Martinez	42	9	2	1	4	3	2	
Miller	4+3		2				0+1	
Millett			0+1					
Mutch	7	1						
Ogden	10		0+1		0+1		1	
Pender	40+1	1			4		3	
Rimmer	27+3				1			
Robertson	14	1	2		2			
Seba	8+12	3	2		0+2		1	
Sharp	20	6			1			

WIMBLEDON (PREM: 14th)

	P/FL App	P/FL Goals	FLC App	FLC Goals	FAC App	FAC Goals	Others App	Others Goals
Ardley	4+2		1		0+2			
Blackwell	8				3			
Blissett	0+4							
Castledine	2+2	1			1+1			
Clarke	9+9	2	0+2	1	1+3	1		
Cunningham	32+1		2		8			
Earle	37	11	2	2	7	1		
Ekoku	28+3	7	1		7	3		
Elkins	7+3		1					

WIMBLEDON cont.

	P/FL App	P/FL Goals	FLC App	FLC Goals	FAC App	FAC Goals	Others App	Others Goals
Euell	4+5	2			1+5			
Fear	4							
Fitzgerald	2+2							
Gayle	21+13	5	2		6+2			
Goodman	9+18	6	0+1		3	3		
Harford	17+4	1	0+1		7			
Heald	18		2					
Holdsworth	31+2	10	2	4	4+1	2		
Jones	27+4	3	2		3			
Kimble	31		1		8			
Leonardsen	28+1	4	1+1		7	1		
McAllister	2							
Pearce	6+1				0+1			
Perry	35+2		2		7			
Reeves	21+3	1	1		6			
Segers	3+1							
Skinner	1							
Sullivan	16				8			
Talboys	3+2		1		1			
Thorn	11+3		1					
Tracey	1							

WOLVERHAMPTON WANDERERS (DIV 1: 20th)

	P/FL App	P/FL Goals	FLC App	FLC Goals	FAC App	FAC Goals	Others App	Others Goals
Atkins	26+6	2	5	2	4			
Birch	5+2		2+1					
Bull	42+2	15	4+1		4	2		
Corica	17							
Cowans	10+6		2					
Crowe	1+1	1						
Daley	16+2	3	4	1	0+1			
Dennison			0+1					
De Wolf	14+1	1	1					
Emblen	30+3	2	1+1	1	3			
Ferguson	26+7	1	4	1	3+1	1		
Foley	1+4		0+1		0+1			
Froggatt	13+5	1						
Goodman	43+1	16	6	3	4	1		
Jones	8		2					
Kelly	3+2							
Law	5+2	1	1+1		1			
Masters	3							
Osborn	21	2			4			
Pearce	3+2		1		1			
Rankine	27+5		6		3+1			
Richards	36+1	1	5		2			
Samways	3							
Shirtliff	2							
Smith	10+3		1					
Stowell	38		4		4			
Thomas	0+2							
Thompson	45	6	6		4			
Venus	19+3		3	1	2			
Williams	5+7	1	2+1	1	1			
Wright	4+3		1+1	1				
Young	30	2	5		4			

WREXHAM (DIV 2: 8th)

	P/FL App	P/FL Goals	FLC App	FLC Goals	FAC App	FAC Goals	Others App	Others Goals
Barnes							0+1	
Brace	16	1	1				1	
Brammer	11	2	1		2		2	
Chalk	19	4						
Connolly	45+1	18	2		4	1	5	2
Cross	4+3						2+1	
Durkan	6+2		1+1		1+1		1	
Futcher							2	
Hardy	41+1		2		4		5	
Hughes	11+11		1		0+3		2	1
Humes	26+1	3			4		3	
Hunter	30+1	3	2		2+1	1	2	
Jones B	39+1		2		4		5	
Jones L	20	8						
McGregor	27+5	1			2+1		3	

WREXHAM cont.

	P/FL App	P/FL Goals	FLC App	FLC Goals	FAC App	FAC Goals	Others App	Others Goals
Marriott	46		2		4		5	
Morris	4+9	3	1+1		1		0+1	
Owen	11+8	2	1				2+1	
Phillips	43+1	5	1+1		4		5	
Russell	37+3	7	2	1	3		2	
Skinner	21+2	3	1		3		3	
Thomas							1	
Ward	33+1	6	1		4		1	1
Watkin	16+13	7	1+1	1	2+1	1	3	

WYCOMBE WANDERERS (DIV 2: 12th)

	P/FL App	P/FL Goals	FLC App	FLC Goals	FAC App	FAC Goals	Others App	Others Goals
Bell	40+1	1	1		2		1+1	
Blissett	4	2						
Brown	38		4		2		2	
Carroll	46	9	4		2		2	
Castledine	7	3						
Clark	1+2							
Cousins	28+2		3		2		2	
Crossley	12	1	3	1				
Desouza	38+5	18	4	2	2		2	
Dykstra	13							
Evans	26+2	3						
Farrell	27+6	5	2		2		2	
Foran	5		2					
Garner	8+5	3	0+2		1+1		1	
Hardyman	12+3		4				1	
Hemmings	0+3		0+2					
Howard	36+3	2	3		2		2	1
Hyde	17		4		2		2	
Lawrence	1+2							
McGavin	22+9	2	2+1		0+1		1+1	
McGorry	0+4		1					
Markman	0+2							
Moussaddik	1		0+1					
Patterson	31+6	1	2		2	1	0+1	
Roberts	15							
Rowbotham	27		2				2	
Ryan	18+5	4						
Skiverton	3+1	1						
Soloman	6+1		1					
Stapleton	1							
Williams	23+6	7	2		1		2	

YORK CITY (DIV 2: 20th)

	P/FL App	P/FL Goals	FLC App	FLC Goals	FAC App	FAC Goals	Others App	Others Goals
Atkin	25+4		1+3				2	
Atkinson	20+2						2	
Baker	11+7	5	2+2	2	1		4	
Barnes	30	15	5	5	1		5	2
Barras	32	3	5	1	1		3+1	1
Bull	15	8						
Bushell	17+6		1				3+2	
Cresswell	9+7	1					1	
Curtis	0+1				0+1		0+1	
Hall	21+2		5				2	
Himsworth	7+1	1						
Jordan	18+8	1	4+1	1			2+3	
Kiely	40		3				3	
McMillan	46		5		1		5	
Matthews	14+3	1			1		3	
Murty	31+4	2	3				3+1	
Naylor	20+5	7	0+1					
Osborne	5+1				1		1	
Oxley	1+1		1					
Pepper	39+1	9	4		1	1	3	
Peverell	11+9	1	3+1	1			2+2	1
Randall	13+3							
Scaife	0+1							
Sharples	10							
Stephenson	24+3	2	2				1+1	1
Tutill	25		5				5	
Warrington	6		2		1		2	
Williams	16+2		4+1		1		3	1

PFA AWARDS 1996

Players' Player of the Year
LES FERDINAND

Young Player of the Year
ROBBIE FOWLER

Special Merit Award
PELE

DIVISIONAL AWARDS

Carling Premier League

David James	Liverpool
Gary Neville	Manchester United
Tony Adams	Arsenal
Ugo Ehiogu	Aston Villa
Alan Wright	Aston Villa
David Ginola	Newcastle United
Robert Lee	Newcastle United
Steve Stone	Nottingham Forest
Ruud Gullit	Chelsea
Les Ferdinand	Newcastle United
Alan Shearer	Blackburn Rovers

Ensleigh League Division 1

Alan Kelly	Sheffield United
Dariusz Kubicki	Sunderland
Dean Richards	Wolverhampton Wanderers
Richard Rufus	Charlton Athletic
Dean Gordon	Crystal Palace
Lee Bowyer	Charlton Athletic
Alex Rae	Millwall
Michael Gray	Sunderland
Garry Parker	Leicester City
Dean Sturridge	Derby County
Steve Claridge	Leicester City

Endsleigh League Division 2

Darren Ward	Notts County
Chris Wilder	Notts County
Shaun Taylor	Swindon Town
Ian Culverhouse	Swindon Town
Paul Bodin	Swindon Town
Neil Lennon	Crewe Alexandra
Michael Mellon	Blackpool
Martyn O'Conner	Walsall
Karl Connolly	Wrexham
Marcus Stewart	Bristol Rovers
Kurt Nogan	Burnley

Endsleigh League Division 3

Jim Stannard	Gillingham
Duncan Jupp	Fulham
Mike Heathcote	Plymouth Argyle
Russell Wilcox	Preston North End
Paul Williams	Plymouth Argyle
Simon Davey	Preston North End
Ian Bryson	Preston North End
Roberto Martinez	Wigan Athletic
Mark Kinsella	Colchester United
Andrew Saville	Preston North End
Carl Dale	Cardiff City

THE TIMES ITF INTERACTIVE TEAM FOOTBALL

IN ASSOCIATION WITH

Listed below are the players' final scoring totals in *The Times* Interactive Team Football at the end of the 1995-96 season

(qualification – a minimum of six Premier League and FA Cup appearances: * denotes total includes appearances for player's previous club)

GOALKEEPERS

			Appearances (League + Cup)
57	D James	Liverpool	38+7
56	P Schmeichel	Man United	36+6
36	D Seaman	Arsenal	38+2
30	M Bosnich	Aston Villa	38+5
13	S Hislop	Newcastle	24
6	D Kharine	Chelsea	26+1
3	I Walker	Tottenham	38+6
-2	N Southall	Everton	38+4
-2	A Miller	Middlesbrough	6
-5	P Srnicek	Newcastle	15+2
-6	C Woods	Sheffield W	8
-13	M Beeney	Leeds	10+1
-14	S Ogrizovic	Coventry	25+3
-17	L Miklosko	West Ham	36+3
-18	K Hitchcock	Chelsea	12+7
-18	G Walsh	Middlesbrough	32+3
-19	J Lukic	Leeds	28+5
-20	D Beasant	Southampton	36+6
-22	T Flowers	Blackburn	37+2
-22	H Sullivan	Wimbledon	16+8
-31	M Crossley	Nottingham F	38+7
-35	J Filan	Coventry	13
-38	P Heald	Wimbledon	18
-39	E Immel	Man City	38+5
-47	K Pressman	Sheffield W	30+1
-48	J Sommer	QPR	33+2
-71	K Branagan	Bolton W	31+2

FULL BACKS

60	R Jones	Liverpool	33+7
56	L Dixon	Arsenal	38+2
56	A Wright	Aston Villa	38+5
54	N Winterburn	Arsenal	36+1
54	D Irwin	Man United	31+6
50	P Neville	Man United	24+7
50	G Charles	Aston Villa	34+5
40	S Campbell	Tottenham	31+6
30	S Harkness	Liverpool	24+1
28	S Pearce	Nottingham F	31+1
26	J Kenna	Blackburn	32+2
26	J Dicks	West Ham	34+3
24	W Barton	Newcastle	31+2
24	J Dodd	Southampton	37+5
22	N Cox	Middlesbrough	35+2
22	G Neville	Man United	31+6
22	C Wilson	Tottenham	28+5
21	A Pickering	Coventry City	30+2
20	D Petrescu	Chelsea	24+7
20	D Lyttle	Nottingham F	33+7
18	H Berg	Blackburn	38+2
18	G Kelly	Leeds	34+5
16	C Morris	Middlesbrough	23+2
15	T Dorigo	Leeds	17+3
13	K Rowland	West Ham	23+2
12	S Staunton	Aston Villa	13+2
12	D Austin	Tottenham	28+4
12	A Myers	Chelsea	20+3
11	S Clarke	Chelsea	22+8
11	M Jackson	Everton	14+2
11	J Beresford	Newcastle	33
10	G Ablett	Everton	13+3
10	F Benali	Southampton	29+1
7	M Hottiger	Everton	9
6	T Phelan	Chelsea	12+8
6	S Charlton	Southampton	26+6
5	J Edinburgh	Tottenham	22+4
5	C Fleming	Middlesbrough	13+1
4	E Barrett	Everton	8
4	D Burrows	Coventry	11+1
3	G Le Saux	Blackburn	14
2	S Minto	Chelsea	10
1	P Parker	Man United	6+2
0	S McCanespie	Bolton W	9
0	A Kimble	Wimbledon	31+8
-1	T Challis	QPR	11+2
-1	R Edghill	Man City	13
-1	Moreno	Middlesbrough	7+1
-2	R Brevett	QPR	27
-2	N Worthington	Leeds	16+3
-4	D Stefanovic	Sheffield W	6+1
-4	A Todd	Bolton W	12
-8	M Hall	Coventry	25+2
-8	G Elkins	Wimbledon	10
-9	S Green	Bolton W	31+2
-9	I Nolan	Sheffield W	29+1
-10	T Breaker	West Ham	22
-10	G Bergsson	Bolton W	34
-12	M Frontzeck	Man City	12+1
-14	K Cunningham	Wimbledon	33+8
-14	D Bardsley	QPR	29+1
-15	P Atherton	Sheffield W	36+1
-16	A Haaland	Nottingham F	17+2
-20	J Phillips	Bolton W	37+2

CENTRAL DEFENDERS

49	J Scales	Liverpool	27+7
45	M Wright	Liverpool	28+7
44	S Bruce	Man United	30+5
44	P Babb	Liverpool	28+4
42	G Pallister	Man United	21+3
41	N Ruddock	Liverpool	20+2
39	U Ehiogu	Aston Villa	36+5
39	D Unsworth	Everton	31+2
37	M Keown	Arsenal	34+2
37	G Mabbutt	Tottenham	32+6
30	P Albert	Newcastle	23+2
30	D May	Man United	16+2
29	D Peacock	Newcastle	34+2
28	P McGrath	Aston Villa	30+4
27	T Adams	Arsenal	21+2
27	D Watson	Everton	34+4
27	C Cooper	Nottingham F	37+5
26	S Howey	Newcastle	28+1
26	D Wetherall	Leeds	34+5
25	C Calderwood	Tottenham	29+4
23	S Bould	Arsenal	19
22	C Hendry	Blackburn	33+2
20	D Lee	Chelsea	31+7
19	A Martin	West Ham	14+1
18	A Linighan	Arsenal	18+1
17	S Vickers	Middlesbrough	32+3
17	K Monkou	Southampton	32+6
16	A Nielson	Southampton	18+2
15	R Hall	Southampton	30+5
15	D Whyte	Middlesbrough	25
14	N Pearson	Middlesbrough	36
14	M Rieper	West Ham	36+3
14	L Daish	Coventry City	11
13	S Potts	West Ham	34+3
13	S Chettle	Nottingham F	37+7
13	K Symons	Man City	38+5
13	C Short	Everton	23+3
13	C Palmer	Leeds	35+6
13	C Coleman	Blackburn	20+2
12	A Stubbs	Bolton W	25+2
10	P Beesley	Leeds	10+4
9	E Johnsen	Chelsea	22+2
8	K Curle	Man City	32+5
8	D Matteo	Liverpool	5+1
6	A MacDonald	QPR	26+2
5	N Marker	Blackburn	9
5	F Sinclair	Chelsea	13
5	D Busst	Coventry	17+3
4	S Bilic	West Ham	13
3	R Jobson	Leeds	12+1
3	I Pearce	Blackburn	12
1	M Duberry	Chelsea	22+8
1	A Pearce	Wimbledon	7+1
0	P Whelan	Middlesbrough	13+3
0	J Newsome	Sheffield W	8
0	D Walker	Sheffield W	36+1
-1	S Coleman	Bolton W	12
-2	A Reeves	Wimbledon	24+6
-3	A Kernaghan	Man City	6
-5	S Nethercott	Tottenham	13+3
-5	K Ready	QPR	22+1
-5	A Thorn	Wimbledon	14
-7	D Rennie	Coventry	11
-9	R Shaw	Coventry	21+3
-10	G Taggert	Bolton W	11+2
-11	S Yates	QPR	30+2

-11	J Pemberton	Leeds	17+2
-13	S Perry	Wimbledon	37+7
-13	D Maddix	QPR	22+2
-15	B Borrows	Coventry	21+1
-20	C Fairclough	Bolton W	33+2

MIDFIELD PLAYERS

82	S McManaman	Liverpool	38+7
81	R Giggs	Man United	33+7
78	A Kanchelskis	Everton	32+4
68	J Barnes	Liverpool	36+7
68	I Woan	Nottingham F	33+7
68	G McAllister	Leeds	36+6
67	R Earle	Wimbledon	37+7
64	M Draper	Aston Villa	36+5
63	P Merson	Arsenal	38+2
62	R Lee	Newcastle	36+1
61	S Stone	Nottingham F	34+6
58	R Gullitt	Chelsea	31+7
57	J Magilton	Southampton	31+6
57	G Kinkladze	Man City	37+4
56	R Fox	Tottenham*	30+6
54	D Wise	Chelsea	35+7
54	D Beckham	Man United	33+3
53	J McAteer	Liverpool*	33+7
49	R Keane	Man United	29+7
49	J Salako	Coventry City	37+3
49	D Ginola	Newcastle	34+2
48	T Sinclair	QPR	37+2
48	I Bishop	West Ham	35+3
48	D Platt	Arsenal	29+1
48	C Bart-Williams	Nottingham F	33+7
47	N Butt	Man United	33+7
47	L Sharpe	Man United	31+6
47	G Southgate	Aston Villa	31+4
45	M Gayle	Wimbledon	34+8
45	G Speed	Leeds	29+4
44	S Lomas	Man City	33+5
44	O Leonhardsen	Wimbledon	29+7
44	D Batty	Newcastle*	34+1
42	M Hughes	West Ham	28+3
42	A Townsend	Aston Villa	33+4
41	N Summerbee	Man City	37+5
41	J Parkinson	Everton	28+2
40	T Sherwood	Blackburn	33+2
40	J Ebbrell	Everton	25+4
40	G Peacock	Chelsea	28+7
40	D Howells	Tottenham	29+2
39	P Telfer	Coventry	31+3
39	I Taylor	Aston Villa	25+3
38	S Gemmill	Nottingham F	31+7
37	S Ripley	Blackburn	28+2
37	L Bohinen	Blackburn*	26+1
37	J Pollock	Middlesbrough	31+3
36	S Barker	QPR	33
36	K Gillespie	Newcastle	28
35	M Pembridge	Sheffield W	25
35	L Clark	Newcastle	28+2
35	A Impey	QPR	29+2
34	S Curcic	Bolton W	28+2
34	K Richardson	Coventry	33+3
34	J Rednapp	Liverpool	23+3
33	S Sellars	Bolton W*	28+1
33	J Dozzell	Tottenham	28+3
33	D Williamson	West Ham	29+3
33	A Hinchcliffe	Everton	28+3
32	M Thomas	Liverpool	27+6
32	E Newton	Chelsea	24+3
32	C Waddle	Sheffield W	32+1
31	D Widdrington	Southampton	21+4
29	S Watson	Newcastle	23+1
29	C Hignett	Middlesbrough	22+1
29	B Horne	Everton	26+4
28	A Limpar	Everton	28+4
27	R Mustoe	Middlesbrough	21
27	N Clough	Man City	15+3
27	I Brightwell	Man City	29+2
26	V Jones	Wimbledon	31+3
26	R Wallace	Leeds	24+4
26	Juninho	Middlesbrough	21+3
26	G Helder	Arsenal	24+2
24	I Holloway	QPR	27+1
24	G Flitcroft	Blackburn*	28+4
24	B Venison	Southampton	22+3
23	L Briscoe	Sheffield W	26
23	C Burley	Chelsea	22+2
22	R Slater	West Ham	22+1
21	R Parlour	Arsenal	22
21	J Moncur	West Ham	20+1
21	D Phillips	Nottingham F	18+6
20	N Heaney	Southampton	17+1
19	A Sinton	Tottenham	9
18	N Maddison	Southampton	16+2
18	G Hyde	Sheffield W	26
18	A Thompson	Bolton W	26+1
16	W McKinlay	Blackburn	19+2
16	J Jensen	Arsenal	15+2
16	G Fenton	Blackburn	14
16	A Grant	Everton	13+1
15	N Spackman	Chelsea	16+3
15	L Radebe	Leeds	13+4
15	J Wilcox	Blackburn	10
14	J Sheridan	Sheffield W	17
11	D Lee	Bolton W	18+1
10	M Holmes	Blackburn	9
10	M Ford	Leeds	12+4
10	D Anderton	Tottenham	8
9	N Quashie	QPR	11+2
9	N Isaias	Coventry	11
9	D Hughes	Southampton	11+1
7	R Elliot	Newcastle	6+2
7	M Walters	Southampton	5+4
7	G McMahon	Tottenham	14+1
6	M Tinkler	Leeds	6
6	C Brown	Man City	21+5
5	G Strachan	Coventry	12+2
4	P Warhurst	Blackburn	10
4	N Ardley	Wimbledon	6+2
3	A Moore	Middlesbrough	12
2	J Moreno	Middlesbrough	7
2	A Couzens	Leeds	14
2	A Clarke	Arsenal	6+2
1	S Davies	Man United	6
1	G Goodridge	QPR	7+1
0	S Howe	Nottingham F	9
0	M Brazier	QPR	11+1

STRIKERS

109	R Fowler	Liverpool	38+7
95	A Shearer	Blackburn	35+2
87	L Ferdinand	Newcastle	37+2
82	E Sheringham	Tottenham	38+6
77	D Yorke	Aston Villa	35+5
74	E Cantona	Man United	30+7
74	C Armstrong	Tottenham	36+6
72	S Collymore	Liverpool	31+7
65	D Dublin	Coventry	34+3
64	N Shipperley	Southampton	37+6
61	S Milosevic	Aston Villa	37+5
60	A Cole	Man United	34+7
55	U Rosler	Man City	36+5
54	J Spencer	Chelsea	28+8
54	I Wright	Arsenal	31+2
53	G Stuart	Everton	29+4
53	A Yeboah	Leeds United	22+6
52	T Cottee	West Ham	33+3
51	E Ekoku	Wimbledon	31+7
51	D Bergkamp	Arsenal	33+1
50	D Hirst	Sheffield W	30+1
49	I Dowie	West Ham	33+3
49	D Holdsworth	Wimbledon	33+5
48	P Beardsley	Newcastle	35+2
48	M Degryse	Sheffield W	34+1
46	N Barmby	Middlesbrough	32+3
46	M Hughes	Chelsea	31+6
46	B Roy	Nottingham F	28+6
45	N Quinn	Man City	32+4
44	B Deane	Leeds	34+6
41	K Gallen	QPR	30
40	P Scholes	Man United	26+2
40	N Whelan	Coventry*	29+3
40	M Le Tissier	Southampton	34+5
40	J McGinlay	Bolton W	32+2
38	K Campbell	Nottingham F	21+7
36	G Whittingham	Sheffield W	29+1
36	D Amokachi	Everton	25+3
34	R Rosenthal	Tottenham	33+5
34	J Fjortoft	Middlesbrough	28
33	P Ndlovu	Coventry	32+1
32	D Dichio	QPR	29+1
31	P Rideout	Everton	25+2
31	J Goodman	Wimbledon	27+3
29	J Lee	Nottingham F	28+4
28	T Johnson	Aston Villa	23+4
28	D Ferguson	Everton	18+2
27	M Bright	Sheffield W	25
27	G Watson	Southampton	25+5
27	F De Freitas	Bolton W	27+1
26	M Newell	Blackburn	30+2
23	T Brolin	Leeds	19+2
22	P Furlong	Chelsea	28+8
22	I Rush	Liverpool	20+4
21	J Hartson	Arsenal	19+1
19	B McClair	Man United	22
18	M Harford	Wimbledon	21+7
18	K Gallagher	Blackburn	16+2
16	A Clarke	Wimbledon	18+4
15	M Hateley	QPR	14+1
15	G Creaney	Man City	15+3
15	F Asprilla	Newcastle	14
12	N Blake	Bolton W	18+2
12	M Paatelainen	Bolton W	15+1
11	E Jess	Coventry	12
11	D Kovacevic	Sheffield W	16+1
8	J Hendrie	Middlesbrough	13
7	R Blinker	Sheffield W	9
7	P Kitson	Newcastle	7+2
7	J Joachim	Aston Villa	11
7	C Sutton	Blackburn	13
7	A Silenzi	Nottingham F	10+3
6	M Stein	Chelsea	8

5	P Wilkinson	Middlesbrough	4+3
5	P Masinga	Leeds	8+1
4	P Dickov	Arsenal	7
3	N Lamptey	Coventry	6+1
2	J Euell	Wimbledon	9+6
0	P McGregor	Nottingham F	14+2

MANAGERS

95	A Ferguson	Manchester United
79	R Evans	Liverpool
70	K Keegan	Newcastle United
63	B Little	Aston Villa
62	G Francis	Tottenham Hotspur
57	F Clark	Nottingham Forest
54	J Royle	Everton
54	B Rioch	Arsenal
52	G Hoddle	Chelsea
48	R Harford	Blackburn Rovers
39	H Rednapp	West Ham United
36	J Kinnear	Wimbledon
34	H Wilkinson	Leeds United
30	D Merrington	Southampton
29	B Robson	Middlesbrough
27	A Ball	Manchester City
25	R Atkinson	Coventry City
21	D Pleat	Sheffield Wednesday
12	R Wilkins	Queens Park Rangers
9	C Todd	Bolton Wanderers

MOST POPULAR CHOICES

The top twenty most popular players/managers selected in a starting line-up.

		Teams
Jamie Redknapp	Liverpool	75651
Roy Keane	Man United	43964
David James	Liverpool	42577
Tim Sherwood	Blackburn	41202
David Platt	Arsenal	40374
Alan Stubbs	Bolton W	39912
David Batty	Blackburn	38067
Gary Neville	Man United	37123
Neville Southall	Everton	33967
David Unsworth	Everton	33675
Sol Campbell	Tottenham	32613
Joe Royle	Everton	31076
Mark Draper	Aston Villa	29659
Mark Hughes	Chelsea	28809
Kevin Keegan	Newcastle	27405
Bruce Rioch	Arsenal	27076
Rob Jones	Liverpool	22569
Warren Barton	Newcastle	22443
Anders Limpar	Everton	21887
Stuart Ripley	Blackburn	21282

Most in demand through transfers

		Moves
Steve Vickers	Middlesbrough	7312
Neil Cox	Middlesbrough	7194
Steve Harkness	Liverpool	6925
Craig Hignett	Middlesbrough	6129
David Beckham	Man United	5739
Les Ferdinand	Newcastle	5602
Mark Draper	Aston Villa	4701
Martin Keown	Arsenal	4659

Shaka Hislop	Newcastle	4525
Gary Walsh	Middlesbrough	4422
Mark Bosnich	Aston Villa	4331
Dwight Yorke	Aston Villa	4331
Tony Yeboah	Leeds	4230
Teddy Sheringham	Tottenham	4217
Mark Wright	Liverpool	3766
Paul Scholes	Man United	3513
Jamie Redknapp	Liverpool	3412
Ugo Ehiogu	Aston Villa	3357
Daniele Dichio	QPR	3344
Lee Clark	Newcastle	3183

The most popular choices in each category in a starting line-up were:

GOALKEEPERS

David James	Liverpool	42577
Neville Southall	Everton	33967
Mark Crossley	Nottingham F	18488
John Lukic	Leeds	14987
Peter Schmeichel	Man United	13535
Ian Walker	Tottenham	12310
David Seaman	Arsenal	9969
Pavel Srnicek	Newcastle	9757
Tim Flowers	Blackburn	9377
Mark Bosnich	Aston Villa	5934

Most in demand through transfers

Shaka Hislop	Newcastle	4525
Gary Walsh	Middlesbrough	4422
Mark Bosnich	Aston Villa	4331
David Seaman	Arsenal	2001
David James	Liverpool	1800

FULL BACKS

Gary Neville	Man United	37123
Sol Campbell	Tottenham	32613
Rob Jones	Liverpool	22569
Warren Barton	Newcastle	22443
Denis Irwin	Man United	18444
Lee Dixon	Arsenal	17351
Stuart Pearce	Nottingham F	14393
Garry Kelly	Leeds	13998
Graham Le Saux	Blackburn	13492
Earl Barrett	Everton	11610

Most in demand through transfers

Neil Cox	Middlesbrough	7194
Steve Harkness	Liverpool	6925
Warren Barton	Newcastle	2869
Lee Dixon	Arsenal	2340
Nigel Winterburn	Arsenal	2292

CENTRAL DEFENDERS

Alan Stubbs	Bolton W	39912
David Unsworth	Everton	33675
Neil Ruddock	Liverpool	17410
Carlton Palmer	Leeds	16645
John Pemberton	Leeds	15713
Phil Babb	Liverpool	14128
Dave Watson	Everton	12920
Ugo Ehiogu	Aston Villa	12007
Steve Bould	Arsenal	11200
Martin Keown	Arsenal	10855

Most in demand through transfers

Steve Vickers	Middlesbrough	7312
Martin Keown	Arsenal	4659
Mark Wright	Liverpool	3766
Ugo Ehiogu	Aston Villa	3357
Steve Bould	Arsenal	2549

MIDFIELD PLAYERS

Jamie Redknapp	Liverpool	75651
Roy Keane	Man United	43964
Tim Sherwood	Blackburn	41202
David Platt	Arsenal	40374
David Batty	Blackburn	38067
Mark Draper	Aston Villa	29659
Anders Limpar	Everton	21887
Stuart Ripley	Blackburn	21282
Andy Impey	QPR	20487
Nicky Butt	Man United	19863

Most in demand through transfers

Craig Hignett	Middlesbrough	6129
David Beckham	Man United	5739
Mark Draper	Aston Villa	4701
Jamie Redknapp	Liverpool	3412
Lee Clark	Newcastle	3183

STRIKERS

Mark Hughes	Chelsea	28809
Kevin Campbell	Nottingham F	18861
Tony Yeboah	Leeds	16770
Dennis Bergkamp	Arsenal	16739
Les Ferdinand	Newcastle	16679
Andy Cole	Man United	15568
Peter Beardsley	Newcastle	15162
Alan Shearer	Blackburn	14447
Matthew Le Tissier	Southampton	12065
Savo Milosevic	Aston Villa	11910

Most in demand through transfers

Les Ferdinand	Newcastle	5602
Dwight Yorke	Aston Villa	4331
Tony Yeboah	Leeds	4230
Teddy Sheringham	Tottenham	4217
Paul Scholes	Man United	3513

MANAGERS

Joe Royle	Everton	31076
Kevin Keegan	Newcastle	27405
Bruce Rioch	Arsenal	27076
Roy Evans	Liverpool	17056
Howard Wilkinson	Leeds	16868
Bryan Robson	Middlesbrough	12197
Frank Clark	Nottingham F	11419
Alex Ferguson	Man United	10469
Glenn Hoddle	Chelsea	8508
Ray Wilkins	QPR	8243

Most in demand through transfers

Bryan Robson	Middlesbrough	2347
Kevin Keegan	Newcastle	2164
Alex Ferguson	Man United	1126
Brian Little	Aston Villa	765
Frank Clark	Nottingham F	661